CASES, MATERIALS, AND COMMENTARY ON THE EUROPEAN CONVENTION ON HUMAN RIGHTS

Cases, Materials, and Commentary on the

EUROPEAN CONVENTION ON HUMAN RIGHTS

Third edition

Alastair Mowbray LLB (Warw), PhD (Edin)
Professor of Public Law,
University of Nottingham

UNIVERSITY PRESS

OXFORD
UNIVERSITY PRESS

Great Clarendon Street, Oxford OX2 6DP
United Kingdom

Oxford University Press is a department of the University of Oxford.
It furthers the University's objective of excellence in research, scholarship,
and education by publishing worldwide. Oxford is a registered trade mark of
Oxford University Press in the UK and in certain other countries

Contains public sector information licensed under the Open Government Licence v1.0
(http://www.nationalarchives.gov.uk/doc/open-government-licence/open-government-licence.htm)

Crown Copyright material reproduced with the permission of the
Controller, HMSO (under the terms of the Click Use licence.)

British Library Cataloguing in Publication Data
Data available

Library of Congress Cataloguing in Publication Data
Library of Congress Control Number: 2011945379

ISBN 978-0-19-957736-1

Printed by CPI Group (UK) Ltd, Croydon, CR0 4YY

PREFACE

In the years since the last edition was published the Convention system has undergone important institutional and procedural reforms. The delayed ratification of Protocol 14 by the Russian Government necessitated the member States agreeing the interim mechanisms of Protocol 14*bis* and the Madrid Agreement. However, Protocol 14 finally came into effect on 1 June 2010. The member States have also embarked on a longer-term process of reforms outlined in the Interlaken Declaration (February 2010) and Izmir Declaration (April 2011). Practical achievements include the Court adopting a new Priority Policy to govern the order in which it will determine applications and the Committee of Ministers introducing a new system for supervising the execution of Court judgments.

The jurisprudence of the Court has also continued to evolve, reflecting contemporary problems such as people trafficking (*Rantsev v Cyprus & Russia*) and indirect forms of discrimination (*D.H. & Others v Czech Republic*). Changes in social attitudes have underpinned the Court's development of Convention rights (e.g. the recognition of long-term gay relationships as constituting 'family life' in *Schalk & Kopf v Austria*), as have alterations in employment relations (reflected in the Court's judgment in *Demir & Baykara v Turkey* that the 'right to form and join trade unions' includes the right to bargain collectively). The use of new technologies by States has continued to be subject to scrutiny by the Court when the relevant actions fall within the ambit of the Convention (including the storing and use of individuals' DNA profiles by law enforcement agencies in *S & Marper v UK*).

In the light of helpful comments received from a selection of different users on the previous edition, this edition focuses on those Articles of the Convention most commonly studied. It has also been necessary to ensure that the extensive new case-law incorporated into this edition did not produce an increase in the length of the text. However, this edition seeks to ensure that important early judgments (like *Ireland v UK*) are retained together with significant new cases. The Court's website provides an updated version of the Convention.

This edition is dedicated to my father, Andrew Mowbray, who like so many of his generation spent their youth fighting (literally) to create a Europe where the Convention could be established and human rights respected (though far too many breaches are still occurring as readers will sadly discover in the ensuing chapters).

I have sought to state the law as it stood on 1 September 2011.

A.R.M.

OUTLINE CONTENTS

DETAILED CONTENTS

ACKNOWLEDGEMENTS

The author would like to thank the European Court of Human Rights and the Council of Europe for permitting the reproductions of extracts from the judgments of the Court and related materials.

Chapter 7 is the author's revision of a chapter originally written by his colleague Emeritus Professor D. J.Harris, CMG.

Grateful acknowledgement is made to all the authors and publishers of copyright material that appears in this book, and in particular to the following for permission to reprint material from the sources indicated:

Cambridge Law Journal and the author: extracts from Colin R. Munro, 'The Value of Commercial Speech' (2003), 62(1), *Cambridge Law Journal* 134.

N. P. Engel Verlag: extract from Peter Leuprecht in M. Nowak, D. Steurer, and H. Tretter (eds), *Progress in the Spirit of Human Rights* (Engle, 1988).

Koninklijke Brill NV: extracts from H. A. Robertson (ed.), *Collected Edition of the 'Travaux Preparatories'*, Vol. 1 (Martinus Nijhoff, The Hague, 1975).

Sweet & Maxwell Ltd: extracts from A.Mowbray, 'The Role of the European Court of Human Rights in the Promotion of Democracy' (1999), *Public Law* 703; and E. Wicks, 'The United Kingdom Government's Perceptions of the European Convention on Human Rights at the Time of Entry' (2000), *Public Law* 438.

Every effort has been made to trace and contact copyright holders prior to publication. If notified, the publisher will undertake to rectify any error or omissions at the earliest opportunity. The author wishes to also thank Tom Young and Heather Smyth together with the other OUP staff and external contractors involved with the production of this book.

TABLE OF STATUTES

Statutory Instruments

International Treaties and Conventions

TABLE OF EUROPEAN LEGISLATION

TABLE OF CASES

1 THE CREATION OF THE CONVENTION

The idea of a regional system of human rights protection operating across European States preceded the formation of the Council of Europe in 1949. In the years following the ending of the Second World War (in 1945) a number of non-governmental groups were established in various West European States to champion European unity. They combined together to form the International Committee of the Movements for European Unity. The Committee organized a major gathering, in The Hague, of politicians (including former leaders such as Winston Churchill (as he then was), current Ministers such as Françoise Mitterrand and future leaders such as Konrad Adenauer), and representatives of civil society including academics, business leaders, trade unionists, and religious leaders. The 'Congress of Europe' lasted from 7 to 10 May 1948 and was attended by about 1,000 persons, mainly drawn from Europe but also with representatives from the United States of America and the Commonwealth. At the end of the gathering the Congress issued the following declaration.

EUROPE IS THREATENED, EUROPE IS DIVIDED, AND THE GREATEST DANGER COMES FROM HER DIVISIONS

Impoverished, overladen with barriers that prevent the circulation of her goods but are no longer able to afford her protection, our disunited Europe marches towards her end. Alone, no one of our countries can hope seriously to defend its independence. Alone, no one of our countries can solve the economic problems of today. Without a freely agreed union our present anarchy will expose us tomorrow to forcible unification whether by the intervention of a foreign empire or usurpation by a political party.

The hour has come to take action commensurate with the danger.

Together with the overseas peoples associated with our destinies, we can tomorrow build the greatest political formation and the greatest economic unit our age has seen. Never will the history of the world have known so powerful a gathering of free men. Never will war, fear and misery have been checked by a more formidable foe.

Between this great peril and this great hope, Europe's mission is clear. It is to unite her peoples in accordance with their genius of diversity and with the conditions of modern community life, and so open the way towards organised freedom for which the world is seeking. It is to revive her inventive powers for the greater protection and respect of the rights and duties of the individual of which, in spite of all her mistakes, Europe is still the greatest exponent.

Human dignity is Europe's finest achievement, freedom her true strength. Both are at stake in our struggle. The union of our continent is now needed not only for the salvation of the liberties we have won, but also for the extension of their benefits to all mankind.

Upon this union depend Europe's destiny and the world's peace.

Let all therefore take note that we Europeans, assembled to express the will of all the peoples of Europe, solemnly declare our common aims in the following five articles, which summarise the resolutions adopted by the Congress:

PLEDGE
1. *We desire a United Europe, throughout whose area the free movement of persons, ideas and goods is restored;*

2. We desire a Charter of Human Rights guaranteeing liberty of thought, assembly and expression as well as the right to form a political opposition;
3. We desire a Court of Justice with adequate sanctions for the implementation of this Charter;
4. We desire a European Assembly where the live forces of all our nations shall be represented;
5. And pledge ourselves in our homes and in public, in our political and religious life, in our professional and trade union circles, to give our fullest support to all persons and governments working for this lofty cause, which offers the last chance of peace and the one promise of a great future for this generation and those that will succeed it.

Subsequently, the International Council of the European Movement sought to develop these Pledges by approving, in February 1949, a 'Declaration of Principles of European Union'. The latter provided, *inter alia*,

No State should be admitted into the European Union which does not accept the fundamental principles of a Charter of Human Rights, and which does not declare itself willing and bound to ensure their application.... the barrier which divides the Free States from the other European nations must not be accepted as permanent. Our aim is the union in freedom of all the peoples of Europe.

The European Movement also established an International Judicial Section chaired by M. Pierre-Henri Teitgen (a former senior French Resistance leader and Minister) together with Sir David Maxwell-Fyfe (a former British Conservative MP, Law Officer, and Deputy Chief Prosecutor at the Nuremberg war crimes trials) and Professor Fernand Dehousse (a Belgian politician and international lawyer) as *rapporteurs*. They produced a draft European Convention on Human Rights and Statute of the European Court of Human Rights. These documents were later given to the Committee of Ministers of the Council of Europe by the European Movement in July 1949.

On the governmental level ten States (Belgium, France, Luxembourg, The Netherlands, UK, Ireland, Italy, Denmark, Norway, and Sweden) signed the Statute of the Council of Europe creating the latter international organization during May 1949. The major aim of the Council of Europe was to achieve greater unity between the member States. A basic condition of membership, elaborated in Article 3 of the Statute, was that: 'Every member of the Council of Europe must accept the principles of the rule of law and the enjoyment by all persons within its jurisdiction of human rights and fundamental freedoms...'

During the summer of 1949 the Committee of Ministers of the Council of Europe (the executive body of the organization, see further, p 12) authorized the Consultative Assembly (comprising of representatives of the national parliaments of member States and now known as the Parliamentary Assembly) to include the topic of the maintenance and further realization of human rights on its agenda. In the ensuing discussions at the first session of the Consultative Assembly both M. Teitgen and Sir David Maxwell-Fyfe made passionate speeches arguing for the creation of an international Convention and Court to protect basic human rights in member States of the Council of Europe.

FIRST SESSION OF THE CONSULTATIVE ASSEMBLY HELD AT STRASBOURG 10TH AUGUST TO 8TH SEPTEMBER 1949 SITTINGS HELD FROM 16TH AUGUST TO 8TH SEPTEMBER 1949

[Taken from *Collected Edition of the 'Travaux Préparatoires'*, Vol I (Martinus Nijhoff, The Hague, 1975)]

M. TEITGEN (France) (Translation).—Mr. President, in Article 1, and later in Article 3, our Statute runs as follows:

'The aim of the Council of Europe is to achieve a greater unity between its Members for the purpose of safeguarding and realising the ideals and principles which are their common heritage and facilitating their economic and social progress.

'Every Member of the Council of Europe must accept the principles of the rule of law and of the enjoyment by all persons within its jurisdiction of human rights and fundamental freedoms, and collaborate sincerely and effectively in the realisation of the aim of the Council as defined in Chapter I.'

This fundamental affirmation is thus inscribed at the very foundation of our union: every man, by reason of his origin, his nature and his destiny, has certain indefensible rights, against which no reason of State may prevail.

And so, Mr. President, at our first meeting, with the friendly agreement of the Committee of Ministers, we are opening a debate with the object of working out proposals which will enable Europe to fulfil its promise.

Europe should in fact be, first and foremost, the land of freedom. The history of our countries tells on every page the price she has had to pay for freedom in the past: nearly twenty centuries of suffering, of struggle, wars, revolutions; tears and bloodshed without end; and ever, above the weariness of its often exhausted peoples, the ceaseless call of the hero and the saint.

Finally, we won our freedom, and our countries became as used to it as to the air they breathed—with the result that they did not perhaps esteem it highly enough.

When the scourges of the modern world descended—Fascism, Hitlerism, Communism—they found us relaxed, sceptical and unarmed. We needed war, and for some of us, enemy occupation, to make us realise afresh the value of our humanism.

Does this mean, Mr. President, that to-day, after the victory, all danger is henceforth banished? Allow me to say that we do not think so. Three things still threaten our freedom. The first threat is the eternal reason of State.

Behind the State, whatever its form, were it even democratic, there ever lurks as a permanent temptation, this reason of State.

Montesquieu said: 'Whoever has power, is tempted to abuse it.' Even parliamentary majorities are in fact sometimes tempted to abuse their power. Even in our democratic countries we must be on guard against this temptation of succumbing to reasons of State.

Then there is the second threat: Fascism and Hitlerism have unfortunately tainted European public opinion. These doctrines of death have infiltrated into our countries. They have left their mark. They have poisoned certain sections of public opinion.

Racialism did not die out with Hitler. I will be even more specific, and say that a certain brand of anti-Communism, which claims to fight Communism not with democratic methods but with dictatorial methods, sometimes puts in jeopardy the very principles of democracy.

Finally, and above all, freedom is in danger in our countries—let us have the courage to admit it—because of the economic and social conditions of the modern world.

Mr. President, freedom, in its bold and conquering youth, meant freedom of the person, of work, and of conscience. It also meant political freedom; it meant economic liberalism, free enterprise, freedom of competition, of profit and of money.

What so often followed, as we must admit, was the formation of a huge proletariat, reduced to undeserved poverty, and for whom freedom and the freedoms had proved a disappointment.

. . .

Very fortunately, the concept of Europe was born before it was too late. Experience has proved to us all that the problem I have just stated is insoluble, on the national plane. It can only be solved by means of a collective effort. The debate now opening is evidence of our wish to make that effort. What is it that we can do?

The task with which we are faced could be undertaken in three stages. Our first decision must be the choice of the distant, near, or immediate objective at which we are going to aim. There is, of course a desirable maximum, a theoretical ideal. It would consist in drawing up for Europe a complete code of all the freedoms and fundamental rights; all the individual freedoms and rights, and all the so-called social freedoms and rights.

A full and complete realisation of this aim would, however, be something beyond our powers.

We should need years of mutual understanding, study, and collective experiments, even to attempt after many years, with any hope of success, to formulate a complete and general definition of all the freedoms and all the rights which Europe should confer on the Europeans. Let us therefore discard for the moment this desirable maximum. Failing this, however, let us be content with the minimum which we can achieve in a very short period, and which consists in defining the seven, eight or ten fundamental freedoms that are essential for a democratic way of life and which our countries should guarantee to all their people. It should be possible to achieve a common definition of these.

If we start to work now and if for example we instruct a Committee of this Assembly, with your permission Mr. President and with that of the Assembly, to prepare this common definition of the essential democratic freedoms, we shall be in a position to propose it to the various Governments in a very short time. The latter could sanction it, and the essential freedoms would thus be guaranteed in the same form by the laws of all our countries. They would be safeguarded by the Court of Justice to which I shall presently refer.

...

But Mr. President, with your permission, we shall not stop there; we shall try, even during this Session, to bring before the peoples and before public opinion an immediate proposal, which we must adopt even before we have defined the essential freedoms for our countries.

The problem can be stated in very simple terms. All the States that have taken part in drawing up, signing and promulgating our Statute have bound themselves to respect the fundamental rights of the human individual. They have accepted the principle of a collective guarantee of fundamental freedoms.

We cannot propose that they should all immediately accept a common definition of these freedoms, but, we can ask them to agree forthwith to a collective guarantee, within the framework of the Council of Europe, of these fundamental freedoms, as they are at present defined in their own respective laws, until the time comes when they can guarantee them in the form of a general and collective definition.

If this principle is accepted by the Assembly, we can immediately make a practical and concrete proposal. We shall tell the Member States, who agreed to including this debate on the Agenda, that we should like them to negotiate forthwith a Convention, which they would all sign and which would be ratified by their Parliaments. It would contain, briefly, the following provisions: the principle of a collective guarantee of the fundamental rights and freedoms, within the framework of the Council of Europe, by all Member States belonging to the Council. For example—security of person; freedom from arbitrary arrest; freedom from slavery and servitude; freedom of speech and expression; freedom of religious belief, practice and teaching; freedom of association and assembly; the natural rights deriving from marriage and paternity and those pertaining to the family, the sanctity of the home, equality before the law, protection from discrimination on account of religion, race, national origin, political or philosophical opinion; freedom from arbitrary deprivation of property.

The foregoing could be taken as examples of the fundamental, undisputed freedoms. I grant you, it is far from complete; there are other freedoms. But we might be content with these to begin with. States would bind themselves by conventions to guarantee these freedoms collectively, within the framework of the Council, by a certain procedure and under the control of a European Court.

They would guarantee these fundamental freedoms in the very near future, in the form of a common definition of each of them, which we could then propose after a period of study.

They would, however, guarantee them immediately, without waiting for this common definition, to the extent that such rights are secured by the constitutions, laws or administrative practice of the respective countries.

They should guarantee these freedoms now, at once, and bind themselves to the observance of the guarantee by an international Convention, signed in the name of Europe.

The same Convention should then create a guaranteeing organ, namely a European Court of Human Rights and a European Commission of Human Rights, within the framework of the Council of Europe.

This Commission could form a kind of barrier—a practical necessity well known to all jurists—which would weed out frivolous or mischievous petitions.

Petitions would be addressed to the Commission which could 'screen' them, retaining only those worthy of serious consideration. These serious petitions would be investigated by the Court. The Court could be composed of nine eminent lawyers, appointed by the Committee of Ministers and by the Consultative Assembly. The Court would give its decision on these petitions. It could set aside governmental decisions, and legislative, administrative or legal measures which were clearly contrary to the principle of the guaranteed rights.

Member States of the Council of Europe, all corporate bodies and all individuals might petition the Court.

The Court would either find that rights and freedoms had been violated, and in that case it would annul the action taken, and, if necessary, prescribe measures for reparation; or it would decide that there had been no violation of the guaranteed rights and freedoms, and that in that case the petition would be dismissed.

...

Mr. President, while I was in the Gestapo prisons, while one of my brothers was at Dachau and one of my brothers-in-law was dying at Mauthausen, my father, who was also a member of our French Parliament, was interned at Buchenwald. He told me that on the monumental gate of the camp was this outrageous inscription: 'Just or unjust, the Fatherland.'

I think that from our first Session we can unanimously proclaim that in Europe there will henceforth only be just fatherlands.

...

Sir David MAXWELL-FYFE (United Kingdom).—In order to appreciate the significance of the proposal which has been put before us so well and so movingly by my friend and colleague in this field, M. Teitgen, it is necessary to envisage the suggestion for a Convention and a Court of Human Rights both in the light of the aims of the Council of Europe and the present position of Europe. This has been the basis of the work of the European Movement on this subject since our conference at The Hague.

With regard to the Council of Europe, three points must be in our minds: the first, as the Statute says, is the method of achieving the aims of the Council and the maintenance and further realisation of human rights and fundamental freedoms. The very word 'further' means that we cannot rest, that we must proceed with this task. Second, it is important to make clear the minimum standard consistent with membership of our body. This is the condition precedent to the general acceptance of the moral basis of our further activities.

Third, Sir, the creation and working of the machinery for the agreement and enforcement of human rights will be an effective method of promoting integration in Europe by means of functional co-operation. Especially will this be so if we accept a means of international assurance that these rights will continue.

From the world point of view we cannot let the matter rest at a declaration of moral principles and pious aspirations, excellent though the latter may be. There must be a binding convention, and we have given you a practical and workable method of bringing this about.

...

Our European Convention is a practical proposition, and will not be faced with the same initial difficulties as a Convention on a world-wide scale. If it can come into existence reasonably soon, it will assist those who are trying to work out a world-wide Convention, by showing them how it will work in practice between States who are accustomed, by legal and political tradition, to enforcing the fundamental rights of man.

With that background in mind, Mr. President, let us consider the most important aspect of our proposals and the criticisms suggested.

In Article I of our project there is set out a short list of basic personal rights. Those rights are all understood, for we are dealing with domestic rights, and negative rights or freedoms which, in any system of law, will be found to be more fundamental than even positive rights. Our list, it is true, contains none of the so-called economic or social rights which appear in the U.N.O. Declaration. Such rights would, in my view, be too controversial and difficult of enforcement even in the changing state of social and international development in Europe, and their inclusion would jeopardise the acceptance of the Convention. Examples, on which I need not expatiate, are the right to free choice of employment, and the right, unknown to you, I am sure, Mr. President, of rest or leisure.

...

Our second Article sets out the fundamental principles of democracy which the contracting States must all respect. It includes, as I have said, the right to organise political opposition, with the implication of the right to nominate opposition candidates at elections.

I have stated that the list has been shortened, and I wish to say a word about the criticism adumbrated by Mr. Ungoed-Thomas that the rights have not been defined with sufficient precision for legal enforcement. I think that this is a highly disputable thesis. The old view that judges took no cognisance of the facts of life is, fortunately, becoming less and less tenable. With some experience in propounding judicial issues before international tribunals, and the experience which we have all had as legislators in clarifying such issues for our national courts, I take leave to doubt whether the task of enforcement would be insurmountable in respect of our draft.

I am entitled to crave in aid the Bill of Rights in the Constitution of the United States as a parallel and a very successful piece of experience. The Supreme Court of the United States of America has not found it difficult to administer and enforce the Bill of Rights in general terms.

...

I come now to the vexed question, which has been so often in our minds during the last few days, of the surrender of sovereignty. Of course this proposal is a new departure. It is an international assurance of what ordinary people want.

Like all treaties, the proposed Convention would involve some voluntary surrender of sovereignty: namely, the sovereign right to suppress liberty and democratic institutions. I cannot imagine that any Member State of the Council of Europe would wish to insist upon this power, or that their citizens would not be happier if it did not exist.

But that is not the only answer. The Governments of the peoples represented here have publicly proclaimed their earnest desire to create a supranational authority. All the Members of U.N.O. are morally bound by the Declaration of Human Rights and committed in principle to trying to make a binding treaty or covenant for the preservation of fundamental human liberties. I have already mentioned our own Statute. Therefore, it is crystal clear that the draft Convention before this Assembly proposes nothing for which the States concerned are not pledged to work, through both U.N.O. and the Council of Europe. The difference—and it is a great one—is that we ask our countries to face up to action at once, which is so simple and practical that it will take effect immediately.

Now let us look for a moment at the criticism from the other end of the scale—that because there is no international police force the Court will be impotent. I point out that under Article 14 the matter can be brought before the Council of Europe, which can take such action as it may consider appropriate. But before we consider such action, I ask my colleagues to estimate the effect of a judgment with the moral prestige of the Court behind it. All Governments are reluctant to be regarded and held up as violators of their people's liberty.

...

The Consultative Assembly established a Committee on Legal and Administrative Questions, chaired by Sir David Maxwell-Fyfe. That Committee produced a report, written by M. Teitgen, advocating the drafting of a Convention protecting ten basic human rights. The Consultative Assembly recommended that the Committee of Ministers should undertake such a process. In November 1949 the Committee of Ministers appointed a committee of government experts to draft a human rights Convention. The experts utilized the Teitgen report and agreed many of the elements of a draft Convention. On some issues (e.g. whether the Convention rights should be defined in detail or expressed in general terms) the experts were divided and in regard to others (such as whether a European Court should be created) the experts decided that they were political decisions that should be left to the Committee of Ministers. The latter body resolved, in April 1950, to hold a conference of senior officials to determine the unresolved issues. In June 1950 the senior officials agreed most of the text of a draft Convention. Some rights were elaborated whilst others were left in general terms. The proposed European Court was given an optional jurisdiction. Whether there should be a right of petition by individual complainants was referred back to the Committee of Ministers. In August 1950 the Committee of Ministers agreed a draft Convention incorporating a conditional right of individual petition and optional jurisdiction for the Court. This draft was weaker than the Consultative Assembly's proposals. Despite further criticisms of the Ministers' draft by the Assembly's Legal Committee, the Committee of Ministers rejected most of them and approved the final text based upon the August draft. The Convention for the Protection of Human Rights and Fundamental Freedoms (subsequently generally referred to as the European Convention on Human Rights) was opened for signature at the Committee of Ministers' meeting in Rome on 4 November 1950.

The Legal Committee's (of the Consultative Assembly) suggestion that three additional rights (encompassing the right to property, the right to education, and political liberties) should be included in the Convention was referred to the government experts by the Committee of Ministers. During 1951 they drafted a Protocol to the Convention, in dialogue with the Consultative Assembly's Legal Committee, guaranteeing protection of property, the right to education, and the right to free elections. The Protocol was opened for signature in May 1952.

From the above account (drawing heavily upon A. H. Robertson's introductory narrative to the *Travaux Préparatoires* of the Convention) we can discern the interaction between the different organs of the nascent Council of Europe during the creation of the Convention. The governments of the member States, acting through the Committee of Ministers, were the dominant actors as they had the final say over the text of the Convention. Nevertheless, the Consultative Assembly through the work of leading figures, including Teitgen and Maxwell-Fyfe, made a significant contribution to the substance of the Convention. From the extracts of the debates in the Consultative Assembly we also gain an understanding of some of the major forces shaping the arguments in favour of the Convention. They include the delegates' personal experiences of the atrocities committed by the Nazis and their allies in the recent past, the current threat to personal liberties posed by the communist regimes in Central and Eastern Europe, and the United Nation's initial steps towards the development of a global system of human rights (for a study of the links between the Universal Declaration of Human Rights and the Convention see A. Mowbray, 'The ECHR' in M. A. Baderin and M. Ssenjonjo (eds), *International Human Rights: Six Decades After the UDHR and Beyond* (Farnham: Ashgate, 2010), ch 14).

Professor A. W. Brian Simpson in his major study of the British contribution to the creation of the Convention noted: '[t]he story, as I tell it, is that the European Convention and its First Protocol were the product of conflicts, compromise, and happenstance. There is no simple answer to the question why the members of the Council of Europe signed the Convention in November 1950 and its First Protocol in 1952', *Human Rights and the End of Empire*

(Oxford: Oxford University Press, 2001), vii. Regarding the conflicts and compromise between States during the creation of the Convention Dr Elizabeth Wicks has observed:

During the process of drafting the ECHR, two opposing schools of thought emerged from the participating states. One group of states approved the approach taken in the draft prepared by the Consultative Assembly of the Council of Europe by which rights were expressed in terms of general principles. Another group of states, including most vociferously the United Kingdom, argued for a more narrowly defined series of rights. The disagreement may be in part a legacy of the different approaches of the common law and civil law systems, although a few states with civil law systems did share the United Kingdom's view (the Netherlands, Norway, Denmark and Greece). The existence of these two schools of thought meant that a compromise was required, but the compromise draft did not seek to bridge the gap between the two opposing views. Instead, the United Kingdom was successful in promoting most of its favoured provisions into the draft with only a few concessions (albeit on matters of great significance, most noticeably individual petition and a permanent European Court of Human Rights).

. . .

Why was the United Kingdom so successful at winning concessions during the negotiation process? Although the representatives of the United Kingdom at no stage explicitly threatened to withdraw from the negotiating process, or to refuse to sign the final Convention, the other negotiators were in no doubt about the strength of feeling on the part of the United Kingdom. For example, the report to the Committee of Ministers submitted by the Committee of Experts (which outlined the views of the United Kingdom government in greater detail than that of other states) quoted the United Kingdom view that precise definitions were an 'essential prerequisite to any Convention' (*Travaux Preparatoires*, vol IV, p. 10) . . .

While the United Kingdom broadly achieved the definition of rights it sought, it was less successful with regard to implementation measures. The acceptance of optional clauses on an individual petitions system and a permanent European Court of Human Rights, both of which the United Kingdom was opposed to at the early stages of negotiations, were the price paid by the United Kingdom for its success on other issues. [E. Wicks, 'The United Kingdom Government's Perceptions of the European Convention on Human Rights at the Time of Entry' [2000] *Public Law* 438 at 439–40.]

According to Professor D. Nicol:

the negotiators were split into two camps with competing ideologies. One camp believed that the ECHR should indeed only serve to protect existing rights, the other camp pursued the more ambitious goal of a cross-frontier Bill of Rights. Some have sought to explain this gulf by reference to the distinction between common law and civil law systems. This may have played a part, but a more compelling explanation relates to constitutional culture. Countries with a strong faith in a written constitution enshrining supra-legislative rights were pitted against countries where the political culture did not favour review of parliamentary legislation. To be sure, there were Left–Right divisions on issues such as property ownership which split even representatives of the same state along party lines. When it came, however, to the overall aim of the ECHR, Assembly members tended to divide on national lines. This indicates the strength of the constitutional culture within each country. [D. Nicol, 'Original Intent and the European Convention on Human Rights' [2005] *Public Law* 152 at 170–1.]

The British (Labour) Government, under Prime Minister Harold Wilson, accepted the right of individuals to petition the European Commission of Human Rights in respect of alleged breaches of their Convention rights by the UK (but not in regard to matters occurring in dependent territories) from 1966. At the same time the British Government also accepted the jurisdiction of the European Court of Human Rights. Lord Lester QC has identified, *inter alios*, Lord McNair (the first President of the European Court of Human Rights) and the Lord Chancellor (Lord Gardiner) as significant figures supporting the taking of these steps by the government (see Lord Lester, 'UK Acceptance of the Strasbourg Jurisdiction: What Really went on in Whitehall in 1965' [1998] *Public Law* 237).

After the adoption of the ECHR and its First Protocol the member States have undertaken a number of modifications to the institutional arrangements provided for in the original Convention (e.g. the creation of the full-time Court under Protocol 11). They have also extended the rights/freedoms that States will respect by creating additional Protocols that individual States can ratify (e.g. abolishing the use of the death penalty in peacetime under Protocol 6). The method of drafting these further Protocols has broadly followed the pattern established during the creation of the Convention. The Committee of Ministers has made the big decisions on matters of principle and policy (such as the decision to replace the European Commission of Human Rights and the part-time Court with a single full-time Court) and utilized a committee of government experts to produce detailed proposals for the draft text of the new Protocol. The Parliamentary Assembly (formerly the Consultative Assembly) has also been involved in these processes of reform (e.g. by agreeing formal Recommendations to the Committee of Ministers). Depending upon the complexity and political sensitivity of the reform proposals it can take many years for the recognition of the need for a new Protocol and the agreeing of its text (over ten years in respect of Protocol 11).

Dr Ed Bates has identified four stages in the development of the Convention. First, the 'genesis' of the Convention, between 1948–50. Secondly, the 'formative phase', from 1950–74, when the Strasbourg enforcement mechanisms were established and began to determine the small number of complaints brought under the ECHR. Thirdly, the 'judicial phase', between 1974–98, when the original Court started to deliver significant judgments and the Convention evolved into a 'European Bill of Rights'. Finally, the era of the permanent Court since 1998. See E. Bates, *The Evolution of the European Convention on Human Rights* (Oxford: Oxford University Press, 2010).

2 THE STRASBOURG SYSTEM FOR DETERMINING APPLICATIONS UNDER THE CONVENTION

Introduction

Three major eras can be distinguished in the development of the Strasbourg institutional system. The original tri-partite structure of the Commission, Court, and Committee of Ministers operated until the full-time Court (Protocol 11 system) began to function in 1998. However, the Protocol 11 system built upon the institutional, procedural, and jurisprudential heritage of the original structures. Therefore, a brief overview of the original decision-making bodies and their processes will be given before the Protocol 11 system is outlined. Then Protocol 14 added new reforms and it became fully operational in June 2010. Finally, we shall consider the process of the Council of Europe contemplating future reforms of the current system.

The original system

As Figure 2.1 reveals, the determination of applications under the original system was the shared responsibility of three institutions: the European Commission of Human Rights, the European Court of Human Rights, and the Committee of Ministers of the Council of Europe.

The European Commission of Human Rights came into existence in 1954 and, under Article 20 (of the pre-Protocol 11 text of the European Convention on Human Rights), it was composed of a number of members equal to the number of States that were parties to the Convention. Individual members of the Commission were elected by the Committee of Ministers from a list (normally of three persons in ranked order) submitted by the Parliamentary Assembly of the Council of Europe. No two members of the Commission could be nationals of the same State. Members were elected for six-year terms of office and could be re-elected. Under the former Article 23 of the Convention, members of the Commission were to sit as independent persons and not as representatives of the States in respect of which they were elected. In 1990 the Convention was amended, by Protocol 8,

Fig. 2.1 The original Strasbourg system for determining applications under the Convention

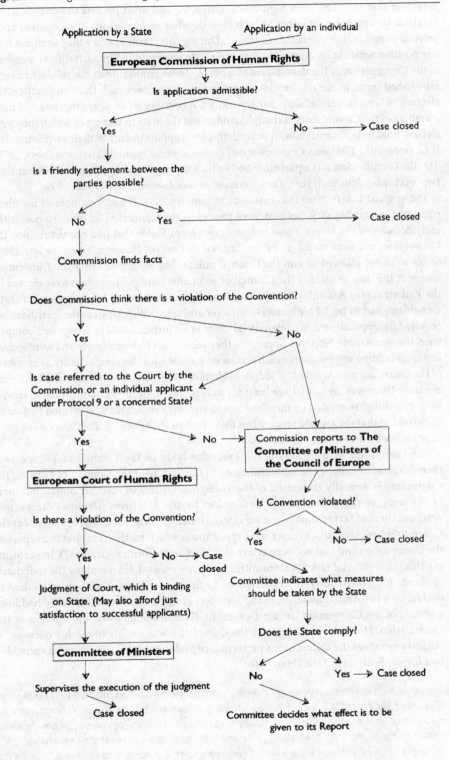

formally to strengthen the stature and independence of the Commission members by requiring that they be: '...of high moral character and must possess the qualifications required for appointment either to high judicial office or be persons of recognised competence in national or international law.... During their term of office they shall not hold any position which is incompatible with their independence and impartiality as members of the Commission or the demands of this office.' These requirements consolidated a well-established trend in the nomination and election of members such that: 'in practice, the election of Government officials has generally not been regarded as appropriate and most members of the Commission, although nationals of the State in respect of which they were elected, hold independent judicial or academic legal appointments in their own countries', F. G. Jacobs, *The European Convention on Human Rights* (Oxford: Clarendon Press, 1975), 217. The Commission was a part-time body which during its final years met for about eight two-weekly sessions each year. The Commission was dissolved in October 1999.

The original Court came into existence in January 1959. It had a number of members equal to the number of States that were parties to the Council of Europe. Hence in the early decades of the Court it had judges drawn from States that had not yet ratified the Convention, but were members of the Council of Europe. However, from the late 1980s States were not allowed to join the Council unless they agreed to ratify the Convention (either at the time of joining the Council or soon afterwards). The judges were elected by the Parliamentary Assembly from a list of candidates nominated by each member State. Candidates had to be, 'of high moral character and must either possess the qualifications required for appointment to high judicial office or be jurisconsults of recognised competence' (former Article 39). Once appointed they were to act independently and were forbidden from holding any position which was incompatible with their impartiality as members of the Court (former Article 40). Judges held office for nine years and were eligible for re-election. There was no formal age limit for judges, although the Parliamentary Assembly (unsuccessfully) requested its members not to vote for candidates who refused to give an undertaking that they would retire when they reached the age of 75. The Court was a part-time body which held sessions each month.

The Committee of Ministers is the executive body of the Council of Europe and, therefore, has its constitutional foundations in the Statute of the Council of Europe. The Committee is formally composed of the Foreign Ministers of member States, but most of the work of the Committee is undertaken by the Ministers' Deputies (ambassadorial members of States' diplomatic services). Under the original Convention system the Committee had, *inter alia*, to determine applications which had been subject to a report by the Commission and had not been referred to the Court (former Article 32). In performing this quasi-judicial task the Committee sat *in camera* and did not allow the individual applicant (or his/her lawyer) to participate in the proceedings. The Committee had to decide, by a two-thirds majority of the members entitled to sit, whether there had been a breach of the Convention. In most cases the Committee followed the opinion of the Commission. However, in a few cases the Committee was unable to reach a decision. A critical analysis of the Committee's performance under the original system was provided by a former Secretary of the Committee.

The Ministers' Deputies are generally career diplomats, namely, the Permanent Representatives of member States at the Council of Europe. They act, in human rights cases as in other matters, on instructions from their capitals. They usually have no special training or competence to deal with human rights issues. They are trained to defend State interests—or what their central authority regards as interests of their State—and, if necessary, to seek compromise solutions; they are not trained to make clear-cut legal pronouncements on human rights issues. When their own State is 'in the dock' they will have a natural inclination to defend it. When other States are concerned they may find it inopportune, embarrassing or even indecent to judge their human rights performance, unless it is considered as being in the interest of their own State to do so, which is not often the case within this group of, in principle, 'likeminded' States. [Peter Leuprecht, 'The Protection of Human Rights By Political Bodies—The Example of the Committee of Ministers of the Council of Europe' in M. Nowak and D. Steurer (eds), *Progress in the Spirit of Human Rights* (Kehl am Rhein: Engel, 1988), 98 and 106–7.]

One of the fundamental improvements in the system of determining applications introduced by Protocol 11 (examined below) was the abolition of the Committee of Ministers' original decision-making role in respect of applications described above. With the ending of the former USSR's domination of Central and Eastern Europe, and the subsequent emergence of many new democracies, the Committee of Ministers now contains representatives from 47 States.

The Protocol 11 system

In the early 1980s the idea began to develop at Strasbourg that it might be desirable for the Commission and the Court to merge into one institution, so as to facilitate greater efficiency in the determination of the increasing number of complaints being brought under the Convention. In 1985 the Swiss Government supported this idea. Four years later a Committee of Experts, which was ultimately accountable to the Committee of Ministers, produced a report which summarized arguments for (e.g. simplifying the control system for applicants) and against (e.g. prejudicing the encouragement of friendly settlements by the Commission) the notion of merging the two bodies. The Committee of Experts concluded that in its view, 'no single and decisive argument for or against a merger has been found' (Document H(89)2, para 57). Subsequently the Committee of Experts drew up an outline structure for a new single full-time Court (Document DH-PR(90)6). Because of political deadlock amongst States over the benefits of creating such a court, the Dutch and Swedish Governments suggested the creation of a two-tier judicial control system:

The central idea in both proposals is that the opinions of the Commission . . . would be transformed into legally binding decisions. In other words, there would be established a two-tier judicial system, i.e. the Commission would operate like a court of first instance from which individual applicants and States would be accorded the right of appeal to the Court against the Commission's decisions on the merits, subject to leave to appeal being granted by the Court . . . [Report to the Steering Committee for Human Rights, 23 March 1992, para 8]

The Committee of Experts was divided over the desirability of the Dutch–Swedish proposal. However, a majority of the Commission supported it. A minority of the Court favoured the creation of a new single Court and this form of institutional reform was also backed by the Parliamentary Assembly of the Council of Europe. [See further, A. Mowbray, 'Reform of the Control System of the European Convention on Human Rights' [1993] *Public Law* 419.]

By May 1993 the Committee of Ministers had reached a political decision to approve the idea of creating a new single Court. However, the price of States' acceptance of the single Court was the demand that the new Court provide a mechanism for the re-hearing of exceptional cases, with the national judge participating in that process. This unusual requirement, that a single court provide the possibility of a second judgment on the merits, was a political compromise analogous to the original Convention agreement concerning the various functions of the Commission, Court, and Committee of Ministers. Some States were reluctant to grant individual applicants the right of direct access to the new Court, however this was also included in Protocol 11. [See further, A. Mowbray, 'A New European Court of Human Rights' [1994] *Public Law* 540.]

Protocol 11 created a new full-time European Court of Human Rights. Although the new Court had the same title as the original Court, it was an entirely different body with new functions, powers, and composition. Judges were elected, by the Parliamentary Assembly, in respect of each State which was a party to the Convention. They were appointed for a six-year term of office and could be re-elected. This reduction in the length of the term of office compared to their predecessors (which was unsuccessfully opposed by the Parliamentary Assembly) was another reflection of States' continuing cautious attitude towards the Strasbourg control system. Judges had to retire when they reached the age of 70. The introduction of a compulsory age limit on judges was opposed by the old Court, but enshrined in Protocol 11 on the grounds that the workload faced by the judges of the full-time Court would be much more demanding than that undertaken by the former part-time judges. The qualifications for office and the obligation to be independent from national States required of the judges were exactly the same as those demanded of the members of the old Court.

The old Court ceased to exist at the end of October 1998. Complex transition arrangements were contained in Protocol 11 for cases pending before the old Court and Commission. The latter body continued to function for one year after the creation of the new Court. Protocol 11 did not alter the definition of inter-State applications (Article 33) or individual applications (Article 34). Likewise, the former admissibility criteria applicable to both types of applications were retained (Article 35). Under Protocol 11, Committees composed of three judges were empowered unanimously to declare inadmissible individual applications. Chambers, consisting of seven judges, would determine the admissibility and merits of inter-State applications and the merits of admissible individual applications. The new Court also assumed responsibility for seeking to secure friendly settlements of cases. When the new Court found a violation of the Convention it could award 'just satisfaction' (Article 41). The Committee of Ministers retained responsibility for supervising the execution of the new Court's judgments (Article 46). See Figure 2.2.

The Protocol 14 system

Background

Within a few months of the full-time Court beginning to operate under the Protocol 11 system President Wildhaber started publicly expressing concern about the rising caseload facing the Court. In June 1999 he issued a press release noting:

> ...The volume of work is already daunting but is set to become more challenging still, especially as applications come in from countries which ratified the ECHR in the late 1990s.

Fig. 2.2 The Protocol 11 Strasbourg system for determining applications under the Convention

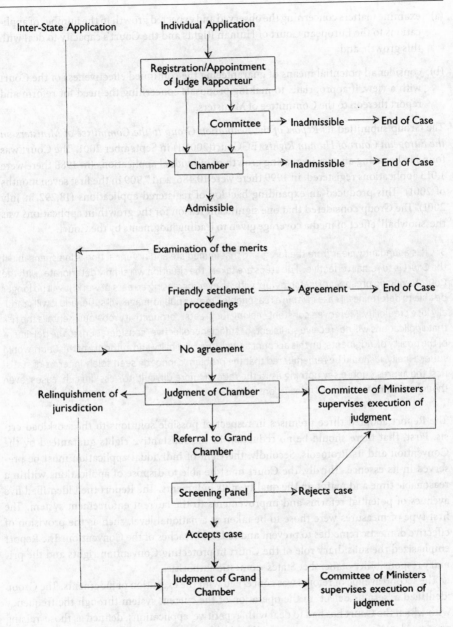

One year later he called upon member States to appoint a 'committee of wise persons' to consider further major reform of the Convention's enforcement system. The Committee of Ministers responded by establishing an Evaluation Group (Chaired by Mr Justin Harman (Ambassador of Ireland to the Council of Europe), President Wildhaber, and

Mr Hans-Christian Kruger (Deputy Secretary General of the Council of Europe), in February 2001 to:

(a) examine matters concerning the observed and expected growth in the number of applications to the European Court of Human Rights and the Court's capacity to deal with this growth; and

(b) consider all potential means of guaranteeing the continued effectiveness of the Court with a view, if appropriate, to making proposals concerning the need for reform and report thereon to the Committee of Ministers.

The Group submitted its *Report of the Evaluation Group to the Committee of Ministers on the European Court of Human Rights* (EGCourt(2001)1) in September 2001. The Court was found to be facing an ever increasing growth of individual applications (in 1988 there were 1,013 applications registered, in 1999 there were 10,486, and 7,909 in the first seven months of 2001). This produced an expanding backlog of registered applications (18,292 in July 2001). The Group considered that one significant reason for the growth in applications was the 'snowball' effect of media coverage given to leading judgments by the Court.

> 3.9. It is abundantly clear from the foregoing that immediate and urgent action is indispensable if the Court is to remain effective. If no steps are taken, the situation will simply deteriorate, with the Court having no prospect of 'catching-up' with its ever-increasing arrears of work. It will no longer be able to determine all cases within a reasonable time, its public image will suffer and it will gradually lose credibility. Moreover, constant seeking for greater 'productivity' obviously entails the risk that applications will not receive sufficient, or sufficient collective, consideration, to the detriment of the quality of judgments; on this account as well, the credibility and authority of the Court would suffer. Finally, it should be remembered that the problem cannot be seen solely in terms of statistics; the figures quoted say nothing as to the ratio of 'more difficult' to 'less difficult' cases, even though it may be that this will remain constant.

The Report adopted three premises in respect of possible solutions to the workload crisis. First, that there should be no reduction in the substantive rights guaranteed by the Convention and its Protocols. Secondly, the right of individual application must be preserved in its essence. Thirdly, the Court must be able to dispose of applications within a reasonable time and maintain the quality of its judgments. The Report then identified five avenues of potential reforms and improvements to the current enforcement system. The first type of measures were those to be taken at a national level, such as the provision of effective domestic remedies to prevent and redress breaches of the Convention. The Report emphasized the subsidiary role of the Court in protecting Convention rights and the primary responsibility of member States' domestic authorities.

The second avenue of reform was concerned with the execution of judgments. The Group identified a 'serious defect' in the operation of the current system through the frequency with which the Court has had to deal with 'repetitive' applications, defined as those 'raising an issue identical or very similar to one already determined in a judgment finding a violation of the Convention'. The Group observed that if appropriate general measures had been taken by the various respondent States after the initial judgments then further applications would not have been necessary. The Report proposed the creation of a special procedure to deal with such cases. When the Court gave a judgment finding a violation in a particular case if the Registry was aware that there were a number of other applications raising a similar issue it would notify the Committee of Ministers. The later body would deal with the execution of the judgment in the lead case by an expedited process. In the meantime all the similar pending applications would be stayed by the Court for an (unspecified) period to allow the respondent State to take the necessary corrective measures. The Group believed that this new procedure would allow the Committee of Ministers 'to exert special pressure on the State concerned and could reduce the need for the Court to deliver a series of purely repetitive judgments on the merits.'

The third category of reforms were those which could be taken by the Court without the need for amendment of the Convention. The Report endorsed proposals emerging from the Court to provide variable levels of treatment for cases depending upon their nature and content; for example applications which were obviously far-fetched and those not satisfying the Rules of Court would no longer be registered. The Report also supported the idea that the Court should become more 'pro-active' in seeking to encourage the friendly settlement of cases; for example financial incentives for applicants to settle 'might be reinforced if there was a practice on the part of the Court of depriving them—in its awards of "just satisfaction"—of part of their costs in cases where they had declined a settlement offer deemed by the Court to be reasonable.'

The fourth avenue of reform was concerned with financial resources. The Report recommended a phased expansion of Registry personnel by approximately 50 per cent over the next four years.

The final, and most dramatic, reforms proposed by the Report involved amendments to the Convention. These were necessary because even if the above procedural reforms and extra resources were implemented the Court would soon reach saturation point and the quality of its judgments could be in danger. The Court should be given the discretion to focus its detailed attention on those cases which merited such consideration. Therefore, the Report recommended that the Convention be amended to empower the Court 'to decline to examine in detail applications which raise no substantial issue under the Convention'. Also, the term of office of the judges should be extended to a single fixed term of not less than nine years. Thereby, strengthening the independence and continuity of the Court.

The Committee of Ministers issued a Declaration *On the protection of Human Rights in Europe Guaranteeing the long-term effectiveness of the European Court of Human Rights* (8 November 2001), 'warmly welcoming' the Report of the Evaluation Group. The Ministers' Deputies were instructed to 'pursue urgent consideration' of the recommendations in the Report. Subsequently, the Steering Committee of Human Rights (CDDH), a group of experts appointed by the Committee of Ministers, began considering detailed reforms. Their *Final Report Containing Proposals of the CDDH* (4 April 2003) identified two main areas of workload problems for the Court. Dealing with thousands of applications which are eventually determined without a judgment on their merits and adjudicating upon repetitive cases. The Report considered that in the light of these statistics a 'thorough reassessment of the manner in which the Convention system works' was needed. The three-judge Committees of the Court, which under Protocol 11 were empowered unanimously to declare an application inadmissible, should have their jurisdiction extended to allow them (unanimously) to rule on the merits of *manifestly well-founded* applications where the subject matter of the particular case is already governed by established jurisprudence of the Court. Hence there would be a considerable efficiency gain in judicial time. The Report accepted that this proposal would end the mandatory participation of the 'national' judge in all cases concerning his/her home State. However, the Report considered that such participation is 'often unnecessary' as these cases would be limited to those governed by established jurisprudence of the Court.

By far the most controversial recommendation in the Report concerning the processing of cases by the Court was directed at adding a further criterion of admissibility for individual applicants. The CDDH rejected the earlier Evaluation Group's suggestion that the Court be granted the power not to examine in detail applications raising no substantial issue under the Convention. In the opinion of the CDDH such a formulation would accord 'too wide a discretion to the Court enabling it to pick and choose the cases it would wish to deal with'. A 'large majority' of the CDDH favoured the addition of the following criterion:

> The Court shall declare inadmissible any individual application…if the applicant has not suffered a significant disadvantage and if the case raises neither a serious question affecting the interpretation or application of the Convention or the protocols thereto, nor a serious issue of general importance.

The thrust behind this proposal was to save the Court from having to determine 'minor' complaints, examples being length of civil proceedings cases involving less than a few hundred euros or disputes between neighbours. 'Several' members of the CDDH favoured a wider definition of the new criterion that would allow the Court to declare inadmissible applications 'if such a decision does not place the applicant at a significant disadvantage…'

The third category of proposed reforms were measures designed to improve and accelerate the execution of judgments. They included developing the procedures of the Committee of Ministers to prioritize the supervision of the execution of Court judgments disclosing systemic defects in member States. Giving the Committee of Ministers the power to institute infringement proceedings, before the Grand Chamber of the Court, against any State which persistently fails to comply with a judgment of the Court. The CDDH envisaged that such a procedure could lead to the Grand Chamber imposing financial penalties on a recalcitrant State.

The Committee of Ministers considered the CDDH Report at its May 2003 meeting and issued a Declaration 'welcoming' and 'endorsing' the Report (*Guaranteeing the long-term effectiveness of the European Court of Human Rights* CM(2003)62). The Committee of Ministers expressed the wish to consider a draft amending Protocol to the Convention, based upon the CDDH recommendations, in one year's time.

The CDDH presented the Committee of Ministers with its *Final Activity Report* in April 2004. The Report contained, *inter alia*, a draft Protocol 14 and an Explanatory Report concerning the draft Protocol. The latter Report explained that the draft Protocol did not make 'radical' changes to the existing Strasbourg enforcement system, but sought to improve the operation of that system so as to allow the Court to concentrate upon the most important cases. The Committee of Ministers invited the Parliamentary Assembly to give its opinion on the draft Protocol. The Assembly delivered its Opinion (No 251, on 28 April 2004), in which it, *inter alia*, criticized the proposed new admissibility criterion and complained that it had only been given two weeks' notice of the draft Protocol. The Committee of Ministers agreed the final text of Protocol 14 at its meeting on 12 May 2004 and the Protocol was opened for signature the next day.

Three significant changes in the Court's handling of cases were introduced in Protocol 14. First, a new decision-making entity 'the single-judge formation' is created under revised Article 26 of the Convention. Such entities, under revised Article 27 of the Convention, are empowered to declare inadmissible or strike out individual applications where such decisions 'can be taken without further examination'. The Explanatory Report notes that single-judge formations will only reach such decisions 'in clear-cut cases, where the inadmissibility of the application is manifest from the outset'. Under revised Article 26 of the Convention, single-judge formations will not determine applications concerning the State in respect of which the judges have been elected. The single-judge formations are assisted by 'rapporteurs' drawn from the Court's Registry. The single judge will have sole responsibility for making determinations but, according to the Explanatory Report:

58....it will be indispensable to create these rapporteur functions in order to achieve the signifi-cant potential increase in filtering capacity which the institution of single-judge formations aims at. The Members of the Registry exercising rapporteur functions will assist the new single-judge formations. In principle, the single judge should be assisted by a rapporteur with knowledge of the language and the legal system of the respondent Party. The function of rapporteur will never be carried out by a judge in this context.

The Court is responsible for determining the number of rapporteurs to be appointed together with the manner and length of their appointments. They may be fixed-term appointments from lawyers having practical experience of member States' legal systems. Of course, according to the Explanatory Report, '...it is understood that the new function of rapporteur should be conferred on persons with a solid legal experience, expertise in the Convention and its case-law and a very good knowledge of at least one of the two official languages of the Council of Europe and who, like the other staff of the Registry, meet the requirements of independence and impartiality.'

The single-judge formation is a novel method of increasing the efficiency of the Court in processing many of the vast majority of applications which are inadmissible. Under Protocol 11, this task had to be undertaken by a three-judge Committee. Hence re-allocating the function to a single-judge formation maximizes the productivity of judges.

The second major change introduced by the Protocol is the expansion of the powers of three-judge Committees. Under revised Article 28 of the Convention these Committees can, unanimously, declare admissible and give a judgment on the merits, at the same time, in respect of cases where the complaint 'is already the subject of well-established case-law of the Court'. The Explanatory Report interprets the phrase as normally meaning: '...case-law which has been consistently applied by a Chamber. Exceptionally, however, it is conceivable that a single judgment on a question of principle may constitute "well-established case-law", particularly when the Grand Chamber has rendered it.' This new power of Committees is aimed at enabling the efficient judicial processing of the numerous admissible cases which raise structural problems in member States that have been previously examined by the Court (e.g. the infamous delays in Italian criminal and civil proceedings breaching the rea-sonable time guarantee contained in Article 6(1) of the Convention). The national judge of the respondent State will not automatically be a member of the Committee as his/her presence is not generally required due to lack of novelty in the substance of the application. However, Committees are given the power to invite the national judge to replace one of the existing members of the Committee. An express factor in Committees' decisions to seek the participation of national judges is whether the respondent State has contested the use of the expedited decision-making process, for example on the ground that the application is materially distinguishable from previous cases. If a Committee is not of the unanimous view that the expedited process should be used then the application is sent to a Chamber, of seven judges, for determination.

The above expansion of the powers of Chambers is another strategy designed to increase the efficiency of the Court by enabling three-judge Committees to determine straightforward applications concerning previously examined structural problems in member States. Applicants should benefit from obtaining swifter judgments on the mer-its of their complaints and States will also be alerted to the ongoing problems in their domestic systems.

The third major reform introduced by Protocol 14 is much more controversial as it involves the addition of a new admissibility criterion for individual applications. The new provision (Article 35(3)(b)) states:

> The Court shall declare inadmissible any individual application submitted under Article 34 if it considers that:…the applicant has not suffered a significant disadvantage, unless respect for human rights as defined in the Convention and the Protocols thereto requires an examination of the application on the merits and provided that no case may be rejected on this ground which has not been duly considered by a domestic tribunal.

It will be for the Grand Chamber and Chambers to elaborate the meaning of 'a significant disadvantage'. Indeed, under Article 20(2) of Protocol 14, for two years following the Protocol's entry into force single-judge formations and Committees will be prevented from utilizing this new criterion. The final element of Article 35(3)(b) is a safeguard that provides, according to the Explanatory Report:

> It will never be possible for the Court to reject an application on account of its trivial nature if the case has not been duly considered by a domestic tribunal. This clause, which reflects the principle of subsidiarity, ensures that, for the purposes of the application of the new admissibility criterion, every case will receive a judicial examination whether at the national level or at the European level.

The Committee on Legal Affairs and Human Rights of the Parliamentary Assembly proposed the addition of this safeguard after noting that many non-governmental organizations (including Amnesty International) were strongly opposed to the creation of a new admissibility criterion (*Report Draft Protocol 14*, Doc 10147, 23 April 2004). The Parliamentary Assembly formally objected to the addition of the new criterion because, '…it is vague, subjective and liable to do the applicant a serious injustice…[i]n addition, it may have the unintended effect of discriminating against female applicants to the Court, by, for example, putting a premium on financial disadvantage suffered', Opinion No 251, at para 11. However, the need to allow the Court greater latitude to focus its resources on the most significant complaints resulted in the Committee of Ministers approving the new criterion with the inclusion of the domestic consideration safeguard.

Protocol 14 also seeks to enhance the effectiveness of the supervision of the execution of the Court's judgments (finding States in breach of the Convention) by the Committee of Ministers. Two new powers are created by the Protocol. First, the Committee of Ministers may, by a vote of two-thirds of representatives, seek a ruling from the Court on the interpretation of a judgment which is problematic (revised Article 46(3) of the Convention). This measure will be used when there is disagreement as to the meaning of the original judgment. Secondly, the ability to bring infringement proceedings against a recalcitrant State has been conferred upon the Committee of Ministers, by revised Article 46(4) of the Convention.

If the Committee of Ministers considers that a High Contracting Party refuses to abide by a final judgment in a case to which it is a party, it may, after serving formal notice on that Party and by a decision adopted by a majority vote of two-thirds of the representatives entitled to sit on the Committee, refer to the Court the question whether that Party has failed to fulfil its obligation under paragraph 1.

The Grand Chamber will then examine whether the respondent State has failed to abide by the original judgment of the Court and inform the Committee of Ministers if there has been a breach of Article 46(1) by the State. According to the Explanatory Report it is envisaged that infringement proceedings will only be necessary in 'exceptional circumstances' but 'the procedure's mere existence, and the threat of using it, should act as an effective new incentive to execute the Court's judgments.' It is noteworthy that the procedure created by Protocol 14 does not authorize the Court, or the Committee of Ministers, to impose any financial penalties if the former concludes that the respondent State has failed to abide by the original judgment. Political pressure on the State generated by the initiation of infringement proceedings and the Grand Chamber's judgment was seen as being sufficient.

Other institutional reforms include according the Council of Europe's Commissioner for Human Rights the right to participate, either via written comments or orally in hearings, in all cases being examined by Chambers or the Grand Chamber. Such interventions may help the Court to identify structural defects in respondent States (and other member States). For example, in *MSS v Belgium and Greece*, judgment of 21 January 2011 (see p 210) the Commissioner expressed his concerns to the Grand Chamber regarding, *inter alia*, Greek legislation and practice governing the determination of claims for asylum. The Convention is also amended to allow the possible future accession of the European Union, though such a development will also require further modifications of the Convention. The term of office of Court judges is altered to a single period of nine years. This is a welcome reversion to the term of office held by judges in the original Court, with the adaptation that under Protocol 14 judges will not be eligible for re-election. Increasing the period of office and preventing re-election should help to enhance the perceived (and possibly the actual) independence of the judges from influence by States. The Parliamentary Assembly has campaigned for a long time for such a period of office.

As Protocol 14 reformed the enforcement system it required the signature and ratification of all member States before it came into effect. By late 2006 all except Russia had ratified, but the Russian Duma blocked the government from doing so (there were suggestions that the Russian political elite was angry about Court judgments finding breaches of the Convention by Russia, especially the case of *Ilascu* (p 67)). Subsequently, leading figures from the Council of Europe, include the President of the Court, publicly called upon Russia to ratify Protocol 14 as the Court desperately needed to be able to utilize the more efficient procedures contained in the Protocol. However, Russia did not ratify. So in October 2008 President Costa suggested to the Committee of Ministers that urgent consideration should be given to developing a mechanism whereby the creation of single-judge formations and the empowering of Committees to determine the merits of repetitive individual applications could be implemented in respect of member States who accepted those reforms. The Committee instructed its expert (CDDH) committee to examine the issue. By spring 2009 CDDH advised that there were two options available. The agreement of all member States to allow individual States formally to accept the provisional use of those reforms in cases brought against them and the creation of a new Protocol that would allow signatory States to approve the use of those reforms in complaints against them. Individual States would be able to choose the option that was most expeditious under their own constitutional arrangements. Protocol 14*bis* was then drafted by the Committee of Ministers and endorsed by the Parliamentary Assembly at the end of April. In early May the Committee of Ministers adopted Protocol 14*bis* and reached the 'Madrid Agreement' whereby parties to Protocol 14 could formally accept the provisional application of the two specified reform measures to complaints against them. This was a remarkably swift agreement of a new Protocol to the Convention (albeit simply containing two of the key components of Protocol 14) and reflected both the desperate workload crisis facing the Court and other States' exasperation with Russia's failure to ratify Protocol 14 (see further A. Mowbray, 'Crisis Measures of Institutional Reform for the European Court of Human Rights' (2009) 9(4) *Human Rights Law Review* 647).

Denmark and Norway immediately ratified Protocol 14*bis* and the UK, Switzerland, Germany, the Netherlands, and Luxembourg made declarations under the Madrid Agreement. Consequently, the first decisions taken by single-judge formations (involving the UK, Germany, the Netherlands, and Denmark) were pronounced during early July

2009 (Press Release by the Registrar: 146 Single Judge decisions adopted, 10 July 2009). December 2009 saw the first judgments on the merits reached by Committees, involving complaints against Germany (Press Release by the Registrar: 21 December 2009). In total 12 States ratified Protocol 14*bis* and ten States made declarations under the Madrid Agreement.

On 18 February 2010, at the beginning of the Interlaken Conference (see p 62), Russia finally ratified Protocol 14. Therefore, Protocol 14*bis* and the Madrid Agreement ceased to be in force on 1 June 2010 when Protocol 14 (and all its reforms) became operational.

Composition of the Court

Under Article 22 of the Convention the appointment of judges to the Court is the shared responsibility of member States and the Parliamentary Assembly of the Council of Europe (composed of members drawn from national legislatures). Each member State must nominate a list of three candidates (who satisfy the criteria under Article 21(1): having 'high moral character' [e.g. not having engaged in acts contrary to the values of the Convention] and either possess the qualifications required for appointment to high judicial office or be 'jurisconsults' [e.g. academics] of recognized competence). The Parliamentary Assembly then elects one of the nominees by means of a majority vote. Significantly, the Convention does not specify how member States should select their nominees. Professor Schermers, a member of the former Commission, was highly critical of the nominations made by some States when the full-time Court was first established.

Some governments nominated candidates who were obviously not fully independent from their governments. Several of the candidates held posts as ambassador...the nominations of several governments convey the impression that political arguments play too important a role in nominations. This harms the reputation of the Court. [H. G. Schermers, 'Election of Judges to the European Court of Human Rights' (1998) 23 *European Law Review* 568 at 574–5.]

He also considered that there had been problems in the Parliamentary Assembly's scrutiny of candidates. The Assembly asked candidates to submit a standard CV and attend an interview before an *ad hoc* sub-committee of the Assembly:

Not all candidates sent their curriculum vitae in accordance with the standard formula. Some candidates thus managed to hide aspects and to underline others. Their curricula vitae were nonetheless accepted.

The interviewing of some 120 candidates proved to be difficult. It was hard to find qualified members for the ad hoc sub-committee charged with the interviewing. Some of the members finally chosen hardly knew the Convention, let alone the case law of the Commission and Court. The interviews were short, between 10 and 15 minutes each.

...The final report of the ad hoc sub-committee was not very satisfactory. Political nominations by some governments, former ambassadors and permanent representatives were accepted...[Schermers, ibid, pp 676–7.]

Subsequently, the Parliamentary Assembly has sought to encourage member States to adopt more open processes for selecting nominees and to enhance the rigour of its own scrutiny of candidates. For example, in 2004 the Assembly passed Recommendation 1649 (2004) Candidates for the European Court of Human Rights [Recommendations are addressed to the Committee of Ministers and their implementation is within the competence of member governments]. The Recommendation stated:

> 2. In order that the European Court of Human Rights continues to command public confidence, it is vital that the process by which judges are selected and appointed must also command confidence.
>
> 3. The Parliamentary Assembly insists that the process of appointment must echo the principles of the democratic method, the rule of law, non-discrimination, accountability and transparency.
>
> ...
>
> 17. ...recalling that the national procedures for selecting candidates are not always satisfactory, it urges member States to publish their procedures for the selection of candidates.
>
> ...
>
> 19. ...the Assembly recommends to the Committee of Ministers to invite the Governments of the member States to ... ensure:
>
>   i. that a call for candidates has been issued through the specialised press;

However, problems still remain in some States regarding the selection process. Consequently, the Parliamentary Assembly agreed Resolution 1646 (2009) Nomination of candidates and election of judges to the European Court of Human Rights which expressed the view that:

> ...Despite a marked improvement in national selection procedures in several countries, there is still significant variance as concerns fairness, transparency and consistency....
>
>   The Assembly also strongly urges the governments of member States which have still not done so, to set up—without delay—appropriate national selection procedures to ensure that the authority and credibility of the Court are not put at risk by ad hoc and politicised processes in the nomination of candidates....

An issue of conflict between the Parliamentary Assembly and some States/the Committee of Ministers has been the under-representation of women on the Court. In 2004 the Parliamentary Assembly formally invited the Committee of Ministers to seek the amendment of the ECHR to include the obligation on member States to include one candidate of each gender on every list of judicial nominations for the Court. The Committee of Ministers replied that it shared the Assembly's desire for a proper balance of the sexes on the Court, but in exceptional circumstances States might only be able to submit a single-gender nominations list if the Article 21 criteria were to be satisfied. The Parliamentary Assembly reacted by passing Resolution 1426 (2005) which stated that:

> 3. The Assembly notes that women are clearly still under-represented in the Court today, as only 11 of the 44 judges currently in office are women.
>
> 5. Accordingly, the Assembly decides to introduce a special rule for considering candidatures for the European Court of Human Rights regarding the under-represented sex in the Court...
>
>   The Assembly decides not to consider lists of candidates where:
>
>   ii. the list does not include at least one candidate of each sex, except when the candidates belong to the sex which is under-represented in the Court, that is the sex to which under 40% of the total number of judges belong.

Applying its new approach the Assembly refused to consider two all-male shortlists submitted by Malta. In response the Maltese Government asked the Committee of Ministers to seek an Advisory Opinion (under Article 47 of the ECHR) from the Court regarding the legality of the gender policy adopted by the Assembly. The Committee made such a request in 2007 asking, *inter alia*:

> can a list of candidates for the post of judge at the European Court of Human Rights, which satisfies the criteria listed in Article 21 of the Convention, be refused solely on the basis of gender-related issues?

After inviting written comments from all the member States and the Parliamentary Assembly, the Grand Chamber delivered its unanimous Advisory Opinion (this was the first substantive Advisory Opinion delivered by the Court) on 12 February 2008: *Advisory Opinion on certain legal questions concerning the lists of candidates submitted with a view to the election of judges to the European Court of Human Rights*. The Grand Chamber considered that whilst States were bound to ensure that all the candidates nominated satisfied the criteria laid down in Article 21, the States could also take into account other criteria; such as a balance between the sexes or different branches of the legal profession. Furthermore:

> 45. ... It is obvious too that the Assembly may take account of additional criteria which it considers relevant for the purposes of choosing between the candidates put forward by a Contracting Party and may, as it has done in a bid to ensure transparency and foreseeability, incorporate those criteria in its resolutions and recommendations. Indeed, neither Article 22 nor the Convention system sets any explicit limits on the criteria which can be employed by the Parliamentary Assembly in choosing between the candidates put forward.

After noting that the Committee of Ministers had not accepted the Parliamentary Assembly's request to amend the Convention regarding the gender of nominees the Advisory Opinion continued:

> 51. In the Court's view, the Contracting Parties, which alone have the power to amend the Convention, have thus set the boundaries which the Assembly may not overstep in its pursuit of a policy aimed at ensuring that the lists include a candidate of the under-represented sex: such a policy must not have the effect of making it more difficult for Contracting Parties to put forward candidates who also satisfy all the requirements of Article 21 § 1, which are accordingly to be given primary consideration ...
>
> 52. ... In any event it is clear that, in not allowing any exceptions to the rule that the under-represented sex must be represented, the current practice of the Parliamentary Assembly is not compatible with the Convention: where a Contracting Party has taken all the necessary and appropriate steps with a view to ensuring that the list contains a candidate of the under-represented sex, but without success, and especially where it has followed the Assembly's recommendations advocating an open and transparent procedure involving a call for candidatures ..., the Assembly may not reject the list in question on the sole ground that no such candidate features on it. Accordingly, exceptions to the principle that lists must contain a candidate of the under-represented sex should be defined as soon as possible.

So the Grand Chamber found that whilst the Committee of Ministers and the Parliamentary Assembly were agreed on the goal of promoting gender equality, the text of the ECHR, combined with States unwillingness to amend it in respect of the gender of judicial nominees, meant that the Assembly's policy was too rigid (see further A. Mowbray, 'The Consideration of Gender in the Process of Appointing Judges to the European Court of Human Rights' (2008) 8(3) *Human Rights Law Review* 549).

In September 2008 the Parliamentary Assembly passed Resolution 1627 (2008), which modified its approach in line with the Advisory Opinion.

The Assembly decides to consider single-sex lists of candidates of the sex that is over-represented in the Court in exceptional circumstances where a Contracting Party has taken all the necessary and appropriate steps to ensure that the list contains a candidate of the under-represented sex, but has not been able to find a candidate of that sex who satisfies the requirements of Article 21 § 1 of the European Convention on Human Rights.

Subsequently a male judge was elected in respect of Malta.

Another unanimous Grand Chamber, on 22 January 2010, delivered a second: *Advisory Opinion on certain legal questions concerning the lists of candidates submitted with a view to the election of judges to the European Court of Human Rights (No 2)*. This concerned the ability of a member State to withdraw its list of judicial nominees before the Parliamentary Assembly had elected the national judge. The origins of the issue had been the Ukrainian Government's attempt to withdraw its whole list after one nominee withdrew (the Ukrainian Council of Judges had expressed the view that one of the nominees had no 'high moral character'!). The Grand Chamber stated that:

49. . . . The High Contracting Parties may withdraw and replace a list of candidates for the post of judge at the Court, but only on condition that they do so before the deadline set for submission of the list to the Parliamentary Assembly. After that date, the High Contracting Parties will no longer be entitled to withdraw their lists.

Therefore Ukraine had been entitled to nominate a new candidate, to replace the one who had withdrawn, but not to submit a new list of three different nominees.

In November 2010, as part of the implementation of the Interlaken Declaration and Action Plan (see p 62), the Committee of Ministers created an Advisory Panel of experts on candidates for election to the Court: Resolution CM/Res(2010)26. This new body was designed to add an extra level of scrutiny into the suitability of State nominees to the Court. The Committee of Ministers appointed seven experts after consultation with the President of the Court. They were: Ms Katarzyna Gonera (Poland, Justice of the Polish Supreme Court); Ms Renate Jaeger (Germany, former Judge at the Strasbourg Court); Chief Justice John L. Murray (Ireland); Mr Matti Pellonpaa (Finland, former Judge at the Strasbourg Court); Professor Sami Selcuk (Turkey, President of the Turkish Supreme Court of Appeal); Professor Luzius Wildhaber (Switzerland, former President of the Strasbourg Court); Mr Valery D. Zorkin (Russian Federation, Chairman of the Constitutional Court of the Russian Federation). The experts serve for three years and can be re-appointed once. Their role is to advise member States if their nominees meet the requirements of Article 21(1). Before a State submits its three nominees to the Parliamentary Assembly it must now send the Panel the CVs of its proposed nominees. If the Panel considers that all the nominees are suitable the State shall be so informed. However, if the Panel has doubts about one or more of the nominees the chair of the Panel will so inform the State. In the light of any comments made by the State the Panel will determine if it considers the nominee(s) not suitable and give (confidential) reasons for such an opinion. The same procedure will be followed for new nominees put forward by the State. The Panel will also give its confidential opinion on nominees' suitability to the Parliamentary Assembly when that body is making the final selection. So, presumably, if a State was to persist in nominating candidates against the 'advice' of the Panel that would be drawn to the attention of the Assembly. The Panel will normally reach its decisions by a written process and adopt opinions on the basis of consensus (failing the latter a majority of five members will be sufficient). Proceedings of the Panel are confidential. If a Panel member is nominated as a candidate for the Court he/she must withdraw from the Panel! This may be a significant (and positive) erosion of some of the discretion States possess to select (unsuitable) nominees.

The full-time Court, sitting in plenary session (under Article 25), elected Luzius Wildhaber as it first President. He had been the Swiss judge on the original Court since 1991. In November 2006, Jean-Paul Costa, the French judge, was elected President to replace the retiring Luzius Wildhaber. Sir Nicolas Bratza, the British judge, who had been a member of the European Commission of Human Rights from 1993 and a judge of the Court since 1998, was elected to succeed the retiring President Costa in November 2011.

Status of the judges

Judges appointed to the Court sit in their individual capacity (Article 21(2)), which means that they are to exercise independent judgement when deciding cases. Their independence is emphasized by the requirement (in Article 21(3)) that during their period of office they must not engage in any activity which is incompatible with their independence (e.g. holding office in a national government). They are also prohibited from taking on any activity which is incompatible with the full-time responsibilities of their office (e.g. any other significant form of work, paid or unpaid). During their term of office judges can only be dismissed by a two-thirds majority of the other judges concluding that a particular judge no longer fulfils the conditions of office (Article 23). This has never occurred.

Organization of the Court

The Court is divided into five Sections. Each Section is balanced in terms of the gender of the judges and the geographical areas of Europe from where they have been nominated. Also, each Section has a membership which takes account of the different legal systems of member States. Each Section is presided over by either a Vice-President of the Court or a Section President (both categories of presidents having been elected by the Court sitting in plenary session). The composition of each Section is fixed for three years. Chambers, composed of seven members, are created within each Section on a rotational basis (the Section President and judge elected in respect of the respondent State always being members of a particular Chamber). Other members of the relevant Section sit as substitute members of the Chamber. Committees, composed of three judges, are established by Chambers for periods of 12 months. The Grand Chamber, composed of 17 members, includes the President, Vice-Presidents, and Section Presidents plus 11 other judges (chosen on a rotational basis).

The Registry of the Court

This body of officials provides legal and administrative support to the Court. The constitutional foundation of the Registry is Article 24 of the Convention. The head of the Registry is the Registrar and he/she is appointed by the plenary Court (under Article 25(e)). The current Registrar, appointed in November 2005, is Erik Fribergh (a Swedish national). Each Section of the Court has a Section Registrar. The Registry is composed of approximately 640 persons (roughly 270 lawyers and 370 support staff, such as administrators and translators). About half the Registry staff are permanent employees of the Council of Europe and the other half are fixed-term employees of the organization. All the staff are required to undertake their work on the basis of independence and impartiality (e.g. they must not seek to favour the interests of their national State). Legally qualified members of the Registry prepare files and analytical notes for the judges (which are highly significant in the processing/determination of applications), but Registry staff do not formally decide cases. In January 2011 a Filtering Section was established within the Registry to streamline the judicial processing of applications from the five States which produce the greatest number of complaints.

Cost of the Court

Under Article 50 the expenditure on the Court shall be borne by the Council of Europe. The budget of the Court is part of the Council of Europe's general budget which is agreed by the Committee of Ministers (member States fund the Council of Europe according to a scheme which takes account of each State's population and Gross National Product). In 2011 the Court's budget amounted to 58.9 million euros. This sum covered the remuneration of judges and staff plus general expenditure (including information technology, translation services, and official journeys), but not the costs of buildings and infrastructure. The judges receive a tax-free salary linked to a specified grade of employment by the Council of Europe (CM/Res(2009)5). In 2011 the salary of a newly elected judge was 187,904 euros (I am grateful to the Court's Press Office for supplying this information). After many years of campaigning by the Court, the judges are now eligible to join medical/social insurance and pension schemes operated by the Council of Europe.

The determination of applications

The Convention provisions dealing with the procedure of the Court have been supplemented by detailed Rules of Court, issued by the plenary Court (composed of all the judges) under Article 25(d). The Rules of Court are regularly revised to take account of changing methods of working by the Court. In 2003 the Court began issuing Practice Directions. The Registry explained that these Directions had two purposes: first, to provide guidance to parties on different facets of their dealings with the Court and, secondly, to introduce more standardized procedures thereby facilitating the Court's processing of cases. They deal with matters including: how requests for interim measures should be communicated to the Court (not by standard post) and the structure of written pleadings (composed of sections replicating judgments of the Court—'facts', 'domestic law and practice', etc). The Practice Directions will be particularly useful for applicants' lawyers who are not experienced in bringing cases at Strasbourg.

In November 2010, the Court issued a Priority Policy which explained that the Court would determine the order in which it adjudicated upon applications on the basis of the importance of the complaint(s) raised. Seven categories of complaints were identified.

1. Urgent applications (in particular risk to life or health of the applicant, other circumstances linked to the personal or family situation of the applicant, particularly where the well-being of a child is at issue, application of Rule 39 of the Rules of Court [i.e. requests for interim measures]).

2. Applications raising questions capable of having an **impact on the effectiveness of the Convention system** (in particular a structural or endemic situation that the Court has not yet examined, pilot-judgment procedure) or applications raising an **important question of**

general interest (in particular a serious question capable of having major implications for domestic legal systems or for the European system), inter-State cases.

3. Applications which on their face raise as main complaints issues under **Articles 2, 3, 4 or 5 § 1** of the Convention ('core rights'), irrespective of whether they are repetitive, and which have given rise to direct threats to the physical integrity and dignity of human beings.

4. Potentially well-founded applications based on other Articles.

5. Applications raising issues already dealt with in a pilot/leading judgment ('repetitive cases').

6. Applications identified as giving rise to a problem of admissibility.

7. Applications which are manifestly inadmissible.

Under this scheme applications falling within higher categories would be examined before those in lower categories (though Chambers retained a discretion to treat a particular application differently). The objective of the policy was to focus the Court's decision-making resources on the most serious complaints and cases revealing new widespread (systemic) problems. Historically, the Court had generally determined applications chronologically according to the date on which they had been lodged.

Fig. 2.3 Protocol 14

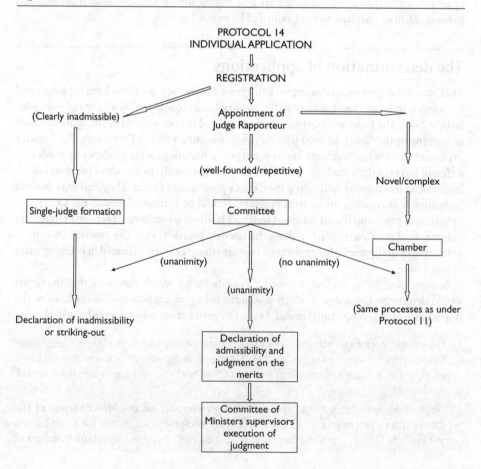

(i) Admissibility

Applications may be brought by member States ('inter-State cases' under Article 33) or persons ('individual applications' under Article 34). Inter-State cases are very rare (only two have resulted in judgments of the Court: *Ireland v UK* A.25 (1978), p 145 and *Cyprus v Turkey* 2001-IV, p 124). This is because the political and economic ties between member States discourage the initiation of 'hostile' applications against a fellow party to the Convention except in the most extreme circumstances (e.g. in *Ireland* where the applicant State alleged widespread violations of Convention rights by the authorities in Northern Ireland and in *Cyprus* where the applicant State alleged that the military occupation of the northern part of Cyprus had resulted in numerous violations of many Convention Articles). The admissibility of inter-State cases is determined by a Chamber (Article 29(2)).

Individual applications are most commonly brought by persons who claim that they have suffered a violation of a right/freedom guaranteed by the Convention. Legal persons may also make an application (e.g. *Krone Verlag GmbH & Co KG v Austria (No 3)*, judgment of 11 December 2003, p 680) as can a non-governmental organization or group of individuals. An example of an applicant that fell within the concept of a non-governmental organization was the *Vereinigung Demokratischer Soldaten Osterreichs* association which published 'The Hedgehog' journal for soldiers, see p 711. Several journalists were considered to be a group of individuals in *Sunday Times v UK* A.30 (1979), p 637. The full-time Court elaborated upon the scope of Article 34 applicants in *Danderyds Kommun v Sweden* (No 52559/99), decision of 7 June 2001. The applicant was a Swedish municipality which sought to challenge the amount of municipal tax it was allocated by the Tax Authority of Stockholm. The Swedish courts refused to hear the challenge. Thereupon, the applicant complained to the Court alleging breaches of its rights under Article 1 of Protocol No 1 and Article 6.

...The Court considers that it should first examine whether, under Article 34 of the Convention, the applicant has locus standi to introduce an application. According to Article 34, the Court may receive applications from 'any person, non-governmental organisation or group of individuals'. The question therefore arises whether the applicant can be deemed to be a non-governmental organisation or a group of individuals within the meaning of that provision.

The applicant notes that previous Convention case-law has emphasised the fact that municipalities perform official duties on behalf of the State, assigned to them by the Constitution and other legislation. However, a Swedish municipality is an independent legal person, acting in its own capacity, which cannot be considered to be exercising its competence on behalf of the Government. Furthermore, in this case the municipalities act with the governmental authorities as their only counterpart. The municipality should therefore be entitled to make an application under Article 34 of the Convention.

The Court notes that the jurisprudence of the Court and the former Commission has already dealt with the question whether a municipality can be considered to be a non-governmental organisation or a group of individuals within the meaning of Article 34 (formerly Article 25) of the Convention (see, e.g. *16 Austrian Communes and some of their Councillors v Austria*, Application Nos 5765/77 et al:, Commission decision of 31 May 1974, Collection 46, p 118; *Commune Rothenthurm v Switzerland*, No. 13252/87, Commission decision of 14 December 1988, Decisions and Reports (DR) 59, p. 251; *The Province of Bari, Sorrentino and Messeni Nemagna v Italy* (dec.), No 41877/98, 22 March 2001; *The Municipal Section of Antilly v France* (dec.), No 45129/98, ECHR 1999-VIII and *Ayuntamiento de Mula v Spain* (dec.), No 55346/00, to be published in ECHR 2001).

According to this jurisprudence it is not only the central organs of the State that are clearly governmental organisations, as opposed to non-governmental organisations, but also decentralised authorities that exercise public functions, notwithstanding the extent of their autonomy vis-à-vis the central organs. This is the case even if the municipality is claiming that in this particular situation it is acting as a private organ.

Moreover, to consider a Swedish municipality a non-governmental organisation is clearly contradicted by the fact that its acts can engage the responsibility of the Swedish State under the Convention. From the Court's perspective the hierarchy between different organs of the State is thus not relevant while examining an application before it. Furthermore, a conflict between a central State organ and a municipality is rather a conflict of jurisdiction which is not for the Court to solve.

Neither can a municipality be considered to be a group of individuals. Such an interpretation would not be compatible with the distinction made between groups of individuals on the one hand and non-governmental organisations on the other.

Turning to the present case, the Court finds that the applicant is clearly a public organ exercising public functions. It must therefore be considered to be a governmental organisation.

It follows that the application is incompatible with the provisions of the Convention within the meaning of Article 35 § 3. The Court must therefore reject the application as being inadmissible *ratione personae*.

Consequently, the unanimous Chamber determined that the application was inadmissible. Hence, it is clear that the Court will not allow disputes between public authorities at different levels of domestic governmental structures to be litigated at Strasbourg. This was confirmed in the later application of ***Demirbas and others v Turkey***, decision of 1 December 2010, where the Chamber declared inadmissible complaints lodged by the former mayor and several councillors concerning the dissolution of a municipal council as a result of legal action brought by the Ministry of the Interior.

All applicants under Article 34 must be claiming that they were the victims of a violation of a right/freedom protected by the Convention (and relevant Protocols) by one (or more) of the member States. The Court elaborated upon the concept of a 'victim' in ***Klass v Germany*** A.28 (1978) (see also p 564) (note, in the original text of the Convention the victim criterion was contained in Article 25). The applicants were lawyers who complained about a German statute, the G10 Act, which allowed the government to authorize the secret interception of designated persons' mail and telecommunications on national security grounds. According to the Court:

...Article 25 requires that an individual applicant should claim to have been actually affected by the violation he alleges... Article 25 does not institute for individuals a kind of *actio popularis* for the interpretation of the Convention; it does not permit individuals to complain against a law *in abstracto* simply because they feel that it contravenes the Convention. In principle, it does not suffice for an individual applicant to claim that the mere existence of a law violates his rights under the Convention; it is necessary that the law should have been applied to his detriment. Nevertheless, as both the Government and the Commission pointed out, a law may by itself violate the rights of an individual if the individual is directly affected by the law in the absence of any specific measure of implementation.

Article 25, which governs the access by individuals to the Commission, is one of the keystones in the machinery for the enforcement of the rights and freedoms set forth in the Convention.... The question arises in the present proceedings whether an individual is to be deprived of the opportunity of lodging an application with the Commission because, owing to the secrecy of the measures objected to, he cannot point to any concrete measure specifically affecting him. In the Court's view, the effectiveness (*l'effet utile*) of the Convention implies in such circumstances some possibility of having access to the Commission. If this were not so, the efficiency of the Convention's enforcement machinery would be materially weakened. The procedural provisions of the Convention must, in view of the fact that the Convention and its institutions were set up to protect the individual, be applied in a manner which serves to make the system of individual applications efficacious. The Court therefore accepts that an individual may, under certain conditions, claim to be the victim of a violation occasioned by the mere existence of secret measures or of legislation permitting secret measures, without having to allege that such measures were in fact applied to him. The relevant conditions are to be determined in each case according to the Convention right or rights alleged to have been infringed, the secret character of the measures objected to, and the connection between the applicant and those measures.

As to the facts of the particular case, the Court observes that the contested legislation institutes a system of surveillance under which all persons in the Federal Republic of Germany can potentially have their mail, post and telecommunications monitored, without their ever knowing this unless there has been either some indiscretion or subsequent notification in the circumstances laid down in the Federal Constitutional Court's judgment... To that extent, the disputed legislation directly affects all users or potential users of the postal and telecommunication services in the Federal Republic of Germany. Furthermore, as the Delegates [of the Commission] rightly pointed out, this menace of surveillance can be claimed in itself to restrict free communication through the postal and telecommunication services, thereby constituting for all users or potential users a direct interference with the right guaranteed by Article 8....

Having regard to the specific circumstances of the present case, the Court concludes that each of the applicants is entitled to '(claim) to be the victim of a violation' of the Convention, even though he is not able to allege in support of his application that he has been subject to a concrete measure of surveillance. [Paras 33, 34, 37, and 38.]

Therefore, generally individual applicants have to show that they were directly affected by some form of State action/inaction if they are to be classified as a 'victim'.

The representatives (family members) of the estates of the deceased terrorists in *McCann v UK* (p 83) were able to lodge their applications against the UK. The full-time Court elaborated upon the circumstances where an application could be continued despite the death of the applicant in *Karner v Austria* (see p 831). The applicant lodged his application with the Commission in July 1997. The application was transferred to the Court in 1998. The applicant died in 2000. During September 2001 the Court declared the application partly admissible. Two months later the applicant's lawyer informed the Court of his client's death and that the applicant's mother had waived her right to succeed to the estate. In the light of the applicant's death and the absence of heirs wishing to continue the case, the government requested the Court to strike out the application (under Article 37(1)). The applicant's lawyer sought the continued examination of the case as he asserted that it involved an important issue of Austrian law. The Chamber held:

22. The Court notes that in a number of cases in which an applicant died in the course of the proceedings it has taken into account the statements of the applicant's heirs or of close family members expressing the wish to pursue the proceedings before the Court (see, among other authorities, *Deweer v Belgium*, judgment of 27 February 1980... and *Raimondo v Italy*, judgment of 22 February 1994, Series A No 281-A, p 8, § 2).23. On the other hand, it has been the Court's practice to strike applications out of the list of cases in the absence of any heir or close relative who has expressed the wish to pursue an application (see *Scherer v Switzerland*, judgment of 25 March 1994, Series A No 287, pp 14–15, § 31; *Öhlinger v Austria*, No 21444/93, Commission's report of 14 January 1997, § 15, unreported; *Malhous v the Czech Republic* (dec.) [GC], No 33071/96, ECHR 2000-XII). Thus, the Court has to determine whether the application in the present case should also be struck out of the list. In formulating an appropriate answer to this question, the object and purpose of the Convention system as such must be taken into account.

24. The Court reiterates that, while Article 33 of the Convention allows each Contracting State to refer to the Court (Commission) 'any alleged breach' of the Convention by another Contracting State, a person, non-governmental organisation or group of individuals must, in order to be able to lodge a petition in pursuance of Article 34, claim 'to be the victim of a violation...of the rights set forth in the Convention or the Protocols thereto'. Thus, in contrast to the position under Article 33—where, subject to the other conditions laid down, the general interest attaching to the observance of the Convention renders admissible an inter-State application—Article 34 requires that an individual applicant should claim to have been actually affected by the violation he alleges (see *Ireland v the United Kingdom*, judgment of 18 January 1978, Series A No 25, pp 90–1, §§ 239–40, and *Klass and Others v Germany*, judgment of 6 September 1978, Series A No 28, pp 17–18, § 33). Article 34 does not institute for individuals a kind of *actio popularis* for the interpretation of the Convention; it does not permit individuals to complain against a law *in abstracto* simply because they feel that it contravenes the Convention (see *Norris v Ireland*, judgment of 26 October 1988, Series A No 142, pp 15–16, § 31, and *Sanles Sanles v Spain (dec.)*, No 48335/99, ECHR 2000-XI).

25. While under Article 34 of the Convention the existence of a 'victim of a violation', that is to say, an individual applicant who is personally affected by an alleged violation of a Convention right, is indispensable for putting the protection mechanism of the Convention into motion, this criterion cannot be applied in a rigid, mechanical and inflexible way throughout the whole proceedings. As a rule, and in particular in cases which primarily involve pecuniary, and, for this reason, transferable claims, the existence of other persons to whom that claim is transferred is an important criterion, but cannot be the only one. As the Court pointed out in *Malhous* (decision cited above), human rights cases before the Court generally also have a moral dimension, which must be taken into account when considering whether the examination of an application after the applicant's death should be continued. All the more so if the main issue raised by the case transcends the person and the interests of the applicant.

26. The Court has repeatedly stated that its 'judgments in fact serve not only to decide those cases brought before the Court but, more generally, to elucidate, safeguard and develop the rules instituted by the Convention, thereby contributing to the observance by the States of the engagements undertaken by them as Contracting Parties' (see *Ireland v the United Kingdom*, cited above, p 62, § 154, and *Guzzardi v Italy*, judgment of 6 November 1980, Series A No 39, p 31, § 86). Although the primary purpose of the Convention system is to provide individual relief, its mission is also to determine issues on public-policy grounds in the common interest, thereby raising the general standards of protection of human rights and extending human rights jurisprudence throughout the community of Convention States.

27. The Court considers that the subject matter of the present application—the difference in treatment of homosexuals as regards succession to tenancies under Austrian law—involves an important question of general interest not only for Austria but also for other States Parties to the Convention. In this connection the Court refers to the submissions made by ILGA-Europe, Liberty and Stonewall, whose intervention in the proceedings as third parties was authorised as it highlights the general importance of the issue. Thus, the continued examination of the present application would contribute to elucidate, safeguard and develop the standards of protection under the Convention.

28. In these particular circumstances, the Court finds that respect for human rights as defined in the Convention and the Protocols thereto requires a continuation of the examination of the case (Article 37 § 1 *in fine* of the Convention) and accordingly rejects the Government's request for the application to be struck out of its list.

The Austrian *ad hoc* Judge dissented as he did not consider the case one of 'general importance'. The judgment in **Karner** is to be welcomed as the Court should be able to determine cases raising significant issues even if the applicant has died during the Strasbourg proceedings and there are no strong personal/family reasons why the case should be struck out.

Article 35(1) imposes two admissibility criteria in respect of both inter-State cases and individual applications. First, the Court can only examine the merits of applications where the applicant (person or State) has exhausted all domestic remedies in regard to the complaint. The Court has explained its approach to this requirement in *Isayeva, Yusupova, Bazayava v Russia*, 24 February 2005 (see p 105).

144. The Court recalls that the rule of exhaustion of domestic remedies referred to in Article 35 § 1 of the Convention obliges applicants first to use the remedies that are normally available and sufficient in the domestic legal system to enable them to obtain redress for the breaches alleged. The existence of the remedies must be sufficiently certain, in practice as well as in theory, failing which they will lack the requisite accessibility and effectiveness. Article 35 § 1 also requires that the complaints intended to be brought subsequently before the Court should have been made to the appropriate domestic body, at least in substance and in compliance with the formal requirements laid down in domestic law, but that no recourse should be had to remedies which are inadequate or ineffective (see the *Aksoy v Turkey* judgment of 18 December 1996, Reports 1996-VI, pp 2275–6, §§ 51–2, and the *Akdivar and Others v Turkey* [1996-IV] p. 1210, §§ 65–7).

145. The Court emphasises that the application of the rule of exhaustion of domestic remedies must make due allowance for the fact that it is being applied in the context of machinery for the protection of human rights that the Contracting States have agreed to set up. Accordingly, it has recognised that Article 35 § 1 must be applied with some degree of flexibility and without excessive formalism. It has further recognised that the rule of exhaustion is neither absolute nor capable of being applied automatically; for the purposes of reviewing whether it has been observed, it is essential to have regard to the circumstances of the individual case. This means, in particular, that the Court must take realistic account not only of the existence of formal remedies in the legal system of the Contracting State concerned but also of the general context in which they operate, as well as the personal circumstances of the applicant. It must then examine whether, in all the circumstances of the case, the applicant did everything that could reasonably be expected of him or her to exhaust domestic remedies (see the *Akdivar and Others* judgment cited above, p 1211, § 69, and the *Aksoy* judgment cited above, p 2276, §§ 53 and 54).

146. The Court observes that Russian law provides, in principle, two avenues of recourse for the victims of illegal and criminal acts attributable to the State or its agents, namely civil procedure and criminal remedies.

147. As regards a civil action to obtain redress for damage sustained through alleged illegal acts or unlawful conduct on the part of State agents, the Court recalls that the Government have relied on two possibilities, namely to lodge a complaint with the Supreme Court or to lodge a complaint with other courts. The Court notes that at the date on which the present application was declared admissible, no decision had been produced to it in which the Supreme Court or other courts were able, in the absence of any results from the criminal investigation, to consider the merits of a claim relating to alleged serious criminal actions. In the instant case, however, the applicants are not aware of the identity of the potential defendant, and so, being dependent for such information on the outcome of the criminal investigation, did not bring such an action.

148. As regards the case of Mr Khashiyev, who had brought a complaint to the Court (No 57942/00), to which the Government refer, it is true that, after receiving the Government's claim that a civil remedy existed, he brought an action before the Nazran District Court in Ingushetia. That court was not able to, and did not, pursue any independent investigation as to the person or persons responsible for the fatal assaults, but it did make an award of damages to Mr Khashiyev on the basis of the common knowledge of the military superiority of the Russian federal forces in the district in question at the relevant time and the State's general liability for the actions by the military.

149. The Court does not consider that that decision affects the effectiveness of a civil action as regards exhaustion of domestic remedies. Despite a positive outcome for Mr Khashiyev in the form of a financial award, it confirms that a civil action is not capable, without the benefit of the conclusions of a criminal investigation, of making any findings as to the identity of the perpetrators of fatal assaults, and still less to establish their responsibility. Furthermore, a Contracting State's obligation under Articles 2 and 13 of the Convention to conduct an investigation capable of leading to the identification and punishment of those responsible in cases of fatal assault might be rendered illusory if, in respect of complaints under those Articles, an applicant would be required to exhaust an action leading only to an award of damages (see *Yaşa v Turkey*, judgment of 2 September 1998, Reports 1998-VI, p 2431, § 74).

150. The Court also notes the practical difficulties cited by the applicants and the fact that the law-enforcement bodies were not functioning properly in Chechnya at the time. In this respect the Court is of the opinion that there existed special circumstances which affected their obligation to exhaust remedies that would otherwise be available under Article 35 § 1 of the Convention.

151. In the light of the above the Court finds that the applicants were not obliged to pursue the civil remedies suggested by the Government in order to exhaust domestic remedies, and the preliminary objection is in this respect unfounded.

152. As regards criminal law remedies, the Court observes that a criminal investigation was instituted into the attack on the refugee convoy, albeit only after a considerable delay—in May 2000, despite the fact that the authorities were aware of it immediately after the incident. The complaints to the authorities made by other victims of the attack, the Committee of the Red Cross and Ms Burdynyuk, in November and December 2000, did not lead to an investigation. The Court further notes that, at least for several years after the incident, the applicants were not questioned about the event, were not granted victim status, had no access to the investigation file and were never informed of its progress. No charges were brought against any individuals.

153. The Court considers that this limb of the Government's preliminary objection raises issues concerning the effectiveness of the criminal investigation in uncovering the facts and responsibility for the attack of which the applicants complain. These issues are closely linked to those raised in the applicant's complaints under Articles 2, 3 and 13 of the Convention. Thus, it considers that these matters fall to be examined under the substantive provisions of the Convention invoked by the applicants. In view of the above, it is not necessary for the Court to decide whether there was indeed a practice of non-investigation of crimes committed by police or military officials, as claimed by the applicants.

Therefore, the Court, unanimously, rejected the Government's claim that the applicants had not satisfied the admissibility criterion of exhausting domestic remedies.

Both the applicant and the respondent State face evidential burdens in seeking to demonstrate that domestic remedies have or have not been exhausted. These were outlined by the Grand Chamber in *Cyprus v Turkey*, 2001-IV (see p 124):

116. The Court further recalls that, in the area of the exhaustion of domestic remedies, there is a distribution of the burden of proof. In the context of the instant case, it is incumbent on the respondent Government claiming non-exhaustion to satisfy the Court that the remedy was an effective one available in theory and in practice at the relevant time, that is to say, that it was accessible, was one which was capable of providing redress in respect of the aggrieved individuals' complaints and offered reasonable prospects of success. However, once this burden of proof has been satisfied it falls to the applicant to establish that the remedy advanced by the respondent Government was in fact exhausted or was for some reason inadequate and ineffective in the particular circumstances

of the case, or that there existed special circumstances absolving the persons concerned from the requirement of exhausting that remedy. One such reason may be constituted by the national authorities remaining totally passive in the face of serious allegations of misconduct or infliction of harm by State agents, for example where they have failed to undertake investigations or offer assistance. In such circumstances it can be said that the burden of proof shifts once again, so that it becomes incumbent on the respondent Government to show what the authorities have done in response to the scale and seriousness of the matters complained of (see, *mutatis mutandis*, the above-mentioned *Akdivar and Others* judgment, p 1211, § 68).

This admissibility criterion emphasizes the subsidiary nature of the Strasbourg system for enforcing Convention rights/freedoms. Member States have the primary responsibility for safeguarding those rights/freedoms within their own domestic legal systems and only where there has been a failure at the national level will the Strasbourg system become a final method of protection. States benefit by being given the opportunity to resolve alleged violations within their domestic institutions (prospective applicants must exhaust domestic remedies to the highest effective level possible within the relevant national legal system: e.g. in *Mogos and Krifka v Germany* (No 78084/01), decision of 27 March 2003, the applicants had not appealed to the German Federal Constitutional Court therefore the European Court determined their application inadmissible for failure to exhaust domestic remedies) and the Court is accorded a degree of shielding from applications which have not been properly pursued at the domestic level.

The Court has held that inter-State applicants are not bound to exhaust domestic remedies, in the respondent State, where the applicant State is alleging an 'administrative practice' of widespread linked breaches of Convention rights/freedoms.

A practice incompatible with the Convention consists of an accumulation of identical or analogous breaches which are sufficiently numerous and inter-connected to amount not merely to isolated incidents or exceptions but to a pattern or system; a practice does not of itself constitute a violation separate from such breaches. It is inconceivable that the higher authorities of a State should be, or at least should be entitled to be, unaware of the existence of such a practice. Furthermore, under the Convention those authorities are strictly liable for the conduct of their subordinates; they are under a duty to impose their will on subordinates and cannot shelter behind their inability to ensure that it is respected.

The concept of practice is of particular importance for the operation of the rule of exhaustion of domestic remedies. This rule, as embodied in Article [35] of the Convention, applies to State applications (Article [33]), in the same way as it does to 'individual' applications (Article [34]), when the applicant State does no more than denounce a violation or violations allegedly suffered by 'individuals' whose place, as it were, is taken by the State. On the other hand and in principle, the rule does not apply where the applicant State complains of a practice as such, with the aim of preventing its continuation or recurrence, but does not ask the Commission or the Court to give a decision on each of the cases put forward as proof or illustrations of that practice. [(Para 159) *Ireland v United Kingdom* A.25 (1978) and see p 145.]

The unanimous Chamber in *Manole and others v Moldova*, judgment of 17 September 2009 (see p 633), applied the administrative practice exemption to individual applicants (journalists) complaining about repeated government interferences with the national TV/radio company.

112. The Court must next examine the Government's preliminary objection about non-exhaustion and the applicants' allegation that there was an administrative practice of censorship and political

control at TRM [Teleradio-Moldova]. The Court has found that, during the period under consideration, one political party dominated the executive and legislative organs of the State and that the
domestic law did not provide adequate safeguards against political interference with and control
over TRM's editorial policy. In these circumstances, there was undoubtedly an increased risk of an
administrative practice of the type alleged by the applicants. Moreover, the Court considers that
the examples of political bias and restrictions on reporting which it has found above are sufficient to
support a conclusion that there was, during the relevant period, a pattern or system of using TRM to
promote the policies of the ruling party, amounting to an administrative practice within the meaning of the Court's case-law. In these circumstances, the applicants were exempted from the usual
rule requiring them to exhaust domestic remedies before lodging their application with the Court.

Hence the scale of the respondent State's breaches justified the Chamber's waiving of the
normal rule governing the exhaustion of domestic remedies.

The second criterion within Article 35(1) is that applicants must lodge their applications
with the Registry of the Court within six months from the date of the final decision by the
highest national authority (usually the constitutional/supreme court) to have considered
their complaints. What is necessary to satisfy this criterion was explained by the Court in
Allan v UK (No 48539/99), decision of 28 August 2001.

The running of the six month time-limit imposed by Article 35(1) is, as a general rule, interrupted by
the first letter from the applicant indicating an intention to lodge an application and giving some
indication of the nature of the complaints made. As regards complaints not included in the initial
application, the running of the six month time-limit is not interrupted until the date when the complaints are first submitted to the Court.

The Court ruled that the applicant's solicitors had not informed the Court of his complaint
regarding an alleged violation of the right to silence until 20 months after the Court of
Appeal had dismissed his appeal. Therefore, that complaint was made outside the six-month
time limit. The Court has, generally, taken a strict approach to this requirement. Hence, in
Walker v UK (No 34979/97), decision of 25 January 2000, the Court ruled that it could apply
this criterion of its own motion, even where the respondent government had not raised it as
a preliminary objection:

... it was recalled that this rule, in reflecting the wish of the Contracting Parties to prevent past
decisions being called into question after an indefinite lapse of time, serves the interests not only
of the respondent Government but also of legal certainty itself. It marks out the temporal limits of
supervision carried out by the organs of the Convention and signals to both individuals and State
authorities the period beyond which supervision is no longer possible.

Consequently, as the applicant had not applied to the Court within six months of the High
Court's determination of his claim for judicial review (the highest domestic remedy available to him) his application was declared inadmissible. Also, if an applicant fails to submit a completed application form within two months of his/her initial letter to the Court
the earlier communication will not be treated as stopping the running of the six-month
time limit: *Kemevuako v Netherlands*, decision of 25 June 2010. However, where there is a
continuing violation of Convention rights this criterion does not apply. So, for example, in
Cyprus v Turkey the Grand Chamber (16 votes to 1) found a continuing violation of Turkey's
procedural obligation under Article 2 to conduct an effective investigation into the fate of
the many hundreds of missing Greek-Cypriots who disappeared in life-threatening circumstances during the military occupation of 1974.

Individual applicants also have to satisfy seven further criteria of admissibility specified under Article 35(2) and (3).

(1) They must not be anonymous, though applicants can request the Court not to disclose their identity in public documentation (as is quite common in complaints invoking Article 8 rights, such as respect for private life: e.g. *KA and AD v Belgium*, 17 February 2005, p 501).

(2) Applications must not be 'substantially the same as a matter' that has already been examined by the Court. This criterion is designed to prevent an applicant making a second application on essentially the same grounds as a previous application. An example of an application being declared inadmissible on the basis of this criterion was *Manuel v Portugal*, decision of 25 September 2003, where the applicant had raised a similar complaint in an earlier application to the former Commission.

(3) Applications which have 'already been submitted to another procedure of international investigation or settlement and contain no relevant new information' are also inadmissible. Although the passage of time has witnessed the emergence of a few international procedures, such as the United Nations Human Rights Committee and the International Labour Organization's Committee on Freedom of Association, these rarely offer a more advantageous form of redress for individuals complaining of serious human rights violations than the Convention. Furthermore, the Court has tended to be reluctant to find this condition satisfied in those rare applications where an applicant has previously invoked another international mechanism. For example, in *Smirnova v Russia* (No 46133/99), decision of 3 October 2002, the respondent government raised the preliminary objection that the first applicant's complaints to the Court should be declared inadmissible as the UN Human Rights Committee was also examining her alleged unlawful arrest. The Court rejected this objection as the applicant's complaints to the Court raised wider factual issues (including being forced to surrender her identity document to the district court) than her complaint to the UN.

(4) Applications must not be 'incompatible with the provisions of the Convention'. This criterion includes applications which are determined to be inadmissible *ratione loci* (i.e. the alleged violations took place at a location outside the jurisdiction of the respondent State) by the Court. For example, in *Yonghong v Portugal* (No 50887/99), decision of 25 November 1999, the Macao Supreme Court had ordered the applicant's extradition to China. From June 1999 the Macao courts had exclusive jurisdiction in the territory and Portuguese administration of the territory was to end in December 1999. Portugal had never made a declaration, under Article 56, extending the Convention to Macao. Therefore, the Court held that the application was inadmissible *ratione loci*. Applications which relate to events that took place before the respondent State had become bound by the Convention are determined to be inadmissible *ratione temporis*. In *Kozak v Ukraine* (No 21291/02), decision of 17 December 2002, the applicant complained about the withdrawal of her title to land in the 1980s. The Court declared her application inadmissible *ratione temporis* as the events had occurred over a decade before the Convention entered into force in regard to Ukraine. Where an applicant seeks to assert a right that is not enshrined within the Convention (or any Protocols binding upon the respondent State) the application will be determined to be inadmissible *ratione materiae*. For example, in *Frette v France* (No 36515/97), decision of 12 June 2001, the applicant alleged, *inter alia*, a breach of Article 12 in conjunction with Article 14 in regard to the authorities' refusal of leave for him to adopt a child. The Court determined that elements of his complaint were inadmissible *ratione materiae* as neither Article guaranteed a right to adopt.

(5) Applications which are 'manifestly ill-founded' are inadmissible. This criterion is concerned with the extent of the evidence applicants have to back up their applications. In

Gongadze v Ukraine (No 34056/02), decision of 22 March 2005, the applicant contended that the respondent State was responsible for the murder of her husband (a journalist). The respondent denied any involvement. The unanimous Chamber stated that:

> The Court considers, in the light of the parties' submissions, that the complaint raises serious issues of fact and law under the Convention, the determination of which requires an examination of the merits. The Court concludes therefore that this complaint is not manifestly ill-founded within the meaning of Article 35 § 3 of the Convention.

So, applicants who cannot satisfy the Court to this standard will have their applications declared manifestly ill-founded.

(6) Applications which the Court considers to be 'an abuse of the right of application' will be declared inadmissible. This criterion covers applicants who make defamatory/abusive comments about members of the Court and its Registry. A dramatic example occurred in *Duringer and others v France* (No 61164/00), decision of 4 February 2003:

> The applications of Messrs Duringer and 'Forest Grunge' were held inadmissible: those applicants had sent numerous communications containing serious accusations against judges of the Court and officials of the Registry and statements without any foundation which were extremely insulting and wild and repeatedly reiterated, and did not fall within the ambit of Article 34 of the Convention. The intolerable conduct of Mr Gérard Duringer and, assuming that he existed, 'Forest Grunge' was contrary to the aim of the right of individual application as provided for by Articles 34 and 35 of the Convention. It was an abuse of the right of application within the meaning of Article 35(3).

If an applicant submits false documentation to the Court, that will also result in the application being declared inadmissible as an abuse of the right of application. For example, in *Jian v Romania* (No 46640/99), decision of 30 March 2004:

> The Court noted that the applicant had, firstly, obscured part of a document in order to conceal the fact that he had decided not to lodge a criminal complaint and had foregone an expert medical report and, secondly, submitted a forged medical certificate in support of his allegations of ill-treatment. The Court stressed that the applicant had thus deliberately sought to mislead it by presenting a distorted view of the most serious part of his application. This was a flagrant and aggravated abuse of the right of application.

Therefore, his application was declared inadmissible.

(7) As we have discussed (p 20) Protocol 14 introduced the additional criterion that the applicant had not suffered a significant disadvantage. Chambers swiftly began applying this new requirement. The first application declared inadmissible under this provision was *Ionescu v Romania*, decision of 28 June 2010. The applicant had brought civil proceedings in Romania against a travel company complaining about his coach trip to Madrid. He sought 90 euros damages from the company. Both the First Instance Court and the High Court dismissed his actions. He then complained to Strasbourg alleging the domestic proceedings had breached his rights to a fair hearing/access to a court under Article 6(1). The Chamber held that:

> 33. Even though the concept of 'significant disadvantage' has not been interpreted to date, it has been referred to in dissenting opinions appended to the judgments in *Debono v Malta* (no. 34539/02, 7 February 2006), *Miholapa v Latvia* (no. 61655/00, 31 May 2007), *O'Halloran and Francis v the United Kingdom* ([GC], nos. 15809/02 and 25624/02, ECHR 2007-VIII) and *Micallef v Malta* ([GC], no. 17056/06, ECHR 2009-...).

34. Those opinions show that the absence of any such disadvantage can be based on criteria such as the financial impact of the matter in dispute or the importance of the case for the applicant. . . .

35. In the present case the Court notes that the applicant's alleged financial loss on account of a failure to perform a contract of carriage was limited. The amount in issue, according to the applicant's own estimation, was 90 euros for all heads of damage, and there is no evidence that his financial circumstances were such that the outcome of the case would have had a significant effect on his personal life.

36. In those circumstances the Court finds that the applicant has not suffered any 'significant disadvantage' in the exercise of his right of access to a court.

As the relevant procedural law in Romania had altered since the applicant's litigation the Chamber did not consider that 'respect for human rights' necessitated an examination of the merits of the applicant's complaints. The substance of his case had been scrutinized by the First Instance Court consequently the case had been 'duly considered by a domestic tribunal'. Therefore a majority (no voting figures were given as it was an admissibility decision) of the Chamber determined that the application should be declared inadmissible as the three elements of the new criterion had been satisfied. This was exactly the type of Strasbourg application (e.g. one involving procedural complaints regarding civil proceedings over trivial amounts of damages) that the drafters of Protocol 14 believed should not be allowed to consume the scarce resources of the Court.

The overwhelming majority of individual applications fail to satisfy all of the above admissibility criteria. In 2010 the Court determined that 38,576 applications were inadmissible whilst 2,474 were found to be admissible. Registered individual applications are allocated to judicial decision-making bodies within the Court. Those that are clearly inadmissible are sent to a single-judge formation for termination (under Article 27). The single-judge formation has a residual power to refer an application to a Committee or Chamber for determination. Where the application (sometimes referred to as a repetitive or clone case) appears admissible and the substance of the complaint has already been the subject of a Court judgment in an earlier case brought by a different applicant, the subsequent application will be referred to a Committee, of three judges, to determine. By a unanimous decision the Committee can declare it admissible and deliver a judgment on the merits (under Article 28). If the Committee is not unanimous then the application will be sent to a Chamber, of seven judges, to determine the admissibility and merits of the case (under Article 29(1)). Complex applications can be sent directly to a Chamber. The admissibility of inter-State applications is always determined by a Chamber, which will also determine the merits if the application is declared admissible (under Article 29(2)).

The determination of admissibility by a Chamber is normally a written procedure, but the Chamber may decide to hold a public hearing to help to resolve difficult issues. Where such a hearing is held the parties will generally also be required to address the merits of the case.

(II) INTERIM MEASURES

The Court, following the practice of the former Commission, has adopted a rule empowering it to indicate interim measures (i.e. actions which should/should not be taken by a party to the proceedings whilst the latter are continuing). A large majority, 14 votes to 3, of a Grand Chamber espoused a radical new approach to the legal status of such measures in *Mamatkulov and Askarov v Turkey*, judgment of 4 February 2005. The applicants were Uzbek nationals who had been arrested in Turkey. The police detained Mamatkulov as he arrived at Istanbul airport under an international police warrant on suspicion of causing injuries by exploding a bomb in Uzbekistan and an attempted terrorist attack on the President of that State. Uzbekistan sought his extradition under a bilateral treaty. Two days after his arrest Mamatkulov was brought before a judge who remanded him in custody. A week later, on 11 March 1999, Mamatkulov, accompanied by his lawyer, was again interviewed by the judge who ordered his extradition under an expedited procedure. On the same day Mamatkulov lodged an application against Turkey with the Court. On 15 March, Mamatkulov appealed to the Bakirkoy Assize Court against the extradition order, but the Assize Court dismissed his appeal on 19 March. Askarov entered Turkey, on a false passport, in December 1998. He was arrested by the police on 5 March 1999 following an extradition request from Uzbekistan, where he was suspected of homicide, causing injuries by a bomb, and an attempted terrorist attack on the President. Two days later a judge remanded Askarov in custody. On 15 March after a hearing the Fatih Criminal Court made an order for the detention of Askarov pending his extradition. The Istanbul Assize Court dismissed his appeal on 26 March. Askarov lodged an application against Turkey with the Court on 22 March.

On 18 March the President of the Chamber of the Court indicated to the Government of Turkey that it was desirable, in the interests of the parties and the smooth progress of the applications before the Court, that the applicants should not be extradited to Uzbekistan before the scheduled meeting of the Chamber (on 23 March). The President acted under Rule 39 of the Rules of Court which provided that:

(1) The Chamber or, where appropriate, its President may, at the request of a party or of any other person concerned, or of its own motion, indicate to the parties any interim measure which it considers should be adopted in the interests of the parties or of the proper conduct of the proceedings before it.

(2) Notice of these measures shall be given to the Committee of Ministers.

(3) The Chamber may request information from the parties on any matter connected with the implementation of any interim measure it has indicated.

However, on 19 March the Government of Turkey ordered the applicants' extradition. When the Chamber met it decided to extend the interim measures until further notice. The applicants were surrendered to the Uzbek authorities on 27 March. The Turkish Government informed the Court, on 19 April, that it had received assurances from the Government of Uzbekistan (prior to the applicants' extradition) that they would not be tortured or sentenced to capital punishment. During July 1999 the Turkish Government notified the Court that the Supreme Court of Uzbekistan had convicted the applicants of the offences for which they had been extradited. Mamatkulov had been sentenced to 20 years' imprisonment and Askarov to 11 years' imprisonment. The applicants' Turkish lawyers informed the Court, in September 1999, that they had not been able to communicate with the applicants, they had not had fair trials, and conditions in Uzbek prisons were bad. During the following month officials from the Turkish embassy in Tashkent visited the applicants in prison and found them to be in good health and they did not complain about their conditions of detention. Whilst relatives of the applicants had been able to visit them during their imprisonment, the Turkish legal representatives of the applicants had been unable to contact them.

The Chamber of the Court determined (by 6 votes to 1), *inter alia*, that the Turkish Government's extradition of the applicants contrary to the Court's indication of interim measures constituted a breach of Article 34 of the Convention. The relevant part of that

Article states, '…the High Contracting Parties undertake not to hinder in any way the effective exercise of this right' (judgment of 6 February 2003).

110.…any State Party to the Convention to which interim measures have been indicated in order to avoid irreparable harm being caused to the victim of an alleged violation must comply with those measures and refrain from any act or omission that will undermine the authority and effectiveness of the final judgment.

111. Consequently, by failing to comply with the interim measures indicated by the Court under Rule 39 of the Rules of Court, Turkey is in breach of its obligations under Article 34 of the Convention.

Subsequently, the Turkish Government applied for the case to be referred to the Grand Chamber of the Court. The request was granted and the President of the Court granted leave for the International Commission of Jurists, Human Rights Watch and the AIRE Centre to submit written observations.

Before the Grand Chamber the applicants' lawyers claimed, *inter alia*, that the Turkish Government's extradition of their clients despite the Court's indication of interim measures constituted a breach of Article 34. This was because once the applicants had been extradited the lawyers were unable to communicate with them. Therefore, the lawyers had been denied the opportunity to obtain further evidence to support their assertions of breaches of the applicants' substantive Convention rights by the Turkish authorities (including a violation of Article 3 by extraditing them to a State where they faced a real risk of ill-treatment contrary to that provision). Consequently, the extradition of the applicants had created an obstacle to the effective presentation of their application to the Court. In response, the Turkish Government argued that under the Convention, member States were not legally obliged to comply with indications of interim measures. This view was supported by the judgment of the original Court in *Cruz Varas v Sweden* A.201 (1991). Furthermore, international courts were governed by the treaties that established them and if a particular treaty did not empower a court to issue binding interim measures then relevant States were not legally bound to obey indications of such measures. The International Commission of Jurists contended that having regard to the general principles of international law, the law of treaties, and international case-law, interim measures indicated by the Court were legally binding upon member States.

The Grand Chamber considered that previous jurisprudence, including *Kurt v Turkey*, 1998-III, established that Article 34 not only prevents States from applying pressure on applicants but also from doing any act which prevents the Court from considering the application. Regarding the indication of interim measures the Court follows the practice of the former Commission and does so only in restricted circumstances. The Court receives a number of requests for interim measures but will only issue them where there is '104.…an imminent risk of irreparable damage'. Requests are usually linked to applications concerning Article 2 and Article 3. Occasionally, other rights are invoked including Article 8. Where the Court has indicated interim measures the cases have mainly involved extradition or deportation proceedings. Interim measures have primarily been directed at governments but they can also be indicated to applicants (e.g. in *Ilascu and Others v Moldova and Russia*, judgment of 8 July 2004, where the President 'urged' one of the applicant/detainees to end his hunger strike; the applicant complied on the same day). It has been very rare for States to disregard interim measures indicated to them. From the late 1950s the former Commission began the practice of requesting States to stay extradition or deportation proceedings where their implementation would undermine pending applications. Then in 1974 the Commission adopted Rule 36 of its Rules of Procedure which provided that:

> The Commission, or when it is not in session, the President may indicate to the parties any interim measure the adoption of which seems desirable in the interest of the parties or the proper conduct of the proceedings before it.

Nine years later the original Court issued a similar Rule:

> 36(1) Before the constitution of a Chamber, the President of the Court may, at the request of a Party, of the Commission, of the applicant or of any other person concerned, or proprio motu, indicate to any Party and, where appropriate, the applicant, any interim measure which it is advisable for them to adopt. The Chamber when constituted or, if the Chamber is not in session, its President shall have the same power.

The Grand Chamber noted that the original Court had held, in *Cruz Varas*, that the indication of interim measures by the Convention organs were not legally binding on parties. However, the Grand Chamber considered that the judgment should be examined in the light of subsequent pronouncements on interim measures by other international bodies. These included the jurisprudence of the Human Rights Committee of the United Nations that a State's failure to comply with interim measures was a breach of its legal obligations under the International Covenant on Civil and Political Rights and the Optional Protocol; the Inter-American Court of Human Rights' rulings that States had to refrain from conduct that may irreversibly violate the rights of alleged victims; and the judgment of the International Court of Justice that its indications of provisional measures were legally binding (*LaGrand (Germany v United States of America)*, judgment of 27 June 2001). The Grand Chamber then sought to place *Cruz Varas* in the context of the historical institutional arrangements at Strasbourg:

> 118....The Court thus confined itself to examining the Commission's power to order interim measures, not its own....

> 119. The Court emphasises in that connection that, unlike the Court and the Committee of Ministers, the Commission had no power to issue a binding decision that a Contracting State had violated the Convention. The Commission's task with regard to the merits was of a preliminary nature and its opinion on whether or not there had been a violation of the Convention was not binding.

Regarding the decision of a Chamber of the full-time Court in *Conka and Others v Belgium* ((dec.) No 51564/99 of 13 March 2001), where the respondent government expelled the Slovakian applicants contrary to the Court's indication of interim measures, the Grand Chamber observed that the Chamber had expressed the view that the government's conduct was 'difficult to reconcile with good faith co-operation with the Court'. After repeating the orthodox principles that the Court should not, without good reason, depart from its own precedents and that the Convention is a living instrument which must be interpreted in the light of contemporary circumstances the Grand Chamber held that:

> 123. In this context, the Court notes that in the light of the general principles of international law, the law of treaties and international case-law, the interpretation of the scope of interim measures cannot be dissociated from the proceedings to which they relate or the decision on the merits they seek to protect. The Court reiterates in that connection that Article 31 § 1 of the Vienna Convention on the Law of Treaties provides that treaties must be interpreted in good faith in the light of their object and purpose... and also in accordance with the principle of effectiveness.

124. The Court observes that the International Court of Justice, the Inter-American Court of Human Rights, the Human Rights Committee and the Committee against Torture of the United Nations, although operating under different treaty provisions to those of the Court, have confirmed in their reasoning in recent decisions that the preservation of the asserted rights of the parties in the face of the risk of irreparable damage represents an essential objective of interim measures in international law. Indeed it can be said that, whatever the legal system in question, the proper administration of justice requires that no irreparable action be taken while proceedings are pending...

It has previously stressed the importance of having remedies with suspensive effect when ruling on the obligations of the State with regard to the right to an effective remedy in deportation or extradition proceedings. The notion of an effective remedy under Article 13 requires a remedy capable of preventing the execution of measures that are contrary to the Convention and whose effects are potentially irreversible. Consequently, it is inconsistent with Article 13 for such measures to be executed before the national authorities have examined whether they are compatible with the Convention (*Čonka v Belgium*, No 51564/99, § 79, ECHR 2002-I). It is hard to see why this principle of the effectiveness of remedies for the protection of an individual's human rights should not be an inherent Convention requirement in international proceedings before the Court, whereas it applies to proceedings in the domestic legal system.

125. Likewise, under the Convention system, interim measures, as they have consistently been applied in practice... play a vital role in avoiding irreversible situations that would prevent the Court from properly examining the application and, where appropriate, securing to the applicant the practical and effective benefit of the Convention rights asserted. Accordingly, in these conditions a failure by a respondent State to comply with interim measures will undermine the effectiveness of the right of individual application guaranteed by Article 34 and the State's formal undertaking in Article 1 to protect the rights and freedoms set forth in the Convention.

Indications of interim measures given by the Court, as in the present case, permit it not only to carry out an effective examination of the application but also to ensure that the protection afforded to the applicant by the Convention is effective; such indications also subsequently allow the Committee of Ministers to supervise execution of the final judgment. Such measures thus enable the State concerned to discharge its obligation to comply with the final judgment of the Court, which is legally binding by virtue of Article 46 of the Convention.

126. Consequently, the effects of the indication of an interim measure to a Contracting State—in this instance the respondent State—must be examined in the light of the obligations which are imposed on the Contracting States by Articles 1, 34 and 46 of the Convention.

127. The facts of the case, as set out above, clearly show that the Court was prevented by the applicants' extradition to Uzbekistan from conducting a proper examination of their complaints in accordance with its settled practice in similar cases and ultimately from protecting them, if need be, against potential violations of the Convention as alleged. As a result, the applicants were hindered in the effective exercise of their right of individual application guaranteed by Article 34 of the Convention, which the applicants' extradition rendered nugatory.

3. CONCLUSION

128. The Court reiterates that by virtue of Article 34 of the Convention Contracting States undertake to refrain from any act or omission that may hinder the effective exercise of an individual applicant's right of application. A failure by a Contracting State to comply with interim measures is to be regarded as preventing the Court from effectively examining the applicant's complaint and as hindering the effective exercise of his or her right and, accordingly, as a violation of Article 34 of the Convention.

129. Having regard to the material before it, the Court concludes that, by failing to comply with the interim measures indicated under Rule 39 of the Rules of Court, Turkey is in breach of its obligations under Article 34 of the Convention.

Judges Caflisch, Turmen, and Klover issued a joint partly dissenting opinion in which they described the majority's judgment as being 'ambiguous'. The dissentients believed that the Court's stance regarding interim measures had been clearly elaborated in *Cruz Varas*. Furthermore, the full-time Court had affirmed that approach in *Conka*. Therefore, the dissentients considered that the majority's view that *Cruz Varas* merely related to the powers of the former European Commission of Human Rights regarding interim measures was 'not very persuasive'. As to the International Court of Justice's ruling in *LaGrand* that could be distinguished as the International Court was interpreting its own constitutive treaty. However, the dissentients did not accept that there was a comparable Article of the Convention that provided for compulsory interim measures.

11. . . . To put it differently, there is a wide difference between the mere interpretation of a treaty and its amendment, between the exercise of judicial functions and international law-making.

12. What the Grand Chamber has done, and the Chamber before it, in their *Mamatkulov and Askarov* judgments is to exercise a legislative function, for the Convention as it stands nowhere prescribes that the States parties to it must recognise the binding force of provisional measures indicated by this Court. That is why, in our view, the Court cannot go down the path shown by the Hague Court and why there is no reason to depart from the existing case-law.

25. . . . To conclude that this Court is empowered, *de lege lata*, to issue binding provisional measures is ultra vires. Such a power may appear desirable; but it is up to the Contracting parties to supply it.

The judgment of the Grand Chamber in *Mamatkulov and Askarov* was a dramatic departure from the previous approach of the Court to the legal effects of indications of interim measures. Prior to this case both the original and full-time Court had not held such measures to be legally binding. The majority's use of Article 34 as the basis for turning interim measures into compulsory obligations was an ingenious route to circumvent the absence of an express power enshrined in the Convention. However, given the persistent refusal of States to add such a power (during the drafting of Protocol 11 both the Commission and the original Court had proposed that the power to order mandatory interim measures be included in the Convention), there is substance in the dissentients' opinion that the majority were legislating in defiance of the clear intention of member States. Whilst the majority could assert that they were seeking to protect vulnerable applicants, it may be concluded that a very desirable procedural reform has been achieved by judicial creativity that extends beyond the permissible limits of Convention interpretation.

In February 2011 President Costa issued a statement expressing the Court's concern regarding the 'alarming rise' in the number of requests for interim measures (in 2006 the Court had received 112 requests whilst during 2010 there had been 4,786 requests). A new Practice Direction governing applications for interim measures was issued in July 2011. Applicants are required, *inter alia*, to provide detailed reasoning justifying their requests.

(III) EXAMINATION OF THE MERITS

Where an application has been declared admissible the Chamber (which will include the judge elected in respect of the respondent State: Article 26(4)) may invite the parties to submit additional evidence and written observations. A hearing may be held, but the Court has increasingly been seeking to determine applications purely on the basis of written submissions as a way of increasing its efficiency. In very exceptional cases, where complicated factual issues cannot be resolved on the basis of documentary evidence, the Court may appoint some of its members to undertake a fact-finding investigation (under Article 38, the procedure is elaborated in an Annex to the Rules of Court) in the respondent State. For example, in *Ilascu and Others v Moldova and Russia*, judgment of 8 July 2004 (and see p 67), the Grand Chamber appointed four of its members as delegates to visit 'Transdniestria' and discover the situation there. The delegates heard 43 witnesses including the imprisoned applicants and members of the Russian Federation armed forces stationed in 'Transdniestria'. Research by P. Leach, C. Paraskeva, and G. Uzelac found that the former Commission and original Court undertook such investigations in 74 cases, but the new Court had only utilized them in 18 cases. The vast majority of fact-finding investigations were in cases involving allegations of unlawful killings/disappearances or ill-treatment. They concluded that:

The Court has shown a more recent tendency not to carry out fact-finding missions, but to find procedural violations, in order to save time and costs. [*International Human Rights & Fact-Finding* (Report by the Human Rights & Social Justice Institute at London Metropolitan University/Nuffield Foundation, 2009), p 80—my thanks to Carla Buckley for providing me with this material.]

Under Article 36(1) member States (which are not the respondent State) have the right to submit written comments and take part in hearings where one of their nationals is an applicant. States do not often participate in individual applications brought by their nationals against other States (most likely for the same reasons that they do not bring inter-State cases). An example where a State asserted its right to submit third party written comments was in *Demades v Turkey*, judgment of 31 July 2003 and see p 548. The President of the Chamber also has the power to invite/grant leave for any member State (which is not a party to the proceedings) or any interested third party to submit written comments and (exceptionally) take part in any hearings (Article 36(2)). Non-governmental organizations (e.g. human rights groups) seek permission to submit written briefs in some cases raising particularly important issues. For example, as we have seen above in *Mamatkulov and Askarov* the International Commission of Jurists, Human Rights Watch, and the AIRE Centre were given permission to submit written comments on the legal significance of interim measures. Article 38 provides that respondent States are required to 'furnish all necessary facilities' to enable the Court to undertake its examination of cases. Occasionally, the Court has been obliged to find a State in breach of this duty; for example in *Dizman v Turkey*, judgment of 20 September 2005, the Chamber found Turkey had violated this provision by repeatedly failing to respond to the Court's requests for documents and information concerning the applicant's complaints of serious ill-treatment by police officers.

A Chamber may, under Article 30, relinquish jurisdiction over a case to the Grand Chamber where it (a) raises a serious question affecting the interpretation of the Convention or (b) where resolution of the case might have a result inconsistent with a previous judgment. The Chamber cannot relinquish jurisdiction if one of the parties to the case objects. Relinquishment is not a common phenomenon. An example of a case where it did take place was *A, B and C v Ireland*, judgment of 16 December 2010 and see p 501, concerning the highly contentious issue of abortion. In 2010, 12 cases were relinquished by Chambers.

(IV) FRIENDLY SETTLEMENTS

Article 39(1) provides that at any stage of the proceedings the Court may place itself at the disposal of the parties concerned with a view to securing a friendly settlement of the matter on the basis of respect for human rights as defined in the Convention. These discussions are confidential (Article 39(2)) and the Registry, not the judges, takes the lead role interacting with the parties. Friendly settlements can be of benefit to the parties as they resolve the dispute without the need for a formal judgment. Individual applicants may gain from a swifter settlement than would arise through a later judgment and States can benefit from avoiding the stigma of a later judgment which finds them to be in breach of the Convention. Friendly settlements also benefit the Court by reducing the number of cases which require a judgment (followed by a possible referral to the Grand Chamber). However, the Court must be satisfied that the proposed settlement between the parties meets the condition of 'respect for human rights'. A rare example of the Court refusing to accept a proposed friendly settlement agreed between the parties occurred in *Ukrainian Media Group v Ukraine*, judgment of 29 March 2005. The applicant published a daily newspaper and had been ordered by the domestic courts to pay compensation to two politicians in respect of critical comments it had published about them. The applicant alleged that the Ukrainian courts had failed to apply Article 10 (especially the Strasbourg jurisprudence on the difference between factual and value comments). A few days before the Court was due to hold a hearing on the merits of the case the parties submitted a friendly settlement proposal to the Court. After examining the proposal the Court rejected it.

36. …the Court took note of the of the serious nature of the complaints made in the case regarding the alleged interference with the applicant's freedom of expression. Because of this, the Court did not find it appropriate to strike the application out of the list of its cases. It considers that there are special circumstances regarding respect for human rights as defined in the Convention and its Protocols which require the further examination of the application on its merits…

As the Court, unanimously, went on to find that '69.…the standards applied by the Ukrainian courts in the present case were not compatible with the principles embodied in Article 10…', we can presume that the Court wished to make clear in a binding judgment how domestic law failed to safeguard the essential freedom of political expression.

Where a friendly settlement is agreed by the parties and approved by the Court, the latter will issue a decision striking the case out and containing a brief statement of the facts and the solution reached (Article 39(3)). A significant minority of admitted cases are resolved by this mechanism; for example in 2010 the Court endorsed 1,223 friendly settlements and unilateral declarations (on the latter see p 48).

A dramatic example of a friendly settlement in the context of a rare inter-State case occurred in *Denmark v Turkey*, judgment of 5 April 2000. Denmark had complained that one of its citizens had been subject to ill-treatment, violating Article 3, whilst detained by the authorities in the latter State during 1996. The Court declared the inter-State application admissible in June 1999. Subsequently, the parties engaged in consultations and proposed an agreed friendly settlement which provided:

1. In order to settle the first part of the application, the respondent Government has agreed to pay to the applicant Government an amount ex gratia of DKK 450,000 which includes legal expenses connected with the case.

2. The applicant Government notes with satisfaction the enclosed declaration of the respondent Government, which constitutes an integral part of the friendly settlement.

3. In the light of the first part of the case, the applicant Government appreciates the acknowledgement and regret expressed by the respondent Government concerning occasional and individual cases of torture and ill-treatment in Turkey.

4. The applicant Government welcomes the steps taken by Turkey in order to combat ill-treatment and torture since the filing of the application on 7 January 1997.

5. The applicant Government and the respondent Government agree that the use of inappropriate police interrogation techniques constitutes a violation of Article 3 of the Convention and that such techniques shall be prevented in the future. The two Governments recognise that this aim can best be attained through training. To this end the applicant Government and the respondent Government recall that the Council of Europe has launched a comprehensive project the objective of which is a re-organisation of the content of the basic, in-service and management training of the police in the member countries. The applicant Government notes with satisfaction the voluntary participation of the respondent Government in this open-ended project. One element of the project is training in police investigation. The project is dependent on funding from Turkey and other members of the Council of Europe. The applicant Government will make a significant financial contribution to this Council of Europe project. Furthermore, the applicant Government will finance a bilateral project. This project—subject to agreement between the two parties—will be aimed at the training of Turkish police officers, in order to achieve further knowledge and practical skills in the field of human rights.

6. On the basis of the Action Plan for the Development of the Bilateral Relations Between Turkey and Denmark which was agreed by the Minister for Foreign Affairs of Denmark and the Minister of Foreign Affairs of Turkey in Copenhagen on 26 November 1999, the Government of Denmark and the Government of Turkey have decided to establish a continuous bilateral Danish–Turkish political dialogue. This dialogue will also focus on human rights issues with a view to improving the human rights situation in concrete fields . . .

DECLARATION BY THE GOVERNMENT OF TURKEY

The Turkish Government regrets the occurrence of occasional and individual cases of torture and ill-treatment despite the resolute action of the Government and existing legislation as well as administrative regulations. New legal and administrative control and punishment regulations have been adopted as a consequence of which such individual acts substantially decreased . . .

The terms of the above agreement reveal how both parties benefited from a friendly settlement. Denmark obtained compensation on behalf of its national, whilst Turkey avoided a potential Court judgment finding it in breach of one of the most important Articles of the Convention. The highly political context of inter-State cases was also illustrated by the meeting between the two States' Foreign Ministers which preceded the agreed friendly settlement of the complaint.

A friendly settlement can also be agreed in regard to the extent of just satisfaction to be paid (and any other necessary remedial measures) following a judgment on the merits. In **Broniowski v Poland**, judgment (Friendly Settlement) of 28 September 2005, the Grand Chamber established the approach to evaluating the acceptability of a friendly settlement agreement subsequent to the delivery of a 'pilot judgment' by the Court. A pilot judgment is one given in relation to an individual application which revealed a systemic or structural problem in the legal order of the respondent State (see p 55). The substantive judgment in Broniowski was the first occasion that the Court had so designated one of its judgments. Following the enactment of new legislation providing for enhanced levels of compensation for all Bug River claimants (approximately 80,000 persons), the government and the applicant agreed a friendly settlement in which the government declared it would, *inter alia*, take practical measures to make the compensation scheme effective and pay 54,000 euros compensation for pecuniary and non-pecuniary damage to the applicant. The Grand Chamber, unanimously, held that:

37. . . . it is appropriate for the Court to have regard not only to the applicant's individual situation but also to measures aimed at resolving the underlying general defect in the Polish legal order identified in the principal judgment as the source of the violation found.

Taking account of both the general and individual measures undertaken by the government in the friendly settlement the Grand Chamber concluded that the agreement was based on 'respect for human rights' and therefore the case should be struck out.

Research by Keller, Forowicz, and Engi distinguished between 'routine' friendly settlements, which occurred in complaints where there was relevant case-law delivered by the Court in previous cases, and 'real' friendly settlements where there was no existing jurisprudence. The researchers found that the Registry followed different procedures in these two categories of complaints. Where the Registry considered that a particular application fell into the first category a letter would be sent to the parties containing the details of a proposed friendly settlement (including the financial compensation to be paid by the respondent State). If one of the parties then sought to query the terms of the proposed settlement the Registry would terminate the friendly settlement process and submit the case for a judgment on the merits.

In these circumstances, the use of the term 'settlement' is a misnomer. Functionally, routine friendly settlements are best understood as *fast track judgments or decisions* in certain areas with established case law. The parties' role is very much limited to an agreement on an accelerated termination of the case, but no more than that. The Registry offers them a proposal and they can take it or leave it. [Keller et al, *Friendly Settlements Before the European Court of Human Rights* (Oxford: Oxford University Press, 2010), 67.]

In respect of the second category of complaints:

In a small group of cases, the parties agree to settle the application. The initiative might come from the parties themselves or from the Registry. Such "real friendly settlements" are the result of a negotiated process assisted by the Registry or conducted only by the parties.... the Registry may sometimes suggest a first draft for the settlement. However, this does not happen on a regular basis and the settlement does not follow a concrete predefined scheme. [Ibid.]

Overall, the authors concluded that:

Friendly settlements take less time than ordinary proceedings, but they do not generally entail higher amounts of compensation. [At p 140.]

These are fascinating insights into a highly secretive aspect of the processing of complaints at Strasbourg. Subsequently, in April 2011, Professor Keller was elected to sit as a judge at the Court in respect of Switzerland.

(v) Striking out

The Court has power, under Article 37(1), to strike out an application at any time where (a) the applicant does not intend to pursue his/her application or (b) the matter has been resolved or (c) for any other reason the Court considers that it is no longer justified to continue the examination of the application. We have already considered (*Karner*) how Article 37(1) has been applied where the applicant has died during the Strasbourg proceedings. Another contentious application of this provision has been where a respondent State makes a unilateral declaration in respect of the application (e.g. apologizing and offering to pay a sum of money ex gratia to the applicant) and then asks the Court to strike the case out, whilst the applicant refuses to accept the unilateral offer and wishes the Court to continue examining the case. A Grand Chamber articulated the principles to be applied to such a situation in *Tahsin Acar v Turkey*, judgment (Preliminary Issue) of 6 May 2003. The applicant made an application to the Commission alleging that his brother had forcibly disappeared at the hands of State agents. The Commission declare the application admissible and it was transferred to the Court when the former body was dissolved. The parties were not able to agree a friendly settlement. The government then requested the Court to strike the case out on the basis of the following unilateral declaration:

> I declare that the Government of the Republic of Turkey offer to pay ex gratia to the applicant, Mr Tahsin Acar, the amount of 70,000 pounds sterling [in respect of] the application registered under No 26307/95.
>
> This sum, which covers any pecuniary and non-pecuniary damage as well as costs, shall be paid in pounds sterling, free of any taxes that may be applicable and to an account named by the applicant. The sum shall be payable within three months from the date of delivery of the judgment by the Court . . . This payment will constitute the final resolution of the case.
>
> The Government regret the occurrence of the actions which have led to the bringing of the present application, in particular the disappearance of the applicant's brother Mr Mehmet Salim Acar and the anguish caused to his family.
>
> It is accepted that unrecorded deprivations of liberty and insufficient investigations into allegations of disappearance constitute violations of Articles 2, 5 and 13 of the Convention. The Government undertake to issue appropriate instructions and adopt all necessary measures with a view to ensuring that all deprivations of liberty are fully and accurately recorded by the authorities and that effective investigations into alleged disappearances are carried out in accordance with their obligations under the Convention.
>
> The Government consider that the supervision by the Committee of Ministers of the execution of Court judgments concerning Turkey in this and similar cases is an appropriate mechanism for ensuring that improvements will be made in this context. To this end, necessary cooperation in this process will continue to take place. . . .

The applicant objected to the government's request. Subsequently, the Chamber, by 6 votes to 1, decided to strike the application out, under Article 37(1)(c):

> 64. The Court has examined carefully the terms of the respondent Government's declaration. Having regard to the nature of the admissions contained in the declaration as well as the scope and extent of the various undertakings referred to therein, together with the amount of compensation proposed, the Court considers that it is no longer justified to continue the examination of the application. [Judgment of 9 April 2002.]

The applicant applied to the Grand Chamber, under Article 43, for the case not to be struck out on the basis that there were substantial grounds for holding that 'respect for human rights' required the Court to continue examining the merits of the case. The Grand Chamber, subject to the dissent of the Turkish *ad hoc* Judge, held that:

> 74. The Court observes at the outset that a distinction must be drawn between, on the one hand, declarations made in the context of strictly confidential friendly-settlement proceedings and, on the other, unilateral declarations—such as the one at issue—made by a respondent Government in public and adversarial proceedings before the Court. In accordance with Article 38 § 2 of the Convention and Rule 62 § 2 of the Rules of Court, the Court will proceed on the basis of the Government's unilateral declaration and the parties' observations submitted outside the framework of friendly-settlement negotiations, and will disregard the parties' statements made in the context of exploring the possibilities for a friendly settlement of the case and the reasons why the parties were unable to agree on the terms of a friendly settlement.

75. The Court considers that, under certain circumstances, it may be appropriate to strike out an application under Article 37 § 1 (c) of the Convention on the basis of a unilateral declaration by the respondent Government even if the applicant wishes the examination of the case to be continued. It will, however, depend on the particular circumstances whether the unilateral declaration offers a sufficient basis for finding that respect for human rights as defined in the Convention does not require the Court to continue its examination of the case (Article 37 § 1 *in fine*).

76. Relevant factors in this respect include the nature of the complaints made, whether the issues raised are comparable to issues already determined by the Court in previous cases, the nature and scope of any measures taken by the respondent Government in the context of the execution of judgments delivered by the Court in any such previous cases, and the impact of these measures on the case at issue. It may also be material whether the facts are in dispute between the parties, and, if so, to what extent, and what prima facie evidentiary value is to be attributed to the parties' submissions on the facts. In that connection it will be of significance whether the Court itself has already taken evidence in the case for the purposes of establishing disputed facts. Other relevant factors may include the question of whether in their unilateral declaration the respondent Government have made any admission(s) in relation to the alleged violations of the Convention and, if so, the scope of such admissions and the manner in which they intend to provide redress to the applicant. As to the last-mentioned point, in cases in which it is possible to eliminate the effects of an alleged violation (as, for example, in some property cases) and the respondent Government declare their readiness to do so, the intended redress is more likely to be regarded as appropriate for the purposes of striking out the application, the Court, as always, retaining its power to restore the application to its list as provided in Article 37 § 2 of the Convention and Rule 44 § 5 of the Rules of Court.

77. The foregoing list is not intended to be exhaustive. Depending on the particulars of each case, it is conceivable that further considerations may come into play in the assessment of a unilateral declaration for the purposes of Article 37 § 1 (c) of the Convention.

78. As to whether it would be appropriate to strike out the present application on the basis of the unilateral declaration made by the Government, the Court notes in the first place that the facts are to a large extent in dispute between the parties. The applicant claimed that his brother had been abducted in 1994 by, or at least with the connivance of, State agents, that he had subsequently been detained at the hands of the State, and that no effective domestic investigation had been conducted into those claims or into the alleged sighting of his brother on television in 2000 by relatives. According to the Government, the abduction and disappearance of the applicant's brother— including the allegations made by relatives against two gendarmes and a village guard, and the subsequent alleged sighting of the applicant's brother on television—did indeed form the subject of effective and ongoing investigations by the competent authorities, albeit without any tangible results to date.

79. Secondly, although the Government on the one hand agreed to state, in their unilateral declaration, that unrecorded deprivations of liberty and insufficient investigations into allegations of disappearance, 'such as in the present case', constituted violations of Articles 2, 5 and 13 of the Convention, on the other hand they subsequently made firm submissions to the effect that their unilateral declaration could in no way be interpreted as entailing any admission of responsibility or liability for any violation of the Convention alleged by the present applicant, who made complaints under Articles 2, 3, 5, 6, 8, 13, 14, 18, 34 and 38 of the Convention. The Government thereby negated the admission of liability contained in their declaration.

. . .

83. In the present case, however, the unilateral declaration made by the Government does not adequately address the applicant's grievances under the Convention. No reference is made to any

measures to deal with his specific complaints, the Government merely undertaking a general obligation to pursue their efforts to prevent future disappearances, without regard to what pertinent and practicable measures might be called for in this particular case.

84. The Court accepts that a full admission of liability in respect of an applicant's allegations under the Convention cannot be regarded as a condition *sine qua non* for the Court's being prepared to strike an application out on the basis of a unilateral declaration by a respondent Government. However, in cases concerning persons who have disappeared or have been killed by unknown perpetrators and where there is prima facie evidence in the case-file supporting allegations that the domestic investigation fell short of what is necessary under the Convention, a unilateral declaration should at the very least contain an admission to that effect, combined with an undertaking by the respondent Government to conduct, under the supervision of the Committee of Ministers in the context of the latter's duties under Article 46 § 2 of the Convention, an investigation that is in full compliance with the requirements of the Convention as defined by the Court in previous similar cases (see, for example, *Kurt v Turkey*, judgment of 25 May 1998, Reports of Judgments and Decisions 1998-III; *Çakıcı v Turkey* [GC], No 23657/94, ECHR 1999-IV; *Ertak v Turkey*, No 20764/92, ECHR 2000-V; *Timurtaş v Turkey*, No 23531/94, ECHR 2000-VI; and *Taş v Turkey*, No 24396/94, 14 November 2000).

85. As the unilateral declaration made by the Government in the present case contains neither any such admission nor any such undertaking, respect for human rights requires that the examination of the case be pursued pursuant to the final sentence of Article 37 § 1 of the Convention. Accordingly, the application cannot be struck out under sub-paragraph (c) of Article 37 § 1 of the Convention since the declaration offers an insufficient basis for holding that it is no longer justified to continue the examination of the application.

86. In conclusion, the Court rejects the Government's request to strike the application out under Article 37 § 1 (c) of the Convention and will accordingly pursue its examination of the merits of the case.

The above judgment indicated that the Grand Chamber took a robust attitude towards whether a respondent State's unilateral declaration was sufficiently comprehensive to justify the Court striking out the case. In the subsequent judgment on the merits in **Tahsin Acar** [judgment of 8 April 2004], the Grand Chamber, unanimously, found a breach of the procedural (investigation) duties required by Article 2.

An example of the Court accepting a respondent State's unilateral declaration as a basis for striking out a case against the wishes of the applicant occurred in **Meriakri v Moldova**, judgment of 1 March 2005. The applicant alleged that whilst he was in prison the authorities opened his correspondence with his lawyer and the Court in breach of Article 8. After the failure of the parties to agree a friendly settlement, the government informed the Court that to settle the case they had made the following declaration:

— the payment to the applicant of the equivalent (at the exchange rate then applying) of 890 euros (14,000 Moldovan Lei (MDL)), as compensation for any non-pecuniary damage caused to him by the interference with his correspondence with the Court and with his lawyer. The government mentioned in this connection that the minimum monthly salary in Moldova was MDL 100;

— an official apology to the applicant for the fact that his correspondence was interfered with by the prison authorities;

— the harmonization of national law with the requirements of the Convention as regards the rights of convicted prisoners to confidentiality for their correspondence with the Court and with other legal bodies.

The Chamber, unanimously, determined that having regard to the scope of the government's undertakings, the amount of compensation to be paid and the Court's established case-law on prisoners' right to respect for their correspondence it was no longer justified to continue the examination of the case.

Keller et al have cautioned that:

The statistics show that in recent years the use of unilateral declarations has become a routine procedure. It is now a well-established practice between some State Agents and the Court. While in 2006 only three unilateral declarations had been issued, this number increased to 47 in 2007 and to 78 in 2008. On the basis of these statistics it becomes all the more apparent that the Court might be too lenient in striking cases from its docket. In some cases, the Court accepted a unilateral declaration based on a questionable offer from the respondent Government. [Above at p 67.]

(VI) JUDGMENT

Where a friendly settlement has not been agreed and the case has not been either relinquished to the Grand Chamber or struck out then the Chamber will deliver its judgment. Chambers determine cases by a majority vote amongst the participating judges. Any judge of the Chamber can issue a separate opinion (concurring or dissenting). The judgment will state the facts as established by the Chamber. The evidential standard applied by the Court is that of 'beyond reasonable doubt'. The full-time Court expressly endorsed this standard in its Grand Chamber judgment in *Cyprus v Turkey*, 2001-IV.

112. The Court also observes that in its assessment of the evidence in relation to the various complaints declared admissible, the Commission applied the standard of proof 'beyond reasonable doubt' as enunciated by the Court in its *Ireland v the United Kingdom* judgment of 18 January 1978 (Series A No 25), it being noted that such proof may follow from the coexistence of sufficiently strong, clear and concordant inferences or of similar unrebutted presumptions of fact (ibid, pp 64–5, § 161).

113. The Court, for its part, endorses the application of this standard, all the more so since it was first articulated in the context of a previous inter-State case and has, since the date of the adoption of the judgment in that case, become part of the Court's established case-law (for a recent example, see *Salman v Turkey* [GC], No 21986/93, § 100, ECHR 2000-VII).

Some applicants and human rights groups have criticized this standard as imposing too high an evidential standard, which enables States to escape findings of liability under the Convention. For example, in *Nachova and Others v Bulgaria*, judgment of 6 July 2005, Interights and the applicant families challenged the use of this standard in discrimination cases involving Article 14. The Grand Chamber upheld the continued use of this standard, but explained how it differed from the domestic criminal law standard in paragraph 147 of its judgment (p 832).

The Chamber will then apply the law of the Convention (i.e. the established legal principles of its jurisprudence regarding the relevant Convention Articles) to the established facts. Where a Chamber finds a breach of the Convention and the applicant has applied for **just satisfaction** (under Article 41) the Chamber will determine whether to make an award. For a study of the evolution of the Court's jurisprudence on this topic, see A. Mowbray, 'The European Court of Human Rights' Approach to Just Satisfaction' [1997] *Public Law* 647. Building upon the foundations laid down in the early cases the Court is now willing to consider awarding just satisfaction in the form of financial compensation to successful applicants for (a) 'pecuniary damage' and (b) 'non-pecuniary damage', sustained as a consequence of the violation of their Convention rights and also (c) for legal costs and expenses incurred in defending those rights. An example of pecuniary damage is depreciation in the value of a person's home attributable to State action or inaction, which is in breach of the Convention. In *Lopez Ostra v Spain* A.303-C (1994) (p 549), the Spanish authorities were found responsible for the serious industrial pollution which constituted a violation of the applicant's right to respect for her home and family life under Article 8. The Court ruled that:

> 65....Mrs Lopez Ostra sustained some damage on account of the violation of Article 8. Her old flat must have depreciated and the obligation to move must have entailed expense and inconvenience....The heads of damage accepted do not lend themselves to precise quantification. Making an assessment on an equitable basis...the Court awards Mrs Lopez Ostra 4 million Ptas.

Victims of maltreatment by State officials infringing Article 3 can claim non-pecuniary damage in respect of the pain and anxiety they suffered. For example in *Ribitsch v Austria* A.308 (1995) (p 174) the applicant successfully complained that he had been assaulted by the police whilst in detention and had suffered bruising to his arm. The Court stated that:

> 46....The Delegate of the Commission argued that a relatively high sum should be awarded in order to encourage people in the same position as Mr Ribitsch to bring court proceedings. The Court considers that the applicant suffered undeniable non-pecuniary damage. Taking the various relevant factors into account, and making its assessment on an equitable basis...it awards him 100,000 Sch.

The key criteria applied by the Court when determining if, and how much, to award successful applicants under Article 41 in respect of their legal costs and expenses incurred in asserting or defending their Convention rights were stated in *McCann v UK* A.324 (1995) (see p 83), as being: '220....only costs which are actually and necessarily incurred and reasonable as to *quantum*...are recoverable under this head.' The requirement that the costs be 'actually' incurred was invoked to deny the applicants any just satisfaction in respect of their legal costs before the Gibraltar inquest, as their legal representatives had acted free of charge. Hence, only those professional costs which applicants are under a legal duty to pay are recoverable under Article 41. Therefore, human rights lawyers must ensure that they bill their clients for ECHR-related work, even if they are disposed on ethical/public interest grounds to waive their fees, because unless successful applicants are formally obliged to pay the fees they will not be recoverable under Article 41. As to the condition that the costs and expenses must have been 'necessarily' incurred in *Tolstoy Miloslavsky v UK* A.323 (1995) (p 701), the applicant claimed, *inter alia*, 104,000 Swiss francs in respect of professional fees and expenses charged by his adviser for handling the application to the Commission. The government asked the Court to take a critical look at the amount of costs claimed. The Court determined that it was '78....not satisfied that all the costs and expenses were necessarily incurred', therefore it awarded a total of 40,000 SF in respect of that part of the applicant's claim for just satisfaction. Also the Court considered that the total amount claimed should be reduced because, 'the applicant has succeeded only in respect of one of his complaints under the Convention' (ibid). This ruling indicates that legal costs and expenses related to unsuccessful aspects of an applicant's case will potentially be ineligible for reimbursement under Article 41. The calculation of the reasonableness of costs was examined by the Court in *Papamichalopoulos v Greece* A.330-B (1995). The applicants had successfully argued that the government's seizure of their land in 1967, and the subsequent failure to make reparation, violate their right to property under Article 1 of Protocol 1. They then sought just satisfaction for, *inter alia*, their legal costs and expenses which they claimed as being approximately 3 billion dr.

47. The Court notes that the applicants calculated the above mentioned sums on the basis of the relevant national scales . . . and in proportion to their claims for pecuniary damage.

. . .

It is settled case law that the Court is not bound by the rules of domestic practice in this area . . .

The Court therefore cannot allow in full the applicants' claims, whose quantum is indisputably very large. However, having regard to the circumstances of the case, the multiplicity and length of the national proceedings, both judicial and administrative, the fact that Counsel for the applicants took part in the negotiations with a view to a friendly settlement, and the special complexity of the question of the application of Article [41], the Court considers it reasonable to award them 65 million dr, including value added tax. [Para 47.]

From this reasoning it is clear that the Court pays close regard to the actual work undertaken (e.g. the amount of time expended) by the applicants' lawyers in assessing the appropriate level of fees. Though national methods of calculating legal costs are not decisive for the Court, it may 'derive some assistance from them' (*Tolstoy Miloslavsky*, para 77). The Court has also been willing to allow applicants to claim for their legal costs and expenses incurred in seeking to protect or defend their Convention rights before national courts. For example, in *Oberschlick v Austria* A.204 (1991) (p 646), the applicant claimed 9,753 schillings in respect of his defence expenditure before the Austrian criminal courts. The Court determined that: '70. . . . these items fall to be taken into account, since they were incurred to prevent or redress the breaches found by the Court. The amount, which was accepted by the Government, appears reasonable to the Court and is therefore awarded in full.'

During 2002, in the light of the adoption of the euro by a number of member States, the Court ruled that: '123. . . . henceforth all just satisfaction awards made under Article 41 of the Convention should in principle be based on the euro as the reference currency' (*Christine Goodwin v UK*, judgment of 11 July 2002). Where the respondent State has a national currency the Court provides that the sum of euros awarded shall be converted into the national currency in accordance with the exchange rate applicable on the day of settlement. Normally the Court gives respondent States three months from date of the award of just satisfaction to pay the specified sums. If a respondent State delays payment beyond the specified date then it will be required to pay simple interest on the award at a rate equal to the marginal lending rate of the European Central Bank during the default period plus three percentage points.

When determining the total amount of just satisfaction to be paid to successful applicants the Court regularly states that it determines the award on 'an equitable basis'. Whilst this creates the potential danger that different Chambers, and now Committees, might diverge in their assessments in similar cases, the Registry established (in 2006) a specialist Just Satisfaction Division to seek to ensure consistency in the calculation of Article 41 awards. During 2010 the Court awarded a total of 64 million euros in just satisfaction. The UK was required to pay a total of 371,160 euros in 13 cases (of which 313,160 euros comprised applicant's legal costs and expenses): Committee of Ministers' 4th Annual Report on the Supervision and Execution of Judgments (April 2011).

In 2004, following a submission by the Court, the Committee of Ministers issued a Resolution, Res (2004)3, inviting the Court to identify:

. . . in its judgments finding a violation of the Convention, what it considers to be an underlying systemic problem and the source of this problem, in particular when it is likely to give rise to numerous applications, so as to assist States in finding the appropriate solution and the Committee of Ministers in supervising the execution of judgments.

For the first time in *Broniowski v Poland*, judgment of 22 June 2004, the Court designated a judgment as a '**pilot judgment**'. This was because the case disclosed a systemic/structural problem in the respondent State's legal order that affected many other persons (up to 80,000 persons were still waiting for compensation to be paid by the government to citizens repatriated from former Polish territory after the end of the Second World War). At the time of the judgment 167 other applications concerning the affected ('Bug River') claimants were pending before the Court. In the Grand Chamber's later just satisfaction judgment in *Broniowski* (28 September 2005) it stated that:

35. The object in designating the principal judgment as a 'pilot judgment' was to facilitate the most speedy and effective resolution of a dysfunction affecting the protection of the right of property in the national—Polish—legal order. One of the relevant factors considered by the Court was the growing threat to the Convention system and to the Court's ability to handle its ever increasing caseload that resulted from large numbers of repetitive cases deriving from, among other things, the same structural or systemic problem. Indeed, the pilot-judgment procedure is primarily designed to assist the Contracting States in fulfilling their role in the Convention system by resolving such problems at national level, thereby securing to the persons concerned the Convention rights and freedoms as required by Article 1 of the Convention, offering to them more rapid redress and, at the same time, easing the burden on the Court which would otherwise have to take to judgment large numbers of applications similar in substance. It will be recalled that in the pilot judgment in Mr Broniowski's application the Court, after finding a violation, also adjourned its consideration of applications deriving from the same general cause 'pending the implementation of the relevant general measures'.

Hence, this exceptional judicial response highlights violations of Convention rights which affect many persons and consequently need swift resolution by the respondent State in order both to safeguard the individuals concerned and to prevent the Court being inundated with applications based on similar breaches.

The application of the pilot judgment procedure was challenged before the Grand Chamber by the respondent State in *Hutten-Czapska v Poland*, judgment of 19 June 2006. The government, *inter alia*, contended that the applicant's circumstances were not those of a typical landlord. The Grand Chamber, by 16 votes to 1, upheld the Chamber's invocation of this procedure:

236. . . . While the number of similar applications pending before the Court currently stands at eighteen—a figure which, in comparison with the *Broniowski* case, may seem insignificant—one of those cases has been lodged by an association of some 200 landlords asserting a breach of their individual rights. At any rate, the identification of a 'systemic situation' justifying the application of the pilot-judgment procedure does not necessarily have to be linked to, or based on, a given number of similar applications already pending. In the context of systemic or structural violations the potential inflow of future cases is also an important consideration in terms of preventing the accumulation of repetitive cases on the Court's docket, which hinders the effective processing of other cases giving rise to violations, sometimes serious, of the rights it is responsible for safeguarding.

So, in determining whether to designate a case as a pilot judgment, the Court will have regard to both the existing number of pending applications concerning the same structural problem and the potential for future applications regarding the problem. Here the relevant

Polish legislation (controlling, *inter alia*, the rents chargeable by landlords) affected about 100,000 landlords and up to 900,000 of their tenants.

In his partly dissenting opinion Judge Zagrebelsky expressed concerns about the 'weakness of the legal basis of the pilot-judgment procedure'. He disagreed with the approach of the majority as he believed the Court's approach interfered with the competence of the Committee of Ministers to supervise the execution of judgments. Nevertheless, the Court has continued to issue pilot judgments on a selective basis. In their study, *Responding to Systemic Human Rights Violations* (Antwerp: Intersentia, 2010), P. Leach, H. Hardman, S. Stephenson, and B. Blitz, identified six cases where the Court had explicitly invoked the pilot judgment procedure. They noted that:

The selection of cases for the application of the procedure will depend upon practical and political considerations, as well as legal factors. The question of whether a state is likely to be co-operative has been a significant factor–the Court Registry gauges the domestic political will to implement change. Concerns have been expressed that the state's non-co-operation may discredit the procedure. However, a state's consent is *not* a prerequisite for the application of the procedure. Indeed, in a number of cases, respondent states have expressly objected to the application of the procedure. [At p 174.]

The UK was subject to the pilot judgment procedure for the first time in *Greens and MT v UK*, judgment of 23 November 2010. The complainants submitted that as convicted prisoners they had been denied the right to vote in domestic and European Parliamentary elections in breach of Article 3 of Protocol 1. They relied on the Grand Chamber judgment in *Hirst v UK (No 2)*, 6 October 2005 (see p 986 of the 2nd edition of this book), where a similar violation had been found. Domestic legislation had not been amended since the *Hirst* judgment. The government sought to object to the application of the pilot judgment procedure by emphasizing, *inter alia*, that the Grand Chamber in *Hirst* had accorded the national authorities a wide margin of appreciation in framing their electoral laws. However, given the 'lengthy delay' (para 105) in the implementation of *Hirst* and the large number of repetitive applications by other prisoners (around 2,500), the Chamber decided to invoke the procedure. Having upheld the applicants complaints under Article 3 of Protocol 1, the united Chamber ruled that (a) the respondent State must bring forward legislative proposals to amend domestic election law so that it would be compliant with the Convention within six months of the present judgment becoming final and (b) to enact the necessary legislation within a period to be determined by the Committee of Ministers. In the meantime all the pending (and future) similar applications would be frozen to await the respondent State's compliance with this pilot judgment. Hence the combination of a five-year delay in a respondent State introducing remedial legislation and a rapidly expanding number of repetitive applications underpinned the Court's resort to the pilot judgment procedure.

From the end of March 2011 a new Rule 61 of the Court regulates the pilot judgment procedure. This provides, *inter alia*, '(1) [t]he Court may initiate a pilot judgment procedure and adopt a pilot judgment where the facts of an application reveal in the Contracting State concerned the existence of a structural or systemic problem or other similar dysfunction which has given rise or may give rise to similar applications.' The Court can initiate the procedure itself or one/both parties may request the application of the procedure. The Court will seek the views of the parties before it has resort to the procedure. Pilot judgments will identify both the particular structural/systemic problem discovered and the type of domestic remedial measures to be taken by the respondent State. The judgment may provide for the adjournment of other similar (repetitive/clone) applications pending the implementation of the remedial measures specified in the pilot judgment. This Rule further enhances the legal foundations of the pilot judgment procedure.

(VII) Referral to the Grand Chamber

Within three months of a judgment being delivered by a Chamber any party to the case may (exceptionally) apply, under Article 43, to the Grand Chamber for the case to be re-heard by the Grand Chamber. This unusual possibility, of a single court providing a second judgment on the merits, was a political comprise that was necessary to secure all the member States' approval of the Protocol 11 reforms. A screening panel (composed of the President of the Court, two Presidents of Sections [designated by rotation], and two judges [elected by the remaining Sections]: Rule 24(5), Rules of Court, June 2010) will only accept the case for re-hearing if it raises: a serious question affecting the interpretation or application of the Convention, or a serious issue of general importance (Article 43(2)). The Grand Chamber has been strict in the application of these criteria. Research by the author disclosed that between 2002–5 the average success rate of requests to the screening panel was only 9 per cent. States were more successful than individual applicants: see A. Mowbray, 'An Examination of the Work of the Grand Chamber of the European Court of Human Rights' [2007] *Public Law* 507. The first acceptance of a request did not take place until October 2000 in *K and T v Finland*, judgment of 12 July 2001 (and see p 537 on the substance of the applicants' complaints under Article 8). In that case the Grand Chamber set out its approach to the scope of its jurisdiction under Article 43.

> 140. The Court would first note that all three paragraphs of Article 43 use the term 'the case' (*'l'affaire'*) for describing the matter which is being brought before the Grand Chamber. In particular, paragraph 3 of Article 43 provides that the Grand Chamber is to 'decide the case'—that is the whole case and not simply 'the serious question' or 'serious issue' mentioned in paragraph 2—'by means of a judgment'. The wording of Article 43 makes it clear that, whilst the existence of 'a serious question affecting the interpretation or application of the Convention or the protocols thereto, or a serious issue of general importance' (paragraph 2) is a prerequisite for acceptance of a party's request, the consequence of acceptance is that the whole 'case' is referred to the Grand Chamber to be decided afresh by means of a new judgment (paragraph 3). The same term 'the case' (*'l'affaire'*) is also used in Article 44(2) which defines the conditions under which the judgments of a Chamber become final. If a request by a party for referral under Article 43 has been accepted, Article 44 can only be understood as meaning that the entire judgment of the Chamber will be set aside in order to be replaced by the new judgment of the Grand Chamber envisaged by Article 43(3). This being so, the 'case' referred to the Grand Chamber necessarily embraces all aspects of the application previously examined by the Chamber in its judgment, and not only the serious 'question' or 'issue' at the basis of the referral. In sum, there is no basis for a merely partial referral of the case to the Grand Chamber.

> 141. The Court would add, for the sake of clarification, that the 'case' referred to the Grand Chamber is the application in so far as it has been declared admissible (see, *mutatis mutandis*, the *Ireland v UK* judgment (1978) A.25 para 157). This does not mean, however, that the Grand Chamber may not also examine, where appropriate, issues relating to the admissibility of the application in the same manner as this is possible in normal Chambers proceedings, for example by virtue of Article 35(4) *in fine* of the Convention (which empowers the Court to 'reject any application which it considers inadmissible . . . at any stage of the proceedings') or where such issues have been joined to the merits or where they are otherwise relevant at the merits stage.

This means that the Grand Chamber will examine all the applicant's admissible complaints *de novo*. The Grand Chamber will allow 'new materials' (i.e. information not presented to the national courts or the Chamber) to be introduced by the parties before the Grand Chamber. Citing judgments of the original Court, including, **Cruz Varas and Others v Sweden** A.201 (1991), the Grand Chamber held that: '146. . . . the Court is not prevented from taking into account any additional information and fresh arguments in determining the merits of the applicants' complaints under the Convention if it considers them relevant.' The Grand Chamber will normally hold a public hearing during the examination of the merits of the case.

A rare example of the Grand Chamber determining that an Article 43 case should be declared inadmissible occurred in **Azinas v Cyprus**, judgment of 28 April 2004. A large majority of the Grand Chamber, 12 votes to 5, accepted the government's submission that the applicant had not exhausted domestic remedies (by failing to raise the issue of the right to property before the Cypriot courts).

The saga of **Hatton and Others v UK** (p 550) illustrates the ability of the Grand Chamber to overrule an earlier judgment of a Chamber. The successes of States in cases such as **Hatton** and **Azinas** reveals why they were so keen to establish the Article 43 referral procedure. Between 2002–5 the Grand Chamber agreed with Chamber judgments in 13 cases and disagreed, at least in part, with ten Chamber judgments: see Mowbray [2007] *Public Law* (above). The Grand Chamber's screening panel accepted 12 cases for referral during 2010.

(VIII) EXECUTION OF JUDGMENTS

Where a Chamber judgment is not subject to referral to the Grand Chamber (or the screening panel refuses to accept the referral) or the Grand Chamber delivers a judgment then the judgment becomes final (under Article 44). The respondent State is bound to abide by that judgment (Article 46(1)). The Committee of Ministers is responsible, under Article 46(2), for supervising the execution of all judgments. The Committee is assisted in this task by a Secretariat of officials in the Department for the Execution of Judgments. Following the promulgation of the Interlaken Declaration and Action Plan (see p 62) the Committee of Ministers agreed a twin-track system of supervision that became effective on 1 January 2011 (1100th meeting of the Ministers' Deputies on 8 December 2010). The new scheme is based on a Report produced by the Department for the Execution of Judgments (CM/Inf/DH(2010), 6 September 2010).

All cases are supervised under the 'standard procedure' unless they demonstrate any of the following characteristics:

— judgments requiring urgent individual measures;
— pilot judgments;
— judgments disclosing major structural and/or complex problems as identified by the Court and/or the Committee of Ministers;
— inter-State cases.

Such judgments are supervised under an 'enhanced procedure'. The standard procedure requires:

12. . . . member States are expected to present an action plan or an action report *as soon as possible* and *in any event not later than six months* after a judgment becomes final. The Committee [of Ministers'] involvement in the standard procedure will be limited to verifying whether or not action plans or action reports have been presented by member States. This formal involvement of the

Committee will not only be necessary for the smooth functioning of the execution process but will also contribute to its transparency and visibility.

13. . . . an action plan is a plan presenting the measures a respondent State intends to take to implement a judgment of the Court. An action report is a report presenting the measures taken by a respondent State to implement a judgment of the Court and explaining why no measures or no further measures are necessary.

14. In practice, there are two possible situations:

— the State concerned considers that it has already taken all the necessary measures to implement a judgment: in such a situation it presents an action report (see a) below);
— the State concerned is in the process of identifying/adopting the measures that are necessary to be taken to implement a judgment: in such a situation it presents an action plan (see b) below).

a) Action report presented (i.e. all measures have been taken):

15. When there is agreement between a member State and the Secretariat on the content of the action report, the case will be presented to the Committee of Ministers with a proposal for closure at the first upcoming 'Human Rights' meeting or in any event not later than six months after the presentation of the action report.

b) Action plan presented (i.e. measures envisaged)

16. Upon reception of the action plan, the Secretariat will make a preliminary assessment on the measures envisaged and the timetable proposed in the action plan and will contact the national authorities if further information and clarifications are necessary.

[The Committee will note the submission of the action plan and invite the respondent State to keep it informed of the progress in implementing the plan.]

18. When the member State informs the Secretariat that it considers that all measures have been taken and that it has complied with its obligation under Article 46 of the Convention, the action plan is turned into an *action report*. The Secretariat will make a *conclusive assessment* of those measures not later than six months after the submission of this information. If the member State and the Secretariat agree on the measures adopted/implemented, the Secretariat will propose that the Committee adopts a final resolution closing the examination of the case.

. . .

C. PRACTICAL MODALITIES OF THE ENHANCED PROCEDURE

20. The supervision under this procedure *does not mean that each and every case should be systematically debated*. It means in particular that the Committee of Ministers entrusts the Secretariat with more intensive and pro-active cooperation with the States concerned by means of:

— assistance in the preparation and/or implementation of action plans;
— expertise assistance as regards the type of measures envisaged;
— bilateral/multilateral cooperation programmes (e.g. seminars, round-tables) in case of complex and substantive issues.

. . .

D. TRANSFER FROM ENHANCED TO STANDARD PROCEDURE OR VICE VERSA

24. A case may be transferred from one procedure to the other by a duly reasoned decision of the Committee of Ministers. A number of situations for transfer of cases are listed below. However, these situations are not exhaustive. The Committee may always decide to transfer a case from

one procedure to the other on grounds other than those listed here. The following situations are envisaged:

a) Enhanced to Standard

25.

— When the Committee of Ministers is satisfied with the action plan presented and/or its implementation;
— When obstacles to the execution no longer exist;
— When required urgent individual measures have been taken.

b) Standard to Enhanced

26. *Failure to present action plan or action reports:* If no action plan or report has been received within six months after a judgment becomes final, the Secretariat will send a reminder to the member State concerned. The Secretariat will also ensure that a list of cases for which no action plan or report has been received is circulated to the delegations before each 'Human Rights' meeting.

[27. If a member State still does not present an action plan or report within three months after the Secretariat's reminder, *and does not provide any explanation for this state of affairs to the Committee of Ministers*, the Secretariat will propose that the case be examined under the enhanced procedure.

28. Consequently, it will be proposed to the Committee that a decision is adopted at the first 'Human Rights' meeting following the expiry of the three months period inviting the member State concerned to provide an action plan/report without any further delay. [As amended by the Ministers' Deputies at their 1100th meeting of the Ministers' Deputies on 8 December 2010.]
...

29. *Disagreement between a member state and the Secretariat on the contents of the action plan or report:* In certain cases, a member State and the Secretariat might have divergent views regarding the necessity or the scope of the measures presented in the action plan or report. When the member State and the Secretariat cannot reach an agreement, the member State and/or the Secretariat can propose that the case is transferred to the enhanced procedure so that the Committee can provide guidance in order to assist the execution process.

30. *Serious delay in the implementation of the measures announced in the action plan:* In cases of serious delays in the implementation of the measures indicated in the action plan, the Committee will be invited to transfer the case concerned for its examination under the enhanced procedure.
...

APPENDIX II: PRACTICAL ARRANGEMENTS FOR SIMPLIFYING THE SUPERVISION OF THE PAYMENT OF JUST SATISFACTION

Operating principles of the simplified system

1. In the light of the Committee of Ministers' discussions and delegations' written contributions, it is proposed that the Committee of Ministers approves the following principles:

— *registration* by the Execution of Judgments Department of payments by States of sums awarded by the Court for just satisfaction;
— *supervision* if the applicant contests the payment or the amount of the sums paid.

2. Registration would therefore become the standard procedure and supervision the exception. Moreover, such registration would make it easier for both governments and the Committee of Ministers to manage situations that may require verification.

3. On this basis:

— States will provide simplified information to permit the registration of payments;
— if the payment is contested, States will agree to provide the necessary information for the Committee of Ministers to exercise its supervision;
— the Secretariat will remain at the Committee of Ministers and States disposal for any questions they might wish to raise.

Action Reports or Plans require respondent States to specify the 'individual measures' (i.e. those concerning the applicant) and the 'general measures' (i.e. those concerning a wider group of persons in a similar situation to the applicant) that have or will be taken to redress the violation(s) found by the judgment of the Court. An example of an individual measure was the granting of indefinite leave to remain in the UK (where he would continue to receive medical treatment/palliative care) to D in *D v UK* (p 206): see Res DH (98)10, adopted on 18 February 1998 by the Committee of Ministers. An illustration of a general measure was the enactment of the Interception of Communications Act 1985 (creating a statutory framework for the interception of postal and telephonic communications) in response to *Malone v UK* (p 564): Res DH (86)1.

The Committee of Ministers relies upon political pressure (and public censure) to require member States fully to comply with judgments. This can be a protracted process, see for example the delays in altering British electoral law to meet the *Hirst* judgment discussed in *Greens and MT* (p 56).

Further reforms

The *Warsaw Declaration* (CM(2005)79final), issued by the Heads of State and Government of the Council of Europe at the conclusion of the Third Summit restated 'the indispensable role' of the ECHR and the Court in formulating, promoting and implementing human rights standards, it is essential to guarantee their effectiveness. Therefore, the Summit agreed, as recommended by the Court, to establish a 'group of wise persons to draw up a comprehensive strategy to secure the effectiveness of the system in the longer term'. In September 2005 the Committee of Ministers announced the names of the 11 wise persons (chaired by Mr Gil Carlos Rodriguez Iglesias, the former President of the European Court of Justice).

Separately from the establishment of the wise persons review of long-term reforms, the Secretary General of the Council of Europe and the President of the Court (in July 2005) invited Lord Woolf (former Lord Chief Justice of England & Wales), assisted by a team of persons with expertise in the administration of courts, to conduct a review of the working methods of the Court. Lord Woolf published his 76-page *Review of the Working Methods of the European Court of Human Rights* during December 2005. The Review was designed to identify administrative steps that could be taken by the Court and its Registry to respond to the growing caseload prior to the implementation of Protocol 14 and future amendments of the Convention. His recommendations included: (a) Satellite Offices of the Registry should be established in Warsaw and two or three other member States from where there are significant numbers of applications (and those States have effective ombudsmen to resolve human rights complaints). These offices would provide advice to persons on the admissibility criteria of the Court and the availability of national remedies. The Offices would also undertake the initial processing of applications made against the relevant State. (b) The Council of Europe and the Court should encourage greater use of national ombudsmen and other methods of alternative dispute resolution to resolve human rights complaints. (c) The Court's use of the pilot judgment procedure should be increased and an 'Article 41 Unit' should be created in the Registry that would produce guidelines on suitable amounts of compensation. We can detect echoes in the Review from Lord Woolf's earlier major examination of English civil law proceedings, *Access to Justice: Final Report* (HMSO, 1996), which led to significant changes in civil cases. For instance, Lord Woolf had advocated the use of alternative dispute resolution procedures, including ombudsmen, as a prelude to persons seeking judicial review of the lawfulness of the decisions of public authorities. As we have already noted, the Court has subsequently delivered a number of pilot judgments and created a Just Satisfaction Division within its Registry.

In November 2006 the Group of Wise Persons (GWP) published its final report (CM(2006)203). Amongst the long-term reform proposals were empowering the Court to provide advisory opinions on the interpretation of the Convention to national supreme courts, thereby increasing the dialogue between these judicial bodies whilst enhancing the 'constitutional' role of the Court. The major institutional reform was the recommendation that a separate 'Judicial Committee' be created to take over the duties of determining the admissibility of applications and the merits of clone cases. Whilst the Committee of Ministers formally welcomed the GWP's report (at their 984th meeting in January 2007), during a subsequent high-level Council of Europe colloquy on the topic (San Marino, March 2007) many participants adopted a cautious attitude towards further major changes to the Strasbourg system and wanted to wait and see the effects of the Protocol 14 reforms (see further A. Mowbray, 'Faltering Steps on the Path to Reform of the Strasbourg Enforcement System' (2007) 7(3) *Human Rights Law Review* 609).

In his speech to mark the start of the judicial year given in January 2009, President Costa called upon member States to hold a conference to (a) re-emphasize their support for the Court and (b) begin the process of implementing long-term reforms of the Strasbourg control system. Switzerland (as incoming Chair of the Committee of Ministers) offered to hold such a gathering in February 2010. At the end of the two-day conference all the member States adopted the *Interlaken Declaration* (hereafter the Declaration) and *Action Plan* by acclamation (19 February 2010).

The Declaration began by expressing the member States' 'strong commitment' to the Convention and the Court. But, the Strasbourg system was subsidiary to the responsibility of domestic bodies (including governments and courts) to guaranteeing Convention rights. Additional measures were 'urgently required' to secure a balance between the number of applications being made to the Court and the number of judgments and decisions given by the Court. Moreover, the Court had to be able to reduce the backlog of pending cases. Therefore, an Action Plan was adopted which provided 'political guidance for the process towards long-term effectiveness of the Convention system'. Whilst reaffirming the 'fundamental importance' of the right of individual petition to the Court, the Action Plan called upon the Committee of Ministers to examine new procedural rules or practices regulating access to the Court. The Action Plan recommended that the Court, in the short term, implement a mechanism 'within the existing bench' to 'ensure effective filtering' of applications. Whilst the Committee of Ministers should consider the creation of a filtering mechanism, 'within the Court going beyond the single judge procedure'. Also, the Committee ought to examine whether the judges responsible for filtering could in the future be empowered to determine repetitive cases. The judges of the Court should have 'knowledge of public international law' and 'the Court's composition should comprise the necessary practical legal experience'. The supervision of the execution of judgments by the Committee of Ministers should be made more 'efficient and transparent' by, *inter alia*, according greater priority to cases disclosing significant structural problems. The Conference also called upon the

Committee of Ministers to examine the feasibility of introducing a simplified mechanism, such as a Statute for the Court, for future reforms of procedural elements of the Convention. A series of deadlines were elaborated. By the end of 2011 State parties should inform the Committee of Ministers of their actions taken to implement the Action Plan. The Committee of Ministers, by June 2011, ought to implement those measures not requiring amendment of the ECHR. The Committee should also authorize its competent bodies to produce specific proposals for measures requiring amendment of the ECHR (including a filtering mechanism and a simplified reform process) by June 2012. Between 2012 and 2015 the Committee of Ministers would assess the effects of Protocol 14 and the implementation of the Action Plan on the workload of the Court. By the end of 2015 the Committee should decide if further action was necessary. Before the end of 2019 the Committee ought to review if the Strasbourg control system is operating on a sustainable basis. If not, then more profound reforms may be necessary.

The *Interlaken Declaration* and *Action Plan* provided the political support for the Court and its need for further institutional reforms sought by President Costa. However, as with previous reforms of the Strasbourg system, agreeing the details is likely to be a complicated process (see further A. Mowbray, 'The Interlaken Declaration—The Beginning of a New Era for the European Court of Human Rights?' (2010) 10(3) *Human Rights Law Review* 519). Nevertheless, the Committee of Ministers responded swiftly and constructively by establishing, in late 2010, an Advisory Panel on candidates for election to the Court and agreeing a new twin-track system for supervising the execution of Court judgments which began operating in January 2011 (discussed p 25 and p 58). In the spring of 2011 the Court also issued a new Rule governing the use of the pilot judgment procedure (p 56).

During April 2011 the Turkish Government organized another high-level conference to assess the achievements of Protocol 14 and progress in the reform process begun at Interlaken. The conference ended with the *Izmir Declaration* (27 April) in which the participants concluded, 'that the provisions introduced by Protocol No. 14, while their potential remains to be fully exploited and the results so far achieved are encouraging, will not provide a lasting and comprehensive solution to the problems facing the Convention system...'. The Committee of Ministers was encouraged to continue examining the desirability of further major institutional reforms including the establishing of new filtering mechanisms for processing individual applications to the Court.

Another strand of reform began in the summer of 2010 when the European Union started formal negotiations with the Council of Europe (as provided for by the EU's Lisbon Treaty and Article 59(2) of the ECHR) to become a party to the ECHR. This will result in EU institutions becoming subject to the jurisdiction of the Strasbourg Court applying the ECHR.

3 ARTICLE 1 OBLIGATION TO RESPECT HUMAN RIGHTS

The case-law of the Court interpreting Article 1 has primarily focused on elaborating when complainants were/are within the jurisdiction of a member State. As *Assanidze* disclosed, the Court mainly adopts a national territorial approach. However, important extensions to the concept of jurisdiction have been recognized such as military control of territory belonging to another (member) State (*Loizidou*) or interception and detention of foreign flagged ships/their crews on the high seas (*Medvedyev*). Inevitably, where a respondent State's actions occur outside its national territory the potential for diplomatic/political conflict with other States is heightened and Strasbourg litigation may become embroiled in these disputes (e.g. Cyprus and Turkey's conflict over the latter's military occupation of northern Cyprus). The Court has adopted a cautious attitude towards complainants' assertions that member States' participation in NATO (*Bankovic*) or United Nations' (*Behrami*) operations fall within the scope of the ECHR. Article 1 has also been used as a jurisprudential brick in the Court's development of positive obligations on member States arising from the Convention.

....

Assanidze v Georgia judgment of 8 April 2004
European Court of Human Rights

The applicant was a Georgian national, and former senior local politician, imprisoned in Batumi, the capital of the Ajarian Autonomous Republic in Georgia (an area historically ruled by the Ottoman and Russian Empires which during the period of the Union of Soviet Socialist Republics had been an autonomous part of Georgia, its precise status within independent Georgia had not been resolved at the time of the Court's judgment). He had been convicted of unlawful financial dealings in 1994 and sentenced to eight years' imprisonment. In 1999 he had been given a pardon suspending the remaining period of his imprisonment by the President of Georgia. The Ajarian authorities did not release him. New criminal charges were brought against him and in 2000 the Ajarian High Court sentenced him to 12 years' imprisonment (backdated to the time of his original arrest/detention in 1993). Assanidze appealed to the Georgian Supreme Court and in 2001 that Court quashed his convictions and ordered his immediate release. Despite numerous requests from the Georgian central government the Ajarian authorities refused to release Assanidze. He complained to the European Court of Human Rights alleging, *inter alia*, a violation of his right to liberty under Article 5.

A crucial aspect of the case concerned the responsibility of the Government of Georgia, under Article 1 of the Convention, for the applicant's continued detention by the Ajarian authorities. The Government accepted that the Ajarian Autonomous Republic was an integral part of Georgia, Ajaria did not have separatist ambitions and apart from the applicant's case (which had significant political elements) there were no problems of judicial cooperation between the central and Ajarian authorities.

The Grand Chamber held that:

137. Article 1 of the Convention requires the State Parties to 'secure to everyone within their jurisdiction the rights and freedoms defined in Section I of th[e] Convention'. It follows from this provision that the State Parties are answerable for any violation of the protected rights and freedoms of anyone within their 'jurisdiction'—or competence—at the time of the violation.

In certain exceptional cases, jurisdiction is assumed on the basis of non-territorial factors, such as: acts of public authority performed abroad by diplomatic and consular representatives of the State; the criminal activities of individuals overseas against the interests of the State or its nationals; acts performed on board vessels flying the State flag or on aircraft or spacecraft registered there; and particularly serious international crimes (universal jurisdiction).

However, as a general rule, the notion of 'jurisdiction' within the meaning of Article 1 of the Convention must be considered as reflecting the position under public international law (*Gentilhomme and Others v France*, Nos 48205/99, 48207/99 and 48209/99, § 20, 14 May 2002; *Bankovic and Others v Belgium and 16 Other Contracting States* (dec.) [GC], No 52207/99, §§ 59–61, ECHR 2001-XII). That notion is 'primarily' or 'essentially' territorial (see *Bankovic* cited above).

138. In addition to the State territory proper, territorial jurisdiction extends to any area which, at the time of the alleged violation, is under the 'overall control' of the State concerned (*Loizidou v Turkey* (preliminary objections) judgment of 23 March 1995, Series A No 310), notably occupied territories (*Cyprus v Turkey* [GC], No 25781/94, ECHR-2001-IV), to the exclusion of areas outside such control (see *Bankovic* cited above).

...

146. ...the sole issue of relevance is the State's international responsibility, irrespective of the national authority to which the breach of the Convention in the domestic system is imputable (see, *mutatis mutandis, Foti and Others v Italy*, judgment of 10 December 1982, Series A No 56, p 21, § 63; *Zimmermann and Steiner v Switzerland*, judgment of 13 July 1983, Series A No 66, p 13, § 32; and *Lingens v Austria*, judgment of 8 July 1986, Series A No 103, p 28, § 46).

Even though it is not inconceivable that States will encounter difficulties in securing compliance with the rights guaranteed by the Convention in all parts of their territory, each State Party to the Convention nonetheless remains responsible for events occurring anywhere within its national territory.

Further, the Convention does not merely oblige the higher authorities of the Contracting States to respect for their own part the rights and freedoms it embodies; it also has the consequence that, in order to secure the enjoyment of those rights and freedoms, those authorities must prevent or remedy any breach at subordinate levels (*Ireland v the United Kingdom*, judgment of 18 January 1978, Series A No 25, pp 90–1, § 239). The higher authorities of the State are under a duty to require their subordinates to comply with the Convention and cannot shelter behind their inability to ensure that it is respected (ibid, p. 64, § 159).

147. Despite the malfunctioning of parts of the State machinery in Georgia and the existence of territories with special status, the Ajarian Autonomous Republic is in law subject to the control of the Georgian State. The relationship existing between the local Ajarian authorities and the central government is such that only a failing on the part of the latter could make the continued breach of the provisions of the Convention at the local level possible. The general duty imposed on the State by Article 1 of the Convention entails and requires the implementation of a national system capable of securing compliance with the Convention throughout the territory of the State for everyone.

That is confirmed by the fact that, firstly, Article 1 does not exclude any part of the member States' 'jurisdiction' from the scope of the Convention and, secondly, it is with respect to their 'jurisdiction' as a whole—which is often exercised in the first place through the Constitution—that Member States are called on to show compliance with the Convention (*United Communist Party of Turkey and Others v Turkey*, judgment of 30 January 1998, Reports 1998-I, pp 17–18, § 29).

...

149. The Court thus emphasises that the higher authorities of the Georgian State are strictly liable under the Convention for the conduct of their subordinates (*Ireland v the United Kingdom*, cited above, p 64, § 159). It is only the responsibility of the Georgian State itself—not that of a domestic authority or organ—that is in issue before the Court. It is not the Court's role to deal with a multiplicity of national authorities or courts or to examine disputes between institutions or over internal politics.

150. The Court therefore finds that the actual facts out of which the allegations of violations arose were within the 'jurisdiction' of Georgia within the meaning of Article 1 of the Convention and that, even though within the domestic system those matters are directly imputable to the local authorities of the Ajarian Autonomous Republic, it is solely the responsibility of the Georgian State that is engaged under the Convention.

In respect of the applicant's continued imprisonment since the Georgian Supreme Court ordered his immediate release in 2001:

173. As to the conformity of the applicant's detention with the aim of Article 5 to protect against arbitrariness, the Court observes that it is inconceivable that in a State subject to the rule of law a person should continue to be deprived of his liberty despite the existence of a court order for his release.

174. As the documents in the case file show, the central State authorities themselves pointed out on a number of occasions that there was no basis for the applicant's detention. The central judicial and administrative authorities were forthright in telling the Ajarian authorities that the applicant's deprivation was arbitrary for the purposes of domestic law and Article 5 of the Convention. However, their numerous reminders and calls for the applicant's release went unanswered...

175. The Court considers that to detain a person for an indefinite and unforeseeable period, without such detention being based on a specific statutory provision or judicial decision, is incompatible with the principle of legal certainty (see, *mutatis mutandis, Jecius v Lithuania*, No 34578/97, § 62, ECHR 2000-IX) and arbitrary, and runs counter to the fundamental aspects of the rule of law.

...

FOR THESE REASONS, THE COURT

...

2. Holds unanimously that the matters complained of are within the 'jurisdiction' of Georgia within the meaning of Article 1 of the Convention and that only the responsibility of the Georgian State is engaged under the Convention (see paragraph 150 above);

...

5. Holds unanimously that since 29 January 2001 the applicant has been held arbitrarily in breach of the provisions of Article 5 (1) of the Convention...

NOTES

1 The Grand Chamber was composed of President Wildhaber and Judges: Rozakis, Costa, Ress, Bratza, Caflisch, Loucaides, Cabral Barreto, Straznicka, Jungwiert, Casadevall, Zupancic, Thomassen, Botoucharova, Ugrekhelidze, Zagrebelsky, and Mularoni.

2 The judgment in *Assanidze* demonstrated that the Court interprets the concept of jurisdiction under Article 1 in accordance with the principles of public international law normally to encompass the national territory of the respondent State. Furthermore, central governments are accountable, under the Convention, for securing respect for Convention rights and freedoms in all parts of their territories and by sub-national tiers of government. These are important rulings as they seek to ensure that persons will be guaranteed their Convention rights and freedoms throughout the territories of member States. It is vital that the central governments of member States ensure that their subordinate authorities fully respect the Convention and *de facto* zones of non-compliance do not emerge within national territories.

3 Another Grand Chamber emphasized the continuing responsibility of a member State under the Convention even in respect of part of its territory which is under the *de facto* control of a separatist regime in *Ilascu and Others v Moldova and Russia*, judgment of 8 July 2004. The four applicants had been arrested, convicted, and detained by the authorities of the 'Moldavian Republic of Transdniestria' (MRT), a region in the east of Moldova which proclaimed its independence in 1991 but which is not recognized by the international community. The Grand Chamber held that:

333. The Court considers that where a Contracting State is prevented from exercising its authority over the whole of its territory by a constraining de facto situation, such as obtains when a separatist regime is set up, whether or not this is accompanied by military occupation by another State, it does not thereby cease to have jurisdiction within the meaning of Article 1 of the Convention over that part of its territory temporarily subject to a local authority sustained by rebel forces or by another State.

Nevertheless such a factual situation reduces the scope of that jurisdiction in that the undertaking given by the State under Article 1 must be considered by the Court only in the light of the Contracting State's positive obligations towards persons within its territory. The State in question must endeavour, with all the legal and diplomatic means available to it vis-à-vis foreign States and international organisations, to continue to guarantee the enjoyment of the rights and freedoms guaranteed by the Convention.

A large majority, 11 votes to 6, consequently determined that the applicants fell within the jurisdiction of Moldova. The majority considered that Moldova had not taken 'effective measures' to bring to an end the continuing detention and mal-treatment of the three applicants who remained in the custody of the MRT after the release of Ilascu in 2001 (note, Judges Casadevall, Ress, Birsan, Tulkens, and Fura-Sandstrom believed that the Government of Moldova had adopted 'a rather acquiescent attitude' towards the plight of the applicants since 1992). Judge Bratza, joined by Judges Rozakis, Hedigan, Thomassen, and Pantiru, dissented regarding the jurisdictional responsibility of Moldova.

8. . . . I have difficulty in accepting the proposition that those within a part of the territory of a State over which, as a result of its unlawful occupation by a separatist administration, the State is prevented from exercising any authority or control may nevertheless be said to be within the 'jurisdiction' of that State according to the autonomous meaning of that term in Article 1 of the Convention, which term presupposes that the State has the power 'to secure to everyone . . . the rights and freedoms' defined therein. I find it equally difficult to accept the conclusion of the majority of the Court that in such a factual situation those within the territory remain 'within [the] jurisdiction' of the State but that the scope of that 'jurisdiction' is reduced, the State continuing to owe positive obligations with regard to the Convention rights of everyone in the territory. The very use of the term 'the positive obligations of the State' and the reliance placed in the judgment on the case-law

of the Court under Article 1 concerning such obligations appears to me to be both misleading and unhelpful in the present context. That case-law—with its references to the fair balance to be struck between the general interest and the interests of the individual and the choices to be made in terms of priorities and resources—was developed in a factual context where the respondent State exercised full and effective control over all parts of its territory and where individuals within that territory were indisputably within the 'jurisdiction' of the State for Convention purposes. The Court's reasoning cannot in my view be readily adapted to the fundamentally different context in which a State is prevented by circumstances outside its control from exercising any authority within the territory and where the very issue is whether individuals within the territory are to be regarded as within the 'jurisdiction' of the State for Convention purposes.

I am unable to accept that in such a situation responsibility for a violation of the Convention rights of individuals within the territory may attach to the State merely because of a failure on its part to establish that it had made sufficient efforts on the legal or diplomatic plane to guarantee those rights. In the specific context of the present case, the responsibility of a State in respect of the wrongful detention of persons detained within territory outside its effective control cannot in my view depend on whether at any particular point of time the State is, in the estimation of the Court, making sufficiently concerted efforts to secure their release. Nor can I accept an interpretation of the Convention which would require the Court to make an assessment, in a complex and fluctuating international situation, as to whether particular legal or diplomatic measures would be effective to restore constitutional rule within the territory, whether such measures were in practice possible and whether they were adequately implemented by the State concerned.

9. I can agree that, where a State is prevented from exercising any authority or control over territory within its borders, the inaction of the State concerned may nevertheless be held to engage its responsibility under the Convention in respect of those within the territory. However, such responsibility could in my view only attach in exceptional circumstances where the evidence before the Court clearly demonstrates such a lack of commitment or effort on the part of the State concerned to reassert its authority or to reinstitute constitutional order within the territory as to amount to a tacit acquiescence in the continued exercise of authority or 'jurisdiction' within the territory by the unlawful administration.

The majority's innovative use of the concept of positive obligations (see further, Note 15) had as its objective the desirable goal, examined above in the comments on *Assanidze*, of seeking to ensure that geographical areas of non-compliance/enforcement are not tolerated within the territories of member States. Do you agree with Judge Bratza's view that the majority's approach requires the Court to become too involved in evaluating governments' diplomatic strategies? For an examination of the jurisdictional responsibility of Russia in respect of the applicants see Note 7.

4   In exceptional situations, a wider notion of jurisdiction applies. For example, in *Loizidou v Turkey (Preliminary Objections)* A.310 (1995) a Grand Chamber held, by 16 votes to 2, that:

62. . . . Bearing in mind the object and purpose of the Convention, the responsibility of a Contracting Party may also arise when as a consequence of military action—whether lawful or unlawful—it exercises effective control of an area outside its national territory.

The obligation to secure, in such an area, the rights and freedoms set out in the Convention derives from the fact of such control whether it be exercised directly, through its armed forces, or through a subordinate local administration.

63. In this connection the respondent Government have acknowledged that the applicant's loss of control of her property stems from the occupation of the northern part of Cyprus by Turkish

troops and the establishment there of the 'TRNC' [Turkish Republic of Northern Cyprus—an entity not recognized by the general international community]. Furthermore, it has not been disputed that the applicant was prevented by Turkish troops from gaining access to her property.

64. It follows that such acts are capable of falling within Turkish 'jurisdiction' within the meaning of Article 1 of the Convention....

In the subsequent judgment on the merits of Mrs Loizidou's complaints (see p 547) the Grand Chamber held, by 11 votes to 6, that:

56. It is not necessary to determine whether, as the applicant and the Government of Cyprus have suggested, Turkey actually exercises detailed control over the policies and actions of the authorities of the 'TRNC'. It is obvious from the large number of troops engaged in active duties in northern Cyprus...that her army exercises effective overall control over that part of the island. Such control, according to the relevant test and in the circumstances of the case, entails her responsibility for the policies and actions of the 'TRNC'...Those affected by such policies or actions therefore come within the 'jurisdiction' of Turkey for the purposes of Article 1 of the Convention. Her obligation to secure to the applicant the rights and freedoms set out in the Convention therefore extends to the northern part of Cyprus.

In view of this conclusion the Court need not pronounce itself on the arguments which have been adduced by those appearing before it concerning the alleged lawfulness or unlawfulness under international law of Turkey's military intervention in the island in 1974 since, as noted above, the establishment of State responsibility under the Convention does not require such an enquiry...It suffices to recall in this context its finding that the international community considers that the Republic of Cyprus is the sole legitimate Government of the island and has consistently refused to accept the legitimacy of the 'TRNC' as a State within the meaning of international law...

57. It follows from the above considerations that the continuous denial of the applicant's access to her property in northern Cyprus and the ensuing loss of all control over the property is a matter which falls within Turkey's 'jurisdiction' within the meaning of Article 1 and is thus imputable to Turkey.

5 In the later, rare, inter-State case of *Cyprus v Turkey*, 2001-IV (see p 124), another Grand Chamber, by 16 votes to 1, confirmed the *Loizidou* approach to jurisdiction in the context of the Turkish military occupation of northern Cyprus.

77. It is of course true that the Court in the Loizidou case was addressing an individual's complaint concerning the continuing refusal of the authorities to allow her access to her property. However, it is to be observed that the Court's reasoning is framed in terms of a broad statement of principle as regards Turkey's general responsibility under the Convention for the policies and actions of the 'TRNC' authorities. Having effective overall control over northern Cyprus, its responsibility cannot be confined to the acts of its own soldiers or officials in northern Cyprus but must also be engaged by virtue of the acts of the local administration which survives by virtue of Turkish military and other support. It follows that, in terms of Article 1 of the Convention, Turkey's 'jurisdiction' must be considered to extend to securing the entire range of substantive rights set out in the Convention and those additional Protocols which she has ratified, and that violations of those rights are imputable to Turkey.

The Grand Chamber, with the dissent of the Turkish *ad hoc* Judge, went on to find breaches of a number of Convention rights including failure to conduct effective investigations into disappeared persons (Articles 2 and 5), the subjection of civilians to trials before military courts in northern Cyprus (Article 6), the denial of access to displaced persons (Greek-Cypriots) to their homes in northern Cyprus (Article 8 and Article 1 of Protocol 1) and unjustifiable restrictions on the freedom to manifest their religion and freedom of expression of Greek-Cypriots in northern Cyprus (Articles 9 and 10).

6 In *Bankovic and Others v Belgium and 16 Other Contracting States*, 2001-XII, the six applicants were nationals of the Federal Republic of Yugoslavia (FYR) whose relatives were among the victims of the firing of a missile by a NATO aircraft at the Radio Television Serbia headquarters in Belgrade on 23 April 1999. The military action was part of a campaign of NATO air strikes on Serbia between March and June 1999 taken because the Government of Serbia refused to accept a political solution to the crisis in Kosovo between Serbian and Kosovar Albanian forces in 1998–9. The attack on the Radio Television Serbia building resulted in the deaths of 16 persons and a similar number of seriously injured persons. The applicants brought a complaint before the Strasbourg Court alleging that the 17 respondent States (who were members of NATO and parties to the Convention) had breached, *inter alia*, their relatives' right to life (Article 2). The respondent States contended that applicants' complaints fell outside their jurisdiction under Article 1 and therefore were inadmissible. The Chamber determining the admissibility of the complaints relinquished the matter to the Grand Chamber. In its decision the latter noted the drafting history of Article 1.

19. The text prepared by the Committee of the Consultative Assembly of the Council of Europe on legal and administrative questions provided, in what became Article 1 of the Convention, that the 'Member States shall undertake to ensure to all persons residing within their territories the rights ...'. The Expert Intergovernmental Committee, which considered the Consultative Assembly's draft, decided to replace the reference to 'all persons residing within their territories' with a reference to persons 'within their jurisdiction'. The reasons were noted in the following extract from the *Collected Edition of the Travaux Préparatoires of the European Convention on Human Rights* (vol III, p 260):

'The Assembly draft had extended the benefits of the Convention to "all persons residing within the territories of the signatory States". It seemed to the Committee that the term "residing" might be considered too restrictive. It was felt that there were good grounds for extending the benefits of the Convention to all persons in the territories of the signatory States, even those who could not be considered as residing there in the legal sense of the word. The Committee therefore replaced the term "residing" by the words "within their jurisdiction" which are also contained in Article 2 of the Draft Covenant of the United Nations Commission.'

20. The next relevant comment prior to the adoption of Article 1 of the Convention, made by the Belgian representative on 25 August 1950 during the plenary sitting of the Consultative Assembly, was to the effect that

'henceforth the right of protection by our States, by virtue of a formal clause of the Convention, may be exercised with full force, and without any differentiation or distinction, in favour of individuals of whatever nationality, who on the territory of any one of our States, may have had reason to complain that [their] rights have been violated'.

21. The *travaux préparatoires* go on to note that the wording of Article 1 including 'within their jurisdiction', did not give rise to any further discussion and the text as it was (and is now) was adopted by the Consultative Assembly on 25 August 1950 without further amendment (the *Collected Edition of the Travaux Préparatoires* (vol VI, p 132)).

The Grand Chamber then held that:

67. In keeping with the essentially territorial notion of jurisdiction, the Court has accepted only in exceptional cases that acts of the Contracting States performed, or producing effects, outside

their territories can constitute an exercise of jurisdiction by them within the meaning of Article 1 of the Convention.

...

71. In sum, the case-law of the Court demonstrates that its recognition of the exercise of extra-territorial jurisdiction by a Contracting State is exceptional: it has done so when the respondent State, through the effective control of the relevant territory and its inhabitants abroad as a consequence of military occupation or through the consent, invitation or acquiescence of the Government of that territory, exercises all or some of the public powers normally to be exercised by that Government.

...

75. ...the applicants suggest a specific application of the 'effective control' criteria developed in the northern Cyprus cases. They claim that the positive obligation under Article 1 extends to securing the Convention rights in a manner proportionate to the level of control exercised in any given extra-territorial situation. The Governments contend that this amounts to a 'cause-and-effect' notion of jurisdiction not contemplated by or appropriate to Article 1 of the Convention. The Court considers that the applicants' submission is tantamount to arguing that anyone adversely affected by an act imputable to a Contracting State, wherever in the world that act may have been committed or its consequences felt, is thereby brought within the jurisdiction of that State for the purpose of Article 1 of the Convention.

...

79. ...the applicants maintain that any failure to accept that they fell within the jurisdiction of the respondent States would defeat the *ordre public* mission of the Convention and leave a regrettable vacuum in the Convention system of human rights' protection.

80. The Court's obligation, in this respect, is to have regard to the special character of the Convention as a constitutional instrument of *European* public order for the protection of individual human beings and its role, as set out in Article 19 of the Convention, is to ensure the observance of the *engagements undertaken* by the Contracting Parties (the above-cited *Loizidou* judgment (*preliminary objections*), at § 93). It is therefore difficult to contend that a failure to accept the extra-territorial jurisdiction of the respondent States would fall foul of the Convention's *ordre public* objective, which itself underlines the essentially regional vocation of the Convention system, or of Article 19 of the Convention which does not shed any particular light on the territorial ambit of that system.

It is true that, in its above-cited *Cyprus v Turkey* judgment (at § 78), the Court was conscious of the need to avoid 'a regrettable vacuum in the system of human-rights protection' in northern Cyprus. However, and as noted by the Governments, that comment related to an entirely different situation to the present: the inhabitants of northern Cyprus would have found themselves excluded from the benefits of the Convention safeguards and system which they had previously enjoyed, by Turkey's 'effective control' of the territory and by the accompanying inability of the Cypriot Government, as a Contracting State, to fulfil the obligations it had undertaken under the Convention.

In short, the Convention is a multi-lateral treaty operating, subject to Article 56 of the Convention, in an essentially regional context and notably in the legal space (*espace juridique*) of the Contracting States. The FRY clearly does not fall within this legal space. The Convention was not designed to be applied throughout the world, even in respect of the conduct of Contracting States. Accordingly, the desirability of avoiding a gap or vacuum in human rights' protection has so far been relied on by the Court in favour of establishing jurisdiction only when the territory in question was one that, but for the specific circumstances, would normally be covered by the Convention.

Consequently, the Grand Chamber was unanimous in determining that there was no jurisdictional link between the applicants' relatives and the respondent States and the application was declared inadmissible.

Happold has commented that:

> Nor is this to say that *Bankovic et al* were legally unprotected. A body of law exists which regulates the conduct of hostilities in international armed conflicts: international humanitarian law. Indeed, there existed a court with jurisdiction over violations of that body of law in the former Yugoslavia at the time of the attack: the International Criminal Tribunal for the Former Yugoslavia. That the Prosecutor of the ICTY declined to bring proceedings with regard to the bombing of [Radio Television Serbia] is not something that can be laid at the door of the European Court of Human Rights, nor should the Court have stepped in to do the Tribunal's work. [M. Happold, 'Bankovic v Belgium and the Territorial Scope of the ECHR' (2003) 3(1) *Human Rights Law Review* 77 at 90.]

7   The Grand Chamber, subject to the dissent of Judge Kovler—the judge of Russian nationality, in *Ilascu and Others* (see Note 3) concluded that the applicants also came within the jurisdiction of Russia.

> 380. The Court observes that during the Moldovan conflict in 1991–92 forces of the former Fourteenth Army (which owed allegiance to the USSR, the CIS and the Russian Federation in turn) stationed in Transdniestria, an integral part of the territory of the Republic of Moldova, fought with and on behalf of the Transdniestrian separatist forces. Moreover, large quantities of weapons from the stores of the Fourteenth Army (which later became the ROG [Russian Operational Group]) were voluntarily transferred to the separatists, who were also able to seize possession of other weapons unopposed by Russian soldiers.
>
> The Court notes that from December 1991 onwards the Moldovan authorities systematically complained, to international bodies among others, of what they called 'the acts of aggression' of the former Fourteenth Army against the Republic of Moldova and accused the Russian Federation of supporting the Transdniestrian separatists.
>
> Regard being had to the principle of States' responsibility for abuses of authority, it is of no consequence that, as the Russian Government submitted, the former Fourteenth Army did not participate as such in the military operations between the Moldovan forces and the Transdniestrian insurgents.
>
> 381. Throughout the clashes between the Moldovan authorities and the Transdniestrian separatists the leaders of the Russian Federation supported the separatist authorities by their political declarations. The Russian Federation drafted the main lines of the ceasefire agreement of 21 July 1992, and moreover signed it as a party.
>
> 382. In the light of all these circumstances the Court considers that the Russian Federation's responsibility is engaged in respect of the unlawful acts committed by the Transdniestrian separatists, regard being had to the military and political support it gave them to help them set up the separatist regime and the participation of its military personnel in the fighting. In acting thus the authorities of the Russian Federation contributed both militarily and politically to the creation of a separatist regime in the region of Transdniestria, which is part of the territory of the Republic of Moldova.
>
> The Court next notes that even after the ceasefire agreement of 21 July 1992 the Russian Federation continued to provide military, political and economic support to the separatist regime, thus enabling it to survive by strengthening itself and by acquiring a certain amount of autonomy vis-à-vis Moldova.
>
> 383. The Court further notes that in the context of the events mentioned above the applicants were arrested in June 1992 with the participation of soldiers of the Fourteenth Army (subsequently the ROG). The first three applicants were then detained on Fourteenth Army premises and guarded

by Fourteenth Army troops. During their detention these three applicants were interrogated and subjected to treatment which could be considered contrary to Article 3 of the Convention. They were then handed over into the charge of the Transdniestrian police.

Similarly, after his arrest by soldiers of the Fourteenth Army, the fourth applicant was handed over to the Transdniestrian separatist police, then detained, interrogated and subjected on police premises to treatment which could be considered contrary to Article 3 of the Convention.

384. The Court considers that on account of the above events the applicants came within the jurisdiction of the Russian Federation within the meaning of Article 1 of the Convention, although at the time when they occurred the Convention was not in force with regard to the Russian Federation.

This is because the events which gave rise to the responsibility of the Russian Federation must be considered to include not only the acts in which the agents of that State participated, like the applicants' arrest and detention, but also their transfer into the hands of the Transdniestrian police and regime, and the subsequent ill-treatment inflicted on them by those police, since in acting in that way the agents of the Russian Federation were fully aware that they were handing them over to an illegal and unconstitutional regime.

In addition, regard being had to the acts the applicants were accused of, the agents of the Russian Government knew, or at least should have known, the fate which awaited them.

385. In the Court's opinion, all of the acts committed by Russian soldiers with regard to the applicants, including their transfer into the charge of the separatist regime, in the context of the Russian authorities' collaboration with that illegal regime, are capable of engaging responsibility for the acts of that regime.

It remains to be determined whether that responsibility remained engaged and whether it was still engaged at the time of the ratification of the Convention by the Russian Federation.

(B) AFTER RATIFICATION OF THE CONVENTION BY THE RUSSIAN FEDERATION

386. With regard to the period after ratification of the Convention, on 5 May 1998, the Court notes the following.

387. The Russian army is still stationed in Moldovan territory in breach of the undertakings to withdraw them completely given by the Russian Federation at the OSCE summits in Istanbul (1999) and Porto (2001). Although the number of Russian troops stationed in Transdniestria has in fact fallen significantly since 1992, the Court notes that the ROG's weapons stocks are still there.

Consequently, in view of the weight of this arsenal, the ROG's military importance in the region and its dissuasive influence persist.

388. The Court further observes that by virtue of the agreements between the Russian Federation, on the one hand, and the Moldovan and Transdniestrian authorities respectively, on the other the 'MRT' authorities were supposed to acquire the infrastructure and arsenal of the ROG at the time of its total withdrawal. It should be noted in that connection that the interpretation given by the Russian Government of the term 'local administrative authorities' of the region of Transdniestria, to be found, among other places, in the agreement of 21 October 1994 is different from that put forward by the Moldovan Government, a fact which enabled the 'MRT' regime to acquire that infrastructure.

389. As regards military relations, the Court notes that the Moldovan delegation to the Joint Control Commission constantly raised allegations of collusion between the ROG personnel and the Transdniestrian authorities regarding transfers of weapons to the latter. It notes that the ROG personnel denied those allegations in the presence of the delegates, declaring that some equipment could have found its way into the separatists' hands as a result of thefts.

Taking into account the accusations made against the ROG and the dangerous nature of its weapons stocks, the Court finds it hard to understand why the ROG troops do not have effective legal resources to prevent such transfers or thefts, as is apparent from their witness evidence to the delegates.

390. The Court attaches particular importance to the financial support enjoyed by the 'MRT' by virtue of the following agreements it has concluded with the Russian Federation:

— the agreement signed on 20 March 1998 between the Russian Federation and the representative of the 'MRT', which provided for the division between the 'MRT' and the Russian Federation of part of the income from the sale of the ROG's equipment;
— the agreement of 15 June 2001, which concerned joint work with a view to using armaments, military technology and ammunition;
— the Russian Federation's reduction by 100 million US dollars of the debt owed to it by the 'MRT'; and
— the supply of Russian gas to Transdniestria on more advantageous financial terms than those given to the rest of Moldova.

The Court further notes the information supplied by the applicants and not denied by the Russian Government to the effect that companies and institutions of the Russian Federation normally controlled by the State, or whose policy is subject to State authorisation, operating particularly in the military field, have been able to enter into commercial relations with similar firms in the 'MRT'.

391. The Court next notes that, both before and after 5 May 1998, in the security zone controlled by the Russian peacekeeping forces, the 'MRT' regime continued to deploy its troops illegally and to manufacture and sell weapons in breach of the agreement of 21 July 1992.

392. All of the above proves that the 'MRT', set up in 1991–1992 with the support of the Russian Federation, vested with organs of power and its own administration, remains under the effective authority, or at the very least under the decisive influence, of the Russian Federation, and in any event that it survives by virtue of the military, economic, financial and political support given to it by the Russian Federation.

393. That being so, the Court considers that there is a continuous and uninterrupted link of responsibility on the part of the Russian Federation for the applicants' fate, as the Russian Federation's policy of support for the regime and collaboration with it continued beyond 5 May 1998, and after that date the Russian Federation made no attempt to put an end to the applicants' situation brought about by its agents, and did not act to prevent the violations allegedly committed after 5 May 1998.

Regard being had to the foregoing, it is of little consequence that since 5 May 1998 the agents of the Russian Federation have not participated directly in the events complained of in the present application.

394. In conclusion, the applicants therefore come within the 'jurisdiction' of the Russian Federation for the purposes of Article 1 of the Convention and its responsibility is engaged with regard to the acts complained of.

This analysis reveals how a member State can be held responsible for actions occurring within the territory of another member State where there has not been a military invasion/occupation.

In his dissenting opinion Judge Kovler stated:

In view of the particular nature of the case, in which the applicants' situation is indissociable from an extremely complex geopolitical context, the Court finds itself in new territory, given the lack of applicable case-law. The Court's judgment in this case could have set a precedent for similar situations in other zones of conflict within the Member States of the Council of Europe, including those which have joined recently. The historical roots of the conflict in which the countries of the region were involved and the 'fragmenting-empire' effect are features which bring to mind conflicts such as the not-so-very distant Balkans or Caucasus have seen.

However, the Court (wrongly in my opinion) preferred to see the situation in terms of a Cyprus-type conflict, following its corresponding case-law and falling into the trap that that case-law represented. To my mind that was a methodological error. The superficial similarities between the present case and the *Loizidou* case are deceptive. The only point in common (to which I will return) is the source of the conflict, namely the prospect for a sizeable community of being attached to another country from which it is radically differentiated by its historical, economic and cultural ties. Hence the reactions and counter-reactions of the participants in the conflict, which took violent forms and led to human tragedies.

He disagreed with the Court's explanation of the historical background to the emergence of the 'MRT' as he traced Russian/Slavic influence over the territory back to the early nineteenth century. Also he considered that Russia could not be held responsible for acts of the 'MRT' as the latter was proclaimed one year before the USSR broke up. Furthermore:

I have not found in the factual material concerning the military, political and economic aspects any valid evidence capable of establishing a limited or continuing intervention by Russia in favour of Transdniestria, or proof of the 'MRT's' military, political or economic dependence on Russia.

See p 169 for further consideration of the case.

8   A unanimous Chamber found that a number of Iraqi shepherds shot and mutilated in northern Iraq at a time when there was a large-scale Turkish military operation, involving over 35,000 ground troops, into Iraq for six weeks in the spring of 1995 were not within the jurisdiction of Turkey in **Issa and Others v Turkey**, judgment of 16 November 2004. The six applicants, wives/mothers of the deceased, claimed that the latter had been killed by Turkish soldiers. The Turkish Government acknowledged that its forces had undertaken an anti-terrorist operation in northern Iraq, but denied that Turkish troops had been in the area where the shepherds had been killed. Applying **Bankovic** and **Loizidou** the Chamber held that:

74. The Court does not exclude the possibility that, as a consequence of this military action, the respondent State could be considered to have exercised, temporarily, effective overall control of a particular portion of the territory of northern Iraq. Accordingly, if there is a sufficient factual basis for holding that, at the relevant time, the victims were within that specific area, it would follow logically that they were within the jurisdiction of Turkey . . .

However, given, *inter alia*, the lack of independent eyewitness accounts of the presence of Turkish forces near the applicant's village the Chamber concluded that it was not satisfied 'beyond reasonable doubt' that the deceased were within the jurisdiction of Turkey at the time of their deaths. This judgment shows that the Court is very circumspect in holding member States liable for acts occurring outside their national territorial boundaries. The judgment in **Issa** also disclosed that at the time of the killings there was intense fighting between the PKK (Kurdistan Workers Party) and KDP (Kurdistan Democratic Party) in the area where the deceased were working.

9 The use of the term 'everyone' in Article 1 means that non-nationals within the jurisdiction of a member State can claim the protection of the rights and guarantees elaborated in the Convention, see for example *Soering v United Kingdom*, p 192.

10 A Grand Chamber examined the overlapping responsibilities of a member State under the Convention and to the European Union in *Bosphorus Hava Yollari Turizm ve Ticaret Anonim Sirketi v Ireland*, judgment of 30 June 2005. The applicant Turkish company had leased two aircraft from Yugoslav Airlines (the national airline of the former Yugoslavia) in 1992. In April 1993 the Security Council of the United Nations adopted a Resolution requiring all States to impound aircraft in their territories in which a controlling interest was held by a person/undertaking from Yugoslavia (this Resolution was part of an ongoing sanctions strategy aimed at the human rights violations taking place in Yugoslavia). The European Community implemented that Resolution by an EC Regulation later that month. In May 1993 the applicant arranged for one of the lease aircraft to be serviced by a company in Ireland. After the aircraft had been serviced (and payment made by the applicant) the Irish Department of Transport impounded the aircraft in accordance with the EC Regulation. The applicant challenged that decision before the Irish courts and the issue was referred to the European Court of Justice for a preliminary ruling as to whether the aircraft came within the Regulation and if so whether the impounding violated the applicant's fundamental rights. The ECJ ruled that the Regulation applied to the aircraft and that the impounding was in furtherance of important international goals and did not constitute a disproportionate measure. Subsequently, the Irish Supreme Court upheld the lawfulness of the impounding. Before the Grand Chamber the applicant company alleged that the actions of the Irish authorities constituted a violation of its rights under Article 1 of Protocol 1. The Government submitted that its compliance with its international obligations in respect of the sanctions imposed upon Yugoslavia justified any interference with the applicant's property rights.

152. The Convention does not, on the one hand, prohibit Contracting Parties from transferring sovereign power to an international (including a supranational) organisation in order to pursue co-operation in certain fields of activity (the *M. & Co.* [*v Germany*, No 13258/87 64 DR 138] at p 144 and *Matthews* [*v UK*, ECHR 1999-I] at § 32. Moreover, even as the holder of such transferred sovereign power, that organisation is not itself held responsible under the Convention for proceedings before, or decisions of, its organs as long as it is not a Contracting Party (see *CFDT v European Communities*, No 8030/77, Commission decision of 10 July 1978, DR 13, p. 231; *Dufay v European Communities*, No 13539/88, Commission decision of 19 January 1989; the above-cited *M. & Co.* case, at p 144 and the above-cited *Matthews* judgment, at § 32).

153. On the other hand, it has also been accepted that a Contracting Party is responsible under Article 1 of the Convention for all acts and omissions of its organs regardless of whether the act or omission in question was a consequence of domestic law or of the necessity to comply with international legal obligations. Article 1 makes no distinction as to the type of rule or measure concerned and does not exclude any part of a Contracting Party's 'jurisdiction' from scrutiny under the Convention (*United Communist Party of Turkey and Others v Turkey* judgment of 30 January 1998, Reports, 1998-I, § 29).

154. In reconciling both these positions and thereby establishing the extent to which State action can be justified by its compliance with obligations flowing from its membership of an international organisation to which it has transferred part of its sovereignty, the Court has recognised that absolving Contracting States completely from their Convention responsibility in the areas covered by such a transfer would be incompatible with the purpose and object of the Convention:

the guarantees of the Convention could be limited or excluded at will thereby depriving it of its peremptory character and undermining the practical and effective nature of its safeguards (*M. & Co.* at p 145 and *Waite and Kennedy* [v *Germany*, ECHR 1999-I] at § 67). The State is considered to retain Convention liability in respect of treaty commitments subsequent to the entry into force of the Convention (*mutatis mutandis*, the above-cited *Matthews v the United Kingdom* judgment, at §§ 29 and 32–4, and *Prince Hans-Adam II of Liechtenstein v Germany* [GC], No 42527/98, § 47, ECHR 2001-VIII).

155. In the Court's view, State action taken in compliance with such legal obligations is justified as long as the relevant organisation is considered to protect fundamental rights, as regards both the substantive guarantees offered and the mechanisms controlling their observance, in a manner which can be considered at least equivalent to that for which the Convention provides (see the above-cited *M. & Co.* decision, at p 145, an approach with which the parties and the European Commission agreed). By 'equivalent' the Court means 'comparable': any requirement that the organisation's protection be 'identical' could run counter to the interest of international co-operation pursued (paragraph 150 above). However, any such finding of equivalence could not be final and would be susceptible to review in the light of any relevant change in fundamental rights' protection.

156. If such equivalent protection is considered to be provided by the organisation, the presumption will be that a State has not departed from the requirements of the Convention when it does no more than implement legal obligations flowing from its membership of the organisation.

However, any such presumption can be rebutted if, in the circumstances of a particular case, it is considered that the protection of Convention rights was manifestly deficient. In such cases, the interest of international co-operation would be outweighed by the Convention's role as a 'constitutional instrument of European public order' in the field of human rights (*Loizidou v Turkey (preliminary objections)*, judgment of 23 March 1995, Series A No 310, § 75).

157. It remains the case that a State would be fully responsible under the Convention for all acts falling outside its strict international legal obligations.

...

158. Since the impugned act constituted solely compliance by Ireland with its legal obligations flowing from membership of the EC, the Court will now examine whether a presumption arises that Ireland complied with its Convention requirements in fulfilling such obligations and whether any such presumption has been rebutted in the circumstances of the present case.

(B) WAS THERE A PRESUMPTION OF CONVENTION COMPLIANCE AT THE RELEVANT TIME?

159. The Court has described (at paragraphs 73–81 above) the fundamental rights guarantees of the EC which govern Member States, Community institutions together with natural and legal persons ('individuals').

While the constituent EC treaty did not initially contain express provisions for the protection of fundamental rights, the ECJ subsequently recognised that such rights were enshrined in the general principles of Community law protected by it and that the Convention had a 'special significance' as a source of such rights. Respect for fundamental rights has become 'a condition of the legality of Community acts' (paragraphs 73–5 above, together with the opinion of the AG in the present case at paragraphs 45–50 above) and in carrying out this assessment the ECJ refers extensively to Convention provisions and to this Court's jurisprudence. At the relevant time, these jurisprudential developments had been reflected in certain treaty amendments (notably those aspects of the Single European Act 1986 and of the TEU . . .).

This evolution has continued thereafter. The Treaty of Amsterdam 1997 is referred to at paragraph 79 above. Although not fully binding, the provisions of the Charter of Fundamental Rights of the European Union were substantially inspired by those of the Convention and the Charter recognises the Convention as establishing the minimum human rights standards. Article I-9 of the later Treaty establishing a Constitution for Europe (not in force) provides for the Charter to become primary law of the European Union and for the Union to accede to the Convention (see paragraphs 80–1 above).

160. However, the effectiveness of such substantive guarantees of fundamental rights depends on the mechanisms of control in place to ensure observance of such rights.

161. The Court has referred (at paragraphs 86–90 above) to the jurisdiction of the ECJ in, *inter alia*, annulment actions (Article 173, now Article 230), in actions against Community institutions for failure to perform Treaty obligations (Article 175, now Article 232), to hear related pleas of illegality under Article 184 (now Article 241) and in cases against Member States for failure to fulfil Treaty obligations (Articles 169, 170, and 171, now Articles 226, 227, and 228).

162. It is true that access of individuals to the ECJ under these provisions is limited: they have no locus standi under Articles 169 and 170; their right to initiate actions under Articles 173 and 175 is restricted as is, consequently, their right under Article 184; and they have no right to take an action against another individual.

163. It nevertheless remains the case that actions initiated before the ECJ by the Community institutions or a Member state constitute important control of compliance with Community norms to the indirect benefit of individuals. Individuals can also bring an action for damages before the ECJ in respect of the non-contractual liability of the institutions.

164. Moreover, it is essentially through the national courts that the Community system provides a remedy to individuals against a Member state or another individual for a breach of EC law. Certain EC Treaty provisions envisaged a complementary role for the national courts in the Community control mechanisms from the outset, notably Article 189 (the notion of direct applicability, now Article 249) and Article 177 (the preliminary reference procedure, now Article 234). It was the development by the ECJ of important notions such as the supremacy of EC law, direct effect, indirect effect and State liability which greatly enlarged the role of the domestic courts in the enforcement of Community law and its fundamental rights' guarantees.

The ECJ maintains its control on the application by national courts of EC law, including its fundamental rights guarantees, through the procedure for which Article 177 of the EC Treaty provides...While the ECJ's role is limited to responding to the interpretative or validity question referred by the domestic court, the response will often be determinative of the domestic proceedings (as, indeed, it was in the present case) and detailed guidelines on the timing and content of a preliminary reference have been laid down by the EC treaty provision and developed by the ECJ in its case-law. The parties to the domestic proceedings have the right to put their case to the ECJ during the Article 177 process. It is further recalled that national courts operate in legal systems into which the Convention has been incorporated, albeit to differing degrees.

165. In such circumstances, the Court finds that the protection of fundamental rights by EC law can be considered to be, and to have been at the relevant time, 'equivalent' (within the meaning of paragraph 155 above) to that of the Convention system. Consequently, the presumption arises that Ireland did not depart from the requirements of the Convention when it implemented legal obligations flowing from its membership of the EC (see paragraph 156).

(C) HAS THAT PRESUMPTION BEEN REBUTTED IN THE PRESENT CASE?

166. The Court has had regard to the nature of the interference, to the general interest pursued by the impoundment and by the sanctions regime and to the ruling of the ECJ (in the light of the opinion

of the AG), a ruling with which the Supreme Court was obliged to and did comply. It considers it clear that there was no dysfunction of the mechanisms of control of the observance of Convention rights.

In the Court's view, therefore, it cannot be said that the protection of the applicant's Convention rights was manifestly deficient with the consequence that the relevant presumption of Convention compliance by the respondent State has not been rebutted.

4. Conclusion under Article 1 of Protocol No 1

167. It follows that the impoundment of the aircraft did not give rise to a violation of Article 1 of Protocol No. 1 to the Convention.

Judges Rozakis, Tulkens, Traja, Botoucharova, Zagrebelsky, and Garlicki issued a joint concurring opinion in which they expressed a more cautious attitude towards the protection of fundamental rights by the EU system.

On the other hand, as the judgment itself acknowledges, individuals' access to the Community court is 'limited' (see paragraph 162). Yet, as the Court reiterated in the *Mamatkulov and Askarov v Turkey* judgment ([GC], Nos 46827/99 and 46951/99, 4 February 2005), the right of individual application 'is one of the keystones in the machinery for the enforcement of the rights and freedoms set forth in the Convention' (see § 122 of that judgment). Admittedly, judicial protection under Community law is based on a plurality of appeals, among which the reference to the Court of Justice for a preliminary ruling has an important role. However, it remains that case that, despite its value, a reference for a preliminary ruling entails an internal, a priori review. It is not of the same nature and does not replace the external, a posteriori supervision of the European Court of Human Rights, carried out following an individual application.

The judgment in **Bosphorus** was intended to maintain a harmonious relationship between the Strasbourg Court and the ECJ. President Wildhaber described it as a 'landmark judgment in the history of the relations between the two European Courts'. However, he noted that as applicants to the Strasbourg Court could seek to argue that in their particular cases they had not received 'equivalent' protection of Convention rights in domestic proceedings implementing EC law such applications were not in principle inadmissible *ratione materiae* (L. Wildhaber, 'The Coordination of the Protection of Fundamental Rights in Europe', Geneva, 8 September 2005).

Subsequently the liability of a member State under the ECHR when utilizing the European Union's system for allocating responsibility for determining asylum claims was examined by another Grand Chamber in *MSS v Belgium and Greece*, judgment of 21 January 2011, see p 210.

11 A later Grand Chamber distinguished **Bosphorus** when considering the potential liability of member States under the Convention in respect of their conduct as participants in UN security ('KFOR'—Kosovo Force) and administrative ('UNMIK'—United Nations Interim Administration Mission in Kosovo") organizations operating in Kosovo following the withdrawal of Yugoslav forces (for the background see Note 6). The applicants in *Behrami v France* and *Saramati v France, Germany and Norway*, decision of 2 May 2007, contended that the respondent States had failed to protect children from being injured by unexploded cluster bombs and unlawfully detained the second applicant. The Grand Chamber (by an undisclosed majority) ruled that:

151. . . . In the present cases, the impugned acts and omissions of KFOR and UNMIK cannot be attributed to the respondent States and, moreover, did not take place on the territory of those States or

by virtue of a decision of their authorities. The present cases are therefore clearly distinguishable from the *Bosphorus* case in terms both of the responsibility of the respondent States under Article 1 and of the Court's competence *ratione personae*.

The underlying concern of the Grand Chamber was to ensure that the application of the Convention did not undermine the effectiveness of UN missions. However, in the later case of *Al-Jedda v UK*, judgment of 7 July 2011, another Grand Chamber rejected the respondent State's contention that its detention of the applicant in Iraq, as a suspected terrorist, fell outside the State's jurisdiction due to the UN Security Council authorizing Multi-National Force action in that country.

80. The Court does not consider that, as a result of the authorisation contained in [UN Security Council] Resolution 1511 [adopted seven months after the military invasion by the Multi-National Force], the acts of soldiers within the Multi-National Force became attributable to the United Nations or—more importantly, for the purposes of this case—ceased to be attributable to the troop-contributing nations…The unified command structure over the force, established from the start of the invasion by the United States and United Kingdom, was not changed as a result of Resolution 1511. Moreover, the United States and the United Kingdom, through the Coalition Provisional Authority which they had established at the start of the occupation, continued to exercise the powers of government in Iraq. Although the United States was requested to report periodically to the Security Council about the activities of the Multi-National Force, the United Nations did not, thereby, assume any degree of control over either the force or any other of the executive functions of the Coalition Provisional Authority.

Consequently, the UK was responsible under Article 1 for the detention of the applicant. By 16 votes to 1 the Grand Chamber found a breach of Article 5(1) as the majority did not accept that any Security Council Resolution, '109.…explicitly or implicitly required the UK to place an individual whom its authorities considered to constitute a risk to the security of Iraq into indefinite detention without charge.' Furthermore, the detention could not be justified under any of the grounds detailed in Article 5(1). This judgment discloses the Court's precise study of Security Council Resolutions when determining if the actions of State personnel are, exceptionally, to be attributed to the UN.

12   A further extension of a State's extraterritorial responsibility under Article 1 was adopted by a Chamber in *Stephens v Malta (no 1)*, judgment of 21 April 2009. The applicant, a British national living in Spain, was suspected of conspiring with others to import drugs into Malta unlawfully. A Maltese court issued a warrant for the applicant's arrest and the Spanish authorities were requested to extradite him to Malta to face trial. He was arrested by the Spanish police and detained pending extradition. Through his Maltese lawyers the applicant began proceedings to challenge the legality of the arrest warrant. On 12 November 2004 the Civil Court in Malta ruled that the warrant had been issued *ultra vires*. The Attorney General appealed and Interpol Malta informed Interpol Spain that the Maltese judgment was not final. Ten days later the Spanish authorities granted the applicant bail. He subsequent lodged a claim at Strasbourg alleging Malta had breached Article 5. Regarding Malta's jurisdictional responsibility the Chamber held that:

52. By setting in motion a request for the applicant's detention pending extradition, the responsibility lay with Malta to ensure that the arrest warrant and extradition request were valid as a matter of Maltese law, both substantive and procedural.…It is to be noted that in the instant case the arrest warrant had been issued by a court which did not have the authority to do so, a technical irregularity which the Spanish court could not have been expected to notice when examining the request

for the applicant's arrest and detention. Accordingly, the act complained of by Mr Stephens having been instigated by Malta on the basis of its own domestic law and followed-up by Spain in response to its treaty obligations, must be attributed to Malta notwithstanding that the act was executed in Spain.

By 6 votes to 1 the Chamber went on to find a breach of Article 5(1) for the duration of the applicant's continued detention between 12 to 22 November 2004. This judgment clearly holds requesting member States liable under the Convention in respect of the detention, in other States, of wanted suspects.

13 The interception of a cargo vessel, suspected of transporting large quantities of illegal drugs, on the high seas by a French naval ship and navy commandos with the subsequent detention of the merchant ship's crew by the French forces was found to have brought the crew within the jurisdiction of France by a unanimous Grand Chamber in *Medvedyev and others v France*, judgment of 29 March 2010. See p 262 for the Article 5 aspects of the judgment.

14 In *Al-Skeini and others v UK*, judgment of 7 July 2011, the Grand Chamber sought to categorize the different forms of jurisdictional responsibility under Article 1. The six applicants alleged that their relatives had been killed by British military personnel during the Multi-National Force's occupation of Iraq and no effective investigations into those deaths had been held. Taking note of the established jurisprudence the Grand Chamber reaffirmed that, '131. A State's jurisdictional competence under Article 1 is primarily territorial…'. Exceptionally, member States could be liable for the extraterritorial effects of their actions, '137.… whenever the State through its agents exercise control and authority over an individual, and thus jurisdiction, the State is under an obligation under Article 1 to secure to that individual the rights and freedoms under Section 1 of the Convention that are relevant to the situation of the individual.' Furthermore, '138. Another exception to the principle that jurisdiction under Article 1 is limited to a State's own territory occurs when, as a consequence of lawful or unlawful military action, a Contracting State exercised effective control of an area outside the national territory.' In such circumstances the controlling member State is liable to secure, '138.…the entire range of substantive rights set out in the Convention and those additional Protocols which it has ratified.' Unanimously, the Grand Chamber determined that the UK was jurisdictionally liable under the first exception above:

149. It can be seen, therefore, that following the removal from power of the Ba'ath regime and until the accession of the Interim Government, the United Kingdom (together with the United States) assumed in Iraq the exercise of some of the public powers normally to be exercised by a sovereign government. In particular, the United Kingdom assumed authority and responsibility for the maintenance of security in South East Iraq. In these exceptional circumstances, the Court considers that the United Kingdom, through its soldiers engaged in security operations in Basrah during the period in question, exercised authority and control over individuals killed in the course of such security operations, so as to establish a jurisdictional link between the deceased and the United Kingdom for the purposes of Article 1 of the Convention.

Whilst the Grand Chamber acknowledged that the deaths of the applicants' relatives had occurred during a 'period when crime and violence were endemic', '164. Nonetheless, the obligation under Article 2 to safeguard life entails that, even in difficult security conditions, all reasonable steps must be taken to ensure an effective, independent investigation is conducted into alleged breaches of the right to life.' In conclusion, there had not been adequate inquiries into the deaths of the relatives of five applicants. This judgment is potentially highly significant for also clarifying that member States' responsibilities for guaranteeing Convention rights will vary according to the type of exceptional extraterritorial actions undertaken.

15 The Court has utilized Article 1 combined with other Articles providing substantive rights as the jurisprudential basis for a number of implied positive obligations upon member States. Examples include the duty to undertake effective investigations into killings first recognized in *McCann v UK* at paragraph 161 (see p 87), and the obligation to take measures to protect vulnerable persons from torture, inhuman or degrading treatment/punishment by other private persons, see *A v UK* at paragraph 22 (p 158). For a detailed analysis of this topic, see A. Mowbray, *The Development of Positive Obligations under the European Convention on Human Rights by the European Court of Human Rights* (Oxford: Hart Publishing, 2004).

4 ARTICLE 2 RIGHT TO LIFE

Although the Court did not have an opportunity to interpret and apply this fundamental Article until 1995 it then made clear that States were liable for the control and actions of their agents. Furthermore, the exceptions contained in Article 2(2) were to be strictly defined. Over the subsequent years the Court has also increased its disapproval of the death penalty with a consequent widening of the application of Article 3 to circumstances where a death penalty may or has been imposed (*Al-Saadoon*). A number of positive obligations have been creatively developed by the Court under Article 2. These encompass both procedural duties (e.g. to conduct effective investigations into killings: *Kelly*) and substantive obligations (e.g. to provide protection to persons known to be at immediate risk of unlawful killing by others: *Opuz*). However, in the face of divided religious/ethical and scientific views the Court has not been willing to recognize a negative aspect (right to die) to Article 2 (*Pretty*) nor to conclusively rule on whether the unborn fall within the protection of this Article (*Vo*).

The Court's general approach

McCann v UK A.324 (1995)
European Court of Human Rights

In early 1988 the British, Spanish, and Gibraltar authorities became aware that the Provisional Irish Republican Army (IRA) were planning a terrorist attack on Gibraltar. Intelligence suggested that it was to centre on the assembly area where the British army changed the guard every Tuesday morning. An advisory group, consisting of, *inter alios*, Special Air Service (SAS) personnel, British Security Service officers, and a bomb-disposal officer, was sent to Gibraltar to assist the Gibraltar Commissioner of Police. Three suspected terrorists (members of an Active Service Unit) were sighted in Malaga (Spain) on 4 March. At midnight on 5 March the Commissioner of Police held a briefing during which representatives of the Security Services stated that in their opinion: the IRA intended to attack the changing of the guard ceremony on 8 March; the ASU comprised Daniel McCann (previously convicted of possessing explosives), Mairead Farrell (previously convicted of causing explosions), and Sean Savage (described as an expert bomb-maker); the attack would be by way of a car bomb; the use of a radio-operated remote-control device to detonate the bomb was thought likely; the placing of a 'blocking' car to reserve a parking space for the car containing the bomb was considered unlikely and the suspects were believed to be dangerous, almost certainly armed, and likely to use their weapons if confronted by the security forces. A detective from Gibraltar went to the Spanish immigration post on the border with Gibraltar to keep a lookout for the suspects. Customs and police officers on duty at the Gibraltar border were not informed of the operation in order to reduce the number of persons with knowledge of the counter-terrorism plan (but an arrest team was located nearby). A person, thought to be Savage, was seen parking a white Renault car in the assembly area at about 12:30 hours. At about 14:00 hours he was confirmed to be Savage. Thirty minutes later Farrell and McCann were identified crossing the border into Gibraltar on foot. At about 15:00 hours the three suspects were seen, by surveillance officers, together looking at the parked car in the assembly area. The police considered whether to arrest the suspects, but they started to move away from the car. The British bomb-disposal adviser spent two minutes looking at the exterior of the car and he noted that the car aerial was out of place (it was rusty while the car was not old). He reported to the Police Commissioner that it was 'a suspect car' (he meant that it was a car parked in suspicious circumstances where there was every reason to believe that it contained a bomb). The Commissioner decided that the suspects should be arrested on suspicion of conspiracy to murder and he signed an order requesting the military to intercept and apprehend the suspects. Two SAS soldiers, in plain clothes and each armed with a pistol, moved within 10 metres behind McCann and Farrell. The former turned round (he may have heard a police car siren in the distance) and Soldier A considered that McCann made an aggressive movement (A thought McCann was going to press a remote-control device to detonate a bomb) so A opened fire on McCann. Soldier A also thought Farrell was reaching for a similar device in her handbag so he fired at her too. Soldier B also shot at both suspects. The two soldiers fired a total of 12 shots. Two other SAS soldiers (also in plain clothes and armed) were following Savage a short distance away. When the shooting began Savage turned around, one of the soldiers shouted out 'Stop' and Savage moved his arm down to his hip. Soldier D believed Savage was going for a radio detonator and so the former opened fire (from a distance of about two to three metres). Likewise soldier C also fired at Savage. Fifteen bullets were fired into Savage. All three suspects were killed. No weapons or detonation devices were found on the suspects' bodies. Nor was a bomb found in the Renault car. However, keys found in Farrell's handbag led Spanish police to another car parked in Marbella which contained an explosive device (consisting of 64 kg of Semtex explosive surrounded by 200 rounds of ammunition—designed to explode as shrapnel—attached to two timers).

An inquest into the killings was held by the Gibraltar Coroner in September 1988. After 19 days of hearings, during which 79 witnesses were heard (including the soldiers, security and police officers involved in the operation), the jury (by 9 to 2) returned verdicts of lawful killing. The applicants, representatives of the estates of the deceased suspects, sought to bring civil actions against the Ministry of Defence in the Northern Ireland High Court; however their action was struck-out. The applicants then complained to the Commission alleging that the planning and execution of the above counter-terrorist operation was in breach of Article 2. By 11 votes 6, the Commission found that there had been no breach.

A. INTERPRETATION OF ARTICLE 2 (ART 2)

1. General approach

146. The Court's approach to the interpretation of Article 2 (art 2) must be guided by the fact that the object and purpose of the Convention as an instrument for the protection of individual human beings requires that its provisions be interpreted and applied so as to make its safeguards practical and effective (see, *inter alia*, the *Soering v UK* judgment of 7 July 1989, Series A No 161, p 34, para 87, and the *Loizidou v Turkey (Preliminary Objections)* judgment of 23 March 1995, Series A No 310, p 27, para 72).

147. It must also be borne in mind that, as a provision (art 2) which not only safeguards the right to life but sets out the circumstances when the deprivation of life may be justified, Article 2

(art 2) ranks as one of the most fundamental provisions in the Convention—indeed one which, in peacetime, admits of no derogation under Article 15 (art 15). Together with Article 3 (art 15+3) of the Convention, it also enshrines one of the basic values of the democratic societies making up the Council of Europe (see the above-mentioned *Soering* judgment, p 34, para 88). As such, its provisions must be strictly construed.

148. The Court considers that the exceptions delineated in paragraph 2 (art 2-2) indicate that this provision (art 2-2) extends to, but is not concerned exclusively with, intentional killing. As the Commission has pointed out, the text of Article 2 (art 2), read as a whole, demonstrates that paragraph 2 (art 2-2) does not primarily define instances where it is permitted intentionally to kill an individual, but describes the situations where it is permitted to 'use force' which may result, as an unintended outcome, in the deprivation of life. The use of force, however, must be no more than 'absolutely necessary' for the achievement of one of the purposes set out in sub-paragraphs (a), (b) or (c) (art 2-2-a, art 2-2-b, art 2-2-c) (see application No 10044/82, *Stewart v UK*, 10 July 1984, Decisions and Reports 39, pp 169–71).

149. In this respect the use of the term 'absolutely necessary' in Article 2 para 2 (art 2-2) indicates that a stricter and more compelling test of necessity must be employed from that normally applicable when determining whether State action is 'necessary in a democratic society' under paragraph 2 of Articles 8 to 11 (art 8-2, art 9-2, art 10-2, art 11-2) of the Convention. In particular, the force used must be strictly proportionate to the achievement of the aims set out in sub-paragraphs 2 (a), (b) and (c) of Article 2 (art 2-2-a-b-c).

150. In keeping with the importance of this provision (art 2) in a democratic society, the Court must, in making its assessment, subject deprivations of life to the most careful scrutiny, particularly where deliberate lethal force is used, taking into consideration not only the actions of the agents of the State who actually administer the force but also all the surrounding circumstances including such matters as the planning and control of the actions under examination.

2. The obligation to protect life in Article 2 para 1 (art 2-1)

(a) Compatibility of national law and practice with Article 2 (art 2) standards

151. The applicants submitted under this head that Article 2 para 1 (art 2-1) of the Convention imposed a positive duty on States to 'protect' life. In particular, the national law must strictly control and limit the circumstances in which a person may be deprived of his life by agents of the State. The State must also give appropriate training, instructions and briefing to its soldiers and other agents who may use force and exercise strict control over any operations which may involve the use of lethal force.

In their view, the relevant domestic law was vague and general and did not encompass the Article 2 (art 2) standard of absolute necessity. This in itself constituted a violation of Article 2 para 1 (art 2-1). There was also a violation of this provision (art 2-1) in that the law did not require that the agents of the State be trained in accordance with the strict standards of Article 2 para 1 (art 2-1).

152. For the Commission, with whom the Government agreed, Article 2 (art 2) was not to be interpreted as requiring an identical formulation in domestic law. Its requirements were satisfied if the substance of the Convention right was protected by domestic law.

153. The Court recalls that the Convention does not oblige Contracting Parties to incorporate its provisions into national law (see, *inter alia*, the *James v UK* judgment of 21 February 1986, Series A No 98, p 47, para 84, and *The Holy Monasteries v Greece* judgment of 9 December 1994, Series A No 301-A, p 39, para 90). Furthermore, it is not the role of the Convention institutions to examine *in abstracto* the compatibility of national legislative or constitutional provisions with the requirements of the Convention (see, for example, the *Klass v Germany* judgment of 6 September 1978, Series A No 28, p 18, para 33).

154. Bearing the above in mind, it is noted that Article 2 of the Gibraltar Constitution . . . is similar to Article 2 (art 2) of the Convention with the exception that the standard of justification for the use of force which results in the deprivation of life is that of 'reasonably justifiable' as opposed to 'absolutely necessary' in paragraph 2 of Article 2 (art 2-2). While the Convention standard appears on its face to be stricter than the relevant national standard, it has been submitted by the Government that, having regard to the manner in which the standard is interpreted and applied by the national courts . . . there is no significant difference in substance between the two concepts.

155. In the Court's view, whatever the validity of this submission, the difference between the two standards is not sufficiently great that a violation of Article 2 para 1 (art 2-1) could be found on this ground alone.

156. As regards the applicants' arguments concerning the training and instruction of the agents of the State and the need for operational control, the Court considers that these are matters which, in the context of the present case, raise issues under Article 2 para 2 (art 2-2) concerning the proportionality of the State's response to the perceived threat of a terrorist attack. It suffices to note in this respect that the rules of engagement issued to the soldiers and the police in the present case provide a series of rules governing the use of force which carefully reflect the national standard as well as the substance of the Convention standard . . .

(b) Adequacy of the inquest proceedings as an investigative mechanism

157. The applicants also submitted under this head . . . that the State must provide an effective *ex post facto* procedure for establishing the facts surrounding a killing by agents of the State through an independent judicial process to which relatives must have full access.

Together with the *amici curiae*, Amnesty International and British-Irish Rights Watch and Others, they submitted that this procedural requirement had not been satisfied by the inquest procedure because of a combination of shortcomings. In particular, they complained that no independent police investigation took place of any aspect of the operation leading to the shootings; that normal scene-of-crime procedures were not followed; that not all eyewitnesses were traced or interviewed by the police; that the Coroner sat with a jury which was drawn from a 'garrison' town with close ties to the military; that the Coroner refused to allow the jury to be screened to exclude members who were Crown servants; that the public interest certificates issued by the relevant Government authorities effectively curtailed an examination of the overall operation.

They further contended that they did not enjoy equality of representation with the Crown in the course of the inquest proceedings and were thus severely handicapped in their efforts to find the truth since, *inter alia*, they had had no legal aid and were only represented by two lawyers; witness statements had been made available in advance to the Crown and to the lawyers representing the police and the soldiers but, with the exception of ballistic and pathology reports, not to their lawyers; they did not have the necessary resources to pay for copies of the daily transcript of the proceedings which amounted to £500–£700.

158. The Government submitted that the inquest was an effective, independent and public review mechanism which more than satisfied any procedural requirement which might be read into Article 2 para 1 (art 2-1) of the Convention. In particular, they maintained that it would not be appropriate for the Court to seek to identify a single set of standards by which all investigations into the circumstances of death should be assessed. Moreover, it was important to distinguish between such an investigation and civil proceedings brought to seek a remedy for an alleged violation of the right to life. Finally, they invited the Court to reject the contention by the intervenors British-Irish Rights Watch and Others that a violation of Article 2 para 1 (art 2-1) will have occurred whenever the Court finds serious differences between the UN Principles on Extra-Legal Executions and the investigation conducted into any particular death . . .

159. For the Commission, the inquest subjected the actions of the State to extensive, independent and highly public scrutiny and thereby provided sufficient procedural safeguards for the purposes of Article 2 (art 2) of the Convention.

160. The Court considers that it is unnecessary to decide in the present case whether a right of access to court to bring civil proceedings in connection with deprivation of life can be inferred from Article 2 para 1 (art 2-1) since this is an issue which would be more appropriately considered under Articles 6 and 13 (art 6, art 13) of the Convention—provisions (art 6, art 13) that have not been invoked by the applicants.

161. The Court confines itself to noting, like the Commission, that a general legal prohibition of arbitrary killing by the agents of the State would be ineffective, in practice, if there existed no procedure for reviewing the lawfulness of the use of lethal force by State authorities. The obligation to protect the right to life under this provision (art 2), read in conjunction with the State's general duty under Article 1 (art 211) of the Convention to 'secure to everyone within their jurisdiction the rights and freedoms defined in [the] Convention', requires by implication that there should be some form of effective official investigation when individuals have been killed as a result of the use of force by, *inter alios*, agents of the State.

162. However, it is not necessary in the present case for the Court to decide what form such an investigation should take and under what conditions it should be conducted, since public inquest proceedings, at which the applicants were legally represented and which involved the hearing of seventy-nine witnesses, did in fact take place. Moreover, the proceedings lasted nineteen days and, as is evident from the inquest's voluminous transcript, involved a detailed review of the events surrounding the killings. Furthermore, it appears from the transcript, including the Coroner's summing-up to the jury, that the lawyers acting on behalf of the applicants were able to examine and cross-examine key witnesses, including the military and police personnel involved in the planning and conduct of the anti-terrorist operation, and to make the submissions they wished to make in the course of the proceedings.

163. In light of the above, the Court does not consider that the alleged various shortcomings in the inquest proceedings, to which reference has been made by both the applicants and the intervenors, substantially hampered the carrying out of a thorough, impartial and careful examination of the circumstances surrounding the killings.

164. It follows that there has been no breach of Article 2 para 1 (art 2-1) of the Convention on this ground.

B. APPLICATION OF ARTICLE 2 (ART 2) TO THE FACTS OF THE CASE

1. General approach to the evaluation of the evidence

165. While accepting that the Convention institutions are not in any formal sense bound by the decisions of the inquest jury, the Government submitted that the verdicts were of central importance to any subsequent examination of the deaths of the deceased. Accordingly, the Court should give substantial weight to the verdicts of the jury in the absence of any indication that those verdicts were perverse or ones which no reasonable tribunal of fact could have reached. In this connection, the jury was uniquely well placed to assess the circumstances surrounding the shootings. The members of the jury heard and saw each of the seventy-nine witnesses giving evidence, including extensive cross-examination. With that benefit they were able to assess the credibility and probative value of the witnesses' testimony. The Government pointed out that the jury also heard the submissions of the various parties, including those of the lawyers representing the deceased.

166. The applicants, on the other hand, maintained that inquests are by their very nature ill-equipped to be full and detailed inquiries into controversial killings such as in the present case. Moreover, the inquest did not examine the killings from the standpoint of concepts such as 'proportionality' or 'absolute necessity' but applied the lesser tests of 'reasonable force' or 'reasonable necessity'. Furthermore, the jury focused on the actions of the soldiers as they opened fire as if it were considering their criminal culpability and not on matters such as the allegedly negligent and reckless planning of the operation.

167. The Commission examined the case on the basis of the observations of the parties and the documents submitted by them, in particular the transcript of the inquest. It did not consider itself bound by the findings of the jury.

168. The Court recalls that under the scheme of the Convention the establishment and verification of the facts is primarily a matter for the Commission (Articles 28 para 1 and 31) (art 28-1, art 31). Accordingly, it is only in exceptional circumstances that the Court will use its powers in this area. The Court is not, however, bound by the Commission's findings of fact and remains free to make its own appreciation in the light of all the material before it (see, *inter alia*, the *Cruz Varas v Sweden* judgment of 20 March 1991, Series A No 201, p 29, para 74, and the *Klaas v Germany* judgment of 22 September 1993, Series A No 269, p 17, para 29).

169. In the present case neither the Government nor the applicants have, in the proceedings before the Court, sought to contest the facts as they have been found by the Commission although they differ fundamentally as to the conclusions to be drawn from them under Article 2 (art 2) of the Convention.

Having regard to the submissions of those appearing before the Court and to the inquest proceedings, the Court takes the Commission's establishment of the facts and findings...to be an accurate and reliable account of the facts underlying the present case.

170. As regards the appreciation of these facts from the standpoint of Article 2 (art 2), the Court observes that the jury had the benefit of listening to the witnesses at first hand, observing their demeanour and assessing the probative value of their testimony.

Nevertheless, it must be borne in mind that the jury's finding was limited to a decision of lawful killing and, as is normally the case, did not provide reasons for the conclusion that it reached. In addition, the focus of concern of the inquest proceedings and the standard applied by the jury was whether the killings by the soldiers were reasonably justified in the circumstances as opposed to whether they were 'absolutely necessary' under Article 2 para 2 (art 2-2) in the sense developed above...

171. Against this background, the Court must make its own assessment whether the facts as established by the Commission disclose a violation of Article 2 (art 2) of the Convention.

172. The applicants further submitted that in examining the actions of the State in a case in which the use of deliberate lethal force was expressly contemplated in writing, the Court should place on the Government the onus of proving, beyond reasonable doubt, that the planning and execution of the operation was in accordance with Article 2 (art 2) of the Convention. In addition, it should not grant the State authorities the benefit of the doubt as if its criminal liability were at stake.

173. The Court, in determining whether there has been a breach of Article 2 (art 2) in the present case, is not assessing the criminal responsibility of those directly or indirectly concerned. In accordance with its usual practice therefore it will assess the issues in the light of all the material placed before it by the applicants and by the Government or, if necessary, material obtained of its own motion (see the *Ireland v UK* judgment of 18 January 1978, Series A No 25, p 64, para 160, and the above-mentioned *Cruz Varas* judgment, p 29, para 75).

2. Applicants' allegation that the killings were premeditated

174. The applicants alleged that there had been a premeditated plan to kill the deceased. While conceding that there was no evidence of a direct order from the highest authorities in the Ministry of Defence, they claimed that there was strong circumstantial evidence in support of their allegation. They suggested that a plot to kill could be achieved by other means such as hints and innuendoes, coupled with the choice of a military unit like the SAS which, as indicated by the evidence given by their members at the inquest, was trained to neutralise a target by shooting to kill. Supplying false information of the sort that was actually given to the soldiers in this case would render a fatal shooting likely. The use of the SAS was, in itself, evidence that the killing was intended.

175. They further contended that the Gibraltar police would not have been aware of such an unlawful enterprise. They pointed out that the SAS officer E gave his men secret briefings to which the Gibraltar police were not privy. Moreover, when the soldiers attended the police station after the shootings, they were accompanied by an army lawyer who made it clear that the soldiers were there only for the purpose of handing in their weapons. In addition, the soldiers were immediately flown out of Gibraltar without ever having been interviewed by the police.

176. The applicants referred to the following factors, among others, in support of their contention:
— The best and safest method of preventing an explosion and capturing the suspects would have been to stop them and their bomb from entering Gibraltar. The authorities had their photographs and knew their names and aliases as well as the passports they were carrying;
— If the suspects had been under close observation by the Spanish authorities from Malaga to Gibraltar, as claimed by the journalist, Mr Debelius, the hiring of the white Renault car would have been seen and it would have been known that it did not contain a bomb...;
— The above claim is supported by the failure of the authorities to isolate the bomb and clear the area around it in order to protect the public. In Gibraltar there were a large number of soldiers present with experience in the speedy clearance of suspect bomb sites. The only explanation for this lapse in security procedures was that the security services knew that there was no bomb in the car;
— Soldier G, who was sent to inspect the car and who reported that there was a suspect car bomb, admitted during the inquest that he was not an expert in radio signal transmission... This was significant since the sole basis for his assessment was that the radio aerial looked older than the car. A real expert would have thought of removing the aerial to nullify the radio detonator, which could have been done without destabilising the explosive, as testified by Dr Scott. He would have also known that if the suspects had intended to explode a bomb by means of a radio signal they would not have used a rusty aerial—which would reduce the capacity to receive a clear signal—but a clean one.... It also emerged from his evidence that he was not an explosives expert either. There was thus the possibility that the true role of Soldier G was to report that he suspected a car bomb in order to induce the Gibraltar police to sign the document authorising the SAS to employ lethal force.

177. In the Government's submission it was implicit in the jury's verdicts of lawful killing that they found as facts that there was no plot to kill the three terrorists and that the operation in Gibraltar had not been conceived or mounted with this aim in view. The aim of the operation was to effect the lawful arrest of the three terrorists and it was for this purpose that the assistance of the military was sought and given. Furthermore, the jury must have also rejected the applicants' contention that Soldiers A, B, C and D had deliberately set out to kill the terrorists, whether acting on express orders or as a result of being given 'a nod and a wink'.

178. The Commission concluded that there was no evidence to support the applicants' claim of a premeditated plot to kill the suspects.

179. The Court observes that it would need to have convincing evidence before it could conclude that there was a premeditated plan, in the sense developed by the applicants.

180. In the light of its own examination of the material before it, the Court does not find it established that there was an execution plot at the highest level of command in the Ministry of Defence or in the Government, or that Soldiers A, B, C and D had been so encouraged or instructed by the superior officers who had briefed them prior to the operation, or indeed that they had decided on their own initiative to kill the suspects irrespective of the existence of any justification for the use of lethal force and in disobedience to the arrest instructions they had received. Nor is there evidence that there was an implicit encouragement by the authorities or hints and innuendoes to execute the three suspects.

181. The factors relied on by the applicants amount to a series of conjectures that the authorities must have known that there was no bomb in the car. However, having regard to the intelligence information that they had received, to the known profiles of the three terrorists, all of whom had a background in explosives, and the fact that Mr Savage was seen to 'fiddle' with something before leaving the car . . . the belief that the car contained a bomb cannot be described as either implausible or wholly lacking in foundation.

182. In particular, the decision to admit them to Gibraltar, however open to criticism given the risks that it entailed, was in accordance with the arrest policy formulated by the Advisory Group that no effort should be made to apprehend them until all three were present in Gibraltar and there was sufficient evidence of a bombing mission to secure their convictions . . .

183. Nor can the Court accept the applicants' contention that the use of the SAS, in itself, amounted to evidence that the killing of the suspects was intended. In this respect it notes that the SAS is a special unit which has received specialist training in combating terrorism. It was only natural, therefore, that in light of the advance warning that the authorities received of an impending terrorist attack they would resort to the skill and experience of the SAS in order to deal with the threat in the safest and most informed manner possible.

184. The Court therefore rejects as unsubstantiated the applicants' allegations that the killing of the three suspects was premeditated or the product of a tacit agreement among those involved in the operation.

3. Conduct and planning of the operation

(a) Arguments of those appearing before the Court

(1) The Applicants

185. The applicants submitted that it would be wrong for the Court, as the Commission had done, to limit its assessment to the question of the possible justification of the soldiers who actually killed the suspects. It must examine the liability of the Government for all aspects of the operation. Indeed, the soldiers may well have been acquitted at a criminal trial if they could have shown that they honestly believed the ungrounded and false information they were given.

186. The soldiers had been told by Officer E (the attack commander) that the three suspects had planted a car bomb in Gibraltar, whereas Soldier G—the bomb-disposal expert—had reported that it was merely a suspect bomb; that it was a remote-control bomb; that each of the suspects could detonate it from anywhere in Gibraltar by the mere flicking of a switch and that they would not hesitate to do so the moment they were challenged. In reality, these 'certainties' and 'facts' were no more than suspicions or at best dubious assessments. However, they were conveyed as facts to soldiers who not only had been trained to shoot at the merest hint of a threat but also, as emerged from the evidence given during the inquest, to continue to shoot until they had killed their target.

In sum, they submitted that the killings came about as a result of incompetence and negligence in the planning and conduct of the anti-terrorist operation to arrest the suspects as well as a failure to maintain a proper balance between the need to meet the threat posed and the right to life of the suspects.

(2) The Government

187. The Government submitted that the actions of the soldiers were absolutely necessary in defence of persons from unlawful violence within the meaning of Article 2 para 2 (a) (art 2-2-a) of the Convention. Each of them had to make a split-second decision which could have affected a large number of lives. They believed that the movements which they saw the suspects make at the moment they were intercepted gave the impression that the terrorists were about to detonate a bomb. This evidence was confirmed by other witnesses who saw the movements in question. If it is accepted that the soldiers honestly and reasonably believed that the terrorists upon whom they opened fire might have been about to detonate a bomb by pressing a button, then they had no alternative but to open fire.

188. They also pointed out that much of the information available to the authorities and many of the judgments made by them proved to be accurate. The three deceased were an IRA active service unit which was planning an operation in Gibraltar; they did have in their control a large quantity of explosives which were subsequently found in Spain; and the nature of the operation was a car bomb. The risk to the lives of those in Gibraltar was, therefore, both real and extremely serious.

189. The Government further submitted that in examining the planning of the anti-terrorist operation it should be borne in mind that intelligence assessments are necessarily based on incomplete information since only fragments of the true picture will be known. Moreover, experience showed that the IRA were exceptionally ruthless and skilled in counter-surveillance techniques and that they did their best to conceal their intentions from the authorities. In addition, experience in Northern Ireland showed that the IRA is constantly and rapidly developing new technology. They thus had to take into account the possibility that the terrorists might be equipped with more sophisticated or more easily concealable radio-controlled devices than the IRA had previously been known to use. Finally, the consequences of underestimating the threat posed by the active service unit could have been catastrophic. If they had succeeded in detonating a bomb of the type and size found in Spain, everyone in the car-park would have been killed or badly maimed and grievous injuries would have been caused to those in adjacent buildings, which included a school and an old-people's home.

190. The intelligence assessments made in the course of the operation were reasonable ones to make in the light of the inevitably limited amount of information available to the authorities and the potentially devastating consequences of underestimating the terrorists' abilities and resources. In this regard the Government made the following observations:

— It was believed that a remote-controlled device would be used because it would give the terrorists a better chance of escape and would increase their ability to maximise the proportion of military rather than civilian casualties. Moreover, the IRA had used such a device in Brussels only six weeks before.

— It was assumed that any remote-control such as that produced to the Court would be small enough to be readily concealed about the person. The soldiers themselves successfully concealed radios of a similar size about their persons.

— As testified by Captain Edwards at the inquest, tests carried out demonstrated that a bomb in the car-park could have been detonated from the spot where the terrorists were shot…

— Past experience strongly suggested that the terrorists' detonation device might have been operated by pressing a single button.

— As explained by Witness O at the inquest, the use of a blocking car would have been unnecessary because the terrorists would not be expected to have any difficulty in finding a free space on 8 March. It was also dangerous because it would have required two trips into Gibraltar, thereby significantly increasing the risk of detection . . .

— There was no reason to doubt the *bona fides* of Soldier G's assessment that the car was a suspect car bomb. In the first place his evidence was that he was quite familiar with car bombs. Moreover, the car had been parked by a known bomb-maker who had been seen to 'fiddle' with something between the seats and the car aerial appeared to be out of place. IRA car bombs had been known from experience to have specially-fitted aerials and G could not say for certain from an external examination that the car did not contain a bomb . . . Furthermore, all three suspects appeared to be leaving Gibraltar. Finally the operation of cordoning off the area around the car began only twenty minutes after the above assessment had been made because of the shortage of available manpower and the fact that the evacuation plans were not intended for implementation until 7 or 8 March.

— It would have been reckless for the authorities to assume that the terrorists might not have detonated their bomb if challenged. The IRA were deeply committed terrorists who were, in their view, at war with the United Kingdom and who had in the past shown a reckless disregard for their own safety. There was still a real risk that if they had been faced with a choice between an explosion causing civilian casualties and no explosion at all, the terrorists would have preferred the former.

(3) The Commission

191. The Commission considered that, given the soldiers' perception of the risk to the lives of the people of Gibraltar, the shooting of the three suspects could be regarded as absolutely necessary for the legitimate aim of the defence of others from unlawful violence. It also concluded that, having regard to the possibility that the suspects had brought in a car bomb which, if detonated, would have occasioned the loss of many lives and the possibility that the suspects could have been able to detonate it when confronted by the soldiers, the planning and execution of the operation by the authorities did not disclose any deliberate design or lack of proper care which might have rendered the use of lethal force disproportionate to the aim of saving lives.

(b) The Court's assessment

(1) Preliminary considerations

192. In carrying out its examination under Article 2 (art 2) of the Convention, the Court must bear in mind that the information that the United Kingdom authorities received that there would be a terrorist attack in Gibraltar presented them with a fundamental dilemma. On the one hand, they were required to have regard to their duty to protect the lives of the people in Gibraltar including their own military personnel and, on the other, to have minimum resort to the use of lethal force against those suspected of posing this threat in the light of the obligations flowing from both domestic and international law.

193. Several other factors must also be taken into consideration.

In the first place, the authorities were confronted by an active service unit of the IRA composed of persons who had been convicted of bombing offences and a known explosives expert. The IRA, judged by its actions in the past, had demonstrated a disregard for human life, including that of its own members.

Secondly, the authorities had had prior warning of the impending terrorist action and thus had ample opportunity to plan their reaction and, in co-ordination with the local Gibraltar authorities, to take measures to foil the attack and arrest the suspects. Inevitably, however, the security authorities could not have been in possession of the full facts and were obliged to formulate their policies on the basis of incomplete hypotheses.

194. Against this background, in determining whether the force used was compatible with Article 2 (art 2), the Court must carefully scrutinise, as noted above, not only whether the force used by the

soldiers was strictly proportionate to the aim of protecting persons against unlawful violence but also whether the anti-terrorist operation was planned and controlled by the authorities so as to minimise, to the greatest extent possible, recourse to lethal force. The Court will consider each of these points in turn.

(2) Actions of the soldiers

195. It is recalled that the soldiers who carried out the shooting (A, B, C and D) were informed by their superiors, in essence, that there was a car bomb in place which could be detonated by any of the three suspects by means of a radio-control device which might have been concealed on their persons; that the device could be activated by pressing a button; that they would be likely to detonate the bomb if challenged, thereby causing heavy loss of life and serious injuries, and were also likely to be armed and to resist arrest...

196. As regards the shooting of Mr McCann and Ms Farrell, the Court recalls the Commission's finding that they were shot at close range after making what appeared to Soldiers A and B to be threatening movements with their hands as if they were going to detonate the bomb...The evidence indicated that they were shot as they fell to the ground but not as they lay on the ground. Four witnesses recalled hearing a warning shout...Officer P corroborated the soldiers' evidence as to the hand movements...Officer Q and Police Constable Parody also confirmed that Ms Farrell had made a sudden, suspicious move towards her handbag...

197. As regards the shooting of Mr Savage, the evidence revealed that there was only a matter of seconds between the shooting at the Shell garage (McCann and Farrell) and the shooting at Landport tunnel (Savage). The Commission found that it was unlikely that Soldiers C and D witnessed the first shooting before pursuing Mr Savage who had turned around after being alerted by either the police siren or the shooting...

Soldier C opened fire because Mr Savage moved his right arm to the area of his jacket pocket, thereby giving rise to the fear that he was about to detonate the bomb. In addition, Soldier C had seen something bulky in his pocket which he believed to be a detonating transmitter. Soldier D also opened fire believing that the suspect was trying to detonate the supposed bomb. The soldiers' version of events was corroborated in some respects by Witnesses H and J, who saw Mr Savage spin round to face the soldiers in apparent response to the police siren or the first shooting...

The Commission found that Mr Savage was shot at close range until he hit the ground and probably in the instant as or after he had hit the ground...This conclusion was supported by the pathologists' evidence at the inquest...

198. It was subsequently discovered that the suspects were unarmed, that they did not have a detonator device on their persons and that there was no bomb in the car...

199. All four soldiers admitted that they shot to kill. They considered that it was necessary to continue to fire at the suspects until they were rendered physically incapable of detonating a device...

200. The Court accepts that the soldiers honestly believed, in the light of the information that they had been given, as set out above, that it was necessary to shoot the suspects in order to prevent them from detonating a bomb and causing serious loss of life...The actions which they took, in obedience to superior orders, were thus perceived by them as absolutely necessary in order to safeguard innocent lives.

It considers that the use of force by agents of the State in pursuit of one of the aims delineated in paragraph 2 of Article 2 (art 2-2) of the Convention may be justified under this provision (art 2-2) where it is based on an honest belief which is perceived, for good reasons, to be valid at the time but which subsequently turns out to be mistaken. To hold otherwise would be to impose an unrealistic burden on the State and its law-enforcement personnel in the execution of their duty, perhaps to the detriment of their lives and those of others.

It follows that, having regard to the dilemma confronting the authorities in the circumstances of the case, the actions of the soldiers do not, in themselves, give rise to a violation of this provision (art 2-2).

201. The question arises, however, whether the anti-terrorist operation as a whole was controlled and organised in a manner which respected the requirements of Article 2 (art 2) and whether the information and instructions given to the soldiers which, in effect, rendered inevitable the use of lethal force, took adequately into consideration the right to life of the three suspects.

(3) Control and organisation of the operation

202. The Court first observes that, as appears from the operational order of the Commissioner, it had been the intention of the authorities to arrest the suspects at an appropriate stage. Indeed, evidence was given at the inquest that arrest procedures had been practised by the soldiers before 6 March and that efforts had been made to find a suitable place in Gibraltar to detain the suspects after their arrest...

203. It may be questioned why the three suspects were not arrested at the border immediately on their arrival in Gibraltar and why, as emerged from the evidence given by Inspector Ullger, the decision was taken not to prevent them from entering Gibraltar if they were believed to be on a bombing mission. Having had advance warning of the terrorists' intentions it would certainly have been possible for the authorities to have mounted an arrest operation. Although surprised at the early arrival of the three suspects, they had a surveillance team at the border and an arrest group nearby... In addition, the Security Services and the Spanish authorities had photographs of the three suspects, knew their names as well as their aliases and would have known what passports to look for...

204. On this issue, the Government submitted that at that moment there might not have been sufficient evidence to warrant the detention and trial of the suspects. Moreover, to release them, having alerted them to the authorities' state of awareness but leaving them or others free to try again, would obviously increase the risks. Nor could the authorities be sure that those three were the only terrorists they had to deal with or of the manner in which it was proposed to carry out the bombing.

205. The Court confines itself to observing in this respect that the danger to the population of Gibraltar—which is at the heart of the Government's submissions in this case—in not preventing their entry must be considered to outweigh the possible consequences of having insufficient evidence to warrant their detention and trial. In its view, either the authorities knew that there was no bomb in the car—which the Court has already discounted... or there was a serious miscalculation by those responsible for controlling the operation. As a result, the scene was set in which the fatal shooting, given the intelligence assessments which had been made, was a foreseeable possibility if not a likelihood.

The decision not to stop the three terrorists from entering Gibraltar is thus a relevant factor to take into account under this head.

206. The Court notes that at the briefing on 5 March attended by Soldiers A, B, C, and D it was considered likely that the attack would be by way of a large car bomb. A number of key assessments were made. In particular, it was thought that the terrorists would not use a blocking car; that the bomb would be detonated by a radio-control device; that the detonation could be effected by the pressing of a button; that it was likely that the suspects would detonate the bomb if challenged; that they would be armed and would be likely to use their arms if confronted...

207. In the event, all of these crucial assumptions, apart from the terrorists' intentions to carry out an attack, turned out to be erroneous. Nevertheless, as has been demonstrated by the Government, on the basis of their experience in dealing with the IRA, they were all possible hypotheses in a situation where the true facts were unknown and where the authorities operated on the basis of limited intelligence information.

208. In fact, insufficient allowances appear to have been made for other assumptions. For example, since the bombing was not expected until 8 March when the changing of the guard ceremony was to take place, there was equally the possibility that the three terrorists were on a reconnaissance mission. While this was a factor which was briefly considered, it does not appear to have been regarded as a serious possibility...

In addition, at the briefings or after the suspects had been spotted, it might have been thought unlikely that they would have been prepared to explode the bomb, thereby killing many civilians, as Mr McCann and Ms Farrell strolled towards the border area since this would have increased the risk of detection and capture... It might also have been thought improbable that at that point they would have set up the transmitter in anticipation to enable them to detonate the supposed bomb immediately if confronted...

Moreover, even if allowances are made for the technological skills of the IRA, the description of the detonation device as a 'button job' without the qualifications subsequently described by the experts at the inquest... of which the competent authorities must have been aware, over-simplifies the true nature of these devices.

209. It is further disquieting in this context that the assessment made by Soldier G, after a cursory external examination of the car, that there was a 'suspect car bomb' was conveyed to the soldiers, according to their own testimony, as a definite identification that there was such a bomb... It is recalled that while Soldier G had experience in car bombs, it transpired that he was not an expert in radio communications or explosives; and that his assessment that there was a suspect car bomb, based on his observation that the car aerial was out of place, was more in the nature of a report that a bomb could not be ruled out...

210. In the absence of sufficient allowances being made for alternative possibilities, and the definite reporting of the existence of a car bomb which, according to the assessments that had been made, could be detonated at the press of a button, a series of working hypotheses were conveyed to Soldiers A, B, C and D as certainties, thereby making the use of lethal force almost unavoidable.

211. However, the failure to make provision for a margin of error must also be considered in combination with the training of the soldiers to continue shooting once they opened fire until the suspect was dead. As noted by the Coroner in his summing-up to the jury at the inquest, all four soldiers shot to kill the suspects... Soldier E testified that it had been discussed with the soldiers that there was an increased chance that they would have to shoot to kill since there would be less time where there was a 'button' device... Against this background, the authorities were bound by their obligation to respect the right to life of the suspects to exercise the greatest of care in evaluating the information at their disposal before transmitting it to soldiers whose use of firearms automatically involved shooting to kill.

212. Although detailed investigation at the inquest into the training received by the soldiers was prevented by the public interest certificates which had been issued... it is not clear whether they had been trained or instructed to assess whether the use of firearms to wound their targets may have been warranted by the specific circumstances that confronted them at the moment of arrest.

Their reflex action in this vital respect lacks the degree of caution in the use of firearms to be expected from law enforcement personnel in a democratic society, even when dealing with dangerous terrorist suspects, and stands in marked contrast to the standard of care reflected in the instructions in the use of firearms by the police which had been drawn to their attention and which emphasised the legal responsibilities of the individual officer in the light of conditions prevailing at the moment of engagement...

This failure by the authorities also suggests a lack of appropriate care in the control and organisation of the arrest operation.

213. In sum, having regard to the decision not to prevent the suspects from travelling into Gibraltar, to the failure of the authorities to make sufficient allowances for the possibility that their intelligence assessments might, in some respects at least, be erroneous and to the automatic recourse to lethal force when the soldiers opened fire, the Court is not persuaded that the killing of the three terrorists constituted the use of force which was no more than absolutely necessary in defence of persons from unlawful violence within the meaning of Article 2 para 2 (a) (art 2-2-a) of the Convention.

214. Accordingly, the Court finds that there has been a breach of Article 2 (art 2) of the Convention....

FOR THESE REASONS, THE COURT

Holds by ten votes to nine that there has been a violation of Article 2 of the Convention;

...

NOTES

1 The Court was composed of Judges: Russo, Spielmann, Valticos, Morenilla, Lopes Rocha, Mifsud Bonnici, Makarczyk, Repik, Kuris, and Lohmus.

2 The nine dissenting judges (President Ryssdal and Judges: Bernhardt, Thor Vilhjalmsson, Gölcüklü, Palm, Pekkanen, Freeland, Baka, and Jambrek) issued a joint dissenting opinion. They disagreed with the majority's evaluation of the planning and control of the counter-terrorism operation in Gibraltar.

8. Before turning to the various aspects of the operation which are criticised in the judgment, we would underline three points of a general nature.

First, in undertaking any evaluation of the way in which the operation was organised and con-trolled, the Court should studiously resist the temptations offered by the benefit of hindsight. The authorities had at the time to plan and make decisions on the basis of incomplete information. Only the suspects knew at all precisely what they intended; and it was part of their purpose, as it had no doubt been part of their training, to ensure that as little as possible of their intentions was revealed. It would be wrong to conclude in retrospect that a particular course would, as things later tran-spired, have been better than one adopted at the time under the pressures of an ongoing anti-terrorist operation and that the latter course must therefore be regarded as culpably mistaken. It should not be so regarded unless it is established that in the circumstances as they were known at the time another course should have been preferred.

9. Secondly, the need for the authorities to act within the constraints of the law, while the suspects were operating in a state of mind in which members of the security forces were regarded as legiti-mate targets and incidental death or injury to civilians as of little consequence, would inevitably give the suspects a tactical advantage which should not be allowed to prevail. The consequences of the explosion of a large bomb in the centre of Gibraltar might well be so devastating that the authorities could not responsibly risk giving the suspects the opportunity to set in train the detona-tion of such a bomb. Of course the obligation of the United Kingdom under Article 2 para 1 (art 2-1) of the Convention extended to the lives of the suspects as well as to the lives of all the many others, civilian and military, who were present in Gibraltar at the time. But, quite unlike those others, the purpose of the presence of the suspects in Gibraltar was the furtherance of a criminal enterprise which could be expected to have resulted in the loss of many innocent lives if it had been successful. They had chosen to place themselves in a situation where there was a grave danger that an irrecon-cilable conflict between the two duties might arise.

10. Thirdly, the Court's evaluation of the conduct of the authorities should throughout take full account of (a) the information which had been received earlier about IRA intentions to mount a major terrorist attack in Gibraltar by an active service unit of three individuals; and (b) the discovery which (according to evidence given to the inquest by Witness O) had been made in Brussels on 21 January 1988 of a car containing a large amount of Semtex explosive and four detonators, with a radio-controlled system—equipment which, taken together, constituted a device familiar in Northern Ireland.

In the light of (a), the decision that members of the SAS should be sent to take part in the operation in response to the request of the Gibraltar Commissioner of Police for military assistance was wholly justifiable. Troops trained in a counter-terrorist role and to operate successfully in small groups would clearly be a suitable choice to meet the threat of an IRA active service unit at large in a densely populated area such as Gibraltar, where there would be an imperative need to limit as far as possible the risk of accidental harm to passers-by.

The detailed operational briefing on 5 March 1988 . . . shows the reasonableness, in the circumstances as known at the time, of the assessments then made. The operational order of the Gibraltar Commissioner of Police, which was drawn up on the same day, expressly proscribed the use of more force than necessary and required any recourse to firearms to be had with care for the safety of persons in the vicinity. It described the intention of the operation as being to protect life; to foil the attempt; to arrest the offenders; and the securing and safe custody of the prisoners . . .

All of this is indicative of appropriate care on the part of the authorities. So, too, is the cautious approach to the eventual passing of control to the military on 6 March 1988 . . .

11. As regards the particular criticisms of the conduct of the operation which are made in the judgment, foremost among them is the questioning (in paragraphs 203–05) of the decision not to prevent the three suspects from entering Gibraltar. It is pointed out in paragraph 203 that, with the advance information which the authorities possessed and with the resources of personnel at their disposal, it would have been possible for them 'to have mounted an arrest operation' at the border.

The judgment does not, however, go on to say that it would have been practicable for the authorities to have arrested and detained the suspects at that stage. Rightly so, in our view, because at that stage there might not be sufficient evidence to warrant their detention and trial. To release them, after having alerted them to the state of readiness of the authorities, would be to increase the risk that they or other IRA members could successfully mount a renewed terrorist attack on Gibraltar. In the circumstances as then known, it was accordingly not 'a serious miscalculation' for the authorities to defer the arrest rather than merely stop the suspects at the border and turn them back into Spain.

12. Paragraph 206 of the judgment then lists certain 'key assessments' made by the authorities which, in paragraph 207, are said to have turned out, in the event, to be erroneous, although they are accepted as all being possible hypotheses in a situation where the true facts were unknown and where the authorities were operating on the basis of limited intelligence information. Paragraph 208 goes on to make the criticism that 'insufficient allowances appear to have been made for other assumptions'.

13. As a first example to substantiate this criticism, the paragraph then states that since the bombing was not expected until 8 March 'there was equally the possibility that the . . . terrorists were on a reconnaissance mission'.

There was, however, nothing unreasonable in the assessment at the operational briefing on 5 March that the car which would be brought into Gibraltar was unlikely, on the grounds then stated, to be a 'blocking' car . . . So, when the car had been parked in the assembly area by one of the suspects and all three had been found to be present in Gibraltar, the authorities could quite properly operate on the working assumption that it contained a bomb and that, as the suspects were unlikely to risk two visits, it was not 'equally' possible that they were on a reconnaissance mission.

In addition, Soldier F, the senior military adviser to the Gibraltar Commissioner of Police, gave evidence to the inquest that, according to intelligence information, reconnaissance missions had been undertaken many times before: reconnaissance was, he had been told, complete and the operation was ready to be run. In these circumstances, for the authorities to have proceeded otherwise than on the basis of a worst-case scenario that the car contained a bomb which was capable of being detonated by the suspects during their presence in the territory would have been to show a reckless failure of concern for public safety.

14. Secondly, it is suggested in the second sub-paragraph of paragraph 208 that, at the briefings or after the suspects had been spotted, 'it might have been thought unlikely that they would have been prepared to explode the bomb, thereby killing many civilians, as Mr McCann and Ms Farrell strolled towards the border area since this would have increased the risk of detection and capture'.

Surely, however, the question is rather whether the authorities could safely have operated on the assumption that the suspects would be unlikely to be prepared to explode the bomb when, even if for the time being moving in the direction of the border, they became aware that they had been detected and were faced with the prospect of arrest. In our view, the answer is clear: certainly, previous experience of IRA activities would have afforded no reliable basis for concluding that the killing of many civilians would itself be a sufficient deterrent or that the suspects, when confronted, would have preferred no explosion at all to an explosion causing civilian casualties. It is relevant that, according to Soldier F's evidence at the inquest, part of the intelligence background was that he had been told that the IRA were under pressure to produce a 'spectacular'. He also gave evidence of his belief that, when cornered, the suspects would have no qualms about pressing the button to achieve some degree of propaganda success: they would try to derive such a success out of having got a bomb into Gibraltar and that would outweigh in their minds the propaganda loss arising from civilian casualties.

15. The second sub-paragraph of paragraph 208 goes on to suggest that it 'might also have been thought improbable that at that point'—that is, apparently, as McCann and Farrell 'strolled towards the border'—'[the suspects] would have set up the transmitter in anticipation to enable them to detonate the supposed bomb immediately if confronted'.

Here, the question ought, we consider, to be whether the authorities could prudently have proceeded otherwise than on the footing that there was at the very least a possibility that, if not before the suspects became aware of detection then immediately afterwards, the transmitter would be in a state of readiness to detonate the bomb.

16. It is next suggested, in the third sub-paragraph of paragraph 208, that 'even if allowances are made for the technological skills of the IRA, the description of the detonation device as a 'button job' without the qualifications subsequently described by the experts at the inquest…, of which the competent authorities must have been aware, over-simplifies the true nature of these devices'. The exact purport of this criticism is perhaps open to some doubt. What is fully clear, however, is that, as the applicants' own expert witness accepted at the inquest, a transmitter of the kind which was thought likely to be used in the present case could be set up so as to enable detonation to be caused by pressing a single button; and in the light of past experience it would have been most unwise to discount the possibility of technological advance in this field by the IRA.

17. Paragraph 209 of the judgment expresses disquiet that the assessment made by Soldier G that there was a 'suspect car bomb' was conveyed to the soldiers on the ground in such a way as to give them the impression that the presence of a bomb had been definitely identified. But, given the assessments which had been made of the likelihood of a remote control being used, and given the various indicators that the car should indeed be suspected of containing a bomb, the actions

which the soldiers must be expected to have taken would be the same whether their understanding of the message was as it apparently was or whether it was in the sense which Soldier G apparently intended. In either case, the existence of the risk to the people of Gibraltar would have been enough, given the nature of that risk, justifiably to prompt the response which followed.

18. Paragraph 209, in referring to the assessment made by Soldier G, also recalls that while he had experience with car bombs, he was not an expert in radio communications or explosives. In considering that assessment, it would, however, be fair to add that, although his inspection of the car was of brief duration, it was enough to enable him to conclude, particularly in view of the unusual appearance of its aerial in relation to the age of the car and the knowledge that the IRA had in the past used cars with aerials specially fitted, that it was to be regarded as a suspect car bomb.

The authorities were, in any event, not acting solely on the basis of Soldier G's assessment. There had also been the earlier assessment, to which we have referred in paragraph 13 above, that a 'blocking' car was unlikely to be used. In addition, the car had been seen to be parked by Savage, who was known to be an expert bomb-maker and who had taken some time (two to three minutes, according to one witness) to get out of the car, after fiddling with something between the seats.

19. Paragraph 210 of the judgment asserts, in effect, that the use of lethal force was made 'almost unavoidable' by the conveyance to Soldiers A, B, C and D of a series of working hypotheses which were vitiated by the absence of sufficient allowances for alternative possibilities and by 'the definite reporting...of a car bomb which..., could be detonated at the press of a button'.

We have dealt in paragraphs 13–16 with the points advanced in support of the conclusion that insufficient allowance was made for alternative possibilities; and in paragraphs 17 and 18 with the question of reporting as to the presence of a car bomb.

We further question the conclusion that the use of lethal force was made 'almost unavoidable' by failings of the authorities in these respects. Quite apart from any other consideration, this conclusion takes insufficient account of the part played by chance in the eventual outcome. Had it not been for the movements which were made by McCann and Farrell as Soldiers A and B closed on them and which may have been prompted by the completely coincidental sounding of a police car siren, there is every possibility that they would have been seized and arrested without a shot being fired; and had it not been for Savage's actions as Soldiers C and D closed on him, which may have been prompted by the sound of gunfire from the McCann and Farrell incident, there is every possibility that he, too, would have been seized and arrested without resort to shooting.

20. The implication at the end of paragraph 211 that the authorities did not exercise sufficient care in evaluating the information at their disposal before transmitting it to soldiers 'whose use of firearms automatically involved shooting to kill' appears to be based on no more than 'the failure to make provision for a margin of error' to which the beginning of the paragraph refers. We have dealt already with the 'insufficient allowances for alternative possibilities' point (see, again, paragraphs 13–16 above), which we take to be the same as the alleged failure to provide for a margin of error which is referred to here. Any assessment of the evaluation by the authorities of the information at their disposal should, in any event, take due account of their need to reckon throughout with the incompleteness of that information (see paragraph 8 above); and there are no cogent grounds for any suggestion that there was information which they ought reasonably to have known but did not.

21. Paragraph 212, after making a glancing reference to the restrictive effect of the public interest certificates and saying that it is not clear 'whether the use of firearms to wound their targets may have been warranted by the specific circumstances that confronted them at the moment of arrest', goes on to say that 'their reflex action in this vital respect lacks the degree of caution...to be expected from law-enforcement personnel in a democratic society, even when dealing with dangerous terrorist suspects, and stands in marked contrast to the standard of care reflected in the instructions in the use of firearms by the police'. It concludes with the assertion that this 'failure

by the authorities also suggests a lack of appropriate care in the control and organisation of the arrest operation'.

22. As regards any suggestion that, if an assessment on the issue had been required by their training or instruction to be carried out by the soldiers, shooting to wound might have been considered by them to have been warranted by the circumstances at the time, it must be recalled that those circumstances included a genuine belief on their part that the suspects might be about to detonate a bomb by pressing a button. In that situation, to shoot merely to wound would have been a highly dangerous course: wounding alone might well not have immobilised a suspect and might have left him or her capable of pressing a button if determined to do so.

23. More generally as regards the training given, there was in fact ample evidence at the inquest to the effect that soldiers (and not only these soldiers) would be trained to respond to a threat such as that which was thought to be posed by the suspects in this case—all of them dangerous terrorists who were believed to be putting many lives at immediate risk—by opening fire once it was clear that the suspect was not desisting; that the intent of the firing would be to immobilise; and that the way to achieve that was to shoot to kill. There was also evidence at the inquest that soldiers would not be accepted for the SAS unless they displayed discretion and thoughtfulness; that they would not go ahead and shoot without thought, nor did they; but they did have to react very fast. In addition, evidence was given that SAS members had in fact been successful in the past in arresting terrorists in the great majority of cases.

24. We are far from persuaded that the Court has any sufficient basis for concluding, in the face of the evidence at the inquest and the extent of experience in dealing with terrorist activities which the relevant training reflects, that some different and preferable form of training should have been given and that the action of the soldiers in this case 'lacks the degree of caution in the use of firearms to be expected of law-enforcement personnel in a democratic society'. (We also question, in the light of the evidence, the fairness of the reference to 'reflex action in this vital respect'—underlining supplied. To be trained to react rapidly and to do so, when the needs of the situation require, is not to take reflex action.)

Nor do we accept that the differences between the guide to police officers in the use of firearms... and the 'Firearms—rules of engagement' annexed to the Commissioner's operational order... when the latter are taken together (as they should be) with the Rules of Engagement issued to Soldier F by the Ministry of Defence... can validly be invoked to support a contention that the standard of care enjoined upon the soldiers was inadequate. Those differences are no doubt attributable to the differences in backgrounds and requirements of the recipients to whom they were addressed, account being taken of relevant training previously given to each group (it is to be noted that, according to the evidence of Soldier F at the inquest, many lectures are given to SAS soldiers on the concepts of the rule of law and the use of minimum force). We fail to see how the instructions for the soldiers could themselves be read as showing a lack of proper caution in the use of firearms.

Accordingly, we consider the concluding stricture, that there was some failure by the authorities in this regard suggesting a lack of appropriate care in the control and organisation of the arrest operation, to be unjustified.

25. The accusation of a breach by a State of its obligation under Article 2 (art 2) of the Convention to protect the right to life is of the utmost seriousness. For the reasons given above, the evaluation in paragraphs 203 to 213 of the judgment seems to us to fall well short of substantiating the finding that there has been a breach of the Article (art 2) in this case. We would ourselves follow the reasoning and conclusion of the Commission in its comprehensive, painstaking and notably realistic report. Like the Commission, we are satisfied that no failings have been shown in the organisation and control of the operation by the authorities which could justify a conclusion that force was used

against the suspects disproportionately to the purpose of defending innocent persons from unlawful violence. We consider that the use of lethal force in this case, however regrettable the need to resort to such force may be, did not exceed what was, in the circumstances as known at the time, 'absolutely necessary' for that purpose and did not amount to a breach by the United Kingdom of its obligations under the Convention.

3   The British Government, and significant sections of the British media, were highly critical of the majority's judgment. In response to a question about the case from the Shadow Attorney General (Mr John Morris), the Attorney General (Sir Nicholas Lyell) stated:

that judgment caused a great deal of proper public unease. I would have expected the right hon and learned Gentleman to have commended the views of the minority in the court. He will remember that the decision was made by only 10 to nine, and that the president of the court took a fundamentally different view from the majority and set it out in concise reasoning with which, in my opinion, every sensible person should agree. [HC Deb 265 (1994–5) col 14.]

Do you think it was significant that the minority was composed of, *inter alios*, the four most senior members of the Court?

4   *McCann* was the first case in which the Court had to interpret and apply Article 2, therefore it is very important to appreciate that all the judges were in agreement about a number of fundamental aspects of the Article. For example, (a) that Article 2(2) applies to non-intentional killings (para 148), (b) the strict test of 'absolutely necessary' force in Article 2(2) (para 149), (c) the need for the Court to examine both the actions of State agents (e.g. police officers or soldiers) who are directly responsible for a death, and the planning and control of those operations when determining if a State is in breach of Article 2 (para 150), (d) that when evaluating the lawfulness of the State agents' actions the Court will have regard to the contemporary honest belief (perceived for good reasons) of those persons regarding the circumstances at the time of the killing (para 200), and (e) that Article 2(1) contains an implied obligation upon States to conduct effective official investigations into the killings of persons by State agents (para 161).

5   The divisions within the Court when applying the above principles to specific circumstances were further illustrated in the later case of *Andronicou and Constantinou v Cyprus*, 1997-VI. Lefteris Andronicou and Elsie Constantinou announced their engagement on 22 December 1993. In the morning of 24 December 1993 neighbours heard a woman calling for help from inside Andronicou's flat. The police were called and Andronicou threatened to shoot the officer unless he left. During the afternoon the local police director called the chief of police about the hostage situation and the latter sent the platoon of Police Special Forces ('MMAD') to deal with the matter. The head of the MMAD platoon informed its members that Andronicou was armed with a double-barrelled hunting gun and that he might have other weapons. The MMAD officers were armed with pistols and machine guns (with torches attached). They were instructed to use proportionate force and fire only if Constantinou or their lives were in danger. Andronicou informed his doctor that he would release Constantinou at midnight and then commit suicide. At 23:00 hours food was delivered to the flat (the police had arranged for the food to be drugged with a sedative). However, Constantinou was still heard screaming that Andronicou was going to kill her. The senior police officers came to the view that Andronicou was planning to kill her and then himself. At 23:55 the MMAD officers forced their way into Andronicou's flat. The first officer to enter was shot, in the shoulder, by Andronicou who then shot

Constantinou (in the hands and shoulder). Two other officers shot Andronicou dead (he was hit by at least 25 bullets). Constantinou was hit by two bullets from the police machine guns. She was taken to hospital in a police car (no ambulance was present at the scene), but despite emergency surgery she died (from injuries caused by the police bullets) several hours later. Subsequently, the government appointed a Commission of Inquiry, chaired by the President of the Supreme Court, Mr Loizou (who also served as a judge at the European Court), to investigate the deaths of Andronicou and Constantinou. The Commission reported, in June 1994, that the MMAD officers had used no more force than was 'absolutely necessary' in order to try and rescue Constantinou and that no criticism could be made of the police operation. The applicants, relatives of the deceased, complained to the Commission alleging, *inter alia*, that the killings violated Andronicou and Constantinou's right to life guaranteed by Article 2. The Commission, by 15 votes to 3, found that the authorities' planning and control of the operation (especially deploying the MMAD unit to end a domestic dispute) violated that Article. A majority, of five judges, of the Chamber that heard the case held that:

182. In carrying out its assessment of the planning and control phase of the operation from the standpoint of Article 2 of the Convention, the Court must have particular regard to the context in which the incident occurred as well as to the way in which the situation developed over the course of the day.

183. As to the context, the authorities clearly understood that they were dealing with a young couple and not with hardened criminals or terrorists. The negotiations and the resolve to negotiate up until the last possible moment clearly indicate that the authorities never lost sight of the fact that the incident had its origins in a 'lovers' quarrel' and that this factor had to be taken into account if, in the final analysis, it transpired that force had to be used to free Elsie Constantinou. It was not unreasonable in view of the context for the authorities to enlist the help of the family and friends of Lefteris Andronicou in order to bring the situation to an end. It is also to be noted that the authorities tried to bring an end to the incident through persuasion and dialogue right up to the last possible moment. The police negotiator continued his attempts in the later phase of the incident to assure Lefteris Andronicou that no harm would come to him if he were to release the young woman. Instructions were in fact given at a meeting which ended at 11pm to delay the involvement of the MMAD officers as much as possible to enable negotiations to continue...This sustained effort by the authorities to resolve the situation through negotiations illustrates a deep concern on the part of the authorities to deploy the MMAD officers only as a last resort. While there may have been shortcomings as regards, for example, the lack of crowd control or the absence of a dedicated telephone line between the police negotiator and Lefteris Andronicou, the Court considers nevertheless that the negotiations were in general conducted in a manner which can be said to be reasonable in the circumstances.

184. Irrespective of the domestic nature of the incident, the situation progressively developed in the eyes of the authorities present into a situation fraught with danger and in which critical decisions had to be taken. Lefteris Andronicou's intransigence in the face of negotiations, his threatening tone as well as the young woman's shouts for help persuaded the authorities that he intended to kill her and commit suicide at midnight. Admittedly, Lefteris Andronicou never announced that he would kill Elsie Constantinou and he only threatened to shoot her if the police broke into his flat. Nevertheless, the authorities could not reasonably ignore her shouts that her life was in danger. It must be emphasised that one hour before midnight she was repeatedly heard screaming that Lefteris Andronicou was going to kill her...and that Lefteris Andronicou had already shown his capacity for violence by beating her...In these circumstances and in the knowledge that Lefteris Andronicou was armed, the authorities could reasonably consider that as midnight approached

the negotiations had failed and that an attempt had to be made to get into the flat, disarm and arrest him and free Elsie Constantinou.

185. In the Court's view the authorities' decision to use the MMAD officers in the circumstances as they were known at the time was justified. Recourse to the skills of a highly professionally trained unit like the MMAD would appear to be quite natural given the nature of the operation which was contemplated. The decision to use the MMAD officers was a considered one of last resort. It was discussed both at the highest possible level in the police chain of command and at ministerial level…and only implemented when the negotiations failed and, as noted above, in view of a reasonably held belief that the young woman's life was in imminent danger. While it is true that the officers deployed were trained to shoot to kill if fired at, it is to be noted that they were issued with clear instructions as to when to use their weapons. They were told to use only proportionate force and to fire only if Elsie Constantinou's life or their own lives were in danger…It is to be noted that no use of weapons was ever intended and in fact the authorities were deeply anxious to avoid any harm to the couple…However, it was not unreasonable to alert the officers to the dangers which awaited them and to direct them carefully on firearms use. Furthermore, it must be stressed that the officers were not in fact informed that Lefteris Andronicou was in possession of weapons in addition to the shotgun. They were told that this possibility could not be excluded…Seen in these terms the message could reasonably be considered to be a warning to the officers to use extreme caution when effecting the operation. As to the decision to arm the officers with machine guns, it must be emphasised once again that the use of any firearm was never intended in the execution of the plan. However, given that Lefteris Andronicou was armed with a double-barrelled shotgun and it was not to be excluded that he had other weapons, the authorities had to anticipate all possible eventualities. It might be added that the machine guns had the advantage that they were fitted with flashlights which would enable the officers to overcome any difficulties encountered in identifying the precise location of the young woman in a dark room filled with tear gas and at the same time leave their hands free to control their weapons in the event of coming under fire. Furthermore, the use by the officers of their machine guns was subject to the same clear instructions as applied to the use of their pistols…

186. Having regard to the above considerations the Court is of the view that it has not been shown that the rescue operation was not planned and organised in a way which minimised to the greatest extent possible any risk to the lives of the couple.

Consequently, the majority determined that there had been no breach of Article 2. The four dissentients considered that the planning and control of the operation did not satisfy the requirements of Article 2. They were particularly concerned about the deployment of the MMAD officers and their use of machine guns to end the hostage taking. 'The use of machine guns in the circumstances of the present case seems to me to be an excessive use of force. The use of that kind of fire power against a frightened young man cannot be considered to be absolutely necessary even if he had the possibility to fire two shots with his hunting gun', *per* Judge Pekkanen, Partly Dissenting Opinion, para 6. Is it possible to reconcile the Court's decisions in **McCann** and **Andronicou and Constantinou**? Is it significant that the MMAD officers only opened fire after they had been shot at by Andronicou? Why did the Cypriot police not remove the public from outside Andronicou's building or have medical facilities on standby at the scene in case persons were injured?

6   The Court was, however, united in finding a breach of Article 2 in respect of the lack of sufficient care in the planning and control of a security forces operation against suspected armed PKK (Workers' Party of Kurdistan) members in **Ergi v Turkey**, 1998-IV. The applicant alleged that his sister (Havva Ergi) had been killed by shots fired by Turkish security

forces when they conducted an ambush of PKK members at the deceased's village. The Commission, unanimously, found a breach of Article 2 regarding, *inter alia*, the planning of the ambush. The Court held that:

79....the responsibility of the State is not confined to circumstances where there is significant evidence that misdirected fire from agents of the State has killed a civilian. It may also be engaged where they fail to take all feasible precautions in the choice of means and methods of a security operation mounted against an opposing group with a view to avoiding and, in any event, to minimising, incidental loss of civilian life. Thus, even though it has not been established beyond reasonable doubt that the bullet which killed Havva Ergi had been fired by the security forces, the Court must consider whether the security forces' operation had been planned and conducted in such a way as to avoid or minimise, to the greatest extent possible, any risk to the lives of the villagers, including from the fire-power of the PKK members caught in the ambush.

80. Turning to the particular circumstances of the case, the Court observes, on the one hand, that the Commission stated that its ability to make an assessment of how the operation had been planned and executed had been limited due to the lack of information provided by the Government. It had no information as to who took part in the operation, in what circumstances the security forces had opened fire and what steps had been taken by the security forces once the clash had developed...On the other hand, the gendarmerie officers' testimonies to the Commission had suggested that the ambush was organised in the north-west of the village without the distance between the village and the ambush being known. It was to be anticipated that PKK terrorists could have approached the village either following the path from the north or proceeding down the river bed to the north-east and in the latter event, they would have been able to penetrate to the edge of the village without being seen by the security forces to the north-west. The Commission found on the evidence that security forces had been present in the south...In these circumstances, the villagers had been placed at considerable risk of being caught in cross-fire between security forces and any PKK terrorists who had approached from the north or north-east. Even if it might be assumed that the security forces would have responded with due care for the civilian population in returning fire against terrorists caught in the approaches to the village, it could not be assumed that the terrorists would have responded with such restraint. There was no information to indicate that any steps or precautions had been taken to protect the villagers from being caught up in the conflict. Accordingly, in the absence of evidence from gendarmes involved in the planning and conduct of the operation, the Commission was not satisfied that the ambush operation carried out close to Kesentas village had been implemented with the requisite care for the lives of the civilian population.

81. The Court, having regard to the Commission's findings...and to its own assessment, considers that it was probable that the bullet which killed Havva Ergi had been fired from the south or south-east, that the security forces had been present in the south and that there had been a real risk to the lives of the civilian population through being exposed to cross-fire between the security forces and the PKK. In the light of the failure of the authorities of the respondent State to adduce direct evidence on the planning and conduct of the ambush operation, the Court, in agreement with the Commission, finds that it can reasonably be inferred that insufficient precautions had been taken to protect the lives of the civilian population.

The judgment is also important for requiring States to have regard to the dangers posed to innocent bystanders from both State personnel and non-State actors (e.g. terrorists or criminals) when planning security force operations. State authorities are under a stringent Convention duty to 'take all feasible precaution' to avoid or minimize 'incidental loss of civilian life' in the planning and implementation of such operations.

7 In two of the full-time Court's initial judgments concerning the actions of Federal military/security forces in Chechnya, a unanimous Chamber found breaches of Russia's obligation to protect the life of the applicants through a lack of the requisite care for civilian life in the planning and execution of military operations against insurgent fighters. In *Isayeva, Yusupova and Bazayeva v Russia*, judgment of 24 February 2005, the applicants were members of a large convoy of vehicles containing persons trying to flee the fighting between Federal forces and insurgents in Grozny during October 1999. The convoy was turned back at a military roadblock and during the return journey two military planes fired 12 air-to-ground missiles at the convoy. The pilots claimed that they were responding to gunfire directed at them from insurgents in the lorries. The missiles caused the deaths of 16 civilians (including two children of the applicants). The Chamber stated that:

178. The Court accepts that the situation that existed in Chechnya at the relevant time called for exceptional measures on behalf of the State in order to regain control over the Republic and to suppress the illegal armed insurgency. These measures could presumably include employment of military aviation equipped with heavy combat weapons. The Court is also prepared to accept that if the planes were attacked by illegal armed groups, that could have justified use of lethal force, thus falling within paragraph 2 of Article 2.

179. However, in the present case, the Government failed to produce convincing evidence which would have supported such findings. The testimonies submitted by the two pilots and the air traffic controller are the only mention of such an attack. These testimonies were collected in October and December 2000, i.e. over a year after the attack. They are incomplete and refer to other statements made by these witnesses during the course of the investigation, which the Government failed to disclose. They are made in almost identical terms and contain a very brief and incomplete account of the events.

Taking account of the 'extremely powerful weapon' used by the military (i.e. missiles which had an impact radius of between 300 and 800 metres, within which thousands of pieces of shrapnel were created by the explosive force of the missiles) in the vicinity of a large convoy of civilian vehicles, the Chamber concluded that the applicants had suffered a violation of Article 2. Similarly, in *Isayeva v Russia*, judgment of 24 February 2005, the applicant and her family were in a civilian vehicle trying to escape from fighting in their home town (where the Federal forces had trapped many armed insurgents). Military planes dropped high explosive bombs which caused the death of the applicant's son and three of her nieces. The Chamber found that:

190. Once the fighters' presence and significant number had become apparent to the authorities, the operation's commanders proceeded with the variant of the plan which involved a bomb and missile strike at Katyr-Yurt [the applicant's home town]. Between 8 and 9 a.m. on 4 February 2000 Major-General Nedobitko called in fighter jets, without specifying what load they should carry. The planes, apparently by default, carried heavy free-falling high-explosion aviation bombs FAB-250 and FAB-500 with a damage radius exceeding 1,000 metres. According to the servicemen's statements, bombs and other non-guided heavy combat weapons were used against targets both in the centre and on the edges of the village.

191. The Court considers that using this kind of weapon in a populated area, outside wartime and without prior evacuation of the civilians, is impossible to reconcile with the degree of caution expected from a law-enforcement body in a democratic society. No martial law and no state of emergency has been declared in Chechnya, and no derogation has been made under Article 15

of the Convention. The operation in question therefore has to be judged against a normal legal background. Even when faced with a situation where, as the Government submit, the population of the village had been held hostage by a large group of well-equipped and well-trained fighters, the primary aim of the operation should be to protect lives from unlawful violence. The massive use of indiscriminate weapons stands in flagrant contrast with this aim and cannot be considered compatible with the standard of care prerequisite to an operation of this kind involving the use of lethal force by State agents.

So, the death of the applicant's relatives amounted to a breach of Article 2. Both these cases reveal the Federal forces using combat weapons in areas with many civilians and with little regard for the protection of the life of ordinary persons, including children.

In the later case of **Abuyeva and others v Russia**, judgment of 2 December 2010, the 29 applicants/their relatives were also victims of the Federal forces' attack subject to the **Isayeva** judgment. The unanimous Chamber found, *inter alia*, that the Russian authorities had failed to undertake an effective investigation into the civilian deaths.

242. . . . However, to this day no independent study of the proportionality and necessity of the use of lethal force has been carried out, nor has there been any attribution of individual responsibility for the aspects of the operation which had caused loss of life and the evaluation of such aspects by an independent body, preferably of a judicial nature.

Therefore, the Chamber concluded that there had been breaches of both the procedural and substantive limbs of Article 2 and that the respondent government should pay the applicants 1.72 million euros compensation for non-pecuniary damage. The Chamber expressed the view that the Committee of Ministers, when supervising the execution of this judgment, would require the Government to conduct a new investigation which met the requirements of Article 2.

8 The Court has found a member State liable for the actions of civilian volunteers acting in association with the professional security forces in **Avsar v Turkey**, judgment of 10 July 2001. The case primarily concerned the actions of village guards who are civilians appointed by the Council of Elders in particular villages or civilians who volunteer themselves and are appointed by provincial governors. Village guards are armed and have the duties of protecting the life, honour, and property of persons within the boundaries of their villages. They have also been used for a wider range of security activities, such as reporting on strangers visiting their villages and preventing attacks on the national infrastructure (roads, bridges, dams etc). The district gendarme commander is responsible for the training and supervision of the village guards in his area. The Avsar family lived in south-east Turkey and they were regarded by the authorities as having a history of involvement with the PKK. In April 1994 Abdulkerim Avsar was in prison awaiting trial on charges of terrorism. On 22 April five village guards accompanied by a former PKK member (a 'confessor') and another unidentified man (who acted with authority as a member of the security forces) entered the Avsar family shop. They insisted that one of the Avsar brothers go with them to make a statement for Abdulkerim. After some resistance Mehmet Avsar agreed to accompany them. He was taken to a gendarmerie. Later he was removed by two of the village guards, the confessor, and the unidentified person. On 7 May the body of Mehmet (he had been shot) was found outside the city of Diyarbakir. Nearly six years later one of the village guards was convicted of murdering Mehmet whilst the other four guards and the confessor were convicted of abduction. The brother of Mehmet complained to Strasbourg alleging, *inter alia*, a breach of Article 2 as Mehmet was in the custody of security officials and killed in circumstances that fell outside Article 2(2). The Court, by 6 votes to 1, upheld this claim.

412. The Court is satisfied that Mehmet Şerif Avşar may be regarded as having died after having been taken into custody by agents of the State. It does not accept the Government's submission that the crime was committed by persons acting in their private capacity without the knowledge of the authorities and thereby beyond the scope of the State's responsibility.

413. The village guards enjoyed an official position, with duties and responsibilities. They had been sent to Diyarbakır to participate in the apprehension of suspects and they held themselves out to the Avşar family as acting on authority. The seventh person, a security officer, also held himself out as acting officially. The participants were, and purported to act as, agents of the State, and made use of their position in forcing Mehmet Şerif Avşar to go with them. In these circumstances, the Government is answerable for their conduct.

414. In that context, the Court has already found that there was a lack of accountability as regarded the security forces in south-east Turkey in or about 1993. . . . This case additionally highlights the risks attaching to the use of civilian volunteers in a quasi-police function. Notwithstanding the official denials that guards were used outside their own villages, it has been established in this case that guards were used regularly on a variety of official operations, including the apprehension of suspects. According to the regulations provided by the Government, village guards were hierarchically subordinate to the district gendarme commander. However, it is not apparent what supervision was, or could be exerted over guards who were engaged in duties outside the jurisdiction of the district gendarme commander. Nor, as the village guards were outside the normal structure of discipline and training applicable to gendarmes and police officers, is it apparent what safeguards there were against wilful or unintentional abuses of position carried out by the village guards either on their own initiative or under the instructions of security officers who themselves were acting outside the law. . . .

416. No justification for the killing of Mehmet Şerif Avşar being provided, the Court concludes that the Government are liable for his death.
  There has accordingly been a breach of Article 2 in this respect.

This ruling is to be welcomed as it seeks to ensure that States are accountable for both the regular security forces and also civilian volunteers. Indeed, the judgment highlights the potential dangers to respect for human rights posed by the latter category of persons. This is increased where the civilian volunteers are armed, operate in areas where they have strong personal relationships with victims and suspects, and are subject to limited supervision. Clearly if States wish to use civilian volunteers they must provide them with rigorous training as to the proper use and limitations of their legal powers and subject them to effective supervision and discipline.

9   Where an applicant alleges that State agents have killed a person in violation of Article 2, the Court will have to be satisfied that there is sufficient evidence 'to enable it to conclude beyond all reasonable doubt' (para 97 of judgment in *Yasa*) that the State was responsible for the death before it can hold the State directly accountable under the Convention. In a number of Turkish cases the Court has been unable to determine who was directly responsible for the killing (e.g. as in *Ergi*) and/or that there was insufficient evidence to hold the State directly accountable for the death(s) (e.g. *Yasa*). The applicant (a newsagent) in *Yasa v Turkey*, 1998-VI, claimed that his uncle had been shot dead by members of the Turkish security forces because the applicant had been selling the pro-Kurdish newspaper *Ozgur Gundem* (see p 632, for the paper's successful complaint under Article 10). The Commission

was not able to establish beyond all reasonable doubt that security or police officers had been implicated in the shooting. Consequently, the Court found Turkey not to have violated Article 2 in regard to the actual shooting. Even though the Court has not always been able to determine who was actually responsible for a particular killing it may find a State liable for breaching other aspects of Article 2 (e.g. failing to take proper care in the planning of a security operation as in *Ergi* or failing to conduct an effective investigation into the death as in *Yasa*).

10 Where a person has been detained by State agents and subsequently disappears without ever being seen again and no body is found, the Court may judge the existence of sufficient circumstantial evidence to determine the State liable under Article 2. For example in *Ipek v Turkey*, judgment of 17 February 2004, the applicant complained about the disappearance of his two sons. The Court found that they were amongst a group of six young men detained by soldiers during a military raid on their village in 1994. The six detainees were taken to a military establishment in a nearby town. On their arrival at the establishment the men were split into two groups of three. Members of one of these groups were released the next day. The other group (including the applicant's sons) were never seen again and their bodies were never found. Citing the earlier judgment of *Timurtas v Turkey*, 2000-VI, the Court held that:

> 166. ... 'Whether the failure on the part of the authorities to provide a plausible explanation as to a detainee's fate, in the absence of a body, might also raise issues under Article 2 of the Convention will depend on all the circumstances of the case, and in particular on the existence of sufficient circumstantial evidence, based on concrete elements, from which it may be concluded to the requisite standard of proof that the detainee must be presumed to have died in custody.... In this respect the period of time which has elapsed since the person was placed in detention, although not decisive in itself, is a relevant factor to be taken into account. It must be accepted that the more time goes by without any news of the detained person, the greater the likelihood that he or she has died. The passage of time may therefore to some extent affect the weight to be attached to other elements of circumstantial evidence before it can be concluded that the person concerned is to be presumed dead....'

Applying this approach the judges went on to find that the applicant's sons were seen being taken away by soldiers, they were subsequently transported to a military establishment and no information regarding their whereabouts has subsequently come to light in over nine years. Therefore, the Court was united in concluding that:

> 168. ... Servet and Ikram Ipek must be presumed dead following their unacknowledged detention by the security forces. Consequently, the responsibility of the respondent State for their death is engaged. Noting that the authorities have not provided any explanation as to what occurred following the Ipek brothers' apprehension, and that they do not rely on any ground of justification in respect of any use of lethal force by their agents, it follows that liability for their death is attributed to the respondent Government. Accordingly, there has been a violation of Article 2 on that account.

Eyewitness testimony, especially from third-parties, supporting applicants' assertions that their relatives were last seen in the custody of State agents coupled with long periods of disappearance are crucial elements in allowing the Court to determine that States should be held liable under this Article in respect of disappeared persons. There have been many successful applications concerning the abduction and disappearance of persons at the hands of the security forces operating in Chechnya: see, for example, *Dzhabirailova and Dzhabrailova v Russia*, judgment of 2 December 2010.

11 A Grand Chamber declined to provide a definitive answer to the question whether an unborn child is a 'person' for the purposes of Article 2 in ***Vo v France***, judgment of 8 July 2004. The applicant, Mrs Thi-Nho Vo, was a 24-year-old French national of Vietnamese origin. In 1991 she went to Lyons General Hospital for a scheduled medical examination as she was six months pregnant. On the same day a Mrs Thi Thanh Van Vo was due to have a coil removed at the hospital. The doctor responsible for the removal of the coil called out the name of 'Mrs Vo' in the waiting room. The applicant answered (the doctor noted that she had problems understanding French). He then consulted the notes for Mrs Van Vo and, without examining the applicant, sought to remove a coil. In undertaking this procedure the doctor pierced the applicant's amniotic sac and caused the loss of considerable fluid with the consequence that the applicant had to undergo an (unwanted) termination of her pregnancy several days later. The applicant, and her partner, made a criminal complaint against the doctor. He was charged with unintentional homicide (of the foetus) and unintentional injury of the applicant. The latter charge was later dropped in the light of a statutory amnesty. Eventually, the Court of Cassation ruled that the former offence had to be construed strictly and did not encompass the foetus. The applicant lodged a complaint at Strasbourg contending, *inter alia*, that the failure of French law to classify the taking of her unborn child's life as unintentional homicide amounted to a breach of Article 2. In her view, a child that had not yet been born was a person. The French Government responded that 'neither metaphysics nor medicine' had provided a definitive answer to when a foetus became a human being and Article 2 did not protect a foetus' right to life as a person. The Court held that:

75. Unlike Article 4 of the American Convention on Human Rights, which provides that the right to life must be protected 'in general, from the moment of conception', Article 2 of the Convention is silent as to the temporal limitations of the right to life and, in particular, does not define 'everyone' ('*toute personne*') whose 'life' is protected by the Convention. The Court has yet to determine the issue of the 'beginning' of 'everyone's right to life' within the meaning of this provision and whether the unborn child has such a right.

To date it has been raised solely in connection with laws on abortion. Abortion does not constitute one of the exceptions expressly listed in paragraph 2 of Article 2 but the Commission has expressed the opinion that it is compatible with the first sentence of Article 2 § 1 in the interests of protecting the mother's life and health because 'if one assumes that this provision applies at the initial stage of the pregnancy, the abortion is covered by an implied limitation, protecting the life and health of the woman at that stage, of the "right to life" of the foetus' (see *X v the United Kingdom*, Commission decision [(1980) 19 DR 244] at p 253).

76. Having initially refused to examine *in abstracto* the compatibility of abortion laws with Article 2 of the Convention (see *X v Norway*, No 867/60, Commission decision of 29 May 1961, Collection of Decisions 6, p. 34, and *X v Austria*, No 7045/75, Commission decision of 10 December 1976, DR 7, p 87), the Commission acknowledged in the case of *Brüggemann and Scheuten v the Federal Republic of Germany* [10 D&R 100 (1977)] that women complaining under Article 8 of the Convention about the Constitutional Court's decision restricting the availability of abortions had standing as victims. It stated on that occasion: 'pregnancy cannot be said to pertain uniquely to the sphere of private life. Whenever a woman is pregnant her private life becomes closely connected with the developing foetus' (ibid, at p 116, § 59). However, the Commission did not find it 'necessary to decide, in this context, whether the unborn child is to be considered as "life" in the sense of Article 2 of the Convention, or whether it could be regarded as an entity which under Article 8 § 2 could justify an interference "for the protection of others"' (ibid, at p 116, § 60). It expressed the opinion that there had been no violation of Article 8 of the Convention because 'not every regulation of the termination of unwanted pregnancies constitutes an interference with the right to respect for the private life of the mother' (ibid, at pp 116–17, § 61), while emphasising: 'There is no evidence that

it was the intention of the Parties to the Convention to bind themselves in favour of any particular solution' (ibid, at pp 117–18, § 64).

...

78. In the case of *H. v Norway*, concerning an abortion carried out on non-medical grounds against the father's wishes, the Commission added that Article 2 required the State not only to refrain from taking a person's life intentionally but also to take appropriate steps to safeguard life (see *H. v Norway* [73 D&R 155 (1992)] at p 167). It considered that it did not have to decide 'whether the foetus may enjoy a certain protection under Article 2, first sentence', but did not exclude the possibility that 'in certain circumstances this may be the case notwithstanding that there is in the Contracting States a considerable divergence of views on whether or to what extent Article 2 protects the unborn life' (ibid). It further noted that in such a delicate area the Contracting States had to have a certain discretion, and concluded that the mother's decision, taken in accordance with Norwegian legislation, had not exceeded that discretion (ibid, p. 168).

79. The Court has only rarely had occasion to consider the application of Article 2 to the foetus. In the case of *Open Door and Dublin Well Woman* [A.246-A (1992)] the Irish Government relied on the protection of the life of the unborn child to justify their legislation prohibiting the provision of information concerning abortion facilities abroad. The only issue that was resolved was whether the restrictions on the freedom to receive and impart the information in question had been necessary in a democratic society, within the meaning of paragraph 2 of Article 10 of the Convention, to pursue the 'legitimate aim of the protection of morals of which the protection in Ireland of the right to life of the unborn is one aspect' (see *Open Door and Dublin Well Woman*, cited above, pp 27–8, § 63), since the Court did not consider it relevant to determine 'whether a right to abortion is guaranteed under the Convention or whether the foetus is encompassed by the right to life as contained in Article 2' (ibid, p 28, § 66). Recently, in circumstances similar to those in the above-mentioned case of *H. v Norway*, where a woman had decided to terminate her pregnancy against the father's wishes, the Court held that it was not required to determine 'whether the foetus may qualify for protection under the first sentence of Article 2 as interpreted [in the case-law relating to the positive obligation to protect life]', and continued: 'Even supposing that, in certain circumstances, the foetus might be considered to have rights protected by Article 2 of the Convention, . . . in the instant case . . . [the] pregnancy was terminated in conformity with section 5 of Law No 194 of 1978'—a law which struck a fair balance between the woman's interests and the need to ensure protection of the foetus (see *Boso v Italy* (dec.), No 50490/99, ECHR 2002-VII).

80. It follows from this recapitulation of the case-law that in the circumstances examined to date by the Convention institutions—that is, in the various laws on abortion—the unborn child is not regarded as a 'person' directly protected by Article 2 of the Convention and that if the unborn do have a 'right' to 'life', it is implicitly limited by the mother's rights and interests. The Convention institutions have not, however, ruled out the possibility that in certain circumstances safeguards may be extended to the unborn child. That is what appears to have been contemplated by the Commission in considering that 'Article 8 §1 cannot be interpreted as meaning that pregnancy and its termination are, as a principle, solely a matter of the private life of the mother' (see *Brüggeman and Scheuten*, cited above, at pp 116–17, § 61) and by the Court in the above-mentioned *Boso* decision. It is also clear from an examination of these cases that the issue has always been determined by weighing up various, and sometimes conflicting, rights or freedoms claimed by a woman, a mother or a father in relation to one another or vis-à-vis an unborn child.

2. APPROACH IN THE INSTANT CASE

81. The special nature of the instant case raises a new issue. The Court is faced with a woman who intended to carry her pregnancy to term and whose unborn child was expected to be viable, at the

very least in good health. Her pregnancy had to be terminated as a result of an error by a doctor and she therefore had to have a therapeutic abortion on account of negligence by a third party. The issue is consequently whether, apart from cases where the mother has requested an abortion, harming a foetus should be treated as a criminal offence in the light of Article 2 of the Convention, with a view to protecting the foetus under that Article. This requires a preliminary examination of whether it is advisable for the Court to intervene in the debate as to who is a person and when life begins, in so far as Article 2 provides that the law must protect 'everyone's right to life'.

82. As is apparent from the above recapitulation of the case-law, the interpretation of Article 2 in this connection has been informed by a clear desire to strike a balance, and the Convention institutions' position in relation to the legal, medical, philosophical, ethical or religious dimensions of defining the human being has taken into account the various approaches to the matter at national level. This has been reflected in the consideration given to the diversity of views on the point at which life begins, of legal cultures and of national standards of protection, and the State has been left with considerable discretion in the matter, as the opinion of the European Group on Ethics at Community level appositely puts it: 'the...Community authorities have to address these ethical questions taking into account the moral and philosophical differences, reflected by the extreme diversity of legal rules applicable to human embryo research....It is not only legally difficult to seek harmonisation of national laws at Community level, but because of lack of consensus, it would be inappropriate to impose one exclusive moral code' [23 November 1998].

It follows that the issue of when the right to life begins comes within the margin of appreciation which the Court generally considers that States should enjoy in this sphere, notwithstanding an evolutive interpretation of the Convention, a 'living instrument which must be interpreted in the light of present-day conditions' (see *Tyrer v the United Kingdom*, judgment of 25 April 1978, Series A No 26, pp 15–16, §31, and subsequent case-law). The reasons for that conclusion are, firstly, that the issue of such protection has not been resolved within the majority of the Contracting States themselves, in France in particular, where it is the subject of debate...and, secondly, that there is no European consensus on the scientific and legal definition of the beginning of life....

83. The Court observes that the French Court of Cassation, in three successive judgments delivered in 1999, 2001 and 2002, considered that the rule that offences and punishment must be defined by law, which required criminal statutes to be construed strictly, excluded acts causing a fatal injury to a foetus from the scope of Article 221–6 of the Criminal Code, under which unintentional homicide of 'another' is an offence. However, if, as a result of unintentional negligence, the mother gives birth to a live child who dies shortly after being born, the person responsible may be convicted of the unintentional homicide of the child. The first-mentioned approach, which conflicts with that of several courts of appeal, was interpreted as an invitation to the legislature to fill a legal vacuum. That was also the position of the Criminal Court in the instant case: 'The court...cannot create law on an issue which [the legislature has] not yet succeeded in defining.' The French parliament attempted such a definition in proposing to create the offence of involuntary termination of pregnancy but the Bill containing that proposal was lost, on account of the fears and uncertainties that the creation of the offence might arouse as to the determination of when life began, and the disadvantages of the proposal, which were thought to outweigh its advantages. The Court further notes that alongside the Court of Cassation's repeated rulings that Article 221–6 of the Criminal Code does not apply to foetuses, the French parliament is currently revising the 1994 bioethics laws, which added provisions to the Criminal Code on the protection of the human embryo and required re-examination in the light of scientific and technological progress. It is clear from this overview that in France, the nature and legal status of the embryo and/or the foetus are currently not defined and that the manner in which it is to be protected will be determined by very varied forces within French society.

84. At European level, the Court observes that there is no consensus on the nature and status of the embryo and/or foetus although they are beginning to receive some protection in the light of

scientific progress and the potential consequences of research into genetic engineering, medically assisted procreation or embryo experimentation. At best, it may be regarded as common ground between States that the embryo/foetus belongs to the human race. The potentiality of that being and its capacity to become a person—enjoying protection under the civil law, moreover, in many States, such as France, in the context of inheritance and gifts, and also in the United Kingdom—require protection in the name of human dignity, without making it a 'person' with the 'right to life' for the purposes of Article 2. The Oviedo Convention on Human Rights and Biomedicine, indeed, is careful not to give a definition of the term 'everyone' and its explanatory report indicates that, in the absence of a unanimous agreement on the definition, the member States decided to allow domestic law to provide clarifications for the purposes of the application of that Convention. The same is true of the Additional Protocol on the Prohibition of Cloning Human Beings and the draft Additional Protocol on Biomedical Research, which do not define the concept of 'human being'. It is worth noting that the Court may be requested under Article 29 of the Oviedo Convention to give advisory opinions on the interpretation of that instrument.

85. Having regard to the foregoing, the Court is convinced that it is neither desirable, nor even possible as matters stand, to answer in the abstract the question whether the unborn child is a person for the purposes of Article 2 of the Convention ('*personne*' in the French text). As to the instant case, it considers it unnecessary to examine whether the abrupt end to the applicant's pregnancy falls within the scope of Article 2, seeing that, even assuming that that provision was applicable, there was no failure on the part of the respondent State to comply with the requirements relating to the preservation of life in the public-health sphere. With regard to that issue, the Court has considered whether the legal protection afforded the applicant by France in respect of the loss of the unborn child she was carrying satisfied the procedural requirements inherent in Article 2 of the Convention.

A large majority of the Grand Chamber, 14 votes to 3, went on to conclude (assuming Article 2 applied) that the option of bringing an action for damages against the doctor/hospital in the French administrative courts, which the applicant had not pursued, would have enabled her to obtain full redress for the damage caused by the doctor's negligence and therefore the procedural requirements were satisfied.

Judge Costa issued a separate opinion in which he expressed the view that:

17. In sum, I see no good legal reason or decisive policy consideration for not applying Article 2 in the present case. On a general level, I believe (in company with many senior judicial bodies in Europe) that there is life before birth, within the meaning of Article 2, that the law must therefore protect such life, and that if a national legislature considers that such protection cannot be absolute, then it should only derogate from it, particularly as regards the voluntary termination of pregnancy, within a regulated framework that limits the scope of the derogation. The actual circumstances of Mrs Vo's case made it all the more appropriate to find that Article 2 was applicable: she was six months pregnant (contrast this—purely for illustration purposes—with the German Federal Constitutional Court's view that life begins after fourteen days gestation), there was every prospect that the foetus would be born viable and, lastly, the pregnancy was clearly ended by an act of negligence, against the applicant's wishes.

18. I have nothing further to add, since, with minor differences, I agree with what the judgment has to say in finding that there has been no violation of Article 2.

Judge Rozakis, joined by Judges Caflisch, Fischbach, Lorenzen, and Thomassen, produced a separate opinion in which he stated that:

It consequently transpires from the present stage of development of the law and morals in Europe that the life of the unborn child, although protected in some attributes, cannot be equated to post-natal life, and, therefore, does not enjoy a right in the sense of 'a right to life', as protected by Article 2 of the Convention.

Judge Ress dissented because:

4. ... Historically, lawyers have understood the notion of 'everyone' as including the human being before birth and, above all, the notion of 'life' as covering all human life commencing with concep-tion, that is to say from the moment an independent existence develops until it ends with death, birth being but a stage in that development.

...

8. There can be no margin of appreciation on the issue of the applicability of Article 2. A margin of appreciation may, in my opinion, exist to determine the measures that should be taken to dis-charge the positive obligation that arises because Article 2 is applicable, but it is not possible to restrict the applicability of Article 2 by reference to a margin of appreciation. The question of the interpretation or applicability of Article 2 (an absolute right) cannot depend on a margin of appre-ciation. If Article 2 is applicable, any margin of appreciation will be confined to the effect thereof.

9. Since I consider that Article 2 applies to human beings even before they are born, an interpreta-tion which seems to me to be consistent with the approach of the Charter of Fundamental Rights of the European Union, and since France does not afford sufficient protection to the foetus against the negligent acts of third parties, I find that there has been a violation of Article 2 of the Convention. As regards the specific measures necessary to discharge that positive obligation, that is a matter for the respondent State, which should either take strict disciplinary measures or afford the protection of the criminal law (against unintentional homicide).

Judge Mularoni, joined by Judge Straznicka, dissented as she considered that the remedy of an action before the French administrative courts did not provide an adequate level of protection for the loss of the applicant's 'child' and:

Although legal personality is only acquired at birth, this does not to my mind mean that there must be no recognition or protection of 'everyone's right to life' before birth. Indeed, this seems to me to be a principle that is shared by all the member States of the Council of Europe, as domestic legislation permitting the voluntary termination of pregnancy would not have been necessary if the foetus was not regarded as having a life that should be protected. Abortion therefore constitutes an exception to the rule that the right to life should be protected, even before birth.

Given the Grand Chamber's findings of the absence of a European consensus regarding the precise time at which the right to life begins or the legal status of embryos/foetuses we can understand why the Court did not feel able to give general rulings on the applicability of Article 2 to such entities. A. Plomer evaluates the judgment in a comparative context in 'A Foetal Right to Life? The Case of Vo France' (2005) 5(2) *Human Rights Law Review* 311. In the later case of *A, B and C v Ireland* (p 501) a majority of the Grand Chamber invoked *Vo* as justification for continuing to accord States a wide margin of appreciation to legislate when abortions would be permitted.

12 Another Grand Chamber followed *Vo* when considering if embryos created during IVF procedures came within Article 2 in *Evans v UK*, judgment of 10 April 2007. After noting that under domestic law an embryo does not have independent rights or interests the Grand Chamber, unanimously, held that:

56. ... the embryos created by the applicant and [her former partner] do not have a right to life within the meaning of Article 2, and that there has not, therefore, been a violation of that provision.

For the Article 8 aspect of the case, see p 520.

13   A Grand Chamber examined the division between the ambit of Article 2 and Article 3 in the context of serious ill-treatment of persons by State agents in ***Ilhan v Turkey***, judgment of 27 June 2000. The applicant's brother ran away when gendarmes came to his village in 1992. A group of gendarmes found him and subjected him to a severe beating, including hitting him with their rifles and kicking him. These injuries resulted in him suffering brain damage resulting in a loss of 60 per cent of the function of his left side. Despite the gravity of these injuries, described as life-threatening by the doctors on his admission to hospital, the gendarmes did not take him to hospital until 36 hours after his arrest/assault. The applicant contended that the assault on his brother constituted a breach of Article 2 as that provision applied to the use of both lethal force and potentially lethal force (i.e. force that could foreseeably result in death). A large majority of the Grand Chamber (12 votes to 5) held that:

> 76. . . . it is only in exceptional circumstances that physical ill-treatment by State officials which does not result in death may disclose a breach of Article 2 of the Convention. . . . In almost all cases where a person is assaulted or maltreated by police or soldiers, their complaints will fall to be examined rather under Article 3 of the Convention.

Therefore, the majority did not consider that the force used by the gendarmes on the applicant's brother was of such a nature or degree to breach Article 2. The dissentients believed that as Article 2 protects the right to life and the injuries inflicted on the applicant's brother were life-threatening that Article was applicable to his maltreatment. Furthermore, given the gravity of the victim's injuries, the dissentients questioned what other 'exceptional circumstances' were required to be present for a serious maltreatment case not resulting in death to be examined under Article 2. The Grand Chamber was, however, unanimous that the applicant's brother had suffered torture (in violation of Article 3) in respect of his severe ill-treatment by the gendarmes and their delay in ensuring that he received proper medical treatment. The majority's approach was essentially to confine Article 2 to cases where officials' maltreatment of persons resulted in the death of the latter. This may be partially explained by the Court's contemporaneous widening of the scope of torture under Article 3 (see p 166).

14   A later example of the Court finding the use of non-lethal force by State agents to have violated Article 2 occurred in ***Makaratzis v Greece***, judgment of 20 December 2004. In September 1995 the applicant drove through red traffic lights, near the American embassy, in central Athens. He was chased by over 30 police officers, some of whom participated of their accord, in cars and on motorcycles. The applicant drove through five police roadblocks and collided with several non-police vehicles, injuring two civilians. The police thereupon opened fire on the applicant's car with handguns and submachine guns. He stopped his car at a petrol station and the police continued to fire at his car. The applicant would not leave his car, so the police forced their way into the car (one officer smashed the windscreen by throwing a plant pot at it). The applicant was then arrested. No weapon was found in his possession. He was taken to hospital and treated for gunshot wounds (he had been injured in the arm, foot, buttock, and chest). Subsequently, he was convicted of, *inter alia*, causing bodily injury to others by his negligence and sentenced to 40 days' imprisonment. An administrative investigation was also carried out and it found 16 bullet holes in the applicant's car. Twenty-nine police officers were identified as having taken part in the operation against the applicant but in addition an unknown number of other officers had participated of their own accord and they had left the scene without identifying themselves or handing in their weapons (to determine if they had been fired). The public prosecutor charged seven of the identified police officers with causing serious bodily harm and unauthorized use of weapons. However, they were later acquitted by the Athens First Instance Criminal Court (because it had not been proven that the accused had injured the applicant and the court held that the police officers had only used their weapons to try and immobilize a car whose driver they believed to be a dangerous criminal). The applicant complained to the European Court alleging breaches of Article 2, because the police had used unnecessary and disproportionate force against him and there had not been an effective investigation into the actions of the police. The Grand Chamber held that:

51. On the other hand, the case-law establishes that it is only in exceptional circumstances that physical ill-treatment by State officials which does not result in death may disclose a violation of Article 2 of the Convention. It is correct that in the proceedings brought under the Convention the criminal responsibility of those concerned in the use of the impugned force is not in issue. Nonetheless, the degree and type of force used and the intention or aim behind the use of force may, among other factors, be relevant in assessing whether in a particular case the State agents' actions in inflicting injury short of death are such as to bring the facts within the scope of the safeguard afforded by Article 2 of the Convention, having regard to the object and purpose pursued by that Article. In almost all cases where a person is assaulted or ill-treated by the police or soldiers, their complaints will rather fall to be examined under Article 3 of the Convention (see *İlhan v Turkey*, cited above, § 76).

52. What the Court must therefore determine in the present case, where State officials were implicated in the applicant's wounding, is whether the force used against the applicant was potentially lethal and what kind of impact the conduct of the officials concerned had not only on his physical integrity but also on the interest which the right to life is intended to protect.

53. It is common ground that the applicant was chased by a large number of police officers who made repeated use of revolvers, pistols and submachine guns.

It is clear from the evidence adduced before the Court that the police used their weapons in order to immobilise the applicant's car and effect his arrest, this being one of the instances contemplated by the second paragraph of Article 2 when the resort to lethal, or potentially lethal, force may be legitimate. As far as the ill-treatment proscribed by Article 3 is concerned, at no time could there be inferred from the police officers' conduct an intention to inflict pain, suffering, humiliation or debasement on him (see, as a recent authority, *Ilascu and Others v Moldova and Russia* [GC], §§ 425–8, ECHR 2004-VII). In particular, on the material before it the Court cannot find that the applicant's allegation as to the shooting of his foot after his removal from his car has been substantiated.

54. The Court likewise accepts the Government's submission that the police did not intend to kill the applicant. It observes, however, that the fact that the latter was not killed was fortuitous. According to the findings of the ballistic report, there were sixteen holes in the car caused by bullets following a horizontal or an upward trajectory to the car driver's level. There were three holes and a mark on the car's front windscreen caused by bullets which came through the rear plate glass; the latter was broken and had fallen in. In the end, the applicant was injured in the right arm, the right foot, the left buttock and the right side of the chest and was hospitalised for nine days. The seriousness of his injuries is not in dispute between the parties.

55. In the light of the above circumstances, and in particular the degree and type of force used, the Court concludes that, irrespective of whether or not the police actually intended to kill him, the applicant was the victim of conduct which, by its very nature, put his life at risk, even though, in the event, he survived. Article 2 is thus applicable in the instant case. Furthermore, given the context in which his life was put at risk and the nature of the impugned conduct of the State officials concerned, the Court is satisfied that the facts call for examination under Article 2.

The Grand Chamber then examined the domestic law governing the use of weapons by police officers and the police operation to arrest the applicant.

62. At the time of the events in issue, however, the applicable legislation was Law No 29/1943, dating from the Second World War when Greece was occupied by the German armed forces. That statute listed a wide range of situations in which a police officer could use firearms without being liable for the consequences. In 1991, a presidential decree authorised the use of firearms in the circumstances set forth in the 1943 statute 'only when absolutely necessary and when all less extreme methods have been exhausted'. No other provisions regulating the use of weapons during police actions and laying down guidelines on planning and control of police operations were contained in Greek law. On its face, the above, somewhat slender, legal framework would not appear sufficient to provide the level of protection 'by law' of the right to life that is required in present-day democratic societies in Europe.

63. This conclusion as to the state of Greek law is confirmed by the evidence before the Court of the bearing which the legal and administrative framework at the material time had on the way in which the potentially lethal police operation culminating in the applicant's arrest was conducted.

64. Turning to the facts of the present case, and having regard to the findings of the domestic court, the Court accepts that the applicant was driving his motor car in the centre of Athens at excessive speed in an uncontrolled and dangerous manner, thereby putting the lives of bystanders and police officers at risk; the police were thus entitled to react on the basis that he was manoeuvring a life-endangering object in a public place. Alternative means to stop him were tried but failed; this was accompanied by an escalation of the havoc that the applicant was causing and by the lethal threat that he was posing by his criminal conduct to innocent people. Further, the police officers pursuing the applicant had been informed by the control centre that he might well be armed and dangerous; they also believed that the movements which they saw the applicant make when he stopped his car were consistent with his being armed.

65. Another important factor must also be taken into consideration, namely the prevailing climate at that time in Greece, which was marked by terrorist activities against foreign interests. For example, a group called the 'Revolutionary Organisation 17 November', established in 1975, had committed, until it was dismantled in 2002, numerous crimes, including the assassination of US officials. This, coupled with the fact that the event took place at night, near the US Embassy, contributed to the applicant being perceived as a greater threat in the eyes of the police.

66. Consequently, like the national court, the Court finds in the circumstances that the police could reasonably have considered that there was a need to resort to the use of their weapons in order to immobilise the car and neutralise the threat posed by its driver, and not merely a need to arrest a motorist who had driven through a red traffic light. Therefore, even though it was subsequently discovered that the applicant was unarmed and that he was not a terrorist, the Court accepts that the use of force against him was based on an honest belief which was perceived, for good reasons, to be valid at the time. To hold otherwise would be to impose an unrealistic burden on the State and its law-enforcement personnel in the execution of their duty, perhaps to the detriment of their lives and those of others (see *McCann and Others v the United Kingdom*, cited above, pp 58–9, § 200).

67. However, although the recourse as such to some potentially lethal force in the present case can be said to have been compatible with Article 2 of the Convention, the Court is struck by the chaotic way in which the firearms were actually used by the police in the circumstances. It may be recalled that an unspecified number of police officers fired volleys of shots at the applicant's car with revolvers, pistols and submachine guns. No less than sixteen gunshot impacts were counted on the car, some being horizontal or even upwards, and not downwards as one would expect if the tyres, and only the tyres, of the vehicle were being shot at by the pursuing police. Three holes and a mark had damaged the car's front windscreen and the rear plate glass was broken and had fallen in. In sum,

it appears from the evidence produced before the Court that large numbers of police officers took part in a largely uncontrolled chase.

68. Serious questions therefore arise as to the conduct and the organisation of the operation. Admittedly some directions were given by the control centre to some police officers who had been expressly contacted, but some others ran of their own accord to their colleagues' assistance, without receiving any instructions. The absence of clear chains of command is a factor which by its very nature must have increased the risk of some police officers shooting erratically.

69. The Court evidently does not overlook the fact that the applicant was injured in the course of an unplanned operation which gave rise to developments to which the police was called upon to react without prior preparation (see, a contrario, *Rehbock v Slovenia*, No 29462/95, §§ 71–2, ECHR 2000-XII). Bearing in mind the difficulties in policing modern societies, the unpredictability of human conduct and the operational choices which must be made in terms of priorities and resources, the positive obligation must be interpreted in a way which does not impose an impossible burden on the authorities (see, *mutatis mutandis*, *Mahmut Kaya v Turkey*, No 22535/93, § 86, ECHR 2000-III).

70. Nonetheless, while accepting that the police officers who were involved in the incident did not have sufficient time to evaluate all the parameters of the situation and carefully organise their operation, the Court considers that the degeneration of the situation, which some of the police witnesses themselves described as chaotic, was largely due to the fact that at that time neither the individual police officers nor the chase, seen as a collective police operation, had the benefit of the appropriate structure which should have been provided by the domestic law and practice. In fact, the Court points out that in 1995, when the event took place, an admittedly obsolete and incomplete law for a modern democratic society was still regulating the use of weapons by State officials. The system in place did not afford to law-enforcement officials clear guidelines and criteria governing the use of force in peacetime. It was thus unavoidable that the police officers who chased and eventually arrested the applicant enjoyed a greater autonomy of action and were able to take unconsidered initiatives, which they would probably not have displayed had they had the benefit of proper training and instructions. The absence of clear guidelines could further explain why other police officers took part in the operation spontaneously without reporting to a central command.

71. In the light of the above, the Court considers that as far as their positive obligation under the first sentence of Article 2 § 1 to put in place an adequate legislative and administrative framework was concerned, the Greek authorities had not, at the relevant time, done all that could be reasonably expected of them to afford to citizens, and in particular to those, such as the applicant, against whom potentially lethal force was used, the level of safeguards required and to avoid real and immediate risk to life which they knew was liable to arise, albeit only exceptionally, in hot-pursuit police operations (see, *mutatis mutandis*, *Osman v United Kingdom*, cited above, p 3160, § 116 *in fine*).

72. Accordingly, the applicant has been the victim of a violation of Article 2 of the Convention on this ground. In view of this conclusion, it is not necessary to examine the life-threatening conduct of the police under the second paragraph of Article 2.

President Wildhaber, joined by Judges Kovler and Mularoni, dissented as they considered that the police had responded to 'the irresponsible and dangerous behaviour of the applicant' and, in their opinion, Greek law laid down 'in an absolutely clear fashion' the standard for the use of force by police officers. However, the Grand Chamber was unanimous in concluding that there had been a procedural breach of Article 2 due to serious defects, including failing to identify all the police officers who participated in the operation against the applicant, in the administrative inquiry into the shooting of the applicant.

The willingness of the overwhelming majority in *Makaratzis* to find a breach of the substantive requirements of Article 2, although the applicant had not been killed, can be explained in terms of both the nature and scale of the police response to his illegal (and dangerous) behaviour (i.e. over 30 officers firing numerous shots at his car) and the existing vague legal restrictions governing the use of firearms by police officers. These features were sufficient for the Grand Chamber to apply the *Ilhan* test of 'exceptional circumstances' to justify the application of Article 2. For an examination of the application of Article 2(2) to the use of firearms resulting in the death of suspects see *Nachova and Others v Bulgaria*, p 141.

15   The outer boundaries of the right to life were delimited in the tragic case of *Pretty v UK*, judgment of 29 April 2002. The applicant was a 43-year-old woman suffering from advanced motor neurone disease (an incurable terminal illness resulting in the progressive weakening of muscles leading to respiratory failure). Mrs Pretty had been diagnosed with the disease in 1999 and it progressed rapidly so that by the time of the Court's judgment she was paralysed from the neck down but her intellect and ability to make decisions were not impaired. She was distressed at the suffering she would endure if the disease was allowed to progress to her death. Therefore, she wished her husband to help her to commit suicide at the time of her choosing (because of the effects of her disease she needed the physical help of another person to commit suicide). She requested the Director of Public Prosecutions to undertake that he would not prosecute her husband (under the Suicide Act 1961 it is an offence to assist another person to commit suicide) if he helped her. The DPP refused to give such an undertaking and the applicant's claim for judicial review of that decision was ultimately rejected by the House of Lords (*R (Pretty) v DPP* [2001] 3 WLR 1598). Before the Court her lawyers contended, *inter alia*, that Article 2 protected not only the right to life but also the right to choose whether to go on living. In a unanimous judgment the Court held that:

37. The Court's case-law accords pre-eminence to Article 2 as one of the most fundamental provisions of the Convention (see the *McCann and Others v the United Kingdom* judgment of 27 September 1995, Series A No 324, §§ 146–7). It safeguards the right to life, without which enjoyment of any of the other rights and freedoms in the Convention is rendered nugatory. It sets out the limited circumstances when deprivation of life may be justified and the Court has applied a strict scrutiny when those exceptions have been invoked by respondent Governments (*McCann and Others v the United Kingdom*, op cit., §§ 149–50).

...

39. The consistent emphasis in all the cases before the Court has been the obligation of the State to protect life. The Court is not persuaded that 'the right to life' guaranteed in Article 2 can be interpreted as involving a negative aspect. While, for example, in the context of Article 11 of the Convention, the freedom of association was found to involve not only a right to join an association but a corresponding right not to be forced to join an association, the Court observes that the notion of a freedom implies some measure of choice as to its exercise (see the *Young, James and Webster v the United Kingdom* judgment of 13 August 1981, Series A No 44, § 52, and *Sigurdur A. Sigurjónsson v Iceland* judgment of 30 June 1993, Series A No 264, pp 15–16, § 35). Article 2 of the Convention is phrased in different terms. It is unconcerned with issues to do with the quality of living or what a person chooses to do with his or her life. To the extent that these aspects are recognised as so fundamental to the human condition that they require protection from State interference, they may be reflected in the rights guaranteed by other Articles of the Convention, or in other international human rights instruments. Article 2 cannot, without a distortion of language, be interpreted as conferring the diametrically opposite right, namely a right to die; nor can it create

a right to self-determination in the sense of conferring on an individual the entitlement to choose death rather than life.

40. The Court accordingly finds that no right to die, whether at the hands of a third person or with the assistance of a public authority, can be derived from Article 2 of the Convention. It is confirmed in this view by the recent Recommendation 1418 (1999) of the Parliamentary Assembly of the Council of Europe.

Consequently, the Court found no breach of Article 2 (or any other right under the Convention). The applicant decided not to request a re-hearing before the Grand Chamber and she died in a hospice a few weeks after the delivery of the above judgment. Her lawyers' attempts to persuade the Court to recognize an implicit 'right to die' within Article 2 would have required the latter to legislate on a very sensitive topic in a manner contrary to the domestic and European consensus (reflected in Recommendation 1418 which sought to uphold 'the prohibition against intentionally taking the life of terminally ill or dying persons...').

Article 2(1)

States' positive obligations

1   The Court implied that Article 2(1) imposed positive obligations upon States to protect the lives of individuals within their jurisdictions in *LCB v UK*, 1998-III. The applicant's father, in his capacity as a catering assistant in the Royal Air Force, was present during four atmospheric nuclear bomb tests conducted at Christmas Island (located in the Pacific Ocean) during 1957–8. The applicant was born in 1966 and during 1970 she was diagnosed as having leukaemia. She received chemotherapy, which lasted until she was 10 years old. In 1992 she became aware of a report, produced by the British Nuclear Tests Veterans' Association, indicating a high incidence of cancers in children of Christmas Island veterans. Thereupon, she complained to the Commission alleging, *inter alia*, that the British Government's failure to warn her parents of the possible risk to her health caused by her father's participation in the nuclear tests violated Article 2. The Commission was unanimous in finding no breach of that provision. The Court was also unanimous in determining that:

36....the first sentence of Article 2 § 1 enjoins the State not only to refrain from the intentional and unlawful taking of life, but also to take appropriate steps to safeguard the lives of those within its jurisdiction (cf the Court's reasoning in respect of Article 8 in the *Guerra v Italy* judgment of 19 February 1998, Reports 1998-I, p 227, § 58, and see also the decision of the Commission on the admissibility of application No 7154/75 of 12 July 1978, Decisions and Reports 14, p 31). It has not been suggested that the respondent State intentionally sought to deprive the applicant of her life. The Court's task is, therefore, to determine whether, given the circumstances of the case, the State did all that could have been required of it to prevent the applicant's life from being avoidably put at risk...

39. Having examined the expert evidence submitted to it, the Court is not satisfied that it has been established that there is a causal link between the exposure of a father to radiation and leukaemia in a child subsequently conceived. As recently as 1993, the High Court judge sitting in the cases of *Reay and Hope v British Nuclear Fuels plc* ([1994] Medical Law Reports 1), having examined a

considerable amount of expert evidence, found that 'the scales tilt[ed] decisively' in favour of a finding that there was no such causal link ... The Court could not reasonably hold, therefore, that, in the late 1960s, the United Kingdom authorities could or should, on the basis of this unsubstantiated link, have taken action in respect of the applicant.

40. Finally, in the light of the conflicting evidence of Dr Bross and Professor Eden ... and as the Commission also found ... it is clearly uncertain whether monitoring of the applicant's health *in utero* and from birth would have led to earlier diagnosis and medical intervention such as to diminish the severity of her disease. It is perhaps arguable that, had there been reason to believe that she was in danger of contracting a life-threatening disease owing to her father's presence on Christmas Island, the State authorities would have been under a duty to have made this known to her parents whether or not they considered that the information would assist the applicant. However, this is not a matter which the Court is required to decide in view of its above findings ...

41. In conclusion, the Court does not find it established that, given the information available to the State at the relevant time ... concerning the likelihood of the applicant's father having been exposed to dangerous levels of radiation and of this having created a risk to her health, it could have been expected to act of its own motion to notify her parents of these matters or to take any other special action in relation to her.

It follows that there has been no violation of Article 2.

2   The nature and extent of States' positive obligations arising from Article 2(1) were elaborated by the Court in ***Osman v UK***, 1998-VIII. The applicants were Mrs Osman and her son, Ahmet. During 1986 the headmaster of the state school attended by Ahmet, who was then 14 years old, noted that one of the teachers (Paul Paget-Lewis) had formed an attachment to Ahmet. After some months the deputy headmaster (Mr Perkins) suggested that Paget-Lewis seek psychiatric help. The police were informed of Paget-Lewis's attachment, but concluded that the matter should be dealt with by the school as there was no sexual element to the attachment. In April 1987, Paget-Lewis changed his name, by deed poll, to Paul Ahmet Yildirim Osman. In May, the police held further discussions with the school during which it was noted that Paget-Lewis had previously adopted that name after a pupil he had taught at another school. Paget-Lewis was seen by an education authority psychiatrist who recommended that he remain teaching at the school, but that he should receive counselling/psychotherapy. The applicants' house and car were attacked. In June Paget-Lewis was designated unfit to work and took medical leave. Throughout the remainder of the year other criminal acts were committed against the applicants' property. In January 1988 Paget-Lewis stole a shotgun. On 7 March Paget-Lewis went to the Osman home and shot dead Mr Osman and seriously wounded Ahmet. He then drove to Mr Perkin's home where he wounded him and killed his son. Paget-Lewis was arrested the next day and subsequently convicted of two charges of manslaughter (he pleaded guilty on grounds of diminished responsibility and was sentenced to be detained, without limit of time, in a secure mental hospital). The applicants sought to sue the Metropolitan Police Commissioner for alleged negligence in failing to prevent Paget-Lewis committing his killings/assaults. The Court of Appeal held that public policy required the police to be immune from such actions (***Osman v Ferguson*** [1993] 4 All ER 344). Later the applicants complained to the Commission alleging, *inter alia*, that the police had failed to protect the lives of Mr Osman and Ahmet as required by Article 2. By 10 votes to 7 the Commission found no breach of that Article. The Court noted:

115. ... that the first sentence of Article 2 § 1 enjoins the State not only to refrain from the intentional and unlawful taking of life, but also to take appropriate steps to safeguard the lives of those within its

jurisdiction (see the *L C B v UK* judgment of 9 June 1998, Reports of Judgments and Decisions 1998-III, p 1403, § 36). It is common ground that the State's obligation in this respect extends beyond its primary duty to secure the right to life by putting in place effective criminal-law provisions to deter the commission of offences against the person backed up by law-enforcement machinery for the prevention, suppression and sanctioning of breaches of such provisions. It is thus accepted by those appearing before the Court that Article 2 of the Convention may also imply in certain well-defined circumstances a positive obligation on the authorities to take preventive operational measures to protect an individual whose life is at risk from the criminal acts of another individual. The scope of this obligation is a matter of dispute between the parties.

116. For the Court, and bearing in mind the difficulties involved in policing modern societies, the unpredictability of human conduct and the operational choices which must be made in terms of priorities and resources, such an obligation must be interpreted in a way which does not impose an impossible or disproportionate burden on the authorities. Accordingly, not every claimed risk to life can entail for the authorities a Convention requirement to take operational measures to prevent that risk from materialising. Another relevant consideration is the need to ensure that the police exercise their powers to control and prevent crime in a manner which fully respects the due process and other guarantees which legitimately place restraints on the scope of their action to investigate crime and bring offenders to justice, including the guarantees contained in Articles 5 and 8 of the Convention. In the opinion of the Court where there is an allegation that the authorities have violated their positive obligation to protect the right to life in the context of their above-mentioned duty to prevent and suppress offences against the person (see paragraph 115 above), it must be established to its satisfaction that the authorities knew or ought to have known at the time of the existence of a real and immediate risk to the life of an identified individual or individuals from the criminal acts of a third party and that they failed to take measures within the scope of their powers which, judged reasonably, might have been expected to avoid that risk. The Court does not accept the Government's view that the failure to perceive the risk to life in the circumstances known at the time or to take preventive measures to avoid that risk must be tantamount to gross negligence or wilful disregard of the duty to protect life . . . Such a rigid standard must be considered to be incompatible with the requirements of Article 1 of the Convention and the obligations of Contracting States under that Article to secure the practical and effective protection of the rights and freedoms laid down therein, including Article 2 (see, *mutatis mutandis*, the . . . *McCann* judgment, p 45, § 146). For the Court, and having regard to the nature of the right protected by Article 2, a right fundamental in the scheme of the Convention, it is sufficient for an applicant to show that the authorities did not do all that could be reasonably expected of them to avoid a real and immediate risk to life of which they have or ought to have knowledge. This is a question which can only be answered in the light of all the circumstances of any particular case. On the above understanding the Court will examine the particular circumstances of this case. . . .

121. In the view of the Court the applicants have failed to point to any decisive stage in the sequence of the events leading up to the tragic shooting when it could be said that the police knew or ought to have known that the lives of the Osman family were at real and immediate risk from Paget-Lewis. While the applicants have pointed to a series of missed opportunities which would have enabled the police to neutralise the threat posed by Paget-Lewis, for example by searching his home for evidence to link him with the graffiti incident or by having him detained under the Mental Health Act 1983 or by taking more active investigative steps following his disappearance, it cannot be said that these measures, judged reasonably, would in fact have produced that result or that a domestic court would have convicted him or ordered his detention in a psychiatric hospital on the basis of the evidence adduced before it. As noted earlier (see paragraph 116 above), the police must discharge their duties in a manner which is compatible with the rights and freedoms of individuals. In the circumstances of the present case, they cannot be criticised for attaching weight to the presumption of innocence or failing to use powers of arrest, search and seizure having regard to their reasonably

held view that they lacked at relevant times the required standard of suspicion to use those powers or that any action taken would in fact have produced concrete results.

122. For the above reasons, the Court concludes that there has been no violation of Article 2 of the Convention in this case.

Seventeen judges agreed with the above conclusion, while three dissentients considered that the British authorities had not complied with their obligations under that Article.

The judgment clearly reveals that States are required by Article 2 to protect persons' right to life by: (a) creating effective criminal law measures, (b) providing policing and criminal justice systems to enforce those measures, and (c) taking reasonable operational measures where there is a 'real and immediate' risk to the life of a particular individual from the criminal acts of another person. However, as the *Osman* case illustrates, the Court is very cautious about finding a breach of the latter requirement.

3 A unanimous Chamber found a violation of the protective obligation in *Opuz v Turkey*, judgment of 9 June 2009. The applicant complained that the domestic authorities had failed to protect her and her mother from persistent violence inflicted by her husband. The latter eventually killed the applicant's mother. The Court held that:

148. Furthermore, in the light of the State's positive obligation to take preventive operational measures to protect an individual whose life is at risk, it might have been expected that the authorities, faced with a suspect known to have a criminal record of perpetrating violent attacks, would take special measures consonant with the gravity of the situation with a view to protecting the applicant's mother. To that end, the local public prosecutor or the judge at the Magistrate's Court could have ordered on his/her initiative one or more of the protective measures [available under domestic law—such as an order requiring a violent family member to leave/not approach the family home]. They could also have issued an injunction with the effect of banning H.O. [the applicant's husband] from contacting, communicating with or approaching the applicant's mother...On the contrary, in response to the applicant's mother's repeated requests for protection, the police and the Magistrate's Court merely took statements from H.O. and released him. While the authorities remained passive for almost two weeks apart from taking statements, H.O. shot dead the applicant's mother.

149. In these circumstances, the Court concludes that the national authorities cannot be considered to have displayed due diligence. They therefore failed in their positive obligation to protect the right to life of the applicant's mother within the meaning of Article 2 of the Convention.

More generally, the Court went on to find that the applicant had produced unchallenged statistical data showing judicial passivity in Turkey towards domestic violence directed against women.

200....the Court considers that the violence suffered by the applicant and her mother may be regarded as gender-based violence which is a form of discrimination against women.

Consequently, there had also been a breach of Article 14 in conjunction with Article 2. This was the first occasion that the Court had reached such a conclusion. Patricia Londono observed, '...most significantly, the Court has acknowledged the extent to which violence against women is an issue of inequality and how this impedes the enjoyment of other rights', in 'Developing Human Rights Principles in Cases of Gender-based Violence (2009) 9(4) *Human Rights Law Review* 657 at 667. In May 2011, at the end of its rotating Chairing of the Committee of Ministers, Turkey oversaw the opening for signature of the Council of Europe's Convention on Preventing and Combating Violence Against Women and Domestic Violence (CETS No 210). Thirteen States, including Turkey, immediately signed the Convention.

4 The positive obligation of protection was applied to a prisoner by a unanimous Chamber in *Paul and Audrey Edwards v UK*, judgment of 14 March 2002. The applicants' 30-year-old son had been remanded in custody by magistrates for making inappropriate comments to women in the street (he had a history of mental illness). He was later transferred to Chelmsford Prison and placed in a cell. Another remand prisoner (Linford), who had previously been diagnosed as suffering from schizophrenia, was also placed in the same cell (because of a shortage of cells). A few hours later Linford killed the applicants' son in a violent attack. Subsequently, Linford was convicted of manslaughter by reason of diminished responsibility. The applicants' contended, *inter alia*, that the relevant authorities had failed to protect the life of their son in breach of their obligations under Article 2. After citing *Osman* the Court held that;

56. In the context of prisoners, the Court has had previous occasion to emphasise that persons in custody are in a vulnerable position and that the authorities are under a duty to protect them.

The judges went on to find that many public agencies (including doctors, the police, the Crown Prosecution Service, and the courts) had failed to pass on information about the health and background of Linford to the prison authorities and the latter had undertaken an inadequate screening of him when he arrived at Chelmsford Prison. Cumulatively, these failures amounted to a breach of the State's obligation to protect the life of the applicants' son under Article 2. The tragic facts of *Edwards* demonstrate that it is not only the police who may be liable to provide protection to persons from the known (or constructively known) real threats posed by others. Where persons are imprisoned, the public authorities (widely drawn in *Edwards*) having responsibility for the care of detainees are under a similar obligation. This is a highly desirable extension of *Osman* as prisoners obviously have limited abilities to protect themselves (e.g. they normally have no choice of with whom they live).

5 A failure by police officers to secure the provision of timely and adequate medical care to a seriously injured detainee, who subsequently died from his injuries, was found to constitute a breach of Article 2 by a unanimous Chamber in *Anguelova v Bulgaria*, judgment of 13 June 2002. The applicant's 17-year-old son had been arrested by the police on suspicion of theft. After a few hours in police detention it became apparent that his health had greatly deteriorated (he had injuries on his forehead and was breathing deeply). The officers at the police station did not call for an ambulance but recalled from patrol those officers who had arrested the detainee. Then the arresting officers went to the hospital and escorted an ambulance back to the police station to collect the detainee. The detainee was found to be dead by the time he arrived at the hospital. The Court found that the behaviour of the police officers and the absence of action taken against those officers by the authorities constituted a violation of '130.... the State's obligation to protect the lives of persons in custody.' The behaviour of the police officers was both suspicious and obviously well below the standard of reasonable care for a seriously ill detainee.

6 A Grand Chamber developed the application of the obligation of protection in the context of a scheme for the early release of prisoners in *Mastromatteo v Italy*, judgment of 24 October 2002. The applicant's son had been shot dead by a bank robber, as the robber tried to escape from the crime scene. The robber and two of his accomplices were serving prison sentences, for violent crimes, at the time of the robbery. However, they had been granted either prison leave or discharge to a semi-custodial regime by the judiciary. The applicant contended that the State had failed to protect the life of his son in breach of its positive obligations under Article 2. After referring to *Osman* and *Edwards* the Court held that:

> 69....The instant case differs from those cases in that it is not a question here of determining whether the responsibility of the authorities is engaged for failing to provide personal protection to [the applicant's son]; what is at issue is the obligation to afford general protection to society against the potential acts of one or of several persons serving a prison sentence for a violent crime and the determination of the scope of that protection.

The judgment acknowledged that whilst one of the basic purposes of imprisonment was to protect society, '72....at the same time the Court recognises the legitimate aim of a policy of progressive social reintegration of persons sentenced to imprisonment.' Taking account of the key features of the Italian prisoner release scheme (including the need for eligible prisoners to have served a minimum period of imprisonment, to have a record of good behaviour whilst in prison, and for a judge to assess the danger to society if a particular prisoner was to be released), together with statistical evidence on the criminal behaviour of prisoners given early release (showing, e.g., that the percentage of prisoners on leave who absconded was about 1 per cent) the Court, unanimously, concluded that the Italian scheme was compatible with the State's obligations under Article 2. Also the individual judicial decisions to grant leave to the prisoners involved in the robbery and subsequent killing of the applicant's son were found to be in conformity with Article 2 because:

> 76. The Court considers that there was nothing in the material before the national authorities to alert them to the fact that the release of M.R. or G.M. would pose a real and immediate threat to life, still less that it would lead to the tragic death of A. Mastromatteo as a result of the chance sequence of events which occurred in the present case. Nor was there anything to alert them to the need to take additional measures to ensure that, once released, the two did not represent a danger to society.

The judgment in *Mastromatteo* sought to achieve a delicate balance between the desirability of promoting social reintegration amongst prisoners and the need to protect the general public from the foreseeable risks of violent crimes being committed by prisoners given early release or home leave. The Court subjected the Italian scheme's criteria and operation to a thorough scrutiny for their conformity with the obligation upon States to protect life under Article 2. Statistically the scheme generated only a very small risk to the public. Furthermore, the Court was careful not to apply the benefit of hindsight when evaluating the release decisions taken by the Italian judiciary.

However, in the subsequent case of *Maiorano and Others v Italy*, judgment of 15 December 2009, a unanimous Chamber found a breach of the protective obligation in respect of the decision to grant day release to a convicted violent prisoner who murdered the wife and daughter of a fellow prisoner whilst he was on release. The Chamber found serious defects in the decision-making process in the light of the prisoner's criminal behaviour whilst serving his initial sentence and the fact that a public prosecutor had been informed that the prisoner was planning further criminal acts but the prosecutor had failed to notify the sentence execution judge (responsible for authorizing the prisoner's day release) of that information. But, the Chamber emphasized that it was not finding a general defect in the Italian prisoner release system.

7   One, of the numerous (see also p 132), complaints made by the applicant State in *Cyprus v Turkey*, 2001-IV, alleged that the authorities in northern Cyprus had failed to provide (or

allowed the receipt of) adequate medical services to the several hundred Greek-Cypriots and Maronites still living in the northern region thereby breaching Article 2. The Grand Chamber, by 16 votes to 1, held that:

219. The Court observes that an issue may arise under Article 2 of the Convention where it is shown that the authorities of a Contracting State put an individual's life at risk through the denial of health care which they have undertaken to make available to the population generally. It notes in this connection that Article 2 § 1 of the Convention enjoins the State not only to refrain from the intentional and unlawful taking of life, but also to take appropriate steps to safeguard the lives of those within its jurisdiction (see the *L.C.B. v the United Kingdom* judgment of 9 June 1998, Reports 1998-III, p 1403, § 36). It notes, however, that the Commission was unable to establish on the evidence that the 'TRNC' [Turkish Republic of Northern Cyprus] authorities deliberately withheld medical treatment from the population concerned or adopted a practice of delaying the processing of requests of patients to receive medical treatment in the south. It observes that during the period under consideration medical visits were indeed hampered on account of restrictions imposed by the 'TRNC' authorities on the movement of the populations concerned and that in certain cases delays did occur. However, it has not been established that the lives of any patients were put in danger on account of delay in individual cases. It is also to be observed that neither the Greek-Cypriot nor Maronite populations were prevented from availing themselves of medical services including hospitals in the north. The applicant Government are critical of the level of health care available in the north. However, the Court does not consider it necessary to examine in this case the extent to which Article 2 of the Convention may impose an obligation on a Contracting State to make available a certain standard of health care. . . .

221. The Court concludes that no violation of Article 2 of the Convention has been established by virtue of an alleged practice of denying access to medical services to Greek Cypriots and Maronites living in northern Cyprus.

Whilst the Court did not find a breach regarding the above health care complaints, the *Cyprus* judgment refined the earlier *LCB* ruling expressly to provide that States may be liable under Article 2 for withholding from an individual life-saving medical care which they have promised to make generally available. The significance of this obligation is that it is left up to particular States to define their own level of health care provision. Only if a State fails to meet its own declared standard, in a life-threatening case, could Article 2 be invoked. However, the Court went on tantalizingly to suggest that Article 2 may also require the provision of a minimum level of health care by member States. Therefore, the positive obligation regarding the provision of medical care by States is at an early stage of development under Article 2.

8   The nature of States' obligations to regulate the provision of private medical services was considered by a Grand Chamber in *Calvelli and Ciglio v Italy*, judgment of 17 January 2002. The applicants' baby had died two days after birth in a private clinic. Six years later the responsible doctor (and joint owner of the clinic) was found guilty of involuntary manslaughter. He successfully appealed against his conviction to the Court of Cassation and by the time his case was sent back for retrial it had become statute barred. The applicants, who had been civil parties to the criminal proceedings, settled their claims against the doctor/clinic when the latter's insurers agreed to pay them 95 million Lire compensation. The applicants claimed that, *inter alia*, the inability to prosecute the doctor, because of delays in the proceedings and the time-bar, constituted a violation of Article 2. After referring to *McCann* and *LCB*, the Court stated that:

49. . . . The aforementioned positive obligations therefore require States to make regulations compelling hospitals, whether public or private, to adopt appropriate measures for the protection of

patients' lives. They also require an effective independent judicial system to be set up so that the cause of death of patients in the care of the medical profession, whether in the public or the private sector, can be determined and those responsible made accountable . . .

The Court then examined the Italian judicial response to the death of the applicants' baby:

51. . . . if the infringement of the right to life or to personal integrity is not caused intentionally, the positive obligation imposed by Article 2 to set up an effective judicial system does not necessarily require the provision of a criminal-law remedy in every case. In the specific sphere of medical negligence the obligation may for instance also be satisfied if the legal system affords victims a remedy in the civil courts, either alone or in conjunction with a remedy in the criminal courts, enabling any liability of the doctors concerned to be established and any appropriate civil redress, such as an order for damages and for the publication of the decision, to be obtained. Disciplinary measures may also be envisaged.

According to a large majority, 14 votes to 3, as the applicants had entered into a voluntary settlement of their civil proceedings against the doctor they had deprived themselves of the best means of a judicial determination of the doctor's responsibility and could no longer claim to be a 'victim' of a breach of the Convention. The determination in *Calvelli and Ciglio* was rather lenient to the State as the delayed and eventually time-barred prosecution of the doctor was not considered to amount to a breach of Article 2. In their joint dissenting opinion Judges Rozakis and Bonello expressed the belief that, '. . . considering civil proceedings as a satisfactory means of recourse satisfying the requirements of Article 2 amounts to a debasement of the protection of the right to life provided for by this Article; it amounts to a "privatisation" of the protection of the right to life.' However, at least the Grand Chamber held that States are under a general obligation to regulate the provision of medical services.

Failures in the domestic legal accountability of a publicly-run nursing home were found to have breached Article 2 in *Dodov v Bulgaria*, judgment of 17 January 2008. The applicant's mother suffered from Alzheimer's disease and needed constant supervision. Whilst resident in a nursing home in Sofia she apparently left an unattended courtyard and was never found (the Court, 12 years later, assumed that she was dead). The applicant initiated criminal proceedings against the relevant staff of the home, but the proceedings were eventually terminated for being time-barred and the applicant's civil action had not even resulted in a first instance judgment after ten years. Therefore, the Court, unanimously, found a violation of Article 2 as the domestic authorities had failed to provide the applicant with the means to bring to account those responsible for his mother's disappearance.

9 A unanimous Grand Chamber found a breach of the positive obligation to protect life in the context of a failure by public authorities to safeguard persons from a lethal explosion at a hazardous waste site in *Oneryildiz v Turkey*, judgment of 30 November 2004. The applicant, his wife, and ten children and his concubine(!) started living in a house, which had been constructed without official authorization on government-owned land, in 1988. The house was located in a 'slum quarter' of a district of Istanbul. Furthermore, the house was next to a municipal household-rubbish tip that had been in operation since the early 1970s. In 1991 the local District Council applied to the District Court for experts to be appointed to examine whether the rubbish tip complied with national environmental regulations. A committee of experts, including a professor of environmental engineering, were appointed. Their report, of May 1991, concluded that the rubbish tip did not comply with the relevant technical regulations and posed a major health risk (involving 20 contagious diseases) to local inhabitants. Also the site had no system for safely burning off the methane gas created by the decomposition of the rubbish and therefore created a serious risk of an explosion occurring. The report stated, 'May God preserve us, as the damage could be very substantial given the neighbouring dwellings…' The four local councils were informed of the report as was the governor and the central government. Two of the local councils applied to the court for the report to be set aside, as they claimed they had not been consulted about the establishment of the expert committee. The national Environment Office recommended, in June 1991, that Istanbul Governor and City Council and local councils take action to remedy the problems identified in the report. In August 1992 one of the local mayors applied to the District Court for temporary orders to prevent other local authorities using the refuse tip. Istanbul Council opposed the request noting that a tender had been invited for redevelopment of the tip. On the morning of 28 April 1993 a methane explosion occurred at the tip causing the eruption of waste and a landslide which covered ten dwellings in the adjoining slum, including the applicant's house. Thirty-nine people died, including the applicant's wife, seven of their children, and his concubine. The applicant complained, *inter alia*, that the authorities, in breach of Article 2, had tolerated the development of the slum dwellings next to the tip, had taken no action to counteract the known dangers posed by the tip, and had not warned the slum residents of those dangers. The Grand Chamber held that:

89. The positive obligation to take all appropriate steps to safeguard life for the purposes of Article 2 entails above all a primary duty on the State to put in place a legislative and administrative framework designed to provide effective deterrence against threats to the right to life…

90. This obligation indisputably applies in the particular context of dangerous activities, where, in addition, special emphasis must be placed on regulations geared to the special features of the activity in question, particularly with regard to the level of the potential risk to human lives. They must govern the licensing, setting up, operation, security and supervision of the activity and must make it compulsory for all those concerned to take practical measures to ensure the effective protection of citizens whose lives might be endangered by the inherent risks.

Among these preventive measures, particular emphasis should be placed on the public's right to information, as established in the case-law of the Convention institutions. The Grand Chamber agrees with the Chamber (see paragraph 84 of the Chamber judgment) that this right, which has already been recognised under Article 8 (see *Guerra and Others* [v Italy 1998-I] § 60), may also, in principle, be relied on for the protection of the right to life…

…

100. The Court considers that neither the reality nor the immediacy of the danger in question is in dispute, seeing that the risk of an explosion had clearly come into being long before it was highlighted in the report of 7 May 1991 and that, as the site continued to operate in the same conditions, that risk could only have increased during the period until it materialised on 28 April 1993.

101. The Grand Chamber accordingly agrees with the Chamber (see paragraph 79 of the Chamber judgment) that it was impossible for the administrative and municipal departments responsible for supervising and managing the tip not to have known of the risks inherent in methanogenesis or of the necessary preventive measures, particularly as there were specific regulations on the matter. Furthermore, the Court likewise regards it as established that various authorities were also aware of those risks, at least by 27 May 1991, when they were notified of the report of 7 May 1991…

It follows that the Turkish authorities at several levels knew or ought to have known that there was a real and immediate risk to a number of persons living near the Ümraniye municipal rubbish tip. They consequently had a positive obligation under Article 2 of the Convention to take such preventive operational measures as were necessary and sufficient to protect those individuals, especially as they themselves had set up the site and authorised its operation, which gave rise to the risk in question.

102. However, it appears from the evidence before the Court that the city council in particular not only failed to take the necessary urgent measures, either before or after 14 March 1991, but also—as the Chamber observed—opposed the recommendation to that effect by the Prime Minister's Environment Office.

103. The city council also opposed the final attempt by the mayor of Ümraniye to apply to the courts, on 27 August 1992, for the temporary closure of the waste-collection site...

Besides that ground, the Government also relied on the conclusions of the *Chapman v the United Kingdom* [2001-I] judgment and criticised the applicant for having knowingly chosen to break the law and live in the vicinity of the rubbish tip.

However, those arguments do not stand up to scrutiny for the following reasons.

104. In the instant case, the Court has examined the provisions of domestic law regarding the transfer to third parties of public property, whether inside or outside the 'slum rehabilitation and clearance zones'...

The Court concludes from these legal considerations that in spite of the statutory prohibitions in the field of town planning, the State's consistent policy on slum areas encouraged the integration of such areas into the urban environment and hence acknowledged their existence and the way of life of the citizens who had gradually caused them to build up since 1960, whether of their own free will or simply as a result of that policy. Seeing that this policy effectively established an amnesty for breaches of town-planning regulations, including the unlawful occupation of public property, it must have created uncertainty as to the extent of the discretion enjoyed by the administrative authorities responsible for applying the measures prescribed by law, which could not therefore have been regarded as foreseeable by the public.

105. This interpretation is, moreover, borne out in the instant case by the administrative authorities' attitude towards the applicant.

The Court observes that between the unauthorised construction of the house in issue in 1988 and the accident of 28 April 1993, the applicant remained in possession of his dwelling, despite the fact that during that time his position remained subject to the rules laid down in Law no. 775, in particular section 18, by which the municipal authorities could have destroyed the dwelling at any time. Indeed, this was what the Government suggested, although they were unable to show that in the instant case the relevant authorities had even envisaged taking any such measure against the applicant.

The authorities let the applicant and his close relatives live entirely undisturbed in their house, in the social and family environment they had created. Furthermore, regard being had to the concrete evidence adduced before the Court and not rebutted by the Government, there is no cause to call into question the applicant's assertion that the authorities also levied council tax on him and on the other inhabitants of the Ümraniye slums and provided them with public services, for which they were charged.

106. In those circumstances, it would be hard for the Government to maintain legitimately that any negligence or lack of foresight should be attributed to the victims of the accident of 28 April 1993, or to rely on the Court's conclusions in the case of *Chapman v the United Kingdom*, in which the British authorities were not found to have remained passive in the face of Mrs Chapman's unlawful actions.

It remains for the Court to address the Government's other arguments relating, in general, to: the scale of the rehabilitation projects carried out by the city council at the time in order to alleviate the problems caused by the Ümraniye waste-collection site; the amount invested, which was said to have influenced the way in which the national authorities chose to deal with the situation at the site; and, lastly, the humanitarian considerations which at the time allegedly precluded any measure entailing the immediate and wholesale destruction of the slum areas.

107. The Court acknowledges that it is not its task to substitute for the views of the local authorities its own view of the best policy to adopt in dealing with the social, economic and urban problems in this part of Istanbul. It therefore accepts the Government's argument that in this respect, an impossible or disproportionate burden must not be imposed on the authorities without consideration being given, in particular, to the operational choices which they must make in terms of priorities and resources (see *Osman* [*v UK*, 1998-VIII] § 116); this results from the wide margin of appreciation which States enjoy, as the Court has previously held, in difficult social and technical spheres such as the one in issue in the instant case (see *Hatton and Others v the United Kingdom* [GC], No 36022/97, §§ 100–1, ECHR 2003-VIII).

However, even when seen from this perspective, the Court does not find the Government's arguments convincing. The preventive measures required by the positive obligation in question fall precisely within the powers conferred on the authorities and may reasonably be regarded as a suitable means of averting the risk brought to their attention. The Court considers that the timely installation of a gas-extraction system at the Ümraniye tip before the situation became fatal could have been an effective measure without diverting the State's resources to an excessive degree in breach of Article 65 of the Turkish Constitution or giving rise to policy problems to the extent alleged by the Government. Such a measure would not only have complied with Turkish regulations and general practice in the area, but would also have been a much better reflection of the humanitarian considerations which the Government relied on before the Court.

108. The Court will next assess the weight to be attached to the issue of respect for the public's right to information (see paragraph 90 above). It observes in this connection that the Government were unable to show that any measures were taken in the instant case to provide the inhabitants of the Ümraniye slums with information enabling them to assess the risks they might run as a result of the choices they had made. In any event, the Court considers that in the absence of more practical measures to avoid the risks to the lives of the inhabitants of the Ümraniye slums, even the fact of having respected the right to information would not have been sufficient to absolve the State of its responsibilities.

109. In the light of the foregoing, the Court cannot see any reason to cast doubt on the domestic investigating authorities' findings of fact and considers that the circumstances examined above show that in the instant case the State's responsibility was engaged under Article 2 in several respects.

Firstly, the regulatory framework proved defective in that the Ümraniye municipal waste-collection site was opened and operated despite not conforming to the relevant technical standards and there was no coherent supervisory system to encourage those responsible to take steps to ensure adequate protection of the public and coordination and cooperation between the various administrative authorities so that the risks brought to their attention did not become so serious as to endanger human lives.

That situation, exacerbated by a general policy which proved powerless in dealing with general town-planning issues and created uncertainty as to the application of statutory measures, undoubtedly played a part in the sequence of events leading to the tragic accident of 28 April 1993, which ultimately claimed the lives of inhabitants of the Ümraniye slums, because the State officials and authorities did not do everything within their power to protect them from the immediate and known risks to which they were exposed.

110. Such circumstances give rise to a violation of Article 2 of the Convention in its substantive aspect...

Hence member States must ensure that they have appropriate domestic laws regulating the location, use, and safety requirements of hazardous facilities/activities. The domestic authorities are also obliged to ensure these provisions are observed and enforced. Local residents must be provided with information about the risks presented by potentially hazardous facilities. Furthermore, States must take reasonable preventive measures (e.g. the installation of methane extraction equipment at waste tips) to protect the lives of persons known to be at risk from such facilities/activities. These legal and operational requirements vividly demonstrate the extensive substantive positive obligations upon States under Article 2.

For an examination of the Court's jurisprudence concerning States' responsibilities in the context of non-lethal environmental pollution, see p 549.

10 The principles derived from *Oneryildiz* were subsequently applied to public authorities' failures to take adequate measures to protect local residents from known natural environmental risks in *Budayeva and others v Russia*, judgment of 29 September 2008. The applicants lived in an area of the central Caucasus subject to regular mudslides. The government had constructed a dam and mud collection facility to reduce the risks. In 1999 the dam was seriously damaged by a mud flow. Subsequently experts warned the local government of the need to repair the dam and establish an early warning system to protect inhabitants from future mudslides. No action was taken and in 2000 a major mudslide caused serious damage to a town where the applicants lived. Several of their relatives were killed or severely injured by the mudslide. The Chamber (unanimously) held that States were to be accorded an even wider margin of appreciation, '135.... in the sphere of emergency relief in relation to a meteorological event, which is as such beyond human control, than in the sphere of dangerous activities of a man-made nature.' But, the failure of the domestic authorities properly to consider repairing the dam or to establish an early warning system amounted to a breach of, '159.... the positive obligation to establish a legislative and administrative framework designed to provide effective deterrence against threats to the right to life as required by Article 2 of the Convention.' This important judgment seeks to ensure that public authorities remain alert and responsive to identified natural hazards which may be increasing as global warming continues.

The duty on States to undertake effective investigations into alleged breaches of the right to life

1 The types of investigations required by this implied duty, derived from the judgment in *McCann*, were elaborated by the Court in *Kaya v Turkey*, 1998-I. The applicant complained to the Commission that his brother (Abdulmenaf Kaya), a farmer, had been deliberately killed by Turkish security forces on 25 March 1993. The Government contended that the deceased was a terrorist who had been killed when he engaged the security forces. The Commission concluded that it was not proved beyond reasonable doubt that Abdulmenaf had been deliberately killed by soldiers in the circumstances alleged by the applicant. However, there had been a breach of Article 2 because of the inadequacy of the investigation conducted by the authorities into Abdulmenaf's death (27 votes to 3). An overwhelming majority of the Court (8 votes to 1) also found that there had been an ineffective investigation.

87. The Court observes that the procedural protection of the right to life inherent in Article 2 of the Convention secures the accountability of agents of the State for their use of lethal force by subjecting their actions to some form of independent and public scrutiny capable of leading to a determination of whether the force used was or was not justified in a particular set of circumstances....

89. The Court is struck in particular by the fact that the public prosecutor would appear to have assumed without question that the deceased was a terrorist who had died in a clash with the security forces. No statements were taken from any of the soldiers at the scene and no attempt was made to confirm whether there were spent cartridges over the area consistent with an intense gun battle having been waged by both sides as alleged. As an independent investigating official he should have been alert to the need to collect evidence at the scene, to make his own independent reconstruction of the events and to satisfy himself that the deceased, despite being dressed as a typical farmer, was in fact a terrorist as alleged. There are no indications that he was prepared in any way to scrutinise the soldiers' account of the incident. His readiness to accept at face value the information given by the military may also explain why no tests were carried out on the deceased's hands or clothing for gunpowder traces or why the weapon was not dusted for fingerprints. In any event, these shortcomings must be considered particularly serious in view of the fact that the corpse was later handed over to villagers, thereby rendering it impossible to conduct any further analyses, including of the bullets lodged in the body. The only exhibits which were taken from the scene for further examination were the weapon and ammunition allegedly used by the deceased. However, whatever the merits of this initiative as an investigative measure at the time, it is to be noted that the public prosecutor issued his decision of non-jurisdiction without awaiting the findings of the ballistics experts... The autopsy report provided the sole record of the nature, severity and location of the bullet wounds sustained by the deceased. The Court shares the concern of the Commission about the incompleteness of this report in certain crucial respects, in particular the absence of any observations on the actual number of bullets which struck the deceased and of any estimation of the distance from which the bullets were fired. It cannot be maintained that the perfunctory autopsy performed or the findings recorded in the report could lay the basis for any effective follow-up investigation or indeed satisfy even the minimum requirements of an investigation into a clear-cut case of lawful killing since they left too many critical questions unanswered. The Court acknowledges that the on-the-spot post-mortem and forensic examination were conducted in an area prone to terrorist violence, which may have made it extremely difficult to comply with standard practices....It is therefore surprising that neither the doctor nor the public prosecutor requested that the body be flown to a safer location to allow more detailed analyses to be made of the body, the clothing and the bullet wounds.

90. No concrete measures were taken thereafter by the public prosecutor to investigate the death of the applicant's brother, for example by verifying whether the deceased was in fact an active member of the PKK or by questioning villagers living in the vicinity of Dolunay to ascertain whether they heard the sound of a gun battle on the day in question or by summoning members of the security forces involved to his office to take statements. The public prosecutor's firm conviction that the deceased was a terrorist killed in an armed clash with the security forces was never in fact tested against any other evidence and the terms of his non-jurisdiction decision effectively excluded any possibility that the security forces might somehow have been culpable, including with respect to the proportionality of the force used in the circumstances of the alleged armed attack...

91. The Court notes that loss of life is a tragic and frequent occurrence in view of the security situation in south-east Turkey...However, neither the prevalence of violent armed clashes nor the high incidence of fatalities can displace the obligation under Article 2 to ensure that an effective, independent investigation is conducted into deaths arising out of clashes involving the security forces, more so in cases such as the present where the circumstances are in many respects unclear.

92. Having regard to the above considerations the Court, like the Commission, concludes that the authorities failed to carry out an effective investigation into the circumstances surrounding the death of the applicant's brother. There has accordingly been a violation of Article 2 of the Convention in that respect.

The Court requires the investigation to be conducted by an independent person exercising a critical assessment of all the relevant evidence (including that provided by State officials). Depending on the circumstances, appropriate forensic tests (such as checks on clothing and bodies for traces of explosives or gunpowder) must also be undertaken. If investigations are to satisfy the requirements of Article 2 they must be genuinely rigorous and not merely ritualistic charades.

2 In *Yasa v Turkey* (p 107), the Court widened the circumstances where States are required to conduct investigations into deaths by holding that:

> the obligation is not confined to cases where it has been established that the killing was caused by an agent of the State. Nor is the issue of whether members of the deceased's family or others have lodged a formal complaint about the killing with the competent investigatory authorities decisive. In the case under consideration, the mere fact that the authorities were informed of the murder of the applicant's uncle gave rise *ipso facto* to an obligation under Article 2 to carry out an effective investigation . . . [Para 100.]

As no 'concrete and credible progress' had been made in the investigation after five years, the Court (by 8 votes to 1) found a violation of Article 2. The above rulings are to be welcomed as they seek to ensure that States conduct effective investigations into killings irrespective of the background/position held by the perpetrator(s) and that duty applies once the State becomes aware of the killing.

3 A Grand Chamber of the full-time Court in *Cyprus v Turkey* (see p 124), further extended the duty to undertake effective investigations to situations where it has not been conclusively established that a person has been killed. The applicant State contended, *inter alia*, that there had been no such investigations into the fate of about 1,500 persons alleged to have be killed or detained by Turkish military forces, or their supporters, during the military occupation of northern Cyprus in 1974. The Grand Chamber did not consider that the evidence before it justified a finding that those persons had been unlawfully killed. But the obligation to conduct an effective investigation, '132. . . . also arises upon proof of an arguable claim that an individual who was last seen in the custody of the state, subsequently disappeared in a context which may be considered life-threatening.' By an overwhelming majority of 16 votes to 1 (the Turkish national judge being the dissentient) the Grand Chamber found that the evidence demonstrated that many persons had been detained by Turkish/Turkish-Cypriot forces during military operations and the context of their detention could be classified as life-threatening. Consequently, the respondent State was under a duty to undertake effective investigations into the claims of the missing persons' relatives that the former had disappeared in life-threatening circumstances. No effective investigations had been held into the whereabouts and fate of the missing Greek-Cypriots, therefore the Grand Chamber found a breach of this duty under Article 2.

In the later case of *Varnava and others v Turkey*, judgment of 18 September 2009, another Grand Chamber, by 16 votes to 1, found, *inter alia*, that Turkey had still failed effectively to investigate the disappearances of the applicants' nine relatives during the 1974 military operations. The Court awarded each relative 12,000 euros for the non-pecuniary damage they had suffered.

4 The Court requires that investigations into arguable claims of killings by State agents must satisfy four institutional and procedural requirements if they are to be classified as effective. These requirements were articulated in *Kelly and Others v UK*, judgment of 4 May 2001.

95.... it may generally be regarded as necessary for the persons responsible for and carrying out the investigation to be independent from those implicated in the events... This means not only a lack of hierarchical or institutional connection but also a practical independence (see, for example, the case of *Ergi v Turkey* judgment of 28 July 1998, Reports 1998-IV, §§ 83–4 where the public prosecutor investigating the death of a girl during an alleged clash showed a lack of independence through his heavy reliance on the information provided by the gendarmes implicated in the incident).

96. The investigation must also be effective in the sense that it is capable of leading to a determination of whether the force used in such cases was or was not justified in the circumstances... and to the identification and punishment of those responsible. This is not an obligation of result, but of means. The authorities must have taken the reasonable steps available to them to secure the evidence concerning the incident, including *inter alia* eye witness testimony, forensic evidence and, where appropriate, an autopsy which provides a complete and accurate record of injury and an objective analysis of clinical findings, including the cause of death... Any deficiency in the investigation which undermines its ability to establish the cause of death or the person responsible will risk falling foul of this standard.

97. A requirement of promptness and reasonable expedition is implicit in this context... It must be accepted that there may be obstacles or difficulties which prevent progress in an investigation in a particular situation. However, a prompt response by the authorities in investigating a use of lethal force may generally be regarded as essential in maintaining public confidence in their adherence to the rule of law and in preventing any appearance of collusion in or tolerance of unlawful acts.

98. For the same reasons, there must be a sufficient element of public scrutiny of the investigation or its results to secure accountability in practice as well as in theory. The degree of public scrutiny required may well vary from case to case. In all cases, however, the next of kin of the victim must be involved in the procedure to the extent necessary to safeguard his or her legitimate interests...

The Court was unanimous in finding a breach of the obligation to hold an effective investigation into the killings of the applicants' nine relatives who had been shot dead by SAS soldiers during an ambush of a terrorist attack on an RUC police station at Loughgall in Northern Ireland. The domestic investigation failed to satisfy the first requirement of independence as it had been undertaken by RUC officers and other members of that force had been involved in the ambush operation. The judgment of the Court indicates that it requires a clear institutional independence of investigators from those State agents implicated in the killing. Public acceptance of the legitimacy of investigations will be enhanced where the investigators are seen to have no connection with the subjects of the investigation.

5 Article 2 can require the effective prosecution of public officials whose gross negligence has contributed to the death of other persons. In *Oneryildiz v Turkey*, see p 126, the applicant contended that there had been a breach of the procedural positive obligation upon Turkey to take effective judicial proceedings against those officials who allowed the refuse tip to continue operating in a dangerous manner. He argued that the Istanbul Criminal Court's fining of two local mayors, the equivalent sum of 9.7 euros (these fines were suspended), for negligent omissions in the performance of their duties regarding the operation of the refuse tip did not satisfy the demands of Article 2. The Grand Chamber held that:

93.... Where it is established that the negligence attributable to State officials or bodies on that account goes beyond an error of judgment or carelessness, in that the authorities in question, fully realising the likely consequences and disregarding the powers vested in them, failed to take measures that were necessary and sufficient to avert the risks inherent in a dangerous activity (see, *mutatis mutandis, Osman,* § 116), the fact that those responsible for endangering life have not been charged with a criminal offence or prosecuted may amount to a violation of Article 2, irrespective of any other types of remedy which individuals may exercise on their own initiative . . .

94. To sum up, the judicial system required by Article 2 must make provision for an independent and impartial official investigation procedure that satisfies certain minimum standards as to effectiveness and is capable of ensuring that criminal penalties are applied where lives are lost as a result of a dangerous activity if and to the extent that this is justified by the findings of the investigation (see, *mutatis mutandis, Hugh Jordan v the United Kingdom,* No 24746/94, §§ 105–9, ECHR 2001-III, and *Paul and Audrey Edwards,* cited above, §§ 69–73). In such cases, the competent authorities must act with exemplary diligence and promptness and must of their own motion initiate investigations capable of, firstly, ascertaining the circumstances in which the incident took place and any shortcomings in the operation of the regulatory system and, secondly, identifying the State officials or authorities involved in whatever capacity in the chain of events in issue.

95. That said, the requirements of Article 2 go beyond the stage of the official investigation, where this has led to the institution of proceedings in the national courts; the proceedings as a whole, including the trial stage, must satisfy the requirements of the positive obligation to protect lives through the law.

96. It should in no way be inferred from the foregoing that Article 2 may entail the right for an applicant to have third parties prosecuted or sentenced for a criminal offence (see, *mutatis mutandis, Perez v France* [GC], No 47287/99, § 70, ECHR 2004-I) or an absolute obligation for all prosecutions to result in conviction, or indeed in a particular sentence (see, *mutatis mutandis, Tanlı v Turkey,* No 26129/95, § 111, ECHR 2001-III).

On the other hand, the national courts should not under any circumstances be prepared to allow life-endangering offences to go unpunished. This is essential for maintaining public confidence and ensuring adherence to the rule of law and for preventing any appearance of tolerance of or collusion in unlawful acts (see, *mutatis mutandis, Hugh Jordan,* cited above, §§ 108 and 136–40). The Court's task therefore consists in reviewing whether and to what extent the courts, in reaching their conclusion, may be deemed to have submitted the case to the careful scrutiny required by Article 2 of the Convention, so that the deterrent effect of the judicial system in place and the significance of the role it is required to play in preventing violations of the right to life are not undermined.

By an overwhelming majority, 16 votes to 1, the Grand Chamber concluded that:

117. Accordingly, it cannot be said that the manner in which the Turkish criminal-justice system operated in response to the tragedy secured the full accountability of State officials or authorities for their role in it and the effective implementation of provisions of domestic law guaranteeing respect for the right to life, in particular the deterrent function of the criminal law.

118. In short, it must be concluded in the instant case that there has been a violation of Article 2 of the Convention in its procedural aspect also, on account of the lack, in connection with a fatal accident provoked by the operation of a dangerous activity, of adequate protection 'by law' safeguarding the right to life and deterring similar life-endangering conduct in future.

Judge Turmen dissented because:

First of all, the majority are of the opinion that there has been a violation of the procedural aspect of Article 2, not because of the lack of an effective investigation, but because of the judicial proceedings or, more precisely, the application of domestic legislation. This is a wholly new approach which does not have any precedent in the Court's case-law.

The effect of the Grand Chamber's judgment is to extend the temporal scope of the implied procedural obligation to encompass the domestic judicial proceedings that should follow where an effective investigation has revealed evidence that State personnel and/or bodies may be guilty of gross negligence in the death(s) of persons. This is a logical development of the positive procedural obligation under Article 2 which has as one of its objectives the deterring of unlawful killings.

The death penalty

Because this judicial penalty was still used in member States when the Convention was drafted (e.g. the death penalty imposed on Marshall Petain, the leader of the Vichy Government in France that collaborated with the Nazis, after the liberation of France see **Lehideux and Isorni v France**, p 655) the power of States to retain its use was enshrined in Article 2(1). Subsequently, as increasing numbers of European States abandoned the death penalty, the Council of Europe developed a policy opposing the death penalty. This development was reflected in Protocol 6 that enables State parties to the ECHR formally to agree to abolish the use of the death penalty in peacetime. Protocol 6 came into effect in March 1985 (when five States had ratified it). The UK ratified it in May 1999. Protocol 13 strengthens the European prohibition on the death penalty by extending the abolition of the penalty to both times of war and peace. It came into force in July 2003 (when ten States had ratified the Protocol). The UK ratified Protocol 13 in October 2003.

Applicants have asked the Court to interpret Article 2, and Article 3, to accord with the contemporary European disapproval of the death penalty. The original Court addressed this issue in **Soering v UK**, see p 192. The full-time Court examined the matter in judgments by a Chamber (given on 12 March 2003) and then a Grand Chamber (under Article 43) in **Ocalan v Turkey**, judgment of 12 May 2005. Abdullah Ocalan, before his arrest, was the leader of the PKK (Workers' Party of Kurdistan) terrorist/political organization. The contentious factual background involved the applicant being expelled from Syria, where he had been resident for several years. He ended up in Greece and was then taken to Kenya. Ocalan was accommodated in the Greek Ambassador's residence.

The Kenyan Ministry of Foreign Affairs announced, on 15 February 1999, that Ocalan had entered Kenyan territory, on 2 February 1999, accompanied by Greek officials without declaring his identity or going through passport control. The Greek Ambassador informed the Kenyan Government that authorities in Athens would arrange for Ocalan's departure from Kenya. The Ambassador told Ocalan that he was free to leave Kenya for the destination of his choice and the Netherlands was willing to accept him. Later that day, Kenyan officials arrived at the Greek Embassy to take Ocalan to the airport. The Ambassador sought to accompany Ocalan, but the latter went in a car driven by a Kenyan official. At Nairobi airport the car transporting Ocalan left the convoy and went through a route reserved for security personnel. He was driven to an aircraft, in which Turkish security personnel were waiting, they arrested him (Turkish courts had issued seven warrants for his arrest in respect of various alleged acts of terrorism) when he boarded the plane (at about 8 pm). During the flight to Turkey Ocalan was handcuffed and blindfolded (according to the Turkish Government the blindfold was removed when the aircraft reached Turkish airspace). A Turkish army doctor was present during the flight. Ocalan claimed that he had been given tranquillizers (probably at the Greek Embassy!).

Ocalan was taken to Imrali prison, located on an island off the coast of Turkey, on 16 February. All the other inmates had just been moved to different prisons. The island was declared to be a prohibited military zone, as the Government considered that special measures were necessary to ensure the safety of Ocalan. Members of the security forces interrogated Ocalan at the prison. Four days later a judge determined, on the basis of the case file, that Ocalan should remain in custody as his interrogation had not been completed. Judges and prosecutors, from the Ankara State Security Court, arrived on the island on 21 February. Ocalan claimed that 16 lawyers instructed by his family were denied access to him on the island on 22 and 23 February. On 22 February 1999 the Public Prosecutor at the Ankara State Security Court questioned the applicant and took a statement from him as an accused. The applicant told the Prosecutor that he was the founder of the PKK and its current leader. Initially, his and the PKK's aim had been to found an independent Kurdish State, but with the passage of time they had changed their objective and sought to secure a share of power for the Kurds as a free people who had played an important role in the founding of the Republic. The applicant confessed that village guards were a prime target for the PKK. He also confirmed that the PKK used violent methods against the civil population, in particular from 1987 onwards; he was personally opposed to such methods and had tried in vain to prevent their being used. He told the Prosecutor that the warlords who wanted to seize power within the PKK had exerted some of their pressure on the Kurdish population; some of them had been tried and found guilty by the PKK and had been executed with his personal approval. He acknowledged that the Turkish Government's estimate of the number of those killed (4,472 civilians, 3,874 soldiers, 247 policemen, and 1,225 village guards from 1978 until the time of Ocalan's arrest) or wounded as a result of the PKK's activities was fairly accurate; that the actual number might even be higher; and that he had ordered the attacks as part of the armed struggle being waged by the PKK. He added that he had decided in 1993 to declare a ceasefire, acting on a request by the Turkish President.

On 23 February Ocalan was brought before a judge of the Ankara State Security Court. He repeated his statement given to the Prosecutor. The judge ordered that Ocalan should be detained pending trial. Ocalan was allowed to see two of his lawyers on 25 February. Ocalan's conversation with his lawyers took place in the presence of a judge and members of the security forces wearing masks. Ocalan claimed that subsequently he had only been allowed to meet with his lawyers twice a week for one hour at a time. He asserted that the discussions were monitored by officials behind glass panels and filmed on video. The Government retorted that no restrictions were placed on the number or length of Ocalan's discussions with his lawyers and that the interviews were held in accordance with the Code of Criminal Procedure.

Delegates of the European Committee for the Prevention of Torture and Inhuman or Degrading Treatment or Punishment (the CPT) visited Imrali prison in early March 1999. They informed the Turkish Government that they had found Ocalan to be physically in good health and that he had told them that he had not been ill-treated since his arrest. His cell was of a high standard. The delegates expressed the view that Ocalan's solitary confinement and limited access to open air could affect him psychologically. Imrali prison was again visited by delegates of the CPT in September 2001. They found Ocalan's cell to have washing and toilet facilities together with an air-conditioning system. He had access to books, newspapers, and a radio. Doctors gave him twice daily medical checks and he was visited by his lawyers once a week.

The Public Prosecutor at the Ankara State Security Court submitted an indictment, on 24 April 1999, accusing Ocalan of activities carried out for the purpose of bringing about the secession of part of Turkish national territory. The Prosecutor sought the death penalty. The case file concerning Ocalan combined seven sets of existing proceedings against him and amounted to 17,000 pages. Ocalan's lawyers were given access to the case file on 7 May, but the authorities did not supply them with a copy (Ocalan's lawyers had to use their own photocopier and it took them until 15 May to copy the case file).

The Ankara State Security Court held two hearings, in Ankara without the presence of Ocalan, at the end of March to determine procedural matters (including requests from third-parties to intervene in the proceedings against Ocalan). The Security Court, composed of two civilian and one military judge, held nine hearings, on the island of Imrali, between 31 May and 29 June 1999. Ocalan attended those hearings. He repeated his statement given to the Prosecutor. His lawyers contended that the Security Court was not an 'independent and impartial tribunal' as required by Article 6 of the Convention. Ocalan stated that he accepted the Security Court's jurisdiction. He promised to halt the PKK's armed struggle. Whilst accepting political responsibility for the PKK's general strategy he denied criminal responsibility for acts of violence which went beyond the organization's declared policy.

On 18 June 1999, the Turkish Parliament amended the constitution to exclude military personnel from being members of State Security Courts. The Security Court hearing the case against Ocalan sat without a military judge from 23 June 1999 (the new additional civilian judge had attended earlier proceedings). Ocalan's counsel unsuccessfully challenged this judge's appointment. The Security Court, on 29 June, found Ocalan guilty of carrying out acts designed to bring about the secession of part of Turkey's territory. It sentenced him to death and Ocalan appealed. In November 1999, the Court of Cassation affirmed the judgment. The European Court requested the Turkish Government to ensure that the death penalty was not implemented in order to enable the Court to examine Ocalan's complaints under the Convention. In January 2000, the Turkish Prime Minister stated that the applicant's file would be sent to the Turkish Parliament, which was empowered to approve/disapprove enforcement of the death penalty, when the Strasbourg proceedings were completed.

In October 2001 the Turkish Constitution was amended to abolish the death penalty except in times of war/imminent threat of war or for acts of terrorism. The Turkish Parliament legislated, in August 2002, to abolish the death penalty in peacetime. The Turkish Government informed the European Court, in September 2002, that Ocalan no longer faced the implementation of the death penalty imposed upon him by the domestic courts. During the following month the Ankara State Security Court commuted Ocalan's death sentence to life imprisonment. In January 2003 Turkey signed Protocol 6 of the Convention and went on to ratify the Protocol in November 2003.

Before the Chamber of the European Court the applicant's lawyers sought to contend, *inter alia*, that Article 2 should be interpreted as no longer permitting capital punishment and that such punishment was inhuman and degrading in violation of Article 3. The Chamber, by 6 votes to 1, found that the imposition of the death penalty on Ocalan, following an unfair trial that breached the requirements of Article 6, amounted to inhuman treatment. Subsequently, both the applicant and the Government requested that the case be referred to the Grand Chamber.

163. The Grand Chamber agrees with the following conclusions of the Chamber...

'...Equally the Court observes that the legal position as regards the death penalty has undergone a considerable evolution since the *Soering* case was decided. The de facto abolition noted in that case in respect of twenty-two Contracting States in 1989 has developed into a de jure abolition in forty-three of the forty-four Contracting States and a moratorium in the remaining State which has not yet abolished the penalty, namely Russia. This almost complete abandonment of the death penalty in times of peace in Europe is reflected in the fact that all the Contracting States have signed Protocol No 6 and forty-one States have ratified it, that is to say, all except Turkey, Armenia and Russia. It is further reflected in the policy of the Council of Europe which requires that new member States undertake to abolish capital punishment as a condition of their admission into the organisation. As a result of these developments the territories encompassed by the member States of the Council of Europe have become a zone free of capital punishment.

'...Such a marked development could now be taken as signalling the agreement of the Contracting States to abrogate, or at the very least to modify, the second sentence of Article 2 § 1, particularly when regard is had to the fact that all Contracting States have now signed Protocol No 6 and that it has been ratified by forty-one States. It may be questioned whether it is necessary to await ratification of Protocol No 6 by the three remaining States before concluding that the death penalty exception in Article 2 has been significantly modified. Against such a consistent background, it can be said that capital punishment in peacetime has come to be regarded as an unacceptable . . . form of punishment which is no longer permissible under Article 2.'

164. The Court notes that by opening for signature Protocol No. 13 concerning the abolition of the death penalty in all circumstances the Contracting States have chosen the traditional method of amendment of the text of the Convention in pursuit of their policy of abolition. At the date of this judgment, three member States have not signed this Protocol and sixteen have yet to ratify it. However, this final step toward complete abolition of the death penalty—that is to say both in times of peace and in times of war—can be seen as confirmation of the abolitionist trend in the practice of the Contracting States. It does not necessarily run counter to the view that Article 2 has been amended in so far as it permits the death penalty in times of peace.

165. For the time being, the fact that there are still a large number of States who have yet to sign or ratify Protocol No. 13 may prevent the Court from finding that it is the established practice of the Contracting States to regard the implementation of the death penalty as inhuman and degrading treatment contrary to Article 3 of the Convention, since no derogation may be made from that provision, even in times of war. However, the Grand Chamber agrees with the Chamber that it is not necessary for the Court to reach any firm conclusion on these points since, for the following reasons, it would be contrary to the Convention, even if Article 2 were to be construed as still permitting the death penalty, to implement a death sentence following an unfair trial.

. . .

169. In the Court's view, to impose a death sentence on a person after an unfair trial is to subject that person wrongfully to the fear that he will be executed. The fear and uncertainty as to the future generated by a sentence of death, in circumstances where there exists a real possibility that the sentence will be enforced, must give rise to a significant degree of human anguish. Such anguish cannot be dissociated from the unfairness of the proceedings underlying the sentence which, given that human life is at stake, becomes unlawful under the Convention.

. . .

173. As to the nature of the applicant's trial, the Court refers to its conclusions on the applicant's complaints under Article 6 of the Convention. It has found that the applicant was not tried by an independent and impartial tribunal within the meaning of Article 6 § 1 and that there has been a breach of the rights of the defence under Article 6 § 1, taken together with Article 6 §§ 3 (b) and (c), as the applicant had no access to a lawyer while in police custody and was unable to communicate with his lawyers out of the hearing of officials, restrictions had been imposed on the number and length of his lawyers' visits to him, he was unable to consult the case-file until an advanced stage of the proceedings and his lawyers did not have sufficient time to consult the file properly.

174. The death penalty has thus been imposed on the applicant following an unfair procedure which cannot be considered to conform with the strict standards of fairness required in cases involving a capital sentence. Moreover, he had to suffer the consequences of the imposition of that sentence for nearly three years.

175. Consequently, the Court concludes that the imposition of the death sentence on the applicant following an unfair trial by a court whose independence and impartiality were open to doubt amounted to inhuman treatment in violation of Article 3.

Four judges dissented as they did not consider there was evidence that Ocalan had suffered fear and anguish after the imposition of the death penalty.

Although the Grand Chamber in *Ocalan* did not find a breach of Article 2, the Court expressed the view that capital punishment in peacetime was unacceptable. Furthermore, the circumstances in which the imposition of a death sentence could violate Article 3 were extended beyond *Soering*.

Subsequently a Chamber developed the Court's opposition to the death penalty in *Al-Saadoon and Mufdhi v UK*, judgment of 2 March 2010. The two applicants were Iraqi nationals and members of the Ba'ath Party, they were arrested and detained by British personnel following the 2003 Multi-National Force invasion of Iraq. An investigation by the British military police discovered evidence that the applicants were members of a group who had captured two British servicemen, rifle-butted the soldiers, and then shot them dead. In 2005 the British authorities referred the criminal case against the applicants to the Iraqi judicial authorities. The latter determined that, as the accusations against the applicants constituted war crimes, the Iraqi High Tribunal (IHT) had jurisdiction. The Iraqi National Assembly created the IHT during 2004 and established the death penalty for specified crimes (including war crimes). The UK Government had requested the Iraqi Government not to re-establish the death penalty. From late 2007, the IHT repeatedly asked the British authorities in Iraq to transfer the applicants to the custody of the Iraqi authorities. The applicants, unsuccessfully, brought judicial review proceedings in England seeking to prohibit their handing-over to the IHT. The British Embassy in Bagdad (with the support of the family of one of the killed soldiers) wrote to the Iraqi authorities asking for the non-imposition of the death penalty in the proceedings against the applicants. The applicants subsequently applied to the Strasbourg Court. On 30 December 2008 the Acting President of the Section granted the applicants' request for an interim measure and informed the British Government that the applicants should not be transferred from British custody. However, the next day the British Government informed the Court that the applicants had been transferred to the IHT earlier that day.

The Chamber expressed the opinion that:

115. . . . Judicial execution involves the deliberate and premeditated destruction of a human being by the State authorities. Whatever the method of execution, the extinction of life involves some physical pain. In addition, the foreknowledge of death at the hands of the State must inevitably give rise to intense psychological suffering. The fact that the imposition and use of the death penalty negates fundamental human rights has been recognised by the Member States of the Council of Europe. In the Preamble to Protocol No. 13 the Contracting States describe themselves as 'convinced that everyone's right to life is a basic value in a democratic society and that the abolition of the death penalty is essential for the protection of this right and for the full recognition of the inherent dignity of all human beings'.

. . .

118. The Court considers that, in respect of those States which are bound by it, the right under Article 1 of Protocol No. 13 not to be subjected to the death penalty, which admits of no derogation and applies in all circumstances, ranks along with the rights in Articles 2 and 3 as a fundamental right, enshrining one of the basic values of the democratic societies making up the Council of Europe. As such, its provisions must be strictly construed . . .

120. It can be seen, therefore, that the Grand Chamber in *Öcalan* did not exclude that Article 2 had already been amended so as to remove the exception permitting the death penalty. Moreover, as noted above, the position has evolved since then. All but two of the Member States have now signed Protocol No. 13 and all but three of the States which have signed have ratified it. These figures, together with consistent State practice in observing the moratorium on capital punishment, are strongly indicative that Article 2 has been amended so as to prohibit the death penalty in all circumstances. Against this background, the Court does not consider that the wording of the second sentence of Article 2 § 1 continues to act as a bar to its interpreting the words "inhuman or degrading treatment or punishment" in Article 3 as including the death penalty (cf. *Soering*, cited above, §§ 102–104).

...

144. The outcome of the applicants' case before the IHT is currently uncertain. While the applicants remain at real risk of execution since their case has been remitted for reinvestigation, it cannot at the present time be predicted whether or not they will be retried on charges carrying the death penalty, convicted, sentenced to death and executed. Whatever the eventual result, however, it is the case that through the actions and inaction of the United Kingdom authorities the applicants have been subjected, since at least May 2006, to the fear of execution by the Iraqi authorities. The Court has held above that causing the applicants psychological suffering of this nature and degree constituted inhuman treatment. It follows that there has been a violation of Article 3 of the Convention.

The Chamber was unanimous in the above conclusion. Significantly, in October 2010, the Screening Panel rejected a request for a referral of the case to the Grand Chamber. Therefore, the Court has reinforced its condemnation of the death penalty and expanded the ability of applicants successfully to invoke Article 3 to challenge proceedings which involve the death penalty.

In **Bader and Others v Sweden**, judgment of 8 November 2005, a unanimous Chamber also applied the deportation element of **Soering** (see p 195) to Article 2. The applicants claimed that if they were deported back to Syria (their country of origin) the first applicant would face execution as he had been convicted and sentenced to death in respect of his (alleged) involvement in the killing of his brother-in-law. The Chamber held that:

42. . . . It follows that an issue may arise under Articles 2 and 3 of the Convention if a Contracting State deports an alien who has suffered or risks suffering a flagrant denial of a fair trial in the receiving State, the outcome of which was or is likely to be the death penalty.

Finding major defects in the Syrian trial of the first applicant, including the absence of him or his lawyer, and the failure of Sweden to secure guarantees that his case would be re-opened with the prosecutor not seeking the death penalty; the Chamber determined that the deportation of the applicants to Syria would breach Articles 2 and 3.

Article 2(2)

Defence of persons from unlawful violence (Article 2(2)(a))

This exception was invoked in *McCann* (above).

A Grand Chamber also found it applied when a *carabiniere* was subject to a 'very violent attack' by a mob during 'anti-globalization' protests in Genoa whilst a G8 summit was being held. In **Giuliani and Gaggio v Italy**, judgment of 24 March 2011, the applicants' son/brother had been attacking a jeep containing three officers. One of the officers drew his handgun and warned the attackers to leave. However, the mob continued to attack the vehicle together with its occupants. The officer then fired two shots, one of which killed the applicants' son/brother. Having seen video/photographic evidence of the incident a large majority of the Grand Chamber (13 votes to 4) determined that:

191. In this extremely tense situation Carlo Giuliani decided to pick up a fire extinguisher which was lying on the ground, and raised it to chest height with the apparent intention of throwing it at the occupants of the vehicle. His actions could reasonably be interpreted by M.P. [the relevant *carabiniere*] as an indication that, despite the latter's shouted warnings and the fact that he had shown his gun, the attack on the jeep was not about to cease or diminish in intensity. Moreover, the vast majority of the demonstrators appeared to be continuing the assault. M.P.'s honest belief that his life was in danger could only have been strengthened as a result. In the Court's view, this served as justification for recourse to a potentially lethal means of defence such as the firing of shots.

...

194. In the light of the foregoing, the Court concludes that in the instant case the use of lethal force was absolutely necessary 'in defence of any person from unlawful violence' within the meaning of Article 2 § 2 (a) of the Convention...

To effect a lawful arrest or to prevent the escape of a person lawfully detained (Article 2(2)(b))

A unanimous Chamber elaborated important limitations upon the use of this exception in **Nachova and Others v Bulgaria**, judgment of 26 February 2004. The applicants complained to the Court about the shooting dead of two of their family members. The deceased were non-violent and unarmed fugitive conscripts, of Roma ethic origin, who had escaped from custody. Four military police officers, equipped with handguns and Kalashnikov automatic rifles, were sent to arrest the fugitives. Military police regulations authorized the use of firearms to apprehend a person serving in the army where, *inter alia*, that person had committed a publicly prosecutable offence, did not surrender, an oral warning had been given, and a warning shot fired in the air. The deceased tried to run away from the house they had been hiding in when the military police arrived. The senior officer, a Major, gave chase and after shouting at the fugitives to stop and firing a warning shot he opened fire with his Kalashnikov rifle killing both fugitives. A neighbour claimed that the Major then pointed the weapon at him and said 'You damn Gypsies!'

103. The Court considers that, balanced against the imperative need to preserve life as a fundamental value, the legitimate aim of effecting a lawful arrest cannot justify putting human life at risk where the fugitive has committed a non-violent offence and does not pose a threat to anyone. Any other approach would be incompatible with the basic principles of democratic societies, as universally accepted today (see the relevant provisions of the United Nations Basic Principles on the Use of Force and Firearms by Law Enforcement Officials... and, *mutatis mutandis*, the Court's reasoning in *Öcalan v Turkey*, No 46221/99, § 196, 12 March 2003).

104. It is only in subparagraphs (a) and (c) of Article 2 § 2 that violence (in the form of unlawful violence, a riot or an insurrection) is expressly made a condition that will justify the use of potentially lethal force. However, the principle of strict proportionality as enshrined in Article 2 of the Convention cannot be read in dissociation from the purpose of that provision: the protection of the right to life. This implies that a similar condition applies to cases under subparagraph (b).

105. The use of potentially lethal firearms inevitably exposes human life to danger even when there are rules designed to minimise the risks. Accordingly, the Court considers that it can in no circumstances be 'absolutely necessary' within the meaning of Article 2 § 2 of the Convention to use such firearms to arrest a person suspected of a non-violent offence who is known not to pose a threat to life or limb, even where a failure to do so may result in the opportunity to arrest the fugitive being lost…

Furthermore, the Chamber believed that excessive force had been used by the military police against the deceased, for example the Major opening fire when other options were available (e.g. using the military police jeep to chase the fugitives) and the Major choosing to fire his rifle in automatic mode when he had a handgun. Hence there had been a breach of Article 2. The Chamber's unequivocal ruling that the use of firearms to arrest non-violent suspects is not lawful under Article 2 should be commended. This provides clear guidance to member States and they must ensure that all their law-enforcement personnel are trained to observe this limitation. The right to life has to take precedence over the risk that non-violent offenders may (temporarily) escape arrest where resort to the use of firearms is prohibited under Article 2. Subsequently, a unanimous Grand Chamber confirmed this approach during a re-hearing of the case under Article 43 in *Nachova and Others v Bulgaria*, judgment of 6 July 2005.

95. Accordingly, and with reference to Article 2(2)(b) of the Convention, the legitimate aim of effecting a lawful arrest can only justify putting human life at risk in circumstances of absolute necessity. The Court considers that in principle there can be no such necessity where it is known that the person to be arrested poses no threat to life or limb and is not suspected of having committed a violent offence, even if a failure to use lethal force may result in the opportunity to arrest the fugitive being lost…

In regard to the alleged racist overtones of the killings in *Nachova*, see p 832.

Action lawfully taken to quell a riot or insurrection (Article 2(2)(c))

1   The Court examined this exception in *Güleç v Turkey*, 1998-IV. The applicant claimed that his 15-year-old son (Ahmet) had been killed by the security forces who opened fire on about 3,000 demonstrators to make them disperse. According to the applicant, Ahmet was trying to return home from school. The Government asserted that Ahmet had been killed by a bullet fired by armed demonstrators shooting at the security forces. The Commission found that the security forces had opened fire, either in the air or at the ground, in order to disperse the demonstrators using a machine gun on an armoured vehicle and that Ahmet had been hit by a fragment of a bullet (that had ricocheted off the ground or a wall) from that weapon. The Commission did not believe the machine gun had been used intentionally to kill demonstrators. However, by 31 votes to 1, the Commission concluded that there had been a breach of Article 2 as the use of a combat weapon to restore order during a

demonstration could not be regarded as proportionate. The Court was unanimous in finding a violation of that Article.

70. The file on the present case has not revealed any reason to cast doubt on the establishment of the facts as set out in the Commission's report. As the Commission rightly pointed out, the demonstration was far from peaceful, as was evidenced by the damage to moveable and immoveable property in the town and the injuries sustained by some gendarmes. Confronted with acts of violence which were, admittedly, serious, the security forces, who were not present in sufficient strength, called for reinforcements, and at least two armoured vehicles were deployed. Whereas the driver of the Condor, warrant-officer Nazim Ayhan, asserted that he had fired into the air, several witnesses, including some of the leading citizens of the town, said that shots had been fired at the crowd. Although this allegation was categorically denied by the Government, it is corroborated by the fact that nearly all the wounded demonstrators were hit in the legs; this would be perfectly consistent with ricochet wounds from bullets with a downward trajectory which could have been fired from the turret of an armoured vehicle.

71. The Court, like the Commission, accepts that the use of force may be justified in the present case under paragraph 2 (c) of Article 2, but it goes without saying that a balance must be struck between the aim pursued and the means employed to achieve it. The gendarmes used a very powerful weapon because they apparently did not have truncheons, riot shields, water cannon, rubber bullets or tear gas. The lack of such equipment is all the more incomprehensible and unacceptable because the province..., as the Government pointed out, is in a region in which a state of emergency has been declared, where at the material time disorder could have been expected.

72. As to the question whether there were armed terrorists among the demonstrators, the Court notes that the Government produced no evidence to support that assertion. In the first place, no gendarme sustained a bullet wound either in the place where the applicant's son died or in other places passed by the demonstration. Secondly, no weapons or spent cartridges supposed to have belonged to PKK members were found on the spot. Moreover, prosecutions brought in the Diyarbakir National Security Court against the owners of thirteen rifles confiscated after the incidents, from which spent cartridges had been collected by the security forces, ended in acquittals, because the defendants had not taken part in the events in issue...

73. In conclusion, the Court considers that in the circumstances of the case the force used to disperse the demonstrators, which caused the death of Ahmet Güleç, was not absolutely necessary within the meaning of Article 2.

Unfortunately, this case provides a dramatic example of excessive (disproportionate) use of force by State personnel.

2   The use of plastic baton rounds, commonly referred to as 'plastic bullets', by the security forces in Northern Ireland to deal with public disorder was considered by the Commission in *Stewart v UK*, 39 DR 162 (1984). The applicant's 13-year-old son (Brian) participated in a riot (with about 150 other persons) directed towards eight soldiers patrolling the Turf Lodge area of Belfast in October 1976. After stones and bottles were thrown by the rioters at the soldiers the Lieutenant, commanding the soldiers, ordered that one baton round be fired. However, this did not stop the rioters, therefore the officer ordered another baton round be fired at the leader of the rioters. The responsible soldier aimed at the leader's legs, but he was struck by two missiles (thrown by the rioters) as he fired. The assaults caused the soldier to jerk and his baton round hit Brian on the head. Brian died several days later as a result of his injuries. Brian's mother sued the Ministry of Defence, but the High Court found that the firing of the baton round was reasonable for the prevention of crime. She then complained

to the Commission arguing that Article 2 had been violated by the security forces using such a deadly and dangerous weapon for crowd control and that the shooting of Brian was not absolutely necessary. Between 1970 and 1975 the security forces in Northern Ireland fired approximately 55,000 'rubber bullets'. Three persons were killed and numerous persons were seriously injured (blinded) by the use of rubber bullets. From 1973 the security forces began to use plastic baton rounds instead of rubber bullets (the former are fired from a more accurate gun). At the time of the Commission's ruling 11 persons (including Brian) had been killed by plastic baton rounds. The Commission based its decision upon the facts found by the domestic courts, no new evidence had been presented to the Commission.

> The Commission notes that the use of the plastic baton round in Northern Ireland has given rise to much controversy and that it is a dangerous weapon which can occasion serious injuries and death, particularly if it strikes the head. However, information provided by the parties concerning casualties, compared with the number of baton rounds discharged, shows that the weapon is less dangerous than alleged.
>
> It recalls that the group of soldiers were confronted with a hostile and violent crowd of 150 persons who were attacking them with stones and other missiles, and, further, that the soldier's aim was disturbed at the moment of discharge when he was struck by several missiles.
>
> The Commission is of the opinion, taking account of all the surrounding circumstances, referred to above, that the death of Brian Stewart resulted from the use of force which was no more than 'absolutely necessary' 'in action lawfully taken for the purpose of quelling a riot . . . [Paras 28–30.]

Therefore, the Commission declared the application inadmissible. This case is also an example of an unintentional killing being evaluated under Article 2 by the Commission.

3 A Chamber found the use of disproportionate force by police and gendarmes, equipped with truncheons, who had been deployed to deal with a disturbance in a prison. The applicants in **Perisan and Others v Turkey**, judgment of 20 May 2010, complained that the deceased had suffered fatal injuries, including fractured skulls, at the hands of the security forces. The Court determined that the Turkish Government's argument that the force used by the police and gendarmes had been proportionate, as the officers had been attacked by prisoners wielding implements such as radiator pipes, was contradicted by the fact that members of the security forces suffered only minor injuries. Consequently, the force used by the officers had not been 'absolutely necessary'.

5 ARTICLE 3 PROHIBITION OF TORTURE

From its early case-law the Court has elaborated the differences between the various forms of conduct prohibited by Article 3. Obviously, torture encompasses the most horrendous forms of maltreatment. The full-time Court sought to widen the scope of this classification (*Selmouni*), however it is still reserved for relatively rare cases of gross abuse (*Gurgurov*). Inhuman treatment has been found in a variety of contexts ranging from officials' physical assaults on detainees (*Tomasi*) to deportations where applicants face a real risk of treatment violating Article 3 in their home State (*D and others v Turkey*). In assessing whether prison conditions (and other detention facilities) meet the minimum requirements of Article 3, the Court has increasingly taken cognizance of the standards and reports produced by the expert European Committee for the Prevention of Torture (*Ilascu and others*), thereby promoting a consistent and harmonious European approach. Strasbourg judgments led to the abolition of corporal punishment in the criminal justice system (*Tyrer*) and were highly significant in the ending of corporal punishment in schools (*Campbell and Cosans*).

The Court has also developed positive obligations under Article 3 including the requirements that States conduct effective investigations into allegations of serious maltreatment by officials (*Assenov*) and give protection to vulnerable persons threatened with Article 3 maltreatment by other private individuals (*Z and others*).

Recent judgments have reinforced the unqualified prohibition of conduct falling within Article 3 irrespective of the threats posed by the victims, whether they be a suspected international terrorist (*Saadi*) or a child killer (*Gafgen*).

The Court's general approach

Ireland v UK A.25 (1978)
European Court of Human Rights

Soon after the creation of the Irish Free State in 1921, six counties in the north opted to remain within the UK. These counties became Northern Ireland and until 1972 it had a separate Parliament (which was constitutionally subordinate to the Westminster Parliament) and Government. In the words of the Court:

Northern Ireland is not a homogeneous society. It consists of two communities divided by deep and long-standing antagonisms. One community is variously termed Protestant, Unionist or Loyalist, the other is generally labelled as Catholic, Republican or Nationalist. About two-thirds of the population of one and a half million belong to the Protestant community, the remaining third to the

Catholic community. The majority group is descended from Protestant settlers who emigrated in large numbers from Britain to Northern Ireland during the seventeenth century. The now traditional antagonism between the two groups is based both on religion and on social, economic and political difference. In particular, the Protestant community has consistently opposed the idea of a united Ireland independent of the United Kingdom, whereas the Catholic community has traditionally supported it. [Para 15.]

From 1963 a campaign for 'civil rights' (demanding the ending of discrimination against Catholics in the allocation of public sector housing, local authority appointments, and the manipulation of electoral boundaries) began to gather momentum in Northern Ireland. Marches in support of the campaign started in 1968 and some ended in rioting. In November 1968 the Northern Ireland Government announced a reform programme to deal with the minority community's grievances. However, the protest marches continued with escalating public disorder in the province. In the spring of 1969 explosive devices were detonated (probably by Loyalist terrorists) at public utility facilities in Northern Ireland and British troops were sent to the province. At about the same time the IRA (the Irish Republican Army, 'a clandestine organisation with quasi-military dispositions') secretly reactivated its members. During 1970 the IRA began a terrorist campaign of bombing buildings and attacking members of the security forces in Northern Ireland. Simultaneously Loyalist terrorists were killing Catholics and bombing their premises. The terrorist violence escalated in 1971 with the IRA being responsible for the majority of incidents. In August 1971 the Government of Northern Ireland, after discussions with the UK Government, brought into operation extra-judicial measures of detention and internment to try and reduce the level of terrorist violence. The authorities introduced these measures because they believed that: (a) the ordinary criminal justice system was unable to deal with IRA terrorism, (b) widespread intimidation of the population made it impossible to secure convictions against IRA terrorists, and (c) the border with the Republic of Ireland made it easy for terrorists to escape from one jurisdiction to the other. In the weeks preceding the introduction of internment, the security forces prepared lists of persons who were suspected of being involved with or having knowledge about IRA terrorism.

Starting at 4 am on Monday 9 August 1971, the army, with police officers occasionally acting as guides, mounted an operation ('Demetrius') to arrest the 452 persons whose names appeared on the final list. In the event some 350 persons were arrested in accordance with the Special Powers Regulations. The arrested persons were taken to one of the three regional holding centres (Malligan Weekend Training Centre in County Londonderry, Ballykinder Weekend Training Centre in County Down, and Girdwood Park Territorial Army Centre in Belfast) that had been set up to receive the prisoners during 48 hours. All those arrested were subjected to interrogation by police officers of the Royal Ulster Constabulary (RUC). One hundred and four persons were released within 48 hours. Those who were to be detained were sent on to the prison ship *Maidstone* or to Crumlin Road prison, both in Belfast. Prior to being lodged in detention, 12 individuals were moved to one or more unidentified centres for 'interrogation in depth' extending over several days (para 39).

Subsequently other persons held and interrogated under the extra-judicial measures were processed at Palace Barracks (Holywood, County Down), Gough (County Armagh), and Girdwood Park and Ballykelly (County Londonderry). Internment resulted in serious rioting and increased terrorist activity. In March 1972, due to the deteriorating security situation, direct rule was established over Northern Ireland by the UK Government (the Northern Ireland Parliament was prorogued and the executive powers of the Northern Ireland Government transferred to the Secretary of State for Northern Ireland). One of the first actions taken under direct rule was to release over 250 detainees. Loyalist terrorism, however, began to increase, especially in the form of sectarian assassinations. In 1973 the first Loyalists were interned. Political reforms were unsuccessfully attempted in Northern Ireland and in 1975 the last extra-judicial detainees were released. By March 1975, according to the UK Government, 1,100 people had been killed, 11,500 injured, and £140 million worth of property destroyed by terrorism and public disorder in Northern Ireland.

In December 1971 the Irish Government lodged a complaint with the Commission against the UK, alleging a number of breaches of the Convention in respect of, *inter alia*, the treatment of persons detained under the extra-judicial powers in Northern Ireland. The applicant Government submitted written evidence in respect of 228 cases concerning incidents between 1971 and 1974. The Commission examined in detail the evidence relating to 16 'illustrative' cases selected by the Irish Government. Also 41 further cases were considered by the Commission. The applicant Government was particularly concerned about the use of 'interrogation in depth' techniques, for several days, on 14 persons in 1971 at unidentified interrogation centres. The 'five techniques' consisted of the following sensory deprivation methods which were used in combination:

(a) wall-standing: forcing the detainees to remain for periods of some hours in a 'stress position', described by those who underwent it as being 'spread-eagled against the wall, with their fingers put high above the head against the wall, the legs spread apart and the feet back, causing them to stand on their toes with the weight of the body mainly on the fingers';

(b) hooding: putting a black or navy coloured bag over the detainees' heads and, at least initially, keeping it there all the time except during interrogation;

(c) subjection to noise: pending their interrogations, holding the detainees in a room where there was a continuous loud, hissing noise;

(d) deprivation of sleep pending their interrogations: depriving the detainees of sleep;

(e) deprivation of food and drink: subjecting the detainees to a reduced diet during their stay at the centre and pending interrogations (para 96).

The applicant Government also made a number of allegations of violent assaults by members of the security forces against detainees. In its report (February 1976) the Commission found, *inter alia*, that the combined use of the five techniques in the cases before it constituted a practice of inhuman treatment and of torture in breach of Article 3 (unanimously).

AS TO THE LAW

...

I. ON ARTICLE 3 (ART 3)

150. Article 3 (art 3) provides that 'no one shall be subjected to torture or to inhuman or degrading treatment or punishment'.

A. PRELIMINARY QUESTIONS

151. In their memorial of 26 October 1976 and at the hearings in February 1977, the United Kingdom Government raised two preliminary questions on the alleged violations of Article 3 (art 3). The first concerns the violations which they no longer contest, the second certain of the violations whose existence they dispute.

1. Preliminary question on the non-contested violations of Article 3 (art 3)

152. The United Kingdom Government contest neither the breaches of Article 3 (art 3) as found by the Commission...nor—a point moreover that is beyond doubt—the Court's jurisdiction to

examine such breaches. However, relying *inter alia* on the case-law of the International Court of Justice (*Northern Cameroons* case, judgment of 2 December 1963, and Nuclear Tests cases, judgments of 20 December 1974), they argue that the European Court has power to decline to exercise its jurisdiction where the objective of an application has been accomplished or where adjudication on the merits would be devoid of purpose. Such, they claim, is the situation here. They maintain that the findings in question not only are not contested but also have been widely publicised and that they do not give rise to problems of interpretation or application of the Convention sufficiently important to require a decision by the Court. Furthermore, for them the subject-matter of those findings now belongs to past history in view of the abandonment of the five techniques (1972), the solemn and unqualified undertaking not to reintroduce these techniques (8 February 1977) and the other measures taken by the United Kingdom to remedy, impose punishment for, and prevent the recurrence of, the various violations found by the Commission.

This argument is disputed by the applicant Government. Neither is it accepted in a general way by the delegates of the Commission; they stated, however, that they would express no conclusion as to whether or not the above-mentioned undertaking had deprived the claim concerning the five techniques of its object.

153. The Court takes formal note of the undertaking given before it, at the hearing on 8 February 1977, by the United Kingdom Attorney-General on behalf of the respondent Government. The terms of this undertaking were as follows:

> 'The Government of the United Kingdom have considered the question of the use of the 'five techniques' with very great care and with particular regard to Article 3 (art 3) of the Convention. They now give this unqualified undertaking, that the 'five techniques' will not in any circumstances be reintroduced as an aid to interrogation.'

The Court also notes that the United Kingdom has taken various measures designed to prevent the recurrence of the events complained of and to afford reparation for their consequences. For example, it has issued to the police and the army instructions and directives on the arrest, interrogation and treatment of persons in custody, reinforced the procedures for investigating complaints, appointed commissions of enquiry and paid or offered compensation in many cases . . .

154. Nevertheless, the Court considers that the responsibilities assigned to it within the framework of the system under the Convention extend to pronouncing on the non-contested allegations of violation of Article 3 (art 3). The Court's judgments in fact serve not only to decide those cases brought before the Court but, more generally, to elucidate, safeguard and develop the rules instituted by the Convention, thereby contributing to the observance by the States of the engagements undertaken by them as Contracting Parties (Article 19) (art 19).

The conclusion thus arrived at by the Court is, moreover, confirmed by paragraph 3 of Rule 47 of the Rules of Court. If the Court may proceed with the consideration of a case and give a ruling thereon even in the event of a 'notice of discontinuance, friendly settlement, arrangement' or 'other fact of a kind to provide a solution of the matter', it is entitled a fortiori to adopt such a course of action when the conditions for the application of this Rule are not present.

155. Accordingly, that part of the present case which concerns the said allegations cannot be said to have become without object; the Court considers that it should rule thereon, notwithstanding the initiatives taken by the respondent State. . . .

B. QUESTIONS OF PROOF

160. In order to satisfy itself as to the existence or not in Northern Ireland of practices contrary to Article 3 (art 3), the Court will not rely on the concept that the burden of proof is borne by one or other of the two Governments concerned. In the cases referred to it, the Court examines all the

material before it, whether originating from the Commission, the Parties or other sources, and, if necessary, obtains material *proprio motu*.

161. The Commission based its own conclusions mainly on the evidence of the one hundred witnesses heard in, and on the medical reports relating to, the sixteen 'illustrative' cases it had asked the applicant Government to select. The Commission also relied, but to a lesser extent, on the documents and written comments submitted in connection with the '41 cases' and it referred to the numerous 'remaining cases' (see paragraph 93 above). As in the *Greek case* (Yearbook of the Convention, 1969, The *Greek* case, p 196, para 30), the standard of proof the Commission adopted when evaluating the material it obtained was proof 'beyond reasonable doubt'.

The Irish Government see this as an excessively rigid standard for the purposes of the present proceedings. They maintain that the system of enforcement would prove ineffectual if, where there was a *prima facie* case of violation of Article 3 (art 3), the risk of a finding of such a violation was not borne by a State which fails in its obligation to assist the Commission in establishing the truth (Article 28, sub-paragraph (a) *in fine*, of the Convention) (art 28-a). In their submission, this is how the attitude taken by the United Kingdom should be described.

The respondent Government dispute this contention and ask the Court to follow the same course as the Commission. The Court agrees with the Commission's approach regarding the evidence on which to base the decision whether there has been violation of Article 3 (art 3). To assess this evidence, the Court adopts the standard of proof 'beyond reasonable doubt' but adds that such proof may follow from the coexistence of sufficiently strong, clear and concordant inferences or of similar unrebutted presumptions of fact. In this context, the conduct of the Parties when evidence is being obtained has to be taken into account.

C. QUESTIONS CONCERNING THE MERITS

162. As was emphasised by the Commission, ill-treatment must attain a minimum level of severity if it is to fall within the scope of Article 3 (art 3). The assessment of this minimum is, in the nature of things, relative; it depends on all the circumstances of the case, such as the duration of the treatment, its physical or mental effects and, in some cases, the sex, age and state of health of the victim, etc.

163. The Convention prohibits in absolute terms torture and inhuman or degrading treatment or punishment, irrespective of the victim's conduct. Unlike most of the substantive clauses of the Convention and of Protocols Nos. 1 and 4 (P1, P4), Article 3 (art 3) makes no provision for exceptions and, under Article 15 para 2 (art 15–2), there can be no derogation therefrom even in the event of a public emergency threatening the life of the nation.

164. In the instant case, the only relevant concepts are 'torture' and 'inhuman or degrading treatment', to the exclusion of 'inhuman or degrading punishment'.

1. The unidentified interrogation centre or centres

(a) The 'five techniques'

165. ... In the Commission's estimation, those facts constituted a practice not only of inhuman and degrading treatment but also of torture. The applicant Government ask for confirmation of this opinion which is not contested before the Court by the respondent Government.

166. The police used the five techniques on fourteen persons in 1971 ... Although never authorised in writing in any official document, the five techniques were taught orally by the English Intelligence Centre to members of the RUC at a seminar held in April 1971. There was accordingly a practice.

167. The five techniques were applied in combination, with premeditation and for hours at a stretch; they caused, if not actual bodily injury, at least intense physical and mental suffering to

the persons subjected thereto and also led to acute psychiatric disturbances during interrogation. They accordingly fell into the category of inhuman treatment within the meaning of Article 3 (art 3). The techniques were also degrading since they were such as to arouse in their victims feelings of fear, anguish and inferiority capable of humiliating and debasing them and possibly breaking their physical or moral resistance.

On these two points, the Court is of the same view as the Commission.

In order to determine whether the five techniques should also be qualified as torture, the Court must have regard to the distinction, embodied in Article 3 (art 3), between this notion and that of inhuman or degrading treatment.

In the Court's view, this distinction derives principally from a difference in the intensity of the suffering inflicted.

The Court considers in fact that, while there exists on the one hand violence which is to be condemned both on moral grounds and also in most cases under the domestic law of the Contracting States but which does not fall within Article 3 (art 3) of the Convention, it appears on the other hand that it was the intention that the Convention, with its distinction between 'torture' and 'inhuman or degrading treatment', should by the first of these terms attach a special stigma to deliberate inhuman treatment causing very serious and cruel suffering.

Moreover, this seems to be the thinking lying behind Article 1 *in fine* of Resolution 3452 (XXX) adopted by the General Assembly of the United Nations on 9 December 1975, which declares:

> 'Torture constitutes an aggravated and deliberate form of cruel, inhuman or degrading treatment or punishment'.

Although the five techniques, as applied in combination, undoubtedly amounted to inhuman and degrading treatment, although their object was the extraction of confessions, the naming of others and/or information and although they were used systematically, they did not occasion suffering of the particular intensity and cruelty implied by the word torture as so understood.

168. The Court concludes that recourse to the five techniques amounted to a practice of inhuman and degrading treatment, which practice was in breach of Article 3 (art 3).

(b) Ill-Treatment alleged to have accompanied the use of the five techniques

...

2. Palace Barracks

173. The Commission came to the view that inhuman treatment had occurred at Palace Barracks in September, October and November 1971 in seven of the nine 'illustrative' cases it examined . . . It considered that these cases, combined with other indications, showed that there had been in these Barracks, in the autumn of 1971, a practice in connection with the interrogation of prisoners by members of the RUC which was inhuman treatment.

The British Government do not contest these conclusions; the Irish Government ask the Court to confirm them but also to supplement them in various respects.

(c) Autumn 1971

174. Insofar as the Commission has found that a practice of inhuman treatment was followed in the autumn of 1971 . . . The evidence before the Court reveals that, at the time in question, quite a large number of those held in custody at Palace Barracks were subjected to violence by members of the RUC. This violence, which was repeated violence occurring in the same place and taking similar forms, did not amount merely to isolated incidents; it definitely constituted a practice. It also led to intense suffering and to physical injury which on occasion was substantial; it thus fell into the category of inhuman treatment.

According to the applicant Government, the violence in question should also be classified, in some cases, as torture.

On the basis of the data before it, the Court does not share this view. Admittedly, the acts complained of often occurred during interrogation and, to this extent, were aimed at extracting confessions, the naming of others and/or information, but the severity of the suffering that they were capable of causing did not attain the particular level inherent in the notion of torture as understood by the Court (see paragraph 167 above)....

3. Other Places

178. According to the applicant Government, a practice or practices in breach of Article 3 (art 3) existed in Northern Ireland from 1971 to 1974, for example at Girdwood Park and at Ballykinler; this allegation is denied by the respondent Government.

The Commission was of the opinion that T 16 and T 7 had been victims of treatment that was both inhuman and degrading and T 11 of treatment that was inhuman: T 16 on 13 August 1971 at Girdwood Park, T 7 on 28 October 1971 in a street in Belfast and T 11 on 20 December 1971 at Albert Street Barracks, also in Belfast. However, the Commission considered that no practice in breach of Article 3 (art 3) had been established in relation to these cases, including the general conditions at Girdwood Park...and, further, that the conditions of detention at Ballykinler did not disclose a violation of that Article (art 3) (ibid).

(a) Ballykinler

...

180. The RUC, with the assistance of the army, used Ballykinler as a holding and interrogation centre for a few days early in August 1971. Some dozens of people arrested in the course of Operation Demetrius were held there in extreme discomfort and were made to perform irksome and painful exercises...

There was thus a practice rather than isolated incidents. The Court found confirmation of this in the judgment of 18 February 1972 in the Moore case.

181. The Court has to determine whether this practice violated Article 3 (art 3). Clearly, it would not be possible to speak of torture or inhuman treatment, but the question does arise whether there was not degrading treatment. The Armagh County Court granted Mr Moore £300 by way of damages, the maximum amount it had jurisdiction to award. This fact shows that the matters of which Mr Moore complained were, if nothing else, contrary to the domestic law then in force in the United Kingdom. Furthermore, the way in which prisoners at Ballykinler were treated was characterised in the judgment of 18 February 1972 as not only illegal but also harsh. However, the judgment does not describe the treatment in detail; it concentrates mainly on reciting the evidence tendered by the witnesses and indicates that the judge rejected that given on behalf of the defence. The Compton Committee for its part considered that, although the exercises which detainees had been made to do involved some degree of compulsion and must have caused hardship, they were the result of lack of judgment rather than an intention to hurt or degrade.

To sum up, the RUC and the army followed at Ballykinler a practice which was discreditable and reprehensible but the Court does not consider that they infringed Article 3 (art 3).

(b) Miscellaneous places

182. There remain the various other places referred to by the Irish Government...The information before the Court concerning these places—for example the large number of cases in which compensation was paid by the British authorities and the many criminal or disciplinary sanctions imposed on members of the security forces...suggests that there must have been individual violations of Article 3 (art 3) in Northern Ireland over and above the breaches already noted by the Court. However, the Commission did not regard this information...as being sufficient to disclose a practice or practices in breach of Article 3 (art 3).

The Court shares this view. Admittedly, the evidence before the Court bears out the Commission's opinion...However, these were incidents insufficiently numerous and inter-connected to amount to a practice…the preventive measures taken by the United Kingdom…at first sight render hardly plausible, especially as regards the period after the introduction of direct rule (30 March 1972), if not the suggestion of individual violations of Article 3 (art 3)—on which the Court does not have to give a specific ruling…at least the suggestion of the continuation or commencement of a practice or practices in breach of that Article (art 3). Furthermore, anyone claiming to be the victim of a breach of Article 3 (art 3) in Northern Ireland is entitled to exercise the domestic remedies open to him (Article 26 the Convention) (art 26) and subsequently, if need be, to apply to the Commission whose competence to receive 'individual' petitions has been recognised by the United Kingdom (Article 25) (art 25); this in fact often happened. Finally, the findings made in connection with the five techniques and Palace Barracks, henceforth embodied in a binding judgment of the Court, provide a far from negligible guarantee against a return to the serious errors of former times.

In these circumstances, the interests protected by the Convention do not compel the Court to undertake lengthy researches that would delay the Court's decision.…

185. In conclusion, the Court does not find, as regards the places concerned, any practice in breach of Article 3 (art 3).

4. The Irish request for a consequential order

186. In a letter dated 5 January 1977, the applicant Government requested the Court to order that the respondent Government

— refrain from reintroducing the five techniques, as a method of interrogation or otherwise;
— proceed as appropriate, under the criminal law of the United Kingdom and the relevant disciplinary code, against those members of the security forces who have committed acts in breach of Article 3 (art 3) referred to in the Commission's findings and conclusions, and against those who condoned or tolerated them.

At the hearings, the applicant Government withdrew the first request following the solemn undertaking given on behalf of the United Kingdom Government on 8 February 1977…on the other hand, the second request was maintained.

187. The Court does not have to consider in these proceedings whether its functions extend, in certain circumstances, to addressing consequential orders to Contracting States. In the present case, the Court finds that the sanctions available to it do not include the power to direct one of those States to institute criminal or disciplinary proceedings in accordance with its domestic law.…

V. ON ARTICLE 50 (ART 50)

…

245. The President, acting on behalf of the Court, instructed the Registrar to ask the Agent of the Irish Government to indicate 'as soon as possible whether it would be correct to assume, particularly in the light' of certain passages in the Commission's decision on the admissibility of the application and in the verbatim report of the public hearings held in February 1977, 'that [his] Government [were not inviting] the Court, should it find a violation of the Convention, to afford just satisfaction within the meaning of Article 50 (art 50)'. This the Registrar did by letter of 8 August 1977. On 14 October 1977, the Agent of the applicant Government replied as follows:

'…the applicant Government, while not wishing to interfere with the *de bene esse* jurisdiction of the Court, have not as an object the obtaining of compensation for any individual person and do not invite the Court to afford just satisfaction under Article 50 (art 50), of the nature of monetary compensation, to any individual victim of a breach of the Convention.…'

246. The Court accordingly considers that it is not necessary to apply Article 50 (art 50) in the present case.

FOR THESE REASONS, THE COURT

I. ON ARTICLE 3 (ART 3)

1. holds unanimously that, although certain violations of Article 3 (art 3) were not contested, a ruling should nevertheless be given thereon;

2. holds unanimously that it has jurisdiction to take cognisance of the cases of alleged violation of Article 3 (art 3) to the extent that the applicant Government put them forward as establishing the existence of a practice;

3. holds by sixteen votes to one that the use of the five techniques in August and October 1971 constituted a practice of inhuman and degrading treatment, which practice was in breach of Article 3 (art 3);

4. holds by thirteen votes to four that the said use of the five techniques did not constitute a practice of torture within the meaning of Article 3 (art 3);

5. holds by sixteen votes to one that no other practice of ill-treatment is established for the unidentified interrogation centres;

6. holds unanimously that there existed at Palace Barracks in the autumn of 1971 a practice of inhuman treatment, which practice was in breach of Article 3 (art 3);

7. holds by fourteen votes to three that the last-mentioned practice was not one of torture within the meaning of Article 3 (art 3);

8. holds unanimously that it is not established that the practice in question continued beyond the autumn of 1971;

9. holds by fifteen votes to two that no practice in breach of Article 3 (art 3) is established as regards other places;

10. holds unanimously that it cannot direct the respondent State to institute criminal or disciplinary proceedings against those members of the security forces who have committed the breaches of Article 3 (art 3) found by the Court and against those who condoned or tolerated such breaches; ...

IV. ON ARTICLE 50 (ART 50)

18. holds unanimously that it is not necessary to apply Article 50 (art 50) in the present case.

...

NOTES

1 The plenary Court was composed of President Balladore Pallieri and Judges: Wiarda, Zekia, Cremona, O'Donoghue, Pedersen, Thor Vilhjalmsson, Ryssdal, Ganshof Van Der Meersch, Fitzmaurice, Bindschedler-Robert, Evrigenis, Teitgen, Lagergren, Liesch, Gölcüklü, and Matscher.

2 Judge Zekia issued a separate opinion in which he set out his conception of torture.

Admittedly the word 'torture' included in Article 3 of the Convention is not capable of an exact and comprehensive definition. It is undoubtedly an aggravated form of inhuman treatment causing intense physical and/or mental suffering. Although the degree of intensity and the length of such suffering constitute the basic elements of torture, a lot of other relevant factors had to be taken into account. Such as: the nature of ill-treatment inflicted, the means and methods employed, the repetition and duration of such treatment, the age, sex and health condition of the person exposed to it, the likelihood that such treatment might injure the physical, mental and psychological condition of the person exposed and whether the injuries inflicted caused serious consequences for short or long duration are all relevant matters to be considered together and arrive at a conclusion whether torture has been committed.

It seems to me permissible, in ascertaining whether torture or inhuman treatment has been committed or not, to apply not only the objective test but also the subjective test.

As an example I can refer to the case of an elderly sick man who is exposed to a harsh treatment—after being given several blows and beaten to the floor, he is dragged and kicked on the floor for several hours. I would say without hesitation that the poor man has been tortured. If such treatment is applied on a wrestler or even a young athlete, I would hesitate a lot to describe it as inhuman treatment and I might regard it as mere rough handling.

3 Judge O'Donoghue, the judge of Irish nationality, dissented on a number of grounds.

For my part I agree with the unanimous finding of the Commission that the use of the five techniques constituted 'torture' in breach of the Convention. . . . One is not bound to regard torture as only present in a mediaeval dungeon where the appliances of rack and thumbscrew or similar devices were employed. Indeed in the present-day world there can be little doubt that torture may be inflicted in the mental sphere.

4 Judge Sir Gerald Fitzmaurice, the judge of British nationality, was the dissenter who did not consider that the five techniques constituted a practice of inhuman and degrading treatment. Generally, he took a more restrictive view of the scope of Article 3 than the Court.

It would be reasonable to suppose that, at the date when the Convention was framed, during the aftermath of war and atrocity, it would have been the severer forms of ill-treatment that the Parties would have had in mind.

Subjection to the five techniques was certainly harsh treatment, ill-treatment, maltreatment, and other descriptions could be found; but the 'inhuman' involves a totally different order or category of concept to which, in my opinion, the five techniques, even used in combination, do not properly belong . . . if standing someone against a wall in a strained position over a considerable period, or keeping him with a hood over his head for a certain time, amounts to 'inhuman' treatment, what language should be used to describe kicking a man in the groin, or placing him in a blacked-out cell in the company of a bevy of starving rats? . . .

In the present context it can be assumed that [degrading treatment] is, or should be, intended to denote something seriously humiliating, lowering as to human dignity, or disparaging, like having one's head shaved, being tarred and feathered, smeared with filth, pelted with muck, paraded naked in front of strangers, forced to eat excreta, deface the portrait of one's sovereign or head of State, or dress up in a way calculated to provoke ridicule or contempt . . .

. . . not only must a certain intensity of suffering be caused before the process can be called torture, but also that torture involves a wholly different order of suffering from what falls short of it. It amounts not to a mere difference of degree but to a difference of kind. If the five techniques are to be regarded as involving torture, how does one characterize eg having one's finger-nails torn out, being slowly impaled on a stake through the rectum, or roasted over an electric grid? . . .

5 Judge Evrigenis took a diametrically opposite approach to Judge Fitzmaurice:

The Court's interpretation in this case seems also to be directed to a conception of torture based on methods of inflicting suffering which have already been overtaken by the ingenuity of modern techniques of oppression. Torture no longer presupposes violence, a notion to which the judgment refers expressly and generically. Torture can be practised—and indeed is practised—by using subtle techniques developed in multidisciplinary laboratories which claim to be scientific. By means of new forms of suffering that have little in common with the physical pain caused by conventional torture it aims to bring about, even if only temporarily, the disintegration of an individual's personality, the shattering of his mental and psychological equilibrium and the crushing of his will. I should very much regret it if the definition of torture which emerges from the judgment could not cover these various forms of technologically sophisticated torture. Such an interpretation would overlook the current situation and the historical prospects in which the European Convention on Human Rights should be implemented.

6   For Judge Matscher:

the distinguishing feature of the notion of torture is the systematic, calculated (hence deliberate) and prolonged application of treatment causing physical or psychological suffering of a certain intensity, the aim of which may be to extort confessions, to obtain information or simply to break a person's will in order to compel him to do something he would not otherwise do, or again, to make a person suffer for other reasons (sadism, aggravation of a punishment, etc.).

7   While the above judicial opinions indicate the difficulties inherent in determining if a particular form of maltreatment falls within any of the specific categories prescribed by Article 3 (for further guidance on how these categories have been applied by the Court see the cases extracted and discussed below), the Court's judgment in *Ireland* emphasizes some of the basic certainties of the Article. Hence a victim's conduct does not permit a State to subject him or her to treatment prohibited by Article 3 (even if the victim is a terrorist or a major criminal). Furthermore, the Article is not subject to exceptions and cannot be derogated from under Article 15 (even where there is a public emergency threatening the life of the nation).

8   The Court's elaboration of the idea of 'a practice' which is incompatible with the Convention and its importance in the determination of the admissibility of a complaint has been examined at p 35.

9   The Commission has expressed the view that legal persons cannot claim to be the victims of a violation of Article 3. In *Verein Kontakt-Information-Therapie and Hagen v Austria*, 57 DR 81 (1988), the first applicant was a private association which ran rehabilitation centres for young drug abusers. The domestic courts ordered two therapists (including the second applicant), employed by the association, to give evidence in criminal proceedings for alleged drug abuse against a former patient. The therapists, with the support of the first applicant, refused to disclose confidential information about the former patient. The courts fined the therapists 5,000 AS each and obliged the association to collect the fine by attachment of their earnings. The applicants complained, *inter alia*, of a breach of Article 3. The Commission declared the application inadmissible noting that the rights protected by Article 3 '…are by their very nature not susceptible of being exercised by a legal person such as a private association' (p 162). Also the treatment of the second applicant involving 'the obligation to give the required evidence did not attain the level of severity which is required by this provision' (p 163). Conceptually it is nonsensical to characterize the treatment of a legal entity as 'torture' or 'inhuman'.

10   The Court has interpreted Article 3 so as to impose a duty on member States to undertake an effective official investigation where a person makes an arguable claim that he or she has been subject to serious maltreatment by public officials. This procedural obligation mirrors the similar duty created by Article 2, in cases where a person has been killed in circumstances governed by that provision (see p 130). In *Assenov and others v Bulgaria*, 1998-VIII, the first applicant was a Bulgarian of Roma origin. In 1992, when he was 14 years old, he was caught gambling in a market square by an off-duty police officer. The officer arrested the applicant and took him to a nearby bus station, where the officer called for additional police help. The applicant's parents were working at the bus station and they sought his release. To show that he would punish the applicant, his father hit the applicant with a strip of plywood. Subsequently, the applicant claimed that he was, *inter alia*, beaten with truncheons by three police officers. The Commission did not find a breach of Article 3 (16 votes to 1) as it was not able to establish who had caused the bruises on the applicant. The Court, unanimously, held that:

102. ... where an individual raises an arguable claim that he has been seriously ill-treated by the police or other such agents of the State unlawfully and in breach of Article 3, that provision, read in conjunction with the State's general duty under Article 1 of the Convention to 'secure to everyone within their jurisdiction the rights and freedoms defined in ... [the] Convention', requires by implication that there should be an effective official investigation. This investigation, as with that under Article 2, should be capable of leading to the identification and punishment of those responsible (see, in relation to Article 2 of the Convention, the *McCann and Others v the United Kingdom* judgment of 27 September 1995, Series A No 324, p 49 ...). If this were not the case, the general legal prohibition of torture and inhuman and degrading treatment and punishment, despite its fundamental importance ... would be ineffective in practice and it would be possible in some cases for agents of the State to abuse the rights of those within their control with virtual impunity.

103. The Court notes that following [the applicant's mother's] complaint, the State authorities did carry out some investigation into the applicant's allegations. It is not, however, persuaded that this investigation was sufficiently thorough and effective to meet the above requirements of Article 3. In this respect it finds it particularly unsatisfactory that the ... investigator was prepared to conclude that Mr Assenov's injuries had been caused by his father ... despite the lack of any evidence that the latter had beaten his son with the force which would have been required to cause the bruising described in the medical certificate. Although this incident had taken place in public view at the bus station, and although, according to the statements of the police officers concerned, it was seen by approximately fifteen to twenty Roma and twenty bus drivers, no attempt appears to have been made to ascertain the truth through contacting and questioning these witnesses in the immediate aftermath of the incident, when memories would have been fresh. Instead, at that time a statement was taken from only one independent witness, who was unable to recall the events in question ...

104. The initial investigation carried out by the regional military prosecution office (RMPO) and that of the general military prosecution office (GMPO) were even more cursory. The Court finds it particularly striking that the GMPO could conclude, without any evidence that Mr Assenov had not been compliant, and without any explanation as to the nature of the alleged disobedience, that 'even if the blows were administered on the body of the juvenile, they occurred as a result of disobedience to police orders' ... To make such an assumption runs contrary to the principle under Article 3 that, in respect of a person deprived of his liberty, recourse to physical force which has not been made strictly necessary by his own conduct is in principle an infringement of his rights ...

...

106. Against this background, in view of the lack of a thorough and effective investigation into the applicant's arguable claim that he had been beaten by police officers, the Court finds that there has been a violation of Article 3 of the Convention.

The articulation of this implicit duty of investigation is valuable for two reasons. First, it seeks to ensure that victims of unlawful maltreatment by public officials will be able to demand an effective domestic inquiry, potentially leading to the punishment of the culpable officials. Secondly, the Convention duty to conduct such an inquiry may act as a deterrent, to prevent ill-treatment, as officials may fear discovery and punishment when an inquiry is held.

A united Chamber also found a breach of this effective investigation obligation in conjunction with Article 14 where the authorities had failed to examine possible racist motivation behind acts of police brutality: *Bekos and Koutropoulos v Greece*, judgment of 13 December 2005.

A broadening of the scope of the effective investigation obligation under this Article to encompass complaints about serious (criminal) ill-treatment by private persons has been endorsed by a unanimous Chamber in *MC v Bulgaria*, judgment of 4 December 2003. The applicant was born in 1980 and she alleged that on 31 July and 1 August 1995, when she was 14 years and 10 months old (the age of consent in Bulgaria is 14), she had been raped by two men. She had been waiting to enter a local disco bar on the evening of 31 July 1995 when three men (P aged 21, A aged 20, and VA of unknown age) arrived in a car. The applicant knew P and A. They invited her to go to another disco bar in a town some distance away and she agreed. On the return journey they went to a reservoir as A wished to swim (the applicant subsequently stated that she had objected to the detour). She remained in the car whilst the men went for a swim. P returned to the car and started kissing her. She claimed that she had refused his advances and asked him to leave her alone. She contended that he then held her hands against her back. She did not have the strength physically to resist or scream. P then had sexual intercourse with her. P later claimed that the applicant had consented to sex. She alleged that afterwards she had been very disturbed and cried. In the early morning of 1 August the group went to a nearby town where relatives of VA had a house. The applicant went into the house with A and VA. She asserted that A had pushed her down on a bed she was sitting on and forced her to have sexual intercourse with him (she claimed that she did not have the strength to resist). The applicant's mother found her in the house and took her directly to the local hospital. The medical examiner confirmed that the applicant had recently lost her virginity. One day later P visited the applicant's home and (according to the applicant and her mother) had asked for forgiveness and promised that he would marry the applicant when she became of age. The applicant's mother considered this a suitable arrangement. Subsequently, the applicant went out with P the following evening. On 10 August the applicant's father returned home. The family then decided to file a complaint with the authorities.

During 11 August 1995 the applicant made a written statement to the police. Later that day the police arrested P and A. The men claimed that she had consented to sex and were subsequently released by the police. On 14 November 1995 the District Prosecutor opened criminal proceedings concerning the alleged rapes and referred the case to an investigator. No action was taken by the authorities for one year and then, in November 1996, the investigator questioned the parties and one month later produced a report recommending the termination of proceedings against P and A (as there was no evidence that they had used threats or violence towards the applicant). The District Prosecutor, in January 1997, ordered a further investigation (as the initial one had not been objective and thorough). The investigator sought the advice of a psychiatrist and a psychologist regarding the behaviour of the applicant at the time of the alleged rapes. They considered that she was psychologically sound but of a credulous nature. She did not appear to have been in a state of shock during the events as she had a clear recollection of them. Her subsequent socializing with P could be explained by the family's wish to present a socially acceptable image of the events. In

February 1997 the investigator produced a second report which again proposed terminating the proceedings (he considered that the experts' opinions did not undermine his earlier finding that there was no evidence of force or threats having been used against the applicant). The District Prosecutor terminated the proceedings in March 1997 as he concluded that the use of force or threats by P and A had not been established beyond reasonable doubt and no resistance by the applicant or attempts to seek help from others had been established. Appeals to the Regional and Chief Public Prosecutor, by the applicant, were rejected.

The applicant contended that, *inter alia*, the authorities had not effectively investigated the events of 31 July and 1 August 1995. The Court held that:

> 151. In a number of cases Article 3 of the Convention gives rise to a positive obligation to conduct an official investigation (see *Assenov v Bulgaria*...). Such positive obligations cannot be considered in principle to be limited solely to cases of ill-treatment by State agents...

The Court went on to find that the Bulgarian authorities had insufficiently investigated the surrounding circumstances of the applicant's allegations and placed undue emphasis on the absence of 'direct' proof of rape (i.e. the lack of evidence that the applicant had 'resisted' the men). Consequently, a violation of the respondent State's positive obligations under Article 3 (and Article 8) were found to have occurred. This extension of *Assenov* is a further enhancement of the procedural protection given to individuals under Article 3. The perpetrators of serious ill-treatment should be sought via effective investigations whether they be State agents or private individuals.

11 Although the vast majority of cases relying upon Article 3 involve allegations against the actions of State officials, the Court has interpreted this provision to require States to take positive steps, such as the enactment of appropriate criminal offences, to protect persons from being subject to Article 3 maltreatment by other private persons. In *A v UK*, 1998-VI, the applicant was a young person born in 1984. In 1993 the applicant's stepfather was charged with assault occasioning actual bodily harm in respect of his beating of the applicant. The stepfather admitted that on several occasions he had caned (i.e. hit on the bottom and back of the legs with a garden cane) the applicant, because the latter was a difficult boy who did not respond to parental or school discipline. To secure a conviction it was necessary for the prosecution to prove that the stepfather's punishment was not reasonable. The jury, by a majority verdict, found the stepfather not guilty. The applicant complained to the Commission alleging, *inter alia*, that the UK Government had failed to protect him from ill-treatment by his stepfather in breach of Article 3. The Commission was unanimous in upholding that claim. The Court was also unanimous in its judgment that the beating of the applicant was sufficiently serious to fall within the scope of Article 3 (note, the Court did not specify what element of Article 3 had been infringed, e.g. whether it was degrading or inhuman treatment or punishment).

> 22. It remains to be determined whether the State should be held responsible, under Article 3, for the beating of the applicant by his stepfather. The Court considers that the obligation on the High Contracting Parties under Article 1 of the Convention to secure to everyone within their jurisdiction the rights and freedoms defined in the Convention, taken together with Article 3, requires States to take measures designed to ensure that individuals within their jurisdiction are not subjected to torture or inhuman or degrading treatment or punishment, including such ill-treatment administered by private individuals (see, *mutatis mutandis*, the *HLR v France* judgment of 29 April 1997, Reports 1997-III, p 758, § 40). Children and other vulnerable individuals, in particular, are entitled to State protection, in the form of effective deterrence, against such serious breaches of personal

integrity (see, *mutatis mutandis*, the *X and Y v Netherlands* judgment of 26 March 1985, Series A No 91, pp 11–13, §§ 21–7; the *Stubbings v UK* judgment of 22 October 1996, Reports 1996-IV, p 1505, §§ 62–4; and also the United Nations Convention on the Rights of the Child, Articles 19 and 37).

23. The Court recalls that under English law it is a defence to a charge of assault on a child that the treatment in question amounted to 'reasonable chastisement' . . . The burden of proof is on the prosecution to establish beyond reasonable doubt that the assault went beyond the limits of lawful punishment. In the present case, despite the fact that the applicant had been subjected to treatment of sufficient severity to fall within the scope of Article 3, the jury acquitted his stepfather, who had administered the treatment.

24. In the Court's view, the law did not provide adequate protection to the applicant against treatment or punishment contrary to Article 3. Indeed, the Government have accepted that this law currently fails to provide adequate protection to children and should be amended. In the circumstances of the present case, the failure to provide adequate protection constitutes a violation of Article 3 of the Convention.

The Court went on to award the applicant £10,000 compensation for non-pecuniary damage. Would it be stretching the reasoning in the above judgment too far to require States to protect individuals from Article 3 maltreatment inflicted by legal persons, for example what of dangerous or humiliating working conditions (the Court used the phrase 'ill-treatment administered by private individuals')?

The Children Act 2004, section 58, removed the defence of reasonable punishment in respect of battery of a child amounting to the offences of wounding and causing grievous bodily harm, assault occasioning actual bodily harm, and cruelty to a person under the age of 16. Also, battery causing actual bodily harm to a child cannot be justified in any civil proceedings as constituting reasonable punishment. These limitations, which apply to England and Wales, the Scottish Parliament having previously introduced similar legislation, came into effect in January 2005. They were designed to allow parents to administer mild physical punishment to their children provided that bruising and cuts were not inflicted. Leading child protection charities, including the NSPCC, criticized the amendments because, *inter alia*, they believed that it was as wrong to hit a child as to hit an adult. Proponents of physical chastisement criticized the legislation as being impossible to police.

12 A unanimous Grand Chamber applied the reasoning in *A v UK* to a local authority's failure to take prompt action to safeguard children from serious neglect by their parents in *Z and Others v UK*, judgment of 10 May 2001. The four applicants were siblings, born between 1982 and 1988. From 1987 their local social services department were aware of concerns about the children's welfare (reports from their neighbours and teachers indicated that the children were not being properly fed and cared for by their parents). In 1989 a social work assistant was assigned to help the parents care for the applicants (social services had concluded that the parents should be aided to look after the applicants rather than the latter being taken away from them into public care). In 1992 the applicants were taken into public care when their mother informed the social services that she could not cope and would 'batter' them. Subsequently, the applicants complained that the social services had failed to protect them from being subject to inhuman and degrading treatment by their parents. The Grand Chamber held that:

73. . . . The obligation on High Contracting Parties under Article 1 of the Convention to secure to everyone within their jurisdiction the rights and freedoms defined in the Convention, taken together with Article 3, requires States to take measures designed to ensure that individuals

within their jurisdiction are not subjected to torture or inhuman or degrading treatment, including such ill-treatment administered by private individuals (see *A v the United Kingdom* judgment of 23 September 1998, Reports of Judgments and Decisions 1998-VI, § 22). These measures should provide effective protection, in particular, of children and other vulnerable persons and include reasonable steps to prevent ill-treatment of which the authorities had or ought to have had knowledge (*mutatis mutandis*, the *Osman v the United Kingdom* judgment of 28 October 1998, Reports 1998-VIII, § 116).

74. There is no dispute in the present case that the neglect and abuse suffered by the four child applicants reached the threshold of inhuman and degrading treatment…This treatment was brought to the local authority's attention, at the earliest in October 1987. It was under a statutory duty to protect the children and had a range of powers available to them, including removal from their home. The children were however only taken into emergency care, at the insistence of the mother, in 30 April 1992. Over the intervening period of four and a half years, they had been subject in their home to what the child consultant psychiatrist who examined them referred to as horrific experiences….The Criminal Injuries Compensation Board had also found that the children had been subject to appalling neglect over an extended period and suffered physical and psychological injury directly attributable to a crime of violence…The Court acknowledges the difficult and sensitive decisions facing social services and the important countervailing principle of respecting and preserving family life. The present case however leaves no doubt as to the failure of the system to protect these child applicants from serious, long-term neglect and abuse.

75. Accordingly, there has been a violation of Article 3 of the Convention.

Each of the applicants was awarded £32,000 non-pecuniary damages in respect of pain and suffering experienced through the local authority's failure to protect them from abuse. In addition they were awarded individual sums, ranging from £4,000 to £100,00 pecuniary damages to compensate them for their loss of employment opportunities and future medical costs attributable to their suffering.

The above judgment expanded the protective measures obligation upon States to encompass the speedy physical intervention of State officials to protect children known to be at risk of serious risk of harm from their parents/carers.

13 The Court has refused to accept that States are under a positive obligation to permit/aid the assisted suicide of a competent adult in the final stages of a terminal illness. In **Pretty v UK**, judgment of 29 April 2002 (and see p 118 for the Article 2 aspects of her case), the applicant submitted that the domestic authorities were under an Article 3 duty to so protect her from death caused by motor neurone disease.

55. The Court cannot but be sympathetic to the applicant's apprehension that without the possibility of ending her life she faces the prospect of a distressing death. It is true that she is unable to commit suicide herself due to physical incapacity and that the state of law is such that her husband faces the risk of prosecution if he renders her assistance. Nonetheless, the positive obligation on the part of the State which is invoked in the present case would not involve the removal or mitigation of harm by, for instance, preventing any ill-treatment by public bodies or private individuals or providing improved conditions or care. It would require that the State sanction actions intended to terminate life, an obligation that cannot be derived from Article 3 of the Convention.

56. The Court therefore concludes that no positive obligation arises under Article 3 of the Convention to require the respondent Government either to give an undertaking not to prosecute the applicant's husband if he assists her to commit suicide or to provide a lawful opportunity for any other form of assisted suicide. There has, accordingly, been no violation of this provision.

This interpretation of Article 3 was a logical consequence of the Court's earlier ruling that there was no right to die recognized under Article 2 of the Convention.

Torture

Aksoy v Turkey 1996-VI
European Court of Human Rights

The applicant was a Turkish national who had been born in 1963 and lived in south-east Turkey. In 1994 he was shot dead, but his father continued his application before the Strasbourg authorities. The applicant alleged that on the night of 24 November 1992 approximately 20 police officers came to his home, accompanied by a detainee who claimed that the applicant was a member of the PKK (Workers' Party of Kurdistan). The applicant was arrested and taken to Mardin Anti-terrorist Headquarters. He was interrogated about the man who identified him (the applicant claimed not to know the man) and threatened with torture. On the second day of his detention the applicant claimed that he was stripped naked, his hands were tied behind his back, and he was strung up by his arms in the form of torture known as 'Palestinian hanging'. While he was hanging, the police connected electrodes to his genitals and threw water over him while they electrocuted him. He was blindfolded during this torture, which lasted for about half an hour. During the next two days he was regularly beaten by the police officers. The applicant claimed that the hanging resulted in him losing the movement of his arms and hands. He asked to see a doctor, but his request was denied. He was released from detention on 10 December 1992 and no charges were brought against him. On the 15 December 1992 he was admitted to the Dicle University Hospital where he was diagnosed as suffering from bilateral radial paralysis (paralysis of both arms caused by nerve damage in the upper arms). He discharged himself on the 31 December 1992, taking his medical file with him. The applicant complained to the Commission alleging, *inter alia*, that he had suffered maltreatment in breach of Article 3 during his detention. Delegates of the Commission held evidentiary hearings in Turkey. The Commission found, *inter alia*, that there was no evidence that the applicant was suffering from any disability prior to his arrest. The medical evidence showed that he was suffering from radial paralysis in both arms (an uncommon condition, but consistent with having been subject to 'Palestinian hanging') soon after his release. The Turkish Government had supplied no alternative explanation for the applicant's injuries. There was insufficient evidence for the Commission to reach any conclusions regarding the applicant's contentions that he had been electrocuted and beaten. By 15 votes to 1 the Commission expressed the opinion that there had been a breach of Article 3.

...THE MERITS...

60. The applicant complained of having been ill-treated in different ways. He claimed to have been kept blindfolded during interrogation, which caused disorientation; to have been suspended from his arms, which were tied together behind his back ('Palestinian hanging'); to have been given electric shocks, which were exacerbated by throwing water over him; and to have been subjected to beatings, slapping and verbal abuse. He referred to medical evidence from Dicle University Medical

Faculty which showed that he was suffering from a bilateral brachial plexus injury at the time of his admission to hospital...This injury was consistent with Palestinian hanging.

He submitted that the treatment complained of was sufficiently severe as to amount to torture; it was inflicted with the purpose of inducing him to admit that he knew the man who had identified him.

In addition, he contended that the conditions in which he was detained...and the constant fear of torture which he suffered while in custody amounted to inhuman treatment.

61. The Court, having decided to accept the Commission's findings of fact...considers that where an individual is taken into police custody in good health but is found to be injured at the time of release, it is incumbent on the State to provide a plausible explanation as to the causing of the injury, failing which a clear issue arises under Article 3 of the Convention (art 3) (see the *Tomasi v France* judgment of 27 August 1992, Series A No 241-A, pp 40–1, paras 108–11 and the *Ribitsch v Austria* judgment of 4 December 1995, Series A No 336, p 26, para 34).

62. Article 3 (art 3), as the Court has observed on many occasions, enshrines one of the fundamental values of democratic society. Even in the most difficult of circumstances, such as the fight against organised terrorism and crime, the Convention prohibits in absolute terms torture or inhuman or degrading treatment or punishment. Unlike most of the substantive clauses of the Convention and of Protocols Nos. 1 and 4 (P1, P4), Article 3 (art 3) makes no provision for exceptions and no derogation from it is permissible under Article 15 (art 15) even in the event of a public emergency threatening the life of the nation (see the *Ireland v the United Kingdom* judgment of 18 January 1978, Series A No 25, p 65, para 163, the *Soering v United Kingdom* judgment of 7 July 1989, Series A No 161, p 34, para 88, and the *Chahal v United Kingdom* judgment of 15 November 1996, Reports 1996-V, p 1855, para 79).

63. In order to determine whether any particular form of ill-treatment should be qualified as torture, the Court must have regard to the distinction drawn in Article 3 (art 3) between this notion and that of inhuman or degrading treatment. As it has remarked before, this distinction would appear to have been embodied in the Convention to allow the special stigma of 'torture' to attach only to deliberate inhuman treatment causing very serious and cruel suffering (see the *Ireland v United Kingdom* judgment previously cited, p 66, para 167).

64. The Court recalls that the Commission found, *inter alia*, that the applicant was subjected to 'Palestinian hanging', in other words, that he was stripped naked, with his arms tied together behind his back, and suspended by his arms...

In the view of the Court this treatment could only have been deliberately inflicted; indeed, a certain amount of preparation and exertion would have been required to carry it out. It would appear to have been administered with the aim of obtaining admissions or information from the applicant. In addition to the severe pain which it must have caused at the time, the medical evidence shows that it led to a paralysis of both arms which lasted for some time...The Court considers that this treatment was of such a serious and cruel nature that it can only be described as torture.

In view of the gravity of this conclusion, it is not necessary for the Court to examine the applicant's complaints of other forms of ill-treatment.

In conclusion, there has been a violation of Article 3 of the Convention (art 3).

...

IV. APPLICATION OF ARTICLE 50 OF THE CONVENTION (ART 50)

110. Under Article 50 of the Convention (art 50),

'If the Court finds that a decision or a measure taken by a legal authority or any other authority of a High Contracting Party is completely or partially in conflict with the obligations arising from the...Convention, and if the internal law of the said Party allows only partial reparation to be made for the consequences of this decision or measure, the decision of the Court shall, if necessary, afford just satisfaction to the injured party.'

111. In his memorial the applicant claimed compensation for pecuniary damage caused by his detention and torture, consisting of medical expenses of 16,635,000 Turkish liras and loss of earnings amounting to £40 (sterling).

In addition he sought non-pecuniary damages of £25,000...

He also requested payment of his legal fees and expenses which totalled £20,710.

112. The Government offered no comment either in its memorial or during the hearing before the Court as regards these claims.

A. DAMAGE

113. In view of the extremely serious violations of the Convention suffered by Mr Zeki Aksoy and the anxiety and distress that these undoubtedly caused to his father, who has continued with the application after his son's death...the Court has decided to award the full amounts of compensation sought as regards pecuniary and non-pecuniary damage. In total this amounts to 4,283,450,000 (four thousand two hundred and eighty-three million, four hundred and fifty thousand) Turkish liras (based on the rate of exchange applicable on the date of adoption of the present judgment).

B. COSTS AND EXPENSES

114. The Court considers that the applicant's claim for costs and expenses is reasonable and awards it in full, less the amounts received by way of legal aid from the Council of Europe which have not already been taken into account in the claim.

FOR THESE REASONS, THE COURT

...

2. Holds by eight votes to one that there has been a violation of Article 3 of the Convention (art 3);...

NOTES

1 The Court was composed of President Ryssdal and Judges: Thor Vilhjalmsson, Gölcüklü, Pettiti, De Meyer, Morenilla, Baka, Makarczyk, and Lohmus.

Judge Gölcüklü, the Judge of Turkish nationality, dissented because he did not believe that the applicant had exhausted domestic remedies. Therefore he was dispensed from considering the merits of the case.

This was the first case where the Court found maltreatment by State officials amounted to torture. Even where the applicant suffered such horrendous treatment the level of compensation payable under Article 50 was not that large in absolute terms. However, the relative value of the just satisfaction award was greater when compared with the applicant's wage level (he claimed only £40 for several weeks' loss of earnings). The effect upon the international reputation of a member State found responsible for acts of torture by the Court is, of course, very significant.

2 The Commission had found a practice of torture inflicted on political detainees by the Athens Security Police in the earlier *Greek Case*, 12 Yearbook of the European Convention on Human Rights (1969). From 1965 until 1967 there was political instability and some public disorder in Greece. During 1967 senior military officers staged a *coup d'etat* and subsequently a number of persons were detained. Widespread allegations of serious ill-treatment of detainees by security officials were made. Denmark, Norway, and Sweden lodged an inter-State application against Greece in respect of the latter's treatment of political detainees. A few days later the Netherlands also made a similar application. The Commission joined the cases and a Sub-Commission went to Greece to conduct on-the-spot inquiries and hear witnesses. The Commission's report found that:

> *Falanga* or *bastinado* has been a method of torture known for centuries. It is the beating of the feet with a wooden or metal stick or bar which, if skilfully done, breaks no bones, makes no skin lesions, and leaves no permanent and recognisable marks, but causes intense pain and swelling of the feet. The use of *falanga* has been described in a variety of situations: on a bench or chair or on a car-seat; with or without shoes on. Sometimes water has been thrown over the feet and sometimes the victim has been made to run around between beatings. Victims have also been gagged....
>
> While *falanga* and severe beatings of all parts of the body are the commonest forms of torture or ill-treatment that appear in the evidence before the Sub-Commission, other forms have been described: for example, the application of electric shock, squeezing of the head in a vice, pulling out of hair from the head or pubic region, or kicking of the male genital organs, dripping water on the head, and intense noises to prevent sleep....
>
> there has since April 1967 been a practice of torture and ill-treatment by the Athens Security Police, Bouboulinas Street, of persons arrested for political reasons, and that:
>
> (a) this torture and ill-treatment has most often consisted in the application of '*falanga*' or severe beatings of all parts of the body;
>
> (b) its purpose has been the extraction of information including confessions concerning the political activities and associations of the victims and other persons considered to be subversive... [Pp 499, 500 and 504.]

The Commission's report was transmitted to the Committee of Ministers on 18 November 1969. On 12 December 1969 the Government of Greece denounced the Convention (under former Article 65 the denunciation would take effect after six months: i.e. 13 June 1970) and refused to participate in further proceedings relating to the report. Therefore, the Committee issued Resolution DH70(1):

> ...Agreeing with the opinion of the Commission, Decides:
>
> (a) that the Government of Greece has violated Articles 3...
>
> 19. Considering that these circumstances and communications clearly established that the Greek Government is not prepared to comply with its continuing obligations under the Convention and thus with the system of collective protection of human rights established thereby, and that accordingly the Committee of Ministers is called upon to deal with the case in conditions which are not precisely those envisaged in the Convention;
>
> 20. Concludes that in the present case there is no basis for further action under paragraph 2 of Article 32 (art 32–2) of the Convention;
>
> 21. Concludes that it must take a decision, in accordance with paragraph 3 of Article 32 (arts 32–3) of the Convention, about the publication of the report of the Commission;
>
> 22. Decides to make public forthwith the report drawn up by the Commission on the above-mentioned Applications;
>
> 23. Urges the Government of Greece to restore, without delay, human rights and fundamental freedoms in Greece, in accordance with the Convention...

24. Also urges the Government of Greece, in particular, to abolish immediately torture and other ill-treatment of prisoners and to release immediately persons detained under administrative order;

25. And accordingly resolves to follow developments in Greece in this respect.

In 1974 constitutional government was restored in Greece and the Government sought readmission to the Council of Europe. The **Greek Case** reveals both the strengths and weaknesses of the Convention system for protecting human rights. The undemocratic military government withdrew from the Council of Europe rather than face censure under the Convention for its practice of torturing political opponents. Yet diplomatic pressures encouraged the restoration of democracy in Greece and readmission to the Council of Europe (together with a renewed accession to the Convention) within a few years.

3   A Grand Chamber of the Court found an act of rape committed by a State official on a detainee to be torture in *Aydin v Turkey*, 1997-VI. The applicant, who was 17 at the time of her detention, had never travelled outside her village before her arrest by the security forces. On the 29 June 1993 she alleged that village guards and a gendarme arrived at her village and arrested her, her father, and her sister-in-law. They were questioned about visits to her family home by members of the PKK (as in *Aksoy*). The three of them were then blindfolded and taken to the gendarmerie headquarters in Derik. The applicant was taken alone into a room, stripped, put in a car tyre and spun round, beaten, sprayed with cold water, and raped by a man in military clothing. The applicant and her relatives were released from custody on 2 July 1993. She complained to the Commission alleging, *inter alia*, a breach of Article 3. Delegates of the Commission visited Turkey to hear witnesses and the Commission found the applicant's allegations to be established beyond reasonable doubt. By 26 votes to 1 the Commission expressed the opinion that there had been a violation of Article 3. A majority of the Court (14 votes to 7) determined that:

83. While being held in detention the applicant was raped by a person whose identity has still to be determined. Rape of a detainee by an official of the State must be considered to be an especially grave and abhorrent form of ill-treatment given the ease with which the offender can exploit the vulnerability and weakened resistance of his victim. Furthermore, rape leaves deep psychological scars on the victim which do not respond to the passage of time as quickly as other forms of physical and mental violence. The applicant also experienced the acute physical pain of forced penetration, which must have left her feeling debased and violated both physically and emotionally.

84. The applicant was also subjected to a series of particularly terrifying and humiliating experiences while in custody at the hands of the security forces at Derik gendarmerie headquarters having regard to her sex and youth and the circumstances under which she was held. She was detained over a period of three days during which she must have been bewildered and disoriented by being kept blindfolded, and in a constant state of physical pain and mental anguish brought on by the beatings administered to her during questioning and by the apprehension of what would happen to her next. She was also paraded naked in humiliating circumstances thus adding to her overall sense of vulnerability and on one occasion she was pummelled with high-pressure water while being spun around in a tyre.

85. The applicant and her family must have been taken from their village and brought to Derik gendarmerie headquarters for a purpose, which can only be explained on account of the security situation in the region . . . and the need of the security forces to elicit information. The suffering inflicted on the applicant during the period of her detention must also be seen as calculated to serve the same or related purposes.

86. Against this background the Court is satisfied that the accumulation of acts of physical and mental violence inflicted on the applicant and the especially cruel act of rape to which she was subjected amounted to torture in breach of Article 3 of the Convention. Indeed the Court would have reached this conclusion on either of these grounds taken separately.

87. In conclusion, there has been a violation of Article 3 of the Convention. ...

The Court went on to award the applicant £25,000 just satisfaction for non-pecuniary damage, 'having regard to the seriousness of the violation of the Convention suffered by the applicant while in custody and the enduring psychological harm which she may be considered to have suffered on account of being raped...' (para 131). The dissenters did not consider that the applicant's allegations had been established with sufficient proof. As a matter of law the Court's decision clearly defines the rape of detainees as a particularly serious breach of Article 3.

4 A Grand Chamber of the full-time Court, unanimously, adopted a new approach to assessing whether particular maltreatment should be classified as torture in *Selmouni v France*, 1999-V. The implication of the Court's statement that in the future 'greater firmness in assessing breaches' (para 101, below) is required, suggests that the Court will be more willing to categorize serious acts of maltreatment as torture. In that case the applicant was a Netherlands and Moroccan national (born in 1942) who had been arrested by the police in France, after he was implicated in drug-trafficking by a fellow suspect. The applicant was held in police custody from 8.30 pm on 25 November 1991 until 7 pm on 28 November 1991. During his detention he was questioned by a number of officers from the Seine-Saint-Denis Criminal Investigation Department. The applicant claimed that during his detention the investigating officers subjected him to a number of forms of serious maltreatment including: repeated assaults (with fists, kicks, and a baseball bat), pulling of his hair, forcing the applicant to kneel down in front of a woman while being verbally abused by an officer, having an officer urinate over him, being threatened with a blowlamp, and having a truncheon inserted into his anus. Later the applicant was convicted of drugs offences and sentenced to 13 years' imprisonment and fined 24 million Francs. The applicant complained to the authorities about the abuse that he had suffered while being questioned and medical reports were obtained. These confirmed that he had many bruises and wounds over his body. However, by the time the applicant alleged that he had been sexually abused by the officers it was too late for medical investigations to establish the truth of his claim. Eventually several police officers were convicted of assaulting and wounding the applicant (the senior officer in charge was sentenced to 18 months' imprisonment—of which 15 months were suspended, another officer was given a 15-month suspended sentence and another a 12-month suspended sentence). The applicant complained to the Commission alleging, *inter alia*, a breach of Article 3. The Commission was unanimous in finding that the deliberate maltreatment of the applicant was of such a serious and cruel nature as to be classified as torture. The Court held that:

96. In order to determine whether a particular form of ill-treatment should be qualified as torture, the Court must have regard to the distinction, embodied in Article 3, between this notion and that of inhuman or degrading treatment. As the European Court has previously found, it appears that it was the intention that the Convention should, by means of this distinction, attach a special stigma to deliberate inhuman treatment causing very serious and cruel suffering (see the *Ireland v United Kingdom* judgment ...).

97. The United Nations Convention against Torture and Other Cruel, Inhuman or Degrading Treatment or Punishment, which came into force on 26 June 1987, also makes such a distinction, as can be seen from Articles 1 and 16:

Article 1:

'1. For the purposes of this Convention, the term "torture" means any act by which severe pain or suffering, whether physical or mental, is intentionally inflicted on a person for such purposes as obtaining from him or a third person information or a confession, punishing him for an act he or a third person has committed or is suspected of having committed, or intimidating or coercing him or a third person, or for any reason based on discrimination of any kind, when such pain or suffering is inflicted by or at the instigation of or with the consent or acquiescence of a public official or other person acting in an official capacity.

...

Article 16, paragraph 1:

'1. Each State Party shall undertake to prevent in any territory under its jurisdiction other acts of cruel, inhuman or degrading treatment or punishment which do not amount to torture as defined in Article 1, when such acts are committed by or at the instigation of or with the consent or acquiescence of a public official or other person acting in an official capacity. In particular, the obligations contained in Articles 10, 11, 12 and 13 shall apply with the substitution for references to torture of references to other forms of cruel, inhuman or degrading treatment or punishment.'

98. The Court finds that all the injuries recorded in the various medical certificates...and the applicant's statements regarding the ill-treatment to which he had been subjected while in police custody...establish the existence of physical and—undoubtedly (notwithstanding the regrettable failure to order a psychological report on Mr Selmouni after the events complained of)—mental pain and suffering. The course of the events also shows that pain and suffering were inflicted on the applicant intentionally for the purpose of, *inter alia*, making him confess to the offence which he was suspected of having committed. Lastly, the medical certificates annexed to the case file show clearly that the numerous acts of violence were directly inflicted by police officers in the performance of their duties.

99. The acts complained of were such as to arouse in the applicant feelings of fear, anguish and inferiority capable of humiliating and debasing him and possibly breaking his physical and moral resistance. The Court therefore finds elements which are sufficiently serious to render such treatment inhuman and degrading (see the *Ireland v UK* judgment, p 66, § 167, and the *Tomasi v France* judgment p 42, § 115). In any event, the Court reiterates that, in respect of a person deprived of his liberty, recourse to physical force which has not been made strictly necessary by his own conduct diminishes human dignity and is in principle an infringement of the right set forth in Article 3 (see the *Ribitsch v Austria* judgment of 4 December 1995, Series A No 336, p 26, § 38)...

100. In other words, it remains to establish in the instant case whether the 'pain or suffering' inflicted on Mr Selmouni can be defined as 'severe' within the meaning of Article 1 of the United Nations Convention. The Court considers that this 'severity' is, like the 'minimum severity' required for the application of Article 3, in the nature of things, relative; it depends on all the circumstances of the case, such as the duration of the treatment, its physical or mental effects and, in some cases, the sex, age and state of health of the victim, etc.

101. The Court has previously examined cases in which it concluded that there had been treatment which could only be described as torture (see the *Aksoy v Turkey* judgment 2279, § 64, and the *Aydin v Turkey* judgment, pp 1892–3, §§ 83–4 and 86). However, having regard to the fact that the

Convention is a 'living instrument which must be interpreted in the light of present-day conditions' (see, among other authorities, the following judgments: *Tyrer v UK*, 25 April 1978, Series A No 26, p 15, § 31; *Soering v UK*, p 40, § 102; and *Loizidou v Turkey*, 23 March 1995, Series A No 310, p 26, § 71), the Court considers that certain acts which were classified in the past as 'inhuman and degrading treatment' as opposed to 'torture' could be classified differently in future. It takes the view that the increasingly high standard being required in the area of the protection of human rights and fundamental liberties correspondingly and inevitably requires greater firmness in assessing breaches of the fundamental values of democratic societies.

102. The Court is satisfied that a large number of blows were inflicted on Mr Selmouni. Whatever a person's state of health, it can be presumed that such intensity of blows will cause substantial pain. Moreover, a blow does not automatically leave a visible mark on the body. However, it can be seen from Dr Garnier's medical report of 7 December 1991 . . . that the marks of the violence Mr Selmouni had endured covered almost all of his body.

103. The Court also notes that the applicant was dragged along by his hair; that he was made to run along a corridor with police officers positioned on either side to trip him up; that he was made to kneel down in front of a young woman to whom someone said 'Look, you're going to hear somebody sing'; that one police officer then showed him his penis, saying 'Look, suck this', before urinating over him; and that he was threatened with a blowlamp and then a syringe . . . Besides the violent nature of the above acts, the Court is bound to observe that they would be heinous and humiliating for anyone, irrespective of their condition.

104. The Court notes, lastly, that the above events were not confined to any one period of police custody during which—without this in any way justifying them—heightened tension and emotions might have led to such excesses. It has been clearly established that Mr Selmouni endured repeated and sustained assaults over a number of days of questioning . . .

105. Under these circumstances, the Court is satisfied that the physical and mental violence, considered as a whole, committed against the applicant's person caused 'severe' pain and suffering and was particularly serious and cruel. Such conduct must be regarded as acts of torture for the purposes of Article 3 of the Convention.

3. Conclusion

There has therefore been a violation of Article 3 . . .

Having regard to the 'extreme seriousness of the violations of the Convention of which Mr Selmouni was a victim' (para 123), the Court awarded him 500,000 Francs just satisfaction in respect of personal and non-pecuniary injury.

This was the first case in which the Court (both in its part-time and current form) found a European Union member State to have committed acts of torture. The judgment indicates the evidential necessity for victims of maltreatment by officials to obtain expeditious and comprehensive medical reports of their physical and mental conditions. If such reports are not obtained the Court is constrained in its ability to determine the occurrence and effects of the maltreatment.

5   A Grand Chamber cited *Selmouni* when it unanimously found that the physical assaults on a young man by gendarmes, which resulted in him suffering considerable permanent brain damage, combined with a 36-hour delay in taking him to a hospital amounted to torture in *Ilhan v Turkey*, judgment of 27 June 2000.

6   Another Grand Chamber, by 16 votes to 1, found Russia liable for, *inter alia*, the torture of the first applicant by the separatist regime of the 'Moldavian Republic of Transdniestria' (MRT) in *Ilascu and Others v Moldova and Russia* (p 67).

434. The applicant was sentenced to death on 9 December 1993 and detained until his release on 5 May 2001.

The Court reiterates that the Convention is not binding on Contracting States save in respect of events that have occurred since its entry into force, the relevant dates being 12 September 1997 for Moldova and 5 May 1998 for the Russian Federation. However, in order to assess the effect on the applicant of his conditions of detention, which remained more or less identical throughout the time he spent in prison, the Court may also take into consideration the whole of the period in question, including that part of it which preceded the Convention's entry into force with regard to each of the respondent States.

435. During the very long period he spent on death row the applicant lived in the constant shadow of death, in fear of execution. Unable to exercise any remedy, he lived for many years, including the time after the Convention's entry into force, in conditions of detention apt to remind him of the prospect of his sentence being enforced.

In particular, the Court notes that after sending a letter to the Moldovan Parliament in March 1999 Mr Ilaşcu was savagely beaten by the warders at Tiraspol Prison, who threatened to kill him. After that incident he was denied food for two days and light for three.

As to the mock executions which took place before the Convention's entry into force, there is no doubt that the effect of such barbaric acts was to increase the anxiety felt by the applicant throughout his detention about the prospect of his execution.

436. The anguish and suffering he felt were aggravated by the fact that the sentence had no legal basis or legitimacy for Convention purposes. The 'Supreme Court of the MRT' which passed sentence on Mr Ilaşcu was set up by an entity which is illegal under international law and has not been recognised by the international community. That 'court' belongs to a system which can hardly be said to function on a constitutional and legal basis reflecting a judicial tradition compatible with the Convention. That is evidenced by the patently arbitrary nature of the circumstances in which the applicants were tried and convicted, as they described them in an account which has not been disputed by the other parties and as described and analysed by the institutions of the OSCE.

437. The judgment of the Supreme Court of Moldova setting aside the applicant's conviction confirmed the unlawful and arbitrary nature of the judgment of 9 December 1993.

438. As regards the applicant's conditions of detention while on death row, the Court notes that Mr Ilaşcu was detained for eight years, from 1993 until his release in May 2001, in very strict isolation: he had no contact with other prisoners, no news from the outside—since he was not permitted to send or receive mail—and no right to contact his lawyer or receive regular visits from his family. His cell was unheated, even in severe winter conditions, and had no natural light source or ventilation. The evidence shows that Mr Ilaşcu was also deprived of food as a punishment and that in any event, given the restrictions on receiving parcels, even the food he received from outside was often unfit for consumption. The applicant could take showers only very rarely, often having to wait several months between one and the next. On this subject the Court refers to the conclusions in the report produced by the CPT following its visit to Transdniestria in 2000, in which it described isolation for so many years as indefensible.

The applicant's conditions of detention had deleterious effects on his health, which deteriorated in the course of the many years he spent in prison. Thus, he did not receive proper care, having been deprived of regular medical examinations and treatment and dietetically appropriate meals. In addition, owing to the restrictions on receiving parcels, he could not be sent medicines and food to improve his health.

439. The Court notes with concern the existence of rules granting a discretionary power in relation to correspondence and prison visits, exercisable by both prison warders and other authorities, and emphasises that such rules are arbitrary and incompatible with the appropriate and effective safeguards against abuses which any prison system in a democratic society must put in place. Moreover, in the present case, such rules made the applicant's conditions of detention even harsher.

440. The Court concludes that the death sentence imposed on the applicant coupled with the conditions he was living in and the treatment he suffered during his detention after ratification, account being taken of the state he was in after spending several years in those conditions before ratification, were particularly serious and cruel and must accordingly be considered acts of torture within the meaning of Article 3 of the Convention.

There has therefore been a failure to observe the requirements of Article 3.

441. As Mr Ilaşcu was detained at the time when the Convention came into force with regard to the Russian Federation, on 5 May 1998, the latter is responsible, for the reasons set out above . . . on account of his conditions of detention, the treatment inflicted on him and the suffering caused to him in prison.

Mr Ilaşcu was released in May 2001 and it is only from that date on that Moldova's responsibility is engaged on account of the acts complained of for failure to discharge its positive obligations . . . Consequently, there has been no violation of Article 3 of the Convention by Moldova with regard to Mr Ilaşcu.

442. In conclusion, the violation of Article 3 of the Convention with regard to Mr Ilaşcu is imputable only to the Russian Federation.

The above findings are a truly appalling catalogue of abuse.

7   A unanimous Chamber found that the forced-feeding of a mentally competent remand prisoner, who was engaging in a hunger strike (to protest about the length and conditions of his detention), constituted torture in *Nevmerzhitsky v Ukraine*, judgment of 5 April 2005.

94. The Court reiterates that a measure which is of therapeutic necessity from the point of view of established principles of medicine cannot in principle be regarded as inhuman and degrading. The same can be said about force-feeding that is aimed at saving the life of a particular detainee who consciously refuses to take food. The Convention organs must nevertheless satisfy themselves that the medical necessity has been convincingly shown to exist (see *Herczegfalvy v Austria*, judgment of 24 September 1992, Series A No 244, p 26, § 83). Furthermore, the Court must ascertain that the procedural guarantees for the decision to force-feed are complied with. Moreover, the manner in which the applicant is subjected to force-feeding during the hunger strike shall not trespass the threshold of a minimum level of severity envisaged by the Court's case law under Article 3 of the Convention. The Court will examine these elements in turn.

95. At the outset, the Court notes that the applicant did not claim that he should have been left without any food or medicine regardless of the possible lethal consequences. However, he claimed that there had been no medical necessity to force-feed him, as there had been no medical examinations, relevant tests or other documents that sufficiently proved that necessity. He claimed that the decision to subject him to force-feeding had been based on the analysis of the acetone level in his urine. He further maintained that the force-feeding had been aimed at his humiliation and punishment, as its purpose had been to make him stop the hunger strike and, in the event of his refusal, to subject him to severe physical suffering.

96. The Court observes the statement of the Government with regard to the satisfactory state of health of the applicant in detention . . . In view of the failure of the Government to provide 'the written report of the medical commission establishing a life-threatening decrease in the state of health of the applicant' and 'the decision of the head of the [detention] institution' that were obligatory under the decree of 4 March 1992 . . . the Court concludes that the Government have not demonstrated that there was a 'medical necessity' established by the domestic authorities to force-feed the applicant. It can only therefore be assumed that the force-feeding was arbitrary. Procedural safeguards were not respected in the face of the applicant's conscious refusal to take food, when dispensing forced treatment against his will. Accordingly, it cannot be said that the authorities acted in the applicant's best interests in subjecting him to force-feeding.

97. As to the manner in which the applicant was fed, the Court assumes, in view of the submissions of the parties, that the authorities complied with the manner of force-feeding prescribed by decree. However, in themselves the restraints applied—handcuffs, a mouth-widener, a special rubber tube inserted into the food channel—in the event of resistance, with the use of force, could amount to torture within the meaning of Article 3 of the Convention, if there is no medical necessity . . .

98. In the instant case, the Court finds that the force-feeding of the applicant, without any medical justification having been shown by the Government, using the equipment foreseen in the decree, but resisted by the applicant, constituted treatment of such a severe character warranting the characterisation of torture.

99. In the light of the above, the Court considers that there has been a violation of Article 3 of the Convention.

Consequently, States must be able to demonstrate that there is a medical necessity to force-feed a detainee in order to preserve his/her life. The respondent State had not provided evidence of the existence of such dire circumstances at the time the decision was made to force-feed the applicant. Furthermore, the relevant domestic procedure, specified in a Decree of the Ministry of Internal Affairs, governing the resort to force-feeding of detainees had not been complied with. For an examination, by the original Court, of the lawfulness under the Convention of the forced-feeding of a mentally ill detainee see *Herczegfalvy v Austria* A.244, see p 186.

8 The placing of a gas mask over the head of a detainee followed by the periodic cutting off of the air supply combined with electric shocks to his ears and the placing of a 32kg weight on his back were held to amount to torture by a united Chamber in *Gurgurov v Moldova*, judgment of 16 June 2009.

Inhuman treatment

Physical violence

As we have already seen in *Ireland v UK* (p 145), the subjection of detainees to physical violence by State officials can amount to inhuman treatment within Article 3. For example, the kicking and punching of detainees by members of the security forces at Palace Barracks was determined to be inhuman treatment by the Court, because the maltreatment led to intense suffering and physical injury (para 174).

Tomasi v France A.241-A (1992)
European Court of Human Rights

In February 1982 the Corsican National Liberation Front (a movement seeking independence from France) claimed responsibility for an armed attack upon a Foreign Legion rest centre in which one soldier was killed and another seriously injured. The applicant, a shopkeeper resident in the same region of Corsica, was an active member of a Corsican political organization. The police suspected the applicant of having taken part in the attack on the rest centre and on 23 March 1983 they arrested him. He was taken to Bastia police station and held for questioning until 25 March. During this period of detention the applicant claimed that the police, *inter alia*, knocked his head against a wall, hit him in the stomach, slapped and kicked him, and left him naked in front of a window for several hours. Medical reports confirmed that he had bruises on different parts of his body. Subsequently he was remanded in custody, by an investigating judge, and in October 1988 he was acquitted of the charge of murder. The applicant complained to the Commission alleging, *inter alia*, that he had suffered inhuman and degrading treatment by the police. The Commission, by 12 votes to 2, found a breach of Article 3.

B. MERITS OF THE COMPLAINT

107. In the circumstances of this case Mr Tomasi's complaint raises two issues, which are separate although closely linked: firstly that of the causal connection between the treatment which the applicant allegedly suffered during his police custody and the injuries noted subsequently by the investigating judge and the doctors; and, secondly and if necessary, the gravity of the treatment inflicted.

1. The causal connection between the treatment complained of and the injuries noted

108. According to the applicant, the observation made on 25 March 1983 by the Bastia investigating judge and the reports drawn up by various doctors at the end of his police custody...confirmed his statements, even though it was, he said, to be regretted that the prison authorities had failed to communicate the X-rays effected on 2 April 1983 at Bastia Hospital...His body had borne marks which had only one origin, the ill-treatment inflicted on him for a period of forty odd hours by some of the police-officers responsible for his interrogation: he had been slapped, kicked, punched and given forearm blows, made to stand for long periods and without support, hands handcuffed behind the back; he had been spat upon, made to stand naked in front of an open window, deprived of food, threatened with a firearm and so on.

109. The Government acknowledged that they could give no explanation as to the cause of the injuries, but they maintained that they had not resulted from the treatment complained of by Mr Tomasi. The medical certificates showed, in their opinion, that the slight bruises and abrasions noted were totally inconsistent with the acts of violence described by the applicant; the certificate of the Chief Medical Officer of Bastia Prison of 4 July 1989 had been drawn up a long time after the event and was in complete contradiction with the earlier certificates. The chronology of the interrogation sessions, which had not been contested by the applicant, in no way corresponded to the allegations. Finally, the five other persons in police custody at the time had neither noticed nor heard anything, and although one of them referred to Mr Tomasi's losing a tooth, this fact was not mentioned by a doctor until six years later. In short, a clear doubt subsisted, which excluded any presumption of the existence of a causal connection.

110. Like the Commission, the Court bases its view on several considerations.

In the first place, no one has claimed that the marks noted on the applicant's body could have dated from a period prior to his being taken into custody or could have originated in an act carried out by the applicant against himself or again as a result of an escape attempt.

In addition, at his first appearance before the investigating judge, he drew attention to the marks which he bore on his chest and his ear; the judge took note of this and immediately designated an expert...

Furthermore, four different doctors—one of whom was an official of the prison authorities—examined the accused in the days following the end of his police custody. Their certificates contain precise and concurring medical observations and indicate dates for the occurrence of the injuries which correspond to the period spent in custody on police premises...

111. This conclusion makes it unnecessary for the Court to inquire into the other acts which it is claimed the officials in question carried out.

2. The gravity of the treatment complained of

112. Relying on the *Ireland v UK* judgment of 18 January 1978 (Series A No 25), the applicant maintained that the blows which he had received constituted inhuman and degrading treatment. They had not only caused him intense physical and mental suffering; they had also aroused in him feelings of fear, anguish and inferiority capable of humiliating him and breaking his physical or moral resistance....

113. The Commission stressed the vulnerability of a person held in police custody and expressed its surprise at the times chosen to interrogate the applicant. Although the injuries observed might appear to be relatively slight, they nevertheless constituted outward signs of the use of physical force on an individual deprived of his liberty and therefore in a state of inferiority. The treatment had therefore been both inhuman and degrading.

114. According to the Government, on the other hand, the 'minimum level of severity' required by the Court's case-law (see the *Ireland v the UK* judgment cited above and the *Tyrer v the UK* judgment of 25 April 1978, Series A No 26) had not been attained. It was necessary to take into account not only that the injuries were slight, but also the other facts of the case: Mr Tomasi's youth and good state of health, the moderate length of the interrogations (fourteen hours, three of which were during the night), 'particular circumstances' obtaining in Corsica at the time and the fact that he had been suspected of participating in a terrorist attack which had resulted in the death of one man and grave injuries to another. In the Government's view, the Commission's interpretation of Article 3 (art 3) in this case was based on a misunderstanding of the aim of that provision.

115. The Court cannot accept this argument...It finds it sufficient to observe that the medical certificates and reports, drawn up in total independence by medical practitioners, attest to the large number of blows inflicted on Mr Tomasi and their intensity; these are two elements which are sufficiently serious to render such treatment inhuman and degrading. The requirements of the investigation and the undeniable difficulties inherent in the fight against crime, particularly with regard to terrorism, cannot result in limits being placed on the protection to be afforded in respect of the physical integrity of individuals.

3. Conclusion

116. There has accordingly been a violation of Article 3 (art 3)....

FOR THESE REASONS, THE COURT UNANIMOUSLY

Holds that there has been a violation of...Article 3...

NOTES

1   The Court was composed of President Ryssdal and Judges: Bernhardt, Gölcüklü, Matscher, Pettiti, Russo, Spielmann, De Meyer, and Morenilla.

The Court awarded the applicant 700,000 Francs just satisfaction in respect of pecuniary and non-pecuniary damage (he had already received 300,000 Francs compensation from the French authorities).

The judgment indicates that the infliction of significant physical violence on a detainee by State officials, even where no serious long-term injuries are caused, will be classified as inhuman treatment. Indeed, Judge De Meyer went further in his concurring opinion where he expressed the view that:

Any use of physical force in respect of a person deprived of his liberty which is not made strictly necessary as a result of his own conduct (for instance in the case of an escape attempt or an act carried out against himself.) violates human dignity and must therefore be regarded as a breach of the right guaranteed under Article 3 of the Convention.

2   In the later case of **Ribitsch v Austria** A.336 (1995), the Court stated that although: '... in principle it is not its task to substitute its own assessment of the facts for that of the domestic courts... it is not bound by the domestic courts' findings any more than it is by those of the Commission.... Its vigilance must be heightened when dealing with rights such as those set forth in Article 3 of the Convention, which prohibits in absolute terms torture and inhuman or degrading treatment or punishment, irrespective of the victim's conduct' (para 32). A majority of the Court, 6 votes to 3, went on to uphold the applicant's claim of inhuman and degrading treatment even though the relevant police officers had been acquitted by the Austrian courts. The applicant had been arrested and his home searched, 0.5g of hashish was found by members of the Security Branch of the Vienna Federal Police Authority who suspected that he had supplied heroin to persons who had died of overdoses. Ribitsch was held in custody at the headquarters of the Security Branch from 12.30 pm on 31 May 1988 until 9.30 am on 2 June 1988. According to Ribitsch while he was being questioned by the police several officers assaulted him (by punching him in the head, kidneys, and on the arm; kicking him; pulling his hair and banging his head on the floor). After his release from police custody the applicant sought medical treatment. A hospital report confirmed that he had several bruises on his right arm. The media gave coverage to Ribitsch's allegations of police maltreatment and in response the police began an inquiry into the officers' conduct. In 1989 the District Criminal Court found one officer guilty of assault occasioning bodily harm (he was given a suspended sentence of two months' imprisonment) and acquitted two other officers. The convicted officer appealed claiming that Ribitsch had sustained his injuries by falling against a car door while being transported during his detention. The Regional Criminal Court allowed the appeal, noting that Ribitsch had been fined for drug offences and was unemployed. The Constitutional Court found that the arrest of Ribitsch, the search of his home, and his detention had been unlawful. However, Ribitsch's allegations of maltreatment by the police had not been proved beyond doubt. The applicant complained to the Commission asserting that he had been subject to inhuman and degrading treatment by the police. By 10 votes to 6 the Commission reported that there had been a breach of Article 3. The Court determined that:

34. It is not disputed that Mr Ribitsch's injuries were sustained during his detention in police custody, which was in any case unlawful, while he was entirely under the control of police officers.

Police Officer Markl's acquittal in the criminal proceedings by a court bound by the principle of presumption of innocence does not absolve Austria from its responsibility under the Convention. The Government were accordingly under an obligation to provide a plausible explanation of how the applicant's injuries were caused. But the Government did no more than refer to the outcome of the domestic criminal proceedings, where the high standard of proof necessary to secure a criminal conviction was not found to have been satisfied. It is also clear that, in that context, significant weight was given to the explanation that the injuries were caused by a fall against a car door. Like the Commission, the Court finds this explanation unconvincing...

On the basis of all the material placed before it, the Court concludes that the Government have not satisfactorily established that the applicant's injuries were caused otherwise than—entirely, mainly or partly—by the treatment he underwent while in police custody.

35. ...a number of witnesses had confirmed that the applicant had sustained physical injuries and was suffering from considerable psychological trauma...

38. The Court emphasises that, in respect of a person deprived of his liberty, any recourse to physical force which has not been made strictly necessary by his own conduct diminishes human dignity and is in principle an infringement of the right set forth in Article 3 of the Convention...

39. In the instant case the injuries suffered by Mr Ribitsch show that he underwent ill-treatment which amounted to both inhuman and degrading treatment.

Ribitsch was awarded 100,000 ATS just satisfaction in respect of non-pecuniary damage. Significantly, the judgment of the Court (of which Judge De Meyer was a member), at paragraph 38, incorporated Judge De Meyer's principle (enunciated in his concurring opinion in *Tomasi*, see Note 1) that the use of any physical force on a detainee, not strictly necessary to respond to actions of the detainee (such as attacking other detainees) is a breach of Article 3. This jurisprudential evolution of Article 3 is a very important Convention safeguard for detainees who are potentially in a highly vulnerable position vis-à-vis the public officials overseeing their detention and questioning.

3   The *Ribitsch* obligation upon States to provide a plausible explanation for injuries sustained by an individual during a period of detention was extended to injuries arising during a person's arrest in *Rehbock v Slovenia*, judgment of 28 November 2000. The applicant was a former German body-building champion whom the Slovenia authorities suspected of being a drug dealer. Therefore, the authorities planned to arrest him in Slovenia during a drug smuggling journey. Given the physical strength of the applicant, 13 police officers were deployed to arrest him. He was arrested by six officers, dressed in black and wearing masks, armed with a shotgun and pistols. After his arrest it was discovered that the applicant had suffered a double fracture to his jaw and facial cuts (subsequently he was sentenced to one year's imprisonment for unauthorized production and dealing in narcotics and of smuggling). A large majority, 6 votes to 1, determined:

76. ...that the Government have not furnished convincing or credible arguments which would provide a basis to explain or justify the degree of force used during the arrest operation. Accordingly, the force used was excessive and unjustified in the circumstances.

77. Such use of force had as a consequence injuries which undoubtedly caused serious suffering to the applicant of a nature amounting to inhuman treatment.

78. There has therefore been a violation of Article 3 of the Convention on account of the treatment to which the applicant was subjected during his arrest.

4 A majority (10 votes to 7) of the Grand Chamber in *Jalloh v Germany*, judgment of 11 July 2006, held that the forced administration of emetics to a suspected drug dealer, in order physically to induce him to regurgitate a packet of cocaine that he had swallowed, amounted to inhuman and degrading treatment.

> 82. Having regard to all the circumstances of the case, the Court finds that the impugned measure attained the minimum level of severity required to bring it within the scope of Article 3. The authorities subjected the applicant to a grave interference with his physical and mental integrity against his will. They forced him to regurgitate, not for therapeutic reasons, but in order to retrieve evidence they could equally have obtained by less intrusive methods. The manner in which the impugned measure was carried out was liable to arouse in the applicant feelings of fear, anguish and inferiority that were capable of humiliating and debasing him. Furthermore, the procedure entailed risks to the applicant's health, not least because of the failure to obtain a proper anamnesis [assessment of his medical history] beforehand. Although this was not the intention, the measure was implemented in a way which caused the applicant both physical pain and mental suffering. He therefore has been subjected to inhuman and degrading treatment contrary to Article 3.

The policy of the public prosecutor in Wuppertal to order the use of emetics to secure evidence against suspected drug offenders was not in accordance with the general practice in member States (only Germany, Luxembourg, Norway, and Macedonia forcibly administered emetics against the wishes of a suspect).

(I) MENTAL SUFFERING

1 In the Court's judgment in *Ireland v UK* (p 145), the deliberate infliction of 'intense physical and mental suffering' leading to 'acute psychiatric disturbances during interrogation' of detainees, by the use of the five techniques, was characterised as inhuman treatment (para 167).

2 The 'severe mental distress and anguish' experienced, over a number of years, by a close relative of a 'disappeared' person was also classified as inhuman treatment by the Commission in *Kurt v Turkey*, 1998-III. The Commission found that in November 1993 gendarmes and village guards conducted an anti-terrorist operation against the PKK in the applicant's village. The last time the applicant, or any other member of her family or the village, saw the applicant's son (Uzeyir Kurt) was on the morning of 25 November 1993, when he was surrounded by members of the security forces. Despite the applicant's subsequent numerous inquiries of various officials, all of them denied any knowledge of the whereabouts or condition of Uzeyir. In May 1994 the applicant complained, on behalf of her son and herself, to the Commission alleging a number of breaches of the Convention. The latter body, by 19 votes to 5, expressed the opinion, *inter alia*, that the applicant had been subject to inhuman and degrading treatment through the 'uncertainty, doubt and apprehension' caused to her by the disappearance of her son for which the Turkish authorities were responsible. The Court, by 6 votes to 3, agreed that there had been a breach of Article 3. But the Court did not specify which particular element of that Article had been infringed.

> 133. The Court notes that ill-treatment must attain a minimum level of severity if it is to fall within the scope of Article 3 . . . It recalls in this respect that the applicant approached the public prosecutor in the days following her son's disappearance in the definite belief that he had been taken into custody. She had witnessed his detention in the village with her own eyes and his non-appearance since that last sighting made her fear for his safety . . . However, the public prosecutor gave no serious consideration to her complaint . . . As a result, she has been left with the anguish of knowing

that her son has been detained and that there is a complete absence of official information as to his subsequent fate. This anguish has endured over a prolonged period of time.

134. Having regard to the circumstances described above as well as to the fact that the complainant was the mother of the victim of a human rights violation and herself the victim of the authorities' complacency in the face of her anguish and distress, the Court finds that the respondent State is in breach of Article 3 in respect of the applicant.

Turkey was ordered to pay the applicant £10,000 compensation.

Regrettably, in the later case of *Cakici v Turkey*, judgment of 8 July 1999, a large majority (14 votes to 3) of a Grand Chamber took a restrictive view of the judgment in *Kurt* by emphasizing that there must be 'special factors' present before a family member of a disappeared person can claim to be a victim of a breach of Article 3. The applicant, a resident of south-east Turkey complained to the Commission (on behalf of his brother Ahmet and himself) regarding the disappearance of Ahmet. The Turkish security authorities suspected Ahmet of being involved in PKK terrorist activities and on 8 November 1993 gendarmes arrested him. Other detainees reported that they had seen Ahmet in a bad condition after he had been tortured. The authorities denied that they had detained Ahmet. Subsequently, the Turkish Government claimed that Ahmet had been killed during a clash between the security forces and the PKK in February 1995. The Commission expressed the opinion that, *inter alia*, there had been a breach of Article 2 in respect of Ahmet (unanimously) and a breach of Article 3 in respect of the applicant (27 votes to 3). The Court held that:

98....in the Kurt case...which concerned the disappearance of the applicant's son during an unacknowledged detention, it found that the applicant had suffered a breach of Article 3 having regard to the particular circumstances of the case. It referred particularly to the fact that she was the mother of a victim of a serious human rights violation and herself the victim of the authorities' complacency in the face of her anguish and distress. The Kurt case does not however establish any general principle that a family member of a 'disappeared person' is thereby a victim of treatment contrary to Article 3. Whether a family member is such a victim will depend on the existence of special factors which gives the suffering of the applicant a dimension and character distinct from the emotional distress which may be regarded as inevitably caused to relatives of a victim of a serious human rights violation. Relevant elements will include the proximity of the family tie—in that context, a certain weight will attach to the parent-child bond—the particular circumstances of the relationship, the extent to which the family member witnessed the events in question, the involvement of the family member in the attempts to obtain information about the disappeared person and the way in which the authorities responded to those enquiries. The Court would further emphasise that the essence of such a violation does not so much lie in the fact of the 'disappearance' of the family member but rather concerns the authorities' reactions and attitudes to the situation when it is brought to their attention. It is especially in respect of the latter that a relative may claim directly to be a victim of the authorities' conduct.

99. In the present case, the applicant was the brother of the disappeared person. Unlike the applicant in the Kurt case, he was not present when the security forces took his brother, as he lived with his own family in another town. It appears also that, while the applicant was involved in making various petitions and enquiries to the authorities, he did not bear the brunt of this task, his father Tevfik Çakici taking the initiative in presenting the petition of 22 December 1993 to the Diyarbakir State Security Court. Nor have any aggravating features arising from the response of the authorities been brought to the attention of the Court in this case. Consequently, the Court perceives no special features existing in this case which would justify finding an additional violation of Article 3 of the Convention in relation to the applicant himself. Accordingly, there has been no breach of Article 3 as concerns the applicant in this case.

Judge Thomassen, joined by Judges Jungwiert and Fischbach, did not express an opinion on the merits of the majority's criterion of the existence of special factors. However, the dissenters considered that this criterion was satisfied in respect of the applicant because, 'a brother can also suffer deeply in face of the uncertainty of the fate of a sibling'.

In *Cicek v Turkey*, judgment of 27 February 2001, a unanimous Chamber found a breach of Article 3 in regard to the authorities' persistent refusals to explain to a mother the whereabouts/fate of her adult sons who had 'disappeared' after being taken into custody by gendarmes.

> 173. It recalls in this respect that the applicant and her daughter made several applications to the public prosecutor and the gendarme commander following her sons' disappearance in the definite belief that they had been kept in custody in the Lice Regional Boarding School [where the gendarmes were based]. However, the public prosecutor and the gendarmerie commander gave no serious consideration to her complaint. The Court observes that the applicant has had no news of her sons for almost six years. She has been living with the fear that her sons are dead and has made attempts before the public prosecutor and requested the authorities to be at least given their bodies. The uncertainty, doubt and apprehension suffered by the applicant over a prolonged and continuing period of time has undoubtedly caused her severe mental distress and anguish.

> 174. Having regard to the circumstances described above as well as to the fact that the complainant is the mother of victims of grave human rights violations and herself the victim of the authorities' complacency in the face of her anguish and distress, the Court finds that the respondent State is in breach of Article 3 in respect of the applicant.

A similar breach was found in the case of a father who had made many attempts to discover the whereabouts/fate of his 'disappeared' sons in *Ipek v Turkey*, judgment of 17 February 2004 (see also p 108 for the Article 2 aspects of this case).

> 182. In the present case, the Court notes that the applicant is the father of the disappeared Ipek brothers. The applicant witnessed the impugned events and his sons being taken away by soldiers almost nine years ago and he has never heard from them since. It further appears from the documents submitted by him that the applicant bore the weight of having to make numerous futile enquiries in order to find out what had happened to his two sons. Despite his tireless endeavours to discover the fate of his sons, the applicant has never received any plausible explanation or information from the authorities as to what became of his sons following their apprehension by the soldiers. Conversely, the authorities' reaction to the applicant's grave concerns was limited to denials that the İpek brothers had ever been detained by the security forces. It is to be noted that the applicant was not even informed of the outcome of the investigations pursued in respect of his complaints. Furthermore, the Court considers that the applicant's anguish about the fate of his sons must have been exacerbated by the destruction of his family home.

> 183. In view of the above, the Court finds that the applicant suffered, and continues to suffer, distress and anguish as a result of the disappearance of his two sons and of his inability to find out what had happened to them. The manner in which his complaints have been dealt with by the authorities must be considered to constitute inhuman treatment contrary to Article 3.
>
> The Court concludes therefore that there has been a violation of Article 3 of the Convention in respect of the applicant.

Hence, the greater the length of time (normally amounting to many years) parents have persisted in their attempts to discover the whereabouts/fate of their 'disappeared' children, combined with lack of cooperation from the authorities, the greater the likelihood that the Court will conclude that the parents have suffered a violation of Article 3.

In **Tanis and Others v Turkey**, judgment of 2 August 2005, a unanimous Chamber found that the wives/partner of two politicians who 'disappeared' after being summoned to a gendarmerie station had suffered inhuman/degrading treatment due to the distress and anxiety caused to them by the authorities' failure over four years to provide a plausible explanation for the fate of their relatives or undertake an effective investigation into the disappearances (the disappearances were found to involve breaches of both substantive and procedural aspects of Article 2).

3   In **V v UK**, 1999-IX, the applicant (born in 1982) had played truant from school with another 10-year-old boy (the applicant in the related case of **T v UK** (1999) 30 EHRR 121) one day during February 1993. While truanting T and V abducted a 2-year-old boy from a shopping centre, took him on a journey of a couple of miles, battered him to death, and then left his body to be run over by a train. The applicants were arrested and charged with murder. Their trial took place in public before Preston Crown Court over three weeks in November 1993.

In the two months preceding the trial, each applicant was taken by social workers to visit the courtroom and was introduced to trial procedures and personnel by way of a 'child witness pack' containing books and games. The trial was preceded and accompanied by massive national and international publicity. Throughout the criminal proceedings, the arrival of the defendants was greeted by a hostile crowd. On occasion, attempts were made to attack the vehicles bringing them to court. In the courtroom, the press benches and public gallery were full. The trial was conducted with the formality of an adult criminal trial. The judge and counsel wore wigs and gowns. The procedure was, however, modified to a certain extent in view of the defendants' age. They were seated next to social workers in a specially raised dock. Their parents and lawyers were seated nearby. The hearing times were shortened to reflect the school day (10.30 am to 3.30 pm, with an hour's lunch break), and a ten-minute interval was taken every hour. During adjournments the defendants were allowed to spend time with their parents and social workers in a play area. The judge made it clear that he would adjourn whenever the social workers or defence lawyers told him that one of the defendants was showing signs of tiredness or stress. This occurred on one occasion.

At the opening of the trial on 1 November 1993 the judge made an order under section 39 of the Children and Young Persons Act 1933, that there should be no publication of the names, addresses, or other identifying details of the applicant or T or publication of their photographs. On the same day, the applicant's counsel made an application for a stay of the proceedings, on the grounds that the trial would be unfair due to the nature and extent of the media coverage. After hearing argument, the judge found that it was not established that the defendants would suffer serious prejudice to the extent that no fair trial could be held. He referred to the warning that he had given to the jury to put out of their minds anything which they might have heard or seen about the case outside the courtroom.

The jury convicted the applicants of murder and the judge sentenced them, as required by law, to detention during Her Majesty's Pleasure. Subsequently, the judge recommended that the applicants serve eight years' detention in order to satisfy the requirements of retribution and deterrence (the 'tariff' period). The Lord Chief Justice recommended a tariff of ten years. The Home Secretary received considerable correspondence from members of the public, including a petition signed by nearly 300,000 people and 21,000 coupons from the *Sun* newspaper calling for the applicants to be detained for the rest of their lives. The Home Secretary allowed the applicants' lawyers to make representations to him and then (July 1994) informed the applicant that his tariff period should be 15 years. The applicant sought to challenge that decision in judicial review proceedings and the House of Lords (by a majority) ruled that the Home Secretary had acted unlawfully by giving weight to the public protests about the applicant's tariff. At the time of the court's judgment the Home Secretary had not set a new tariff for the applicant (in part because he was still awaiting representations from T). The applicant complained to the Commission alleging, *inter alia*, that his trial before an adult court in public and his sentence amounted to inhuman and degrading treatment in breach of Article 3. The Commission, by 17 votes to 2, found no breach of that provision. A majority of the Court (12 votes to 5 and 10 votes to 7) also found no violations of Article 3 in respect of the applicant's trial or sentence.

63. The applicant alleged that the cumulative effect of the age of criminal responsibility, the accusatorial nature of the trial, the adult proceedings in a public court, the length of the trial, the jury of twelve adult strangers, the physical lay-out of the courtroom, the overwhelming presence of the media and public, the attacks by the public on the prison van which brought him to court and the disclosure of his identity, together with a number of other factors linked to his sentence . . . gave rise to a breach of Article 3 . . . .

72. The Court has considered first whether the attribution to the applicant of criminal responsibility in respect of acts committed when he was ten years old could, in itself, give rise to a violation of Article 3. In doing so, it has regard to the principle, well established in its case-law that, since the Convention is a living instrument, it is legitimate when deciding whether a certain measure is acceptable under one of its provisions to take account of the standards prevailing among the member States of the Council of Europe (see the *Soering* judgment . . . p 40, § 102; and also the *Dudgeon v UK* judgment of 22 October 1981, Series A No 45, and the *X, Y and Z v UK* judgment of 22 April 1997, Reports 1997-II).

73. In this connection, the Court observes that, at the present time, there is not yet a commonly accepted minimum age for the imposition of criminal responsibility in Europe. While most of the Contracting States have adopted an age-limit which is higher than that in force in England and Wales, other States, such as Cyprus, Ireland, Liechtenstein and Switzerland, attribute criminal responsibility from a younger age. Moreover, no clear tendency can be ascertained from examination of the relevant international texts and instruments . . . Rule 4 of the Beijing Rules which, although not legally binding, might provide some indication of the existence of an international consensus, does not specify the age at which criminal responsibility should be fixed but merely invites States not to fix it too low, and Article 40(3)(a) of the UN Convention requires States Parties to establish a minimum age below which children shall be presumed not to have the capacity to infringe the criminal law, but contains no provision as to what that age should be.

74. The Court does not consider that there is at this stage any clear common standard among the member States of the Council of Europe as to the minimum age of criminal responsibility. Even if England and Wales is among the few European jurisdictions to retain a low age of criminal responsibility, the age of ten cannot be said to be so young as to differ disproportionately from the age-limit followed by other European States. The Court concludes that the attribution of criminal responsibility to the applicant does not in itself give rise to a breach of Article 3 of the Convention.

75. The second part of the applicant's complaint under Article 3 concerning the trial relates to the fact that the criminal proceedings took place over three weeks in public in an adult Crown Court with attendant formality, and that, after his conviction, his name was permitted to be published.

76. The Court notes in this connection that one of the minimum guarantees provided by Article 40(2)(b) of the UN Convention to children accused of crimes is that they should have their privacy fully respected at all stages of the proceedings. Similarly, Rule 8 of the Beijing Rules states that 'the juvenile's privacy shall be respected at all stages' and that 'in principle, no information that may lead to the identification of a juvenile offender shall be published'. Finally, the Committee of Ministers

of the Council of Europe recommended in 1987 that member States should review their law and practice with a view to avoiding committing minors to adult courts where juvenile courts exist and to recognising the right of juveniles to respect for their private lives...

77. The Court considers that the foregoing demonstrates an international tendency in favour of the protection of the privacy of juvenile defendants, and it notes in particular that the UN Convention is binding in international law on the United Kingdom in common with all the other member States of the Council of Europe...Moreover, Article 6 § 1 of the Convention states that 'the press and public may be excluded from all or part of the trial...where the interests of juveniles...so require'. However, while the existence of such a trend is one factor to be taken into account when assessing whether the treatment of the applicant can be regarded as acceptable under the other Articles of the Convention, it cannot be determinative of the question whether the trial in public amounted to ill-treatment attaining the minimum level of severity necessary to bring it within the scope of Article 3...

78. The Court recognises that the criminal proceedings against the applicant were not motivated by any intention on the part of the State authorities to humiliate him or cause him suffering. Indeed, special measures were taken to modify the Crown Court procedure in order to attenuate the rigours of an adult trial in view of the defendants' young age...

79. Even if there is evidence that proceedings such as those applied to the applicant could be expected to have a harmful effect on an eleven-year-old child...the Court considers that any proceedings or inquiry to determine the circumstances of the acts committed by T. and the applicant, whether such inquiry had been carried out in public or in private, attended by the formality of the Crown Court or informally in the Youth Court, would have provoked in the applicant feelings of guilt, distress, anguish and fear. The psychiatric evidence shows that before the trial commenced he was suffering from the post-traumatic effects of the offence; that he cried inconsolably and found it difficult and distressing when asked to talk about what he and T. had done to the two-year-old, and that he suffered fears of punishment and terrible retribution...While the public nature of the proceedings may have exacerbated to a certain extent these feelings in the applicant, the Court is not convinced that the particular features of the trial process as applied to him caused, to a significant degree, suffering going beyond that which would inevitably have been engendered by any attempt by the authorities to deal with the applicant following the commission by him of the offence in question...

80. In conclusion, therefore, the Court does not consider that the applicant's trial gave rise to a violation of Article 3 of the Convention....

93. The applicant argued that, in view of his age at the time of the offence, the sentence of detention during Her Majesty's pleasure was severely disproportionate and in breach of Article 3 of the Convention...

98. The Court recalls that States have a duty under the Convention to take measures for the protection of the public from violent crime (see, for example, the *A v UK* judgment of 23 September 1998, Reports 1998-VI, p 2699, § 22, and the *Osman v UK* judgment of 28 October 1998, Reports 1998-VIII, p 3159, § 115). It does not consider that the punitive element inherent in the tariff approach itself gives rise to a breach of Article 3, or that the Convention prohibits States from subjecting a child or young person convicted of a serious crime to an indeterminate sentence allowing for the offender's continued detention or recall to detention following release where necessary for the protection of the public (see the *Hussain* judgment...p 269, § 53).

99. The applicant has not yet reached the stage in his sentence where he is able to have the continued lawfulness of his detention reviewed with regard to the question of dangerousness, and although he has not yet been notified of any new tariff, it can be assumed that he is currently detained for the

purposes of retribution and deterrence. Until a new tariff has been set, it is not possible to draw any conclusions regarding the length of punitive detention to be served by the applicant. At the time of adoption of the present judgment he has been detained for six years since his conviction in November 1993. The Court does not consider that, in all the circumstances of the case including the applicant's age and his conditions of detention, a period of punitive detention of this length can be said to amount to inhuman or degrading treatment.

100. Finally, the Court observes that it cannot be excluded, particularly in relation to a child as young as the applicant at the time of his conviction, that an unjustifiable and persistent failure to fix a tariff, leaving the detainee in uncertainty over many years as to his future, might also give rise to an issue under Article 3. In the present case, however, in view of the relatively short period of time during which no tariff has been in force and the need to seek the views, *inter alia*, of both the applicant and T.... no such issue arises.

101. It follows that there has been no violation of Article 3 in respect of the applicant's sentence.

The above judgment indicates that the effects of a trial and a subsequent sentence of imprisonment on a person's mental well-being will have to be devastating before the Court is likely to find suffering of an intensity that violates Article 3 (note, the Court found the applicant's trial and the setting of his tariff to be in breach of Articles 6 and 5).

In February 2000 a new Practice Note (Crown Court: trial of children and young persons) was issued [2000] 2 All ER 284. The Direction emphasized that all possible steps should be taken to assist the young defendant to understand and participate in his/her trial. The proceedings should not expose the defendant to avoidable intimidation, humiliation, or distress. Special arrangements should be made for the trials of juveniles in the Crown Court including: counsel not wearing robes and wigs, police presence in the courtroom should not normally be recognizable, and restricting the number of reporters present in the courtroom (if appropriate the proceedings could be relayed to another room to which the media would have access). In March 2000 the Home Secretary (Mr Jack Straw) referred the cases of Robert Thompson and Jon Venables to the Lord Chief Justice for the latter to determine the tariff to be served before their cases would be considered by the Parole Board.

In October 2000 Lord Woolf ruled that the parole process could begin for both Thompson and Venables. During June 2001 the Parole Board authorized their release on life licences as they were no longer deemed to pose a danger to society. However, because of their notoriety and threats made against them they were given new secret identities on their release.

Jon Venables was recalled to prison, by the Justice Secretary (Mr Straw in another ministerial role), in February 2010 on suspicion of having child abuse images on his computer. Subsequently, in July 2010, he admitted child pornography offences and was sentenced to two years' imprisonment. Because of 'compelling evidence' of threats to the safety of Venables, the trial judge ruled that Venables' new identity must be kept secret.

The Committee of Ministers issued lengthy Guidelines on Child Friendly Justice on 17 November 2010. They provided, *inter alia*, that 'children' were persons under the age of 18 and:

23. The minimum age of criminal responsibility should not be too low and should be determined by law.

63. As far as possible, specialist courts (or court chambers), procedures and institutions should be established for children in conflict with the law. This could include the establishment of specialised units within the police, the judiciary, the court system and the prosecutor's office.

Hence, no European consensus had emerged as to the precise minimum age of criminal responsibility.

4 The tragic background to *Gafgen v Germany*, judgment of 1 June 2010, resembled the factual scenario in a jurisprudence seminar where the issue for debate was whether the police should be able to torture a suspect in order to gain information to try and save a victim's life. Gafgen, a law student, had befriended a wealthy family and then murdered the family's 11-year-old son and hid his body. Gafgen demanded a one million euros ransom for the return of the son. The police arrested Gafgen after he collected the ransom. Later that evening Gafgen told the police that other kidnappers were holding the boy. The next morning the Deputy Chief of Frankfurt police ordered another officer to threaten (and if necessary inflict) considerable physical pain on Gafgen if he did not disclose where the boy was being held. The officer told Gafgen that a specially trained person would come and cause him great pain if he did not provide the required information regarding the boy. A few minutes later Gafgen disclosed the location of the boy's body. Subsequently, Gafgen was convicted of murder and kidnapping and given a life sentence. The Deputy Chief of Police was convicted of inciting a subordinate to commit coercion and given a suspended fine (later he was appointed Chief of the Police Headquarters for Technology). The junior officer was convicted of coercion and also given a suspended fine. Gafgen complained that he had been subject to torture. The Grand Chamber held that:

107. In this connection, the Court accepts the motivation for the police officers' conduct and that they acted in an attempt to save a child's life. However, it is necessary to underline that, having regard to the provision of Article 3 and to its long-established case-law, the prohibition on ill-treatment of a person applies irrespective of the conduct of the victim or the motivation of the authorities. Torture, inhuman or degrading treatment cannot be inflicted even in circumstances where the life of an individual is at risk. No derogation is allowed even in the event of a public emergency threatening the life of the nation. Article 3, which has been framed in unambiguous terms, recognises that every human being has an absolute, inalienable right not to be subjected to torture or to inhuman or degrading treatment under any circumstances, even the most difficult. The philosophical basis underpinning the absolute nature of the right under Article 3 does not allow for any exceptions or justifying factors or balancing of interests, irrespective of the conduct of the person concerned and the nature of the offence at issue.

108. ... a threat of torture can amount to torture, as the nature of torture covers both physical pain and mental suffering. In particular, the fear of physical torture may itself constitute mental torture. However, there appears to be broad agreement, and the Court likewise considers, that the classification of whether a given threat of physical torture amounted to psychological torture or to inhuman or degrading treatment depends upon all the circumstances of a given case, including, notably, the severity of the pressure exerted and the intensity of the mental suffering caused. Contrasting the applicant's case to those in which torture has been found to be established in its case-law, the Court considers that the method of interrogation to which he was subjected in the circumstances of this case was sufficiently serious to amount to inhuman treatment prohibited by Article 3, but that it did not reach the level of cruelty required to attain the threshold of torture.

Hence the Court's answer to the jurisprudential conundrum is unequivocal—not only is torture prohibited to elicit such information but so are all other types of maltreatment falling within Article 3. For a criticism of this ruling see S. Greer, 'Should Police Threats to Torture Suspects Always be Severely Punished? Reflections on the Gafgen Case' (2011) 11(1) *Human Rights Law Review* 67.

(II) DESTRUCTION OF HOMES

The Court, by 8 votes to 1, has held that the burning of people's homes, by members of the security forces of a member State, can be so serious in its effects as to amount to inhuman treatment. In *Selcuk and Asker v Turkey*, 1998-II, the Court determined that:

77. ...Mrs Selçuk and Mr Asker were aged respectively 54 and 60 at the time and had lived in the village...all their lives...Their homes and most of their property were destroyed by the security forces, depriving the applicants of their livelihoods and forcing them to leave their village. It would appear that the exercise was premeditated and carried out contemptuously and without respect for the feelings of the applicants. They were taken unprepared; they had to stand by and watch the burning of their homes; inadequate precautions were taken to secure the safety of Mr and Mrs Asker; Mrs Selçuk's protests were ignored, and no assistance was provided to them afterwards.

78. Bearing in mind in particular the manner in which the applicants' homes were destroyed...and their personal circumstances, it is clear that they must have been caused suffering of sufficient severity for the acts of the security forces to be categorised as inhuman treatment within the meaning of Article 3.

79. The Court recalls that the Commission made no finding as regards the underlying motive for the destruction of the applicants' property. However, even if it were the case that the acts in question were carried out without any intention of punishing the applicants, but instead to prevent their homes being used by terrorists or as a discouragement to others, this would not provide a justification for the ill-treatment.

80. In conclusion, the Court finds that the particular circumstances of this case disclose a violation of Article 3.

In the light of the applicants' property losses the Court awarded Mrs Selcuk £17,760 and Mr Asker £22,408 compensation for pecuniary damage. In addition Turkey was ordered to pay each applicant £10,000 in respect of non-pecuniary damage to compensate for their suffering. Where the circumstances and effects of the deliberate destruction of homes is not quite so traumatic the Court will find such conduct to be a breach of Article 8 (right to respect for a person's home), see p 557.

(III) CONDITIONS OF DETENTION

1 A unanimous Chamber found the severe regime of imprisonment in which a convicted multiple child murderer had been held for over three years amounted to inhuman and degrading treatment in *Iorgov v Bulgaria*, judgment of 11 March 2004. The applicant who had been sentenced to death, but after the introduction of a *de facto* moratorium on executions, was imprisoned alone in a cell for 23 hours per day. Food was served in his cell and he was not allowed to eat with other prisoners. Apart from two visits per month, his only contact with other persons was with prison staff and conversations with other prisoners during a daily one-hour walk.

84. The Court notes that although the damaging effects of the impoverished regime to which the applicant was subject were known, that regime was maintained for many years...Furthermore, it is significant that the Government have not invoked any particular security reasons requiring the applicant's isolation and have not mentioned why it was not possible to revise the regime of prisoners in the applicant's situation so as to provide them with adequate possibilities for human contact and sensible occupation...

86. In sum, the Court considers that the stringent custodial regime to which the applicant was subjected after 1995 and the material conditions in which he was detained must have caused him suffering exceeding the unavoidable level inherent in detention. The Court thus concludes that the minimum threshold of severity under Article 3 of the Convention has been reached and that the applicant has been subjected to inhuman and degrading treatment.

2 A Chamber was very divided on the issue whether the detention of the notorious terrorist Ilich Ramirez, popularly known as 'Carlos the Jackal', in solitary confinement for over eight years amounted to inhuman treatment. In *Ramirez Sanchez v France*, judgment of 27 January 2005, the applicant complained about his detention in a 7 sq m cell; he was allowed two hours of walking in a prison exercise yard per day and access to newspapers and television. He was not allowed to associate with other prisoners but was visited by a doctor twice a week, a cleric once a month, and his lawyer (who had become his partner) visited him 640 times during five years. The applicant was in good physical and mental health. The authorities sought to justify the stringent conditions of detention because of the exceptional level of danger he posed (he was deemed to be the most dangerous terrorist in the world at the time of his capture in the mid-1990s; in 1997 he had been sentenced to life imprisonment for the murder of three French police officers in 1975—part of his terrorists group's campaign of violence which included the seizure of OPEC ministers and the hijacking of an Air France aeroplane). The Chamber, by 4 votes to 3, found that given his personality and the extreme level of danger he posed the conditions of his detention did not amount to inhuman treatment. On a referral under Article 43 the Grand Chamber (judgment of 4 July 2006) by a large majority (12 votes to 5) found that, having regard to the applicant's character and the danger he posed, his solitary confinement did not amount to a breach of Article 3. However, the Grand Chamber emphasized that solitary confinement should not be imposed on a prisoner indefinitely. Since the beginning of 2006 he had been detained under normal prison conditions and the Grand Chamber expressed the view that that should continue.

3 The routine subjection of a prisoner to strip-searches, combined with a very strict security regime (e.g. limited physical contact allowed with visiting close family members), was found to constitute inhuman or degrading treatment by a united Chamber in *Van Der Ven v Netherlands*, judgment of 4 February 2003. The applicant was detained on remand, in an ordinary prison, during September 1995 accused of having committed murder, rape, and narcotics offences. The next month he was transferred to an 'Extra-Security Institution' (EBI) after the authorities concluded that he was planning to escape from custody. The EBI was part of a large prison complex. As the applicant had threatened to commit suicide if transferred to the EBI he was placed under a high security regime in the institution. His cell was searched at least on a weekly basis and each time that occurred he was subject to a strip-search (involving an external inspection of his body orifices—including an anal inspection—by an officer of the same gender in a closed room). The applicant was subject to this regime for over three and a half years. The European Committee for the Prevention of Torture had reported that in its view the systematic strip-searching of detainees in the EBI did not appear to be justified in accordance with legitimate security requirements.

61. In the present case, the Court is struck by the fact that the applicant was submitted to the weekly strip-search in addition to all the other strict security measures within the EBI. In view of the fact that the domestic authorities, through the reports drawn up by the Psychological Department of their Penitentiary Selection Centre, were well aware that the applicant was experiencing serious difficulties coping with the regime, and bearing in mind that at no time

during the applicant's stay in the EBI did it appear that anything untoward was found in the course of a strip-search, the Court is of the view that the systematic strip-searching of the applicant required more justification than has been put forward by the Government in the present case.

62. The Court considers that in the situation where the applicant was already subjected to a great number of control measures, and in the absence of convincing security needs, the practice of weekly strip-searches that was applied to the applicant for a period of approximately three and a half years diminished his human dignity and must have given rise to feelings of anguish and inferiority capable of humiliating and debasing him. The applicant himself confirmed that this was indeed the case in a meeting with a psychiatrist, during which he also stated that he would forsake, for instance, going to the hairdresser's so as not to have to undergo a strip-search . . .

63. Accordingly, the Court concludes that the combination of routine strip-searching with the other stringent security measures in the EBI amounted to inhuman or degrading treatment in violation of Article 3 of the Convention. There has thus been a breach of this provision.

The above judgment does not prevent States from subjecting detainees to strip-searches but recourse to them must be justifiable on legitimate security grounds in the case of each person undergoing such a search (see also *Iwanczuk v Poland*, p 215). More generally, once again, in *Van Der Ven* it was the prison regime, rather than the physical conditions of incarceration, that led the Court to find a breach of Article 3.

4 The forced-feeding, physical restraint, and forced administration of sedatives to a mentally ill person who was compulsorily detained in a psychiatric hospital and a special prison were found not to have breached Article 3 in *Herczegfalvy v Austria* A.242-B (1992). The applicant had been proven to have assaulted fellow prisoners and prison wardens together with threatening judges, but the Court found that he was 'dangerous and not criminally responsible for his acts' due to a mental illness (paranoia querulans). Therefore, he was detained in a special prison and later a psychiatric hospital.

After several weeks of the applicant being on a hunger strike the director of the hospital ordered that he be force fed. The applicant was also given sedatives, against his will, on a number of occasions. For two days he was also attached to a security bed by means of straps and a net. The applicant claimed that this treatment was inhuman. The Commission, unanimously, agreed that it was in breach of Article 3. However, the Court, also unanimously, took a different view.

79. Mr Herczegfalvy also complained of his medical treatment. In that he had been forcibly administered food and neuroleptics [tranquillizers], isolated and attached with handcuffs to a security bed . . . he had been subjected to brutal treatment incompatible with Article 3 . . .

80. The Commission considered that the manner in which the treatment was administered had not complied with the requirements of Article 3 (art 3): the various measures complained of had been violent and excessively prolonged, and taken together had amounted to inhuman and degrading treatment, and even contributed to the worsening of the patient's condition.

81. In the Government's opinion, on the other hand, the measures were essentially the consequence of the applicant's behaviour, as he had refused medical treatment which was urgent in view of the deterioration in his physical and mental health.

Thus when Mr Herczegfalvy returned to the hospital on 10 September 1979 it proved to be necessary to feed him artificially, in view of his extremely weak state caused by his refusal to take any food . . . Later on, it was partly at his own request that he was fed through a tube, while continuing—at least ostensibly—with his hunger strike.

Similarly, it was only his resistance to all treatment, his extreme aggressiveness and the threats and acts of violence on his part against the hospital staff which explained why the staff had used coercive measures including the intramuscular injection of sedatives and the use of handcuffs and the security bed. These measures had been agreed to by Mr Herczegfalvy's curator, their sole aim had always been therapeutic, and they had been terminated as soon as the state of the patient permitted this.

Finally, the Government claimed that the isolation complained of had in fact consisted of being placed in an individual cell, in accordance with Mr Herczegfalvy's wishes. He had had contact with doctors and nurses, and had been able to receive visits and even walk in the garden.

82. The Court considers that the position of inferiority and powerlessness which is typical of patients confined in psychiatric hospitals calls for increased vigilance in reviewing whether the Convention has been complied with. While it is for the medical authorities to decide, on the basis of the recognised rules of medical science, on the therapeutic methods to be used, if necessary by force, to preserve the physical and mental health of patients who are entirely incapable of deciding for themselves and for whom they are therefore responsible, such patients nevertheless remain under the protection of Article 3 (art 3), whose requirements permit of no derogation.

The established principles of medicine are admittedly in principle decisive in such cases; as a general rule, a measure which is a therapeutic necessity cannot be regarded as inhuman or degrading. The Court must nevertheless satisfy itself that the medical necessity has been convincingly shown to exist.

83. In this case it is above all the length of time during which the handcuffs and security bed were used…which appears worrying. However, the evidence before the Court is not sufficient to disprove the Government's argument that, according to the psychiatric principles generally accepted at the time, medical necessity justified the treatment in issue. Moreover, certain of the applicant's allegations are not supported by the evidence. This is the case in particular with those relating to…the extent of the isolation.

84. No violation of Article 3 (art 3) has thus been shown.

Hence the Court will permit the compulsory medical treatment of mentally ill patients who cannot make rational decisions about their own treatment. But, States will have to be able to show that any particular course of treatment was medically necessary. The Court's 'vigilance' in ensuring that the Convention rights of these patients have been respected is a vital European safeguard to prevent States abusing their extensive domestic powers over a potentially vulnerable group.

5   The failure of the authorities to provide a detained person, who had been injured during his arrest, with prompt medical treatment was considered to be inhuman treatment by the Commission, unanimously, in **Hurtado v Switzerland** A.280A (1994). The applicant, a suspected member of a drug smuggling gang, had been arrested by a police special task force who used a stun grenade in order to overpower him. Two days after his arrest and detention the applicant asked to see a doctor. However, he was not examined by a doctor for another six days at which time X-rays revealed that the applicant had a fracture of the ninth left rib.

The Commission considers that in a situation of such gravity, resulting from the use of force by the police, Article 3 of the Convention requires the State authorities to adopt measures to safeguard the physical well-being of a person placed in the charge of the police, judicial or prison authorities. Under Article 3 of the Convention the State has a specific positive obligation to protect the physical well-being of persons deprived of their liberty. The lack of adequate medical treatment in such a situation must be classified as inhuman treatment. [Para 79.]

Later the applicant and the respondent State agreed a friendly settlement in which the latter paid the former an ex gratia sum of 14,000 SF (while not admitting that there had been a breach of the Convention).

6 The Court applied *Hurtado* when determining that the lack of appropriate specialist medical care, together with the imposition of a disciplinary period of solitary confinement, for a prisoner with a long history of serious mental illness who committed suicide amounted to inhuman and degrading treatment in *Keenan v UK*, judgment of 3 April 2001. The applicant's son, Mark, had a history of mental illness, including symptoms of paranoia, violence, and deliberate self-harm. In April 1993 he was convicted of assaulting his former girlfriend and sentenced to four months' imprisonment. He was admitted to Exeter Prison and sent to the prison health centre. The prison's senior doctor consulted the psychiatrist who had been treating Mark. Several attempts were made to transfer Mark to the ordinary cells but he resisted (by barricading himself in the ward on one occasion). At the end of April the prison's visiting psychiatrist recommended a change in Mark's medication. The next day Mark's condition deteriorated and a prison doctor, with no psychiatric training, ordered a return to his original medication. Later that day Mark assaulted two prison hospital officers (one was seriously injured). The next day another prison doctor, who had six months' psychiatric training, certified Mark as being fit for disciplinary proceedings in respect of the assaults and for placement in the segregation unit within the prison's punishment block. A deputy governor ordered Mark's placement in the segregation unit, where he was locked up for 23 hours each day. He was visited each day by a doctor, the prison chaplain, and the prison governor. Mark asked to see a prisoner trained by the Samaritans (to counsel inmates who may be suicidal) and threatened to harm himself. He was put on a 15-minute watch by prison staff. Prison doctors recorded that he was a hazard to staff. No further entries were made in Mark's medical record from 3 May 1993. However, the segregation unit's occurrence book had several entries regarding his behaviour, stating that he was being aggressive to staff and acting strangely. On 14 May he was subject to a disciplinary adjudication, after being certified as medically fit for the hearing by one of the prison doctors, and found guilty of assaulting the officers. The deputy governor sentenced him to 28 additional days in prison and seven days in the segregation unit. During the next day Mark was visited by a friend and he appeared to be in good spirits. However, that evening Mark was found hanged in his cell (the relevant prison officer had been absent in the toilet for a few minutes prior to the discovery of Mark's suicide). The applicant contended that, *inter alia*, there had been wholly insufficient psychiatric care given to her son whilst in prison and that violated his rights under Article 3. The Court, by 5 votes to 2, held that:

110. It is relevant in the context of the present application to recall also that the authorities are under an obligation to protect the health of persons deprived of liberty (*Hurtado v Switzerland*, Comm. Report 8 July 1993, Series A No 280, p 16, § 79). The lack of appropriate medical treatment may amount to treatment contrary to Article 3 (see *Ilhan v Turkey* [GC] No 22277/93, ECHR 2000-VII, § 87). In particular, the assessment of whether the treatment or punishment concerned is incompatible with the standards of Article 3 has, in the case of mentally ill persons, to take into consideration their vulnerability and their inability, in some cases, to complain coherently or at all about how they are being affected by any particular treatment (see e.g. the *Herczegfalvy v Austria* judgment of 24 September 1992, Series A no. 244, § 82; the *Aerts v Belgium* judgment of 30 July 1998, Reports 1998-V, p 1966, § 66).

113. In this case, the Court is struck by the lack of medical notes concerning Mark Keenan, who was an identifiable suicide risk and undergoing the additional stresses that could be foreseen from

segregation and, later, disciplinary punishment. From 5 May to 15 May 1993, when he died, there were no entries in his medical notes. Given that there were a number of prison doctors who were involved in caring for Mark Keenan, this shows an inadequate concern to maintain full and detailed records of his mental state and undermines the effectiveness of any monitoring or supervision process. The Court does not find the explanation of Dr Keith—that an absence of notes indicates that there was nothing to record—a satisfactory answer in the light of the occurrence book entries for the same period.

114. Further, while the prison senior medical officer consulted Mark Keenan's doctor on admission and the visiting psychiatrist, who also knew Mark Keenan, had been called to see Mark Keenan on 29 April 1993, the Court notes that there was no subsequent reference to a psychiatrist. Even though Dr Rowe had warned on 29 April 1993 that Mark Keenan should be kept from association until his paranoid feelings had died down, the question of returning to normal location was raised with him the next day. When his condition proceeded to deteriorate, a prison doctor, unqualified in psychiatry, reverted to Mark Keenan's previous medication without reference to the psychiatrist who had originally recommended a change. The assault on the two prison officers followed. Though Mark Keenan asked the prison doctor to point out to the governor at the adjudication that the assault occurred after a change in medication, there was no reference to a psychiatrist for advice either as to his future treatment or his fitness for adjudication and punishment.

115. The lack of effective monitoring of Mark Keenan's condition and the lack of informed psychiatric input into his assessment and treatment disclose significant defects in the medical care provided to a mentally ill person known to be a suicide risk. The belated imposition on him in those circumstances of a serious disciplinary punishment—seven days' segregation in the punishment block and an additional twenty-eight days to his sentence imposed two weeks after the event and only nine days before his expected date of release—which may well have threatened his physical and moral resistance, is not compatible with the standard of treatment required in respect of a mentally ill person. It must be regarded as constituting inhuman and degrading treatment and punishment within the meaning of Article 3 of the Convention.

Accordingly, the Court finds a violation of this provision.

This judgment is important for indicating the Court's increasing concern that States must provide adequate medical care for mentally ill prisoners, especially those who may commit suicide.

7　The failure accurately to monitor and adequately to treat a new inmate experiencing serious withdrawal symptoms from heroin addiction were found to constitute inhuman and degrading treatment in *McGlinchey and Others v UK*, judgment of 29 April 2003. The applicants were the mother and children of Judith McGlinchey, born in 1968, who had a long history of drug addiction. On 7 December 1998 she was sentenced to four months' imprisonment for theft. On her arrival, at New Hall Prison Wakefield, she weighed 50 kg and complained of withdrawal symptoms (she was vomiting frequently). The next day the prison doctor examined her and prescribed medication to reduce the symptoms of withdrawal. On 9 December her weight was recorded as 43 kg and she was given an anti-nausea drug. The following day she telephoned her mother to complain about the lack of treatment she was receiving. On 11 December she was found to be 'opiate positive'. For the next two days her pulse and blood pressure readings were within normal limits. However, on 14 December she collapsed and was taken to hospital. Subsequently she suffered a cardiac arrest and died on 3 January 1999. The autopsy found brain damage and multiple organ failure and recorded her weight as being 41 kg. An inquest jury was unanimous in reaching an open verdict in respect of her death. The applicants complained that the authorities subjected Judith to inhuman and degrading treatment by, *inter alia*, permitting her to dehydrate and leaving her to clean up her vomit. The Chamber, by 6 votes to 1, concluded that:

57. The evidence indicates to the Court that by the morning of 14 December 1998 Judith McGlinchey, a heroin addict whose nutritional state and general health were not good on admission to prison, had suffered serious weight loss and was dehydrated. This was the result of a week of largely uncontrolled vomiting symptoms and an inability to eat or hold down fluids. This situation, in addition to causing Judith McGlinchey distress and suffering, posed very serious risks to her health, as shown by her subsequent collapse. Having regard to the responsibility owed by prison authorities to provide the requisite medical care for detained persons, the Court finds that in the present case there was a failure to meet the standards imposed by Article 3 of the Convention. It notes in this context the failure of the prison authorities to provide accurate means of establishing Judith McGlinchey's weight loss, which was a factor that should have alerted the prison to the seriousness of her condition, but was largely discounted due to the discrepancy of the scales. There was a gap in the monitoring of her condition by a doctor over the weekend when there was a further significant drop in weight and a failure of the prison to take more effective steps to treat Judith McGlinchey's condition, such as her admission to hospital to ensure the intake of medication and fluids intravenously, or to obtain more expert assistance in controlling the vomiting.

58. The Court concludes that the prison authorities' treatment of Judith McGlinchey contravened the prohibition against inhuman or degrading treatment contained in Article 3 of the Convention.

In this case, as in *Keenan*, the victim sadly died.

8   The full-time Court found no breach of Article 3 in respect of the forced medical treatment of a convicted murder being held on 'death row' (his sentence was commuted to life imprisonment four years later) in *Naumenko v Ukraine*, judgment of 10 February 2004. During his detention on death row he was diagnosed as being psychopathic, he attempted suicide several times and was aggressive. A psychiatrist prescribed neuroleptic and psychoactive drugs. The applicant complained, *inter alia*, that he was being subject to radiation from a 'psychoactive drugs generator'. A delegation from the Court took evidence from the applicant and witnesses at the prison where he was being held. In its judgment the Court repeated that domestic authorities were under a duty to protect the health of prisoners and therapeutic treatment, no matter how disagreeable, could not be regarded as breaching Article 3 if it was shown to be necessary on medical grounds. Although the Court was critical of the lack of detail in the medical records kept on the applicant by the prison authorities, the judges were unanimous in finding no credible evidence that the authorities had acted wrongly in making the applicant take the above medication. Also, there was no evidence that he had been subject to treatment from a 'psychoactive drugs generator'. This judgment adopted a similar approach to the compulsory treatment of a mentally ill detainee as that applied by the original Court in *Herczegfalvy* (see Note 4).

9   In *Iorgov v Bulgaria* (see Note 1) the applicant also alleged that surgery on a swollen gland had been unduly delayed because of hostility to him by the prison medical staff and administration. The Court stated that:

85. As regards the quality of the health care provided to the applicant, the Court notes that his health was regularly monitored and in most cases the necessary treatment was provided. However, the evidence about the treatment of the applicant's swollen salivary gland, although not conclusive, suggests that there had been an unwarranted delay in providing adequate medical assistance. It must be stressed in this respect that the applicant's alleged rude behaviour towards medical staff

and, indeed, any violation of prison rules and discipline by a detainee, can in no circumstances warrant a refusal to provide medical assistance.

Clearly, denial or delay in the provision of necessary medical care must not be used as a form of (official or unofficial) punishment of detainees.

10 A united Grand Chamber determined that the high security conditions in which the former leader of a terrorist/political organization (described as a 'warlord' by President Wildhaber in his joint partly dissenting opinion) was serving his life sentence did not constitute inhuman or degrading treatment in *Ocalan v Turkey*, see p 135.

192. In the present case, it is true that the applicant's detention posed exceptional difficulties for the Turkish authorities. The applicant, as the leader of a large, armed separatist movement, is considered in Turkey to be the most dangerous terrorist in the country. Reactions to his arrest and differences of opinion that have come to light within his own movement show that his life is genuinely at risk. It is also a reasonable presumption that his supporters will seek to help him escape from prison. In those circumstances, it is understandable that the Turkish authorities should have found it necessary to take extraordinary security measures to detain the applicant.

193. The applicant's prison cell is indisputably furnished to a standard that is beyond reproach. From the photographs in its possession and the findings of the delegates of the CPT [European Committee for the Prevention of Torture], who inspected the applicant's prison during their visit to Turkey from 2 to 14 September 2001, the Court notes that the cell which the applicant occupies alone is large enough to accommodate a prisoner and furnished with a bed, table, armchair and bookshelves. It is also air-conditioned, has washing and toilet facilities and a window overlooking an inner courtyard. The applicant appears to be under medical supervision that is both strict and regular. The Court considers that these conditions do not give rise to any issue under Article 3 of the Convention.

194. Further, the Court considers that the applicant cannot be regarded as being kept in sensory isolation or cellular confinement. It is true that, as the sole inmate, his only contact is with prison staff. He has books, newspapers and a radio at his disposal. He does not have access to television programmes or a telephone. He does, however, communicate with the outside world by letter. He sees a doctor every day and his lawyers and members of his family once a week (his lawyers were allowed to see him twice a week during the trial). The difficulties in gaining access to İmralı Prison in adverse weather conditions appear to have been resolved, as the prison authorities were provided with a suitable craft at the end of 2004.

195. The Court notes the CPT's recommendations that the applicant's relative social isolation should not be allowed to continue for too long and that its effects should be attenuated by giving him access to a television and to telephone communications with his lawyers and close relatives. However, like the Chamber, the Grand Chamber is also mindful of the Government's concerns that the applicant may seek to take advantage of communications with the outside world to renew contact with members of the armed separatist movement of which he was the leader. These concerns cannot be said to be unfounded. An added consideration is the Government's fear that it would be difficult to protect the applicant's life in an ordinary prison.

196. While concurring with the CPT's recommendations that the long-term effects of the applicant's relative social isolation should be attenuated by giving him access to the same facilities as other high security prisoners in Turkey, such as television and telephone contact with his family, the Grand Chamber agrees with the Chamber that the general conditions in which he is being detained at İmralı Prison have not thus far reached the minimum level of severity required to constitute inhuman or degrading treatment within the meaning of Article 3 of the Convention. Consequently, there has been no violation of that provision on that account.

11   The chaining of the legs of unconscious prisoners (undertaking a hunger strike) to their beds in a hospital was held to constitute inhuman treatment by a unanimous Chamber in *Avci and Others v Turkey*, judgment of 27 June 2006. The Court found that given their weak medical condition the risk of the prisoners absconding was non-existent (they were also guarded by gendarmes) and therefore the restraint was disproportionate.

12   The imprisonment of a 15-year-old youth in an adult prison together with a failure to provide adequate medical care for his serious psychological problems (manifested through several attempted suicides) was held to amount to inhuman and degrading treatment by a unanimous Chamber in *Guvec v Turkey*, judgment of 20 January 2009.

(IV) EXTRADITION OR DEPORTATION

Soering v United Kingdom   A.161 (1989)
European Court of Human Rights

The applicant, Jens Soering, is a German national born in 1966. In March 1985 the parents of his girlfriend were brutally killed in their home in Virginia, USA. The applicant and his girlfriend disappeared together from Virginia in October 1985 and were subsequently arrested in England, during April 1986, in connection with cheque fraud. The applicant was interviewed, in England, by a Virginia police officer and admitted that he had killed his girlfriend's parents because they were opposed to his relationship with her. In June 1986 a Virginia grand jury indicted Soering on capital murder charges in respect of the killings. Two months later the Government of the United States of America requested the applicant's extradition (and that of the girlfriend) under the terms of the 1972 Extradition Treaty between the USA and the UK. The UK Government began extradition proceedings against the applicant in September 1986 and shortly afterwards the British Embassy in Washington made the following request of the US authorities:

> Because the death penalty has been abolished in Great Britain, the Embassy has been instructed to seek an assurance, in accordance with the terms of . . . the Extradition Treaty, that, in the event of Mr Soering being surrendered and being convicted of the crimes for which he has been indicted . . . , the death penalty, if imposed, will not be carried out. Should it not be possible on constitutional grounds for the United States Government to give such an assurance, the United Kingdom authorities ask that the United States Government undertake to recommend to the appropriate authorities that the death penalty should not be imposed or, if imposed, should not be executed.

In December 1986 a German prosecutor interviewed the applicant and in February 1987 a court in Bonn issued a warrant for Soering's arrest in respect of the alleged murders. This was followed by the German Government requesting his extradition to Germany under the terms of the 1872 Extradition Treaty between Germany and the UK. The UK Government replied that as the US authorities had already submitted a request for Soering's extradition those proceedings should be allowed to continue. The prosecuting attorney in Virginia swore an affidavit that:

> I hereby certify that should Jens Soering be convicted of the offence of capital murder as charged in Bedford County, Virginia . . . a representation will be made in the name of the United Kingdom to the judge at the time of sentencing that it is the wish of the United Kingdom that the death penalty should not be imposed or carried out.

However, he intended to seek the death penalty. After a hearing the Chief Magistrate at Bow Street Magistrates' Court committed the applicant to await the Home Secretary's order for his return to the USA. Soering was unsuccessful in challenging that decision in judicial review proceedings. While awaiting extradition, in July 1987, Soering applied to the Commission alleging that if he was to be extradited to the USA there was a serious likelihood that he would be sentenced to death and that consequently he would be subject to inhuman and degrading treatment and punishment contrary to Article 3 (particularly through exposure to the 'death row phenomenon'). The Commission requested the UK not to extradite Soering until the application had been determined. Subsequently, the Commission (by 6 votes to 5) expressed the opinion that there had been no breach of Article 3. The Commission, UK and German Governments referred the case to the Court.

A. APPLICABILITY OF ARTICLE 3 (ART 3) IN CASES OF EXTRADITION

81. The alleged breach derives from the applicant's exposure to the so-called 'death row phenomenon'. This phenomenon may be described as consisting in a combination of circumstances to which the applicant would be exposed if, after having been extradited to Virginia to face a capital murder charge, he were sentenced to death.

82. In its report (at paragraph 94) the Commission reaffirmed 'its case-law that a person's deportation or extradition may give rise to an issue under Article 3 (art 3) of the Convention where there are serious reasons to believe that the individual will be subjected, in the receiving State, to treatment contrary to that Article (art 3)'.

The Government of the Federal Republic of Germany supported the approach of the Commission, pointing to a similar approach in the case-law of the German courts.

The applicant likewise submitted that Article 3 (art 3) not only prohibits the Contracting States from causing inhuman or degrading treatment or punishment to occur within their jurisdiction but also embodies an associated obligation not to put a person in a position where he will or may suffer such treatment or punishment at the hands of other States. For the applicant, at least as far as Article 3 (art 3) is concerned, an individual may not be surrendered out of the protective zone of the Convention without the certainty that the safeguards which he would enjoy are as effective as the Convention standard.

83. The United Kingdom Government, on the other hand, contended that Article 3 (art 3) should not be interpreted so as to impose responsibility on a Contracting State for acts which occur outside its jurisdiction. In particular, in their submission, extradition does not involve the responsibility of the extraditing State for inhuman or degrading treatment or punishment which the extradited person may suffer outside the State's jurisdiction. To begin with, they maintained, it would be straining the language of Article 3 (art 3) intolerably to hold that by surrendering a fugitive criminal the extraditing State has 'subjected' him to any treatment or punishment that he will receive following conviction and sentence in the receiving State. Further arguments advanced against the approach of the Commission were that it interferes with international treaty rights; it leads to a conflict with the norms of international judicial process, in that it in effect involves adjudication on the internal affairs of foreign States not Parties to the Convention or to the proceedings before the Convention institutions; it entails grave difficulties of evaluation and proof in requiring the examination of alien systems of law and of conditions in foreign States; the practice of national courts and the international community cannot reasonably be invoked to support it; it causes a serious risk of harm in the Contracting State which is obliged to harbour the protected person, and leaves criminals untried, at large and unpunished.

In the alternative, the United Kingdom Government submitted that the application of Article 3 (art 3) in extradition cases should be limited to those occasions in which the treatment or punishment abroad is certain, imminent and serious. In their view, the fact that by definition the matters complained of are only anticipated, together with the common and legitimate interest of all States in bringing fugitive criminals to justice, requires a very high degree of risk, proved beyond reasonable doubt, that ill-treatment will actually occur.

84. The Court will approach the matter on the basis of the following considerations.

85. As results from Article 5 § 1 (f) (art 5-1-f), which permits 'the lawful...detention of a person against whom action is being taken with a view to...extradition', no right not to be extradited is as such protected by the Convention. Nevertheless, in so far as a measure of extradition has consequences adversely affecting the enjoyment of a Convention right, it may, assuming that the consequences are not too remote, attract the obligations of a Contracting State under the relevant Convention guarantee (see, *mutatis mutandis*, the *Abdulaziz, Cabales and Balkandali* judgment of 25 May 1985, Series A No 94, pp 31–2, §§ 59–60—in relation to rights in the field of immigration). What is at issue in the present case is whether Article 3 (art 3) can be applicable when the adverse consequences of extradition are, or may be, suffered outside the jurisdiction of the extraditing State as a result of treatment or punishment administered in the receiving State.

86. Article 1 (art 1) of the Convention, which provides that 'the High Contracting Parties shall secure to everyone within their jurisdiction the rights and freedoms defined in Section I', sets a limit, notably territorial, on the reach of the Convention. In particular, the engagement undertaken by a Contracting State is confined to 'securing' ('reconnaitre' in the French text) the listed rights and freedoms to persons within its own 'jurisdiction'. Further, the Convention does not govern the actions of States not Parties to it, nor does it purport to be a means of requiring the Contracting States to impose Convention standards on other States. Article 1 (art 1) cannot be read as justifying a general principle to the effect that, notwithstanding its extradition obligations, a Contracting State may not surrender an individual unless satisfied that the conditions awaiting him in the country of destination are in full accord with each of the safeguards of the Convention. Indeed, as the United Kingdom Government stressed, the beneficial purpose of extradition in preventing fugitive offenders from evading justice cannot be ignored in determining the scope of application of the Convention and of Article 3 (art 3) in particular.

In the instant case it is common ground that the United Kingdom has no power over the practices and arrangements of the Virginia authorities which are the subject of the applicant's complaints. It is also true that in other international instruments cited by the United Kingdom Government—for example the 1951 United Nations Convention relating to the Status of Refugees (Article 33), the 1957 European Convention on Extradition (Article 11) and the 1984 United Nations Convention against Torture and Other Cruel, Inhuman and Degrading Treatment or Punishment (Article 3)—the problems of removing a person to another jurisdiction where unwanted consequences may follow are addressed expressly and specifically.

These considerations cannot, however, absolve the Contracting Parties from responsibility under Article 3 (art 3) for all and any foreseeable consequences of extradition suffered outside their jurisdiction.

87. In interpreting the Convention regard must be had to its special character as a treaty for the collective enforcement of human rights and fundamental freedoms (see the *Ireland v UK* judgment of 18 January 1978, Series A No 25, p 90, § 239). Thus, the object and purpose of the Convention as an instrument for the protection of individual human beings require that its provisions be interpreted and applied so as to make its safeguards practical and effective (see, *inter alia*, the *Artico* judgment of 13 May 1980, Series A No 37, p 16, § 33). In addition, any interpretation of the rights and freedoms guaranteed has to be consistent with 'the general spirit of the Convention, an instrument designed to maintain and promote the ideals and values of a democratic society' (see the *Kjeldsen, Busk Madsen and Pedersen* judgment of 7 December 1976, Series A No 23, p 27, § 53).

88. Article 3 (art 3) makes no provision for exceptions and no derogation from it is permissible under Article 15 (art 15) in time of war or other national emergency. This absolute prohibition of torture and of inhuman or degrading treatment or punishment under the terms of the Convention shows that Article 3 (art 3) enshrines one of the fundamental values of the democratic societies making up the Council of Europe. It is also to be found in similar terms in other international instruments such as the 1966 International Covenant on Civil and Political Rights and the 1969 American Convention on Human Rights and is generally recognised as an internationally accepted standard.

The question remains whether the extradition of a fugitive to another State where he would be subjected or be likely to be subjected to torture or to inhuman or degrading treatment or punishment would itself engage the responsibility of a Contracting State under Article 3 (art 3). That the abhorrence of torture has such implications is recognised in Article 3 of the United Nations Convention Against Torture and Other Cruel, Inhuman or Degrading Treatment or Punishment, which provides that 'no State Party shall... extradite a person where there are substantial grounds for believing that he would be in danger of being subjected to torture'. The fact that a specialised treaty should spell out in detail a specific obligation attaching to the prohibition of torture does not mean that an essentially similar obligation is not already inherent in the general terms of Article 3 (art 3) of the European Convention. It would hardly be compatible with the underlying values of the Convention, that 'common heritage of political traditions, ideals, freedom and the rule of law' to which the Preamble refers, were a Contracting State knowingly to surrender a fugitive to another State where there were substantial grounds for believing that he would be in danger of being subjected to torture, however heinous the crime allegedly committed. Extradition in such circumstances, while not explicitly referred to in the brief and general wording of Article 3 (art 3), would plainly be contrary to the spirit and intendment of the Article, and in the Court's view this inherent obligation not to extradite also extends to cases in which the fugitive would be faced in the receiving State by a real risk of exposure to inhuman or degrading treatment or punishment proscribed by that Article (art 3).

89. What amounts to 'inhuman or degrading treatment or punishment' depends on all the circumstances of the case (see paragraph 100 below). Furthermore, inherent in the whole of the Convention is a search for a fair balance between the demands of the general interest of the community and the requirements of the protection of the individual's fundamental rights. As movement about the world becomes easier and crime takes on a larger international dimension, it is increasingly in the interest of all nations that suspected offenders who flee abroad should be brought to justice. Conversely, the establishment of safe havens for fugitives would not only result in danger for the State obliged to harbour the protected person but also tend to undermine the foundations of extradition. These considerations must also be included among the factors to be taken into account in the interpretation and application of the notions of inhuman and degrading treatment or punishment in extradition cases.

90. It is not normally for the Convention institutions to pronounce on the existence or otherwise of potential violations of the Convention. However, where an applicant claims that a decision to extradite him would, if implemented, be contrary to Article 3 (art 3) by reason of its foreseeable consequences in the requesting country, a departure from this principle is necessary, in view of the serious and irreparable nature of the alleged suffering risked, in order to ensure the effectiveness of the safeguard provided by that Article (art 3) (see paragraph 87 above).

91. In sum, the decision by a Contracting State to extradite a fugitive may give rise to an issue under Article 3 (art 3), and hence engage the responsibility of that State under the Convention, where substantial grounds have been shown for believing that the person concerned, if extradited, faces a real risk of being subjected to torture or to inhuman or degrading treatment or punishment in the requesting country. The establishment of such responsibility inevitably involves an assessment of

conditions in the requesting country against the standards of Article 3 (art 3) of the Convention. Nonetheless, there is no question of adjudicating on or establishing the responsibility of the receiving country, whether under general international law, under the Convention or otherwise. In so far as any liability under the Convention is or may be incurred, it is liability incurred by the extraditing Contracting State by reason of its having taken action which has as a direct consequence the exposure of an individual to proscribed ill-treatment.

B. APPLICATION OF ARTICLE 3 (ART 3) IN THE PARTICULAR CIRCUMSTANCES OF THE PRESENT CASE

92. The extradition procedure against the applicant in the United Kingdom has been completed, the Secretary of State having signed a warrant ordering his surrender to the United States authorities... this decision, albeit as yet not implemented, directly affects him. It therefore has to be determined on the above principles whether the foreseeable consequences of Mr Soering's return to the United States are such as to attract the application of Article 3 (art 3). This inquiry must concentrate firstly on whether Mr Soering runs a real risk of being sentenced to death in Virginia, since the source of the alleged inhuman and degrading treatment or punishment, namely the 'death row phenomenon', lies in the imposition of the death penalty. Only in the event of an affirmative answer to this question need the Court examine whether exposure to the 'death row phenomenon' in the circumstances of the applicant's case would involve treatment or punishment incompatible with Article 3 (art 3).

1. Whether the applicant runs a real risk of a death sentence and hence of exposure to the 'death row phenomenon'

93. The United Kingdom Government, contrary to the Government of the Federal Republic of Germany, the Commission and the applicant, did not accept that the risk of a death sentence attains a sufficient level of likelihood to bring Article 3 (art 3) into play. Their reasons were fourfold.

Firstly, as illustrated by his interview with the German prosecutor where he appeared to deny any intention to kill... the applicant has not acknowledged his guilt of capital murder as such.

Secondly, only a prima facie case has so far been made out against him. In particular, in the United Kingdom Government's view the psychiatric evidence... is equivocal as to whether Mr Soering was suffering from a disease of the mind sufficient to amount to a defence of insanity under Virginia law...

Thirdly, even if Mr Soering is convicted of capital murder, it cannot be assumed that in the general exercise of their discretion the jury will recommend, the judge will confirm and the Supreme Court of Virginia will uphold the imposition of the death penalty... The United Kingdom Government referred to the presence of important mitigating factors, such as the applicant's age and mental condition at the time of commission of the offence and his lack of previous criminal activity, which would have to be taken into account by the jury and then by the judge in the separate sentencing proceedings.

Fourthly, the assurance received from the United States must at the very least significantly reduce the risk of a capital sentence either being imposed or carried out...

At the public hearing the Attorney General nevertheless made clear his Government's understanding that if Mr Soering were extradited to the United States there was 'some risk', which was 'more than merely negligible', that the death penalty would be imposed.

94. As the applicant himself pointed out, he has made to American and British police officers and to two psychiatrists admissions of his participation in the killings of the Haysom parents, although he appeared to retract those admissions somewhat when questioned by the German prosecutor... It is not for the European Court to usurp the function of the Virginia courts by ruling that a defence of insanity would or would not be available on the psychiatric evidence as it

stands. The United Kingdom Government are justified in their assertion that no assumption can be made that Mr Soering would certainly or even probably be convicted of capital murder as charged . . . Nevertheless, as the Attorney General conceded on their behalf at the public hearing, there is 'a significant risk' that the applicant would be so convicted.

95. Under Virginia law, before a death sentence can be returned the prosecution must prove beyond reasonable doubt the existence of at least one of the two statutory aggravating circumstances, namely future dangerousness or vileness (see paragraph 43 above). In this connection, the horrible and brutal circumstances of the killings . . . would presumably tell against the applicant, regard being had to the case-law on the grounds for establishing the 'vileness' of the crime . . .

Admittedly, taken on their own the mitigating factors do reduce the likelihood of the death sentence being imposed. No less than four of the five facts in mitigation expressly mentioned in the Code of Virginia could arguably apply to Mr Soering's case. These are a defendant's lack of any previous criminal history, the fact that the offence was committed while a defendant was under extreme mental or emotional disturbance, the fact that at the time of commission of the offence the capacity of a defendant to appreciate the criminality of his conduct or to conform his conduct to the requirements of the law was significantly diminished, and a defendant's age . . .

96. These various elements arguing for or against the imposition of a death sentence have to be viewed in the light of the attitude of the prosecuting authorities.

97. The Commonwealth's Attorney for Bedford County, Mr Updike, who is responsible for conducting the prosecution against the applicant, has certified that 'should Jens Soering be convicted of the offence of capital murder as charged . . . a representation will be made in the name of the United Kingdom to the judge at the time of sentencing that it is the wish of the United Kingdom that the death penalty should not be imposed or carried out' . . . The Court notes, like Lord Justice Lloyd in the Divisional Court . . . that this undertaking is far from reflecting the wording of Article IV of the 1972 Extradition Treaty between the United Kingdom and the United States, which speaks of 'assurances satisfactory to the requested Party that the death penalty will not be carried out' . . . However, the offence charged, being a State and not a Federal offence, comes within the jurisdiction of the Commonwealth of Virginia; it appears as a consequence that no direction could or can be given to the Commonwealth's Attorney by any State or Federal authority to promise more; the Virginia courts as judicial bodies cannot bind themselves in advance as to what decisions they may arrive at on the evidence; and the Governor of Virginia does not, as a matter of policy, promise that he will later exercise his executive power to commute a death penalty . . . This being so, Mr Updike's undertaking may well have been the best 'assurance' that the United Kingdom could have obtained from the United States Federal Government in the particular circumstances. According to the statement made to Parliament in 1987 by a Home Office Minister, acceptance of undertakings in such terms 'means that the United Kingdom authorities render up a fugitive or are prepared to send a citizen to face an American court on the clear understanding that the death penalty will not be carried out . . . It would be a fundamental blow to the extradition arrangements between our two countries if the death penalty were carried out on an individual who had been returned under those circumstances' . . . Nonetheless, the effectiveness of such an undertaking has not yet been put to the test.

98. The applicant contended that representations concerning the wishes of a foreign government would not be admissible as a matter of law under the Virginia Code or, if admissible, of any influence on the sentencing judge.

Whatever the position under Virginia law and practice . . . and not withstanding the diplomatic context of the extradition between the United Kingdom and the United States, objectively it cannot be said that the undertaking to inform the judge at the sentencing stage of the wishes of the United Kingdom eliminates the risk of the death penalty being imposed. In the independent exercise of his discretion the Commonwealth's Attorney has himself decided to seek and to persist in seeking the death penalty because the evidence, in his determination, supports such action...If the national authority with responsibility for prosecuting the offence takes such a firm stance, it is hardly open to the Court to hold that there are no substantial grounds for believing that the applicant faces a real risk of being sentenced to death and hence experiencing the 'death row phenomenon'.

99. The Court's conclusion is therefore that the likelihood of the feared exposure of the applicant to the 'death row phenomenon' has been shown to be such as to bring Article 3 (art 3) into play.

2. Whether in the circumstances the risk of exposure to the 'death row phenomenon' would make extradition a breach of Article 3 (art 3)

(a) General considerations

100. As is established in the Court's case-law, ill-treatment, including punishment, must attain a minimum level of severity if it is to fall within the scope of Article 3 (art 3). The assessment of this minimum is, in the nature of things, relative; it depends on all the circumstances of the case, such as the nature and context of the treatment or punishment, the manner and method of its execution, its duration, its physical or mental effects and, in some instances, the sex, age and state of health of the victim (see the...*Ireland v UK* judgment, Series A No 25, p 65, § 162; and the *Tyrer* judgment of 25 April 1978, Series A No 26, pp 14–15, §§ 29 and 30).

Treatment has been held by the Court to be both 'inhuman' because it was premeditated, was applied for hours at a stretch and 'caused, if not actual bodily injury, at least intense physical and mental suffering', and also 'degrading' because it was 'such as to arouse in [its] victims feelings of fear, anguish and inferiority capable of humiliating and debasing them and possibly breaking their physical or moral resistance' (see the above-mentioned *Ireland v UK* judgment, p 66, § 167). In order for a punishment or treatment associated with it to be 'inhuman' or 'degrading', the suffering or humiliation involved must in any event go beyond that inevitable element of suffering or humiliation connected with a given form of legitimate punishment (see the *Tyrer* judgment, loc. cit.). In this connection, account is to be taken not only of the physical pain experienced but also, where there is a considerable delay before execution of the punishment, of the sentenced person's mental anguish of anticipating the violence he is to have inflicted on him.

101. Capital punishment is permitted under certain conditions by Article 2 § 1 (art 2-1) of the Convention, which reads:

> 'Everyone's right to life shall be protected by law. No one shall be deprived of his life intentionally save in the execution of a sentence of a court following his conviction of a crime for which this penalty is provided by law.'

In view of this wording, the applicant did not suggest that the death penalty per se violated Article 3 (art 3). He, like the two Government Parties, agreed with the Commission that the extradition of a person to a country where he risks the death penalty does not in itself raise an issue under either Article 2 (art 2) or Article 3 (art 3). On the other hand, Amnesty International in their written comments...argued that the evolving standards in Western Europe regarding the existence and use of the death penalty required that the death penalty should now be considered as an inhuman and degrading punishment within the meaning of Article 3 (art 3).

102. Certainly, 'the Convention is a living instrument which...must be interpreted in the light of present-day conditions'; and, in assessing whether a given treatment or punishment is to be regarded as inhuman or degrading for the purposes of Article 3 (art 3), 'the Court cannot but be influenced by the developments and commonly accepted standards in the penal policy of the member States of the Council of Europe in this field' (see the above-mentioned *Tyrer* judgment, Series A No 26, pp 15–16, § 31). *De facto* the death penalty no longer exists in time of peace in the Contracting States to the Convention. In the few Contracting States which retain the death penalty in law for some peacetime offences, death sentences, if ever imposed, are nowadays not carried

out. This 'virtual consensus in Western European legal systems that the death penalty is, under current circumstances, no longer consistent with regional standards of justice', to use the words of Amnesty International, is reflected in Protocol No 6 (P6) to the Convention, which provides for the abolition of the death penalty in time of peace. Protocol No 6 (P6) was opened for signature in April 1983, which in the practice of the Council of Europe indicates the absence of objection on the part of any of the Member States of the Organisation; it came into force in March 1985 and to date has been ratified by thirteen Contracting States to the Convention, not however including the United Kingdom.

Whether these marked changes have the effect of bringing the death penalty *per se* within the prohibition of ill-treatment under Article 3 (art 3) must be determined on the principles governing the interpretation of the Convention.

103. The Convention is to be read as a whole and Article 3 (art 3) should therefore be construed in harmony with the provisions of Article 2 (art 2) (see, *mutatis mutandis*, the *Klass* judgment of 6 September 1978, Series A No 28, p 31, § 68). On this basis Article 3 (art 3) evidently cannot have been intended by the drafters of the Convention to include a general prohibition of the death penalty since that would nullify the clear wording of Article 2 § 1 (art 2-1).

Subsequent practice in national penal policy, in the form of a generalised abolition of capital punishment, could be taken as establishing the agreement of the Contracting States to abrogate the exception provided for under Article 2 § 1 (art 2-1) and hence to remove a textual limit on the scope for evolutive interpretation of Article 3 (art 3). However, Protocol No 6 (P6), as a subsequent written agreement, shows that the intention of the Contracting Parties as recently as 1983 was to adopt the normal method of amendment of the text in order to introduce a new obligation to abolish capital punishment in time of peace and, what is more, to do so by an optional instrument allowing each State to choose the moment when to undertake such an engagement. In these conditions, notwithstanding the special character of the Convention (see paragraph 87 above), Article 3 (art 3) cannot be interpreted as generally prohibiting the death penalty.

104. That does not mean however that circumstances relating to a death sentence can never give rise to an issue under Article 3 (art 3). The manner in which it is imposed or executed, the personal circumstances of the condemned person and a disproportionality to the gravity of the crime committed, as well as the conditions of detention awaiting execution, are examples of factors capable of bringing the treatment or punishment received by the condemned person within the proscription under Article 3 (art 3). Present-day attitudes in the Contracting States to capital punishment are relevant for the assessment whether the acceptable threshold of suffering or degradation has been exceeded.

(b) The particular circumstances

105. The applicant submitted that the circumstances to which he would be exposed as a consequence of the implementation of the Secretary of State's decision to return him to the United States, namely the 'death row phenomenon', cumulatively constituted such serious treatment that his extradition would be contrary to Article 3 (art 3). He cited in particular the delays in the appeal and review procedures following a death sentence, during which time he would be subject to increasing tension and psychological trauma; the fact, so he said, that the judge or jury in determining sentence is not obliged to take into account the defendant's age and mental state at the time of the offence; the extreme conditions of his future detention on 'death row' in Mecklenburg Correctional Center, where he expects to be the victim of violence and sexual abuse because of his age, colour and nationality; and the constant spectre of the execution itself including the ritual of execution. He also relied on the possibility of extradition or deportation, which he would not oppose, to the Federal Republic of Germany as accentuating the disproportionality of the Secretary of State's decision.

The Government of the Federal Republic of Germany took the view that, taking all the circumstances together, the treatment awaiting the applicant in Virginia would go so far beyond treatment inevitably connected with the imposition and execution of a death penalty as to be 'inhuman' within the meaning of Article 3 (art 3).

On the other hand, the conclusion expressed by the Commission was that the degree of severity contemplated by Article 3 (art 3) would not be attained.

The United Kingdom Government shared this opinion. In particular, they disputed many of the applicant's factual allegations as to the conditions on death row in Mecklenburg and his expected fate there.

I. Length of detention prior to execution

106. The period that a condemned prisoner can expect to spend on death row in Virginia before being executed is on average six to eight years . . . This length of time awaiting death is, as the Commission and the United Kingdom Government noted, in a sense largely of the prisoner's own making in that he takes advantage of all avenues of appeal which are offered to him by Virginia law. The automatic appeal to the Supreme Court of Virginia normally takes no more than six months . . . The remaining time is accounted for by collateral attacks mounted by the prisoner himself in habeas corpus proceedings before both the State and Federal courts and in applications to the Supreme Court of the United States for *certiorari* review, the prisoner at each stage being able to seek a stay of execution . . . The remedies available under Virginia law serve the purpose of ensuring that the ultimate sanction of death is not unlawfully or arbitrarily imposed.

Nevertheless, just as some lapse of time between sentence and execution is inevitable if appeal safeguards are to be provided to the condemned person, so it is equally part of human nature that the person will cling to life by exploiting those safeguards to the full. However well-intentioned and even potentially beneficial is the provision of the complex of post-sentence procedures in Virginia, the consequence is that the condemned prisoner has to endure for many years the conditions on death row and the anguish and mounting tension of living in the ever-present shadow of death.

II. Conditions on death row

107. As to conditions in Mecklenburg Correctional Center, where the applicant could expect to be held if sentenced to death, the Court bases itself on the facts which were uncontested by the United Kingdom Government, without finding it necessary to determine the reliability of the additional evidence adduced by the applicant, notably as to the risk of homosexual abuse and physical attack undergone by prisoners on death row . . .

. . . In this connection, the United Kingdom Government drew attention to the necessary requirement of extra security for the safe custody of prisoners condemned to death for murder. While it might thus well be justifiable in principle, the severity of a special regime such as that operated on death row in Mecklenburg is compounded by the fact of inmates being subject to it for a protracted period lasting on average six to eight years.

III. The applicant's age and mental state

108. At the time of the killings, the applicant was only 18 years old and there is some psychiatric evidence, which was not contested as such, that he 'was suffering from [such] an abnormality of mind . . . as substantially impaired his mental responsibility for his acts' . . .

Unlike Article 2 (art 2) of the Convention, Article 6 of the 1966 International Covenant on Civil and Political Rights and Article 4 of the 1969 American Convention on Human Rights expressly prohibit the death penalty from being imposed on persons aged less than 18 at the time of commission of the offence. Whether or not such a prohibition be inherent in the brief and general language of Article 2 (art 2) of the European Convention, its explicit enunciation in other, later international instruments, the former of which has been ratified by a large number of States Parties to the European Convention, at the very least indicates that as a general principle the youth of the person concerned is a circumstance which is liable, with others, to put in question the compatibility with Article 3 (art 3) of measures connected with a death sentence.

It is in line with the Court's case-law (as summarised above at paragraph 100) to treat disturbed mental health as having the same effect for the application of Article 3 (art 3).

109. Virginia law, as the United Kingdom Government and the Commission emphasised, certainly does not ignore these two factors. Under the Virginia Code account has to be taken of mental disturbance in a defendant, either as an absolute bar to conviction if it is judged to be sufficient to amount to insanity or, like age, as a fact in mitigation at the sentencing stage . . . Additionally, indigent capital murder defendants are entitled to the appointment of a qualified mental health expert to assist in the preparation of their submissions at the separate sentencing proceedings . . . These provisions in the Virginia Code undoubtedly serve, as the American courts have stated, to prevent the arbitrary or capricious imposition of the death penalty and narrowly to channel the sentencer's discretion . . . They do not however remove the relevance of age and mental condition in relation to the acceptability, under Article 3 (art 3), of the 'death row phenomenon' for a given individual once condemned to death.

Although it is not for this Court to prejudge issues of criminal responsibility and appropriate sentence, the applicant's youth at the time of the offence and his then mental state, on the psychiatric evidence as it stands, are therefore to be taken into consideration as contributory factors tending, in his case, to bring the treatment on death row within the terms of Article 3 (art 3).

IV. Possibility of extradition to the Federal Republic of Germany

110. For the United Kingdom Government and the majority of the Commission, the possibility of extraditing or deporting the applicant to face trial in the Federal Republic of Germany . . . where the death penalty has been abolished under the Constitution . . . is not material for the present purposes. Any other approach, the United Kingdom Government submitted, would lead to a 'dual standard' affording the protection of the Convention to extraditable persons fortunate enough to have such an alternative destination available but refusing it to others not so fortunate.

This argument is not without weight. Furthermore, the Court cannot overlook either the horrible nature of the murders with which Mr Soering is charged or the legitimate and beneficial role of extradition arrangements in combating crime. The purpose for which his removal to the United States was sought, in accordance with the Extradition Treaty between the United Kingdom and the United States, is undoubtedly a legitimate one. However, sending Mr Soering to be tried in his own country would remove the danger of a fugitive criminal going unpunished as well as the risk of intense and protracted suffering on death row. It is therefore a circumstance of relevance for the overall assessment under Article 3 (art 3) in that it goes to the search for the requisite fair balance of interests and to the proportionality of the contested extradition decision in the particular case (see paragraphs 89 and 104 above).

(c) Conclusion

111. For any prisoner condemned to death, some element of delay between imposition and execution of the sentence and the experience of severe stress in conditions necessary for strict incarceration are inevitable. The democratic character of the Virginia legal system in general and the positive features of Virginia trial, sentencing and appeal procedures in particular are beyond doubt. The Court agrees with the Commission that the machinery of justice to which the applicant would be subject in the United States is in itself neither arbitrary nor unreasonable, but, rather, respects the rule of law and affords not inconsiderable procedural safeguards to the defendant in a capital trial. Facilities are available on death row for the assistance of inmates, notably through provision of psychological and psychiatric services . . . However, in the Court's view, having regard to the very long period of time spent on death row in such extreme conditions, with the ever present and mounting anguish of awaiting execution of the death penalty, and to the personal circumstances of the applicant, especially his age and mental state at the time of the offence, the applicant's extradition to the United States would expose him to a real risk of treatment going beyond the threshold set by Article 3 (art 3). A further consideration of relevance is that in the particular instance the legitimate

purpose of extradition could be achieved by another means which would not involve suffering of such exceptional intensity or duration.

Accordingly, the Secretary of State's decision to extradite the applicant to the United States would, if implemented, give rise to a breach of Article 3 (art 3).

This finding in no way puts in question the good faith of the United Kingdom Government, who have from the outset of the present proceedings demonstrated their desire to abide by their Convention obligations, firstly by staying the applicant's surrender to the United States authorities in accord with the interim measures indicated by the Convention institutions and secondly by themselves referring the case to the Court for a judicial ruling...

FOR THESE REASONS, THE COURT UNANIMOUSLY

I. Holds that, in the event of the Secretary of State's decision to extradite the applicant to the United States of America being implemented, there would be a violation of Article 3; ...

NOTES

1 The plenary Court was composed of President Ryssdal and Judges: Cremona, Thor Vilhjalmsson, Gölcüklü, Matscher, Pettiti, Walsh, Evans, Macdonald, Russo, Bernhardt, Spielmann, De Meyer, Carrillo Salcedo, Valticos, Martens, Palm, and Foighel.

Soering was eventually extradited to the USA after the UK received an assurance that he would not be prosecuted on capital charges.

The British Parliament abolished the death penalty for the remaining civilian offences of treason and piracy (Crime and Disorder Act 1998) and for military offences, in times of peace and war (Human Rights Act 1998) during 1998. Subsequently, the UK ratified Protocol 6 (abolition of the death penalty in peacetime) on 20 May 1999 and Protocol 13 (abolition of the death penalty in all circumstances) on 10 October 2003.

2 The **Soering** principle has been extended by the Court to cover member States' decisions to deport or expel aliens in *Cruz Varas v Sweden* A.201 (1991). The applicants were a husband, wife, and their son all of whom held Chilean citizenship. The husband arrived in Sweden in January 1987 and applied for political asylum. At first he claimed that he had been a member of various left-wing political groups in Chile in the 1960s and 1970s, but that he left Chile for financial reasons. The Swedish National Immigration Board and the Government rejected his request for asylum. Some months later he informed the Swedish authorities that he had been tortured by members of the Chilean security forces in 1986. The Swedish Government decided to continue with his expulsion and he was expelled from Sweden (to Chile) in October 1989. He complained to the Commission alleging, *inter alia*, a breach of Article 3. A majority of that body, 8 votes to 5, found no breach of Article 3. The Court held:

69. In its *Soering* judgment of 7 July 1989 the Court held that the decision by a Contracting State to extradite a fugitive may give rise to an issue under Article 3 (art 3), and hence engage the responsibility of that State under the Convention, where substantial grounds have been shown for believing that the person concerned, if extradited, faces a real risk of being subjected to torture or to inhuman or degrading treatment or punishment in the requesting country (Series A No 161, p 35, § 91).

Although the establishment of such responsibility involves an assessment of conditions in the requesting country against the standards of Article 3 (art 3), there is no question of adjudicating on or establishing the responsibility of the receiving country, whether under general international law, under the Convention or otherwise. In so far as any liability under the Convention is or may be incurred, it is liability incurred by the extraditing Contracting State by reason of its having taken action which has as a direct consequence the exposure of an individual to proscribed ill-treatment (ibid, p 36, § 91).

70. Although the present case concerns expulsion as opposed to a decision to extradite, the Court considers that the above principle also applies to expulsion decisions and a fortiori to cases of actual expulsion.

75. In determining whether substantial grounds have been shown for believing in the existence of a real risk of treatment contrary to Article 3 (art 3) the Court will assess the issue in the light of all the material placed before it or, if necessary, material obtained proprio motu (see the *Ireland v UK* judgment of 18 January 1978, Series A No 25, p 64, § 160).

76. Since the nature of the Contracting States' responsibility under Article 3 (art 3) in cases of this kind lies in the act of exposing an individual to the risk of ill-treatment, the existence of the risk must be assessed primarily with reference to those facts which were known or ought to have been known to the Contracting State at the time of the expulsion; the Court is not precluded, however, from having regard to information which comes to light subsequent to the expulsion. This may be of value in confirming or refuting the appreciation that has been made by the Contracting Party or the well-foundedness or otherwise of an applicant's fears.

A majority of the Court, 18 votes to 1, went on to find that the principle's requirements had not been satisfied in this case because, *inter alia*, of doubts regarding the credibility of the applicant's claims regarding his alleged maltreatment in Chile, the re-emergence of democracy in Chile, and the thorough examination of the applicant's case by the Swedish immigration authorities. Therefore, no breach of Article 3 had occurred.

3   The Court has held that mere membership of a minority group, which is caught up in a foreign civil conflict, is not of itself enough to satisfy the **Soering** principle. The evidence must show that there were substantial grounds for believing that the particular applicant was at real risk of being subject to prohibited treatment if he/she was to be deported back to the State where the conflict was occurring. In **Vilvarajah v UK** A.215 (1991), the applicants were Sri Lankan citizens of Tamil ethnic origin. Tamils make up about 20 per cent of the population of Sri Lanka and there has been ethnic conflict between the majority Sinhalese and the minority Tamils for several decades. The applicants were refused political asylum in the UK and returned to Sri Lanka where several of them claimed to have been seriously mistreated by security officials (one applicant alleged that he was beaten with belts and kicked for about half an hour by police officers). Subsequently, the British authorities allowed them to return to stay in the UK. The Commission, on the casting vote of the President, expressed the opinion that there had been no breach of Article 3 in respect of the UK's original decisions to deport the applicants. A majority of the Court, 8 votes to 1, upheld that finding.

111. The evidence before the Court concerning the background of the applicants, as well as the general situation, does not establish that their personal position was any worse than the generality of other members of the Tamil community or other young male Tamils who were returning to their country. Since the situation was still unsettled there existed the possibility that they might be detained and ill-treated as appears to have occurred previously in the cases of some of the applicants . . . A mere possibility of ill-treatment, however, in such circumstances, is not in itself sufficient to give rise to a breach of Article 3.

During 2007 the security situation in Sri Lanka deteriorated and more Tamils sought asylum in the UK. The Court granted interim measures in over 340 cases preventing the UK from returning the applicants prior to a determination of their Strasbourg complaints. In a lead case **NA v UK**, judgment of 17 July 2008, a unanimous Chamber held that assessing the Article 3 risk of maltreatment if a particular applicant was to be returned to Sri Lanka had to be undertaken on an individual basis. The Court endorsed the UK's use of a list of 'risk factors' including: a record as a suspected/actual member of the Liberation Tigers of Tamil Eelam (Tamil Tigers), having relatives in the Tigers, and having made an asylum claim.

In May 2009 the Sri Lankan Government proclaimed military victory over the Tamil Tigers.

4 The Court ruled in **Chahal v UK**, 1996-V, that the conduct of the individual was not a relevant factor in the application of the **Soering** principle. Mr Chahal is an Indian citizen who illegally entered the UK in 1971. Three years later he was given indefinite leave to remain under the terms of an amnesty for illegal entrants. Subsequently he married another Indian citizen and she came to live with him in the UK. They had two children born in the UK (who have British citizenship). In the early 1980s Mr Chahal visited the Punjab province and was baptised into Sikhism. At this time there was considerable violence taking place between Sikh separatists, who wanted an independent State, and Indian security forces; since 1984 over 20,000 people have been killed in this conflict. When he returned to the UK Mr Chahal became a leading figure in the Sikh community and he organized protests against the Indian Government. He was arrested several times, on suspicion of conspiring to kill the Indian Prime Minister and moderate Sikhs in the UK, but he was released without charge. In 1990 the Home Secretary decided that Mr Chahal ought to be deported as his presence in the UK was contrary to the public good for reasons of national security and the international fight against terrorism. The Secretary ordered the detention of Chahal who sought, unsuccessfully, to challenge that decision before an advisory panel and in judicial review proceedings. Chahal complained to the Commission and it requested the UK to stay the deportation of the applicant. Later the Commission expressed the unanimous opinion that, *inter alia*, there would be a breach of Article 3 if the applicant were to be deported to India because of the applicant's notoriety and the level of violence against Sikh separatists and their supporters in that country. Before the Court, the British Government argued that the guarantees under Article 3 were not absolute where the applicant posed a threat to the national security of the member State. However, this limitation was not accepted by the Court:

79. Article 3 (art 3) enshrines one of the most fundamental values of democratic society (see…*Soering* judgment, p 34, para 88). The Court is well aware of the immense difficulties faced by States in modern times in protecting their communities from terrorist violence. However, even in these circumstances, the Convention prohibits in absolute terms torture or inhuman or degrading treatment or punishment, irrespective of the victim's conduct. Unlike most of the substantive clauses of the Convention and of Protocols Nos. 1 and 4 (P1, P4), Article 3 (art 3) makes no provision for exceptions and no derogation from it is permissible under Article 15 (art 15) even in the event of a public emergency threatening the life of the nation (see the *Ireland v UK* judgment of 18 January 1978, Series A No 25, p 65, para 163, and also the *Tomasi v France* judgment of 27 August 1992, Series A No 241-A, p 42, para 115).

80. The prohibition provided by Article 3 (art 3) against ill-treatment is equally absolute in expulsion cases. Thus, whenever substantial grounds have been shown for believing that an individual would face a real risk of being subjected to treatment contrary to Article 3 (art 3) if removed to another State, the responsibility of the Contracting State to safeguard him or her against such treatment is engaged in the event of expulsion (see the … *Vilvarajah* judgment, p 34, para 103). In these circumstances, the activities of the individual in question, however undesirable or dangerous, cannot be a material consideration…

81. Paragraph 88 of the Court's above-mentioned *Soering* judgment, which concerned extradition to the United States, clearly and forcefully expresses the above view. It should not be inferred from the Court's remarks concerning the risk of undermining the foundations of extradition, as set out in paragraph 89 of the same judgment, that there is any room for balancing the risk of ill-treatment against the reasons for expulsion in determining whether a State's responsibility under Article 3 (art 3) is engaged.

82. It follows from the above that it is not necessary for the Court to enter into a consideration of the Government's untested, but no doubt bona fide, allegations about the first applicant's terrorist activities and the threat posed by him to national security.

C. APPLICATION OF ARTICLE 3 (ART 3) IN THE CIRCUMSTANCES OF THE CASE

1. The point of time for the assessment of the risk

83. Although there were differing views on the situation in India and in Punjab . . . it was agreed that the violence and instability in that region reached a peak in 1992 and had been abating ever since. For this reason, the date taken by the Court for its assessment of the risk to Mr Chahal if expelled to India is of importance.

84. The applicant argued that the Court should consider the position in June 1992, at the time when the decision to deport him was made final . . . The purpose of the stay on removal requested by the Commission . . . was to prevent irremediable damage and not to afford the High Contracting Party with an opportunity to improve its case. Moreover, it was not appropriate that the Strasbourg organs should be involved in a continual fact-finding operation.

85. The Government, with whom the Commission agreed, submitted that because the responsibility of the State under Article 3 of the Convention (art 3) in expulsion cases lies in the act of exposing an individual to a real risk of ill-treatment, the material date for the assessment of risk was the time of the proposed deportation. Since Mr Chahal had not yet been expelled, the relevant time was that of the proceedings before the Court.

86. . . . as far as the applicant's complaint under Article 3 (art 3) is concerned, the crucial question is whether it has been substantiated that there is a real risk that Mr Chahal, if expelled, would be subjected to treatment prohibited by that Article (art 3). Since he has not yet been deported, the material point in time must be that of the Court's consideration of the case. It follows that, although the historical position is of interest in so far as it may shed light on the current situation and its likely evolution, it is the present conditions which are decisive . . .

A majority of the Court, 12 votes to 7, went on to determine that the evidence showed that the contemporary involvement of the Indian security forces in killings and serious human rights violations associated with the problems in the Punjab meant that there was a real risk of Mr Chahal being subject to treatment contrary to Article 3 if he were to be deported to India. Therefore, the UK would violate Article 3 if it were to implement the Home Secretary's deportation order.

In addition to reinforcing the absolute nature of the guarantees contained in Article 3, the above judgment also provides valuable guidance regarding the time at which the risk to the applicant should be assessed. Where the applicant has been extradited/deported the date of that action will be appropriate, but where the applicant has not yet been expelled the Court will consider the risk at the time of the determination of the case at Strasbourg.

With the continued growth of international terrorism some member States became increasingly unhappy with the restrictions *Chahal* placed on their ability to deport/extradite foreign nationals from their territories. In *Saadi v Italy*, judgment of 28 February 2008, the British Government intervened as a third party to argue (with the support of the Italian Government) that *Chahal* had caused governments many difficulties in practice and that the Court should adopt a new test that took account of the threat posed by the foreign national to the host member State. The unanimous Grand Chamber responded that whilst:

137. ...It cannot therefore underestimate the scale of the danger of terrorism today and the threat it presents to the community. That must not, however, call into question the absolute nature of Article 3.

138. ...It must therefore reaffirm the principle stated in the *Chahal* judgment that it is not possible to weigh the risk of ill-treatment against the reasons put forward for the expulsion in order to determine whether the responsibility of a State is engaged under Article 3, even where such treatment is inflicted by another State. In that connection, the conduct of the person concerned however undesirable or dangerous, cannot be taken into account...

Consequently, as the applicant had established a real risk that he would suffer severe maltreatment by the authorities if he was deported to Tunisia, the Grand Chamber determined a breach of Article 3 would occur if his deportation was to be implemented.

    Saadi demonstrated the Court's unwillingness to reduce the level of protection granted by Article 3, for further analysis of the judgment, see D. Moeckli, '*Saadi v Italy*: The Rules of the Game Have Not Changed' (2008) 8(3) *Human Rights Law Review* 534.

5   The nature and sources of the prohibited forms of treatment which fall within the *Soering* principle were defined very broadly by the unanimous Court in *D v UK*, 1997-III. The applicant was a citizen of St Kitts who was in the terminal stages of AIDS (Acquired Immunodeficiency Syndrome). He had sought to enter the UK in 1993, but was found to be in possession of a large quantity of cocaine. He was formally refused entry to the UK and arrested. Subsequently, he pleaded guilty to being knowingly involved in the fraudulent evasion of the prohibition on the importation of controlled drugs into the UK. He was sentenced to six years' imprisonment. While in prison it was discovered that the applicant was HIV (Human Immunodeficiency Virus) positive, the infection appeared to have occurred at some time prior to his arrival in the UK. He was given medical treatment and allowed a period of compassionate leave in 1995. Prior to his release from prison in January 1996 (on licence because of his good behaviour) the immigration authorities gave directions for his deportation to St Kitts. The applicant's lawyers sought leave for him to remain in the UK on compassionate grounds as they argued that he would not be able to receive the same specialist medical care in St Kitts that he was currently receiving in the UK, thereby shortening his life expectancy. The Chief Immigration Officer refused the request and judicial review proceedings were also unsuccessful. The applicant complained to the Commission and it requested the UK not to deport him while his case was being examined. The Commission, by 11 votes to 7, expressed the opinion that there would be a breach of Article 3 if the applicant were to be deported. Before the Court, the applicant's lawyers argued that his removal to St Kitts would condemn him to an even earlier death in conditions of squalor and destitution (as he had no close relatives or friends to care for him and expensive drug therapies were not available to patients with HIV/AIDS in St Kitts).

B. THE COURT'S ASSESSMENT

46. The Court recalls at the outset that Contracting States have the right, as a matter of well-established international law and subject to their treaty obligations including the Convention, to control the entry, residence and expulsion of aliens. It also notes the gravity of the offence which was

committed by the applicant and is acutely aware of the problems confronting Contracting States in their efforts to combat the harm caused to their societies through the supply of drugs from abroad. The administration of severe sanctions to persons involved in drug trafficking, including expulsion of alien drug couriers like the applicant, is a justified response to this scourge.

47. However, in exercising their right to expel such aliens Contracting States must have regard to Article 3 of the Convention (art 3), which enshrines one of the fundamental values of democratic societies. It is precisely for this reason that the Court has repeatedly stressed in its line of authorities involving extradition, expulsion or deportation of individuals to third countries that Article 3 (art 3) prohibits in absolute terms torture or inhuman or degrading treatment or punishment and that its guarantees apply irrespective of the reprehensible nature of the conduct of the person in question...

48. The Court observes that the above principle is applicable to the applicant's removal under the Immigration Act 1971. Regardless of whether or not he ever entered the United Kingdom in the technical sense...is to be noted that he has been physically present there and thus within the jurisdiction of the respondent State within the meaning of Article 1 of the Convention (art 1) since 21 January 1993. It is for the respondent State therefore to secure to the applicant the rights guaranteed under Article 3 (art 3) irrespective of the gravity of the offence which he committed.

49. It is true that this principle has so far been applied by the Court in contexts in which the risk to the individual of being subjected to any of the proscribed forms of treatment emanates from intentionally inflicted acts of the public authorities in the receiving country or from those of non-State bodies in that country when the authorities there are unable to afford him appropriate protection...Aside from these situations and given the fundamental importance of Article 3 (art 3) in the Convention system, the Court must reserve to itself sufficient flexibility to address the application of that Article (art 3) in other contexts which might arise. It is not therefore prevented from scrutinising an applicant's claim under Article 3 (art 3) where the source of the risk of proscribed treatment in the receiving country stems from factors which cannot engage either directly or indirectly the responsibility of the public authorities of that country, or which, taken alone, do not in themselves infringe the standards of that Article (art 3). To limit the application of Article 3 (art 3) in this manner would be to undermine the absolute character of its protection. In any such contexts, however, the Court must subject all the circumstances surrounding the case to a rigorous scrutiny, especially the applicant's personal situation in the expelling State.

50. Against this background the Court will determine whether there is a real risk that the applicant's removal would be contrary to the standards of Article 3 (art 3) in view of his present medical condition. In so doing the Court will assess the risk in the light of the material before it at the time of its consideration of the case, including the most recent information on his state of health...

51. The Court notes that the applicant is in the advanced stages of a terminal and incurable illness. At the date of the hearing, it was observed that there had been a marked decline in his condition and he had to be transferred to a hospital. His condition was giving rise to concern...The limited quality of life he now enjoys results from the availability of sophisticated treatment and medication in the United Kingdom and the care and kindness administered by a charitable organisation. He has been counselled on how to approach death and has formed bonds with his carers.

52. The abrupt withdrawal of these facilities will entail the most dramatic consequences for him. It is not disputed that his removal will hasten his death. There is a serious danger that the conditions of adversity which await him in St Kitts will further reduce his already limited life expectancy and subject him to acute mental and physical suffering. Any medical treatment which he might hope to receive there could not contend with the infections which he may possibly contract on account of his lack of shelter and of a proper diet as well as exposure to the health and sanitation problems which beset the population of St Kitts...While he may have a cousin in St Kitts...no evidence has

been adduced to show whether this person would be willing or in a position to attend to the needs of a terminally ill man. There is no evidence of any other form of moral or social support. Nor has it been shown whether the applicant would be guaranteed a bed in either of the hospitals on the island which, according to the Government, care for AIDS patients...

53. In view of these exceptional circumstances and bearing in mind the critical stage now reached in the applicant's fatal illness, the implementation of the decision to remove him to St Kitts would amount to inhuman treatment by the respondent State in violation of Article 3 (art 3).

The Court also notes in this respect that the respondent State has assumed responsibility for treating the applicant's condition since August 1994. He has become reliant on the medical and palliative care which he is at present receiving and is no doubt psychologically prepared for death in an environment which is both familiar and compassionate. Although it cannot be said that the conditions which would confront him in the receiving country are themselves a breach of the standards of Article 3 (art 3), his removal would expose him to a real risk of dying under most distressing circumstances and would thus amount to inhuman treatment...

54. Against this background the Court emphasises that aliens who have served their prison sentences and are subject to expulsion cannot in principle claim any entitlement to remain in the territory of a Contracting State in order to continue to benefit from medical, social or other forms of assistance provided by the expelling State during their stay in prison.

However, in the very exceptional circumstances of this case and given the compelling humanitarian considerations at stake, it must be concluded that the implementation of the decision to remove the applicant would be a violation of Article 3 (art 3)...

Clearly the Court was motivated by the extreme plight of the applicant's situation in concluding that deportation to his country of birth would amount to inhuman treatment. Given the increase in HIV/AIDS in many countries it is, sadly, not surprising that other non-nationals infected with HIV (or suffering from alternative serious medical conditions) subsequently contended that their deportation from a variety of member States to their home States would violate Article 3. However a Grand Chamber confirmed that *D v UK* applied only in the most exceptional circumstances: *N v UK*, judgment of 27 May 2008. The applicant in the latter case was a Ugandan national who entered the UK in 1998. She was immediately admitted to hospital where she was diagnosed as HIV positive. Over the following nine years she received extensive medical treatment from the National Health Service, whilst she unsuccessfully sought asylum. That medical treatment greatly improved her health and the use of antiretroviral drugs stabilized her HIV. Before the Court she contended that her deportation would breach Article 3 as her home town hospital was unable to cope with AIDS and she was too weak to work or pay for medication. The Grand Chamber noted that since *D v UK* the Court had never upheld a health-related deportation challenge under Article 3.

42. In summary, the Court observes that since *D. v the United Kingdom* it has consistently applied the following principles.

Aliens who are subject to expulsion cannot in principle claim any entitlement to remain in the territory of a Contracting State in order to continue to benefit from medical, social or other forms of assistance and services provided by the expelling State. The fact that the applicant's circumstances, including his life expectancy, would be significantly reduced if he were to be removed from the Contracting State is not sufficient in itself to give rise to breach of Article 3. The decision to remove an alien who is suffering from a serious mental or physical illness to a country where the facilities for the treatment of that illness are inferior to those available in the Contracting State may raise an issue under Article 3, but only in a very exceptional case, where the humanitarian grounds against the removal are compelling. In the *D.* case the very exceptional circumstances were that the applicant was critically ill and appeared to be close to death, could not be guaranteed any nursing or medical care in his country of origin and had no family there willing or able to care for him or provide him with even a basic level of food, shelter or social support.

43. The Court does not exclude that there may be other very exceptional cases where the humanitarian considerations are equally compelling. However, it considers that it should maintain the high threshold set in *D. v the United Kingdom* and applied in its subsequent case-law, which it regards as correct in principle, given that in such cases the alleged future harm would emanate not from the intentional acts or omissions of public authorities or non-State bodies, but instead from a naturally occurring illness and the lack of sufficient resources to deal with it in the receiving country.

A large majority, 14 votes to 3, concluded that as the applicant was not critically ill her situation could be distinguished from that of *D*, therefore the UK would not be in breach of Article 3 if the applicant was to be deported to Uganda. Consequently, only a foreign national who is facing deportation during the final stages of a terminal illness and who will not receive any suitable care in his/her home State is likely to succeed with an Article 3 complaint.

6   One day after giving judgment in the case of *D v UK*, the Court further broadened the scope of the *Soering* principle by stating that the source of the risk of an applicant being subject to treatment contrary to Article 3 could arise from the actions of private persons, such as organized criminals. In *HLR v France*, 1997–III, the applicant was a Colombian national who was arrested at a French airport in possession of 580g of cocaine. While being questioned by the police the applicant provided officers with information on other persons involved in the smuggling of drugs. This information facilitated the conviction of another person for drug smuggling in Germany. The applicant was convicted of drug offences and sentenced to five years' imprisonment and permanent exclusion from French territory. After the applicant had served his sentence the French authorities began the process of deporting him. He complained to the Commission alleging that if he were to be returned to Colombia he would face a real risk of serious injury or death at the hands of the drug traffickers on whom he had informed. The Commission, by 19 votes to 10, expressed the opinion that if France were to deport the applicant in these circumstances it would amount to a breach of Article 3. The Court held that:

40. Owing to the absolute character of the right guaranteed, the Court does not rule out the possibility that Article 3 of the Convention (art 3) may also apply where the danger emanates from persons or groups of persons who are not public officials. However, it must be shown that the risk is real and that the authorities of the receiving State are not able to obviate the risk by providing appropriate protection.

41. Like the Commission, the Court can but note the general situation of violence existing in the country of destination. It considers, however, that this circumstance would not in itself entail, in the event of deportation, a violation of Article 3 (art 3).

42. The documents from various sources produced in support of the applicant's memorial provide insight into the tense atmosphere in Colombia, but do not contain any indication of the existence of a situation comparable to his own. Although drug traffickers sometimes take revenge on informers, there is no relevant evidence to show in H.L.R.'s case that the alleged risk is real. His aunt's letters cannot by themselves suffice to show that the threat is real. Moreover, there are no documents to support the claim that the applicant's personal situation would be worse than that of other Colombians, were he to be deported.

Amnesty International's reports for 1995 and 1996 do not provide any information on the type of situation in which the applicant finds himself. They describe acts of the security forces and guerrilla movements. Only in the 1995 report is there any reference, in a context which is not relevant to the present case, to criminal acts attributable to drug trafficking organisations.

43. The Court is aware, too, of the difficulties the Colombian authorities face in containing the violence. The applicant has not shown that they are incapable of affording him appropriate protection.

44. In the light of these considerations, the Court finds that no substantial grounds have been established for believing that the applicant, if deported, would be exposed to a real risk of being subjected to inhuman or degrading treatment within the meaning of Article 3 (art 3). It follows that there would be no violation of Article 3 (art 3) if the order for the applicant's deportation were to be executed.

Six judges dissented as they believed that the risk to the applicant was sufficient to satisfy the *Soering* test.

The deportation of aliens may also raise Convention issues under Article 8 (right to respect for family life), see p 531.

7   In *D and Others v Turkey*, judgment of 22 June 2006, a unanimous Chamber held that the deportation of a married woman (together with her husband and child) to her home State of Iran where she had been sentenced to 100 lashes for fornication (she had married her husband in a Sunni ceremony without the consent of her father, a Shia) would constitute inhuman treatment. The Chamber expressed the view that where a legal system permitted such physical violence, even if it was imposed by a symbolic punishment using a special lash with 100 tails, the sentence was 'inhuman'.

For earlier case-law involving corporal punishment see the section below on Degrading punishment.

8   The operation of the European Union's system of allocating responsibility for determining asylum applications was the background to the Grand Chamber's consideration of Article 3 in *MSS v Belgium and Greece*, judgment of 21 January 2011. Under the EU's 'Dublin Regulation' (Council No 343/2003) where an asylum seeker irregularly entered the territory of a member State of the EU, from a third State, that EU State had responsibility for determining the asylum seeker's claim (even if he/she travelled on to another EU member State). The applicant was an Afghan national who entered Greece from Turkey. He was detained, for a week, and then ordered to leave Greece (he did not claim asylum in Greece). Two months later he claimed asylum in Belgium. The Belgian authorities notified the Greek authorities that, under the Dublin Regulation, it was for the latter to determine the applicant's claim. Whilst the applicant's appeals against being deported to Greece were pending, the United Nations High Commissioner for Refugees wrote to the Belgian Government recommending the suspension of such transfers to Greece because of deficiencies in Greek procedures for determining asylum claims and the poor living conditions of asylum seekers in that country. Nevertheless, after the rejection of the applicant's appeals he was transferred to Greece. After three days' detention the applicant was released by the Greek authorities and he claimed that he then had to live in a public park for many months with no accommodation or material support given to him by the Greek authorities (local people and the church gave him some assistance). By large majorities (16 votes to 1 and 15 votes to 2) the Grand Chamber concluded that Belgium had violated Article 3 by deporting

the applicant to Greece when the Belgian authorities knew or ought to have known that there was a real risk that his asylum claim would not be properly determined and he would be exposed to degrading living conditions. A key factor underlying the Grand Chamber's conclusions was the UNCHR's letter. The judgment was significant for confirming that State parties to the ECHR who were also members of the EU could not automatically apply the Dublin Regulation mechanism to deal with claims for asylum, they also had to ensure that any transfer of an asylum seeker to another EU member State respected the asylum seeker's rights under Article 3. In his concurring opinion Judge Rozakis, the judge of Greek nationality, observed:

> ... almost 88% of the immigrants (and among them asylum seekers) entering the EU today cross the Greek borders to land in our continent. In these circumstances it is clear that the EU immigration policy ... does not reflect the present realities, or do justice to the disproportionate burden that falls to the Greek immigration authorities.

Inhuman punishment

Chember v Russia judgment of 3 July 2008
European Court of Human Rights

The applicant had been called up for military service, after passing medical tests, in the Ministry of Internal Affairs forces. He claimed that he injured his spine carrying an axle for a lorry during his service. A couple of weeks later he was transferred to another unit and he complained to a medical officer and a Lieutenant D about constant pains in his knees. During the next month a Sergeant, with Lieutenant D present, ordered the applicant (and fellow servicemen) to do 350 knee bends as punishment for failing to clean their barracks sufficiently. After many knee bends the applicant collapsed and he was taken to the medical unit. After several weeks of treatment in a medical university, the applicant was discharged from military service due to spinal injury acquired during that service. The applicant contended that he had been subject to inhuman treatment and punishment.

> 50. ... the State has a duty to ensure that a person performs military service in conditions which are compatible with respect for his human dignity, that the procedures and methods of military training do not subject him to distress or suffering of an intensity exceeding the unavoidable level of hardship inherent in military discipline and that, given the practical demands of such service, his health and well-being are adequately secured by, among other things, providing him with the medical assistance he requires (see, *mutatis mutandis, Kılınç and Others v Turkey*, no. 40145/98, § 41, 7 June 2005, and *Álvarez Ramón v Spain* (dec.), no. 51192/99, 3 July 2001). The State has a primary duty to put in place rules geared to the level of risk to life or limb that may result not only from the nature of military activities and operations, but also from the human element that comes into play when a State decides to call up ordinary citizens to perform military service. Such rules must require the adoption of practical measures aimed at the effective protection of conscripts against the dangers inherent in military life and appropriate procedures for identifying shortcomings and errors liable to be committed in that regard by those in charge at different levels ...

52. Even though challenging physical exercise may be part and parcel of military discipline, the Court reiterates that, to remain compatible with Article 3 of the Convention, it should not go beyond the level above which it would put in danger the health and well-being of conscripts or undermine their human dignity. In the present case the applicant—who was known to have painful knees—was ordered to do 350 knee bends which appears to be a particularly demanding workout. However, the Court sees no need to determine *in abstracto* whether that particular order was compatible with the requirements of Article 3, for it will have regard to the following elements of the case which it considers crucial for its assessment of compliance with Article 3.

53. The applicant was ordered to do knee bends as punishment for insufficiently thorough cleaning of the barracks. The order emanated from his acting commander Junior Sergeant Ch. It was tacitly endorsed by the higher commander Lieutenant D. who was present at the scene but did not contradict the order. It follows that the treatment complained about was applied on the applicant deliberately.

54. It is obvious from the statements collected in the framework of the domestic inquiry that both Lieutenant D. and Junior Sergeant Ch. were well aware of the applicant's knee-related health problems from the moment of his arrival at the military base. . . . Notwithstanding their awareness of the applicant's specific health problems, the commanders forced the applicant to do precisely the kind of exercise that put great strain on his knees and spine. In these circumstances, the Court cannot but find that the treatment was both deliberate and calculated to cause the applicant physical suffering. The severity of the punishment cannot obviously be accounted for by any requirements of military service or discipline or said to have contributed to the specific mission of the armed force . . .

55. As regards the consequences of the punishment at issue, the Court notes that the applicant collapsed on the spot and lost control of his legs. Despite the emergency treatment he received first in a military and then in a civilian hospital, the injury resulted in long-term damage to his health. The applicant was discharged from the military service and assigned the second category of disability.

56. Assessing the above elements as a whole, the Court finds that in the present case the applicant was subjected to forced physical exercise to the point of physical collapse. This punishment was applied deliberately by his commanders, in full knowledge of the applicant's specific health problems and without there being any military necessity which might have called for that course of action. The Court is of the opinion that in these circumstances that punishment caused the applicant intense physical suffering and went beyond the threshold of a minimum level of severity.

57. Having regard to the above considerations, the Court finds that the applicant was subjected to inhuman punishment in breach of Article 3 of the Convention. There has therefore been a violation of that provision under its substantive limb.

NOTES

1 The unanimous Chamber was composed of President Rozakis and Judges: Vajic, Klover, Steiner, Hajiyev, Malinverni, and Nicolaou.

2 The key findings in the above judgment were that the onerous physical exercises required to be undertaken by the applicant were deliberately imposed as a form of punishment by his superiors, who knew of his health problems, and the consequent serious disability that was inflicted on him. That was a far too brutal measure of military discipline.

Degrading treatment

....

Yankov v Bulgaria judgment of 11 December 2003
European Court of Human Rights

The applicant, a Bulgarian national born in 1943, had a doctorate in economics and was the executive director of an agricultural investment fund and a financial company. In March 1996 he had been arrested and detained in respect of alleged criminal dereliction of his professional duties. He was subsequently held in custody pending his trial. Whilst in prison, on 10 March 1998, prior to a meeting with his lawyers the applicant was searched. The officers found and confiscated a manuscript from the applicant. The manuscript was read and it contained an account of the applicant's prosecution and imprisonment by the authorities. Parts of the manuscript were highly critical of officials: for example 'The search [in the apartment] was conducted by police officer [B]. His inexperience was betrayed by his behaviour, he was a provincial parvenu...The [prison] wardens, most of whom are simple villagers and are better paid than teachers, doctors and engineers, "work" 24 hours and then have a 72-hour rest...' On the same day the prison governor ordered that the applicant be placed in an isolation cell for seven days as punishment for having made offensive remarks about public officials. The applicant contended that the manuscript was the draft of a book he had been writing and he had merely intended to read parts of the manuscript to his lawyers, while the prison officer who seized the manuscript claimed that the applicant had planned to transmit it to his lawyer. Prior to being placed in the isolation cell, the applicant's head was shaved (no other prisoners had witnessed the shaving). Two days after being released from the isolation cell the applicant was brought before a public hearing of the District Court and the fact that his head had been shaved was noticeable. Subsequently the applicant lodged a complaint with the Strasbourg authorities alleging, *inter alia*, that the shaving of his head amounted to a breach of Article 3.

105. In considering whether treatment is 'degrading' within the meaning of Article 3, the Court will have regard to whether its object is to humiliate and debase the person concerned and whether, as far as the consequences are concerned, it adversely affected his or her personality in a manner incompatible with Article 3. Even the absence of such a purpose cannot conclusively rule out a finding of a violation of Article 3 (see, for example, *Peers v Greece*, No 28524/95, § 74, ECHR 2001-III; and *Kalashnikov v Russia*, No 47095/99, § 101, ECHR 2002-VI).

106. Ill-treatment must attain a minimum level of severity if it is to fall within the scope of Article 3 of the Convention. The assessment of this minimum level of severity is relative; it depends on all the circumstances of the case, such as the duration of the treatment, its physical and mental effects and, in some cases, the sex, age and state of health of the victim (see *Ireland v the United Kingdom*, judgment of 18 January 1978, Series A No 25, p. 65, § 162).

107. The Court has consistently stressed that the suffering and humiliation involved must go beyond that inevitable element of suffering or humiliation connected with a given form of legitimate treatment or punishment. Measures depriving a person of his liberty may often involve such an element. The State must ensure that a person is detained in conditions which are compatible with respect for his human dignity, that the manner and method of the execution of the measure do not subject him to distress or hardship of an intensity exceeding the unavoidable level of suffering inherent in detention and that, given the practical demands of imprisonment, his health and well-being are adequately secured (*Kudła v Poland* [GC], No 30210/96, §§ 93–4, ECHR 2000-XI).

2. Application of those principles in the present case

108. The Court notes that the applicant's hair was shaved off before his placement in an isolation cell.

109. The Court has not had occasion to rule on whether or not the forced shaving off of a prisoner's hair may constitute degrading treatment contrary to Article 3 of the Convention.

...

112. A particular characteristic of the treatment complained of, the forced shaving off of a prisoner's hair, is that it consists in a forced change of the person's appearance by the removal of his hair. The person undergoing that treatment is very likely to experience a feeling of inferiority as his physical appearance is changed against his will.

113. Furthermore, for at least a certain period of time a prisoner whose hair has been shaved off carries a mark of the treatment he has undergone. The mark is immediately visible to others, including prison staff, co-detainees and visitors or the public, if the prisoner is released or brought into a public place soon thereafter. The person concerned is very likely to feel hurt in his dignity by the fact that he carries a visible physical mark.

114. The Court thus considers that the forced shaving off of detainees' hair is in principle an act which may have the effect of diminishing their human dignity or may arouse in them feelings of inferiority capable of humiliating and debasing them. Whether or not the minimum threshold of severity is reached and, consequently, whether or not the treatment complained of constitutes degrading treatment contrary to Article 3 of the Convention will depend on the particular facts of the case, including the victim's personal circumstances, the context in which the impugned act was carried out and its aim.

115. The Court rejects as being unsubstantiated the Government's allegation that the applicant's hair was shaved off as a hygienic measure. It has not been alleged that a problem of infestation existed in the particular detention facility. It is also unclear why the hygienic requirements for entry into the isolation cell would differ from those concerning other cells in the same detention facility.

116. The Government have not offered any other explanation. Therefore, even assuming that there was a practice of shaving off of the hair of prisoners punished by confinement in an isolation cell...the act complained of had no legal basis and valid justification.

117. The Court thus considers that even if it was not intended to humiliate, the removal of the applicant's hair without specific justification contained in itself an arbitrary punitive element and was therefore likely to appear in his eyes to be aimed at debasing and/or subduing him.

118. Furthermore, in the particular case the applicant must have had reasons to believe that the aim had been to humiliate him, given the fact that his hair was shaved off by the prison administration in the context of a punishment imposed on him for writing critical and offensive remarks about prison warders, among others.

119. Additional factors to be taken into consideration in the present case are the applicant's age— 55 at the relevant time—and the fact that he appeared at a public hearing nine days after his hair had been shaved off.

120. Having regard to the foregoing, the Court considers that in the particular circumstances of the present case the shaving off of the applicant's hair in the context of his punishment by confinement in an isolation cell for writing critical and offensive remarks about prison warders and State organs constituted an unjustified treatment of sufficient severity to be characterised as degrading within the meaning of Article 3 of the Convention.

121. It follows that there has been a violation of Article 3 of the Convention on account of the forced removal of the applicant's hair.

FOR THESE REASONS, THE COURT UNANIMOUSLY

1. Holds that there has been a violation of Article 3 of the Convention;

NOTES

1 The Court was composed of President Rozakis and Judges: Tulkens, Vajic, Levits, Botoucharova, Kovler, and Zagrebelsky.

2 *Yankov* reveals that degrading treatment can occur via intentionally humiliating acts or by subjecting a person to degrading conditions. For a consideration of the Article 10 aspects of the judgment, see p 653.

3 An example of State officials intentionally subjecting a person to degrading treatment occurred in *Iwanczuk v Poland*, judgment of 15 November 2001. The applicant was a remand prisoner awaiting trial on charges of misappropriation. At 9.30 pm on 19 September 1993 he asked the Wroclaw prison authorities to allow him to visit the voting facilities in the prison, so that he might cast his vote in the parliamentary elections. A prison officer took him to the guards' room and four guards told him that he would have to undress and undergo a body search in order to be allowed to vote. The applicant removed all his clothes, except his underwear, and the guards verbally abused him (in part by making humiliating comments about his body). The guards ordered that he strip naked. The applicant refused. He also refused to undergo a body search. Consequently the guards denied him the opportunity to vote and took him back to his cell. Iwanczuk subsequently lodged a complaint with the Strasbourg authorities alleging, *inter alia*, that the guards' behaviour constituted degrading treatment in breach of Article 3. The Court determined that the guards' order that the applicant undergo a body search as a precondition to being allowed to enter the voting area in the prison was not necessary. Relevant factors included his peaceful behaviour during his entire period of detention, the nature of the charges against him (not involving allegations of violence), and the absence of previous convictions against the applicant. The Court held that:

59....whilst strip searches may be necessary on occasions to ensure prison security or prevent disorder in prisons, they must be conducted in an appropriate manner. In the present case, the prison's guards verbally abused and derided the applicant. Their behaviour was intended to cause in the applicant feelings of humiliation and inferiority. This, in the Court's view, showed a lack of respect for the applicant's human dignity.

Therefore, by 6 votes to 1, the Court determined that the applicant had been subjected to degrading treatment. Here the guards' behaviour was unjustified/unprofessional and suggests that they were seeking to humiliate him as a response to his request to vote during the late evening. For the Court's consideration of a high security regime involving regular strip-searches see *Van Der Ven v Netherlands* (p 185).

4 The Court has found that poor physical conditions of detention in a number of States constituted degrading treatment even though there was no intention to humiliate detainees. Examples include: *Dougoz v Greece*, judgment of 6 March 2001, where a convicted foreign drug offender was held for ten months in Drapetsona detention centre and for eight months in Alexandras Avenue police headquarters (both locations were severely overcrowded and there were no beds, mattresses or blankets). The Court, unanimously, determined that:

46.... conditions of detention may sometimes amount to inhuman or degrading treatment. In the Greek case (Yearbook of the European Convention on Human Rights No 12, 1969), the Commission reached this conclusion regarding overcrowding and inadequate facilities for heating, sanitation, sleeping arrangements, food, recreation and contacts with the outside world. When assessing conditions of detention, account has to be taken of the cumulative effects of these conditions, as well as of specific allegations made by the applicant. In the present case, although the Court has not conducted an on-site visit, it notes that the applicant's allegations are corroborated by the conclusions of the CPT [the European Committee for the Prevention of Torture and Inhuman or Degrading Treatment or Punishment] report of 29 November 1994 regarding the Police Headquarters in Alexandras Avenue. In its report the CPT stressed that the cellular accommodation and detention regime in that place were quite unsuitable for a period in excess of a few days, the occupancy levels being grossly excessive and the sanitary facilities appalling. Although the CPT had not visited the Drapetsona detention centre at that time, the Court notes that the Government had described the conditions in Alexandras as being the same as in Drapetsona, and the applicant himself conceded that the former were slightly better with natural light, air in the cells and adequate hot water.

47. Furthermore, the Court does not lose sight of the fact that in 1997 the CPT visited both the Alexandras Police Headquarters and the Drapetsona detention centre and felt it necessary to renew its visit to both places in 1999. The applicant was detained in the interim from July 1997 to December 1998.

48. In the light of the above, the Court considers that the conditions of detention of the applicant in the Alexandras Police Headquarters and the Drapetsona detention centre, in particular the serious overcrowding and absence of sleeping facilities, combined with the inordinate length of the period during which he was detained in such conditions, amounted to degrading treatment contrary to Article 3.

Shortly afterwards the segregation unit of Koridallos prison was found to breach this element of Article 3 in *Peers v Greece*, judgment of 19 April 2001. The applicant was a British drug addict who had been convicted of drug offences. He was detained in the segregation unit for two months while he underwent drug withdrawal. During that time he had to share a single person cell with another prisoner and they had to use an open toilet (with no screen from the sleeping area) in their cell. A united Court concluded that:

74. ... in the present case there is no evidence that there was a positive intention of humiliating or debasing the applicant. However, the Court notes that, although the question whether the purpose of the treatment was to humiliate or debase the victim is a factor to be taken into account, the absence of any such purpose cannot conclusively rule out a finding of violation of Article 3 (*V. v the United Kingdom* [GC], No 24888/94, § 71, ECHR-IX).

75. Indeed, in the present case, the fact remains that the competent authorities have taken no steps to improve the objectively unacceptable conditions of the applicant's detention. In the Court's view, this omission denotes lack of respect for the applicant. The Court takes particularly into account that, for at least two months, the applicant had to spend a considerable part of each 24-hour period practically confined to his bed in a cell with no ventilation and no window which would at times become unbearably hot. He also had to use the toilet in the presence of another inmate and be present while the toilet was being used by his cellmate. The Court is not convinced by the Government's allegation that these conditions have not affected the applicant in a manner incompatible with Article 3. On the contrary, the Court is of the opinion that the prison conditions complained of diminished the applicant's human dignity and arose in him feelings of anguish and inferiority capable of humiliating and debasing him and possibly breaking his physical or moral resistance. In sum, the Court considers that the conditions of the applicant's detention in the segregation unit of the Delta wing of the Koridallos prison amounted to degrading treatment within the meaning of Article 3 of the Convention.

The terrible conditions of detention for asylum seekers in Greece, including detainees having to drink water from toilets, led the Court to find a detainee had suffered degrading treatment in *MSS v Belgium and Greece*, see p 210.

A few days' detention of a severely disabled person was found to breach this provision in *Price v UK*, judgment of 10 July 2001. The applicant was a four-limb deficient victim of thalidomide. In 1995 she refused to answer questions regarding her financial position during civil proceedings. The judge found her in contempt of court and ordered that she be committed to prison for seven days. She was held in the cells of Lincoln police station that night, as it was too late to send her to a prison. Price had to sleep in her wheelchair (she claimed that she could not sleep on the wooden bed as it would have been too painful for her hips) and was cold (extra blankets were provided and a doctor attended her). The next day she was moved to the health centre of New Hall Women's Prison, in Wakefield. Her cell had a wider wheelchair door access, hand pulls on the toilet, and a hydraulic hospital bed. Constant nursing care was provided. Male officers were required to help the nurse lift Price on and off the toilet. She was released after four days (due to the rules on remission of sentences). Price alleged that her treatment during detention breached Article 3. The Court, unanimously, found that:

30. There is no evidence in this case of any positive intention to humiliate or debase the applicant. However, the Court considers that to detain a severely disabled person in conditions where she is dangerously cold, risks developing sores because her bed is too hard or unreachable, and is unable to go to the toilet or keep clean without the greatest of difficulty, constitutes degrading treatment contrary to Article 3.

The judgment in *Price* indicates that States must ensure that the conditions of detention are appropriate for disabled detainees (the Court was critical of the domestic judge for not checking to confirm that there would be suitable facilities for the care of Price before he ordered her incarceration).

The dire conditions of detention in Russia were first examined by the Court in *Kalashnikov v Russia*, judgment of 15 July 2002. The applicant, a businessman charged with fraud, had been held on remand in a detention centre in Magadan for over four years. His cell was so overcrowded that the inmates had to share each bed amongst three detainees (on an eight-hour shift system), the light was constantly on in the cell, and between 11 and 24 inmates had to share the toilet in the corner of the cell. Furthermore, the cell was infested with pests and some of the inmates had serious contagious diseases (e.g. tuberculosis). Consequently, the Court, unanimously, ruled that:

102....the applicant's conditions of detention, in particular the severely overcrowded and insanitary environment and its detrimental effect on the applicant's health and well-being, combined with the length of the period during which the applicant was detained in such conditions, amounted to degrading treatment.

Very significantly during the Strasbourg proceedings the respondent government had acknowledged that the conditions of the applicant's detention were no worse than those of most detainees in Russia and that, because of economic difficulties, such conditions were below those acceptable to the Council of Europe.

In the subsequent case of *Poltoratskiy v Ukraine*, judgment of 29 April 2003, the Court held that a State's economic problems cannot be used to justify bad conditions of detention which infringe Article 3. The applicant was convicted, in December 1995, of the murder of four persons. He was sentenced to death. In February 1996 he was moved to one of the cells in Ivano-Frankivsk prison where convicted prisoners awaiting execution were detained. A moratorium on executions was announced by the President of Ukraine in March 1997 and in December 1999 the Constitutional Court of Ukraine ruled that the death penalty was contrary to the Constitution. In June 2000 the applicant's sentence was commuted to life imprisonment. He alleged a number of breaches of his Convention rights before the Strasbourg authorities.

145. The Court views with particular concern the fact that, until at earliest May 1998, the applicant, in common with other prisoners detained in the prison under a death sentence, was locked up for 24 hours a day in cells which offered only a very restricted living space, that the windows of the cells were covered with the consequence that there was no access to natural light, that there was no provision for any outdoor exercise and that there was little or no opportunity for activities to occupy himself or for human contact. In common with the observations of the CPT concerning the subjection of death row prisoners in Ukraine to similar conditions, the Court considers that the detention of the applicant in unacceptable conditions of this kind amounted to degrading treatment in breach of Article 3 of the Convention. In the case of the present applicant, the situation was aggravated by the fact that in the period between 24 February and 24 March 1998, he was detained in a cell where there was no water tap or washbasin but only a small pipe on the wall near the toilet, and where the water supply could only be turned on from the corridor, where the walls were covered with faeces and where the bucket for flushing the toilet had been taken away. The applicant' situation was further aggravated by the fact that he was throughout the period in question subject to a death sentence, although...a moratorium had been in effect since 11 March 1997.

146. The Court considers that in the present case there is no evidence that there was a positive intention of humiliating or debasing the applicant. However, although the question whether the purpose of the treatment was to humiliate or debase the victim is a factor to be taken into account, the absence of any such purpose cannot conclusively rule out a finding of a violation of Article 3 of the Convention (see *V. v the United Kingdom* [GC], No 24888/94, § 71, ECHR 1999-IX; and *Kalashnikov*, cited above, § 101). It considers that the conditions of detention, which the applicant had to endure in particular until May 1998, must have caused him considerable mental suffering, diminishing his human dignity.

147. The Court acknowledges that following May 1998 substantial and progressive improvements had taken place, both in the general conditions of the applicant's detention and in the regime applied within the prison. In particular, the coverings over the windows of the cells were removed, daily outdoor walks were introduced and the rights of prisoners to receive visits and to correspond were enhanced. Nevertheless, the Court observes that, by the date of introduction of these improvements, the applicant had already been detained in these deleterious conditions for a period of nearly 30 months, including a period of 8 months after the Convention had come into force in respect of Ukraine.

148. The Court has also borne in mind, when considering the material conditions in which the applicant was detained and the activities offered to him, that Ukraine encountered serious socio-economic problems in the course of its systemic transition and that prior to the summer of 1998 the prison authorities were both struggling under difficult economic conditions and occupied with the implementation of new national legislation and related regulations. However, the Court observes that lack of resources cannot in principle justify prison conditions which are so poor as to reach the threshold of treatment contrary to Article 3 of the Convention. Moreover, the economic problems faced by Ukraine cannot in any event explain or excuse the particular conditions of detention which it has found in paragraph 145 to be unacceptable in the present case.

149. There has, accordingly, been a violation of Article 3 of the Convention in this respect.

If the Court had allowed a plea of State economic hardship to justify very poor prison conditions it would have undermined the potential protection of Article 3 for many detainees across Europe and reduced the external incentive upon States to improve their conditions of detention.

Prison overcrowding resulting in a non-smoking prisoner being imprisoned in cells with smoking inmates for several years, during which time he developed chronic health problems, was found to have breached Article 3 in *Elefteriadis v Romania*, judgment of 25 January 2011.

We can note that in many of the above prison condition cases the judgments have reflected a symbiotic relationship between the Court's role in applying and interpreting the Convention rights of detainees and the work of it sister organization the European Committee for the Prevention of Torture and Inhuman or Degrading Treatment or Punishment (CPT). Published reports by the latter on its inspections of particular places of detention are of great help to the Court in reaching findings of fact in respect of applicants who allege breaches of their Convention rights concerning their treatment in those institutions. Also adverse comments by the CPT regarding conditions in an institution may encourage the Court to find a breach of Article 3 where an inmate, who has suffered from those conditions, lodges a complaint under the Convention.

5   The conditions in which a prisoner was repeatedly transported from a remand facility to the courthouse were held to violate Article 3 by a unanimous Chamber in *Khudoyorov v Russia*, judgment of 8 November 2005. On 205 occasions the applicant was transported to and from the Regional Court, a journey that took an hour, in a prison van where he occupied a compartment of about 1 sq m. The applicant had to share that compartment with another prisoner, there was only one seat, and the occupants had to take turns sitting on the other's lap. During the days that he was taken to the Regional Court the applicant was given no food or outdoor exercise. The Chamber had regard to the CPT's published views that transportation compartments for individual prisoners up to 0.8 sq m were unsuitable (irrespective of the duration of the journey). Therefore, given the size of the compartment used to transport the applicant and another prisoner, the lack of adequate seating, and the absence of food and exercise the Chamber concluded that Article 3 had been breached. The Court did not specify which element of the Article had been violated. Again, we see the significance of the CPT's expertise being used by the Court in the application of Article 3.

6   The delayed release of a very ill elderly prisoner was found to constitute degrading treatment by a Chamber (6 votes to 1) in *Farbtuhs v Latvia*, judgment of 2 December 2004. The applicant had been sentenced to five years' imprisonment in 2000, when he was aged 84, in respect of acts of genocide and crimes against humanity he committed when an official of the Soviet Union after the latter's annexation of Latvia in 1940. Prior to beginning his imprisonment he was examined by medical experts who reported that he was paraplegic and suffered from a number of other serious ailments. Because of his ill-health he was detained in the prison infirmary. In February 2001 the medical experts recommended that, given his ill-health and age, he should be released on licence. Three days later the prison governor applied for the applicant's release to the District Court. His request was refused. In March 2002 the Regional Court authorized the applicant's release in the light of evidence that he had developed two further illnesses, including diabetes, whilst in prison. The applicant was then released. The Chamber expressed grave concern that the applicant's release from prison had been delayed for over one year despite expert medical advice that his declining health merited immediate release. Furthermore, the Chamber was critical of the limited professional medical care given to Farbtuhs whilst he was being detained. Outside working hours he had

to rely on fellow prisoners, sometimes acting on a voluntary basis, to care for him. This judgment indicates that States ought not to continue the detention of persons where independent medical opinion clearly supports their immediate release on health grounds.

7   Latvia's failure to provide adequate food to a remand prisoner on the days when he was taken to court for hearings constituted degrading treatment according to the unanimous Chamber in *Moisejevs v Latvia*, judgment of 15 June 2006. The applicant was taken to court for hearings on 72 days and on those occasions he was not given a normal lunch, but only a slice of bread, an onion, and a piece of fish or a meatball. The Chamber considered that this was insufficient nutrition to meet his needs (especially having regard to the stresses he faced during trial hearings). Furthermore, on the hearing days when he was returned to prison in the evening he frequently was not given a meal, but just a bread roll.

8   In *Hurtado v Switzerland* A.280A (1994), p 187, the effects of the stun grenade and the police officers' use of physical force to arrest the applicant were to cause him to defecate in his trousers. He was not allowed to change into clean clothing for over 24 hours, during which time he was questioned by the police and brought before an investigating judge. The Commission, by 15 votes to 1, found this treatment to be degrading contrary to Article 3.

67. The Commission reiterates that treatment is considered 'degrading' when it is such as to arouse in its victims feelings of fear, anguish and inferiority capable of humiliating and debasing them and possibly breaking their physical or moral resistance (Court's judgments in *Ireland v UK* p 66 para 167 and *Soering v UK* p 39 para 100).

68. The Commission considers that the conduct of the authorities, who neglected to take the most elementary hygiene measures by failing to make available to the applicant clean clothes to replace those soiled as a result of their action, was humiliating and debasing for the applicant and therefore degrading within the meaning of Article 3 of the Convention.

9   The routine handcuffing of a life-sentence prisoner every time he was taken out of his cell (during a 13-year period) was found to amount to degrading treatment by a unanimous Chamber in *Kashavelov v Bulgaria*, judgment of 20 January 2011. There was no evidence that the applicant had attempted to harm others or escape from custody.

10   A unanimous Chamber found the confining of a non-violent defendant in a metal cage during his criminal trial, for alleged economic crimes, amounted to degrading treatment in *Khodorkovskiy v Russia*, judgment of 31 May 2011. Prior to his arrest the applicant had been one of the richest businessmen in Russia, he had also supported opposition political groups and expressed concerns about anti-democratic trends in the country. The Chamber determined that the Government had not identified any specific security risk that justified such confinement.

126. In sum, the security arrangements in the courtroom, given their cumulative effect, were, in the circumstances, excessive and could have been reasonably perceived by the applicant and the public as humiliating. There was, therefore, a violation of Article 3 of the Convention in that the treatment was degrading within the meaning of this provision.

The Chamber also found several breaches of Article 5, but he had failed to substantiate his claim that his prosecution (and conviction) had been politically motivated.

11   The Commission found racial discrimination in British immigration restrictions amounted to degrading treatment in *East African Asians v UK* (1973) 3 EHRR 76. By the 1960s there were several hundred thousand citizens of the UK and colonies, many of whom

were of Asian ethnic origin, resident in East Africa. As British colonies in that region gained their independence their new national governments began various 'Africanization' policies; the effects of these programmes were to deprive many of the Asians of their livelihoods (e.g. by withdrawing their trading licences) and render them destitute. Consequently, significant numbers of the Asians sought to enter and settle in the UK. In 1968 Parliament enacted the Commonwealth Immigrants Act 1968 which had the effect of prohibiting the East African Asians from entering or settling in the UK. Twenty-five such persons, who had been refused entry into the UK, complained to the Commission alleging, *inter alia*, a breach of Article 3. In its report the Commission concluded that:

207....the legislation applied in the present case discriminated against the applicants on the grounds of their colour or race. It has also confirmed the view, which it expressed at the admissibility stage, that discrimination based on race could, in certain circumstances, of itself amount to degrading treatment within the meaning of Article 3 of the Convention. The Commission recalls in this connection that, as generally recognised, a special importance should be attached to discrimination based on race; that publicity [sic] to single out a group of persons for differential treatment on the basis of race might, in certain circumstances, constitute a special form of affront to human dignity; and that differential treatment of a group of persons on the basis of race might therefore be capable of constituting degrading treatment when differential treatment on some other ground would raise no such question.

208. The Commission considers that the racial discrimination, to which the applicants have been publicly subjected by the application of the above immigration legislation, constitutes an interference with their human dignity which, in the special circumstances described above, amounted to 'degrading treatment' in the sense of Article 3 of the Convention.

209. It therefore concludes, by six votes against three votes [in addition two other members of the Commission, who were not present when the vote was taken, expressed their agreement with the majority], that Article 3 has been violated in the present case.

The special circumstances identified by the Commission included the fact that the applicants were not aliens in British law, yet the 1968 Act denied them entry to the UK, and the difficult situation the applicants faced in East Africa because of the local 'Africanization' programmes. Subsequently the British Government allowed the applicants to enter the UK and introduced a special voucher scheme that allowed entry for other persons in the same predicament. In 1977 the Committee of Ministers was unable to reach a two-thirds majority decision on the application and, therefore, resolved that no further action was called for (Res DH(77)2). In 1994, at the request of the British Government, the Committee of Ministers finally resolved formally to publish the above report of the Commission (Res DH(94)30). The failure of the Committee of Ministers to reach a conclusive determination of the case illustrates the problematic role played by that institution under the former Strasbourg supervisory system.

12   The Court did not find racial or sexual discrimination which breached Article 3 in *Abdulaziz, Cabales and Balkandali v UK* A.94 (1985), and see p 530. The applicants, who were aliens, were lawfully resident in the UK and under existing immigration rules they were unable to gain entry to the UK for their foreign husbands. The Court, unanimously, held that: '...the difference of treatment complained of did not denote any contempt or lack of respect for the personality of the applicants and that it was not designed to, and did not, humiliate or debase...' (para 91). Hence, the Court will examine the justifications and effects of any alleged discriminatory action when assessing if it is serious enough to constitute degrading treatment.

13 A unanimous Chamber of the full-time Court determined that racially discriminatory comments by domestic courts and public officials against members of the minority Roma community contributed towards the latter suffering degrading treatment in *Moldovan and Others v Romania (No 2)*, judgment of 12 July 2005. The seven Roma applicants had their homes and personal property destroyed by a mob, including police officers, who also murdered three Roma involved in a fight with non-Roma villagers which had led to the death of a villager. For many years after the destruction of their homes the applicants were forced to live in hen-houses, pigsties, and cellars. During the criminal proceedings against the villagers the court stated that, *inter alia*, the Roma living in the village '…rejected the moral values accepted by the rest of the population…Most of the Roma have no occupation and earn their living by doing odd jobs, stealing and engaging in all kinds of illicit activity.' The applicants complained to Strasbourg. The Chamber held that:

111. In addition, the remarks concerning the applicants' honesty and way of life made by some authorities dealing with the applicants' grievances…appear to be, in the absence of any substantiation on behalf of those authorities, purely discriminatory. In this connection the Court reiterates that discrimination based on race can of itself amount to degrading treatment within the meaning of Article 3 of the Convention (see *East African Asians v the United Kingdom*, Commission Report, 14 December 1973, DR 78, p 5, at p 62).

Such remarks should therefore be taken into account as an aggravating factor in the examination of the applicants' complaint under Article 3 of the Convention.

…

113. In the light of the above, the Court finds that the applicants' living conditions and the racial discrimination to which they have been publicly subjected by the way in which their grievances were dealt with by the various authorities, constitute an interference with their human dignity which, in the special circumstances of this case, amounted to 'degrading treatment' within the meaning of Article 3 of the Convention.

114. Accordingly, there has also been a violation of Article 3 of the Convention.

14 The types of discrimination which can potentially violate Article 3 were extended to encompass sexual orientation in *Smith and Grady v UK* (1999) 29 EHRR 493, extracted and discussed at p 492. The Court, unanimously, held that:

121. …Moreover, the Court would not exclude that treatment which is grounded upon a predisposed bias on the part of a heterosexual majority against a homosexual minority of the nature described above could, in principle, fall within the scope of Article 3 (see *mutatis mutandis*, the *Addulaziz, Cabales and Balkandali v UK* A.94 p 42, paras 90–1).

122. However, while accepting that the policy, together with the investigation and discharge which ensued, were undoubtedly distressing and humiliating for each of the applicants, the Court does not consider, having regard to all the circumstances of the case, that the treatment reached the minimum level of severity which would bring it within the scope of Article 3 of the Convention.

15 The deliberate delaying of a pregnant woman undergoing amniocentesis, in order to confirm whether her foetus was suffering from a serious genetic abnormality, by doctors opposed to abortion, was found to have breached Article 3 in *RR v Poland*, judgment of 26 May 2011. The applicant was 18 weeks pregnant when an ultrasound scan disclosed the potential abnormality. However, it took the applicant six weeks to find a doctor willing to undertake the genetic testing and produce the results. By then it was too late for her to have a lawful abortion and her child was subsequently born with Turner syndrome. By 6 votes to 1 the Chamber held that:

160. The Court is further of the view that the applicant's suffering, both before the results of the tests became known and after that date, could be said to have been aggravated by the fact that the diagnostic services which she had requested early on were at all times available and that she was entitled as a matter of domestic law to avail herself of them.

It is a matter of great regret that the applicant was so shabbily treated by the doctors dealing with her case. The Court can only agree with the Polish Supreme Court's view that the applicant had been humiliated ...

161. The Court is of the view that the applicant's suffering reached the minimum threshold of severity under Article 3 of the Convention.

For the lack of care another pregnant woman had received from Polish doctors opposed to abortion see *Tysiac*, p 501.

Degrading punishment

Tyrer v UK A.26 (1978)
European Court of Human Rights

The applicant was born on the Isle of Man (a dependency of the British Crown with its own government, legislature, and courts) in 1956. In early March 1972 he pleaded guilty to a charge of unlawful assault occasioning actual bodily harm to a fellow pupil at school (who had earlier reported the applicant for bringing beer into the school). The juvenile court sentenced him to three strokes of the birch (local regulations specified that the birch rod should have a maximum length of 40 inches with a spray circumference not exceeding 6 inches). The applicant appealed against the sentence to the High Court of Justice of the Isle of Man. On the morning of 28 April 1972 the court ordered Tyrer to be examined by a doctor to determine if he was fit to receive the punishment. The doctor reported that he was fit. In the afternoon the court dismissed Tyrer's appeal. After waiting in a police station for some time for a doctor to arrive, Tyrer was birched later that day. The doctor and Tyrer's father were present. Tyrer was made to take down his trousers and underpants and bend over a table; he was held by two policemen while a third officer administered the birching. After the first stroke pieces of the birch rod were broken by the force of the impact on Tyrer. The applicant's father thereupon 'went for' one of the policemen and had to be restrained. The birching did not cut the applicant's skin, but he was sore for about one and a half weeks after the punishment. Judicial corporal punishment of adults and juveniles was abolished in England, Wales and Scotland in 1948 and in Northern Ireland in 1968. The applicant complained to the Commission in 1972 arguing, *inter alia*, that his punishment violated Article 3. In January 1976 the applicant sought to withdraw his application. However, the Commission refused his request because, 'the case raised questions of a general character affecting the observance of the Convention which necessitated a further examination of the issues involved.' Thereafter the applicant took no further part in the proceedings. In its December 1976 report the Commission, by 14 votes to 1, found the punishment to be degrading and in breach of Article 3.

II. ON ARTICLE 3 (ART 3)

29. The Court shares the Commission's view that Mr Tyrer's punishment did not amount to 'torture' within the meaning of Article 3 (art 3). The Court does not consider that the facts of this particular case reveal that the applicant underwent suffering of the level inherent in this notion as it was interpreted and applied by the Court in its judgment of 18 January 1978 (*Ireland v UK*, Series A No 25, pp 66–67 and 68, paras 167 and 174).

That judgment also contains various indications concerning the notions of 'inhuman treatment' and 'degrading treatment' but it deliberately left aside the notions of 'inhuman punishment' and 'degrading punishment' which alone are relevant in the present case (ibid, p 65, para 164). Those indications accordingly cannot, as such, serve here. Nevertheless, it remains true that the suffering occasioned must attain a particular level before a punishment can be classified as 'inhuman' within the meaning of Article 3 (art 3). Here again, the Court does not consider on the facts of the case that that level was attained and it therefore concurs with the Commission that the penalty imposed on Mr Tyrer was not 'inhuman punishment' within the meaning of Article 3 (art 3). Accordingly, the only question for decision is whether he was subjected to a 'degrading punishment' contrary to that Article (art 3).

30. The Court notes first of all that a person may be humiliated by the mere fact of being criminally convicted. However, what is relevant for the purposes of Article 3 (art 3) is that he should be humiliated not simply by his conviction but by the execution of the punishment which is imposed on him. In fact, in most if not all cases this may be one of the effects of judicial punishment, involving as it does unwilling subjection to the demands of the penal system.

However, as the Court pointed out in its judgment of 18 January 1978 in the case of *Ireland v UK* (Series A No 25, p 65, para 163), the prohibition contained in Article 3 (art 3) of the Convention is absolute: no provision is made for exceptions and, under Article 15 (2) (art 15-2) there can be no derogation from Article 3 (art 3). It would be absurd to hold that judicial punishment generally, by reason of its usual and perhaps almost inevitable element of humiliation, is 'degrading' within the meaning of Article 3 (art 3). Some further criterion must be read into the text. Indeed, Article 3 (art 3), by expressly prohibiting 'inhuman' and 'degrading' punishment, implies that there is a distinction between such punishment and punishment in general.

In the Court's view, in order for a punishment to be 'degrading' and in breach of Article 3 (art 3), the humiliation or debasement involved must attain a particular level and must in any event be other than that usual element of humiliation referred to in the preceding subparagraph. The assessment is, in the nature of things, relative: it depends on all the circumstances of the case and, in particular, on the nature and context of the punishment itself and the manner and method of its execution.

31. The Attorney-General for the Isle of Man argued that the judicial corporal punishment at issue in this case was not in breach of the Convention since it did not outrage public opinion in the Island. However, even assuming that local public opinion can have an incidence on the interpretation of the concept of 'degrading punishment' appearing in Article 3 (art 3), the Court does not regard it as established that judicial corporal punishment is not considered degrading by those members of the Manx population who favour its retention: it might well be that one of the reasons why they view the penalty as an effective deterrent is precisely the element of degradation which it involves. As regards their belief that judicial corporal punishment deters criminals, it must be pointed out that a punishment does not lose its degrading character just because it is believed to be, or actually is, an effective deterrent or aid to crime control. Above all, as the Court must emphasise, it is never permissible to have recourse to punishments which are contrary to Article 3 (art 3), whatever their deterrent effect may be.

The Court must also recall that the Convention is a living instrument which, as the Commission rightly stressed, must be interpreted in the light of present-day conditions. In the case now before it the Court cannot but be influenced by the developments and commonly accepted standards in the penal policy of the member States of the Council of Europe in this field. Indeed, the Attorney-General for the Isle of Man mentioned that, for many years, the provisions of Manx legislation concerning judicial corporal punishment had been under review.

32. As regards the manner and method of execution of the birching inflicted on Mr Tyrer, the Attorney-General for the Isle of Man drew particular attention to the fact that the punishment was carried out in private and without publication of the name of the offender.

Publicity may be a relevant factor in assessing whether a punishment is 'degrading' within the meaning of Article 3 (art 3), but the Court does not consider that absence of publicity will necessarily prevent a given punishment from falling into that category: it may well suffice that the victim is humiliated in his own eyes, even if not in the eyes of others.

The Court notes that the relevant Isle of Man legislation, as well as giving the offender a right of appeal against sentence, provides for certain safeguards. Thus, there is a prior medical examination; the number of strokes and dimensions of the birch are regulated in detail; a doctor is present and may order the punishment to be stopped; in the case of a child or young person, the parent may attend if he so desires; the birching is carried out by a police constable in the presence of a more senior colleague.

33. Nevertheless, the Court must consider whether the other circumstances of the applicant's punishment were such as to make it 'degrading' within the meaning of Article 3 (art 3).

The very nature of judicial corporal punishment is that it involves one human being inflicting physical violence on another human being. Furthermore, it is institutionalised violence, that is in the present case violence permitted by the law, ordered by the judicial authorities of the State and carried out by the police authorities of the State . . . Thus, although the applicant did not suffer any severe or long-lasting physical effects, his punishment—whereby he was treated as an object in the power of the authorities—constituted an assault on precisely that which it is one of the main purposes of Article 3 (art 3) to protect, namely a person's dignity and physical integrity. Neither can it be excluded that the punishment may have had adverse psychological effects.

The institutionalised character of this violence is further compounded by the whole aura of official procedure attending the punishment and by the fact that those inflicting it were total strangers to the offender.

Admittedly, the relevant legislation provides that in any event birching shall not take place later than six months after the passing of sentence. However, this does not alter the fact that there had been an interval of several weeks since the applicant's conviction by the juvenile court and a considerable delay in the police station where the punishment was carried out. Accordingly, in addition to the physical pain he experienced, Mr Tyrer was subjected to the mental anguish of anticipating the violence he was to have inflicted on him.

34. In the present case, the Court does not consider it relevant that the sentence of judicial corporal punishment was imposed on the applicant for an offence of violence. Neither does it consider it relevant that, for Mr Tyrer, birching was an alternative to a period of detention: the fact that one penalty may be preferable to, or have less adverse effects or be less serious than, another penalty does not of itself mean that the first penalty is not 'degrading' within the meaning of Article 3 (art 3).

35. Accordingly, viewing these circumstances as a whole, the Court finds that the applicant was subjected to a punishment in which the element of humiliation attained the level inherent in the notion of 'degrading punishment' as explained at paragraph 30 above. The indignity of having the punishment administered over the bare posterior aggravated to some extent the degrading character of the applicant's punishment but it was not the only or determining factor.

The Court therefore concludes that the judicial corporal punishment inflicted on the applicant amounted to degrading punishment within the meaning of Article 3 (art 3) of the Convention.

FOR THESE REASONS, THE COURT

…

2. holds by six votes to one that the judicial corporal punishment inflicted on Mr Tyrer amounted to degrading punishment within the meaning of Article 3; …

NOTES

1 The Court was composed of President Balladore Pallieri and Judges: Cremona, Pedersen, Vilhjalmsson, Teitgen, and Matscher.

Judge Fitzmaurice dissented as he did not consider that judicial corporal punishment was degrading when applied to juveniles. Furthermore:

9. The 'other' circumstances (Judgment, paragraph 33 et seq.)—I have noted the following:

(i) In paragraph 33, much stress is placed on the fact that the 'violence' was 'institutionalised', ie 'permitted by law' and 'carried out by the police authorities'. For my part, I cannot see the relevance of this criterion, ie that the punishment was degrading because 'institutionalised', or more degrading on that account that if it had not been.

To be 'institutionalised' is, in an ordered society, inseparable from any punishment for crime, since non-institutionalised punishment, except such as the law tolerates, must be illegal. Therefore I do not follow (and it is not explained) why institutionalised violence must necessarily be degrading, if non-institutionalised is not, or be more degrading than the latter. Indeed, it is not at all clear what form of non-institutionalised violence the Court had in mind which, by comparison, would not be regarded as degrading to the recipient. Possibly it was desired to imply (though this is not stated) that, for instance, a beating administered by a parent to a child would not degrade the latter,— whereas a 'judicial' one would. I do not believe in these subtleties. In my view neither punishment (so long as administered in private) can be considered as inherently degrading where a juvenile is concerned, unless other factors over and above the beating as such are involved. The State is, in a certain sense, in loco parentis in such a situation.

(ii) Next (third section of paragraph 33), the alleged effect of the institutionalisation is said to be 'compounded' by 'the whole aura of official procedure attending the punishment'—(but how could the procedure not be official if there was institutionalisation?—the one is, or entails, the other)— and also compounded 'by the fact that those inflicting [the punishment] were total strangers to the offender'. As to this last objection, leaving aside the question whether, in the restricted community of Castletown, Isle of Man, the police officers concerned were 'total strangers' to the boy, I for my part fail to see how it can be any more degrading to be beaten by strangers than non-strangers. Many would, I believe, think it less so.

…

11. … . Modern opinion has come to regard corporal punishment as an undesirable form of punishment; and this, whatever the age of the offender. But the fact that a certain form of punishment is an undesirable form of punishment does not automatically turn it into a degrading one. A punishment may well have an undesirable character without being in the least degrading—or at any rate not more so than punishment in general is. And hitherto, whatever may have been felt about corporal punishment from such standpoints as whether it really deters, whether it may not have a brutalising effect, whether it harms the psyche of those who carry it out, etc., it has not been generally regarded as degrading when applied to juveniles and young offenders, in the same way as it is considered so to be in the case of adults. In that respect, the two things have never been regarded as being quite of the same order or as being on the same plane. This last is the real point—for to put it in terms of the criterion adopted by the Court, and assuming that corporal punishment does involve some degree of degradation, it has never been seen as doing so for a juvenile to anything

approaching the same manner or extent as for an adult. Put in terms of the Convention and of the Court's criterion, therefore, such punishment does not, in the case of a juvenile, attain the level of degradation needed to constitute it a breach of Article 3 (art 3), unless of course seriously aggravating circumstances are present over and above the simple fact of the corporal character of the punishment. This is why I could have understood it if the Court had regarded the infliction of the blows on the bare posterior as bringing matters up to the required level of degradation. I would not necessarily have agreed with that view, but it would have been tenable. However, the Court held that this was not a determining element: the punishment was in any event degrading. This means, in effect, that any judicial corporal punishment meted out to a juvenile is degrading and a breach of Article 3 (art 3). It is this view (in my opinion far too dogmatic and sweeping) that I cannot agree with. That such punishments may be undesirable and ought perhaps to be abolished is, as I have said, quite another matter: they are not ipso facto degrading on that account in the case of juvenile offenders.

12. I have to admit that my own view may be coloured by the fact that I was brought up and educated under a system according to which the corporal punishment of schoolboys (sometimes at the hands of the senior ones—prefects or monitors—sometimes by masters) was regarded as the normal sanction for serious misbehaviour, and even sometimes for what was much less serious. Generally speaking, and subject to circumstances, it was often considered by the boy himself as preferable to probable alternative punishments such as being kept in on a fine summer's evening to copy out 500 lines or learn several pages of Shakespeare or Virgil by heart, or be denied leave of absence on a holiday occasion. Moreover, these beatings were carried out without any of the safeguards attendant on Mr Tyrer's: no parents, nurses or doctors were ever present. They also not infrequently took place under conditions of far greater intrinsic humiliation than in his case. Yet I cannot remember that any boy felt degraded or debased. Such an idea would have been thought rather ridiculous. The system was the same for all until they attained a certain seniority. If a boy minded, and resolved not to repeat the offence that had resulted in a beating, this was simply because it had hurt, not because he felt degraded by it or was so regarded by his fellows: indeed, such is the natural perversity of the young of the human species that these occasions were often seen as matters of pride and congratulation,—not unlike the way in which members of the student corps in the old German universities regarded their duelling scars as honourable—(though of course that was, in other respects, quite a different case).

13. In conclusion, I must insist that I am not seeking to maintain that the state of affairs I have just described was necessarily a good one, though it had, and has, many supporters. I am not advocating corporal punishment. I am simply saying that it is not degrading for juvenile offenders—or (to such extent as it is), does not, in their case, involve the level of degradation required to constitute it a breach of Article 3 (art 3) of the European Human Rights Convention, when inflicted under proper restrictions and safeguards in consequence of a regularly pronounced judicial sentence, traditionally sanctioned for certain offences by the law of the community to which the offender belongs, and by its public opinion. No juvenile is or need feel 'degraded' under those conditions....

The dissent is notable for the candour with which Sir Gerald Fitzmaurice acknowledged the effects of his public school upbringing upon his personal conception of degrading punishment. For a contrasting (and later) account of the consequences of corporal punishment in a British non-state school see *Costello-Roberts*, Note 3.

In 1993 the Parliament of the Isle of Man (Tynwald) enacted legislation abolishing judicial corporal punishment.

The judgment of the Court in *Tyrer* also has an enduring importance, extending beyond the definition of Article 3, through the judiciary's articulation of the 'living instrument' doctrine regarding the interpretation and application of the rights guaranteed by the Convention. This evolutionary approach enables the Court to take account of changes in social and economic relationships, cultural values, and governmental structures since the time of the Convention's drafting in the immediate post-Second World War era.

In an analysis of the doctrine I have observed that it has been used by the Court to:

> ...creatively update the interpretation of a number of Convention Articles in varied situations. These judgment have, *inter alia*, prohibited judicial corporal punishment (*Tyrer v UK*), limited the role of a government minister in determining the release of a prisoner (*Stafford v UK*), contributed to reducing the 'democratic deficit' in the European Union (*Matthews v UK*), recognised a right not to be compelled to belong to a trade union/employers' association (*Sigurjonsson v Iceland*) and required the legal recognition of the new identity of post-operative transsexuals (*Christine Goodwin v UK*). In utilising this doctrine the Court has had regard to a wide range of factors when determining what contemporary conditions necessitate. The common approach of member States has been relied upon (e.g. in *Tyrer* and *Pretty v UK*), whilst similar developments in a number of non-member States were noted in *Christine Goodwin*. The rulings of other international bodies were cited in support of the Court's interpretation of Article 11 in *Sigurjonsson*. ['The Creativity of the European Court of Human Rights' (2005) 5(1) *Human Rights Law Review* 57 at 69.]

2   Corporal punishment in state-funded schools was challenged by two Scottish mothers in *Campbell and Cosans v UK* A.48 (1982). Mrs Campbell's son, who was aged 6 at the time of the application to the Commission, attended a Roman Catholic primary school in the Strathclyde Region Education Authority area. The school used corporal punishment, in the form of striking the palm of the pupil's hand with a leather strap called a tawse, for disciplinary purposes. Mrs Campbell's son never received such punishment while he attended that school, but the Authority refused her request that it guarantee that he would not be so punished. Mrs Cosans' son, Jeffrey who was born in 1961, attended a High School in the Fife Region Education Authority area. In September 1976 Jeffrey was ordered to report to the Assistant Headmaster to receive corporal punishment (the tawse) for having tried to take a prohibited route, through a cemetery, on his way home from school. On his father's advice, Jeffrey reported to the Assistant Headmaster, but refused to accept the punishment. Jeffrey was immediately suspended from the school and he never returned as his parents continued to object to him receiving corporal punishment (in May 1977 he ceased to be of compulsory school age). Both mothers complained to the Commission that the use of corporal punishment in the schools attended by their sons violated, *inter alia*, Article 3. By 13 votes to 1, the Commission found no breach of that Article. The Court was unanimous in also finding no violation of that provision on the facts of the applicants' cases.

> 25. Neither Gordon Campbell nor Jeffrey Cosans was, in fact, strapped with the tawse. Accordingly, the Court does not in the present case have to consider under Article 3 (art 3) an actual application of corporal punishment.
>
> 26. However, the Court is of the opinion that, provided it is sufficiently real and immediate, a mere threat of conduct prohibited by Article 3 (art 3) may itself be in conflict with that provision. Thus, to threaten an individual with torture might in some circumstances constitute at least 'inhuman treatment'.
>
> 27. Although the system of corporal punishment can cause a certain degree of apprehension in those who may be subject to it, the Court nevertheless shares the Commission's view that the situation in which the applicants' sons found themselves did not amount to 'torture' or 'inhuman treatment', within the meaning of Article 3 (art 3): there is no evidence that they underwent suffering of the level inherent in these notions as they were interpreted and applied in the Court's *Ireland v UK* judgment of 18 January 1978 (Series A No 25, pp 66–7 and 68, paras 167 and 174).

28. The Court's judgment of 25 April 1978 in the *Tyrer* case does indicate certain criteria concerning the notion of 'degrading punishment' (Series A No 26, p 15, par 30). In the present case, no 'punishment' has actually been inflicted. Nevertheless, it follows from that judgment that 'treatment' itself will not be 'degrading' unless the person concerned has undergone—either in the eyes of others or in his own eyes (ibid, p 16, para 32)—humiliation or debasement attaining a minimum level of severity. That level has to be assessed with regard to the circumstances of the case (see the above-mentioned *Ireland v UK* judgment, p 65, para 162, p 66, para 167, and pp 69–70, paras 179–181).

29. Corporal chastisement is traditional in Scottish schools and, indeed, appears to be favoured by a large majority of parents . . . Of itself, this is not conclusive of the issue before the Court for the threat of a particular measure is not excluded from the category of 'degrading', within the meaning of Article 3 (art 3), simply because the measure has been in use for a long time or even meets with general approval (see, *mutatis mutandis*, the above-mentioned *Tyrer* judgment, p 15, para 31).

However, particularly in view of the above-mentioned circumstances obtaining in Scotland, it is not established that pupils at a school where such punishment is used are, solely by reason of the risk of being subjected thereto, humiliated or debased in the eyes of others to the requisite degree or at all.

30. As to whether the applicants' sons were humiliated or debased in their own eyes, the Court observes first that a threat directed to an exceptionally insensitive person may have no significant effect on him but nevertheless be incontrovertibly degrading; and conversely, an exceptionally sensitive person might be deeply affected by a threat that could be described as degrading only by a distortion of the ordinary and usual meaning of the word. In any event, in the case of these two children, the Court, like the Commission, notes that is has not been shown by means of medical certificates or otherwise that they suffered any adverse psychological or other effects . . .

Jeffrey Cosans may well have experienced feelings of apprehension or disquiet when he came close to an infliction of the tawse . . . but such feelings are not sufficient to amount to degrading treatment, within the meaning of Article 3 (art 3).

The same applies, a fortiori, to Gordon Campbell since he was never directly threatened with corporal punishment . . . It is true that counsel for his mother alleged at the hearings that group tension and a sense of alienation in the pupil are induced by the very existence of this practice but, even if this be so, these effects fall into a different category from humiliation or debasement.

31. To sum up, no violation of Article 3 (art 3) is established . . .

Hence the fact that neither of the applicants' sons had actually received corporal punishment was the decisive element in the Court's determination that the minimum threshold of Article 3 had not been infringed in these circumstances. However, the applicants succeeded in their claims that the school authorities had failed to respect the parents' 'religious and philosophical convictions' during the education of their children; thereby breaching Article 2 of Protocol 1.

Subsequently, a number of other complaints were made to the Commission by parents, and their children, concerning the existence and use of corporal punishment in state funded schools. These cases, where admissible, were subject to friendly settlements. A major component in the friendly settlements was the enactment of the Education (No 2) Act 1986, which ended corporal punishment in state-funded schools (by abolishing teachers' reasonable punishment defence to criminal charges or civil actions brought in respect of corporal punishment in such schools). See, for example, **Durairaj, Townend and Brant v UK** (1987), European Commission of Human Rights, *Stock-taking on the ECHR: Supplement 1987,* p 26.

3   Corporal punishment in non-state-funded schools, where the parents paid for the education of their children, was considered by the Court in *Costello-Roberts v UK* A.247-C (1993). In September 1985 Mrs Costello-Roberts sent her son, Jeremy, aged 7, to an independent boarding preparatory school (the school received no financial support from the government). The school's prospectus stated that a high standard of discipline was maintained, but it did not mention the use of corporal punishment. In fact the school operated a demerit marks system whereby pupils were given demerit marks each time they broke a school rule. When five demerit marks had been accumulated the pupil was subject to corporal punishment. By early October 1985 Jeremy had acquired five demerit marks, for talking in the corridor and being late for bed. The headmaster discussed the matter with colleagues and decided to punish Jeremy. Three days later the headmaster 'whacked' Jeremy three times on the bottom through his shorts with a rubber-soled gym shoe. No other person was present when the punishment was administered. Afterwards, Jeremy wrote to his mother several times complaining about the 'slippering'. In early November Mrs Costello-Roberts wrote to the school's governors expressing her 'grave concern' about the use of such a 'barbaric practice'. She also informed the headmaster that she did not want her son to be subject to any further corporal punishment. He replied that as she wished Jeremy to be exempt from the 'framework of discipline and punishment that is acceptable to all other parents at the school' it would be best if Jeremy were to be removed from the school at the end of term. Mrs Costello-Roberts also complained to the police regarding Jeremy's punishment, but they said that action could not be taken as there was no evidence of bruising on his buttocks. Jeremy was removed from the school in November 1985 by his mother. Mrs Costello-Roberts and Jeremy complained to the Commission alleging, *inter alia*, that the headmaster's punishment violated Article 3. The Commission declared Mrs Costello-Roberts' application inadmissible and that Jeremy had not suffered a breach of Article 3 (by 9 votes to 4). The Court held that the government was responsible under the Convention for the actions of the school because, *inter alia*, States are obliged (by Article 2 of Protocol 1) to secure to children their right to education and they cannot absolve themselves from responsibility by devolving authority to private persons/bodies. However, a majority, of five judges, determined that there had been no breach of Article 3.

31. The circumstances of the applicant's punishment may be distinguished from those of Mr Tyrer's which was found to be degrading within the meaning of Article 3 (art 3). Mr Costello-Roberts was a young boy punished in accordance with the disciplinary rules in force within the school in which he was a boarder. This amounted to being slippered three times on his buttocks through his shorts with a rubber-soled gym shoe by the headmaster in private ... Mr Tyrer, on the other hand, was a young man sentenced in the local juvenile court to three strokes of the birch on the bare posterior. His punishment was administered some three weeks later in a police station where he was held by two policemen while a third administered the punishment, pieces of the birch breaking at the first stroke.

32. Beyond the consequences to be expected from measures taken on a purely disciplinary plane, the applicant has adduced no evidence of any severe or long-lasting effects as a result of the treatment complained of. A punishment which does not occasion such effects may fall within the ambit of Article 3 (art 3) (see the *Tyrer* judgment, Series A No 26, pp 16–17, para 33), provided that in the particular circumstances of the case it may be said to have reached the minimum threshold of severity required. While the Court has certain misgivings about the automatic nature of the punishment and the three-day wait before its imposition, it considers that minimum level of severity not to have been attained in this case.

Accordingly, no violation of Article 3 (art 3) has been established.

Is the Court's distinction between the context and nature of the punishments in the above case and *Tyrer* convincing? Four judges dissented.

> However, in the present case, the ritualised character of the corporal punishment is striking. After a three-day gap, the headmaster of the school 'whacked' a lonely and insecure 7-year-old boy. A spanking on the spur of the moment might have been permissible, but in our view, the official and formalised nature of the punishment meted out, without adequate consent of the mother, was degrading to the applicant and violated Article 3 (art 3).

The School Standards and Framework Act 1998 abolished corporal punishment in all schools.

4   Yutaka Arai-Takahashi has commented that:

> Degrading treatment or punishment, set as the 'lowest' form of an absolute right on the graded scale of ill-treatment under Article 3 of the ECHR, offers a string of practical advantages to the decision-making policy of the Strasbourg organs. First, in view of its low intensity requirement, degrading treatment or punishment allows the Court to address multiple issues in diverse fields, some of which may never be condemned as worthy of a stigma associated with the inkling of torture. Second, since the ascertainment of a minimum threshold of severity is a malleable process susceptible to evolving perceptions of common European human rights standards, the benchmark of degrading treatment can be adapted to capture a greater number of claims, including even those that were previously declared inadmissible *ratione materiae* in the initial screening phase . . . . Third, an extensive coverage of issues under the rubric of degrading treatment can be undertaken without compromising the non-derogable nature of Article 3. ['Grading Scale of Degradation: Identifying the Threshold of Degrading Treatment or Punishment Under Article 3 ECHR' (2003) 21(3) *Netherlands Quarterly of Human Rights* 385 at 420–1.]

ARTICLE 4 PROHIBITION OF SLAVERY AND FORCED LABOUR

There has not been a large amount of litigation involving Article 4. Nevertheless in recent judgments the Court has ruled that this Article applies to contemporary forms of servitude (onerous/unpaid 'domestic' labour in *Siliadin*) and to human trafficking (*Rantsev*). Adapting it jurisprudence concerning Articles 2 and 3, that we have examined in previous chapters, the Court imposed positive obligations under Article 4 on member States to, *inter alia*, enact and implement legislation criminalizing such mistreatment of others and to provide practical help to the victims of those abusers.

Van der Mussele v Belgium A.70 (1983)
European Court of Human Rights

The profession of avocat in Belgium is regulated by the Ordre des avocats, a public law body that is independent of the executive. The Ordre determines who is qualified to be entered on the register of avocats. Avocats, including pupil avocats, enjoy an exclusive right of audience before the courts. At the time of this case the Belgian Judicial Code subjected the Ordre to a duty to make provision for the assistance of persons of insufficient means by establishing a 'Legal Advice and Defence Office'. In criminal cases the Office had to make an officially appointed ('pro Deo') avocat available to any indigent accused who so requested at least three days before his/her hearing. The Office generally appointed pupil avocats and they would normally spend about one quarter of their working time dealing with such cases during their three years of training. Appointed avocats were not entitled to remuneration or reimbursement of their expenses incurred in defending the poor. If a pupil advocat had not acted as an officially appointed avocat for a sufficient number of defendants the Ordre would not register that person as a qualified avocat.

The applicant was enrolled as a pupil avocat in September 1976. During July 1979, the Legal Advice and Defence Office of the Antwerp Bar appointed him to defend a Gambian national (Ebrima) arrested on suspicion of theft. The applicant represented Ebrima throughout his trial and appeal. After the latter was released from prison in December 1979, following representations from the applicant, the Office discharged the applicant from the case. Although the applicant had spent about 18 hours working for Ebrima he was allocated no fees or expenses (the applicant calculated these involving: 250BF for preparation of the case file, 1,800BF for correspondence, 1,300BF for travel to and from the prison and courts, and 50BF in respect of court costs) by the Office due to Ebrima's impecuniosity. The applicant was registered as a qualified avocat by the Ordre in October 1979. During his three years of pupillage he handled about 250 cases of which approximately 50 were in the capacity as an officially appointed avocat.

In 1980 an Act was passed that provided for governmental funding to pay pupil avocats for their defence work undertaken at the direction of the Legal Advice and Defence Office. However, because of budgetary reasons, the Act had not been implemented at the time of the Court's judgment.

The applicant complained to the Commission that his appointment by the Office to represent Ebrima, without remuneration and with sanctions in respect of his career if he refused, amounted to forced or compulsory labour contrary to Article 4. By 10 votes to 4, the Commission found no breach of that Article.

II. RESPONSIBILITY OF THE BELGIAN STATE

28. Before the Commission and in their memorial to the Court, the Government submitted that there was no primary or subordinate legislation that obliged avocats to accept work entrusted to them by a Legal Advice and Defence Office: their duty to act for indigent persons was said to derive solely from professional rules freely adopted by the Ordres des avocats themselves. According to the Government, the Belgian State did not prescribe either how appointments were to be made or their effects; it was therefore not answerable for any infringements of the Convention's guarantees that might be occasioned by implementation of the professional rules.

29. This argument, to which counsel for the Government did not revert at the hearings before the Court, was not accepted by the applicant or the Commission. Neither does it convince the Court.

Under the Convention, the obligation to grant free legal assistance arises, in criminal matters, from Article 6 § 3 (c) (art 6-3-c); in civil matters, it sometimes constitutes one of the means of ensuring a fair trial as required by Article 6 § 1 (art 6-1) (see the *Airey* judgment of 9 October 1979, Series A No 32, pp 14–16, § 26). This obligation is incumbent on each of the Contracting Parties. The Belgian State—and this was not contested by the Government—lays the obligation by law on the Ordres des avocats, thereby perpetuating a state of affairs of long standing; under Article 455, first paragraph, of the Judicial Code, the Councils of the Ordres are to make provision for the assistance of indigent persons by setting up Legal Advice and Defence Offices . . . As was pointed out by the applicant, the Councils have 'no discretion as regards the principle itself': legislation 'compels them to compel' members of the Bar to 'defend indigent persons'. Such a solution cannot relieve the Belgian State of the responsibilities it would have incurred under the Convention had it chosen to operate the system itself.

Moreover, the Government recognised at the hearings that 'the obligation', for pupil avocats, 'to act as defence counsel in cases assigned by the Legal Advice and Defence Office' arose from Article 455 of the Judicial Code; in paragraph 21 of their memorial, they had already conceded that Belgian law, by not making any provision for indemnifying pupil avocats, acknowledged at least implicitly that the latter have to bear the expenses incurred in dealing with the cases in question.

In addition, the Belgian Bars, bodies that are associated with the exercise of judicial power, are, without prejudice to the basic principle of independence necessary for the accomplishment of their important function in the community, subject to the requirements of the law. The relevant legislation states their objects and establishes their institutional organs; it endows with legal personality in public law each of the Councils of the twenty-seven local Ordres and the General Council of the National Ordre . . .

30. The responsibility of the Belgian State being thus engaged in the present case, it has to be ascertained whether that State complied with the provisions of the Convention and of Protocol No 1 art 4, art 14, P1-1) relied on by Mr Van der Mussele.

III. ALLEGED VIOLATION OF ARTICLE 4 OF THE CONVENTION, TAKEN ALONE (ART 4)

31. The applicant maintained that he had had to perform forced or compulsory labour incompatible with Article 4 (art 4) of the Convention. Under that Article (art 4) . . .

Four members of the Commission considered that this had been the case, but a majority of ten of their colleagues arrived at the opposite conclusion. The Government contended, as their principal submission, that the labour in question was not 'forced or compulsory' or, in the alternative, that it formed part of the applicant's 'normal civic obligations'.

32. Article 4 (art 4) does not define what is meant by 'forced or compulsory labour' and no guidance on this point is to be found in the various Council of Europe documents relating to the preparatory work of the European Convention.

As the Commission and the Government pointed out, it is evident that the authors of the European Convention—following the example of the authors of Article 8 of the draft International Covenant on Civil and Political Rights—based themselves, to a large extent, on an earlier treaty of the International Labour Organisation, namely Convention No 29 concerning Forced or Compulsory Labour.

Under the latter Convention (which was adopted on 28 June 1930, entered into force on 1 May 1932 and was modified—as regards the final clauses—in 1946), States undertook 'to suppress the use of forced or compulsory labour in all its forms within the shortest possible period' (Article 1 § 1); with a view to 'complete suppression' of such labour, States were permitted to have recourse thereto during a 'transitional period', but 'for public purposes only and as an exceptional measure, subject to the conditions and guarantees' laid down in Articles 4 *et seq.* (Article 1 § 2). The main aim of the Convention was originally to prevent the exploitation of labour in colonies, which were still numerous at that time. Convention No 105 of 25 June 1957, which entered into force on 17 January 1959, complemented Convention No 29, by prescribing 'the immediate and complete abolition of forced or compulsory labour' in certain specified cases.

Subject to Article 4 § 3 (art 4-3), the European Convention, for its part, lays down a general and absolute prohibition of forced or compulsory labour.

The Court will nevertheless take into account the above-mentioned ILO Conventions—which are binding on nearly all the member States of the Council of Europe, including Belgium—and especially Convention No 29. There is in fact a striking similarity, which is not accidental, between paragraph 3 of Article 4 (art 4-3) of the European Convention and paragraph 2 of Article 2 of Convention No 29. Paragraph 1 of the last-mentioned Article provides that 'for the purposes' of the latter Convention, the term 'forced or compulsory labour' shall mean 'all work or service which is exacted from any person under the menace of any penalty and for which the said person has not offered himself voluntarily'. This definition can provide a starting-point for interpretation of Article 4 (art 4) of the European Convention. However, sight should not be lost of that Convention's special features or of the fact that it is a living instrument to be read 'in the light of the notions currently prevailing in democratic States' (see, *inter alia,* the *Guzzardi* judgment of 6 November 1980, Series A No 39, p 34, § 95).

33. It was common ground between those appearing before the Court that the services rendered by Mr Van der Mussele to Mr Ebrima amounted to 'labour' for the purposes of Article 4 § 2 (art 4-2). It is true that the English word 'labour' is often used in the narrow sense of manual work, but it also bears the broad meaning of the French word 'travail' and it is the latter that should be adopted in the present context. The Court finds corroboration of this in the definition included in Article 2 § 1 of Convention No 29 ('all work or service', 'tout travail ou service'), in Article 4 § 3 (d) (art 4-3-d) of the European Convention ('any work or service', 'tout travail ou service') and in the very name of the International Labour Organisation (Organisation internationale du Travail), whose activities are in no way limited to the sphere of manual labour.

34. It remains to be ascertained whether there was 'forced or compulsory' labour. The first of these adjectives brings to mind the idea of physical or mental constraint, a factor that was certainly absent in the present case. As regards the second adjective, it cannot refer just to any form of legal compulsion or obligation. For example, work to be carried out in pursuance of a freely negotiated contract cannot be regarded as falling within the scope of Article 4 (art 4) on the sole ground that one of the parties has undertaken with the other to do that work and will be subject to sanctions if he does not honour his promise. On this point, the minority of the Commission agreed with the majority. What there has to be is work 'exacted . . . under the menace of any penalty' and also performed against the will of the person concerned, that is work for which he 'has not offered himself voluntarily'.

35. The definition given in Article 2 § 1 of ILO Convention No 29 leads the Court to inquire firstly whether there existed in the circumstances of the present case 'the menace of any penalty'.

Had Mr Van der Mussele refused without good reason to defend Mr Ebrima, his refusal would not have been punishable with any sanction of a criminal character. On the other hand, he would have run the risk of having the Council of the Ordre strike his name off the roll of pupils or reject his application for entry on the register of avocats . . . these prospects are sufficiently daunting to be capable of constituting 'the menace of [a] penalty', having regard both to the use of the adjective 'any' in the definition and to the standards adopted by the ILO on this point ('Abolition of Forced Labour': General Survey by the Committee of Experts on Application of Conventions and Recommendations, 1979, paragraph 21).

36. It must next be determined whether the applicant 'offered himself voluntarily' for the work in question.

According to the majority of the Commission, the applicant had consented in advance to the situation he complained of, so that it ill became him to object to it subsequently. Their argument ran as follows. On the eve of embarking on his career, the future avocat will make 'a kind of prospective assessment': he will weigh up the pros and cons, setting the 'advantages' of the profession against the 'drawbacks' it entails. And here the drawbacks were 'perfectly foreseeable' by the future avocat since he was not unaware either of the existence or of the scope of the obligations he would have to bear as regards defending clients free of charge, obligations that were 'limited' both in quantity (about fourteen cases each year) and in time (the period of pupillage). He also had knowledge of the corresponding advantages: the freedom he would enjoy in carrying out his duties and the opportunity he would have of familiarising himself with life in the courts and of 'establishing for himself a paying clientele'. One of the distinctive features of compulsory labour was therefore lacking and this was sufficient to establish that there had not been a violation of Article 4 § 2 (art 4-2).

This argument, which was supported by the Government, correctly reflects one aspect of the situation; nevertheless, the Court cannot attach decisive weight thereto. Mr Van der Mussele undoubtedly chose to enter the profession of avocat, which is a liberal profession in Belgium, appreciating that under its rules he would, in accordance with a long-standing tradition, be bound on occasions to render his services free of charge and without reimbursement of his expenses. However, he had to accept this requirement, whether he wanted to or not, in order to become an avocat and his consent was determined by the normal conditions of exercise of the profession at the relevant time. Nor should it be overlooked that what he gave was an acceptance of a legal régime of a general character.

The applicant's prior consent, without more, does not therefore warrant the conclusion that the obligations incumbent on him in regard to legal aid did not constitute compulsory labour for the purposes of Article 4 § 2 (art 4-2) of the Convention. Account must necessarily also be taken of other factors.

37. On the basis of jurisprudence of its own which dates back to 1963 (admissibility decision on application No 1468/62, *Iversen v Norway*, Yearbook of the Convention, vol. 6, pp 327–9) and which it has subsequently re-affirmed, the Commission expressed the opinion that for there to be forced

or compulsory labour, for the purposes of Article 4 § 2 (art 4-2) of the European Convention, two cumulative conditions have to be satisfied: not only must the labour be performed by the person against his or her will, but either the obligation to carry it out must be 'unjust' or 'oppressive' or its performance must constitute 'an avoidable hardship', in other words be 'needlessly distressing' or 'somewhat harassing'. After examining the issue 'as a supplementary consideration', the Commission concluded by a majority that the second condition was no more satisfied than the first condition.

The Court would observe that the second criterion thus applied is not stated in Article 2 § 1 of ILO Convention No 29. Rather it is a criterion that derives from Article 4 and the following Articles of that Convention, which are not concerned with the notion of forced or compulsory labour but lay down the requirements to be met for the exaction of forced or compulsory labour during the transitional period provided for under Article 1 § 2 (see 'ILO-internal minute—January 1966', paragraph 2).

Be that as it may, the Court prefers to adopt a different approach. Having held that there existed a risk comparable to 'the menace of [a] penalty' (see paragraph 35 above) and then that relative weight is to be attached to the argument regarding the applicant's 'prior consent' (see paragraph 36 above), the Court will have regard to all the circumstances of the case in the light of the underlying objectives of Article 4 (art 4) of the European Convention in order to determine whether the service required of Mr Van der Mussele falls within the prohibition of compulsory labour. This could be so in the case of a service required in order to gain access to a given profession, if the service imposed a burden which was so excessive or disproportionate to the advantages attached to the future exercise of that profession, that the service could not be treated as having been voluntarily accepted beforehand; this could apply, for example, in the case of a service unconnected with the profession in question.

38. The structure of Article 4 (art 4) is informative on this point. Paragraph 3 (art 4-3) is not intended to 'limit' the exercise of the right guaranteed by paragraph 2 (art 4-2), but to 'delimit' the very content of this right, for it forms a whole with paragraph 2 (art 4-2) and indicates what 'the term 'forced or compulsory labour' shall not include' (ce qui 'n'est pas considéré comme "travail forcé ou obligatoire"'). This being so, paragraph 3 (art 4-3) serves as an aid to the interpretation of paragraph 2 (art 4-2).

The four sub-paragraphs of paragraph 3 (art 4-3-a, art 4-3-b, art 4-3-c, art 4-3-d), notwithstanding their diversity, are grounded on the governing ideas of the general interest, social solidarity and what is in the normal or ordinary course of affairs. The final sub-paragraph, namely sub-paragraph (d) (art 4-3-d) which excludes 'any work or service which forms part of normal civil obligations' from the scope of forced or compulsory labour, is of especial significance in the context of the present case.

39. When viewed in the light of the foregoing considerations, the circumstances complained of can be seen to be characterised by several features, each of which provides a standard of evaluation.

The services to be rendered did not fall outside the ambit of the normal activities of an avocat; they differed from the usual work of members of the Bar neither by their nature nor by any restriction of freedom in the conduct of the case.

Secondly, a compensatory factor was to be found in the advantages attaching to the profession, including the exclusive right of audience and of representation enjoyed by avocats in Belgium as in several other countries...

In addition, the services in question contributed to the applicant's professional training in the same manner as did the cases in which he had to act on the instructions of paying clients of his own or of his pupil-master. They gave him the opportunity to enlarge his experience and to increase his reputation. In this respect, a certain degree of personal benefit went hand in hand with the general interest which was foremost.

Moreover, the obligation to which Mr Van der Mussele objected constituted a means of securing for Mr Ebrima the benefit of Article 6 § 3 (c) (art 6-3-c) of the Convention. To this extent, it was founded on a conception of social solidarity and cannot be regarded as unreasonable. By the same token, it was an obligation of a similar order to the 'normal civic obligations' referred to in Article 4 § 3 (d) (art 4-3-d). The Court is not required on the present occasion to rule on the correctness of the argument of the minority of the Commission to the effect that the almost routine allocation of pro-Deo cases to pupil avocats might not be fully consonant with the need to provide effective legal aid to impecunious litigants (see the *Artico* judgment of 13 May 1980, Series A No 37, pp 15–16, § 33).

Finally, the burden imposed on the applicant was not disproportionate. According to his own evidence, acting for Mr Ebrima accounted for only seventeen or eighteen hours of his working time...Even if one adds to this the other cases in which he was appointed to act during his pupillage—about fifty in three years, representing, so he said, a total of some seven hundred and fifty hours...—it can be seen that there remained sufficient time for performance of his paid work (approximately two hundred cases).

40. In point of fact, the applicant did not challenge the principle, as such, of the obligation in question; his complaint was limited to two aspects of the manner in which the obligation was implemented, namely the absence of fees and more especially the non-reimbursement of incurred expenditure...He felt it unjust—and on this the minority of the Commission concurred with him—to entrust the free representation of the most needy citizens to pupil avocats who themselves were in receipt of insufficient resources and to make them bear the cost of a public service instituted by law. He drew attention to the fact that for many years the successive chairmen of the Ordre des avocats in Belgium have regarded such a state of affairs as intolerable.

For their part, the Government acknowledged that the practice complained of was inspired by a 'paternalism' that was now 'outmoded'. They asserted that the traditional stance of a profession jealous of its independence accounted for the fact that Belgium had delayed in 'endeavouring', by means of the Act of 9 April 1980...'to bring its standards' in this sphere to 'the level of other States, notably European': until recent times, so the Government stated, the Bar had viewed with 'distrust' State-payment of pupil avocats, the idea of an official scale of fees inspiring deep-rooted hostility among its members.

The Commission also described as unfortunate a legal situation which in its opinion, while being compatible with Article 4 (art 4), no longer meets 'the requirements of modern life'. Pointing out that if pupil avocats were remunerated their professional training would not suffer thereby, the Commission expressed the wish for a prompt and effective implementation of the Act of 9 April 1980.

The Court has not overlooked this aspect of the problem. While remunerated work may also qualify as forced or compulsory labour, the lack of remuneration and of reimbursement of expenses constitutes a relevant factor when considering what is proportionate or in the normal course of affairs. In this connection, it is noteworthy that the respective laws of numerous Contracting States have evolved or are evolving, albeit in varying degrees, towards the assumption by the public purse of the cost of paying lawyers or trainee lawyers appointed to act for indigent litigants. The Belgian Act of 9 April 1980 is an example of this development; that Act, once it has been implemented, should bring about a significant improvement, without thereby threatening the independence of the Bar.

At the relevant time, the state of affairs complained of undoubtedly caused Mr Van der Mussele some prejudice by reason of the lack of remuneration and of reimbursement of expenses, but that prejudice went hand in hand with advantages (see paragraph 39 above) and has not been shown to be excessive. The applicant did not have a disproportionate burden of work imposed on him (ibid) and the amount of expenses directly occasioned by the cases in question was relatively small...

The Court would recall that Mr Van der Mussele had voluntarily entered the profession of avocat with knowledge of the practice complained of. This being so, a considerable and unreasonable imbalance between the aim pursued—to qualify as an avocat—and the obligations undertaken in order to achieve that aim would alone be capable of warranting the conclusion that the services exacted of Mr Van der Mussele in relation to legal aid were compulsory despite his consent. No such imbalance is disclosed by the evidence before the Court, notwithstanding the lack of remuneration and of reimbursement of expenses—which in itself is far from satisfactory.

Having regard, furthermore, to the standards still generally obtaining in Belgium and in other democratic societies, there was thus no compulsory labour for the purposes of Article 4 § 2 (art 4-2) of the Convention.

41. In view of this conclusion, the Court need not determine whether the work in question was in any event justified under Article 4 § 3 (d) (art 4-3-d) as such and, in particular, whether the notion of 'normal civic obligations' extends to obligations incumbent on a specific category of citizens by reason of the position they occupy, or the functions they are called upon to perform, in the community.

IV. ALLEGED VIOLATION OF ARTICLE 14 OF THE CONVENTION, TAKEN TOGETHER WITH ARTICLE 4 (ART 14+4)

42. The applicant also invoked Article 14 read in conjunction with Article 4 (art 14+4)

...

43. Article 14 (art 14) complements the other substantive provisions of the Convention and the Protocols. It may be applied in an autonomous manner as breach of Article 14 (art 14) does not presuppose breach of those other provisions. On the other hand, it has no independent existence since it has effect solely in relation to 'the enjoyment of the rights and freedoms' safeguarded by the other substantive provisions (see, *inter alia*, the *Marckx* judgment of 13 June 1979, Series A No 31, pp 15–16, § 32). As the Court has found that there was no forced or compulsory labour for the purposes of Article 4 (art 4), the question arises whether the facts in issue fall completely outside the ambit of that Article (art 4) and, hence, of Article 14 (art 14). However, such reasoning would be met by one major objection. The criteria which serve to delimit the concept of compulsory labour include the notion of what is in the normal course of affairs (see paragraph 38 above). Work or labour that is in itself normal may in fact be rendered abnormal if the choice of the groups or individuals bound to perform it is governed by discriminatory factors, which was precisely what the applicant contended had occurred in the present circumstances.

Consequently, this is not a case where Article 14 (art 14) should be held inapplicable; the Government, moreover, did not contest the point.

44. In a memorial of 27 October 1980 filed before the Commission, Mr Van der Mussele stated that he was not complaining of any discrimination between pupil avocats and avocats entered on the register. He did not alter his attitude before the Court, and the Court sees no reason for examining the issue of its own motion.

45. On the other hand, in the applicant's submission, Belgian avocats are subject, in respect of the matters under consideration, to less favourable treatment than that of members of a whole series of other professions. In legal aid cases, the State accords remuneration to judges and registrars, pays the emoluments of interpreters (Article 184 bis of the Code of Criminal Procedure and Article 691 of the Judicial Code) and, 'in lieu of the legally aided person', advances 'the travel and subsistence expenses of judicial, public or publicly appointed officers, the costs and fees of experts, the allowances of witnesses..., the disbursements and one quarter of the salaries of bailiffs as well as the disbursements of other public or publicly appointed officers' (Article 692 of the Judicial Code)...Medical practitioners, veterinary surgeons, pharmacists and dentists, for their part, are not required to provide their services free of charge to indigent persons. According to the applicant, these all represented instances of arbitrary inequality, being devoid of any 'objective and reasonable justification' (see the judgment of 23 July 1968 in the '*Belgian Linguistic*' case, Series A No

6, p 34, § 10); they thereby contravened Articles 14 and 4 (art 14+14) taken together. The minority of the Commission shared this view, at least to a large extent.

46. Article 14 (art 14) safeguards individuals, placed in analogous situations, from discrimination (see the above-mentioned *Marckx* judgment, Series A No 31, p 15, § 32). Yet between the Bar and the various professions cited by the applicant, including even the judicial and parajudicial professions, there exist fundamental differences to which the Government and the majority of the Commission rightly drew attention, namely differences as to legal status, conditions for entry to the profession, the nature of the functions involved, the manner of exercise of those functions, etc. The evidence before the Court does not disclose any similarity between the disparate situations in question: each one is characterised by a corpus of rights and obligations of which it would be artificial to isolate one specific aspect.

On the basis of the applicant's grievances, the Court accordingly does not find any breach of Articles 14 and 4 taken together (art 14+4).

...

FOR THESE REASONS, THE COURT UNANIMOUSLY

Holds that there has been no breach of Article 4 of the Convention, taken on its own or in conjunction with Article 14...

NOTES

1   The Court was composed of President Wiarda and Judges: Ryssdal, Thor Vilhjalmsson, Ganshof van der Meersch, Bindschedler-Robert, Evrigenis, Lagergren, Liesch, Gölcüklü, Matscher, Garcia de Enterria, Pettiti, Walsh, Evans, Russo, and Gersing.

The judgment is very important for explaining the origins of the terms used in Article 4 and the way in which they should be interpreted. The Court also set out the relationship between the constituent paragraphs of the Article. The judges were not willing to follow the Commission's established approach to Article 4(2) and introduced a proportionality test as an element in assessing the extent and lawfulness of the burdens placed upon individuals required to undertake work by States.

2   The notion of 'servitude' in Article 4(1) was considered in the case of ***Van Droogenbroeck v Belgium*** A.44 (1982). The applicant was a recidivist who had been convicted of a number of thefts. In 1970 he was sentenced to two years' imprisonment for theft and also 'placed at the Government's disposal' for ten years pursuant to the Social Protection Act 1964. The latter order was classified as a penalty, but had the objective of trying to rehabilitate frequent offenders. After the applicant completed his prison sentence the authorities attempted to secure training and employment for the applicant on a number of occasions, however he continued to engage in criminal activity and was recalled to prison a number of times during the period of his placement. The applicant complained to the Commission alleging, *inter alia*, that he had been held in servitude and forced to work contrary to paragraphs (1) and (2) of Article 4. The Commission was unanimous in finding no breach of Article 4. Likewise the Court was united in rejecting the applicant's complaints under this Article:

58. The applicant's first allegation was that by being placed at the Government's disposal he was held in 'servitude', contrary to paragraph 1, in that he was subjected 'to the whims of the administration'.

The situation complained of did not violate Article 5 par. 1 [as it was justified under Article 5(1)(a), being a lawful detention after conviction by a competent court]. Accordingly, it could have been regarded as servitude only if it involved a 'particularly serious' form of 'denial of freedom' (see paragraphs 79–80 of the Commission's report), which was not so in the present case.

59. Mr Van Droogenbroeck further complained that, contrary to paragraph 2 of Article 4 (art 4-2), he was 'forced' to work in order to save 12,000 BF. According to the Government, he was simply 'invited' to work.

The Court considers that it may leave this question of fact open. In practice, once release is conditional on the possession of savings from pay for work done in prison . . . one is not far away from an obligation in the strict sense of the term.

However, it does not follow that the complaint is well-founded . . . the latter Article authorises, in paragraph 3 (a) (art 4-3-a), work required to be done in the ordinary course of detention which has been imposed, as was here the case, in a manner that does not infringe paragraph 1 of Article 5 (art 5-1). Moreover, the work which Mr Van Droogenbroeck was asked to do did not go beyond what is 'ordinary' in this context since it was calculated to assist him in reintegrating himself into society and had as its legal basis provisions which find an equivalent in certain other member States of the Council of Europe . . .

60. Accordingly, the Belgian authorities did not fail to observe the requirements of Article 4 (art 4).

Hence, forms of punishment and prison work which are within the bounds of contemporary European practices will not generally violate Article 4.

3 A unanimous Chamber of the full-time Court held that States are under positive obligations to adopt and effectively implement criminal law provisions prohibiting the practices proscribed by Article 4 in *Siliadin v France*, judgment of 26 July 2005. In 1994, when she was 15 years old, the applicant, a Togolese national, was brought to France by a relative of her father. The relative, who had acquired French nationality, had undertaken to regularize the applicant's immigration status in France and arrange for her education. In return the applicant was to undertake housework for the relative until she had earned enough to pay back the cost of her airfare to France. The relative confiscated the applicant's passport. Ten months after the applicant arrived in France the relative 'lent' the applicant to a couple of friends in order that she could help them with household tasks. The applicant was retained by the couple as a 'maid of all work' for nearly four years. During that time she worked from 7.30 am to 10.30 pm, with no days off (she was given permission to attend church on certain Sundays) for no pay. She slept on a mattress on the floor and wore old clothes. Eventually, the applicant informed a neighbour of her situation and the matter was referred to the public prosecutor. The couple were charged and convicted of, *inter alia*, wrongfully obtaining unpaid services from a vulnerable person. The couple successfully appealed against their conviction. However, they were ordered to pay the applicant 15,000 euros in damages and an employment tribunal later awarded her 31,000 euros in salary arrears against them. The Chamber characterized the treatment of the applicant as amounting to forced labour in that she was required to work for years, against her will, on behalf of the couple without being paid. Furthermore, given the applicant's status as a minor and the coercion exercised over her by the couple (her passport had been confiscated, her immigration status had never been regularized, and she was afraid of being arrested by the police) the Chamber found that she had also been held in servitude. Given the couple's acquittal and subsequent criticism of the relevant criminal law provisions by the National Assembly, the Chamber concluded that there had been a breach of Article 4 by the respondent State as its law had not provided the applicant with adequate protection. The horrifying facts of this case amply illustrate why States must take appropriate measures to ensure that vulnerable persons within their jurisdiction are not abused by other exploitative persons.

4   A unanimous Chamber significantly extended the ambit of Article 4 to encompass the phenomenon of people trafficking in ***Rantsev v Cyprus and Russia***, judgment of 7 January 2010. The applicant's 20-year-old daughter (Oxana) had left Russia to work as an 'artiste' in a Cypriot nightclub. The Cypriot authorities granted about 4,000 visas/work permits annually to enable foreign persons to work, for three to six months, in designated night clubs (in a subsequent report the Cypriot Ombudsman noted that most of the women taking up these visas came from East European States and were aware that their real work involved prostitution). After a few days work in the nightclub Oxana left her residence (in a note she said she wanted to return to Russia). However, she was seen in another nightclub a few evenings later. The manager of her nightclub went and took Oxana to the police (he wanted her to be detained/deported so that he could replace her with another foreign 'artiste'). Later that night the manager was called back to the police station and Oxana was handed over to him, they were told she should be taken to the immigration office in the daytime. The manager took Oxana to the (duplex) flat of an employee. He slept on the lower floor while Oxana was in a bedroom on the upper floor. A short time later Oxana was found dead on the ground beneath the fifth-floor balcony of her room. A later inquest found that Oxana, '…in an attempt to escape from the aforementioned apartment and in strange circumstances, jumped into the void as a result of which she was fatally injured.… There is no evidence… that suggests criminal liability of a third person for her death.'

The applicant contended that Cyprus and Russia had violated Article 4 by failing to protect Oxana from being trafficked and undertaking effective investigations into the nature of her work in Cyprus. The Chamber held that:

282. There can be no doubt that trafficking threatens the human dignity and fundamental freedoms of its victims and cannot be considered compatible with a democratic society and the values expounded in the Convention. In view of its obligation to interpret the Convention in light of present-day conditions, the Court considers it unnecessary to identify whether the treatment about which the applicant complains constitutes 'slavery', 'servitude' or 'forced and compulsory labour'. Instead, the Court concludes that trafficking itself, within the meaning of Article 3(a) of the Palermo Protocol and Article 4(a) of the Anti-Trafficking Convention, falls within the scope of Article 4 of the Convention.

The Palermo Protocol defined trafficking as encompassing:

…the recruitment, transportation, transfer, harbouring or receipt of persons, by means of the threat or use of force or other forms of coercion, of abduction, of fraud, of deception, of the abuse of power or of a position of vulnerability or of the giving or receiving of payments or benefits to achieve the consent of a person having control over another person, for the purpose of exploitation. Exploitation shall include, at a minimum, the exploitation of the prostitution of others or other forms of sexual exploitation, forced labour or services, slavery or practices similar to slavery, servitude or the removal of organs.

Under Article 4 of the ECHR States were required to satisfy three positive obligations to combat people trafficking in the judgment of the Court. First, member States had to enact domestic regulatory frameworks that:

284.…ensure the practical and effective protection of the rights of victims or potential victims of trafficking. Accordingly, in addition to criminal law measures to punish traffickers, Article 4 requires member States to put in place adequate measures regulating businesses often used as a cover for human trafficking. Furthermore, a State's immigration rules must address relevant concerns relating to encouragement, facilitation or tolerance of trafficking…

Secondly, States should provide specific protection to individuals at imminent risk of being trafficked where:

286. ... the State authorities were aware, or ought to have been aware, of circumstances giving rise to a credible suspicion that an identified individual had been, or was at real and immediate risk of being, trafficked or exploited within the meaning of Article 3(a) of the Palermo Protocol and Article 4(a) of the Anti-Trafficking Convention. In the case of an answer in the affirmative, there will be a violation of Article 4 of the Convention where the authorities fail to take appropriate measures within the scope of their powers to remove the individual from that situation or risk ...

Finally, States were obliged to conduct effective investigations into allegations that trafficking was occurring in their territories and to cooperate with other States where the allegations involved cross-border trafficking.

Applying these obligations the Chamber found significant weaknesses in the Cypriot system of granting 'artiste' visas as the authorities knew, from the 1970s, that there was a major problem of foreign women being brought into the country to work as prostitutes. Also the Cypriot authorities had failed to give adequate protection to Oxana when they ought to have appreciated that there was a real risk that she had been subject to trafficking. The Russian authorities were found to have breached Article 4 by failing to investigate how she had been recruited in Russia.

The above judgment demonstrated the Court interpreting the language of Article 4 to embrace modern forms of slave-like maltreatment of persons. It, therefore, represents yet another example of the Court applying the living instrument/evolutive approach to update the Convention's protections to reflect contemporary needs. Additionally, the Court built upon the implied positive obligations developed under Articles 2 and 3 to establish further safeguards in respect of people trafficking.

In June 2010 the Council of Europe's Commissioner for Human Rights (Thomas Hammarberg), following a visit to Cyprus, wrote to the Cypriot Minister of Interior welcoming the abolition of the Cypriot artiste visa. However, the Commissioner expressed concern that other types of work permits (e.g. for barmaids) could be used to facilitate people trafficking.

5 The Court interpreted Article 4(3)(d) as encompassing the duty on men to serve in the local fire brigade, or pay a financial contribution instead of actual service, in Baden-Wurttemberg: *Schmidt v Germany* A.291-B (1994).

23. Like the participants in the proceedings, the Court considers that compulsory fire service such as exists in Baden-Württemberg is one of the 'normal civic obligations' envisaged in Article 4 para 3 (d) (art 4-3-d). It observes further that the financial contribution which is payable—in lieu of service—is, according to the Federal Constitutional Court ... a 'compensatory charge'. The Court therefore concludes that, on account of its close links with the obligation to serve, the obligation to pay also falls within the scope of Article 4 para 3 (d) (art 4-3-d).

By holding that the liability for the financial payment was also covered by Article 4 the Court was able to go on and find unlawful sex discrimination in breach of Article 14, because only men were liable (see p 823).

6 The approach of the original Court to the interpretation of paragraph 3 of Article 4 in *Schmidt* was followed by the Chamber in *Zarb Adami v Malta*, judgment of 20 June 2006.

In the latter case the applicant complained that men were much more likely to be called for jury service than women (in 1996, 147 women were placed on the lists of jurors whilst 4,298 men were placed on the lists). The Chamber (6 votes to 1) held that:

46. . . . Therefore, the fact that a situation corresponds to the notion of a normal civic obligation within the meaning of paragraph 3 is not an obstacle to the applicability of Article 4 of the Convention, read in conjunction with Article 14.

47. Like the participants in the proceedings, the Court considers that compulsory jury service such as exists in Malta is one of the 'normal civic obligations' envisaged in Article 4 § 3(d). It observes further that the applicant did not offer himself voluntarily for jury service and that his failure to appear led to the imposition of a fine, which could be converted into a term of imprisonment. On account of its close links with the obligation to serve, the obligation to pay the fine also falls within the scope of Article 4 § 3(d) (see, *mutatis mutandis, Karlheinz Schmidt*, judgment cited above, p 32, § 23).

. . .

49. It follows that the facts in issue fall within the ambit of Article 4. Article 14 of the Convention is accordingly applicable.

The Chamber then found that the Maltese Government had not been able to provide any proper justification for the low number of women registered on the lists of jurors and consequently there had been a breach of Article 14 read in conjunction with Article 4(3)(d). However, several judges expressed varying degrees of disquiet about the established interpretation of the ambit of Article 4. Judge Bratza in his concurring opinion stated that he did not find the reasoning in **Schmidt** 'to be entirely convincing or satisfactory'. Whilst Judge Garlicki in his concurring opinion was not convinced by the earlier reasoning. He believed that:

. . . it is possible to read Article 4, taken as a whole, in a broader way, not only as prohibiting any forms of forced or compulsory labour but also as regulating State prerogatives in establishing different forms of compulsory works and services. In other words, Article 4 may also be read as setting a general framework of duties which may be imposed on an individual. Article 4 empowers the State to establish such duties and services, but—by the very fact of their enumeration—Article 4 also absorbs (includes) them into the realm of the Convention. One of the consequences of such inclusion is that those duties and services must be formulated in a manner compatible with the Convention, its Article 14 included. It should not be forgotten that Article 4 is drafted in a particular manner: no other substantive provision of the Convention contains enumerations of such kind. This may suggest that the drafters of the Convention envisaged that Article 4 might be interpreted in a particular way.

Several arguments may warrant this broad reading of Article 4. First of all, it would reflect the particular rank of Article 4 as 'one of the fundamental values of democratic societies'. Secondly, it would correspond better to the concept of positive duties of the State: the State is not only prohibited from introducing any form of forced or compulsory labour, but is also required to regulate the scope and manner of what remains imposable on individual citizens. Finally, it would respond to the developing trends of modern societies: whilst it is now very difficult to find situations of 'classic' forced labour or servitude (the 2005 *Siliadin v France* case being the only recent example), there may be more controversies surrounding obligations enumerated in paragraph 3 of Article 4.

Judge Casadevall dissented:

2. Like the dissenting judges in the case of *Karlheinz Schmidt* (a judgment that is now twelve years old), I fail to see how Article 14, which is dependent for its existence on a recognised right (see

paragraph 42 of the judgment), can be linked to subparagraph (d) of Article 4 § 3 for the following reasons:

(a) subparagraph (d) actually constitutes an exception to the general rule prohibiting forced or compulsory labour;
(b) the expression 'forced or compulsory labour' in Article 4 does not include 'any work or service which forms part of normal civic obligations' (see paragraph 43 of the judgment); and
(c) it is accepted that the obligation to serve as a juror in Malta forms part of the 'normal civic obligations' (see paragraph 47 of the judgment).

3. It is quite clear that Mr Zarb Adami has not been required to perform forced or compulsory labour within the meaning of Article 4 § 2 and that the service he was asked to perform constituted a civic obligation, such as serving the administration of criminal justice. Since the applicant is unable to assert a substantive right protected by the Convention (Article 4 does not prohibit civic obligations of this type) Article 14 cannot come into play.

Furthermore, he considered the applicant's complaint to be 'frivolous'. Given these diverging views in the Chamber, the Grand Chamber may reconsider the interpretation of Article 4(2) and (3) in the future.

7   The contemporary approach of the Court to persons claiming conscientious objection to compulsory military service was elaborated in *Bayatyan v Armenia*, p 609.

ARTICLE 5 RIGHT TO LIBERTY AND SECURITY

The lengthy and detailed text of Article 5 has generated extensive case-law. The Court has sought to elaborate the concept of liberty protected by this Article (*Guzzardi*) whilst also emphasizing that States can only justify infringements of liberty by reference to the specific grounds elaborated in Article 5(1). These exceptions have been applied to contemporary issues, such as the detention of HIV positive individuals (*Enhorn*). However, the Court has required States to demonstrate the proportionality of detention measures (*Vasileva*). The right to be informed of the reasons for your detention, granted by Article 5(2), has been extended to cover both criminal and civil forms of detention (*Van der Leer*). The Court has been very firm in requiring detained criminal suspects to be brought swiftly before a judicial officer to enable, *inter alia*, an independent review of the lawfulness of such persons' detention (*Brogan*). Furthermore, the ambiguous wording of Article 5(3) has been clarified to require States to justify both the reasons for and the length of time detainees have been held on remand awaiting their criminal trials (*Wemhoff*). The Court has become increasingly strict in its assessment of these requirements (*Kalashnikov*). Domestic courts have been obliged, under Article 5(4), to conduct regular reviews of the need for the continued detention of, *inter alios*, the mentally ill (*Winterwerp*) and life sentence prisoners (*Thynne*). Alongside the express duties imposed on States by Article 5 the Court has also found implied positive obligations (*Kurt*).

The concept of liberty

Guzzardi v Italy A.39 (1980)
European Court of Human Rights

The applicant was suspected by the police of engaging in very serious illegal activities and belonging to a band of Mafia. Under legislation making provision for various preventive measures which could be taken against 'persons presenting a danger for security and public morality', the Milan Regional Court directed that the applicant be placed under special supervision and combined this with an obligation of confinement to a part of an island (Asinara) allocated for compulsory residents. Accordingly, for 16 months the applicant was confined to a special area of approximately 2.5 sq km, viz a hamlet (Cala Reale) on the island consisting of a former medical establishment and certain other buildings, including a police station where he had to report twice daily. He was subject to a curfew between 10 pm and 7 am but otherwise there were significant elements of the confinement which distinguished it from normal prison detention.

The applicant alleged breaches of Articles 3, 8, 9, and Article 2 of Protocol 1. The Commission of its own initiative examined the case from the perspective of Article 5. It was unanimously of the opinion that there had been a breach of Article 5(1), but not of any other Articles.

JUDGMENT OF THE COURT

92. The Court recalls that in proclaiming the 'right to liberty', paragraph 1 of Article 5 is contemplating the physical liberty of the person; its aim is to ensure that no one should be dispossessed of this liberty in an arbitrary fashion. As was pointed out by those appearing before the Court, the paragraph is not concerned with mere restrictions on liberty of movement; such restrictions are governed by Article 2 of Protocol No 4 which has not been ratified by Italy. In order to determine whether someone has been 'deprived of his liberty' within the meaning of Article 5, the starting point must be his concrete situation and account must be taken of a whole range of criteria such as the type, duration, effects and manner of implementation of the measure in question (see the *Engel* judgment of 8 June 1976, Series A No 22, p 24, §§ 58–9).

93. The difference between deprivation of and restriction upon liberty is nonetheless merely one of degree or intensity, and not one of nature or substance. Although the process of classification into one or other of these categories sometimes proves to be no easy task in that some borderline cases are a matter of pure opinion, the Court cannot avoid making the selection upon which the applicability or inapplicability of Article 5 depends.

94. As provided for under the 1956 Act . . . , special supervision accompanied by an order for compulsory residence in a specified district does not of itself come within the scope of Article 5. The Commission acknowledged this: it focused its attention on Mr Guzzardi's 'actual position' at Cala Reale . . . and pointed out that on 5 October 1977 it had declared inadmissible application no 7960/77 lodged by the same individual with regard to his living conditions at Force . . .

[However it] does not follow that 'deprivation of liberty' may never result from the manner of implementation of such a measure, and in the present case the manner of implementation is the sole issue that falls to be considered . . . .

95. The Government's reasoning is not without weight. It demonstrates very clearly the extent of the difference between the applicant's treatment on Asinara and classic detention in prison or strict arrest imposed on a serviceman (see the above-mentioned *Engel* judgment, p 26, § 63). Deprivation of liberty may, however, take numerous other forms. Their variety is being increased by developments in legal standards and in attitudes; and the Convention is to be interpreted in the light of the notions currently prevailing in democratic States (see notably the *Tyrer* judgment of 25 April 1978, Series A No 26, pp 15–16, § 31).

Whilst the area around which the applicant could move far exceeded the dimensions of a cell and was not bounded by any physical barrier, it covered no more than a tiny fraction of an island to which access was difficult and about nine-tenths of which was occupied by a prison. Mr Guzzardi was housed in part of the hamlet of Cala Reale which consisted mainly of the buildings of a former medical establishment which were in a state of disrepair or even dilapidation, a carabinieri station, a school and a chapel. He lived their principally in the company of other persons subjected to the same measure and of policemen. The permanent population of Asinara resided almost entirely at Cala d'Oliva, which Mr Guzzardi could not visit, and would appear to have made hardly any use of its right to go to Cala Reale. Consequently, there were few opportunities for social contacts available to the applicant other than with his near family, his fellow 'residents' and the supervisory staff. Supervision was carried out strictly and on an almost constant basis. Thus, Mr Guzzardi was not able to leave his dwelling between 10 pm and 7 am without giving prior notification to the authorities in due time. He had to report to the authorities twice a day and inform them of the name and number of his correspondent whenever he wished to use the telephone. He needed the consent of the authorities for each of his trips to Sardinia or the mainland, trips which were rare and, understandably, made under the strict supervision of the carabinieri. He was liable to punishment by 'arrest' if he failed to comply with any of his obligations. Finally, more than sixteen months elapsed between his arrival at Cala Reale and his departure for Force...

It is admittedly not possible to speak of 'deprivation of liberty' on the strength of any one of these factors taken individually, but cumulatively and in combination they certainly raise an issue of categorisation from the viewpoint of Article 5. In certain respects the treatment complained of resembles detention in an 'open prison' or committal to a disciplinary unit (see the above-mentioned *Engel* judgment, p 26, § 64)...

The Court considers on balance that the present case is to be regarded as one involving deprivation of liberty...

96. It remains to be determined whether the situation was one of those, exhaustively listed in Article 5 § 1 of the Convention (see the *Winterwerp* judgment of 24 October 1979, Series A No 33, p 16, § 37), in which the Contracting States reserve the right to arrest or detain individuals...

The Court rejected a government argument that the applicant was a vagrant within Article 5(1)(e).

100. On a true analysis, the order for Mr Guzzardi's compulsory residence was not a punishment for a specific offence but a preventive measure taken on the strength of indications of a propensity to crime...

In the Court's opinion, comparison of Article 5 § 1(a) with Articles 6 § 2 and 7 § 1 shows that for Convention purposes there cannot be a 'condamnation' (in the English text: 'conviction') unless it has been established in accordance with the law that there has been an offence—either criminal or, if appropriate, disciplinary (see the above-mentioned *Engel* judgment, p 27, § 68). Moreover, to use 'conviction' for a preventive or security measure would be consonant neither with the principle of narrow interpretation to be observed in this area (see paragraph 98 above) nor with the fact that that word implies a finding of guilt....

101. The deprivation of liberty complained of was not covered by sub-paragraph (b) either.

Admittedly, under the procedure laid down by the 1956 Act judicial decisions are a kind of sanction for failure to heed a prior warning (deffida), but the warning is not indispensable if, as in the present case, recourse is had to the 1965 Act; moreover, the warning is issued by the Chief of Police and so does not constitute an 'order of a court'....

As regards the words 'to secure the fulfilment of any obligation prescribed by law', they concern only those cases where the law permits the detention of a person to compel him to fulfil a 'specific and concrete' obligation which he has failed to satisfy (see the above-mentioned *Engel* judgment, p 28, § 69). However, as the Commission rightly emphasised, the 1956 and 1965 Acts impose general obligations...

102. Neither was the applicant in one of the situations dealt with by sub-paragraph (c).

It is true that there was 'reasonable suspicion of [his] having committed an offence' and that he remained subject to charges throughout the time he spent on Asinara, but the decisions of the Regional Court (30 January 1975), the Court of Appeal (12 March 1975) and the Court of Cassation (6 October 1975) [authorising his detention as Asinara] had no connection in law with the investigation being pursued in his respect: they were based on the 1956 and 1965 Acts which are applicable irrespective of whether or not there has been a charge and do not prescribe any subsequent appearance 'before the competent legal authority'...

At first sight, a more likely hypothesis is that the measure complained of was taken because it was 'reasonably considered necessary to prevent [Mr Guzzardi's] committing an offence' or, at the outside, 'fleeing after having done so'. However, in that case as well a question would arise as to the measure's 'lawfulness' since, solely on the basis of the 1956 and 1965 Acts, an order for compulsory residence as such, leaving aside the manner of its implementation, does not constitute deprivation of liberty (see paragraph 94 above). It would also be necessary to consider whether the requirements of paragraph 3 of Article 5 had been observed (see the *Lawless* judgment of 1 July 1961, Series A No 3, pp 51–3, §§ 13–14). In any event, the phrase under examination is not adapted to a policy of general prevention directed against an individual or a category of individuals who, like mafiosi, present a danger on account of their continuing propensity to crime; it does no more than afford the Contracting States a means of preventing a concrete and specific offence. This can be seen both from the use of the singular ('an offence', 'celle-ci' in the French text; see the *Matznetter* judgment of 10 November 1969, Series A No 10, pp 40 and 43, separate opinions of Mr Balladore Palliere and Mr Zekia) and from the object of Article 5, namely to ensure that no one should be dispossessed of his liberty in an arbitrary fashion (see the above-mentioned *Winterwerp* judgment, p 16, § 37)....

FOR THESE REASONS, THE COURT...

4. Holds by eleven votes to seven that there was in the instant case deprivation of liberty within the meaning of Article 5 of the Convention;

5. Holds unanimously that the said deprivation of liberty was not justified under sub-paragraph (e) of Article 5 § 1 or under sub-paragraph (b);

6. Holds by sixteen votes to two that the said deprivation of liberty was also not justified under sub-paragraph (a);

7. Holds by twelve votes to six that the said deprivation of liberty was not justified under sub-paragraph (c) either;

8. Holds, to sum up, by ten votes to eight, that from 8 February 1975 to 22 July 1976 the applicant was the victim of a breach of Article 5 § 1;...

Dissenting Opinion of Judge Sir Gerald Fitzmaurice:

8. Basically what happened to the applicant was not that he was imprisoned or confined, but that he was banished to an island on which he was assigned a place of residence (an ordinary house) and restricted to an area sufficiently big for him to be able to live a normal life except that he could not leave it without permission, and was (and for that purpose had to be) under surveillance. To me all this has very much more the flavour of Article 2 of the [Fourth] Protocol than of Article 5 of the Convention, even if a residue of doubt may remain—but in that event, is it right to condemn a Government for breach of the Convention in the presence of a very reasonable doubt as to whether any has occurred?...

11. In this connexion, and in general, I consider that the Court failed to give any adequate weight— if weight at all—to the fact that the applicant was a terrorist and mafioso. Naturally these factors would not justify treating him in a manner clearly, or at any rate substantially, contrary to the Convention. But where there are grounds for genuine doubt whether any contravention has in fact occurred, such factors, though in no way conclusive per se, may legitimately be taken into account (I do not put it any higher than that) in deciding how to set about resolving the doubt— again I put it no higher. In the present case, however, the Court completely ignored the plea of the Italian Government to the effect that public order in Italy at this time was seriously menaced by threats coming essentially from political terrorism and the mafia, and that the authorities were under strong pressure to combat these evils by draconian measures—pressure which they had so far resisted, as was exemplified in the case of Guzzardi by the relative leniency of his original treatment as described in paragraph 8 above....

12. The process of simply ignoring the whole context in which a case occurs is bound to lead to injustices and absurdities ... The present case in fact bristles with absurdities. Another instance of this is that, as pointed out by the Italian Government, whereas by reason of sub-paragraph (e) of Article 5 § 1 of the Convention, a vagrant can, merely by reason of his being such, be placed under detention without any contravention of the Convention, a known terrorist cannot even have his movements restricted under the conditions applied to Guzzardi without such a breach resulting— if the judgment of the Court is correct. To be sure, modern terrorism was an evil not specifically present to the minds of those who drafted the Convention, or they would doubtless have provided for it. Again, it is admittedly for governments and none other to remedy this defect: the Court cannot do so by deeming a terrorist to be a vagrant even though he is in fact much worse than a vagrant (who may well be a harmless individual, which a terrorist never is). But this does not alter the fact that, according to the order of things resulting from the Court's judgment, a terrorist may be much better off than a vagrant. (He may even be paid a million lire!). All these absurdities could have been avoided by an attitude of greater realism against the background of the case, leading to the conclusion—for which there was ample warrant on the facts—that the case was basically one of restriction on movement and place of residence and not one of deprivation of liberty under Article 5 of the Convention, interpreted, as it has to be, in the light of the existence of Article 2 of Protocol No 4.

NOTES

1   The Court was composed of President Wiarda and Judges: Balladore Pallieri, Zekia, Cremona, Vilhjálmsson, Ryssdal, Ganshof van der Meersch, Sir Gerald Fitzmaurice, Bindschedler-Robert, Evrigenis, Teitgen, Lagergren, Liesch, Gölcüklü, Matscher, Pinheiro Farinha, García de Enterría, and Walsh. In addition to Judge Fitzmaurice dissenting opinions were given by Judges: Balladore Pallieri, Zekia, Cremona, Bindschedler-Robert, Teitgen and García de Enterría, and Pinheiro Farinha. Judge Matscher issued a partly dissenting opinion.

2   As the *Guzzardi* case indicates, the distinction between the deprivation of liberty in the sense of Article 5, ECHR and a limitation upon freedom of movement, which is subject only to Article 2, Protocol 4 to the ECHR, is a matter of the 'degree and intensity' of the confinement. In Application 7960/77, to which the Court refers, the same applicant had been restricted to a village on the mainland where his living conditions were those of other inhabitants. The Commission considered that this case did not involve sufficiently close detention for Article 5 to apply.

3   There are other cases in which the closeness of confinement has been an issue. In *Engel v Netherlands* A.22 (1976), in the context of disciplinary offences, the detention of a soldier in a locked cell ('strict arrest') fell within Article 5, but confinement during off-duty hours to an unlocked building in the barracks ('aggravated arrest') did not.

4   In *Amuur v France*, 1996-III, the applicant Somali nationals arrived at Orly airport in Paris, having fled from Somalia (via Syria) in fear of their lives after a revolution. They were refused entry into France because their passports were false. While their applications for asylum were being considered, they were kept in the international transit area at the airport. After 20 days, their applications were refused and they were put on a flight back to Syria. During the whole of this time, they were free to leave the airport on a flight of their choice for another State that would receive them. The European Court held unanimously that the applicants were being detained in the sense of Article 5 during the 20-day period. It stated:

43. Holding aliens in the international zone does indeed involve a restriction upon liberty, but one which is not in every respect comparable to that which obtains in centres for the detention of aliens pending deportation. Such confinement, accompanied by suitable safeguards for the persons concerned, is acceptable only in order to enable States to prevent unlawful immigration while complying with their international obligations, particularly under the 1951 Geneva Convention Relating to the Status of Refugees and the European Convention on Human Rights. States' legitimate concern to foil the increasingly frequent attempts to circumvent immigration restrictions must not deprive asylum-seekers of the protection afforded by these conventions.

Such holding should not be prolonged excessively, otherwise there would be a risk of it turning mere restriction on liberty—inevitable with a view to organising the practical details of the alien's repatriation or, where he has requested asylum, while his application for leave to enter the territory for that purpose is considered—into a deprivation of liberty. In that connection account should be taken of the fact that the measure is applicable not to those who have committed criminal offences but to aliens who, often fearing for their lives, have fled from their own country.

Although by the force of circumstances the decision to order holding must necessarily be taken by the administrative or police authorities, its prolongation requires speedy review by the courts, the traditional guardians of personal liberties. Above all, such confinement must not deprive the asylum-seeker of the right to gain effective access to the procedure for determining refugee status....

45. The Court notes that for the greater part of the above period [20 days] the applicants, who claimed to be refugees, were left to their own devices. They were placed under strict and constant police surveillance and had no legal and social assistance—particularly with a view to completing the formalities relating to an application for political refugee status—until 24 March, when a humanitarian association, which had in the meantime been informed of their presence in the international zone, put them in contact with a lawyer. Moreover, until 26 March neither the length nor the necessity of their confinement were reviewed by a court....

48. The mere fact that it is possible for asylum-seekers to leave voluntarily the country where they wish to take refuge cannot exclude a restriction on liberty, the right to leave any country, including one's own, being guaranteed, moreover, by Protocol No 4 to the Convention. Furthermore, this possibility becomes theoretical if no other country offering protection comparable to the protection they expect to find in the country where they are seeking asylum is inclined or prepared to take them in.

Sending the applicants back to Syria only became possible, apart from the practical problems of the journey, following negotiations between the French and Syrian authorities. The assurances of the latter were dependent on the vagaries of diplomatic relations, in view of the fact that Syria was not bound by the Geneva Convention relating to the Status of Refugees.

49. The Court concludes that holding the applicants in the transit zone of Paris-Orly Airport was equivalent in practice, in view of the restrictions suffered, to a deprivation of liberty. Article 5 § 1 is therefore applicable to the case....

The Court then held unanimously that Article 5(1) had been infringed. It stated:

50....In laying down that any deprivation of liberty must be effected 'in accordance with a procedure prescribed by law', Article 5 § 1 primarily requires any arrest or detention to have a legal basis in domestic law. However, these words do not merely refer back to domestic law; like the expressions 'in accordance with the law' and 'prescribed by law' in the second paragraphs of Articles 8 to 11, they also relate to the quality of the law, requiring it to be compatible with the rule of law, a concept inherent in all the Articles of the Convention.

In order to ascertain whether a deprivation of liberty has complied with the principle of compatibility with domestic law, it therefore falls to the Court to assess not only the legislation in force in the field under consideration, but also the quality of the other legal rules applicable to the persons concerned. Quality in this sense implies that where a national law authorises deprivation of liberty—especially in respect of a foreign asylum-seeker—it must be sufficiently accessible and precise, in order to avoid all risk of arbitrariness. These characteristics are of fundamental importance with regard to asylum-seekers at airports, particularly in view of the need to reconcile the protection of fundamental rights with the requirements of States' immigration policies....

52. The Court notes that even though the applicants were not in France within the meaning of the Ordinance of 2 November 1945, holding them in the international zone of Paris-Orly Airport made them subject to French law.

Despite its name, the international zone does not have extraterritorial status. In its decision of 25 February 1992 the Constitutional Council did not challenge the legislature's right to lay down rules governing the holding of aliens in that zone. For example, the Law of 6 July 1992...provides, *inter alia*, for the intervention of the ordinary courts to authorise holding for more than four days, the assistance of an interpreter and a doctor and the possibility of communicating with a lawyer. The Decree of 15 December 1992...lays down the procedural rules applicable to proceedings brought in accordance with that Law. The Decree of 2 May 1995...gives the delegate of the United Nations High Commissioner for Refugees or his representatives and humanitarian associations permanent access to the zone.

However, these rules—which postdate the facts of the case—were not applicable at the time to the applicants.

53. The Court emphasises that from 9 to 29 March 1992 the applicants were in the situation of asylum-seekers whose application had not yet been considered. In that connection, neither the Decree of 27 May 1982 nor the—unpublished—circular of 26 June 1990 (the only text at the material time which specifically dealt with the practice of holding aliens in the transit zone) constituted a 'law' of sufficient 'quality' within the meaning of the Court's case-law; there must be adequate legal protection in domestic law against arbitrary interferences by public authorities with the rights safeguarded by the Convention (see the *Malone v UK* judgment of 2 August 1984, Series A No 82, p 32, § 67). In any event, the Decree of 27 May 1982 did not concern holding aliens in the international zone. The above-mentioned circular consisted, by its very nature, of instructions given by the Minister of the Interior to Prefects and Chief Constables concerning aliens refused leave to enter at the frontiers. It was intended to provide guidelines for immigration control at ports and airports. Moreover, the brief section it devoted to holding in the international zone and aliens' rights contains no guarantees comparable to those introduced by the Law of 6 July 1992. At the material time none of these texts allowed the ordinary courts to review the conditions under which aliens were held or, if necessary, to impose a limit on the administrative authorities as regards the length of time for which they were held or, if necessary, to impose a limit on the administrative authorities as regards the length of time for which they were held. They did not provide for legal, humanitarian and social assistance, nor did they lay down procedures and time-limits for access to such assistance so that asylum seekers like the applicants could take the necessary steps.

54. The French legal rules in force at the time, as applied in the present case, did not sufficiently guarantee the applicants' right to liberty.

There has accordingly been a breach of Article 5(1).

In the later case of **Riad and Idiab v Belgium**, judgment of 24 January 2008, a unanimous Chamber found the detention of the two applicants (Palestinian asylum seekers) for 12 days in the transit zone of Brussels-National airport pending their deportation breached both Article 5 and Article 3 (inhuman and degrading treatment). The Court expressed the opinion that the transit zone was not a suitable place for the length of detention the applicants were subject to.

5   A unanimous Chamber held that the deprivation of liberty under Article 5 involved both objective and subjective elements in **Storck v Germany**, judgment of 16 June 2005. When the applicant was 18 years old, in 1977, she was placed in a private psychiatric clinic (located in Bremen) at the demand of her father. She was forced to remain in the clinic and receive medication for nearly two years. During that period she was brought back to the clinic by the police after she escaped. She contended that during her time in the clinic she was given psychotropic drugs and had been physically attached to beds, chairs, and radiators. Subsequently, she received extensive medical treatment at a number of hospitals and at the Bremen clinic. From 1980 until 1991 she lost the ability to speak. In the 1990s she obtained two reports from expert psychiatrists that she had never suffered from schizophrenia and that in the 1970s she had had experienced an 'identity crisis'. At the time of the proceedings before the Court she was classified as 100 per cent handicapped and received an invalidity pension. After a number of actions in the lower courts the German Constitutional Court determined that she had not demonstrated a violation of her constitutional rights in respect of her treatment in the private clinic. The Chamber ruled that:

74. However, the notion of deprivation of liberty within the meaning of Article 5 § 1 does not only comprise the objective element of a person's confinement to a certain limited place for a not negligible length of time. A person can only be considered as being deprived of his or her liberty if, as an additional subjective element, he has not validly consented to the confinement in question (see, *mutatis mutandis, H.M. v Switzerland* [ECHR 2002-II] § 46). The Court notes that in the present case, it is disputed between the parties whether the applicant had consented to her stay in the clinic.

75. Having regard to the national courts' related findings of fact and to the factors which are undisputed between the parties, the Court observes that the applicant had attained majority at the time of her admission to the clinic and had not been placed under guardianship. Therefore, she had been considered to have the capacity to consent or object to her admission and treatment in hospital. It is undisputed that she had not signed the clinic's admission form prepared on the day of her arrival. It is true that she had presented herself to the clinic, accompanied by her father. However, the right to liberty is too important in a democratic society for a person to lose the benefit of the Convention protection for the single reason that he may have given himself up to be taken into detention (see *De Wilde, Ooms and Versyp v Belgium*, judgment of 18 June 1971, Series A No 12, p. 36, § 65; *H.L. v the United Kingdom* [ECHR 2004-IX] § 90).

76. Having regard to the continuation of the applicant's stay in the clinic, the Court considers the key factor in the present case to be that—which is uncontested—the applicant, on several occasions, had tried to flee from the clinic. She had to be fettered in order to prevent her from absconding and had to be brought back to the clinic by the police when she had managed to escape on one occasion. Under these circumstances, the Court is unable to discern any factual basis for the assumption that the applicant—presuming her capacity to consent—had agreed to her continued stay in the clinic. In the alternative, assuming that the applicant had no longer been capable of consenting following her treatment with strong medicaments, she could, in any event, not be considered as having validly agreed to her stay in the clinic.

77. Indeed, a comparison of the facts of this case with those in *H.L. v the United Kingdom* (cited above) cannot but confirm this finding. That case concerned the confinement of an individual who was of age but lacked the capacity to consent in a psychiatric institution which he had never attempted to leave, and in which the Court had found that there had been a deprivation of liberty. In the present case, *a fortiori*, a deprivation of liberty must be found. The applicant's lack of consent must also be regarded as the decisive feature distinguishing the present case from the case of *H.M. v Switzerland* (cited above, § 46). In that case, it was held that the placing of an elderly person

in a foster home, to ensure necessary medical care, had not amounted to a deprivation of liberty. However, that applicant, who had been legally capable of expressing a view, had been undecided as to whether or not she wanted to stay in the nursing home. The clinic could then draw the conclusion that she did not object.

78. The Court therefore concludes that the applicant had been deprived of her liberty within the meaning of Article 5 § 1 of the Convention.

The Chamber then found that the State was responsible, under Article 5, for the applicant's deprivation of liberty in the private clinic on several grounds. First, through the involvement of public authorities, as the police had returned her to the clinic after she had escaped. Secondly, the German courts had failed to interpret the civil law in accordance with the 'spirit' of Article 5 in the actions brought by the applicant. Thirdly, through the State's failure to comply with its positive obligation to protect the applicant's liberty from being interfered with by private persons.

101. The Court has consistently held that the responsibility of a State is engaged if a violation of one of the rights and freedoms defined in the Convention is the result of non-observance by that State of its obligation under Article 1 to secure those rights and freedoms in its domestic law to everyone within its jurisdiction (see, *inter alia*, *Costello-Roberts v the United Kingdom*, judgment of 25 March 1993, Series A No 247-C, p 57, § 26; *Woś v Poland* (dec.), No 22860/02, § 60, 1 March 2005). Consequently, the Court has expressly found that Article 2 (see, amongst others, *L.C.B. v the United Kingdom*, judgment of 9 June 1998, Reports of Judgments and Decisions 1998-III, p 1403, § 36), Article 3 (see, *inter alia*, *Costello-Roberts*, cited above, pp 57–8, §§ 26 and 28) and Article 8 of the Convention (see, *inter alia*, *X and Y v The Netherlands*, judgment of 26 March 1985, Series A No 91, p 11, § 23; *Costello-Roberts*, ibid) enjoin the State not only to refrain from an active infringement by its representatives of the rights in question, but also to take appropriate steps to provide protection against an interference with those rights either by State agents or private parties.

102. Having regard to this, the Court considers that Article 5 § 1, first sentence, of the Convention must equally be considered as laying down a positive obligation on the State to protect the liberty of its citizens. Any conclusion to the effect that this was not the case would not only be inconsistent with the Court's case-law, notably under Articles 2, 3 and 8 of the Convention. It would, moreover, leave a sizeable gap in the protection from arbitrary detention, which would be inconsistent with the importance of personal liberty in a democratic society. The State is, therefore, obliged to take measures providing effective protection of vulnerable persons, including reasonable steps to prevent a deprivation of liberty of which the authorities have or ought to have knowledge (see, *mutatis mutandis*, *Z and Others v the United Kingdom* [GC], No 29392/95, § 73, ECHR 2001-V; *Ilaşcu and Others v Moldova and Russia* [GC], No 48787/99, §§ 332–52, 464, ECHR 2004-VII).

105. Turning to the present case, the Court notes that, under German law, the confinement of a person to a psychiatric hospital had to be ordered by a judge if the person concerned either did not or was unable to consent. In this case, the competent health authority also had supervisory powers to control the execution of these court orders. However, in the applicant's case, the clinic, despite the lack of the applicant's consent, had not obtained the necessary court order. Therefore, no public health officer had ever assessed whether the applicant—what was more than doubtful—posed a serious threat to public safety or order within the meaning of Article 2 of the Act of the Land Bremen on the detention of mentally insane persons, mentally deficient persons and drug addicts. Consequently, the State also did not exercise any supervisory control over the lawfulness of the applicant's detention in the clinic for some 20 months.

106. It is true, though, that, with deprivation of liberty being a crime punishable with up to ten years' imprisonment, German law retrospectively provided sanctions with a deterring effect. Moreover, a victim could, under German civil law, claim compensation in tort for damage caused by an unlawful detention. However, the Court, having regard to the importance of the right to liberty, does not consider such retrospective measures alone as providing effective protection for individuals in such a vulnerable position as the applicant. It notes that particularly in the Act of the Land Bremen on the detention of mentally insane persons, mentally deficient persons and drug addicts, there were numerous—necessary—safeguards for persons detained in a mental institution following a court order. However, these safeguards did not apply in the more critical cases of persons confined to a psychiatric institution without such an order. It must be borne in mind that the applicant, once detained and treated with strong antipsychotic medicaments, had no longer been in a position to secure independent outside help.

106. The lack of any effective State control is most strikingly shown by the fact that on 4 March 1979 the police, by the use of force, had brought back the applicant to her place of detention from which she had escaped. Thereby, public authorities, as already shown above, had been involved in the applicant's detention in the clinic, without her flight and obvious unwillingness to return having entailed any control of the lawfulness of her forced stay in the clinic. This discloses the great danger of abuse in this field, notably in cases like that of the applicant, in which family conflicts and an identity crisis had been at the root of her troubles and long detention in a psychiatric hospital. The Court is therefore not convinced that the control exercised by State authorities merely in connection with the issuing of a licence for the conduct of a private clinic pursuant to Section 30 of the Act regulating the Conduct of Trade sufficed to ensure a competent and regular supervisory control against a deprivation of liberty in such a clinic. Moreover, Section 30 of the Act regulating the Conduct of Trade as such had not been in force at the beginning of the applicant's detention in the clinic.

107. The Court observes that shortly after the end of the applicant's detention in the private clinic, further safeguards have been introduced by Section 34 of the Act on Measures of Aid and Protection with respect to Mental Disorders for individuals detained in psychiatric institutions, responding to the lack of sufficient protection in this field. In particular, visiting commissions were created to inspect psychiatric institutions, to control whether the rights of patients were respected and to give patients the opportunity to raise complaints. However, these mechanisms came too late for the applicant.

108. Therefore, the Court concludes that the respondent State has violated its existing positive obligation to protect the applicant against interferences with her liberty carried out by private persons from July 1977 to April 1979. Consequently, there has been a violation of Article 5 § 1, first sentence, of the Convention.

The Chamber went on to conclude that the applicant's detention in the private clinic could not be justified under Article 5(1)(e) as it had not been 'lawful' due to the fact that she had not consented and no court order had been obtained (as was required by *Länder* law).

The judgment in **Storck** should be welcomed for the robust protection of the right to liberty taken by the Chamber. It is particularly noteworthy that the Chamber decisively rejected the German Government's assertion that it was 'questionable' whether States were under a positive obligation to protect persons from being deprived of their liberty by other private persons. Paragraph 102 of the judgment elaborates the scope of this positive obligation in terms similar to those of analogous obligations under other Articles, therefore it should not be unduly burdensome for States.

The obligation to account for a person in custody

Kurt v Turkey 1998-III
European Court of Human Rights

The facts of this case are set out above, p 176.

JUDGMENT OF THE COURT

122. The Court notes at the outset the fundamental importance of the guarantees contained in Article 5 for securing the right of individuals in a democracy to be free from arbitrary detention at the hands of the authorities. It is precisely for that reason that the Court has repeatedly stressed in its case-law that any deprivation of liberty must not only have been effected in conformity with the substantive and procedural rules of national law but must equally be in keeping with the very purpose of Article 5, namely to protect the individual from arbitrariness (see, among many other authorities, the *Chahal v UK* judgment of 15 November 1996, Reports 1996-IV, p 1864, § 118). This insistence on the protection of the individual against any abuse of power is illustrated by the fact that Article 5 § 1 circumscribes the circumstances in which individuals may be lawfully deprived of their liberty, it being stressed that these circumstances must be given a narrow interpretation having regard to the fact that they constitute exceptions to the most basic guarantee of individual freedom (see, *mutatis mutandis*, the *Quinn v France* judgment of 22 March 1995, Series A No 311, p 17, § 42).

123. It must also be stressed that the authors of the Convention reinforced the individual's protection against arbitrary deprivation of his or her liberty by guaranteeing a corpus of substantive rights which are intended to minimise the risks of arbitrariness by allowing the act of deprivation of liberty to be amenable to independent judicial scrutiny and by securing the accountability of the authorities for that act. The requirements of Article 5 §§ 3 and 4 with their emphasis on promptitude and judicial control assume particular importance in this context. Prompt judicial intervention may lead to the detection and prevention of life-threatening measures or serious ill-treatment which violate the fundamental guarantees contained in Articles 2 and 3 of the Convention (see, *mutatis mutandis*, the above-mentioned *Aksoy* judgment, p 2282, § 76). What is at stake is both the protection of the physical liberty of individuals as well as their personal security in a context which, in the absence of safeguards, could result in a subversion of the rule of law and place detainees beyond the reach of the most rudimentary forms of legal protection.

124. The Court emphasises in this respect that the unacknowledged detention of an individual is a complete negation of these guarantees and a most grave violation of Article 5. Having assumed control over that individual it is incumbent on the authorities to account for his or her whereabouts. For this reason, Article 5 must be seen as requiring the authorities to take effective measures to safeguard against the risk of disappearance and to conduct a prompt effective investigation into an arguable claim that a person has been taken into custody and has not been seen since.

125. Against that background, the Court recalls that it has accepted the Commission's finding that Üzeyir Kurt was held by soldiers and village guards on the morning of 25 November 1993. His detention at that time was not logged and there exists no official trace of his subsequent whereabouts or fate. That fact in itself must be considered a most serious failing since it enables those responsible for the act of deprivation of liberty to conceal their involvement in a crime, to cover their tracks and to escape accountability for the fate of the detainee. In the view of the Court, the absence of holding data recording such matters as the date, time and location of detention, the name of the detainee

as well as the reasons for the detention and the name of the person effecting it must be seen as incompatible with the very purpose of Article 5 of the Convention.

126. Furthermore, the Court considers that having regard to the applicant's insistence that her son was detained in the village the public prosecutor should have been alert to the need to investigate more thoroughly her claim. He had the powers under the Code of Criminal Procedure to do so.... However, he did not request her to explain why she was so adamant in her belief that he was in detention. She was neither asked to provide a written statement nor interviewed orally. Had he done so he may have been able to confront the military personnel involved in the operation in the village with her eye-witness account. However, that line of enquiry was never opened and no statements were taken from any of the soldiers or village guards present in the village at the time. The public prosecutor was unwilling to go beyond the gendarmerie's assertion that the custody records showed that Üzeyir Kurt had neither been held in the village nor was in detention. He accepted without question the explanation that Üzeyir Kurt had probably been kidnapped by the PKK during the military operation and this explanation shaped his future attitude to his enquiries and laid the basis of his subsequent non-jurisdiction decision.

127. The Court, like the Commission, also considers that the alleged PKK involvement in the disappearance of the applicant's son lacked any firm and plausible evidentiary basis. As an explanation it was advanced too hastily by the gendarmerie in the absence of any corroborating evidence; nor can it be maintained that the statements given by the three villagers to the gendarme officers on 28 February 1994 lent credence to what was in effect mere supposition as to the fate of Üzeyir Kurt. The questions put to the villagers can only be described as formulated in a way designed to elicit responses which could enhance the credibility of the PKK kidnapping theory...Furthermore, and as noted earlier..., the Government's other contention that the applicant's son had left the village to join the PKK also lacks any firm evidentiary basis.

128. Having regard to these considerations, the Court concludes that the authorities have failed to offer any credible and substantiated explanation for the whereabouts and fate of the applicant's son after he was detained in the village and that no meaningful investigation was conducted into the applicant's insistence that he was in custody and that she was concerned for his life. They have failed to discharge their responsibility to account for him and it must be accepted that he has been held in unacknowledged detention in the complete absence of the safeguards contained in Article 5.

129. The Court, accordingly, like the Commission, finds that there has been a particularly grave violation of the right to liberty and security of person guaranteed under Article 5 raising serious concerns about the welfare of Üzeyir Kurt....

FOR THESE REASONS, THE COURT ...

5. Holds by six votes to three that there has been a violation of Article 5 of the Convention; ...

NOTES

1 The Court was composed of President Bernhardt and Judges: Foighel, Morenilla, Bonnici, Jungwiert, and Lohmus. Judges Matscher, Gölcüklü, and Pettiti issued dissenting opinions in which they expressed the view that the applicant had not established the truth of her allegations beyond all reasonable doubt.

2 In most cases under Article 5, the State acknowledges that the person concerned is in its custody. In the *Kurt* case, the Court accepted the Commission's finding of fact the son had been detained by State agents, despite the State's denial. In this situation, the question is not one of testing compliance with the particular guarantees listed in Article 5, but of a

State obligation to account for a person in its detention that is implicit in Article 5. Following from this general obligation, are particular implied obligations to keep records of persons detained and to investigate allegations of detention.

3   A unanimous Chamber found a breach of the **Kurt** record-keeping obligation in **Anguelova v Bulgaria**, judgment of 13 June 2002 (see above, p 123 for the Article 2 aspect of this case). The police station's register did not contain an original record of the detention of the applicant's son and a forged entry was later added to the register. Accordingly, the Chamber found a violation of the '157. . . . requirements implicit in Article 5 of the Convention for the proper recording of deprivations of liberty.'

4   Grave systematic failings were found in the custody records of Turkish gendarme stations in **Orhan v Turkey**, judgment of 18 June 2002. The applicant contended that three of his close relatives had been taken away by gendarmes in 1994 and those persons had never been seen again. The Chamber was united in concluding that serious deficiencies were present in the practice of recording custody in gendarme stations.

372. . . . The first established deficiency is not allowed by domestic law namely, the gendarme practice of detaining persons for various reasons in their stations without being entered in the custody records. The second and third failing further underline the unreliability of custody records as those records will not show whether one is apprehended by military forces and may not show the date of release from the gendarme station. These three deficiencies attest to the absence of effective measures to safeguard against the risk of disappearances of individuals in detention.

Consequently, the Court concluded that the applicant's two brothers and son had been held in unacknowledged detention in violation of Article 5. The above findings indicated both weaknesses in the scope of domestic custody records and a flouting of existing requirements by military personnel.

5   A Grand Chamber held that the implied obligation upon States to undertake effective investigations into the whereabouts and fate of persons whom, it is arguably claimed, have disappeared after being detained by State agents is a continuing duty in **Cyprus v Turkey**, judgment of 10 May 2001 (and see above, p 132 for the Article 2 aspects of the case). The applicant government asserted that the Turkish authorities had failed effectively to investigate (in both occupied northern Cyprus and in Turkey) the detention and subsequent disappearance of many hundreds of Greek-Cypriots who had disappeared during the military invasion of 1974. The Grand Chamber, subject to the dissent of the Turkish *ad hoc* judge, determine that, '150. . . . there has been a continuing violation of Article 5 of the Convention by virtue of the failure of the authorities of the respondent State to conduct an effective investigation in to the whereabouts and fate of the missing Greek-Cypriot persons in respect of whom there is an arguable claim that they were in custody at the time they disappeared.' This was an important clarification of the extent of the effective investigation duty and ought to provide some satisfaction to the relatives of 'disappeared' persons whose legitimate wish to discover the fate of their family members is an enduring goal.

6   In the autumn of 2005 reports began to appear in the US media (led by the *Washington Post*) of secret Central Intelligence Agency (CIA) detention centres in European States (Romania and Poland were named) where suspects in the US 'War on Terror' were being held and interrogated. The Legal Affairs Committee of the Parliamentary Assembly (Council of Europe) appointed Senator Dick Marty, a former prosecutor, to undertake an inquiry into alleged secret detentions in member States. Allegations also emerged of clandestine CIA aircraft flights using European airports and airspace for the transportation of detainees as part of the US global programme of 'extraordinary rendition', involving terrorist suspects being secretly sent for interrogation by officials in other States where they have no rights under US law. In November 2005 the Council of Europe's Secretary General, Terry Davis, invoked his (rarely used) power under Article 52 of the ECHR to request all member States to inform him how their domestic laws prevented the unacknowledged deprivation of liberty and the giving of aid to foreign agents to undertake such acts. Article 52 provides that: 'On receipt of a request from the Secretary General of the Council of Europe any High Contracting Party shall furnish an explanation of the manner in which its internal law ensures the effective implementation of any of the provisions of the Convention.' The Secretary General published his report (1 March 2006) on the replies received. He stated:

> ...I strongly support cooperation between Europe and the United States of America on all issues and especially the fight against terrorism but I also insist that European governments should have sufficient confidence to participate in such cooperation as equal partners and not play the role of the proverbial three brass monkeys [who could not hear, see or speak].
>
> ...For the time being, the analysis of the replies received already indicates that there are several areas of general concern. Firstly, it would appear that most of Europe is a happy hunting ground for foreign security services. Whilst most of our member States have mechanisms to supervise the activities of their domestic intelligence agencies as well as the presence of foreign police officers on their territory, hardly any country, with the exception of Hungary, has any legal provisions to ensure an effective oversight over the activities of foreign security services on their territory....
>
> The second concern is that Europe's skies appear to be excessively open. Very few countries seem to have adopted an adequate and effective way to monitor who and what is transiting through their airports and airspace. Indeed, no member State appears to have established any kind of procedure in order to assess whether civil aircraft are used for purposes which would be incompatible with internationally recognised human rights standards. This is alarming because the explanations provided on the specific point of controls over aircraft allegedly used for rendition show that existing procedures do not provide adequate safeguards against abuse.
>
> The third general concern arising from the analysis of the replies is related to the existing rules on jurisdiction and state immunity, which create considerable obstacles for effective law enforcement in relation to the activities of foreign agents, especially when they are accredited as diplomatic or consular agents....

The Secretary General considered that the replies by Bosnia and Herzegovina, Italy, the former Yugoslav republic of Macedonia, and Poland were not adequate. He intended to continue his inquiries in respect of those States and more generally to consider what action the Council of Europe should take to deal with the problems identified in his report.

At a meeting of the Legal Affairs Committee, on 7 June 2006, Mr Marty reported that his investigations had found 'converging elements' indicating that 'landing points in Romania and Poland were detainee drop-off points near to secret detention centres'. In his opinion '...the authorities in several European countries actively participated with the CIA in these unlawful activities. Other countries ignored them knowingly, or did not want to know.' Spain, Turkey, Germany, and Cyprus provided 'staging posts' for rendition operations and the UK, Portugal, Ireland, and Greece were 'stopping-off points' during the transportation of detainees. Italy, Sweden, Macedonia, and Bosnia-Herzegovina allowed the Americans to abduct persons from their territories. On the same day, BBC News reported that it was unlikely that any secret US detention centres were still operating in Europe and they had probably been relocated to northern Africa.

In August 2009 Mr Marty reported that his sources suggested that Lithuania had also hosted a secret CIA prison.

So far it has been the parliamentary and administrative institutions of the Council of Europe that have played the leading roles in the investigations into these serious allegations. Presumably, the nature of the US detention and treatment of any individual detainees has created practical obstacles preventing them from invoking the judicial remedies under the ECHR. However, in November 2010, the British Government reached a confidential settlement in civil proceedings brought against it by around a dozen British citizens or residents who alleged that British security officials had colluded in their transfer and detention overseas by the USA. The British Government did not admit that its officials colluded in maltreatment of the claimants. The BBC reported that the 'significant' compensation paid was in the millions of pounds (BBC News online, 16 November 2010).

In accordance with a procedure prescribed by law

Article 5 requires that all deprivations of liberty must satisfy this condition. A unanimous Grand Chamber of the full-time Court explained the meaning of this requirement in *Ocalan v Turkey*, see p 135. The following extracts deal with the applicant's complaint that his detention in Kenya amounted to abduction by Turkish officials in breach of international law.

83....On the question whether detention is 'lawful', including whether it complies with 'a procedure prescribed by law', the Convention refers back essentially to national law and lays down the obligation to conform to the substantive and procedural rules thereof. However, it requires in addition that any deprivation of liberty should be consistent with the purpose of Article 5, namely to protect individuals from arbitrariness. What is at stake here is not only the 'right to liberty' but also the 'right to security of person' (see, among other authorities, *Bozano* [v *France*, A.111 (1986)], p 23, § 54; and *Wassink v The Netherlands*, judgment of 27 September 1990, Series A No 185-A, p 11, § 24).

84. It is in the first place for the national authorities, notably the courts, to interpret and apply domestic law. However, since under Article 5 § 1 failure to comply with domestic law entails a breach of the Convention, it follows that the Court can and should exercise a certain power to review whether this law has been complied with (see *Benham v the United Kingdom*, judgment of 10 June 1996, Reports of Judgments and Decisions 1996-III, p 753, § 41; and *Bouamar v Belgium*, judgment of 29 February 1988, Series A No 129, p 21, § 49).

85. An arrest made by the authorities of one State on the territory of another State, without the consent of the latter, affects the person concerned's individual rights to security under Article 5 § 1 (see, to the same effect, *Stocké v Germany*, 12 October 1989, Series A No 199, opinion of the Commission, p 24, § 167).

86. The Convention does not prevent cooperation between States, within the framework of extradition treaties or in matters of deportation, for the purpose of bringing fugitive offenders to justice, provided that it does not interfere with any specific rights recognised in the Convention (see *Stocké*, opinion of the Commission cited above, pp 24–5, § 169).

87. As regards extradition arrangements between States when one is a party to the Convention and the other not, the rules established by an extradition treaty or, in the absence of any such treaty, the cooperation between the States concerned are also relevant factors to be taken into account for determining whether the arrest that has led to the subsequent complaint to the Court was lawful. The fact that a fugitive has been handed over as a result of cooperation between States does not in itself make the arrest unlawful or, therefore, give rise to any problem under Article 5 (see *Freda*

v Italy, No 8916/80, Commission decision of 7 October 1980, DR 21, p 250; *Klaus Altmann (Barbie) v France*, No 10689/83, Commission decision of 4 July 1984, DR 37, p 225; *Luc Reinette v France*, No 14009/88, Commission decision of 2 October 1989, DR 63, p 189).

88. Inherent in the whole of the Convention is a search for a fair balance between the demands of the general interest of the community and the requirements of the protection of the individual's fundamental rights. As movement about the world becomes easier and crime takes on a larger international dimension, it is increasingly in the interest of all nations that suspected offenders who flee abroad should be brought to justice. Conversely, the establishment of safe havens for fugitives would not only result in danger for the State obliged to harbour the protected person but also tend to undermine the foundations of extradition (see *Soering v the United Kingdom*, judgment of 7 July 1989, Series A No 161, p. 35, § 89).

89. The Convention contains no provisions concerning the circumstances in which extradition may be granted, or the procedure to be followed before extradition may be granted. Subject to its being the result of cooperation between the States concerned and provided that the legal basis for the order for the fugitive's arrest is an arrest warrant issued by the authorities of the fugitive's State of origin, even an atypical extradition cannot as such be regarded as being contrary to the Convention (see *Illich Ramirez Sánchez [v France*, Commission Decision of 24 June 1996, DR 86], p. 155).

90. Irrespective of whether the arrest amounts to a violation of the law of the State in which the fugitive has taken refuge—a question which only falls to be examined by the Court if the host State is a party to the Convention—the Court requires proof in the form of concordant inferences that the authorities of the State to which the applicant has been transferred have acted extra-territorially in a manner that is inconsistent with the sovereignty of the host State and therefore contrary to international law (see, *mutatis mutandis*, *Stocké v Germany*, judgment of 19 March 1991, Series A No 199, p 19, § 54). Only then will the burden of proving that the sovereignty of the host State and international law have been complied with shift to the respondent Government. However, the applicant is not required to adduce proof 'beyond all reasonable doubt' on this point, as was suggested by the Chamber (judgment of 12 March 2003, § 92).

(b) Application of the principles to the present case

(i) Whether the arrest complied with Turkish law

91. The Court notes that the applicant was arrested by members of the Turkish security forces inside an aircraft registered in Turkey in the international zone of Nairobi Airport.

It is common ground that, directly after being handed over to the Turkish officials by the Kenyan officials, the applicant was under effective Turkish authority and therefore within the 'jurisdiction' of that State for the purposes of Article 1 of the Convention, even though in this instance Turkey exercised its authority outside its territory. It is true that the applicant was physically forced to return to Turkey by Turkish officials and was under their authority and control following his arrest and return to Turkey (see, in this respect, the aforementioned decisions in the cases of *Illich Ramirez Sánchez v France* and *Freda v Italy*; and, by converse implication, the *Banković and Others v Belgium and 16 Other Contracting States* decision ((dec.) [GC], No 52207/99, ECHR 2001-XII)).

92. As to whether the arrest complied with Turkish domestic law, the Court notes that the Turkish criminal courts had issued seven warrants for the applicant's arrest while Interpol had circulated a wanted notice ('red notice'). In each of these documents, the applicant was accused of criminal offences under the Turkish Criminal Code, namely founding an armed gang with a view to undermining the territorial integrity of the State and instigating a series of terrorist acts that had resulted in the loss of life. Following his arrest and on the expiry of the statutory period for which he could be held in police custody the applicant was brought before a court. Subsequently, he was charged, tried and convicted of offences under Article 125 of the Criminal Code. It follows that his arrest and detention complied with orders that had been issued by the Turkish courts 'for the purpose of bringing him before the competent legal authority on reasonable suspicion of having committed an offence'.

(ii) Interception by Kenyan agents

93. The Court must decide in the light of the parties' arguments whether the applicant's interception in Kenya immediately before he was handed over to Turkish officials on board the aircraft at Nairobi Airport was the result of acts by Turkish officials that violated Kenyan sovereignty and international law (as the applicant submitted) or of cooperation between the Turkish and Kenyan authorities in the absence of any extradition treaty between Turkey and Kenya laying down a formal procedure (as the Government submitted).

94. The Court will begin by examining the evidence on the role in fact played by the Kenyan authorities in the present case. The applicant entered Kenya without declaring his identity to the immigration officers. However, once they had been informed of the applicant's presence at the Greek Embassy in Nairobi, the Kenyan authorities invited the Greek Ambassador, with whom the applicant was staying in Nairobi, to arrange for the applicant to leave Kenyan territory. Shortly before the applicant was due to leave Kenya, more precisely as he was being transferred from the Greek Embassy to the airport, Kenyan officials intervened and separated the applicant from the Greek Ambassador. The car in which the applicant was travelling was driven by a Kenyan official, who took him to the aircraft in which Turkish officials were waiting to arrest him.

95. The Kenyan authorities did not perceive the applicant's arrest by the Turkish officials on board an aircraft at Nairobi Airport as being in any way a violation of Kenyan sovereignty. In sum, neither aspect of the applicant's detention—whether his interception by the Kenyan authorities before his transfer to the airport, or his arrest by the Turkish officials in the aircraft—led to an international dispute between Kenya and Turkey or to any deterioration in their diplomatic relations. The Kenyan authorities did not lodge any protest with the Turkish Government on these points or claim any redress from Turkey, such as the applicant's return or compensation.

96. The Kenyan authorities did, however, issue a formal protest to the Greek Government, accompanied by a demand for the Greek Ambassador's immediate recall, on the grounds that the applicant had entered Kenya illegally with the help of Greek officials and was unlawfully staying there. The applicant was not welcome in Kenya and the Kenyan authorities were anxious for him to leave.

97. These aspects of the case lead the Court to accept the Government's version of events: it considers that at the material time the Kenyan authorities had decided either to hand the applicant over to the Turkish authorities or to facilitate such a handover.

98. The applicant has not adduced evidence enabling concordant inferences (see paragraph 90 above) to be drawn that Turkey failed to respect Kenyan sovereignty or to comply with international law in the present case. The Grand Chamber agrees with the Chamber's finding that:

> '...The Court is not persuaded by the statement by the Kenyan Minister of Foreign Affairs on 16 February 1999 that, contrary to what the applicant maintained, the Kenyan authorities had had no involvement in the applicant's arrest or transfer... While it is true that the applicant was not arrested by the Kenyan authorities, the evidence before the Court indicates that Kenyan officials had played a role in separating the applicant from the Greek Ambassador and in transporting him to the airport immediately preceding his arrest on board the aircraft.' (see paragraph 100 of the Chamber judgment)

99. Consequently, the applicant's arrest on 15 February 1999 and his detention were in accordance with 'a procedure prescribed by law' for the purposes of Article 5 § 1 of the Convention. There has, therefore, been no violation of that provision.

Hence, this phrase demands that States comply with national law and international law, where appropriate (e.g. when extraditing individuals), regarding the detention of persons. Also, States must not act in an 'arbitrary' manner, that is contrary to the ethos of the right to liberty guaranteed by Article 5 (see *Bozano*, p 292). Do you agree with the Grand Chamber that the Turkish authorities did not violate these standards in *Ocalan*?

Another Grand Chamber was deeply divided as to whether international law provided a legal basis for the French navy detaining the crew of a merchant vessel suspected of transporting illegal drugs on the high seas in *Medvedyev and others v France*, judgment of 29 March 2010. Having secured the authorization of the flag State of the suspect vessel (Cambodia) 'to intercept, inspect and take legal action against the ship' (via a diplomatic note), French commandos boarded the vessel off the west coast of Africa. The ship and its crew were then escorted to a French port where the crew were charged with conspiracy to attempt to import narcotics illegally. Several of them were subsequently convicted and given lengthy prison sentences. Before the Court it was argued that the French authorities did not have authority under international law to detain the applicant crew members. A majority of the Grand Chamber (ten judges) determined that the 1982 UN Convention on the Law of the Sea did not provide a basis for the French action and Cambodia was not a party to the Convention. Furthermore, the diplomatic note referred to action against the ship:

> 99.…Evidently, therefore, the fate of the crew was not covered sufficiently clearly by the note and so it is not established that their deprivation of liberty was the subject of an agreement between the two States that could be considered to represent a 'clearly defined law' within the meaning of the Court's case-law.

Therefore, the Grand Chamber concluded that the applicants' detention had not been lawful and a breach of Article 5(1) had occurred. The seven dissentients, led by President Costa, considered that the diplomatic note should be interpreted as logically extending to authorizing French action being taken against the crew on board the ship. They did not believe the French authorities had acted in an arbitrary manner.

The majority in *Medvedyev* identified the lacunae in public international law:

> 101. It is regrettable, in the Court's view, that the international effort to combat drug trafficking on the high seas is not better coordinated bearing in mind the increasingly global dimension of the problem.…Having regard to the gravity and enormity of the problem posed by illegal drug trafficking, developments in public international law which embrace the principle that all States have jurisdiction as an exception to the law of the flag State would be a significant step in the fight against illegal trade in narcotics. This would bring international law on drug trafficking into line with what has already existed for many years now in respect of piracy.

Article 5(1): permissible grounds for arrest and detention

Article 5(1)(a): conviction by a competent court

Van Droogenbroeck v Belgium A.50 (1982)
European Court of Human Rights

The applicant was convicted of theft by the Bruges criminal court and sentenced to two years' imprisonment. In the light of prior convictions, he was also ordered by the court to be 'placed at the Government's disposal' for a further ten years as a recidivist, pursuant to the 1964 Social Protection Act. The first instance decision was confirmed by the Ghent Court of Appeal. On completion of his two-year sentence, the applicant was released. Thereafter, within the prescribed ten-year period, he was detained and released several times by the Minister of Justice under the court order because of later offences of theft and his failure to respond to rehabilitation measures.

The applicant alleged breaches, *inter alia*, of Articles 5(1) and 5(4) resulting respectively from the periods of detention ordered by the Minister of Justice and the absence of satisfactory remedies to challenge their legality. The Commission expressed the opinion unanimously that there had been a violation of Article 5(4), but, by ten votes to two, that the detention could be justified under Article 5(1)(a).

JUDGMENT OF THE COURT

35. The Court has to determine whether those periods of detention occurred 'after conviction' by the Ghent Court of Appeal.

Having regard to the French text, the word 'conviction', for the purposes of Article 5 § 1(a), has to be understood as signifying both a 'finding of guilt', after 'it has been established in accordance with the law that there has been an offence' (see the *Guzzardi* judgment of 6 November 1980, Series A No 39, p 37, § 100), and the imposition of a penalty or other measure involving deprivation of liberty. These conditions are satisfied in the instant case.

The word 'after' does not simply mean that the 'detention' must follow the 'conviction' in point of time: in addition, the 'detention' must result from, 'follow and depend upon' or occur 'by virtue of' the 'conviction' (see the *X v UK* judgment of 5 November 1981, Series A No 46, p 17, § 39; the *Engel* judgment of 8 June 1976, Series A, No 22, p 27, § 68) . . .

37. The Ministerial decisions . . . revoking the conditional release granted to Mr Van Droogenbroeck did order that he be 'detained' . . .

38. Be that as it may, one must look beyond the appearances and the language used and concentrate on the realities of the situation (see notably, *mutatis mutandis*, the *Deweer* judgment of 27 February 1980, Series A No 35, p 23, § 44).

This is a matter in which the Government enjoy a wide measure of discretion. Case-law and practice certainly confirm the meaning suggested by the text of section 25 of the 1964 Act ('if necessary') and the actual phrase 'placing at disposal'. In a judgment of 4 April 1978, the Belgian Court of Cassation observed that 'execution of the penalty' in question 'is to a large extent a matter for the discretion' of the Minister of Justice (*Pasicrisie* 1978, I, p 861). One finds that far less fetters are imposed on Ministerial decisions by a court's decision to apply the Social Protection Act than in the analogous area of the system of placing vagrants 'at the Government's disposal' (Act of 27 November 1891; see the *De Wilde, Ooms and Versyp* judgment of 18 June 1971, Series A No 12, pp 24–25, § 37, and pp 33–34, § 61). In short, to adopt the language used by the Commission's Delegate, 'the court decision does not order the detention' of recidivists and habitual offenders: it 'authorises' it.

39. In these circumstances, the Court has to consider whether there was a sufficient connection, for the purposes of Article 5, between the last-mentioned decision and the deprivation of liberty at issue.

This question must receive an affirmative reply since the Minister's discretion is exercised within a framework set both by the Act and by the sentence pronounced by the 'competent court'. In this respect, the Court notes that, according to Belgian case-law, a judgment which sentences the person concerned to imprisonment and, by way of a supplementary or accessory penalty, places him at the Government's disposal pursuant to section 22 or section 23 of the 1964 Act constitutes 'an inseparable whole' (Court of Cassation, 17 June 1975, *Pasicrisie* 1975, I, p 999). There are two components to the judgment: the first is a penalty involving deprivation of liberty which the offender must undergo for a period specified in the court decision, and the second is the placing of the offender at the Government's disposal, the execution of which may take different forms ranging from remaining at liberty under supervision to detention.

The choice between these forms of execution is a matter for the discretion of the Minister of Justice. Nevertheless he does not enjoy an unlimited power in making his decision: within the bounds laid down by the Act, he must assess the degree of danger presented by the individual concerned and the short- to medium-term prospects of reintegrating him into society.

40. In fact, sight must not be lost of what the title and general structure of the 1964 Act, the drafting history and Belgian case-law show to be the objectives of this statute, that is to say not only 'to protect society against the danger presented by recidivists and habitual offenders' but also 'to provide [the Government] with the possibility of endeavouring to reform [them]' (Court of Cassation, 11 December 1933, *Pasicrisie* 1934, I, p 99). Attempting to achieve these objectives requires that account be taken of circumstances that, by their nature, differ from case to case and are susceptible of modification. At the time of its decision, the court can, in the nature of things, do no more than estimate how the individual will develop in the future. The Minister of Justice, for his part, is able, through and with the assistance of his officials, to monitor that development more closely and at frequent intervals but this very fact means that with the passage of time the link between his decisions not to release or to re-detain and the initial judgment gradually becomes less strong. The link might eventually be broken if a position were reached in which those decisions were based on grounds that had no connection with the objectives of the legislature and the court or on an assessment that was unreasonable in terms of those objectives. In those circumstances, a detention that was lawful at the outset would be transformed into a deprivation of liberty that was arbitrary and, hence, incompatible with Article 5 (see, notably, the above-mentioned *X v UK* judgment, Series A No 46, p 19, § 43).

Such a situation did not obtain in the present case. The Belgian authorities showed patience and trust towards Mr Van Droogenbroeck: notwithstanding his conduct, they gave him several opportunities to mend his ways.... The manner in which they exercised their discretion respected the requirements of the Convention, which allows a measure of indeterminacy in sentencing and does not oblige the Contracting States to entrust to the courts the general supervision of the execution of sentences....

42. There has accordingly been no violation of Article 5 § 1....

FOR THESE REASONS, THE COURT UNANIMOUSLY

1. Holds that there has not been a violation of Article 5(1) of the Convention;
2. Holds that there has been a violation of Article 5(4);...

NOTES

1 The Court was composed of President Wiarda and Judges: Zekia, Cremona, Van der Meersch, Bindschedler-Robert, Evrigenis, Lagergren, Liesch, Gölcüklü, Matscher, Pinheiro Farinha, García de Enterría, Pettiti, Walsh, Sir Vincent Evans, Russo, Bernhardt, and Gersing.

2 The 'sufficient connection' test that was adopted by the Court in the **Van Droogenbroeck** case was followed in **Weeks v UK**, the facts of which are summarized at p 330, where the case is considered under Article 5(4). The **Weeks** case concerned the recall by the Home Secretary of a convicted person who had been given a discretionary life sentence. Holding that Article 5(1) had not been infringed, the Court stated:

46.... The intention [in giving him a discretionary life sentence] was to make the applicant, who was qualified both by the trial judge and by the Court of Appeal as a 'dangerous young man', subject to a continuing security measure in the interests of public safety'.

... In substance, Mr Weeks was being put at the disposal of the State because he needed continued supervision in custody for an unforeseeable length of time and, as a corollary, periodic reassessment in order to ascertain the most appropriate manner of dealing with him.

The grounds expressly relied on by the sentencing courts for ordering this form of deprivation of liberty against Mr Weeks are by their very nature susceptible of change with the passage of time, whereas the measure will remain in force for the whole of his life. In this, his sentence differs from a life sentence imposed on a person because of the gravity of the offence.

47. In this sense, the measure ordered against Mr Weeks is thus comparable to the Belgian measure at issue in the *Van Droogenbroeck* case, that is the placing of a recidivist or habitual offender at the disposal of the Government—although in the present case the placement was for a whole lifetime and not for a limited period (Series A No 50, especially at pp 21–2, § 40). The legitimate aim (of social protection and the rehabilitation of offenders) pursued by the measure and its effect on the convicted person are substantially the same in both cases....

49. Applying the principles stated in the *Van Droogenbroeck* judgment, the formal legal connection between Mr Weeks' conviction in 1966 and his recall to prison some ten years later is not on its own sufficient to justify the contested detention under Article 5 § 1(a). The causal link required by sub-paragraph (a)... might eventually be broken if a position were reached in which a decision not to release or to re-detain was based on grounds that were inconsistent with the objectives of the sentencing court. 'In those circumstances, a detention that was lawful at the outset would be transformed into a deprivation of liberty that was arbitrary and, hence, incompatible with Article 5' (Series A No 50, pp 21–2, § 40)...

It remains to examine the sufficiency of the grounds on which his re-detention in June 1977 and thereafter was based. In this area, as in many others, the national authorities are to be recognised as having a certain discretion since they are better placed than the international judge to evaluate the evidence in a particular case (see, *inter alia*, the *X v UK* judgment of 5 November 1981, Series A No 46, p 20, § 43, and the *Luberti* judgment of 23 February 1984, Series A No 75, p 12, § 27)....

51.... In view of [his] unstable, disturbed and aggressive behaviour, there were grounds for the Home Secretary to have considered that the applicant's continued liberty would constitute a danger to the public and to himself. The Minister's decision to re-detain remained.

In the Court's judgment, therefore, a sufficient connection, for the purposes of sub-paragraph (a) of Article 5 § 1, existed between his conviction in 1966 and his recall to prison in 1977.

3   In ***Monnell and Morris v UK*** A.115 (1987), the Court of Appeal directed that the time between a conviction and the rejection of a frivolous appeal should not count towards the sentence. The European Court held that detention during the period of the appeal was justified under Article 5(1)(a) since it followed from the conviction.

4   In ***Tsirlis and Kouloumpas v Greece***, 1997-III, the applicants were ministers of the Jehovah's Witnesses who were convicted for insubordination by a military tribunal and sentenced to four years' imprisonment for refusing to perform military service, the tribunal considering that Jehovah's Witnesses were not a 'known religion'. In convicting the applicants, the tribunal ignored Greek judicial decisions establishing that Jehovah's Witnesses were a 'known religion', so that their ministers were exempt from military service. Eventually, the applicants' convictions were quashed by the Supreme Administrative Court and the applicants were released after detention for 13 and 12 months respectively.

Holding that the applicants' detention was not 'lawful' under Article 5(1)(a), the European Court stated:

56. It must therefore be established whether Mr Tsirlis's detention between 30 April 1990 and 30 May 1991 as well as Mr Kouloumpas's detention between 30 May 1990 and 29 May 1991 were 'in accordance with a procedure prescribed by law' and 'lawful' within the meaning of Article 5 § 1 of the Convention. The Court reiterates that the Convention here essentially refers back to domestic law and states the obligation to conform to the substantive and procedural rules thereof; but it requires in addition that any deprivation of liberty should be consistent with the purpose of Article 5, namely to protect individuals from arbitrariness (see, among many other authorities, the *Bozano v France* judgment of 18 December 1986, Series A No 111, p 23, § 54, and the *Lukanov v Bulgaria* judgment of 20 March 1997, Reports of Judgments and Decisions 1997-II, pp 543–4, § 41).

57. It is in the first place for the national authorities, notably the courts, to interpret and apply domestic law. However, since under Article 5 § 1 failure to comply with domestic law entails a breach of the Convention, it follows that the Court can and should exercise a certain power to review whether this law has been complied with (see the *Bouamar v Belgium* judgment of 29 February 1988, Series A No 129, p 21, § 49).

58. Detention will in principle be lawful if it is carried out pursuant to a court order. A subsequent finding that the court erred under domestic law in making the order will not necessarily retrospectively affect the validity of the intervening period of detention. For this reason, the Strasbourg organs have consistently refused to uphold applications from persons convicted of criminal offences who complain that their convictions or sentences were found by the appellate courts to have been based on errors of fact or law (see the *Benham v UK* judgment of 10 June 1996, Reports 1996-III, p 753, § 42).

59. The Court notes that section 6 of the 1988 Law refers to ministers of all 'known religions'. As early as 1975, the Supreme Administrative Court acknowledged that the Jehovah's Witnesses were to be considered as such, and this case-law could unquestionably be regarded as established by 1990. . . . It was not disputed throughout the domestic proceedings that the applicants were ministers of that religion. However, in deciding on the issue of the applicants' criminal liability, and thus on the lawfulness of their detention, the military authorities blatantly ignored this case-law. As a result, Mr Tsirlis and Mr Kouloumpas spent thirteen and twelve months in detention respectively.

60. Furthermore, the relevant authorities' persistence not to recognise Jehovah's Witnesses as a 'known religion' and the disregard of the applicants' right to liberty that followed, were of a discriminatory nature when contrasted with the way in which ministers of the Greek Orthodox Church obtain exemption . . .

61. It is no answer to these failings that, as the Government have submitted, the question of the applicants' position as ministers of religion lay outside the scope of the case before the military courts, whose jurisdiction only extended itself to the alleged offence of insubordination. . . . In the first place, it is clear from the repeated adjournments of the applicants' cases by the Military Appeal Court in order to clarify whether Jehovah's Witnesses ministers were under an obligation to perform military service . . . that this latter issue was of central importance to the appeals. In the second place, the appellate courts acquitted the applicants immediately after the Supreme Administrative Court had quashed the Director for Recruitment's decision not to grant exemption from military duties on the grounds that the applicants were ministers of a 'known religion'.

62. Against this background, the Court finds that the applicants' detention following their conviction on charges of insubordination had no basis under domestic law and was arbitrary. It cannot accordingly be considered to have been 'lawful' for the purposes of Article 5 § 1.

5 A Grand Chamber found that the detention of the applicants after their 'conviction', following an arbitrary trial, by a 'court' established by a separatist regime not recognized by the international community violated Article 5(1)(a) in *Ilascu and Others v Moldova and Russia*, judgment of 8 July 2004 (and see above, p 67 in respect of Article 3 aspects of the case).

461. The requirement of lawfulness laid down by Article 5 § 1 (a) ('lawful detention' ordered 'in accordance with a procedure prescribed by law') is not satisfied merely by compliance with the relevant domestic law; domestic law must itself be in conformity with the Convention, including the general principles expressed or implied in it, particularly the principle of the rule of law, which is expressly mentioned in the Preamble to the Convention. The notion underlying the expression 'in accordance with a procedure prescribed by law' is one of fair and proper procedure, namely that any measure depriving a person of his liberty should issue from and be executed by an appropriate authority and should not be arbitrary (see, among other authorities, *Winterwerp v The Netherlands*, judgment of 24 October 1979, Series A No 33, § 45).

In addition, as the purpose of Article 5 is to protect the individual from arbitrariness (see, among other authorities, *Stafford v the United Kingdom* [GC], No 46295/99, § 63, ECHR 2002-IV), a 'conviction' cannot be the result of a flagrant denial of justice (see, *mutatis mutandis*, *Drozd and Janousek v France and Spain*, judgment of 26 June 1992, Series A No 240, § 110).

The Court also refers to its conclusions under Article 3 of the Convention regarding the nature of the proceedings in the 'Supreme Court of the MRT'.

462. The Court accordingly finds that none of the applicants was convicted by a 'court', and that a sentence of imprisonment passed by a judicial body such as the 'Supreme Court of the MRT' at the close of proceedings like those conducted in the present case cannot be regarded as 'lawful detention' ordered 'in accordance with a procedure prescribed by law'.

463. That being so, the deprivation of liberty suffered by the applicants during the period covered by the Court's jurisdiction *ratione temporis* in respect of the respondent States (namely, as regards Mr Ilaşcu, from 12 September 1997 to 5 May 2001 for Moldova, and from 5 May 1998 to 5 May 2001 for Russia and, as regards the other applicants, from the date of ratification by each of the respondent States to the present date) cannot satisfy the conditions laid down in paragraph 1 (a) of Article 5 of the Convention.

It follows that there was a violation of Article 5 § 1 of the Convention until May 2001 as regards Mr Ilaşcu [when he was released], and that there has been and continues to be a violation of that provision as regards the three applicants still detained.

464. Having regard to the fact that the applicants were detained at the time of the Convention's entry into force with regard to the Russian Federation, and taking into account its findings above... the Court concludes that the conduct constituting a violation of Article 5 is imputable to the Russian Federation as regards all the applicants.

Taking into account its conclusion above... that the responsibility of the Republic of Moldova by virtue of its positive obligations is engaged from May 2001, the Court concludes that there has been no violation of Article 5 by Moldova as regards Mr Ilaşcu. On the other hand, there has been a violation of that provision by Moldova as regards the other three applicants.

Hence trials and 'convictions' by bodies that fail to comply with the constitutional and procedural norms of the Convention will not be recognized by the Court as justifying the detention of persons under Article 5.

6 In several cases the imposition of additional periods of prevention detention, on prisoners deemed to pose a continuing risk to society, by German criminal courts have been found to violate this provision; examples include *M v Germany*, judgment of 17 December

2009 and *Kallweit, Mautes,* and *Schummer v Germany,* judgments of 13 January 2011. The defects in the German system were that the additional periods had not been ordered by the sentencing courts and the length of the preventive detention had been increased retrospectively (which also constituted a breach of Article 7(1)). In May 2011 the German Federal Constitutional Court declared all the legislation on the retrospective extension of preventive detention incompatible with the Basic Law. That ruling was welcomed by a unanimous chamber in *Schmitz v Germany,* judgment of 9 June 2011.

Article 5(1)(b): non-compliance with a court order or failure to fulfil an obligation prescribed by law

Gatt v Malta judgment of 27 July 2010
European Court of Human Rights

In 2001 the applicant was granted bail, pending prosecution for alleged drug trafficking, on a personal guarantee of 23,300 euros. His bail was subject to a number of conditions including a curfew in his house (he was allowed to take his son to and from school). In 2006 the Criminal Court determined that he had breached his bail by being seen outside his home one evening. He was ordered to pay the personal guarantee to the Government. The applicant did not have the funds to pay and so the court, in accordance with the Criminal Code, converted the sum into a period of 2,000 days' detention. After unsuccessful appeals the applicant complained to the court alleging, *inter alia,* a breach of Article 5.

36. In the present case, the Government submitted that the detention was in accordance with Article 5 § 1 (b) under both its first and second limbs.

37. The first limb refers to detention for 'non-compliance with the lawful order of a court', already made against the individual. The Convention organs have applied it to include, *inter alia,* failure to pay a court fine (see *Airey v Ireland,* Decisions and Reports (DR) no. 8), failure to undergo medical examinations ordered by a court (see *X v Austria,* DR no. 18, and *X v FRG,* no.6659/74, DR no. 3), failure to comply with a decision to hand over children to a parent (see *Paradis v Germany,* (dec). no. 4065/04, 4 September 2007), failure to observe residence restrictions imposed by a judicial decision (see *Freda v Italy,* DR no. 21) and failure to observe binding-over orders (see, for example, *Steel and Others v the United Kingdom,* 23 September 1998, § 69, Reports 1998-VII).

38. The Court notes that the applicant did not comply with the court order of 6 June 2006 ordering him to pay EUR 23,300 and was consequently imprisoned for two thousand (2,000) days.

. . .

40. The Court reiterates that Article 5 § 1 of the Convention requires in the first place that the detention be 'lawful', which includes the condition of compliance with a procedure prescribed by law. The Convention here essentially refers back to national law and states the obligation to conform to the substantive and procedural rules thereof, but it requires in addition that any deprivation of liberty should be consistent with the purpose of Article 5, namely to protect individuals from arbitrariness. A period of detention will in principle be lawful if it is carried out pursuant to a court order (see *Benham v the United Kingdom,* §§ 40 and 42, 10 June 1996, Reports 1996-III). However, the domestic

authorities must strike a fair balance between the importance in a democratic society of securing compliance with a lawful order of a court, and the importance of the right to liberty (see *Paradis v France*, (dec.) cited above). The Court considers that in such circumstances issues such as the purpose of the order, the feasibility of compliance with the order, and the duration of the detention are matters to be taken into consideration. The issue of proportionality assumes particular significance in the overall scheme of things.

...

42. The purpose of the court order was to secure payment of an amount due to the authorities by way of a penalty for breaching bail conditions. The Court considers that monetary guarantees are indispensable to ensure respect for the right to liberty when considering remand in custody. It notes however that in 2006 the applicant was indigent and unable to pay the said amount, although he might have been able to do so when he assented to the obligation in 2001. Indeed, it would have been reasonable for the applicant to assume that the proceedings against him would not have lasted over five years. The Court observes that the applicant had been under strict bail conditions for nearly five years. Thus, it is plausible to conclude that he had been unable to earn a living during that period. In such circumstances, it was unrealistic to expect that the applicant would be able to comply with the court order.

43. The Court further notes that in the cases examined under the first limb of Article 5 § 1 (b) the duration of the detention amounted to short periods, such as four days (see, *Airey v Ireland,* Commission decision, cited above) or one week (see *Freda*, and *Steel and Others*, both cited above) and at maximum six months (see *Paradis*, cited above). In the present case, the detention for non-compliance with a court order has so far amounted to over four years and is set to last for over five years and six months in total. Moreover, this period was not subject to remission, as would have been the case had the applicant been detained after conviction (Article 5 § 1 (a)). Nor was this period of detention subject to the guarantees of Article 5 § 3, as would have been the case had the applicant been remanded in custody on suspicion of having committed a crime (Article 5 § 1 (c)). In light of the above, the Court considers that a period of detention of more than five years and six months (two thousand days) for failure to comply with a court order to pay EUR 23,300 as a result of a one-time breach of curfew imposed as a bail condition cannot be considered to strike a fair balance between the importance in a democratic society of securing compliance with a lawful order of a court and the importance of the right to liberty.

44. In consequence, in so far as it is based on this ground, the applicant's entire period of detention cannot be said to have been in accordance with Article 5 § 1 of the Convention.

45. The Court must nevertheless consider whether the detention was Convention compatible on the basis of the second ground invoked by the Government, namely the second limb of Article 5 § 1 (b) 'in order to secure the fulfilment of any obligation prescribed by law'.

46. The Court reiterates that the second limb of Article 5 § 1 (b) allows for detention to secure the fulfilment of a specific and concrete obligation prescribed by law, which is already incumbent on the person concerned. The arrest and detention must be for the purpose of securing its fulfilment and not punitive in character. Moreover, a balance must be struck between the importance in a democratic society of securing the immediate fulfilment of the obligation in question and the importance of the right to liberty. In this assessment the nature of the obligation arising from the relevant legislation including its underlying object and purpose, the person being detained, the particular circumstances leading to the detention and the length of the detention are relevant (see *Vasileva v Denmark*, no. 52792/99, §§ 36–38, 25 September 2003).

47. The Court considers that the obligation undertaken by the applicant on 14 August 2001 to pay EUR 23,300 in the event that he breached his bail conditions was concrete and sufficiently precise.

48. As to the purpose of detention, the Court notes that at that stage it was no longer to ensure compliance with bail conditions, but simply to ensure the payment of the sum guaranteed. The Court has previously held that imprisonment in default of payment (of a customs fine) was not a means of enforcing the fine, but a penalty (see *Jamil v France*, 8 June 1995, § 32, Series A no. 317-B, and *Göktan* [*v France*, no. 33402/96] § 48) and the Government have acknowledged that in the present case the measure was punitive in nature. The Court sees no reason to differ. In particular, it notes that, imprisonment in default as applied to the failure to pay a guarantee following a breach of bail conditions, may give rise to a situation where an individual is imprisoned for a longer time than the term he would have served had he been found guilty of the crime he was charged with. The situation would be even more paradoxical if the individual were to be acquitted of such charges. The Court, furthermore, has difficulty in accepting that the detention of the applicant could secure the fulfilment of the obligation as his indigent state will undoubtedly persist and quite plausibly increase while he remains in jail.

...

51. In conclusion, the Court considers that in the circumstances of the present case, and especially on account of its duration, the applicant's detention was disproportionate. In particular, the law and its application to the applicant, failed to strike a balance between the importance in a democratic society of securing the immediate fulfilment of the obligation in question and the importance of the right to liberty.

...

FOR THESE REASONS THE COURT UNANIMOUSLY

2. *Holds* that there has been a violation of Article 5(1) of the Convention;

NOTES

1 The Court was composed of President Bratza and Judges: Garlicki, Bonello, Mijovic, Thor Bjorgvinsson, Bianku, and Poalelungi.

2 The judgment in **Gatt** clearly sets out the nature of the two limbs of Article 5(1)(b). The Court subjected detention under either limb to a test of proportionality.

3 In **Benham v UK**, 1996-III, a magistrates' court ordered the applicant to be imprisoned for one month because his failure to pay his community charge had been due to his culpable neglect. On appeal, the Divisional Court held that the magistrates' court had been mistaken: there was no evidence on the basis of which they could properly have found culpable neglect. The European Court held that the applicant's detention on the basis of the court order was justified by Article 5(1)(b), and that this was so even though the order had been set aside on appeal. It stated:

42. A period of detention will in principle be lawful if it is carried out pursuant to a court order. A subsequent finding that the court erred under domestic law in making the order will not necessarily retrospectively affect the validity of the intervening period of detention. For this reason, the Strasbourg organs have consistently refused to uphold applications from persons convicted of criminal offences who complain that their convictions or sentences were found by the appellate courts to have been based on errors of fact or law (see the *Bozano v France* judgment of 18 December 1986, Series A No 111, p 23, § 55, and the report of the Commission of 9 March 1978 on application no 7629/76, *Krzycki v Germany*, Decisions and Reports 13, pp 60–1).

43. It was agreed by those appearing before the Court that the principles of English law which should be taken into account in this case distinguished between acts of a magistrates' court which

were within its jurisdiction and those which were in excess of jurisdiction. The former were valid and effective unless or until they were overturned by a superior court, whereas the latter were null and void from the outset. . . .

46. It cannot be said with any degree of certainty that . . . the magistrates acted in excess of jurisdiction within the meaning of English law. It follows that the Court does not find it established that the order for detention was invalid, and thus that the detention which resulted from it was unlawful under national law (see the above-mentioned *Bouamar* judgment p 21, § 49). The mere fact that the order was set aside on appeal did not in itself affect the lawfulness of the detention (see paragraph 42 above).

47. Nor does the Court find that the detention was arbitrary. It has not been suggested that the magistrates who ordered Mr Benham's detention acted in bad faith, nor that they neglected to attempt to apply the relevant legislation correctly (see the above-mentioned *Bozano* judgment, pp 25–6, § 59). . . .
   Accordingly, the Court finds no violation of Article 5 § 1 of the Convention.

In the later case of ***Beet and Others v UK***, judgment of 1 March 2005, a unanimous Chamber applied **Benham** to determine that as the magistrates had failed to undertake a proper inquiry into the applicant's means, before imprisoning her due to her arrears in the payment of the community charge, this omission resulted in the magistrates' order being made in excess of jurisdiction. Consequently, it was unlawful and therefore the applicant had been detained in breach of Article 5(1).

4   A unanimous Chamber found a violation of this provision in ***Vasileva v Denmark***, judgment of 25 September 2003. The applicant was a 67-year-old Bulgarian citizen. On 11 August 1995 she had a dispute with a ticket inspector on a bus in Arhus. The inspector accused her of travelling without a valid ticket and sought to issue her with a penalty fare. However, she refused to disclose her identity. The police were called and they requested that she disclose her identity, under section 750 of the Administration of Justice Act everyone is under a duty to disclose his/her name, address, and date of birth to the police upon request (failure to do so is punishable with a fine). She refused to provide the police with this information and so they arrested her, under the same Act, at 9.30 pm. She was taken to the police station and placed in a waiting room. Vasileva continued to refuse to identify herself (and she had no documents in her possession which contained such information). At 11 pm she was placed in a cell. From 6.30 am the next day the police sought to persuade the applicant to disclose her identity. She eventually did so at 10.45 am and she was then released at 11 am. Immediately after her release she collapsed and was hospitalized for three days diagnosed with high blood pressure. She was not charged with the offence of refusing to provide details of her identity to the police. After failing to secure compensation from the police in the domestic courts, she complained to Strasbourg alleging a breach of Article 5. The Danish Government sought to justify her detention under Article 5(1)(b) in order to secure the fulfilment of her specific legal obligation under Danish law to identify herself to the police when so requested. The Court held that:

36. . . . detention is authorised under sub-paragraph (b) of Article 5 § 1 only to 'secure the fulfilment' of the obligation prescribed by law. It follows that, at the very least, there must be an unfulfilled obligation incumbent on the person concerned and the arrest and detention must be for the purpose of securing its fulfilment and not punitive in character. As soon as the relevant obligation has been fulfilled, the basis for detention under Article 5 § 1 (b) ceases to exist.

37. Finally, a balance must be drawn between the importance in a democratic society of securing the immediate fulfilment of the obligation in question, and the importance of the right to liberty...The duration of detention is also a relevant factor in drawing such a balance (see *McVeigh and Others v the United Kingdom*, Applications Nos 8022/77, 8025/77, 8027/77, Commission decision of 18 March 1981, DR 25, pp 37–8 and 42; *Johansen v Norway*, Application No 10600/83, Commission decision of 14 October 1985, DR 44, p 162).

...

41....In the present case the applicant was deprived of her liberty for thirteen and a half hours. The Court notes that the police several times in vain requested that she reveal her identity in the period from 9.30 until 11.00 p.m. on 11 August 1995, and from 6.30 until 10.45 a.m. on 12 August 1995, and relying on the findings of the domestic courts, the Court is satisfied that the applicant was not in possession of any documentation, which could have revealed her identity. Also, it notes that it appears to be common ground that no efforts were made to identify her in the period between 11.00 p.m. and 6.30 a.m. The Government allege that the reason therefore can be attributed to considerations as to the applicant's need for sleep. While accepting that such considerations may be relevant in certain circumstances, it is in the Court's opinion not established that this was so in the present case. Furthermore, the Court would be reluctant to accept that such considerations could generally be given priority over the obligation to secure that the detention did not exceed a period proportionate to the cause of the detention. The Court notes in addition, having regard to the fact that the Chief Constable of Århus on 18 July 1996 found reason to regret that the applicant during her detention had not been attended to by a doctor as promised, that the involvement of such a third person might have broken the impasse, which the communication between the police and the applicant obviously had reached. Moreover, having regard to its finding above as to the applicant and the circumstances leading to her detention, and to the fact that the applicant's failure to comply with the obligation prescribed in section 750 of the Administration of Justice Act was a minor offence, which could carry only a fine, the Court considers that her detention in any event should not have been maintained for a longer period of time. It finds that the deprivation of the applicant's liberty for thirteen and a half hours exceeded a period proportionate to the cause of her detention.

42. In the light of the above elements, the Court considers that the authorities by extending the applicant's detention to thirteen and a half-hour failed to strike a fair balance between the need to ensure the fulfilment of the obligation and the right to liberty.

43. There has, accordingly, been a violation of Article 5 § 1 of the Convention.

The obligation upon the applicant to identify herself to the police was a clear example of the type of specific duty falling within the second limb of Article 5(1)(b). In assessing the proportionality of a period of detention utilized to secure the fulfilment of such a duty the Court examined, *inter alia*, the nature/purpose of the obligation, the action/inaction of the police to secure the fulfilment of that obligation during the period of detention, and the duration of the period of detention. Here the combination of the minor nature of the applicant's suspected criminal conduct, the overnight hiatus in the attempts by the police to discover the applicant's identity, and the length of her detention resulted in the Court finding a breach of Article 5. Do you agree with the Court's assessment that the police were at fault for allowing the applicant to sleep during the night and for not continuing to try and discover her identity?

Article 5(1)(c): reasonable suspicion of a criminal offence, etc

Fox, Campbell and Hartley v UK A.182 (1990)
European Court of Human Rights

The applicants were arrested in Northern Ireland by a police constable exercising his statutory power under section 11 of the Northern Ireland (Emergency Provisions) Act 1978 'to arrest without warrant any person whom he suspects of being a terrorist'. This power had been interpreted in *McKee v Chief Constable for Northern Ireland* [1984] 1 WLR 1358, HL, as incorporating a subjective test, so that an arrest was permissible if the policeman had an 'honestly held suspicion'. On their arrest, the applicants were told only that they were being arrested under section 11 on suspicion of being terrorists; they were given no facts in support of the suspicion. The applicants claimed, *inter alia*, that Articles 5(1)(c) and 5(2) had been infringed. In its report, the Commission expressed the opinion, by 7 votes to 5, that both provisions had been infringed in respect of all three applicants.

JUDGMENT OF THE COURT

32. The 'reasonableness' of the suspicion on which an arrest must be based forms an essential part of the safeguard against arbitrary arrest and detention which is laid down in Article 5 § 1(c). The Court agrees with the Commission and the Government that having a 'reasonable suspicion' presupposes the existence of facts or information which would satisfy an objective observer that the person concerned may have committed the offence. What may be regarded as 'reasonable' will however depend upon all the circumstances.

In this respect, terrorist crime falls into a special category. Because of the attendant risk of loss of life and human suffering, the police are obliged to act with utmost urgency in following up all information, including information from secret sources. Further, the police may frequently have to arrest a suspected terrorist on the basis of information which is reliable but which cannot, without putting in jeopardy the source of the information, be revealed to the suspect or produced in court to support a charge.

As the Government pointed out, in view of the difficulties inherent in the investigation and prosecution of terrorist-type offences in Northern Ireland, the 'reasonableness of the suspicion justifying such arrests cannot always be judged according to the same standards as are applied in dealing with conventional crime'. Nevertheless, the exigencies of dealing with terrorist crime cannot justify stretching the notion of 'reasonableness' to the point where the essence of the safeguard secured by Article 5 § 1(c) is impaired.

...

34. Certainly Article 5 § 1(c) of the Convention should not be applied in such a manner as to put disproportionate difficulties in the way of the police authorities of the Contracting States in taking effective measures to counter organised terrorism (see, *mutatis mutandis*, the *Klaas* judgment of 6 September 1978, Series A No 28, pp 27 and 30–1, §§ 58 and 68). It follows that the Contracting States cannot be asked to establish the reasonableness of the suspicion grounding the arrest of a suspected terrorist by disclosing the confidential sources of supporting information or even facts which would be susceptible to indicating such sources or their identity.

Nevertheless the Court must be enabled to ascertain whether the essence of the safeguard afforded by Article 5 § 1(c) has been secured. Consequently the respondent Government have to furnish at least some facts or information capable of satisfying the Court that the arrested person was reasonably suspected of having committed the alleged offence. This is all the more necessary where, as in the present case, the domestic law does not require reasonable suspicion, but sets a lower threshold by merely requiring honest suspicion.

35. The Court accepts that the arrest and detention of each of the present applicants was based on a bona fide suspicion that he or she was a terrorist, and that each of them, including Mr Hartley, was questioned during his or her detention about specific terrorist acts of which he or she was suspected.

The fact that Mr Fox and Ms Campbell both have previous convictions for acts of terrorism connected with the IRA..., although it could reinforce a suspicion linking them to the commission of terrorist-type offences, cannot form the sole basis of a suspicion justifying their arrest in 1986, some seven years later.

The fact that all the applicants, during their detention, were questioned about specific terrorist acts, does no more than confirm that the arresting officers had a genuine suspicion that they had been involved in those acts, but it cannot satisfy an objective observer that the applicants may have committed these acts.

The aforementioned elements on their own are insufficient to support the conclusion that there was 'reasonable suspicion'. The Government have not provided any further material on which the suspicion against the applicants was based. Their explanations therefore do not meet the minimum standard set by Article 5(1)(c) for judging the reasonableness of a suspicion for the arrest of an individual....

FOR THESE REASONS, THE COURT

1. Holds by four votes to three that there has been a breach of Article 5 § 1;...

JOINT DISSENTING OPINION OF JUDGES SIR VINCENT EVANS, BERNHARDT AND PALM

We are unable to agree with the finding of the majority of the Court that there has been a violation of Article 5 § 1(c) in this case...

The majority accept—and on this we agree—that the arrest and detention of each of the applicants was based on a bona fide suspicion that he or she was a terrorist and that each of them was questioned during his or her detention about specific terrorist acts of which he or she was suspected. But, in the opinion of the majority, the latter fact does no more than confirm that the arresting officers had a genuine suspicion and a genuine suspicion was not the equivalent of a reasonable suspicion.

In our view the 'genuine suspicion' on the part of the arresting officers that the applicants were involved in the specific terrorist acts about which they were questioned must have had some basis in information received by them, albeit from sources which the Government maintain that they are unable to disclose for security reasons. In the situation in Northern Ireland the police must have a responsibility to follow up such information of involvement in terrorist activities and, if circumstances so warrant, to arrest and detain the suspect for further investigation.

In cases such as these it is not possible to draw a sharp distinction between genuine suspicion and reasonable suspicion. Having regard to all the circumstances and to the facts and information between the Court, including in the case of Mr Fox and Ms Campbell the fact that they had previously been involved in and convicted of terrorist activities, we are satisfied that there were reasonable grounds for suspicion justifying the arrest and detention of the applicants in accordance with Article 5 § 1(c)....

NOTES

1 The Court was composed of President Ryssdal and Judges: Cremona, Pinheiro Farinha, Sir Vincent Evans, Bernhardt, Martens, and Palm.

2   The *Fox, Campbell and Hartley* case spell out the meaning of 'reasonable suspicion' in Article 5(1)(c). The objective test that it states was not complied with on the facts, even with the special allowance that the Court was prepared to make in the special context of terrorist offences. The test was complied with in the later terrorist case of *Murray (Margaret) v UK* A.300 (1994). In that case, the first applicant was arrested by a member of the armed forces under section 14 of the Northern Ireland (Emergency Provisions) Act 1978 on suspicion of having committed an offence involving the collection of funds for the Provisional IRA. Confirming the approach it had taken in the *Fox, Campbell and Hartley* case, and adding that the length of time for which the person might be detained (four hours maximum under section 14) was relevant to the level of suspicion required, the Court stated:

61. It cannot be excluded that all or some of the evidence adduced before the national courts in relation to the genuineness of the suspicion on the basis of which Mrs Murray was arrested may also be material to the issue whether the suspicion was 'reasonable' for the purposes of Article 5 § 1(c) of the Convention. At the very least the honesty and bona fides of a suspicion constitute one indispensable element of its reasonableness.

In the action brought by Mrs Murray against the Ministry of Defence for false imprisonment and other torts, the High Court judge, after having heard the witnesses and assessed their credibility, found that she had genuinely been suspected of having been involved in the collection of funds for the purchase of arms in the USA for the Provisional IRA.... The judge believed the evidence of the arresting officer, Corporal D, who was described as a 'transparently honest witness', as to what she had been told at her briefing before the arrest.... Likewise as found by the judge, although the interview at the Army centre was later in time than the arrest, the line of questioning pursued by the interviewer also tends to support the conclusion that Mrs Murray herself was suspected of the commission of a special criminal offence....

62. Some weeks before her arrest two of Mrs Murray's brothers had been convicted in the USA of offences connected with purchase of arms for the Provisional IRA.... As she disclosed in her evidence to the High Court, she had visited the USA and had contacts with her brothers there.... The offences of which her brothers were convicted were ones that implied collaboration with 'trustworthy' persons residing in Northern Ireland.

63. Having regard to the level of factual justification required at the stage of suspicion and to the special exigencies of investigating terrorist crime, the Court finds, in the light of all the above considerations, that there did exist sufficient facts or information which would provide a plausible and objective basis for a suspicion that Mrs Murray may have committed the offence of involvement in the collection of funds for the Provisional IRA. On the particular facts of the present case, therefore, the Court is satisfied that, notwithstanding the lower standard of suspicion under domestic law, Mrs Murray can be said to have been arrested and detained on 'reasonable suspicion' of the commission of a criminal offence, within the meaning of sub-paragraph (c) of Article 5 § 1.

3   In *Brogan v UK*, p 302, it was held that Article 5(1)(c) may justify an arrest or detention even though no criminal proceedings are eventually brought, provided that there is 'reasonable suspicion' that an offence has been committed when the arrest is made.

4   The 'prevention of an offence' ground for arrest or detention in Article 5(1)(c) does not authorize preventive detention: see the *Guzzardi* case, p 245, and *Lawless v Ireland* A.1 (1961).

5   A 'breach of the peace' is an 'offence' for the purposes of Article 5(1)(c) even though it is not a criminal offence in English law: *Steel v UK*, 1998-VII.

6 The full-time Court examined another Northern Irish suspected terrorist arrest in *O'Hara v UK*, judgment of 16 October 2001. The applicant was a well-known member of 'Sinn Fein'. In November 1985 a German national, Kurt Konig, who worked for the caterers supplying food to police stations in Londonderry was murdered (the Provisional IRA claimed responsibility for his killing). The Northern Irish Special Branch received intelligence from four informants (none of whom had criminal records and whose previous information had proved reliable) stating that the applicant and three other persons were responsible for the murder of Konig. The Special Branch briefed Detective Superintendent R of the Royal Ulster Constabulary that the applicant was a member of the Provisional IRA and had been implicated in the murder. Superintendent R subsequently briefed Inspector B who then briefed Detective Constable S. On 28 December 1985 the latter went to the applicant's home and arrested him. The applicant was informed by S that he was being arrested under section 12(1)(b) of the Prevention of Terrorism (Temporary Provisions) Act 1984 (which authorized a police officer to arrest a person whom he had reasonable grounds for suspecting of being concerned in the commission, preparation, or instigation of acts of terrorism). The applicant was taken to Castlereagh Detention Centre and held for six days and 13 hours during which time he was interviewed 34 times (he did not answer any questions). He was released without charge. The applicant sued the Chief Constable for, *inter alia*, seizure of documents and unlawful arrest. The High Court in Northern Ireland heard evidence from Detective Constable S that Inspector B had, prior to the arrest of the applicant, briefed him that there were reasonable grounds for suspecting the applicant to be involved in the murder of Konig. The trial judge considered that he only had 'scanty' evidence of the matters disclosed to Detective Constable S but that he was 'just satisfied' of the legality of the arrest. On appeal both the Court of Appeal and the House of Lords upheld the lawfulness of the arrest. Before the Court the applicant contended that he had never been a member of the IRA or been involved in the murder of Konig and therefore the police could not have received reliable information to that effect.

34. The Court emphasises that the 'reasonableness' of the suspicion on which an arrest must be based forms an essential part of the safeguard against arbitrary arrest and detention laid down in Article 5 § 1 (c) of the Convention. This requires the existence of some facts or information which would satisfy an objective observer that the person concerned may have committed the offence, though what may be regarded as reasonable will depend on all the circumstances of the case (see *Fox, Campbell and Hartley v the United Kingdom*, judgment of 30 August 1990, Series A No 182, p 16, § 32).

35. In that context, terrorist crime poses particular problems, as the police may be called upon, in the interests of public safety, to arrest a suspected terrorist on the basis of information which is reliable but which cannot be disclosed to the suspect or produced in court without jeopardising the informant. However, though Contracting States cannot be required to establish the reasonableness of the suspicion grounding the arrest of a suspected terrorist by disclosing confidential sources of information, the Court has held that the exigencies of dealing with terrorist crime cannot justify stretching the notion of 'reasonableness' to the point where the safeguard secured by Article 5 § 1 (c) is impaired. Even in those circumstances, the respondent Government have to furnish at least some facts or information capable of satisfying the Court that the arrested person was reasonably suspected of having committed the alleged offence (see *Fox, Campbell and Hartley*, cited above, pp 16–18, §§ 32–4).

36. It may also be observed that the standard imposed by Article 5 § 1 (c) does not presuppose that the police have sufficient evidence to bring charges at the time of arrest. The object of questioning

during detention under sub-paragraph (c) of Article 5 § 1 is to further the criminal investigation by way of confirming or dispelling the concrete suspicion grounding the arrest. Thus facts which raise a suspicion need not be of the same level as those necessary to justify a conviction, or even the bringing of a charge which comes at the next stage of the process of criminal investigation (see *Brogan and Others v the United Kingdom*, judgment of 29 November 1988, Series A No 145-B, p 29, § 53, and *Murray v the United Kingdom*, judgment of 28 October 1994, Series A No 300-A, p 27, § 55).

...

42. The suspicion in the present case was based on information passed on at a police briefing by informers who identified the applicant as one of a number of persons suspected of involvement in a specific terrorist event, the murder of Mr Konig. There is no basis in the material provided for the Court to reject the Government's submissions on this point. The arrest was therefore a pre-planned operation, more akin to the arrest in Murray, and was based on slightly more specific detail than in Fox, Campbell and Hartley. In these circumstances...the Court considers that the domestic courts' approach—that the judge was entitled on the sparse materials before him to infer the existence of reasonable grounds of suspicion—was not incompatible with the standard imposed by Article 5 § 1 (c) of the Convention.

43. The applicant argued, with some force, that police officers should not be able to hide behind references to anonymous informants by way of justifying abuse of their power of arrest. The Court reiterates, however, that in the domestic proceedings the applicant did not attempt to raise any complaints concerning bad faith or oppression. His claim was based on the narrow legal argument concerning the state of mind of the arresting officer relevant under section 12(1)(b) of the 1984 Act. Nor is the Court persuaded that there was any immunity conferred on other police officers, as a result of the finding by the domestic courts, that the arresting officer had the required suspicion. If the briefing officer or any other superior officer had deliberately passed on misleading or inaccurate information to the arresting officer, the police authorities would have been liable for wrongful arrest or false imprisonment in respect of that misconduct.

44. The Court does not find, therefore, that the approach of the domestic courts to the standard of suspicion in this case removed the accountability of the police for arbitrary arrest, or conferred on the police any impunity with regard to arrests conducted on the basis of confidential information. In the circumstances, the suspicion against the applicant reached the required level as it was based on specific information that he was involved in the murder of Kurt Konig and the purpose of the deprivation of liberty was to confirm or dispel that suspicion. The applicant can accordingly be said to have been arrested and detained on 'reasonable suspicion' of a criminal offence, within the meaning of subparagraph (c) of Article 5 § 1.

Accordingly, there has been no violation of that provision.

Judge Loucaides dissented as he considered that:

...this case is nearer to *Fox, Campbell and Hartley* than to *Murray*, the reason being that both in this case and in the first-mentioned case no grounds at all in support of the reasonableness of the suspicion were submitted to the domestic courts, while in Murray certain facts in support of the suspicion were in fact adduced in the competent national courts.

The judgment in **O'Hara** reveals the Court treading a fine line between requiring the production of information justifying the reasonableness of an arrest of a suspected terrorist by States and recognition of the security implications of such disclosures in the increasingly important battle against all forms of terrorism. Do you agree with the Court's assessment of the sufficiency of the information against O'Hara?

Article 5(1)(d): educational supervision, etc, of minors

Bouamar v Belgium A.129 (1988)
European Court of Human Rights

The applicant was a seriously disturbed, delinquent 16-year-old who was detained by court order in a remand prison that provided no educational facilities for periods amounting to 119 days during most of one year. The orders were made under a 1965 Act, the purpose of which was to cause juveniles who committed criminal offences to be placed in juvenile reformatories with educational facilities instead of being tried and convicted by a criminal court. The Act allowed a juvenile to be placed in a remand prison for up to 15 days when it was 'materially impossible' to find him a place in a reformatory immediately. In the applicant's case, no open reformatory with the necessary educational facilities was willing to take him because of his behavioural problems and there was no suitable closed reformatory in the French-speaking region. In these circumstances, orders for his detention in a remand prison for 15-day periods were regularly renewed.

The applicant alleged that his detention was in breach of Article 5(1), not being justifiable under Article 5(1)(d). Having found that the detention was not in breach of Belgian law (since 'material impossibility' had been interpreted as extending to the juvenile's behavioural problems) and hence was not unlawful contrary to Article 5(1) on this basis, the Court continued as follows.

JUDGMENT OF THE COURT

50. 'Lawfulness', however, also implies that the deprivation of liberty is in keeping with the purpose of the restrictions permissible under Article 5 § 1 of the Convention....

The Court notes that the confinement of a juvenile in a remand prison does not necessarily contravene sub-paragraph (d), even if it is not in itself such as to provide for the person's 'educational supervision'. As is apparent from the words 'for the purpose of' ('pour'), the 'detention' referred to in the text is a means of ensuring that the person concerned is placed under 'educational supervision', but the placement does not necessarily have to be an immediate one. Just as Article 5 § 1 recognises—in subparagraphs (c) and (a)—the distinction between pre-trial detention and detention after conviction, so sub-paragraph (d) does not preclude an interim custody measure being used as a preliminary to a regime of supervised education, without itself involving any supervised education. In such circumstances, however, the imprisonment must be speedily followed by actual application of such a regime in a setting (open or closed) designed and with sufficient resources for the purpose.

51. In the instant case the applicant was, as it were, shuttled to and fro between the remand prison at Lantin and his family. In 1980 alone, the juvenile courts ordered his detention nine times and then released him on or before the expiry of the statutory limit of fifteen days; in all, he was thus deprived of his liberty for 119 days during the period of 291 days from 18 January to 4 November 1980....

52. In the Government's submission, the placements complained of were part of an educative programme initiated by the courts, and Mr Bouamar's behaviour during the relevant time enabled them to gain a clearer picture of his personality.

The Court does not share this view. The Belgian State chose the system of educational supervision with a view to carrying out its policy on juvenile delinquency. Consequently it was under an obligation to put in place appropriate institutional facilities which met the demands of security and the educational objectives of the 1965 Act, in order to be able to satisfy the requirements of

Article 5 § 1(d) of the Convention (see, among other authorities and *mutatis mutandis*, the *Guincho* judgment of 10 July 1984, Series A No 81, p 16, § 38, and the *De Cubber* judgment of 26 October 1984, Series A No 86, p 20, § 35).

Nothing in the evidence, however, shows that this was the case. At the time of the events in issue, Belgium did not have—at least in the French-speaking region in which the applicant lived—any closed institution able to accommodate highly disturbed juveniles (see paragraph 28 above). The detention of a young man in a remand prison in conditions of virtual isolation and without the assistance of staff with educational training cannot be regarded as furthering any educational aim....

53. The Court accordingly concludes that the nine placement orders, taken together, were not compatible with sub-paragraph (d). Their fruitless repetition had the effect of making them less and less 'lawful' under sub-paragraph (d), especially as Crown Counsel never instituted criminal proceedings against the applicant in respect of the offences alleged against him.

There was therefore a breach of Article 5 § 1 of the Convention....

FOR THESE REASONS, THE COURT

1. Holds unanimously that there was a breach of paragraph 1 of Article 5; ...

NOTES

1 The Court was composed of President Ryssdal and Judges: Vilhjálmsson, Walsh, Sir Vincent Evans, Macdonald, Russo, and De Meyer.

2 The full-time Court followed the approach of **Bouamar** in the case of **DG v Ireland**, judgment of 16 May 2002. The applicant had been in the care of public authorities since he was two years old due to his father's imprisonment for life and his mother's inability to care for him or his siblings. The applicant committed a number of crimes and after serving several periods of detention he was released in March 1997 when he was 16 years old. A case conference determined that he needed to live in a high-support therapeutic unit for 16–18–year-olds but that no such facility existed in Ireland. In the following month his guardian *ad litem* brought judicial review proceedings against the authorities claiming that in failing to provide him with suitable care and accommodation they were violating his constitutional rights. The High Court initially ordered that the applicant be accommodated in a hostel but that option became impossible when the applicant made threats of violence. Thereupon the High Court concluded that as the applicant had a serious personality order, which meant that he was a danger to himself and others, and as no secure therapeutic unit existed in Ireland he should be detained in St Patrick's Institution (an institution for the detention of males between 16 and 21 years of age being held on remand or after sentencing). The applicant was detained in St Patrick's from 27 June to 28 July 1997 when he was placed in special accommodation under 24-hour supervision. The applicant complained to Strasbourg that his detention in St Patrick's violated Article 5(1)(d). The Irish Government responded that his detention there had been for the lawful purpose of 'educational supervision'. The Court was unanimous in holding that:

80. It is also accepted that, in the context of the detention of minors, the words 'educational supervision' must not be equated rigidly with notions of classroom teaching: in the context of a young person in local authority care, educational supervision must embrace many aspects of the exercise, by the local authority, of parental rights for the benefit and protection of the person concerned...

81. However, the Court does not consider, and indeed, it does not appear to be argued by the Government, that St Patrick's itself constituted 'educational supervision'. As noted above, it was

a penal institution and the applicant was subjected to its disciplinary regime. The educational and other recreation services were entirely voluntary and the applicant's history was demonstrative of an unwillingness to cooperate with the authorities: indeed the Government accept that he did not avail himself of the educational facilities. There is no entry in the applicant's 'prison' file, in the medical or psychiatric reports submitted or any specific submission by the Government detailing any instruction received by the applicant during his detention in St Patrick's. The only indication of his participation in recreational activities is a brief reference to his playing football in a medical report. Most importantly, the High Court itself was convinced that St Patrick's could not guarantee his constitutional educational right or provide the special care he required: even with the special conditions the High Court attached to his detention, the High Court considered St Patrick's to be the best of four inappropriate options and that, accordingly, his detention there should be temporary.

Consequently, the applicant's detention was not compatible with Article 5(1)(d).

This judgment, again, demonstrates the need for States to establish specialist facilities for the care and education of severely disturbed young persons.

Article 5(1)(e): infectious diseases, unsound mind, alcoholics, vagrants, etc

Enhorn v Sweden judgment of 25 January 2005
European Court of Human Rights

The applicant, born in 1947, was a homosexual. In 1994 he was diagnosed as being infected with the HIV virus. It was also discovered that he had infected a 19-year-old, with whom he had first had sex in 1990. In September 1994 the relevant county medical officer issued a number of instructions to the applicant, under the Infectious Diseases Act 1988, designed to minimize the risks of the applicant transmitting the virus to other persons (they included: not to have sexual intercourse without first telling his partner about his HIV infection, using a condom, abstaining from consuming alcohol in amounts that would impair his judgment, informing medical staff about his condition if he had to have an operation, etc, and to attend medical appointments scheduled by the county medical officer). At first the applicant attended his scheduled medical appointments, but he then failed to attend five appointments in October and November 1994. In February 1995 the county medical officer applied to the County Administrative Court, under the 1988 Act, for an order that the applicant be compulsorily isolated in a hospital for three months (on the grounds that he was not complying with the practical instructions issued to him to prevent the spreading of a 'disease dangerous to society' and there was a 'manifest risk of the infection being spread'). The Administrative Court granted the order. The applicant failed to go to the hospital and some weeks later he was arrested by the police and taken there. The domestic courts regularly renewed the compulsory isolation orders until December 2001. However, during those years the applicant absconded from the hospital on a number of occasions and he actually spent a total of one-and-a-half years in compulsory isolation. During the remainder of the time, when he was absent without permission from the hospital, he claimed that he had not had any sexual relationships and there was no evidence that he had infected any other persons. In his complaint to the European Court the applicant contended that the issuing of the compulsory isolation orders against him had not been a proportionate response to his situation. The Swedish Government replied that the orders had been made with the aim of supporting a person having a dangerous infection to change their lifestyle and that no coercive medical treatment had been given to the applicant whilst he was isolated in the hospital.

43. Moreover, Article 5 § 1(e) of the Convention refers to several categories of individuals, namely persons spreading infectious diseases, persons of unsound mind, alcoholics, drug addicts and vagrants. There is a link between all those persons in that they may be deprived of their liberty either in order to be given medical treatment or because of considerations dictated by social policy, or on both medical and social grounds. It is therefore legitimate to conclude from this context that a predominant reason why the Convention allows the persons mentioned in paragraph 1(e) of Article 5 to be deprived of their liberty is not only that they are dangerous for public safety but also that their own interests may necessitate their detention (see *Guzzardi v Italy*, judgment of 6 November 1980, Series A No 39, pp. 36–7, § 98 *in fine*, and *Witold Litwa* [*v Poland* ECHR 2000-III] § 60).

44. Taking the above principles into account, the Court finds that the essential criteria when assessing the 'lawfulness' of the detention of a person 'for the prevention of the spreading of infectious diseases' are whether the spreading of the infectious disease is dangerous for public health or safety, and whether detention of the person infected is the last resort in order to prevent the spreading of the disease, because less severe measures have been considered and found to be insufficient to safeguard the public interest. When these criteria are no longer fulfilled, the basis for the deprivation of liberty ceases to exist.

45. Turning to the instant case, it is undisputed that the first criterion was fulfilled, in that the HIV virus was and is dangerous for public health and safety.

46. It thus remains to be examined whether the applicant's detention could be said to be the last resort in order to prevent the spreading of the virus, because less severe measures had been considered and found to be insufficient to safeguard the public interest.

47. In a judgment of 16 February 1995, the County Administrative Court ordered that the applicant should be kept in compulsory isolation for up to three months under section 38 of the 1988 Act. Thereafter, orders to prolong his deprivation of liberty were continuously issued every six months until 12 December 2001, when the County Administrative Court turned down the county medical officer's application for an extension of the detention order. Accordingly, the order to deprive the applicant of his liberty was in force for almost seven years.

Admittedly, since the applicant absconded several times, his actual deprivation of liberty lasted from 16 March 1995 until 25 April 1995, 11 June 1995 until 27 September 1995, 28 May 1996 until 6 November 1996, 16 November 1996 until 26 February 1997, and 26 February 1999 until 12 June 1999—almost one and a half years altogether.

48. The Government submitted that a number of voluntary measures had been attempted in vain during the period between September 1994 and February 1995 to ensure that the applicant's behaviour would not contribute to the spread of the HIV infection. Also, they noted the particular circumstances of the case, notably as to the applicant's personality and behaviour, as described by various physicians and psychiatrists; his preference for teenage boys; the fact that he had transmitted the HIV virus to a young man; and the fact that he had absconded several times and refused to cooperate with the staff at the hospital. Thus, the Government found that the involuntary placement of the applicant in hospital had been proportionate to the purpose of the measure, namely to prevent him from spreading the infectious disease.

49. The Court notes that the Government have not provided any examples of less severe measures which might have been considered for the applicant in the period from 16 February 1995 until 12 December 2001, but were apparently found to be insufficient to safeguard the public interest.

50. It is undisputed that the applicant failed to comply with the instruction issued by the county medical officer on 1 September 1994, which stated that he should visit his consulting physician

again and keep to appointments set up by the county medical officer. Although he kept to three appointments with the county medical officer in September 1994 and one in November 1994, and received two home visits by the latter, on five occasions during October and November 1994 the applicant failed to appear as summoned.

51. Another of the practical instructions issued by the council medical officer on 1 September 1994 was that, if the applicant was to have a physical examination, an operation, a vaccination or a blood test or was bleeding for any reason, he was obliged to tell the relevant medical staff about his infection. Also, he was to inform his dentist about his HIV infection. In April 1999, before the County Administrative Court, the county medical officer stated that during the last two years, while on the run, the applicant had sought medical treatment twice and that it had been established that both times he had said that he had the HIV virus, as opposed to the period when he had absconded between September 1995 and May 1996, during which the applicant had failed on three occasions to inform medical staff about his virus.

52. Yet another of the practical instructions issued by the county medical officer on 1 September 1994 required the applicant to abstain from consuming such an amount of alcohol that his judgment would thereby be impaired and others put at risk of being infected with HIV. However, there were no instructions to abstain from alcohol altogether or to undergo treatment against alcoholism. Nor did the domestic courts justify the deprivation of the applicant's liberty with reference to his being an 'alcoholic' within the meaning of Article 5 § 1(e) and the requirements deriving from that provision.

53. Moreover, although the county medical officer stated before the County Administrative Court in February 1995 that, in his opinion, it was necessary for the applicant to consult a psychiatrist in order to alter his behaviour, undergoing psychiatric treatment was not among the practical instructions issued by the county medical officer on 1 September 1994. Nor did the domestic courts during the proceedings justify the deprivation of the applicant's liberty with reference to his being of 'unsound mind' within the meaning of Article 5 § 1(e) and the requirements deriving from that provision.

54. The instructions issued on 1 September 1994 prohibited the applicant from having sexual intercourse without first having informed his partner about his HIV infection. Also, he was to use a condom. The Court notes in this connection that, despite his being at large for most of the period from 16 February 1995 until 12 December 2001, there is no evidence or indication that during that period the applicant transmitted the HIV virus to anybody, or that he had sexual intercourse without first informing his partner about his HIV infection, or that he did not use a condom, or that he had any sexual relationship at all for that matter. It is true that the applicant infected the 19-year-old man with whom he had first had sexual contact in 1990. This was discovered in 1994, when the applicant himself became aware of his infection. However, there is no indication that the applicant transmitted the HIV virus to the young man as a result of intent or gross neglect, which in many of the Contracting States, including Sweden, would have been considered a criminal offence under the Criminal Code.

55. In these circumstances, the Court finds that the compulsory isolation of the applicant was not a last resort in order to prevent him from spreading the HIV virus because less severe measures had been considered and found to be insufficient to safeguard the public interest. Moreover, the Court considers that by extending over a period of almost seven years the order for the applicant's compulsory isolation, with the result that he was placed involuntarily in a hospital for almost one and a half years in total, the authorities failed to strike a fair balance between the need to ensure that the HIV virus did not spread and the applicant's right to liberty.

56. There has accordingly been a violation of Article 5 § 1 of the Convention.

...

FOR THESE REASONS, THE COURT UNANIMOUSLY

1. Holds that there has been a violation of Article 5(1) of the Convention;

...

NOTES

1   The Court was composed of President Costa and Judges: Baka, Cabral Barreto, Turmen, Ugrekhelidze, Fura-Sandstrom, and Jociene.

2   This was the first case where the Court examined, in detail, the infectious diseases ground of detention. The judgment clearly demonstrates that even in respect of a serious infection, such as HIV, compulsory hospitalization is a measure of last resort. Such an approach is in conformity with the UN *International Guidelines on HIV/Aids and Human Rights* (1998) which state that: '112. In exceptional cases involving objective judgments concerning deliberate and dangerous behaviour, restrictions on liberty may be imposed. Such exceptional cases should be handled under ordinary provisions of public health, or criminal laws, with appropriate due process protection.'

Johnson v UK 1997-VII
European Court of Human Rights

After being diagnosed as suffering from 'mental illness' and in accordance with the appropriate procedures under the Mental Health Act 1983, the applicant was transferred from Leicester Prison to Rampton Hospital, a maximum security psychiatric institution.

The applicant's detention was reviewed regularly by a Mental Health Review Tribunal. On the basis of psychiatric reports, in 1989 the Tribunal ruled that although no longer suffering from mental illness, the applicant, having been a resident at Rampton for five years, had an unrealistic opinion of his ability to live on his own and that he required rehabilitation under medical supervision in a hostel environment. In the interests of the applicant himself and of the public, a conditional discharge was ordered, one condition of which was residence in an approved hostel under psychiatric supervision.

Discharge from Rampton proved impossible, however, because, despite considerable efforts, a suitable hostel that was willing to take the applicant could not be found. A trial period in a less secure hospital began in September 1990 but the applicant was returned to Rampton six weeks later after a drinking bout which led to the assault of one patient and the terrorizing of nursing staff. Thereafter, in the continued absence of a suitable hostel, the applicant remained in detention in Rampton until the Tribunal ordered his absolute discharge into the community in 1993.

JUDGMENT OF THE COURT

50. The applicant complained that his detention between 15 June 1989, the date when the Tribunal first found him to be no longer suffering from mental illness, and 12 January 1993, the date when his absolute discharge was ordered, was in violation of Article 5 § 1 of the Convention....

58. The Court considers at the outset that it is appropriate to examine the lawfulness of the applicant's continued detention after 15 June 1989 under Article 5 § 1(e) alone of the Convention, even if the lawfulness of his detention, at least up until that date, could also possibly be grounded on Article 5 § 1(a) since it resulted from a 'conviction' by a 'competent court' within the meaning of

that sub-paragraph. While the applicability of one ground listed in Article 5 § 1 does not necessarily preclude the applicability of another and a detention may be justified under more than one sub-paragraph of that provision (see the *Eriksen v Norway* judgment of 27 May 1997, Reports of Judgments and Decisions 1997-III, pp 861–2, § 76), it is to be noted that the applicant was detained at Rampton Hospital on the basis of a hospital and a restriction order without limit in time made under the Mental Health Act 1983 in order to undergo psychiatric treatment...

59. The Court also notes that those appearing before it have not contested that the applicant's continued detention was lawful under domestic law, having regard to the Tribunal's powers under section 73(2) and (7) of the 1983 Act to impose conditions on the discharge of patients who are no longer mentally ill within the meaning of section 1(2) of that Act and to defer a discharge until those conditions have been fulfilled. ...

60. The Court stresses, however, that the lawfulness of the applicant's continued detention under domestic law is not in itself decisive. It must also be established that his detention after 15 June 1989 was in conformity with the purpose of Article 5 § 1 of the Convention, which is to prevent persons from being deprived of their liberty in an arbitrary fashion (see, among many authorities, the *Wassink v Netherlands* judgment of 27 September 1990, Series A No 185-A, p 11, § 24) and with the aim of the restriction contained in sub-paragraph (e) (see the above-mentioned *Winterwerp* judgment, p 17, § 39). In this latter respect the Court recalls that, according to its established case-law, an individual cannot be considered to be of 'unsound mind' and deprived of his liberty unless the following three minimum conditions are satisfied: firstly, he must reliably be shown to be of unsound mind; secondly, the mental disorder must be of a kind or degree warranting compulsory confinement; thirdly, and of sole relevance to the case at issue, the validity of continued confinement depends upon the persistence of such a disorder (see the *Winterwerp* judgment cited above, pp 21–2, § 40; and the *Luberti v Italy* judgment of 23 February 1984, Series A No 75, pp 12–13, § 27).

61. By maintaining that the 1989 Tribunal was satisfied that he was no longer suffering from the mental illness which led to his committal to Rampton Hospital, Mr Johnson is arguing that the above-mentioned third condition as to the persistence of mental disorder was not fulfilled and he should as a consequence have been immediately and unconditionally released from detention.

The Court cannot accept that submission. In its view it does not automatically follow from a finding by an expert authority that the mental disorder which justified a patient's compulsory confinement no longer persists, that the latter must be immediately and unconditionally released into the community...

62. It is to be recalled in this respect that the Court in its *Luberti* judgment (cited above, pp 13–15, § 29) accepted that the termination of the confinement of an individual who has previously been found by a court to be of unsound mind and to present a danger to society is a matter that concerns, as well as that individual, the community in which he will live if released. Having regard to the pressing nature of the interests at stake, and in particular the very serious nature of the offence committed by Mr Luberti when mentally ill, it was accepted in that case that the responsible authority was entitled to proceed with caution and needed some time to consider whether to terminate his confinement, even if the medical evidence pointed to his recovery.

63. In the view of the Court it must also be acknowledged that a responsible authority is entitled to exercise a similar measure of discretion in deciding whether in the light of all the relevant circumstances and the interests at stake it would in fact be appropriate to order the immediate and absolute discharge of a person who is no longer suffering from the mental disorder which led to his confinement. That authority should be able to retain some measure of supervision over the progress of the person once he is released into the community and to that end make his discharge subject to conditions. It cannot be excluded either that the imposition of a particular condition may

in certain circumstances justify a deferral of discharge from detention, having regard to the nature of the condition and to the reasons for imposing it. It is, however, of paramount importance that appropriate safeguards are in place so as to ensure that any deferral of discharge is consonant with the purpose of Article 5 § 1 and with the aim of the restriction in sub-paragraph (e) (see paragraph 60 above) and, in particular, that discharge is not unreasonably delayed.

64. Having regard to the above considerations, the Court is of the opinion that the 1989 Tribunal could in the exercise of its judgment properly conclude that it was premature to order Mr Johnson's absolute and immediate discharge from Rampton Hospital....

It was not...unreasonable for the Tribunal to consider, having regard to the views of Dr Wilson and Dr Cameron, that the applicant should be placed under psychiatric and social-worker supervision and required to undergo a period of rehabilitation in a hostel on account of the fact that 'the recurrence of mental illness requiring recall to hospital cannot be excluded'... The Tribunal was also in principle justified in deferring the applicant's release in order to enable the authorities to locate a hostel which best suited his needs and provided him with the most appropriate conditions for his successful rehabilitation....

66. However, while imposing the hostel residence requirement on the applicant and deferring his release until the arrangements had been made to its satisfaction, the Tribunal lacked the power to guarantee that the applicant would be relocated to a suitable post-discharge hostel within a reasonable period of time. The onus was on the authorities to secure a hostel willing to admit the applicant. It is to be observed that they were expected to proceed with all reasonable expedition in finalising the arrangements for a placement.... While the authorities made considerable efforts to this end, these efforts were frustrated by the reluctance of certain hostels to accept the applicant as well as by the latter's negative with respect to the options available.... They were also constrained by the limited number of available placements. Admittedly, a suitable hostel may have been located within a reasonable period of time had the applicant adopted a more positive approach to his rehabilitation. However, this cannot refute the conclusion that neither the Tribunal nor the authorities possessed the necessary powers to ensure that the condition could be implemented within a reasonable time....

67. In these circumstances, it must be concluded that the imposition of the hostel residence condition by the June 1989 Tribunal led to the indefinite deferral of the applicant's release from Rampton Hospital, especially since the applicant was unwilling after October 1990 to co-operate further with the authorities in their efforts to secure a hostel, thereby excluding any possibility that the condition could be satisfied. While the 1990 and 1991 Tribunals considered the applicant's case afresh, they were obliged to order his continued detention since he had not yet fulfilled the terms of the conditional discharge imposed by the June 1989 Tribunal.

Having regard to the situation which resulted from the decision taken by the latter Tribunal and to the lack of adequate safeguards, including provision for judicial review to ensure that the applicant's release from detention would not be unreasonably delayed, it must be considered that his continued confinement after 15 June 1989 cannot be justified on the basis of Article 5 § 1(e) of the Convention (see paragraph 63 above).

For these reasons, the Court concludes that the applicant's continued detention after 15 June 1989 constituted a violation of Article 5 § 1 of the Convention...

FOR THESE REASONS, THE COURT UNANIMOUSLY

1. Holds that there has been a breach of Article 5 § 1 of the Convention....

NOTES

1 The Court was composed of President Ryssdal and Judges: Gölcüklü, Spielmann, Valticos, Sir John Freeland, Baka, Kuris, Levits, and Van Dijk.

2   The three requirements justifying the detention of persons of 'unsound mind' (see para 60, judgment) were first set out by the Court in the *Winterwerp* case, p 322.

3   Although Article 5(1) does not guarantee a right to treatment (see the *Winterwerp* case, p 322), a person of 'unsound mind' must be detained in an appropriate institution. In *Aerts v Belgium*, 1998-V, there was a breach of Article 5(1) when there was some delay in finding the applicant an appropriate hospital. The Court stated:

46....there must be some relationship between the ground of permitted deprivation of liberty relied on and the place and conditions of detention. In principle, the 'detention' of a person as a mental health patient will only be 'lawful' for the purposes of subparagraph (e) of paragraph 1 if effected in a hospital, clinic or other appropriate institution (see the *Ashingdane v UK* judgment of 28 May 1985, Series A No 93, p 21, § 44).

47. In the present case, on 15 January 1993, the Committals Chamber decided to order Mr Aerts's detention and stated that, pending a decision by the Mental Health Board designating the institution in which he was to be detained, he would be detained provisionally in the psychiatric wing of Lantin Prison. On 22 March 1993 the Mental Health Board designed the Paifve Social Protection Centre as the place of detention. As there were no spare places at Paifve, the applicant continued to be detained at Lantin for seven months, his transfer not being effected until 27 October 1993....

48. The Court notes that the length of provisional detention pending transfer is not specified by any statutory or other provision. Nevertheless, it must determine whether, in view of the purpose of the detention order, the continuation of provisional detention for such a lengthy period can be regarded as lawful.

49. The reports of 10 and 15 January 1990, which reflect the situation obtaining in 1990..., the CPT's [the European Committee for the Prevention of Torture's] report...and the observations on that report made by the Belgian Government...show sufficiently clearly that the Lantin psychiatric wing could not be regarded as an institution appropriate for the detention of persons of unsound mind, the latter not receiving either regular medical attention or a therapeutic environment. On 2 August 1993, in response to an application for leave lodged by Mr Aerts, the Mental Health Board expressed the view that the situation was harmful to the applicant, who was not receiving the treatment required by the condition that had given rise to his detention. Moreover, the Government did not deny that the applicant's treatment in Lantin had been unsatisfactory from a therapeutic point of view. The proper relationship between the aim of the detention and the conditions in which it took place was therefore deficient.

See also on the detention of persons of 'unsound mind' *Ashingdane v UK* A.93 (1985).

4   A unanimous Chamber found the English practice of detaining mentally incapacitated persons as 'informal' patients under common law failed to satisfy the procedural safeguards inherent within Article 5(1) in *HL v UK*, judgment of 5 October 2004. The applicant had suffered from autism since his birth in 1949. He cannot speak and has limited understanding. Therefore, he is unable to consent/object to medical treatment. He is often agitated and prone to self-harm. For over 30 years he was cared for in a national health service hospital (Bournewood). Since 1977 his responsible medical officer has been Dr M (a Consultant Psychiatrist). In 1994 he was discharged to reside with paid carers, though the hospital remained responsible for his care and treatment. HL attended a weekly day-care centre run by his local authority. On 22 July 1997, whilst at the day-care centre, he became very agitated (hitting his head against the wall and with his fists). His carers could not be contacted so the centre called a local doctor who administered a sedative to HL. He was then taken to the accident and emergency unit of the hospital where an Acting

Consultant Psychiatrist assessed HL as requiring in-patient treatment. HL was moved, with the physical support of two members of staff, to the hospital's intensive behavioural unit. HL made no attempt to leave the unit. Dr M decided not to order the compulsory detention of HL under the Mental Health Act 1983 as he had not resisted his admission to the hospital. He was therefore, admitted as an 'informal' patient. Dr M decided to discourage HL's carers from visiting him to prevent him, and them, becoming distressed. In August 1997 Dr M reported to the local health authority that the hospital was coming to the view that HL suffered from a mood disorder as well as autism and that his immediate discharge would be against medical opinion. Another Consultant Psychiatrist, who examined HL on behalf of his carers, reached similar conclusions but recommended closer cooperation between HL's doctors and his carers. In September 1997 the applicant, via his cousin, applied for judicial review of the hospital's decision to admit him in July. The High Court rejected the application finding that HL had been informally admitted to the hospital and the common law principle of necessity had been satisfied. On appeal the Court of Appeal found that as the applicant did not have the capacity to consent to his admission he had been detained unlawfully. On the same day a doctor ordered HL's compulsory detention under the Mental Health Act 1983. That decision was confirmed by two other doctors in accordance with the statutory procedure two days later. At the beginning of November 1997 HL's carers were allowed to visit him for the first time since his hospitalization. In December 1997 the hospital formally discharged HL to his carers. Subsequently, the House of Lords allowed an appeal by the health authority against the judgment of the Court of Appeal.

Before the Court the applicant contended that his detention in the hospital between July and October 1997 as an 'informal' patient violated Article 5(1) as he was not of unsound mind, the common law principle of necessity lacked precision, and there had been inadequate safeguards against arbitrary detention. The UK Government responded that the admission of informal patients (who were incapacitated) respected their dignity and the authorities wished to avoid having to utilize formal statutory procedures of compulsory committal wherever possible. The Court considered that HL had been deprived of his liberty, for the purposes of Article 5(1) because:

91....the health care professionals treating and managing the applicant exercised complete and effective control over his care and movements from the moment he presented acute behavioural problems on 22 July 1997 to the date he was compulsorily detained on 29 October 1997.

Applying the well-established test, derived from *Winterwerp v Netherlands*, the Court found that he was of unsound mind as the evidence established HL:

101....to have been suffering from a mental disorder of a kind or degree warranting compulsory confinement which persisted during his detention between 22 July and 5 December 1997.

The Court did not reach a conclusion in regard to the applicant's argument that the common law doctrine of necessity was too vague to satisfy the requirement of reasonable foreseeability under Article 5(1). This was because the judges found the common law provided insufficient safeguards against the arbitrary detention of informal patients.

120. In this latter respect, the Court finds striking the lack of any fixed procedural rules by which the admission and detention of compliant incapacitated persons is conducted. The contrast between this dearth of regulation and the extensive network of safeguards applicable to psychiatric committals covered by the 1983 [Mental Health] Act is, in the Court's view, significant.

In particular and most obviously, the Court notes the lack of any formalised admission procedures which indicate who can propose admission, for what reasons and on the basis of what kind of medical and other assessments and conclusions. There is no requirement to fix the exact purpose of admission (for example, for assessment or for treatment) and, consistently, no limits in terms of time, treatment or care attach to that admission. Nor is there any specific provision requiring a continuing clinical assessment of the persistence of a disorder warranting detention. The nomination of a representative of a patient who could make certain objections and applications on his or her behalf is a procedural protection accorded to those committed involuntarily under the 1983 Act and which would be of equal importance for patients who are legally incapacitated and have, as in the present case, extremely limited communication abilities.

121. As a result of the lack of procedural regulation and limits, the Court observes that the hospital's health care professionals assumed full control of the liberty and treatment of a vulnerable incapacitated individual solely on the basis of their own clinical assessments completed as and when they considered fit...While the Court does not question the good faith of those professionals or that they acted in what they considered to be the applicant's best interests, the very purpose of procedural safeguards is to protect individuals against any 'misjudgements and professional lapses' (Lord Steyn [in the House of Lords judgment]).

...

123. The Government's submission that detention could not be arbitrary within the meaning of Article 5 § 1 because of the possibility of a later review of its lawfulness disregards the distinctive and cumulative protections offered by paragraphs 1 and 4 of Article 5 of the Convention: the former strictly regulates the circumstances in which one's liberty can be taken away whereas the latter requires a review of its legality thereafter.

124. The Court therefore finds that this absence of procedural safeguards fails to protect against arbitrary deprivations of liberty on grounds of necessity and, consequently, to comply with the essential purpose of Article 5 § 1 of the Convention. On this basis, the Court finds that there has been a violation of Article 5 § 1 of the Convention.

The domestic rights of vulnerable persons were enhanced by the Mental Capacity Act 2005 and the Mental Health Act 2007.

Witold Litwa v Poland judgment of 4 April 2000
European Court of Human Rights

Accompanied by a friend, the applicant, whose sight was severely impaired, went with his guide dog to the Post Office to check his post box. Finding that it was open and empty, he complained to the Post Office clerks, who then called the police alleging that the applicant was drunk and had behaved offensively. Since the applicant smelt of alcohol, the police took him to the Krakow Sobering-up Centre. After being medically examined by a doctor and assessed to be 'moderately intoxicated', he was detained at the Centre for six-and-a-half hours. The Commission was of the opinion, by 21 votes to 5, that the detention was justified under Article 5(1)(e) on the basis that the applicant was lawfully detained as an alcoholic.

JUDGMENT OF THE COURT

57. The Court affirms that, in ascertaining the Convention meaning of the term 'alcoholics', it will be guided by Articles 31 to 33 of the Vienna Convention of 23 May 1969 on the Law of Treaties, as it has

repeatedly been in other cases where an interpretation of the Convention was required (see, for instance, the *Johnston v Ireland* judgment of 18 December 1986, Series A No 112, p 24, § 51 *et seq* and the *Lithgow v UK* judgment of 8 July 1986, Series A No 102, p 48 § 114 *in fine* and p 49 § 117).

58. In that respect, the Court reiterates that, in the way it is presented in the general rule of interpretation laid down in Article 31 of the Vienna Convention, the process of discovering and ascertaining the true meaning of the terms of the treaty is a unity, a single combined operation. This general rule, closely integrated, places on the same footing the various elements enumerated in the four paragraphs of that Article (see the *Golder v UK* judgment of 21 February 1975, Series A No 18, p 14, §§ 29–30).

59. The sequence in which those elements are listed in Article 31 of the Vienna Convention stipulates, however, the order which the process of interpretation of the treaty should follow. That process must start from ascertaining the ordinary meaning of the terms of a treaty—in their context and in the light of its object and purpose, as laid down in paragraph 1 of Article 31. This is particularly so in relation to the provisions which, like Article 5 § 1 of the Convention, refer to exceptions to a general rule and which, for this very reason, cannot be given an extensive interpretation (see the *De Wilde, Ooms and Versyp v Belgium* judgment of 18 June 1971, Series A No 12, p 37, § 68 and the *Winterwerp v Netherlands* judgment of 24 October 1979, Series A No 33, p 16, § 37).

60. The Court observes that the word 'alcoholics', in its common usage, denotes persons who are addicted to alcohol. On the other hand, in Article 5 § 1 of the Convention this term is found in a context that includes a reference to several other categories of individuals, that is, persons spreading infectious diseases, persons of unsound mind, drug addicts and vagrants. There is a link between all those persons in that they may be deprived of their liberty either in order to be given medical treatment or because of considerations dictated by social policy, or on both medical and social grounds. It is therefore legitimate to conclude from this context that a predominant reason why the Convention allows the persons mentioned in paragraph 1(e) of Article 5 to be deprived of their liberty is not only that they are dangerous for public safety but also that their own interests may necessitate their detention (see the *Guzzardi v Italy* judgment of 6 November 1980, Series A No 39, p 37, § 98 *in fine*).

61. This *ratio legis* indicates how the expression 'alcoholics' should be understood in the light of the object and purpose of Article 5 § 1(e) of the Convention. It indicates that the object and purpose of this provision cannot be interpreted as only allowing the detention of 'alcoholics' in the limited sense of persons in a clinical state of 'alcoholism'. The Court considers that, under Article 5 § 1(e) of the Convention, persons who are not medically diagnosed as 'alcoholics', but whose conduct and behaviour under the influence of alcohol pose a threat to public order or themselves, can be taken into custody for the protection of the public or their own interests, such as their health or personal safety.

62. That does not mean that Article 5 § 1(e) of the Convention can be interpreted as permitting the detention of an individual merely because of his alcohol intake. However, the Court considers that in the text of Article 5 there is nothing to suggest that this provision prevents that measure from being applied by the State to an individual abusing alcohol, in order to limit the harm caused by alcohol to himself and the public, or to prevent dangerous behaviour after drinking. On this point, the Court observes that there can be no doubt that the harmful use of alcohol poses a danger to society and that a person who is in a state of intoxication may pose a danger to himself and others, regardless of whether or not he is addicted to alcohol.

63. The Court further finds that this meaning of the term 'alcoholics' is confirmed by the preparatory work of the Convention. . . . In that regard, the Court observes that in the commentary on the preliminary draft Convention it is recorded that the text of the relevant Article covered the right of the

signatory States to take measures to combat vagrancy and 'drunkenness' ('l'alcoolisme' in French). It is further recorded that the Committee of Experts had no doubt that this could be agreed 'since such restrictions were justified by the requirements of public morality and order'.

64. On this basis, the Court concludes that the applicant's detention fell within the ambit of Article 5 § 1(e) of the Convention. . . .

72. The Court reiterates that under Article 5 of the Convention any deprivation of liberty must be 'lawful', which includes a requirement that it must be effected 'in accordance with a procedure prescribed by law'. On this point, the Convention essentially refers to national law and lays down an obligation to comply with its substantive and procedural provisions.

73. It also requires that any measure depriving the individual of his liberty must be compatible with the purpose of Article 5, namely to protect the individual from arbitrariness (see the *K-F v Germany* judgment of 27 November 1997, Reports 1997-VII, p 2674, § 63).

74. In the present case, the Court notes that there is no dispute as to the fact that the police, when arresting the applicant and taking him to the sobering-up centre, followed the procedure provided for by Section 40 of the Law of 26 October 1982. The Court considers therefore that the applicant's detention had a legal basis in Polish law.

75. The Court further notes that the essential statutory conditions for the application of the measures laid down in Section 40 of the Law of 26 October 1982 are, first, that the person concerned is intoxicated and, second, that either his behaviour is offensive or his condition is such as to endanger his own or other persons' life or health. . . .

76. It is not for the Court to review whether the domestic authorities have taken correct decisions under Polish law. Its task is to establish whether the applicant's detention was 'the lawful detention' of an 'alcoholic', within the autonomous meaning of the Convention as the Court has explained it above in paragraphs 57 to 63.

77. In this respect, the Court entertains serious doubts as to whether it can be said that the applicant behaved in such a way, influenced by alcohol, that he posed a threat to the public or himself, or that his own health, well-being or personal safety were endangered. The Court's doubts are reinforced by the rather trivial factual basis for the detention and the fact that the applicant is almost blind.

78. The Court reiterates that a necessary element of the 'lawfulness' of the detention within the meaning of Article 5 § 1(e) is the absence of arbitrariness. The detention of an individual is such a serious measure that it is only justified where other, less severe measures have been considered and found to be insufficient to safeguard the individual or public interest which might require that the person concerned be detained. That means that it does not suffice that the deprivation of liberty is executed in conformity with national law but it must also be necessary in the circumstances.

79. However, in the applicant's case no consideration appears to have been given to the fact that Section 40 of the Law of 26 October 1982 provides for several different measures which may be applied to an intoxicated person, among which detention in a sobering-up centre is the most extreme one. Indeed, under that section, an intoxicated person does not necessarily have to be deprived of his liberty since he may well be taken by the police to a public-care establishment or to his place of residence. . . .

80. The absence of any such considerations in the present case, although expressly foreseen by the domestic law, has finally persuaded the Court that the applicant's detention cannot be considered 'lawful' under Article 5 § 1(e). There has therefore been a breach of that provision. . . .

FOR THESE REASONS THE COURT

Holds by six votes to one that there has been a violation of Article 5 § 1 of the Convention.

. . .

NOTES

1   The Court was composed of President of the Chamber Fischbach and Judges: Conforti, Bonello, Stráznická, Tsatsa-Nivolovska, Baka, and Levits. Judge Baka issued a dissenting opinion in which he agreed with the Court's interpretation of the term 'alcoholics' but he considered that there had been an adequate basis for the detention of the applicant (he had been causing a public nuisance and a doctor diagnosed him as being moderately intoxicated).

2   The *Litwa* concept of 'alcoholics' was subsequently applied in *Hilda Hafsteinsdottir v Iceland*, judgment of 8 June 2004. The applicant was a woman in her forties who developed a habit of going, when intoxicated, to her local police station and verbally/physically abusing the police officers! On each occasion she was arrested, detained overnight, and then released without charge. She contended that she had suffered violations of Article 5(1) as the deprivation of her liberty had not been authorized under any statutory provisions. The Court found:

> 42. . . . it established that the applicant's conduct and behaviour were under the strong influence of alcohol and could reasonably be considered to entail a threat to public order. It is further satisfied that the purpose of the measures was to avert that kind of threat. In other words, the matter was covered by the notion of 'alcoholic' in sub-paragraph (e), which is therefore applicable.

As to whether her detention was 'lawful' the Court stated that:

> 51. . . . where deprivation of liberty is concerned it is particularly important that the general principle of legal certainty be satisfied. It is therefore essential that the conditions for deprivation of liberty under domestic law be clearly defined and that the law itself be foreseeable in its application, so that it meets the standard of 'lawfulness' set by the Convention, a standard which requires that all law be sufficiently accessible and precise to allow the person—if necessary with appropriate advice—to foresee, to a degree that is reasonable in the circumstances the consequences which a given action may entail . . .

A large majority of the Court, 5 votes to 2, concluded that:

> 56. . . . at the time of the six disputed events, in one essential respect, namely the duration of the relevant type of detention, the scope and the manner of exercise of the police's discretion were governed by administrative practice alone and, in the absence of precise statutory provisions or case-law, lacked the necessary regulatory framework (see the *Kruslin v France* and *Huvig v France* judgments of 24 April 1990, Series A No 176-A and -B, respectively §§ 35 and 34). Moreover, it appears that, at the time of the first event in January 1988, before the entry into force on 1 July 1988 of the 1988 Rules, not only the duration of the detention but also the decision to detain suffered from that defect.
>
> Moreover the Court is not convinced that the more detailed provisions contained in the above-mentioned instructions had been made accessible to the public.
>
> For these reasons, the Court is not satisfied that the law, as applicable at the material time, was sufficiently precise and accessible to avoid all risk of arbitrariness. Accordingly, it finds that the applicant's deprivation of liberty was not 'lawful' within the autonomous meaning of Article 5 § 1 of the Convention, which has therefore been violated.

The judgments in *Litwa* and *Hafsteinsdottir* demonstrate the Court adopting a broad and purposive interpretation of the term 'alcoholics', but this is counterbalanced by the strict examination of the question whether the detention of such persons was 'lawful', that is, was it a proportional response to the danger those persons posed to others or themselves and was the domestic law sufficiently clear/accessible. This is a well-balanced analytical framework that seeks to protect the interests of both society and intoxicated persons.

3 On the detention of vagrants consistently with Article 5(1)(e), see the *Vagrancy* cases, p 315.

Article 5(1)(f): deportation or extradition

Bozano v France A.111 (1986)
European Court of Human Rights

The applicant, an Italian national, was tried in absentia by an Italian court for abduction and murder and sentenced to life imprisonment. Three years later, he was arrested in France by the police, but a formal request for extradition was refused by the Limoges Court of Appeal as the conviction in absentia was incompatible with French public policy. The applicant remained in residence in the Limoges area awaiting trial by the French courts for other offences. On the day that an order was made committing him for trial, the applicant was abducted by French policemen, served with a deportation order (which was over one month old) and forcibly taken to the Swiss border where he was handed over to the Swiss authorities. Following proceedings in Switzerland, he was extradited to Italy, under a standing agreement between the two countries, where he was imprisoned for the conviction by the Italian courts.

After his abduction, the applicant's lawyers pursued various remedies in the French courts, including the summoning of the Minister of the Interior before the Paris Tribunal de grande instance where they sought an injunction requiring him to apply for the applicant's return. Although the tribunal held that it had no competence to meet the request, it noted the 'manifest and very serious irregularities' behind what appeared 'not a straightforward expulsion on the basis of the deportation order, but…a prearranged handing over to the Swiss police…'. The Limoges Administrative Court subsequently quashed the deportation order on the basis that the Minister of the Interior had committed 'a manifest error of judgment' and the administrative authorities an 'abuse of powers'.

The Commission concluded, by 11 votes to 2, that there had been a violation of Article 5(1).

JUDGMENT OF THE COURT

58. Where the Convention refers directly back to domestic law, as in Article 5, compliance with such law is an integral part of Contracting States' 'engagements' and the Court is accordingly competent to satisfy itself of such compliance where relevant (Article 19); the scope of its task in this connection, however, is subject to limits inherent in the logic of the European system of protection, since it is in the first place for the national authorities, notably the courts, to interpret and apply domestic law (see, *inter alia* and *mutatis mutandis*, the *Winterwerp* judgment of 24 October 1976 Series A No 33, p 20, § 46).

Several points of French law have been disputed in the instant case. Even if the arguments of those appearing before the Court and the other information in the file are not absolutely conclusive in the Court's view, they provide sufficient material for the Court to have the gravest doubts whether the contested deprivation of liberty satisfied the legal requirements in the respondent State.

59. 'Lawfulness', in any event, also implies absence of any arbitrariness.... In this respect, the Court attaches great weight to the circumstances in which the applicant was forcibly conveyed to the Swiss border.

Firstly, the relevant authorities waited for more than a month before serving the deportation order of 17 September 1979 on Mr Bozano, although there was no difficulty about finding him in Limoges, where he was in pre-trial detention until 19 September and subsequently under judicial supervision.... The authorities thus prevented him from making any effective use of the remedies theoretically available to him.

What is more serious is that the authorities gave every appearance of having wanted to ensure that Mr Bozano did not find out about the action they were preparing to take against him, so that they could the more effectively face him with a fait accompli thereafter....

To this must be added the suddenness with which the applicant was apprehended by the police on the evening of 26 October and, more striking still, the way in which the Minister of the Interior's decision was carried out. From what their own Agent himself indicated, the Government had contacted only Switzerland, a State which had an extradition treaty with Italy and where since April 1976 there had been a warrant out for the applicant's arrest with a view to extradition, as was recorded in the Swiss Police Gazette (*Moniteur suisse de police*).... Mr Bozano was not even able to speak to his wife or his lawyer and at no time was any offer made to him that he should be expelled—if necessary under supervision—across the frontier of his choice or even across the nearest frontier, the Spanish border. On the contrary, he was forced to travel from Limoges to the customs post at Moillesulaz—some twelve hours and several hundred kilometres away—, handcuffed and flanked by policemen who in due course handed him over to Swiss colleagues.... Mr Bozano's precise, detailed description of the events strongly suggests that this is what happened. His account seems plausible in the absence of any evidence or explanation to the contrary....

60. Viewing the circumstances of the case as a whole and having regard to the volume of material pointing in the same direction, the Court consequently concludes that the applicant's deprivation of liberty in the night of 26 to 27 October 1975 was neither 'lawful', within the meaning of Article 5 § 1(f), nor compatible with the 'right to security of person'. Depriving Mr Bozano of his liberty in this way amounted in fact to a disguised form of extradition designed to circumvent the negative ruling of 15 May 1979 by the Indictment Division of the Limoges Court of Appeal, and not to 'detention' necessary in the ordinary course of 'action...taken with a view to deportation'. The findings of the presiding judge of the Paris tribunal de grande instance—even if *obiter*—and of the Limoges Administrative Court, even if that court had only to determine the lawfulness of the order of 17 September 1979, are of the utmost importance in the Court's view; they illustrate the vigilance displayed by the French courts....

FOR THESE REASONS, THE COURT UNANIMOUSLY

...

Holds that there has been a breach of Article 5(1) of the Convention.

...

NOTES

1 The Court was composed of President Ryssdal and Judges: Cremona, Pinheiro Farinha, Pettiti, Sir Vincent Evans, Russo, and Gersing.

2 The *Bozano* case concerned the 'lawfulness' of the detention pending deportation. Although the grounds for deporting or extraditing a person who is detained pending his removal may not be challenged under Article 5, the unreasonable length of time taken to complete deportation or extradition proceedings may mean that the detention is not justified by Article 5(1)(f). In *Quinn v France* A.311 (1995), the applicant was detained for almost two years while extradition proceedings were pending. The applicant alleged that the reason for this was to keep him in detention after a French court had ordered his release on bail in connection with criminal proceedings against him which later led to his conviction and a sentence of imprisonment, which he completed before he was extradited. The Court found a breach of Article 5(1). Holding that the detention was not justified by Article 5(1)(f), it stated:

47....Unlike the Commission, the Court does not discern in the present case any evidence to suggest that the detention pending extradition pursued an aim other than that for which it was ordered and that it was pre-trial detention in disguise. In particular the circumstances of Mr Quinn's arrest and the fact that proceedings were conducted concurrently cannot in themselves warrant the conclusion that there was abuse, for purposes relating to national law, of the extradition procedure and accordingly that the detention ordered in response to the request of the Geneva investigating judge was unlawful.

48. The Court notes nevertheless that the applicant's detention with a view to extradition was unusually long. He was detained in connection with the extradition proceedings from 4 August 1989 to 10 July 1991, almost two years.... Thereafter he served the sentence imposed by the Paris Court of Appeal until 24 September 1992, on which date he was surrendered to the Swiss authorities pursuant to the order of 24 January 1991.

It is clear from the wording of both the French and the English versions of Article 5 § 1(f) that deprivation of liberty under this sub-paragraph will be justified only for as long as extradition proceedings are being conducted. It follows that if such proceedings are not being prosecuted with due diligence, the detention will cease to be justified under Article 5 § 1(f). The Court notes that, at the different stages of the extradition proceedings, there were delays of sufficient length to render the total duration of those proceedings excessive: the first decision on the merits, a preliminary decision, was given on 2 November 1989, three months after the applicant had been placed in detention pending extradition, and the extradition order was not made until 24 January 1991, ten months after the Indictment Division's favourable opinion.... The remedies of which Mr Quinn availed himself over this period (three appeals on points of law against the decisions dismissing applications for release and one appeal on points of law against the Indictment Division's opinion)...did not significantly delay the proceedings.

The detention with a view to extradition continued until 10 July 1991, well after the adoption of the extradition order, as the applicant's surrender to the Swiss authorities was postponed, in accordance with Article 19 § 1 of the European Convention on Extradition, on account of the criminal proceedings conducted in France at the same time. It is not the Court's role to determine what measures the national authorities should have taken in these circumstances to ensure that the detention pending extradition, which had already exceeded a reasonable time by 24 January 1991, did not last even hours after the Indictment Division's decision directing that he be released 'forthwith', without that decision being notified to him or any move being made to commence its execution.

Mr Quinn's continued detention on 4 August 1989 was clearly not covered by subparagraph (c) of paragraph 1 of Article 5 and did not fall within the scope of any other of the sub-paragraphs of that provision.

3   In contrast, the detention of the applicant for three-and-a-half years pending deportation in *Chahal v UK*, 1996-IV, did not prevent the detention being justifiable under Article 5(1)(f). There was, however, a breach of Article 5(4): see p 319. For the facts of the case, see p 204. On compliance with Article 5(1)(f), the Court stated:

115....As regards the decisions taken by the Secretary of State to refuse asylum, it does not consider that the periods (that is, 16 August 1990–27 March 1991 and 2 December 1991–1 June 1992) were excessive, bearing in mind the detailed and careful consideration required for the applicant's request for political asylum and the opportunities afforded to the latter to make representations and submit information....

116. In connection with the judicial review proceedings before the national courts, it is noted that Mr Chahal's first application was made on 9 August 1991 and that a decision was reached on it by Mr Justice Popplewell on 2 December 1991. He made a second application on 16 July 1992, which was heard between 18 and 21 December 1992, judgment being given on 12 February 1993. The Court of Appeal dismissed the appeal against this decision on 22 October 1993 and refused him leave to appeal to the House of Lords. The House of Lords similarly refused leave to appeal on 3 March 1994....

117. As the Court has observed in the context of Article 3, Mr Chahal's case involves considerations of an extremely serious and weighty nature. It is neither in the interests of the individual applicant nor in the general public interest in the administration of justice that such decisions be taken hastily, without due regard to all the relevant issues and evidence.

Against this background, and bearing in mind what was at stake for the applicant and the interest that he had in his claims being thoroughly examined by the courts, none of the periods complained of can be regarded as excessive, taken either individually or in combination. Accordingly, there has been no violation of Article 5 § 1(f) of the Convention on account of the diligence, or lack of it, with which the domestic procedures were conducted.

118. It also falls to the Court to examine whether Mr Chahal's detention was 'lawful' for the purposes of Article 5 § 1(f), with particular reference to the safeguards provided by the national system....

119. There is no doubt that Mr Chahal's detention was lawful under national law and was effected 'in accordance with a procedure prescribed by law'.... However, in view of the extremely long period during which Mr Chahal has been detained, it is also necessary to consider whether there existed sufficient guarantees against arbitrariness.

120. In this context, the Court observes that the applicant has been detained since 16 August 1990 on the ground, essentially, that successive Secretaries of State have maintained that, in view of the threat to national security represented by him, he could not safely be released.... The applicant has, however, consistently denied that he posed any threat whatsoever to national security, and has given reasons in support of this denial....

121. The Court further notes that, since the Secretaries of State asserted that national security was involved, the domestic courts were not in a position effectively to control whether the decisions to keep Mr Chahal in detention were justified, because the full material on which these decisions were based was not made available to them....

122. However, in the context of Article 5 § 1 of the Convention, the advisory panel procedure... provided an important safeguard against arbitrariness. This panel, which included experienced judicial figures... was able fully to review the evidence relating to the national security threat represented by the applicant. Although its report has never been disclosed, at the hearing before the Court the Government indicated that the panel had agreed with the Home Secretary that Mr Chahal ought to be deported on national security grounds. The Court considers that this procedure provided an adequate guarantee that there were at least prima facie grounds for believing that, if Mr Chahal were at liberty, national security would be put at risk and thus that the executive had not acted arbitrarily when it ordered him to be kept in detention.

123. In conclusion, the Court recalls that Mr Chahal has undoubtedly been detained for a length of time which is bound to give rise to serious concern. However, in view of the exceptional circumstances of the case and the facts that the national authorities have acted with due diligence

throughout the deportation proceedings against him and that there were sufficient guarantees against the arbitrary deprivations of his liberty, this detention complied with the requirements of Article 5 § 1(f).

4 *Chahal* was distinguished by a united Grand Chamber in *A and others v UK*, judgment of 19 February 2009. Following the Al'Qaeda attacks in the USA during September 2001, the British Parliament had enacted the Anti-Terrorism, Crime and Security Act 2001 which, *inter alia*, established a system of detention for foreign nationals resident in the UK whom the Home Secretary considered to be a risk to British national security through their involvement in international terrorism. Such persons were to be held in detention where they could not be deported to their home States as there was a real risk that they would be subject to Article 3 maltreatment in those countries. The British Government, in December 2001, lodged a derogation under Article 15 of the ECHR in respect of the application of Article 5(1) to the above powers of detention. The 11 applicants (including Omar Othman aka 'Abu Qatada') who were or had been detained under these powers complained to the Court. The Grand Chamber held that, unlike in *Chahal*, the British authorities were not actively seeking to deport nine of the applicants (because of the risks to them in their home States) and therefore their detention was not justified under Article 5(1)(f). Furthermore, the derogation was not valid and, consequently, did not protect the action of the authorities (see p 862).

5 A unanimous chamber of the full-time Court found that the use of deception by public authorities to secure the attendance at a police station of illegal immigrants, so that the latter could be arrested and detained pending deportation was a breach of Article 5(1) in *Conka v Belgium*, judgment of 5 February 2002. The applicants were a family of Slovakian nationals of Roma ethnicity. Their claims for political asylum in Belgium had been rejected but the applicants did not leave that country. Therefore, the authorities planned a large-scale operation to deport many Slovakian Roma living illegally in Ghent back to Slovakia. The Roma were each sent a letter inviting them to attend Ghent police station to enable their files to be completed. At the station the Roma were arrested and, whilst some were released, 70, including the applicants, were detained and then deported a few days later.

38. The Court notes that it is common ground that the applicants were arrested so that they could be deported from Belgium. Article 5 § 1(f) of the Convention is thus applicable in the instant case. Admittedly, the applicants contest the necessity of their arrest for that purpose; however, Article 5 § 1(f) does not require that the detention of a person against whom action is being taken with a view to deportation be reasonably considered necessary, for example to prevent his committing an offence or fleeing. In this respect, Article 5 § 1(f) provides a different level of protection from Article 5 § 1(c): all that is required under sub-paragraph (f) is that 'action is being taken with a view to deportation' (see *Chahal v the United Kingdom*, judgment of 15 November 1996, Reports of Judgments and Decisions 1996-V, p 1862, § 112).

39. Where the 'lawfulness' of detention is in issue, including the question whether 'a procedure prescribed by law' has been followed, the Convention refers essentially to the obligation to conform to the substantive and procedural rules of national law, but it requires in addition that any deprivation of liberty should be in keeping with the purpose of Article 5, namely to protect the individual from arbitrariness (see, among other authorities, *Bozano v France*, judgment of 18 December 1986, Series A No 111, p 23, § 54, and *Chahal*, cited above, p 1864, § 118).

40. In the present case, the applicants received a written notice at the end of September 1999 inviting them to attend Ghent police station on 1 October to 'enable the file concerning their application

for asylum to be completed'. On their arrival at the police station they were served with an order to leave the territory dated 29 September 1999 and a decision for their removal to Slovakia and for their arrest for that purpose. A few hours later they were taken to a closed transit centre at Steenokkerzeel.

41. The Court notes that, according to the Government, while the wording of the notice was admittedly unfortunate, as had indeed been publicly recognised by the Minister of the Interior ... that did not suffice to vitiate the entire arrest procedure, or to warrant its being qualified as an abuse of power.

While the Court has reservations about the compatibility of such practices with Belgian law, particularly as the practice in the instant case was not reviewed by a competent national court, the Convention requires that any measure depriving an individual of his liberty must be compatible with the purpose of Article 5, namely to protect the individual from arbitrariness (see paragraph 39 above). Although the Court by no means excludes its being legitimate for the police to use stratagems in order, for instance, to counter criminal activities more effectively, acts whereby the authorities seek to gain the trust of asylum-seekers with a view to arresting and subsequently deporting them may be found to contravene the general principles stated or implicit in the Convention.

In that regard, there is every reason to consider that while the wording of the notice was 'unfortunate', it was not the result of inadvertence; on the contrary, it was chosen deliberately in order to secure the compliance of the largest possible number of recipients. At the hearing, counsel for the Government referred in that connection to a 'little ruse', which the authorities had knowingly used to ensure that the 'collective repatriation' they had decided to arrange was successful.

42. The Court reiterates that the list of exceptions to the right to liberty secured in Article 5 § 1 is an exhaustive one and only a narrow interpretation of those exceptions is consistent with the aim of that provision (see, *mutatis mutandis, K.-F. v Germany*, judgment of 27 November 1997, Reports 1997-VII, p. 2975, § 70). In the Court's view, that requirement must also be reflected in the reliability of communications such as those sent to the applicants, irrespective of whether the recipients are lawfully present in the country or not. It follows that, even as regards overstayers, a conscious decision by the authorities to facilitate or improve the effectiveness of a planned operation for the expulsion of aliens by misleading them about the purpose of a notice so as to make it easier to deprive them of their liberty is not compatible with Article 5.

...

Consequently, there has been a violation of Article 5 § 1 of the Convention.

The above judgment also discloses that States have wider powers of arrest/detention in respect of persons arrested/detained under Article 5(1)(f) than with regard to suspected criminals arrested/detained under Article 5(1)(c).

6 A Grand Chamber held that States could detain asylum seekers (and other types of foreign nationals seeking entry) for short periods of time whilst their applications for entry were being determined in *Saadi v UK*, judgment of 28 January 2008. The applicant was detained in Oakington Reception Centre for seven days whilst his claim was considered via a fast-track procedure.

66. While holding, however, that the first limb of Article 5 § 1(f) permits the detention of an asylum seeker or other immigrant prior to the State's grant of authorisation to enter, the Court emphasises that such detention must be compatible with the overall purpose of Article 5, which is to safeguard the right to liberty and ensure that no-one should be dispossessed of his or her liberty in an arbitrary fashion.

74. To avoid being branded as arbitrary, therefore, such detention must be carried out in good faith; it must be closely connected to the purpose of preventing unauthorised entry of the person to the

country; the place and conditions of detention should be appropriate, bearing in mind that 'the measure is applicable not to those who have committed criminal offences but to aliens who, often fearing for their lives, have fled from their own country' (see *Amuur*, § 43); and the length of the detention should not exceed that reasonably required for the purpose pursued.

A large majority (11 votes to 6) found the applicant's detention had been lawful given its duration and the facilities available to detainees in the specialist centre. Furthermore, the government had introduced the fast-track process in good faith so as to deal with the large numbers of asylum applications being made at that time (over 80,000 per year).

Article 5(2): reasons for detention

....

Fox, Campbell and Hartley v UK A.182 (1990)
European Court of Human Rights

For the facts of this case, see above, p 273.

JUDGMENT OF THE COURT

40. Paragraph 2 of Article 5 contains the elementary safeguard that any person arrested should know why he is being deprived of his liberty. This provision is an integral part of the scheme of protection afforded by Article 5: by virtue of paragraph 2 any person arrested must be told, in simple, non-technical language that he can understand, the essential legal and factual grounds for his arrest, so as to be able, if he sees fit, to apply to a court to challenge its lawfulness in accordance with paragraph 4.... Whilst this information must be conveyed 'promptly' (in French: 'dans le plus court delai'), it need not be related in its entirety by the arresting officer at the very moment of the arrest. Whether the content and promptness of the information conveyed were sufficient is to be assessed in each case according to its special features....

41. On being taken into custody, Mr Fox, Ms Campbell and Mr Hartley were simply told by the arresting officer that they were being arrested under section 11(1) of the 1978 Act on suspicion of being terrorists.... This bare indication of the legal basis for the arrest, taken on its own, is insufficient for the purposes of Article 5 § 2, as the Government conceded.

However, following their arrest all of the applicants were interrogated by the police about their suspected involvement in specific criminal acts and their suspected membership of proscribed organisations.... There is no ground to suppose that these interrogations were not such as to enable the applicants to understand why they had been arrested. The reasons why they were suspected of being terrorists were thereby brought to their attention during their interrogation.

42. Mr Fox and Ms Campbell were arrested at 3.40 pm on 5 February 1986 at Woodbourne RUC station and then separately questioned the same day between 8.15 pm and 10.00 pm at Castlereagh Police Office.... Mr Hartley, for his part, was arrested at his home at 7.55 am on 18 August 1986 and taken to Antrim Police Station where he was questioned between 11.05 am and 12.15 pm.... In the context of the present case these intervals of a few hours cannot be regarded as falling outside the constraints of time imposed by the notion of promptness in Article 5 § 2....

FOR THESE REASONS, THE COURT...

Holds unanimously that there has been no breach of Article 5 § 2;...

NOTES

1   For the composition of the Court, see above, p 274.

2   The *Fox, Campbell and Hartley* case was followed on the matter of the information to be given to the arrested person in the *Murray (Margaret)* case, above, p 275, another Northern Ireland terrorist case. There the arrested person was only told at the time of arrest of the section of the 1978 Act under which she was arrested, but the questions put to her during interrogation some two hours later meant that overall Article 5(2) was complied with. The Court stated:

> In the Court's view, it must have been apparent to Mrs Murray that she was being questioned about her possible involvement in the collection of funds for the purchase of arms for the Provisional IRA by her brothers in the United States. Admittedly, 'there was never any probing examination of her collecting money'—to use the words of the trial judge—but, as the national courts noted, this was because of Mrs Murray's declining to answer any questions at all beyond giving her name. The Court therefore finds that the reasons for her arrest were sufficiently brought to her attention during her interview.

3   Should it be sufficient, as the Court allows in the *Fox, Campbell and Hartley* case, that a person may infer the information required by Article 5(2) from what might be said during questioning? Might the Court have been unduly influenced by the terrorist context of the case when stating what appears to intend to be an interpretation of Article 5(2) of general application?

4   The original Court greatly widened the scope of this obligation to encompass persons detained under civil law powers in *Van der Leer v Netherlands* A.170 (1990). The applicant was detained in a psychiatric hospital on the orders of the local Burgomaster. A few days later the District Court refused to confirm his order. However, the applicant remained in the hospital as a voluntary patient. Two months later another court, at the request of the applicant's husband, ordered her compulsory confinement in the hospital for six months. The applicant was not told of the order and only learned of it ten days later when she was placed in isolation within the hospital. She immediately contacted her lawyer and after various court proceedings the order was revoked some months later. Before the Court, the Dutch Government submitted that Article 5(2) only applied to detentions under criminal law. The unanimous Court held that:

> 27. The Court is not unmindful of the criminal-law connotation of the words used in Article 5(2). However, it agrees with the Commission that they should be interpreted 'autonomously', in particular in accordance with the aim and purpose of Article 5, which are to protect everyone from arbitrary deprivations of liberty. Thus the 'arrest' referred to in paragraph 2 of Article 5 extends beyond the realm of criminal-law measures. Similarly, in using the words 'any charge' ('tout accusation') in this provision, the intention of the drafters was not to lay down a condition for its applicability, but to indicate an eventuality of which it takes account.

> 28. The close links between paragraphs 2 and 4 of Article 5 supports this interpretation. Any person who is entitled to take proceedings to have the lawfulness of his detention decided speedily cannot make effective use of that right unless he is promptly and adequately informed of the reasons why he has been deprived of his liberty . . .

> Paragraph 4 does not make any distinction as between persons deprived of their liberty on the basis of whether they have been arrested or detained. There are therefore no grounds for excluding the latter from the scope of paragraph 2.

The Court concluded that neither the manner nor timing of the applicant becoming aware of the order satisfied the requirements of Article 5(2). This judgment represented a valuable expansion of the ambit of this provision to potentially vulnerable persons being detained under civil law powers.

5 A unanimous Grand Chamber found a breach of this obligation when the immigration authorities took 76 hours to inform an asylum seeker of the reasons why he was being detained in a special immigration centre for the fast processing of his claim: *Saadi v UK* (see above, p 297).

Article 5(3): pre-trial detention and trial within a reasonable time

Right to be brought promptly before a judge

Assenov and others v Bulgaria 1998-VIII
European Court of Human Rights

The applicant alleged, *inter alia*, that he had not been brought promptly before 'a judge or other officer authorised to exercise judicial power', as required by Article 5(3). The facts of the case, so far as relevant to this allegation, are set out in the following extract.

JUDGMENT OF THE COURT

32. In January 1995, Mr Assenov was questioned by the Shoumen prosecuting authorities in connection with an investigation into a series of thefts and robberies.

33. He was arrested on 27 July 1995 and the following day, in the presence of his lawyer and a prosecutor ('K'), he was questioned by an investigator and formally charged with ten or more burglaries, allegedly committed between 9 January and 2 May 1995, and six robberies committed between 10 September 1994 and 24 July 1995, all involving attacks on passers-by on the street. Mr Assenov admitted most of the burglaries but denied having committed the robberies.

The decision was taken to detain him on remand. This decision was approved the same day by another prosecutor, 'A.' ...

144. The Government submitted that the various prosecutors who considered Mr Assenov's applications for release were 'officer[s] authorised by law to exercise judicial power' within the meaning of Article 5 § 3, since under Bulgarian law a prosecutor was fully independent, under a duty to protect the public interest and authorised to decide on a number of questions arising in criminal proceedings, including whether or not to detain an accused on remand.

145. The Commission, with whom the applicant agreed, noted that although under Bulgarian law investigators were institutionally independent, in practice they were subject to the control of prosecutors with regard to every question concerning the conduct of an investigation, including whether or not to detain a suspect on remand. There was, therefore, a strong objective appearance that the investigator who dealt with Mr Assenov lacked independence from the prosecuting authorities, which were subsequently to act as the opposing party in criminal proceedings.

146. The Court reiterates that judicial control of interferences by the executive with the individual's right to liberty is an essential feature of the guarantee embodied in Article 5 § 3 (see the above-mentioned *Aksoy* judgment, p 2282, § 76). Before an 'officer' can be said to exercise 'judicial power' within the meaning of this provision, he or she must satisfy certain conditions providing a guarantee to the person detained against any arbitrary or unjustified deprivation of liberty (see the *Schiesser v Switzerland* judgment of 4 December 1979, Series A No 34, p 13, § 31).

Thus, the 'officer' must be independent of the executive and the parties (ibid). In this respect, objective appearances at the time of the decision on detention are material: if it appears at that time that the 'officer' may later intervene in subsequent criminal proceedings on behalf of the prosecuting authority, his independence and impartiality may be open to doubt (see the *Huber v Switzerland* judgment of 23 October 1990, Series A No 188, p 18, § 43 and the *Brincat v Italy* judgment of 26 November 1992, Series A No 249-A, p 12, § 21). The 'officer' must hear the individual brought before him in person and review, by reference to legal criteria, whether or not the detention is justified. If it is not so justified, the 'officer' must have the power to make a binding order for the detainee's release (see the above-mentioned *Schiesser* judgment, pp 13–14, § 31, and the *Ireland v UK* judgment of 18 January 1978, Series A No 25, p 76, § 199).

147. The Court notes at the outset that Mr Assenov's application for release was not considered by a judge until 19 September 1995...three months into his detention. This was clearly insufficiently 'prompt' for the purposes of Article 5 § 3 (see, for example, the *Brogan v UK* judgment of 29 November 1988, Series A No 145, p 33, § 62), and indeed it has not been argued that this procedure was adequate to satisfy the requirements of this provision.

148. The Court recalls that on 28 July 1995 Mr Assenov was brought before an investigator who questioned him, formally charged him, and took the decision to detain him on remand....It notes that, under Bulgarian law, investigators do not have the power to make legally binding decisions as to the detention or release of a suspect. Instead, any decision made by an investigator is capable of being overturned by the prosecutor, who may also withdraw a case from an investigator if dissatisfied with the latter's approach....It follows that the investigator was not sufficiently independent properly to be described as an 'officer authorised by law to exercise judicial power' within the meaning of Article 5 § 3.

149. Mr Assenov was not heard in person by prosecutor A, who approved the investigator's decision...or by any of the other prosecutors who later decided that he should continue to be detained. In any case, since any one of these prosecutors could subsequently have acted against the applicant in criminal proceedings...they were not sufficiently independent or impartial for the purposes of Article 5 § 3.

150. The Court considers, therefore, that there has been a violation of Article 5 § 3 on the grounds that the applicant was not brought before an 'officer authorised by law to exercise judicial power'....

FOR THESE REASONS THE COURT...

Holds unanimously that there has been a violation of Article 5(3) of the Convention in that Mr Assenov was not brought promptly before a judge or other officer authorised by law to exercise judicial power....

NOTES

1 The Court was composed of President Bernhardt and Judges: Petitti, Palm, Baka, Bonnici, Makarczyk, Gotchev, Van Dijk, and Toumanov.

2 In the Bulgarian system of criminal investigation under examination in the *Assenov* case, the investigation into offences was the responsibility of investigators from the state-funded central investigation service or the competent regional investigation department, which

were institutionally separate from the police and the prosecutor's department. However, as the European Court judgment notes, the investigators were subject to the control of the prosecutor's department in the conduct of the investigation and the taking of remand decisions. Bulgarian law has been reformed so that remand decisions are now taken by a judge.

3 In *Hood v UK*, 1999-I, the Court held that a decision by his commanding officer ordering the detention of a soldier pending trial was in breach of Article 5(3). The Court stated:

> 57. As to the applicant's substantive complaint about the commanding officer's impartiality in the context of the Rule 4 hearing, according to the case-law of the Convention bodies, if it appears at the time the decision on pre-trial detention is taken that the 'officer authorised by law to exercise judicial power' is liable to intervene in the subsequent proceedings as a representative of the prosecuting authority, then he could not be regarded as independent of the parties at that preliminary stage as it is possible for him to become one of the parties at a later stage (see the *Huber v Switzerland* judgment of 23 October 1990, Series A No 188, p 18, §§ 42–3 and the *Brincat v Italy* judgment of 26 November 1992, Series A No 249-A, pp 11–12, §§ 20–1).
>
> The Court has noted the powers and duties of the commanding officer outlined, in particular, at paragraphs 23, 27, 28, 32 and 34 above, which would arise subsequent to that officer's conduct of the hearing pursuant to Rule 4 of the 1972 Rules. This being so, the commanding officer was liable to play a central role in the subsequent prosecution of the case against the applicant. Although the unit adjutant often carries out certain of these functions of the commanding officer (and, indeed, did so in the present case), it is clear that the adjutant does so on behalf of the commanding officer to whom he is directly subordinate in rank. Moreover, the judge advocate confirmed during the applicant's court martial that the unit adjutant is generally nominated prosecuting or assistant prosecuting officer and, in the present case, he carried out the latter function.
>
> In such circumstances, the Court concludes that the applicant's misgivings about his commanding officer's impartiality must be taken to be objectively justified.
>
> 58. The Court also considers, as did the Commission, that the commanding officer's concurrent responsibility for discipline and order in his command would provide an additional reason for an accused reasonably to doubt that officer's impartiality when deciding on the necessity of the pre-trial detention of an accused in his command. This view is reinforced by paragraph 6.005 of the Queen's Regulations (see paragraph 36 above), which allows for the commanding officer to refuse the pre-trial release of an accused if he is of the view that it is undesirable 'in the interests of discipline' that the accused be at large or be allowed to consort with his comrades.

Brogan v UK A.145 (1988)
European Court of Human Rights

The four applicants were arrested by the police in Northern Ireland under section 12 of the Prevention of Terrorism (Temporary Provisions) Act 1984 as persons suspected on reasonable grounds of being 'concerned in the commission, preparation or instigation of acts of terrorism' connected with the affairs of Northern Ireland. They were then questioned in respect of specific criminal offences resulting from terrorist activities and of membership of proscribed organizations. All four applicants were later released without being charged with any offence, having been detained for periods ranging from four days and six hours to six days and 16-and-a-half hours. Under the 1984 Act, it was lawful to detain a person for an initial period of 48 hours and, on the authorization of the Secretary of State for Northern Ireland, for up to five more days, making a total of seven days' detention, without bringing him before a magistrate. In this case, the applicants alleged, *inter alia*, breaches of Article 5(1)(c), 5(3), 5(4), and 5(5). As to Article 5(4), the Court held, unanimously, that habeas corpus provided the remedy required by Article 5(4). The following extract from the Court's judgment concerns Article 5(3), (5). The Commission had expressed the opinion in its report that Article 5(3) had been infringed in respect of the two applicants who had been detained for over five days because they had not been brought 'promptly before a judge', but not in respect of the two who had been detained for four to five days. The Commission had also expressed the opinion that Article 5(5) had been infringed in respect of the first two applicants.

JUDGMENT OF THE COURT

57. The Commission, in its report, cited its established case-law to the effect that a period of four days in cases concerning ordinary criminal offences and of five days in exceptional cases could be considered compatible with the requirement of promptness in Article 5 § 3 (see respectively the admissibility decisions in application no 2864/66, *X v Netherlands*, Yearbook of the Convention, Vol 9, p 568 [1966], and in application No 4960/71, *X v Belgium*, Collection of Decisions, Vol 42, pp 54–5 [1973]). In the Commission's opinion, given the context in which the applicants were arrested and the special problems associated with the investigation of terrorist offences, a somewhat longer period of detention than in normal cases was justified. The Commission concluded that the periods of four days and six hours (Mr McFadden) and four days and eleven hours (Mr Tracey) did satisfy the requirement of promptness, whereas the periods of five days and eleven hours (Mr Brogan) and six days and sixteen and a half hours (Mr Coyle) did not.

58. The fact that a detained person is not charged or brought before a court does not in itself amount to a violation of the first part of Article 5 § 3. No violation of Article 5 § 3 can arise if the arrested person is released 'promptly' before any judicial control of his detention would have been feasible (see the *de Jong, Baljet and van den Brink* judgment of 22 May 1984, Series A No 77, p 25, § 52). If the arrested person is not released promptly, he is entitled to a prompt appearance before a judge or judicial officer.

The assessment of 'promptness' has to be made in the light of the object and purpose of Article 5.... The Court has regard to the importance of this Article in the Convention system: it enshrines a fundamental human right, namely the protection of the individual against arbitrary interferences by the State with his right to liberty (see the *Bozano* judgment of 18 December 1986, Series A No 111, p 23, § 54). Judicial control of interferences by the executive with the individual's right to liberty is an essential feature of the guarantee embodied in Article 5 § 3, which is intended to minimise the risk of arbitrariness....

59. The obligation expressed in English by the word 'promptly' and in French by the word 'aussitôt' is clearly distinguishable from the less strict requirement in the second part of paragraph 3 ('reasonable time'/'délai raisonnable') and even from that in paragraph 4 of Article 5 ('speedily'/'à bref délai'). The term 'promptly' also occurs in the English text of paragraph 2, where the French text uses the words 'dans le plus court délai'. As indicated in the *Ireland v UK* judgment (18 January 1978, Series A No 25, p 76, § 199), 'promptly' in paragraph 3 may be understood as having a broader significance than 'aussitôt', which literally means immediately. Thus confronted with versions of a law-making treaty which are equally authentic but not exactly the same, the Court must interpret them in a way that reconciles them as far as possible and is most appropriate in order to realise the aim and achieve the object of the treaty (see, *inter alia*, the *Sunday Times* judgment of 26 April 1979, Series A No 30, p 30, § 48, and Article 33 § 4 of the Vienna Convention of 23 May 1969 on the Law of Treaties).

The use in the French text of the word 'aussitôt', with its constraining connotation of immediacy, confirms that the degree of flexibility attaching to the notion of 'promptness' is limited, even if the attendant circumstances can never be ignored for the purposes of the assessment under paragraph 3. Whereas promptness is to be assessed in each case according to its special features (see the above-mentioned *de Jong, Baljet and van den Brink* judgment, Series A No 77, p 25, § 52), the significance to be attached to those features can never be taken to the point of impairing the very essence of the right guaranteed by Article 5 § 3, that is to the point of effectively negating the State's obligation to ensure a prompt release or a prompt appearance before a judicial authority.

60. The instant case is exclusively concerned with the arrest and detention, by virtue of powers granted under special legislation, of persons suspected of involvement in terrorism in Northern Ireland. . . . There is no call to determine in the present judgment whether in an ordinary criminal case any given period, such as four days, in police or administrative custody would as a general rule be capable of being compatible with the first part of Article 5 § 3.

None of the applicants was in fact brought before a judge or judicial officer during his time in custody. The issue to be decided is therefore whether, having regard to the special features relied on by the Government, each applicant's release can be considered as 'prompt' for the purposes of Article 5 § 3.

61. The investigation of terrorist offences undoubtedly presents the authorities with special problems. . . . The Court takes full judicial notice of the factors adverted to by the Government in this connection. It is also true that in Northern Ireland the referral of police requests for extended detention to the Secretary of State and the individual scrutiny of each police request by a Minister do provide a form of executive control. . . . In addition, the need for the continuation of the special powers has been constantly monitored by Parliament and their operation regularly reviewed by independent personalities. . . . The Court accepts that, subject to the existence of adequate safeguards, the context of terrorism in Northern Ireland has the effect of prolonging the period during which the authorities may, without violating Article 5 § 3, keep a person suspected of serious terrorist offences in custody before bringing him before a judge or other judicial officer.

The difficulties, alluded to by the Government, of judicial control over decisions to arrest and detain suspected terrorists may affect the manner of implementation of Article 5 § 3, for example in calling for appropriate procedural precautions in view of the nature of the suspected offences. However, they cannot justify, under Article 5 § 3, dispensing altogether with 'prompt' judicial control.

62. As indicated above (paragraph 59), the scope for flexibility in interpreting and applying the notion of 'promptness' is very limited. In the Court's view, even the shortest of the four periods of detention, namely the four days and six hours spent in police custody by Mr McFadden . . . , falls outside the strict constraints as to time permitted by the first part of Article 5 § 3. To attach such importance to the special features of this case as to justify so lengthy a period of detention without appearance before a judge or other judicial officer would be an unacceptably wide interpretation of the plain meaning of the word 'promptly'. An interpretation to this effect would import into Article 5 § 3 a serious weakening of a procedural guarantee to the detriment of the individual and would entail consequences impairing the very essence of the right protected by this provision. The Court thus has to conclude that none of the applicants was either brought 'promptly' before a judicial authority or released 'promptly' following his arrest. The undoubted fact that the arrest and detention of the applicants were inspired by the legitimate aim of protecting the community as a whole from terrorism is not on its own sufficient to ensure compliance with the specific requirements of Article 5 § 3.

There has thus been a breach of Article 5 § 3 in respect of all four applicants. . . .

FOR THESE REASONS, THE COURT . . .

Holds by twelve votes to seven that there has been a violation of Article 5 § 3 in respect of all four applicants; . . .

NOTES

1 The Court was composed of President Ryssdal and Judges: Cremona, Vilhjálmsson, Bindschedler-Robert, Gölcüklü, Matscher, Pinheiro Farinha, Pettiti, Walsh, Evans, Macdonald, Russo, Bernhardt, Spielmann, Meyer, Carrilo Salcedo, Valticos, Martens, and Palm. A joint dissenting opinion was issued by Judges: Vilhjálmsson, Bindschedler-Robert, Gölcüklü, Matscher, and Valticos in which they expressed the view that taking account of the exceptional situation in Northern Ireland assessed against the established case-law of the Commission they considered the applicants' periods of detention were justifiable.

2 The UK's response to the decision in the *Brogan* case was to derogate under Article 15 from its obligations under, *inter alia*, Article 5(3) in respect of the public emergency which it judged to exist in Northern Ireland. The UK had on several occasions previously derogated under Article 15 in respect of Northern Ireland. No such derogation was in operation at the time of the *Brogan* case. The UK decided upon this response to the *Brogan* case after failing to find a way of bringing its law into line with the judgment that was consistent with its traditions and that also allowed it to counteract sufficiently the threat posed by terrorism in Northern Ireland. In *Brannigan and McBride v UK* A.258-B (1993) (see p 850 for the Article 15 aspects of this judgment), the Court held that the UK derogation notice was valid, so that the applicants could not complain that the detention of terrorist suspects under the same power as in the *Brogan* case and for similar periods was in breach of Article 5(3).

In February 2001 the Permanent Representative of the UK at the Council of Europe issued a Note Verbale to the Secretary General withdrawing the above derogation. This withdrawal was based upon the enactment of the Terrorism Act 2000 which provided, *inter alia*, that police officers could arrest and detain for up to 48 hours any person reasonably suspected of being concerned in the commission, preparation, or instigation of acts of terrorism. Thereafter, a judicial authority could extend the period of detention for up to a further five days (by section 306 of the Criminal Justice Act 2003 this period was increased to a maximum of 14 days and, after intense controversy, this period was further extended to 28 days by section 23 of the Terrorism Act 2006).

3 In *Aksoy v Turkey*, 1996-VI, the Court held that an Article 15 notice of derogation could not justify the applicant's detention for 14 days without being brought before a judicial officer: it was not required by 'the exigencies of the situation' (Article 15(1)). The Court stated:

78. Although the Court is of the view—which it has expressed on several occasions in the past (see, for example, the above-mentioned *Brogan and Others* judgment)—that the investigation of terrorist offences undoubtedly presents the authorities with special problems, it cannot accept that it is necessary to hold a suspect for fourteen days without judicial intervention. This period is exceptionally long, and left the applicant vulnerable not only to arbitrary interference with his right to liberty but also to torture (see paragraph 64 above). Moreover, the Government have not adduced any detailed reasons before the Court as to why the fight against terrorism in South-East Turkey rendered judicial intervention impracticable....

82. In its above-mentioned *Brannigan and McBride* judgment..., the Court was satisfied that there were effective safeguards in operation in Northern Ireland which provided an important measure of protection against arbitrary behaviour and incommunicado detention. For example, the remedy of habeas corpus was available to test the lawfulness of the original arrest and detention, there was an absolute and legally enforceable right to consult a solicitor forty-eight hours after the time of arrest and detainees were entitled to inform a relative or friend about their detention and to have access to a doctor (*op cit* pp 55–6, §§ 62–3).

83. In contrast, however, the Court considers that in this case insufficient safeguards were available to the applicant, who was detained over a long period of time. In particular, the denial of access to a lawyer, doctor, relative or friend and the absence of any realistic possibility of being brought before a court to test the legality of the detention meant that he was left completely at the mercy of those holding him.

4 The full-time Court applied its predecessor's approach to assessing the promptness of the release of a suspected terrorist in *O'Hara v UK* (see p 276).

46. The Court notes that the Government have not disputed that the applicant was held for six days and thirteen hours before his eventual release and that this was not in compliance with the requirement to bring an arrested person promptly before an appropriate judicial officer. Having regard to its case-law (in particular *Brogan and Others* ... where detention periods exceeding four days for terrorists suspects were found not to be compatible with the requirement of prompt judicial control), the Court finds that there has in this respect been a violation of Article 5(3) of the Convention.

5 However, by a majority of one, a Grand Chamber concluded that the detention of suspected drugs traffickers for 13 days, on board their ship as it was taken thousands of kilometres to France, before the detainees were brought before an investigating judge satisfied the promptness duty within Article 5(3) in *Medvedyev and others v France*, see p 262.

131. ... There was nothing to indicate that it took any longer than necessary to escort [their ship] to France, particularly in view of the weather conditions and the poor state of repair of the [ship], which made it impossible for it to travel any faster.

The eight dissenters considered that the French authorities had failed to consider whether there were other methods of bringing the applicants before a judge more swiftly.

6 A Grand Chamber identified two elements within Article 5(3) in *McKay v UK*, judgment of 3 October 2006.

31. ... the early stages following an arrest when an individual is taken into the power of the authorities and the period pending eventual trial before a criminal court during which the suspect may be detained or released with or without conditions. These two limbs confer distinct rights and are not on their face logically or temporarily linked.

...

40. The initial automatic review of arrest and detention accordingly must be capable of examining lawfulness issues and whether or not there is a reasonable suspicion that the arrested person had committed an offence, in other words, that detention falls within the permitted exception set out in Article 5(1)(c). When the detention does not, or is unlawful, the judicial officer must then have the power to release.

As to the second stage when the main issue was whether the suspect should be granted bail:

47. In order to ensure that the right guaranteed is practical and effective, not theoretical and illusory, it is not only good practice, but highly desirable in order to minimise delay, that the judicial officer who conducts the first automatic review of lawfulness and the existence of a ground for detention also has the competence to consider release on bail. It is not however a requirement of the Convention and there is no reason in principle why the issues cannot be dealt with by two judicial officers, within the requisite time-frame.

Applying these requirements to the applicant's complaint that the magistrate who conducted the review of the lawfulness of his arrest on suspicion of robbery (two days after he had been arrested) did not have the power (because of the security situation in Northern Ireland) to grant bail in respect of persons arrested in respect of scheduled offences (which included robbery), the Grand Chamber concluded, by 16 votes to 1, there had been no breach of Article 5(3). The Court noted that the applicant had been able (successfully) to apply to the High Court for bail on the next day.

Five members of the Grand Chamber issued a separate opinion in which they expressed the view that:

> ...the reasoning of the majority in concluding that no automatic bail review is required on the first appearance before a judicial officer is not in conformity with the very purpose of Article 5(3)...

Nevertheless, the judgment makes it clear that judicial officers must promptly review the merits of a suspect's detention and the need for the suspect's continued incarceration.

Granting of bail

Wemhoff v Federal Republic of Gemany A.7 (1968)
European Court of Human Rights

The applicant, a West German national, was arrested on 9 November 1961, on suspicion of complicity in offences of breach of trust. The investigation of the case by the West Berlin Prosecutor's Office was completed on 24 February 1964. An indictment was filed on 23 April 1964, and on 17 July 1964 the applicant was committed for trial. The trial began in the Regional Court of Berlin on 9 November 1964, and the applicant was convicted on 7 April 1965 of a 'particularly serious case of prolonged abetment to breach of trust' for which he was sentenced to six-and-a-half years' penal servitude. The period of time spent in detention pending trial was counted as a part of this sentence. The applicant's appeal against conviction was rejected on 17 December 1965. The applicant had remained in detention since he was first arrested. The case was very complicated. It involved 12 other accused and required the examination of a mass of bank accounts and transactions. The Commission admitted the application for consideration on its merits in respect of alleged violations by West Germany of Articles 5(3) and 6(1). In its report, the Commission expressed the opinion, by 7 votes to 3, that Article 5(3) had been violated because the applicant had not been brought to trial 'within a reasonable time' and, unanimously, that there had been no violation of the 'reasonable time' guarantee in Article 6(1). The Commission referred the case to the Court. The following extracts concern Article 5(3). The Court held unanimously that Article 6 had not been infringed.

JUDGMENT OF THE COURT

4. ...As the word 'reasonable' applies to the time within which a person is entitled to trial, a purely grammatical interpretation would leave the judicial authorities with a choice between two obligations, that of conducting the proceedings until judgment within a reasonable time or that of releasing the accused pending trial, if necessary against certain guarantees.

5. The Court is quite certain that such an interpretation would not conform to the intention of the High Contracting Parties. It is inconceivable that they should have intended to permit their judicial

authorities, at the price of release of the accused, to protract proceedings beyond a reasonable time. This would, moreover, be flatly contrary to the provision in Article 6(1) cited above....

Article 5, which begins with an affirmation of the right of everyone to liberty and security of person, goes on to specify the situations and conditions in which derogations from this principle may be made.... It is thus mainly in the light of the fact of the detention of the person being prosecuted that national courts, possibly followed by the European Court, must determine whether the time that has elapsed, for whatever reason, before judgment is passed on the accused has at some stage exceeded a reasonable limit, that is to say imposed a greater sacrifice than could, in the circumstances of the case, reasonably be expected of a person presumed to be innocent.

In other words it is the provisional detention of accused persons which must not, according to Article 5(3), be prolonged beyond a reasonable time....

6. Another question relating to the interpretation of Article 5(3) ... is that of the period of detention covered by the requirement of a 'reasonable time....'

The representative of the German Government expounded the reasons which led him to maintain the interpretation, accepted in the Commission's Report, that it is the time of appearance before the trial court that marks the end of the period with which Article 5(3) is concerned.

7. The Court cannot accept this restrictive interpretation. It is true that the English text of the Convention allows such an interpretation....

But while the English text permits two interpretations the French version, which is of equal authority, allows only one. According to it the obligation to release an accused person within a reasonable time continues until that person has been 'jugée,' that is until the day of the judgment that terminates the trial. Moreover, he must be released 'pendant la procédure,' a very broad expression which indubitably covers both the trial and the investigation.

8. Thus confronted with two versions of a treaty which are equally authentic but not exactly the same the Court must, following established international law precedents, interpret them in a way that will reconcile them as far as possible. Given that it is a law-making treaty, it is also necessary to seek the interpretation that is most appropriate in order to realise the aim and achieve the object of the treaty, not that which would restrict to the greatest possible degree the obligations undertaken by the Parties. It is impossible to see why the protection against unduly long detention on remand which Article 5 seeks to ensure for persons suspected of offences should not continue up to delivery of judgment rather than cease at the moment the trial opens.

9. It remains to ascertain whether the end of the period of detention with which Article 5(3) is concerned is the day on which a conviction becomes final or simply that on which the charge is determined, even if only by a court of first instance.

The Court finds for the latter interpretation.

One consideration has appeared to it as decisive, namely that a person convicted at first instance, whether or not he has been detained up to this moment, is in the position provided for by Article 5(1)(2)(a) which authorises deprivation of liberty 'after conviction.' This last phrase cannot be interpreted as being restricted to the case of a final conviction, for this would exclude the arrest at the hearing of convicted persons who appeared for trial while still at liberty, whatever remedies are still open to them. Now, such a practice is frequently followed in many Contracting States and it cannot be believed that they intended to renounce it. It cannot be overlooked moreover that the guilt of a person who is detained during the appeal or review proceedings, has been established in the course of a trial conducted in accordance with requirements of Article 6.... A person who has cause to complain of the continuation of his detention after conviction because of delay in determining his appeal, cannot avail himself of Article 5(3) but could possibly allege a disregard of the 'reasonable time' provided for by Article 6(1)....

10. The reasonableness of an accused person's continued detention must be assessed in each case according to its special features. The factors which may be taken into consideration are extremely

diverse. Hence the possibility of wide differences in opinion in the assessment of the reasonableness of a given detention. . . .

13. The arrest warrant taken out in Wemhoff's name on 9 November 1961 was based on the fear that if he were left at liberty, he would abscond and destroy the evidence against him, in particular by communicating with persons who might be involved. . . . Both of these reasons continued to be invoked until 5 August 1963 in the decisions of the courts rejecting Wemhoff's many applications for release pending trial.

On that date, however, although the investigation had yet to be concluded, the Court of Appeal accepted that there was some doubt as to whether any danger of suppression of evidence still existed, but it considered that the other reason was still operative . . . , and the same reasoning was repeated in later decisions dismissing the Applicant's appeals.

14. With regard to the existence of a danger of suppression of evidence, the Court regards this anxiety of the German courts to be justified in view of the character of the offences of which Wemhoff was suspected and the extreme complexity of the case.

As to the danger of flight, the Court is of opinion that, while the severity of the sentence which the accused may expect in the event of conviction may legitimately be regarded as a factor encouraging him to abscond—though the effect of such fear diminishes as detention continues and, consequently, the balance of the sentence which the accused may expect to have to serve is reduced, nevertheless the possibility of a severe sentence is not sufficient in this respect. The German courts have moreover been careful to support their affirmations that a danger of flight existed by referring at an early stage in the proceedings to certain circumstances relating to the material position and the conduct of the accused. . . .

15. The Court wishes, however, to emphasise that the concluding words of Article 5(3) of the Convention show that, when the only remaining reason for continued detention is the fear that the accused will abscond and thereby subsequently avoid appearing for trial, his release pending trial must be ordered if it is possible to obtain from him guarantees that will ensure such appearance.

It is beyond doubt that, in a financial case such as that in which Wemhoff was involved, an essential factor in such guarantees should have been the deposit by him of bail or the provision of security for a large amount. The positions successfully taken up by him on this matter (statement of the facts, paras 5 and 14) [in August 1962, the applicant offered to deposit 200,000 DM but withdrew the offer two days later, apparently before the court had considered it. After his conviction, an offer of 100,000 DM was accepted by the court, but then replaced by a much lower one which the court could not accept] are not such as to suggest that he would have been prepared to furnish such guarantees.

16. In these circumstances the Court could not conclude that there had been any breach of the obligations imposed by Article 5(3) unless the length of Wemhoff's provisional detention between 9 November 1961 and 7 April 1965 had been due either (a) to the slowness of the investigation, which was only completed at the end of February 1964, or (b) to the lapse of time which occurred either between the closing of the investigation and the preferment of the indictment (April 1964) or between then and the opening of the trial (9 November 1964) or finally (c) to the length of the trial (which lasted until 7 April 1965). It cannot be doubted that, even when an accused person is reasonably detained during these periods for reasons of the public interest, there may be a violation of Article 5(3) if, for whatever cause, the proceedings continue for a considerable length of time.

17. On this point the Court shares the opinion of the Commission that no criticism can be made of the conduct of the case by the judicial authorities. The exceptional length of the investigation and of the trial are justified by the exceptional complexity of the case and by further unavoidable reasons for delay. . . .

FOR THESE REASONS, THE COURT

Holds, by six votes to one, that there has been no breach of Article 5(3) of the Convention; . . .

INDIVIDUAL DISSENTING OPINION OF JUDGE ZEKIA

The legal system of a country, governing the provisions of the criminal law and procedure relating to pre-trial proceedings—such as preliminary enquiries, investigation and arraignment—as well as the presentation of a case to the court and the power of the court itself in reopening investigations, has a lot to do with the time taken in the conclusion of a trial....

In [a common law system]...it is the police and the prosecution who conduct the enquiries and collect the evidence. They present the case to a court either for trial or—in indictable offences—for preliminary enquiries for the purpose of committal before the Assizes. Under [a civil law]...system the investigation is carried out by a judge and the trial of the accused is started after judicial investigations are closed and after the decision is taken for remitting the case before trial....

While in the former system sufficient evidence to build up a prima facie case against the suspected person is normally expected to be available before he is charged and is taken into custody, in the latter case, ie continental system, it appears that the availability of such evidence at an early stage is not essential. Information to the satisfaction of the judicial officials seems to be sufficient for the arrest and detention of a suspect.

As a consequence of these basic divergences inherent in the two systems, suspected persons are, as a rule, kept in detention considerably longer on the continent than in the case of those in England or other countries where the system of common law prevails.

...My intention is neither to touch on the merits or demerits of either system. My digression from the track is to emphasise the fact that—if in England, a Member of the Council of Europe—the concept of 'reasonable time' regarding the period of detention of an unconvicted person awaiting his trial does not allow us to stretch the time beyond six months even in an exceptionally difficult and complicated case, could we say that, in the continent in a similar case, the period of detention might be six times longer and yet it could be considered as reasonable and therefore compatible with the Convention?

...it may fairly be inferred that the Governments' signatories of the Convention, intended amongst other things, to set a common standard of right to liberty, the scope of which could not differ so vastly from one country to another....

If a man, presumably innocent, is kept in custody for years, this is bound to ruin him. It is true in the case of Wemhoff that the trial ended with a conviction, but it might have ended with an acquittal as well...

I believe that in all systems of law there exist always ways and means of avoiding unreasonably long delayed trials....

NOTES

1   The Court was composed of President Rolin and Judges: Rodenberg, Wold, Mosler, Zekia, Favre, and Bilge.

2   In deciding that the 'reasonable time' guarantee in Article 5(3) provided a basis for reviewing the *grounds* upon which a person detained pending trial under Article 5(1)(c) continues to be detained after his initial arrest as well as providing a means of control over the *length* of the procedure against a person detained pending trial, the Court clearly filled what would otherwise have been a significant gap in the Convention and made sense of an obscure text.

3   In *Stögmüller v Austria* A.9 (1969), the Court expressed the general test that should be applied in deciding whether the danger of the accused disappearing is too great to permit his release as follows:

There must be a whole set of circumstances...which give reason to suppose that the consequences and hazards of flight will seem to him [the accused] to be a lesser evil than continued imprisonment.

Apart from the dangers of flight and of the suppression of evidence, the Court also, in *Matznetter v Austria* A.10 (1969) by 4 votes to 3, accepted prevention of crime as a permissible ground for detention 'in the special circumstances of the case'. These would seem to have been that there was good reason to believe that the accused, if released, would have committed an offence or offences of the same and serious kind as those with which he was already charged, although there was no particular offence which could be identified at the time that the question of release arose as one which it was reasonably believed he would commit.

4 In *Cabellero v UK*, 2000-II, the European Court accepted a UK Government concession that the automatic refusal of bail to the applicant, who was charged with attempted rape, under section 25 of the Criminal Justice and Public Order Act 1994 was a breach of Article 5(3). Under section 25, an accused charged with murder, manslaughter, or rape, or attempted murder or rape, 'shall not be granted bail... only if he has been previously convicted... of any such offence or of culpable homicide and, in the case of a previous conviction of manslaughter or culpable homicide, if he was then sentenced to imprisonment or, if he was then a child or young person, to long term detention.'

Subsequently, in *SCB v UK*, judgment of 19 June 2001, the Court examined the compatibility of section 25 with the requirements of Article 5(3) in the context of a person refused bail for six months who was subsequently acquitted of all the charges against him. Despite the Government, again, conceding a breach of Article 5(3) the Court determined that it should consider the applicant's complaints.

21. As to the merits of those complaints, the Court recalls that the Government's concession in the *Caballero* case was made following the adoption of the Commission's report in that case which concluded that the application of section 25 of the 1994 Act constituted a violation of Article 5 §§ 3 and 5 of the Convention.

22. The reasoning of the Commission in its report can be summarised as follows. It noted that judicial control of interference by the executive with an individual's right to liberty was an essential feature of the guarantees embodied in Article 5 § 3, the purpose being to minimise the risk of arbitrariness in the pre-trial detention of accused persons. Certain procedural and substantive guarantees ensure that judicial control: the judge (or other officer) before whom the accused is 'brought promptly' must be seen to be independent of the executive and of the parties to the proceedings; that judge, having heard the accused himself, must examine all the facts arguing for and against the existence of a genuine requirement of public interest justifying, with due regard to the presumption of innocence, a departure from the rule of respect for the accused's liberty, and that judge must have the power to order an accused's release. It not being disputed that Mr Caballero fell within the scope of section 25 of the 1994 Act, the Commission found that the possibility of any consideration by a Magistrate of his pre-trial release on bail had been excluded in advance by the legislature by section 25 of the 1994 Act. This removal of the judicial control of pre-trial detention required by Article 5 § 3 of the Convention was found by the Commission to amount to a violation of that Article....

23. The Court sees no reason to disagree with the conclusions reached by the Commission in relation to Articles 5 and 13 in its report in the *Cabellero* case and, in this context, it finds no material difference between the relevant facts of the cases of Mr Caballero and the present applicant. It considers that section 25 of the 1994 Act applied in the applicant's case and that, by its terms, it removed the judicial control of his pre-trial detention which is required by Article 5 § 3 of the Convention.

24. Accordingly, the Court concludes that there has been a violation of Article 5 §§ 3 and 5 of the Convention.

Parliament had amended section 25 in 1998 (by the Crime and Disorder Act 1998, section 56) so that, in respect of the listed charges, 'bail shall be granted . . . only if the court, or as the case may be, the constable, considering the grant of bail is satisfied that there are exceptional circumstances which justify it.'

5   A Grand Chamber was deeply divided over the imposition of a three million euros guarantee as a condition for the granting of bail to a foreign captain of a merchant ship which suffered accidental damage in Spanish waters causing a massive oil spill and consequential serious environmental damage in *Mangouras v Spain*, judgment of 28 September 2010. All the members of the Court were in agreement that:

78. . . . the guarantee provided for by Article 5(3) of the Convention is designed to ensure not the reparation of loss but, in particular, the appearance of the accused at the hearing. Its amount must therefore be assessed principally 'by reference to [the accused], his assets and his relationship with the persons who are to provide the security . . .'

However, the majority (ten judges) considered that growing international concern with environmental offences meant that:

87. . . . It cannot therefore be ruled out that, in a situation such as that in the present case, the professional environment which forms the setting for the activity in question should be taken into consideration in determining the amount of bail, in order to ensure that the measure retains its effectiveness.

After noting that the applicant was released on bail, after 83 days, when the ship-owner's insurance company paid the guarantee, the majority found no breach of Article 5(3) because:

92. In these circumstances the Court considers that the domestic courts, in fixing the amount of bail, took sufficient account of the applicant's personal situation, and in particular his status as an employee of the ship's owner, his professional relationship with the persons who were to provide the security, his nationality and place of permanent residence and also his lack of ties in Spain and his age. In view of the particular context of the case and the disastrous environmental and economic consequences of the oil spill, the courts were justified in taking into account the seriousness of the offences in question and the amount of the loss imputed to the applicant.

Whereas, the seven dissentients considered that the Spanish courts had not followed the principles of Article 5(3), by fixing the applicant's bail at an exorbitant amount. The ship's owner and insurers paid 22.7 million euros compensation for the civil damages they were liable for.

....

Kalashnikov v Russia judgment of 15 July 2002
European Court of Human Rights

The applicant was the president of a bank in 1995. In February of that year criminal proceedings were begun against him in respect of embezzlement of bank funds and misappropriation of shares. In June 1995 he was arrested and held in detention on remand by order of the prosecutor, as it was alleged that Kalashnikov had obstructed the criminal investigation. Subsequently, the applicant's lawyer made numerous unsuccessful applications to the courts for Kalashnikov to be released on bail. In August 1999 he was convicted, by the Magadan

City Court, of one count and acquitted on two others. The court sentenced him to five-and-a-half years' imprisonment (starting from the time of his detention in 1995). He was released from prison, under an amnesty, in May 2000.

The applicant complained to the Court that, *inter alia*, his lengthy pre-trial detention violated Article 5(3).

114. The Court recalls that the question of whether or not a period of detention is reasonable cannot be assessed in the abstract. Whether it is reasonable for an accused to remain in detention must be examined in each case according to its special features. Continued detention can be justified in a given case only if there are specific indications of a genuine requirement of public interest which, notwithstanding the presumption of innocence, outweighs the rule of respect for individual liberty laid down in Article 5 of the Convention . . .

It falls in the first place to the national judicial authorities to ensure that, in a given case, the pre-trial detention of an accused person does not exceed a reasonable time. To this end they must, paying due regard to the principle of the presumption of innocence, examine all the facts arguing for or against the existence of the above-mentioned requirement of public interest justifying a departure from the rule in Article 5, and must set them out in their decisions on the applications for release. It is essentially on the basis of the reasons given in these decisions, and any well-documented facts stated by the applicant in his appeals, that the Court is called upon to decide whether or not there has been a violation of Article 5 § 3 . . .

The persistence of a reasonable suspicion that the person arrested has committed an offence is a condition sine qua non for the lawfulness of the continued detention, but after a certain lapse of time it no longer suffices. The Court must then establish whether the other grounds given by the judicial authorities continued to justify the deprivation of liberty. Where such grounds were 'relevant' and 'sufficient', the Court must also be satisfied that the national authorities displayed 'special diligence' in the conduct of the proceedings. The complexity and special characteristics of the investigation are factors to be considered in this respect . . .

(ii) Application of the above principles to the present case

(a) Grounds for detention

115. During the period covered by the Court's jurisdiction ratione temporis the Magadan City Court, in refusing to release the applicant, relied on the gravity of the charges against him and the danger of his obstructing the establishment of the truth while at liberty. The Court observes that similar grounds had been cited by the City Court earlier—on 27 December 1996 and 8 August 1997—to justify the applicant's continued detention.

It further notes that the principal reason for the decision to place the applicant in detention on remand on 29 June 1995 was that he had obstructed the investigation of the case by refusing to turn over certain bank documents necessary for the investigation, he had brought pressure to bear on witnesses and had allegedly tampered with the evidence. The decision also had regard to the gravity of the charges.

116. The Court recalls that the existence of a strong suspicion of the involvement of a person in serious offences, while constituting a relevant factor, cannot alone justify a long period of pre-trial detention . . . As regards the other ground relied on by the Magadan City Court in prolonging the applicant's detention, namely the danger of obstructing the examination of the case, the Court notes that, unlike the order of the investigator of 29 June 1995, the City Court did not mention any factual circumstances underpinning its conclusions, which were identical both in 1996, 1997 and 1999. There is no reference in its rulings to any factor capable of showing that the risk relied on actually persisted during the relevant period.

117. The Court accepts that the interference with the investigation, along with the suspicion that the applicant had committed the offences with which he was charged, could initially suffice to

warrant the applicant's detention. However, as the proceedings progressed and the collection of the evidence became complete that ground inevitably became less relevant.

118. In sum, the Court finds that the reasons relied on by the authorities to justify the applicant's detention, although relevant and sufficient initially, lost this character as time passed.

(b) Conduct of the proceedings

119. As regards the duration of the criminal investigation, the Court notes the findings of the domestic courts that the case was not particularly complex and that the investigation of the case had been of poor quality contributing to a delay in the proceedings. The Court finds no reason to come to a different conclusion. It also observes that, according to the domestic courts, the investigators had unjustifiably attempted to increase the number of counts in the indictment—a reproach which is borne out by the fact that only one of the nine charges against the applicant was found to be substantiated in the judgment of the Magadan City Court on 3 August 1999.

120. As regards the subsequent judicial proceedings, the Court observes that there were significant delays in the proceedings before the Magadan City Court. The trial, which had began on 11 November 1996, was adjourned on 7 May 1997 due to the removal from office of the presiding judge. It did not resume until 15 April 1999, although certain procedural steps were taken in July–August 1997 (the appointment of a new judge and scheduling of a hearing), May and July 1998 (the transfer of the case to another court), November 1998 (the scheduling of a hearing), January and March 1998 (decisions on the need for further investigation).

While it is true that the hearing scheduled for 8 August 1997 had to be postponed on account of the absence of the applicant's lawyer and the applicant objected to the transfer of his case to another court—a move destined to expedite the proceedings—the Court finds that the applicant did not substantially contribute to the length of the proceedings between the two trial periods, where there was no progress in the case.

It is thus apparent that the protracted proceedings are attributable neither to the complexity of the case nor the conduct of the applicant. Having regard to the characteristics of the investigation and the substantial delays in the court proceedings, the Court considers that the authorities did not act with all due expedition.

(g) Conclusion

121. Against the above background, the Court finds that the period spent by the applicant in detention pending trial exceeded a 'reasonable time'. There has thus been a violation of Article 5 § 3 of the Convention.

…

FOR THESE REASONS, THE COURT UNANIMOUSLY

…

2. Holds that there has been a violation of Article 5(3) of the Convention;

NOTES

1 The Court was composed of President Costa and Judges: Fuhrmann, Loucaides, Bratza, Greve, Traja, and Kovler.

2 The judgment demonstrates the contemporary approach of the full-time Court to assessing whether a (lengthy) period of pre-trial detention on remand is reasonable under Article 5(3). The Court will subject the reasons for the detention given by the domestic judiciary to a close and strict evaluation. National authorities must grant detainees bail unless there are convincing public interest grounds justifying pre-trial detention. Where such grounds exist the domestic courts must monitor the continuance of those grounds and order the detainees release as soon as they end. Furthermore, the prosecution and judicial authorities must process cases with reasonable expedition.

3   For the Article 3 aspects of *Kalashnikov,* see p 217.

Article 5(4): remedy to challenge the legality of detention

De Wilde, Ooms and Versyp v Belgium (the 'Vagrancy' cases) A.12 (1971)
European Court of Human Rights

The applicants reported voluntarily to the police declaring that they had no home and were destitute. They were brought before a police court composed of a single magistrate who verified the 'identity, age, physical and mental state and manner of life' of the individuals and, after giving them an opportunity to reply, decided they were 'vagrants' as defined by Belgian law. Under an 1891 Act 'for the suppression of vagrancy and begging' the magistrate was therefore obliged to place the applicants 'at the disposal of the Government'. De Wilde and Versyp were ordered by the magistrate 'to be detained in a vagrancy centre for two years' (the minimum requirement) and Ooms was ordered 'to be detained in an assistance home' (under special provisions in the Act for alcoholism or begging). Although an appropriate note was put on their criminal records, domestic law did not treat the court's decision as a criminal conviction. For this reason, no challenge or appeal was possible as legally the magistrate's decision was viewed an administrative act, not a judgment.

Soon after their respective detention orders were issued, the applicants made a series of unsuccessful representations to the Minister of Justice complaining, *inter alia*, of the regime and conditions of work to which they were subject and requesting their release, *inter alia*, because of their changed circumstances, including the prospect of work in the community and the money that they had earned for their work in detention. The 1891 Act required release on the expiry of the term given by the court or at the discretion of the Minister of Justice, or additionally, for those detained in assistance homes only (i.e. Ooms), when an amount stated in advance by the Minister of Justice had been saved.

The applicants alleged, *inter alia*, breaches of Article 5(1) and (4). The Commission expressed the opinion, *inter alia*, that there had been a violation of Article 5(4) (9 votes to 2), but not of Article 5(1) (10 votes to 1).

In the following extract, the Court first considered whether the detention of the applicants could be justified under Article 5(1)(e) on the basis that they were 'vagrants'. It then examined how Article 5(4) should be applied in a case where the detention is ordered not by a policeman or an administrator, but by a body that qualifies as a court in the sense of Article 5(4).

JUDGMENT OF THE COURT

64. The government stressed that the applicants had reported voluntarily to the police and that their admission to Wortel and Merksplas had been the result 'of an express or implicit request' on their part, express for Versyp and Ooms, implicit for De Wilde. According to the Government,

such a 'voluntary reporting' can scarcely amount to being 'deprived of liberty' within the meaning of Article 5. From this it concluded that the Court ought to rule out forthwith any idea of a failure to comply with the requirements of the Convention, as regards both 'the detention itself' and 'the conditions of detention'.

65. The Court is not persuaded by this line of argument.

Temporary distress or misery may drive a person to give himself up to the police to be detained. This does not necessarily mean that the person so asking is in a state of vagrancy and even less that he is a professional beggar or that his state of vagrancy results from one of the circumstances— idleness, drunkenness or immorality—which, under Section 13 of the Belgian Act of 1891, may entail a more severe measure of detention.

Insofar as the wishes of the applicants were taken into account, they cannot in any event remove or disguise the mandatory, as opposed to contractual, character of the decisions complained of; this mandatory character comes out unambiguously in the legal texts (Sections 8, 13, 15, 16 and 18 of the 1891 Act) and in the documents before the Court.

Finally and above all, the right to liberty is too important in a 'democratic society' within the meaning of the Convention for a person to lose the benefit of the protection of the Convention for the single reason that he gives himself up to be taken into detention. Detention might violate Article 5 even although the person concerned might have agreed to it. When the matter is one which concerns ordre public within the Council of Europe, a scrupulous supervision by the organs of the Convention of all measures capable of violating the rights and freedoms which it guarantees is necessary in every case. Furthermore, Section 12 of the 1891 Act acknowledges the need for such supervision at national level: it obliges the magistrates to 'ascertain the identity, age, physical and mental state and manner of life of persons brought before the police court for vagrancy'. Nor does the fact that the applicants 'reported voluntarily' in any way relieve the Court of its duty to see whether there has been a violation of the Convention....

67. The applicants were provisionally deprived of their freedom by the police superintendent to whom they presented themselves and they were brought by him within 24 hours, as provided by section 3 of the Act of 1 May 1849, before the magistrate, who placed them at the disposal of the Government....

The lawfulness of the action of the police superintendents has not been challenged; as the persons concerned reported voluntarily and indicated that they were in a state of vagrancy, it was only normal that they should be brought before the magistrate for a decision. This action, moreover, was of a purely preliminary nature.

It was by virtue of the magistrates' orders that the detention took place. It is therefore by reference to these orders that the lawfulness of the detention of the three applicants must be assessed.

68. The Convention does not contain a definition of the term 'vagrant'. The definition in article 347 of the Belgian Criminal Code reads: 'vagrants are persons who have no fixed abode, no means of subsistence and no regular trade or profession'. Where these three conditions are fulfilled, they may lead the competent authorities to order that the persons concerned be placed at the disposal of the Government as vagrants. The definition quoted does not appear to be in any way irreconcilable with the usual means of the term 'vagrant', and the Court considers that a person who is a vagrant under the terms of Article 347 in principle falls within the exception provided for in article 5(1)(e) of the Convention.

In the present cases, the want of a fixed abode and of means of subsistence resulted not merely from the action of the persons concerned in reporting voluntarily to the police but from their own declarations made at the time: all three stated that they were without any employment....As to the habitual character of this lack of employment, the magistrates at Charleroi, Namur and Brussels were in a position to deduce this from the information available to them concerning the respective applicants....

69. Having thus the character of a 'vagrant', the applicants could, under Article 5(1)(e) of the Convention, be made the subject of a detention provided that it was ordered by the competent authorities and in accordance with the procedure prescribed by Belgian law.

The Court then examined the procedures that had been followed and concluded that Belgian law had been complied with.

70. The Court has, therefore, not found either irregularity or arbitrariness in the placing of the three applicants at the disposal of the Government and it has no reason to find the resulting detention incompatible with Article 5(1)(e) of the Convention....

73. Although the Court has not found in the present cases any incompatibility with paragraph (1) of Article 5...this finding does not dispense it from now proceeding to examine whether there has been any violation of paragraph (4). The latter is, in effect, a separate provision, and its observance does not result *eo ipso* from the observance of the former: 'everyone who is deprived of his liberty', lawfully or not, is entitled to a supervision of lawfulness by a court; a violation can therefore result either from a detention incompatible with paragraph (1) or from the absence of any proceedings satisfying paragraph (4), or even from both at the same time....

75. The applicants were detained in execution of the magistrates' orders: their arrest by the police was merely a provisional act and no other authority intervened in the three cases....A first question consequently arises. Does Article 5(4) require that two authorities should deal with the cases falling under it, that is, one which orders the detention and a second, having the attributes of a court, which examines the lawfulness of this measure on the application of the person concerned? Or, as against this, is it sufficient that the detention should be ordered by an authority which had the elements inherent in the concept of a 'court' within the meaning of Article 5(4)?

76. At first sight, the wording of Article 5(4) might make one think that it guarantees the right of the detainee always to have supervised by a court the lawfulness of a previous decision which has deprived him of his liberty. The two official tests do not however use the same terms, since the English text speaks of 'proceedings' and not of 'appeal', 'recourse' or 'remedy' (compare Articles 13 and 26). Besides, it is clear that the purpose of Article 5(4) is to assure to persons who are arrested and detained the right to a judicial supervision of the lawfulness of the measure to which they are thereby subjected; the word 'court' ('tribunal') is there found in the singular and not in the plural. Where the decision depriving a person of his liberty is one taken by an administrative body, there is no doubt that Article 5(4) obliges the Contracting States to make available to the person detained a right of recourse to a court; but there is nothing to indicate that the same applies when the decision is made by a court at the close of judicial proceedings. In the latter case the supervision required by Article 5(4) is incorporated in the decision; this is so, for example, where a sentence of imprisonment is pronounced after 'conviction by a competent court' (Article 5(1)(a) of the Convention). It may therefore be concluded that Article 5(4) is observed if the arrest or detention of a vagrant, provided for in paragraph (1)(e), is ordered by a 'court' within the meaning of paragraph (4).

It results, however, from the purpose and object of Article 5, as well as from the very terms of paragraph (4) ('proceedings'/'recours'), that in order to constitute such a 'court' an authority must provide the fundamental guarantee of procedure applied in matters of deprivation of liberty....

77. The Court has therefore enquired whether in the present case the magistrate possessed the character of a 'court' within the meaning of Article 5(4), and especially whether the applicants enjoyed, when appearing before him, the guarantees mentioned above. There is no doubt that, from an organisational point of view, the magistrate is a 'court'....The magistrate is independent both of the executive and of the parties to the case...

78.…The forms of the procedure required by the Convention need not, however, necessarily be identical in each of the cases where the intervention of a court is required. In order to determine whether a proceeding provides adequate guarantees, regard must be had to the particular nature of the circumstances in which such proceeding takes place. Thus, in the *Neumeister* case, the Court considered that the competent courts remained 'courts' in spite of the lack of 'equality of arms' between the prosecution and an individual who requested provisional release (ibidem); nevertheless, the same might not be true in a different context and, for example, in another situation which is also governed by Article 5(4).

79.…The deprivation of liberty complained of by De Wilde, Ooms and Versyp resembles that imposed by a criminal court. Therefore, the procedure applicable should not have provided guarantees markedly inferior to those existing in criminal matters in the member States of the Council of Europe.

According to Belgian law, every individual found in a state of vagrancy is arrested and then brought—within twenty-four hours as a rule—before the police court (Section 8 of the 1891 Act and Section 3 of the Act of 1st May 1849). Regarding the interrogation of this individual, the 1891 Act limits itself to specifying in Section 12 that the magistrate ascertains the identity, age, physical and mental state and manner of life of the person brought before him. Regarding the right of defence, the only relevant provision is found in Section 3 of the Act of 1st May 1849, which provides that the person concerned is granted a three-day adjournment if he so requests. According to information provided by the Government, the Code of Criminal Procedure does not apply to the detention of vagrants.

The procedure in question is affected by the administrative nature of the decision to be given. It does not ensure guarantees comparable to those which exist as regards detention in criminal cases, notwithstanding the fact that the detention of vagrants is very similar in many respects. It is hard to understand why persons arrested for simple vagrancy have to be content with such a summary procedure.… This procedure undoubtedly presents certain judicial features, such as the hearing taking place and the decision being given in public, but they are not sufficient to give the magistrate the character of a 'court' within the meaning of Article 5(4) when due account is taken of the seriousness of what is at stake, namely a long deprivation of liberty attended by various shameful consequences. Therefore it does not by itself satisfy the requirements of Article 5(4) and the Commission was quite correct in considering that a remedy should have been open to the applicants. The Court, however, has already held that De Wilde, Ooms and Versyp had no access either to a superior court or, at least in practice, to the Conseil d'Etat.…

80. The Court therefore reaches the conclusion that on the point now under consideration there has been a violation of Article 5(4) in that the three applicants did not enjoy the guarantees contained in that paragraph.…

FOR THESE REASONS, THE COURT,

Holds unanimously that the 'voluntary reporting' by the applicants does not suffice to establish the absence of any violation of the Convention;

Holds unanimously that there has been no breach of Article 5(1);

Holds by nine votes to seven that there has been a breach of Article 5(4) in that the applicants had no remedy open to them before a court against the decision ordering their detention;…

NOTES

1 The Court was composed of President Sir Humphrey Waldock and Judges: Rolin, Cassin, Holmback, Verdross, Rodenbourg, Ross, Wold, Balladore Pallieri, Mosler, Zekia, Favre, Cremona, Bilge, Wiarda, and Sigurjónsson. Judges Balladore Pallieri and Verdross issued a joint separate opinion in which they considered that the possibility of the applicants'

appealing to the Conseil d'Etat against the decisions of the magistrates satisfied the requirements of Article 5(4). A similar conclusion was reached in the collective separate opinion of Judges: Holmback, Rodenbourg, Ross, Favre, and Bilge.

2   The *Vagrancy* cases establish that where the decision to detain an individual is taken by a court—not by a police officer or an administrator—the judicial decision on the legality of the detention required by Article 5(4) is incorporated in the initial decision to detain. For the purpose of this 'incorporation' rule, and generally under Article 5(4), a 'court' is a body that is 'independent both of the executive and of the parties to the case': *Neumeister v Austria* A.8 (1968). It must also be able to take a binding decision. This last requirement and the need for the remedy to be able to cover all aspects of the justification for detention led to the finding of a breach of Article 5(4) in *Chahal v UK*, 1996-IV. The Court stated:

129. The notion of 'lawfulness' in Article 5 § 1(f) does not refer solely to the obligation to conform to the substantive and procedural rules of national law; it requires in addition that any deprivation of liberty should be in keeping with the purpose of Article 5. . . . The question therefore arises whether the available proceedings to challenge the lawfulness of Mr Chahal's detention and to seek bail provided an adequate control by the domestic courts.

130. The Court recollects that, because national security was involved, the domestic courts were not in a position to review whether the decisions to detain Mr Chahal and to keep him in detention were justified on national security grounds. . . . Furthermore, although the procedure before the advisory panel undoubtedly provided some degree of control, bearing in mind that Mr Chahal was not entitled to legal representation before the panel, that he was only given an outline of the grounds for the notice of intention to deport, that the panel had no power of decision and that its advice to the Home Secretary was not binding and was not disclosed . . . , the panel could not be considered as a 'court' within the meaning of Article 5 § 4 (see, *mutatis mutandis*, the *X v UK* judgment of 5 November 1981, Series A No 46, p 26, § 61).

131. The Court recognises that the use of confidential material may be unavoidable where national security is at stake. This does not mean, however, that the national authorities can be free from effective control by the domestic courts whenever they choose to assert that national security and terrorism are involved (see, *mutatis mutandis*, the *Fox, Campbell and Hartley v UK* judgment of 30 August 1990, Series A No 182, p 17, § 34, and the *Murray v UK* judgment of 28 October 1994, Series A No 300-A, p 27, § 58). The Court attaches significance to the fact that, as the intervenors pointed out in connection with Article 13 . . . , in Canada a more effective form of judicial control has been developed in cases of this type. This example illustrates that there are techniques which can be employed which both accommodate legitimate security concerns about the nature and sources of intelligence information and yet accord the individual a substantial measure of procedural justice.

132. It follows that the Court considers that neither the proceedings for habeas corpus and for judicial review of the decision to detain Mr Chahal before the domestic courts, nor the advisory panel procedure, satisfied the requirements of Article 5 § 4. This shortcoming is all the more significant given that Mr Chahal has undoubtedly been deprived of his liberty for a length of time which is bound to give rise to serious concern. . . .

3   As established in the *Vagrancy* cases, and confirmed, *inter alia*, in the *Chahal* case, the 'court' before which a detained person must have a remedy is required to provide appropriate procedural guarantees, which may vary according to the kind of detention (of an accused, a person of 'unsound mind', a person being deported, etc). In *A and others v UK* (see p 296) the Grand Chamber had to consider the procedures followed by the Special Immigration Appeals Commission (SIAC). This was a tribunal, composed of independent

judges, with a right of appeal to the higher courts, created to address the breach found in *Chahal*. Under the Anti-Terrorism, Crime and Security Act 2001 it was given jurisdiction to undertake reviews of the detention of foreign nationals authorized by the Home Secretary. SIAC adopted a special procedure whereby open material was disclosed to detainees/their lawyers whilst closed material (which because of national security needs could not be made public) was only disclosed to security-cleared counsel ('special advocates') appointed by the Solicitor General to act on behalf of each detainee. The applicants contended that this procedure did not meet the requirements of Article 5(4).

219. The Court considers that SIAC, which was a fully independent court and which could examine all the relevant evidence, both closed and open, was best placed to ensure that no material was unnecessarily withheld from the detainee. In this connection, the special advocate could provide an important, additional safeguard through questioning the State's witnesses on the need for secrecy and through making submissions to the judge regarding the case for additional disclosure. On the material before it, the Court has no basis to find that excessive and unjustified secrecy was employed in respect of any of the applicants' appeals or that there were not compelling reasons for the lack of disclosure in each case.

220. The Court further considers that the special advocate could perform an important role in counterbalancing the lack of full disclosure and the lack of a full, open, adversarial hearing by testing the evidence and putting arguments on behalf of the detainee during the closed hearings. However, the special advocate could not perform this function in any useful way unless the detainee was provided with sufficient information about the allegations against him to enable him to give effective instructions to the special advocate. While this question must be decided on a case-by-case basis, the Court observes generally that, where the evidence was to a large extent disclosed and the open material played the predominant role in the determination, it could not be said that the applicant was denied an opportunity effectively to challenge the reasonableness of the Secretary of State's belief and suspicions about him. In other cases, even where all or most of the underlying evidence remained undisclosed, if the allegations contained in the open material were sufficiently specific, it should have been possible for the applicant to provide his representatives and the special advocate with information with which to refute them, if such information existed, without his having to know the detail or sources of the evidence which formed the basis of the allegations. An example would be the allegation made against several of the applicants that they had attended a terrorist training camp at a stated location between stated dates; given the precise nature of the allegation, it would have been possible for the applicant to provide the special advocate with exonerating evidence, for example of an alibi or of an alternative explanation for his presence there, sufficient to permit the advocate effectively to challenge the allegation. Where, however, the open material consisted purely of general assertions and SIAC's decision to uphold the certification and maintain the detention was based solely or to a decisive degree on closed material, the procedural requirements of Article 5 § 4 would not be satisfied.

The Grand Chamber went on to conclude that there had been breaches of Article 5(4) in the SIAC proceedings concerning four of the applicants, but no breaches in five of the applicants' cases. Hence the special advocates/closed material procedure is only compatible with Article 5(4) if sufficient information is disclosed to the detainee that enables him/her to mount an effective challenge to his/her detention with the assistance of the special advocate. The appointment of the latter does not of itself make up for an insufficient disclosure of material asserted to justify the detention of the relevant person.

4   In *Kampanis v Greece* A.325 (1995), the prosecutor was allowed to appear before the court deciding on the renewal of detention on remand when the accused was not.

The European Court held that this lack of 'equality of arms' infringed Article 5(4). It stated:

56. The Court must bear in mind that the prosecutor essentially represents the interests of society in criminal proceedings. In connection with the application in issue, his task was to suggest to the Indictment Division either that the accused's detention be prolonged or that he be released. In the instant case he always submitted that detention should be prolonged.

57. Secondly, the Court acknowledges that the applicant filed a number of applications for release and a number of pleadings in support of them, both during the investigation and even after it had been closed. His arguments, which mostly concerned the legal classification of the offences he was accused of and the reasons given for his detention, were undoubtedly known to the prosecutor and the Indictment Division.

However, when he lodged the application in question, Mr Kampanis had been in prison for 25 months and 10 days pursuant to three successive orders, each of which fixed a different starting point for the calculation of his detention on remand; in two of these cases detention had been prolonged up to the maximum permitted under the Constitution. Moreover, in this particular application he criticised, *inter alia*, the incompatibility of the length of his detention with the Constitution and the Convention.

58. In the light of these considerations, the Court is of the view that to ensure equality of arms it was necessary to give the applicant the opportunity to appear at the same time as the prosecutor so that he could reply to his arguments.

5   In *Reinprecht v Austria*, judgment of 15 November 2005, a unanimous Chamber held that Article 5(4) does not impose a general requirement for the hearing of reviews of the lawfulness of pre-trial detention to be held in public. The applicant brought several challenges to his pre-trial detention before the Regional Court. The latter held hearings, at which the applicant and his lawyer were present, after which the Regional Court ordered the applicant's continued detention. He complained to Strasbourg arguing that Article 5(4) required the hearings to be held in public. The Helsinki Foundation for Human Rights, as a third party, supported his claim as they believed that public scrutiny of such hearings would help to verify the independence of the court and ensure the absence of arbitrariness. The Austrian Government contended that requiring these hearings to be held in public could well cause delays (the hearings were often held in remand prisons and if the prisoner had to be taken to a court building for a public hearing that might result in delays). The Chamber concluded that the Court's existing case-law did not oblige these hearings to be held in public and there was 'some force' in the Government's argument that requiring public hearings could have a negative impact on the speediness of reviews. Therefore, no breach of Article 5(4) had occurred.

6   The speediness of the judicial determination of a detainee's challenge to the lawfulness of his detention was examined by the full-time Court in *Rehbock v Slovenia*, judgment of 28 November 2000 (and see p 175 for the Article 3 aspects of the case). The applicant was arrested by Slovenian police on 8 September 1995 for suspected drug smuggling. On 10 September an investigating judge of the Slovenj Gradec Regional Court remanded him in custody. On 3 October the applicant, via his lawyer, lodged a request for his release on bail (he offered a security of 50,000 DEM). The Slovenj Gradec Regional Court dismissed his request on 26 October (the Court did not consider the applicant's offer of security as a sufficient guarantee that he would attend his trial). The Strasbourg Court was unanimous in concluding that the 23 days taken by the Regional Court to determine the applicant's request for release did not satisfy the requirement of speediness contained in Article 5(4).

Winterwerp v Netherlands A.33 (1979)
European Court of Human Rights

In 1968, after events in which it was apparent that he was in some distress, the applicant was committed for a short-term period to a psychiatric hospital by the direction of the local burgomaster in accordance with an emergency procedure provided for in Dutch law. Six weeks later, on his wife's application and following a medical report, the applicant was confined on a longer term basis following non-emergency procedures to the same hospital under an order made by the District Court. Thereafter the applicant regularly requested that he be discharged. His requests were passed by the hospital authorities to the public prosecutor. In 1969, in the exercise of his discretion, the public prosecutor referred the applicant's first request to the Regional Court where it was dismissed. As the law allowed, the prosecutor declined to refer the requests to the Regional Court in 1971, 1972, and again in 1973 on the basis that upon the evidence it appeared manifestly impossible that the Regional Court would grant the request.

The Commission expressed the unanimous opinion that there had been no breach of Article 5(1) but that there had been for Article 5(4). In the following extract, the Court considered whether the applicant's detention could be justified under Article 5(1)(e) on the basis that he was 'of unsound mind' and whether the failure to refer the applicant's requests for release to a court after 1969 amounted to a breach of Article 5(4) in a case where the facts for justifying the detention may change.

JUDGMENT OF THE COURT

37. The Convention does not state what is to be understood by the words 'persons of unsound mind'. This term is not one that can be given a definitive interpretation: as was pointed out by the Commission, the Government and the applicant, it is a term whose meaning is continually evolving as research in psychiatry progresses, an increasing flexibility in treatment is developing and society's attitude to mental illness changes, in particular so that a greater understanding of the problems of mental patients is becoming more wide-spread.

In any event, sub-paragraph (e) of Article 5 § 1 obviously cannot be taken as permitting the detention of a person simply because his views or behaviour deviate from the norms prevailing in a particular society. To hold otherwise would not be reconcilable with the text of Article 5 § 1 which sets out an exhaustive list (see the *Engel* judgment of 8 June 1976, Series A No 22, p 24, § 57, and the *Ireland v UK* judgment of 18 January 1978, Series A No 25, p 74, § 194) of exceptions calling for a narrow interpretation (see, *mutatis mutandis*, the *Klass* judgment of 6 September 1978, Series A No 28, p 21, § 42, and the *Sunday Times* judgment of 26 April 1979, Series A No 30, p 41, § 65). Neither would it be in conformity with the object and purpose of Article 5 § 1, namely to ensure that no one should be dispossessed of his liberty in an arbitrary fashion (see the *Lawless* judgment of 1 July 1961, Series A No 3, p 52, and the above-mentioned *Engel* judgment, p 25, § 58). Moreover, it would disregard the importance of the right to liberty in a democratic society (see the *De Wilde, Ooms and Versyp* judgment of 18 June 1971, Series A No 12, p 36, § 65, and the above-mentioned *Engel* judgment, p 35, § 82 *in fine*).

38. Just as the Convention does not give any definition of 'persons of unsound mind', so the Netherlands legislation does not define 'mentally ill persons' (krankzinnige); what the legislation does is to lay down the grounds for committing such persons to a psychiatric hospital....

The Court examined the relevant Dutch law and practice.

Having regard to the above-mentioned practice, the law in force does not appear to be in any way incompatible with the meaning that the expression 'persons of unsound mind' is to be given in the context of the Convention. The Court therefore considers that an individual who is detained under the Netherlands Mentally Ill Persons Act in principle falls within the ambit of Article 5 § 1(e).

39. The next issue to be examined is the 'lawfulness' of the detention for the purposes of Article 5 § 1(e). Such 'lawfulness' presupposes conformity with the domestic law in the first place and also, as confirmed by Article 18, conformity with the purpose of the restrictions permitted by Article 5 § 1(e); it is required in respect of both the ordering and the execution of the measures involving deprivation of liberty (see the above-mentioned *Engel* and others judgment, p 28, § 68, *in fine*).

As regards the conformity with the domestic law, the Court points out that the term 'lawful' covers procedural as well as substantive rules. There thus exists a certain overlapping between this term and the general requirement stated at the beginning of Article 5 § 1, namely observance of 'a procedure prescribed by law'....

Indeed, these two expressions reflect the importance of the aim underlying Article 5 § 1 (see paragraph 37 above): in a democratic society subscribing to the rule of law (see the *Golder* judgment of 21 February 1975, Series A No 18, pp 16–17, § 34, and the above-mentioned *Klass* judgment, p 25, § 55), no detention that is arbitrary can ever be regarded as 'lawful'.

The Commission likewise stresses that there must be no element of arbitrariness; the conclusion it draws is that no one may be confined as 'a person of unsound mind' in the absence of medical evidence establishing that his mental state is such as to justify his compulsory hospitalisation.... The applicant and the Government both express similar opinions.

The Court fully agrees with this line of reasoning. In the Court's opinion, except in emergency cases, the individual concerned should not be deprived of his liberty unless he has been reliably shown to be of 'unsound mind'. The very nature of what has to be established before the competent authority—that is, a true mental disorder—calls for objective medical expertise. Further, the mental disorder must be of a kind or degree warranting compulsory confinement. What is more, the validity of continued confinement depends upon the persistence of such a disorder (see, *mutatis mutandis*, the *Stögmüller* judgment of 10 November 1969, Series A No 9, pp 39–40, § 4, and the above-mentioned *De Wilde, Ooms and Versyp* judgment, p 43, § 82).

40. The Court undoubtedly has the jurisdiction to verify the 'lawfulness' of the detention (see the above-mentioned *Engel* judgment, p 29, § 69). Mr Winterwerp in fact alleges unlawfulness by reason of procedural defects in the making of three of the detention orders under consideration. Those allegations are dealt with below in connection with the closely linked issue of compliance with 'a procedure prescribed by law'.... In the present context it suffices to add the following: in deciding whether an individual should be detained as a 'person of unsound mind', the national authorities are to be recognised as having a certain discretion since it is in the first place for the national authorities to evaluate the evidence adduced before them in a particular case; the Court's task is to review under the Convention the decisions of those authorities (see notably, *mutatis mutandis*, the *Handyside* judgment of 7 December 1976, Series A No 24, pp 22 and 23, §§ 48 and 50, the above-mentioned *Klass* judgment, p 23, § 49, and the above-mentioned *Sunday Times* judgment, p 36, § 59).

41. As to the facts of the instant case, the medical evidence submitted to the courts indicated in substance that the applicant showed schizophrenic and paranoiac reactions, that he was unaware of his pathological condition and that, on several occasions, he had committed some fairly serious acts without appreciating their consequences. In addition, various attempts at his gradual rehabilitation into society have failed....

42. Mr Winterwerp criticises the medical reports as unsatisfactory for the purposes of Article 5 § 1(e). In addition, he queries whether the burgomaster's initial direction to detain was founded on psychiatric evidence.

In the Court's view, the events that prompted the burgomaster's direction in May 1968 ... are of a nature to justify an 'emergency' confinement of the kind provided for at that time under section 14 of the Netherlands Act. While some hesitation may be felt as to the need for such confinement to continue for as long as six weeks, the period is not so excessive as to render the detention 'unlawful'. Despite the applicant's criticisms, the Court has no reason whatsoever to doubt the objectivity and reliability of the medical evidence on the basis of which the Netherlands courts, from June 1968 onwards, have authorised his detention as a person of unsound mind. Neither is there any indication that the contested deprivation of liberty was effected for a wrongful purpose.

43. The Court accordingly concludes that Mr Winterwerp's confinement, during all the various phases under consideration, constituted 'the lawful detention' of [a person] of unsound mind', within the meaning of sub-paragraph (e) of Article 5 § 1....

51. Mr Winterwerp argues that Article 5 § 1(e) entails, for any individual confined as a 'person of unsound mind', the right to appropriate treatment in order to ensure that he is not detained longer than absolutely necessary. As to his own situation, he complains that the meetings with his psychiatrist were too short and infrequent and that the medication administered to him was unduly made up of tranquillisers.

The Government categorically deny these allegations.

The Court considers, as does the Commission, that a mental patient's right to treatment appropriate to his condition cannot as such be derived from Article 5 § 1(e). Furthermore, the evidence contains no suggestion, as regards treatment, of a breach of any other provision in the Convention....

53. The applicant also relies on paragraph 4 of Article 5....

55. In the above-mentioned *De Wilde, Ooms and Versyp* judgment of 18 June 1971 (p 40, § 76), the Court stated:

> 'Where the decision depriving a person of his liberty is one taken by an administrative body, ... Article 5 § 4 obliges the Contracting States to make available to the person detained a right of recourse to a court; but there is nothing to indicate that the same applies when the decision is made by a court at the close of judicial proceedings. In the latter case the supervision required by Article 5 § 4 is incorporated in the decision; ...'

Citing its own case-law, the Commission puts forward the view that, as it stands, this conclusion by the Court cannot be sustained in the case of confinement of persons on the ground of 'unsound mind', at any rate when the confinement is for an indefinite period (see paragraph 95 of the report).

As is indicated earlier in the present judgment, ... the reasons initially warranting confinement of this kind may cease to exist.... Consequently, it would be contrary to the object and purpose of Article 5 ... to interpret paragraph 4 thereof, read in its context, as making this category of confinement immune from subsequent review of lawfulness merely provided that the initial decision issued from a court. The very nature of the deprivation of liberty under consideration would appear to require a review of lawfulness to be available at reasonable intervals. However, as the Commission states in paragraph 95 of its report, further examination of this question is superfluous without first establishing whether the relevant decisions affecting Mr Winterwerp were in fact take after 'proceedings [before] a court' ('recours devant un tribunal') within the meaning of Article 5 § 4.

56. Neither the burgomaster, who made the initial direction to detain, nor the public prosecutor, who prolonged its validity, can be regarded as possessing the characteristics of a 'court'. In contrast, there is no doubt that the District Court and the Regional Courts, which issued the various detention orders, are 'courts' from an organisational point of view: they are 'independent both of

the executive and of the parties to the case' (see the above-mentioned *De Wilde, Ooms and Versyp* judgment, p 41, § 77).

57. Nevertheless, the intervention of such a body will satisfy Article 5 § 4 only on condition that 'the procedure followed has a judicial character and gives to the individual concerned guarantees appropriate to the kind of deprivation of liberty in question'; 'in order to determine whether a proceeding provides adequate guarantees, regard must be had to the particular nature of the circumstances in which such proceeding takes place' (see the last-mentioned judgment, pp 41 and 42, §§ 76 *in fine* and 78).

As the Government rightly stress, the 'detention of persons of unsound mind' (Article 5 § 1(e) constitutes a special category....'

60. The judicial proceedings referred to in Article 5 § 4 need not, it is true, always be attended by the same guarantees as those required under Article 6 § 1 for civil or criminal litigation (see the above-mentioned *De Wilde, Ooms and Versyp* judgment, p 42, § 78 *in fine*). Nonetheless, it is essential that the person concerned should have access to a court and the opportunity to be heard either in person or, where necessary, through some form of representation, failing which he will not have been afforded 'the fundamental guarantees of procedure applied in matters of deprivation of liberty' (see the last-mentioned judgment, p 41, § 76). Mental illness may entail restricting or modifying the manner of exercise of such a right (see, as regards Article 6 § 1, the above-mentioned *Golder* judgment, p 19, § 39), but it cannot justify impairing the very essence of the right. Indeed, special procedural safeguards may prove called for in order to protect the interests of persons who, on account of their mental disabilities, are not fully capable of acting for themselves.

61. Under sections 17, 23 and 24 of the Mentally Ill Persons Act as in force at the relevant times, neither the District Court nor the Regional Court was obliged to hear the individual whose detention was being sought....

As to the particular facts, the applicant was never associated either personally or through a representative, in the proceedings leading to the various detention orders made against him: he was never notified of the proceedings or of their outcome; neither was he heard by the courts or given the opportunity to argue his case.

In this fundamental respect, the guarantees demanded by Article 5 § 4 of the Convention were lacking both in law and in practice. In spite of presenting some judicial features, the procedure followed by the District Court and the Regional Court for deciding the applications for his detention did not entitle Mr Winterwerp 'to take proceedings ... [before] a court', within the meaning of Article 5 § 4 (see paragraph 57 above). Without in any way underestimating the value of the many guarantees provided under the Mentally Ill Persons Act, the Court finds that the said procedure did not meet the requirements of Article 5 § 4.

62. As concerns the applicant's requests for discharge [the] Government rightly insist on the need to take a comprehensive view of the whole system established under the Mentally Ill Persons Act. It therefore remains to determine whether the foregoing lacunae found by the Court are remedied in the procedure governing requests for discharge....

63. While section 29 of the Act allows the person concerned to seek a review of his detention, his request for discharge is not necessarily decided on by a court. The request has to be addressed to the hospital authorities who transmit it, if they have received an unfavourable medical opinion, to the public prosecutor. The public prosecutor will in principle then refer the request to the Regional Court, but in certain cases he is not obliged to do so, in particular where it appears manifestly impossible to grant the request. The public prosecutor's decision can in no way be regarded as issuing from a court for the purposes of Article 5 § 4 of the Convention. Admittedly, limitations as to the intervals between applications for release may, according to the circumstances, constitute legitimate restrictions on access to the courts by persons of unsound mind (see paragraph 60 above).

However, each time the public prosecutor declines to communicate a request to the Regional Court on the ground that it appears evidently ill-founded he is not merely restricting but effectively denying the right to court proceedings as embodied in Article 5 § 4.

The Regional Court, in those instances where the request has come before it for decision, is completely free in judging the desirability of hearing the detained person. A power of this kind does not assure the fundamental guarantees of procedure to be applied in matters of deprivation of liberty (see paragraphs 60 and 61 above).

64. Mr Winterwerp was in fact heard by the Regional Court in February 1969 when it examined his first request for release.... To this extent, he had been able to take proceedings before a court in order to test the lawfulness of his confinement.

In contrast, his subsequent requests in April 1971, July 1972 and February 1973 were not forwarded to the Regional Court since the public prosecutor rejected them as being devoid of any prospects of success.... The public prosecutor heard Mr Winterwerp each time and his decisions may well have been justified on the basis of the information at his disposal, but they cannot be qualified as decisions taken by a 'court' within the meaning of Article 5 § 4.

67. To sum up, the various decisions ordering or authorising Mr Winterwerp's detention issued from bodies which either did not possess the characteristics of a 'court' or, alternatively, failed to furnish the guarantees of judicial procedure required by Article 5 § 4; neither did the applicant have access to a 'court' or the benefit of such guarantees when his request which was rejected by the Regional Court in February 1969. Mr Winterwerp was accordingly the victim of a breach of Article 5 § 4.

FOR THESE REASONS, THE COURT UNANIMOUSLY

Holds that there has been no breach of Article 5(1);
  Holds that there has been a breach of Article 5(4); ...

NOTES

1 The Court was composed of President Pedersen and Judges: Wiarda, Evrigenis, Teitgen, Lagergren, Liesch, and Gölcüklü.

2 In the **Winterwerp** case the Court recognized that in some cases Article 5(4) requires a continuing remedy at reasonable intervals to check that the reasons justifying a person's detention continue to apply. The cases that follow in the remainder of this section are all concerned with this continuing remedy requirement.

X v UK A.46 (1981)
European Court of Human Rights

Following his conviction by Sheffield Assizes in 1968 of wounding with intent to cause grievous bodily harm, X was ordered by the court to be detained in Broadmoor Hospital as a restricted offender patient under section 85 of the Mental Health Act 1959. In 1971, the Home Secretary, acting under section 66 of the 1959 Act, ordered X's conditional discharge on the ground that X's condition had improved. After some three years of normal life, X was recalled to Broadmoor by the Home Secretary, acting under section 66 of the 1959 Act, in the light of evidence that his condition had deteriorated. X at once applied to the High Court for habeas corpus, but his application was unsuccessful. After six months' detention following his recall, X was entitled by section 66 to apply to the Mental Health Tribunal for a recommendation that he be released, which he did without success. Had the Tribunal recommended in his favour, the Home Secretary would have retained a discretion whether or not to accept the recommendation.

The applicant alleged breaches, *inter alia*, of Article 5(1) and (4). The Commission expressed the opinion, by 14 votes to 2, that X's recall had not violated Article 5(1). It was of the unanimous opinion that Article 5(4) had been violated, since X had not been entitled to take proceedings by which the lawfulness of his detention consequent on his recall to hospital could be decided speedily by a court. In particular, an appeal to the Mental Health Review Tribunal to challenge the recall was only possible six months after it had occurred.

The Court held unanimously that Article 5(1) was not infringed. In the following passage from its judgment, the Court considered whether there was a breach of Article 5(4).

JUDGMENT OF THE COURT

50. As their main submission, the Government contended that the requirements of Article 5 § 4 were met by the proceedings before the Sheffield Assizes in 1968. In this connection, they relied on a passage from the *De Wilde, Ooms and Versyp* judgment of 18 June 1971 (Series A No 12, p 40, § 76):

'At first sight, the wording of Article 5 § 4 might make one think that it guarantees the right of the detainee always to have supervised by a court the lawfulness of a previous decision which has deprived him of his liberty....Where [this] decision...is one taken by an administrative body, there is no doubt that Article 5 § 4 obliges the Contracting States to make available to the person detained a right of recourse to a court; but there is nothing to indicate that the same applies when the decision is made by a court at the close of judicial proceedings. In the latter case the supervision required by Article 5 § 4 is incorporated in the decision; this is so, for example, where a sentence of imprisonment is pronounced after 'conviction by a competent court' (Article 5 § 1(a) of the Convention).'

51. In point of fact, this passage speaks only of 'the decision depriving a person of his liberty'; it does not purport to deal with an ensuing period of detention in which new issues affecting the lawfulness of the detention might subsequently arise. The judgment of 18 June 1971 considered, for the purposes of Article 5 § 4, not only the initial decisions ordering detention for vagrancy taken in respect of three applicants (ibid, pp 40, 43, §§ 74–80), but also the procedure governing the examination of the applicants' requests for release (ibid, pp 43–4, §§ 81–4).

52. Furthermore, as the Government themselves pointed out the content of the obligation imposed on the Contracting States by Article 5 § 4 will not necessarily be the same in all circumstances and as regards every category of deprivation of liberty (see, *mutatis mutandis*, the above-mentioned *De Wilde, Ooms and Versyp* judgment, pp 41–2, § 78).

X's detention fell within the ambit of sub-paragraph (e) of Article 5 § 1 at least as much as within that of sub-paragraph (a)....The 'detention of persons of unsound mind' constitutes a special category with its own specific problems (see *Winterwerp* judgment, pp 23–24, §§ 57 and 60). In particular, 'the reasons initially warranting confinement of this kind may cease to exist'. This leads, so the *Winterwerp* judgment noted, to a consequence of some importance (p 23, § 55):

'...it would be contrary to the object and purpose of Article 5...to interpret paragraph 4...as making this category of confinement immune from subsequent review of lawfulness merely provided that the initial decision issued from a court. The very nature of the deprivation of liberty under consideration would appear to require a review of lawfulness to be available at reasonable intervals'.

By virtue of Article 5 § 4, a person of unsound mind compulsorily confined in a psychiatric institution for an indefinite or lengthy period is thus in principle entitled, at any rate where there is no automatic periodic review of a judicial character, to take proceedings at reasonable intervals before a court to put in issue the 'lawfulness'—within the meaning of the Convention (see paragraph 57 below)—of his detention, whether that detention was ordered by a civil or criminal court or by some other authority.

53. It is not within the province of the Court to inquire into what would be the best or most appropriate system of judicial review in this sphere, for the Contracting States are free to choose different methods of performing their obligations. Thus, in Article 5 § 4 the word 'court' is not necessarily to be understood as signifying a court of law of the classic kind, integrated within the standard judicial machinery of the country. This term, as employed in several Articles of the Convention including Article 5 § 4, serves to denote 'bodies which exhibit not only common fundamental features, of which the most important is independence of the executive and of the parties to the case . . . , but also the guarantees'—'appropriate to the kind of deprivation of liberty in question'—'of [a] judicial procedure', the forms of which may vary from one domain to another (see the above-mentioned *De Wilde, Ooms and Versyp* judgment, pp 41–2, §§ 76 and 78).

54. To sum up, during the period of his detention subsequent to his readmission to Broadmoor Hospital in April 1974 X should have been enabled to take proceedings attended by such 'guarantees'. At that stage, the proceedings that had been held in 1968 before the Sheffield Assizes were no longer sufficient to satisfy the requirements of Article 5 § 4. . . .

55. The Government maintained, in the alternative, that the 'lawfulness' of the said detention had in fact been 'decided speedily by a court', namely by the Divisional Court of the Queen's Bench Division when hearing X's application for a writ of habeas corpus. . . .

56. The habeas corpus proceedings brought by X are described above. . . . The case was considered by the Divisional Court on the basis of affidavits, including one by the applicant. Such medical evidence as there was before the Divisional Court . . . was obtained by X's solicitors. The Home Secretary was himself under no obligation to produce material justification for X's detention.

All this, however, followed from the nature of the remedy provided. In habeas corpus proceedings, in examining an administrative decision to detain, the court's task is to inquire whether the detention is in compliance with the requirements stated in the relevant legislation and with the applicable principles of the common law. According to these principles, such a decision—even though technically legal on its face—may be upset, *inter alia*, if the detaining authority misused its powers by acting in bad faith or capriciously or for a wrongful purpose, or if the decision is supported by no sufficient evidence or is one which no reasonable person could have reached in the circumstances. Subject to the foregoing, the court will not be able to review the grounds or merits of a decision taken by an administrative authority to the extent that under the legislation in question these are exclusively a matter for determination by that authority. As X's case well exemplifies, when the terms of a statute afford the executive a discretion, whether wide or narrow, the review exercisable by the courts in habeas corpus proceedings will bear solely upon the conformity of the exercise of that discretion with the empowering statute.

In the present case, once it was established that X was a patient who had been conditionally discharged whilst still subject to a restriction order, the statutory requirements for recall by warrant under section 66 § 3 of the 1959 Act were satisfied. This being so, it was then effectively up to X to show, within the limits permitted by English law, some reason why the apparently legal detention was unlawful. The evidence adduced by X did not disclose any such reason and the Divisional Court had no option but to dismiss the application.

57. Although X had access to a court which ruled that his detention was 'lawful' in terms of English law, this cannot of itself be decisive as to whether there was a sufficient review of 'lawfulness' for the purposes of Article 5 § 4. In paragraph 1(e) of Article 5 as interpreted by the Court (see the above-mentioned *Winterwerp* judgment, pp 17–18, § 39), . . . the Convention itself makes the 'lawfulness' of the kind of deprivation of liberty undergone by X subject to certain requirements over

and above conformity with domestic law. Article 5 must be read as a whole and there is no reason to suppose that in relation to one and the same deprivation of liberty the significance of 'lawfulness' differs from paragraph 1(e) to paragraph 4.

58. Notwithstanding the limited nature of the review possible in relation to decisions taken under section 66 § 3 of the 1959 Act, the remedy of habeas corpus can on occasions constitute an effective check against arbitrariness in this sphere. It may be regarded as adequate, for the purposes of Article 5 § 4, for emergency measures for the detention of persons on the ground of unsoundness of mind. Such measures, provided they are of short duration (see the above-mentioned *Winterwerp* judgment, p 19, § 42), are capable of being 'lawful' under Article 5 § 1(e) even though not attended by the usual guarantees such as thorough medical examination (see paragraph 41 above). The authority empowered to order emergency detention of this kind must, in the nature of things, enjoy a wide discretion, and this inevitably means that the role of the courts will be reduced.

On the other hand, in the Court's opinion, a judicial review as limited as that available in the habeas corpus procedure in the present case is not sufficient for a continuing confinement such as the one undergone by X. Article 5 § 4, the Government are quite correct to affirm, does not embody a right to judicial control of such scope as to empower the court, on all aspects of the case, to substitute its own discretion for that of the decision-making authority. The review should, however, be wide enough to bear on those conditions which, according to the Convention, are essential for the 'lawful' detention of a person on the ground of unsoundness of mind, especially as the reasons capable of initially justifying such a detention may cease to exist.... This means that in the instant case, Article 5 § 4 required an appropriate procedure allowing a court to examine whether the patient's disorder still persisted and whether the Home Secretary was entitled to think that a continuation of the compulsory confinement was necessary in the interests of public safety (see, *mutatis mutandis*, the above-mentioned *De Wilde, Ooms and Versyp* judgment, pp 43–4, §§ 82–3).

59. The habeas corpus proceedings brought by X in 1974 did not therefore secure him the enjoyment of the right guaranteed by Article 5 § 4; this would also have been the case had he made any fresh application at a later date....

61. The Government drew the Court's attention to four ways by which the continued need for detention may come to be reviewed by the Home Office, namely a recommendation from the responsible medical officer that the patient be discharged, the intervention of a Member of Parliament with the Home Secretary, a direct request by the patient to the Home Secretary asking for release or for his case to be referred to a Mental Health Review Tribunal....

The first three do not, however, bring into play any independent review procedure, whether judicial or administrative.

The fourth calls for closer examination since, in relation to the confinement of restricted patients, the 1959 Act provides the opportunity for a periodic review on a comprehensive factual basis by Mental Health Review Tribunals. There is nothing to preclude a specialised body of this kind being considered as a 'court' within the meaning of Article 5 § 4 provided it enjoys the necessary independence and offers sufficient procedural safeguards appropriate to the category of deprivation of liberty being dealt with (see paragraph 59 above and the above-mentioned *Winterwerp* judgment, p 24, § 20). Nonetheless, even supposing Mental Health Review Tribunals fulfilled these conditions, they lack the competence to decide 'the lawfulness of [the] detention' and to order release if the detention is unlawful, as they have advisory functions only....

Therefore, without underestimating the undoubted value of the safeguards thereby provided, the Court does not find that the other machinery adverted to by the Government serves to remedy the inadequacy, for the purposes of Article 5 § 4, of the habeas corpus proceedings.

62. In conclusion, there has been a breach of Article 5 § 4....

FOR THESE REASONS, THE COURT UNANIMOUSLY...

Holds that there has been a breach of Article 5(4); ...

NOTES

1 The Court was composed of President Wiarda and Judges: Zekia, Evrigenis, Matscher, Pinheiro Farinha, Walsh, and Jennings (*ad hoc* Judge).

2 To comply with Article 5(4), a remedy must allow a person to challenge the grounds for his detention as well as the legality of the procedures followed. Thus, in *X v UK*, habeas corpus was not a sufficient remedy. Nor was the possibility of recourse to a Mental Health Review Tribunal because, as the Court indicated, the Tribunal could only make a recommendation to the Home Secretary who took the final decision. In its report in the case, the Commission had expressed the opinion that the Tribunal remedy was insufficient also because it was only available after six months' detention, so that the question of release was not decided 'speedily'. The Mental Health (Amendment) Act 1982 redressed the defects found in *X v UK*.

Weeks v UK A.114 (1987)
European Court of Human Rights

In 1966, when aged 17, the applicant had been given a discretionary life sentence for armed robbery after having stolen 35 pence from a shop with a starting pistol. The sentence had been imposed because the alternative was a definite term of imprisonment for a number of years and the judge had considered that the more merciful approach was to impose a life sentence so that the emotionally immature applicant could be released on licence when it was considered appropriate (i.e. when he was sufficiently responsible) and this might be earlier than in the case of a determinate sentence. In fact, the applicant was released by the Home Secretary, following a Parole Board recommendation, only in 1976 after a ten-year spell in detention. In 1977, following incidents involving minor offences, the Parole Board confirmed an order by the Home Secretary for the applicant's recall. Thereafter the applicant was twice released and recalled, following the same procedures and as a result of minor offences. The Court held that the recalls could be justified under Article 5(1)(a): see p 264. In this extract the Court considered whether the remedies available to challenge the legality of the recall satisfied Article 5(4).

JUDGMENT OF THE COURT

58. The Court has already held in the context of paragraph 1(a) of Article 5 that the stated purpose of social protection and rehabilitation for which the 'indeterminate' sentence was passed on Mr Weeks, taken together with the particular circumstances of the offence for which he was convicted, places the sentence in a special category . . . : unlike the case of a person sentenced to life imprisonment because of the gravity of the offence committed, the grounds relied on by the sentencing judges for deciding that the length of the deprivation of Mr Weeks' liberty should be subject to the discretion of the executive for the rest of his life are by their nature susceptible of change with the passage of time. The Court inferred from this that if the decisions not to release or to re-detain were based on grounds inconsistent with the objectives of the sentencing court, Mr Weeks' detention would no longer be 'lawful' for the purposes of sub-paragraph (a) of paragraph 1 of Article 5.

It follows that, by virtue of paragraph 4 of Article 5, Mr Weeks was entitled to apply to a 'court' having jurisdiction to decide 'speedily' whether or not his deprivation of liberty had become 'unlawful' in this sense; this entitlement should have been exercisable by him at the moment of any return to custody after being at liberty and also at reasonable intervals during the course of his imprisonment (see, *mutatis mutandis*, the above-mentioned *Van Droogenbroeck* judgment, Series A No 50, p 26, § 48 *in fine*).

59. Article 5 § 4 does not guarantee a right to judicial control of such scope as to empower the 'court', on all aspects of the case, including questions of expediency, to substitute its own discretion for that of the decision-making authority. The review should, however, be wide enough to bear on those conditions which, according to the Convention, are essential for the lawful detention of a person subject to the special kind of deprivation of liberty ordered against Mr Weeks (ibid, p 26, § 49)....

60. The Government submitted in the alternative that the requirements of Article 5 § 4 were sufficiently met by the Parole Board's jurisdiction, supplemented as it was by the availability of judicial review before the High Court. Both the applicant and the Commission disagreed with this analysis....

61. The 'court' referred to in Article 5 § 4 does not necessarily have to be a court of law of the classic kind integrated within the standard judicial machinery of the country (see the above-mentioned *X v UK* judgment, Series A No 46, p 23, § 53). The term 'court' serves to denote 'bodies which exhibit not only common fundamental features, of which the most important is independence of the executive and of the parties to the case . . . , but also the guarantees'—'appropriate to the kind of deprivation of liberty in question'—'of [a] judicial procedure', the forms of which may vary from one domain to another (see the above-mentioned *De Wilde, Ooms and Versyp* judgment, Series A No 12, pp 41–2, §§ 76 and 78). In addition, as the text of Article 5 § 4 makes clear, the body in question must not have merely advisory functions but must have the competence to 'decide' the 'lawfulness' of the detention and to order release if the detention is unlawful.

There is thus nothing to preclude a specialised body such as the Parole Board being considered as a 'court' within the meaning of Article 5 § 4, provided it fulfils the foregoing conditions (see the above-mentioned *X v UK* judgment, Series A No 46, p 26, § 61)....

62. The applicant maintained that the Parole Board is not independent of the Home Secretary, primarily because he appoints the members of the Board, provides its staff and makes the rules under which it conducts its procedures.

The Parole Board sits in small panels, each of which in the case of life prisoners includes a High Court judge and a psychiatrist.... The manner of appointment of the Board's members does not, in the Court's opinion, establish a lack of independence on the part of the members (see, *mutatis mutandis*, the *Campbell and Fell* judgment of 28 June 1984, Series A No 80, p 40, § 79). Furthermore, the Court is satisfied that the judge member and the other members of the Board remain wholly independent of the executive and impartial in the performance of their duties.

There remains the question whether the Board presents an appearance of independence, notably to persons whose liberty it considers (ibid, pp 39–41, §§ 78 and 81). On this point, as the Government stated, the functions of the Board do not bring it into contact with officials of the prisons or of the Home Secretary in such a way as to identify it with the administration of the prison or of the Home Office.

The Court therefore sees no reason to conclude that the Parole Board and its members are not independent and impartial.

63. The Commission, together with the applicant, took the view that the Board lacked the necessary powers and procedural guarantees for the purposes of Article 5 § 4. The applicant further contended that the Board's proceedings were not 'speedy'. He pointed out that, whereas his licence was revoked in June 1977, the Board did not give its decision until December 1977....

64. According to the wording of the 1967 Act, the duty of the Parole Board is to 'advise' the Home Secretary on the exercise of his powers to release prisoners on licence and to revoke such licences, and its decisions take the form of 'recommendations' to the Home Secretary (sections 59(3), 61(1) and 62(1) and (5))....

The Board's functions are without doubt purely advisory, both in law and in substance, as regards the periodic review that it carries out in relation to the question of the possible release on licence of a detained person serving a sentence of life imprisonment (section 61(1) of the 1967 Act). The Home Secretary may not, it is true, release on licence a life prisoner unless recommended to do so by the Parole Board (ibid). However, where the Board does recommend release of such prisoners, the Home Secretary must also consult the Lord Chief Justice, together with the trial judge if available (ibid); and, as demonstrated by the facts of Mr Weeks' own case . . . , the Home Secretary is free, in the light of all the material before him, not to accept the Board's recommendation. Quite apart from any consideration of procedural guarantees, the Board therefore lacks the power of decision required by Article 5 § 4 when dealing with this category of case.

On the other hand, the Board's recommendation to release is binding on the Home Secretary when the Board has to consider, as it did in December 1977 in relation to Mr Weeks, recall to prison after release on licence (section 62(5) of the 1967 Act). . . . The procedure applicable in the event of recall must therefore be examined. . . .

65. The language of Article 5 § 4 speaks of the detained individual being entitled to initiate proceedings. Under the British system of parole of life prisoners, although only the Home Secretary may refer a case to the Board, referral is obligatory in recall cases except where a person recalled after a recommendation to that effect by the Board has chosen not to make written representations (section 62(4) of the 1967 Act). . . . In these circumstances, the recalled person can be considered as having sufficient access to the Parole Board for the purposes of Article 5 § 4 (see the above-mentioned *X v UK* judgment, Series A No 46, p 23, § 52).

66. The Board deals with individual cases on consideration of the documents supplied to it by the Home Secretary and of any reports, information or interviews with the individual concerned it has itself called for (section 59(4) and (5) of the 1967 Act). . . . The prisoner is entitled to make representations with respect to his recall, not only in writing to the Board but also orally to a member of the Local Review Committee (sections 59(5)–(6) and 62(3) of the 1967 Act). . . . The individual is free to take legal advice in preparing such representations. Furthermore, he must be sufficiently informed of the reasons for his recall in order to enable him to make sensible representations (section 62(3) of the 1967 Act and the judgments in the *Gunnell* and *Wilson* cases—ibid).

Whilst these safeguards are not negligible, there remains a certain procedural weakness in the case of a recalled prisoner. Thus, the Court of Appeal established in the *Gunnell* case that the duty on the Board to act fairly, as required under English law by the principles of natural justice, does not entail an entitlement to full disclosure of the adverse material which the Board has in its possession. . . . The procedure followed does not therefore allow proper participation of the individual adversely affected by the contested decision, this being one of the principal guarantees of a judicial procedure for the purposes of the Convention, and cannot therefore be regarded as judicial in character (see, *mutatis mutandis*, the *Sanchez-Reisse* judgment of 21 October 1986, Series A No 107, p 19, § 51).

67. In view of this finding, the Court does not consider it necessary to rule on the remaining points raised by the applicant and the Commission, that is: firstly, whether, in relation to the special category of deprivation of liberty ordered against Mr Weeks, this requirement of a proper procedure calls for the holding of an oral hearing in addition to the existing possibility of making written submissions (see, *mutatis mutandis*, the above-mentioned *Sanchez-Reisse* judgment, Series A No 107, p 19, § 51); and, secondly, whether the proceedings before the Board were 'speedy'. . . .

68. Consequently, neither in relation to consideration of Mr Weeks' recall to prison in 1977 nor in relation to periodic examination of his detention with a view to release on licence can the Parole Board be regarded as satisfying the requirements of Article 5 § 4. . . .

69. The Court has in previous cases recognised the need to take a comprehensive view of the system in issue before it, as apparent short-comings in one procedure may be remedied by safeguards available in other procedures (see, for example, the above-mentioned *X v UK* judgment, Series A

No 46, p 26, § 60). In this connection, an application for judicial review undoubtedly represents a useful supplement to the procedure before the Parole Board: it enables the individual concerned to obtain a control by the ordinary courts of both the Parole Board's decisions (see, for example, the judgment of the Queen's Bench Division in the *Wilson* case...) and the Home Secretary's decisions.

The applicant, adopting conclusions reached by the Commission in its report, argued that the remedy of judicial review did not meet the requirements of accessibility and effectiveness under Article 5 § 4 (see the above-mentioned *Van Droogenbroeck* judgment, Series A No 50, p 30, § 54).

The grounds on which judicial review lies, as summarised by Lord Diplock in his speech in the Council of Civil Service Unions case, are 'illegality', 'irrationality' and 'procedural impropriety'. By 'illegality' is meant incorrect application of the law governing the decision-making power and, in particular, breach of the relevant statutory requirements; 'irrationality' covers a decision that is so outrageous in its defiance of logic or of accepted moral standards that no sensible person who had applied his mind to the question to be decided could have arrived at it; and 'procedural impropriety' is a failure to observe expressly laid down procedural rules, a denial of natural justice or a lack of procedural fairness...

As the Commission pointed out, the scope of the control afforded is thus not wide enough to bear on the conditions essential for the 'lawfulness', in the sense of Article 5 § 4 of the Convention, of Mr Weeks' detention, that is to say, whether it was consistent with and therefore justified by the objectives of the indeterminate sentence imposed on him (see paragraphs 58 and 59 above). In the Court's view, having regard to the nature of the control it allows, the remedy of judicial review can neither itself provide the proceedings required by Article 5 § 4 nor serve to remedy the inadequacy, for the purposes of that provision, of the procedure before the Parole Board....

FOR THESE REASONS, THE COURT...

Holds, by thirteen votes to four, that there has been a breach of Article 5 § 4;

NOTES

1 The Court was composed of President Ryssdal and Judges: Cremona, Thor Vilhjálmsson, Bindschedler-Robert, Lagergren, Gölcüklü, Matscher, Pinheiro Farinha, Pettiti, Walsh, Sir Vincent Evans, Macdonald, Russo, Bernhardt, Gersing, Spielman, and De Mayer. Judges Vilhjalmsson, Lagergren, Evans, and Gersing issued a joint partly concurring/dissenting opinion in which they expressed the view that Weeks' original trial combined with the possibility of him challenging his recall via an action for judicial review satisfied the demands of Article 5(4).

2 The *Weeks* case was the first in a series of cases in which the European Court applied the continuing remedy requirement in Article 5(4) to the arrangements in English discretionary or indeterminate life sentences, mandatory life sentences, and to the detention of juveniles during Her Majesty's Pleasure. As will be seen, the involvement of the Home Secretary, who clearly was not a 'court', became increasingly problematic and untenable in the judgments of the Court.

....

Thynne, Wilson and Gunnell v UK A.190 (1990)
European Court of Human Rights

The applicants had been convicted of very grave sex offences for which they would have been sentenced to long terms of imprisonment had definite terms been imposed. Instead, since the applicants were regarded as unstable and likely to commit other offences if released, they were, in accordance with established sentencing policy, given discretionary life sentences, which contained a number of years (the tariff period) calculated as punishment for the offence committed and thereafter were justified in terms of the public interest in keeping dangerous criminals secure. In all three cases, the applicants had moved from the punishment to the security phase of their life sentences and could be released on licence by the Home Secretary on the recommendation of the Parole Board if they were no longer thought a danger to society. The Commission expressed the opinion, by 10 votes to 2, that the remedies available to the applicant to challenge their continued detention after the end of the tariff period did not satisfy Article 5(4).

JUDGMENT OF THE COURT

68. It was held in the *De Wilde, Ooms and Versyp* judgment of 18 June 1971 that where a sentence of imprisonment is imposed after 'conviction by a competent court', the supervision required by Article 5 § 4 is incorporated in the decision of the court (Series A No 12, p 40, § 76). In subsequent cases the Court made it clear that this finding related only to 'the initial decision depriving a person of his liberty' and did not purport 'to deal with an ensuing period of detention in which new issues affecting the lawfulness of the detention might arise' (see, *inter alia*, the above-mentioned *Weeks* judgment, Series A No 114, p 28, § 56). In this connection the concept of lawfulness under Article 5 § 4 requires that the detention be in conformity not only with domestic law but also with the text of the Convention, the general principles embodied therein and the aim of the restrictions permitted by Article 5 § 1 (ibid, p 23, § 42, and p 28, § 57).

69. In cases concerning detention of persons of unsound mind under Article 5 § 1(e) where the reasons initially warranting detention may cease to exist the Court has held that 'it would be contrary to the object and purpose of Article 5 ... to interpret paragraph 4 ... as making this category of confinement immune from subsequent review of lawfulness merely provided that the initial decision issued from a court ...' (see the *X v UK* judgment of 5 November 1981, Series A No 46, pp 22–3, § 52). This interpretation of Article 5 § 4 has also, in certain circumstances, been applied to detention 'after conviction by a competent court' under Article 5 § 1(a) (see, *inter alia*, the *Van Droogenbroeck* judgment of 24 June 1982, Series A No 50, pp 23–7, §§ 44–9, the above-mentioned *Weeks* judgment, Series A No 114, pp 28–9, §§ 55–9, and the *E v Norway* judgment of 29 August 1990, Series A No 181-A, pp 21–2, § 50). What is of importance in this context is the nature and purpose of the detention in question, viewed in the light of the objectives of the sentencing court, and not the category to which it belongs under Article 5 § 1 (see the above-mentioned *Van Droogenbroeck* judgment, p 24, § 47).

70. Mr Weeks received a discretionary life sentence not because of the gravity of his offence but because of his dangerous and unstable personality and to enable the Home Secretary to monitor his progress and release him when he was no longer judged to represent a danger to the community (see Series A No 114, especially at pp 10–11, §§ 14–15).

The Court considered that the measure ordered against him was comparable to the measure of placement at the Government's disposal at issue in the *Van Droogenbroeck* case and, further, that the protective purpose underlying the life sentence, taken together with the particular circumstances of the offence for which he was convicted, placed the sentence in a special category to which Article 5 § 4 was applicable (ibid, pp 24–5, §§ 46–7, and pp 28–9, § 58). It was an important feature of this category that the grounds relied on by the sentencing judges as the reason for imposing a life sentence on Mr Weeks, namely his mental instability and dangerousness, were, by their nature, susceptible of change with the passage of time. The Court inferred from this that, if the decisions not to release or to re-detain were based on grounds inconsistent with the objectives of the sentencing court, his detention would no longer be 'lawful' for the purposes of Article 5 § 1(a) and the Court concluded that Mr Weeks was entitled, by virtue of Article 5 § 4, to have recourse to a court to decide on the lawfulness of his deprivation of liberty at the moment of any return to custody after being at liberty as well as at reasonable intervals during the course of his imprisonment (ibid, p 29, § 58).

71. The Court has had regard to the reasons given by the courts for the sentences imposed on each of the applicants in the present case and the nature and purpose of the discretionary life sentence under English law.

72. Mr Thynne was found to have a personality disorder which required observation and possibly operative treatment. The sentencing judge indicated that but for the psychiatric reports he would have imposed a very long prison sentence. . . . However, the Court of Appeal said that it did not 'see the life sentence in this case as necessarily involving detention in custodial conditions for a very long period of time'; it added that this was a case in which the offences were very grave indeed and society needed to be protected against 'outbursts of this nature which would very seriously affect other persons'. . . .

The Court made similar analyses of the other two applicants' cases.

Each of the applicants was thus sentenced to life imprisonment because, in addition to the need for punishment, he was considered by the courts to be suffering from a mental or personality disorder and to be dangerous and in need of treatment. Life imprisonment was judged to be the most appropriate sentence in the circumstances since it enabled the Secretary of State to assess their progress and to act accordingly. Thus the courts' sentencing objectives were in that respect similar to those in *Weeks*, but also took into account the much greater gravity of the offences committed.

73. As regards the nature and purpose of the discretionary life sentence under English law, the Government's main submission was that it is impossible to disentangle the punitive and security components of such sentences. The Court is not persuaded by this argument: the discretionary life sentence has clearly developed in English law as a measure to deal with mentally unstable and dangerous offenders; numerous judicial statements have recognised the protective purpose of this form of life sentence (see, in particular, the remarks by Lord Chief Justice Lane and Lord Justice Stuart-Smith in *R v Wilkinson* and *R v Secretary of State, ex p Bradley*, . . .). Although the dividing line may be difficult to draw in particular cases, it seems clear that the principles underlying such sentences, unlike mandatory life sentences, have developed in the sense that they are composed of a punitive element and subsequently of a security element designed to confer on the Secretary of State the responsibility for determining when the public interest permits the prisoner's release. This view is confirmed by the judicial description of the 'tariff' as denoting the period of detention considered necessary to meet the requirements of retribution and deterrence. . . .

75. It is clear from the judgments of the sentencing courts that in their view the three applicants, unlike Mr Weeks, had committed offences of the utmost gravity meriting lengthy terms of imprisonment. Nevertheless, the Court is satisfied that in each case the punitive period of the discretionary life sentence has expired. . . .

76. Having regard to the foregoing, the Court finds that the detention of the applicants after the expiry of the punitive periods of their life sentences is comparable to that at issue in the *Van Droogenbroeck* and *Weeks* cases: the factors of mental instability and dangerousness are susceptible to change over the passage of time and new issues of lawfulness may thus arise in the course of detention. It follows that at that phase in the execution of their sentences, the applicants were entitled under Article 5 § 4 to take proceedings to have the lawfulness of their continued detention decided by a court at reasonable intervals and to have the lawfulness of any re-detention determined by a court.

77. The applicants and the Commission submitted that Article 5 § 4 should be considered to apply throughout the whole of the applicants' imprisonment because of the uncertainty of the 'tariff' period, which was not communicated directly to the applicants. Furthermore the applicants attached weight to the fact that the 'tariff' or punitive period was not stated in open court and subject to the normal process of appeal.

The Government argued that a life prisoner should not be placed in a better position than a prisoner who received a fixed-term sentence. The length of the 'tariff' can be deduced from the date when the first review is set. Article 5 § 4 should only apply, if at all, following the expiry of the 'tariff' period.

78. The Court does not consider that it is necessary to decide this question in the present case since it is clear that the punitive period of the three applicants' life sentences has expired (see paragraph 75 above). Accordingly the applicants were entitled to subsequent judicial control as guaranteed by Article 5 § 4. . . .

79. Article 5 § 4 does not guarantee a right to judicial control of such scope as to empower the 'court' on all aspects of the case, including questions of expediency, to substitute its own discretion for that of the decision-making authority; the review should, nevertheless, be wide enough to bear on those conditions which, according to the Convention, are essential for the lawful detention of a person subject to the special type of deprivation of liberty ordered against these three applicants (see, *inter alia*, the above-mentioned *Weeks* judgment, Series A No 114, p 29, § 59, and the above-mentioned *E v Norway* judgment, Series A No 181-A, pp 21–2, § 50).

80. The Court sees no reason to depart from its finding in the *Weeks* judgment (pp 29–33, §§ 60–9) that neither the Parole Board nor judicial review proceedings—no other remedy of a judicial character being available to the three applicants—satisfy the requirements of Article 5 § 4. Indeed, this was not disputed by the Government. . . .

FOR THESE REASONS, THE COURT

Holds by eighteen votes to one that there has been a violation of Article 5(4) in the case of all three applicants;

NOTES

1 The Court was composed of President Ryssdal and Judges: Cremona, Vilhjálmsson, Gölcüklü, Matchser, Pinheiro Farinha, Pettiti, Walsh, Sir Vincent Evans, MacDonald, Russo, Bernhardt, Spielmann, De Meyer, Valticos, Martens, Pekkanen, Loizou, and Morenilla Rodriguez. Judge Vilhjálmsson issued a dissenting opinion in which he stated that he considered the applicants' original trials provided the judicial review required by Article 5(4).

2 In *Oldham v UK*, judgment of 26 September 2000, the applicant, a post-tariff discretionary life prisoner, claimed the two-year period between reviews of his continuing detention did not satisfy the requirements of Article 5(4). Oldham had been convicted of manslaughter, whilst suffering from a mental abnormality induced by alcohol, in 1970. He was released and recalled to prison several times from the late 1980s. In July 1996 he was recalled by the Home Secretary on the ground that he had injured his partner after a drinking binge. The Parole Board Discretionary Lifer Panel that examined his recall expressed the view that he should remain in custody, as he posed a risk to the public and that he should undertake work in respect of alcohol abuse and the management of anger. The Home Secretary informed Oldham that the Parole Board would review his detention in two years' time. Within eight months of his recall Oldham completed courses on the specified topics. In 1998 the applicant had another hearing before the Discretionary Lifer Panel and it recommended his release (the Home Secretary duly released him on licence). Oldham contended that the

delay in reviewing his detention was unreasonable and thereby violated Article 5(4). The Court stated that:

> 31. It is true that the question of whether periods comply with the requirement must—as with the reasonable time stipulation in Article 5 § 3 and Article 6 § 1—be determined in the light of the circumstances of each case (see the *Sanchez-Reisse v Switzerland* judgment of 21 October 1986, Series A No 107, p 55, § 55). It is therefore not for this Court to attempt to rule as to the maximum period of time between reviews which should automatically apply to this category of life prisoner as a whole. It notes that the system as applied in this case has a flexibility which must reflect the realities of the situation, namely, that there are significant differences in the personal circumstances of the prisoners under review.

After observing that Oldham had completed his courses within eight months of the previous review the Court concluded that his having to wait a further 16 months before having his case reconsidered by the Discretionary Lifer Panel was not reasonable, hence the lawfulness of his continuing detention had not been decided 'speedily' as mandated by Article 5(4). This judgment indicates that national review procedures should not be primarily governed by automatic timetables but by the personal conditions of individual prisoners.

3   In the *Thynne, Wilson and Gunnell* cases, para 73, the European Court drew a distinction between discretionary and mandatory life sentences in the English system, with the result that a continuing remedy was not required under Article 5(4) in the case of the latter. The original Court confirmed this view in its ruling, by 18 votes to 1, in *Wynne v UK* A.294 (1994), which concerned a mandatory life sentence. The Court stated:

> 35. ... However, the fact remains that the mandatory sentence belongs to a different category from the discretionary sentence in the sense that it is imposed automatically as the punishment for the offence of murder irrespective of considerations pertaining to the dangerousness of the offender. ... That mandatory life prisoners do not actually spend the rest of their lives in prison and that a notional tariff period is also established in such cases—facts of which the Court was fully aware in *Thynne, Wilson and Gunnell* (*loc cit*, p 29, § 74)—does not alter this essential distinction between the two types of life sentence.
>
> As observed by the House of Lords in *R v Secretary of State, ex p Doody*, while the two types of life sentence may now be converging there remains nonetheless, on the statutory framework, the underlying theory and the current practice, a substantial gap between them. ... This is borne out by the very facts *inter alia* relied on by the applicant to support his case, namely that in mandatory life sentences the release of the prisoner is entirely a matter within the discretion of the Secretary of State who is not bound by the judicial recommendation as to the length of the tariff period and who is free under English law to have regard to other criteria than dangerousness, following the expiry of the 'tariff' period, in deciding whether the prisoner should be released. ... It is further reflected in the decision of Parliament to limit the application of the new procedures in the 1991 Act to discretionary life sentences only, even in cases like the present where the prisoner is serving both a mandatory and a discretionary life sentence. ...
>
> 36. Against the above background, the Court sees no cogent reasons to depart from the finding in the *Thynne, Wilson and Gunnell* case that, as regards mandatory life sentences, the guarantee of Article 5 § 4 was satisfied by the original trial and appeal proceedings and confers no additional right to challenge the lawfulness of continuing detention or re-detention following revocation of the life licence (see, *mutatis mutandis*, the *Cossey v UK* judgment of 27 September 1990, Series A No 184, p 14, § 35). Accordingly, in the circumstances of the present case, there are no new issues of lawfulness which entitle the applicant to a review of his continued detention under the original mandatory life sentence. ...

However, in 2002 a Grand Chamber of the full-time Court declined to follow the approach in *Wynne*. *Stafford v UK*, judgment of 28 May 2002 concerned a person convicted of murder in 1967. He was released on licence in 1979 but broke his parole conditions by leaving the country. During 1989 he returned to the UK and was arrested in possession of a false passport. He was fined and remained in custody because his licence had been revoked. After 18 months' imprisonment the Parole Board recommended his release on licence. The Home Secretary authorized Stafford's release. In 1994 he was convicted of conspiracy to forge travellers' cheques and passports and sentence to six years' imprisonment. His licence was again revoked. In 1996 the Parole Board recommended his release on licence as it considered the risk of him re-offending was low. Nevertheless, the Home Secretary refused to release him. In July 1997 the applicant would have been released from prison in respect of his fraud sentence but he remained in custody due to the revocation of his life sentence licence. The Home Secretary approved his release on licence in December 1998. Stafford contended that the Court should reconsider the judgment in *Wynne* and hold that Article 5(4) required a judicial body to determine the continuing need for a mandatory lifer to be held in custody. The Court observed that:

78. ... The abolition of the death penalty in 1965 and the conferring on the Secretary of State of the power to release convicted murderers represented, at that time, a major and progressive reform. However, with the wider recognition of the need to develop and apply, in relation to mandatory life prisoners, judicial procedures reflecting standards of independence, fairness and openness, the continuing role of the Secretary of State in fixing the tariff and in deciding on a prisoner's release following its expiry, has become increasingly difficult to reconcile with the notion of separation of powers between the executive and the judiciary, a notion which has assumed growing importance in the case-law of the Court (*mutatis mutandis*, the *Incal v Turkey* judgment of 9 June 1998, Reports 1998–IV).

79. The Court considers that it may now be regarded as established in domestic law that there is no distinction between mandatory life prisoners, discretionary life prisoners and juvenile murderers as regards the nature of tariff-fixing. It is a sentencing exercise. The mandatory life sentence does not impose imprisonment for life as a punishment. The tariff, which reflects the individual circumstances of the offence and the offender, represents the element of punishment. The Court concludes that the finding in Wynne that the mandatory life sentence constituted punishment for life can no longer be regarded as reflecting the real position in the domestic criminal justice system of the mandatory life prisoner.

Furthermore, the Grand Chamber determined that after the expiry of the tariff the continued detention of mandatory lifers depended upon:

87. ... elements of dangerousness and risk associated with the objectives of the original sentence of murder. These elements may change with the course of time, and thus new issues of lawfulness arise requiring determination by a body satisfying the requirements of Article 5 § 4. It can no longer be maintained that the original trial and appeal proceedings satisfied, once and for all, issues of compatibility of subsequent detention of mandatory life prisoners with the provisions of Article 5 § 1 of the Convention.

Consequently the Grand Chamber unanimously found a breach of Article 5(4) as Stafford had not had access to such a judicial body.

President Wildhaber speaking extra-judicially observed that in *Stafford*:

The Court took judicial notice of the evolving position of the British courts as to the nature of life sentences in an interesting example of a two-way process whereby developments in the domestic legal system influence Strasbourg to change its case-law, which in turn results in the consolidation of the evolution at national level, what one might call jurisprudential osmosis. [Speech by President Luzius Wildhaber to mark the opening of the judicial year: Strasbourg, 23 January 2003.]

The Court's decision in **Stafford** can be welcomed on both constitutional and public policy grounds as individual sentencing decisions should be left to the independent judiciary and not rest with a minister subject to political pressures.

The Criminal Justice Act 2003 created a new system of sentencing adults subject to mandatory life sentences with the trial court determining the minimum term of imprisonment, having regard to the severity of the crime(s) assessed in the light of statutory criteria (Chapter 7 of and Schedule 21 to the Act).

....

Hussain v UK 1996-I
European Court of Human Rights

At the age of 16, the applicant was convicted of murdering his 2-year-old brother. As he was a juvenile, he automatically received a mandatory sentence of detention 'during Her Majesty's Pleasure' pursuant to section 53(1) of the Children and Young Persons Act 1933. The effect was that he was 'liable to be detained in such a place and under such conditions as the [Home Secretary] may direct'. The release procedure for this type of detention was the same as for adults who had received mandatory life sentences, that is, only after the expiry of the tariff (here 15 years, as determined by the Home Secretary) and on the decision of the Home Secretary. The Parole Board undertook periodical reviews of the applicant's position with a view to his release on licence, but could only make recommendations to the Home Secretary. Following an English court decision in another case, the applicant was allowed to see the reports on him that had been placed before the Parole Board, but he was still not given the opportunity to appear in person before it. By the time the case reached the European Court the applicant had been detained for 17 years.

JUDGMENT OF THE COURT

50. The Court notes at the outset that, as has been commonly accepted, the central issue in the present case is whether detention during Her Majesty's pleasure, given its nature and purpose, should be assimilated, under the case-law on the Convention, to a mandatory sentence of life imprisonment or rather to a discretionary sentence of life imprisonment. In dealing with this issue the Court must therefore decide whether the substance of a sentence of detention under section 53 is more closely related to that at the heart of the cases of *Weeks v UK* (judgment of 2 March 1987, Series A No 114) and *Thynne, Wilson and Gunnell* or to that in the more recent *Wynne* case....

51. It is true, as submitted by the Government, that a sentence of detention during Her Majesty's pleasure is mandatory: it is fixed by law and is imposed automatically in all cases where persons under the age of 18 are convicted of murder, the trial judge having no discretion. It is also the case that the 1991 Act as well as recent policy statements treat the sentence at issue in the present case in an identical manner to mandatory life sentences as regards proceedings for release on licence and recall....

On the other hand, it is undisputed that, in its statutory origins, the expression 'during Her Majesty's pleasure' had a clearly preventive purpose and that—unlike sentences of life custody or life imprisonment—the word 'life' is not mentioned in the description of the sentence.

52. Nevertheless, important as these arguments may be for the understanding of the sentence of detention under section 53 in English law, the decisive issue in the present context is whether the

nature and, above all, the purpose of that sentence are such as to require the lawfulness of the continued detention to be examined by a court satisfying the requirements of Article 5 § 4.

53. It is recalled that the applicant was sentenced to be detained during Her Majesty's pleasure because of his young age at the time of the commission of the offence. In the case of young persons convicted of serious crimes, the corresponding sentence undoubtedly contains a punitive element and accordingly a tariff is set to reflect the requirements of retribution and deterrence. However an indeterminate term of detention for a convicted young person, which may be as long as that person's life, can only be justified by considerations based on the need to protect the public.

These considerations, centred on an assessment of the young offender's character and mental state and of his or her resulting dangerousness to society, must of necessity take into account any developments in the young offender's personality and attitude as he or she grows older. A failure to have regard to the changes that inevitably occur with maturation would mean that young persons detained under section 53 would be treated as having forfeited their liberty for the rest of their lives, a situation which, as the applicant and the Delegate of the Commission pointed out, might give rise to questions under Article 3 of the Convention.

54. Against this background the Court concludes that the applicant's sentence, after the expiration of his tariff, is more comparable to a discretionary life sentence. This was, albeit in a different context, the view expressed by the Divisional Court in its judgment of 20 April 1993 (*R v Secretary of State for the Home Department, ex p Prem Singh*)....

The decisive ground for the applicant's continued detention was and continues to be his dangerousness to society, a characteristic susceptible to change with the passage of time. Accordingly, new issues of lawfulness may arise in the course of detention and the applicant is entitled under Article 5 § 4 to take proceedings to have these issues decided by a court at reasonable intervals (see, *mutatis mutandis*, the above-mentioned *Thynne, Wilson and Gunnell* judgment, p 30, § 76)....

58. As in *Thynne, Wilson and Gunnell* (p 30, § 80) and despite the new policy allowing persons detained under section 53 of the 1933 Act the opportunity to see the material before the Parole Board..., the Court sees no reason to depart from its findings in the case of *Weeks* (cited above, pp 29–33, §§ 60–69) that the Parole Board does not satisfy the requirements of Article 5 § 4. Indeed, to the extent to which the Parole Board cannot order the release of a prisoner this is not contested by the Government. However, the lack of adversarial proceedings before the Parole Board also prevents it from being regarded as a court or court-like body for the purposes of Article 5 § 4.

59. The Court recalls in this context that, in matters of such crucial importance as the deprivation of liberty and where questions arise which involve, for example, an assessment of the applicant's character or mental state, it has held that it may be essential to the fairness of the proceedings that the applicant be present at an oral hearing (see, *mutatis mutandis*, the *Kremzow v Austria* judgment of 21 September 1993, Series A No 268-B, p 45, § 67).

60. The Court is of the view that, in a situation such as that of the applicant, where a substantial term of imprisonment may be at stake and where characteristics pertaining to his personality and level of maturity are of importance in deciding on his dangerousness, Article 5 § 4 requires an oral hearing in the context of an adversarial procedure involving legal representation and the possibility of calling and questioning witnesses.

61. It is not an answer to this requirement that the applicant might have been able to obtain an oral hearing by instituting proceedings for judicial review. In the first place, Article 5 § 4 presupposes the existence of a procedure in conformity with its requirements without the necessity of instituting separate legal proceedings in order to bring it about. In the second place, like the Delegate of the

Commission, the Court is not convinced that the applicant's possibility of obtaining an oral hearing by way of proceedings for judicial review is sufficiently certain to be regarded as satisfying the requirements of Article 5 § 4 of the Convention....

FOR THESE REASONS, THE COURT UNANIMOUSLY

Holds that there has been a violation of Article 5 § 4 of the Convention in that the applicant, after the expiry of his punitive period, was unable to bring the case of his continued detention before a court; ...

NOTES

1   The Court was composed of President Ryssdal and Judges: Gölcüklü, MacDonald, Spielmann, Valticos, Palm, Bigi, Sir John Freeland, and Jambrek.

2   The *Hussain* case concerned remedies under Article 5(4) after the end of the tariff period. In *T v UK*, judgment of 16 December 1999, the Court held that Article 5(4) also required a continuing remedy to challenge the detention of a juvenile during Her Majesty's Pleasure before the tariff period expired because the tariff had been set not by a court but by the Home Secretary. The Court stated:

118. The Court recalls that where a national court, after convicting a person of a criminal offence, imposes a fixed sentence of imprisonment for the purposes of punishment, the supervision required by Article 5 § 4 is incorporated in that court decision (see the *De Wilde, Ooms and Versyp v Belgium* judgment of 18 June 1971, Series A No 12, pp 40–1, § 76, and the *Wynne* judgment cited above, p 15, § 36). This is not the case, however, in respect of any ensuing period of detention in which new issues affecting the lawfulness of the detention may arise (see the *Weeks* judgment cited above, p 28, § 56, and the *Thynne, Wilson and Gunnell v UK* judgment of 25 October 1990, Series A No 190-A, pp 26–7, § 68). Thus, in the *Hussain* judgment (*op cit*, pp 269–70, § 54), the Court decided in respect of a young offender detained during Her Majesty's pleasure that, after the expiry of the tariff period, Article 5 § 4 required that he should be able periodically to challenge the continuing legality of his detention since its only justification could be dangerousness, a characteristic subject to change. In the *Hussain* case the Court was not called upon to consider the position under Article 5 § 4 prior to the expiry of the tariff (*op cit*, p 266, § 44).

119. The Court has already determined that the failure to have the applicant's tariff set by an independent tribunal within the meaning of Article 6 § 1 gives rise to a violation of that provision (see paragraph 113 above). Accordingly, given that the sentence of detention during Her Majesty's pleasure is indeterminate and that the tariff was initially set by the Home Secretary rather than the sentencing judge, it cannot be said that the supervision required by Article 5 § 4 was incorporated in the trial court's sentence (cf the *De Wilde, Ooms and Versyp* judgment and the *Wynne* judgment cited in paragraph 118 above).

120. Moreover, the Home Secretary's decision setting the tariff was quashed by the House of Lords on 12 June 1997 and no new tariff has since been substituted. This failure to set a new tariff means that the applicant's entitlement to access to a tribunal for periodic review of the continuing lawfulness of his detention remains inchoate.

121. It follows that the applicant has been deprived, since his conviction in November 1993, of the opportunity to have the lawfulness of his detention reviewed by a judicial body in accordance with Article 5 § 4. Against this background, the Court finds a violation of that Article.

Article 5(5): right to compensation

Brogan v UK A.145 (1988)
European Court of Human Rights

As we have examined (p 302), the plenary Court found a violation of Article 5(3), the applicants further contended that as they could not claim compensation under domestic law in respect of this violation there had also been a breach of Article 5(5).

VI. ALLEGED BREACH OF ARTICLE 5 PARA. 5

66. The applicants further alleged breach of Article 5 para. 5 which reads:

> 'Everyone who has been the victim of arrest or detention in contravention of the provisions of this Article shall have an enforceable right to compensation.'

A claim for compensation for unlawful deprivation of liberty may be made in the United Kingdom in respect of a breach of domestic law. As Article 5 is not considered part of the domestic law of the United Kingdom, no claim for compensation lies for a breach of any provision of Article 5 which does not at the same time constitute a breach of United Kingdom law.

The Government argued, *inter alia*, that the aim of paragraph 5 is to ensure that the victim of an 'unlawful' arrest or detention should have an enforceable right to compensation. In this regard, they have also contended that 'lawful' for the purposes of the various paragraphs of Article 5 is to be construed as essentially referring back to domestic law and in addition as excluding any element of arbitrariness. They concluded that even in the event of a violation being found of any of the first four paragraphs, there has been no violation of paragraph 5 because the applicants' deprivation of liberty was lawful under Northern Ireland law and was not arbitrary.

67. The Court, like the Commission, considers that such a restrictive interpretation is incompatible with the terms of paragraph 5 which refers to arrest or detention 'in contravention of the provisions of this Article'.

In the instant case, the applicants were arrested and detained lawfully under domestic law but in breach of paragraph 3 of Article 5. This violation could not give rise, either before or after the findings made by the European Court in the present judgment, to an enforceable claim for compensation by the victims before the domestic courts; this was not disputed by the Government.

Accordingly, there has also been a breach of paragraph 5 in this case in respect of all four applicants.

...

FOR THESE REASONS, THE COURT

...

4. Holds by thirteen votes to six that there has been a violation of Article 5 para. 5 in respect of all four applicants;

...

NOTES

1 The Court's rejection of the Government's narrow interpretation of Article 5(5) favours victims of breaches of earlier parts of this Article and is in accordance with the language of paragraph 5.

2   The Dutch Government was, however, successful in arguing that applicants must be able to show that they have suffered damage as a consequence of breaches of Article 5 rights if they are to be entitled to compensation under paragraph 5 in *Wassink v Netherlands* A.185-A (1990). The applicant had been subject to confinement in a psychiatric hospital by his local burgomaster under emergency powers (he had attacked members of his family and a neighbour). A few days later the President of the District Court authorized the applicant's continued confinement in the hospital after a hearing, which the applicant and his representative had attended. Subsequently, the applicant challenged the lawfulness of the District Court's decision, before the Strasbourg authorities, arguing that it violated Article 5(1) as a registrar had not been present to record the proceedings in accordance with Dutch law. The Strasbourg Court found a breach of Article 5(1) by a large majority (6 votes to 1).

36. The applicant alleged a violation of Article 5 § 5, according to which:

'Everyone who has been the victim of arrest or detention in contravention of the provisions of this Article shall have an enforceable right to compensation.'

In his opinion, the sole provision of Netherlands law which he could have relied on in order to obtain compensation, Article 1401 of the Civil Code, only applied where damage could be shown. In this case, the existence of damage would have been almost impossible to prove because it could not be affirmed with absolute certainty that proceedings conducted in conformity with Article 5 of the Convention would have led to the desired result.

37. Unlike the Commission, the Government did not subscribe to this view. They considered that the right to compensation guaranteed in paragraph 5 of Article 5 was restricted to persons who had sustained damage, whether pecuniary or non-pecuniary, on account of the violation of another of the paragraphs of the Article; this was clear, in particular, from the use of the word 'victim'. Article 1401 of the Civil Code was therefore fully consistent with the Convention.

38. In the Court's view, paragraph 5 of Article 5 is complied with where it is possible to apply for compensation in respect of a deprivation of liberty effected in conditions contrary to paragraphs 1, 2, 3 or 4 (art. 5-1, art. 5-2, art. 5-3, art. 5-4). It does not prohibit the Contracting States from making the award of compensation dependent upon the ability of the person concerned to show damage resulting from the breach. In the context of Article 5 § 5, as for that of Article 25 (see, *inter alia*, the *Huvig* [v *France*] judgment of 24 April 1990, Series A No 176-B, pp 56–7, § 35), the status of 'victim' may exist even where there is no damage, but there can be no question of 'compensation' where there is no pecuniary or non-pecuniary damage to compensate.

    More generally, the evidence provided to the Court does not lead to the conclusion that an action based on Article 1401 of the Netherlands Civil Code would have failed to satisfy the requirements of Article 5 § 5 of the Convention.

Therefore, the Court was unanimous in finding no breach of Article 5(5).

3   The full-time Court found a breach of Article 5(5) in *Beet and Others v UK*, p 271. The UK Government submitted that from 2 October 2000, the date when the Human Rights Act 1998 came into force, anyone imprisoned in violation of Article 5(1) had a domestic right to claim compensation from the Crown.

8

ARTICLE 6   RIGHT TO A FAIR TRIAL

Article 6(1)

The Court has delivered more judgments concerning this Article than any other right/ freedom guaranteed by the Convention. This is a consequence of both systemic failures in member States to organize their domestic judicial systems in ways which meet the minimum requirements of Article 6 (e.g. failing to ensure criminal courts are independent of the administration (*Incal*) or tolerating excessive delays in the judicial determination of cases (*Rumpf*)) and the breadth of the rights encompassed by Article 6. From its early case-law the Court has ruled that the concepts of 'civil rights and obligations' and a 'criminal charge' have autonomous meanings with the Strasbourg judiciary having the final say on whether particular proceedings fall within the protected categories. The Court has elaborated a number of requirements derived from the general obligation upon member States, under Article 6(1), to provide 'fair' hearings before domestic courts, extending from an effective right of access to a court (*Lawyer Partners AS*) to a right to silence for criminal suspects/defendants (*John Murray*). The requirement that domestic courts be independent and impartial has been firmly applied by the Strasbourg Court, for example in *Micallef*, where a national Chief Justice was found to have breached the objective test of impartiality. The Article 6(2) presumption of innocence of criminal defendants has been protected against adverse comments by both judges and senior public officials (*Allenet de Ribermont*). The specific Article 6(3) rights of criminal defendants have been interpreted and applied by the Court in ways that seek to ensure practical benefits for individuals, for example through the development of an implied right of access to a lawyer for suspects being interrogated by the police (*Salduz*).

Civil rights and obligations

Ringeisen v Austria A.13 (1971)
European Court of Human Rights

The applicant was an insurance agent and also dealt in real estate between 1958 and 1963. In 1961 he obtained general powers of attorney from Mr and Mrs Roth, who owned agricultural land in Upper Austria, and later that year he acquired an option to purchase their land. During February 1962 he made a contract with the Roths to purchase the land. From early 1962 Ringeisen had begun to sell part of the relevant land to various purchasers for building plots. In March 1962 Ringeisen submitted the Roths' contract for sale to the District Commission for its approval; this public authority had to be satisfied that the sale of agricultural land was in the public interest according to the Upper Austria Real Property Transactions Act. The District Commission refused to grant permission in September 1962 (it concluded the sale was for speculative building). Ringeisen then appealed to the Regional Real Property Transactions Commission, headed by a judge and seven other appointed persons. In May 1963 the Regional Commission dismissed his appeal. Ringeisen then successfully challenged the Regional Commission's conduct (some of the members had not fully participated in all the Commission's meetings) before the Constitutional Court. Ringeisen's appeal was remitted to the Regional Commission. He sought to challenge the composition of the Commission on the ground of bias, for example claiming that certain of the members had participated in the previous appeal. Ringeisen's challenges were dismissed and in February 1965 the Regional Commission rejected his appeal.

By early 1963 several persons, including the Roths, had laid criminal charges against Ringeisen in respect of his property dealings. The investigating judge first interviewed Ringeisen in February of that year. The indictment, containing charges of aggravated fraud and fraudulent conversion, was laid against him in April 1965. The trial began in December 1965 and was concluded in January 1966. Ringeisen was convicted of 78 counts of fraud and sentenced to three years' severe imprisonment. After several appeals, the Supreme Court upheld his convictions in February 1968.

Ringeisen complained to the Commission alleging, *inter alia*, breaches of Article 6 in respect of both the civil proceedings he had brought to challenge the authorities' refusal to approve his contract with the Roths and the criminal proceedings brought against him. By 7 votes to 5, the Commission expressed the opinion that Article 6(1) did not apply to the contract approval proceedings as they were not concerned with 'civil rights and obligations'. The Commission was also unanimous in concluding that the criminal proceedings against Ringeisen had been concluded within a reasonable time.

(c) As to the question whether the present complaint involves the determination of civil rights and obligations

94. For Article 6, paragraph (1) (art 6-1), to be applicable to a case ('contestation') it is not necessary that both parties to the proceedings should be private persons, which is the view of the majority of the Commission and of the Government. The wording of Article 6, paragraph (1) (art 6-1), is far wider; the French expression 'contestations sur (des) droits et obligations de caractère civil' covers all proceedings the result of which is decisive for private rights and obligations. The English text 'determination of... civil rights and obligations', confirms this interpretation.

The character of the legislation which governs how the matter is to be determined (civil, commercial, administrative law, etc.) and that of the authority which is invested with jurisdiction in the matter (ordinary court, administrative body, etc.) are therefore of little consequence.

In the present case, when Ringeisen purchased property from the Roth couple, he had a right to have the contract for sale which they had made with him approved if he fulfilled, as he claimed to do, the conditions laid down in the Act. Although it was applying rules of administrative law, the Regional Commission's decision was to be decisive for the relations in civil law ('de caractère civil') between Ringeisen and the Roth couple. This is enough to make it necessary for the Court to decide whether or not the proceedings in this case complied with the requirements of Article 6, paragraph (1) (art 6-1), of the Convention.

(c) As to whether the complaint that article 6, paragraph (1) (art 6-1), was not observed is well-founded

95. The Court has not found any facts to prove that Ringeisen was not given a 'fair hearing' of his case. Besides, the Court observes that the Regional Commission is a 'tribunal' within the meaning of Article 6, paragraph (1) (art 6-1), of the Convention as it is independent of the executive and also of the parties, its members are appointed for a term of five years and the proceedings before it

afford the necessary guarantees (see, *mutatis mutandis*, the *Neumeister* judgment of 27th June 1968, Series A, p 44, paragraph 24, and the *De Wilde, Ooms and Versyp* judgment of 18th June 1971, paragraph 78).

96. The applicant, however, accused six members of the Regional Commission of bias; when these complaints were brought before it, the Constitutional Court did not find it necessary to examine their substance for the reason that, as stated in its judgment of 27th September 1965, the question of bias had no bearing on the competence of the Regional Commission which was the only question submitted to its supervision...

97. It is not the function of the European Court to pronounce itself on the interpretation of Austrian law on which the said judgment is based or to express an opinion on the manner in which it was substantiated; on the other hand, it is the Court's duty to examine the grounds relied upon by Ringeisen and to determine whether or not the Regional Commission respected the rule of impartiality laid down in Article 6, paragraph (1) (art 6-1).

   The Court finds that even if Ringeisen's assertions were in fact true they would not support the conclusion that there was bias on the part of the Regional Commission. In the case of such a board with mixed membership comprising, under the presidency of a judge, civil servants and representatives of interested bodies, the complaint made against one member for the single reason that he sat as nominee of the Upper Austrian Chamber of Agriculture cannot be said to bear out a charge of bias. The same holds true for the complaint made against a member who was alleged by Ringeisen to have made certain statements the precise tenor of which the Regional Commission was, moreover, at pains to restore... As to the twofold fact that the president had represented the Regional Commission before the Constitutional Court in 1964 and that another member had been heard as a witness, this is obviously immaterial. Nor, finally, can any grounds of legitimate suspicion be found in the fact that two other members had participated in the first decision of the Regional Commission, for it cannot be stated as a general rule resulting from the obligation to be impartial that a superior court which sets aside an administrative or judicial decision is bound to send the case back to a different jurisdictional authority or to a differently composed branch of that authority.

98. Article 6, paragraph (1) (art 6-1), is not limited, however, to ensuring that in every determination of civil rights and obligations there must be a fair hearing within a reasonable time; it also requires, at least as a general rule, that the case be heard and the judgment pronounced in public.

   The Court could have verified, even proprio motu—and subject to the reopening of the hearings on this point—whether the District and Regional Commissions had complied with this rule or whether they were entitled to depart from it.

   The Court has not undertaken this examination because Austria's ratification of the Convention was made subject to the following reservation:

   '...The provisions of Article 6 (art 6) of the Convention shall be so applied that there shall be no prejudice to the principles governing public court hearings (im gerichtlichen Verfahren) laid down in Article 90 of the 1929 version of the Federal Constitution Law....'

The said Article 90 is worded as follows:

   'Hearings in civil and criminal cases (in Zivil- und Strafrechtssachen) by the trial court shall be oral and public. Exceptions may be prescribed by law....'

This reservation does not refer expressly to administrative proceedings but only to civil and criminal cases, that is, no doubt, the cases dealt with by the civil or criminal courts. Yet it must be accepted that the reservation covers a fortiori proceedings before administrative authorities where their subject matter is the determination of civil rights and where, therefore, the said authorities are considered to be tribunals within the meaning of Article 6, paragraph (1) (art 6-1). This is the case of the proceedings commenced by Ringeisen's request for approval on 30th March 1962.

99. For these reasons, the Court reaches the conclusion that there was no violation of Article 6, paragraph (1) (art 6-1), in the proceedings relating to that request.

...

III. AS TO THE QUESTION WHETHER THE DURATION OF THE CRIMINAL PROCEEDINGS AGAINST RINGEISEN EXCEEDED THE LIMITS OF A REASONABLE TIME AS LAID DOWN IN ARTICLE 6, PARAGRAPH (1) (ART 6-1)

110. The Court shares the Commission's opinion that the length of the fraud proceedings—preliminary investigations were opened on 21st February 1963 and the final decision was taken on 24th April 1968—resulted from both the complexity of the case and the innumerable requests and appeals made by Ringeisen not merely for his release, but also challenging most of the competent judges and for the transfer of the proceedings to different court areas.... The Court therefore reaches the conclusion that there was no violation of Article 6, paragraph (1) (art 6-1).

FOR THESE REASONS, THE COURT,

I. As to the question whether Ringeisen was the victim of a violation of Article 6, paragraph (1) (art 6-1), in the proceedings he introduced to obtain approval of a transfer of real property consisting of farmland...

3. Holds unanimously that Article 6, paragraph (1) (art 6-1), was applicable to the proceedings in question;

4. Holds unanimously that in the proceedings in question there has been no violation of Article 6, paragraph (1) (art 6-1); ...

III. As to the question whether the duration of the criminal proceedings against Ringeisen exceeded the limits of a reasonable time as laid down in Article 6, paragraph (1) (art 6-1)

8. Holds unanimously that in the proceedings in question there has been no violation of Article 6, paragraph (1) (art 6-1).

NOTES

1 The Court was composed of President Rolin and Judges: Holmback, Verdross, Wold, Zekia, Favre, and Sigurjonsson.

2 The above judgment is crucial for articulating the essence of the Court's conception of what types of rights and duties fall within the Convention notion of 'civil rights and obligations'. The Court focuses upon the substance of the rights/duties at issue to determine if they are 'private rights and obligations', such as the contractual and property rights being asserted by Ringeisen. Furthermore, the Court held that all forms of legal proceedings, including those before administrative authorities and courts exercising public law jurisdictions, could fall within the ambit of Article 6(1) where their determinations were decisive for this class of rights and obligations (see further, Note 9).

3 The Court elaborated upon its conception of 'civil rights and obligations' in the subsequent case of *König v Germany* A.27 (1978). The applicant opened a clinic, where he performed plastic surgery, at Bad Homburg in 1960. In 1962 the Regional Medical Society began proceedings against Dr Konig for unprofessional conduct and in 1964 he was declared unfit to practise. In April 1967 the Regierungsprasident in Wiesbaden (the senior officer of the provincial government), at the request of the Regional Medical Society, withdrew the applicant's authorization to run his clinic (an inspection had revealed numerous irregularities, including poor medical record-keeping and an unclean operating theatre). The applicant filed an objection, which was rejected, and then he appealed (in November 1967) to the Frankfurt Administrative Court against the Regierungsprasident's decision. The appeal was dismissed in June 1977. Konig's appeal to the Hessen Administrative Court of Appeal was still pending when the European Court gave its judgment. In May 1971 the Regierungsprasident in Darmstadt withdrew Konig's authorization to practise medicine. Konig's objection to that decision was dismissed in September 1971, and he then appealed to the Administrative Court (it was referred to another division of the Frankfurt Administrative Court). His appeal was dismissed in June 1976 (a further appeal by Konig to the Hessen Administrative Court of Appeal had not been finalized by the time of the European Court's decision). Konig complained to the Commission alleging that the dilatory nature of the Frankfurt Administrative Court's proceedings violated his right to the determination of his civil rights and obligations within a reasonable time as guaranteed by Article 6(1). The Commission, by 9 votes to 6—with 1 abstention, found a breach of that provision.

(a) On the applicability of Article 6 para 1 (art 6-1) of the Convention

86. The majority of the Commission is of the opinion that Article 6 para 1 (art 6-1) is applicable to the rights claimed by the applicant before the Frankfurt Administrative Court, namely the right to run his clinic and the right to exercise his profession of medical practitioner; it considers these rights to be 'civil' ...

The correctness of this opinion is disputed by the Government.

87. The Court notes at the outset that, as is not contested, under the legislation of the State concerned the actions brought by the applicant before the German courts concern 'rights'. The difference of view between Commission and Government relates only to the question whether the present case involves disputes ('contestations') over civil rights within the meaning of Article 6 para 1 (art 6-1) of the Convention.

88. Both the Commission and the Government agree that the concept of 'civil rights and obligations' cannot be interpreted solely by reference to the domestic law of the respondent State.

The problem of the 'autonomy' of the meaning of the expressions used in the Convention, compared with their meaning in domestic law, has already been raised before the Court on several occasions. Thus, it has decided that the word 'charge' appearing in Article 6 para 1 (art 6-1) has to be understood 'within the meaning of the Convention' (*Neumeister* judgment of 27 June 1968, Series A No 8, p 41, para 18, as compared with the second sub-paragraph on p 28 and the first sub-paragraph on p 35; see also *Wemhoff* judgment of 27 June 1968, Series A No 7, pp 26–7, para 19; *Ringeisen* judgment of 16 July 1971, Series A No 13, p 45 para 110; *Engel* judgment of 8 June 1976, Series A No 22, p 34 para 81). The Court has also recognised, in the context of the case of Engel, the 'autonomy' of the concept of 'criminal' within the meaning of Article 6 para 1 (art 6-1) (above-mentioned *Engel* judgment, p 34, para 81). Again, the Court has already acknowledged, implicitly, that the concept of 'civil rights and obligations' is autonomous (above-mentioned *Ringeisen* judgment, p 39, para 94).

The Court confirms this case-law on the present occasion. Hence, it considers that the same principle of autonomy applies to the concept in question; any other solution might lead to results incompatible with the object and purpose of the Convention (see, *mutatis mutandis*, the above-mentioned *Engel* and others judgment, p 34, para 81).

89. While the Court thus concludes that the concept of 'civil rights and obligations' is autonomous, it nevertheless does not consider that, in this context, the legislation of the State concerned is without importance. Whether or not a right is to be regarded as civil within the meaning of this expression in the Convention must be determined by reference to the substantive content and effects of the right—and not its legal classification—under the domestic law of the State concerned. In the

exercise of its supervisory functions, the Court must also take account of the object and purpose of the Convention and of the national legal systems of the other Contracting States (see, *mutatis mutandis*, the above-mentioned *Engel* and others judgment, p 35, para 82).

90. The Government submit that Article 6 para 1 (art 6-1) covers private-law disputes in the traditional sense, that is disputes between individuals or between an individual and the State to the extent that the latter had been acting as a private person, subject to private law; among other things, disputes between an individual and the State acting in its sovereign capacity would be excluded from the ambit of that Article (art 6-1).

As regards the field of application of Article 6 para 1 (art 6-1), the Court held in its *Ringeisen* judgment of 16 July 1971 that 'for Article 6 para 1 (art 6-1) to be applicable to a case ('contestation') it is not necessary that both parties to the proceedings should be private persons...The wording of Article 6 para 1 (art 6-1) is far wider; the French expression 'contestations sur (des) droits et obligations de caractère civil' covers all proceedings the result of which is decisive for private rights and obligations. The English text, 'determination of...civil rights and obligations', confirms this interpretation. The character of the legislation which governs how the matter is to be determined...and that of the authority which is invested with jurisdiction in the matter...are therefore of little consequence' (Series A No 13, p 39, para 94).

If the case concerns a dispute between an individual and a public authority, whether the latter had acted as a private person or in its sovereign capacity is therefore not conclusive.

Accordingly, in ascertaining whether a case ('contestation') concerns the determination of a civil right, only the character of the right at issue is relevant.

91. The Court recalls firstly that the applicant's appeals before the German administrative courts do not concern the right to be authorised to run a clinic and to be authorised to exercise the medical profession...in challenging the withdrawal of his authorisations ordered by the competent authorities, Dr König is claiming the right to continue his professional activities for which he had obtained the necessary authorisations. If the proceedings before the administrative courts were successful, the applicant would not be granted new authorisations: the Court would simply annul the withdrawal decisions taken by the Regierungspräsidenten in Wiesbaden and Darmstadt...

Therefore, it remains to be ascertained whether Dr König's right to continue to run a private clinic and his right to continue to exercise the medical profession are civil rights within the meaning of Article 6 para 1 (art 6-1).

92. The Court notes that, in the Federal Republic of Germany, the running of a private clinic is in certain respects a commercial activity carried on with a view to profit, classified by German law as a 'Gewerbe'. This activity is carried on in the private sector through the conclusion of contracts between the clinic and its patients and resembles the exercise of a private right in some ways akin to the right of property. Private clinics are certainly subject to supervision effected by the authorities in the public interest in order, *inter alia*, to protect health; supervision in the public interest, which moreover exists as a general rule for all private professional activities in the member States of the Council of Europe, cannot of itself lead to the conclusion that the running of a private clinic is a public-law activity. An activity presenting, under the law of the State concerned, the character of a private activity cannot automatically be converted into a public-law activity by reason of the fact that it is subject to administrative authorisations and supervision, including if appropriate the withdrawal of authorisations, provided for by law in the interests of public order and public health. The Court recalls in this context the Ringeisen case in which supervision by the public authorities concerned a contract for sale between private individuals: the Court nonetheless concluded that the right at issue had a civil character (above-mentioned judgment, p 39, para 94).

93. The medical profession counts, in the Federal Republic of Germany, among the traditional liberal professions...Even under the national health scheme, the medical profession is not a public

service: once authorised, the doctor is free to practise or not, and he provides treatment for his patients on the basis of a contract made with them. Of course, besides treating his patients, the medical practitioner, in the words of the above-mentioned Act, 'has the care of the health of the community as a whole'. This responsibility, which the medical profession bears towards society at large, does not, however, alter the private character of the medical practitioner's activity: while of great importance from the social point of view, that responsibility is accessory to his activity and its equivalent is to be found in other professions whose nature is undeniably private.

94. In these conditions, it is of little consequence that here the cases concern administrative measures taken by the competent bodies in the exercise of public authority. Neither does it appear pertinent that, under the law of the State concerned, it is for administrative courts to give the decision on these cases and to do so in proceedings which leave to the court the responsibility for the investigation and for the conduct of the trial. All that is relevant under Article 6 para 1 (art 6-1) of the Convention is the fact that the object of the cases in question is the determination of rights of a private nature.

95. Since it thus considers the rights affected by the withdrawal decisions and forming the object of the cases before the administrative courts to be private rights, the Court concludes that Article 6 para 1 (art 6-1) is applicable, without it being necessary in the present case to decide whether the concept of 'civil rights and obligations' within the meaning of that provision extends beyond those rights which have a private nature.

96. Before the Commission, the applicant claimed, in the alternative, that, in view of the nature of the complaints which led to the decisions he contests, he is in reality faced with a 'criminal charge' within the meaning of Article 6 para 1 (art 6-1) of the Convention.... However, the Court does not consider that it has to examine whether in this case paragraph 1 of Article 6 (art 6-1) is also relevant under the 'criminal charge' head. For, although the requirements of Article 6 (art 6) as regards cases ('contestations') concerning civil rights are less onerous than they are for criminal charges, this difference is of no consequence here: all proceedings covered by Article 6 (art 6) are subject to the requirement of a 'reasonable time', whose observance by the German courts remains to be examined.

(b) On the observance of Article 6 para 1 (art 6-1) of the Convention

97. According to the Commission, the duration of the proceedings instituted by the applicant before the administrative courts exceeded the 'reasonable time' stipulated by Article 6 para 1 (art 6-1) of the Convention. Before the Court, the Agent of the Government conceded that the length of those proceedings was a serious matter. She referred, moreover, to certain proposals under discussion in the Federal Republic of Germany designed to accelerate the procedure before the administrative courts. Although she questions whether, in the circumstances of the case, it is possible to speak of a violation of the Convention, she leaves it to the Court to assess whether the duration of the proceedings was reasonable.

98. In order to be able to arrive at a decision, the Court must first specify the period to be taken into account in the application of Article 6 para 1 (art 6-1).

According to the Government and the Commission, time starts to run from the date of the filing of the appeals with the Administrative Court of first instance. The Court does not share this view. As the Court stated in its *Golder* judgment of 21 February 1975, 'it is conceivable...that in civil matters the reasonable time may begin to run, in certain circumstances, even before the issue of the writ commencing proceedings before the court to which the plaintiff submits the dispute' (Series A No 18, p 15, para 32). This is the situation in the applicant's case, since he could not seise the competent court before having the lawfulness and the expediency of the impugned administrative acts examined in preliminary proceedings (Vorverfahren) before the administrative authority... Consequently, in the present case, the reasonable time stipulated by Article 6 para 1 (art 6-1) starts to run on the day on which Dr König lodged an objection against the withdrawals of his authorisations.

As regards the period to which Article 6 (art 6) is applicable, the Court has held that in criminal matters this period covers the whole of the proceedings in question, including appeal proceedings (above-mentioned *Wemhoff* judgment, pp 26 and 27, paras 18 and 20; above-mentioned *Neumeister* judgment, p 41, para 19; *Delcourt* judgment of 17 January 1970, Series A No 11, pp 13–15, paras 25 and 26). The position—as, moreover, the Government concede—is no different in the case of disputes ('contestations') over civil rights and obligations for which Article 6 para 1 (art 6-1) likewise requires that there be—at first instance, on appeal or in cassation—a determination.

99. The reasonableness of the duration of proceedings covered by Article 6 para 1 (art 6-1) of the Convention must be assessed in each case according to its circumstances. When enquiring into the reasonableness of the duration of criminal proceedings, the Court has had regard, *inter alia*, to the complexity of the case, to the applicant's conduct and to the manner in which the matter was dealt with by the administrative and judicial authorities (above-mentioned *Neumeister* judgment, pp 42–3, paras 20–1; above-mentioned *Ringeisen* judgment, p 45, para 110). The Court, like those appearing before it, considers that the same criteria must serve in the present case as the basis for its examination of the question whether the duration of the proceedings before the administrative courts exceeded the reasonable time stipulated by Article 6 para 1 (art 6-1).

100. Before embarking upon this examination, the Court wishes to emphasise that it is not its function to express an opinion on the German system of procedure before administrative courts which, as the Agent of the Government stated, enjoys a long tradition. Admittedly, the present system may appear complex on account of the number of courts and remedies but the Court is not unaware that the explanation for this situation is to be found in the eminently praiseworthy concern to reinforce the guarantees of individual rights. Should these efforts result in a procedural maze, it is for the State alone to draw the conclusions and, if need be, to simplify the system with a view to complying with Article 6 para 1 (art 6-1) of the Convention.

(i) The proceedings relative to the withdrawal of the authorisation to run the clinic

101. These proceedings, which began on 13 July 1967 when the applicant filed an objection against the withdrawal of the authorisation...have still not been concluded: the Hessen Administrative Court of Appeal has not yet ruled on Dr König's appeal against the judgment of 22 June 1977 of the 4th Chamber of the Frankfurt Administrative Court.

102. It is clearly a matter for serious concern—as the Government moreover admit—that more than ten years and ten months have elapsed without a decision on the merits of the case and that it was necessary to wait for almost ten years for the judgment at first instance.

It is true—and on this point the Court shares the Government's opinion—that the 4th Chamber of the Administrative Court encountered great difficulties in tracing witnesses several of whom had in the meantime changed name or address...

105. In an overall assessment of the various factors, the Court concludes that the delays occasioned by the difficulties in the investigation and by the applicant's behaviour do not of themselves justify the length of the proceedings. Without attaching decisive importance to any one step taken by the 4th Chamber rather than to another, the Court is in fact of the opinion that the principal reason for the length of the proceedings is to be found in the conduct of the case. The Court finds that it would have been possible for the 4th Chamber to bring the proceedings to an end at an earlier date. Taking into account the fact that the proceedings began on 13 July 1967 and ended on 22 June 1977, the Court concludes that the 'reasonable time' stipulated by Article 6 para 1 (art 6-1) was exceeded.

The Government stressed that Dr König's appeal had the effect of suspending enforcement of the withdrawal of the authorisation to run his clinic...and that this feature of the proceedings might have been to his advantage. The Court recognises that this suspensive effect may have a bearing on the interpretation of the concept of 'reasonable time'. However, in view of the total duration of the proceedings and the prolonged uncertainty in which the applicant found himself, the Court cannot depart, on the ground of the appeal's suspensive effect, from the assessment at which it has arrived above.

(ii) The proceedings relative to the withdrawal of the authorisation to practise

106. These proceedings began on 18 May 1971 when the applicant lodged his objection against the withdrawal of the authorisation to practise. The 2nd Chamber of the Frankfurt Administrative Court gave judgment on 9 June 1976, that is after more than five years of proceedings, and the Hessen Administrative Court of Appeal on 2 May 1978.

107. Although the length of these particular proceedings is not as great as that of the action relative to the withdrawal of the authorisation to run the clinic, it does not appear to the Court to be less serious.

This action seems less complex than the action before the 4th Chamber of the Administrative Court: not only did the 2nd Chamber encounter fewer difficulties as regards the hearing of the witnesses summoned, but also the enquiry was facilitated by the fact that, as early as 14 October 1970, the Regional Tribunal for the Medical Profession had declared Dr König unfit to practise...

111. In an overall assessment of the various factors and taking into account what was at stake in the proceedings, namely, Dr König's whole professional livelihood, the Court considers that, notwithstanding the delays attributable to the applicant's behaviour, the investigation of the case was not conducted with the necessary expedition....

Accordingly, the Court considers that in this case the 'reasonable time' stipulated by Article 6 para 1 (art 6-1) of the Convention was exceeded.

...

FOR THESE REASONS, THE COURT

1. holds by fifteen votes to one that Article 6 para 1 (art 6-1) is applicable to the proceedings relative to the withdrawal of the applicant's authorisation to run his clinic;

2. holds by fourteen votes to two that Article 6 para 1 (art 6-1) is applicable to the proceedings relative to the withdrawal of the applicant's authorisation to practise;

3. holds by fifteen votes to one that there has been a violation of Article 6 para 1 (art 6-1) as regards the duration of the proceedings relative to the withdrawal of the authorisation to run the clinic;

4. holds by fifteen votes to one that there has been a violation of Article 6 para 1 (art 6-1) as regards the duration of the proceedings relative to the withdrawal of the authorisation to practise;...

By the time of this judgment the Court was willing to express openly the ruling that the concept of 'civil rights and obligations' was an autonomous one (for the identical approach to the notion of 'criminal charge' see the extracts in the following section of this chapter).

4 Domestic proceedings determining the existence of a right to a licence can also come within this limb of Article 6(1) according to the Court. In **Benthem v Netherlands** A.97 (1985), the applicant had owned a garage, and during 1976 he applied to the municipal authority for a licence to build and operate a liquid petroleum gas installation at his garage. The municipal authority granted him the licence, however the Regional Health Inspector lodged an appeal with the Crown (i.e. central government) against the grant of the licence. The appeal was considered by the Administrative Litigation Division of the Council of State, which sought information from the Minister of Public Health and held a hearing (at which the applicant was heard). In June 1979 the Administrative Litigation Division sent an opinion to the Minister of Health recommending that the licence should be refused. A few weeks later the Crown issued a Decree quashing the municipal authority's decision to grant the licence to Benthem. The applicant complained to the Commission alleging that the dispute over his civil rights and obligations had not been heard by an independent and impartial tribunal in breach of Article 6(1). By 9 votes to 8, the Commission considered that provision was not applicable to Benthem's case. After citing its understanding of 'civil rights and obligations' expressed in *Ringeisen* and *Konig*, the Court applied those principles to the facts of these proceedings.

36. The grant of the licence to which the applicant claimed to be entitled was one of the conditions for the exercise of part of his activities as a businessman. It was closely associated with the right to use one's possessions in conformity with the law's requirements. In addition, a licence of this kind has a proprietary character, as is shown, *inter alia*, by the fact that it can be assigned to third parties.

According to the Government, Mr Benthem was prevented only from exploiting an LPG installation on a site of his own choosing, and could have obtained a licence for another locality. The Court is not persuaded by this argument: a change of this kind—which anyway would have involved an element of chance since it would have required a fresh application whose success was in no way guaranteed in advance—might have had adverse effects on the value of the business and of the goodwill and also on Mr Benthem's contractual relations with his customers and his suppliers. This confirms the existence of direct links between the grant of the licence and the entirety of the applicant's commercial activities.

In consequence, what was at stake was a 'civil' right, within the meaning of Article 6 para 1 (art 6-1). That provision was therefore applicable to the proceedings in the appeal to the Crown.

II. COMPLIANCE WITH ARTICLE 6 PARA 1 (ART 6-1)

37. In order to determine whether the proceedings complained of were in conformity with Article 6 para 1 (art 6-1), two institutions fall to be considered, namely the Administrative Litigation Division of the Council of State and the Crown.

A. THE ADMINISTRATIVE LITIGATION DIVISION OF THE COUNCIL OF STATE

38. The applicant relied on the fact that the Division merely tendered an advice, which had no binding force; in addition, it did not, in his submission, constitute an independent and impartial tribunal. On technical matters, it consulted the department of the competent Minister; the latter could request the Division to reconsider its draft Decree and was entitled, as a last resort, not to approve it. Moreover, the Division was not obliged to give its views within a specified time-limit and the text of its advice remained secret, being communicated neither to the appellant nor to the licence-holder nor to the issuing authority.

39. According to the Government, one had to look beyond the appearances in order to determine whether the proceedings in appeals to the Crown satisfied the requirements of Article 6 para 1 (art 6-1). Although the Division was not empowered to determine the dispute, it took cognisance of all the aspects of the case and not only of questions of law; in fact, it acted like a court, and only very rarely did the competent Minister not follow the Division's proposals to the letter.

40. The Court does not agree with this argument. It is true that, in order to decide whether the Convention rights have been infringed, one must frequently look beyond the appearances and the language used and concentrate on the realities of the situation (see, *inter alia*, as regards Article 5 para 1 (art 5-1), the *Van Droogenbroeck* judgment of 24 June 1982, Series A No 50, p 20, para 38). However, a power of decision is inherent in the very notion of 'tribunal' within the meaning of the

Convention (see the *Sramek* judgment of 22 October 1984, Series A No 84, p 17, para 36). Yet the Division tenders only an advice. Admittedly, that advice is—as happened on the present occasion—followed in the great majority of cases, but this is only a practice of no binding force, from which the Crown can depart at any moment... The proceedings before the Administrative Litigation Division of the Council of State thus do not provide the 'determination by a tribunal of the matters in dispute' which is required by Article 6 para 1 (art 6-1) (see notably the... *Albert and Le Compte* judgment, Series A No 58, p 16, para 29 *in fine*).

B. THE CROWN

41. According to the applicant, the proceedings in appeals to the Crown were of an administrative and not of a judicial nature, since there was a review not only of the lawfulness but also of the expediency of the decisions challenged.

In the present case, the appellant was the Regional Health Inspector; his superior was the Director General for Environmental Protection, and that official was also responsible for the department dealing with appeals to the Crown. Again, the technical opinion on which the Royal Decree was based reflected the provisional view of the Ministry and not of independent and impartial experts.

42. For the Government, on the other hand, the Crown was here exercising a function of an essentially judicial nature. Save very exceptionally, it followed the advice tendered by the Administrative Litigation Division of the Council of State and, indeed, had done so on this occasion. As for the Regional Inspector, he acted independently of the Minister where the entering of appeals was concerned.

43. It is true that the Crown, unlike the Administrative Litigation Division, is empowered to determine the dispute, but the Convention requires more than this: by the word 'tribunal', it denotes 'bodies which exhibit...common fundamental features', of which the most important are independence and impartiality, and 'the guarantees of judicial procedure'. The Court refers on this point to its established case-law, and notably to its *De Wilde, Ooms and Versyp* judgment of 18 June 1971 (Series A No 12, p 41, para 78).

However, the Royal Decree by which the Crown, as head of the executive, rendered its decision constituted, from the formal point of view, an administrative act and it emanated from a Minister who was responsible to Parliament therefor. Moreover, the Minister was the hierarchical superior of the Regional Health Inspector, who had lodged the appeal, and of the Ministry's Director General, who had submitted the technical report to the Division.

Finally, the Royal Decree was not susceptible to review by a judicial body as required by Article 6 para 1 (art 6-1).

C. CONCLUSION

44. There was accordingly a violation of Article 6 para 1 (art 6-1)....

5 The ownership of real property, which was also an element in **Benthem**, has been held to be a 'civil right' in **Zander v Sweden** A.279-B (1993). The applicants owned a piece of land which contained a well from which they drew their drinking water. In 1986 the National Licensing Board for Protection of the Environment granted a company permission to expand its household/industrial waste dump on land adjacent to the applicants' property. Under Swedish law there was no opportunity for the applicants to challenge that decision before the domestic courts. Therefore, the applicants complained to Strasbourg alleging a breach of Article 6(1). Both the Commission and the Court were unanimous in finding a breach of that provision. The Court held that, 'the right of property is clearly a "civil right" within the meaning of Article 6(1)...' (para 27).

6 The Court has held that an increasing range of social insurance and welfare assistance entitlements can be classified as 'civil rights' for the purposes of Article 6. This trend began with **Feldbrugge v Netherlands** A.99 (1986). During March 1978 the applicant's occupational insurance association determined that she was fit to resume work and therefore stopped paying her a sickness allowance. The applicant appealed, but the President of the Appeals Board, after considering medical reports, rejected her appeal. Mrs Feldbrugge also lost a further domestic appeal. She complained to the Commission alleging a breach of Article 6(1) in that she had not had a fair hearing of her appeals. The Commission, by 8 votes to 6, considered that her case did not fall within this Article. After citing its previous judgments in **Ringeisen** and **Konig**, the Court stated that:

27. As in previous cases, the Court does not consider that it has to give on this occasion an abstract definition of the concept of 'civil rights and obligations.'

This being the first time that the Court has had to deal with the field of social security, and more particularly the sickness insurance scheme in the Netherlands, the Court must identify such relevant factors as are capable of clarifying or amplifying the principles stated above.

(b) Supplementary factors disclosed by the subject matter of the litigation

28. Under Netherlands legislation, the right in issue is treated as a public-law right . . . This classification, however, provides only a starting point (see notably, *mutatis mutandis*, the *Engel* judgment of 8 June 1976, Series A No 22, p 35, para 82); it cannot be conclusive of the matter unless corroborated by other factors. In its *König* judgment of 28 June 1978, the Court stated in particular:

'Whether or not a right is to be regarded as civil . . . must be determined by reference to the substantive content and effects of the right—and not its legal classification—under the domestic law of the State concerned. In the exercise of its supervisory functions, the Court must also take account of the object and purpose of the Convention and of the national legal systems of the other Contracting States . . .' (Series A No 27, p 30, para 89)

29. There exists great diversity in the legislation and case-law of the member States of the Council of Europe as regards the juridical nature of the entitlement to health insurance benefits under social security schemes, that is to say as regards the category of law to which such entitlement belongs. Some States—including the Netherlands—treat it as a public-law right, whereas others, on the contrary, treat it as a private-law right; others still would appear to operate a mixed system. What is more, even within the same legal order differences of approach can be found in the case-law. Thus, in some States where the public-law aspect is predominant, some court decisions have nonetheless held Article 6 para 1 (art 6-1) to be applicable to claims similar to the one in issue in the present case (for example, the judgment of 11 May 1984 by the Brussels Labour Court, Journal des Tribunaux 1985, pp 168–169). Accordingly, there exists no common standard pointing to a uniform European notion in this regard.

30. An analysis of the characteristics of the Netherlands system of social health insurance discloses that the claimed entitlement comprises features of both public law and private law.

(i) Features of public law

31. A number of factors might tend to suggest that the dispute in question should be considered as one falling within the sphere of public law.

(1) Character of the legislation

32. The first such factor is the character of the legislation. The legal rules governing social security benefits in the context of health insurance differ in many respects from the rules which apply to insurance in general and which are part of civil law. The Netherlands State has assumed the responsibility of regulating the framework of the health insurance scheme and of overseeing the operation of that scheme. To this end, it specifies the categories of beneficiaries, defines the limits of the protection afforded, lays down the rates of the contributions and the allowances, etc.

In several cases (see notably *König*; *Le Compte, Van Leuven and De Meyere*; *Benthem*), State intervention by means of a statute or delegated legislation has nonetheless not prevented the Court from finding the right in issue to have a private, and hence civil, character. In the present case likewise, such intervention cannot suffice to bring within the sphere of public law the right asserted by the applicant.

(2) Compulsory nature of the insurance

33. A second factor of relevance is the obligation to be insured against illness or, more precisely, the fact of being covered by insurance in the event of fulfilling the conditions laid down by the legislation (see paragraph 38 below). In other words, those concerned can neither opt out of the benefits nor avoid having to pay the relevant contributions.

Comparable obligations can be found in other fields. Examples are provided by the rules making insurance cover compulsory for the performance of certain activities—such as driving a motor vehicle—or for householders. Yet the entitlement to benefits to which this kind of insurance contract gives rise cannot be qualified as a public-law right. The Court does not therefore discern why the obligation to belong to a health insurance scheme should change the nature of the corresponding right.

(3) Assumption by the State of responsibility for social protection

34. One final aspect to be considered is the assumption, by the State or by public or semi-public institutions, of full or partial responsibility for ensuring social protection. This was what happened in the present case by virtue of the health insurance scheme operated by the Occupational Association of the Banking and Insurance, Wholesale Trade and Self-Employment Sector in Amsterdam. Whether viewed as the culmination of or a stage in the development of the role of the State, such a factor implies, prima facie, an extension of the public-law domain....

35. In sum, even taken together the three foregoing factors, on analysis, do not suffice to establish that Article 6 (art 6) is inapplicable.

(ii) Features of private law

36. In contrast, various considerations argue in favour of the opposite conclusion.

(1) Personal and economic nature of the asserted right

37. To begin with, Mrs Feldbrugge was not affected in her relations with the public authorities as such, acting in the exercise of discretionary powers, but in her personal capacity as a private individual. She suffered an interference with her means of subsistence and was claiming a right flowing from specific rules laid down by the legislation in force.

For the individual asserting it, such a right is often of crucial importance; this is especially so in the case of health insurance benefits when the employee who is unable to work by reason of illness enjoys no other source of income. In short, the right in question was a personal, economic and individual right, a factor that brought it close to the civil sphere.

(2) Connection with the contract of employment

38. Secondly, the position of Mrs Feldbrugge was closely linked with the fact of her being a member of the working population, having been a salaried employee. The applicant was admittedly unemployed at the relevant time, but the availability of the health benefits was determined by reference to the terms of her former contract of employment and the legislation applicable to that contract.

The legal basis of the work that she had performed was a contract of employment governed by private law. While it is true that the insurance provisions derived directly from statute and not from an express clause in the contract, these provisions were in a way grafted onto the contract. They thus formed one of the constituents of the relationship between employer and employee.

In addition, the sickness allowance claimed by Mrs Feldbrugge was a substitute for the salary payable under the contract, the civil character of this salary being beyond doubt. This allowance shared the same nature as the contract and hence was also invested with a civil character for the purposes of the Convention.

(3) Affinities with insurance under the ordinary law

39. Finally, the Netherlands health insurance is similar in several respects to insurance under the ordinary law. Thus, under the Netherlands health insurance scheme recourse is had to techniques of risk covering and to management methods which are inspired by those current in the private insurance sphere. In the Netherlands, the occupational associations conduct their dealings, notably with those insured, in the same way as a company providing insurance under the ordinary law, for example as regards collection of contributions, calculation of risks, verification of fulfilment of the conditions for receipt of benefits, and payment of allowances.

There exists a further feature of relevance. Complementary insurance policies, taken out with friendly societies or private insurance companies, allow employees to improve their social protection at the price of an increased or fresh financial outlay; such policies constitute in sum an optional extension of compulsory insurance cover. Proceedings instituted in their connection are incontestably civil proceedings. Yet in both cases the risk insured against (for example, ill-health) is the same and, while the extent of the cover increases, the nature of the cover does not change.

Such differences as may exist between private sector insurance and social security insurance do not affect the essential character of the link between the insured and the insurer. Finally, the Court would draw attention to the fact that in the Netherlands, as in some other countries, the insured themselves participate in the financing of all or some of the social security schemes. Deductions at source are made from their salaries, which deductions establish a close connection between the contributions called for and the allowances granted. Thus, when Mrs Feldbrugge was working, her employer withheld from her pay a sum paid over to the Occupational Association...In addition, her employer also bore a portion of the insurance contributions, which were included in the firm's accounts under the head of social insurance expenses. The Netherlands State, for its part, was not involved in the financing of the scheme.

(c) Conclusion

40. Having evaluated the relative cogency of the features of public law and private law present in the instant case, the Court finds the latter to be predominant. None of these various features of private law is decisive on its own, but taken together and cumulatively they confer on the asserted entitlement the character of a civil right within the meaning of Article 6 para 1 (art 6-1) of the Convention, which was thus applicable....

This view was supported by ten judges, while seven dissented arguing that the applicant's entitlement was not a 'civil right'. The majority went on to find a breach of Article 6(1) as the president of the Appeals Board had not allowed Mrs Feldbrugge to participate in the proceedings (by either oral or written pleadings). In the later case of *Salesi v Italy* A.257-E (1990), a unanimous Court applied the majority's analytical framework developed in *Feldbrugge* to a non-contributory welfare assistance entitlement. Mrs Salesi was refused a monthly disability allowance by the government. During February 1986 she began legal proceedings, in the Rome magistrate's court, to challenge that decision. The Court of Cassation finally determined the case in March 1992. She complained to the Commission claiming that the domestic courts had not determined her 'civil rights' within a reasonable time as required by Article 6(1). By 13 votes to 8 the Commission upheld her complaint.

19. The Court is here once again confronted with the issue of the applicability of Article 6 para 1 (art 6-1) to social security disputes. The question arose earlier in the cases of *Feldbrugge v the Netherlands* and *Deumeland v Germany*, in which it gave judgment on 29 May 1986 (Series A nos 99 and 100). At that time the Court noted that there was great diversity in the legislation and practice

of the member States of the Council of Europe as regards the nature of the entitlement to insurance benefits under social security schemes. Nevertheless, the development in the law that was initiated by those judgments and the principle of equality of treatment warrant taking the view that today the general rule is that Article 6 para 1 (art 6-1) does apply in the field of social insurance.

In the present case, however, the question arises in connection with welfare assistance and not, as in the cases previously cited, social insurance. Certainly there are differences between the two, but they cannot be regarded as fundamental at the present stage of development of social security law. This justifies following, in relation to the entitlement to welfare allowances, the opinion which emerges from the aforementioned judgments as regards the classification of the right to social insurance benefits, namely that State intervention is not sufficient to establish that Article 6 para 1 (art 6-1) is inapplicable.

As in the two cases previously referred to, other considerations argue in favour of the applicability of Article 6 para 1 (art 6-1) in the instant case. The most important of these lies in the fact that despite the public law features pointed out by the Government, Mrs Salesi was not affected in her relations with the administrative authorities as such, acting in the exercise of discretionary powers; she suffered an interference with her means of subsistence and was claiming an individual, economic right flowing from specific rules laid down in a statute giving effect to the Constitution...

The protection of this basic right is, moreover, organised in such a way that at the judicial stage disputes over it come within the jurisdiction of the ordinary court, the labour magistrate's court (pretore del lavoro).

In sum, the Court sees no convincing reason to distinguish between Mrs Salesi's right to welfare benefits and the rights to social insurance benefits asserted by Mrs Feldbrugge and Mr Deumeland.

Article 6 para 1 (art 6-1) therefore applies in the instant case....

As the domestic proceedings were not complex and the applicant had not contributed to the delay, the Court found that they had not been completed within a 'reasonable' time. In terms of the Court's application of the concept of 'civil rights' in the above cases the decisive consideration was that private law factors outweighed those of public law. How significant do you think it was that both Mrs Feldbrugge and Mrs Salesi had rights under domestic law to the social insurance and welfare assistance benefits they were claiming? The Court has also utilized the *Feldbrugge* method of analysis to determine that compulsory contributions to a social insurance scheme could be classified as 'civil rights and obligations' in *Schouten and Meldrum v Netherlands* A.304 (1994). The applicants were physiotherapists and their occupational insurance association demanded that they pay health and disability insurance contributions in respect of other physiotherapists who used their premises. According to the applicants, the time taken by the domestic tribunals to determine their appeals breached Article 6(1). The Court unanimously found that the duration of the proceedings (four years, three months and three years, three months) exceeded the 'reasonable time' requirement laid down in that provision.

The full-time Court has adopted an expansive approach to the classification of welfare benefits as 'possessions' falling within Article 1 of Protocol No 1: *Stec and Others v UK*, decision of 6 July 2005.

7 The Court's approach to determining if civil servants can bring their employment disputes within Article 6(1) has undergone dramatic changes during recent times. In *Pellegrin v France*, judgment of 8 December 1999, a Grand Chamber sought to clarify the existing case-law by providing a new functional categorization of when particular civil servants would fall outside the protection of Article 6(1) (those whose duties '66....typify the specific activities of the public service in so far as the latter is acting as the depository of public

authority responsible for protecting the general interests of the State or other public authorities'). However, a few years later another Grand Chamber effectively replaced that test with a new one in *Vilho Eskelinen and others v Finland*, judgment of 19 April 2007. The applicants were police officers and a civilian office assistant who disputed the removal of wage supplements from them when their police district was re-organized. Their appeals up to the Supreme Administrative Court took seven years. They subsequently lodged a complaint at Strasbourg alleging, *inter alia*, a breach of the reasonable time guarantee in Article 6(1). The Finnish Government contended that applying the *Pellegrin* test the police officer applicants fell outside the scope of Article 6(1). A larger majority of the Grand Chamber, 12 voted to 5, held that:

55. The Court can only conclude that the functional criterion, as applied in practice, has not simplified the analysis of the applicability of Article 6 in proceedings to which a civil servant is a party or brought about a greater degree of certainty in this area as intended . . .

56. It is against this background and for these reasons that the Court finds that the functional criterion adopted in the case of *Pellegrin* must be further developed.

. . .

62. To recapitulate, in order for the respondent State to be able to rely before the Court on the applicant's status as a civil servant in excluding the protection embodied in Article 6, two conditions must be fulfilled. Firstly, the State in its national law must have expressly excluded access to a court for the post or category of staff in question. Secondly, the exclusion must be justified on objective grounds in the State's interest. The mere fact that the applicant is in a sector or department which participates in the exercise of power conferred by public law is not in itself decisive. In order for the exclusion to be justified, it is not enough for the State to establish that the civil servant in question participates in the exercise of public power or that there exists, to use the words of the Court in the *Pellegrin* judgment, a 'special bond of trust and loyalty' between the civil servant and the State, as employer. It is also for the State to show that the subject matter of the dispute in issue is related to the exercise of State power or that it has called into question the special bond. Thus, there can in principle be no justification for the exclusion from the guarantees of Article 6 of ordinary labour disputes, such as those relating to salaries, allowances or similar entitlements, on the basis of the special nature of relationship between the particular civil servant and the State in question. There will, in effect, be a presumption that Article 6 applies. It will be for the respondent Government to demonstrate, first, that a civil-servant applicant does not have a right of access to a court under national law and, second, that the exclusion of the rights under Article 6 for the civil servant is justified.

As all the applicants had the right to bring actions in the domestic courts regarding their wage supplements the Grand Chamber determined that Article 6(1) was applicable and there had been a breach caused by unreasonable delays in the Finnish proceedings.

The five dissentients, led by President Costa and former President Wildhaber, issued a joint opinion in which they criticized the analysis of the majority.

6. In any event, we fail to see what theoretical or practical necessity required the Court to abandon the *Pellegrin* case-law in the present case. It has been applied by the Court for seven years without any real problem and, as could have been expected and desired, it has extended rather than restricted the application of the guarantees secured under Article 6(1). . . .

7. In conclusion, the Court has overturned its well-established case-law. Admittedly, it is entitled to do so (even if the case-law in question is relatively recent). In general, however, the Court takes this

step where there are new developments and where a new need arises. This is not the case here. Abandoning a solid precedent in such conditions creates legal uncertainty and, in our opinion, will make it difficult for the States to identify the extent of their obligations.

This is a fascinating example of strong disagreements amongst Grand Chamber judges as to whether certainty in the Court's jurisprudence required the maintenance of an existing interpretation or the development of a new one (see further A. Mowbray, 'An Examination of the European Court of Human Rights' Approach to Overruling its Previous Case Law' (2009) 9(2) *Human Rights Law Review* 179). Civil servants will, however, be pleased that the **Vilho** criteria make it more difficult for governments successfully to contend that public servants fall outside the scope of the civil rights and obligations limb of Article 6(1).

8 A Grand Chamber, by 11 votes to 6, confirmed the established approach of the Strasbourg institutions that tax proceedings do not fall within the scope of 'civil rights and obligations' in **Ferrazzini v Italy**, judgment of 12 July 2001. The applicant claimed that, *inter alia*, his capital-gains tax liabilities had not been determined by the domestic authorities in a reasonable time as required by Article 6(1).

21. The Government argued that Article 6 was inapplicable to the proceedings in question, considering that they did not concern a 'civil right'. The existence of an individual's tax obligation vis-à-vis the State belonged, in their submission, exclusively to the realm of public law. That obligation was part of the civic duties imposed in a democratic society and the purpose of the specific provisions of public law was to support national economic policy.

22. The applicant, for his part, stressed the pecuniary aspect of his claims and contended that the proceedings accordingly concerned 'civil rights and obligations'.

23. As it is common ground that there was a 'dispute' (contestation), the Court's task is confined to determining whether it was over 'civil rights and obligations'.

24. According to the Court's case-law, the concept of 'civil rights and obligations' cannot be interpreted solely by reference to the domestic law of the respondent State. The Court has on several occasions affirmed the principle that this concept is 'autonomous', within the meaning of Article 6 § 1 of the Convention (see, among other authorities, *König v Germany*, judgment of 28 June 1978, Series A No 27, pp 29–30, §§ 88–9, and *Baraona v Portugal*, judgment of 8 July 1987, Series A No 122, pp 17–18, § 42). The Court confirms this case-law in the instant case. It considers that any other solution is liable to lead to results that are incompatible with the object and purpose of the Convention (see, *mutatis mutandis*, *König*, cited above, pp 29–30, § 88, and *Maaouia v France* [GC], No 39652/98, § 34, ECHR 2000-X).

25. Pecuniary interests are clearly at stake in tax proceedings, but merely showing that a dispute is 'pecuniary' in nature is not in itself sufficient to attract the applicability of Article 6 § 1 under its 'civil' head (see *Pierre-Bloch v France*, judgment of 21 October 1997, Reports of Judgments and Decisions 1997-VI, p 2223, § 51, and *Pellegrin v France* [GC], No 28541/95, § 60, ECHR 1999-VIII; cf. *Editions Périscope v France*, judgment of 26 March 1992, Series A No 234-B, p 66, § 40). In particular, according to the traditional case-law of the Convention institutions:

'There may exist "pecuniary" obligations vis-à-vis the State or its subordinate authorities which, for the purpose of Article 6 § 1, are to be considered as belonging exclusively to the realm of public law and are accordingly not covered by the notion of "civil rights and obligations". Apart from fines imposed by way of "criminal sanction", this will be the case, in particular, where an obligation which is pecuniary in nature derives from tax legislation or is otherwise part of normal civic duties in a democratic society'. (See, among other authorities, *Schouten and Meldrum v*

The Netherlands, judgment of 9 December 1994, Series A No 304, p 21, § 50; *Company S. and T. v Sweden*, No 11189/84, Commission decision of 11 December 1986, Decisions and Reports (DR) 50, p 121, at p 140; and *Kustannus oy Vapaa Ajattelija AB, Vapaa-Ajattelijain Liitto—Fritänkarnas Förbund r.y. and Kimmo Sundström v Finland*, No 20471/92, Commission decision of 15 April 1996, DR 85-A, p 29, at p 46).

26. The Convention is, however, a living instrument to be interpreted in the light of present-day conditions (see, among other authorities, *Johnston and Others v Ireland*, judgment of 18 December 1986, Series A No 112, pp 24–5, § 53), and it is incumbent on the Court to review whether, in the light of changed attitudes in society as to the legal protection that falls to be accorded to individuals in their relations with the State, the scope of Article 6 § 1 should not be extended to cover disputes between citizens and public authorities as to the lawfulness under domestic law of the tax authorities' decisions.

27. Relations between the individual and the State have clearly evolved in many spheres during the fifty years which have elapsed since the Convention was adopted, with State regulation increasingly intervening in private-law relations. This has led the Court to find that procedures classified under national law as being part of 'public law' could come within the purview of Article 6 under its 'civil' head if the outcome was decisive for private rights and obligations, in regard to such matters as, to give some examples, the sale of land, the running of a private clinic, property interests, the granting of administrative authorisations relating to the conditions of professional practice or of a licence to serve alcoholic beverages (see, among other authorities, *Ringeisen v Austria*, judgment of 16 July 1971, Series A No 13, p 39, § 94; *König*, cited above, p 32, §§ 94–5; *Sporrong and Lönnroth v Sweden*, judgment of 23 September 1982, Series A No 52, p 29, § 79; *Allan Jacobsson v Sweden (no. 1)*, judgment of 25 October 1989, Series A No 163, pp 20–1, § 73; *Benthem v The Netherlands*, judgment of 23 October 1985, Series A No 97, p 16, § 36; and *Tre Traktörer AB v Sweden*, judgment of 7 July 1989, Series A No 159, p 19, § 43). Moreover, the State's increasing intervention in the individual's day-to-day life, in terms of welfare protection for example, has required the Court to evaluate features of public law and private law before concluding that the asserted right could be classified as 'civil' (see, among other authorities, *Feldbrugge v The Netherlands*, judgment of 29 May 1986, Series A No 99, p 16, § 40; *Deumeland v Germany*, judgment of 29 May 1986, Series A No 100, p 25, § 74; *Salesi v Italy*, judgment of 26 February 1993, Series A No 257-E, pp 59–60, § 19; and *Schouten and Meldrum*, cited above, p 24, § 60).

28. However, rights and obligations existing for an individual are not necessarily civil in nature. Thus, political rights and obligations, such as the right to stand for election to the National Assembly (see *Pierre-Bloch*, cited above, p 2223, § 50), even though in those proceedings the applicant's pecuniary interests were at stake (ibid, § 51), are not civil in nature, with the consequence that Article 6 § 1 does not apply. Neither does that provision apply to disputes between administrative authorities and those of their employees who occupy posts involving participation in the exercise of powers conferred by public law (see *Pellegrin*, cited above, §§ 66–7). Similarly, the expulsion of aliens does not give rise to disputes (contestations) over civil rights for the purposes of Article 6 § 1 of the Convention, which accordingly does not apply (see *Maaouia*, cited above, §§ 37–8).

29. In the tax field, developments which might have occurred in democratic societies do not, however, affect the fundamental nature of the obligation on individuals or companies to pay tax. In comparison with the position when the Convention was adopted, those developments have not entailed a further intervention by the State into the 'civil' sphere of the individual's life. The Court considers that tax matters still form part of the hard core of public-authority prerogatives, with the public nature of the relationship between the taxpayer and the community remaining predominant. Bearing in mind that the Convention and its Protocols must be interpreted as a whole, the Court also observes that Article 1 of Protocol No 1, which concerns the protection of property, reserves

the right of States to enact such laws as they deem necessary for the purpose of securing the payment of taxes (see, *mutatis mutandis, Gasus Dosier und Fördertechnik GmbH v The Netherlands*, judgment of 23 February 1995, Series A No 306-B, pp. 48–9, § 60). Although the Court does not attach decisive importance to that factor, it does take it into account. It considers that tax disputes fall outside the scope of civil rights and obligations, despite the pecuniary effects which they necessarily produce for the taxpayer.

30. The principle according to which the autonomous concepts contained in the Convention must be interpreted in the light of present-day conditions in democratic societies does not give the Court power to interpret Article 6 § 1 as though the adjective 'civil' (with the restriction that that adjective necessarily places on the category of 'rights and obligations' to which that Article applies) were not present in the text.

31. Accordingly, Article 6 § 1 of the Convention does not apply in the instant case.

Of course, if penal tax proceedings satisfy the *Engel* criteria (see p 368) they can be classified as involving a 'criminal charge' and fall under that limb of Article 6: see, for example, *Bendenoun v France*, judgment of 24 February 1994, where the Court found proceedings involving the imposition of substantial tax surcharges (totalling nearly £100,000) should be so categorized.

9 In order to be able to invoke this limb of Article 6(1) applicants must be able to satisfy the Court that there is (or had been) a 'contestation' (dispute) regarding their 'civil rights and obligations' at the domestic level. The Court elaborated its understanding of this requirement in *Le Compte, Van Leuven and De Meyere v Belgium* A.43 (1981). The applicants were medical doctors who had been found to have breached professional rules, governing contempt for the Ordre and fellow doctors, by the Provincial Council and Appeals Council of the Ordre des medecins (Belgian Medical Association). The applicants' appeals to the courts against those findings and the related suspensions of their rights to practise (three months for Dr Le Compte and 15 days for the other applicants) were unsuccessful. They complained to the Commission alleging, *inter alia*, breaches of their right to a fair hearing under Article 6(1) in respect of the domestic proceedings. The Commission, by 8 votes to 3, found a violation of the right to a public hearing contained in that provision.

1. The existence of 'contestations' (disputes) over 'civil rights and obligations'

44. In certain respects, the meaning of the words 'contestations' (disputes) over 'civil rights and obligations' has been clarified in the Ringeisen judgment of 16 July 1971 and the *König* judgment of 28 June 1978.

According to the first of these judgments, the phrase in question covers 'all proceedings the result of which is decisive for private rights and obligations', even if the proceedings concern a dispute between an individual and a public authority acting in its sovereign capacity; the character 'of the legislation which governs how the matter is to be determined' and of the 'authority' which is invested with jurisdiction in the matter are of little consequence (Series A No 13, p 39, par 94).

The very notion of 'civil rights and obligations' lay at the heart of the *König* case. The rights at issue included the right 'to continue his professional activities' as a medical practitioner 'for which he had obtained the necessary authorisations'. In the light of the circumstances of that case, the Court classified this right as private, and hence as civil for the purposes of Article 6 par 1 (art 6-1) (*loc. cit.*, pp 29–32, par 88–91 and 93–5).

The ramifications of this line of authority are again considerably extended as a result of the *Golder* judgment of 21 February 1975. The Court concluded that 'Article 6 par 1 (art 6-1) secures to everyone the right to have any claim relating to his civil rights and obligations brought before a court or tribunal' (Series A No 18, p 18, par 36). One consequence of this is that Article 6 par 1 (art 6-1) is not applicable solely to proceedings which are already in progress: it may also be relied on by anyone who considers that an interference with the exercise of one of his (civil) rights is unlawful and complains that he has not had the possibility of submitting that claim to a tribunal meeting the requirements of Article 6 par 1 (art 6-1).

45. In the present case, a preliminary point needs to be resolved: can it be said that there was a veritable 'contestation' (dispute), in the sense of 'two conflicting claims or applications' (oral submissions of counsel for the Government)?

Conformity with the spirit of the Convention requires that this word should not be construed too technically and that it should be given a substantive rather than a formal meaning; besides, it has no counterpart in the English text of Article 6 par 1 (art 6-1) ('In the determination of his civil rights and obligations'; cf Article 49 (art 49): 'dispute').

Even if the use of the French word 'contestation' implies the existence of a disagreement, the evidence clearly shows that there was one in this case. The Ordre des médecins alleged that the applicants had committed professional misconduct rendering them liable to sanctions and they denied those allegations. After the competent Provincial Council had found them guilty of that misconduct and ordered their suspension from practice—decisions that were taken in absentia in the case of Dr Le Compte (West Flanders) and after hearing submissions on issues of fact and of law from Dr Van Leuven and Dr De Meyere in their cases (East Flanders)—the applicants appealed to the Appeals Council. They all appeared before that Council where, with the assistance of lawyers, they pleaded among other things Articles 6 par 1 and 11 (art 6-1, art 11). In most respects their appeals proved unsuccessful, whereupon they turned to the Court of Cassation relying once more, *inter alia*, on the Convention . . .

46. In addition, it must be shown that the 'contestation' (dispute) related to 'civil rights and obligations', in other words that the 'result of the proceedings' was 'decisive' for such a right (see the above-mentioned *Ringeisen* judgment).

According to the applicants, what was at issue was their right to continue to exercise their profession; they maintained that this had been recognised to be a 'civil' right in the *König* judgment of 28 June 1978 (*loc. cit.*, pp 31–2, paragraphs 91 and 93).

According to the Government, the decisions of the Provincial and Appeals Councils had but an 'indirect effect' in the matter. It was argued that these organs, unlike the German administrative courts in the *König* case, did not review the lawfulness of an earlier measure withdrawing the right to practise but had instead to satisfy themselves that breaches of the rules of professional conduct, of a kind justifying disciplinary sanctions, had actually occurred. A 'contestation' (dispute) over the right to continue to exercise the medical profession was said to have arisen, if at all, 'at a later stage', that is when Dr Le Compte, Dr Van Leuven and Dr De Meyere contested before the Court of Cassation the lawfulness of the measures imposed on them. The Government further submitted that this right was not 'civil' and invited the Court not to follow the decision which it took in this respect in the *König* judgment.

47. As regards the question whether the dispute related to the above-mentioned right, the Court considers that a tenuous connection or remote consequences do not suffice for Article 6 par 1 (art 6-1), in either of its official versions ('contestation sur', 'determination of'): civil rights and obligations must be the object—or one of the objects—of the 'contestation' (dispute); the result of the proceedings must be directly decisive for such a right.

While the Court agrees with the Government on this point, it does not agree that in the present case there was not this kind of direct relationship between the proceedings in question and the right to continue to exercise the medical profession. The suspensions ordered by the Provincial Council on 30 June 1971 (Dr Le Compte) and on 24 October 1973 (Dr Van Leuven and Dr De Meyere) were to deprive them temporarily of their rights to practise. That right was directly in issue before the Appeals Council and the Court of Cassation, which bodies had to examine the applicants' complaints against the decisions affecting them.

48. Furthermore, it is by means of private relationships with their clients or patients that medical practitioners in private practice, such as the applicants, avail themselves of the right to continue to practise; in Belgian law, these relationships are usually contractual or quasi-contractual and, in any event, are directly established between individuals on a personal basis and without any intervention of an essential or determining nature by a public authority. Accordingly, it is a private right that is at issue, notwithstanding the specific character of the medical profession—a profession which is exercised in the general interest—and the special duties incumbent on its members.

The Court thus concludes that Article 6 par 1 (art 6-1) is applicable; as in the *König* case (see the above-mentioned judgment, p 32, par 95), it does not have to determine whether the concept of 'civil rights' extends beyond those rights which have a private nature.

49. Two members of the Commission, Mr Frowein and Mr Polak, emphasised in their dissenting opinion that the present proceedings did not concern a withdrawal of the authorisation to practise, as did the König case, but a suspension for a relatively short period—three months for Dr Le Compte and fifteen days for Dr Van Leuven and Dr de Meyere. These members maintained that a suspension of this kind did not impair a civil right but was to be regarded as no more than a limitation inherent therein.

The Court is not convinced by this argument, which the Government adopted as a further alternative plea in paragraph 19 of their memorial. Unlike certain other disciplinary sanctions that might have been imposed on the applicants (warning, censure and reprimand...), the suspension of which they complained undoubtedly constituted a direct and material interference with the right to continue to exercise the medical profession. The fact that the suspension was temporary did not prevent its impairing that right (see, *mutatis mutandis*, the above-mentioned *Golder* judgment, p 13, par 26); in the 'contestations' (disputes) contemplated by Article 6 par 1 (art 6-1) the actual existence of a 'civil' right may, of course, be at stake but so may the scope of such a right or the manner in which the beneficiary may avail himself thereof.

50. Since the dispute over the decisions taken against the applicants has to be regarded as a dispute relating to 'civil rights and obligations', it follows that they were entitled to have their case (in French: 'cause') heard by 'a tribunal' satisfying the conditions laid down in Article 6 par 1 (art 6-1) (see the above-mentioned *Golder* judgment, p 18, par 36).

51. In fact, their case was dealt with by three bodies—the Provincial Council, the Appeals Council and the Court of Cassation. The question therefore arises whether those bodies met the requirements of Article 6 par 1 (art 6-1).

(a) The Court does not consider it indispensable to pursue this point as regards the Provincial Council. While Article 6 par 1 (art 6-1) embodies the 'right to a court' (see paragraph 44 above), it nevertheless does not oblige the Contracting States to submit 'contestations' (disputes) over 'civil rights and obligations' to a procedure conducted at each of its stages before 'tribunals' meeting the Article's various requirements. Demands of flexibility and efficiency, which are fully compatible with the protection of human rights, may justify the prior intervention of administrative or professional bodies and, a fortiori, of judicial bodies which do not satisfy the said requirements in every respect; the legal tradition of many Member states of the Council of Europe may be invoked in support of such a system...

(b) Once the Provincial Council had imposed on Dr Le Compte, Dr Van Leuven and Dr De Meyere a temporary ban on the exercise of their profession, they appealed to the Appeals Council which thus had to determine the dispute over the right in question.

According to the Government, the Appeals Council nevertheless did not have to meet the conditions contained in Article 6 par 1 (art 6-1) since an appeal on a point of law against its decision lay to the Court of Cassation and that Court's procedure certainly did satisfy those conditions.

The Court does not agree. For civil cases, just as for criminal charges (see the *Deweer* judgment of 27 February 1980, Series A No 35, pp 24–5, par 48), Article 6 par 1 (art 61) draws no distinction between questions of fact and questions of law. Both categories of question are equally crucial for the outcome of proceedings relating to 'civil rights and obligations'. Hence, the 'right to a court' (see the above-mentioned *Golder* judgment, p 18, par 36) and the right to a judicial determination of the dispute (see the above-mentioned *König* judgment, p 34, par 98 *in fine*) cover questions of fact just as much as questions of law. Yet the Court of Cassation does not have jurisdiction to rectify factual errors or to examine whether the sanction is proportionate to the fault... It follows that Article 6 par 1 (art 6-1) was not satisfied unless its requirements were met by the Appeals Council itself....

B. COMPLIANCE WITH ARTICLE 6 PAR 1 (ART 6-1)

54. Having regard to the conclusion at paragraph 51 above, it has to be established whether in the exercise of their jurisdiction both the Appeals Council and the Court of Cassation met the conditions laid down by Article 6 par 1 (art 6-1), the former because it alone fully examined measures affecting a civil right and the latter because it conducted a final review of the lawfulness of those measures...

59. Under the Royal Decree of 6 February 1970, all publicity before the Appeals Council is excluded in a general and absolute manner, both for the hearings and for the pronouncement of the decision...

Article 6 par 1 (art 6-1) of the Convention does admittedly provide for exceptions to the rule requiring publicity—at least in respect of the trial of the action—, but it makes them subject to certain conditions. However, there is no evidence to suggest that any of these conditions was satisfied in the present case. The very nature both of the misconduct alleged against the applicants and of their own complaints against the Ordre was not concerned with the medical treatment of their patients. Consequently, neither matters of professional secrecy nor protection of the private life of these doctors themselves or of patients were involved; the Court does not concur with the Government's argument to the contrary. Furthermore, there is nothing to indicate that other grounds, among those listed in the second sentence of Article 6 par 1 (art 61), could have justified sitting in camera; the Government, moreover, did not rely on any such ground.

Dr Le Compte, Dr Van Leuven and Dr de Meyere were thus entitled to have the proceedings conducted in public. Admittedly, neither the letter nor the spirit of Article 6 par 1 (art 6-1) would have prevented them from waiving this right of their own free will, whether expressly or tacitly (cf the above-mentioned *Deweer* judgment, p 26, par 49); conducting disciplinary proceedings of this kind in private does not contravene the Convention, provided that the person concerned consents. In the present case, however, the applicants clearly wanted and claimed a public hearing. To refuse them such a hearing was not permissible under Article 6 par 1 (art 6-1), since none of the circumstances set out in its second sentence existed.

60. The public character of the proceedings before the Belgian Court of Cassation cannot suffice to remedy this defect. In fact, the Court of Cassation 'shall not take cognisance of the merits of cases' (Article 95 of the Constitution and Article 23 of Royal Decree No 79); this means that numerous issues arising in 'contestations' (disputes) concerning 'civil rights and obligations' fall outside its jurisdiction... On the issues of this nature arising in the present case, there was neither a public hearing nor a decision pronounced publicly as required by Article 6 par 1 (art 6-1).

61. To sum up, the applicants' case (in French: 'cause') was not heard publicly by a tribunal competent to determine all the aspects of the matter. In this respect, there was, in the particular circumstances, a breach of Article 6 par 1 (art 6-1)....

Sixteen judges agreed with the above conclusion and four dissented. The Court was willing to find the existence of a 'contestation' regarding 'civil rights and obligations' where domestic proceedings were decisive for a range of issues associated with such entitlements and duties (including the scope and availability of these provisions). The Article 11 aspects of this case are also examined at p 753.

In *Micallef v Malta*, judgment of 15 October 2009, a Grand Chamber held that interim measures (such as interlocutory injunctions) issued by civil courts would be treated as falling within Article 6(1) where (a) the proceedings concerned 'civil rights and obligations' and (b) the granting of the interim measure effectively determined the dispute between the parties. The Grand Chamber explained this change in the jurisprudence because, *inter alia*:

> 79....the exclusion of interim measures from the ambit of Article 6 has so far been justified by the fact that they do not in principle determine civil rights and obligations. However, in circumstances where many Contracting States face considerable backlogs in their overburdened justice systems leading to excessively long proceedings, a judge's decision on an injunction will often be tantamount to a decision on the merits of the claim for a substantial period of time, even permanently in exceptional cases. It follows that, frequently, interim and main proceedings decide the same 'civil rights or obligations' and have the same resulting long lasting or permanent effects.

Furthermore, many member States and the European Court of Justice, applied fair trial guarantees to interlocutory proceedings. Consequently, the granting of an interlocutory injunction against the applicant's sister in an action brought by her neighbour, over the hanging out of washing to dry, was determined to be subject to Article 6(1). A breach was found (see p 445).

10   The full-time Court, unanimously, found disciplinary proceedings taken against the applicant (a former accountant) by the Chamber of Accountants fell within the civil limb of Article 6(1) and breached the reasonable time guarantee as they took nearly 11 years to be concluded in *Luksch v Austria*, judgment of 13 December 2001.

11   A unanimous Grand Chamber announced a new approach to the analysis under Article 6(1) of civil party proceedings, claims for compensation by the victims lodged during criminal cases, available in several continental jurisdiction in *Perez v France*, judgment of 12 February 2004. The applicant filed a criminal complaint with her local gendarmerie that her son and daughter had injected her with a sedative drug (Valium). During the subsequent judicial investigation she applied to join the proceedings as a civil party. The investigating judge determined that there was no case to answer, as there was insufficient evidence of a crime having been committed. The applicant unsuccessfully challenged the judge's ruling before the Court of Cassation. She then complained to Strasbourg that the procedure and judgment of the Court of Cassation had violated Article 6(1). The Grand Chamber held that:

> 56. The Court thus wishes to end the uncertainty surrounding the applicability of Article 6 § 1 to civil-party proceedings, particularly since a number of other High Contracting Parties to the Convention have similar systems.
>
> **3. A new approach**
>
> 57. The Court notes that although it has found the concept of 'civil rights and obligations' to be autonomous, it has also held that, in this context, the legislation of the State concerned is not

without importance. (see *König v Germany*, judgment of 28 June 1987, Series A No 27, p 30, § 89). Whether or not a right is to be regarded as civil within the meaning of that term in the Convention must be determined by reference not only to its legal classification but also to its substantive content and effects under the domestic law of the State concerned. Moreover the Court, in the exercise of its supervisory function, must also take account of the object and purpose of the Convention.

58. The Court considers it necessary to examine the domestic legislation on civil-party applications in the French criminal courts.

59. In French law victims of an offence may, under Article 4 § 1 of the Code of Criminal Procedure, pursue a civil action separately from the prosecution, in the civil courts. They may also pursue it in the criminal courts simultaneously with the prosecution, under Article 3 § 1 of that Code. Article 3 § 2 specifies that a civil claim is admissible in respect of all the damage caused by the offence being prosecuted.

60. French law thus gives the victim of an offence the option of choosing between civil and criminal proceedings. Under the civil option, the fact that the damage is caused by a criminal offence means that civil procedure is only applied subject to certain rules: irrevocability of the choice (Article 5 of the Code of Criminal Procedure), the principle whereby 'civil proceedings must await the outcome of criminal proceedings' and 'a final criminal judgment prevails over a civil claim'.

61. The criminal option, with which the Court is concerned here, is exercised by way of a civil-party complaint, which is subject to certain conditions and produces certain consequences. Civil-party proceedings are brought either 'by intervention', after the prosecution has already started, by means of an application to the investigating judge or the trial court for leave to join the proceedings, or 'by instigation', or in other words by means of a civil-party complaint or a direct summons before the trial court. Although a civil-party victim faces certain constraints in as much as he can no longer testify and is exposed to sanctions for failure or abuse, he enjoys the benefit of being a party to the criminal trial, is kept informed of the steps in the proceedings, may file requests for documents and lodge appeals and, above all, may obtain compensation from the criminal courts for the damage he has suffered.

62. In view of the foregoing, there can be no doubt that civil-party proceedings constitute, in French law, a civil action for reparation of damage caused by an offence. In these circumstances the Court therefore sees no reason, a priori, to consider it otherwise for the purposes of applying Article 6 § 1 of the Convention.

The Grand Chamber went on to rule that in general, except where the applicant was seeking to bring the proceedings for the purposes of 'private revenge' or as an *actio popularis*, civil party proceedings should be classified as within the 'civil rights and obligations' limb of Article 6(1). However, in the applicant's case there had been no breach of the requirements of Article 6(1) by the Court of Cassation. This judgment demonstrates the complex intertwining that may exist between civil rights and criminal proceedings in member States.

12 A unanimous Chamber held that the claims of Polish victims of forced labour under Nazi Germany seeking compensation from the Polish–German Reconciliation Foundation (established under a 1991 agreement between the Federal Republic of Germany and Poland) were asserting a civil right in *Wos v Poland*, judgment of 8 June 2006. As the Polish courts had declined to review the determinations of the Foundation (whose adjudicative bodies did not meet the requirements of Article 6(1)) the Chamber held that the applicant had been denied the right of access to a court in breach of Article 6(1).

Criminal charge

Engel v The Netherlands A.22 (1976)
European Court of Human Rights

The five applicants were conscript soldiers serving in the Dutch armed forces. Under the Military Discipline Act 1903 they were subject to disciplinary law, which was a separate body of law from that of military criminal law. Each of the applicants was found to be in breach of disciplinary law and punished by the relevant military authorities. Mr Engel was sentenced, by the Supreme Military Court, to two days' 'strict arrest' (i.e. locked in a cell) for disregarding previous lesser punishments (imposed for having been absent without authorization). Mr van der Wiel was sentenced, by the Supreme Military Court, to four days' 'light arrest' (i.e. confined to barracks, during off-duty hours he could freely move around the barracks and use the facilities, such as the camp cinema) for being four hours late for duty. The same Court sentenced Mr de Wit to 12 days' 'aggravated arrest' (i.e. confined to a specially designated, but unlocked, place in the barracks during off-duty hours) for failures to observe discipline, including driving a military jeep in an irresponsible manner. Messrs Dona and Schul were committed to a disciplinary unit (a separate military establishment where soldiers were subject to a stricter disciplinary regime and locked in cells during the night) for three months, by the Supreme Military Court, for editing a journal (published by the Conscript Servicemen's Association) considered to undermine military discipline. The applicants complained to the Commission alleging breaches of a number of Convention provisions, including Article 6 in respect of the proceedings before the Supreme Military Court in each of their cases. By 10 votes to 1, the Commission concluded that Article 6 was not applicable to any of the disciplinary proceedings against the applicants.

79. ...the Court will first investigate whether the said proceedings concerned 'any criminal charge' within the meaning of this text; for, although disciplinary according to Netherlands law, they had the aim of repressing through penalties offences alleged against the applicants, an objective analogous to the general goal of the criminal law.

1. ON THE APPLICABILITY OF ARTICLE 6 (ART 6)

(a) On the existence of 'any criminal charge'

80. All the Contracting States make a distinction of long standing, albeit in different forms and degrees, between disciplinary proceedings and criminal proceedings. For the individuals affected, the former usually offer substantial advantages in comparison with the latter, for example as concerns the sentences passed. Disciplinary sentences, in general less severe, do not appear in the person's criminal record and entail more limited consequences. It may nevertheless be otherwise; moreover, criminal proceedings are ordinarily accompanied by fuller guarantees.

It must thus be asked whether or not the solution adopted in this connection at the national level is decisive from the standpoint of the Convention. Does Article 6 (art 6) cease to be applicable just because the competent organs of a Contracting State classify as disciplinary an act or omission and the proceedings it takes against the author, or does it, on the contrary, apply in certain cases notwithstanding this classification? This problem, the importance of which the Government acknowledge, was rightly raised by the Commission; it particularly occurs when an act or omission is treated by the domestic law of the respondent State as a mixed offence, that is both criminal and disciplinary, and where there thus exists a possibility of opting between, or even cumulating, criminal proceedings and disciplinary proceedings.

81. The Court has devoted attention to the respective submissions of the applicants, the Government and the Commission concerning what they termed the 'autonomy' of the concept of a 'criminal charge'...

In the *Neumeister* judgment of 27 June 1968, the Court has already held that the word 'charge' must be understood 'within the meaning of the Convention' (Series A No 8, p 41, para 18...)...

The question of the 'autonomy' of the concept of 'criminal' does not call for exactly the same reply.

The Convention without any doubt allows the States, in the performance of their function as guardians of the public interest, to maintain or establish a distinction between criminal law and disciplinary law, and to draw the dividing line, but only subject to certain conditions. The Convention leaves the States free to designate as a criminal offence an act or omission not constituting the normal exercise of one of the rights that it protects. This is made especially clear by Article 7 (art 7). Such a choice, which has the effect of rendering applicable Articles 6 and 7 (art 6, art 7), in principle escapes supervision by the Court.

The converse choice, for its part, is subject to stricter rules. If the Contracting States were able at their discretion to classify an offence as disciplinary instead of criminal, or to prosecute the author of a 'mixed' offence on the disciplinary rather than on the criminal plane, the operation of the fundamental clauses of Articles 6 and 7 (art 6, art 7) would be subordinated to their sovereign will. A latitude extending thus far might lead to results incompatible with the purpose and object of the Convention. The Court therefore has jurisdiction, under Article 6 (art 6) and even without reference to Articles 17 and 18 (art 17, art 18), to satisfy itself that the disciplinary does not improperly encroach upon the criminal.

In short, the 'autonomy' of the concept of 'criminal' operates, as it were, one way only.

82. Hence, the Court must specify, limiting itself to the sphere of military service, how it will determine whether a given 'charge' vested by the State in question—as in the present case—with a disciplinary character nonetheless counts as 'criminal' within the meaning of Article 6 (art 6).

In this connection, it is first necessary to know whether the provision(s) defining the offence charged belong, according to the legal system of the respondent State, to criminal law, disciplinary law or both concurrently. This however provides no more than a starting point. The indications so afforded have only a formal and relative value and must be examined in the light of the common denominator of the respective legislation of the various Contracting States.

The very nature of the offence is a factor of greater import. When a serviceman finds himself accused of an act or omission allegedly contravening a legal rule governing the operation of the armed forces, the State may in principle employ against him disciplinary law rather than criminal law. In this respect, the Court expresses its agreement with the Government.

However, supervision by the Court does not stop there. Such supervision would generally prove to be illusory if it did not also take into consideration the degree of severity of the penalty that the person concerned risks incurring. In a society subscribing to the rule of law, there belong to the 'criminal' sphere deprivations of liberty liable to be imposed as a punishment, except those which by their nature, duration or manner of execution cannot be appreciably detrimental. The seriousness of what is at stake, the traditions of the Contracting States and the importance attached by the Convention to respect for the physical liberty of the person all require that this should be so (see, *mutatis mutandis*, the *De Wilde, Ooms and Versyp* judgment of 18 June 1971, Series A No 12, p 36, last sub-paragraph, and p 42 *in fine*).

83. It is on the basis of these criteria that the Court will ascertain whether some or all of the applicants were the subject of a 'criminal charge' within the meaning of Article 6 para 1 (art 6-1).

In the circumstances, the charge capable of being relevant lay in the decision of the commanding officer as confirmed or reduced by the complaints officer. It was undoubtedly this decision that settled once and for all what was at stake, since the tribunal called upon to give a ruling, that is the Supreme Military Court, had no jurisdiction to pronounce a harsher penalty...

84. The offences alleged against Mr Engel, Mr van der Wiel, Mr de Wit, Mr Dona and Mr Schul came within provisions belonging to disciplinary law under Netherlands legislation (the 1903 Act and Regulations on Military Discipline), although those to be answered for by Mr Dona and Mr Schul (Article 147 of the Military Penal Code), and perhaps even by Mr Engel and Mr de Wit (Articles 96 and 114 of the said Code according to Mr van der Schans, hearing on 28 October 1975), also lent themselves to criminal proceedings. Furthermore, all the offences had amounted, in the view of the military authorities, to contraventions of legal rules governing the operation of the Netherlands armed forces. From this aspect, the choice of disciplinary action was justified.

85. The maximum penalty that the Supreme Military Court could pronounce consisted in four days' light arrest for Mr van der Wiel, two days' strict arrest for Mr Engel (third punishment) and three or four months' committal to a disciplinary unit for Mr de Wit, Mr Dona and Mr Schul.

Mr van der Wiel was therefore liable only to a light punishment not occasioning deprivation of liberty...

For its part, the penalty involving deprivation of liberty that in theory threatened Mr Engel was of too short a duration to belong to the 'criminal' law. He ran no risk, moreover, of having to undergo this penalty at the close of the proceedings instituted by him before the Supreme Military Court on 7 April 1971, since he had already served it from 20 to 22 March...

On the other hand, the 'charges' against Mr de Wit, Mr Dona and Mr Schul did indeed come within the 'criminal' sphere since their aim was the imposition of serious punishments involving deprivation of liberty... The Supreme Military Court no doubt sentenced Mr de Wit to twelve days' aggravated arrest only, that is to say, to a penalty not occasioning deprivation of liberty... but the final outcome of the appeal cannot diminish the importance of what was initially at stake.

The Convention certainly did not compel the competent authorities to prosecute Mr de Wit, Mr Dona and Mr Schul under the Military Penal Code before a court martial... a solution which could have proved less advantageous for the applicants. The Convention did however oblige the authorities to afford them the guarantees of Article 6 (art 6).

...

88. In short, it is the duty of the Court to examine under Article 6 (art 6) the treatment meted out to Mr de Wit, Mr Dona and Mr Schul, but not that complained of by Mr Engel and Mr van der Wiel.

2. ON COMPLIANCE WITH ARTICLE 6 (ART 6)

89. The Supreme Military Court, before which appeared Mr de Wit, Mr Dona and Mr Schul, constitutes an 'independent and impartial tribunal established by law'... and there is nothing to indicate that it failed to give them a 'fair hearing'. For its part, the 'time' that elapsed between the 'charge' and the final decision appears 'reasonable'. It did not amount to six weeks for Mr Dona and Mr Schul (8 October–17 November 1971) and hardly exceeded two months for Mr de Wit (22 February–28 April 1971). Furthermore, the sentence was 'pronounced publicly'.

In contrast, the hearings in the presence of the parties had taken place *in camera* in accordance with the established practice of the Supreme Military Court in disciplinary proceedings... In point of fact, the applicants do not seem to have suffered on that account; indeed the said Court improved the lot of two of their number, namely Mr Schul and, to an even greater extent, Mr de Wit. Nevertheless, in the field it governs, Article 6 para 1 (art 6-1) requires in a very general fashion that judicial proceedings be conducted in public. Article 6 (art 6) of course makes provision for exceptions which it lists, but the Government did not plead, and it does not emerge from the file, that the circumstances of the case amounted to one of the occasions when the Article allows 'the press and the public (to be) excluded'. Hence, on this particular point, there has been violation of paragraph 1 of Article 6 (art 6-1).

...

FOR THESE REASONS, THE COURT,

… Holds, by eleven votes to two, that Article 6 was not applicable to Mr Engel on the ground of the words 'criminal charge';

Holds, unanimously, that neither was it applicable to Mr van der Wiel;

Holds, by eleven votes to two, that there was a breach of Article 6 para 1 in the case of Mr de Wit, Mr Dona and Mr Schul insofar as hearings before the Supreme Military Court took place *in camera*; …

NOTES

1 The Court was composed of President Mosler and Judges: Verdross, Wiarda, Vilhjalmsson, Petren, Bozer, Ganshof van der Meersch, Bindschedler-Robert, and Evrigenis. Judges O'Donoghue and Pedersen issued a separate opinion in which they expressed the view that the proceedings against all the applicants were 'predominantly' disciplinary offences and therefore fell outside the ambit of criminal charges under Article 6. Judges Zekia and Cremona also produced separate opinions in which they argued that where soldiers were charged with an offence punishable with loss of liberty (even of short duration) Article 6(1) was applicable to those proceedings.

2 The Court's judgment in *Engel* is very important because it establishes the autonomous nature of the Convention term 'criminal'. As the Court explained, in paragraph 81, where domestic law does not characterize a charge as being criminal that of itself is not decisive for the application of Article 6 by the Strasbourg control system. In such circumstances the Court will make its own assessment as to whether the national proceedings should be classified as criminal. In reaching such a determination the Court has regard to the three criteria identified in paragraph 82, of the above judgment. First, the type of national law embodying the relevant offence (and how other member States' legal systems characterize similar offences). Secondly, the nature of the conduct prohibited by the offence. Finally, the severity of the punishment attached to the offence (more than minimal loss of liberty is likely to result in the Court ruling that the offence is criminal). Having regard to these criteria, especially the last one, do you agree with the majority's determination that the proceedings against Engel did not involve a criminal charge? The Article 10 aspects of *Engel* are examined at p 710.

3 In subsequent cases the Court has applied the three criteria established in *Engel* to decide if particular domestic proceedings fall within Article 6's 'criminal' category. The second criterion was accorded greater significance, than the first, when the Court evaluated the German programme of decriminalization of minor road traffic offences in *Öztürk v Germany* A.73 (1984). The applicant, a Turkish citizen living and working in Germany, drove his car into another car and caused DM5,000 worth of damage. The owner of the other car called the police and they sent a report on the incident to the local administrative authority (Heilbronn). Two months later, in April 1978, the administrative authorities imposed a fine (of DM60) on the applicant for careless driving under the authority of the Regulatory Offences Act 1968/1975. The Act removed petty offences from the sphere of the criminal law and substituted 'regulatory offences', which were punishable by the imposition of fines. The applicant, through his lawyer, lodged an objection against the administrative authority's decision in his case. In August 1978, the Heilbronn District Court heard the applicant, who was assisted by an interpreter, and three witnesses. Thereupon the applicant withdrew his objection. The District Court ordered that the applicant should bear the court costs (DM185, of which DM64 related to the interpreter's fees) and his own expenses. The applicant appealed against his liability to pay the interpreter's fees based upon Article 6(3)(e) of the Convention. However, his appeal was dismissed. The court costs, including the interpreter's fees, were paid by the applicant's insurance company. The applicant complained to the Commission alleging that the order to pay the interpreter's fees violated his right to free interpretation in criminal proceedings guaranteed by Article 6. A majority of the Commission, 8 votes to 5, found a violation of subparagraph (3)(e). Before the Court, the German Government contended that Article 6 was not applicable to Mr Ozturk as he had not been charged with a criminal offence. The decriminalization of minor road traffic offences meant that he had been found liable for a 'regulatory offence', which was subject to a different procedure and consequences, than an ordinary criminal offence.

48. The Court was confronted with a similar issue in the case of Engel and others, which was cited in argument by the representatives. The facts of that case admittedly concerned penalties imposed on conscript servicemen and treated as disciplinary according to Netherlands law. In its judgment delivered on 8 June 1976 in that case, the Court was careful to state that it was confining its attention to the sphere of military service (Series A No 22, p 34, § 82). The Court nevertheless considers that the principles set forth in that judgment (ibid, §§ 80–2) are also relevant, *mutatis mutandis*, in the instant case.

49. The Convention is not opposed to States, in the performance of their task as guardians of the public interest, both creating or maintaining a distinction between different categories of offences for the purposes of their domestic law and drawing the dividing line, but it does not follow that the classification thus made by the States is decisive for the purposes of the Convention.

By removing certain forms of conduct from the category of criminal offences under domestic law, the law-maker may be able to serve the interests of the individual (see, *mutatis mutandis*, the above-mentioned *Engel and others* judgment, ibid, p 33, § 80) as well as the needs of the proper administration of justice, in particular in so far as the judicial authorities are thereby relieved of the task of prosecuting and punishing contraventions—which are numerous but of minor importance—of road traffic rules. The Convention is not opposed to the moves towards 'decriminalisation' which are taking place—in extremely varied forms—in the member States of the Council of Europe. The Government quite rightly insisted on this point. Nevertheless, if the Contracting States were able at their discretion, by classifying an offence as 'regulatory' instead of criminal, to exclude the operation of the fundamental clauses of Articles 6 and 7 (art 6, art 7), the application of these provisions would be subordinated to their sovereign will. A latitude extending thus far might lead to results incompatible with the object and purpose of the Convention.

50. Having thus reaffirmed the 'autonomy' of the notion of 'criminal' as conceived of under Article 6 (art 6), what the Court must determine is whether or not the 'regulatory offence' committed by the applicant was a 'criminal' one within the meaning of that Article (art 6). For this purpose, the Court will rely on the criteria adopted in the above-mentioned *Engel and others* judgment (ibid, pp 34–5, § 82). The first matter to be ascertained is whether or not the text defining the offence in issue belongs, according to the legal system of the respondent State, to criminal law; next, the nature of the offence and, finally, the nature and degree of severity of the penalty that the person concerned risked incurring must be examined, having regard to the object and purpose of Article 6 (art 6), to the ordinary meaning of the terms of that Article (art 6) and to the laws of the Contracting States.

51. Under German law, the facts alleged against Mr Öztürk—non-observance of Regulation 1 § 2 of the Road Traffic Regulations—amounted to a 'regulatory offence' (Regulation 49 § 1, No 1, of the same Regulations). They did not fall within the ambit of the criminal law, but of section 17 of the Ordnungswidrigkeitengesetz and of section 24 sub-section 2 of the Road Traffic Act ... The 1968/1975

legislation marks an important step in the process of 'decriminalisation' of petty offences in the Federal Republic of Germany. Although legal commentators in Germany do not seem unanimous in considering that the law on 'regulatory offences' no longer belongs in reality to criminal law, the drafting history of the 1968/1975 Act nonetheless makes it clear that the offences in question have been removed from the criminal law sphere by that Act (see Deutscher Bundestag, Drucksache V/1269 and, *inter alia*, the judgment of 16 July 1969 by the Constitutional Court, Entscheidungen des Bundesverfassungsgerichts, vol 27, pp 18–36).

While the Court thus accepts the Government's arguments on this point, it has nonetheless not lost sight of the fact that no absolute partition separates German criminal law from the law on 'regulatory offences', in particular where there exists a close connection between a criminal offence and a 'regulatory offence'...Nor has the Court overlooked that the provisions of the ordinary law governing criminal procedure apply by analogy to 'regulatory' proceedings...notably in relation to the judicial stage, if any, of such proceedings.

52. In any event, the indications furnished by the domestic law of the respondent State have only a relative value. The second criterion stated above—the very nature of the offence, considered also in relation to the nature of the corresponding penalty—represents a factor of appreciation of greater weight.

In the opinion of the Commission—with the exception of five of its members—and of Mr Öztürk, the offence committed by the latter was criminal in character.

For the Government in contrast, the offence in question was beyond doubt one of those contraventions of minor importance—numbering approximately five million each year in the Federal Republic of Germany—which came within a category of quite a different order from that of criminal offences. The Government's submissions can be summarised as follows. By means of criminal law, society endeavoured to safeguard its very foundations as well as the rights and interests essential for the life of the community. The law on Ordnungswidrigkeiten, on the other hand, sought above all to maintain public order. As a general rule and in any event in the instant case, commission of a 'regulatory offence' did not involve a degree of ethical unworthiness such as to merit for its perpetrator the moral value-judgment of reproach (Unwerturteil) that characterised penal punishment (Strafe). The difference between 'regulatory offences' and criminal offences found expression both in procedural terms and in relation to the attendant penalties and other legal consequences.

In the first place, so the Government's argument continued, in removing 'regulatory offences' from the criminal law the German legislature had introduced a simplified procedure of prosecution and punishment conducted before administrative authorities save in the event of subsequent appeal to a court. Although general laws on criminal procedure were in principle applicable by analogy, the procedure laid down under the 1968/1975 Act was distinguishable in many respects from criminal procedure. For example, prosecution of Ordnungswidrigkeiten fell within the discretionary power of the competent authorities and the 1968/1975 Act greatly limited the possibilities of restricting the personal liberty of the individual at the stage of the preliminary investigations...

In the second place, instead of a penal fine (Geldstrafe) and imprisonment the legislature had substituted a mere 'regulatory' fine (Geldbusse...). Imprisonment was not an alternative (Ersatzfreiheitsstrafe) to the latter type of fine as it was to the former and no coercive imprisonment (Erzwingungshaft) could be ordered unless the person concerned had failed to pay the sum due without having established his inability to pay...Furthermore, a 'regulatory offence' was not entered in the judicial criminal records but solely, in certain circumstances, on the central traffic register...

The reforms accomplished in 1968/1975 thus, so the Government concluded, reflected a concern to 'decriminalise' minor offences to the benefit not only of the individual, who would no longer be answerable in criminal terms for his act and who could even avoid all court proceedings, but also of the effective functioning of the courts, henceforth relieved in principle of the task of dealing with the great majority of such offences.

53. The Court does not underestimate the cogency of this argument. The Court recognises that the legislation in question marks an important stage in the history of the reform of German criminal law and that the innovations introduced in 1968/1975 represent more than a simple change of terminology.

Nonetheless, the Court would firstly note that, according to the ordinary meaning of the terms, there generally come within the ambit of the criminal law offences that make their perpetrator liable to penalties intended, *inter alia*, to be deterrent and usually consisting of fines and of measures depriving the person of his liberty.

In addition, misconduct of the kind committed by Mr Öztürk continues to be classified as part of the criminal law in the vast majority of the Contracting States, as it was in the Federal Republic of Germany until the entry into force of the 1968/1975 legislation; in those other States, such misconduct, being regarded as illegal and reprehensible, is punishable by criminal penalties.

Moreover, the changes resulting from the 1968/1975 legislation relate essentially to procedural matters and to the range of sanctions, henceforth limited to Geldbussen. While the latter penalty appears less burdensome in some respects than Geldstrafen, it has nonetheless retained a punitive character, which is the customary distinguishing feature of criminal penalties. The rule of law infringed by the applicant has, for its part, undergone no change of content. It is a rule that is directed, not towards a given group possessing a special status—in the manner, for example, of disciplinary law—but towards all citizens in their capacity as road-users; it prescribes conduct of a certain kind and makes the resultant requirement subject to a sanction that is punitive. Indeed, the sanction—and this the Government did not contest—seeks to punish as well as to deter. It matters little whether the legal provision contravened by Mr Öztürk is aimed at protecting the rights and interests of others or solely at meeting the demands of road traffic. These two ends are not mutually exclusive. Above all, the general character of the rule and the purpose of the penalty, being both deterrent and punitive, suffice to show that the offence in question was, in terms of Article 6 (art 6) of the Convention, criminal in nature.

The fact that it was admittedly a minor offence hardly likely to harm the reputation of the offender does not take it outside the ambit of Article 6 (art 6). There is in fact nothing to suggest that the criminal offence referred to in the Convention necessarily implies a certain degree of seriousness. In this connection, a number of Contracting States still draw a distinction, as did the Federal Republic at the time when the Convention was opened for the signature of the Governments, between the most serious offences (crimes), lesser offences (délits) and petty offences (contraventions), while qualifying them all as criminal offences. Furthermore, it would be contrary to the object and purpose of Article 6 (art 6), which guarantees to 'everyone charged with a criminal offence' the right to a court and to a fair trial, if the State were allowed to remove from the scope of this Article (art 6) a whole category of offences merely on the ground of regarding them as petty. Nor does the Federal Republic deprive the presumed perpetrators of Ordnungswidrigkeiten of this right since it grants them the faculty—of which the applicant availed himself—of appealing to a court against the administrative decision.

54. As the contravention committed by Mr Öztürk was criminal for the purposes of Article 6 (art 6) of the Convention, there is no need to examine it also in the light of the final criterion stated above (at paragraph 50). The relative lack of seriousness of the penalty at stake . . . cannot divest an offence of its inherently criminal character.

55. The Government further appeared to consider that the applicant did not have the status of a person 'charged with a criminal offence' because the 1968/1975 Act does not provide for any 'Beschuldigung' ('charge') and does not employ the terms 'Angeschuldigter' ('person charged') or 'Angeklagter' ('the accused'). On this point, the Court would simply refer back to its well-established case-law holding that 'charge', for the purposes of Article 6 (art 6), may in general be defined as 'the official notification given to an individual by the competent authority of an allegation that he has committed a criminal offence', although 'it may in some instances take the form of other

measures which carry the implication of such an allegation and which likewise substantially affect the situation of the suspect' (see, as the most recent authorities, the *Foti* judgment of 10 December 1982, Series A No 56, p 18, § 52, and the *Corigliano* judgment of the same date, Series A No 57, p 13, § 34). In the present case, the applicant was 'charged' at the latest as from the beginning of April 1978 when the decision of the Heilbronn administrative authorities was communicated to him …

56. Article 6 § 3 (e) (art 6-3-e) was thus applicable in the instant case. It in no wise follows from this, the Court would want to make clear, that the very principle of the system adopted in the matter by the German legislature is being put in question. Having regard to the large number of minor offences, notably in the sphere of road traffic, a Contracting State may have good cause for relieving its courts of the task of their prosecution and punishment. Conferring the prosecution and punishment of minor offences on administrative authorities is not inconsistent with the Convention provided that the person concerned is enabled to take any decision thus made against him before a tribunal that does offer the guarantees of Article 6 …

II. COMPLIANCE WITH ARTICLE 6 § 3 (E) (ART 6-3-E)

57. Invoking the above-cited *Luedicke, Belkacem and Koç* judgment of 28 November 1978 [(A.29)], the applicant submitted that the decision whereby the Heilbronn District Court had made him bear the costs incurred in having recourse to the services of an interpreter at the hearing on 3 August 1978 was in breach of Article 6 § 3 (e) (art 6-3-e).

The Commission's opinion was to the same effect. The Government, for their part, maintained that there had been no violation, but concentrated their arguments on the issue of the applicability of Article 6 § 3 (e) (art 6-3-e), without discussing the manner in which the Court had construed this text in 1978.

58. On the basis of the above-cited judgment, the Court finds that the impugned decision of the Heilbronn District Court violated the Convention: 'the right protected by Article 6 § 3 (e) (art 6-3-e) entails, for anyone who cannot speak or understand the language used in court, the right to receive the free assistance of an interpreter, without subsequently having claimed back from him the payment of the costs thereby incurred' (Series A No 29, p 19, § 46).

…

FOR THESE REASONS, THE COURT

…

Holds, by twelve votes to six, that there has been a breach of the said Article (6(3)(e)); …

The judgment reveals that when applying the second *Engel* criterion, the nature of the offence at issue, the Court is likely to conclude that the proceedings are 'criminal' where the provision applies to a large section of the public and the relevant sanction has a punitive aim. From a wider policy perspective the Court, in paragraph 56, upheld the ability of States to engage in decriminalization programmes regarding the determination and punishment of less serious offences, provided that affected individuals have an ultimate right of recourse to a body complying with the institutional and procedural safeguards laid down by Article 6. This is a fair balance between the efficiency goals of governments and the due process rights of individuals.

4   The Court was, however, united in determining that breach of privilege proceedings brought by a national parliament against a satirical journalist were 'criminal' in **Demicoli v Malta** A.210 (1991). The applicant edited a political periodical in which he published a satirical review of a parliamentary debate. The article, headed 'The Parliamentary Clown',

ridiculed the speeches of two members of the Maltese House of Representatives (Mr Debono Grech and Mr Bartolo). The two members brought the article to the attention of the House and the Speaker found it to be a prima facie case of breach of privilege. The same day the House, on a proposal from Mr Debono Grech, passed a resolution holding the article to be in breach of parliamentary privilege. Several weeks later the House passed a motion, seconded by Mr Debono Grech, summoning the applicant to appear before the House '...to state why he should not be found guilty of breach of privilege...'. Together with his lawyer, the applicant appeared before the House; however he refused to answer whether he was guilty or not. The House found him guilty. After the Constitutional Court upheld the legality of the House's proceedings, the latter body fined Demicoli 250 Maltese liri and ordered him to publish details of the House's findings in his periodical. The two criticized members participated in the House proceedings against Demicoli. The Commission expressed the unanimous view that Maltese proceedings violated the applicant's right to a fair trial under Article 6(1). The Court began by applying the ***Engel*** criteria.

32. It must first be ascertained whether the provisions defining the offence in issue belong, according to the legal system of the respondent State, to criminal law, disciplinary law or both concurrently.

The legal basis of the proceedings taken against Mr Demicoli was provided by section 11 of the Ordinance... The applicant argued that the origin of the Maltese law of Parliamentary privilege is to be found in United Kingdom law and that breaches of privilege are referred to as crimes in certain textbooks on English law. As noted by the Commission and the Government, breach of Parliamentary privilege is not formally classified as a crime in Maltese law... The Constitutional Court, in its judgment of 13 October 1986, did not find it necessary to decide whether 'the act constituting the contempt or breach of privilege amounts to a criminal act or not.'

33. However... the indication afforded by national law is not decisive for the purpose of Article 6 (art 6). A factor of greater importance is 'the very nature of the offence' in question (see, *inter alia*, the... *Campbell and Fell* judgment, Series A No 80, p 36, para 71...

In this context the applicant quoted from the records of the Parliamentary sittings of 4, 17, 18 and 19 March 1986 to highlight the fact that certain Members of the House equated the proceedings taken against him with criminal proceedings...

The Government, on the other hand, submitted that, although some breaches of privilege may also constitute criminal offences, Parliamentary privilege, being concerned with respect for the dignity of the House, pursued a different aim from that of the criminal law....

Mr Demicoli was not a Member of the House. In the Court's view, the proceedings taken against him in the present case for an act of this sort done outside the House are to be distinguished from other types of breach of privilege proceedings which may be said to be disciplinary in nature in that they relate to the internal regulation and orderly functioning of the House. Section 11(1)(k) potentially affects the whole population since it applies whether the alleged offender is a Member of the House or not and irrespective of where in Malta the publication of the defamatory libel takes place. For the offence thereby defined the Ordinance provides for the imposition of a penal sanction and not a civil claim for damages. From this point of view, therefore, the particular breach of privilege in question is akin to a criminal offence...

34. The third criterion is the degree of severity of the penalty that the person concerned risks incurring. The Court notes that in the present case, while the House imposed a fine of 250 Maltese liri on the applicant which has not yet been paid or enforced, the maximum penalty he risked was imprisonment for a period not exceeding sixty days or a fine not exceeding 500 Maltese liri or both. What was at stake was thus sufficiently important to warrant classifying the offence with which the applicant was charged as a criminal one under the Convention...

35. In conclusion, Article 6 applied in the present case.

B. COMPLIANCE WITH ARTICLE 6 PARA 1 (ART 6-1)

36. The applicant submitted that in the proceedings before the House of Representative she did not receive a fair hearing by an independent and impartial tribunal. The political context in which the proceedings against him were conducted 'made a mockery of the whole concept of the independence and the impartiality of the judiciary'. This, he claimed, was evident from statements made by Members of the House in relation to his case in the official record of the Parliamentary sittings... He maintained that in breach of privilege proceedings Members of Parliament sit as victims, accusers, witnesses and judges. In his case it was the privilege of the individual Members concerned that was in issue and not, as the Government suggested, that of the whole House. Even if the Government's view on this point were accepted, that would mean, in his view, that 'each and every Member of the House of Representatives is a *judex in causa sua*'.

37. The Government argued that the House of Representatives was 'an independent and impartial tribunal established by law' for the purpose of hearing the disciplinary charge against Mr Demicoli. The Maltese House of Representatives was an independent authority 'par excellence'. The House was independent of the executive and of the parties, its Members were elected for a term of five years and its proceedings afforded the necessary guarantees. Accordingly it fulfilled all the requirements of a tribunal set out in the *Ringeisen* judgment of 16 July 1971 (Series A No 13, p 39, para 95). The independence of the House was sufficient to exclude any legitimate doubt as to its impartiality. Moreover, the Members directly satirised by the article intervened to defend the dignity of the House and not just their own reputations.

38. The Commission took the view that the House of Representatives could not be considered to be a court and did not fulfil the requirements of the Convention as to independence or impartiality.

39. The Court, like the Commission, notes that the power of the Maltese Parliament to impose disciplinary measures and to govern its own internal affairs is not in issue. Moreover, the Court's task is not to review the relevant law and practice *in abstracto*, but to determine whether the manner in which the proceedings against Mr Demicoli were conducted gave rise to a violation of Article 6 para 1 (art 6-1).

According to its case-law, 'a 'tribunal' is characterised in the substantive sense of the term by its judicial function, that is to say determining matters within its competence on the basis of rules of law and after proceedings conducted in a prescribed manner... It must also satisfy a series of further requirements—independence, in particular of the executive; impartiality; duration of its members' terms of office; guarantees afforded by its procedure—several of which appear in the text of Article 6 para 1 (art 6-1) itself' (see the *Belilos* judgment of 29 April 1988, Series A No 132, p 29, para 64).

40. In the circumstances of the present case the House of Representatives undoubtedly exercised a judicial function in determining the applicant's guilt. The central issue raised in this case is whether the requirement of impartiality was duly respected. For the purposes of Article 6 para 1 (art 6-1) this must be determined according to a subjective test, that is on the basis of the personal conviction or interest of a particular judge in a given case, and according to an objective test, namely ascertaining whether the judge offered guarantees sufficient to exclude any legitimate doubt in this respect. In this context even appearances may be of a certain importance, particularly as far as criminal proceedings are concerned (see, among other authorities, the *Hauschildt* judgment of 24 May 1989, Series A No 154, p 21, paras 46–8).

41. The two Members of the House whose behaviour in Parliament was criticised in the impugned article and who raised the breach of privilege in the House... participated throughout in the proceedings against the accused, including the finding of guilt and (except for one of them who had meanwhile died) the sentencing.

Already for this reason, the impartiality of the adjudicating body in these proceedings would appear to be open to doubt and the applicant's fears in this connection were justified...

42. Accordingly, there has been a breach of Article 6 para 1 (art 6-1) of the Convention on the point considered. It is therefore not necessary to go into other aspects of this provision....

The decisive factors in the Court classifying these proceedings as 'criminal' were the general applicability of the privilege norms (i.e. they encompassed the public outside the House, rather than being internal principles governing members' behaviour) and the potential severity of the punishments available (including imprisonment for up to almost two months).

5   The Court has also decided that the term 'charge' has an autonomous meaning (i.e. the Court is not bound to accept national interpretations of the concept). The authoritative definition of this term was given in ***Deweer v Belgium*** A.35 (1980). The applicant had owned a butcher's shop in Louvain since 1935. On 18 September 1974 an official from the Economic Inspectorate General visited the shop. The inspector concluded that the applicant had not reduced the price of his pigmeat by 6.5 per cent as required by a Ministerial Decree issued a few weeks earlier. The applicant claimed that he had made a mistake in good faith and immediately reduced the price. The inspector later produced a formal report (called a *pro-justitia*) of his visit and sent it to the procureur du Roi attached to the Louvain Court of First Instance. On 30 September the procureur ordered the provisional closure of the applicant's shop within 48 hours of the notification of his decision, under powers granted by the Economic Regulation and Prices Act 1945. The same day the procureur wrote a letter to the applicant informing him of the closure order and stating that if he paid 10,000F, as a friendly settlement, the closure order would be terminated. The police delivered the letter to the applicant on the 1 October and he replied on 3 October. The applicant wrote that he was paying the sum to avoid the costs of closure of his business pending a subsequent criminal trial. The applicant complained to the Commission alleging that the procureur's making of the provisional closure order combined with the offer of a financial settlement violated his right to a fair hearing in the determination of any criminal charge against him guaranteed by Article 6(1). The Commission unanimously found a breach of that right. The Court held that:

46. ... The 'charge' could, for the purposes of Article 6 par 1 (art 6-1), be defined as the official notification given to an individual by the competent authority of an allegation that he has committed a criminal offence. In several decisions and opinions the Commission has adopted a test that appears to be fairly closely related, namely whether 'the situation of the [suspect] has been substantially affected' (*Neumeister* case, Series B No 6, p 81; case of *Huber v Austria*, Yearbook of the Convention, vol 18, p 356, 67; case of *Hätti v Federal Republic of Germany*, ibid, vol 19, p 1064, 50, etc). Under these circumstances, the Court considers that as from 30 September 1974 the applicant was under a 'criminal charge'.

Furthermore, the Court was unanimous that the procureur's actions had deprived the applicant of his right to a fair trial and thereby breached Article 6(1). We have already seen the Court's utilization of this definition of a criminal 'charge' in the context of German road traffic proceedings: ***Ozturk*** para 55 (above).

6   In ***V v UK*** (see p 179), the Court held that in criminal cases Article 6(1) covers the whole of the proceedings, including the determination of sentence. The Court, therefore, concluded that the Home Secretary's role in determining the tariff period (i.e. the minimum term of imprisonment necessary to satisfy the requirements of retribution and deterrence) of juvenile murderers, sentenced to detention during Her Majesty's Pleasure, violated the 'independent tribunal' element of Article 6(1). As the Court noted, the Home Secretary 'was clearly not independent of the executive' (para 114).

7   Two convicted prisoners successfully contended that the power of English prison governors to determine 'disciplinary' offences and award extra days custody (i.e. to delay their final release date) of prisoners found guilty, amounted to the determination of 'criminal charges' within the meaning of Article 6(1) in *Ezeh and Connors v UK*, Chamber judgment of 15 July 2002 and Grand Chamber Judgment of 9 October 2003. The first applicant was alleged to have threatened to kill his probation officer during a meeting with her in prison. His case was heard by a prison governor who refused the applicant's request to have legal representation. The governor found him guilty of using threatening words (this was his seventh offence of threatening to kill or injure a member of staff) and sentenced him to, *inter alia*, 40 days' additional custody. The second applicant was charged with assaulting a prison officer, by deliberately running into him in the exercise yard of the prison. The prison governor also refused his request for legal representation. The governor found him guilty (it was Connors' 37th offence against discipline) and awarded him seven days' additional custody. Both applicants complained to Strasbourg alleging a breach of the right to legal representation in respect of persons charged with a criminal offence under Article 6(3)(c). The Chamber, unanimously, applied the *Engel* criteria to classify the proceedings before the governors as involving 'criminal charges' and concluded that Article 6(3)(c) had been violated. The U Government petitioned the Grand Chamber to re-hear the case under Article 43 on the ground that Article 6 did not apply to these proceedings. Before the Grand Chamber, the Government argued that the Chamber, when applying the *Engel* criteria, had not accorded sufficient weight to the needs of maintaining effective discipline within prisons. The Court, by 11 votes to 6, held that:

85. . . . as in the *Campbell and Fell* [v UK A.80 (1984)] judgment, the Grand Chamber agrees with the Chamber that it is correct to apply the '*Engel* criteria' to the facts of the present cases in determining where to place the dividing line between the 'criminal' and the 'disciplinary'. The Court will do so in a manner consistent with the object and purpose of Article 6 of the Convention, while making 'due allowance' for the prison context and for the 'practical reasons and reasons of policy' in favour of establishing a special prison disciplinary regime.

86. In addition, it is the Court's established jurisprudence that the second and third criteria laid down in the Engel judgment are alternative and not necessarily cumulative: for Article 6 to be held applicable, it suffices that the offence in question is by its nature to be regarded as 'criminal' from the point of view of the Convention, or that the offence made the person liable to a sanction which, by its nature and degree of severity, belongs in general to the 'criminal' sphere (*Öztürk v Germany*, judgment of 21 February 1984, Series A No 73, § 54, and *Lutz v Germany*, judgment of 25 August 1987, Series A No 123, § 55). This does not exclude that a cumulative approach may be adopted where separate analysis of each criterion does not make it possible to reach a clear conclusion as to the existence of a criminal charge (*Bendenoun v France*, judgment of 24 February 1994, Series A No 284, § 47; *Benham v the United Kingdom*, judgment of 10 June 1996, Reports of Judgments and Decisions 1996-III, § 56; *Garyfallou AEBE v Greece*, judgment of 24 September 1997, Reports 1997-V, § 33; *Lauko v Slovakia*, judgment of 2 September 1998, Reports 1998-VI, § 57).

87. The Court would also make certain observations on the more general submissions of the parties concerning the application of the *Engel* criteria to a prison environment.

88. In the first place, the Court notes that the Government's central submission was that the necessity of maintaining an effective prison disciplinary regime had to weigh heavily in determining

where the dividing line between the criminal and disciplinary lay. As in its *Campbell and Fell* judgment, the Court would not question the importance of preserving an effective system of order and control in prison. However, it does not find compelling the Government's argument that the loss by the governor of the power to award 'additional days' would undermine the prison disciplinary regime in England and Wales.

In this regard, the Court notes that other sanctions were available to the governor at the relevant times (including forfeiture of privileges, exclusion from associated work and cellular confinement) and that the range and severity of sanctions other than additional days has been extended and increased since the applicants' adjudication proceedings, most recently in August 2002. The Court considers that it has not been convincingly explained why these other sanctions would not have an impact comparable to awards of additional days in maintaining the effectiveness of the prison disciplinary system, including the authority of the prison management. In this regard, the Government did not address how a sanction with immediate application would be less effective than an award of additional days which is not served until a prisoner's early release date (set pursuant to section 33 of the [Criminal Justice] 1991 Act) and which in many cases will be therefore served some time, even years, after the adjudication hearing. Further, the Court does not consider that the Government have convincingly demonstrated significant material differences between the disciplinary needs in Scottish prisons, where use of additional days was suspended almost two years ago, and those needs in prisons in England and Wales.

...

2. The first of the *Engel* criteria—the domestic classification of the offences

90. The offences with which the applicants were charged were classified by domestic law as disciplinary: paragraphs 1 and 17 of Rule 47 state that the relevant conduct on the part of a prisoner shall be 'an offence against discipline' and the Prison Rules go on to provide how such offences shall be dealt with under the prison disciplinary regime by adjudication before the governor.

Thus, as the Chamber noted, according to national law the adjudication of such offences was treated as a disciplinary matter and was designed to maintain order within the confines of the prison. The fact, as pointed out by the Government, that a governor's findings would not form part of the applicants' criminal records is simply a natural consequence of the disciplinary classification of the offence.

91. However, the indications so afforded by the national law have only a formal and relative value; the 'very nature of the offence is a factor of greater import' (the above-cited *Engel and Others* judgment, at § 82).

3. The second of the *Engel* criteria—the nature of the charge

...

103. In the present cases, the Court notes, in the first place, that the offences in question were directed towards a group possessing a special status, namely prisoners, as opposed to all citizens. However, the Court does not accept the Government's submission that this fact renders the nature of the offences prima facie disciplinary. It is but one of the 'relevant indicators' in assessing the nature of the offence (the *Campbell and Fell* judgment, cited above, at § 71).

104. Secondly, it was not disputed before the Grand Chamber that the charge against the first applicant corresponded to an offence in the ordinary criminal law (sections 4 and 5 of the [Public Order] 1986 Act). It is also clear that the charge of assault against the second applicant is an offence under the criminal law as well as under the Prison Rules. It is true that the latter charge involved a relatively minor incident of deliberately colliding with a prison officer which may not necessarily have led to prosecution outside the prison context. It is also true that the extreme gravity of the offence may be indicative of its criminal nature, as indicated in the *Campbell and Fell* judgment. However, that does

not conversely mean that the minor nature of an offence can, of itself, take it outside of the ambit of Article 6 as there is nothing in the Convention to suggest that the criminal nature of an offence, within the meaning of the second of the *Engel* criteria, necessarily requires a certain degree of seriousness (the above-cited *Öztürk* judgment, § 53). The reliance on the severity of the penalty in the *Campbell and Fell* judgment (at § 72) was a matter relevant to the third of the Engel criteria as opposed to a factor defining the nature of the offence.

Relying on Convention case-law, the Government contested the weight to be attached to this concurrent criminal and disciplinary liability. However, in the case most directly in point, the *Campbell and Fell* judgment (at § 71), the Court referred to even a 'theoretical' possibility of the impugned acts being the subject of concurrent criminal and disciplinary pursuit as a relevant factor in the assessment of the nature of the offence and it did so independently of the gravity of the offences in question. Accordingly, and even noting the prison context of the charges, the theoretical possibility of concurrent criminal and disciplinary liability is, at the very least, a relevant point which tends to the classification of the nature of both offences as 'mixed' offences.

105. Thirdly, the Government submit that disciplinary rules and sanctions in prison are designed primarily to ensure the successful operation of a system of early release so that the 'punitive' element of the offence is secondary to the primary purpose of 'prevention' of disorder. The Court considers that awards of additional days were, on any view, imposed after a finding of culpability (*Benham v the United Kingdom*, cited above, at § 56) to punish the applicants for the offences they had committed and to prevent further offending by them and other prisoners. It does not find persuasive the Government's argument distinguishing between the punishment and deterrent aims of the offences in question, these objectives not being mutually exclusive (the above-cited *Öztürk* judgment, at § 53) and being recognised as characteristic features of criminal penalties).

106. Accordingly, the Court considers that these factors, even if they were not of themselves sufficient to lead to the conclusion that the offences with which the applicants were charged are to be regarded as 'criminal' for Convention purposes, clearly gives them a certain colouring which does not entirely coincide with that of a purely disciplinary matter.

107. The Court finds, as did the Chamber, that it is therefore necessary to turn to the third criterion: the nature and degree of severity of the penalty that the applicants risked incurring (the *Engel and Others* judgment, § 82, and the *Campbell and Fell* judgment, § 72, both cited above).

4. The third of the *Engel* criteria—the nature and severity of the penalty

...

123. ... The reality of awards of additional days was that prisoners were detained in prison beyond the date on which they would otherwise have been released, as a consequence of separate disciplinary proceedings which were legally unconnected to the original conviction and sentence.

124. Accordingly, the Court finds that awards of additional days by the governor constitute fresh deprivations of liberty imposed for punitive reasons after a finding of culpability (see paragraph 105 above). The Court finds further support for this view in the provisions of Rule 54(1) of the Prison Rules which allow for the imposition of additional days during a prisoner's detention on remand and, therefore, prior to any conviction, although such days would not be served in the event of acquittal.

125. This being so, the mere fact, emphasised by the Government, that at the time of the governor's decision the applicants were prisoners serving a lawfully imposed prison sentence does not, in the view of the Court, serve to distinguish their case from that of civilians or military personnel at liberty. It is, moreover, for this reason that the question of the procedural protections to be accorded to prison adjudication proceedings is one properly considered under Article 6 and not, as the Government suggest, under the provisions of Article 5 of the Convention.

It is true that in its *Campbell and Fell* judgment the Court concluded that the penalty imposed 'came close to, even if it did not technically constitute' a deprivation of liberty. However, the Court was constrained to so frame its finding since it was examining a 'loss of remission' as opposed to an 'award of additional days' for which the later 1991 Act provided.

126. It is recalled that, in its *Engel and Others* judgment, the Court found (at § 82) as follows:

'In a society subscribing to the rule of law, there belong to the "criminal" sphere deprivations of liberty liable to be imposed as a punishment, except those which by their nature, duration or manner of execution cannot be appreciably detrimental. The seriousness of what is at stake, the traditions of the Contracting States and the importance attached by the Convention to respect for the physical liberty of the person all require that this should be so.'

Accordingly, given the deprivations of liberty, liable to be and actually imposed on the present applicants, there is a presumption that the charges against them were criminal within the meaning of Article 6, a presumption which could be rebutted entirely exceptionally, and only if those deprivations of liberty could not be considered 'appreciably detrimental' given their nature, duration or manner of execution.

127. As to whether the presumption can be rebutted in the present cases, the Chamber could not find much guidance from the Court's *Campbell and Fell* judgment and the Grand Chamber agrees. In that judgment the Court concluded that the level of 'remission lost' by Mr Campbell (570 days) involved 'such serious consequences as regards the length of his detention' that that penalty had to be regarded as 'criminal' for the purposes of Article 6 of the Convention. It was not therefore relevant, in the *Campbell and Fell* case, to apply the 'appreciably detrimental' test.

128. In the present cases, it is observed that the maximum number of additional days which could be awarded to each applicant by the governor was 42 for each offence (Rule 50 of the Prison Rules). The first applicant was awarded 40 additional days and this was to be his twenty-second offence against discipline and his seventh offence involving violent threats. The second applicant was awarded 7 additional days' detention and this was to be his thirty-seventh offence against discipline. The awards of 40 and 7 additional days constituted the equivalent, in duration, of sentences handed down by a domestic court of approximately 11 and 2 weeks' imprisonment, respectively, given the provisions of section 33 (1) of the 1991 Act.

The Court also observes that there was nothing before the Chamber, and nothing was submitted to the Grand Chamber, to suggest that awards of additional days would be served other than in prison and under the same prison regime as would apply until the normal release date set by section 33 of the 1991 Act.

129. In these circumstances, the Court finds that the deprivations of liberty which were liable to be, and which were actually, imposed on the applicants cannot be regarded as sufficiently unimportant or inconsequential as to displace the presumed criminal nature of the charges against them.

The Court notes that the maximum penalty that could have been awarded against Mr Engel and the actual penalty imposed on him—2 days' strict arrest in both respects—was found to be of too short a duration to belong to the criminal sphere. However, it observes that, in any event even the lowest penalty imposed in the present cases was substantially greater than that in Mr Engel's case.

5. The Court's conclusion

130. In such circumstances, the Court concludes as did the Chamber that the nature of the charges together with the nature and severity of the penalties, were such that the charges against the applicants constituted criminal charges within the meaning of Article 6 of the Convention, which Article applied to their adjudication hearings.

The Court went on to conclude that Article 6(3)(c) had been breached in the governors' proceedings against both applicants.

In his dissenting opinion Judge Pellonpaa (joined by President Wildhaber and Judges Palm and Caflisch) stated:

> ...I also disagree with the view of the majority that 'the mere fact' that 'the applicants were prisoners serving a lawfully imposed sentence does not... serve to distinguish their case from that of civilians or military personnel at liberty' (paragraph 125). To me, the difference is fundamental. This also leads me to conclude that the additional days awarded cannot be regarded as 'appreciably detrimental' within the meaning of paragraph 82 of the *Engel* judgment. I note that even the imposition of the maximum penalty of 42 days would not as such have prevented the applicants' release long—indeed, several years—before the expiry of their respective sentences.

The British Government is to be credited for swiftly responding to the Chamber's judgment in *Ezeh and Connors* by introducing a revised system of prison discipline in August 2002. If the governor considered that a charge against a prisoner was serious enough to warrant the imposition of additional days' punishment if proven the governor should refer the case to an independent adjudicator (a District Judge) appointed by the Justice Secretary. Prisoners were given the opportunity to be legally represented before adjudicators. Adjudicators could impose an award of up to 42 additional days in prison (together with any other punishment available to governors, e.g. loss of privileges) where they found a prisoner guilty. Charges not meriting the award of additional days continued to be determined by governors.

8   Lustration proceedings to determine if a person had collaborated with the security services of a State during the era of communist totalitarianism were held to fall within the criminal limb of Article 6 by a unanimous Chamber in *Matyjek v Poland*, decision of 29 June 2006. The applicant, a former member of the Polish Parliament, submitted a lustration declaration, as required by legislation passed in 1997, stating that he had not collaborated with the communist security services. Later, the Warsaw Court of Appeal ruled that he had lied in his lustration declaration and, in accordance with the 1997 legislation, he was prohibited from holding a number of specified public positions for ten years. The Chamber considered that having regard to the nature and severity of the penalty imposed on the applicant, the lustration proceedings should be classified as criminal under Article 6 and his complaints about the fairness of the domestic hearings would be declared admissible. The application of Article 8 to lustration proceedings conducted by another former communist State are considered below in *Turek v Slovakia* (see p 507).

Fair hearing

(I) RIGHT TO A COURT

Golder v UK A.18 (1975)
European Court of Human Rights

In 1965 the applicant had been sentenced to 15 years' imprisonment for robbery. During October 1969 a serious disturbance took place in Parkhurst prison where Golder was serving his sentence. After the authorities had restored order in the prison, one officer (Laird) made a statement identifying Golder as a participant in the violence. A few days later that officer qualified his accusation against Golder and another officer reported that Golder had not participated in the prisoners' violence. The authorities did not bring any disciplinary charges against Golder. Subsequently he applied to the Home Secretary for permission to consult a solicitor with a view to suing Laird for libel in respect of the latter's accusations against him. The Home Secretary refused Golder's request. The applicant then complained to the Commission alleging, *inter alia*, that the Home Secretary's refusal violated his right of access to a court guaranteed by Article 6(1). The Commission, unanimously, upheld his complaint.

27. One point has not been put in issue and the Court takes it for granted: the 'right' which Golder wished, rightly or wrongly, to invoke against Laird before an English court was a 'civil right' within the meaning of Article 6 para 1 (art 6-1).

28. Again, Article 6 para 1 (art 6-1) does not state a right of access to the courts or tribunals in express terms. It enunciates rights which are distinct but stem from the same basic idea and which, taken together, make up a single right not specifically defined in the narrower sense of the term. It is the duty of the Court to ascertain, by means of interpretation, whether access to the courts constitutes one factor or aspect of this right.

29. The submissions made to the Court were in the first place directed to the manner in which the Convention, and particularly Article 6 para 1 (art 6-1), should be interpreted. The Court is prepared to consider, as do the Government and the Commission, that it should be guided by Articles 31 to 33 of the Vienna Convention of 23 May 1969 on the Law of Treaties. That Convention has not yet entered into force and it specifies, at Article 4, that it will not be retroactive, but its Articles 31 to 33 enunciate in essence generally accepted principles of international law to which the Court has already referred on occasion. . . .

30. In the way in which it is presented in the 'general rule' in Article 3l of the Vienna Convention, the process of interpretation of a treaty is a unity, a single combined operation . . .

31. The terms of Article 6 para 1 (art 6-1) of the European Convention, taken in their context, provide reason to think that this right is included among the guarantees set forth.

32. The clearest indications are to be found in the French text, first sentence. In the field of 'contestations civiles' (civil claims) everyone has a right to proceedings instituted by or against him being conducted in a certain way—'équitablement' (fairly), 'publiquement' (publicly), 'dans un délai raisonnable' (within a reasonable time), etc—but also and primarily 'à ce que sa cause soit entendue' (that his case be heard) not by any authority whatever but 'par un tribunal' (by a court or tribunal) within the meaning of Article 6 para 1 (art 6-1) (*Ringeisen* judgment of 16 July 1971, Series A No 13, p 39, para 95). The Government have emphasised rightly that in French 'cause' may mean 'procès qui se plaide' (Littré, *Dictionnaire de la langue française*, tome I, p 509, 5°). This, however, is not the sole ordinary sense of this noun; it serves also to indicate by extension 'l'ensemble des intérêts à soutenir, à faire prévaloir' (Paul Robert, *Dictionnaire alphabétique et analogique de la langue française*, tome I, p 666, II–2°). Similarly, the 'contestation' (claim) generally exists prior to the legal proceedings and is a concept independent of them. As regards the phrase 'tribunal indépendant et impartial établi par la loi' (independent and impartial tribunal established by law), it conjures up the idea of organisation rather than that of functioning, of institutions rather than of procedure.

The English text, for its part, speaks of an 'independent and impartial tribunal established by law'. Moreover, the phrase 'in the determination of his civil rights and obligations', on which the Government have relied in support of their contention, does not necessarily refer only to judicial proceedings already pending; as the Commission have observed, it may be taken as synonymous with 'wherever his civil rights and obligations are being determined' (paragraph 52 of the report). It too would then imply the right to have the determination of disputes relating to civil rights and obligations made by a court or 'tribunal'.

The Government have submitted that the expressions 'fair and public hearing' and 'within a reasonable time', the second sentence in paragraph 1 ('judgment', 'trial'), and paragraph 3 of Article 6 (art 6-1, art 6-3) clearly presuppose proceedings pending before a court.

While the right to a fair, public and expeditious judicial procedure can assuredly apply only to proceedings in being, it does not, however, necessarily follow that a right to the very institution of such proceedings is thereby excluded…Besides, in criminal matters, the 'reasonable time' may start to run from a date prior to the seisin of the trial court, of the 'tribunal' competent for the 'determination…of (the) criminal charge' (*Wemhoff* judgment of 27 June 1968, Series A No 7, pp 26–7, para 19; *Neumeister* judgment of 27 June 1968, Series A No 8, p 41, para 18; *Ringeisen* judgment of 16 July 1971, Series A No 13, p 45, para 110). It is conceivable also that in civil matters the reasonable time may begin to run, in certain circumstances, even before the issue of the writ commencing proceedings before the court to which the plaintiff submits the dispute.…

34. As stated in Article 31 para 2 of the Vienna Convention, the preamble to a treaty forms an integral part of the context. Furthermore, the preamble is generally very useful for the determination of the 'object' and 'purpose' of the instrument to be construed.

In the present case, the most significant passage in the Preamble to the European Convention is the signatory Governments declaring that they are 'resolved, as the Governments of European countries which are like-minded and have a common heritage of political traditions, ideals, freedom and the rule of law, to take the first steps for the collective enforcement of certain of the Rights stated in the Universal Declaration' of 10 December 1948.…And in civil matters one can scarcely conceive of the rule of law without there being a possibility of having access to the courts.

35.…The principle whereby a civil claim must be capable of being submitted to a judge ranks as one of the universally 'recognised' fundamental principles of law; the same is true of the principle of international law which forbids the denial of justice. Article 6 para 1 (art 6-1) must be read in the light of these principles.

Were Article 6 para 1 (art 6-1) to be understood as concerning exclusively the conduct of an action which had already been initiated before a court, a Contracting State could, without acting in breach of that text, do away with its courts, or take away their jurisdiction to determine certain classes of civil actions and entrust it to organs dependent on the Government. Such assumptions, indissociable from a danger of arbitrary power, would have serious consequences which are repugnant to the aforementioned principles and which the Court cannot overlook (*Lawless* judgment of 1 July 1961, Series A No 3, p 52, and *Delcourt* judgment of 17 January 1970, Series A No 11, pp 14–15).

It would be inconceivable, in the opinion of the Court, that Article 6 para 1 (art 6-1) should describe in detail the procedural guarantees afforded to parties in a pending lawsuit and should not first protect that which alone makes it in fact possible to benefit from such guarantees, that is, access to a court. The fair, public and expeditious characteristics of judicial proceedings are of no value at all if there are no judicial proceedings.

36. Taking all the preceding considerations together, it follows that the right of access constitutes an element which is inherent in the right stated by Article 6 para 1 (art 6-1). This is not an extensive interpretation forcing new obligations on the Contracting States: it is based on the very terms of the first sentence of Article 6 para 1 (art 6-1) read in its context and having regard to the object and purpose of the Convention, a lawmaking treaty (see the *Wemhoff* judgment of 27 June 1968, Series A No 7, p 23, para 8), and to general principles of law.

The Court thus reaches the conclusion, without needing to resort to 'supplementary means of interpretation' as envisaged at Article 32 of the Vienna Convention, that Article 6 para 1 (art 6-1) secures to everyone the right to have any claim relating to his civil rights and obligations brought before a court or tribunal. In this way the Article embodies the 'right to a court', of which the right of access, that is the right to institute proceedings before courts in civil matters, constitutes one aspect only. To this are added the guarantees laid down by Article 6 para 1 (art 6-1) as regards both the organisation and composition of the court, and the conduct of the proceedings. In sum, the whole makes up the right to a fair hearing. The Court has no need to ascertain in the present case whether and to what extent Article 6 para 1 (art 6-1) further requires a decision on the very substance of the dispute (English 'determination', French 'décidera').

B. ON THE 'IMPLIED LIMITATIONS'

37. Since the impediment to access to the courts...affected a right guaranteed by Article 6 para 1 (art 6-1), it remains to determine whether it was nonetheless justifiable by virtue of some legitimate limitation on the enjoyment or exercise of that right.

38. The Court considers, accepting the views of the Commission and the alternative submission of the Government, that the right of access to the courts is not absolute. As this is a right which the Convention sets forth (see Articles 13, 14, 17 and 25) (art 13, art 14, art 17, art 25) without, in the narrower sense of the term, defining, there is room, apart from the bounds delimiting the very content of any right, for limitations permitted by implication....

39. The Government and the Commission have cited examples of regulations, and especially of limitations, which are to be found in the national law of states in matters of access to the courts, for instance regulations relating to minors and persons of unsound mind. Although it is of less frequent occurrence and of a very different kind, the restriction complained of by Golder constitutes a further example of such a limitation.

It is not the function of the Court to elaborate a general theory of the limitations admissible in the case of convicted prisoners, nor even to rule *in abstracto* on the compatibility of...the Prison Rules 1964 with the Convention. Seised of a case which has its origin in a petition presented by an individual, the Court is called upon to pronounce itself only on the point whether or not the application of those Rules in the present case violated the Convention to the prejudice of Golder (*De Becker* judgment of 27 March 1962, Series A No 4, p 26).

40. In this connection, the Court confines itself to noting what follows.

In petitioning the Home Secretary for leave to consult a solicitor with a view to suing Laird for libel, Golder was seeking to exculpate himself of the charge made against him by that prison officer on 25 October 1969 and which had entailed for him unpleasant consequences...Furthermore, the contemplated legal proceedings would have concerned an incident which was connected with prison life and had occurred while the applicant was imprisoned. Finally, those proceedings would have been directed against a member of the prison staff who had made the charge in the course of his duties and who was subject to the Home Secretary's authority.

In these circumstances, Golder could justifiably wish to consult a solicitor with a view to instituting legal proceedings. It was not for the Home Secretary himself to appraise the prospects of the action contemplated; it was for an independent and impartial court to rule on any claim that might be brought. In declining to accord the leave which had been requested, the Home Secretary failed to respect, in the person of Golder, the right to go before a court as guaranteed by Article 6 para 1 (art 6-1)....

FOR THESE REASONS, THE COURT,
Holds by nine votes to three that there has been a breach of Article 6(1); ...

NOTES

1   The Court was composed of President Balladore Pallieri and Judges: Mosler, Rodenbourg, Cremona, Pedersen, Vilhjalmsson, Ryssdal, Bozer, and Ganshof van der Meersch. Judges Verdross, Zekia, and Fitzmaurice issued dissenting opinions in which they concluded that if the contracting States had intended to include a right of access to the civil courts in the Convention, they would have expressly embodied such a provision in the text of the Convention.

2   The above judgment is very significant for a number of reasons. First, it revealed the general principles and methodology the Court will utilize to interpret the rights contained within the Convention (particularly relying upon the guidelines elaborated by the Vienna Convention on the Law of Treaties). Secondly, the Court's interpretation of Article 6(1) demonstrated a generous approach that facilitated the protection of implicit, as well as express, rights concerned with a fair hearing/trial. Thirdly, the decision reflected a concern to protect the rights of prisoners, a group of persons who have historically not possessed many domestic legal rights in States such as the UK (for further cases involving prisoners, see p 568).

3   The Court refined the right of access to a domestic court in its subsequent jurisprudence and ruled that Article 6(1) guaranteed effective access. This elaboration of the right could necessitate positive action by States, to facilitate individuals' access to their courts. In *Airey v Ireland* A.32 (1979), the applicant was a married woman, of humble background and modest means (her net weekly wage was £40), who had been trying for a number of years to obtain a decree of judicial separation from her husband (who had been convicted of assaulting her). Under Irish law such an order could only be obtained from the High Court and the legal costs involved varied between £500–1,200. As there was no civil legal aid in Ireland the applicant had not been able to find a lawyer willing to act for her. She, therefore, complained to the Commission alleging, *inter alia*, that her right of access to a court was effectively denied to her by the Irish legal system. The Commission was unanimous in finding a breach of Article 6(1). By 5 votes to 2, the Court also upheld her claim.

24. The Government contend that the applicant does enjoy access to the High Court since she is free to go before that court without the assistance of a lawyer.

The Court does not regard this possibility, of itself, as conclusive of the matter. The Convention is intended to guarantee not rights that are theoretical or illusory but rights that are practical and effective (see, *mutatis mutandis*, the judgment of 23 July 1968 in the '*Belgian Linguistic*' case, Series A No 6, p 31, paras 3 *in fine* and 4; the above-mentioned *Golder* judgment, p 18, para 35)...This is particularly so of the right of access to the courts in view of the prominent place held in a democratic society by the right to a fair trial...It must therefore be ascertained whether Mrs Airey's appearance before the High Court without the assistance of a lawyer would be effective, in the sense of whether she would be able to present her case properly and satisfactorily.

Contradictory views on this question were expressed by the Government and the Commission during the oral hearings. It seems certain to the Court that the applicant would be at a disadvantage if her husband were represented by a lawyer and she were not. Quite apart from this eventuality, it is not realistic, in the Court's opinion, to suppose that, in litigation of this nature, the applicant could effectively conduct her own case, despite the assistance which, as was stressed by the Government, the judge affords to parties acting in person.

In Ireland, a decree of judicial separation is not obtainable in a District Court, where the procedure is relatively simple, but only in the High Court. A specialist in Irish family law, Mr Alan J Shatter, regards the High Court as the least accessible court not only because 'fees payable for representation before it are very high' but also by reason of the fact that 'the procedure for instituting proceedings...is complex particularly in the case of those proceedings which must be commenced by a petition', such as those for separation (*Family Law in the Republic of Ireland*, Dublin 1977, p 21).

Furthermore, litigation of this kind, in addition to involving complicated points of law, necessitates proof of adultery, unnatural practices or, as in the present case, cruelty; to establish the facts, expert evidence may have to be tendered and witnesses may have to be found, called and examined. What is more, marital disputes often entail an emotional involvement that is scarcely compatible with the degree of objectivity required by advocacy in court.

For these reasons, the Court considers it most improbable that a person in Mrs Airey's position...can effectively present his or her own case. This view is corroborated by the Government's replies to the questions put by the Court, replies which reveal that in each of the 255 judicial separation proceedings initiated in Ireland in the period from January 1972 to December 1978, without exception, the petitioner was represented by a lawyer...

The Court concludes from the foregoing that the possibility to appear in person before the High Court does not provide the applicant with an effective right of access...

25. The Government seek to distinguish the *Golder* case on the ground that, there, the applicant had been prevented from having access to court by reason of the positive obstacle placed in his way by the State in the shape of the Home Secretary's prohibition on his consulting a solicitor. The Government maintain that, in contrast, in the present case there is no positive obstacle emanating from the State and no deliberate attempt by the State to impede access; the alleged lack of access to court stems not from any act on the part of the authorities but solely from Mrs Airey's personal circumstances, a matter for which Ireland cannot be held responsible under the Convention.

Although this difference between the facts of the two cases is certainly correct, the Court does not agree with the conclusion which the Government draw therefrom. In the first place, hindrance in fact can contravene the Convention just like a legal impediment (above-mentioned *Golder* judgment, p 13, para 26). Furthermore, fulfilment of a duty under the Convention on occasion necessitates some positive action on the part of the State; in such circumstances, the State cannot simply remain passive and 'there is...no room to distinguish between acts and omissions' (see, *mutatis mutandis*, the above-mentioned *Marckx* judgment, p 15, para 31)...The obligation to secure an effective right of access to the courts falls into this category of duty.

26. The Government's principal argument rests on what they see as the consequence of the Commission's opinion, namely that, in all cases concerning the determination of a 'civil right', the State would have to provide free legal aid. In fact, the Convention's only express provision on free legal aid is Article 6 para 3 (c) (art 6-3-c) which relates to criminal proceedings and is itself subject to limitations; what is more, according to the Commission's established case law, Article 6 para 1 (art 6-1) does not guarantee any right to free legal aid as such. The Government add that since Ireland, when ratifying the Convention, made a reservation to Article 6 para 3 (c) (art 6-3-c) with the intention of limiting its obligations in the realm of criminal legal aid, a fortiori it cannot be said to have implicitly agreed to provide unlimited civil legal aid. Finally, in their submission, the Convention should not be interpreted so as to achieve social and economic developments in a Contracting State; such developments can only be progressive.

The Court is aware that the further realisation of social and economic rights is largely dependent on the situation—notably financial—reigning in the State in question. On the other hand, the Convention must be interpreted in the light of present-day conditions (above-mentioned *Marckx* judgment, p 19, para 41) and it is designed to safeguard the individual in a real and practical way as regards those areas with which it deals (see paragraph 24 above). While the Convention sets forth what are essentially civil and political rights, many of them have implications of a social or economic nature. The Court therefore considers, like the Commission, that the mere fact that an interpretation of the Convention may extend into the sphere of social and economic rights should not be a decisive factor against such an interpretation; there is no watertight division separating that sphere from the field covered by the Convention.

The Court does not, moreover, share the Government's view as to the consequence of the Commission's opinion.

It would be erroneous to generalise the conclusion that the possibility to appear in person before the High Court does not provide Mrs Airey with an effective right of access; that conclusion does not hold good for all cases concerning 'civil rights and obligations' or for everyone involved therein. In certain eventualities, the possibility of appearing before a court in person, even without a lawyer's assistance, will meet the requirements of Article 6 para 1 (art 6-1); there may be occasions when such a possibility secures adequate access even to the High Court. Indeed, much must depend on the particular circumstances.

In addition, while Article 6 para 1 (art 6-1) guarantees to litigants an effective right of access to the courts for the determination of their 'civil rights and obligations', it leaves to the State a free choice of the means to be used towards this end. The institution of a legal aid scheme—which Ireland now envisages in family law matters . . . constitutes one of those means but there are others such as, for example, a simplification of procedure. In any event, it is not the Court's function to indicate, let alone dictate, which measures should be taken; all that the Convention requires is that an individual should enjoy his effective right of access to the courts in conditions not at variance with Article 6 para 1 (art 6-1) . . .

The conclusion appearing at the end of paragraph 24 above does not therefore imply that the State must provide free legal aid for every dispute relating to a 'civil right'.

To hold that so far-reaching an obligation exists would, the Court agrees, sit ill with the fact that the Convention contains no provision on legal aid for those disputes, Article 6 para 3 (c) (art 6-3-c) dealing only with criminal proceedings. However, despite the absence of a similar clause for civil litigation, Article 6 para 1 (art 6-1) may sometimes compel the State to provide for the assistance of a lawyer when such assistance proves indispensable for an effective access to court either because legal representation is rendered compulsory, as is done by the domestic law of certain Contracting States for various types of litigation, or by reason of the complexity of the procedure or of the case.

As regards the Irish reservation to Article 6 para 3 (c) (art 6-3-c), it cannot be interpreted as affecting the obligations under Article 6 para 1 (art 6-1); accordingly, it is not relevant in the present context.

27. The applicant was unable to find a solicitor willing to act on her behalf in judicial separation proceedings. The Commission inferred that the reason why the solicitors she consulted were not prepared to act was that she would have been unable to meet the costs involved. The Government question this opinion but the Court finds it plausible and has been presented with no evidence which could invalidate it.

28. Having regard to all the circumstances of the case, the Court finds that Mrs Airey did not enjoy an effective right of access to the High Court for the purpose of petitioning for a decree of judicial separation. There has accordingly been a breach of Article 6 para 1 . . .

The Court's focus upon the practicality of a specific person's right of access to a court was a very welcome development. The full-time Court's analysis of the circumstances where States are obliged to provide legal assistance for impecunious civil defendants can be seen in **Steel and Morris v UK**, p 411.

4 The Court's approach to restrictions on persons' right of access to a court was explained in **Stubbings v UK**, 1996-IV. Ms Stubbings was born in 1957 and adopted when she was 3 years old. From 1976 she experienced serious psychological problems and in 1984, following treatment by a family psychiatrist, she allegedly realized that there might be a connection between her mental health problems and childhood sexual abuse that she claimed to have suffered from members of her adoptive family. In 1987 she commenced civil proceedings against her adoptive father and brother seeking damages for the alleged assaults. The defendants sought to have her claim dismissed as time-barred under the Limitation Act 1980. Eventually, the House of Lords determined that her claim was subject to a six-year limitation period that began on her 18th birthday. As she had only begun her action in 1987, her claim was dismissed as being out of time (**Stubbings v Webb** [1993] 1 All ER 322). She, and three other women whose alleged sexual abuse claims were also dismissed as time-barred, complained to the Commission alleging breaches of their right of access to a court. The Commission, unanimously, found a breach of Article 14 in combination with Article 6(1). The Court, by 7 votes to 2, stated that:

47. The applicants submitted that the very essence of their right of access to court had been impaired by the limitation period of six years from the age of majority applied in their cases. One of the effects of the sexual abuse each applicant suffered was to prevent her from appreciating that it was the cause of her psychological problems until after the expiry of the limitation period...Expert evidence showed that the victims of child sexual abuse might commonly be unable to perceive the causal connection between the abuse and their psychological problems without medical assistance. Thus, each applicant's claim for damages for the injuries caused by the abuse became time-barred before she had even realised she had a cause of action....

50. The Court recalls that Article 6 para 1 (art 6-1) embodies the 'right to a court', of which the right of access, that is, the right to institute proceedings before a court in civil matters, constitutes one aspect.

However, this right is not absolute, but may be subject to limitations; these are permitted by implication since the right of access by its very nature calls for regulation by the State. In this respect, the Contracting States enjoy a certain margin of appreciation, although the final decision as to the observance of the Convention's requirements rests with the Court. It must be satisfied that the limitations applied do not restrict or reduce the access left to the individual in such a way or to such an extent that the very essence of the right is impaired. Furthermore, a limitation will not be compatible with Article 6 para 1 (art 6-1) if it does not pursue a legitimate aim and if there is not a reasonable relationship of proportionality between the means employed and the aim sought to be achieved...

51. It is noteworthy that limitation periods in personal injury cases are a common feature of the domestic legal systems of the Contracting States. They serve several important purposes, namely to ensure legal certainty and finality, protect potential defendants from stale claims which might be difficult to counter and prevent the injustice which might arise if courts were required to decide upon events which took place in the distant past on the basis of evidence which might have become unreliable and incomplete because of the passage of time.

52. In the instant case, the English law of limitation allowed the applicants six years from their eighteenth birthdays in which to initiate civil proceedings. In addition, subject to the need for sufficient evidence, a criminal prosecution could be brought at any time and, if successful, a compensation order could be made...Thus, the very essence of the applicants' right of access to a court was not impaired.

53. The time-limit in question was not unduly short; indeed it was longer than the extinction periods for personal injury claims set by some international treaties...Moreover, it becomes clear that the rules applied were proportionate to the aims sought to be achieved (see paragraph 50 above) when it is considered that if the applicants had commenced actions shortly before the expiry of the period, the courts would have been required to adjudicate on events which had taken place approximately twenty years earlier.

54. The time bar in the applicants' cases commenced from the age of majority and could not be waived or extended...It appears from the material available to the Court that there is no uniformity among the member States of the Council of Europe with regard either to the length of civil limitation periods or the date from which such periods are reckoned. In many States, the period is calculated from the date of the accrual of the cause of action, while in other jurisdictions time only starts to run from the date when the material facts in the case were known, or ought to have been known, to the plaintiff. This second principle applies in England and Wales to civil claims based on negligence (sections 11 (4) (b) and 14 of the 1980 Act...). However, it cannot be said at the present time that this principle is commonly accepted in European States in cases such as that in issue.

55. The Contracting States properly enjoy a margin of appreciation in deciding how the right of access to court should be circumscribed. It is clear that the United Kingdom legislature has devoted a substantial amount of time and study to the consideration of these questions. Since 1936, there have been four statutes to amend and reform the law of limitation and six official bodies have reviewed aspects of it . . . The decision of the House of Lords, of which the applicants complain . . . that a fixed six-year period should apply in cases of intentionally caused personal injury, was not taken arbitrarily, but rather followed from the interpretation of the Limitation Act 1980 in the light of the report of the Tucker Committee upon which the Act had been based . . .

56. There has been a developing awareness in recent years of the range of problems caused by child abuse and its psychological effects on victims, and it is possible that the rules on limitation of actions applying in member States of the Council of Europe may have to be amended to make special provision for this group of claimants in the near future.

   However, since the very essence of the applicants' right of access was not impaired and the restrictions in question pursued a legitimate aim and were proportionate, it is not for the Court to substitute its own view for that of the State authorities as to what would be the most appropriate policy in this regard.

57. Accordingly, taking into account in particular the legitimate aims served by the rules of limitation in question and the margin of appreciation afforded to States in regulating the right of access to a court (see paragraphs 50–1 above), the Court finds that there has been no violation of Article 6 para 1 of the Convention taken alone (art 6-1) . . .

The Court, by 8 votes to 1, also found no breach of Article 14 taken in conjunction with Article 6(1). To what extent do you think the above judgment was influenced by the lack of consensus among member States regarding the starting time and duration of limitation periods for civil actions? A unanimous Court applied the criteria outlined in paragraph 50 of the *Stubbings* judgment when evaluating ministerial certificates preventing the continuation of alleged religious/political discrimination proceedings in Northern Ireland. The applicants in *Tinnelly & Sons Ltd and McElduff v UK*, 1998-IV, complained to the Fair Employment Commission/Fair Employment Tribunal that they had been refused contracts or security clearance with public bodies because of religious/political discrimination contrary to the Fair Employment (Northern Ireland) Act 1976. The Secretary of State issued certificates under section 42 of the Act stating that action taken in respect of the applicants had been done 'for the purposes of safeguarding national security'. The certificates had the effect of terminating the applicants' complaints before domestic tribunals/courts. The Commission, unanimously, found a violation of Article 6(1). The Court held that:

61. . . . the 1976 Act guaranteed persons a right not to be discriminated against on grounds of religious belief or political opinion in the job market including, and of relevance to the instant case, when bidding for a public works contract or subcontract. In the opinion of the Court that clearly defined statutory right, having regard to the context in which it applied and to its pecuniary nature, can be classified as a 'civil right' within the meaning of Article 6(1) of the Convention. . . .

77. . . . the conclusive nature of the section 42 certificates had the effect of preventing a judicial determination of the merits of the applicants' complaints that they were victims of unlawful discrimination. The Court would observe that such a complaint can properly be submitted for an independent judicial determination even if national security considerations are present and constitute a highly material aspect of the case. The right guaranteed to an applicant under Article 6 § 1 of the Convention to submit a dispute to a court or tribunal in order to have a determination of questions of both fact and law cannot be displaced by the *ipse dixit* of the executive . . .

Therefore, the issuing of the certificates constituted a disproportionate restriction on the applicants' right of access to a court. Clearly, the absolute effect of the certificates on the applicants' domestic proceedings was a dominant factor in the Court's determination. A similar conclusion was reached by the Court in respect of the public policy immunity of the English police from negligence actions concerning the investigation and suppression of crime. In *Osman v UK* (see p 120), the Court was united in finding a breach of Article 6(1):

150. Although the aim of such a rule may be accepted as legitimate in terms of the Convention, as being directed to the maintenance of the effectiveness of the police service and hence to the prevention of disorder or crime, the Court must nevertheless, in turning to the issue of proportionality, have particular regard to its scope and especially its application in the case at issue. While the Government have contended that the exclusionary rule of liability is not of an absolute nature . . . and that its application may yield to other public-policy considerations, it would appear to the Court that in the instant case the Court of Appeal proceeded on the basis that the rule provided a watertight defence to the police and that it was impossible to prise open an immunity which the police enjoy from civil suit in respect of their acts and omissions in the investigation and suppression of crime.

151. The Court would observe that the application of the rule in this manner without further enquiry into the existence of competing public-interest considerations only serves to confer a blanket immunity on the police for their acts and omissions during the investigation and suppression of crime and amounts to an unjustifiable restriction on an applicant's right to have a determination on the merits of his or her claim against the police in deserving cases. . . .

Once again, it was the comprehensive nature of the immunity which led the Court to determine that there had been a disproportionate limitation on the applicants' right of access to a court. However, in the later case of *Z and others v UK* (p 159) a majority of the Grand Chamber did not follow *Osman* because of clarifications in the law of negligence by the domestic courts.

5   Three important judgments on the relationship between the international law rules on State (sovereign) immunity and the implied right of access to court were given by Grand Chambers on the same day in November 2001. In *Al-Adsani v UK*, judgment of 21 November 2001, the applicant was a dual British/Kuwaiti national. He claimed that during 1991 he went to Kuwait to assist in its defence against invasion by Iraq. After the latter's invasion he remained in Kuwait as a member of the resistance movement. He came into possession of sexual video tapes involving Sheikh Jaber Al-Sabah (a relative of the Emir of Kuwait). Somehow those tapes were circulated and the Sheikh held the applicant responsible for their distribution. In May 1991, after the Iraqi's had been expelled from Kuwait, the Sheikh together with two other persons entered the applicant's house, beat him, and forced him to accompany them in a government vehicle. He was taken to the Kuwait State Security Prison and repeatedly beaten by guards over several days. Soon after his release the applicant was again forced to accompany the Sheikh in a government car to the palace of the Emir's brother. The applicant's head was held under the water of a swimming pool containing corpses and he was then taken to a room where the Sheikh set fire to the furniture causing Al-Adsani to receive burns on a quarter of his body's surface. Later that month the applicant returned to the UK for medical treatment. In August 1992 the applicant began civil proceedings against the Sheikh and the Government of Kuwait in respect of the injuries allegedly inflicted upon him in Kuwait. In December of that year Al-Adsani obtained a default judgment against the Sheikh. In 1993 the proceedings were re-issued to include two named individuals as defendants. In August the High Court

granted the applicant leave to serve the proceedings upon the named individual defendants, but not on the Government of Kuwait. Subsequently the Court of Appeal granted the applicant leave to serve the writ on the Kuwait Government. However, the latter applied for an order striking the proceedings out on the grounds of State immunity. The UK has ratified, with seven other States, the Council of Europe's 1972 European Convention on State Immunity (Basle Convention) which provides that contracting States are entitled to immunity unless the proceedings relate to stated exceptions. Domestic law was brought into conformity with the Basle Convention by the State Immunity Act 1978. During 1996 the Court of Appeal held that the Government of Kuwait were entitled to assert State immunity under the 1978 Act.

The applicant later lodged a complaint at Strasbourg asserting that the striking out of his claim against the Government of Kuwait violated his right of access to a court for the determination of his civil rights guaranteed by Article 6(1) of the Convention. The Court held that his claim was for damages in respect of personal injuries, a well-established cause of action in England. Consequently, there existed a genuine dispute over 'civil rights' within the meaning of Article 6(1). The British Government argued that the restriction on the applicant's right of access was for the legitimate aim of complying with the universally applicable principles of public international law on State immunity as embodied in the Basle Convention. The Court acknowledged that:

53. The right of access to court is not, however, absolute, but may be subject to limitations; these are permitted by implication since the right of access by its very nature calls for regulation by the State. In this respect, the Contracting States enjoy a certain margin of appreciation, although the final decision as to the observance of the Convention's requirements rests with the Court. It must be satisfied that the limitations applied do not restrict or reduce the access left to the individual in such a way or to such an extent that the very essence of the right is impaired. Furthermore, a limitation will not be compatible with Article 6 § 1 if it does not pursue a legitimate aim and if there is no reasonable relationship of proportionality between the means employed and the aim sought to be achieved...

A bare majority (9 votes to 8) determined that the striking out of the applicant's claim by the English courts was for a legitimate aim and proportionate to that objective. The former criterion was satisfied because,

54. ... the grant of sovereign immunity to a State in civil proceedings pursues the legitimate aim of complying with international law to promote comity and good relations between States through the respect of another State's sovereignty.

As to the latter, the Court considered that:

55. ... The Convention should so far as possible be interpreted in harmony with other rules of international law of which it forms part, including those relating to the grant of State immunity.

56. It follows that measures taken by a High Contracting Party which reflect generally recognised rules of public international law on State immunity cannot in principle be regarded as imposing a disproportionate restriction on the right of access to court as embodied in Article 6 § 1. Just as the right of access to court is an inherent part of the fair trial guarantee in that Article, so some restrictions on access must likewise be regarded as inherent, an example being those limitations generally accepted by the community of nations as part of the doctrine of State immunity.

The majority, however, rejected the applicant's contention that public international law now recognized a peremptory norm (*jus cogens*) that prevented States from claiming State immunity from civil proceedings in another State regarding acts of torture committed in the territory of the former.

61. While the Court accepts, on the basis of these authorities, that the prohibition of torture has achieved the status of a peremptory norm in international law, it observes that the present case concerns not, as in the [*Prosecutor v*] *Furundzija* [ICTY: (1999) 38 ILM 317] and *Pinochet* [*R v Bow Street Metropolitan Stipendiary Magistrate and Others, ex parte Pinochet Ugarte (No 3)* [2000] AC 147] decisions, the criminal liability of an individual for alleged acts of torture, but the immunity of a State in a civil suit for damages in respect of acts of torture within the territory of that State. Notwithstanding the special character of the prohibition of torture in international law, the Court is unable to discern in the international instruments, judicial authorities or other materials before it any firm basis for concluding that, as a matter of international law, a State no longer enjoys immunity from civil suit in the courts of another State where acts of torture are alleged. In particular, the Court observes that none of the primary international instruments referred to (Article 5 of the Universal Declaration of Human Rights, Article 7 of the International Covenant on Civil and Political Rights and Articles 2 and 4 of the United Nations Convention against Torture) relates to civil proceedings or to State immunity.

62. It is true that in its Report on Jurisdictional Immunities of States and their Property the Working Group of the International Law Commission noted, as a recent development in State practice and legislation on the subject of immunities of States, the argument increasingly put forward that immunity should be denied in the case of death or personal injury resulting from acts of a State in violation of human rights norms having the character of jus cogens, particularly the prohibition on torture. However, as the Working Group itself acknowledged, while national courts had in some cases shown some sympathy for the argument that States were not entitled to plead immunity where there had been a violation of human rights norms with the character of jus cogens, in most cases (including those cited by the applicant in the domestic proceedings and before the Court) the plea of sovereign immunity had succeeded.

66. The Court, while noting the growing recognition of the overriding importance of the prohibition of torture, does not accordingly find it established that there is yet acceptance in international law of the proposition that States are not entitled to immunity in respect of civil claims for damages for alleged torture committed outside the forum State. The 1978 Act, which grants immunity to States in respect of personal injury claims unless the damage was caused within the United Kingdom, is not inconsistent with those limitations generally accepted by the community of nations as part of the doctrine of State immunity.

67. In these circumstances, the application by the English courts of the provisions of the 1978 Act to uphold Kuwait's claim to immunity cannot be said to have amounted to an unjustified restriction on the applicant's access to court.

It follows that there has been no violation of Article 6 § 1 in this case.

A dissenting opinion was given by Judges Rozarkis and Caflisch, joined by Judges Wildhaber, Costa, Cabral Barreto, and Vajic. They disagreed with the majority's distinction between criminal and civil proceedings involving allegations of State torture. In the dissentients' view it was significant that the British courts had not relied upon that distinction. Furthermore:

...the distinction made by the majority between civil and criminal proceedings, concerning the effect of the rule of the prohibition of torture, is not consonant with the very essence of the operation of the *jus cogens* rules. It is not the nature of the proceedings which determines the effects that a *jus cogens* rule has upon another rule of international law, but the character of the rule as a peremptory norm and its interaction with a hierarchically lower rule. The prohibition of torture, being a rule of *jus cogens*, acts in the international sphere and deprives the rule of sovereign immunity of all its legal effects in that sphere. The criminal or civil nature of the domestic proceedings is immaterial. The jurisdictional bar is lifted by the very interaction of the international rules involved, and the national judge cannot admit a plea of immunity raised by the defendant State as an element preventing him from entering into the merits of the case and from dealing with the claim of the applicant for the alleged damages inflicted upon him.

Under these circumstances we believe that the United Kingdom courts have erred in considering that they had no jurisdiction to entertain the applicant's claim because of the procedural bar of State immunity and the consequent application of the 1978 Act. Accordingly, the applicant was deprived of his right to have access to the British court to entertain his claim of damages for the alleged torture suffered by him in Kuwait, and Article 6 § 1, has, in our view, been violated.

The above case revealed the Court to be very divided in its assessments of the requirements of public international law regarding claims of State immunity in the context of allegations of State torture. The same Grand Chamber was, however, much more united in its assessment of the rules of State immunity regarding civil claims involving the employment of persons by foreign embassies. In *Fogarty v UK*, judgment of 21 November 2001, the applicant was an Irish national. Between November 1993 and February 1995 she had been employed as an administrative assistant in the Foreign Broadcasting Information Service (a subsidiary organization of the Central Intelligence Agency) at the US Embassy in London. Following her dismissal she brought proceedings against the US Government before an industrial tribunal alleging that her dismissal had been the result of sex discrimination (contrary to the Sex Discrimination Act 1975). She claimed that she had been the victim of persistent sexual harassment by her supervisor. In June 1995 she obtained a 12-month contract as an administrative assistant with the Foreign Building Operations section of the US Embassy. The US Government did not claim State immunity before the industrial tribunal and in May 1996 the tribunal upheld the applicant's claim. Compensation of £12,000 was agreed between the parties. In June and August 1996 the applicant unsuccessfully applied for secretarial posts within the US Embassy. During September 1996 the applicant made a further application to the industrial tribunal asserting that the embassy's refusals to re-employ her were a consequence of her successful earlier sex discrimination claim and therefore constituted further acts of discrimination and victimization contrary to the 1975 Act. Lawyers acting for the US Government informed the tribunal that the Government intended to claim immunity from these subsequent proceedings under the State Immunity Act 1978. The latter provides for the immunity of States in respect of the employment of members of foreign missions and consular facilities. Likewise the Basle Convention expressly preserves the privileges and immunities of diplomatic missions. Consequently, counsel advised the applicant that the US Government was entitled to assert immunity and that she had no remedy in domestic law.

Before the Court the applicant complained that the doctrine of State immunity recognized by English law denied her access to a court in breach of Article 6(1). Following the method of analysis used in *Al-Adsani*, the Court first examined whether the applicant had been seeking to assert a 'civil right' in the proceedings before the industrial tribunal.

26. Section 6 of the Sex Discrimination Act 1975 creates a statutory right which arises, *inter alia*, when an employer refuses to employ a woman on grounds of sex discrimination or by reason of the fact that she has already taken proceedings under the 1975 Act. Thus, the proceedings which the applicant intended to pursue were for damages for a cause of action well known to English law.

The Court does not accept the Government's plea that because of the operation of State immunity she did not have a substantive right under domestic law....

Secondly, did the restriction on the applicant's right to bring those proceedings against the US Government pursue a legitimate aim? The Court held that it did because:

34....sovereign immunity is a concept of international law, developed out of the principle *par in parem non habet imperium*, by virtue of which one State shall not be subject to the jurisdiction of another State. The Court considers that the grant of sovereign immunity to a State in civil proceedings pursues the legitimate aim of complying with international law to promote comity and good relations between States through the respect of another State's sovereignty.

Thirdly, it was necessary to determine if the restriction was a proportionate measure. An overwhelming majority (16 votes to 1) considered that it was.

38....Questions relating to the recruitment of staff to missions and embassies may by their very nature involve sensitive and confidential issues, related, *inter alia*, to the diplomatic and organisational policy of a foreign State. The Court is not aware of any trend in international law towards a relaxation of the rule of State immunity as regards issues of recruitment to foreign missions....

39. In these circumstances, the Court considers that, in conferring immunity on the United States in the present case by virtue of the provisions of the 1978 Act, the United Kingdom cannot be said to have exceeded the margin of appreciation allowed to States in limiting an individual's access to court.

It follows that there has been no violation of Article 6 § 1 in this case.

Judge Loucaides dissented on the ground that the application of the doctrine of State immunity to the applicant's sex discrimination claim resulted in an absolute blocking of her proceedings without any consideration of the substance of her claim or the balancing of competing interests. He considered that such an absolute bar to proceedings was not a proportionate limitation of the right of access to a court.

The distinction between **Fogarty** and **Al-Adsani** was that in the former case the relevant rules of international law on State immunity, in respect of the recruitment of embassy staff, were much more certain. Therefore, the Court was almost unanimous in holding that they were a legitimate and proportionate restriction on the Convention right of access to a court.

In **McElhinney v Ireland**, judgment of 21 November 2001, the Court was faced with a respondent State that was not a party to the Basle Convention. The applicant was a police officer in Ireland. Late one evening in March 1991, whilst off-duty, the applicant drove a vehicle pulling a trailer into the barrier of a UK vehicle checkpoint in County Derry (Northern Ireland). The checkpoint was staffed by armed British soldiers. A corporal in the military police approached the applicant's vehicle and was hit by the trailer. The applicant drove off into Ireland and the soldier climbed onto the tow-bar of the applicant's vehicle. The soldier fired six shots, hitting the exhaust pipe and rear window of the applicant's vehicle. The applicant claimed that he heard the shots and believed that he was under attack from a terrorist. Therefore, he drove for about two miles until he reached an Irish police station. When he stopped the soldier ordered him, and his passengers, to stand against a wall with their hands in the air. According to the applicant the soldier tried to shoot him, but his gun jammed. The applicant was arrested by Irish police officers on suspicion of driving having consumed excess alcohol. He refused to provide either blood or urine samples and was later convicted for failing to do so. The applicant alleged that he suffered severe post-traumatic shock as a result of the soldier's actions. In 1993 he began an action in the Irish High Court against the soldier and the (British) Secretary of State for Northern Ireland claiming damages for assault. In 1994 the Secretary of State applied for the summons to be set aside on the ground of sovereign immunity. The High Court granted the Secretary's request. On appeal the Supreme Court upheld the lower court's ruling, as the soldier was carrying out governmental/sovereign activities at the checkpoint his actions had to be regarded as *de jure imperii*. Furthermore, it had not been established that the principles of sovereign immunity in public international law no longer applied to the tortious acts of a foreign State's agent within the sphere of *de jure imperii*. The applicant did not pursue his action against the corporal nor did he initiate civil proceedings in the courts of Northern Ireland.

At Strasbourg the Court held that the applicant had been seeking to assert 'civil rights' in his action against the British Government, because his claims of assault, trespass to the person, negligence, and breach of duty were well-known causes of action in Ireland. However, the setting aside of his proceedings had been for the legitimate aim of complying with international law. A large majority of the Court (12 votes to 5) also concluded that the Irish courts' termination of the proceedings, in deference to the doctrine of sovereign immunity, was a proportionate measure.

38. The Court observes that, on the material before it ... there appears to be a trend in international and comparative law towards limiting State immunity in respect of personal injury caused by an act or omission within the forum State, but that this practice is by no means universal. Further, it appears ... that the trend may primarily refer to 'insurable' personal injury, that is incidents arising out of ordinary road traffic accidents, rather than matters relating to the core area of State sovereignty such as the acts of a soldier on foreign territory which, of their very nature, may involve sensitive issues affecting diplomatic relations between States and national security. Certainly, it cannot be said that Ireland is alone in holding that immunity attaches to suits in respect of such torts committed by *acta jure imperii* or that, in affording this immunity, Ireland falls outside any currently accepted international standards. The Court agrees with the Supreme Court in the present case ... that it is not possible, given the present state of the development of international law, to conclude that Irish law conflicts with its general principles.

40. In these circumstances, the decisions of the Irish courts upholding the United Kingdom's claim to immunity cannot be said to have exceeded the margin of appreciation allowed to States in limiting an individual's right to access to court.

It follows that there has been no violation of Article 6 § 1 in this case.

Judges Caflisch, Cabral Barreto, and Vajic issued a dissenting opinion in which they expressed the belief that international law had evolved further in the limitation of claims of sovereign immunity than the position recognized by the majority. In his dissent Judge Loucaides emphasized the distinct nature of the Convention's legal regime and sought to distance it from the universal principles of international law.

In the above three cases the variable sizes of the majorities and minorities in the Court reflected the different contexts in which claims for State/sovereign immunity were being claimed and the judges' disagreements over the requirements of contemporary international law. The fact that the latter body of law is evolving in its treatment of State/sovereign immunity claims added to the complexity of the task facing the Court. Nevertheless, in the later case of *Cudak v Lithuania*, judgment of 23 March 2010, the Grand Chamber was united in finding a breach of Article 6(1). The applicant, a Lithuanian national, had been employed for two years as a secretary at the Polish Embassy in Vilnius. After a complaint by the applicant, the Lithuanian Equal Opportunities Ombudsman reported that she had been a victim of sexual harassment by a work colleague (a member of the diplomatic staff). The applicant was on sick leave for several weeks but when she returned to work the embassy refused her entry and she was notified that she had been dismissed for failing to attend for work. The applicant lodged a civil claim seeking compensation for unlawful dismissal but the Polish Government successfully asserted State immunity before the Lithuanian courts. The applicant complained to Strasbourg alleging a breach of her right of access to a court.

The Grand Chamber considered that her case could be distinguished from *Fogarty* as it concerned a complaint about dismissal (not recruitment). Furthermore, customary international law, as reflected in the International Law Commission's Draft Article on employment contracts and State immunity, provided that a State should not enjoy immunity in respect of complaints such as the applicant's.

74. In conclusion, by upholding in the present case an objection based on State immunity and by declining jurisdiction to hear the applicant's claim, the Lithuanian courts, in failing to preserve a reasonable relationship of proportionality, overstepped their margin of appreciation and thus impaired the very essence of the applicant's right of access to a court.

Cudak was awarded 10,000 euros compensation for pecuniary/non-pecuniary damage by the Grand Chamber. Similarly, another Grand Chamber was united in finding a breach of this right in respect of the inability of a French national to challenge the termination of his employment, as an accountant, at the Kuwait Embassy in Paris before the domestic courts: *Sabeh El Leil v France*, judgment of 29 June 2011.

6 The absolute privilege given to debates in the House of Commons, by Article 9 of the Bill of Rights 1689, was challenged in *A v UK*, judgment of 17 December 2002. The applicant's Member of Parliament (MP) initiated a debate on public sector housing in which he described the applicant and her family as neighbours from hell giving detailed allegations of anti-social behaviour caused by her family. The MP identified the applicant and gave her address in his speech. The speech was given wide publicity in the local press and subsequently the applicant received hate mail and was harassed to the extent that she was re-housed. She contended that her inability to bring civil proceedings against the MP violated her right of access to court. The Chamber, by 6 votes to 1, held that:

77. The Court concludes that the parliamentary immunity enjoyed by the MP in the present case pursued the legitimate aims of protecting free speech in Parliament and maintaining the separation of powers between the legislature and the judiciary.

78. The Court must next assess the proportionality of the immunity enjoyed by the MP. In this regard, the Court notes that the immunity concerned was absolute in nature and applied to both criminal and civil proceedings. The Court agrees with the applicant's submission that the broader an immunity, the more compelling must be its justification in order that it can be said to be compatible with the Convention. However, ... its absolute nature cannot be decisive. Thus, for example, in the above-mentioned *Al-Adsani* case, the Court stated that measures taken by signatory States which reflected generally recognised rules of public international law on State immunity could not in principle be regarded as imposing a disproportionate restriction on the right of access to court as embodied in Article 6 § 1 (see also *Fogarty v the United Kingdom* [GC], No 37112/97, § 36, ECHR 2001-XI; *McElhinney v Ireland* [GC], No 31253/96, § 37, ECHR 2001-XI).

79. It is also recalled that, in the recent case of *Jerusalem v Austria* (No 26958/95, §§ 36 and 40, ECHR 2001-II), the Court stated that, while freedom of expression is important for everybody, it is especially so for an elected representative of the people. He or she represents the electorate,

draws attention to their preoccupations and defends their interests. In a democracy, Parliament or such comparable bodies are the essential fora for political debate. Very weighty reasons must be advanced to justify interfering with the freedom of expression exercised therein.

80. The Court notes that most, if not all, signatory States to the Convention have in place some form of immunity for members of their national legislatures. In particular, the domestic law of each of the eight States to have made a third-party intervention in the present case makes provision for such an immunity … although the precise detail of the immunities concerned varies.

81. Measures are also in place granting privileges and immunities to, *inter alios*, Representatives to the Consultative Assembly of the Council of Europe and Members of the European Parliament.

…

83. In light of the above, the Court believes that a rule of parliamentary immunity, which is consistent with and reflects generally recognised rules within signatory States, the Council of Europe and the European Union, cannot in principle be regarded as imposing a disproportionate restriction on the right of access to court as embodied in Article 6 § 1 (see, *mutatis mutandis*, the above-mentioned *Al-Adsani* judgment, § 56). Just as the right of access to court is an inherent part of the fair trial guarantee in that Article, so some restrictions on access must likewise be regarded as inherent, an example being those limitations generally accepted by signatory States as part of the doctrine of parliamentary immunity (ibid).

84. Furthermore, the immunity afforded to MPs in the United Kingdom appears to the Court to be in several respects narrower than that afforded to members of national legislatures in certain other signatory States and those afforded to Representatives to the Consultative Assembly of the Council of Europe and Members of the European Parliament. In particular, the immunity attaches only to statements made in the course of parliamentary debates on the floor of the House of Commons or House of Lords. No immunity attaches to statements made outside Parliament, even if they amount to a repetition of statements made during the course of Parliamentary debates on matters of public interest. Nor does any immunity attach to an MP's press statements published prior to parliamentary debates, even if their contents are repeated subsequently in the debate itself.

85. The absolute immunity enjoyed by MPs is moreover designed to protect the interests of Parliament as a whole as opposed to those of individual MPs. This is illustrated by the fact that the immunity does not apply outside Parliament. In contrast, the immunity which protects those engaged in the reporting of parliamentary proceedings, and that enjoyed by elected representatives in local government, are each qualified in nature.

86. The Court observes that victims of defamatory misstatement in Parliament are not entirely without means of redress. In particular, such persons can, where it is their own MP who has made the offending remarks, petition the House through any other MP with a view to securing a retraction. In extreme cases, deliberately misleading statements may be punishable by Parliament as a contempt. General control is exercised over debates by the Speaker of each House. The Court considers that all of these factors are of relevance to the question of proportionality of the immunity enjoyed by the MP in the present case.

87. It follows that, in all the circumstances of this case, the application of a rule of absolute Parliamentary immunity cannot be said to exceed the margin of appreciation allowed to States in limiting an individual's right of access to court.

88. The Court agrees with the applicant's submissions to the effect that the allegations made about her in the MP's speech were extremely serious and clearly unnecessary in the context of a debate about municipal housing policy. The MP's repeated reference to the applicant's name and address was particularly regrettable. The Court considers that the unfortunate consequences

of the MP's comments for the lives of the applicant and her children were entirely foreseeable. However, these factors cannot alter the Court's conclusion as to the proportionality of the parliamentary immunity at issue, since the creation of exceptions to that immunity, the application of which depended upon the individual facts of any particular case, would seriously undermine the legitimate aims pursued.

89. There has, accordingly, been no violation of Article 6 § 1 of the Convention as regards the parliamentary immunity enjoyed by the MP.

The concluding comments of the Court indicate that it did not approve of the way in which the MP (Michael Stern) had used his freedom of speech in Parliament.

The Court has not always upheld claims of parliamentary immunity. For example, in the subsequent case of *Cordova (No 1) v Italy*, judgment of 30 January 2003, the applicant was a prosecutor who had been investigating a person associated with Francesco Cossiga (a former President of Italy and a 'senator for life'). Cossiga sent the applicant several sarcastic letters and toys. The applicant lodged criminal and civil complaints against Cossiga for allegedly insulting a public official. However, the Senate considered that Cossiga's acts were covered by a constitutional immunity as his opinions had been expressed in the performance of his parliamentary duties. Therefore, the court held that Cossiga had no case to answer. The Strasbourg Court was unanimous in concluding that the absence of an obvious link between Cossiga's acts and any kind of parliamentary activity meant that the resolution of the Senate and ruling of the court that he had no case to answer upset the fair balance between the interests of the community and the rights of the applicant and consequently a breach of Article 6(1) had occurred. Hence, only comments/actions directly connected with parliamentary affairs are likely to be recognized as deserving absolute immunity by the Court.

A Grand Chamber dealt with the novel challenge to parliamentary immunity by a member of parliament who contended that the immunity prevented him from defending his reputation in suspended criminal proceedings brought against him. The applicant in *Kart v Turkey*, judgment of 3 December 2009, worked as a lawyer prior to being elected to the Turkish Parliament. Criminal proceedings had been initiated against him concerning his professional conduct. However, once he was elected those proceedings were suspended because of his parliamentary immunity. The applicant, unsuccessfully, requested the parliamentary authorities to lift his immunity. Before the Grand Chamber he argued that he had been deprived of the right to a fair trial because of the application of parliamentary immunity. The Grand Chamber, by 13 votes to 4, determined that there had been no breach of Article 6(1) as the application of parliamentary immunity to Kart had merely suspended the criminal proceedings against him and that in standing for election (on successive occasions) the applicant had been aware of the effect of parliamentary immunity. This was the first time that the beneficiary of parliamentary immunity had sought to challenge it before the Court.

7   In *Roche v UK*, judgment of 19 October 2005, the Grand Chamber confirmed the distinction, under Article 6(1), between 'substantive' and 'procedural' limitations on the right of access to a civil court. The former concern the existence and scope of 'civil rights' within national law, whilst the latter govern the ability of litigants to bring proceedings in domestic courts to enforce 'civil rights'. The Grand Chamber repeated that Article 6(1) does not guarantee any particular content of 'civil rights', that is a matter for national law. Hence, national law delimiting the scope of a particular 'civil right' will not constitute a breach of the right of access to a court. Whereas, procedural limitations on the

enforcement of a recognized 'civil right' may breach Article 6(1); as in *Tinnelly*, see Note 4. Roche complained that section 10 of the Crown Proceedings Act 1947, which prevented military personnel from generally suing the Crown in respect of alleged torts, violated his right of access to a court. The Grand Chamber was deeply divided on whether section 10 should be classified as a substantive or procedural limitation. The majority, of nine judges, accorded significant weight to the unanimous decision of the House of Lords in *Matthews v Ministry of Defence* [2003] UKHL 4, that section 10 was a substantive limitation that did not infringe Article 6(1).

120. In assessing therefore whether there is a civil 'right' and in determining the substantive or procedural characterisations to be given to the impugned restriction, the starting point must be the provisions of the relevant domestic law and their interpretation by the domestic courts ...

Consequently, the majority found no breach of Article 6(1). Whereas, the eight dissentients believed that section 10 should be classified as a procedural limitation that violated Article 6(1) by denying Roche access to the courts to challenge the lawfulness of the poison gas tests he had been subject to whilst serving in the British army during the 1960s.

Providing for a condition such as certification by the Secretary of State, rather than defining a series of exceptions and leaving the question of their existence in any particular case to be decided by the courts, lends support to the view that the relevant restriction on the right of access to the court is procedural in nature.

Roche vividly disclosed how difficult it can be in practice to distinguish between substantive and procedural limitations. Indeed, Judge Zupancic, one of the dissenters, described it as being an 'artificial separation'.

8   Excessive court fees have been found to violate the right of access to a court. For example, in *Kreuz v Poland*, judgment of 19 June 2001, the applicant was a businessman who sued his local council regarding its refusal to confirm his planning permission to construct a car wash. The domestic court ordered that he pay 100 million PLZ (roughly the average annual salary in Poland at that time) as a fee for lodging his claim. Despite his contention that he could not afford that sum, the court ruled that as a businessman he should have ensured that he had adequate funds available to conduct litigation concerning his venture. He did not pay the fee and his proceedings were terminated. In response to his claim of a breach of Article 6(1) the Court, unanimously, held that:

60. ... the requirement to pay fees to civil courts in connection with claims they are asked to determine cannot be regarded as a restriction on the right of access to a court that is incompatible per se with Article 6(1) of the Convention. It reiterates, however, that the amount of the fees assessed in the light of the particular circumstances of a given case, including the applicant's ability to pay them, and the phase of the proceedings at which that restriction has been imposed are factors which are material in determining whether or not a person enjoyed his right of access ...

66. Assessing the facts of the case as a whole and having regard to the prominent place held by the right to a court in a democratic society, the Court considers that the judicial authorities have failed to secure a proper balance between, on the one hand, the interest of the State in collecting court fees for dealing with claims and, on the other hand, the interest of the applicant in vindicating his claim through the courts.

The fee required from the applicant for proceeding with his action was excessive. It resulted in his desisting from his claim and in his case never being heard by a court. That, in the Court's opinion, impaired the very essence of his right of access.

67. For the above reasons, the Court concludes that the imposition of the court fees on the applicant constituted a disproportionate restriction on his right of access to a court. It accordingly finds that there has been a breach of Article 6(1) of the Convention.

The Polish courts had clearly failed to give sufficient weight to the actual financial resources available to Kreuz when determining the amount of fees he should be required to pay to bring his action.

9 The failure of State authorities to take adequate steps to enforce court judgments is another type of breach. For example, in *Sirbu and Others v Moldova*, judgment of 15 June 2004, the six applicants were civil servants who had obtained final court judgments against the Ministry of Internal Affairs requiring the payment to them of allowances. Despite the issuing of enforcement warrants the Ministry refused to pay the sums due because of alleged lack of funds. After the applicants lodged their complaints at Strasbourg the Ministry executed the judgments (over five years after the domestic judgments against the Ministry). The Court, unanimously, ruled that:

23. . . . Article 6 § 1 secures to everyone the right to have any claim relating to his civil rights and obligations brought before a court or tribunal; in this way it embodies the 'right to a court', of which the right of access, that is the right to institute proceedings before courts in civil matters, constitutes one aspect. However, that right would be illusory if a Contracting State's domestic legal system allowed a final, binding judicial decision to remain inoperative to the detriment of one party. It would be inconceivable that Article 6 § 1 should describe in detail procedural guarantees afforded to litigants—proceedings that are fair, public and expeditious—without protecting the implementation of judicial decisions; to construe Article 6 as being concerned exclusively with access to a court and the conduct of proceedings would be likely to lead to situations incompatible with the principle of the rule of law which the Contracting States undertook to respect when they ratified the Convention. Execution of a judgment given by any court must therefore be regarded as an integral part of the 'trial' for the purposes of Article 6 (see the *Hornsby v Greece* judgment of 19 March 1997, Reports 1997-II, p 510, § 40).

24. It is not open to a State authority to cite lack of funds as an excuse for not honouring a judgment. Admittedly, a delay in the execution of a judgment may be justified in particular circumstances. But the delay may not be such as to impair the essence of the right protected under Article 6 § 1 of the Convention (see *Immobiliare Saffi v Italy* [GC], No 22774/93, § 74, ECHR 1999-V). In the instant case, the applicants should not have been prevented from benefiting from the success of the litigation, which concerned the payment of compensation.

25. The Court notes that the Centru District Court's judgments of 1 and 18 August 1997 remained unenforced for more than five years and a half (until after the cases had been communicated to the Government by the Court, on 15 May 2003).

26. By failing for years to take the necessary measures to comply with the final judgments in the instant case, the Moldovan authorities deprived the provisions of Article 6 § 1 of the Convention of all useful effect.

27. There has accordingly been a violation of Article 6 § 1 of the Convention. It is noteworthy that the Court expressly rejected the suggestion that lack of public funds is an excuse for domestic authorities not complying with a financial judgment against them.

10 Technological limitations regarding the filing of court documents were found to violate the right of access to a court by a unanimous Chamber in *Lawyer Partners AS v Slovakia*, judgment of 16 June 2009. The applicant company acquired the right, from Slovak Radio, to recover unpaid receiver licences. The applicant company then prepared civil debt actions against over 70,000 persons. These documents were generated by computer software and recorded on DVDs (in physical form they would have occupied over 40 million pages of text). The company then sought to file those actions with several district courts in 2006. The courts refused to register the applications and the Ministry of Justice announced that ordinary courts did not have the facilities to accept electronic applications. During 2008 the Ministry published (on its website) details of how electronic submissions could be filed. The Chamber found that as domestic law had provided, from 2002, for the possibility of electronic filing, the refusal of the district courts to accept the applicant's DVDs amounted to a disproportionate limitation on the company's right of access to a court.

(II) EQUALITY OF ARMS

Rowe and Davis v UK 2000-II
European Court of Human Rights

During the night of 15–16 December 1988 a series of serious offences occurred in Surrey. Around 1.30 am two men were attacked in a field near Fickleshall, one of the men (Hurburgh) was killed. The victim's car was also stolen. Two hours later three masked men armed with a knife and a gun entered a house in Oxted, robbed the occupants of jewellery, stabbed one occupant (Timothy Napier) and stole the latter's car. Hurburgh's car was abandoned near the Napier home. A few hours afterwards three masked men broke into a house in Fetcham, bound the occupants, stole jewellery and a car. Timothy's car was left nearby. There was great media coverage of these crimes and a large reward (£25,000) offered for information leading to the conviction of the offenders. On 18 December information was given to the police that the offenders were living in a specific house in south London. The police obtained search warrants and carried out a search of the premises (flats) on 19 December. The premises were occupied by Rowe and Davis (who were black) and the 'Jobbins group' (Jobbins, Duncan, and Griffin; all of whom had criminal records and were white). A brooch from the Fetcham robbery was found in Rowe's wastepaper basket together with a blood-stained jacket. Rowe, Davis, Jobbins, and Griffin were arrested on suspicion of aggravated burglary. Rowe's 16-year-old girlfriend gave the police other items of jewellery stolen from the Fetcham robbery which she claimed Rowe had given her. Johnson was arrested, carrying a gun, a couple of weeks later and he admitted that he had been at the south London house on the night of the offences, but he denied any involvement in the crimes. Rowe, Davis, and Johnson were tried at the Old Bailey in February 1990. The prosecution relied heavily on the evidence of the Jobbins group having helped the defendants to commit the crimes on the night in question. The defendants denied involvement in the offences. The jury, unanimously, found the defendants guilty of murder, grievous bodily harm, and robbery. They were given life sentences. On appeal the prosecution gave the court a document which the defendants/appellants were not allowed to see. The Court of Appeal refused to order disclosure of the document and dismissed the appeal. In 1997 the new Criminal Cases Commission ordered an investigation into the case and it was revealed that one member of the Jobbins group (Duncan) was a long-standing police informant who had provided the police with the information about the applicants. Duncan received £10,000 reward and immunity from prosecution in respect of his involvement in the crimes. These facts had not been disclosed to the defence on grounds of public interest immunity. The Criminal Cases Commission referred the applicants' convictions back to the Court of Appeal. The applicants complained to the

European Commission alleging that the prosecution's failure to disclose the information about Duncan undermined their right to a fair trial. The Commission was unanimous in finding a breach of Article 6(1) in conjunction with Article 6(3)(b) and (d).

59. The Court recalls that the guarantees in paragraph 3 of Article 6 are specific aspects of the right to a fair trial set out in paragraph 1 ... In the circumstances of the case it finds it unnecessary to examine the applicants' allegations separately from the standpoint of paragraph 3(b) and (d), since they amount to a complaint that the applicants did not receive a fair trial. It will therefore confine its examination to the question whether the proceedings in their entirety were fair ...

60. It is a fundamental aspect of the right to a fair trial that criminal proceedings, including the elements of such proceedings which relate to procedure, should be adversarial and that there should be equality of arms between the prosecution and defence. The right to an adversarial trial means, in a criminal case, that both prosecution and defence must be given the opportunity to have knowledge of and comment on the observations filed and the evidence adduced by the other party (see the *Brandstetter v Austria* judgment of 28 August 1991, Series A No 211, §§ 66, 67). In addition Article 6 § 1 requires, as indeed does English law ... that the prosecution authorities should disclose to the defence all material evidence in their possession for or against the accused ...

61. However, as the applicants recognised ... the entitlement to disclosure of relevant evidence is not an absolute right. In any criminal proceedings there may be competing interests, such as national security or the need to protect witnesses at risk of reprisals or keep secret police methods of investigation of crime, which must be weighed against the rights of the accused (see, for example, the *Doorson v Netherlands* judgment of 26 March 1996, Reports of Judgments and Decisions 1996-II, § 70). In some cases it may be necessary to withhold certain evidence from the defence so as to preserve the fundamental rights of another individual or to safeguard an important public interest. However, only such measures restricting the rights of the defence which are strictly necessary are permissible under Article 6 § 1 (see the *Van Mechelen v Netherlands* judgment of 23 April 1997, Reports 1997-III, § 58). Moreover, in order to ensure that the accused receives a fair trial, any difficulties caused to the defence by a limitation on its rights must be sufficiently counterbalanced by the procedures followed by the judicial authorities (see the above-mentioned *Doorson* judgment, § 72 and the above-mentioned *Van Mechelen* judgment, § 54).

62. In cases where evidence has been withheld from the defence on public interest grounds, it is not the role of this Court to decide whether or not such non-disclosure was strictly necessary since, as a general rule, it is for the national courts to assess the evidence before them ... Instead, the European Court's task is to ascertain whether the decision-making procedure applied in each case complied, as far as possible, with the requirements of adversarial proceedings and equality of arms and incorporated adequate safeguards to protect the interests of the accused.

63. During the applicants' trial at first instance the prosecution decided, without notifying the judge, to withhold certain relevant evidence on grounds of public interest. Such a procedure, whereby the prosecution itself attempts to assess the importance of concealed information to the defence and weigh this against the public interest in keeping the information secret, cannot comply with the above-mentioned requirements of Article 6 § 1. Indeed this principle is recognised by the English case-law from the Court of Appeal's judgment in *Ward* (*R v Ward* [1993] 2 All ER 577) onwards ...

64. It is true that at the commencement of the applicants' appeal prosecution counsel notified the defence that certain information had been withheld, without however revealing the nature of this material, and that on two separate occasions the Court of Appeal reviewed the undisclosed evidence and, in ex parte hearings with the benefit of submissions from the Crown but in the absence of the defence, decided in favour of non-disclosure.

65. However, the Court does not consider that this procedure before the appeal court was sufficient to remedy the unfairness caused at the trial by the absence of any scrutiny of the withheld information by the trial judge. Unlike the latter, who saw the witnesses give their testimony and was fully versed in all the evidence and issues in the case, the judges in the Court of Appeal were dependent for their understanding of the possible relevance of the undisclosed material on transcripts of the Crown Court hearings and on the account of the issues given to them by prosecuting counsel. In addition, the first instance judge would have been in a position to monitor the need for disclosure throughout the trial, assessing the importance of the undisclosed evidence at a stage when new issues were emerging, when it might have been possible through cross-examination seriously to undermine the credibility of key witnesses and when the defence case was still open to take a number of different directions or emphases. In contrast, the Court of Appeal was obliged to carry out its appraisal *ex post facto* and may even, to a certain extent, have unconsciously been influenced by the jury's verdict of guilty into underestimating the significance of the undisclosed evidence.

66. In conclusion, therefore, the prosecution's failure to lay the evidence in question before the trial judge and to permit him to rule on the question of disclosure deprived the applicants of a fair trial...It follows that there has been a violation of Article 6 § 1 of the Convention.

...

FOR THESE REASONS THE COURT UNANIMOUSLY

Holds that there has been a violation of Article 6(1) of the Convention...

NOTES

1 The Court was composed of President Wildhaber and Judges: Palm, Ferrari Bravo, Caflisch, Costa, Fuhrmann, Jungwiert, Fischbach, Zupanoio, Vajio, Hedigan, Thomassen, Tsatsa-Nikolovska, Pantiru, Levits, Traja, and Laws.

2 The Criminal Procedure and Investigations Act 1996 introduced a new system of prosecution disclosures and defence statements for trials in England and Wales. Under the statutory scheme, prosecution disclosure decisions could be challenged by the defence and reviewed by the trial judge.

3 In July 2000, the Court of Appeal quashed the convictions of Rowe, Davis, and Johnson. The court ruled that the collusion between the police and Duncan was one of three 'material irregularities' that made the jury's verdicts unsafe. However, the court stated that the case against all three was 'formidable' and in respect of the charge of robbery against Rowe the evidence was 'overwhelming'. The Lords Justices expressed the view that the court's judgment 'is not a finding of innocence, far from it'. The court also considered the relationship between the European Court of Human Rights' finding of a breach of Article 6(1) in an English criminal case and the Court of Appeal's duty to determine the 'safety' of that conviction. Mantell LJ ruled that: '...a finding of a breach of Article 6(1) would not lead inexorably to the quashing of the conviction. The effect of any unfairness upon the safety of a conviction would vary according to its nature and degree': *R v Davis*, *R v Rowe* and *R v Johnson* (2000) *The Times*, 25 July.

4 Two persons who had been convicted, after their trial judges allowed *ex parte* applications by the prosecution to withhold evidence from the defence on public interest grounds, successfully invoked Article 6(1) to challenge their inability during their trials to establish whether the involvement of *agents provocateurs* in the alleged offences made the proceedings against them unfair in *Edwards and Lewis v UK*, judgment of 22 July 2003. The first applicant had been arrested, following a police undercover operation, in a van with nearly 5 kg of heroin accompanied by 'Graham' (an undercover police officer). Edwards subsequently came to suspect that a number of the other participants in the drug transaction were either undercover police officers or police informers. He was sentenced to nine years' imprisonment for possessing a Class A drug with intent to supply. The second applicant was arrested when he showed two undercover police officers counterfeit notes that he was willing to supply. Lewis was sentenced to four-and-a-half years' imprisonment. Before the Chamber the applicants contended that their trials had been unfair as their trial judges, who had to determine if the applicants had been entrapped, had heard prosecution requests for the withholding of evidence without any adversarial processes.

49. The applicants claim to have been victims of entrapment. The Court recalls that, although the admissibility of evidence is primarily a matter for regulation by national law, the requirements of a fair criminal trial under Article 6 entail that the public interest in the fight against crime cannot justify the use of evidence obtained as a result of police incitement... In *Teixeira de Castro* [v *Portugal*, Reports 1998-IV] the Court found that the activities of the two police officers had gone beyond that of undercover agents, in that they had not 'confined themselves to investigating the applicant's criminal activity in an essentially passive manner', but had 'exercised an influence such as to incite the commission of the offence'. Their actions had 'gone beyond those of undercover agents because they instigated the offence and there is nothing to suggest that without their intervention it would have been committed' (ibid, § 39).

In arriving at this conclusion the Court laid stress on a number of features of the case before it, particularly the facts that the intervention of the two officers had not been part of a judicially supervised operation and that the national authorities had had no good reason to suspect the applicant of prior involvement in drug trafficking: he had no criminal record and there was nothing to suggest that he had a predisposition to become involved in drug dealing until he was approached by the police (ibid, §§ 37–8).

50. Under English law, although entrapment does not constitute a substantive defence to a criminal charge, it does place the judge under a duty either to stay the proceedings as an abuse of process or to exclude any evidence obtained by entrapment on the grounds that its admission would have such an adverse effect on the fairness of the proceedings that the court could not admit it (see *R. v Looseley* [[2001] UKHL 53], and the earlier case-law referred to therein).

51. As the applicants point out, it is impossible for this Court to determine whether or not either applicant was the victim of entrapment, contrary to Article 6, because the relevant information has not been disclosed by the prosecuting authorities. It is, therefore, essential that the Court examine the procedure whereby the plea of entrapment was determined in each case, to ensure that the rights of the defence were adequately protected...

52. It is in any event a fundamental aspect of the right to a fair trial that criminal proceedings, including the elements of such proceedings which relate to procedure, should be adversarial and that there should be equality of arms between the prosecution and defence. The right to an adversarial trial means, in a criminal case, that both prosecution and defence must be given the opportunity to have knowledge of and comment on the observations filed and the evidence adduced by the other party... In addition Article 6 § 1 requires that the prosecution authorities should disclose to the defence all material evidence in their possession for or against the accused...

53. The entitlement to disclosure of relevant evidence is not, however, an absolute right. In any criminal proceedings there may be competing interests, such as national security or the need to protect witnesses at risk of reprisals or keep secret police methods of investigation of crime, which must be weighed against the rights of the accused. In some cases it may be necessary to withhold certain evidence from the defence so as to preserve the fundamental rights of another individual or

to safeguard an important public interest. Nonetheless, only such measures restricting the rights of the defence which are strictly necessary are permissible under Article 6 § 1. Furthermore, in order to ensure that the accused receives a fair trial, any difficulties caused to the defence by a limitation on its rights must be sufficiently counterbalanced by the procedures followed by the judicial authorities...

54. In cases where evidence has been withheld from the defence on public interest grounds, it is not the role of this Court to decide whether or not such non-disclosure was strictly necessary since, as a general rule, it is for the national courts to assess the evidence before them. In any event, in many cases, including the present, where the evidence in question has never been revealed, it would not be possible for the Court to attempt to weigh the public interest in non-disclosure against that of the accused in having sight of the material. It must therefore scrutinise the decision-making procedure to ensure that, as far as possible, the procedure complied with the requirements to provide adversarial proceedings and equality of arms and incorporated adequate safeguards to protect the interests of the accused...

57. In the present case, however, it appears that the undisclosed evidence related, or may have related, to an issue of fact decided by the trial judge. Each applicant complained that he had been entrapped into committing the offence by one or more undercover police officers or informers, and asked the trial judge to consider whether prosecution evidence should be excluded for that reason. In order to conclude whether or not the accused had indeed been the victim of improper incitement by the police, it was necessary for the trial judge to examine a number of factors, including the reason for the police operation, the nature and extent of police participation in the crime and the nature of any inducement or pressure applied by the police...Had the defence been able to persuade the judge that the police had acted improperly, the prosecution would, in effect, have had to be discontinued. The applications in question were, therefore, of determinative importance to the applicants' trials, and the public interest immunity evidence may have related to facts connected with those applications.

58. Despite this, the applicants were denied access to the evidence. It was not, therefore, possible for the defence representatives to argue the case on entrapment in full before the judge. Moreover, in each case the judge, who subsequently rejected the defence submissions on entrapment, had already seen prosecution evidence which may have been relevant to the issue....

59. In these circumstances, the Court does not consider that the procedure employed to determine the issues of disclosure of evidence and entrapment complied with the requirements to provide adversarial proceedings and equality of arms and incorporated adequate safeguards to protect the interests of the accused. It follows that there has been a violation of Article 6 § 1 in this case.

The unanimous judgment was another condemnation by the Court of the common law procedure governing disclosure of evidence. The Government sought a referral of the Chamber's judgment in *Edwards and Lewis* for a re-hearing by a Grand Chamber under Article 43. The latter granted permission in December 2003. However, in April 2004 the Government wrote to the Grand Chamber that:

Having now had the opportunity to give even fuller consideration to the judgment of the Chamber of the Court of 22 July 2003 and its implications, the Government have decided that they no longer wish to pursue the referral of this application to the Grand Chamber which was accepted on 3 December 2002 at the request of the Government.

In the circumstances the Government accept that it is open to the Grand Chamber to endorse the judgment of the Chamber of 22 July 2003, and confirm that they are content that the Grand Chamber should now do so.

Subsequently, the Grand Chamber, unanimously ruled that:

48. Having examined the issues raised by the case in the light of the Chamber's judgment, the Grand Chamber sees no reason to depart from the Chamber's findings. It therefore concludes that there has been a violation of Article 6 § 1, for the reasons elaborated by the Chamber.

We may speculate that the Government decided not to pursue the re-hearing because of the House of Lords' judgment, pronounced on 5 February 2004, in *R v H and R v C* [2004] UKHL 3. The House, unanimously, endorsed the appointment of special counsel to represent the interests of defendants in criminal trials where the prosecution sought non-disclosure of sensitive information to the defendants or their ordinary lawyers. But, according to their Lordships:

22. . . . Such an appointment will always be exceptional, never automatic; a course of last and never first resort. It should not be ordered unless and until the trial judge is satisfied that no other course will adequately meet the overriding requirement of fairness to the defendant. . . .

5 The principle of equality of arms is not only concerned with matters of court procedure but also institutional arrangements. For example, in *Borgers v Belgium* A.214-A (1991), the applicant complained about the role of the avocat general in the determination of cases by the Belgian Court of Cassation. The avocat general provided advice to the court on whether a particular appeal should be allowed or dismissed and participated in the court's deliberations. The applicant's appeal against his forgery conviction was opposed by the avocat general and dismissed by the Court of Cassation. He then alleged that the functions of the avocat general violated the equality of arms principle (the Commission found a breach of Article 6(1) by 14 votes to 1). A large majority of the Court, 18 votes to 4, also found a violation.

26. No one questions the objectivity with which the procureur général's department at the Court of Cassation discharges its functions. This is shown by the consensus which has existed in Belgium in relation to it since its inception and by its approval by Parliament on various occasions.

Nevertheless the opinion of the procureur général's department cannot be regarded as neutral from the point of view of the parties to the cassation proceedings. By recommending that an accused's appeal be allowed or dismissed, the official of the procureur général's department becomes objectively speaking his ally or his opponent. In the latter event, Article 6 para 1 (art 6-1) requires that the rights of the defence and the principle of equality of arms be respected.

27. In the present case the hearing on 18 June 1985 before the Court of Cassation concluded with the avocat général's submissions to the effect that Mr Borger's appeal should not be allowed . . . At no time could the latter reply to those submissions: before hearing them, he was unaware of their contents because they had not been communicated to him in advance; thereafter he was prevented from doing so by statute. Article 1107 of the Judicial Code prohibits even the lodging of written notes following the intervention of the member of the procureur général's department . . .

The Court cannot see the justification for such restrictions on the rights of the defence. Once the avocat général had made submissions unfavourable to the applicant, the latter had a clear interest in being able to submit his observations on them before argument was closed. The fact that the Court of Cassation's jurisdiction is confined to questions of law makes no difference in this respect.

28. Further and above all, the inequality was increased even more by the avocat général's participation, in an advisory capacity, in the Court's deliberations. Assistance of this nature, given with total objectivity, may be of some use in drafting judgments, although this task falls in the first place

to the Court of Cassation itself. It is however hard to see how such assistance can remain limited to stylistic considerations, which are in any case often indissociable from substantive matters, if it is in addition intended, as the Government also affirmed, to contribute towards maintaining the consistency of the case-law. Even if such assistance was so limited in the present case, it could reasonably be thought that the deliberations afforded the avocat général an additional opportunity to promote, without fear of contradiction by the applicant, his submissions to the effect that the appeal should be dismissed.

29. In conclusion, having regard to the requirements of the rights of the defence and of the principle of the equality of arms and to the role of appearances in determining whether they have been complied with, the Court finds a violation of Article 6 para 1 (art 6-1)....

In the very early case of **Delcourt v Belgium** A.11 (1970), the Court had upheld the independence and impartiality of the Court of Cassation and its procureur general's department. However, the Court adopted a more rigorous stance in **Borgers**, because the concept of a fair trial, '…has undergone a considerable evolution in the Court's case-law, notably in respect of the importance attached to appearances and to the increased sensitivity of the public to the fair administration of justice…' (para 24).

6 The Court has held that the principle of equality of arms extends to civil proceedings. In **Dombo Beheer BV v Netherlands** A.274 (1993), the applicant company had sued its bank after the latter had allegedly frozen Dombo's accounts. The bank disputed the company's allegations. Before the domestic courts Dombo sought to call its former managing director as a witness (he had been directly involved in the company's dealing with the bank). The bank objected to the admissibility of his evidence (under the Civil Code a person who was substantively a party to litigation could not be heard as a witness in his/her own case). The court agreed with the bank and refused to allow the former managing director to testify. However, the bank was able to call its local bank manager to give evidence on its behalf. The Dutch courts decided in favour of the bank. Dombo then complained to the Commission alleging a breach of the equality of arms principle. By 14 votes to 5, the Commission upheld the complaint. The Court determined that:

32. The requirements inherent in the concept of 'fair hearing' are not necessarily the same in cases concerning the determination of civil rights and obligations as they are in cases concerning the determination of a criminal charge. This is borne out by the absence of detailed provisions such as paragraphs 2 and 3 of Article 6 (art 6-2, art 6-3) applying to cases of the former category. Thus, although these provisions have a certain relevance outside the strict confines of criminal law (see, *mutatis mutandis*, the *Albert and Le Compte v Belgium* judgment of 10 February 1983, Series A No 58, p 20, para 39), the Contracting States have greater latitude when dealing with civil cases concerning civil rights and obligations than they have when dealing with criminal cases.

33. Nevertheless, certain principles concerning the notion of a 'fair hearing' in cases concerning civil rights and obligations emerge from the Court's case-law. Most significantly for the present case, it is clear that the requirement of 'equality of arms', in the sense of a 'fair balance' between the parties, applies in principle to such cases as well as to criminal cases...

The Court agrees with the Commission that as regards litigation involving opposing private interests, 'equality of arms' implies that each party must be afforded a reasonable opportunity to present his case—including his evidence—under conditions that do not place him at a substantial disadvantage vis-à-vis his opponent.

It is left to the national authorities to ensure in each individual case that the requirements of a 'fair hearing' are met.

34. In the instant case, it was incumbent upon the applicant company to prove that there was an oral agreement between it and the Bank to extend certain credit facilities. Only two persons had been present at the meeting at which this agreement had allegedly been reached, namely Mr van Reijendam (the former managing director) representing the applicant company and Mr van W. representing the Bank. Yet only one of these two key persons was permitted to be heard, namely the person who had represented the Bank. The applicant company was denied the possibility of calling the person who had represented it, because the Court of Appeal identified him with the applicant company itself.

35. During the relevant negotiations Mr van Reijendam and Mr van W. acted on an equal footing, both being empowered to negotiate on behalf of their respective parties. It is therefore difficult to see why they should not both have been allowed to give evidence.

The applicant company was thus placed at a substantial disadvantage vis-à-vis the Bank and there has accordingly been a violation of Article 6 para 1 (art 6-1)....

Four judges dissented as they considered that the applicant company had an equal opportunity to submit its evidence (both written and oral) during the domestic proceedings. Two months after Dombo lost its final appeal before the Supreme Court, the Dutch Civil Code was amended to allow parties to give evidence as witnesses in their own cases.

7   The full-time Court has followed *Dombo Beheer*, for example in *Komanicky v Slovakia*, judgment of 4 June 2002. The applicant was involved in protracted litigation concerning his former employment. The domestic courts held several hearings at which the applicant was not present (even when he had given prior notice of his inability to attend due to ill-health). A unanimous Chamber held that:

45. The Court recalls that the principle of equality of arms—one of the elements of the broader concept of fair trial—requires that each party should be afforded a reasonable opportunity to present his or her case under conditions that do not place him or her at a substantial disadvantage vis-à-vis his or her opponent (see the *Dombo Beheer B.V. v The Netherlands* judgment of 27 October 1993, Series A No 274, p. 19, § 33; *Ankerl v Switzerland* judgment of 23 October 1996, Reports of Judgments and Decisions 1996-V, pp 1567–8, § 38).

46. The concept of a fair hearing also implies the right to adversarial proceedings, according to which the parties must have the opportunity not only to make known any evidence needed for their claims to succeed, but also to have knowledge of, and comment on, all evidence adduced or observations filed, with a view to influencing the court's decision (see the *Nideröst-Huber v Switzerland* judgment of 18 February 1997, Reports 1997-I, p 108, § 24, and the *Mantovanelli v France* judgment of 18 March 1997, Reports 1997-II, p 436, § 33).

47. The Court's role is to ascertain whether the proceedings considered as a whole were fair as required by Article 6 § 1. In this context, importance is to be attached to the appearance of the fair administration of justice. However, it is not the Court's function to deal with errors of fact or law allegedly committed by a national court unless and in so far as they may have infringed rights and freedoms protected by the Convention. Moreover, while Article 6 of the Convention guarantees the right to a fair hearing, it does not lay down any rules on the admissibility of evidence or the way it should be assessed, which are therefore primarily matters for regulation by national law and the national courts (see, *mutatis mutandis*, the *Schenk v Switzerland* judgment of 12 July 1988, Series A No 140, p 29, § 46; the *Borgers v Belgium* judgment of 30 October 1991, Series A No 214-B, p 31, § 24 and the *Garcia Ruiz v Spain* judgment of 21 January 1999, Reports 1999-I, pp 98–9, § 28).

...

55. In these circumstances, and having regard to the requirements of the principle of the equality of arms and to the role of appearances in determining whether they have been complied with, the Court finds that the procedure followed did not enable the applicant to participate properly in the proceedings and thus deprived him of a fair hearing within the meaning of Article 6 § 1 of the Convention. In conclusion, there has been a violation of this provision.

8 A unanimous Chamber found a breach of the equality of arms principle in the well-publicized case of *Steel and Morris v UK*, judgment of 15 February 2005 (often referred to as the '*McLibel*' case in the British media). The applicants were two campaigners (on low income/state benefits) who, according to the High Court, were responsible for the publication of several thousand copies of a leaflet, distributed in the UK, which made serious allegations about, *inter alia*, the health and environmental implications of eating McDonald's food and the working practices within the company. In 1990 the US and UK divisions of McDonald's brought libel proceedings against the applicants claiming £100,000 damages for the alleged defamation caused by the production and distribution of the leaflets. Civil legal aid was not available for defamation proceedings in England and the applicants had to defend themselves, with some pro bono assistance from various lawyers, in what became the longest trial (civil or criminal) in English legal history. The High Court proceedings involved 313 court days (with 40,000 pages of documentary evidence, 130 witnesses gave oral evidence, and it was estimated that McDonald's spent over £10 million on their legal expenses/representation for the action). In June 1997, after six months' deliberation, the judge delivered his 762-page judgment finding that a number of the allegations in the leaflets were untrue and he awarded McDonald's damages of £60,000 against the applicants (McDonald's did not seek to require the applicants to pay their legal costs as they could have). The applicants appealed to the Court of Appeal and after a hearing of 23 days the Court of Appeal delivered its 301-page judgment in March 1999. The Court of Appeal allowed some of the applicants' grounds of appeal. Before the European Court the applicants contended, *inter alia*, that the denial of legal aid to help them to defend themselves from McDonald's resulted in them facing an unfair trial. The Court held that:

61. The question whether the provision of legal aid is necessary for a fair hearing must be determined on the basis of the particular facts and circumstances of each case and will depend *inter alia* upon the importance of what is at stake for the applicant in the proceedings, the complexity of the relevant law and procedure and the applicant's capacity to represent him or herself effectively…

McDonald's were seeking substantial damages against the applicants, the case involved complex factual and legal issues, and whilst the applicants were articulate and resourceful:

69. …the disparity between the respective levels of legal assistance enjoyed by the applicants and McDonald's was of such a degree that it could not have failed, in this exceptionally demanding case, to have given rise to unfairness, despite the best efforts of the judges at first instance and on appeal.

…

72. In conclusion, therefore, the Court finds that the denial of legal aid to the applicants deprived them of the opportunity to present their case effectively before the court and contributed to an unacceptable inequality of arms with McDonald's. There has, therefore, been a violation of Article 6(1).

Whilst the above judgment maintains the approach of the original Court, that States are not obliged to establish general civil legal aid schemes under Article 6, it demonstrates that gross inequalities in the resources of parties can require the authorities to provide legal assistance for impecunious defendants in specific cases.

(III) THE RIGHT TO SILENCE/PRIVILEGE AGAINST SELF-INCRIMINATION

John Murray v UK 1996-I
European Court of Human Rights

The applicant was arrested in a house by Northern Irish police officers at 5.40 pm on 7 January 1990. He was cautioned that he did not have to say anything, but that adverse inferences might be drawn at his trial if he failed to mention any facts he later relied on as part of his defence. Almost as soon as he arrived at the police station he stated that he wished to consult a solicitor. Half an hour later, a detective superintendent authorized the delaying of the applicant's access to a solicitor for 48 hours under powers granted by emergency legislation. Murray was subsequently interviewed by the police on ten occasions. He did not answer any of the questions put to him. After 48 hours he was allowed to consult a solicitor. Afterwards he continued to refuse to reply to police questions. In May 1991, Murray was tried (before the Lord Chief Justice of Northern Ireland) on charges of, *inter alia*, conspiracy to murder and unlawful imprisonment. Murray did not give any evidence and no witnesses were called on his behalf. The prosecution alleged that Murray was one of a group of persons who had imprisoned a suspected IRA informer, interrogated him, and planned to have him killed. Murray had been arrested in the house where the police also found the victim. The Lord Chief Justice found Murray guilty of unlawful imprisonment and in doing so drew 'very strong inferences against' his failure to explain to the police his presence in the house and give evidence in his own defence. Under the Criminal Evidence (Northern Ireland) Order 1988, a defendant could not be convicted solely on the basis of adverse inferences from silence, but trial courts could take account of such inferences in specified circumstances (e.g. where a defendant failed to explain his/her presence at a particular place). Murray was sentenced to eight years' imprisonment. He later complained to the Commission alleging that he was deprived of the right to silence in breach of Article 6(1) and that delaying his access to a solicitor violated Article 6(3). The Commission rejected the first complaint (by 15 votes to 2) and upheld the latter (by 13 votes to 4).

45. Although not specifically mentioned in Article 6 (art 6) of the Convention, there can be no doubt that the right to remain silent under police questioning and the privilege against self-incrimination are generally recognised international standards which lie at the heart of the notion of a fair procedure under Article 6 (art 6) (see the *Funke v France* judgment [A.256-A (1993)]). By providing the accused with protection against improper compulsion by the authorities these immunities contribute to avoiding miscarriages of justice and to securing the aims of Article 6 (art 6).

46. The Court does not consider that it is called upon to give an abstract analysis of the scope of these immunities and, in particular, of what constitutes in this context 'improper compulsion'. What is at stake in the present case is whether these immunities are absolute in the sense that the exercise by an accused of the right to silence cannot under any circumstances be used against him at trial or, alternatively, whether informing him in advance that, under certain conditions, his silence may be so used, is always to be regarded as 'improper compulsion'.

47. On the one hand, it is self-evident that it is incompatible with the immunities under consideration to base a conviction solely or mainly on the accused's silence or on a refusal to answer questions or to give evidence himself. On the other hand, the Court deems it equally obvious that these immunities cannot and should not prevent that the accused's silence, in situations which clearly call for an explanation from him, be taken into account in assessing the persuasiveness of the evidence adduced by the prosecution.

Wherever the line between these two extremes is to be drawn, it follows from this understanding of 'the right to silence' that the question whether the right is absolute must be answered in the negative.

It cannot be said therefore that an accused's decision to remain silent throughout criminal proceedings should necessarily have no implications when the trial court seeks to evaluate the evidence against him. In particular, as the Government have pointed out, established international standards in this area, while providing for the right to silence and the privilege against self-incrimination, are silent on this point.

Whether the drawing of adverse inferences from an accused's silence infringes Article 6 (art 6) is a matter to be determined in the light of all the circumstances of the case, having particular regard to the situations where inferences may be drawn, the weight attached to them by the national courts in their assessment of the evidence and the degree of compulsion inherent in the situation.

48. As regards the degree of compulsion involved in the present case, it is recalled that the applicant was in fact able to remain silent. Notwithstanding the repeated warnings as to the possibility that inferences might be drawn from his silence, he did not make any statements to the police and did not give evidence during his trial. Moreover under Article 4 (5) of the Order he remained a non-compellable witness... Thus his insistence in maintaining silence throughout the proceedings did not amount to a criminal offence or contempt of court. Furthermore, as has been stressed in national court decisions, silence, in itself, cannot be regarded as an indication of guilt...

49. The facts of the present case accordingly fall to be distinguished from those in *Funke*... where criminal proceedings were brought against the applicant by the customs authorities in an attempt to compel him to provide evidence of offences he had allegedly committed. Such a degree of compulsion in that case was found by the Court to be incompatible with Article 6 (art 6) since, in effect, it destroyed the very essence of the privilege against self-incrimination.

50. Admittedly a system which warns the accused—who is possibly without legal assistance (as in the applicant's case)—that adverse inferences may be drawn from a refusal to provide an explanation to the police for his presence at the scene of a crime or to testify during his trial, when taken in conjunction with the weight of the case against him, involves a certain level of indirect compulsion. However, since the applicant could not be compelled to speak or to testify, as indicated above, this factor on its own cannot be decisive. The Court must rather concentrate its attention on the role played by the inferences in the proceedings against the applicant and especially in his conviction.

51. In this context, it is recalled that these were proceedings without a jury, the trier of fact being an experienced judge. Furthermore, the drawing of inferences under the Order is subject to an important series of safeguards designed to respect the rights of the defence and to limit the extent to which reliance can be placed on inferences.

In the first place, before inferences can be drawn under Article 4 and 6 of the Order appropriate warnings must have been given to the accused as to the legal effects of maintaining silence.... The question in each particular case is whether the evidence adduced by the prosecution is sufficiently strong to require an answer. The national court cannot conclude that the accused is guilty merely because he chooses to remain silent. It is only if the evidence against the accused 'calls' for an explanation which the accused ought to be in a position to give that a failure to give any explanation 'may as a matter of common sense allow the drawing of an inference that there is no explanation and that the accused is guilty'. Conversely if the case presented by the prosecution had so little evidential value that it called for no answer, a failure to provide one could not justify an inference of guilt...In sum, it is only common-sense inferences which the judge considers proper, in the light of the evidence against the accused, that can be drawn under the Order.

In addition, the trial judge has a discretion whether, on the facts of the particular case, an inference should be drawn. As indicated by the Court of Appeal in the present case, if a judge accepted that an accused did not understand the warning given or if he had doubts about it, 'we are confident that he would not activate Article 6 against him'...Furthermore in Northern Ireland, where trial judges sit without a jury, the judge must explain the reasons for the decision to draw inferences and the weight attached to them. The exercise of discretion in this regard is subject to review by the appellate courts.

52. In the present case, the evidence presented against the applicant by the prosecution was considered by the Court of Appeal to constitute a 'formidable' case against him...It is recalled that when the police entered the house some appreciable time after they knocked on the door, they found the applicant coming down the flight of stairs in the house where Mr L had been held captive by the IRA. Evidence had been given by Mr L—evidence which in the opinion of the trial judge had been corroborated—that he had been forced to make a taped confession and that after the arrival of the police at the house and the removal of his blindfold he saw the applicant at the top of the stairs. He had been told by him to go downstairs and watch television. The applicant was pulling a tape out of a cassette. The tangled tape and cassette recorder were later found on the premises. Evidence by the applicant's co-accused that he had recently arrived at the house was discounted as not being credible...

53. The trial judge drew strong inferences against the applicant under Article 6 of the Order by reason of his failure to give an account of his presence in the house when arrested and interrogated by the police. He also drew strong inferences under Article 4 of the Order by reason of the applicant's refusal to give evidence in his own defence when asked by the court to do so...

54. In the Court's view, having regard to the weight of the evidence against the applicant, as outlined above, the drawing of inferences from his refusal, at arrest, during police questioning and at trial, to provide an explanation for his presence in the house was a matter of common sense and cannot be regarded as unfair or unreasonable in the circumstances.

57. Against the above background, and taking into account the role played by inferences under the Order during the trial and their impact on the rights of the defence, the Court does not consider that the criminal proceedings were unfair or that there had been an infringement of the presumption of innocence...

58. Accordingly, there has been no violation of Article 6 paras 1 and 2 (art 6-1, art 6-2) of the Convention.

B. ACCESS TO LAWYER

59. The applicant submitted that he was denied access to a lawyer at a critical stage of the criminal proceedings against him. He pointed out that in Northern Ireland the initial phase of detention is of crucial importance in the context of the criminal proceedings as a whole because of the possibility of inferences being drawn under Articles 3, 4 and 6 of the Order....

62. The Court observes that it has not been disputed by the Government that Article 6 (art 6) applies even at the stage of the preliminary investigation into an offence by the police....

63. National laws may attach consequences to the attitude of an accused at the initial stages of police interrogation which are decisive for the prospects of the defence in any subsequent criminal

proceedings. In such circumstances Article 6 (art 6) will normally require that the accused be allowed to benefit from the assistance of a lawyer already at the initial stages of police interrogation. However, this right, which is not explicitly set out in the Convention, may be subject to restrictions for good cause. The question, in each case, is whether the restriction, in the light of the entirety of the proceedings, has deprived the accused of a fair hearing.

64. In the present case, the applicant's right of access to a lawyer during the first 48 hours of police detention was restricted under section 15 of the Northern Ireland (Emergency Provisions) Act 1987 on the basis that the police had reasonable grounds to believe that the exercise of the right of access would, *inter alia*, interfere with the gathering of information about the commission of acts of terrorism or make it more difficult to prevent such an act....

66. The Court is of the opinion that the scheme contained in the Order is such that it is of paramount importance for the rights of the defence that an accused has access to a lawyer at the initial stages of police interrogation. It observes in this context that, under the Order, at the beginning of police interrogation, an accused is confronted with a fundamental dilemma relating to his defence. If he chooses to remain silent, adverse inferences may be drawn against him in accordance with the provisions of the Order. On the other hand, if the accused opts to break his silence during the course of interrogation, he runs the risk of prejudicing his defence without necessarily removing the possibility of inferences being drawn against him.

Under such conditions the concept of fairness enshrined in Article 6 (art 6) requires that the accused has the benefit of the assistance of a lawyer already at the initial stages of police interrogation. To deny access to a lawyer for the first 48 hours of police questioning, in a situation where the rights of the defence may well be irretrievably prejudiced, is—whatever the justification for such denial—incompatible with the rights of the accused under Article 6 (art 6)....

70. There has therefore been a breach of Article 6 para 1 in conjunction with paragraph 3 (c) (art 6-1 art 6-3-c) of the Convention as regards the applicant's denial of access to a lawyer during the first 48 hours of his police detention.

...

FOR THESE REASONS, THE COURT

Holds by fourteen votes to five that there has been no violation of Article 6(1) and (2) of the Convention arising out of the drawing of adverse inferences on account of the applicant's silence;

Holds by twelve votes to seven that there has been a violation of Article 6(1) in conjunction with 6(3)(c) as regards the applicant's lack of access to a lawyer during the first 48 hours of his police detention;...

NOTES

1 The Court was composed of Judges: Bernhardt, Pettiti, Walsh, Valticos, Martens, Pekkanen, Loizou, Bigi, Lopes Rocha, Makarczyk, Gotchev, and Lohmus. President Ryssdal and Judges: Matscher, Palm, Foighel, Freeland, Wildhaber, and Jungwiert issued a joint partly dissenting opinion in which they expressed the view that in the context of the terrorist situation prevailing in Northern Ireland during the 1990s it was not unreasonable for senior police officers to possess a statutory power to delay arrested terrorist suspects access to a lawyer for not more than 48 hours.

2 The Court's judgment in **Murray** reflects a deft balancing exercise. Adverse inferences can in certain circumstances (relevant factors are elaborated in paragraph 47) be drawn in respect of a suspect/defendant's silence. However, where national law allows such inferences to be drawn in regard to a suspect's refusal to answer police questions then there is a corresponding implied right for suspects to have access to a lawyer (paragraph 63).

3 The Court first recognized the implied right to silence/privilege against self-incrimination in *Funke v France* A.256-A (1993). French courts had ordered Mr Funke to produce foreign bank account details to the customs authorities (they suspected him of unlawful foreign financial dealings) and imposed a daily fine of 50 Francs payable by him until he delivered the documents to the authorities. By 8 votes to 1, the Court found a breach of Article 6(1).

44. The Court notes that the customs secured Mr Funke's conviction in order to obtain certain documents which they believed must exist, although they were not certain of the fact. Being unable or unwilling to procure them by some other means, they attempted to compel the applicant himself to provide the evidence of offences he had allegedly committed. The special features of customs law … cannot justify such an infringement of the right of anyone 'charged with a criminal offence', within the autonomous meaning of this expression in Article 6, to remain silent and not to contribute to incriminating himself.

It is interesting to observe that the Court in *Funke* provided no clear justification for recognizing these implicit rights/privileges. But in *Murray* the Court was more forthcoming (see paragraph 45) about the origins and objectives of these implied safeguards.

4 In the later case of *Saunders v UK*, 1996-VI, the Court referred to the 'right' not to incriminate oneself and elaborated the purposes served by this provision. The applicant had been the chief executive of Guinness plc during its contentious take-over of another drinks company (Distillers Company plc). Rumours of misconduct during the take-over led the Secretary of State for Trade and Industry to appoint inspectors to investigate the affair. The inspectors had statutory powers to require witnesses to answer their questions. The applicant, accompanied by his lawyers, was interviewed by the inspectors on nine occasions. Subsequently he was charged with a number of financial crimes. During his trial the prosecution read out extracts of the applicant's answers to the inspectors' questions. The jury convicted him of 12 counts of conspiracy, false accounting, and theft. He was sentenced to five years' imprisonment. The Commission upheld his complaint under Article 6(1), by 14 votes to 1. Likewise the Court, by 16 votes to 4, determined that there was a violation of that provision.

68. The Court recalls that, although not specifically mentioned in Article 6 of the Convention (art 6), the right to silence and the right not to incriminate oneself are generally recognised international standards which lie at the heart of the notion of a fair procedure under Article 6 (art 6). Their rationale lies, *inter alia*, in the protection of the accused against improper compulsion by the authorities thereby contributing to the avoidance of miscarriages of justice and to the fulfilment of the aims of Article 6 (art 6) (see the … *John Murray* judgment, p 49, para 45, and the … *Funke* judgment, p 22, para 44). The right not to incriminate oneself, in particular, presupposes that the prosecution in a criminal case seek to prove their case against the accused without resort to evidence obtained through methods of coercion or oppression in defiance of the will of the accused. In this sense the right is closely linked to the presumption of innocence contained in Article 6 para 2 of the Convention (art 6-2).

69. The right not to incriminate oneself is primarily concerned, however, with respecting the will of an accused person to remain silent. As commonly understood in the legal systems of the Contracting Parties to the Convention and elsewhere, it does not extend to the use in criminal proceedings of material which may be obtained from the accused through the use of compulsory powers but which has an existence independent of the will of the suspect such as, *inter alia*, documents acquired pursuant to a warrant, breath, blood and urine samples and bodily tissue for the purpose of DNA testing.

In the present case the Court is only called upon to decide whether the use made by the prosecution of the statements obtained from the applicant by the inspectors amounted to an unjustifiable infringement of the right. This question must be examined by the Court in the light of all the circumstances of the case. In particular, it must be determined whether the applicant has been subject to compulsion to give evidence and whether the use made of the resulting testimony at his trial offended the basic principles of a fair procedure inherent in Article 6 para 1 (art 6-1) of which the right not to incriminate oneself is a constituent element.

70. It has not been disputed by the Government that the applicant was subject to legal compulsion to give evidence to the inspectors. He was obliged under sections 434 and 436 of the Companies Act 1985 . . . to answer the questions put to him by the inspectors in the course of nine lengthy interviews of which seven were admissible as evidence at his trial. A refusal by the applicant to answer the questions put to him could have led to a finding of contempt of court and the imposition of a fine or committal to prison for up to two years . . . and it was no defence to such refusal that the questions were of an incriminating nature . . .

However, the Government have emphasised, before the Court, that nothing said by the applicant in the course of the interviews was self-incriminating and that he had merely given exculpatory answers or answers which, if true, would serve to confirm his defence. In their submission only statements which are self-incriminating could fall within the privilege against self-incrimination.

71. The Court does not accept the Government's premise on this point since some of the applicant's answers were in fact of an incriminating nature in the sense that they contained admissions to knowledge of information which tended to incriminate him . . . In any event, bearing in mind the concept of fairness in Article 6 (art 6), the right not to incriminate oneself cannot reasonably be confined to statements of admission of wrongdoing or to remarks which are directly incriminating. Testimony obtained under compulsion which appears on its face to be of a non-incriminating nature—such as exculpatory remarks or mere information on questions of fact—may later be deployed in criminal proceedings in support of the prosecution case, for example to contradict or cast doubt upon other statements of the accused or evidence given by him during the trial or to otherwise undermine his credibility. Where the credibility of an accused must be assessed by a jury the use of such testimony may be especially harmful. It follows that what is of the essence in this context is the use to which evidence obtained under compulsion is put in the course of the criminal trial.

72. In this regard, the Court observes that part of the transcript of answers given by the applicant was read to the jury by counsel for the prosecution over a three-day period despite objections by the applicant. The fact that such extensive use was made of the interviews strongly suggests that the prosecution must have believed that the reading of the transcripts assisted their case in establishing the applicant's dishonesty. This interpretation of the intended impact of the material is supported by the remarks made by the trial judge in the course of the *voir dire* concerning the eighth and ninth interviews to the effect that each of the applicant's statements was capable of being a 'confession' for the purposes of section 82(1) of the Police and Criminal Evidence Act 1984 . . . Similarly, the Court of Appeal considered that the interviews formed 'a significant part' of the prosecution's case against the applicant . . . Moreover, there were clearly instances where the statements were used by the prosecution to incriminating effect in order to establish the applicant's knowledge of payments to persons involved in the share-support operation and to call into question his honesty . . . They were also used by counsel for the applicant's co-accused to cast doubt on the applicant's version of events . . .

In sum, the evidence available to the Court supports the claim that the transcripts of the applicant's answers, whether directly self-incriminating or not, were used in the course of the proceedings in a manner which sought to incriminate the applicant. . . .

74. Nor does the Court find it necessary, having regard to the above assessment as to the use of the interviews during the trial, to decide whether the right not to incriminate oneself is absolute or whether infringements of it may be justified in particular circumstances.

It does not accept the Government's argument that the complexity of corporate fraud and the vital public interest in the investigation of such fraud and the punishment of those responsible could justify such a marked departure as that which occurred in the present case from one of the basic principles of a fair procedure. Like the Commission, it considers that the general requirements of fairness contained in Article 6 (art 6), including the right not to incriminate oneself, apply to criminal proceedings in respect of all types of criminal offences without distinction from the most simple to the most complex. The public interest cannot be invoked to justify the use of answers compulsorily obtained in a non-judicial investigation to incriminate the accused during the trial proceedings. It is noteworthy in this respect that under the relevant legislation statements obtained under compulsory powers by the Serious Fraud Office cannot, as a general rule, be adduced in evidence at the subsequent trial of the person concerned. Moreover the fact that statements were made by the applicant prior to his being charged does not prevent their later use in criminal proceedings from constituting an infringement of the right.

75. It follows from the above analysis and from the fact that section 434(5) of the Companies Act 1985 authorises, as noted by both the trial judge and the Court of Appeal, the subsequent use in criminal proceedings of statements obtained by the inspectors that the various procedural safeguards to which reference has been made by the respondent Government...cannot provide a defence in the present case since they did not operate to prevent the use of the statements in the subsequent criminal proceedings.

76. Accordingly, there has been an infringement in the present case of the right not to incriminate oneself.

Mr Saunders was controversially given early release from prison, on the grounds of ill-health, and subsequently resumed working in the world of business. In September 2000 three of Saunders' co-defendants successfully argued that the prosecution's use of statements, which they had been compelled to give to the DTI inspectors, violated their right to a fair trial: *IJL, GMR and AKP v UK* (judgments of 19 September 2000). The applicants were identified by *The Times* (20 September 2000) as Jack Lyons, Gerald Ronson, and Anthony Parnes. The applicants were businessmen whom the prosecution alleged had engaged in an illegal share support operation designed to help Guinness to acquire Distillers. In the light of the Court's earlier ruling in *Saunders*, the British Government conceded that the prosecution's use of the statements violated Article 6(1). The Court rejected the applicants' other complaints. Significantly, the Court did not award the applicants any compensation for pecuniary or non-pecuniary damage. Under Schedule 3 to the Youth Justice and Criminal Evidence Act 1999, which came into effect during April 2000, the prosecution were generally prohibited from using statements obtained from defendants under compulsory powers in the field of company and business inquiries.

5   A unanimous Court found a breach of the right to silence where an English judge failed to direct a jury to exercise sufficient caution when drawing adverse inferences from the silence of two suspects, who were undergoing heroin withdrawal symptoms, while being questioned by the police. The husband and wife applicants in *Condron v UK*, judgment of 2 May 2000, were suspected of aiding a neighbour in the supply of unlawful drugs (police videos showed them passing suspicious items between their adjoining flats). The applicants were arrested and 16 'wraps' (individual sachets) of heroin were found in their flat. Several hours later when the police proposed to interview the applicants, at the police station, their solicitor formed the view that because the applicants were undergoing the effects of drug

withdrawal (they were both heroin addicts) they were unfit to be questioned. However, the force's doctor examined the applicants and determined that they were fit to be questioned. Each of the applicants was cautioned by the police that 'you do not have to say anything but it may harm your defence if you do not mention when questioned something which you later rely on in court....' The police also advised them that if they felt unwell during the interviews they could ask for them to be stopped. Their solicitor was present throughout the separate interviews of each applicant. Both applicants replied 'no comment' when asked about their activities with their neighbour. They were tried on charges of possession and supply of heroin. The applicants gave evidence at their trial that the heroin in the flat was for their own consumption and they had not helped their neighbour to supply drugs. They stated that they had not answered the police questions because their solicitor had advised them that they were not fit to do so. The judge directed the jury that under the Criminal Justice and Public Order Act 1994: 'The law is...that you may draw such inferences as appear proper from a defendant's failure to mention the points...referred to in their respective interviews....You do not have to hold it against him or her. It is for you to decide whether it is proper to do so. Failure to mention the points in interview cannot on its own prove guilt but depending on the circumstances you may hold it against him or her when deciding whether he or she is guilty....' Both applicants were convicted by majority (9 to 1) verdicts and sentenced to four and three years' imprisonment. Although the Court of Appeal expressed some criticism of the judge's direction it upheld the applicants' convictions. The European Court reiterated its approach to the right to silence articulated in *Murray*.

57. The Court observes that there are features of the applicants' case which distinguish it from that of the applicant John Murray. In particular, unlike John Murray, the applicants gave evidence at their trial and their case was conducted before a jury which required direction by the trial judge on how to approach the issue of their silence during police interview. Moreover, the applicants, contrary to the stance adopted by John Murray at his trial, offered an explanation at their trial for their silence at the police station. For the Court, these and other distinguishing features fall to be considered from the standpoint of 'all the circumstances of the case'...Accordingly, the fact that the applicants' exercised their right to silence at the police station is relevant to the determination of the fairness issue. However, that fact does not of itself preclude the drawing of an adverse inference, it being observed that the principles laid down in the *John Murray* judgment addressed the drawing of inferences under both Articles 4 and 6 of the Criminal Evidence (Northern Ireland) Order 1988. Similarly, the fact that the issue of the applicants' silence was left to a jury cannot of itself be considered incompatible with the requirements of a fair trial. It is, rather, another relevant consideration to be weighed in the balance when assessing whether or not it was fair to do so in the circumstances....

60. It must also be observed that the applicants' solicitor was present throughout the whole of their interviews and was able to advise them not to volunteer any answers to the questions put to them. The fact that an accused person who is questioned under caution is assured access to legal advice, and in the applicants' case the physical presence of a solicitor during police interview, must be considered a particularly important safeguard for dispelling any compulsion to speak which may be inherent in the terms of the caution....

61. It is to be noted that the trial judge directed the jury on the issue of the applicants' silence in accordance with the terms of the relevant specimen direction at the time...The Court notes, however, that the formula employed by the trial judge cannot be said to reflect the balance which the Court in its *John Murray* judgment sought to strike between the right to silence and the circumstances in which an adverse inference may be drawn from silence, including by a jury. It reiterates that the Court stressed in that judgment that, provided appropriate safeguards were in place, an

accused's silence, in situations which clearly call for an explanation, could be taken into account in assessing the persuasiveness of the evidence adduced by the prosecution against him...The Court further noted, with reference to Articles 4 and 6 of the Criminal Evidence (Northern Ireland) Order 1988, that those provisions only permitted a judge to draw common-sense inferences which he considered proper in the light of the evidence against the accused...However, in the instant case the applicants put forward an explanation for their failure to mention during the police interview why certain items were exchanged between them and their co-accused, Mr Curtis...They testified that they acted on the strength of the advice of their solicitor who had grave doubts about their fitness to cope with police questioning...Their solicitor confirmed this in his testimony in the *voir dire* proceedings...Admittedly the trial judge drew the jury's attention to this explanation. However he did so in terms which left the jury at liberty to draw an adverse inference notwithstanding that it may have been satisfied as to the plausibility of the explanation. It is to be observed that the Court of Appeal found the terms of the trial judge's direction deficient in this respect...In the Court's opinion, as a matter of fairness, the jury should have been directed that if it was satisfied that the applicants' silence at the police interview could not sensibly be attributed to their having no answer or none that would stand up to cross-examination it should not draw an adverse inference....

The judgment reveals that the Court demands clear guidance be given by trial judges on the limited circumstances where it is permissible for juries to draw adverse inferences from defendants' silences. In England, the Judicial Studies Board provides guideline directions, taking account of the Court of Appeal's evolving case-law on the 1994 Act, for judges to use when juries may have to consider a particular defendant's silence.

6 The full-time Court, unanimously, rejected the Irish Government's defence that the fight against Irish terrorism justified compelling arrested persons to explain their conduct during a specified period of time in ***Heaney and McGuinness v Ireland***, judgment of 21 December 2000. The applicants had been arrested in connection with a bombing of a nearby checkpoint on the border with Northern Ireland at which a number of persons had been killed. The applicants refused to answer police questions whereupon the latter invoked section 52 of the Offences Against the State Act 1939 (which provided that if detainees held under the Act refused to account for their movements and actions during a specified time frame they were guilty of an offence punishable with up to six months' imprisonment). The applicants failed to provide the required information and were subsequently convicted and sentenced to the maximum term of imprisonment. In response to the applicants' contention that they had suffered an infringement of their right to silence under Article 6(1) the Government submitted that section 52 was a proportionate response to the continuing threat from terrorism. However, the Court held that:

55....the 'degree of compulsion', imposed on the applicants by s.52 of the 1939 Act with a view to compelling them under that Act, in effect, destroyed the very essence of their privilege against self-incrimination and their right to remain silent.

...

58. The Court, accordingly, finds that the security and public order concerns of the Government cannot justify a provision which extinguishes the very essence of the applicants' right to silence and against self-incrimination guaranteed by Article 6(1) of the Convention.

59. It concludes therefore that there has been a violation of the applicants' right to silence and their right not to incriminate themselves guaranteed by Article 6(1) of the Convention.

This case can be distinguished from *John Murray* because in the former the applicants had been convicted and punished for remaining silent as opposed to having adverse inferences drawn from their silence in respect of a specific substantive crime.

7   The contentious issue of whether the registered keepers of vehicles caught exceeding the speed limit by cameras can be legally obliged to inform the police who was driving the vehicle at the relevant time (so that person can be prosecuted) was addressed by a Grand Chamber in *O'Halloran and Francis v UK*, judgment of 29 June 2007. The first applicant complied with such a notice served on him by the police and he was subsequently convicted of speeding (he received a fine and penalty points on his driving licence). The second applicant refused to provide any information after being served with a notice. He was later convicted of failing to comply with the notice (and received a large fine and penalty points). The applicants complained to Strasbourg alleging that their treatment amounted to a breach of the right to silence and the privilege against self-incrimination. The Government contended that the right/privilege were not absolute and could be limited in the public interest. Indeed, the Privy Council had rejected an Article 6 challenge to such a notice in *Brown v Stott* [2001] 2 WLR 817. The Grand Chamber, by 15 votes to 2, determined that:

57.... The Court notes that although both the compulsion and the underlying offences were 'criminal' in nature, the compulsion flowed from the fact, as Lord Bingham expressed it in the Privy Council in the case of *Brown v Stott*, that 'All who own or drive motor cars know that by doing so they subject themselves to a regulatory regime. This regime is imposed not because owning or driving cars is a privilege or indulgence granted by the State but because the possession and use of cars (like, for example, shotguns...) are recognised to have the potential to cause grave injury'. Those who choose to keep and drive motor cars can be taken to have accepted certain responsibilities and obligations as part of the regulatory regime relating to motor vehicles, and in the legal framework of the United Kingdom, these responsibilities include the obligation, in the event of suspected commission of road traffic offences, to inform the authorities of the identity of the driver on that occasion.

...

62. Having regard to all the circumstances of the case, including the special nature of the regulatory regime at issue and the limited nature of the information sought by a notice under section 172 of the Road Traffic Act 1988, the Court considers that the essence of the applicants' right to remain silent and their privilege against self-incrimination has not been destroyed.

63. Accordingly, there has been no violation of Article 6 § 1 of the Convention.

In his dissent Judge Pavlovschi stated:

In my opinion, the majority has committed a fundamental mistake in accepting the Government's position that obtaining self-incriminating statements under the threat of criminal prosecution can be considered as a permissible method of prosecution in certain very specific circumstances, such as those of the present case. This is not only wrong, but is also an extremely dangerous approach.

...

    The security and public order concerns relied on by the Government cannot justify a provision which extinguishes the very essence of the applicants' rights to silence and against self-incrimination guaranteed by Article 6 § 1 of the Convention (see *Heaney and McGuiness*, cited above, § 58).

    In my view, the provisions of section 172 of the Road Traffic Act 1988 amount to a deviation from the principle of prohibition of 'compulsory self-incrimination' and a breach of the right to silence, and can be considered as subjecting the individuals concerned to a legal compulsion to give evidence against themselves. Moreover, the applicants in this case were actually subjected to legal compulsion to give evidence which incriminated them.

What would have been the effect on the use of speed/safety cameras if the applicants had been successful?

8 A large majority (11 votes to 6) of the Grand Chamber in *Jalloh v Germany* (see p 176) considered that allowing the use at the applicant's trial of evidence (a packet of cocaine he had swallowed) obtained by the forced application of emetics to him was both an infringement of his right to a fair trial and his right not to incriminate himself.

105. As noted above, the use of evidence obtained in violation of Article 3 in criminal proceedings raises serious issues as to the fairness of such proceedings. The Court has not found in the instant case that the applicant was subjected to torture. In its view, incriminating evidence—whether in the form of a confession or real evidence—obtained as a result of acts of violence or brutality or other forms of treatment which can be characterised as torture—should never be relied on as proof of the victim's guilt, irrespective of its probative value. Any other conclusion would only serve to legitimate indirectly the sort of morally reprehensible conduct which the authors of Article 3 of the Convention sought to proscribe or, as it was so well put in the US Supreme Court's judgment in the *Rochin* [v *California* (342 U.S. 165 (1952)] case, to 'afford brutality the cloak of law'. It notes in this connection that Article 15 of the UN Convention against Torture and Other Cruel, Inhuman or Degrading Treatment or Punishment provides that statements which are established to have been made as a result of torture shall not be used in evidence in proceedings against the victim of torture.

106. Although the treatment to which the applicant was subjected did not attract the special stigma reserved to acts of torture, it did attain in the circumstances the minimum level of severity covered by the ambit of the Article 3 prohibition. It cannot be excluded that on the facts of a particular case the use of evidence obtained by intentional acts of ill-treatment not amounting to torture will render the trial against the victim unfair irrespective of the seriousness of the offence allegedly committed, the weight attached to the evidence and the opportunities which the victim had to challenge its admission and use at his trial.

107. In the present case, the general question whether the use of evidence obtained by an act qualified as inhuman and degrading treatment automatically renders a trial unfair can be left open. The Court notes that, even if it was not the intention of the authorities to inflict pain and suffering on the applicant, the evidence was obtained by a measure which breached one of the core rights guaranteed by the Convention. Furthermore, it was common ground between the parties that the drugs obtained by the impugned measure were the decisive element in securing the applicant's conviction. It is true that, as was equally uncontested, the applicant was given the opportunity, which he took, of challenging the use of the drugs obtained by the impugned measure. However, any discretion on the part of the national courts to exclude that evidence could not come into play as they considered the administration of emetics to be authorised by the domestic law. Moreover, the public interest in securing the applicant's conviction cannot be considered to have been of such weight as to warrant allowing that evidence to be used at the trial. As noted above, the measure targeted a street dealer selling drugs on a relatively small scale who was finally given a six months' suspended prison sentence and probation.

108. In these circumstances, the Court finds that the use in evidence of the drugs obtained by the forcible administration of emetics to the applicant rendered his trial as a whole unfair.

Regarding the principle against self-incrimination, the majority considered that the extent of force used on the applicant '118.... significantly interfered with his physical and mental integrity'. He was only suspected of small-scale drug dealing and the evidence obtained by the use of emetics was decisive in securing his conviction. Therefore, the obtaining of this evidence could be distinguished from the permissible compulsory acquisition of blood etc samples mentioned in paragraph 69 of **Saunders** (above). As we have discovered in respect of the Article 3 aspect of **Jalloh**, the forcible use of emetics to obtain physical evidence from inside the bodies of suspects in some regions of Germany was contrary to the practice of the overwhelming majority of member States.

In the later case of **Gafgen v Germany** (see p 183), the Grand Chamber was divided upon the issue whether the use of real evidence obtained by a breach of Article 3 should always be found to violate Article 6(1). The majority (of 11 judges) observed that:

173. The Court is therefore called upon to examine the consequences for a trial's fairness of the admission of real evidence obtained as a result of an act qualified as inhuman treatment in breach of Article 3, but falling short of torture. As shown above, in its case-law to date, it has not yet settled the question whether the use of such evidence will always render a trial unfair, that is, irrespective of other circumstances of the case. It has, however, found that both the use in criminal proceedings of statements obtained as a result of a person's treatment in breach of Article 3—irrespective of the classification of that treatment as torture, inhuman or degrading treatment—and the use of real evidence obtained as a direct result of acts of torture made the proceedings as a whole automatically unfair, in breach of Article 6.

174. The Court notes that there is no clear consensus among the Contracting States to the Convention, the courts of other States and other human-rights monitoring institutions about the exact scope of application of the exclusionary rule. In particular, factors such as whether the impugned evidence would, in any event, have been found at a later stage, independently of the prohibited method of investigation, may have an influence on the admissibility of such evidence.

The majority considered that as the German courts had convicted the applicant on the basis of his confession made during his trial there had not been a breach of Article 6(1). However, Judge Rozakis (joined by Judges: Tulkens, Jebens, Ziemele, Bianku, and Power) issued a partly dissenting opinion criticizing the analysis of the majority.

2....The Court could have answered that question categorically by asserting, in an unequivocal manner, that irrespective of the conduct of an accused, fairness, for the purpose of Article 6, presupposes respect for the rule of law and requires, as a self-evident proposition, the exclusion of any evidence that has been obtained in violation of Article 3. A criminal trial which admits and relies, to any extent, upon evidence obtained as a result of breaching such an absolute provision of the Convention cannot *a fortiori* be a fair one. The Court's reluctance to cross that final frontier and to establish a clear or 'bright-line' rule in this core area of fundamental human rights is regrettable.

3....Regrettably, the answer now given and the reasoning adopted by the majority risks undermining the effectiveness of the absolute rights guaranteed by Article 3. A distinction has been introduced into the Court's jurisprudence between the admissibility of statements obtained in breach of the absolute prohibition of inhuman and degrading treatment and the admissibility of other evidence obtained in the same manner. Such a distinction is difficult to sustain.

This is topic where the Strasbourg case-law may evolve further, especially if a consensus on the exclusion of real evidence obtained by inhuman or degrading treatment develops.

(IV) THE RIGHT OF DEFENDANTS TO PARTICIPATE EFFECTIVELY IN THEIR CRIMINAL TRIALS

V v UK 1999-IX
European Court of Human Rights

The background to this case has already been explained (p 179). One of the applicant's complaints was that he had not received a fair trial. The Commission, by 15 votes to 4, agreed that there had been a breach of Article 6(1).

85. The Court notes that Article 6, read as a whole, guarantees the right of an accused to participate effectively in his criminal trial (see the *Stanford* judgment [*Stanford v UK*, A.282-A (1994)]). It has not until the present time been called upon to consider how this Article 6 § 1 guarantee applies to criminal proceedings against children, and in particular whether procedures which are generally considered to safeguard the rights of adults on trial, such as publicity, should be abrogated in respect of children in order to promote their understanding and participation...

86. The Court recalls its above findings that there is not at this stage any clear common standard among the member States of the Council of Europe as to the minimum age of criminal responsibility and that the attribution of criminal responsibility to the applicant does not in itself give rise to a breach of Article 3 of the Convention...Likewise, it cannot be said that the trial on criminal charges of a child, even one as young as eleven, as such violates the fair trial guarantee under Article 6 § 1. The Court does, however, agree with the Commission that it is essential that a child charged with an offence is dealt with in a manner which takes full account of his age, level of maturity and intellectual and emotional capacities, and that steps are taken to promote his ability to understand and participate in the proceedings.

87. It follows that, in respect of a young child charged with a grave offence attracting high levels of media and public interest, it would be necessary to conduct the hearing in such a way as to reduce as far as possible his or her feelings of intimidation and inhibition. In this connection it is noteworthy that in England and Wales children charged with less serious crimes are dealt with in special Youth Courts, from which the general public is excluded and in relation to which there are imposed automatic reporting restrictions on the media...Moreover, the Court has already referred to the international tendency towards the protection of the privacy of child defendants...It has considered carefully the Government's argument that public trials serve the general interest in the open administration of justice...and observes that, where appropriate in view of the age and other characteristics of the child and the circumstances surrounding the criminal proceedings, this general interest could be satisfied by a modified procedure providing for selected attendance rights and judicious reporting.

88. The Court notes that the applicant's trial took place over three weeks in public in the Crown Court. Special measures were taken in view of the applicant's young age and to promote his understanding of the proceedings: for example, he had the trial procedure explained to him and was taken to see the courtroom in advance, and the hearing times were shortened so as not to tire the defendants excessively. Nonetheless, the formality and ritual of the Crown Court must at times have seemed incomprehensible and intimidating for a child of eleven, and there is evidence that certain of the modifications to the courtroom, in particular the raised dock which was designed to enable the defendants to see what was going on, had the effect of increasing the applicant's sense of discomfort during the trial, since he felt exposed to the scrutiny of the press and public. The trial generated extremely high levels of press and public interest, both inside and outside the courtroom, to the extent that the judge in his summing-up referred to the problems caused to witnesses by the blaze of publicity and asked the jury to take this into account when assessing their evidence.

89. There is considerable psychiatric evidence relating to the applicant's ability to participate in the proceedings. Thus, Dr Susan Bailey (a consultant psychiatrist from the Adolescent Forensic Service of the Home Office) gave evidence during the trial in November 1993 that on each occasion when she had seen the applicant prior to the trial he had cried inconsolably and had not been able to talk about the circumstances of the offence in any useful way...Dr Bentovim (a defence expert from the Great Ormond Street Hospital for Children) similarly found in his report of September 1993 that the applicant was suffering from post-traumatic effects and found it very difficult and distressing to think or talk about the events in question, making it impossible to ascertain many aspects...Subsequent to the trial, in January 1995, the applicant told Dr Bentovim that he had been terrified of being looked at in court and had frequently found himself worrying what people were thinking about him. He had not been able to pay attention to the proceedings and had spent time counting in his head or making shapes with his shoes. Dr Bentovim considered that, in view of V.'s immaturity, it was 'very doubtful' that he understood the situation and was able to give informed instruction to his lawyers...The report of Dr Bailey dated November 1997 also described the applicant's attempts to distract himself during the trial, his inability to listen to what was said and the distress caused to him by the public nature of the proceedings...

90. In such circumstances the Court does not consider that it was sufficient for the purposes of Article 6 § 1 that the applicant was represented by skilled and experienced lawyers. This case is different from that of *Stanford*...where the Court found no violation arising from the fact that the accused could not hear some of the evidence given at trial, in view of the fact that his counsel, who could hear all that was said and was able to take his client's instructions at all times, chose for tactical reasons not to request that the accused be seated closer to the witnesses. Here, although the applicant's legal representatives were seated, as the Government put it, 'within whispering distance', it is highly unlikely that the applicant would have felt sufficiently uninhibited, in the tense courtroom and under public scrutiny, to have consulted with them during the trial or, indeed, that, given his immaturity and his disturbed emotional state, he would have been capable outside the courtroom of cooperating with his lawyers and giving them information for the purposes of his defence.

91. In conclusion, the Court considers that the applicant was unable to participate effectively in the criminal proceedings against him and was, in consequence, denied a fair hearing in breach of Article 6 § 1.

NOTES

1 The Court was composed of President Wildhaber and Judges: Palm, Rozakis, Pastor Ridruejo, Ress, Makarczyk, Kuris, Turmen, Costa, Tulkens, Birsan, Lorenzen, Fischbach, Butkevych, Casadevall, and Reed. Judge Baka dissented because in his opinion the authorities had sufficiently adapted the ordinary court proceedings to take account of the applicant's young age.

2 The changes in the institutional arrangements and procedures for dealing with subsequent trials of juvenile defendants facing serious criminal charges have been outlined during our previous examination of the Article 3 aspects of this case. The modified process was found by a Chamber, 5 votes to 2, not to satisfy the right to participate effectively of an 11-year-old with a limited intellectual capacity in *SC v UK*, judgment of 15 June 2004. The applicant, with a 14-year-old accomplice, attempted to snatch the bag of an elderly woman causing her to fracture her arm. He was charged with attempted robbery. Having regard to his previous criminal history (including robbery, burglary, and arson) the Youth Court committed him for trial at the Crown Court. Two expert reports were commissioned and one found that he was capable of entering a pleas whilst another determined that he had a

significant degree of learning difficulty (with cognitive abilities of a 6- to 8-year-old). The judge ruled that he should stand trial in the Crown Court adopting an informal procedure (SC did not sit in the dock and was accompanied by his social worker, wigs and gowns were dispensed with, and frequent breaks were taken by the court). The trial lasted one day and the applicant gave evidence (he was legally represented). He was convicted and sentenced to two-and-a-half years' detention. The Chamber held that:

29. The Court accepts the Government's argument that Article 6 § 1 does not require that a child on trial for a criminal offence should understand or be capable of understanding every point of law or evidential detail. Given the sophistication of modern legal systems, many adults of normal intelligence are unable fully to comprehend all the intricacies and exchanges which take place in the courtroom: this is why the Convention, in Article 6 § 3(c), emphasises the importance of the right to legal representation. However, 'effective participation' in this context presupposes that the accused has a broad understanding of the nature of the trial process and of what is at stake for him or her, including the significance of any penalty which may be imposed. It means that he or she, if necessary with the assistance of, for example, an interpreter, lawyer, social worker or friend, should be able to understand the general thrust of what is said in court. The defendant should be able to follow what is said by the prosecution witnesses and, if represented, to explain to his own lawyers his version of events, point out any statements with which he disagrees and make them aware of any facts which should be put forward in his defence...

35. The Court considers that, when the decision is taken to deal with a child, such as the applicant, who risks not being able to participate effectively because of his young age and limited intellectual capacity, by way of criminal proceedings rather than some other form of disposal directed primarily at determining the child's best interests and those of the community, it is essential that he be tried in a specialist tribunal which is able to give full consideration to and make proper allowance for the handicaps under which he labours, and adapt its procedure accordingly.

36. ...Dr Brennan found that, 'on balance', the applicant probably did have sufficient intelligence to understand that what he had done was wrong, and that he was therefore fit to plead. The Court is not, however, convinced, in the circumstances of the present case, that it follows that the applicant was capable of participating effectively in his trial to the extent required by Article 6(1).

37. There has therefore been a violation of that provision.

Judges Pellonpaa and Bratza dissented as they believed that sufficient precautions had been taken to accommodate the applicant's youth and mental development. Whilst SC's trial had not been accompanied by any of the media interest or public outrage present in V's, the very low intellectual development of the former was the decisive factor for the majority in concluding that SC had not been accorded a trial process in which he was able to participate effectively. Is it realistic to expect that young children/juveniles can participate effectively as defendants in trials held by the ordinary criminal courts?

3   In the earlier case of *Stanford v UK* A.282-A (1994), the Court articulated its understanding of the basis and scope of this implied right in the following terms:

Nor is it in dispute that Article 6, read as whole, guarantees the right of an accused to participate effectively in a criminal trial. In general this includes, *inter alia*, not only his right to be present but also, to hear and follow the proceedings. Such rights are implicit in the very notion of an adversarial procedure and can also be derived from the guarantees contained in sub-paragraphs (c), (d) and (e) of paragraph 3 of Article 6... [Para 26.]

Stanford had been tried at Norwich Crown Court in respect of a number of serious sexual and violent crimes. During his trial he sat in a glass-fronted dock and he was unable to hear all the witnesses' testimony. He complained about the poor acoustics to his solicitor and counsel but, for tactical reasons, they did not pass his concern on to the trial judge. Stanford was convicted of rape, kidnapping, and making threats to kill for which he was sentenced to a total of ten years' imprisonment. The Court was unanimous in finding no breach of Article 6 because, *inter alia*, he was represented by experienced counsel who heard all the testimony and was able to discuss it with him and expert reports indicated that the glass screen only caused a minimal loss of sound in the courtroom. The practical significance of the judgment was that the increasing need for more elaborate security features in domestic criminal courtrooms would not be allowed by the Court to undermine defendants' basic right of participation either personally or via their lawyers.

4   A unanimous Chamber found a breach of this requirement in *Ziliberberg v Moldova*, judgment of 1 February 2005. The applicant, a student, had been fined by the Centru District Court for participating in an unauthorized demonstration. He appealed against that decision. However, he did not receive notification of the date/time of his appeal hearing until after it had taken place. Consequently, he was unable to attend the hearing. The appeal court considered his appeal, in his absence, and dismissed it. The Chamber found that the applicant had thereby been denied the opportunity to participate in his appeal and that constituted a breach of Article 6(1).

(v) Overall assessment

When determining if there has been a breach of the right to a fair hearing the Court makes an evaluation of the fairness of the entire domestic proceedings. For example, in *Barberà, Messegué and Jabardo v Spain* A.146 (1988), the applicants made a number of complaints about the trial that led to their conviction and imprisonment for involvement in a terrorist murder. The Court determined that:

89. Having regard to the belated transfer of the applicants from Barcelona to Madrid, the unexpected change in the court's membership immediately before the hearing opened, the brevity of the trial and, above all, the fact that very important pieces of evidence were not adequately adduced and discussed at the trial in the applicants' presence and under the watchful eye of the public, the Court concludes that proceedings in question, taken as a whole, did not satisfy the requirements of a fair and public hearing. Consequently, there was a violation of Article 6(1).

This approach also enables the Court to consider whether defects in first instance proceedings have been rectified by subsequent appellate hearings. In *Edwards v UK* A.247-B (1992), the applicant had been convicted at Sheffield Crown Court of robbery and burglary. Subsequently, Edwards complained to the Home Secretary about the conduct of the police investigation into those crimes. The Home Secretary referred Edwards' case back to the Court of Appeal. The latter found that police officers testifying at Edwards' trial had not stated that another person's (the neighbour's) fingerprints had been found at the crime scene, however the applicant's conviction was not 'unsafe or unsatisfactory'. Edwards then alleged a breach of Article 6 before the Strasbourg authorities. The Court found no violation because, '...the defects of the original trial were remedied by the subsequent procedure before the Court of Appeal...' (para 39).

In *Taxquet v Belgium*, judgment of 16 November 2010, the applicant complained that there had been a breach of his right to a fair trial as the Assize Court, which had convicted him of having killed/attempted to kill a government minister, had not given reasons for the guilty verdict nor was the applicant able to appeal to a court with a full jurisdiction. The Governments of Ireland, France, and the UK submitted third party comments to the Grand Chamber because the case was perceived as involving a challenge to the lawfulness of the jury system(s) under the ECHR. The unanimous Grand Chamber noted that ten member States utilized a traditional jury system and 24 member States used a collaborative system (where professional judges and jurors collectively determine, *inter alia*, the guilt/innocence of the defendant). Given the diversity of criminal justice systems across the member States, the Grand Chamber acknowledged that it was not the Court's role to seek to harmonize them.

83. ... A State's choice of a particular criminal justice system is in principle outside the scope of the supervision carried out by the Court...

84. Accordingly, the institution of the lay jury cannot be called into question in this context. The Contracting States enjoy considerable freedom in the choice of the means calculated to ensure that their judicial systems are in compliance with the requirements of Article 6.

...

90. ... the Convention does not require jurors to give reasons for their decision and that Article 6 does not preclude a defendant from being tried by a lay jury even where reasons are not given for the verdict. Nevertheless, for the requirements of a fair trial to be satisfied, the accused, and indeed the public, must be able to understand the verdict that has been given; this is a vital safeguard against arbitrariness....

92. In the case of assize courts sitting with a lay jury, any special procedural features must be accommodated, seeing that the jurors are usually not required—or not permitted—to give reasons for their personal convictions... In these circumstances likewise, Article 6 requires an assessment of whether sufficient safeguards were in place to avoid any risk of arbitrariness and to enable the accused to understand the reasons for his conviction (see paragraph 90 above). Such procedural safeguards may include, for example, directions or guidance provided by the presiding judge to the jurors on the legal issues arising or the evidence adduced, and precise, unequivocal questions put to the jury by the judge, forming a framework on which the verdict is based or sufficiently offsetting the fact that no reasons are given for the jury's answers (see *Papon* [v *France* ((dec.), no. 54210/00, ECHR 2001-XII]). Lastly, regard must be had to any avenues of appeal open to the accused.

Having regard to the circumstances of the applicant's trial the Grand Chamber found that the jurors had been required to answer 32 questions regarding the eight defendants; four of the questions related to the applicant. But those questions did not enable the applicant to understand why he had been found guilty.

97. ... Thus, the applicant was unable, for example, to make a clear distinction between the co-defendants as to their involvement in the commission of the offence; to ascertain the jury's perception of his precise role in relation to the other defendants; to understand why the offence had been classified as premeditated murder (assassinat) rather than murder (meurtre); to determine what factors had prompted the jury to conclude that the involvement of two of the co-defendants in the alleged acts had been limited, carrying a lesser sentence; or to discern why the aggravating factor of premeditation had been taken into account in his case as regards the attempted murder of [the victim's] partner. This shortcoming was all the more problematic because the case was both factually and legally complex...

Furthermore, the applicant had no opportunity to appeal against the verdict of the Assize Court. Therefore, overall, the Grand Chamber concluded that he had suffered a violation of his right to a fair trial. States using jury systems will be relieved that the Court accepted their legitimacy under the ECHR, but clearly professional judges have a central role in ensuring juries are given precise guidance on their decision-making in order to guarantee defendants a fair hearing. For an insightful analysis from a criminal jurisprudence perspective see P. Roberts, 'Does Article 6 of the ECHR Require Reasoned Verdicts in Criminal Trials?' (2011) 11(2) *Human Rights Law Review* 213.

Public hearing

We have already examined several cases which involved this right. The Court found a breach of this provision in *Le Compte, Van Leuven and De Meyere v Belgium* (p 362), because the disciplinary hearings before the Provincial Council and the Appeals Council of the Belgian Medical Association were held in private. The Court noted that if the disciplinary charges had involved allegations of malpractice involving patients (rather than accusations of contempt of the Association) then it would have been appropriate to invoke the Article 6(1) exception to a public hearing for the 'protection of the private life' of the patients. Conversely, in *Campbell and Fell v UK* A.80 (1984), the Court held that the prison authorities were justified, on the grounds of 'public order and security', in excluding the press and public from the disciplinary hearings involving prisoners conducted inside prisons. We should also note that the wide access of the public and press to the trial of the juvenile defendant in *V v UK* (p 424), was one of the factors which led the Court to conclude that he had been unable to participate effectively in his trial.

The full-time Court revealed a far more protective attitude than its predecessor towards the right to public hearings of prisoners facing criminal charges in *Riepan v Austria*, judgment of 14 February 2001. The applicant had been convicted of murder and during his subsequent imprisonment he was alleged to have made a number of threats against prison officers. The authorities responded by charging him with the crime of dangerous menace. The local Regional Court decided to hold the applicant's trial in the closed area of the prison where he was serving his existing sentence. As usual, in the week before the trial, the Public Prosecutor's Office at the Regional Court distributed a list of forthcoming cases (and their locations) including the applicant's to the media and made the list available to the public. The hearing took place in a small room within the prison. The applicant, represented by counsel, pleaded not guilty. After hearing from the relevant prison officers the judge found the applicant guilty and sentenced him to ten months' imprisonment. The trial lasted about half an hour and no members of the media/public were present. Before the Court the applicant complained that his trial breached the public hearing obligation under Article 6(1). A united Court held that:

27. ... The public character of the proceedings assumes particular importance in a case such as the present where the defendant in the criminal proceedings is a prisoner, where the charges relate to the making of threats against prison officers and where the witnesses are officers of the prison in which the defendant is detained.

28. It was undisputed in the present case, that the publicity of the hearing was not formally excluded. However, hindrance in fact can contravene the Convention just like a legal impediment (see the *Airey v Ireland* judgment of 9 October 1979, Series A No 32, p. 14, § 25). The Court considers that the mere fact that the trial took place in the precincts of Garsten Prison does not lead necessarily to

the conclusion that it lacked publicity. Nor did the fact that any potential spectators would have had to undergo certain identity and possibly security checks in itself deprive the hearing of its public nature...

29. Nevertheless, it must be borne in mind that the Convention is intended to guarantee not rights that are theoretical or illusory but rights that are practical and effective (see the *Artico v Italy* judgment of 13 May 1980, Series A No 37, p 16, § 33). The Court considers a trial will only comply with the requirement of publicity if the public is able to obtain information about its date and place and if this place is easily accessible to the public. In many cases these conditions will be fulfilled by the simple fact that a hearing is held in a regular court room large enough to accommodate spectators. However, the Court observes that the holding of a trial outside a regular court room, in particular in a place like a prison to which the general public on principle has no access, presents a serious obstacle to its public character. In such a case, the State is under an obligation to take compensatory measures in order to ensure that the public and the media are duly informed about the place of the hearing and are granted effective access.

The Court did not find that such measures, for example directions in a special public/media notice issued by the Public Prosecutor as to how the media/public could reach the prison and what access conditions would apply, had been taken. Consequently, the Court determined that there had been a violation of the public hearing requirement of Article 6(1). Although *Riepan* concerned a criminal trial being held in a prison and *Campbell and Fell* dealt with 'criminal' disciplinary charges the full-time Court was, rightfully, concerned to ensure that adequate publicity and accessibility applied to proceedings involving a serious charge of misbehaviour against a prisoner.

An examination, by the full-time Court, of the obligation to hold public hearings for civil proceedings occurred in *B and P v UK*, judgment of 24 July 2001. The applicants were fathers whose children resided with their mothers. Both applicants applied to the courts for residency orders in respect of their sons. The applicants requested that the proceedings be conducted in open court, however their requests were rejected by the judges as the Children Act 1989 established a presumption that such proceedings should be conducted in private. The applicants complained that the presumption violated the right to a public hearing in Article 6(1). The Court explained the justification for the public hearing obligation as being:

36. ... The public character of proceedings protects litigants against the administration of justice in secret with no public scrutiny; it is also one of the means whereby confidence in the courts can be maintained. By rendering the administration of justice visible, publicity contributes to the achievement of the aim of Article 6 § 1, a fair hearing, the guarantee of which is one of the foundations of a democratic society...

As to whether States could establish predetermined exceptions to the public hearing obligation the Court was divided. A majority, 5 votes to 2, held that:

39. ... while the Court agrees that Article 6 § 1 states a general rule that civil proceedings, *inter alia*, should take place in public, it does not find it inconsistent with this provision for a State to designate an entire class of case as an exception to the general rule where considered necessary in the interests of morals, public order or national security or where required by the interests of juveniles or the protection of the private life of the parties... although the need for such a measure must always be subject to the Court's control... The English procedural law can therefore be seen as a specific reflection of the general exceptions provided for by Article 6 § 1.

From this perspective there had been no violation of the applicants' right to a public hearing. However, the dissentients, Judges Loucaides and Tulkens, believed that, '…the general legal rule against public hearings applied in these cases is incompatible not only with the wording but also with the basic objective and philosophy of the requirement for public hearings under Article 6…' The approach of the majority allows States considerable freedom to establish broad class exemptions from the obligation to hold public hearings, but individuals should be able to apply to the national courts for their particular cases to be heard in public (as the applicants were able to do in this case). If the individuals consider that the domestic procedural rulings are not compatible with Article 6(1), for example their cases do not fall within the exceptions specified in the Article, then they have the possibility of making a complaint to Strasbourg.

Within a reasonable time

1   The criteria that the Court applies when evaluating whether a civil or criminal court has determined proceedings (falling within Article 6(1)) within a reasonable time were articulated in paragraph 99 of the *Konig* judgment (p 351). That case also established that where national legal systems provide appellate courts which are competent to determine 'civil rights and obligations' or 'criminal charges' their proceedings come within this Convention right.

2   In *Robins v UK*, 1997-V, the Court ruled that judicial decisions regarding legal costs, made after the substantive dispute had been decided, could be subject to this right. During May 1991 Exeter County Court gave judgment against the applicants in a civil action they had brought against their neighbours over alleged sewage pollution. Subsequent hearings were held into the applicants' liability to pay the defendants' legal costs. In November 1992 the County Court ordered that the applicants should pay approximately £10,000 to the defendants. The applicants appealed to the Court of Appeal which confirmed the costs award in June 1995. The applicants complained that their liability to pay costs had not been determined within a reasonable time. In a unanimous judgment:

> 28. The Court recalls that Article 6(1) requires that all stages of legal proceedings for the 'determination of…civil rights and obligations', not excluding stages subsequent to judgment on the merits, be resolved within a reasonable time…
>
> 29. The Court observes that the legal costs which formed the subject matter of the proceedings in question were incurred during the resolution of a dispute between neighbours which undoubtedly involved 'the determination of…civil rights and obligations'…the Court considers that the costs proceedings, even though separately decided, must be seen as a continuation of the substantive litigation and accordingly as part of a 'determination of…civil rights and obligations'…

The Court went on to find a violation of this right due to two periods (lasting ten months and 16 months) of inactivity by the State authorities preceding the Court of Appeal's resolution of the appeal.

3   The State that has been found to be in breach of the reasonable time guarantee most frequently is Italy. In *Bottazzi v Italy*, 1999-V, a Grand Chamber found the continuing failure of Italian courts to determine cases within a reasonable time amounted to a 'practice' in breach of the Convention. The applicant complained that it had taken the Court of Audit nearly seven years to determine his claim for a pension.

22. The Court notes at the outset that Article 6 § 1 of the Convention imposes on the Contracting States the duty to organise their judicial systems in such a way that their courts can meet the requirements of this provision (see the *Salesi v Italy* judgment of 26 February 1993, Series A No 257-E, p 60, § 24). It wishes to reaffirm the importance of administering justice without delays which might jeopardise its effectiveness and credibility (see the *Katte Klitsche de la Grange v Italy* judgment of 27 October 1994, Series A No 293-B, p 39, § 61). It points out, moreover, that the Committee of Ministers of the Council of Europe, in its Resolution DH (97) 336 of 11 July 1997 (Length of civil proceedings in Italy: supplementary measures of a general character), considered that 'excessive delays in the administration of justice constitute an important danger, in particular for the respect of the rule of law'.

The Court next draws attention to the fact that since 25 June 1987, the date of the *Capuano v Italy* judgment (Series A No 119), it has already delivered 65 judgments in which it has found violations of Article 6 § 1 in proceedings exceeding a 'reasonable time' in the civil courts of the various regions of Italy. Similarly, under former Articles 31 and 32 of the Convention, more than 1,400 reports of the Commission resulted in resolutions by the Committee of Ministers finding Italy in breach of Article 6 for the same reason.

The frequency with which violations are found shows that there is an accumulation of identical breaches which are sufficiently numerous to amount not merely to isolated incidents. Such breaches reflect a continuing situation that has not yet been remedied and in respect of which litigants have no domestic remedy.

This accumulation of breaches accordingly constitutes a practice that is incompatible with the Convention.

Therefore, the judges were united in concluding that the applicant had suffered a breach of Article 6(1). Unfortunately, the number of complaints against Italy alleging breaches of this guarantee (in respect of both civil and criminal proceedings) continued to grow.

The 'Pinto Act' was enacted by Italy in 2001 to enable persons subject to excessive delays in domestic courts to seek compensation. But the implementation of that measure in turn generated complaints to the Court. In **Riccardi Pizzati v Italy**, judgment of 29 March 2006 (one of nine joined Grand Chamber judgments involving the Pinto Act). The Court was confronted with an elderly applicant (aged 82) who had waited 26 years for a first instance court to determine her civil claim against a neighbour in respect of sewage pollution. She had applied, in October 2001, under the Pinto Act for compensation of 103,000 euros (in respect of non-pecuniary damage). In January 2002 the Court of Appeal found that the first instance proceedings had been excessively long and awarded her 5,000 euros compensation. She appealed the level of damages to the Court of Cassation which dismissed her appeal, for being out of time, in November 2002. The authorities did not pay her compensation until December 2003. Before the Grand Chamber, the Italian Government disputed the existence of a 'practice' of unreasonable delays in Italian trials given the enactment of the Pinto Act. The Grand Chamber was unanimous in finding that:

115. . . . Like the applicant, the Court does not see how the introduction of the Pinto remedy at domestic level has solved the problem of excessively lengthy proceedings. It has admittedly saved the Court the trouble of finding these violations, but the task has simply been transferred to the courts of appeal, which were already overburdened. . . .

116. The Court emphasises once again that Article 6(1) of the Convention obliges the Contracting States to organise their legal systems so as to enable the courts to comply with its various requirements. It wishes to reaffirm the importance of administering justice without delays which might jeopardise its effectiveness and credibility (see *Bottazzi*, para 22). Italy's position in this regard has

not changed sufficiently to call into question the conclusion that this accumulation of breaches constitutes a practice that is incompatible with the Convention.

Regarding the payment of compensation in respect of lengthy proceedings the Grand Chamber held that:

88....The Court can accept that the authorities need time in which to make payment. However, in respect of a compensatory remedy designed to redress the consequences of excessively lengthy proceedings that period should not generally exceed six months from the date on which the decision awarding compensation becomes final.

Overall, the Grand Chamber concluded that the complainant's first instance proceedings had not been determined in a reasonable time and that breach of Article 6(1) had been aggravated by the delay in the payment of (inadequate) compensation under the Pinto Act. As there were 'hundreds' of cases pending before the Court in respect of awards made under the Pinto Act the Grand Chamber invited Italy, '127....to take all measures necessary to ensure that the domestic decisions are not only in conformity with the case-law of this Court but also executed within six months of being deposited with the registry.'

So, the Grand Chamber found serious defects in the Italian remedial measure designed to compensate victims of lengthy proceedings. Yet, the Italian authorities continue to have major difficulties in paying Pinto compensation within an acceptable timeframe. In **Gaglione and others v Italy**, judgment of 21 December 2010, a Chamber dealt with applications involving 475 cases where 65 per cent of the applicants had waited at least 19 months for payment of their Pinto compensation. The Chamber considered that general measures were needed in Italy to deal with this growing problem (including allocating budget funds to pay Pinto compensation), as the number of applications to Strasbourg were increasing rapidly (over 3,900 applications were pending). The Chamber found, *inter alia*, a breach of Article 6(1).

The Court has also concluded that other States have systemic problems in their judicial systems causing unreasonable delays. For example, in **Rumpf v Germany**, judgment of 2 September 2010, a unanimous Chamber ruled that:

70....the violations found in the present judgment were neither prompted by an isolated incident nor were they attributed to a particular turn of events in this case, but were the consequence of shortcoming of the respondent State. Accordingly, the situation in the present case must be qualified as resulting from a practice incompatible with the Convention (see *Bottazzi v Italy*, ECHR 1999-V).

The German civil courts had taken over 13 years to determine the applicant's claims regarding a gun licence and he had no domestic remedy enabling him to challenge the delays in the administrative courts. It is a sad reflection that it was the judgment in **Konig v Germany**, pronounced during 1978, that elaborated the criteria for assessing whether a case has been determined within a reasonable time, but the German legal system was still repeatedly failing to deliver expeditious justice by 2010.

In December 2010, the Court (for the first time) applied the pilot judgment procedure to Greece because of excessive delays in administrative law proceedings. The applicants' litigation regarding their army pensions had lasted for over 13 years in **Vassilios Athanasiou and others v Greece**, judgment of 21 December 2010. The Chamber noted the chronic problem of unreasonable delays in Greek judicial proceedings (especially administrative ones) demonstrated by the fact that the Court had given judgments finding such breaches of Article 6(1) in about 300 cases against Greece between 1999–2009 (and 200 more were pending before the Court). Therefore, the Court ruled that the national authorities should introduce, within one year, an effective remedy to deal with excessive delays in judicial proceedings.

A similar requirement was imposed on Bulgaria in *Dimitrov and Hamanov v Bulgaria* and *Finger v Bulgaria*, judgments of 10 May 2011. The Chamber, unanimously, applied the pilot judgment procedure (for the first time) to Bulgaria finding there were systemic problems causing unreasonable delays in both criminal and civil proceedings. The Chamber noted that the Court had already found over eight breaches of the reasonable time guarantee in respect of Bulgarian criminal proceedings and nearly 50 violations concerning civil proceedings. There were over 700 further cases alleging unreasonable delays pending against Bulgaria.

An independent and impartial tribunal

McGonnell v UK 2000-II
European Court of Human Rights

In 1982 the applicant bought the Calais Vinery on Guernsey. A few years later he started to live in a converted packing shed on that land. During 1988, through an advocate, he made representations to a planning inquiry that was considering the draft Detailed Development Plan No 6 (DDP6). The inspector rejected the applicant's arguments that his land should be subject to development. In 1990 the States of Deliberation (the Parliament of Guernsey) presided over by the Deputy Bailiff (the Bailiff is President of the States of Deliberation, President of the island's Royal Court, and a senior figure in the Government of Guernsey), Mr Graham Dorey, adopted DDP6 and continued to zone the applicant's land as agricultural. In 1995 the applicant brought legal proceedings to challenge the authorities' refusal to allow him to build on his land. His appeal was heard by the Royal Court, composed of its President (the new Bailiff, Sir Graham Dorey) and seven Jurats (lay persons). The appeal was dismissed unanimously. The applicant complained to the Commission alleging that his appeal had not been heard by an independent and impartial tribunal because of the participation of the Bailiff. By 25 votes to 5 the Commission considered that there had been a breach of Article 6(1).

46. The applicant pointed to the non-judicial functions of the Bailiff, contending that they gave rise to such close connections between the Bailiff as a judicial officer and the legislative and executive functions of government that the Bailiff no longer had the independence and impartiality required by Article 6....

48. The Court recalls that it found in its *Findlay v UK* judgment (judgment of 25 February 1997, Reports 1997-I, p 198, § 73) that:

in order to establish whether a tribunal can be considered as 'independent', regard must be had, *inter alia*, to the manner of appointment of its members and their term of office, the existence of guarantees against outside pressures and the question whether the body presents an appearance of independence...

As to the question of 'impartiality', there are two aspects to this requirement. First, the tribunal must be subjectively free of personal prejudice or bias. Secondly, it must also be impartial from an objective viewpoint, that is, it must offer sufficient guarantees to exclude any legitimate doubt in this respect... The concepts of independence and objective impartiality are closely linked...

49. In the present case, too, the concepts of independence and objective impartiality are closely linked, and the Court will consider them together.

50. The Court first observes that there is no suggestion in the present case that the Bailiff was subjectively prejudiced or biased when he heard the applicant's planning appeal in June 1995. It has not been alleged that the Bailiff's participation as Deputy Bailiff in the adoption of DDP6 in 1990 gives rise to actual bias on his part: the applicant states that it is not possible to ascertain whether there was actual bias because of the Bailiff's various functions, but he does not contend that the Bailiff was subjectively biased or prejudiced.

51. The Court can agree with the Government that neither Article 6 nor any other provision of the Convention requires States to comply with any theoretical constitutional concepts as such. The question is always whether, in a given case, the requirements of the Convention are met. The present case does not, therefore, require the application of any particular doctrine of constitutional law to the position in Guernsey: the Court is faced solely with questions of whether the Bailiff had the required 'appearance' of independence, or the required 'objective' impartiality.

52. In this connection, the Court notes that the Bailiff's functions are not limited to judicial matters, but that he is also actively involved in non-judicial functions on the island. The Court does not accept the Government's analysis that when the Bailiff acts in a non-judicial capacity he merely occupies positions rather than exercising functions: even a purely ceremonial constitutional role must be classified as a 'function'. The Court must determine whether the Bailiff's functions in his non-judicial capacity were, or were not, compatible with the requirements of Article 6 as to independence and impartiality.

53. The Court observes that the Bailiff in the present case had personal involvement with the planning matters at the heart of the applicant's case on two occasions. The first occasion was in 1990, when, as Deputy Bailiff, he presided over the States of Deliberation at the adoption of DDP6. The second occasion was on 6 June 1995, when he presided over the Royal Court in the determination of the applicant's planning appeal.

55. ... As the Court has noted above, the Bailiff's non-judicial constitutional functions cannot be accepted as being merely ceremonial. With particular respect to his presiding, as Deputy Bailiff, over the States of Deliberation in 1990, the Court considers that any direct involvement in the passage of legislation, or of executive rules, is likely to be sufficient to cast doubt on the judicial impartiality of a person subsequently called on to determine a dispute over whether reasons exist to permit a variation from the wording of the legislation or rules at issue. ...

57. The Court thus considers that the mere fact that the Deputy Bailiff presided over the States of Deliberation when DDP6 was adopted in 1990 is capable of casting doubt on his impartiality when he subsequently determined, as the sole judge of the law in the case, the applicant's planning appeal. The applicant therefore had legitimate grounds for fearing that the Bailiff may have been influenced by his prior participation in the adoption of DDP6. That doubt in itself, however slight its justification, is sufficient to vitiate the impartiality of the Royal Court, and it is therefore unnecessary for the Court to look into the other aspects of the complaint. It follows that there has been a breach of Article 6 § 1. ...

NOTES

1 The unanimous Court was composed of President Costa and Judges: Kuris, Tulkens, Fuhrmann, Jungwiert, Greve, and Laws.

2 In advance of the full implementation of the Human Rights Act 1998, the Lord Chancellor, Lord Irvine of Lairg, announced that he would not sit in the Judicial Committee of the House of Lords when it heard cases involving legislation which he had been directly concerned with or cases directly involving the Government (HL Deb, vol 610, col WA33: 23 February 2000). The Constitutional Reform Act 2005 provided, *inter alia*, for the creation of a Supreme Court of the United Kingdom to replace the Judicial Committee of the House of Lords. The Lord Chancellor, who need no longer be a qualified lawyer, is not a member of the new Supreme Court. The Supreme Court began its judicial work on 1 October 2009.

3 *McGonnell* was distinguished in the subsequent case of *Pabla Ky v Finland*, judgment of 22 June 2004. The applicant company had unsuccessfully sued its landlord in the special-ist Housing Court Division of the Court of Appeal (composed of two experts and three professional judges). The applicant company subsequently challenged the objective impar-tiality of one of the expert members (MP) of the Court of Appeal on the basis that he was a member of the Finnish Parliament at the time of the judgment. The Strasbourg Court, by 6 votes to 1, held that:

29. This case also raises issues concerning the role of a member of the legislature in a judicial con-text. Although the notion of the separation of powers between the political organs of government and the judiciary has assumed growing importance in the Court's case-law (see *Stafford v the United Kingdom* [GC], No 46295/99, § 78, ECHR 2002-IV), neither Article 6 nor any other provision of the Convention requires States to comply with any theoretical constitutional concepts regard-ing the permissible limits of the powers' interaction. The question is always whether, in a given case, the requirements of the Convention are met. As in the other cases examined by the Court, the present case does not, therefore, require the application of any particular doctrine of consti-tutional law. The Court is faced solely with the question whether, in the circumstances of the case, the Court of Appeal had the requisite 'appearance' of independence, or the requisite 'objective' impartiality (see *McGonnell v the United Kingdom*, No 28488/95, ECHR 2000-II, § 51 . . .

31. The Court notes, first of all, that there is no indication that M.P. was actually, or subjectively, biased against the applicant when sitting in the Court of Appeal in his case. The only issue is whether due to his position as a member of the legislature his participation cast legitimate doubt on the objective impartiality or structural impartiality of the court which decided the applicant's appeal.

32. There is no objection per se to expert lay members participating in the decision-making in a court. The domestic legislation of the Council of Europe's member States affords many examples of tribunals in which professional judges sit alongside specialists in a particular sphere whose knowl-edge is desirable and even essential in settling the disputes (see, e.g., *Ettl v Austria*, judgment of 23 April 1994, Series A No 117, §§ 38–40 *Debled v Belgium*, judgment of 22 September 1994, Series A No 292-B, §36). The Court recalls that M.P. had sat on the Court of Appeal as an expert in rental matters since 1974 and had, in the Government's view, accrued considerable experience valuable in contributing to adjudicating in these types of cases. The Court notes in that regard that two expert members sat alongside a majority of three judges in the composition of the Court of Appeal in such cases.

33. While the applicant points to M.P.'s political affiliation, the Court does not find that there is any indication in the present case that M.P.'s membership of a particular political party had any connec-tion or link with any of the parties in the proceedings or the substance of the case before the Court of Appeal (*mutatis mutandis, Holm v Sweden*, judgment of 25 November 1995, Series A No 279-A, §§ 32–3). Nor is there any indication that M.P. played any role in respect of the legislation which was in issue in the case. The Act on Commercial Leases had been submitted by the Government for

adoption by Parliament on 21 November 1994 and it had been adopted on 17 February 1995 before M.P. had been elected for his second term of office on 19 March 1995. Even assuming therefore that participation by a Member of Parliament in, for example, the adoption of a general legislative measure could cast doubts on later judicial functions, it cannot be asserted in this case that M.P. was involved in any other capacity with the subject-matter of the applicant's case through his position as Member of Parliament.

34. Accordingly, the Court concludes that, unlike the situation examined by it in the cases of *Procola v Luxembourg* 28 September 1985, Series A No 326, and *McGonnell v the United Kingdom*, cited above, M.P. had not exercised any prior legislative, executive or advisory function in respect of the subject-matter or legal issues before the Court of Appeal for decision in the applicant's appeal. The judicial proceedings therefore cannot be regarded as involving 'the same case' or 'the same decision' in the sense which was found to infringe Article 6 § 1 in the two judgments cited above. The Court is not persuaded that the mere fact that M.P. was a member of the legislature at the time when he sat on the applicant's appeal is sufficient to raise doubts as to the independence and impartiality of the Court of Appeal. While the applicant relies on the theory of separation of powers, this principle is not decisive in the abstract.

35. In these circumstances, the Court is of the opinion that the applicant's fear as to a lack of independence and impartiality of the Court of Appeal, due to the participation of an expert member who was also a Member of Parliament, cannot be regarded as being objectively justified. Consequently, there has been no violation of Article 6 § 1 of the Convention.

The dissentient, Judge Borrego Borrego, stated:

I would refer here to Montesquieu, father of the theory of separation of powers:

'Nor is there liberty if the power of judging is not separate from legislative power and from executive power. If it were joined to legislative power, the power over the life and liberty of the citizens would be arbitrary, for the judge would be the legislator. If it were joined to executive power, the judge could have the force of an oppressor'.

I believe that this is the first time the Court has examined a complaint concerning the simultaneous exercise of legislative and judicial functions by the same person. I consider—humbly, as befits a minority voice, yet with strong conviction—that in the present case the requirement of independence of the courts from the legislature, as set forth in our case-law, was not observed.

Do you agree with the pragmatic approach of the majority?

4   The conflicting functions of court martial 'convening officers' were at the heart of the *Findlay v UK*, 1997-I, case. The applicant was a former Lance-Sergeant who in 1990, after a heavy drinking session, held members of his unit at gunpoint and threatened to kill some of them and himself. Subsequent, psychiatric evidence disclosed that he was suffering from post-traumatic stress disorder caused by his experiences in the Falklands War. The General Officer Commanding London District, a Major-General, assumed the duties of convening officer (including remanding the applicant for trial on eight charges, appointing the members of the court martial, appointing the prosecuting and defending officers) and later confirming the sentence. The applicant pleaded guilty to seven charges (including threatening to kill) and was sentenced by the court martial to, *inter alia*, two years' imprisonment. The Major-General confirmed this sentence. The applicant complained that because of the influence of the convening officer over the court martial process he had not received a fair hearing by an independent and impartial tribunal. The Commission,

unanimously, found a breach of Article 6(1). Likewise the Court upheld his complaint because:

76. In order to maintain confidence in the independence and impartiality of the court, appearances may be of importance. Since all the members of the court martial which decided Mr Findlay's case were subordinate in rank to the convening officer and fell within his chain of command, Mr Findlay's doubts about the tribunal's independence and impartiality could be objectively justified...

77. In addition, the Court finds it significant that the convening officer also acted as 'confirming officer'. Thus, the decision of the court martial was not effective until ratified by him, and he had the power to vary the sentence imposed as he saw fit... This is contrary to the well-established principle that the power to give a binding decision which may not be altered by a non-judicial authority is inherent in the very notion of 'tribunal' and can also be seen as a component of the 'independence' required by Article 6 para 1....

80. For all these reasons, and in particular the central role played by the convening officer in the organisation of the court martial, the Court considers that Mr Findlay's misgivings about the independence and impartiality of the tribunal which dealt with his case were objectively justified....

The Armed Forces Act 1996 abolished the role of convening officer and allocated the functions to separate bodies within the military (a 'higher authority' decided whether a case should be referred to a prosecuting authority within the Services' legal branches and court administration officers (independent of the higher and prosecuting authorities) were responsible for organizing individual court martial hearings).

4 The revised court martial systems, as used by the different armed services, received mixed responses in subsequent cases at Strasbourg. In *Morris v UK*, judgment of 26 February 2002, a Chamber was unanimous in finding structural violations of Article 6(1) in the army system. These included the absence of sufficient safeguards to guarantee the independence of the two junior officers who sat *ad hoc* on the applicant's court martial: '72. In particular, it notes that those officers had no legal training, that they remained subject to arm discipline and reports, and that there was no statutory or other bar to their being made subject to external army influence when sitting on the case.' However, the next year in *Cooper v UK*, judgment of 16 December 2003, a Grand Chamber, unanimously, found no breach of Article 6(1) in respect of a Royal Air Force court martial. The Grand Chamber took account of new submissions by the Government and concluded that it should depart from the conclusions in *Morris*. Regarding the independence of the *ad hoc* officers the Grand Chamber found that they were provided with detailed written guidance on their roles prior to the trial and that they could not be subject to disciplinary reporting on their judicial performance: '126. For these reasons, the Court finds that there were sufficient safeguards of the independence of the ordinary members of the applicant's court martial.' But, the same Grand Chamber was united in finding a breach of Article 6(1) by a Royal Navy court martial in *Grieves v UK*, judgment of 16 December 2003. The applicant, a former member of the Royal Navy, had been convicted of malicious wounding by a court martial and sentenced to three years' imprisonment and dismissal from the service.

74. The present applicant raised the same complaint as in the *Cooper* case but in relation to a naval court-martial. Naval courts-martial differ in certain important respects from the air-force system examined in the *Cooper* case and the Court has considered whether those distinctions are such as to lead to a conclusion in the present case different from that in the *Cooper* judgment.

...

80. Fourthly, the post of PPCM [Permanent President of Court-Martial] does not exist in the naval system, the President of a naval court-martial being appointed for each court-martial as it is convened. The applicant pointed out that, as a result, the entire court-martial was convened on an ad hoc basis. The Government explained that, since there were less naval courts-martial, there was no need for a group of officers with the sole task of acting as PPCMs and considered that the naval court-martial complied with Article 6 § 1 even without PPCMs.

81. The Court considers that the absence of a full-time PPCM, with no hope of promotion and no effective fear of removal and who was not subject to report on his judicial decision-making (the *Cooper* judgment, § 118) deprives naval courts-martial of what was considered, in the air-force context, to be an important contribution to the independence of an otherwise ad hoc tribunal.

82. Fifthly, and most importantly, the Judge Advocate [the legal expert to the court-martial] in a naval court-martial is a serving naval officer who, when not sitting in a court-martial, carries out regular naval duties. In contrast, the Judge Advocate in the air-force is a civilian working full-time on the staff of the Judge Advocate General, himself a civilian.

83. The applicant considered this distinction sufficient of itself to conclude as to the lack of independence of naval courts-martial. He maintained that it was inevitable that the JAF's [Judge Advocate of the Fleet] comments on the Judge Advocate's conduct of the court-martial would be taken into account in the wider service evaluation of that officer for promotion. Whether or not there was at the time a regulation excluding reporting in the service on a Judge Advocate's judicial decision-making, he submitted that it was unreal to consider that the service would genuinely separate his judicial and other service functions....

84. The Government maintained that a service Judge Advocate is no less a safeguard than the civilian one sitting in air-force courts-martial because, *inter alia*, of the following matters: the Judge Advocate is ticketed [appointed] only with the consent of the JAF (a civilian judge), he can only be removed by the JAF and on the same grounds as those for a civilian judge; he is responsible solely to the JAF in the performance of his duties as Judge Advocate; he receives no extra pay for acting as Judge Advocate and neither his pay nor promotion are affected by his performance as a Judge Advocate; the Judge Advocate in the applicant's court-martial was not reported on as regards his performance as Judge Advocate (a practice now enshrined in Queen's Regulation 3630)...there is de facto security of tenure since a ticketed Judge Advocate remains as such indefinitely; a Judge Advocate takes a particular form of oath; he sits apart from court-martial members and his only contact with them (apart from deliberations on sentence) is in open court...

85. The Court notes that, as in the air-force, the naval Judge Advocate fulfils a pivotal role in the court-martial but that, unlike his air-force equivalent, he is a serving naval officer in a post which may or may not be a legal one and who, although 'ticketed' indefinitely, sits in courts-martial only from time to time. As to the Government's reliance on the involvement of a civilian JAF, the Court observes that the JAF has no input into naval court-martial proceedings, his principal role being to report to the Reviewing Authority on those proceedings. Further, it is not the JAF but the CNJA [Chief Naval Judge Advocate] (a naval officer) who is responsible for the initial 'ticketing' of a Judge Advocate (albeit with the agreement of the JAF).

86. Moreover, the Court notes with some concern certain reporting practices as regards Judge Advocates which applied at the relevant time. The JAF could pass comments about a Judge Advocate's court-martial performance to the CNJA. It may be that the CNJA had no control over promotions but the CNJA remained a senior service officer whose main functions included the appointment of legally trained service officers to legal posts in the service and who was answerable as regards those duties to the senior Admiral responsible for personnel policy. In addition, at the relevant time the JAF's report on a Judge Advocate's judicial performance could be forwarded

to the Judge Advocate's service reporting officer. While this may not actually have happened in the present case, the Judge Advocate took up his duties in the applicant's court-martial at a time when his performance in those proceedings could, in principle, have been the subject of a report to his evaluating service officer....

87. For these reasons, the Court considers that, even if the naval Judge Advocate appointed to the applicant's court-martial could be considered to have been independent despite the reporting matters highlighted in the preceding paragraph, the position of naval Judge Advocates cannot be considered to constitute a strong guarantee of the independence of a naval court-martial.

88. Moreover, the Court finds unconvincing the Government's explanations as to why a serving officer was to be preferred as Judge Advocate in naval courts-martial whereas the JAG and the Judge Advocates involved air-force courts-martial were civilians.

The Government referred, in the first place, to the relatively small number of naval courts-martial. However, the Court considers that this only means that fewer naval Judge Advocates would be required. They also relied upon the knowledge a naval officer would have of the unique language, customs and environment of the Royal Navy. However, since the essential function of the Judge Advocate is to ensure the lawfulness and fairness of the court-martial and to direct the court on points of law, it is difficult to understand why a detailed knowledge of the way of life and language of the navy should be called for, particularly where, as in the present case, the offence with which the applicant was charged was the ordinary criminal offence of malicious wounding. In any event, the Court is not persuaded that a civilian Judge Advocate would have more difficulty in following naval language or customs than a trial judge would have with complex expert evidence in a civilian case.

The Government further relied on the need for the naval court-martial system to be 'flexible' and 'portable' because of the particularly mobile nature of the navy. Naval Judge Advocates were therefore preferable as, *inter alia*, they would have 'ready access' to the area in question and would be better prepared for the difficulties and dangers of working at sea. However, the Court does not find this relevant given the Government's clarification (in response to questions at the oral hearing) that naval courts-martial have in fact been held on land since 1986 in two trial centres (Portsmouth and Plymouth) regardless of the part of the world in which the offence was alleged to have been committed.

89. Accordingly, the lack of a civilian in the pivotal role of Judge Advocate deprives a naval court-martial of one of the most significant guarantees of independence enjoyed by other services' courts-martial (army and air-force court-martial systems being the same for all relevant purposes—the *Cooper* judgment, § 107), for the absence of which the Government have offered no convincing explanation.

90. Sixthly and finally, the Court considers the Briefing Notes sent to members of naval courts-martial to be substantially less detailed and significantly less clear than the CMAU (RAF) Briefing Notes examined in detail in the above-cited *Cooper* case (see paragraphs 45–62 of that judgment). The Court considers that they are consequently less effective in safeguarding the independence of the ordinary members of courts-martial from inappropriate outside influence.

91. The Court accordingly finds that the distinctions between the air-force court-martial system assessed in the above-cited *Cooper* case and naval court-martial system at issue in the present case are such that the present applicant's misgivings about the independence and impartiality of his naval court-martial, convened under the 1996 Act, can be considered to be objectively justified. His court-martial proceedings were consequently unfair (see, for example, *Smith and Ford v the United Kingdom*, Nos 37475/97 and 39036/97, § 25, 29 September 1999 and *Moore and Gordon v the United Kingdom*, Nos 36529/97 and 37393/97, § 24, 29 September 1999).

There has therefore been a violation of Article 6 § 1 of the Convention.

The Armed Forces Act 2006 created a harmonized system of service law applying to all three armed forces. The institutional changes included: the appointment of a Director of Service Prosecutions to replace the three single-service prosecution authorities; the merger of the offices of Judge Advocate General and Judge Advocate of the Fleet; the establishment of a standing court (the court martial) to replace the previous ad hoc Courts Martial; and the setting up of a Service Appeal Court to take over the appellate work of the former single-service Summary Appeal Courts.

5   The subjective and objective approaches to evaluating whether a particular judge/tribunal is impartial were explained, in the context of a continental criminal trial, in *Piersack v Belgium* A.53 (1982). The applicant had been arrested on suspicion of murder. His prosecution was handled by a section of the office of the Brussels public prosecutor. Mr Van de Walle was the head of that section. Subsequently, Mr Van de Walle was appointed to the Brussels Court of Appeal and presided over the applicant's trial (the jury found him guilty by a majority of 7 votes to 5). Judge Van de Walle sentenced the applicant to 18 years' hard labour. The Commission was unanimous in finding a breach of the independent and impartial tribunal guarantee. A united Court held that:

30. While impartiality normally denotes absence of prejudice or bias, its existence or otherwise can, notably under Article 6 § 1 (art 6-1) of the Convention, be tested in various ways. A distinction can be drawn in this context between a subjective approach, that is endeavouring to ascertain the personal conviction of a given judge in a given case, and an objective approach, that is determining whether he offered guarantees sufficient to exclude any legitimate doubt in this respect.

(a) As regards the first approach, the Court notes that the applicant is pleased to pay tribute to Mr Van de Walle's personal impartiality; it does not itself have any cause for doubt on this score and indeed personal impartiality is to be presumed until there is proof to the contrary (see the *Le Compte, Van Leuven and De Meyere* judgment of 23 June 1981, Series A No 43, p 25, § 58).

However, it is not possible to confine oneself to a purely subjective test. In this area, even appearances may be of a certain importance (see the *Delcourt* judgment of 17 January 1970, Series A No 11, p 17, § 31). As the Belgian Court of Cassation observed in its judgment of 21 February 1979 . . . any judge in respect of whom there is a legitimate reason to fear a lack of impartiality must withdraw. What is at stake is the confidence which the courts must inspire in the public in a democratic society.

(b) It would be going too far to the opposite extreme to maintain that former judicial officers in the public prosecutor's department were unable to sit on the bench in every case that had been examined initially by that department, even though they had never had to deal with the case themselves. So radical a solution, based on an inflexible and formalistic conception of the unity and indivisibility of the public prosecutor's department, would erect a virtually impenetrable barrier between that department and the bench. It would lead to an upheaval in the judicial system of several Contracting States where transfers from one of those offices to the other are a frequent occurrence. Above all, the mere fact that a judge was once a member of the public prosecutor's department is not a reason for fearing that he lacks impartiality; the Court concurs with the Government on this point. . . .

31. . . . Yet previously and until November 1977, Mr Van de Walle had been the head of section B of the Brussels public prosecutor's department, which was responsible for the prosecution instituted against Mr Piersack. As the hierarchical superior of the deputies in charge of the file, Mrs del Carril and then Mr De Nauw, he had been entitled to revise any written submissions by them to the courts, to discuss with them the approach to be adopted in the case and to give them advice on points of law . . . Besides, the information obtained by the Commission and the Court . . . tends to confirm that Mr Van de Walle did in fact play a certain part in the proceedings. . . . It is sufficient to find that the impartiality of the 'tribunal' which had to determine the merits (in the French text: 'bien-fondé') of the charge was capable of appearing open to doubt.

32. In this respect, the Court therefore concludes that there was a violation of Article 6 § 1 (art 6-1)...

The acceptability under the Convention of transfers between domestic prosecution services and the judiciary, provided that judges do not hear cases in which they had a prior involvement as a prosecutor, is very important for those member States that have a career judicial system in which transfers between these organizations is a common occurrence.

6 Assize Court judges were found not to have been subjectively impartial when convicting a defence lawyer for contempt in the face of the court in *Kyprianou v Cyprus*, judgment of 15 December 2005. The Assize Court had questioned the way the applicant was cross-examining a prosecution witness and he had retorted that the judges had been passing 'ravasakia' (translated as love letters/notes) amongst themselves. After a short adjournment the judges found the applicant (who had been practising law for 40 years with an unblemished professional reputation) guilty of contempt and sentenced him to five days' imprisonment (to begin immediately). This was the first time that a lawyer had been imprisoned for contempt of court in Cyprus. Subsequently, before the Grand Chamber, the applicant contended that the Assize judges had acted with personal bias when convicting him.

130. This limb of the applicant's complaint was therefore directed at the judges' personal conduct. The Court will accordingly examine a number of aspects of the judges' conduct which are capable of raising an issue under the subjective test.

Firstly, the judges in their decision sentencing the applicant acknowledged that they had been 'deeply insulted' 'as persons' by the applicant. Even though the judges proceeded to say that this had been the least of their concerns, in the Court's view this statement in itself shows that the judges had been personally offended by the applicant's words and conduct and indicates personal embroilment on the part of the judges.

Secondly, the emphatic language used by the judges throughout their decision conveyed a sense of indignation and shock, which runs counter to the detached approach expected of judicial pronouncements. In particular, the judges stated that they could not 'conceive of another occasion of such a manifest and unacceptable contempt of court by any person, let alone an advocate' and that 'if the court's reaction is not immediate and drastic, we feel that justice will have suffered a disastrous blow'.

Thirdly, they then proceeded to impose a sentence of five days' imprisonment, enforced immediately, which they deemed to be the 'only adequate response'. In the judges' opinion, 'an inadequate reaction on the part of the lawful and civilised order, as expressed by the courts would mean accepting that the authority of the courts be demeaned'.

Fourthly, the judges expressed the opinion early on in their discussion with the applicant that they considered him guilty of the criminal offence of contempt of court. After deciding that the applicant had committed the above offence they gave the applicant the choice, either to maintain what he had said and to give reasons why a sentence should not be imposed on him or to retract. He was, therefore, in fact asked to mitigate 'the damage he had caused by his behaviour' rather than defend himself.

131. Although the Court does not doubt that the judges were concerned with the protection of the administration of justice and the integrity of the judiciary and that for this purpose they felt it appropriate to initiate the *instanter* summary procedure, it finds, in view of the above considerations, that they did not succeed in detaching themselves sufficiently from the situation.

132. This conclusion is reinforced by the speed with which the proceedings were carried out and the brevity of the exchanges between the judges and Mr Kyprianou.

132. Against this background and having regard in particular to the different elements of the judges' personal conduct taken together, the Court finds that the misgivings of Mr Kyprianou about the impartiality of the Limassol Assize Court were also justified under the subjective test.

This was a rare example of an allegation of subjective bias being upheld by the European Court. Indeed, the Grand Chamber observed that, '119.... the Court has recognised the difficulty of establishing a breach of Article 6 on account of subjective partiality and for this reason has in the vast majority of cases raising impartiality issues focused on the objective test.' In *Kyprianou* the Grand Chamber also found that the Assize judges had violated the objective standard of impartiality. However, the Grand Chamber emphasized that it was only ruling on the facts of this case and '125.... the Court does not regard it as necessary or desirable to review generally the law on contempt and the practice of summary proceedings in Cyprus and other common law systems.' Thereby leaving open the potential lawfulness under Article 6 of trial court judges dealing summarily with certain types of contempt in the face of the court (e.g. the refusal of a witness to give evidence).

In the later case of *Panovits v Cyprus*, judgment of 11 December 2008, a Chamber found that the trial of Mr Kyprianou's client had also breached Article 6(1) due to the above behaviour of the judges.

98.... The Court considers that the personal conduct of the judges in the case undermined the applicant's confidence that his trial would be conducted in a fair manner. Although the contempt proceedings were separate from the applicant's main trial, the fact that the judges were offended by the applicant's lawyer when he complained about the manner in which his cross-examination was received by the bench undermined the conduct of the applicant's defence.

...

101. In these circumstances, the Court concludes that the Assize Court's handling of the confrontation with the applicant's defence counsel rendered the trial unfair.

7   All the judges were united in finding that the Home Secretary's determination of the tariff (period of imprisonment for the purposes of retribution and deterrence) for juvenile murderers violated the 'independent' tribunal requirement in *V v UK* (p 424).

114. The Court notes that Article 6(1) guarantees, *inter alia*, 'a fair...hearing...by an independent and impartial tribunal...'. 'Independent' in this context means independent of the parties to the case and also of the executive... The Home Secretary, who set the applicant's tariff, was clearly not independent of the executive, and it follows that there has been a violation of Article 6(1).

8   A majority of the Court, 12 votes to 8, found a violation of the right to an independent and impartial tribunal when an opposition politician was tried before a special court (composed of two civilian judges and a military judge) for distributing a leaflet critical of the authorities' treatment of Kurds: *Incal v Turkey* (see p 649).

67. The Court notes that the status of military judges sitting as members of National Security Courts provides certain guarantees of independence and impartiality. For example, military judges follow the same professional training as their civilian counterparts, which gives them the status of regular members of the Military Legal Service. When sitting as members of National Security Courts, military judges enjoy constitutional safeguards identical to those of civilian judges...as full members of a National Security Court they sit as individuals, according to the Constitution, they must be independent and no public authority may give them instructions concerning their judicial activities or influence them in the performance of their duties.

68. On the other hand, other aspects of these judges' status make it questionable. Firstly, they are servicemen who still belong to the army, which in turn takes its orders from the executive. Secondly, they remain subject to military discipline and assessment reports are compiled on them by the army for that purpose...Decisions pertaining to their appointment are to a great extent taken by the army's administrative authorities...Lastly, their term of office as National Security Court judges is only four years and can be renewed.

72....the Court attaches great importance to the fact that a civilian had to appear before a court composed, even if only in part, of members of the armed forces. It follows that the applicant could legitimately fear that because one of the judges of the Izmir National Security Court was a military judge it might allow itself to be unduly influenced by considerations which had nothing to do with the nature of the case....

73. In conclusion, the applicant had legitimate cause to doubt the independence and impartiality of the Izmir national Security Court....

Do you think the nature of the accusations against the applicant exacerbated the dangers of the military judge undermining the independence and impartiality of the National Security Court?

Subsequently, a number of other persons convicted by the Turkish Security Courts successfully invoked this aspect of Article 6 before the European Court. In *Ocalan v Turkey*, see p 135, the applicant complained that a judge holding the military rank of a colonel sat as one of the members of the State Security Court that tried and convicted him. The Turkish Government responded that the military judge was replaced by a civilian judge during the course of the trial. The Grand Chamber, 11 votes to 6, found that the applicant had not been tried by an independent and impartial tribunal.

112. The Court has consistently held that certain aspects of the status of military judges sitting as members of the State Security Courts made their independence from the executive questionable (see *Incal v Turkey*, judgment of 9 June 1998, Reports 1998-IV, § 68; and *Çiraklar v Turkey*, judgment of 28 October 1998, Reports of Judgments and Decisions 1998-VII, § 39).

113. It is understandable that the applicant—prosecuted in a State Security Court for serious offences relating to national security—should have been apprehensive about being tried by a bench which included a regular army officer belonging to the military legal service. On that account he could legitimately fear that the State Security Court might allow itself to be unduly influenced by considerations which had nothing to do with the nature of the case (see, among other authorities, *Iprahim Ülger v Turkey*, No 57250/00, 29 July 2004).

114. As to whether the military judge's replacement by a civilian judge in the course of the proceedings before the verdict was delivered remedied the situation, the Court considers, firstly, that the question whether a court is seen to be independent does not depend solely on its composition when it delivers its verdict. In order to comply with the requirements of Article 6 regarding independence, the court concerned must be seen to be independent of the executive and the legislature at each of the three stages of the proceedings, namely the investigation, the trial and the verdict (those being the three stages in Turkish criminal proceedings according to the Government).

115. Secondly, when a military judge has participated in one or more interlocutory decisions that continue to remain in effect in the criminal proceedings concerned, the accused has reasonable cause for concern about the validity of the entire proceedings, unless it is established that the procedure subsequently followed in the state security court sufficiently disposed of that concern. More specifically, where a military judge has participated in an interlocutory decision that forms an

integral part of proceedings against a civilian the whole proceedings are deprived of the appearance of having been conducted by an independent and impartial court.

116. In its previous judgments, the Court attached importance to the fact that a civilian had to appear before a court composed, even if only in part, of members of the armed forces (see, among other authorities, *Incal*, cited above, § 72). Such a situation seriously affects the confidence which the courts must inspire in a democratic society (see, *mutatis mutandis*, *Piersack v Belgium*, judgment of 1 October 1982, Series A No 53, pp 14–15, § 30).

117. In the instant case, the Court notes that before his replacement on 23 June 1999 the military judge was present at two preliminary hearings and six hearings on the merits when interlocutory decisions were taken. It further notes that none of the decisions were renewed after the replacement of the military judge and that all were validated by the replacement judge.

118. In these circumstances, the Court cannot accept that the replacement of the military judge before the end of the proceedings disposed of the applicant's reasonably held concern about the trial court's independence and impartiality. Insofar as the decision or reasoning in the case of *Imrek v Turkey* [(dec.) No 57175/00, 28 January 2003] may be regarded as inconsistent with this conclusion, the Grand Chamber would not follow the decision and the reasoning in that case.

Consequently, there has been a violation of Article 6 § 1 on this point.

President Wildhaber, joined by Judges: Costa, Caflisch, Turmen, Garlicki, and Borrego Borrego, issued a joint partly dissenting opinion in which they expressed the view that:

8. In addition, in Mr Oçalan's case, and without departing from the principles established in the *Incal* judgment itself, it is hard to agree with what is said in paragraph 116 of the judgment. The applicant is there described as a civilian (or equated to a civilian). However, he was accused of instigating serious terrorist crimes leading to thousands of deaths, charges which he admitted at least in part. He could equally well be described as a warlord, which goes a long way to putting into perspective the fact that at the start of his trial one of the three members of the court before which he appeared was himself from the military.

During 2006 the Istanbul Assize Court, after examining the merits, dismissed Ocalan's application for the reopening of the criminal proceedings against him. The Assize Court considered that even if the breaches found by the European Court of Human Rights had not occurred, the sentence imposed on him would have been the same. Subsequently Ocalan's complaint to Strasbourg that the reopening proceedings had violated Article 6 was (unanimously) declared inadmissible by a Chamber decision of 16 July 2010.

9 The presiding over a civil Court of Appeal hearing by the Chief Justice in a case where one party's lawyers were the brother and nephew of the Chief Justice was found to violate the objective test of impartiality by a Grand Chamber in *Micallef v Malta*, p 366.

102....The Grand Chamber is of the view that close family ties between the opposing party's advocate and the Chief Justice sufficed to objectively justify fears that the presiding judge lacked impartiality. It cannot be overlooked that Malta is a small country and that entire families practising law are a common phenomenon. Indeed, the Government have also acknowledged that this had become a recurring issue which necessitated action resulting in an amendment to the relevant law, which now includes sibling relationships as a ground for withdrawal.

This is a stark example of a very senior judge being found to have breached the impartiality guarantee contained within Article 6(1).

10 The range of bodies classified as 'tribunals' for the purposes of this provision has been drawn widely by the Court. For example, we have already seen that the Court found a lack of impartiality on the part of the Maltese House of Representatives in seeking to punish a journalist in *Demicoli v Malta* (p 375). The Court's conception of a 'tribunal' was explained in paragraph 39 of that judgment.

Public pronouncement of judgment

1 The Court was unanimous in finding no breach of this requirement in respect of the Italian Court of Cassation's procedure of depositing its judgments in the court registry (members of the public could consult/obtain copies of judgments from the registry): *Pretto v Italy* A.71 (1983). The first applicant, a tenant farmer, had brought proceedings in the Vicenza Regional Court and the Venice Court of Appeal to acquire the land he farmed. The latter court decided in favour of the landlord and Mr Pretto appealed on points of law to the Court of Cassation. His appeal was dismissed and the Court of Cassation deposited its full judgment in the court registry. The applicant complained to the Commission alleging, *inter alia*, a breach of this right. By 12 votes to 3 the Commission found no violation of this provision. The Court held that:

21. The public character of proceedings before the judicial bodies referred to in Article 6 § 1 (art 6-1) protects litigants against the administration of justice in secret with no public scrutiny; it is also one of the means whereby confidence in the courts, superior and inferior, can be maintained. By rendering the administration of justice visible, publicity contributes to the achievement of the aim of Article 6 § 1 (art 6-1), namely a fair trial, the guarantee of which is one of the fundamental principles of any democratic society, within the meaning of the Convention (see the *Golder* judgment of 21 February 1975, Series A No 18, p 18, § 36, and also the *Lawless* judgment of 14 November 1960, Series A No 1, p 13).

22. While the member States of the Council of Europe all subscribe to this principle of publicity, their legislative systems and judicial practice reveal some diversity as to its scope and manner of implementation, as regards both the holding of hearings and the 'pronouncement' of judgments. The formal aspect of the matter is, however, of secondary importance as compared with the purpose underlying the publicity required by Article 6 § 1 (art 6-1). The prominent place held in a democratic society by the right to a fair trial impels the Court, for the purposes of the review which it has to undertake in this area, to examine the realities of the procedure in question . . .

24. In accordance with Article 133 of the Code of Civil Procedure, the judgment adopted on 19 October 1976 by the Court of Cassation was simply deposited in the court registry, with written notification of the operative provisions being given to the parties, but not pronounced in open court . . . It therefore has to be determined whether, as the applicants and a minority of the Commission contended, this state of affairs violated the Convention.

25. The terms used in the second sentence of Article 6 § 1 (art 6-1)—'judgment shall be pronounced publicly', 'le jugement sera rendu publiquement'—might suggest that a reading out aloud of the judgment is required. Admittedly the French text employs the participle 'rendu' (given), whereas the corresponding word in the English version is 'pronounced' (prononcé), but this slight difference is not sufficient to dispel the impression left by the language of the provision in question: in French, 'rendu publiquement'—as opposed to 'rendu public' (made public)—can very well be regarded as the equivalent of 'prononcé publiquement'.

At first sight, Article 6 § 1 (art 6-1) of the European Convention would thus appear to be stricter in this respect than Article 14 § 1 of the 1966 International Covenant on Civil and Political Rights, which provides that the judgment 'shall be made public', 'sera public'.

26. However, many member States of the Council of Europe have a long-standing tradition of recourse to other means, besides reading out aloud, for making public the decisions of all or some of their courts, and especially of their courts of cassation, for example deposit in a registry accessible to the public. The authors of the Convention cannot have overlooked that fact, even if concern to take it into account is not so easily identifiable in their working documents as in the *travaux préparatoires* of the 1966 Covenant (see, for instance, document A/4299 of 3 December 1959, pp 12, 15 and 19, §§ 38 (b), 53 and 63 (c) *in fine*).

The Court therefore does not feel bound to adopt a literal interpretation. It considers that in each case the form of publicity to be given to the 'judgment' under the domestic law of the respondent State must be assessed in the light of the special features of the proceedings in question and by reference to the object and purpose of Article 6 § 1 (art 6-1).

27....the Court of Cassation took its decision after holding public hearings and, although the judgment dismissing the appeal on points of law was not delivered in open court, anyone may consult or obtain a copy of it on application to the court registry...

In the opinion of the Court, the object pursued by Article 6 § 1 (art 6-1) in this context—namely, to ensure scrutiny of the judiciary by the public with a view to safeguarding the right to a fair trial—is, at any rate as regards cassation proceedings, no less achieved by a deposit in the court registry, making the full text of the judgment available to everyone, than by a reading in open court of a decision dismissing an appeal or quashing a previous judgment, such reading sometimes being limited to the operative provisions.

28. The absence of public pronouncement of the Court of Cassation's judgment therefore did not contravene the Convention in the present case....

Hence the Court, sensibly, focused upon the substantive goal of ensuring that the domestic court's reasoning and decision was subject to public scrutiny.

2 A majority of the full-time Court, 5 votes to 2, found the English system of restricted access to civil judgments concerning children to be compatible with the public judgments obligation in *B and P v UK*, judgment of 24 July 2001 (and see p 430 in respect of the public hearing aspect of the case). Generally court orders and judgments concerning children are not made public, but any person with a legitimate interest can apply to the relevant court for permission to see and copy the text of orders and judgments. Also judgments of legal importance are published, in an anonymous form, in the law reports. In the light of these practices the Court held that:

48....a literal interpretation of the terms of Article 6 § 1 concerning the pronouncement of judgments would not only be unnecessary for the purposes of public scrutiny but might even frustrate the primary aim of Article 6 § 1, which is to secure a fair hearing...

49. The Court thus concludes that the Convention did not require making available to the general public the residence judgments in the present cases, and that there has been no violation of Article 6 § 1 in this respect.

Judges Loucaides and Tulkens dissented as they considered that the obligation to pronounce judgments was expressed in unqualified terms by Article 6(1).

In an ideal world all judgments should be made generally available to the public (technically more feasible in the modern digital era) with appropriate deletions of sensitive information (e.g. the identities of persons in family disputes).

Article 6(2): presumption of innocence

Minelli v Switzerland A.62 (1983)
European Court of Human Rights

The applicant was a journalist who published an article in a Swiss newspaper in January 1972 accusing a company, Tele-Repertoire SA, and its director, Mr Vass, of fraud. The accusation involved the same allegations as another journalist, Mr Furst, had published a few days earlier in a different newspaper. The company and Mr Vass brought a criminal complaint of defamation against both journalists. Proceedings against the applicant were suspended in July 1974, at the request of Mr Vass, until the complaint against Mr Furst had been completed. In September 1975 Mr Furst was convicted, fined, and ordered to pay costs. In May 1976 the Zurich Assize Court held that it could not hear the complaint against the applicant because the absolute limitation period of four years had expired. However, the court ordered that he should pay two-thirds of the court's costs and 1,200 SF towards the costs incurred by the complainants, because if it had not been for the expiry of the limitation period the complaint would 'very probably have led to the conviction of the accused...'. The applicant complained to the Commission that the court's order to pay costs amounted to a violation of the presumption of innocence contained in Article 6(2). The Commission was unanimous in finding a violation of that right.

30. In the Court's opinion, Article 6 § 2 (art 6-2) governs criminal proceedings in their entirety, irrespective of the outcome of the prosecution, and not solely the examination of the merits of the charge...

In the Canton of Zürich, a decision on the apportionment of costs is a normal part of criminal proceedings for defamation and is designed to settle certain consequences thereof. In this connection, it is of little moment that the decision was adopted after the ruling on the merits or that its text appears in a separate document.

II. COMPLIANCE WITH ARTICLE 6 § 2 (ART 6-2)

A. Limits of the Court's task

34. The applicant and the Government agreed that the case raised a question of principle: is it consonant with the presumption of innocence to direct that a person shall pay court costs and compensation in respect of expenses where he has been acquitted or where the case has been discontinued, discharged or, as here, terminated on account of limitation?

As the Government emphasised by way of alternative plea, the system which permits the adoption of such a solution in certain cases is deeply rooted in Swiss legal tradition: it is enshrined in Federal legislation and in that of most Cantons, including the Canton of Zürich, and has been developed by case-law and practice. According to Mr Minelli, on the other hand, it is the State which should bear all the risks of criminal proceedings, not only as regards evidence but also as regards costs.

In the Commission's view, the system in question could not of itself run counter to Article 6 § 2 (art 6-2) of the Convention; however, a problem arose if the reasons for the court's decision or some other precise and conclusive evidence showed that the apportionment of costs resulted from an appraisal of the guilt of the accused.

35. The Court in principle concurs with the Commission. However, it would point out, in conformity with its established jurisprudence, that in proceedings originating in an individual application, it has to confine itself, as far as possible, to an examination of the concrete case before it … Accordingly, it has to give a ruling not on the Zürich legislation and practice *in abstracto* but solely on the manner in which they were applied to the applicant.

…

37. In the Court's judgment, the presumption of innocence will be violated if, without the accused's having previously been proved guilty according to law and, notably, without his having had the opportunity of exercising his rights of defence, a judicial decision concerning him reflects an opinion that he is guilty. This may be so even in the absence of any formal finding; it suffices that there is some reasoning suggesting that the court regards the accused as guilty. The Court has to ascertain whether this was the case on 12 May 1976.

38. The Chamber of the Assize Court based its decision on Article 293 of the Zürich Code of Criminal Procedure, which, in the case of a private prosecution for defamation, permits a departure, in special circumstances, from the rule that the losing party is to bear the court costs and pay compensation to the other party in respect of his expenses … In the light of Zürich case-law, it found that in the present case 'the incidence of the costs and expenses should depend on the judgment that would have been delivered' had the statutory period of limitation not expired. To decide this point, it had regard to four matters … the fact that the case was virtually identical to that of the journalist Fust, which had resulted on 2 September 1975 in a conviction … the seriousness of the applicant's accusations against Mr Vass; the applicant's failure to verify his allegations; and the negative outcome of the 1972 prosecution of Mr Vass …

For these reasons, which were set out at length and cannot be dissociated from the operative provisions … the Chamber of the Assize Court concluded that, in the absence of limitation, the 'National Zeitung' article complained of would 'very probably have led to the conviction' of the applicant. In setting out those reasons, the Chamber treated the conduct denounced by the private prosecutors as having been proved; furthermore, the reasons were based on decisions taken in two other cases to which, although they concerned the same facts, Mr Minelli had not been a party and which, in law, were distinct from his case.

In this way the Chamber of the Assize Court showed that it was satisfied of the guilt of Mr Minelli, an accused who, as the Government acknowledged, had not had the benefit of the guarantees contained in paragraphs 1 and 3 of Article 6 (art 6-1, art 6-3). Notwithstanding the absence of a formal finding and despite the use of certain cautious phraseology ('in all probability', 'very probably'), the Chamber proceeded to make appraisals that were incompatible with respect for the presumption of innocence.

…

41. Accordingly, there has been a violation of Article 6(2). …

NOTES

1 The Court was composed of President Wiarda and Judges: Bindschedler-Robert, Lagergren, Gölcüklü, Matscher, Macdonald, and Russo.

2 Subsequently, the Court has held that statements by public officials, as well as judicial determinations, can violate this right. In *Allenet de Ribemont v France* A.308 (1995), on 24 December 1976 a member of the French Parliament was murdered outside the applicant's home. The applicant had financial dealings with the victim. On 29 December the Paris police arrested the applicant in connection with the murder. During that day the Minister of the Interior held a press conference regarding the police budget. He was accompanied by senior police officers involved in the murder investigation. During the conference a journalist asked who was the key figure in the case and Mr Ducret, Director of the Paris Criminal Investigation Department, replied 'The instigator, Mr De Varga, and his acolyte, Mr de Ribemont, were the instigators of the murder.' On 14 January 1977 the applicant was charged with aiding and abetting intentional homicide. Three years later a discharge order was issued against him. The applicant complained that the comments made at the press conference infringed Article 6(2). The Commission unanimously upheld his complaint.

32. The Government contested, in substance, the applicability of Article 6 para 2 (art 6-2), relying on the *Minelli v Switzerland* judgment of 25 March 1983 (Series A No 62). They maintained that the presumption of innocence could be infringed only by a judicial authority, and could be shown to have been infringed only where, at the conclusion of proceedings ending in a conviction, the court's reasoning suggested that it regarded the defendant as guilty in advance.

33. The Commission acknowledged that the principle of presumption of innocence was above all a procedural safeguard in criminal proceedings, but took the view that its scope was more extensive, in that it imposed obligations not only on criminal courts determining criminal charges but also on other authorities.

34. The Court's task is to determine whether the situation found in this case affected the applicant's right under Article 6 para 2 . . .

35. The presumption of innocence enshrined in paragraph 2 of Article 6 (art 6-2) is one of the elements of the fair criminal trial that is required by paragraph 1 (art 6-1) (see, among other authorities, the . . . *Minelli* judgment previously cited, p 15, para 27). It will be violated if a judicial decision concerning a person charged with a criminal offence reflects an opinion that he is guilty before he has been proved guilty according to law. It suffices, even in the absence of any formal finding, that there is some reasoning suggesting that the court regards the accused as guilty (see the *Minelli* judgment previously cited, p 18, para 37).

   However, the scope of Article 6 para 2 (art 6-2) is not limited to the eventuality mentioned by the Government . . . Moreover, the Court reiterates that the Convention must be interpreted in such a way as to guarantee rights which are practical and effective as opposed to theoretical and illusory . . .

36. The Court considers that the presumption of innocence may be infringed not only by a judge or court but also by other public authorities.

37. At the time of the press conference of 29 December 1976 Mr Allenet de Ribemont had just been arrested by the police . . . Although he had not yet been charged with aiding and abetting intentional homicide . . . his arrest and detention in police custody formed part of the judicial investigation begun a few days earlier by a Paris investigating judge and made him a person 'charged with a criminal offence' within the meaning of Article 6 para 2 (art 6-2). The two senior police officers present were conducting the inquiries in the case. Their remarks, made in parallel with the judicial investigation and supported by the Minister of the Interior, were explained by the existence of that investigation and had a direct link with it. Article 6 para 2 (art 6-2) therefore applies in this case.

B. COMPLIANCE WITH ARTICLE 6 PARA 2 (ART 6-2)

1. Reference to the case at the press conference

38. Freedom of expression, guaranteed by Article 10 (art 10) of the Convention, includes the freedom to receive and impart information. Article 6 para 2 (art 6-2) cannot therefore prevent the authorities from informing the public about criminal investigations in progress, but it requires that they do so with all the discretion and circumspection necessary if the presumption of innocence is to be respected.

2. Content of the statements complained of

39. Like the applicant, the Commission considered that the remarks made by the Minister of the Interior and, in his presence and under his authority, by the police superintendent in charge of the inquiry and the Director of the Criminal Investigation Department, were incompatible with the presumption of innocence. It noted that in them Mr Allenet de Ribemont was held up as one of the instigators of Mr de Broglie's murder.

40. The Government maintained that such remarks came under the head of information about criminal proceedings in progress and were not such as to infringe the presumption of innocence, since they did not bind the courts and could be proved false by subsequent investigations. The facts of the case bore this out, as the applicant had not been formally charged until two weeks after the press conference and the investigating judge had eventually decided that there was no case to answer.

41. The Court notes that in the instant case some of the highest-ranking officers in the French police referred to Mr Allenet de Ribemont, without any qualification or reservation, as one of the instigators of a murder and thus an accomplice in that murder... This was clearly a declaration of the applicant's guilt which, firstly, encouraged the public to believe him guilty and, secondly, prejudged the assessment of the facts by the competent judicial authority. There has therefore been a breach of Article 6 para 2 (art 6-2)....

Do you think the Court would have found a breach if the statements had been made by a junior police officer?

3 Comments made by the Chairman of the Lithuanian Seimas (Parliament) were found to violate this provision in *Butkevicius v Lithuania*, judgment of 26 March 2002. The applicant was the Minister of Defence and a Member of the Seimas from 1996 to 2000. In 1997 he was arrested by intelligence officers while accepting $15,000 from a businessman. After criminal proceedings were initiated against Butkevicius the Chairman made several comments to the press about him including calling him a 'bribe-taker'. The applicant was later convicted and sentenced to five years' imprisonment for attempting to obtain property by deception. The Court, unanimously, accepted that:

50. ... the fact that the applicant was an important political figure at the time of the alleged offence required the highest State officials, including the Prosecutor General and the Chairman of the Seimas, to keep the public informed of the alleged offence and the ensuing criminal proceedings. However, it cannot agree with the Government's argument that this circumstance could justify any use of words chosen by the officials in their interviews with the press.

...

53. ... While the impugned remarks of the Chairman of the Seimas were in each case brief and made on separate occasions, in the Court's opinion they amounted to declarations by a public official of

the applicant's guilt, which served to encourage the public to believe him guilty and prejudged the assessment of the facts by the competent judicial authority.

54. There has therefore been a breach of Article 6(2) of the Convention.

Clearly, the Chairman's position as a State office holder brought him within the ambit of Article 6(2). Similar comments by a political opponent of the applicant would not have infringed this provision.

4 A united Chamber found a complete disregard for the presumption of innocence of the applicant, the Minister for Economic Development at the time of his arrest, in press releases issued by the Prosecutor General and two government Ministers soon after the applicant had been detained and charged: *Farhad Aliyev v Azerbaijan*, judgment of 9 November 2010.

5 The Court has also ruled that presumptions of law or fact imposed on persons in defined circumstances by domestic criminal law provisions may be compatible with Article 6(2). For example, in *Salabiaku v France* A.141-A (1988), the applicant had gone to collect a parcel at Roissy airport. He was unable to find the parcel but was directed to a trunk (which had not been collected and had no name on it). An airline official advised him to leave the trunk where it was. However, the applicant removed the trunk and took it through the 'green' (nothing to declare) customs exit. He was detained by customs officials outside the airport building who opened the trunk and found a false bottom with 10 kg of cannabis hidden inside. The applicant was eventually convicted of the customs offence of smuggling prohibited goods because: '...any person in possession of goods which he or she has brought into France without declaring them to customs is presumed to be legally liable unless he or she can prove specific event of *force majeure* exculpating him; such *force majeure* may arise only as a result of an event beyond human control which could be neither foreseen nor averted...'. The applicant complained that his conviction under the Customs Code violated Article 6(2). The Commission, by 9 votes to 4, found no breach of this right. A united Court rejected the applicant's complaint.

27. As the Government and the Commission have pointed out, in principle the Contracting States remain free to apply the criminal law to an act where it is not carried out in the normal exercise of one of the rights protected under the Convention (*Engel* judgment of 8 June 1976, Series A No 22, p 34, para 81) and, accordingly, to define the constituent elements of the resulting offence. In particular, and again in principle, the Contracting States may, under certain conditions, penalise a simple or objective fact as such, irrespective of whether it results from criminal intent or from negligence. Examples of such offences may be found in the laws of the Contracting States.

...

28. ....Presumptions of fact or of law operate in every legal system. Clearly, the Convention does not prohibit such presumptions in principle. It does, however, require the Contracting States to remain within certain limits in this respect as regards criminal law. If, as the Commission would appear to consider (paragraph 64 of the report), paragraph 2 of Article 6 (art 6-2) merely laid down a guarantee to be respected by the courts in the conduct of legal proceedings, its requirements would in practice overlap with the duty of impartiality imposed in paragraph 1 (art 6-1). Above all, the national legislature would be free to strip the trial court of any genuine power of assessment and deprive the presumption of innocence of its substance, if the words 'according to law' were construed exclusively with reference to domestic law. Such a situation could not be reconciled with the object and purpose of Article 6 (art 6), which, by protecting the right to a fair trial and in particular the right to be presumed innocent, is intended to enshrine the fundamental principle

of the rule of law (see, *inter alia*, the *Sunday Times* judgment of 26 April 1979, Series A No 30, p 34, para 55).

Article 6 para 2 (art 6-2) does not therefore regard presumptions of fact or of law provided for in the criminal law with indifference. It requires States to confine them within reasonable limits which take into account the importance of what is at stake and maintain the rights of the defence. The Court proposes to consider whether such limits were exceeded to the detriment of Mr Salabiaku.

...

30. ...It is clear from the judgment of 27 March 1981 and that of 9 February 1982, that the courts in question were careful to avoid resorting automatically to the presumption laid down in Article 392 para 1 of the Customs Code. As the Court of Cassation observed in its judgment of 21 February 1983, they exercised their power of assessment 'on the basis of the evidence adduced by the parties before [them]'. They inferred from the 'fact of possession a presumption which was not subsequently rebutted by any evidence of an event responsibility for which could not be attributed to the perpetrator of the offence or which he would have been unable to avoid'...Moreover, as the Government said, the national courts identified in the circumstances of the case a certain 'element of intent', even though legally they were under no obligation to do so in order to convict the applicant.

It follows that in this instance the French courts did not apply Article 392 para 1 of the Customs Code in a way which conflicted with the presumption of innocence....

Hence, offences of strict liability will not necessarily be incompatible with the Convention.

6 An example of the Court finding an unacceptable re-allocation of the burden of proof onto the defence occurred in *Telfner v Austria*, judgment of 20 March 2001. A person had been slightly injured one night after being hit by a car. The victim had noted the registration number of the car, but he had not been able to identify the driver. The next morning the police found the car, registered to the applicant's mother, outside the family home. The mother informed the police that she had not been driving the car and the applicant was not yet home. She said that the car was frequently used by different members of her family. Subsequently the applicant was charged with causing injury by negligence. He pleaded not guilty and stated that he had not been driving the car at the time of the accident. His mother and sister exercised their right not to testify. The District Court found the applicant guilty on the basis that, according to the local police, '...it was common knowledge that the vehicle in question was mainly driven by the accused'. Therefore, the District Court concluded that the applicant was the driver who caused the accident/injury. He was sentenced to a fine of 24,000 Austrian schillings. His appeal was dismissed by the Regional Court. The European Court, unanimously, determined that:

18. In the present case, both the District Court and the Regional Court relied in essence on a report of the local police station that the applicant was the main user of the car and had not been home on the night of the accident. However, the Court cannot find that these elements of evidence, which were moreover not corroborated by evidence taken at the trial in an adversarial manner, constituted a case against the applicant which would have called for an explanation from his part. In this context, the Court notes, in particular, that the victim of the accident had not been able to identify the driver, nor even to say whether the driver had been male or female, and that the Regional Court, after supplementing the proceedings, found that the car in question was also used by the applicant's sister. In requiring the applicant to provide an explanation although they had not been able to establish a convincing prima facie case against him, the courts shifted the burden of proof from the prosecution to the defence.

...

20. In conclusion, the Court finds that there has been a violation of Article 6(2) of the Convention.

7 The Court, by a large majority of 5 to 2, concluded that Article 6(2) did not apply to financial confiscation proceedings brought against a convicted drugs smuggler in *Phillips v UK*, judgment of 5 July 2001. The applicant had been found guilty of importing a large amount of cannabis resin into the UK and sentenced to nine years' imprisonment. Soon after his conviction, in June 1996, the Customs and Excise began confiscation proceedings, under the Drug Trafficking Act 1994, against the applicant. Under that Act all property held or expenditure by a convicted drug trafficker up to six years prior to the start of the criminal proceedings was assumed to have been obtained from the proceeds of drug trafficking. The value of that property/expenditure was liable to be confiscated by the court that tried the offender unless the latter was able to establish, on the balance of probabilities, that the property/expenditure was not so obtained. In December 1996 the trial court ordered that the applicant should pay £91,400 compensation in respect of property acquired as a result of drug trafficking (or serve a further two years' imprisonment in default of payment). The applicant contended before the European Court that the statutory assumption utilized by the trial court violated his right to the presumption of innocence. The Court held that:

34. ...the purpose of the procedure under the 1994 Act was to enable the national court to assess the amount at which the confiscation order should properly be fixed. The Court considers that this procedure was analogous to the determination by a court of the amount of a fine or the length of a period of imprisonment to impose upon a properly convicted offender....

35. ...Once an accused has properly been proved guilty of that offence, Article 6(2) can have no application in relation to allegations made about the accused's character and conduct as part of the sentencing process, unless such accusations are of such a nature and degree as to amount to the bringing of a new 'charge' within the autonomous Convention meaning...

36. In conclusion, therefore, the Court holds that Article 6(2) was not applicable to the confiscation proceedings brought against the applicant.

For an examination of the Court's consideration of earlier financial confiscation powers applicable to drug offenders under Article 7, see p 483.

8 The relationship between criminal and compensation proceedings relating to the same event was examined in *Y v Norway*, judgment of 11 February 2003. The applicant, when aged 18, was alleged to have committed a violent sexual assault on his 17-year-old cousin which resulted in her death. He was convicted of her homicide by the District Court and sentenced to 14 years' imprisonment. The District Court ordered him to pay the victim's parents 100,000 NOK compensation under the Damage Compensation Act 1969. The Act provided that, *inter alios*, the parents of a deceased person could claim compensation, for pecuniary/non-pecuniary damage, from the alleged perpetrator who had caused the death intentionally or by gross negligence. Regardless of the outcome of criminal proceedings against the alleged perpetrator, in the compensation proceedings the claimants bore the burden of proof, on the balance of probabilities. The applicant appealed to the High Court where the jury found him not guilty. However, after submissions by counsel for the victim's parents and the applicant the High Court ordered that the District Court's compensation award should be upheld. The applicant's appeal to the Supreme Court was rejected. He then lodged a complaint at Strasbourg contending that the upholding of the compensation award against him violated his presumption of innocence under Article 6(2). A united Chamber held that:

39. The Court reiterates that the concept of a 'criminal charge' in Article 6 is an autonomous one. According to its established case-law there are three criteria to be taken into account when deciding whether a person was 'charged with a criminal offence' for the purposes of Article 6, namely the classification of the proceedings under national law, their essential nature and the type and severity of the penalty that the applicant risked incurring (see *Phillips v the United Kingdom* ...). Moreover, the scope of Article 6 § 2 is not limited to criminal proceedings that are pending (see *Allenet de Ribemont v France*, judgment of 10 February 1995, Series A No 308, p 16, § 35). In certain instances, the Court has also found the provision applicable to judicial decisions taken after the discontinuation of such proceedings (see in particular the following judgments: *Minelli v Switzerland*, 25 March 1983, Series A No 62, and *Lutz, Englert and Nölkenbockhoff v Germany*, 25 August 1987, Series A No 123), or following an acquittal ... Those judgments concerned proceedings related to such matters as an accused's obligation to bear court costs and prosecution expenses, a claim for reimbursement of his (or his heirs') necessary costs, or compensation for detention on remand, and which were found to constitute a consequence and the concomitant of the criminal proceedings.

Accordingly, the Court will examine whether the compensation proceedings in the present case gave rise to a 'criminal charge' against the applicant and, in the event that this was not the case, whether the compensation case nevertheless was linked to the criminal trial in such a way as to fall within the scope of Article 6 § 2.

40. Turning to the first of the above-mentioned criteria, the classification of the proceedings under national law, the Court notes the applicant's argument that, formally speaking, he remained 'charged' until the acquittal gained legal force. However, this concerned only the initial criminal charges of which he was acquitted; it was of no relevance to the compensation claim. The Court notes that the latter had its legal basis in Chapter 3 of the Damage Compensation Act 1969, which sets out the general principles of the national law on torts applicable to personal injuries. It is clear from both the wording of Article 3-5 and Norwegian case-law that criminal liability is not a prerequisite for liability to pay compensation. Even where, as here, the victim had opted for joining the compensation claim to the criminal trial, pursuant to Article 3 of the Code of Criminal Procedure, the claim would still be considered a 'civil' one. This also transpires from the Supreme Court's judgment in the applicant's case, which described the claim as 'civil'. Thus, the Court finds that the compensation claim in issue was not viewed as a 'criminal charge' under the relevant national law.

41. As regard the second and third criteria, the nature of the proceedings and the type and severity of the 'penalty' (i.e. in the instant case the allegedly punitive award of compensation), the Court observes that, while the conditions for civil liability could in certain respects overlap, depending on the circumstances, with those for criminal liability, the civil claim was nevertheless to be determined on the basis of the principles that were proper to the civil law of tort. The outcome of the criminal proceedings was not decisive for the compensation case. The victim had a right to claim compensation regardless of whether the defendant was convicted or, as here, acquitted, and the compensation issue was to be the subject of a separate legal assessment based on criteria and evidentiary standards which in several important respects differed from those applicable to criminal liability.

In the view of the Court, the fact that an act which may give rise to a civil compensation claim under the law of tort is also covered by the objective constitutive elements of a criminal offence could not, notwithstanding its gravity, provide a sufficient ground for regarding the person allegedly responsible for the act in the context of a tort case as being 'charged with a criminal offence'. Nor could the fact that evidence from the criminal trial is used to determine civil law consequences of the act warrant such characterisation. Otherwise, as rightly pointed out by the Government, Article 6 § 2 would give a criminal acquittal the undesirable effect of pre-empting the victim's possibilities of claiming compensation under the civil law of tort, entailing an arbitrary and disproportionate limitation on his or her right of access to court under Article 6 § 1 of the Convention. This again could give an acquitted perpetrator, who would be deemed responsible according the civil burden of proof, the undue advantage of avoiding any responsibility for his or her actions. Such an extensive interpretation would not be supported either by the wording of Article 6 § 2 or any common ground in the national legal systems within the Convention community. On the contrary, in a significant number of Contracting States, an acquittal does not preclude establishing civil liability in relation to the same facts.

Thus, the Court considers that, while the acquittal from criminal liability ought to be maintained in the compensation proceedings, it should not preclude the establishment of civil liability to pay compensation arising out of the same facts on the basis of a less strict burden of proof (see, *mutatis mutandis, X v Austria*, No 9295/81, Commission decision of 6 October 1992, Decisions and Reports (D.R.) 30, p 227; *M.C. v the United Kingdom*, No 11882/85, decision of 7 October 1987, D.R. 54, p 162).

42. However, if the national decision on compensation contains a statement imputing the criminal liability of the respondent party, this could raise an issue falling within the ambit of Article 6 § 2 of the Convention.

43. The Court will therefore examine the question whether the domestic courts acted in such a way or used such language in their reasoning as to create a clear link between the criminal case and the ensuing compensation proceedings as to justify extending the scope of the application of Article 6 § 2 to the latter.

44. The Court notes that the High Court opened its judgment with the following finding:

> 'Considering the evidence adduced in the case as a whole, the High Court **finds it clearly probable that [the applicant] has committed the offences against Ms T.** with which he was charged and that an award of compensation to her parents should be made under Article 3-5 (2) of the Damage Compensation Act. . . .' (emphasis added)

45. This judgment was upheld by the majority of the Supreme Court, albeit using more careful language. However, that judgment, by not quashing the former, did not rectify the issue, which in the Court's opinion, thereby arises.

46. The Court is mindful of the fact that the domestic courts took note that the applicant had been acquitted of the criminal charges. However, in seeking to protect the legitimate interests of the purported victim, the Court considers that the language employed by the High Court, upheld by the Supreme Court, overstepped the bounds of the civil forum, thereby casting doubt on the correctness of that acquittal. Accordingly, there was a sufficient link to the earlier criminal proceedings which was incompatible with the presumption of innocence.

47. In the light of these considerations, the Court concludes that Article 6 § 2 was applicable to the proceedings relating to the compensation claim against the present applicant and that this provision was violated in the instant case.

So, civil actions based on events which have been the subject of criminal proceedings will not infringe Article 6(2) provided the courts determining the civil claims do not attribute criminal liability to parties who have not been convicted by the criminal courts. The Court delivered similar judgments in the parallel cases of *O v Norway* and *Hammern v Norway*, judgments of 11 February 2003.

Article 6(3)

Article 6(3)(a): defendant's right to be informed of the accusation

....

Brozicek v Italy A.167 (1989)
European Court of Human Rights

The applicant had been born in the former Czechoslovakia and was now a German national living in the latter country. In August 1975 he was arrested by the Italian police in Savona for allegedly tearing down flags erected by a political party. One of the police officers who detained him was allegedly injured by the applicant. In February 1976 the Savona Public Prosecutor's Office sent a registered letter, written in Italian, to the applicant's home in Germany informing him that criminal proceedings had been initiated against him for, *inter alia*, resisting the police and wounding. The applicant returned the letter to the prosecutor with a letter, written in German, requesting that the Italian authorities write to him in his mother tongue or one of the official languages of the United Nations. The prosecutor did not reply and continued to send correspondence to the applicant written in Italian. In July 1981 the applicant was convicted, *in absentia*, by the Savona Regional Court. A majority of the Commission upheld the applicant's claim of a breach of Article 6(3)(a).

41. In the Court's opinion, it is necessary to proceed on the basis of the following facts. The applicant was not of Italian origin and did not reside in Italy. He informed the relevant Italian judicial authorities in an unequivocal manner that because of his lack of knowledge of Italian he had difficulty in understanding the contents of their communication. He asked them to send it to him either in his mother tongue or in one of the official languages of the United Nations.

On receipt of this request, the Italian judicial authorities should have taken steps to comply with it so as to ensure observance of the requirements of Article 6 § 3 (a) (art 6-3-a), unless they were in a position to establish that the applicant in fact had sufficient knowledge of Italian to understand from the notification the purport of the letter notifying him of the charges brought against him.

No such evidence appears from the documents in the file or the statements of the witnesses heard on 23 April 1989... On this point there has therefore been a violation of Article 6 § 3 (a) (art 6-3-a).

42. On the other hand, the Court considers the allegation that the judicial notification of 23 February 1976 did not identify 'in detail... the nature and cause of the accusation' to be unfounded. This communication was intended to inform Mr Brozicek of the institution of proceedings against him; it sufficiently listed the offences of which he was accused, stated the place and the date thereof, referred to the relevant Articles of the Criminal Code and mentioned the name of the victim....

NOTES

1   The Court was composed of President Ryssdal and Judges: Cremona, Bindschedler-Robert, Gölcüklü, Matscher, Pinheiro-Farinha, Walsh, Evans, Macdonald, Bernhardt, Spielmann, Carrillo Salcedo, Martens, Palm, and Foighel.

2 Judges Thor Vilhjalmsson, Pettiti, Russo, De Meyer, and Valticos issued a joint dissenting opinion in which they expressed the view that the applicant had not exhausted domestic remedies in Italy.

Article 6(3)(b): defendant's right to adequate time/facilities to prepare defence

A dramatic example of a breach of this provision was found by a unanimous Grand Chamber in *Ocalan v Turkey*, see p 135. The Grand Chamber determined, *inter alia*, that the applicant/defendant was only given access to the case file against him (which comprised 17,000 pages) on 4 June 1999 and his trial was concluded on 29 June 1999. Furthermore, Ocalan's lawyers were only given access to the case file on the 7 May 1999 (they were not given a copy and it took them until 15 May 1999 to photocopy the contents of the case file).

Article 6(3)(c): legal assistance

Artico v Italy A.37 (1980)
European Court of Human Rights

The applicant was an accountant who had been convicted and imprisoned for various dishonesty offences. He appealed against his convictions and requested the Court of Cassation to provide him with free legal aid. In August 1972 the President of the Second Criminal Section of the court accepted the request and appointed a lawyer (Mr Della Rocca) as the applicant's legal aid lawyer. During the next month Mr Della Rocca informed the applicant that he could not accept the appointment due to other commitments. Subsequently, Mr Della Rocca stated that health reasons prevented him from taking on the onerous task of representing the applicant. Despite the applicant's numerous requests to the Court of Cassation for the appointment of another legal aid lawyer none was appointed. The Commission was unanimous in upholding the applicant's complaint under Article 6(3)(c).

32. Paragraph 3 of Article 6 (art 6-3) contains an enumeration of specific applications of the general principle stated in paragraph 1 of the Article (art 6-1). The various rights of which a non-exhaustive list appears in paragraph 3 reflect certain of the aspects of the notion of a fair trial in criminal proceedings... When compliance with paragraph 3 is being reviewed, its basic purpose must not be forgotten nor must it be severed from its roots.

33. ...Mr Artico claimed to be the victim of a breach of this obligation. The Government, on the other hand, regarded the obligation as satisfied by the nomination of a lawyer for legal aid purposes, contending that what occurred thereafter was in no way the concern of the Italian Republic. According to them, although Mr Della Rocca declined to undertake the task entrusted to him on 8 August 1972 by the President of the Second Criminal Section of the Court of Cassation, he continued to the very end and 'for all purposes' to be the applicant's lawyer. In the Government's view, Mr Artico was, in short, complaining of the failure to appoint a substitute but this amounted to claiming a right which was not guaranteed.

The Court recalls that the Convention is intended to guarantee not rights that are theoretical or illusory but rights that are practical and effective; this is particularly so of the rights of the defence in view of the prominent place held in a democratic society by the right to a fair trial, from which they derive (see the *Airey* judgment of 9 October 1979, Series A No 32, pp 12–13, par 24, and paragraph 32 above). As the Commission's Delegates correctly emphasised, Article 6 par 3 (c) (art 6-3-c) speaks of 'assistance' and not of 'nomination'. Again, mere nomination does not ensure effective assistance since the lawyer appointed for legal aid purposes may die, fall seriously ill, be prevented for a protracted period from acting or shirk his duties. If they are notified of the situation, the authorities must either replace him or cause him to fulfil his obligations. Adoption of the Government's restrictive interpretation would lead to results that are unreasonable and incompatible with both the wording of sub-paragraph (c) (art 6-3-c) and the structure of Article 6 (art 6) taken as a whole; in many instances free legal assistance might prove to be worthless.

In the present case, Mr Artico did not have the benefit of Mr Della Rocca's services at any point of time. From the very outset, the lawyer stated that he was unable to act. He invoked firstly the existence of other commitments and subsequently his state of health...The Court is not called upon to enquire into the relevance of these explanations. It finds, as did the Commission...that the applicant did not receive effective assistance before the Court of Cassation; as far as he was concerned, the above-mentioned decision of 8 August 1972 remained a dead letter.

34. Sub-paragraph (c) of Article 6 par 3 (art 6-3-c) does, nevertheless, make entitlement to the right it sets forth dependent on two conditions. While here there was no argument over the first condition—that the person charged with a criminal offence does not have sufficient means—, the Government denied that the second condition was satisfied: on their view, the 'interests of justice' did not require that Mr Artico be provided with free legal aid. The subject-matter of the Court of Cassation proceedings was, so the Government claimed, crystallized by the grounds adduced in support of the applications to quash, grounds that were filed by the applicant in December 1971 with the assistance of a lawyer of his own choice, Mr Ferri. However, the Government continued, the grounds related to an issue—the regularity of the summons to appear in court—that was of the utmost simplicity, so much so that the public prosecutor pleaded in July 1973 that the applications were manifestly ill-founded...hence, a lawyer would have played but a 'modest' rôle, limited to receiving notification to the effect that the Court of Cassation would take its decision in chambers...

In any event, here the interests of justice did require the provision of effective assistance. This would, according to Mr Della Rocca, have been a very demanding and onerous task...At any rate, the written procedure, which is of prime importance before the Italian Court of Cassation, had not been concluded by 8 August 1972. A qualified lawyer would have been able to clarify the grounds adduced by Mr Artico and, in particular, to give the requisite emphasis to the crucial issue of statutory limitation which had hardly been touched on in the 'voluminous and verbose' declarations of 14/15 March 1972...In addition, only a lawyer could have countered the pleadings of the public prosecutor's department by causing the Court of Cassation to hold a public hearing devoted, among other things, to a thorough discussion of this issue...

36....In reality, Mr Artico doggedly attempted to rectify the position: he multiplied his complaints and representations both to his official lawyer—to the extent of importuning and even finally exasperating him—and to the Court of Cassation...Admittedly, a State cannot be held responsible for every shortcoming on the part of a lawyer appointed for legal aid purposes but, in the particular circumstances, it was for the competent Italian authorities to take steps to ensure that the applicant enjoyed effectively the right to which they had recognised he was entitled. Two courses were open to the authorities: either to replace Mr Della Rocca or, if appropriate, to cause him to fulfil his obligations...They chose a third course—remaining passive—, whereas compliance with the Convention called for positive action on their part (see the above-mentioned *Airey* judgment, p 14, par 25 *in fine*).

37. The Court thus concludes that there has been a breach of the requirements of Article 6 par 3 (c) (art 6-3-c)...

NOTES

1 The Court was composed of President Wiarda and Judges: Balladore Pallieri, Zekia, Bindschedler-Robert, Liesch, Gölcüklü, and Pinheiro-Farinha. The Court's focus upon the reality of whether the applicant had been provided with effective legal assistance was to be commended. If States could satisfy the requirements of this provision merely by designating a legal aid lawyer the guarantee could become worthless in practice; as happened in the applicant's case.

2 In *Benham v UK*, 1996-III (see p 270), the Grand Chamber was unanimous in holding that, '61.... where deprivation of liberty is at stake, the interests of justice in principle call for legal representation'. As Benham was liable to be imprisoned for failing to pay his community charge ('poll tax') the Grand Chamber concluded that he should have received free legal representation and consequently the absence of such representation for him before the magistrates resulted in a breach of Article 6(3)(c). A unanimous Chamber of the full-time Court reached a similar conclusion in *Beet and Others v UK*, judgment of 1 March 2005. Legal aid was made available for such proceedings from 1 June 1997.

3 As we have already seen in *John Murray v UK* (p 412), the denial of access to a lawyer for the first 48 hours of questioning (and detention) of a terrorist suspect was held to amount to a violation of this provision (at least where adverse inferences could be drawn from the detainee's silence).

4 A united Grand Chamber strengthened the right of access to a lawyer for suspects when being questioned by the police in *Salduz v Turkey*, judgment of 27 November 2008. The 17-year-old applicant was arrested for having allegedly participated in an illegal demonstration (supporting the PKK). Legislation provided that persons accused of offences falling within the jurisdiction of the State security courts did not have a right to legal advice. The applicant admitted his participation in the illegal demonstration to the police. Later he was sentenced to two-and-a-half years' imprisonment by a State security court. The Grand Chamber held that:

55....in order for the right to a fair trial to remain sufficiently 'practical and effective' Article 6(1) requires that, as a rule, access to a lawyer should be provided as from the first interrogation of a suspect by the police, unless it is demonstrated in the light of the particular circumstances of each case that there are compelling reasons to restrict this right. Even where compelling reasons may exceptionally justify denial of access to a lawyer, such restriction—whatever its justification— must not unduly prejudice the rights of the accused under Article 6... The rights of the defence will in principle be irretrievably prejudiced when incriminating statements made during police interrogation without access to a lawyer are used for a conviction.

...

60. Finally, the Court notes that one of the specific elements of the instant case was the applicant's age....the Court stresses the fundamental importance of providing access to a lawyer where the person in custody is a minor.

Therefore, a breach of Article 6(3)(c) had occurred. Judges Bratza, Zagrebelsky, Casadevall, and Turmen believed that Court should have gone further and proclaimed the principle that suspects are entitled to legal assistance 'from the moment he is taken into police custody or pre-trial detention'.

5   In *Krombach v France*, judgment of 13 February 2001, the respondent government submitted that the term 'assistance' should be given a strict interpretation and distinguished from 'representation'; with the consequence that the applicant did not have a right to have his lawyer represent him at his trial when he was absent. A unanimous Chamber rejected this narrow interpretation:

89. ... Although not absolute, the right of everyone charged with a criminal offence to be effectively defended by a lawyer, assigned officially if need be, is one of the fundamental features of a fair trial. A person charged with a criminal offence does not loose the benefit of this right merely on account of not being present at the trial. Even if the legislature must be able to discourage unjustified absences, it cannot penalise them by creating exceptions to the right to legal assistance.

The Court concluded that the penalization of the applicant for his non-attendance at his trial by barring his lawyer from making any submissions on behalf of the applicant was 'manifestly disproportionate' and amounted to a breach of Article 6(1) in conjunction with Article 6(3)(c).

6   In *Ezeh and Connors v UK*, judgment of 9 October 2003 (see p 379), the Grand Chamber concluded, by 11 votes to 6, that there had been a breach of Article 6(3)(c) because of the governors' refusals to allow the applicant prisoners to have legal representation during the disciplinary hearings. However, the Grand Chamber declined to consider the applicants' contention that the interests of justice required that they should have been given free legal assistance under this provision.

7   In *Ocalan v Turkey*, see p 135, the Grand Chamber emphasized the need for privileged communications between a defendant and his/her lawyers.

132. ... the Grand Chamber endorses the Chamber's findings:

'...the applicant's first visit from his lawyers took place under the supervision and within sight and hearing of members of the security forces and a judge, all of whom were present in the same room as the applicant and his lawyers. The security forces restricted the visit to twenty minutes. The record of the visit was sent to the State Security Court.

'...As regards subsequent visits, ...the Court accepts that meetings between the applicant and his lawyers after the initial visit took place within hearing of members of the security forces, even though the security officers concerned were not in the room where the meetings took place.'

133. The Grand Chamber agrees with the Chamber's assessment of the effects of the applicant's inability to consult his lawyers out of the hearing of third parties:

'...an accused's right to communicate with his legal representative out of hearing of a third person is part of the basic requirements of a fair trial in a democratic society and follows from Article 6 § 3 (c) of the Convention. If a lawyer were unable to confer with his client and receive confidential instructions from him without such surveillance, his assistance would lose much of its usefulness, whereas the Convention is intended to guarantee rights that are practical and effective (*S. v Switzerland*, judgment of 28 November 1991, Series A No 220, p. 16 § 48). The importance to the rights of the defence of ensuring confidentiality in meetings between the accused and his lawyers has been affirmed in various international instruments, including European instruments (see *Brennan v the United Kingdom*, No 39846/98, §§ 38–40, ECHR 2001-X). However, as stated above ... restrictions may be imposed on an accused's access to his lawyer if good cause exists. The relevant issue is whether, in the light of the proceedings taken as a whole, the restriction has deprived the accused of a fair hearing.

> '...In the present case, the Court accepts...that the applicant and his lawyers were unable to consult out of hearing of the authorities at any stage. It considers that the inevitable consequence of that restriction, which was imposed during both the preliminary investigation and the trial, was to prevent the applicant from conversing openly with his lawyers and asking them questions that [might prove] important to the preparation of his defence. The rights of the defence were thus significantly affected.
>
> '...The Court observes in that connection that the applicant had already made statements by the time he conferred with his lawyers and made further statements at hearings before the State Security Court after consulting them. If his defence to the serious charges he was required to answer was to be effective, it was essential that those statements be consistent. Accordingly, the Court considers that it was necessary for the applicant to be able to speak with his lawyers out of hearing of third parties.
>
> '...As to the Government's contention that the supervision of the meetings between the applicant and his lawyers was necessary to ensure the applicant's security, the Court observes that the lawyers had been retained by the applicant himself and that there was no reason to suspect that they had threatened their client's life. They were not permitted to see the applicant until they had undergone a series of searches. Mere visual surveillance by the prison officials, accompanied by other measures, would have sufficed to ensure the applicant's security.'

Consequently, the Court held that the fact that it was impossible for the applicant to confer with his lawyers out of the hearing of members of the security forces infringed the rights of the defence. The Grand Chamber, unanimously, went on to find a violation of Article 6(3)(c).

8 A unanimous Grand Chamber found a breach of this provision where a convicted murderer was only given 15 minutes' consultation with his legal aid lawyer, via a video-link, prior to the commencement of his appeal. The applicant in *Sakhnovskiy v Russia*, judgment of 2 November 2010, was being detained in a prison facility 3000 km away from the Supreme Court located in Moscow. The Supreme Court ruled that his appeal should be conducted via a video-link with the legal aid lawyer being present in the Moscow courtroom. The Grand Chamber concluded that:

> 106. The Court notes that the Government did not explain why it was impossible to make different arrangements for the applicant's legal assistance. It accepts that transporting the applicant from Novosibirsk to Moscow for a meeting with his lawyer would have been a lengthy and costly operation...While emphasising the central importance of an effective legal assistance, the Court must examine whether in view of this particular geographic obstacle the respondent Government undertook measures which sufficiently compensated for the limitations of the applicant's rights. The Court notes in this respect that nothing prevented the authorities from organising at least a telephone conversation between the applicant and Ms A. [the applicant's designated legal aid lawyer] more in advance of the hearing. Nothing prevented them from appointing a lawyer from Novosibirsk who could have visited the applicant in the detention centre and have been with him during the hearing. Furthermore, it is unclear why the Supreme Court did not confer the representation of the applicant to the lawyer who had already defended him before the first-instance court and prepared the original statement of appeal. Finally, the Supreme Court could have adjourned the hearing on its own motion so as to give the applicant sufficient time to discuss the case with Ms A.
>
> 107. The Court concludes that the arrangements made by the Supreme Court were insufficient and did not secure effective legal assistance to the applicant...

So whilst States may use technological means to enable defendants/appellants to receive legal assistance, the domestic authorities must still ensure the assistance made available is of adequate effectiveness.

Article 6(3)(d): examination of witnesses

Van Mechelen v The Netherlands 1997-III
European Court of Human Rights

The police received information that the four applicants were involved in a series of armed robberies. Teams of officers were deployed to keep the suspects under observation. The officers saw the applicants go, in three cars, to a post office where a robbery took place and the police gave chase. The robbers opened fire, with a sub-machine gun, on the police and some officers were wounded. Subsequently, the applicants were arrested and charged with attempted murder/manslaughter and robbery. The prosecution relied on written statements of anonymous police officers identifying the applicants as the persons involved in the robbery and shootings. The Regional Court convicted the applicants of attempted manslaughter and robbery. Each applicant was sentenced to ten years' imprisonment. The applicants appealed to the Hertogenbosch Court of Appeal. The court ordered that the anonymous police officers should be questioned by the defence and prosecution through a sound link (the police witness was in one room with an investigating judge and registrar while the defendants, their lawyers, and prosecution were in another room). Each anonymous police witnesses stated that he wished to remain anonymous to protect himself/his family. The officers repeated their evidence that the applicants had been participants in the robbery and shootings. The investigating judge reported that the officers appeared to be truthful. The Court of Appeal convicted the applicants of attempted murder and robbery and sentenced each of them to 14 years' imprisonment. The applicants complained that their convictions, based to a decisive extent on the evidence of the anonymous police officers, violated Articles 6(1) and 6(3)(d). By 20 votes to 8, the Commission found no breach of the Convention.

49. As the requirements of Article 6 para 3 (art 6-3) are to be seen as particular aspects of the right to a fair trial guaranteed by Article 6 para 1 (art 6-1), the Court will examine the complaints under Article 6 paras 1 and 3 (d) taken together (art 6-1+6-3-d) (see, among many other authorities, the above-mentioned *Doorson* judgment, pp 469–70, para 66).

50. The Court reiterates that the admissibility of evidence is primarily a matter for regulation by national law and as a general rule it is for the national courts to assess the evidence before them. The Court's task under the Convention is not to give a ruling as to whether statements of witnesses were properly admitted as evidence, but rather to ascertain whether the proceedings as a whole, including the way in which evidence was taken, were fair (see, among other authorities, the…*Doorson* judgment [*Doorson v The Netherlands*, 1996-II], p 470, para 67).

51. In addition, all the evidence must normally be produced at a public hearing, in the presence of the accused, with a view to adversarial argument. There are exceptions to this principle, but they must not infringe the rights of the defence; as a general rule, paragraphs 1 and 3 (d) of Article 6 (art 6-1, art 6-3-d) require that the defendant be given an adequate and proper opportunity to challenge and question a witness against him, either when he makes his statements or at a later stage…

52. As the Court had occasion to state in its *Doorson* judgment (ibid, p 470, para 69), the use of statements made by anonymous witnesses to found a conviction is not under all circumstances incompatible with the Convention.

53. In that same judgment the Court noted the following:

> It is true that Article 6 (art 6) does not explicitly require the interests of witnesses in general, and those of victims called upon to testify in particular, to be taken into consideration. However, their life, liberty or security of person may be at stake, as may interests coming generally within the ambit of Article 8 of the Convention (art 8). Such interests of witnesses and victims are in principle protected by other, substantive provisions of the Convention, which imply that Contracting States should organise their criminal proceedings in such a way that those interests are not unjustifiably imperilled. Against this background, principles of fair trial also require that in appropriate cases the interests of the defence are balanced against those of witnesses or victims called upon to testify. (See the above-mentioned *Doorson* judgment, p 470, para 70.)

54. However, if the anonymity of prosecution witnesses is maintained, the defence will be faced with difficulties which criminal proceedings should not normally involve. Accordingly, the Court has recognised that in such cases Article 6 para 1 taken together with Article 6 para 3 (d) of the Convention (art 6-1+6-3-d) requires that the handicaps under which the defence labours be sufficiently counterbalanced by the procedures followed by the judicial authorities (ibid, p 471, para 72).

55. Finally, it should be recalled that a conviction should not be based either solely or to a decisive extent on anonymous statements (ibid, p 472, para 76).

2. Application of the above principles

56. In the Court's opinion, the balancing of the interests of the defence against arguments in favour of maintaining the anonymity of witnesses raises special problems if the witnesses in question are members of the police force of the State. Although their interests—and indeed those of their families—also deserve protection under the Convention, it must be recognised that their position is to some extent different from that of a disinterested witness or a victim. They owe a general duty of obedience to the State's executive authorities and usually have links with the prosecution; for these reasons alone their use as anonymous witnesses should be resorted to only in exceptional circumstances. In addition, it is in the nature of things that their duties, particularly in the case of arresting officers, may involve giving evidence in open court.

57. On the other hand, the Court has recognised in principle that, provided that the rights of the defence are respected, it may be legitimate for the police authorities to wish to preserve the anonymity of an agent deployed in undercover activities, for his own or his family's protection and so as not to impair his usefulness for future operations . . .

58. Having regard to the place that the right to a fair administration of justice holds in a democratic society, any measures restricting the rights of the defence should be strictly necessary. If a less restrictive measure can suffice then that measure should be applied.

59. In the present case, the police officers in question were in a separate room with the investigating judge, from which the accused and even their counsel were excluded. All communication was via a sound link. The defence was thus not only unaware of the identity of the police witnesses but were also prevented from observing their demeanour under direct questioning, and thus from testing their reliability . . .

60. It has not been explained to the Court's satisfaction why it was necessary to resort to such extreme limitations on the right of the accused to have the evidence against them given in their presence, or why less far-reaching measures were not considered.

In the absence of any further information, the Court cannot find that the operational needs of the police provide sufficient justification . . .

61. Nor is the Court persuaded that the Court of Appeal made sufficient effort to assess the threat of reprisals against the police officers or their families. It does not appear from that court's judgment that it sought to address the question whether the applicants would have been in a position to carry out any such threats or to incite others to do so on their behalf. Its decision was based exclusively on the seriousness of the crimes committed...In this connection, it is to be noted that Mr Engelen, a civilian witness who in the early stages of the proceedings had made statements identifying one of the applicants as one of the perpetrators, did not enjoy the protection of anonymity and it has not been claimed that he was at any time threatened.

62. It is true—as noted by the Government and the Commission...—that the anonymous police officers were interrogated before an investigating judge, who had himself ascertained their identity and had, in a very detailed official report of his findings, stated his opinion on their reliability and credibility as well as their reasons for remaining anonymous.

However these measures cannot be considered a proper substitute for the possibility of the defence to question the witnesses in their presence and make their own judgment as to their demeanour and reliability. It thus cannot be said that the handicaps under which the defence laboured were counterbalanced by the above procedures.

63. Moreover, the only evidence relied on by the Court of Appeal which provided positive identification of the applicants as the perpetrators of the crimes were the statements of the anonymous police officers. That being so the conviction of the applicants was based 'to a decisive extent' on these anonymous statements.

64. In the Court's view, the present case falls to be distinguished from that of *Doorson*: in the latter case it was decided on the basis of information contained in the case file itself that the witnesses Y.15 and Y.16—who were both civilians, and who knew the accused personally—had sufficient reason to believe that he might resort to violence, and they were heard in the presence of counsel (see the above-mentioned *Doorson* judgment, pp 454–5, para 25, pp 455–6, para 28, and pp 470–1, paras 71 and 73).

In addition, in the latter case other evidence providing positive identification of the accused as the perpetrator of the crimes charged was available from sources unrelated to the anonymous witnesses (ibid, pp 458–9, para 34, and p 472, para 76).

65. Against this background the Court cannot find that the proceedings taken as a whole were fair.

C. CONCLUSION

66. There has been a violation of Article 6 para 1 taken together with Article 6 para 3 (d)...

NOTES

1 The Court was composed of President Bernhardt and Judges: Russo, Foighel, Repik, Jungwiert, and Levits. Judges Matscher and Valticos issued a joint dissenting opinion in which they expressed the view that the case was a 'borderline' one. However, they found no violation of Article 6 because, '...this was a case of armed robbery and it is understandable that the witnesses—even though they were police officers—should be in fear of reprisals from trigger-happy criminals.' In his dissenting opinion Judge Van Dijk concluded that the applicants had received a fair trial as, *inter alia*, the police officers had been interrogated by the investigating judge and the Court of Appeal had assessed the threat of reprisals against the officers.

2 Should police officers generally be expected to identify themselves and give evidence in open court?

3 The fundamental criterion applied by the Court in the above judgment was that articulated in paragraph 55.

4 In the earlier case of *Doorson v Netherlands*, 1996-II, the police had launched an investigation into drug trafficking in Amsterdam. Drug users would only give the police information on their suppliers if the informants remained anonymous (in the light of past experience they feared violence from the suppliers). Information was given to the police regarding the applicant and he was arrested. He was eventually convicted, by the Amsterdam Regional Court, of drug trafficking on the basis of an identified witness who appeared in court and was subject to defence and prosecution questioning (his evidence was very equivocal) and two anonymous witnesses (Y.15 and Y.16) who had been heard by the investigating judge (the applicant's lawyer had left the hearing before they arrived, late, to give their evidence). The applicant appealed to the Amsterdam Court of Appeal and his lawyer was able to question Y.15 and Y.16 in the presence of the investigating judge (however their identities were not disclosed). Both these witnesses stated that the applicant had sold them illegal drugs. The Court of Appeal found the applicant guilty of selling heroin and cocaine on the basis of, *inter alia*, the evidence of Y.15 and Y.16, police information regarding his illegal activities, and the evidence of the identified witness before the Regional Court. The applicants complaint of a breach of Articles 6(1) and 6(3)(d) was rejected by the Commission (by 15 votes to 12). A large majority of the Court (7 votes to 2) also found no breach of these provisions.

73. In the instant case the anonymous witnesses were questioned at the appeals stage in the presence of counsel by an investigating judge who was aware of their identity . . . even if the defence was not. She noted, in the official record of her findings dated 19 November 1990, circumstances on the basis of which the Court of Appeal was able to draw conclusions as to the reliability of their evidence . . . Counsel was not only present, but he was put in a position to ask the witnesses whatever questions he considered to be in the interests of the defence except in so far as they might lead to the disclosure of their identity, and these questions were all answered . . .

74. While it would clearly have been preferable for the applicant to have attended the questioning of the witnesses, the Court considers, on balance, that the Amsterdam Court of Appeal was entitled to consider that the interests of the applicant were in this respect outweighed by the need to ensure the safety of the witnesses. More generally, the Convention does not preclude identification—for the purposes of Article 6 para 3 (d) (art 6-3-d)—of an accused with his counsel . . .

75. In addition, although it is normally desirable that witnesses should identify a person suspected of serious crimes in person if there is any doubt about his identity, it should be noted in the present case that Y.15 and Y.16 identified the applicant from a photograph which he himself had acknowledged to be of himself . . . moreover, both gave descriptions of his appearance and dress . . .
  It follows from the above considerations that in the circumstances the 'counterbalancing' procedure followed by the judicial authorities in obtaining the evidence of witnesses Y.15 and Y.16 must be considered sufficient to have enabled the defence to challenge the evidence of the anonymous witnesses and attempt to cast doubt on the reliability of their statements, which it did in open court by, among other things, drawing attention to the fact that both were drug addicts . . .

76. Finally, it should be recalled that even when 'counterbalancing' procedures are found to compensate sufficiently the handicaps under which the defence labours, a conviction should not be based either solely or to a decisive extent on anonymous statements. That, however, is not the case here: it is sufficiently clear that the national court did not base its finding of guilt solely or to a decisive extent on the evidence of Y.15 and Y.16 . . .
  Furthermore, evidence obtained from witnesses under conditions in which the rights of the defence cannot be secured to the extent normally required by the Convention should be

treated with extreme care. The Court is satisfied that this was done in the criminal proceedings leading to the applicant's conviction, as is reflected in the express declaration by the Court of Appeal that it had treated the statements of Y.15 and Y.16 'with the necessary caution and circumspection'...

The applicant, through his lawyer, clearly had a greater opportunity to challenge the testimony and credibility of the anonymous witnesses (Y.15 and Y.16) in this case than the applicants did in *Van Mechelen* regarding the anonymous police officers.

5 The Committee of Ministers promulgated a Recommendation to member States ('Concerning Intimidation of Witnesses and the Rights of the Defence', R (97) 13) in 1997 to guide the latters' formulation of domestic criminal policy and legislation. The Recommendation stated that:

...10. Where available and in accordance with domestic law, anonymity of persons who might give evidence should be an exceptional measure. Where the guarantee of anonymity has been requested by such persons and/or temporarily granted by the competent authorities, criminal procedural law should provide for a verification procedure to maintain a fair balance between the needs of criminal proceedings and the rights of the defence. The defence should, through this procedure, have the opportunity to challenge the alleged need for anonymity of the witness, his credibility and the origin of his knowledge.

11. Anonymity should only be granted when the competent judicial authority, after hearing the parties, finds that:

i.   the life or freedom of the person involved is seriously threatened or, in the case of an under-cover agent, his potential to work in the future is seriously threatened; and
ii. the evidence is likely to be significant and the person appears to be credible.

12. Where appropriate, further measures should be available to protect witnesses giving evidence, including preventing identification of the witness by the defence eg by using screens, disguising his face or distorting his voice.

13. When anonymity has been granted, the conviction shall not be based solely or to a decisive extent on the evidence of such persons.

14. Where appropriate, special programmes, such as witness protection programmes, should be set up and made available to witnesses who need protection. The main objective of these programmes should be to safeguard the life and personal security of witnesses, their relatives and other persons close to them.

15. Witness protection programmes should offer various methods of protection; this may include giving witnesses and their relatives and other persons close to them an identity change, relocation, assistance in obtaining new jobs, providing them with bodyguards and other physical protection....

6 The full-time Court has followed the approach of its predecessor to Article 6(3)(d), for example in *Birutis and Others v Lithuania*, judgment of 28 June 2002. The three applicants/prisoners were charged with organizing and participating in a prison riot. The evidence against the first applicant consisted of written statements obtained by the investigating authorities from 17 anonymous witnesses, mostly other prisoners, statements made by three co-accused, and evidence given at his trial by five members of the prison staff. The evidence against the second applicant was broadly the same, however the only evidence against the third applicant comprised of written statements by six anonymous witnesses. The trial court

convicted all the applicants and imposed long prison sentences on them. The European Court held that:

> 28....as a general rule, paragraphs 1 and 3(d) of Article 6 require that the defendant be given an adequate and proper opportunity to challenge and question a witness against him, either when he makes his statements or at a later stage...

The judges were united in concluding that the conviction of the third applicant solely on the basis of anonymous evidence violated the **Doorson** principle. Furthermore, the trial court had failed to implement counterbalancing procedures, such as questioning the anonymous witnesses or scrutinizing how their evidence had been obtained, to safeguard the defence rights of the first and second applicants. Therefore, the Court found a breach of Article 6(3)(d) had occurred in respect of each applicant.

Article 6(3)(e): provision of free interpretation

Luedicke, Belkacem and Koc v Germany A.29 (1978)
European Court of Human Rights

The three applicants were non-German nationals (respectively a British citizen, an Algerian citizen, and a Turkish citizen) who had been convicted of various offences (a road traffic offence, assault, and grievous bodily harm) by German courts. They were not fluent in German therefore interpreters had been provided for their trials. After conviction the courts ordered the applicants to pay the costs of interpretation. The applicants complained to the Commission which was unanimous in finding a violation of Article 6(3)(e).

> 38....In its report, the Commission expressed the unanimous opinion that the decisions challenged by the applicants were in breach of Article 6 para 3(e) (art 6-3-e). The Commission takes this provision to mean that every accused person who 'cannot understand or speak the language used in court' must be granted the free assistance of an interpreter and may not have payment of the resulting costs subsequently claimed back from him.
>
> The Government contest the correctness of this opinion. They submit that while Article 6 para 3(e) (art 6-3-e) exempts the accused from paying in advance for the expenses incurred by using an interpreter, it does not prevent him from being made to bear such expenses once he has been convicted.
>
> 39. For the purposes of interpreting Article 6 para 3(e) (art 6-3-e), the Court will be guided, as also were the Government and the Commission, by Articles 31 to 33 of the Vienna Convention of 23 May 1969 on the Law of Treaties (see the *Golder* judgment of 21 February 1975, Series A No 18, p 14, para 29). In order to decide the issue arising in the present proceedings, the Court will therefore seek to ascertain 'the ordinary meaning to be given to the terms' of Article 6 para 3(e) (art 6-3-e) 'in their context and in the light of its object and purpose' (Article 31 para 1 of the Vienna Convention).
>
> 40. The Court finds, as did the Commission, that the terms 'gratuitement'/'free' in Article 6 para 3(e) (art 6-3-e) have in themselves a clear and determinate meaning. In French, 'gratuitement' signifies 'd'une manière gratuite, qu'on donne pour rien, sans rétribution' (Littré, *Dictionnaire de la langue française*), 'dont on jouit sans payer' (Hatzfeld et Darmesteter, *Dictionnaire général de la langue française*), 'à titre gratuit, sans avoir rien à payer', the opposite of 'à titre onéreux' (Larousse, *Dictionnaire de la langue française*), 'd'une manière gratuite; sans rétribution, sans contrepartie'

(Robert, *Dictionnaire alphabétique et analogique de la langue française*). Similarly, in English, 'free' means 'without payment, gratuitous' (*Shorter Oxford Dictionary*), 'not costing or charging anything, given or furnished without cost or payment' (Webster's *Third New International Dictionary*).

Consequently, the Court cannot but attribute to the terms 'gratuitement' and 'free' the unqualified meaning they ordinarily have in both of the Court's official languages: these terms denote neither a conditional remission, nor a temporary exemption, nor a suspension, but a once and for all exemption or exoneration. It nevertheless remains to be determined whether, as the Government contend, the context as well as the object and purpose of the provision in issue negative the literal interpretation.

41. According to the Government, all the rights enumerated in Article 6 para 3 (art 6-3) are concerned with criminal proceedings and become devoid of substance once those proceedings, the fair conduct of which they are to guarantee, have been terminated by a final and binding judgment. The Government submitted that what are involved are certain minimum rights which—in specifying the content of the right to a fair trial as enshrined in Article 6 para 1 (art 6-1)—are granted only to an accused ('everyone charged with a criminal offence', 'tout accusé'). The Government likewise place reliance on the presumption of innocence, which is enunciated in Article 6 para 2 (art 6-2) and which is rebutted on the final and binding conviction of the accused. Their reasoning is that the various guarantees of a fair trial, because they are intended to enable the accused to preserve the presumption of innocence, lapse at the same time as that presumption. In the Government's submission, the costs of the proceedings constitute a consequence of the conviction and accordingly fall entirely outside the ambit of Article 6 (art 6).

42. The Court notes that, for the purpose of ensuring a fair trial, paragraph 3 of Article 6 (art 6-3) enumerates certain rights ('minimum rights'/'notamment') accorded to the accused (a person 'charged with a criminal offence'). Nonetheless, it does not thereby follow, as far as sub-paragraph (e) is concerned, that the accused person may be required to pay the interpretation costs once he has been convicted. To read Article 6 para 3(e) (art 6-3-e) as allowing the domestic courts to make a convicted person bear these costs would amount to limiting in time the benefit of the Article and in practice, as was rightly emphasised by the Delegates of the Commission, to denying that benefit to any accused person who is eventually convicted. Such an interpretation would deprive Article 6 para 3(e) (art 6-3-e) of much of its effect, for it would leave in existence the disadvantages that an accused who does not understand or speak the language used in court suffers as compared with an accused who is familiar with that language—these being the disadvantages that Article 6 para 3(e) (art 6-3-e) is specifically designed to attenuate.

Furthermore, it cannot be excluded that the obligation for a convicted person to pay interpretation costs may have repercussions on the exercise of his right to a fair trial as safeguarded by Article 6 (art 6) (see the *Golder* judgment of 21 February 1975, Series A No 18, p 18, para 36), even if, as in the Federal Republic of Germany, an interpreter is appointed as a matter of course to assist every accused person who is not conversant with the language of the court. Making such an appointment admittedly eliminates in principle the serious drawbacks that would arise were an accused to defend himself in person in a language he did not master or fully master rather than incurring additional costs. Nevertheless, as was pointed out by the Delegates of the Commission, the risk remains that in some borderline cases the appointment or not of an interpreter might depend on the attitude taken by the accused, which might in turn be influenced by the fear of financial consequences.

Hence, it would run counter not only to the ordinary meaning of the terms 'free'/'gratuitement' but also to the object and purpose of Article 6 (art 6), and in particular of paragraph 3(e) (art 6-3-e) thereof, if this latter paragraph were to be reduced to the guarantee of a right to provisional exemption from payment—not preventing the domestic courts from making a convicted person bear the interpretation costs—, since the right to a fair trial which Article 6 (art 6) seeks to safeguard would itself be adversely affected....

48. Before the Court a difference of opinion emerged between the Government and the Commission as to which costs come within the scope of Article 6 para 3(e) (art 6-3-e). In the Government's submission, Article 6 para 3(e) (art 6-3-e) 'unambiguously and expressly settles the assistance of an interpreter at the oral hearing (audience)' but does not apply to other interpretation costs.

The Government's contention, the correctness of which is contested by the Delegates, cannot be accepted by the Court. Article 6 para 3(e) (art 6-3-e) does not state that every accused person has the right to receive the free assistance of an interpreter at the oral hearing (à l'audience); it states that this right is accorded to him 'if he cannot understand or speak the language used in court' ('s'il ne comprend pas ou ne parle pas la langue employée à l'audience'). As was pointed out by the Delegates, the latter words do no more than indicate the conditions for the granting of the free assistance of an interpreter. Furthermore, the English text 'used in court', being wider than the French expression 'employée à l'audience' (literally translated as 'used at the hearing'), furnishes an additional argument in this respect.

Construed in the context of the right to a fair trial guaranteed by Article 6, paragraph 3(e) (art 6-3-e) signifies that an accused who cannot understand or speak the language used in court has the right to the free assistance of an interpreter for the translation or interpretation of all those documents or statements in the proceedings instituted against him which it is necessary for him to understand in order to have the benefit of a fair trial.

49. In this connection, certain differences exist between the three cases.

Mr Luedicke had to pay DM 225.40 by way of interpretation costs, including DM 154.60 in respect of the oral hearing ... The representatives appearing before the Court did not provide any details as to the nature of the remaining balance; accordingly, the Court cannot conclude that this balance falls outside the scope of the guarantee in Article 6 para 3(e) (art 6-3-e).

As regards Mr Koç, the interpretation costs are exclusively attributed to three hearings before the Assize Court attached to the Aachen Regional Court and amount respectively to DM 311.50 and DM 510.50 and DM 112.50 ... Therefore, these costs indisputably come within the ambit of Article 6 para 3(e) (art 6-3-e).

The interpretation costs awarded against Mr Belkacem result from four distinct procedural steps, namely, the accused's appearance before the judge (DM 33.25), the review of his detention on remand (DM 67.60), the translation of the indictment (DM 90.20) and the trial hearing (DM 130.90) (see paragraph 22 above). In the Court's opinion, Article 6 para 3(e) (art 6-3-e) covers all these costs.

50. Accordingly, the Court concludes that the contested decisions of the German courts were in breach of Article 6 para 3(e) (art 6-3-e) of the Convention. . . .'

NOTES

1 The Court was composed of President Wiarda and Judges: Mosler, Pedersen, Bindschedler-Robert, Evrigenis, Teitgen, and Lagergren.

2 The Court's unwillingness to accept the German Government's narrow conception of the scope of this right should be commended. In the Court's judgment the right encompasses the provision of translation/interpretation facilities covering more than just the oral aspects of a criminal trial (paragraph 48) and it is not conditional on the defendant being acquitted (paragraph 42). Once again, the Court's ruling sought to make Convention rights effective in practice.

3 The Court also found Germany to be in breach of this right in *Öztürk* (p 371).

4 The full-time Court has emphasized the fundamental role of trial judges in ensuring that defendants who do not understand the language of the court are provided with

effective interpretation assistance. In *Cuscani v UK*, judgment of 24 September 2002, the applicant was an Italian national with a very limited command of English. He had been the manager of a restaurant in Newcastle-upon-Tyne. The authorities charged him with various offences involving the alleged evasion of hundreds of thousands of pounds of taxes. He was granted legal aid and represented by a Queen's Counsel, junior counsel, and solicitors. At his trial Cuscani pleaded guilty, on the advice of his counsel. During that hearing his counsel informed the judge of Cuscani's poor English and asked the court to direct that an interpreter be present at subsequent hearings. The court so ordered. However, when the trial resumed a few weeks later for sentencing no interpreter was present. Cuscani's counsel accepted that the hearing should proceed without an interpreter. The judge asked if there was anyone in court who knew the defendant and was fluent in Italian and English. Cuscani's counsel, without consulting him, replied that Cuscani's brother (who was present) could provide translation if required. In fact the brother was never asked to provide any interpretation during the subsequent hearing at which Cuscani was sentenced to four years' imprisonment. The European Court was unanimous in finding that those proceedings violated Article 6(3)(e).

38.... in the Court's opinion the verification of the applicant's need for interpretation facilities was a matter for the judge to determine in consultation with the applicant, especially since he had been alerted to counsel's own difficulties in communicating with the applicant.

9

ARTICLE 7   NO PUNISHMENT WITHOUT LAW

Whilst there has not been a large amount of case-law regarding this Article, the Court has provided significant rulings. The Court has endorsed the ability of domestic judges to develop the scope of criminal offences to reflect changing conditions (*CR*). Also, as we have seen in previous chapters regarding other Convention provisions, the Court has held that key elements of this Article have an autonomous meaning (e.g. *Welch*). The Court has had to adjudicate on domestic criminal proceedings brought against former leaders (*Streletz*) and military personnel (*Korbely*) of the communist totalitarian regimes previously controlling many of the newer member States.

Article 7(1)

CR v UK A.335-C (1995)
European Court of Human Rights

The applicant married his wife in 1984. They separated for a short time in 1987, but were reconciled. On 21 October 1989 the applicant's wife left their home, with their son, and went to live with her parents. She left a note for the applicant informing him that she intended to seek a divorce. On 12 November 1989 the applicant forced his way into the parents' house and attempted to have sexual intercourse with the wife against her will. In the course of the attempt he assaulted her, by squeezing her neck with his hands. The applicant was charged with attempted rape (under section 1(1) of the Sexual Offences (Amendment) Act 1976 rape was defined as occurring when a man 'has unlawful sexual intercourse with a woman who at the time of the intercourse does not consent to it...') and assault occasioning actual bodily harm. At his trial, in the summer of 1990, the applicant submitted that the charge of rape was not one which was known to the law because the victim was his wife. He relied upon a statement by Sir Matthew Hale CJ in his *History of the Pleas of the Crown* (published in 1736): 'But the husband cannot be guilty of rape committed by himself upon his lawful wife, for by their matrimonial consent and contract the wife hath given up herself in this kind unto her husband, which she cannot retract.' However, the trial judge, Owen J, cited more recent cases to support the view that in certain circumstances wives could revoke their consent to sexual intercourse with their husbands. He identified three such situations: (a) by a court order, (b) by agreement between the parties, and (c) a withdrawal of either party from cohabitation accompanied by a clear indication that consent to sexual intercourse had been terminated. The judge considered that both (b) and (c) applied to the wife of the applicant. In the light of this ruling the applicant pleaded guilty and was sentenced to three years' imprisonment. His appeal was dismissed by a unanimous Court of Appeal. The House of Lords was also united in rejecting his final appeal (*R v R* [1991] 4 All ER 481). On behalf of the House, Lord Keith of Kinkel stated that:

> For over 150 years after the publication of Hale's work there appeared to have been no reported case in which judicial consideration was given to his proposition. The first such case was *R v Clarence* [1888] 22 Queen's Bench Division 23, [1886–90] All England Law Reports 133 . . . It may be taken that the proposition was generally regarded as an accurate statement of the common law of England. The common law is, however, capable of evolving in the light of changing social, economic and cultural developments. Hale's proposition reflected the state of affairs in these respects at the time it was enunciated. Since then the status of women, and particularly of married women, has changed out of all recognition in various ways which are very familiar and upon which it is unnecessary to go into detail. Apart from property matters and the availability of matrimonial remedies, one of the most important changes is that marriage is in modern times regarded as a partnership of equals, and no longer one in which the wife was the subservient chattel of the husband. Hale's proposition involves that by marriage a wife gives her irrevocable consent to sexual intercourse with her husband under all circumstances and irrespective of the state of her health or how she happens to be feeling at the time. In modern times any reasonable person must regard that conception as quite unacceptable. . . .
>
> The position then is that that part of Hale's proposition which asserts that a wife cannot retract the consent to sexual intercourse which she gives on marriage has been departed from in a series of decided cases. On grounds of principle there is no good reason why the whole proposition should not be held inapplicable in modern times. The only question is whether section 1(1) of the 1976 Act presents an insuperable obstacle to that sensible course. The argument is that 'unlawful' in that subsection means outside the bond of marriage.
>
> . . . The fact is that it is clearly unlawful to have sexual intercourse with any woman without her consent, and that the use of the word in the subsection adds nothing. In my opinion there are no rational grounds for putting the suggested gloss on the word, and it should be treated as being mere surplusage in this enactment . . .
>
> I am therefore of the opinion that section 1 (1) of the 1976 Act presents no obstacle to this House declaring that in modern times the supposed marital exception in rape forms no part of the law of England. The Court of Appeal, Criminal Division, took a similar view [in the present case]. Towards the end of the judgment of that court Lord Lane CJ said . . . :
>
> > The remaining and no less difficult question is whether, despite that view, this is an area where the court should step aside to leave the matter to the parliamentary process. This is not the creation of a new offence, it is the removal of a common law fiction which has become anachronistic and offensive and we consider that it is our duty having reached that conclusion to act upon it.
>
> I respectfully agree. [Pp 483–490.]

The applicant complained to the Commission alleging a breach of Article 7 in that he had been convicted of conduct, attempted rape of his wife, which he argued did not constitute a criminal offence at that time. By 14 votes to 3, the Commission considered that there had been no breach of Article 7. The Court held that:

A. GENERAL PRINCIPLES

32. The guarantee enshrined in Article 7 (art 7), which is an essential element of the rule of law, occupies a prominent place in the Convention system of protection, as is underlined by the fact that no

derogation from it is permissible under Article 15 (art 15) in time of war or other public emergency. It should be construed and applied, as follows from its object and purpose, in such a way as to provide effective safeguards against arbitrary prosecution, conviction and punishment.

33. Accordingly, as the Court held in its *Kokkinakis v Greece* judgment of 25 May 1993 (Series A No 260-A, p 22, para 52), Article 7 (art 7) is not confined to prohibiting the retrospective application of the criminal law to an accused's disadvantage: it also embodies, more generally, the principle that only the law can define a crime and prescribe a penalty (*nullum crimen, nulla poena sine lege*) and the principle that the criminal law must not be extensively construed to an accused's detriment, for instance by analogy. From these principles it follows that an offence must be clearly defined in the law. In its aforementioned judgment the Court added that this requirement is satisfied where the individual can know from the wording of the relevant provision and, if need be, with the assistance of the courts' interpretation of it, what acts and omissions will make him criminally liable. The Court thus indicated that when speaking of 'law' Article 7 (art 7) alludes to the very same concept as that to which the Convention refers elsewhere when using that term, a concept which comprises written as well as unwritten law and implies qualitative requirements, notably those of accessibility and foreseeability (see, as a recent authority, the *Tolstoy Miloslavsky v UK* judgment of 13 July 1995, Series A No 316-B, pp 71–2, para 37).

34. However clearly drafted a legal provision may be, in any system of law, including criminal law, there is an inevitable element of judicial interpretation. There will always be a need for elucidation of doubtful points and for adaptation to changing circumstances. Indeed, in the United Kingdom, as in the other Convention States, the progressive development of the criminal law through judicial law-making is a well entrenched and necessary part of legal tradition. Article 7 (art 7) of the Convention cannot be read as outlawing the gradual clarification of the rules of criminal liability through judicial interpretation from case to case, provided that the resultant development is consistent with the essence of the offence and could reasonably be foreseen.

B. APPLICATION OF THE FOREGOING PRINCIPLES

35. The applicant maintained that the general common law principle that a husband could not be found guilty of rape upon his wife, albeit subject to certain limitations, was still effective on 12 November 1989, when he committed the acts which gave rise to the charge of attempted rape...A succession of court decisions before and also after that date...had affirmed the general principle of immunity. It was clearly beyond doubt that as at 12 November 1989 no change in the law had been effected, although one was being mooted. The removal of the immunity by the Court of Appeal on 14 March 1991 and the House of Lords on 23 October 1991 occurred by way of direct reversal, not clarification, of the law.

When the House of Commons debated the Bill for the Sexual Offences (Amendment) Act 1976...different views on the marital immunity were expressed. On the advice of the Minister of State to await a report of the Criminal Law Revision Committee, an amendment that would have abolished the immunity was withdrawn and never voted upon. In its report, which was not presented until 1984, the Criminal Law Revision Committee recommended that the immunity should be maintained and that a new exception should be created.

In 1988, when considering certain amendments to the 1976 Act, Parliament had the opportunity to take out the word 'unlawful' in section 1(1)(a)...or to introduce a new provision on marital intercourse, but took no action in this respect.

On 17 September 1990 the Law Commission provisionally recommended that the immunity rule be abolished...However, the debate was pre-empted by the Court of Appeal's and the House of Lords' rulings in the applicant's case...In the applicant's submission, these rulings altered the law retrospectively, which would not have been the case had the Law Commission's proposal been implemented by Parliament. Consequently, he concluded, when Parliament in 1994 removed the word 'unlawful' from section 1 of the 1976 Act...it did not merely restate the law as it had been in 1976.

36. The applicant further argued that in examining his complaint under Article 7 para 1 (art 7-1) of the Convention, the Court should not consider his conduct in relation to any of the exceptions to the immunity rule. The issue was never resolved by the national courts, as the sole ground on which the applicant's conviction rested was in fact the removal of the common law fiction by the Court of Appeal and the House of Lords.

37. Should a foreseeability test akin to that under Article 10 para 2 (art 10-2) apply in the instant case, the applicant was of the opinion that it had not been satisfied. Although the Court of Appeal and the House of Lords did not create a new offence or change the basic ingredients of the offence of rape, they were extending an existing offence to include conduct which until then was excluded by the common law. They could not be said to have adapted the law to a new kind of conduct but rather to a change of social attitudes. To extend the criminal law, solely on such a basis, to conduct which was previously lawful was precisely what Article 7 (art 7) of the Convention was designed to prevent. Moreover, the applicant stressed, it was impossible to specify with precision when the change in question had occurred. In November 1989, change by judicial interpretation was not foreseen by the Law Commission, which considered that a parliamentary enactment would be necessary.

38. The Government and the Commission were of the view that by November 1989 there was significant doubt as to the validity of the alleged marital immunity for rape. This was an area where the law had been subject to progressive development and there were strong indications that still wider interpretation by the courts of the inroads on the immunity was probable. In particular, given the recognition of women's equality of status with men in marriage and outside it and of their autonomy over their own bodies, the adaptation of the ingredients of the offence of rape was reasonably foreseeable, with appropriate legal advice, to the applicant. He was not convicted of conduct which did not constitute a criminal offence at the time when it was committed.

In addition, the Government pointed out, on the basis of agreed facts Mr Justice Owen had found that there was an implied agreement between the applicant and his wife to separation and to withdrawal of the consent to intercourse. The circumstances in his case were thus covered by the exceptions to the immunity rule already stated by the English courts.

39. The Court notes that the applicant's conviction for attempted rape was based on the statutory offence of rape in section 1 of the 1956 Act, as further defined in section 1(1) of the 1976 Act...The applicant does not dispute that the conduct for which he was convicted would have constituted attempted rape within the meaning of the statutory definition of rape as applicable at the time, had the victim not been his wife. His complaint under Article 7 (art 7) of the Convention relates solely to the fact that he could not avail himself of the marital immunity under common law because, so he submitted, it had been retrospectively abolished.

40. It is to be observed that a crucial issue in the judgment of the Court of Appeal...related to the definition of rape in section 1(1)(a) of the 1976 Act: 'unlawful sexual intercourse with a woman who at the time of the intercourse does not consent to it'. The question was whether 'removal' of the marital immunity would conflict with the statutory definition of rape, in particular whether it would be prevented by the word 'unlawful'. The Court of Appeal carefully examined various strands of interpretation of the provision in the case-law, including the argument that the term 'unlawful' excluded intercourse within marriage from the definition of rape. In this connection, the Court recalls that it is in the first place for the national authorities, notably the courts, to interpret and apply national law (see, for instance, the *Kemmache v France (No 3)* judgment of 24 November 1994, Series A No 296-C, pp 86–7, para 37). It sees no reason to disagree with the Court of Appeal's conclusion, which was subsequently upheld by the House of Lords...that the word 'unlawful' in the definition of rape

was merely surplusage and did not inhibit them from 'removing a common law fiction which had become anachronistic and offensive' and from declaring that 'a rapist remains a rapist subject to the criminal law, irrespective of his relationship with his victim'...

41. The decisions of the Court of Appeal and then the House of Lords did no more than continue a perceptible line of case-law development dismantling the immunity of a husband from prosecution for rape upon his wife...There was no doubt under the law as it stood on 12 November 1989 that a husband who forcibly had sexual intercourse with his wife could, in various circumstances, be found guilty of rape. Moreover, there was an evident evolution, which was consistent with the very essence of the offence, of the criminal law through judicial interpretation towards treating such conduct generally as within the scope of the offence of rape. This evolution had reached a stage where judicial recognition of the absence of immunity had become a reasonably foreseeable development of the law...

42. The essentially debasing character of rape is so manifest that the result of the decisions of the Court of Appeal and the House of Lords—that the applicant could be convicted of attempted rape, irrespective of his relationship with the victim—cannot be said to be at variance with the object and purpose of Article 7 (art 7) of the Convention, namely to ensure that no one should be subjected to arbitrary prosecution, conviction or punishment (see paragraph 32 above). What is more, the abandonment of the unacceptable idea of a husband being immune against prosecution for rape of his wife was in conformity not only with a civilised concept of marriage but also, and above all, with the fundamental objectives of the Convention, the very essence of which is respect for human dignity and human freedom.

43. Having reached this conclusion, the Court does not find it necessary to enquire into whether the facts in the applicant's case were covered by the exceptions to the immunity rule already made by the English courts before 12 November 1989.

44. In short, the Court, like the Government and the Commission, finds that the national courts' decisions that the applicant could not invoke immunity to escape conviction and sentence for attempted rape upon his wife did not give rise to a violation of his rights under Article 7 para 1 (art 7-1) of the Convention.

FOR THESE REASONS, THE COURT UNANIMOUSLY

Holds that there has been no violation of Article 7 para 1 (art 7-1) of the Convention.

NOTES

1 The Court was composed of President Ryssdal and Judges: Gölcüklü, Russo, De Meyer, Martens, Bigi, Freeland, Jambrek, and Lohmus.

2 The Court's judgment in *CR* upholds the 'gradual clarification' of rules of criminal liability, provided the evolution is 'consistent with the essence of the offence and could reasonably be foreseen', as being compatible with the requirements of Article 7(1). However, determining whether a particular evolution is within these broad parameters is not an easy task. To what extent do you think the Court's conclusion in the above case was influenced by its abhorrence of the act of rape?

3 Parliament adopted a new, and wider, statutory definition of rape in the Criminal Justice and Public Order Act 1994: '1(1) It is an offence for a man to rape a woman or another man. (2) A man commits rape if—(a) he has sexual intercourse with a person...who at the time of the intercourse does not consent to it...'

4 The case of *Kokkinakis v Greece* is examined below (at p 598). The Court, by 8 votes to 1, found that the Greek offence of proselytism defined by Law No 1363/1938 did not breach the certainty requirements of Article 7(1).

5 A Grand Chamber, by 15 votes to 2, found a breach of Article 7 because of ambiguities in the law and practice governing the actual duration of a life sentence in *Kafkaris v Cyprus*, judgment of 12 February 2008. The applicant was convicted of three murders (a 'contract' killing of a father and his two children) in 1989. The Assize Court ruled that this meant imprisonment for the rest of the applicant's life. However, when the applicant went to prison he was given a notice stating that he would be eligible for release in 2002 (if he maintained good conduct in prison). He was not released in 2002. The Grand Chamber held that:

> 150. ... at the time the applicant committed the offence, the relevant Cypriot law taken as a whole was not formulated with sufficient precision as to enable the applicant to discern, even with appropriate advice, to a degree that was reasonable in the circumstances, the scope of the penalty of life imprisonment and the manner of its execution. Accordingly, there has been a violation of Article 7 of the Convention in this respect.

Hence, domestic law must provide adequate clarity in respect of both the definition of offences and their penalties.

....

Streletz, Kessler and Krenz v Germany judgment of 22 March 2001
European Court of Human Rights

The applicants were the former Deputy Defence Minister (from 1979 to 1989), the Minister of Defence (from 1985 to 1989), and President of the Council of State and the National Defence Council (October–December 1989) of the former German Democratic Republic (GDR). Between 1949 and the construction of the Berlin Wall in 1961 approximately two-and-a-half million persons fled from East Germany to the Federal Republic of Germany (FRG). Thereafter, the GDR authorities maintained a highly sophisticated security system along the border with West Germany including anti-personnel minefields and automatic-fire installations. East German border guards through their training and political instruction were under orders 'not to permit border crossings, to arrest border violators or to annihilate them and to protect the State borders at all costs...' (para 19 of the judgment). Western estimates of the number of persons killed whilst trying to cross the border varied between 264 and 938 due to the secrecy surrounding these events by the GDR authorities. Following the collapse of the GDR, in the autumn of 1989, a newly elected parliament requested the FRG to ensure that criminal prosecutions would be initiated against persons who had committed injustices under the rule of the East German Communist Party. In October 1990 Germany was reunited (under the FRG). Subsequently, during 1993, the Berlin Regional Court sentenced the first and second applicants to periods of imprisonment (five years and seven years) for incitement to commit intentional homicide on the grounds of shared responsibility for the deaths of a number of young persons killed (by anti-personnel mines or shot by border guards) between 1971 and 1989. The Regional Court initially applied the Criminal Code of the former GDR to determine the applicants' guilt and then substituted the FRG's Criminal Code as it was more lenient. The convictions were upheld by the Federal Court of Justice and the Federal Constitutional Court. The third applicant was sentenced to six years' imprisonment for intentional homicide as an indirect principal, on the basis of his participation in decisions of the Political Bureau and the National Defence Council (between 1984 and 1986) on the GDR's border-policing regime and the consequent deadly shooting of four young persons trying to cross to the West between 1984 and 1989. The Berlin Regional Court's decision was also upheld on appeal.

The applicants petitioned the former Commission alleging that their actions did not constitute offences, at the times when they were committed, under either national (i.e. GDR) or international law; and their convictions by FRG courts breached, *inter alia*, Article 7 (no punishment without law). The applications were transferred to the new Court where a Chamber, none of the parties objecting, relinquished them to the Grand Chamber. Before the Court the applicants argued that Article 7 had been violated because, *inter alia*, (a) their convictions after reunification were not foreseeable, (b) their actions did not constitute offences under GDR criminal law, and (c) neither did their actions amount to offences under international law (in the majority of States access to borders was forbidden/strictly regulated and the use of firearms by border guards authorized).

51.…it notes that one special feature of the present case is that its background is the transition between two States governed by two different legal systems, and that after reunification the German courts convicted the applicants for crimes they had committed in their capacity as leaders of the GDR.

…

(a) National law

73. The Court considers that recourse to anti-personnel mines and automatic-fire systems, in view of their automatic and indiscriminate effect, and the categorical nature of the border guards' orders to 'annihilate border violators (*Grenzverletzer*) and protect the border at all costs', flagrantly infringed the fundamental rights enshrined in Articles 19 and 30 of the GDR's Constitution, which were essentially confirmed by the GDR's Criminal Code (Article 213) and successive statutes on the GDR's borders (section 17(2) of the People's Police Act 1968 and section 27(2) of the State Borders Act 1982). This State practice was also in breach of the obligation to respect human rights and the other international obligations of the GDR, which, on 8 November 1974, had ratified the International Covenant on Civil and Political Rights, expressly recognising the right to life and to the freedom of movement…regard being had to the fact that it was almost impossible for ordinary citizens to leave the GDR legally. Even though the use of anti-personnel mines and automatic-fire systems had ceased in about 1984, the border guards' orders remained unchanged until the fall of the Berlin Wall in November 1989.

74. The Court further notes that, in justification, the applicants relied on the order to fire which they themselves had issued to the border guards and on the ensuing practice, on account of which they had been convicted. However, according to the general principles of law, defendants are not entitled to justify the conduct which has given rise to their conviction simply by showing that such conduct did in fact take place and therefore formed a practice.

75. Moreover, irrespective of the GDR's responsibility as a State, the applicants' acts as individuals were defined as criminal by Article 95 of the GDR's Criminal Code, which already provided in its 1968 version, in terms repeated in 1977: 'Any person whose conduct violates human or fundamental rights…may not plead statute law, an order or written instructions in justification; he shall be held criminally responsible.'

76. There is accordingly no doubt that the applicants bore individual responsibility for the acts in question.

77. However, the applicants argued that in view of the reality of the situation in the GDR their conviction by the German courts had not been foreseeable and that it had been absolutely impossible

for them to foresee that they would one day be called to account in a criminal court because of a change of circumstances.

78. The Court is not convinced by that argument. The broad divide between the GDR's legislation and its practice was to a great extent the work of the applicants themselves. Because of the very senior positions they occupied in the State apparatus, they evidently could not have been ignorant of the GDR's Constitution and legislation, or of its international obligations and the criticisms of its border-policing regime that had been made internationally...Moreover, they themselves had implemented or maintained that regime, by superimposing on the statutory provisions, published in the GDR's Official Gazette, secret orders and service instructions on the consolidation and improvement of the border-protection installations and the use of firearms. In the order to fire given to border guards they had insisted on the need to protect the GDR's borders 'at all costs' and to arrest 'border violators' or 'annihilate' them...The applicants were therefore directly responsible for the situation which obtained at the border between the two German States from the beginning of the 1960s until the fall of the Berlin Wall in 1989.

79. Moreover, the fact that the applicants had not been prosecuted in the GDR, and were not prosecuted and convicted by the German courts until after the reunification, on the basis of the legal provisions applicable in the GDR at the material time, does not in any way mean that their acts were not offences according to the law of the GDR.

80. In that connection, the Court notes that the problem Germany had to deal with after reunification as regards the attitude to adopt vis-à-vis persons who had committed crimes under a former regime has also arisen for a number of other States which have gone through a transition to a democratic regime.

81. The Court considers that it is legitimate for a State governed by the rule of law to bring criminal proceedings against persons who have committed crimes under a former regime; similarly, the courts of such a State, having taken the place of those which existed previously, cannot be criticised for applying and interpreting the legal provisions in force at the material time in the light of the principles governing a State subject to the rule of law.

...

84. It should also be pointed out that the parliament of the GDR democratically elected in 1990 had expressly requested the German legislature to ensure that criminal prosecutions would be brought in respect of the injustices committed by the SED [East German Communist Party]. That makes it reasonable to suppose that, even if the reunification of Germany had not taken place, a democratic regime taking over from the SED regime in the GDR would have applied the GDR's legislation and prosecuted the applicants, as the German courts did after reunification.

85. Moreover, regard being had to the pre-eminence of the right to life in all international instruments on the protection of human rights...including the Convention itself, in which the right to life is guaranteed by Article 2, the Court considers that the German courts' strict interpretation of the GDR's legislation in the present case was compatible with Article 7 § 1 of the Convention....

87. The Court considers that a State practice such as the GDR's border-policing policy, which flagrantly infringes human rights and above all the right to life, the supreme value in the international hierarchy of human rights, cannot be covered by the protection of Article 7 § 1 of the Convention. That practice, which emptied of its substance the legislation on which it was supposed to be based, and which was imposed on all organs of the GDR, including its judicial bodies, cannot be described as 'law' within the meaning of Article 7 of the Convention.

88. The Court accordingly takes the view that the applicants, who, as leaders of the GDR, had created the appearance of legality emanating from the GDR's legal system but then implemented or

continued a practice which flagrantly disregarded the very principles of that system, cannot invoke the protection of Article 7 § 1 of the Convention. To reason otherwise would run counter to the object and purpose of that provision, which is to ensure that no one is subjected to arbitrary prosecution, conviction or punishment.

89. Having regard to all of the above considerations, the Court holds that at the time when they were committed the applicants' acts constituted offences defined with sufficient accessibility and foreseeability in GDR law.

(b) International law

i. Applicable rules

90. The Court considers that it is its duty to examine the present case from the standpoint of the principles of international law also, particularly those relating to the international protection of human rights, especially because the German courts used arguments grounded on those principles...

91. It is therefore necessary to consider whether, at the time when they were committed, the applicants' acts constituted offences defined with sufficient accessibility and foreseeability under international law, particularly the rules of international law on the protection of human rights.

ii. International protection of the right to life

92. The Court notes in the first place that in the course of the development of that protection the relevant conventions and other instruments have constantly affirmed the pre-eminence of the right to life.

93. Article 3 of the Universal Declaration on Human Rights of 10 December 1948, for example, provides: 'Everyone has the right to life.' That right was confirmed by the International Covenant on Civil and Political Rights of 16 December 1966, ratified by the GDR on 8 November 1974, Article 6 of which provides: 'Every human being has the inherent right to life' and 'No one shall be arbitrarily deprived of his life'. It is also included in the Convention, Article 2 § 1 of which provides:

> 'Everyone's right to life shall be protected by law. No one shall be deprived of his life intentionally save in the execution of a sentence of a court following his conviction of a crime for which this penalty is provided by law.'

94. The convergence of the above-mentioned instruments is significant: it indicates that the right to life is an inalienable attribute of human beings and forms the supreme value in the hierarchy of human rights.

95. However, the applicants alleged that their actions had been justified by the exceptions in Article 2 § 2 of the Convention, which provides:

> 'Deprivation of life shall not be regarded as inflicted in contravention of this article when it results from the use of force which is no more than absolutely necessary:
> '(a) in defence of any person from unlawful violence;
> '(b) in order to effect a lawful arrest or to prevent the escape of a person lawfully detained;
> '(c) in action lawfully taken for the purpose of quelling a riot or insurrection.'

96. The Court considers that, regard being had to the arguments set out above, the deaths of the fugitives were in no sense the result of a use of force which was 'absolutely necessary'; the State practice implemented in the GDR by the applicants did not protect anyone against unlawful violence, was not pursued in order to make any arrest that could be described as 'lawful' according to the law of the GDR and had nothing to do with the quelling of a riot or insurrection, as the fugitives' only aim was to leave the country.

97. It follows that the applicants' acts were not justified in any way under Article 2 § 2 of the Convention.

iii. International protection of the freedom of movement

98. Like Article 2 § 2 of Protocol No. 4 to the Convention, Article 12 § 2 of the International Covenant on Civil and Political Rights provides: 'Everyone shall be free to leave any country, including his own.' Restrictions on that right are authorised only where they are provided by law, are necessary to protect national security, public order, public health or morals or the rights and freedoms of others, and are consistent with the other rights recognised in the Covenant.

99. The applicants relied on those restrictions to justify the introduction and continued operation the GDR's border-policing regime.

100. However, the Court considers that in the present case none of the above exceptions applied. Firstly, the acts in issue were orders, given and executed, which were not compatible with either the Constitution or statute law. Secondly, it cannot be contended that a general measure preventing almost the entire population of a State from leaving was necessary to protect its security, or for that matter the other interests mentioned. Lastly, the way in which the GDR put into practice the prohibition barring its nationals from leaving the country and punished contravention of that policy was contrary to another right secured under the Covenant, namely the right to life guaranteed by Article 6, for those who were its victims.

101. Still in connection with the right to freedom of movement, the Court points out that when Hungary opened its border with Austria on 11 September 1989 it denounced a bilateral agreement between itself and the GDR, referring expressly to Articles 6 and 12 of the International Covenant and to Article 62 (fundamental change of circumstances) of the Vienna Convention on the Law of Treaties.

iv. The GDR's State responsibility and the applicants' individual responsibility

102. Thus, by installing anti-personnel mines and automatic-fire systems along the border, and by ordering border guards to 'annihilate border violators and protect the border at all costs', the GDR had set up a border-policing regime that clearly disregarded the need to preserve human life, which was enshrined in the GDR's Constitution and legislation, and the right to life protected by the above-mentioned international instruments; that regime likewise infringed the right to the freedom of movement mentioned in Article 12 of the International Covenant on Civil and Political Rights.

103. The State practice in issue was to a great extent the work of the applicants themselves, who, as political leaders, knew—or should have known—that it infringed both fundamental rights and human rights, since they could not have been ignorant of the legislation of their own country. Articles 8 and 19 § 2 of the 1968 Constitution already provided, respectively: 'The generally recognised rules of international law intended to promote peace and peaceful cooperation between peoples are binding on the State and every citizen' and 'Respect for and protection of the dignity and liberty of the person are required of all State bodies, all forces in society and every citizen'. Furthermore, as early as 1968 the first chapter of the Special Part of the Criminal Code included an introduction that provided: 'The merciless punishment of crimes against...humanity and human rights...is an indispensable prerequisite for stable peace in the world, for the restoration of faith in fundamental human rights and the dignity and worth of human beings, and for the preservation of the rights of all.' Similarly, as noted above (paragraph 78), the applicants could not have been ignorant of the international obligations entered into by the GDR or of the repeated international criticism of its border-policing regime.

104. If the GDR still existed, it would be responsible from the viewpoint of international law for the acts concerned. It remains to be established that alongside that State responsibility the applicants individually bore criminal responsibility at the material time. Even supposing that such responsibility

cannot be inferred from the above-mentioned international instruments on the protection of human rights, it may be deduced from those instruments when they are read together with Article 95 of the GDR's Criminal Code, which explicitly provided, and from as long ago as 1968 moreover, that individual criminal responsibility was to be borne by those who violated the GDR's international obligations or human rights and fundamental freedoms.

105. In the light of all of the above considerations, the Court considers that at the time when they were committed the applicants' acts also constituted offences defined with sufficient accessibility and foreseeability by the rules of international law on the protection of human rights.

106. In addition, the applicants' conduct could be considered, likewise under Article 7 § 1 of the Convention, from the standpoint of other rules of international law, notably those concerning crimes against humanity. However, the conclusion reached by the Court (see paragraph 105 above) makes consideration of that point unnecessary.

(c) Conclusion

107. Accordingly, the applicants' conviction by the German courts after the reunification was not in breach of Article 7 § 1.

108. In the light of that finding, the Court is not required to consider whether their convictions were justified under Article 7 § 2 of the Convention.

...

FOR THESE REASONS, THE COURT UNANIMOUSLY

1. Holds that there has been no violation of Article 7(1) of the Convention.

NOTES

1 The Grand Chamber was composed of President Wildhaber and Judges: Palm, Rozakis, Ress, Costa, Ferrari Bravo, Caflisch, Loucaides, Cabral Barreto, Jungwiert, Bratza, Zupancic, Vajic, Pellonpaa, Tsatsa-Nikolovska, Levits, and Kovler.

2 The judgment of the Grand Chamber, in the year of the fortieth anniversary of the construction of the Berlin Wall, revealed a clear condemnation of the practical failure of the former GDR regime to respect the basic human rights (enshrined in international, regional, and domestic legal rules) of its citizens. The irony of the applicants' complaints was that they were in essence challenging the application of their own regime's formal laws (retrospectively) to determine their criminal culpability. Of course, as the judgment vividly demonstrates, one of the great lies of the former communist regimes of Eastern Europe was the fundamental difference between the formal legal provisions in those States and the norms actually applied. In contrast the value of the Strasbourg system is that it seeks to ensure that member States give practical effect to those Convention rights that they have guaranteed to observe in their treatment of all persons within their jurisdictions. Consequently, the Court is a vital mechanism in ensuring that member governments do not develop a corrosive bifurcation between the public espousal of human rights and the neglect, or deliberate undermining, of those norms in official practices.

3 The same Grand Chamber delivered a similar judgment in the parallel case of **K-HW v Germany**, judgment of 22 March 2001. In this case the applicant was a former GDR border guard who, when aged 20, in 1972 had shot dead a person trying to swim across the border from East Berlin. The applicant was awarded an Order of Merit and given a bonus of 150 Marks by the GDR authorities for his actions. After the re-unification of Germany, he was convicted in 1993 of intentional homicide by the Berlin Regional Court and sentenced to one year and ten months' juvenile detention suspended on probation. The Grand Chamber, by 14 votes to 3, rejected the applicant's claim that his conviction violated Article 7. The dissentients, Judges Cabral Barreto, Pellonpaa, and Zupancic considered the applicant to be a low-level official who was a victim of the oppressive communist regime.

4   A Grand Chamber found that the domestic courts had not considered all the international law elements of a 'crime against humanity' when the applicant had been convicted of that offence for his actions in helping to suppress the 1956 Hungarian Revolution. At that time he was a military officer who had been commanded to go, with his subordinates, and recover control of the police building which had been occupied by armed revolutionaries. Three revolutionaries were shot dead by the applicant and his men. In 1994 the applicant was charged with a crime against humanity (by violating Article 3(1) of the Geneva Convention governing the Protection of Civilian Persons in Time of War (1949)) and ultimately sentenced to five years' imprisonment. He alleged a breach of Article 7 in *Korbely v Hungary*, judgment of 19 September 2008. By a large majority, 11 votes to 6, the Grand Chamber determined that the Hungarian courts had not examined, *inter alia*, whether the applicant's conduct was part of 'State action or policy', with the consequence that there had been a breach of Article 7 as it had '95. . . . not been shown that it was foreseeable that the applicant's acts constituted a crime against humanity under international law'. The dissenters criticized the majority for substituting their own findings of fact for those of the domestic courts. These divergent views within the Court reveal the complexity of scrutinizing highly sensitive criminal proceedings brought decades after the contested events.

5   In *Ould Dah v France*, decision of 30 March 2009, a Mauritanian army officer complained that his conviction for torturing prisoners in Mauritania, by a French court (after he went to France for a military training course), despite the fact that he had received an amnesty in Mauritania violated the foreseeability requirement of Article 7. The Court determined that his complaint was manifestly ill-founded as such amnesty laws were incompatible with the duty on States to investigate acts of torture. The applicant had fled France whilst on bail and was sentenced to ten years' imprisonment *in absentia*.

....

Welch v UK A.307-A (1995)
European Court of Human Rights

The applicant was arrested for suspected drugs offences in November 1986. On the day following his arrest he was charged with offences involving the importation of large amounts of cannabis. In February 1987 he was further charged with the offence of possession with intent to supply cocaine (alleged to have taken place on 3 November 1986) and in May 1987 he was also charged with conspiracy to obtain cocaine with intent to supply (between January and November 1986). In August 1987 he was found guilty on five counts and sentenced to 22 years' imprisonment. The judge also imposed a confiscation order, under the Drug Trafficking Offences Act 1986, on the applicant in the sum of £66,914 (in default of payment the applicant would be liable to serve a further period of two years' imprisonment). The Act came into force on 12 January 1987 and enabled the Crown Court to make confiscation orders in respect of 'any payment or other reward in connection with drug trafficking' received (whether before or after the commencement of the Act) by a person convicted of a drug trafficking offence after 12 January 1987. Subsequently, the Court of Appeal slightly reduced his sentence and the amount of the confiscation order. The applicant complained to the Commission alleging that the imposition of the confiscation order on him amounted to a retrospective criminal penalty in breach of Article 7(1). By 7 votes to 7 with the casting vote of the Acting President, the Commission found no violation of that Article. The Court determined that:

26. The Court first observes that the retrospective imposition of the confiscation order is not in dispute in the present case. The order was made following a conviction in respect of drugs offences which had been committed before the 1986 Act came into force... The only question to be determined therefore is whether the order constitutes a penalty within the meaning of Article 7 para 1 (art 7-1), second sentence.

27. The concept of a 'penalty' in this provision is, like the notions of 'civil rights and obligations' and 'criminal charge' in Article 6 para 1 (art 6-1), an autonomous Convention concept... To render the protection offered by Article 7 (art 7) effective, the Court must remain free to go behind appearances and assess for itself whether a particular measure amounts in substance to a 'penalty' within the meaning of this provision...

28. The wording of Article 7 para 1 (art 7-1), second sentence, indicates that the starting-point in any assessment of the existence of a penalty is whether the measure in question is imposed following conviction for a 'criminal offence'. Other factors that may be taken into account as relevant in this connection are the nature and purpose of the measure in question; its characterisation under national law; the procedures involved in the making and implementation of the measure; and its severity.

29. As regards the connection with a criminal offence, it is to be observed that before an order can be made under the 1986 Act the accused must have been convicted of one or more drug-trafficking offences (see section 1(1) of the 1986 Act)... This link is in no way diminished by the fact that, due to the operation of the statutory presumptions concerning the extent to which the applicant has benefited from trafficking, the court order may affect proceeds or property which are not directly related to the facts underlying the criminal conviction. While the reach of the measure may be necessary to the attainment of the aims of the 1986 Act, this does not alter the fact that its imposition is dependent on there having been a criminal conviction.

30. In assessing the nature and purpose of the measure, the Court has had regard to the background of the 1986 Act, which was introduced to overcome the inadequacy of the existing powers of forfeiture and to confer on the courts the power to confiscate proceeds after they had been converted into other forms of assets... The preventive purpose of confiscating property that might be available for use in future drug-trafficking operations as well as the purpose of ensuring that crime does not pay are evident from the ministerial statements that were made to Parliament at the time of the introduction of the legislation... However it cannot be excluded that legislation which confers such broad powers of confiscation on the courts also pursues the aim of punishing the offender. Indeed the aims of prevention and reparation are consistent with a punitive purpose and may be seen as constituent elements of the very notion of punishment.

31. In this connection, confiscation orders have been characterised in some United Kingdom court decisions as constituting 'penalties' and, in others, as pursuing the aim of reparation as opposed to punishment... Although on balance these statements point more in the direction of a confiscation order being a punitive measure, the Court does not consider them to be of much assistance since they were not directed at the point at issue under Article 7 (art 7) but rather made in the course of examination of associated questions of domestic law and procedure.

32. The Court agrees with the Government and the Commission that the severity of the order is not in itself decisive, since many non-penal measures of a preventive nature may have a substantial impact on the person concerned.

33. However, there are several aspects of the making of an order under the 1986 Act which are in keeping with the idea of a penalty as it is commonly understood even though they may also be considered as essential to the preventive scheme inherent in the 1986 Act. The sweeping statutory assumptions in section 2 (3) of the 1986 Act that all property passing through the offender's hands over a six-year period is the fruit of drug trafficking unless he can prove otherwise...the fact that the confiscation order is directed to the proceeds involved in drug dealing and is not limited to actual enrichment or profit (see sections 1 and 2 of the 1986 Act...); the discretion of the trial judge, in fixing the amount of the order, to take into consideration the degree of culpability of the accused...and the possibility of imprisonment in default of payment by the offender...are all elements which, when considered together, provide a strong indication of, *inter alia*, a regime of punishment.

34. Finally, looking behind appearances at the realities of the situation, whatever the characterisation of the measure of confiscation, the fact remains that the applicant faced more far-reaching detriment as a result of the order than that to which he was exposed at the time of the commission of the offences for which he was convicted (see, *mutatis mutandis*, the *Campbell and Fell v UK* judgment of 28 June 1984, Series A No 80, p 38, para 72).

35. Taking into consideration the combination of punitive elements outlined above, the confiscation order amounted, in the circumstances of the present case, to a penalty. Accordingly, there has been a breach of Article 7 para 1 (art 7-1).

36. The Court would stress, however, that this conclusion concerns only the retrospective application of the relevant legislation and does not call into question in any respect the powers of confiscation conferred on the courts as a weapon in the fight against the scourge of drug trafficking.

. . .

FOR THESE REASONS, THE COURT UNANIMOUSLY

1. Holds that there has been a violation of Article 7 para 1 (art 7-1) of the Convention

. . .

NOTES

1   The Court was composed of President Ryssdal and Judges: Matscher, Macdonald, De Meyer, Foighel, Pekkanen, Freeland, Wildhaber, and Jungwiert. The judgment in *Welch* is important for the Court's ruling that the concept of a penalty is an autonomous one, which enables the Court to reach its own determination of whether a particular sanction falls within Article 7.

2   In a separate judgment (*Welch v UK*, 1996-II) dealing with the applicant's claims for just satisfaction, the Court noted that the British authorities had not, and were not going to, enforce the compensation order against Welch. The Court dismissed the applicant's request for pecuniary and non-pecuniary damages.

3   In *Scoppola v Italy (No 2)*, judgment of 17 September 2009, a Grand Chamber adopted a new approach to applying Article 7 where after the commission of a crime legislative changes provide for a more lenient criminal penalty. The applicant was charged with the murder of his wife and the attempted murder of one of his sons. Those crimes carried a penalty of life imprisonment with daytime isolation. In February 2000 he requested that he be tried under a summary procedure whereby, according to the Code of Criminal Procedure, if he were to be convicted his sentence of life imprisonment would be replaced by a sentence of 30 years' imprisonment. On 24 November 2000 he was convicted and given the latter sentence. Subsequently, the prosecutor appealed arguing that on 24 November

2000 a Legislative Decree entered into force which substituted life imprisonment (for life imprisonment with daytime isolation) in respect of persons convicted under the summary procedure. The Rome Court of Appeal replaced the applicant's sentence with that of life imprisonment.

The Grand Chamber noted that in *X v Germany*, decision of 6 March 1978, the European Commission had expressed the opinion that Article 7 did not guarantee the right to a more lenient penalty enacted subsequent to the time of the offence and that the Court had followed that interpretation. However:

> 106. …a consensus has gradually emerged in Europe and internationally around the view that application of a criminal law providing for a more lenient penalty, even one enacted after the commission of the offence, has become a fundamental principle of criminal law.
>
> …
>
> 109. In the light of the foregoing considerations the Court takes the view that it is necessary to depart from the case-law established by the Commission in the case of *X. v Germany* and affirm that Article 7(1) of the Convention guarantees not only the principle of non-retrospectiveness of more stringent criminal laws but also, and implicitly, the principle of retrospectiveness of the more lenient criminal law. That principle is embodied in the rule that where there are differences between the criminal law in force at the time of the commission and subsequent criminal laws enacted before a final judgment is rendered, the courts must apply the law whose provisions are most favourable to the defendant.

Consequently, by 11 votes to 6, the Grand Chamber found that the applicant had suffered a breach of Article 7. The dissentients criticized the majority for 'overstepping the limits' of interpretation. Certainly, the judgment in *Scoppola* is a significant enhancement of the rights of defendants.

Article 7(2)

The framers of the Convention included this provision to protect national laws enacted in the aftermath of the Second World War to punish war crimes and other serious offences committed during that war.

In *Kononov v Latvia*, judgment of 17 May 2010, a Grand Chamber, by 14 votes to 3, determined that there had been no violation of Article 7 in respect of the applicant's conviction (in 2004) of war crimes committed during 1944. The Latvian courts found that the applicant had been in command of a group of 'Red Partisans', members of the Soviet Army, who had killed nine villagers (including three women) in German-occupied Belarus, as the partisans believed that the villagers had betrayed some of their comrades to the Germans. Given his current age (81) and poor health the Latvian courts sentenced him to one year and eight months' imprisonment. The Grand Chamber concluded that:

> 238. …having regard to the flagrantly unlawful nature of the ill-treatment and killing of the nine villagers in the established circumstances of the operation on 27 May 1944, even the most cursory reflection by the applicant, would have indicated that, at the very least, the impugned acts risked being counter to the laws and customs of war as understood at that time and, notably, risked

constituting war crimes for which, as commander, he could be held individually and criminally accountable.

...

244. In the light of all of the above considerations, the Court concludes that, at the time when they were committed, the applicant's acts constituted offences defined with sufficient accessibility and foreseeability by the laws and customs of war.

10 ARTICLE 8 RIGHT TO RESPECT FOR PRIVATE AND FAMILY LIFE

There is an enormous body of jurisprudence involving Article 8, reflecting both the range of rights guaranteed by Article 8(1) and the limitations States seek to invoke under Article 8(2). The Court has consistently refrained from providing a comprehensive definition of 'private life' (*Niemietz*), but we shall explore the ever-expanding boundaries of the concept (e.g. to include the storage of a person's DNA profile by the police: *S and Marper*). Echoing social changes, the Court has regularly widened the spectrum of relationships that have been classified as falling within the protected category of 'family life' to encompass, amongst others, single parents and their children (*Marckx*), transsexuals and their partners/children (*X, Y and Z*), and cohabiting homosexuals (*Schalk and Kopf*). Protection of a person's home has been extended to second properties (*Demades*) and business premises (*Societe Colas Est*). Furthermore, States have been subject to a positive obligation to protect homes against serious pollution (*Hatton*). The types of communications safeguarded as 'correspondence' have been updated in line with evolving technology to include, for example, emails in *Liberty*. The Court has also elaborated the requirements of the limitations contained in Article 8(2), for example by explaining the elements of interferences being 'in accordance with the law' (*Silver*).

Article 8(1)

Private life

Niemietz v Germany A.251B (1992)
European Court of Human Rights

A fax was sent from the Freiburg post office to a District Court judge, who was hearing a criminal case involving the alleged non-payment of church tax. The fax accused the judge of abusing his office, by his conduct in the tax case, and was sent by 'Klaus Wegner' of the 'Freiburg Bunte Liste' (a local political party). The Munich public prosecutor's office began criminal proceedings against Wegner for insulting behaviour, but they were unable to serve a summons on him as his whereabouts was unknown and his identity may also have been false. Consequently, the prosecutor obtained a judicial warrant to search the law office of

Mr Niemietz, a local lawyer and chairman of the Bunte Liste, because mail for the party was sent to his office and it was believed that Niemietz might have documents revealing the identity of Wegner. Police officers and officials from the public prosecutor's office carried out the search, which lasted for just over one hour. During the search a number of filing cabinets, containing details of clients' legal affairs, and the client index were examined. No documents disclosing any details of Wegner were found and nothing was seized by the authorities. Later, criminal proceedings were discontinued against Wegner for lack of evidence. Niemietz complained to the Commission that he had suffered a violation of his rights under Articles 8, 13 and Article 1, Protocol 1. He also acknowledged that he had hidden and then destroyed documents identifying Wegner. The Commission expressed the unanimous opinion that Niemietz's rights to respect for his private life and home in Article 8 had been infringed. The Commission did not consider it necessary to examine the other complaints.

A. WAS THERE AN 'INTERFERENCE'?

29. The Court does not consider it possible or necessary to attempt an exhaustive definition of the notion of 'private life'. However, it would be too restrictive to limit the notion to an 'inner circle' in which the individual may live his own personal life as he chooses and to exclude therefrom entirely the outside world not encompassed within that circle. Respect for private life must also comprise to a certain degree the right to establish and develop relationships with other human beings.

There appears, furthermore, to be no reason of principle why this understanding of the notion of 'private life' should be taken to exclude activities of a professional or business nature since it is, after all, in the course of their working lives that the majority of people have a significant, if not the greatest, opportunity of developing relationships with the outside world. This view is supported by the fact that, as was rightly pointed out by the Commission, it is not always possible to distinguish clearly which of an individual's activities form part of his professional or business life and which do not. Thus, especially in the case of a person exercising a liberal profession, his work in that context may form part and parcel of his life to such a degree that it becomes impossible to know in what capacity he is acting at a given moment of time.

To deny the protection of Article 8 on the ground that the measure complained of related only to professional activities—as the Government suggested should be done in the present case—could moreover lead to an inequality of treatment, in that such protection would remain available to a person whose professional and non-professional activities were so intermingled that there was no means of distinguishing between them. In fact, the Court has not heretofore drawn such distinctions: it concluded that there had been an inference with private life even where telephone tapping covered both business and private calls (see the *Huvig v France* judgment of 24 April 1990, Series A No 176-B, p 41, § 8, and p 52, § 25); and where a search was directed solely against business activities, it did not rely on that fact as a ground for excluding the applicability of Article 8 under the head of 'private life' (see the *Chappell v UK* judgment of 30 March 1989, Series A No 152-A, pp 12–13, § 26, and pp 21–2, § 51.)

30. As regards the word 'home', appearing in the English text of Article 8, the Court observes that in certain Contracting States, notably Germany..., it has been accepted as extending to business premises. Such an interpretation is, moreover, fully consonant with the French text, since the word 'domicile' has a broader connotation than the word 'home' and may extend, for example, to a professional person's office.

In this context also, it may not always be possible to draw precise distinctions, since activities which are related to a profession or business may well be conducted from a person's private residence and activities which are not so related may well be carried on in an office or commercial premises. A narrow interpretation of the words 'home' and 'domicile' could therefore give rise to the same risk of inequality of treatment as a narrow interpretation of the notion of 'private life' (see paragraph 29 above).

31. More generally, to interpret the words 'private life' and 'home' as including certain professional or business activities or premises would be consonant with the essential object and purpose of Article 8, namely to protect the individual against arbitrary interference by the public authorities (see, for example, the *Marckx v Belgium* judgment of 13 June 1979, Series A No 31, p 15, § 31). Such an interpretation would not unduly hamper the Contracting States, for they would retain their entitlement to 'interfere' to the extent permitted by paragraph 2 of Article 8; that entitlement might well be more far-reaching where professional or business activities or premises were involved than would otherwise be the case.

...

33. Taken together, the foregoing reasons lead the Court to find that the search of the applicant's office constituted an interference with his rights under Article 8.

...

D. WAS THE INTERFERENCE 'NECESSARY IN A DEMOCRATIC SOCIETY'?

37. [The Court] has formed the opinion that, as was contended by the applicant and as was found by the Commission, the measure complained of was not proportionate to those aims.

It is true that the offence in connection with which the search was effected, involving as it did not only an insult to but also an attempt to bring pressure on a judge, cannot be classified as no more than minor. On the other hand, the warrant was drawn in broad terms, in that it ordered a search for and seizure of 'documents', without any limitation, revealing the identity of the author of the offensive letter; this point is of special significance where, as in Germany, the search of a lawyer's office is not accompanied by any special procedural safeguards, such as the presence of an independent observer. More importantly, having regard to the materials that were in fact inspected, the search impinged on professional secrecy to an extent that appears disproportionate in the circumstances; it has, in this connection, to be recalled that, where a lawyer is involved, an encroachment on professional secrecy may have repercussions on the proper administration of justice and hence on the rights guaranteed by Article 6 of the Convention. In addition, the attendant publicity must have been capable of affecting adversely the applicant's professional reputation, in the eyes both of his existing clients and of the public at large.

...

FOR THESE REASONS, THE COURT UNANIMOUSLY [9-0]

1. Holds that there has been a violation of Article 8 of the Convention; ...

NOTES

1 The Chamber was composed of President Ryssdal and Judges: Bernhardt, Pettiti, Walsh, Russo, Spielmann, Valticos, Loizou, and Freeland.

2 Although the Court made clear in **Niemietz** that it was not going to provide a comprehensive definition of the concept of 'private life', other cases help to delimit the wide boundaries of this flexible notion.

3 In *X and Y v Netherlands*, A.191 (1985), the Court unanimously held that: '... private life', [is] a concept which covers the physical and moral integrity of the person, including his or her sexual life' (para 22). In that case Article 8 was found to have been violated by the failure of Dutch criminal law to provide effective protection for a mentally handicapped 16-year-old who had been subjected to a serious sexual assault. For further details of this case, see p 570.

4 Similarly, in *Dudgeon v UK* A.45 (1981), the Court treated a person's sexual life as an essential aspect of his/her private life. A majority (15 to 4) ruled that the criminal prohibition on homosexual conduct between consenting adults in private existing in Northern Ireland; '...constitutes a continuing interference with the applicant's right to respect for his private life (which includes his sexual life) within the meaning of Article 8(1)' (para 41). Furthermore, the majority did not consider that the interference could be justified under Article 8(2). Subsequently, analogous criminal laws were found by the Court to breach homosexuals' right to respect for their private lives in *Norris v Ireland* A.142 (1988) and *Modinos v Cyprus* A.259 (1993).

In *Sutherland v UK* (1997) 24 EHRR CD22, the applicant successfully challenged the age of consent for male homosexuals in England before the Commission. Sutherland, who was born in 1977, became aware of attraction to other boys at about the age of 12 and had his first homosexual sexual relations (with another person of his own age) when he was 16. Under the Sexual Offences Act 1967, male homosexual acts were decriminalized where the parties were aged 21 or over and the conduct took place in private. By virtue of the earlier Sexual Offences Act 1956, the heterosexual age of consent is 16 and this also applies to sexual relations between lesbians. In 1981 the Policy Advisory Committee on Sexual Offences recommended to the Home Secretary that, in accordance with medical advice on the sexual maturity of males, the age of consent for male homosexuals should be reduced to 18. The Government did not act on this suggestion. However, in 1994 the British Medical Association, responding to new research that showed that sexual orientation is usually established before the age of puberty and growing concern that young male homosexuals were especially at risk from sexually transmitted infections (including HIV), recommended that the age of consent for male homosexuals should be reduced to 16. That year the House of Commons, on a free vote, passed an amendment to reduce the homosexual age of consent to 18 (by 427 votes to 162) and that was implemented by the Criminal Justice and Public Order Act 1994. The applicant complained to the Commission that the 1994 Act's homosexual age of consent was discriminatory when compare with the heterosexual (and lesbian) minimum age of 16 and therefore breached his rights under Articles 8 and 14. Even though Sutherland had not been threatened with prosecution, applying the Court's reasoning in *Dudgeon*, the Commission concluded that the applicant had been directly affected by the age of consent legislation and it constituted an interference with his right to respect for his private life. Consequently, it was necessary to examine whether the legislation was compatible with Articles 8(2) and 14. The Commission believed that the different ages of consent for heterosexual and homosexual sexual relations were a difference that fell within Article 14 as being based on 'sex' or 'other status' and that as this different treatment '...impinges on a most intimate aspect of affected individuals' private lives, the margin of appreciation must be relatively narrow' (para 57). While the Commission acknowledged that it had upheld the 21-year-old age of homosexual consent in *X v UK* 19 DR 66 (1975), it considered that it was now time to reconsider its earlier case-law in the light of modern circumstances. A majority of the Commission (14 votes to 4) then found that (having regard to *inter alia* the view of the BMA and the fact that '...equality of treatment in respect of the age of consent is now recognised by the great majority of member States of the Council of Europe' (para 59)) there had been a violation of Article 8 taken in conjunction with Article 14. In the majority's opinion, '...no objective and reasonable justification exists for the maintenance of a higher minimum age of consent to male homosexual, than to heterosexual, acts and that the application discloses discriminatory treatment in the exercise of the applicant's right to respect for private life under Article 8 of the Convention' (para 66). The dissenters felt that the homosexual age of consent established by Parliament in 1994 was within the domestic margin of appreciation and they also did not consider that there was a common European standard regarding the age of consent. In June 1998 the British Government reached an agreement with Sutherland and the House of Commons was given an opportunity to hold a free vote (on an amendment to the Crime and Disorder Bill) to reduce the homosexual age of consent to 16. The amendment was passed by the Commons but rejected by the House of Lords. Consequently, during December 1998, the Government introduced the Sexual Offences (Amendment) Bill which sought, *inter alia*, to harmonize the age of consent for homosexual and heterosexual relations at 16 for England, Wales, and Scotland (it provided that in Northern Ireland the homosexual age of consent should be 17 as that is the existing heterosexual age of consent in the Province). However, the House of Lords, again, refused to pass the Bill.

The Government responded by invoking the rarely used Parliament Acts 1911 and 1949 procedure (whereby approval by the House of Lords can be dispensed with). The House of Commons enacted (with Royal Assent) the Sexual Offences (Amendment) Act 2000 which implemented the above changes to the homosexual age of consent. In January 2001, after the Act was brought into effect, Sutherland applied to the Court for his case to be struck out. A unanimous Grand Chamber did so in *Sutherland v UK*, judgment of 27 March 2001, after noting the legislative changes and that the applicant's legal costs had been paid by the Government, the Court was satisfied that the complaint had been resolved.

The full-time Court, unanimously, found a breach of Article 14 in combination with Article 8 when a 41-year-old man had been prosecuted in 1998 (after the Commission gave its Opinion in *Sutherland*) for alleged buggery with a 16-year-old male. In *BB v UK*, judgment of 10 February 2004, the applicant had complained to the police, in January 1998, that he had been attacked by the 16-year-old male. However, it was BB who was prosecuted (he was formally acquitted in 1999 when the young person refused to testify). The Court found that, '25. ... the existence of, and the applicant's prosecution under, the legislation applicable at the relevant time constituted a violation of Article 14 taken in conjunction with Article 8 of the Convention.'

5 The Court has unanimously found a breach of Article 8 in respect of the investigations into the sexual orientation and the subsequent discharge from the British armed forces of a number of homosexual (gay and lesbian) personnel: *Smith and Grady v UK*, 1999-VI and in the simultaneous case *Lustig-Prean and Beckett v UK* (1999) 29 EHRR 548. Jeanette Smith joined the Royal Air Force, for a nine-year engagement, in 1989 as a nurse and she obtained the rank of senior aircraft woman. In June 1994 a woman telephoned the air force Provost and Security Service (the service police) alleging that Ms Smith was homosexual and was sexually harassing the caller. Subsequently, Smith was interviewed by the service police. Smith admitted that she was homosexual (she had her initial lesbian relationship during her first year in the RAF) and that she had a current homosexual relationship (which had begun 18 months previously) with a civilian. The service police then sought to question Smith about the intimate aspects of her homosexual relationships (the police stated that they had to verify Smith's statement about her sexual orientation in order to ensure that she was not seeking to obtain an early discharge from the service). She was asked, *inter alia*, the names of her previous partners, the extent of her relationship with her current partner, whether she and her current partner had a sexual relationship with their foster daughter, whether she had thought about HIV, and whether she liked 'girlie games' such as hockey. Her partner was, voluntarily, also interviewed and she confirmed that they were involved in a full sexual relationship. A few months later Smith was given an administrative discharge from the RAF in accordance with the armed forces' policy that homosexuality (male or female) is incompatible with service in the forces. The RAF had assessed Smith's trade proficiency

and personal qualities as very good and her conduct as exemplary. Graeme Grady joined the RAF in 1980 and by 1993 he was a sergeant working as chief clerk to the British Defence Intelligence Liaison Service in Washington DC. In June 1994 the nanny to the wife of the head of the Liaison Service made disclosures which resulted in Sergeant Grady being sent back to a British air base and his questioning by the service police. At his first interview Grady denied he was homosexual. The next day, after seeking legal advice and ascertaining his financial position if he was to be given an administrative discharge, he admitted his homosexuality (he confirmed that he began homosexual relationships in the previous year). The police asked him a number of intimate questions including whether his wife knew he was homosexual, the names of his sexual partners, and the nature of his relationships with them. In December 1994 Mr Grady was given an administrative discharge, his service record noted that he had displayed sound personal qualities and integrity throughout his service. The applicants sought to challenge their discharges through judicial review proceedings but the High Court and the Court of Appeal found that the authorities' actions did not violate the principles of legality including *Wednesbury* unreasonableness/irrationality (*R v Ministry of Defence, ex p Smith* [1996] 1 All ER 257). The applicants then complained to the Strasbourg institutions alleging a breach of their Convention rights including their right to respect for their private lives under Article 8. The Government accepted that there had been such interferences.

> ...In these circumstances, the Court is of the view that the investigations by the military police into the applicants' homosexuality, which included detailed interviews with each of them and with third parties on matters relating to their sexual orientation and practices, together with the preparation of a final report for the armed forces' authorities on the investigations, constituted a direct interference with the applicants' right to respect for their private lives. Their consequent administrative discharge on the sole ground of their sexual orientation also constituted an interference with that right (see the *Dudgeon v UK* judgment of 22 October 1981, Series A No 45, pp 18–19, § 41, and, *mutatis mutandis*, the *Vogt v Germany* judgment of 26 September 1995, Series A No 323, p 23, § 44). [Para 71.]

As the armed forces' policy of discharging homosexuals was endorsed by section 146 of the Criminal Justice and Public Order Act 1994, the Court found that the interferences were 'in accordance with the law'. Furthermore the authorities' actions pursued the legitimate aims of 'the interests of national security' and 'the prevention of disorder' under Article 8(2) as the Government contended that its policy towards homosexuality in the armed forces maintained the morale of service personnel and consequently the fighting power of the armed forces. The contentious issue was whether the interferences were 'necessary in a democratic society'. The Government, relying particularly on a 1996 internal review of the policy conducted by the 'Homosexuality Policy Assessment Team' (HPAT), argued that, *inter alia*, admitting homosexuals to the armed forces at the present time would have a significant and negative effect on the morale of those forces and that it was within the State's margin of appreciation to impose such limitations on the private lives of service personnel. The applicants contended, *inter alia*, that the Government had not produced any objective evidence to support its assertion that service morale would be damaged by altering the policy towards homosexuals.

(c) The Court's assessment

(i) Applicable general principles

87. An interference will be considered 'necessary in a democratic society' for a legitimate aim if it answers a pressing social need and, in particular, is proportionate to the legitimate aim pursued

(see the *Norris* judgment..., p 18, § 41). Given the matters at issue in the present case, the Court would underline the link between the notion of 'necessity' and that of a 'democratic society', the hallmarks of the latter including pluralism, tolerance and broadmindedness (see the *Vereinigung Demokratischer Soldaten Österreichs and Gubi* judgment...above, p 17, § 36, and the Dudgeon judgment...p 21, § 53).

88. The Court recognises that it is for the national authorities to make the initial assessment of necessity, though the final evaluation as to whether the reasons cited for the interference are relevant and sufficient is one for this Court. A margin of appreciation is left open to Contracting States in the context of this assessment, which varies according to the nature of the activities restricted and of the aims pursued by the restrictions (see the *Dudgeon* judgment...pp 21 and 23, §§ 52 and 59).

89. Accordingly, when the relevant restrictions concern 'a most intimate part of an individual's private life', there must exist 'particularly serious reasons' before such interferences can satisfy the requirements of Article 8 § 2 of the Convention (see the *Dudgeon* judgment...p 21, § 52). When the core of the national security aim pursued is the operational effectiveness of the armed forces, it is accepted that each State is competent to organise its own system of military discipline and enjoys a certain margin of appreciation in this respect (see the *Engel* judgment p 25, § 59). The Court also considers that it is open to the State to impose restrictions on an individual's right to respect for his private life where there is a real threat to the armed forces' operational effectiveness, as the proper functioning of an army is hardly imaginable without legal rules designed to prevent service personnel from undermining it. However, the national authorities cannot rely on such rules to frustrate the exercise by individual members of the armed forces of their right to respect for their private lives, which right applies to service personnel as it does to others within the jurisdiction of the State. Moreover, assertions as to a risk to operational effectiveness must be 'substantiated by specific examples' (see, *mutatis mutandis*, the *Vereinigung Demokratischer Soldaten Österreichs and Gubi* judgment..., p 17, §§ 36 and 38, and the *Grigoriades* judgment...pp 2589–90, § 45).

(ii) Application to the facts of the case

90. It is common ground that the sole reason for the investigations conducted and for the applicants' discharge was their sexual orientation. Concerning as it did a most intimate aspect of an individual's private life, particularly serious reasons by way of justification were required (see paragraph 89 above). In the case of the present applicants, the Court finds the interferences to have been especially grave for the following reasons.

91. In the first place, the investigation process...was of an exceptionally intrusive character. Anonymous telephone calls to Ms Smith and to the service police, and information supplied by the nanny of Mr Grady's commander, prompted the investigations into their sexual orientation, a matter which, until then, each applicant had kept private. The investigations were conducted by the service police, whose investigation methods were, according to the HPAT, based on criminal procedures and whose presence the HPAT described as widely publicised and strongly resented among the forces...Once the matter was brought to the attention of the service authorities, Mr Grady was required to return immediately (without his wife or children) to the United Kingdom. While he was in the United Kingdom, detailed investigations into his homosexuality began in the United States and included detailed and intrusive interviews about his private life with his wife, a colleague, the latter's husband and the nanny who worked with his commander's family. Both applicants were interviewed and asked detailed questions of an intimate nature about their particular sexual practices and preferences. Certain lines of questioning of both applicants were, in the Court's view, particularly intrusive and offensive and, indeed, the Government conceded that they could not defend the question put to Ms Smith about whether she had had a sexual relationship with her foster daughter. Ms Smith's partner was also interviewed. Mr Grady's accommodation was searched, many personal items (including a letter to his homosexual partner) were seized and he was later questioned in detail on the content of these items. After the interviews, a service

police report was prepared for the air force authorities on each applicant's homosexuality and related matters.

92. Secondly, the administrative discharge of the applicants had, as Sir Thomas Bingham MR described, a profound effect on their careers and prospects. Prior to the events in question, both applicants enjoyed relatively successful service careers in their particular field. Ms Smith had over five years' service in the air force; she had been recommended for promotion, had been accepted for a training course which would facilitate this promotion and was about to complete the course final examinations. Her evaluations prior to and after her discharge were very positive. Mr Grady had served in the air force for fourteen years, being promoted to sergeant and posted to a high-security position in Washington in 1991. His evaluations prior to and after his discharge were also very positive with recommendations for further promotion. The Government accepted in their observations that neither the service records nor the conduct of the applicants gave any grounds for complaint and the High Court described their service records as 'exemplary'. The Court notes, in this respect, the unique nature of the armed forces (underlined by the Government in their pleadings before the Court) and, consequently, the difficulty in directly transferring essentially military qualifications and experience to civilian life. The Court recalls, in this respect that one of the several reasons why the Court considered Mrs Vogt's dismissal from her post as a school teacher to be a 'very severe measure', was its finding that school teachers in her situation would 'almost certainly be deprived of the opportunity to exercise the sole profession for which they have a calling, for which they have been trained and in which they have acquired skills and experience' (*Vogt* judgment...p 29, § 60). In this regard, the Court accepts that the applicants' training and experience would be of use in civilian life. However, it is clear that the applicants would encounter difficulty in obtaining civilian posts in their areas of specialisation which would reflect the seniority and status which they had achieved in the air force.

93. Thirdly, the absolute and general character of the policy which led to the interferences in question is striking (see the *Dudgeon* judgment...p 24, § 61, and the *Vogt* judgment...p 28, § 59). The policy results in an immediate discharge from the armed forces once an individual's homosexuality is established and irrespective of the individual's conduct or service record. With regard to the Government's reference to the Kalaç judgment, the Court considers that the compulsory retirement of Mr Kalaç is to be distinguished from the discharge of the present applicants, the former being dismissed on grounds of his conduct while the applicants were discharged on grounds of their innate personal characteristics.

94. Accordingly, the Court must consider whether, taking account of the margin of appreciation open to the State in matters of national security, particularly convincing and weighty reasons exist by way of justification for the interferences with the applicants' right to respect for their private lives.

95. The core argument of the Government in support of the policy is that the presence of open or suspected homosexuals in the armed forces would have a substantial and negative effect on morale and, consequently, on the fighting power and operational effectiveness of the armed forces. The Government rely in this respect on the report of the HPAT and, in particular, on Section F of the report. Although the Court acknowledges the complexity of the study undertaken by the HPAT, it entertains certain doubts as to the value of the HPAT report for present purposes. The independence of the assessment contained in the report is open to question given that it was completed by Ministry of Defence civil servants and service personnel...In addition, on any reading of the report and the methods used...only a very small proportion of the armed forces' personnel participated in the assessment. Moreover, many of the methods of assessment (including the consultation with policy-makers in the Ministry of Defence, one-to-one interviews and the focus group discussions) were not anonymous. It also appears that many of the questions in the attitude survey suggested answers in support of the policy.

96. Even accepting that the views on the matter which were expressed to the HPAT may be considered representative, the Court finds that the perceived problems which were identified in the HPAT report as a threat to the fighting power and operational effectiveness of the armed forces were founded solely upon the negative attitudes of heterosexual personnel towards those of homosexual orientation. The Court observes, in this respect, that no moral judgment is made on homosexuality by the policy, as was confirmed in the affidavit of the Vice Chief of the Defence Staff... It is also accepted by the Government that neither the records nor conduct of the applicants nor the physical capability, courage, dependability and skills of homosexuals in general are in any way called into question by the policy.

97. The question for the Court is whether the above-noted negative attitudes constitute sufficient justification for the interferences at issue. The Court observes from the HPAT report that these attitudes, even if sincerely felt by those who expressed them, ranged from stereotypical expressions of hostility to those of homosexual orientation, to vague expressions of unease about the presence of homosexual colleagues. To the extent that they represent a predisposed bias on the part of a heterosexual majority against a homosexual minority, these negative attitudes cannot, of themselves, be considered by the Court to amount to sufficient justification for the interferences with the applicants' rights outlined above any more than similar negative attitudes towards those of a different race, origin or colour.

98. The Government emphasised that the views expressed in the HPAT report served to show that any change in the policy would entail substantial damage to morale and operational effectiveness. The applicants considered these submissions to be unsubstantiated.

99. The Court notes the lack of concrete evidence to substantiate the alleged damage to morale and fighting power that any change in the policy would entail. Thorpe LJ in the Court of Appeal found that there was no actual or significant evidence of such damage as a result of the presence of homosexuals in the armed forces... and the Court further considers that the subsequent HPAT assessment did not, whatever its value, provide evidence of such damage in the event of the policy changing. Given the number of homosexuals dismissed between 1991 and 1996 [30 officers and 331 persons of other rank] the number of homosexuals who were in the armed forces at the relevant time cannot be said to be insignificant. Even if the absence of such evidence can be explained by the consistent application of the policy, as submitted by the Government, this is insufficient to demonstrate to the Court's satisfaction that operational effectiveness problems of the nature and level alleged can be anticipated in the absence of the policy (see the *Vereinigung Demokratischer Soldaten Österreichs and Gubi* judgment... p 17, § 38).

100. However, in the light of the strength of feeling expressed in certain submissions to the HPAT and the special, interdependent and closely knit nature of the armed forces' environment, the Court considers it reasonable to assume that some difficulties could be anticipated as a result of any change in what is now a long-standing policy. Indeed, it would appear that the presence of women and racial minorities in the armed forces led to relational difficulties of the kind which the Government suggest admission of homosexuals would entail...

101. The applicants submitted that a strict code of conduct applicable to all personnel would address any potential difficulties caused by negative attitudes of heterosexuals. The Government, while not rejecting the possibility out of hand, emphasised the need for caution given the subject matter and the armed forces context of the policy and pointed out that this was one of the options to be considered by the next Parliamentary Select Committee in 2001.

102. The Court considers it important to note, in the first place, the approach already adopted by the armed forces to deal with racial discrimination and with racial and sexual harassment and bullying... The January 1996 Directive, for example, imposed both a strict code of conduct on every soldier together with disciplinary rules to deal with any inappropriate behaviour and conduct. This

dual approach was supplemented with information leaflets and training programmes, the army emphasising the need for high standards of personal conduct and for respect for others. The Government, nevertheless, underlined that it is 'the knowledge or suspicion of homosexuality' which would cause the morale problems and not conduct, so that a conduct code would not solve the anticipated difficulties. However, in so far as negative attitudes to homosexuality are insufficient, of themselves, to justify the policy (see paragraph 97 above), they are equally insufficient to justify the rejection of a proposed alternative. In any event, the Government themselves recognised during the hearing that the choice between a conduct code and the maintenance of the policy lay at the heart of the judgment to be made in this case. This is also consistent with the Government's direct reliance on Section F of the HPAT's report where the anticipated problems identified as posing a risk to morale were almost exclusively problems related to behaviour and conduct... The Government maintained that homosexuality raised problems of a type and intensity that race and gender did not. However, even if it can be assumed that the integration of homosexuals would give rise to problems not encountered with the integration of women or racial minorities, the Court is not satisfied that the codes and rules which have been found to be effective in the latter case would not equally prove effective in the former. The 'robust indifference' reported by the HPAT of the large number of British armed forces' personnel serving abroad with allied forces to homosexuals serving in those foreign forces, serves to confirm that the perceived problems of integration are not insuperable...

103. The Government highlighted particular problems which might be posed by the communal accommodation arrangements in the armed forces. Detailed submissions were made during the hearing, the parties disagreeing as to the potential consequences of shared single-sex accommodation and associated facilities. The Court notes that the HPAT itself concluded that separate accommodation for homosexuals would not be warranted or wise and that substantial expenditure would not, therefore, have to be incurred in this respect. Nevertheless, the Court remains of the view that it has not been shown that the conduct codes and disciplinary rules referred to above could not adequately deal with any behavioural issues arising on the part either of homosexuals or of heterosexuals.

104. The Government, referring to the relevant analysis in the HPAT report, further argued that no worthwhile lessons could be gleaned from the relatively recent legal changes in those foreign armed forces which now admitted homosexuals. The Court disagrees. It notes the evidence before the domestic courts to the effect that the European countries operating a blanket legal ban on homosexuals in their armed forces are now in a small minority. It considers that, even if relatively recent, the Court cannot overlook the widespread and consistently developing views and associated legal changes to the domestic laws of Contracting States on this issue (see the *Dudgeon* judgment..., pp 23–4, § 60).

105. Accordingly, the Court concludes that convincing and weighty reasons have not been offered by the Government to justify the policy against homosexuals in the armed forces or, therefore, the consequent discharge of the applicants from those forces.

106. While the applicants' administrative discharges were a direct consequence of their homosexuality, the Court considers that the justification for the investigations into the applicants' homosexuality requires separate consideration in so far as those investigations continued after the applicants' admissions of homosexuality. In Ms Smith's case her admission was immediate and Mr Grady admitted his homosexuality when his interview of 26 May 1994 commenced.

107. The Government maintained that investigations, including the interviews and searches, were necessary in order to detect false claims of homosexuality by those seeking administrative discharges from the armed forces. The Government cited five examples of individuals in the armed forces who had relatively recently made such false claims in order to obtain discharge. However, and despite the fact that Mr Grady's family life could have led to some doubts about the

genuineness of the information received as to his homosexuality, it was and is clear, in the Court's opinion, that at the relevant time both Ms Smith and Mr Grady wished to remain in the air force. Accordingly, the Court does not find that the risk of false claims of homosexuality could, in the case of the present applicants, provide any justification for their continued questioning.

108. The Government further submitted that the medical, security and disciplinary concerns outlined by the HPAT justified certain lines of questioning of the applicants. However, the Court observes that, in the HPAT report, security issues relating to those suspected of being homosexual were found not to stand up to close examination as a ground for maintaining the policy. The Court is, for this reason, not persuaded that the risk of blackmail, being the main security ground canvassed by the Government, justified the continuation of the questioning of either of the present applicants. Similarly, the Court does not find that the clinical risks (which were, in any event, substantially discounted by the HPAT as a ground for maintaining the policy) justified the extent of the applicants' questioning. Moreover, no disciplinary issue existed in the case of either applicant.

109. The Government, referring to the cautions given to the applicants at the beginning of their interviews, further argued that the applicants were not obliged to participate in the interview process. Moreover, Ms Smith was asked to consent to her partner being interviewed and Mr Grady agreed to the search of his accommodation and to hand over his electronic diary. The Court considers, however, that the applicants did not have any real choice but to cooperate in this process. It is clear that the interviews formed a standard and important part of the investigation process which was designed to verify to 'a high standard of proof' the sexual orientation of the applicants... Had the applicants not cooperated with the interview process, including with the additional elements of this process outlined above, the Court is satisfied that the authorities would have proceeded to verify the suspected homosexuality of the applicants by other means which were likely to be less discreet. That this was the alternative open to the applicants in the event of their failing to cooperate was made clear to both applicants, and in particularly forthright terms to Mr Grady.

110. In such circumstances, the Court considers that the Government have not offered convincing and weighty reasons justifying the continued investigation of the applicants' sexual orientation once they had confirmed their homosexuality to the air force authorities.

111. In sum, the Court finds that neither the investigations conducted into the applicants' sexual orientation, nor their discharge on the grounds of their homosexuality in pursuance of the Ministry of Defence policy, were justified under Article 8 § 2 of the Convention.

112. Accordingly, there has been a violation of Article 8 of the Convention.

Clearly, the Court was not satisfied that the Government had provided credible justification for the armed forces' treatment of homosexual personnel. In reaching that conclusion the Court may have been influenced by a number of *dicta* in the domestic proceedings where several of the judges (including Simon Brown LJ and Thorpe LJ) expressed doubts about the durability of the armed forces' policy towards homosexuals. Within hours of the Court's judgment the Defence Secretary, Lord Robertson, announced that the armed forces would suspend current actions against homosexual personnel. After consulting the chiefs of the armed forces, ministers would make recommendations to Parliament regarding the policy to be adopted towards homosexuals in the forces. In January 2000, the new Defence Secretary (Geoffrey Hoon) announced to Parliament that the ban on homosexuals serving in the British armed forces had been ended. All service personnel would now be subject to a code of social conduct which prohibits 'social misconduct'. Commanding officers will be obliged to investigate the personal lives of their subordinates where the latter's actions or behaviour 'adversely impacted... on the efficiency or operational effectiveness of the Service'. The code covers all forms of sexual activity and expressly prohibits, *inter alia*, 'displays of affection which might cause offence to others' or 'taking sexual advantage of subordinates'. On the same day as the Defence Secretary made the above announcement the Chief of the Defence Staff (General Sir Charles Guthrie) gave an interview (to *The Times* newspaper) in which he expressed his full support for the new policy. He described the code of conduct as 'sensible and pragmatic', and acknowledged that some of the earlier military police investigations into the sexual practices of service personnel 'went too far'. In July 2000, the Court awarded Ms Smith and Mr Grady £19,000 each in non-pecuniary damages to compensate them for 'the profoundly destabilising events' experienced during their investigations and discharges from the military. Smith was also awarded £59,000 pecuniary damages (in respect of past and future loss of earnings, loss of service pension benefits, and interest), while Grady was allocated £40,000 in pecuniary damages (under the same heads). For other cases applying the Convention to military personnel, see p 710.

6　However, the Court has indicated in *obiter dicta* that there are limits as to the types of sexual conduct that fall within the protected concept of 'private life'. ***Laskey, Jaggard and Brown v UK***, 1997-I, concerned the conviction of a number of homosexual men for assaults occasioning actual bodily as a result of organized 'consensual' sadomasochistic encounters involving over 40 men during a ten-year period.

> The Court observes that not every sexual activity carried out behind closed doors necessarily falls within the scope of Article 8. In the present case, the applicants were involved in consensual sado-masochistic activities for purposes of sexual gratification. There can be no doubt that sexual orientation and activity concern an intimate aspect of private life (see, *Dudgeon v UK*, A45 (1981)). However, a considerable number of people were involved in the activities in question which included, *inter alia*, the recruitment of new 'members', the provision of several specially-equipped 'chambers', and the shooting of many video-tapes which were distributed among the 'members'. It may thus be open to question whether the sexual activities of the applicants fell entirely within the notion of 'private life' in the particular circumstances of the case. [Para 36.]

But, as neither the British Government nor the Commission had raised this point, the Court was not willing to examine it of its own motion. Instead, the unanimous Court decided that the interferences with the applicants' private lives, brought about by the convictions, could be justified under Article 8(2) as being necessary in a democratic society for the protection of health (the applicants' conduct resulted in the flow of blood and left scarring). Moran has criticized the Court's judgment: 'In the final instance the decision appears to suggest that in matters of particular complexity specifically when concerned with morality or presented in terms of the protection of the vulnerable, the Strasbourg Court will be reluctant to intervene, thereby giving a State's paternalistic policy, decisions considerable latitude and the gloss of legitimacy associated with human rights' (1998) 61 MLR 82.

In the later case of ***ADT v UK***, 2000-IX, a Chamber of the Court determined that consensual homosexual activity between five adult men in the applicant's home was a matter of private sexual behaviour protected by Article 8. During a lawful search of the applicant's home the police discovered video tapes which showed the applicant and up to four other men engaged in acts of oral sex and mutual masturbation (no physical harm was involved in the conduct). The applicant was subsequently convicted of gross indecency (prohibited by section 13 of the Sexual Offences Act 1956) and conditionally discharged for two years plus the seized materials were ordered to be destroyed. Under section 1 of the Sexual Offences Act 1967, if more than two persons take part or are present when consensual male homosexual acts occur those acts are deemed not to have taken place in private and are criminal. English law does not criminalize private homosexual acts between consenting adult women nor heterosexual acts between consenting adults. In response to the applicant's complaints that section 13 of the 1956 Act when combined with section 1 of the 1967 Act and his conviction violated his right to respect for his private life under Article 8, the Government sought to argue that following **Laskey** the applicant's sexual activity fell outside the scope of 'private life'. The Court was unanimous in rejecting the Government's contention:

25. As to the Government's comments in connection with the scope of 'private life' within the meaning of Article 8 of the Convention, the Court recalls that there was no dispute between the parties in the case of *Laskey, Jaggard and Brown* as to the existence of an interference...In that case, the Court's comments did not go beyond raising a question 'whether the sexual activities of the applicants fell entirely within the notion of "private life"'. The sole element in the present case which could give rise to any doubt about whether the applicants' private lives were involved is the video recording of the activities. No evidence has been put before the Court to indicate that there was any actual likelihood of the contents of the tapes being rendered public, deliberately or inadvertently. In particular, the applicant's conviction related not to any offence involving the making or distribution of the tapes, but solely to the acts themselves. The Court finds it most unlikely that the applicant, who had gone to some lengths not to reveal his sexual orientation, and who has repeated his desire for anonymity before the Court, would knowingly be involved in any such publication.

26. The Court thus considers that the applicant has been the victim of an interference with his right to respect for his private life both as regards the existence of legislation prohibiting consensual sexual acts between more than two men in private, and as regards the conviction for gross indecency.

The Court went on to conclude that neither the legislation nor the applicant's conviction were 'necessary in a democratic society'.

37. The Court can agree with the Government that, at some point, sexual activities can be carried out in such a manner that State interference may be justified, either as not amounting to an interference with the right to respect for private life, or as being justified for the protection, for example, of health or morals. The facts of the present case, however, do not indicate any such circumstances. The applicant was involved in sexual activities with a restricted number of friends in circumstances in which it was most unlikely that others would become aware of what was going on. It is true that the activities were recorded on video tape, but the Court notes that the applicant was prosecuted for the activities themselves, and not for the recording, or for any risk of it entering the public domain. The activities were therefore genuinely 'private', and the approach of the Court must be to adopt the same narrow margin of appreciation as it found applicable in other cases involving intimate aspects of private life (as, for example, in the *Dudgeon* judgment, p 21, § 52).

38. Given the narrow margin of appreciation afforded to the national authorities in the case, the absence of any public health considerations and the purely private nature of the behaviour in the present case, the Court finds that the reasons submitted for the maintenance in force of legislation criminalising homosexual acts between men in private, and a fortiori the prosecution and conviction in the present case, are not sufficient to justify the legislation and the prosecution.

39. There has therefore been a violation of Article 8 of the Convention.

Significantly, the Government did not contest the applicant's claim for over £20,000 in just satisfaction, including £10,000 in respect of non-pecuniary loss. The Court considered his claim to be reasonable and awarded the full amount sought. This case can be distinguished from **Laskey** on a number of grounds, such as the nature of the sexual activities and numbers of persons involved. A few days before the Court issued its judgment in **ADT**, the Government published a report (*Setting the Boundaries*) from a group of experts it had appointed to review the law on sexual offences. The report made 62 recommendations for reform, including abolishing the offence of gross indecency. Most of these recommendations, including the abolition of the offence of gross indecency, were implemented by the Sexual Offences Act 2003.

In *KA and AD v Belgium*, judgment of 17 February 2005, a unanimous Chamber ruled that there had to be 'particularly serious reasons' to justify a State interfering with matters of sexuality. The first applicant, a judge, had been convicted of assault occasioning actual bodily harm and incitement to prostitution/immorality by facilitating his wife being used as a 'slave' for violent and extremely cruel sadomasochistic practices at a sadomasochism club. The second applicant, a doctor, had been convicted of assault occasioning actual bodily harm in respect of the sadomasochistic acts in which he engaged with the first applicant's wife at the club. The domestic court found that videotape evidence disclosed that the applicants had ignored the wife's pleas for the violent conduct to stop. The Chamber held that the applicants' freedom to engage in sexual behaviour had to respect the wishes of the 'victims' of such activities and that this had not occurred in the violent treatment of the first applicant's wife. Therefore, the applicants' convictions did not amount to a disproportionate interference with their right to respect for their private lives.

7   Given the diverse views across Europe regarding abortion, the Court for many years avoided giving a clear ruling as to whether women had a right to an abortion under Article 8. For example, in *Tysiac v Poland*, judgment of 20 March 2007, the applicant, who had a long-standing eye disability, sought to gain permission from the medical authorities for an abortion because of the risk of further damage to her eyes caused by giving birth. A GP provided such a certificate, but the head of the local hospital gynaecology department would not give his authorization. The applicant had the child and her eyesight significantly deteriorated soon afterwards. Before the Court she claimed a breach of Article 8 through the authorities' failures to provide her with a therapeutic abortion and a comprehensive legal framework to safeguard her rights. The Court determined that:

104....the applicable Polish law, the 1993 Act, while it prohibits abortion, provides for certain exceptions. In particular, under section 4 (a) 1 (1) of that Act, abortion is lawful where pregnancy poses a threat to the woman's life or health, certified by two medical certificates, irrespective of the stage reached in pregnancy. Hence, it is not the Court's task in the present case to examine whether the Convention guarantees a right to have an abortion.

However, as regards the applicant's complaint concerning the absence of a system enabling her to challenge the consultant's refusal to authorize an abortion:

124. The Court concludes that it has not been demonstrated that Polish law as applied to the applicant' case contained any effective mechanisms capable of determining whether the conditions for obtaining a lawful abortion had been met in her case. It created for the applicant a situation of prolonged uncertainty. As a result, the applicant suffered severe distress and anguish when contemplating the possible negative consequences of her pregnancy and upcoming delivery for her health.

Therefore, subject to a dissent, the Chamber found the applicant had suffered a violation of her right to respect for her private life. But a Grand Chamber finally directly addressed this issue in *A, B and C v Ireland*, judgment of 16 December 2010. For the background to the Irish constitutional limitations upon abortion see *Open Door and Dublin Well Woman*, p 715. The three applicants claimed that they been forced to go to the UK to obtain abortions as Irish law only permitted abortions where the woman's life was at serious risk. The Irish Government submitted that the restrictions contained in domestic law were justified under Article 8(2) as reflecting the moral values of Irish society. The Grand Chamber held that:

213. . . . The woman's right to respect for her private life must be weighed against other competing rights and freedoms invoked including those of the unborn child (*Tysiqc v Poland* judgment, cited above, § 106 . . .).

214. While Article 8 cannot, accordingly, be interpreted as conferring a right to abortion, the Court finds that the prohibition in Ireland of abortion where sought for reasons of health and/or well-being about which the first and second applicants complained, and the third applicant's alleged inability to establish her qualification for a lawful abortion in Ireland, come within the scope of their right to respect for their private lives and accordingly Article 8.

A majority of the Grand Chamber (11 votes) went on to find no breach of Article 8 in respect of A and B, because the Court should allow considerable discretion to States when balancing the competing interests.

233. There can be no doubt as to the acute sensitivity of the moral and ethical issues raised by the question of abortion or as to the importance of the public interest at stake. A broad margin of appreciation is, therefore, in principle to be accorded to the Irish State in determining the question whether a fair balance was struck between the protection of that public interest, notably the protection accorded under Irish law to the right to life of the unborn, and the conflicting rights of the first and second applicants to respect for their private lives under Article 8 of the Convention.

The majority believed that this wide margin of appreciation was not curtailed by the existence of a consensus amongst a substantial majority of member States to permit abortions on grounds of the woman's health or well-being (at least 35 member States would have allowed A and B to have abortions within their jurisdictions).

237. Of central importance is the finding in the above-cited *Vo* case [see p 109], that the question of when the right to life begins came within the States' margin of appreciation because there was no European consensus on the scientific and legal definition of the beginning of life, so that it was impossible to answer the question whether the unborn was a person to be protected for the purposes of Article 2. Since the rights claimed on behalf of the foetus and those of the mother are inextricably interconnected (see the review of the Convention case law at paragraphs 75–80 in the above-cited *Vo v France* [GC] judgment), the margin of appreciation accorded to a State's protection of the unborn necessarily translates into a margin of appreciation for that State as to how it balances the conflicting rights of the mother. It follows that, even if it appears from the national laws referred to that most Contracting Parties may in their legislation have resolved those conflicting rights and interests in favour of greater legal access to abortion, this consensus cannot be a decisive factor in the Court's examination of whether the impugned prohibition on abortion in Ireland for health and well-being reasons struck a fair balance between the conflicting rights and interests, notwithstanding an evolutive interpretation of the Convention (*Tyrer v the United Kingdom*, § 31; and *Vo v France* [GC], § 82, both cited above).

However, the six dissentients criticized the approach of the majority:

6. Yet in the case before us a European consensus (and indeed, a strong one) exists. We believe that this will be one of the rare times in the Court's case-law that Strasbourg considers that such consensus does not narrow the broad margin of appreciation of the State concerned; . . . [Joint Partly Dissenting Opinion of Judges Rozakis, Tulkens, Fura, Hirvela, Malinverni and Poalelungi.]

Echoing the judgment in *Tysiac*, the Grand Chamber was united in finding a breach of C's right to respect for her private life as Irish law had failed to provide an accessible procedure whereby she could ascertain if she was entitled to an abortion within Ireland.

Hence the Court has now held that Article 8 does not provide women with a right to an abortion. Nevertheless, it may be possible for pregnant women successfully to claim that domestic law violates their right to respect for their private life if the restrictions on abortion are imprecise and/or no effective system of adjudicating requests for abortion is available. But, the Grand Chamber's judgment in *A, B and C* reveals the Court adopting a highly circumspect stance when evaluating the lawfulness of national abortion provisions.

8   Another facet of private life is a person's name. In *Burghartz v Switzerland* A.280B (1994), the applicant complained that his rights under Article 8 and Article 14 had been violated by the Swiss authorities' refusal to register his surname as Schnyder Burghartz after his family surname had been recorded as Burghartz (his wife's surname). A majority (6 to 3) of the Court held that:

> Unlike some other international instruments, such as the International Covenant on Civil and Political Rights (Article 24(2)), the Convention on the Rights of the Child of 20 November 1989 (Articles 7 and 8) or the American Convention on Human Rights (Article 18), Article 8 of the Convention does not contain any explicit provisions on names. As a means of personal identification and of linking to a family, a person's name none the less concerns his or her private and family life. The fact that society and the State have an interest in regulating the use of names does not exclude this, since these public-law aspects are compatible with private life conceived of as including, to a certain degree, the right to establish and develop relationships with other human beings, in professional or business contexts as in others (see, *Niemietz v Germany* A.251B (1992)). In the instant case, the applicant's retention of the surname by which, according to him, he has become known in academic circles may significantly affect his career. Article 8 therefore applies. [Para 24.]

By a bare majority of one (5 to 4) the Court went on to decide that Switzerland had violated the applicant's rights under Article 14 taken together with Article 8, as there was no objective and reasonable justification why men could not combine their surnames with their wives' surnames when Swiss law allowed married women to combine their surnames with their husbands' surnames.

In a later case the Court did not find a violation of Article 8 when a man was refused permission to change his surname, despite the fact that he claimed other people often misspelt his name. The unanimous view of the Court was that States had a wide margin of appreciation in regulating the changing of names, because there was little common ground in the domestic practices of member States: see *Stjerna v Finland* A.299B (1994).

In *Guillot v France*, 1996-V, the Court held that forenames fall within the ambit of 'private life'. However, by a majority (7 to 2) the Court found that France had not violated the parents' rights, under Article 8, by refusing to register their daughter as 'Fleur de Marie' (a forename which was not listed in any calendar of saints' days). Instead, the authorities had registered the child's name as 'Fleur-Marie' and the majority considered that this did not cause the applicants sufficient inconvenience as to amount to a breach of their Convention rights.

A unanimous Chamber of the full-time Court ruled that the tradition of demonstrating family unity by married women being obliged to adopt the surname of their husbands was no longer compatible with the Convention in *Unal Tekeli v Turkey*, judgment of 16 November 2004. The applicant married in 1990 and took her husband's surname in accordance with

Turkish law. In 1995 she applied to the domestic courts for permission to use her maiden name (Unal). Her application was dismissed. In 1997 the Turkish Civil Code was amended to enable married women to put their maiden name before their husband's surname if they so wished (this provision was re-enacted in 2001). This reform did not satisfy the applicant's wish only to use her maiden name. She complained to the Court alleging a breach of Article 8 and Article 14. The Chamber held that:

61. Moreover, the Court notes the emergence of a consensus among the Contracting States of the Council of Europe in favour of choosing the spouses' family name on an equal footing.

Of the member States of the Council of Europe Turkey is the only country which legally imposes—even where the couple prefers an alternative arrangement—the husband's name as the couple's surname and thus the automatic loss of the woman's own surname on her marriage. Married women in Turkey cannot use their maiden name alone even if both spouses agree to such an arrangement. The possibility made available by the Turkish legislature on 22 November 2001 of putting the maiden name in front of the husband's surname does not alter that position. The interests of married women who do not want their marriage to affect their name have not been taken into consideration.

62. The Court observes, moreover, that Turkey does not position itself outside the general trend towards placing men and women on an equal footing in the family. Prior to the relevant legislative amendments, particularly those of 22 November 2001, the man's position in the family was the dominant one. The reflection of family unity through the husband's surname corresponded to the traditional conception of the family maintained by the Turkish legislature until then. The aim of the reforms of November 2001 was to place married women on an equal footing with their husband in representing the couple, in economic activities and in the decisions to be taken affecting the family and children. Among other things the husband's role as head of the family has been abolished. Both married partners have acquired the power to represent the family. Despite the enactment of the Civil Code in 2001, however, the provisions concerning the family name after marriage, including those obliging married women to take their husband's name, have remained unchanged.

63. The first question for the Court is whether the tradition of reflecting family unity through the husband's name can be regarded as a decisive factor in the present case. Admittedly, that tradition derives from the man's primordial role and the woman's secondary role in the family. Nowadays the advancement of the equality of the sexes in the member States of the Council of Europe, including Turkey, and in particular the importance attached to the principle of non-discrimination, prevent States from imposing that tradition on married women.

64. In this context it should be recalled that while family unity can be reflected by choosing the husband's surname as the family name, it can be reflected just as well by choosing the wife's surname or a joint name chosen by the couple (see *Burghartz*, cited above, § 28).

65. The second question that the Court is asked to address is whether family unity has to be reflected by a joint family name and whether, in the event of disagreement between the married partners, one partner's surname can be imposed on the other.

66. The Court observes in this regard that, according to the practice of the Contracting States, it is perfectly conceivable that family unity will be preserved and consolidated where a married couple chooses not to bear a joint family name. Observation of the systems applicable in Europe supports this finding. The Government have not shown in the present case that concrete or substantial hardship for married partners and/or third parties or detriment to the public interest would be likely to flow from the lack of reflection of family unity through a joint family name. In these circumstances the Court considers that the obligation on married women, in the name of family unity, to bear their

husband's surname—even if they can put their maiden name in front of it—has no objective and reasonable justification.

67. The Court does not underestimate the important repercussions which a change in the system, involving a transition from the traditional system of family name based on the husband's surname to other systems allowing the married partners either to keep their own surname or freely choose a joint family name, will inevitably have for keeping registers of births, marriages and deaths. However, it considers that society may reasonably be expected to tolerate a certain inconvenience to enable individuals to live in dignity and worth in accordance with the name they have chosen (see, *mutatis mutandis, Christine Goodwin v the United Kingdom* [GC], No 28957/95, § 91, ECHR 2002-VI).

68. Consequently, the objective of reflecting family unity through a joint family name cannot provide a justification for the gender-based difference in treatment complained of in the instant case.

Accordingly, the difference in treatment in question contravenes Article 14 taken in conjunction with Article 8.

69. Having regard to that conclusion, the Court does not consider it necessary to determine whether there has also been a breach of Article 8 taken alone.

This judgment discloses that the margin of appreciation for member States to regulate the choice of family names has now been eliminated where national regulations are based upon gender discrimination. Another Chamber was unanimous in finding a breach of Article 14 in combination with Article 8 where a foreign husband was unable to retain his surname after marriage to a Swiss national: *Losonci Rose and Rose v Switzerland*, judgment of 9 November 2010.

Whilst confirming that States have a wide margin of appreciation to regulate the choice of forenames a united Chamber concluded that the authorities had violated Article 8 by refusing to register the applicants' son with the forename Axl in *Johansson v Finland*, judgment of 6 September 2007. The Court found that the name was not ridiculous, could be pronounced in Finnish, and three other persons had been registered with that name in Finland.

9 The keeping and use of secret files on individuals by governmental bodies amounts to an interference with such persons' private lives. In *Leander v Sweden* A.116 (1987), the applicant had been prevented from continuing to work at a naval museum—this job involved access to a neighbouring naval base—when the military authorities refused him a personnel control after seeing the contents of a secret file on him maintained by the National Police Board. Despite Leander's complaints to the authorities they would not allow him to see or comment upon the file concerning him. During proceedings before the Commission Leander explained that some years earlier he had been a member of the Swedish Communist Party, he had also been active in the soldiers' union, and more recently in the Swedish Building Workers' Association. His only criminal conviction was for being late for a military parade. The Court held that:

It is uncontested that the secret police-register contained information relating to Mr Leander's private life. Both the storing and the release of such information, which were coupled with a refusal to allow Mr Leander an opportunity to refute it, amounted to an interference with his right to respect for private life as guaranteed by Article 8(1). [Para 48.]

However, the Court, unanimously, went on to find that the Swedish secret police-register was necessary for the protection of national security and had sufficient procedural safeguards (including the involvement of parliamentarians) to satisfy the requirements of Article 8(2).

The Commission expressed the opinion that:

>...secret surveillance activities for the purpose of gathering and storing on file information concerning a person's private life also constitutes an interference with this right. [*Hewitt and Harman v UK* 14 EHRR 657 at 663.]

The applicants, former senior officers working for the National Council for Civil Liberties (now known as 'Liberty'), complained that the British Security Service had subjected them to secret surveillance and had kept files on them as 'communist sympathizers' and 'subversives'. A majority of the Commission (13 to 2) concluded that the likely actions of the Security Service violated the applicants' rights under Article 8(1) and could not be brought within the exceptions in Article 8(2), because the Security Service did not operate within a legal framework that was 'in accordance with the law'. The Committee of Ministers agreed with the Commission's opinion. However, it noted that the British Parliament had subsequently enacted the Security Service Act 1989, which placed the Service on a statutory basis and established an independent Commissioner and Tribunal to determine complaints against the Service; therefore, no further action was required by the Committee. In *Christie v UK* 78A DR E Com HR 119 (1994), the Commission declared inadmissible a complaint by a trade unionist, who had links with the former communist authorities of Eastern Europe, regarding alleged surveillance of him by the British Security Service. The Commission considered that in his case the provisions of the 1989 Act satisfied the requirements of Article 8(2). In July 1998 the British Government disclosed, for the first time, the number of files held by the British Security Service. The Home Secretary stated that the Service held a total of 440,000 files. Of those, 290,000 files related to persons who had at some time been the subject of inquiry or investigation by the Service; 75,000 concerned people or groups who had not been investigated by the Service, but had some connection with its work (e.g. they had been given security advice by the Service); and 40,000 involved organizations and subjects studied by the Service. About 20,000 files were active dossiers of which one-third related to foreign nationals (e.g. members of foreign intelligence services) and the rest to British nationals (of whom over half were suspected terrorists): (1998) *The Times*, 30 July.

The practice of the Swiss Federal Government compiling a card index of persons who had, *inter alia*, been in contact with staff at the former Soviet Embassy was found to be in breach of Article 8 in the case of **Amann v Switzerland**, judgment of 16 February 2000. The applicant was a businessman who sold depilatory appliances. During 1981 a woman telephoned him from the former Soviet Embassy in Berne to order one of his appliances. The telephone call was secretly intercepted by the Federal Public Prosecutor's Office, which then instigated an investigation into the applicant and his business. As a result of the investigation a card on the applicant was placed in the national security card index. The card stated 'from the Zurich Intelligence Service: A. identified as a contact with the Russian embassy according to...'. In 1990 the applicant became aware of the index and sought a copy of his card. Subsequently, he brought legal proceedings against the Swiss Government for compiling and retaining the card, but the Federal Court dismissed his claims. He then complained to the Commission which, by 9 votes to 8, concluded that there had been a breach of the applicant's rights under Article 8. The Court was unanimous in concluding that:

>...both the creation of the impugned card by the Public Prosecutor's Office and the storing of it in the Confederation's card index amounted to interference with the applicant's private life which cannot be considered to be 'in accordance with the law' since Swiss law does not indicate with sufficient clarity the scope and conditions of exercise of the authorities' discretionary power in the

area under consideration. It follows that there has been a violation of Article 8 of the Convention. [Para 80.]

Hence, the storing of information regarding persons, and their businesses, by public authorities amounts to an 'interference' with their right to respect for their private lives, which States must justify under the conditions laid down in Article 8(2).

A Chamber has held that where member States have introduced schemes to determine if persons have collaborated with former totalitarian regimes ('lustration measures') then affected persons should generally have access to the secret files upon which such decisions have been made. In *Turek v Slovakia*, judgment of 14 February 2006, the applicant had been issued with a certificate stating that he had collaborated with the former State Security Agency (StB) of Czechoslovakia. He challenged the certificate before the Slovak courts but they ruled that he had not proved that he not collaborated with the StB. The Chamber held that:

115. The Court recognises that, particularly in proceedings related to the operations of state security agencies, there may be legitimate grounds to limit access to certain documents and other materials. However, in respect of lustration proceedings, this consideration loses much of its validity. In the first place, lustration proceedings are, by their very nature, oriented towards the establishment of facts dating back to the communist era and are not directly linked to the current functions and operations of the security services. Thus, unless the contrary is shown on the facts of a specific case, it cannot be assumed that there remains a continuing and actual public interest in imposing limitations on access to materials classified as confidential under former regimes. Secondly, lustration proceedings inevitably depend on the examination of documents relating to the operations of the former communist security agencies. If the party to whom the classified materials relate is denied access to all or most of the materials in question, his or her possibilities to contradict the security agency's version of the facts would be severely curtailed. Finally, under the relevant laws, it is typically the security agency itself that has the power to decide what materials should remain classified and for how long. Since, it is the legality of the agency's actions which is in question in lustration proceedings, the existence of this power is not consistent with the fairness of the proceedings, including the principle of equality of arms. Thus, if a State is to adopt lustration measures, it must ensure that the persons affected thereby enjoy all procedural guarantees under the Convention in respect of any proceedings relating to the application of such measures.

By a large majority, 6 votes to 1, the Chamber concluded that an unrealistic burden had been placed on the applicant to disprove his alleged collaboration with the StB and consequently he had not had access to a procedure which effectively protected his right to respect for his private life. This judgment is potentially very significant for ensuring that those States with lustration schemes provide adequate procedural safeguards for affected persons.

When States maintain secret security files on individuals the Court has held that the storage of such information must be supported by relevant and sufficient reasons. In a contemporary case involving the Swedish system a unanimous Chamber found that, *inter alia*, the retention of a record that a person participated in a political meeting in Poland during 1967 was no longer justified as regards the protection of national security and constituted a breach of Article 8: *Segerstedt-Wiberg and Others v Sweden*, judgment of 6 June 2006.

10 The disclosure of medical records and information concerning patients by State authorities will in principle amount to a breach of the right to respect for a person's 'private life' and can only be justified if the conditions of Article 8(2) are satisfied. In *Z v Finland*, 1997-I, the applicant had been married to a man (X) who was originally charged with a series of serious sexual offences, later the prosecutors also charged him with several counts of attempted manslaughter on the basis that he knew/ought to have known that he was HIV positive at the time of the sexual crimes. A central element of the trial concerned the issue of when X became aware that he was HIV positive. The applicant exercised her right under Finnish law not to give evidence in a case concerning a spouse. Thereupon, the court ordered Z's doctor to provide evidence about her health and he disclosed that she too was HIV positive (all the proceedings were conducted *in camera*). Later the prosecution ordered the seizing and copying of the applicant's medical records. The court convicted X of three counts of attempted manslaughter and one count of rape, and sentenced him to seven years' imprisonment. Records of the proceedings were ordered by the court to be kept confidential for ten years. On appeal the Helsinki Court of Appeal gave a judgment, a copy of which was provided to the press, which found X guilty of five counts of attempted manslaughter and increased his sentence to 11-and-a-half years' imprisonment. The judgment identified the applicant by name and disclosed her HIV status. This information was published by several newspapers. She complained to the Commission which, unanimously, found a breach of Article 8. The Court also found breaches of that Article. The judgment focused on whether the Finnish authorities could justify their interferences with the applicant's right to respect for her privacy under Article 8(2).

In this connection, the Court will take into account that the protection of personal data, not least medical data, is of fundamental importance to a person's enjoyment of his or her right to respect for private and family life as guaranteed by Article 8 of the Convention. Respecting the confidentiality of health data is a vital principle in the legal systems of all the Contracting Parties to the Convention. It is crucial not only to respect the sense of privacy of a patient but also to preserve his or her confidence in the medical profession and in the health services in general.

Without such protection, those in need of medical assistance may be deterred from revealing such information of a personal and intimate nature as may be necessary in order to receive appropriate treatment and even, from seeking such assistance, thereby endangering their own health and, in the case of transmissible diseases, that of the community.

The domestic law must therefore afford appropriate safeguards to prevent any such communication or disclosure of personal health data as may be inconsistent with the guarantees in Article 8 of the Convention. The above considerations are especially valid as regards protection of the confidentiality of information about a person's HIV infection. The disclosure of such data may dramatically affect his or her private and family life, as well as social and employment situation, by exposing him or her to opprobrium and the risk of ostracism...

In view of the highly intimate and sensitive nature of information concerning a person's HIV status, any state measures compelling communication or disclosure of such information without the consent of the patient call for the most careful scrutiny on the part of the Court, as do the safeguards designed to secure an effective protection.

At the same time, the Court accepts that the interests of a patient and the community as a whole in protecting the confidentiality of medical data may be outweighed by the interest in investigation and prosecution of crime and in the publicity of court proceedings. [Paras 95–7.]

A majority of the Court (8 votes to 1) held that (a) the Finnish court's requirement for Z's doctors to give evidence regarding her medical condition and (b) the prosecution's seizure/copying of Z's medical records, were proportionate actions under Article 8(2) directed at the 'prevention of crime' and 'the protection of the rights and freedoms of others'. However, the Court, unanimously, found that (c) the limited (ten-year) time limit on the confidentiality of the trial court's records and (d) the Court of Appeal's public judgment, could not be justified under Article 8(2). The exceptional circumstances of X's criminal behaviour and the trial court's confidential hearings undoubtedly constituted significant factors in the Court's application of Article 8 in this case. Indeed, the Court noted that the Committee of Ministers of the Council of Europe had issued guidance to member States on the importance of confidentiality of medical data regarding HIV infections (Recommendation No R(89)14: 'The ethical issues of HIV infection in the health care and social settings'). States will also have to justify, under Article 8(2), any disclosure of medical records from public health bodies to other agencies of the State. In *MS v Sweden*, 1997-IV, the applicant allegedly injured herself at work and sought treatment at her regional hospital. She was unable to return to work because of serious back pain and later she received a disability pension. In 1991 she applied to the State Social Insurance Office for compensation regarding her alleged injury under the terms of the Industrial Injury Insurance Act. The Office obtained her medical records from the hospital, these included details of her subsequent treatments including an abortion. In the light of these medical details the Office rejected her claim on the basis that her ill health had not been caused by an industrial injury. The applicant complained to the Commission that the disclosure of her medical details to the Social Insurance Office by the hospital without her express consent amounted to a violation of her right to respect for her private life. The Commission (by 22 votes to 5) found no violation. The Court (unanimously) also rejected her claim. However, the Court held that the disclosure of her medical records to a wider circle of public servants (albeit subject to similar duties of confidence regarding the contents of the records) combined with the different use of the data by the Social Insurance Office, amounted to a interference with the applicant's right to privacy under Article 8(1). But the Swedish authorities were able to justify the interference as being necessary for 'the protection of the economic well-being of the country' under Article 8(2), because they were seeking to ensure that public funds were only allocated to deserving claimants. The Court considered that all the medical records disclosed to the Office were relevant to determining the applicant's claim. Presumably, therefore, if State authorities disclose irrelevant confidential medical information to other public agencies, the individual concerned might be able to claim that the disclosure was not a proportionate interference and fell outside Article 8(2). For an individual's right of access to his/her own social or medical files see, *Gaskin* and *McGinley and Egan* (pp 577–79).

11 The covert recording of the voices of two suspects whilst at a police station, for the purposes of voice analysis to determine if they were involved in a planned robbery, was held to fall within the scope of private life in *PG and JH v UK*, judgment of 25 September 2001. Whilst the applicants were responding to formal charges and were talking in their cells their voices were secretly recorded. They were subsequently convicted of conspiracy to commit armed robbery and sentenced to 15 years' imprisonment. The Chamber, unanimously, ruled that:

59. The Court's case-law has, on numerous occasions, found that the covert taping of telephone conversations falls within the scope of Article 8 in both aspects of the right guaranteed, namely, respect for private life and correspondence. While it is generally the case that the recordings were made for the purpose of using the content of the conversations in some way, the Court is not persuaded that recordings taken for use as voice samples can be regarded as falling outside the scope of the protection afforded by Article 8. A permanent record has nonetheless been made of the person's voice and it is subject to a process of analysis directly relevant to identifying that person in the context of other personal data. Though it is true that when being charged the applicants answered formal questions in a place where police officers were listening to them, the recording and analysis of their voices on this occasion must still be regarded as concerning the processing of personal data about the applicants.

60. The Court concludes therefore that the recording of the applicants' voices when being charged and when in their police cell discloses an interference with their right to respect for private life within the meaning of Article 8 § 1 of the Convention.

No precise domestic law authorized the police to make the recordings and therefore the Chamber found that the interference with the applicants' private lives had not been in accordance with the law as required by Article 8(2). Part II of the Regulation of Investigatory Powers Act 2000 sought to fill this lacuna by establishing a statutory scheme of authorizations for such forms of directed surveillance by senior police officers and independent Surveillance Commissioners (persons who hold or have held high judicial office). For an examination of the case-law on the interception of telephone calls. see p 561.

12   A unanimous Chamber found that the disclosure to the media of pictures, derived from a closed circuit television system (CCTV) covering a town centre, by the local authority operating the system breached the right to respect for his private life of a person shown attempting to commit suicide in *Peck v UK*, judgment of 28 January 2003. The Council's CCTV operator saw a man walking down the High Street carrying a knife. The police were alerted and officers took the knife from the man (the applicant), gave him medical help, and took him to the police station where he was detained under the Mental Health Act 1983. After being treated by a doctor he was released without charge. Subsequently, as part of the Council's policy to publicize the effectiveness of the CCTV system, the local authority authorized the release of photos taken by the CCTV cameras showing the applicant (but not him cutting his wrists) and the police response. These pictures were published in two local papers and on regional and national television programmes. The applicant's face was not masked in all these publications/broadcasts and people who knew him were able to identify the applicant from the pictures. The High Court found that the Council had acted lawfully, under the Criminal Justice Act 1994 and the Local Government Act 1972. The Chamber considered that:

59. The monitoring of the actions of an individual in a public place by the use of photographic equipment which does not record the visual data does not, as such, give rise to an interference with the individual's private life (see, for example, *Herbecq and the association 'Ligue des droits de l'homme' v Belgium*, applications Nos 32200/96 and 32201/96, Commission decision of 14 January 1998, DR 92-B, p 92). On the other hand, the recording of the data and the systematic or permanent nature of the record may give rise to such considerations. Accordingly, in both *Rotaru* and *Amann* (to which *P.G. and J.H.* [v UK ECHR 2001-IX] referred) the compilation of data by security services on particular individuals, even without the use of covert surveillance methods, constituted an interference with the applicants' private lives (*Rotaru v Romania* [GC], No 28341/95, §§ 43–4, ECHR 2000-V, and *Amann v Switzerland* [GC], No 27798/95, §§ 65–7, ECHR 2000-II). While the permanent recording of the voices of P.G. and J.H. was made while they answered questions in a police cell as police officers listened to them, the recording of their voices for further analysis was regarded as the processing of personal data about them amounting to an interference with their right to respect for their private lives (see *P.G. and J.H.*, cited above, §§ 59–60).

60. However, the Court notes that the present applicant did not complain that the collection of data through the CCTV-camera monitoring of his movements and the creation of a permanent record of itself amounted to an interference with his private life. Indeed, he admitted that that function of the CCTV system, together with the consequent involvement of the police, may have saved his life. Rather, he argued that it was the disclosure of that record of his movements to the public in a manner in which he could never have foreseen which gave rise to such an interference.

...

62. The present applicant was in a public street but he was not there for the purposes of participating in any public event and he was not a public figure. It was late at night, he was deeply perturbed and in a state of distress. While he was walking in public wielding a knife, he was not later charged with any offence. The actual suicide attempt was neither recorded nor therefore disclosed. However, footage of the immediate aftermath was recorded and disclosed by the Council directly to the public in its CCTV News publication. In addition, the footage was disclosed to the media for further broadcasting and publication purposes. Those media included the audiovisual media: Anglia Television broadcast locally to approximately 350,000 people and the BBC broadcast nationally, and it is 'commonly acknowledged that the audiovisual media have often a much more immediate and powerful effect than the print media' (*Jersild v Denmark*, judgment of 23 September 1994, Series A No 298, pp 23–4, § 31). The *Yellow Advertiser* was distributed in the applicant's locality to approximately 24,000 readers. The applicant's identity was not adequately, or in some cases not at all, masked in the photographs and footage so published and broadcast. He was recognised by certain members of his family and by his friends, neighbours and colleagues.

As a result, the relevant moment was viewed to an extent which far exceeded any exposure to a passer-by or to security observation (as in *Herbecq and the association 'Ligue des droits de l'homme'*, cited above) and to a degree surpassing that which the applicant could possibly have foreseen when he walked in Brentwood on 20 August 1995.

63. Accordingly, the Court considers that the disclosure by the Council of the relevant footage constituted a serious interference with the applicant's right to respect for his private life.

The Chamber found that the Council's disclosure was in accordance with the law, as it had a statutory basis and was foreseeable. Also it had a legitimate aim under Article 8(2) of promoting public safety, the prevention of disorder, and crime and the protection of the rights of others. However the Chamber did not consider that the disclosure was necessary in a democratic society.

85. In sum, the Court does not find that, in the circumstances of this case, there were relevant or sufficient reasons which would justify the direct disclosure by the Council to the public of stills from the footage in its own CCTV News article without the Council obtaining the applicant's consent or masking his identity, or which would justify its disclosures to the media without the Council taking steps to ensure so far as possible that such masking would be effected by the media. The crime-prevention objective and context of the disclosures demanded particular scrutiny and care in these respects in the present case.

...

87. Accordingly, the Court considers that the disclosures by the Council of the CCTV material in the CCTV News and to the *Yellow Advertiser*, Anglia Television and the BBC were not accompanied by sufficient safeguards to prevent disclosure inconsistent with the guarantees of respect for the applicant' private life contained in Article 8. As such, the disclosure constituted a disproportionate and therefore unjustified interference with his private life and a violation of Article 8 of the Convention.

The Chamber awarded the applicant £11,800 compensation in respect of non-pecuniary damage.

Given the rapid expansion of public CCTV systems (and those of private sector bodies) over recent years the judgment in **Peck** is very important for articulating the Court's approach to the installation and use of such technology. Clearly the recording of images from such systems and their retention or distribution potentially fall within the ambit of relevant persons' private lives. In such circumstances the judgment requires that, *inter alia,* adequate procedural steps are taken to protect the identity of such persons from improper public disclosure.

Subsequently, another Chamber examined the modification and use of images obtained from a CCTV system located inside a police station in *Perry v UK*, judgment of 17 July 2003. The applicant had been arrested on suspicion of committing a number of armed robberies. Later he failed to attend several identification parades. So the police arranged to have the surveillance camera at one of their custody suites adjusted to record detailed pictures. The applicant was then brought to the custody area and his picture was recorded by the camera. The recording was used by the police to compile a video identification and that evidence was used in his trial. He was convicted of three counts of robbery and sentenced to five years' imprisonment. Before the Court he argued that the filming of him in the above circumstances violated his right to respect for his private life. The Chamber, unanimously, held that:

40. As stated above, the normal use of security cameras *per se* whether in the public street or on premises, such as shopping centres or police stations where they serve a legitimate and foreseeable purpose, do not raise issues under Article 8 § 1 of the Convention. Here, however, the police regulated the security camera so that it could take clear footage of the applicant in the custody suite and inserted it in a montage of film of other persons to show to witnesses for the purposes of seeing whether they identified the applicant as the perpetrator of the robberies under investigation. The video was also shown during the applicant's trial in a public court room. The question is whether this use of the camera and footage constituted a processing or use of personal data of a nature to constitute an interference with respect for private life.

41. The Court recalls that the applicant had been brought to the police station to attend an identity parade and that he had refused to participate. Whether or not he was aware of the security cameras running in the custody suite, there is no indication that the applicant had any expectation that footage was being taken of him within the police station for use in a video identification procedure and, potentially, as evidence prejudicial to his defence at trial. This ploy adopted by the police went beyond the normal or expected use of this type of camera, as indeed is demonstrated by the fact that the police were required to obtain permission and an engineer had to adjust the camera. The permanent recording of the footage and its inclusion in a montage for further use may therefore be regarded as the processing or collecting of personal data about the applicant.

42. The Government argued that the use of the footage was analogous to the use of photos in identification albums, in which circumstance the Commission had stated that no issue arose where they were used solely for the purpose of identifying offenders in criminal proceedings (*Lupker v The Netherlands*, No 18395/91, Commission decision of 7 December 1992, unreported). However, the Commission emphasised in that case that the photographs had not come into the possession of the police through any invasion of privacy, the photographs having been submitted voluntarily to the authorities in passport applications or having been taken by the police on the occasion of a previous arrest. The footage in question in the present case had not been obtained voluntarily or in circumstances where it could be reasonably anticipated that it would be recorded and used for identification purposes.

43. The Court considers therefore that the recording and use of the video footage of the applicant in this case discloses an interference with his right to respect for private life.

As the actions of the police were in breach of the requirements of the Code of Practice, issued under the Police and Criminal Evidence Act 1984, governing identification videos, the Chamber concluded that the measures taken against the applicant were not in accordance with the law and therefore violated Article 8. Perry was awarded 1,500 euros compensation in respect of non-pecuniary damage.

So, whilst the normal use of surveillance cameras within police stations (which may help to ensure the proper treatment of detainees as officers know their actions are being recorded and conversely help to protect officers from false accusations by detainees) will not fall within the scope of Article 8(1) their covert use, as in *Perry*, may do so.

13 The full-time Court has held that resolving questions of disputed paternity falls within the scope of the child's private life in *Mikulic v Croatia*, judgment of 7 February 2002. The applicant was born out of an extra-marital relationship in November 1996. Two months later she and her mother filed a paternity suit against a named man alleged to be her father. On six occasions the Zagreb Municipal Court scheduled appointments for that man to undergo DNA tests, to determine if he was the applicant's father. The man did not attend any of the appointments to provide a specimen of his DNA for analysis. In November 2001, the Municipal Court gave judgment finding that the man was the applicant's father, based upon his repeated avoidance of the DNA tests and the testimony of the applicant's mother. The man then appealed against the judgment. The applicant complained to the Strasbourg Court alleging, *inter alia*, that the Croatian judicial system had been inefficient in determining her paternity claim and thereby left her uncertain as to her personal identity in breach of her right to respect for her private life under Article 8. The Court accepted that her claim fell within the ambit of that right.

53....There appears, furthermore, to be no reason of principle why the notion of 'private life' should be taken to exclude the determination of the legal relationship between a child born out of wedlock and her natural father.

The Court then examined whether Croatia had complied with its positive obligations under Article 8. Having regard to the diversity of paternity procedures and evidential rules in member States the Court concluded that Article 8 did not require States to compel alleged fathers to undergo DNA testing. However, if such testing was not compulsory in a particular State the legal system must provide '64....alternative means enabling an independent authority to determine the paternity claim speedily.' That had not happened in the applicant's case therefore Article 8 had been violated.

In *Shofman v Russia*, judgment of 24 November 2005, a unanimous Chamber extended the ruling in *Mikulic* to encompass the 'private life' of a man who disputed his parentage of the child of his former wife. Under the law of the former Russian Soviet Federalist Socialist Republic, subsequently amended, actions contesting paternity were subject to a time limit of one year from the date the man was informed that he had been registered as the father. The applicant received no indications that his wife's child was not his until two years after he had been registered as the father. He then disputed paternity in the courts. Despite DNA evidence that the applicant was not the father, the courts applied the time limit to reject the applicant's claim. The Chamber concluded that there had been a breach of the applicant's right to respect for his private life as the Russian Soviet law had not struck a fair balance between his interest and that of the general interest regarding legal certainty of family relationships.

For cases where persons seek information about their natural parents which is in the possession of public authorities, see p 577.

14 A unanimous Chamber determined that a gynaecological examination of a detainee, undertaken against her wishes, constituted an unlawful interference with her private life in *YF v Turkey*, judgment of 22 July 2003. The applicant and his wife were arrested by the police on suspicion of aiding the PKK. After four days' detention the police took the applicant's wife to a gynaecologist and requested an examination to determine if she had been subject to sexual intercourse during her time in custody. The wife refused to consent to the examination, but the police officers insisted that it be undertaken and remained on the premises whilst the examination took place (the wife was examined in private). The doctor reported that there was no evidence of sexual intercourse having taken place during the period of detention. The applicant complained to the Court, on behalf of his wife. The Court held:

> 33. ... It reiterates in this connection that a person's body concerns the most intimate aspect of one's private life. Thus, a compulsory medical intervention, even if it is of minor importance, constitutes an interference with this right ...
>
> 43. ... Finally, while the Court accepts the Government's submission that the medical examination of detainees by a forensic medical doctor can prove to be a significant safeguard against sexual harassment or ill-treatment, it considers that any interference with the physical integrity of a person must be prescribed by law and requires the consent of that person. Otherwise, a person in a vulnerable situation, such as a detainee, would be deprived of legal guarantees against arbitrary acts. In the light of the foregoing, the Court finds that the interference at issue was not 'in accordance with the law'.
>
> 44. That finding suffices for the Court to hold that there has been a violation of Article 8.

This is obviously an important ruling that is designed to protect the dignity of detainees. In the later case of *Storck v Germany*, see p 252 for the factual background and Article 5 aspects of the case, the Chamber found that the medical treatment of the applicant against her will in a private clinic also constituted a violation of her right to respect for her private life.

15 A Grand Chamber applied Article 8 in the politically highly sensitive context of the withdrawal of former Soviet Union military forces from the territory of an independent State that had previously been part of the Union of Soviet Socialist Republics (USSR) in *Slivenko v Latvia*, judgment of 9 October 2003. The first applicant, Tatjana Slivenko, had been born during 1959 in Estonia to the wife of a military officer serving in the forces of the USSR. One month after her birth the family moved to Latvia where her father was posted. Tatjana met her future husband in Latvia during the late 1970s and they married there in 1980. He was stationed in Latvia as an officer of the USSR military. Their daughter, Karina (the second applicant), was born in Latvia during 1981. Tatjana's father retired from military service in 1986 and remained living in Latvia. During 1991 Latvia regained its independence from the USSR and on 28 January 1992 the Russian Federation took control of the military forces of the former USSR. The applicants and Tatjana's parents were recorded as 'ex-USSR citizens' in the register of Latvian residents in March 1993. Tatjana's husband became a Russian citizen on an unspecified date in the early 1990s and continued to serve in the Russian army, based in Latvia, until his discharge in 1994. A treaty was signed between Latvia and Russia on 30 April 1994 providing for the complete withdrawal of Russian military troops (and members of their families) by 31 August 1994. Under the treaty the discharge of military personnel after 28 January 1992 (the date Russia assumed control over former USSR forces) was not to be regarded as constituting their withdrawal from Latvia.

In October 1994 Tatjana's husband applied to the Latvian Citizenship and Migration Authority (CMA) for a temporary residence permit in Latvia based on his marriage to a permanent resident of Latvia. The CMA refused his application as the Authority considered that he was a Russian military officer who was obliged to leave Latvia under the terms of the above treaty. Soon afterwards the CMA cancelled the applicants' entry in the register of Latvian residents on the basis of Tatjana's husband's status. He challenged the CMA's decision to refuse him a temporary residence permit in the Latvian courts. Eventually, in 1996, the Riga Regional Court upheld the lawfulness of the CMA's decision on the ground that he had been a Russian officer until June 1994 and therefore he was obliged to leave Latvia under the treaty. In August 1996 the Latvian immigration authorities issued a deportation order against the applicants and two days later the local authority issued an eviction order against them in respect of the flat that they rented (this order was never enforced). Tatjana's husband moved to Russia on an unspecified date in 1996.

The applicants brought legal proceedings in the Latvian courts arguing that they were permanent residents and could not be removed. Their claims were upheld by Riga District and Regional Courts but rejected by the Supreme Court (on the basis that the applicants had been provided with a flat in Russia and that they were subject to the 1994 treaty). In early October 1998 Tatjana submitted an appeal to the immigration authorities in respect of the deportation order against her and Karina. However, late on the evening of 28 October the police arrested the applicants at their flat on the basis that they had no valid documents justifying their presence in Latvia. They were released the next day following the intervention of the Director of the CMA. The latter wrote to the applicants in early February 1999 informing them that they were required to leave Latvia immediately. On 16 March 1999 the police arrested Karina, at her grandparents' home, and she was detained in a centre for illegal immigrants for 30 hours. The applicants moved to Russia, to join Tatjana's husband/Karina's father, on 11 July 1999. They adopted Russian citizenship in 2001. Tatjana's parents continued to live, lawfully, in Latvia. The Latvian authorities issued the applicants with visas allowing them to visit their parents/grandparents in late 2001.

The applicants complained to the Court that, *inter alia*, their removal from Latvia violated their right to respect for their private/family life and their home guaranteed by Article 8. In their contention they had been completely integrated into Latvian society (Tatjana had lived there since she was one month old, she had been educated in Latvia, and had worked there since she was 17; Katrina had been born and educated in Latvia). The Government of Russia joined the proceedings as a third party intervener under Article 36 of the Convention. The Chamber decided to relinquish jurisdiction over the complaint to the Grand Chamber in accordance with Article 30.

The Latvian Government submitted that the applicants' removal should be considered in the context of '76. . . . the eradication of the consequences of the illegal occupation of Latvia by the Soviet Union, which had been completed by the withdrawal of Russian troops from the territory of Latvia.' Furthermore, their removal had been in accordance with the Latvian–Russian treaty of 1994 governing the withdrawal of the latter's troops and any interference with the applicants' rights had the legitimate aims, under Article 8(2) of the Convention, of protecting Latvian national security and preventing crime or disorder. The Latvian Government asserted that the applicants had never been integrated into Latvian society because: they had not chosen to live in Latvia but had been there in connection with the military service of members of their family, in their everyday life they had not had to deal with local inhabitants/authorities as their basic services (such as medical care) had been provided by the USSR military authorities, and the applicants were not proficient in the Latvian language. The Russian Government claimed that the applicants had been completely integrated into Latvian society as they had been nationals of the Latvian Soviet Socialist Republic and had lived almost all their lives in the country.

The Grand Chamber began its judgment by considering whether the applicants could claim that they had a 'private life', 'family life', or 'home' in Latvia.

96. . . . It is undisputed that the applicants left Latvia against their own will, as a result of the unsuccessful outcome of the legal proceedings concerning the legality of their stay in Latvia. They were

thus removed from the country where they had developed, uninterruptedly since birth, the network of personal, social and economic relations that make up the private life of every human being. Furthermore, as a result of the removal the applicants lost the flat in which they had lived in Riga. In these circumstances, the Court cannot but find that the applicants' removal from Latvia constituted an interference with their 'private life' and their 'home' within the meaning of Article 8 paragraph 1 of the Convention.

However, the Grand Chamber did not consider that the removal of the applicants from Latvia was directed at breaking–up their 'family life'. This was because the whole family (husband, wife, and daughter) were deported in consequence of the Latvian–Russian treaty.

97. . . . Furthermore, the existence of 'family life' could not be relied on by the applicants in relation to the first applicant's elderly parents, adults who did not belong to the core family and who have not been shown to have been dependent members of the applicants' family, the applicants' arguments in this respect not having been sufficiently substantiated. Nonetheless, the impact of the impugned measures on the applicants' family life—notably their ultimate enforced migration as a family unit to the Russian Federation—is a relevant factor for the Court's assessment of the case under Article 8 of the Convention. The Court will also take into account the applicants' link with the first applicant's parents (the second applicant's grandparents) under the head of the applicants' 'private' life within the meaning of Article 8 paragraph 1 of the Convention.

The Grand Chamber went on to find that the applicants' removal was 'in accordance with the law' under Article 8(2) on the basis that the Latvian court decisions concerning them were applying the Latvian–Russian treaty. As to whether the removal was for the legitimate aim, under Article 8(2), of safeguarding Latvia's national security:

111. The Court considers that the aim of the particular measures taken in respect of the applicants cannot be dissociated from the wider context of the constitutional and international law arrangements made after Latvia regained its independence in 1991. In this context it is not necessary to deal with the previous situation of Latvia under international law. It is sufficient to note that after the dissolution of the USSR former Soviet military troops remained in Latvia under Russian jurisdiction, at the time when both Latvia and Russia were independent States. The Court therefore accepts that by the Latvian-Russian treaty on the withdrawal of Russian troops and the measures for the implementation of this treaty, the Latvian authorities sought to protect the interest of the country's national security.

Therefore, the key issue for the Court was whether the applicants' removal was 'necessary in a democratic society'.

116. In the Court's view, the withdrawal of the armed forces of one independent State from the territory of another, following the dissolution of the State to which they both formerly belonged, constitutes, from the point of view of the Convention, a legitimate means of dealing with the various political, social and economic problems arising from that dissolution. The fact that in the present case the Latvian-Russian treaty provided for the withdrawal of all military officers who after 28 January 1992 had been placed under Russian jurisdiction, including those who had been discharged from the armed forces prior to the entry into force of the treaty (which in this respect therefore had retroactive effect), and that it also obliged their families to leave the country, is not in itself objectionable from the point of view of the Convention and in particular Article 8. Indeed, it can be said that this arrangement respected the family life of the persons concerned in that it did

not interfere with the family unit and obliged Russia to accept the whole family within its territory, irrespective of the origin or nationality of the individual family members.

117. In so far as the withdrawal of the Russian troops interfered with the private life and home of the persons concerned, this interference would normally not appear disproportionate, having regard to the conditions of service of military officers. This is true in particular in the case of active servicemen and their families. Their withdrawal can be treated as akin to a transfer to another place of service, which might have been ordered on other occasions in the course of their normal service. Moreover, it is evident that the continued presence of active servicemen of a foreign army, with their families, may be seen as being incompatible with the sovereignty of an independent State and as a threat to national security. The public interest in the removal of active servicemen and their families from the territory will therefore normally outweigh the individual's interest in staying. However, even in respect of such persons it is not to be excluded that the specific circumstances of their case might render the removal measures unjustified from the point of view of the Convention.

118. The justification of removal measures does not apply to the same extent to retired military officers and their families. After their discharge from the armed forces a requirement to move for reasons of service will normally no longer apply to them. While their inclusion in the treaty does not as such appear objectionable (see paragraph 116 above), the interests of national security will in the Court's view carry less weight in respect of this category of persons, while more importance must be attached to their legitimate private interests.

The Grand Chamber noted that the applicants' husband/father had retired from the Russian military by mid-1994. Also the Latvian authorities had permitted about 900 Latvian citizens/close relatives of Latvian citizens to remain in Latvia despite the fact that they were family members of Russian military personnel obliged to leave under the terms of the Latvian–Russian treaty.

122. The Court considers that schemes such as the present one for the withdrawal of foreign troops and their families, based on a general finding that their removal is necessary for national security, cannot as such be deemed to be contrary to Article 8 of the Convention. However, application of such a scheme without any possibility of taking into account the individual circumstances of persons not exempted by the domestic law from removal is in the Court's view not compatible with the requirements of that Article. In order to strike a fair balance between the competing interests of the individual and the community the removal of a person should not be enforced where such measure is disproportionate to the legitimate aim pursued. In the present case the question is whether the applicants' specific situation was such as to outweigh any danger to national security based on their family ties with former foreign military officers.

A large majority of the Grand Chamber, 11 votes to 6, concluded that the Latvian authorities had not achieved such a balance in forcing the applicants to leave Latvia. The majority found that the applicants had been integrated into Latvian society (they did not live in army barracks, nor did they work or study in a military institution, and their language skills in Latvian were sufficient to allow them to participate in everyday life). The Latvian Government's refusal to make an exception in respect of the applicants' removal was because they were the daughter/granddaughter of a former USSR officer. However, the majority was unable to accept that this fact created a danger to the national security of Latvia (the applicants' father/grandfather was allowed to remain in Latvia). Consequently, the majority found a breach of Article 8, respect for private life/home, as the applicants' removal was not 'necessary in a democratic society'.

The applicants claimed 400,000 euros in respect of non-pecuniary damage caused by their enforced removal from their motherland. The Russian Government supported this claim, whilst the Latvian Government submitted that it was exorbitant. The Court, by 11 votes to 6, awarded each applicant the much smaller sum of 10,000 euros compensation.

The six dissentients (President Wildhaber and Judges: Ress, Bratza, Cabral Barreto, Greve, and Maruste) issued a joint dissenting opinion in which they emphasized the significance of the origins and terms of the Latvian–Russian treaty as the decisive factors in assessing the proportionality, under Article 8 of the Convention, of the removal measures taken against the applicants.

> 4. We note at the outset the specific historical context and purpose for which the treaty was signed, namely the elimination of the consequences of the Soviet rule of Latvia. In the preamble of the treaty both parties to the agreement—Latvia and Russia—accepted that the withdrawal of the Russian troops was intended "to eradicate the negative consequences of their common history. The legitimacy of this purpose of the treaty is, in our view, of foremost importance in assessing the justification for an interference with the rights of individual members of the forces and of their families, who were subject to removal from the country under the treaty.
>
> It is also significant to note that the treaty itself did not impose on the Latvian authorities an obligation to justify each measure taken by reference to the actual danger posed to national security by the specific individual concerned, particularly in relation to non-military family members. General schemes such as the present one for the withdrawal of foreign troops and their families do not easily accommodate procedures of individual, particularised justification on the merits of each and every case (see, *mutatis mutandis*, *James and Others v the United Kingdom*, judgment of 21 February 1986, Series A No 98, pp 41–2, § 68). In our view the approach of defining in the governing instrument the broad categories of troops, and the accompanying members of their family, to be withdrawn without reference to their personal history strikes the requisite fair balance between the competing interests of the individual and the community.

The dissenters also stressed the applicants' ties with Russia including the facts that: they were of Russian national origin, Russian speaking, had attended Russian-speaking educational institutions, and eventually became Russian citizens.

> 11. In these circumstances, we are unable to conclude that the Latvian authorities overstepped the margin of appreciation afforded to them under Article 8 of the Convention in the particular context of the withdrawal of the Russian armed forces from the territory of Latvia after almost 50 years of Soviet presence there. The Latvian authorities were in our view entitled to consider that the impugned interference with the applicants' right to respect for their private life and their home was 'necessary in a democratic society'.

The dissenters placed the agreed removal of Russian forces (and their family members) from Latvia above the interests of the applicants being able to remain in Latvia. Given the seniority of many of the dissenters in the hierarchy of the Court (including the President of the Court and two Section Presidents) their views merit our respect, but the dissenting opinion may be unduly dismissive of the applicants' links with Latvia (the first applicant had spent all her life, bar one month, living in Latvia and the second applicant had been born there and lived all her life in that country). Prior to their removal, which they vigorously contested in the Latvian courts over several years, the applicants had not demonstrated any desire to relocate to Russia. If their ties with Russia were as great as the dissenters contended then surely the applicants would have been keener to move to their true motherland?

16 A unanimous Chamber determined that the administration of diamorphine to a chronically ill 12-year-old (who was severely mentally and physically disabled) by doctors, against the wishes of the child's mother, amounted to an interference with the former's '70. . . . right to respect for his private life, and in particular his right to physical integrity': in *Glass v UK*, judgment of 9 March 2004. The child had been admitted to hospital following respiratory failure and the doctors considered that he was dying from lung disease. To relieve his distress the doctors ordered that he be given diamorphine. The next day the child's condition had deteriorated significantly and his mother resuscitated him, whilst other family members assaulted the doctors. The child's condition subsequently improved and he was discharged from hospital later that day. The Chamber found a breach of Article 8 because the hospital authorities had not sought a ruling from the domestic court's regarding the appropriateness of treating the child with diamorphine against the wishes of his mother.

83. The Court considers that, having regard to the circumstances of the case, the decision of the authorities to override the [mother's] objection to the proposed treatment in the absence of authorisation by a court resulted in a breach of Article 8 of the Convention.

17 The interpretation of 'private life' to encompass professional/business activities given in *Niemietz* was developed and applied by a Chamber of the full-time Court in *Sidabras and Dziautas v Lithuania*, judgment of 27 July 2004. The applicants had been employees of the Lithuanian branch of the KGB (Soviet Security Service) during the 1980s at a time when Lithuania had been a member of the USSR. Following the independence of Lithuania the applicants became a tax inspector and a public prosecutor. In 1998 the Lithuanian Parliament enacted a law which prohibited former members of the KGB from working as public officials and for banks, credit institutions, security companies, and a number of other private sector businesses for ten years beginning in 1998. The applicants were dismissed from their public employment under the terms of the legislation. They then complained to the Court that the statutory ban on them working in the designated private sector businesses and occupations violated their rights under Article 8 in combination with Article 14. The Court held that:

47. Nevertheless, having regard in particular to the notions currently prevailing in democratic states, the Court considers that a far-reaching ban on taking up private-sector employment does affect 'private life'. It attaches particular weight in this respect to the text of Article 1 § 2 of the European Social Charter and the interpretation given by the European Committee of Social Rights as well as to the texts adopted by the ILO [International Labour Organization]. It further recalls that there is no watertight division separating the sphere of social and economic rights from the field covered by the Convention (see, *Airey v Ireland*, judgment of 9 October 1979, Series A No 32, § 26).

A majority of the Court, 5 votes to 2, went on to find a breach of Article 14 in conjunction with Article 8 as the restrictions upon the applicants' employment were not proportionate to the legitimate aims of protecting national security and the economic well-being of Lithuania.

57. Even assuming that their lack of loyalty had been undisputed, it must be noted that the applicants' employment prospects were restricted not only in the State service but also in various spheres of the private sector. The Court reiterates that the requirement of an employee's loyalty to the State is an inherent condition of employment with State authorities responsible for protecting and securing the general interest. However, such a requirement is not inevitably the case for employment with private companies. Although the economic activities of private-sector actors

undoubtedly affect and contribute to the functioning of the State, they are not depositaries of the sovereign power vested in the State. Moreover, private companies may legitimately engage in activities, notably financial and economic, which compete with the goals fixed for public authorities or State-run companies.

58. For the Court, State-imposed restrictions on the possibility for a person to find employment with a private company for reasons of lack of loyalty to the State cannot be justified from the Convention point of view in the same manner as restrictions governing access to their employment in the public service, regardless of the private company's importance to the State's economic, political or security interests.

The majority were also concerned that the legislation had not been enacted until eight years after Lithuania had regained its independence. The Court awarded each applicant 7,000 euros compensation for pecuniary and non-pecuniary damage. The two dissentients, Judges Loucaides and Thomassen believed that Article 8 alone had been violated.

Article 1(2) of the European Social Charter, referred to in the above judgment, provides that: 'With a view to ensuring the effective exercise of the right to work, the Parties undertake… to protect effectively the right of the worker to earn his living in an occupation freely entered upon.'

18 The seizure and retention of a national's passport for several years whilst criminal proceedings were pending against him was found to violate Article 8 in *Iletmis v Turkey*, judgment of 6 December 2005. The applicant had registered as a student at a German university in 1975. He married a Turkish national in 1979 and they had two children who lived with them in Germany. In 1984 a judicial investigation was opened by the Turkish authorities into the applicant's political activities. Whilst visiting his family in Turkey, during 1992, the applicant was arrested and his passport seized. He was charged, with separatist activities, and released on bail a few weeks later. However, the authorities would not return his passport. In 1999 he was acquitted and supplied with a passport. The Chamber unanimously determined that the confiscation of the applicant's passport amounted to an interference with the applicant's right to respect for his private life and that it was a disproportionate act (given that he had no criminal record, there was never any evidence that he was a danger to national security, and his family lived in Germany).

19 A Grand Chamber held that the right to respect for a person's private life 'incorporates the right to respect for both the decisions to become and not to become a parent' in *Evans v UK*, judgment of 10 April 2007. The majority, 13 votes to 4, went on to conclude that, given the lack of a European consensus regarding the regulation of *in vitro* fertilization treatment, the legislature's enactment of a clear rule that both the male and female partners could withdraw their consent to the implantation of an embryo at any time prior to implantation did not breach Article 8 regarding a woman whose former partner withdrew his consent with the consequence that she would not be able to have a child to whom she was biologically related. However, another Grand Chamber, by 12 votes to 5, found a breach of this aspect of Article 8 where the prison authorities refused to allow a prisoner, serving a life sentence with a tariff of 15 years' imprisonment, facilities for the artificial insemination of his older wife (who he had met and married whilst serving his sentence) in *Dickson v UK*, judgment of 4 December 2007. The majority concluded that the authorities' policy, of only providing such facilities in exceptional cases, failed to strike a fair balance between the competing public and private interests. Whilst uncertainty in the domestic legislation regulating medical assistance for women wishing to give birth at home was also held to breach this aspect of respect for a person's private life in *Ternovszky v Hungary*, judgment of 14 December 2010.

20   A unanimous Grand Chamber ruled that the retention of fingerprints, cellular samples (usually collected from a mouth swab), and the resultant DNA profile (a digital code derived from an analysis of cellular samples from a person) by the police amounted to an interference with the relevant person's private life in *S and Marper v UK*, judgment of 4 December 2008. The first applicant, when he was 11, was arrested and charged with attempted robbery. His fingerprints and DNA samples were taken by the police. Later he was acquitted of the charge, but the police retained his fingerprints, cellular sample, and DNA profile (on the national DNA police database) in accordance with English law. The second, adult, applicant was also arrested and charged with harassment of his partner. Similar DNA/fingerprint information was taken from him. The case against him was discontinued, but his DNA/fingerprint data was also retained. The British Government sought to justify the retention of such materials/data under Article 8(2) as being necessary to prevent crime/disorder and protect the rights of others. However, the Grand Chamber noted that:

110....England, Wales and Northern Ireland appear to be the only jurisdictions within the Council of Europe to allow the indefinite retention of fingerprint and DNA material of any person of any age suspected of any recordable offence.

...

125. In conclusion, the Court finds that the blanket and indiscriminate nature of the powers of retention of the fingerprints, cellular samples and DNA profiles of persons suspected but not convicted of offences, as applied in the case of the present applicants, fails to strike a fair balance between the competing public and private interests and that the respondent State has overstepped any acceptable margin of appreciation in this regard. Accordingly, the retention at issue constitutes a disproportionate interference with the applicants' right to respect for private life and cannot be regarded as necessary in a democratic society. This conclusion obviates the need for the Court to consider the applicants' criticism regarding the adequacy of certain particular safeguards, such as too broad an access to the personal data concerned and insufficient protection against the misuse or abuse of such data.

126. Accordingly, there has been a violation of Article 8 of the Convention in the present case.

For an examination of the Court's interaction with scientific developments see T. Murphy and G. O. Cuinn, 'Works in Progress: New Technologies and the European Court of Human Rights' (2010) 10(4) *Human Rights Law Review* 601.

21   The government's contention that police stop and search powers exercised in public places did not amount to an interference with the private life of the relevant person was decisively rejected by a united Chamber in *Gillan and Quinton v UK*, judgment of 12 January 2010. Under the Terrorism Act 2000 senior police officers, with the approval of the Home Secretary, could designate geographical areas where uniformed police officers could stop and search persons/vehicles for 'articles of a kind which could be used in connection with terrorism'. The whole of London had been subject to the exercise of this power, on a rolling basis, since 2001. In 2003 the first applicant was stopped and searched on his way to join a protest against a defence/arms exhibition in east London. Nothing incriminating was found on him. The second applicant, a press photographer, was also stopped and searched near the event (she had nothing incriminating in her possession). In the view of the Court:

63....Irrespective of whether in any particular case correspondence or diaries or other private documents are discovered and read or other intimate items are revealed in the search, the Court considers that the use of the coercive powers conferred by the legislation to require an individual to submit to a detailed search of his person, his clothing and his personal belongings amounts to a clear interference with the right to respect for private life. Although the search is undertaken in a public place, this does not mean that Article 8 is inapplicable. Indeed, in the Court's view, the public nature of the search may, in certain cases, compound the seriousness of the interference because of an element of humiliation and embarrassment. Items such as bags, wallets, notebooks and diaries may, moreover, contain personal information which the owner may feel uncomfortable about having exposed to the view of his companions or the wider public.

Furthermore, the Court did not accept that the powers were compatible with Article 8(2):

80. The Court notes at the outset that the senior police officer referred to in section 44(4) of the Act is empowered to authorise any constable in uniform to stop and search a pedestrian in any area specified by him within his jurisdiction if he 'considers it expedient for the prevention of acts of terrorism'. However, 'expedient' means no more than 'advantageous' or 'helpful'. There is no requirement at the authorisation stage that the stop and search power be considered 'necessary' and therefore no requirement of any assessment of the proportionality of the measure. The authorisation is subject to confirmation by the Secretary of State within 48 hours. The Secretary of State may not alter the geographical coverage of an authorisation and although he or she can refuse confirmation or substitute an earlier time of expiry, it appears that in practice this has never been done. Although the exercise of the powers of authorisation and confirmation is subject to judicial review, the width of the statutory powers is such that applicants face formidable obstacles in showing that any authorisation and confirmation are *ultra vires* or an abuse of power.

81. The authorisation must be limited in time to 28 days, but it is renewable. It cannot extend beyond the boundary of the police force area and may be limited geographically within that boundary. However, many police force areas in the United Kingdom cover extensive regions with a concentrated populations. The Metropolitan Police Force Area, where the applicants were stopped and searched, extends to all of Greater London. The failure of the temporal and geographical restrictions provided by Parliament to act as any real check on the issuing of authorisations by the executive are demonstrated by the fact that an authorisation for the Metropolitan Police District has been continuously renewed in a 'rolling programme' since the powers were first granted.

82. An additional safeguard is provided by the Independent Reviewer. However, his powers are confined to reporting on the general operation of the statutory provisions and he has no right to cancel or alter authorisations, despite the fact that in every report from May 2006 onwards he has expressed the clear view that 'section 44 could be used less and I expect it to be used less'.

83. Of still further concern is the breadth of the discretion conferred on the individual police officer. The officer is obliged, in carrying out the search, to comply with the terms of the Code. However, the Code governs essentially the mode in which the stop and search is carried out, rather than providing any restriction on the officer's decision to stop and search. That decision is, as the House of Lords made clear, one based exclusively on the 'hunch' or 'professional intuition' of the officer concerned. Not only is it unnecessary for him to demonstrate the existence of any reasonable suspicion; he is not required even subjectively to suspect anything about the person stopped and searched. The sole proviso is that the search must be for the purpose of looking for articles which could be used in connection with terrorism, a very wide category which could cover many articles commonly carried by people in the streets. Provided the person concerned is stopped for the purpose of searching for such articles, the police officer does not even have to have grounds for suspecting the presence of such articles. As noted by Lord Brown in the House of Lords, the stop and search power provided for by section 44 'radically... departs from our traditional understanding of the limits of police power.'

84. In this connection the Court is struck by the statistical and other evidence showing the extent to which resort is had by police officers to the powers of stop and search under section 44 of the

Act. The Ministry of Justice recorded a total of 33,177 searches in 2004/5, 44,545 in 2005/6, 37,000 in 2006/7 and 117,278 in 2007/8. In his Report into the operation of the Act in 2007, Lord Carlile [the Independent Reviewer] noted that while arrests for other crimes had followed searches under section 44, none of the many thousands of searches had ever related to a terrorism offence; in his 2008 Report Lord Carlile noted that examples of poor and unnecessary use of section 44 abounded, there being evidence of cases where the person stopped was so obviously far from any known terrorism profile that, realistically, there was not the slightest possibility of him/her being a terrorist, and no other feature to justify the stop.

85. In the Court's view, there is a clear risk of arbitrariness in the grant of such a broad discretion to the police officer. While the present cases do not concern black applicants or those of Asian origin, the risks of the discriminatory use of the powers against such persons is a very real consideration, as the judgments of Lord Hope, Lord Scott and Lord Brown recognised. The available statistics show that black and Asian persons are disproportionately affected by the powers, although the Independent Reviewer has also noted, in his most recent report, that there has also been a practice of stopping and searching white people purely to produce greater racial balance in the statistics. There is, furthermore, a risk that such a widely framed power could be misused against demonstrators and protestors in breach of Article 10 and/or 11 of the Convention.

86. The Government argue that safeguards against abuse are provided by the right of an individual to challenge a stop and search by way of judicial review or an action in damages. But the limitations of both actions are clearly demonstrated by the present case. In particular, in the absence of any obligation on the part of the officer to show a reasonable suspicion, it is likely to be difficult if not impossible to prove that the power was improperly exercised.

87. In conclusion, the Court considers that the powers of authorisation and confirmation as well as those of stop and search under sections 44 and 45 of the 2000 Act are neither sufficiently circumscribed nor subject to adequate legal safeguards against abuse. They are not, therefore, 'in accordance with the law' and it follows that there has been a violation of Article 8 of the Convention.

Despite the extensive misuse of this excessively broad power by the police detailed in the above judgment it is highly significant that the domestic courts (including a unanimous House of Lords) had rejected the applicants' complaints.

Family life

X, Y and Z v UK 1997-II
European Court of Human Rights

X was born in 1955 and is a female-to-male transsexual. In 1975, he (the male pronoun is used in accordance with the Court's judgment) began hormone treatment and started to live as a man. During 1979 he began to cohabit with Y, a 20-year-old woman, and a few months later he underwent gender reassignment surgery. Since that time X and Y have lived in a permanent and stable union. In 1990, X and Y applied for permission, from a hospital ethics committee, for Y to undergo Artificial Insemination by Donor (AID). After an appeal the committee granted permission and asked that X acknowledge himself to be the father of the child under section 28 of the Human Fertilisation and Embryology Act 1990 (which provides that where an unmarried woman gives birth as a result of AID with the involvement of her male partner, the latter, rather than the donor of the sperm, shall be treated for legal purposes as the father of the child). In 1992 Y gave birth to a girl (applicant Z). X sought to be registered as Z's father on her birth certificate. However, the Registrar General refused as he considered that only a biological man could be regarded as a father for the purpose of registration. In the register Z was given X's surname, while the identity of her father was left blank. The applicants petitioned the European Commission alleging that the refusal to register X as the father of Z amounted to a violation of Article 8 and unlawful discrimination (Articles 14 and 8). The Commission found a breach of Article 8 (13 votes to 5) and that it was not necessary to examine Article 14.

...

A. THE EXISTENCE OF 'FAMILY LIFE'

33. The applicants submitted that they had shared a 'family life' within the meaning of Article 8 since Z's birth. They emphasised that, according to the jurisprudence of the Commission and the Court, social reality, rather than formal legal status, was decisive. Thus, it was important to note that X had irrevocably changed many of his physical characteristics and provided financial and emotional support to Y and Z. To all appearances, the applicants lived as a traditional family.

34. The Government did not accept that the concept of 'family life' applied to the relationships between X and Y or X and Z. They reasoned that X and Y had to be treated as two women living together, because X was still regarded as female under domestic law and a complete change of sex was not medically possible. Case-law of the Commission indicated that a 'family' could not be based on two unrelated persons of the same sex, including a lesbian couple (see the Commission's decisions on admissibility in *X and Y v UK* application No 9369/81, Decisions and Reports 32, p 220, and *Kerkhoven v Netherlands*, application No 15666/89). Nor could X be said to enjoy 'family life' with Z since he was not related to the child by blood, marriage or adoption.

At the hearing before the Court, counsel for the Government accepted that if X and Y applied for and were granted a joint residence order in respect of Z ..., it would be difficult to maintain that there was no 'family life' for the purposes of Article 8.

35. The Commission considered that the relationship between X and Y could not be equated with that of a lesbian couple, since X was living in society as a man, having undergone gender reassignment surgery. Aside from the fact that X was registered at birth as a woman and was therefore under a legal incapacity to marry Y or be registered as Z's father, the applicants' situation was indistinguishable from the traditional notion of 'family life'.

36. The Court recalls that the notion of 'family life' in Article 8 is not confined solely to families based on marriage and may encompass other de facto relationships (see the *Marckx v Belgium* judgment of 13 June 1979, Series A No 31, p 14, § 31; the *Keegan v Ireland* judgment of 26 May 1994, Series A No 290, p 17, § 44; and the *Kroon v Netherlands* judgment of 27 October 1994, Series A No 297-C, pp 55–6, § 30). When deciding whether a relationship can be said to amount to 'family life', a number of factors may be relevant, including whether the couple live together, the length of their relationship and whether they have demonstrated their commitment to each other by having children together or by any other means (see, for example, the above-mentioned *Kroon* judgment, *loc cit*).

37. In the present case, the Court notes that X is a transsexual who has undergone gender reassignment surgery. He has lived with Y, to all appearances as her male partner, since 1979. The couple applied jointly for, and were granted, treatment by AID to allow Y to have a child. X was involved throughout that process and has acted as Z's 'father' in every respect since the birth. ... In these circumstances, the Court considers the de facto family ties link the three applicants.

It follows that Article 8 is applicable.

B. COMPLIANCE WITH ARTICLE 8

...

2. The Court's general approach

44. The Court observes that there is no common European standard with regard to the granting of parental rights to transsexuals. In addition, it has not been established before the Court that there exists any generally shared approach amongst the High Contracting Parties with regard to the manner in which the social relationship between a child conceived by AID and the person who performs the role of father should be reflected in law. Indeed, according to the information available to the Court, although the technology of medically assisted procreation has been available in Europe for several decades, many of the issues to which it gives rise, particularly with regard to the question of filiation, remain the subject of debate. For example, there is no consensus amongst the member States of the Council of Europe on the question whether the interests of a child conceived in such a way are best served by preserving the anonymity of the donor of the sperm or whether the child should have the right to know the donor's identity.

Since the issues in the case, therefore, touch on areas where there is little common ground amongst the member States of the Council of Europe and, generally speaking, the law appears to be in a transitional stage, the respondent State must be afforded a wide margin of appreciation...

3. Whether a fair balance was struck in the instant case

45. The applicants, with whom the Commission agreed, argued that a number of consequences flowed from the lack of legal recognition of X's role as father. Perhaps most importantly, the child's sense of security within the family might be undermined. Furthermore, the absence of X's name on her birth certificate might cause distress on those occasions when a full-length certificate had to be produced, for example on registration with a doctor or school, if an insurance policy was taken out on her life or when she applied for a passport. Although Z was a British citizen by birth and could trace connection through her mother in immigration and nationality matters, problems could still arise if X sought to work abroad. For example, he had already had to turn down an offer of employment in Botswana because he had been informed that Y and Z would not have been recognised as his 'dependants' and would not, therefore, have been entitled to receive certain benefits (see paragraph 19 above). Moreover, in contrast to the position where a parent–child relationship was recognised by law, Z could not inherit from Y on intestacy or succeed to certain tenancies on X's death. The possibility of X obtaining a residence order in respect of Z...did not satisfy the requirement of respect, since this would entail the incurring of legal expense and an investigation by a court welfare officer which might distress the child.

In their submission, it was apparent that the legal recognition sought would not interfere with the rights of others or require any fundamental reorganisation of the United Kingdom system of registration of births, since the Human Fertility [sic] and Embryology Act 1990 allowed a man who was not a transsexual to be registered as the father of a child born to his female partner by AID...

46. The Government pointed out that the applicants were not restrained in any way from living together as a 'family' and they asserted that the concerns expressed by them were highly theoretical. Furthermore, X and Y could jointly apply for a residence order, conferring on them parental rights and duties in relation to Z...

47. First, the Court observes that the community as a whole has an interest in maintaining a coherent system of family law which places the best interests of the child at the forefront. In this respect, the Court notes that, whilst it has not been suggested that the amendment to the law sought by the applicants would be harmful to the interests of Z or of children conceived by AID in general, it is not clear that it would necessarily be to the advantage of such children.

In these circumstances, the Court considers that the State may justifiably be cautious in changing the law, since it is possible that the amendment sought might have undesirable or unforeseen ramifications for children in Z's position. Furthermore, such an amendment might have implications in other areas of family law. For example, the law might be open to criticism on the ground of inconsistency if a female-to-male transsexual were granted the possibility of becoming a 'father' in law while still being treated for other legal purposes as female and capable of contracting marriage to a man.

48. Against these general interests, the Court must weigh the disadvantages suffered by the applicants as a result of the refusal to recognise X in law as Z's 'father'.

The applicants identify a number of legal consequences flowing from this lack of recognition (see paragraph 45 above). For example, they point to the fact that if X were to die intestate, Z would have no automatic right of inheritance. The Court notes, however, that the problem could be solved in practice if X were to make a will. No evidence has been adduced to show that X is the beneficiary of any transmissible tenancies of the type referred to; similarly, since Z is a British citizen by birth and can trace connection through her mother in immigration and nationality matters, she will not be disadvantaged in this respect by the lack of a legal relationship with X.

The Court considers, therefore, that these legal consequences would be unlikely to cause undue hardship given the facts of the present case.

49. In addition, the applicants claimed that Z might suffer various social or developmental difficulties. Thus, it was argued that she would be caused distress on those occasions when it was necessary to produce her birth certificate.

In relation to the absence of X's name on the birth certificate, the Court notes, first, that unless X and Y choose to make such information public, neither the child nor any third party will know that this absence is a consequence of the fact that X was born female. It follows that the applicants are in a similar position to any other family where, for whatever reason, the person who performs the role of the child's 'father' is not registered as such. The Court does not find it established that any particular stigma still attaches to children or families in such circumstances.

Secondly, the Court recalls that in the United Kingdom a birth certificate is not in common use for administrative or identification purposes and that there are few occasions when it is necessary to produce a full length certificate . . .

50. The applicants were also concerned, more generally, that Z's sense of personal identity and security within her family would be affected by the lack of legal recognition of X as father.

In this respect, the Court notes that X is not prevented in any way from acting as Z's father in the social sense. Thus, for example, he lives with her, providing emotional and financial support to her and Y, and he is free to describe himself to her and others as her 'father' and to give her his surname. . . . Furthermore, together with Y, he could apply for a joint residence order in respect of Z, which would automatically confer on them full parental responsibility for her in English law . . .

51. It is impossible to predict the extent to which the absence of a legal connection between X and Z will affect the latter's development. As previously mentioned, at the present time there is uncertainty with regard to how the interests of children in Z's position can best be protected (see paragraph 44 above) and the Court should not adopt or impose any single viewpoint.

52. In conclusion, given that transsexuality raises complex scientific, legal, moral and social issues, in respect of which there is no generally shared approach among the Contracting States, the Court is of the opinion that Article 8 cannot, in this context, be taken to imply an obligation for the respondent State formally to recognise as the father of a child a person who is not the biological father. That being so, the fact that the law of the United Kingdom does not allow special legal recognition of the relationship between X and Z does not amount to a failure to respect family life within the meaning of that provision.

It follows that there has been no violation of Article 8 of the Convention.

. . .

FOR THESE REASONS, THE COURT

1. Holds unanimously that Article 8 of the Convention is applicable in the present case;
2. Holds by fourteen votes to six that there has been no violation of Article 8; . . .

NOTES

1 The majority of the Grand Chamber on the Article 8 aspect of the case was comprised of President Ryssdal and Judges: Bernhardt, Matscher, Pettiti, Spielmann, De Meyer, Valticos, Freeland, Baka, Lopes Rocha, Jungwiert, Kuris, Lohmus, and Levits. Six judges dissented for various reasons. Casadevall J (joined by Russo and Makarczyk JJ) considered that the UK was in breach of Article 8 because it had authorized, and financed, X's gender reassignment together with Y's AID, and 'it must accept the consequences and take all the measures needed to enable the applicants to live normal lives, without discrimination, under their new identity and with respect for their right to private and family life.' Thor Vilhjalmsson J based his dissent on the consideration that the register of births may now lawfully contain statements that are not in conformity with biological facts (i.e. the identity of the 'father' of a child created via AID). Therefore, he felt that to refuse to register X as Z's 'father' amounted to a lack of respect for the applicants' family life. Foighel J believed that the Government had not been able to justify its refusal to register X, an act which would have benefited him and harmed no other person. Gotchev J held that as *de facto* family ties existed between the applicants, the Government was under a duty to facilitate Z's integration into the family unit, which entailed X being able to be recognized in law as her father.

2 The Court's willingness to recognize a broad spectrum of *de facto* relationships as capable of falling within the protected category of 'family life' under Article 8, demonstrates that the judges are interpreting this concept in accordance with evolving patterns of social behaviour. A dynamic interpretation helps to ensure that the rights guaranteed do not become redundant through social change. However, this evolutionary approach is counterbalanced by the judiciary's granting of a wide margin of appreciation (note, this judicial creation is discussed at p 633) to States in cases concerning social mores where there is no European consensus in the legal and administrative regulation of such relationships. In this case, the margin of appreciation was particularly extensive as the subject matter involved both transsexualism and the rapidly developing medical technology of AID. On the Court's jurisprudence regarding transsexuals, see further p 574.

3 In *Kroon v Netherlands* A.297-C (1994), the applicants challenged the Dutch birth registration system. The first applicant (Mrs Kroon) had married a Moroccan national (Mr Omar M'Hallem-Driss) in 1979. By the end of 1980 the marriage had broken down and Mrs Kroon lived apart from her husband (official records showed that he left Amsterdam in 1986 and his whereabouts have remained unknown since that time). The second applicant (Mr Ali Zerrouk, also a Moroccan national) developed a stable relationship with the first applicant, although they did not live together, and in 1987 the third applicant (Samir M'Hallem-Driss) was born of the relationship. He was entered in the register of births as the son of Mrs Kroon and Mr M'Hallem-Driss. Mrs Kroon and Mr Zerrouk applied to the registrar for Samir to be registered as the son of Mr Zerrouk (his biological father), however their application was refused because under Dutch law only the married husband (Mr M'Hallem-Driss) could bring proceedings to deny the paternity of a child born to his wife. The applicants alleged that this ruling failed to respect their right to family life under Article 8. The Commission, by 12 votes to 6, found a breach. The Court rejected the Dutch Government's argument that the applicants' relationship did not amount to 'family life' under Article 8(1).

Although, as a rule, living together may be a requirement for such a relationship, exceptionally other factors may also serve to demonstrate that a relationship has sufficient constancy to create de facto 'family ties'; such is the case here, as since 1987 four children have been born to Mrs Kroon and Mr Zerrouk. [Para 30.]

A majority, 7 votes to 2, went on to find in favour of the applicants because:

In the Court's opinion, 'respect' for 'family life' requires that biological and social reality prevail over a legal presumption which, as in the present case, flies in the face of both established fact and the wishes of those concerned without actually benefiting anyone. Accordingly, the Court concludes that, even having regard to the margin of appreciation left to the State, the Netherlands has failed to secure to the applicants the 'respect' for their family life to which they are entitled under the Convention. [Para 40.]

4   In *Marckx v Belgium* A.31 (1979), an unmarried mother and her infant daughter complained, *inter alia*, about the status of illegitimate children in Belgian law. Illegitimate children were only recognized as the children of their mothers if the latter formally recognized their maternity and, in law, such children remained strangers to their parents' families. The Court held that:

By guaranteeing the right to respect for family life, Article 8 presupposes the existence of a family. The Court concurs entirely with the Commission's established case-law on a crucial point, namely that Article 8 makes no distinction between the 'legitimate' and the 'illegitimate' family. Such a distinction would not be consonant with the word 'everyone', and this is confirmed by Article 14 with its prohibition, in the enjoyment of the rights and freedoms enshrined in the Convention, of discrimination grounded on 'birth'. In addition, the Court notes that the Committee of Ministers of the Council of Europe regards the single woman and her child as one form of family no less than others (Resolution (70) 15 of 15 May 1970). . . . In the Court's opinion, 'family life' within the meaning of Article 8, includes at least the ties between near relatives, for instance those between grandparents and grandchildren, since such relatives may play a considerable part in family life. [Paras 31 and 45.]

By varying majorities the Court then held that Belgian law, regarding affiliation rules and family relationships, violated the applicants' rights under Article 8. A similar approach was followed in *Johnston v Ireland* A.112 (1986). The first applicant separated from his wife, they were unable to obtain a divorce as that was prohibited by the Irish Constitution, and since 1971 he had been living with the second applicant. The third applicant was their daughter who had been born in 1978. The applicants complained, *inter alia*, of a violation of Article 8 due to the lack of respect for their family life on account of the third applicant's status under Irish law (e.g. the first applicant's lack of parental rights in regard to her, the impossibility of the third applicant to be jointly adopted by her parents, and her limited succession rights in respect of her parents). The Court, unanimously, held that:

As it observed in its above-mentioned *Marckx* judgment, 'respect' for family life, understood as including the ties between near relatives, implies an obligation for the State to act in a manner calculated to allow these ties to develop normally. And in the present case the normal development of the natural family ties between the first and second applicants and their daughter requires, in the Court's opinion, that she should be placed, legally and socially, in a position akin to that of a legitimate child. Examination of the third applicant's present legal situation, seen as a whole, reveals, however, that it differs considerably from that of a legitimate child; in addition, it has not been shown that there are any means available to her or her parents to eliminate or reduce the differences. Having regard to the particular circumstances of this case and notwithstanding the wide margin of appreciation enjoyed by Ireland in this area...the absence of an appropriate legal regime reflecting the third applicant's natural family ties amounts to a failure to respect her family life. Moreover, the close and intimate relationship between the third applicant and her parents is such that there is of necessity also a resultant failure to respect the family life of each of the latter.

There is accordingly, as regards all three applicants, a breach of Article 8...[Paras 74–6.]

However, as we have seen (p 514) in *Slivenko v Latvia*, judgment of 9 October 2003, a Grand Chamber of the full-time Court took a narrower view of family life. The Grand Chamber refused to accept that the relationship between a daughter/granddaughter and their parents/grandparents amounted to family life as the latter were not dependent upon the former (paragraph 97 of the judgment). Judge Kovler, the judge of Russian nationality, in his partly concurring and partly dissenting opinion disagreed with the majority's restrictive approach.

In my humble opinion, in paragraph 97 of its judgment the Court has narrowed the concept of 'family life' by taking it to cover ties within the 'core family' only. In other words, the Court has opted for the traditional concept of a family based on the conjugal covenant—that is to say, a conjugal family consisting of a father, a mother and their children below the age of majority, while adult children and grandparents are excluded from the circle. That might be correct within the strict legal meaning of the term as used by European countries in their civil legislation, but the manner in which the Court has construed Article 8 § 1 in its case-law opens up other horizons by placing the emphasis on broader family ties.

In the actual text of the *Marckx* judgment cited in the instant case, the Court observed that ' "family life", within the meaning of Article 8, includes at least the ties between near relatives, for instance those between grandparents and grandchildren, since such relatives may play a considerable part in family life' and concluded that ' "respect" for a family life so understood implies an obligation for the State to act in a manner calculated to allow these ties to develop normally' (see *Marckx v Belgium*, judgment of 13 June 1979, Series A No 31, p. 21, § 45; see also *Scozzari and Giunta v Italy* [GC], Nos 39221/98 and 41963/98, § 221, ECHR 2000-VIII). To put it another way, the Court could at least have made a more careful distinction between the 'family' in the strict legal sense of the term and the broader concept of 'family life' set out in the *Marckx* judgment.

Accordingly, the assertion in the present judgment that 'the existence of "family life" could not be relied on by the applicants in relation to the first applicant's elderly parents, adults who did not belong to the core family' departs from the case-law referred to above and does not take into account the sociological and human aspects of contemporary European families (I am deliberately leaving aside Muslim and African families since my reasoning relates solely to the geographical area within the Court's jurisdiction). Reference may be made, for example, to the Littré *Dictionnaire de la langue française*, which defines 'famille' ('family') as 'l'ensemble des individus de même sang qui vivent les uns à côté des autres' ('a group of persons related by blood who live together'). Even if that concept is not necessarily a legal one, it reflects the perception of those subject to our courts' jurisdiction.

The restrictive concept of a conjugal family (known as a 'nuclear family' in legal anthropology) is becoming obsolete in the light of the obvious changes reflected in family legislation recently enacted in a number of European States. At the same time, the tradition of the 'extended family', so strong in east and southern European countries, is enshrined in those countries' basic laws. For example, the Constitution of the Russian Federation—the State of which the applicants are now nationals—provides: 'Children over eighteen years of age who are able to work shall provide for their parents who are unfit for work' (Article 38 § 3). There are similar provisions in the Constitutions of Ukraine (Article 51 § 2), Moldova (Article 48 § 4) and other countries. This means that in those countries the tradition of helping one's elderly parents is firmly established as a moral imperative written into the Constitution. Those were essentially the considerations guiding the applicants in their ultimately unsuccessful request to the Latvian authorities not to separate them from their elderly, sick ascendants. 'Family life' was plainly inconceivable for them if they were denied the possibility of looking after those relatives. What could be more natural or more humane?

It follows, in my opinion, that the applicants' removal amounted to unjustified interference not only with their 'private life' and 'home' but also, and above all, with their 'family life'.

5   The applicants in *Abdulaziz, Cabales and Balkandali v UK* A.94 (1985), claimed that the refusal of the British immigration authorities to allow their foreign husbands to join them in the UK amounted to, *inter alia*, a breach of their right to family life under Article 8. The British Government, as part of its defence, asserted that Mrs Cabales' marriage was void under Philippine law, the State where the marriage ceremony took place, because it had not been solemnized with a licence. Nevertheless, the Court ruled that:

... by guaranteeing the right to respect for family life, Article 8 'presupposes the existence of a family'. However, this does not mean that all intended family life falls entirely outside its ambit. Whatever else the word 'family' may mean, it must at any rate include the relationship that arises from a lawful and genuine marriage, such as that contracted by Mr and Mrs Abdulaziz and Mr and Mrs Balkandali. ... Mr and Mrs Cabales had gone through a ceremony of marriage and the evidence before the Court confirms that they believed themselves to be married and that they genuinely wished to cohabit and lead a normal family life. And indeed they subsequently did so. In the circumstances, the committed relationship thus established was sufficient to attract the application of Article 8. [Paras 62 and 63.]

Hence, the Court was more concerned with the substance of a relationship than its formal status. The Court, unanimously, went on to find that the applicants' rights under Article 8 had not been violated because, 'the duty imposed by Article 8 cannot be considered as extending to a general obligation on the part of a Contracting State to respect the choice by married couples of the country of their matrimonial residence and to accept the non-national spouses for settlement in that country' (para 68). But the UK was in breach of Article 14 taken together with Article 8 as its immigration rules had unjustifiably discriminated against the applicants on the ground of their gender (males were able to gain entry for their foreign female partners more easily).

6   A united Grand Chamber (in *Serife Yigit v Turkey*, judgment of 2 November 2010) held that, '102. ... Article 8 cannot be interpreted as imposing an obligation on the State to recognise religious marriage'. Furthermore, as the domestic authorities had not imposed any civil or criminal penalties on the applicant during the 26 years of her religious (Islamic) marriage there had been no interference with her family life. See p 838, for the Article 14 aspect of the judgment.

7   Until 2010 the case-law did not recognize same-sex relationships as falling within the concept of family life. However, in *Schalk and Kopf v Austria*, judgment of 24 June 2010, the Chamber noted that during the previous decade, '93. ... a rapid evolution of social attitudes towards same-sex couples has taken place in many member States'. Additionally, aspects of EU law had recognized such relationships as constituting a family.

94. In view of this evolution the Court considers it artificial to maintain the view that, in contrast to a different-sex couple, a same-sex couple cannot enjoy 'family life' for the purposes of Article 8. Consequently the relationship of the applicants, a co-habiting same-sex couple living in a stable *de facto* partnership, falls within the notion of 'family life', just as the relationship of a different-sex couple in the same situation would.

But, by a bare majority of 4 votes to 3, the Chamber found the inability of the applicants to marry or have their relationship recognized by Austrian law did not constitute a breach of Article 14 in conjunction with Article 8. The majority reasoned that as Article 12 did not oblige member States to grant a right to marry to same-sex couples (see p 792) Articles 14/8 should not be interpreted as creating such a right. The dissentients considered that same-sex couples ought to be provided with a legal framework, in domestic law, granting similar types of rights/benefits as marriage. The extension of family life to same-sex couples in the above judgment was another vivid demonstration of the Court reflecting social dynamics.

8 The nature of the relationship between a divorced parent and his/her child and the concept of 'family life' was examined by the Court in *Berrehab v Netherlands* A.138 (1988). The applicant was a Moroccan citizen who had married a Dutch national (Mrs Koster) in 1977. After the marriage the Dutch authorities granted him permission to enter, and work, in the Netherlands 'for the sole purpose of enabling him to live with his Dutch wife'. In 1979 they were divorced and soon afterwards she gave birth to their daughter. Despite, the divorce Mr Berrehab had regular contact with his daughter (he saw her four times a week for several hours each time) and he provided financial contributions towards her maintenance and education. In 1983 he was deported from the Netherlands as his reason for being allowed to stay in the country had ended. Two years later he remarried Mrs Koster and was subsequently given permission to reside in the Netherlands in order to live with his wife. Mr Berrehab claimed that his deportation amounted to a violation of his (and his daughter's) right to respect for their family life. In its judgment the Court:

...does not see cohabitation as a *sine qua non* of family life between parents and minor children. It has held that the relationship created between the spouses by a lawful and genuine marriage—such as that contracted by Mr and Mrs Berrehab—has to be regarded as 'family life' (see *Abdulaziz v UK* A.94 (1985)). It follows from the concept of family on which Article 8 is based that a child born of such a union is *ipso jure* part of that relationship: hence, from the moment of the child's birth and by the very fact of it, there exists between him and his parents a bond amounting to 'family life', even if the parents are not then living together. Subsequent events, of course, may break that tie, but this was not so in the instant case.

...Mr Berrehab saw his daughter four times a week...the frequency and regularity of his meetings with her prove that he valued them very greatly. It cannot therefore be maintained that the ties of 'family life' between them had been broken. [Para 21.]

A majority of the Court (6 to 1) concluded that given the close ties between Mr Berrehab and his daughter, the deportation was not a proportionate response by the Dutch authorities and their actions could not be justified as necessary to preserve the economic well-being of the Netherlands under Article 8(2).

9 The Court has also been faced with a number of cases where aliens have been convicted of criminal behaviour, and ordered to be deported/excluded for a specified time, and the aliens claim that their removal has (or will) infringe their right to respect for their family (and private) lives. A Grand Chamber confirmed the factors that would be evaluated in determining the lawfulness of the deportation/exclusion under Article 8 in *Uner v Netherlands*, judgment of 18 October 2006. The applicant had been born in Turkey but moved to the Netherlands, with his mother and two brothers, when he was 12 years old to be with his father. He was initially given a renewable residence permit and then a permanent one. In his early twenties he was convicted of violence against the person. He began cohabiting with a Dutch national and in 1992 they had a son. However, in 1994 he was convicted of manslaughter and given a seven-year prison sentence. His partner visited him at least every week in prison and another child was born to them in 1996. The Deputy Minister of Justice determined that the applicant should be deported at the end of his imprisonment and be excluded from returning to the Netherlands for ten years to protect public safety in the country. Subsequently the applicant complained that his deportation/exclusion violated Article 8. The Grand Chamber noted the criteria identified by a Chamber in *Boultif v Switzerland*, 2001-IX, when assessing whether an expulsion measure was necessary in a democratic society and proportionate.

57....

- the nature and seriousness of the offence committed by the applicant;
- the length of the applicant's stay in the country from which he or she is to be expelled;
- the time elapsed since the offence was committed and the applicant's conduct during that period;
- the nationalities of the various persons concerned;
- the applicant's family situation, such as the length of the marriage, and other factors expressing the effectiveness of a couple's family life;
- whether the spouse knew about the offence at the time when he or she entered into a family relationship;
- whether there are children of the marriage, and if so, their age; and
- the seriousness of the difficulties which the spouse is likely to encounter in the country to which the applicant is to be expelled.

58. The Court would wish to make explicit two criteria which may already be implicit in those identified in the *Boultif* judgment:

- the best interests and well-being of the children, in particular the seriousness of the difficulties which any children of the applicant are likely to encounter in the country to which the applicant is to be expelled; and
- the solidity of social, cultural and family ties with the host country and with the country of destination.

As to whether a resident alien could bring him/herself within Article 8(1):

59....it must be accepted that the totality of social ties between settled migrants and the community in which they are living constitute part of the concept of 'private life' within the meaning of Article 8. Regardless of the existence or otherwise of a 'family life', therefore, the Court considers that the expulsion of a settled migrant constitutes interference with his or her right to respect for private life. It will depend on the circumstances of the particular case whether it is appropriate for the Court to focus on the 'family life' rather than the 'private life' aspect.

The Grand Chamber found that the impugned measures constituted an interference with Uner's family life in the Netherlands. However, a large majority (14 votes to 3) concluded that given the seriousness of the offences he had been convicted of and his criminal propensities those factors outweighed the practical difficulties involved in his partner joining him in Turkey. Therefore, no breach of Article 8 had occurred. Judges Costa, Zupancic, and Turmen issued a joint dissenting opinion in which they expressed the wish for the Court's case-law to develop, '18....towards increased protection for foreign nationals (even criminals) rather than towards increased penalties which target them specifically'.

In the later Grand Chamber case of *Maslov v Austria*, judgment of 23 June 2008, President Costa and his fellow judges enhanced the protection given to juvenile aliens against deportation/exclusion orders. The applicant, a Bulgarian national, had lawfully moved to Austria, with his parents and two siblings, when he was 6 years old. When he was 15 he was convicted of 22 counts of aggravated gang burglary. He was sentenced to imprisonment and ordered to undergo drug therapy. A year later he was convicted of 18 counts of aggravated burglary. The Vienna Juvenile Court found that he had not undertaken the required drug therapy. He was given a 15-month prison sentence. Later, the Vienna Police Authority imposed a ten-year exclusion order on the applicant and he was deported to Bulgaria once he completed his sentence. The Grand Chamber held that:

75. In short, the Court considers that for a settled migrant who has lawfully spent all or the major part of his or her childhood and youth in the host country very serious reasons are required to justify expulsion. This is all the more so where the person concerned committed the offences underlying the expulsion measure as a juvenile.

The majority determined that there had been a breach of the applicant's right to respect for his private and family life because:

100. Having regard to the foregoing considerations, in particular the—with one exception—non-violent nature of the offences committed when a minor and the State's duty to facilitate his reintegration into society, the length of the applicant's lawful residence in Austria, his family, social and linguistic ties with Austria and the lack of proven ties with his country of origin, the Court finds that the imposition of an exclusion order, even of a limited duration, was disproportionate to the legitimate aim pursued, 'the prevention of disorder or crime'. It was therefore not 'necessary in a democratic society'.

Judge Steiner dissented as she considered the measure was a proportionate response to the applicant's criminal behaviour. In a subsequent public lecture President Costa described the *Maslov* judgment as demonstrating the 'evolutionary approach' of the Court: 'Immigration and human rights in the case law of the ECHR', Inner Temple, London, 23 March 2009.

10 A number of applicants have challenged various aspects of State authorities' decisions regarding the assumption of public care over their children. In *W v UK* A.121-A (1987), the applicant challenged the decision-making process followed by a local authority to assume the parental rights of the applicant and his wife in respect of their youngest child (S) and subsequently to place S with long-term foster parents while denying W (and his wife) access to S. The applicant and his wife had a history of serious marital and financial difficulties. S was born in October 1978 and his parents placed him in the voluntary care of the local authority in March 1979 (as his mother was suffering from post-natal depression and alcoholism). In August 1979 the local authority passed resolutions assuming parental rights over S, but the applicant and his wife were not informed that such resolutions were being considered. Early in 1980 an unidentified official in the authority's Social Services Department determined that S should be placed with foster parents on a long-term basis with a view to adoption. In March 1980 the authority's Adoption and Foster Care Committee, without consulting the applicant (or his wife), approved the proposal to place S with long-term foster parents and restrict access to him by his natural parents. During the next month the Area Director of Social Services decided that W (and his wife) should not be allowed to visit S (in order to avoid jeopardizing S developing a good relationship with his foster parents). W and his wife began legal proceedings to challenge the local authority's actions, but in June 1981 the High Court held that it would not be in S's best interests to be returned to their care. The Court of Appeal confirmed that decision in October 1981. Subsequently, the Local Ombudsman upheld the applicant's complaint of maladministration in respect of the decision-making procedure followed by the local authority. In 1984 the High Court approved an application by the foster parents to adopt S. W complained to the Commission alleging, *inter alia*, that the procedures followed by the local authority had violated his right to respect for his family life. By 13 votes to 1 the Commission found a breach of Article 8. The plenary Court began its judgment by observing that:

> The mutual enjoyment by parent and child of each other's company constitutes a fundamental element of family life. Furthermore, the natural family relationship is not terminated by reason of the fact that the child is taken into public care. It follows—and this was not contested by the Government—that the Authority's decisions resulting from the procedures at issue amounted to interferences with the applicant's right to respect for his family life. [Para 59.]

The Court found that the interferences were 'in accordance with the law' and had the legitimate aim of protecting the health or rights and freedoms of others (i.e. S). Therefore, the contentious issue was whether the authority's conduct was 'necessary in a democratic society'.

> The Court recognises that, in reaching decisions in so sensitive an area, local authorities are faced with a task that is extremely difficult. To require them to follow on each occasion an inflexible procedure would only add to their problems. They must therefore be allowed a measure of discretion in this respect.
>
> On the other hand, predominant in any consideration of this aspect of the present case must be the fact that the decisions may well prove to be irreversible: thus, where a child has been taken away from his parents and placed with alternative carers, he may in the course of time establish with them new bonds which it might not be in his interests to disturb or interrupt by reversing a previous decision to restrict or terminate parental access to him. This is accordingly a domain in which there is an even greater call than usual for protection against arbitrary interferences.
>
> It is true that Article 8 contains no explicit procedural requirements, but this is not conclusive of the matter. The local authority's decision-making process clearly cannot be devoid of influence on the substance of the decision, notably by ensuring that it is based on the relevant considerations and is not one-sided and, hence, neither is nor appears to be arbitrary. Accordingly, the Court is entitled to have regard to that process to determine whether it has been conducted in a manner that, in all the circumstances, is fair and affords due respect to the interests protected by Article 8....
>
> The relevant considerations to be weighed by a local authority in reaching decisions on children in its care must perforce include the views and interests of the natural parents. The decision-making process must therefore, in the Court's view, be such as to secure that their views and interests are made known to and duly taken into account by the local authority and that they are able to exercise in due time any remedies available to them....
>
> There are three factors which have a bearing on the practicalities of the matter. Firstly, as the Commission pointed out, there will clearly be instances where the participation of the natural parents in the decision-making process either will not be possible or will not be meaningful—as, for example, where they cannot be traced or are under a physical or mental disability or where an emergency arises. Secondly, decisions in this area, while frequently taken in the light of case reviews or case conferences, may equally well evolve from a continuous process of monitoring on the part of the local authority's officials. Thirdly, regular contacts between the social workers responsible and the parents often provide an appropriate channel for the communication of the latter's views to the authority.
>
> In the Court's view, what therefore has to be determined is whether, having regard to the particular circumstances of the case and notably the serious nature of the decisions to be taken, the parents have been involved in the decision-making process, seen as a whole, to a degree sufficient to provide them with the requisite protection of their interests. If they have not, there will have been a failure to respect their family life and the interference resulting from the decision will not be capable of being regarded as 'necessary' within the meaning of Article 8....the Court considers that in

conducting its review in the context of Article 8 it may also have regard to the length of the local authority's decision-making process and of any related judicial proceedings. As the Commission has rightly pointed out, in cases of this kind there is always the danger that any procedural delay will result in the de facto determination of the issue submitted to the court before it has held its hearing. And an effective respect for family life requires that future relations between parent and child be determined solely in the light of all relevant considerations and not by the mere effluxion of time. [Paras 62–5.]

These principles were applied by the Court and led it to conclude that the local authority had not involved the applicant sufficiently in the decisions it had taken, early in 1980, regarding S. The length of the domestic court proceedings was also a subsidiary factor in the Court's application of Article 8. Consequently, a unanimous Court found a violation of that provision. The judgment of the Court was highly significant in requiring public authorities to follow fair procedures that ensured that parents were properly involved in decision-making regarding the care of their children. However, having regard to the diverse range of situations in which public authorities have to reach decisions regarding the care of children, the Court did not mandate a specific form of procedure, but instead focused upon the duty on the relevant State agencies to ensure that the parents' opinions were adequately considered. The Court found breaches of this requirement in the similar cases of *B v UK* A.121-B (1987) and *R v UK* A.121-C (1987). The law in England and Wales was subject to major reforms by the Children Act 1989 which provided, *inter alia*, local authorities would have to apply to the courts for care orders, such orders would automatically include provisions allowing reasonable contact with parents and disputes about contact and its termination would be resolved by the courts. Procedural aspects of the Scottish system of child welfare protection were considered in *McMichael v UK* A.307-B (1995). The first and second applicants were married in 1990 and both had a history of mental illness. In November 1987 the second applicant gave birth to a son (A) whom she denied was the son of the first applicant (although both applicants were living together at the time). The Reporter to the local Children's Panel arranged for a children's hearing to be convened (this was before a tribunal of independent members drawn from the Panel) to consider the need for compulsory care of A, because the second applicant's doctors had found that she was suffering from a recurrence of her mental illness. In December the children's hearing granted a warrant for A to be kept in a place of safety by the local authority. In February 1988 the children's hearing held a session at which the second applicant attended, and the first applicant was also present as her representative. The children's hearing had a report on A, compiled by the local social work department. In accordance with the Children's Hearings (Scotland) Rules 1986, the applicants were not given copies of the report (or other documents before the hearing), but the chairman informed them of the substance of the relevant documents. The children's hearing decided that A was in need of compulsory care. In 1993 the Sheriff granted an application by A's foster parents to adopt him. The applicants complained to the Commission alleging, *inter alia*, that they had not had a fair hearing before the children's hearing in breach of Article 8. A unanimous Commission upheld that claim. After citing its decision in *W v UK*, the Court sought to elaborate the different procedural rights granted by Articles 6(1) and 8.

Thus, Article 6(1) affords a procedural safeguard, namely the 'right to a court' in the determination of one's 'civil rights and obligations' (see *Golder v UK* A.18); whereas not only does the procedural requirement inherent in Article 8 cover administrative procedures as well as judicial proceedings, but it is ancillary to the wider purpose of ensuring proper respect for, *inter alia*, family life...The difference between the purpose pursued by the respective safeguards afforded by Articles 6(1) and 8 may, in the light of the particular circumstances, justify the examination of the same set of facts under both Articles...[Para 91.]

Because of the applicants' inability to have access to some of the documents before the children's hearing, the Court found a breach of their right to respect for their family life (unanimously in the case of the second applicant and by 6 votes to 3 in the case of the first applicant).

A unanimous Grand Chamber has held that governmental authorities in possession of relevant information concerning a child subject to public care measures must generally make that material available to the parent(s) without the latter having formally to seek its disclosure. In *TP and KM v UK*, judgment of 10 May 2001 the first applicant was a young single mother with a daughter (the second applicant) nearly 5 years old. The local authority became concerned that the daughter was the victim of sexual abuse. An interview, recorded on video, was conducted with the daughter (in the absence of the first applicant) by a consultant child psychiatrist (employed by the local health authority) and a social worker (employed by the local social services) in November 1987. The child revealed that she had been abused by a man named X. The first applicant's current boyfriend shared the same forename (XY). Later that day, the local authority applied to the magistrates' court for a place of safety order in respect of the daughter on the basis that she was being abused at home by XY. The court granted that order and she was taken into public care. During the following year the first applicant was only allowed very limited access to her daughter. In subsequent judicial proceedings the consultant and the health authority objected to the video of the second applicant's interview being disclosed to the first applicant. In November 1988 the first applicant's solicitors were given a transcript of the daughter's interview and it became apparent that the person she had identified as her abuser was not XY. Subsequently, the High Court granted leave for the second applicant to be returned to live with the first applicant. The applicants complained to Strasbourg that, *inter alia*, the unjustifiable taking into care of the second applicant had violated their right to respect for their family life. Before the Court, the Government contended that the first applicant could have applied to the High Court for an order obliging the local authority to disclose the video tape of the interview at any time after the second applicant had been taken into public care. However, the Court considered that this possibility did not satisfy the duties incumbent upon domestic authorities.

82....The positive obligation on the Contracting State to protect the interests of the family requires that this material be made available to the parent concerned, even in the absence of any request by the parent. If there were doubts as to whether this posed a risk to the welfare of the child, the matter should have been submitted to the court by the local authority at the earliest stage in the proceedings possible for it to resolve the issue involved.

Hence there had been a breach of Article 8. The decision in *TP* is a further important strengthening of parental rights under Article 8, as it places the primary responsibility for disclosure upon those public authorities that possess the relevant materials. Given that many parents experiencing the compulsory taking of their children into care are likely to be in a distressed state, at that time, requiring the public authorities to take the initiative in disclosing relevant information will reduce the burden upon the parents and, perhaps, enable them to gain a better understanding of the situation.

Judicial authorities of member States are also required to disclose relevant evidence to parents. For example, in *Buchberger v Austria*, judgment of 20 December 2001, the applicant was a single mother who had two young children. Her job was delivering papers in the morning. One day she was 45 minutes late returning from work (because she claimed she had been unwell) and a neighbour had contacted the local authority as she had seen the applicant's 2-year-old son wandering around in his garden wearing only pyjamas despite the freezing temperature. The local Youth Welfare Office took the applicant's two young sons into provisional care and applied to the District Court for the transfer of custody of the boys to the Office. After a hearing, at which the applicant was assisted by counsel, the District Court ordered the prompt return of the boys to the applicant. In subsequent appellate proceedings the Office submitted a report to the Regional Court. The Regional Court also obtained several court files concerning other civil and criminal proceedings against the applicant. She was not informed of this further evidence. Custody of the boys was transferred to the Office by the Regional Court as it found that their living conditions with the applicant were desolate and chaotic. The European Court was unanimous in determining that the procedure followed by the Regional Court violated the applicant's right to respect for her family life.

43. ... It is not in dispute that this additional evidence has not been brought to the applicant's attention. However, in the circumstances of the case the Regional Court should not have decided without having given the applicant an opportunity to react thereto. The additional evidence was of particular importance to the proceedings as the Regional Court considered it sufficiently strong to overturn the first instance decision. The Regional Court did not merely rely on the outcome of previous court proceedings but considered the further contents of the case-file. Moreover, it relied on a recent report by the Youth Welfare Office, a document which the applicant had never seen.

44. In the Court's opinion, the failure of the Regional Court to inform the applicant of the additional evidence obtained during the appeal proceedings which deprived her of the possibility to react thereto reveals an insufficient involvement of her in the decision-making process.

A Grand Chamber of the full-time Court elaborated limitations on the rights of parents to participate in official decision-making procedures concerning the custody and care of their children in *K and T v Finland*, judgment of 12 July 2001. This was also the first occasion on which a Grand Chamber gave a re-hearing judgment (under Article 43) following an earlier Chamber judgment on the same facts. K was the mother of two children (P, born in 1986 and M, born in 1988) by different fathers. From the summer of 1991 she had been cohabiting with T. K had a history of serious mental illness involving periods of compulsory and voluntary hospitalization. During March 1993, when K was pregnant with T's child, her mother informed the social welfare authorities that K's mental health was bad (K had allegedly destroyed family photographs by piercing the eyes of the persons appearing in them). K was subsequently placed in voluntary psychiatric care for several weeks. M was showing signs of behavioural problems and the social welfare authorities decided to place him in a children's home for three months (K and T did not object to this placement). On 18 June 1993 K went into hospital where she gave birth to a daughter (J). The local Social Director, exercising statutory powers, issued an emergency care order taking J into public care. The order was served on the hospital and immediately after J's birth she was taken from K to the children's ward. Three days later the Social Director issued another emergency order placing M in public care. In July 1993 the local Social Welfare Board made 'normal' public care orders in respect of M and J. K was only allowed to see the children when she was accompanied by her personal nurse. Both K and T had been able to express their opposition to the making of these orders before the Board reached its decisions. During the summer of 1993 T spent much time with J caring for her in the hospital and later in a family centre. In the autumn of 1993 the County Administrative Court confirmed the care orders in respect of J and M. At the start of 1994 J and M were placed, by the Board, with a foster family in a city 120 km from the applicant's home. The applicants were restricted, by the authorities, to visiting their children once a month. From January 2001 M and J have been allowed unsupervised visits to and by the applicants once a month.

The applicants complained to the former Commission in 1994 and their case was referred to the new Court in 1998. The Chamber, in a judgment given on 27 April 2000, unanimously found, *inter alia*, a breach of the applicants' right to respect for their family life under Article 8 in respect of the Finnish authorities' decisions to take M and J into care and the failure to take appropriate measures to reunite the family. Just a few days before the expiry of the three-month deadline for seeking a referral to the Grand Chamber under Article 43, the respondent State sought a re-examination of those matters where the Chamber had found a violation of the Convention. The applicants did not contest the request. In October 2000 the five-member Grand Chamber Panel accepted the Finnish request and the Grand Chamber held a hearing in the spring of 2001.

The Grand Chamber adopted a more precise framework of analysis when applying Article 8 than that utilized by the Chamber. The latter examined the taking of M and J into care as a whole. Whereas:

160. The Grand Chamber, for its part, considers it appropriate to examine the emergency care order and the normal care order for each child separately as they were different kinds of decision, which had different consequences—an emergency care order being of short, limited duration and a normal care order being of a more permanent nature—and which were the product of separate decision-making processes, even though one measure followed immediately after the other. In the Grand Chamber's view there are substantive and procedural differences to be taken into account which warrant examining the two sets of decisions separately.

A large majority of the Grand Chamber (14 votes to 3) determined that the emergency order taking J into care as soon as she had been born was not necessary in a democratic society and therefore in breach of Article 8.

168. ...the taking of a new-born baby into public care at the moment of its birth is an extremely harsh measure. There must be extraordinarily compelling reasons before a baby can be physically removed from the care of its mother, against her will, immediately after birth as a consequence of a procedure in which neither she nor her partner has been involved. The shock and disarray felt by even a perfectly healthy mother are easy to imagine. ... The reasons relied on by the national authorities were relevant but, in the Court's view, not sufficient to justify the serious intervention in the family life of the applicants. Even having regard to the national authorities' margin of appreciation, the Court considers that the making of the emergency care order in respect of J. and the methods used in implementing that decision were disproportionate in their effects on the applicants' potential for enjoying a family life with their new-born child as from her birth. This being so, whilst there may have been a 'necessity' to take some precautionary measures to protect the child J., the interference in the applicants' family life entailed in the emergency care order made in respect of J. cannot be regarded as having been 'necessary' in a democratic society.

Regarding the emergency care order in respect of M the Grand Chamber, by 13 votes to 4, decided that there had not been a breach of Article 8. The majority considered that this order did not have the same impact on the applicants' family life as J's order. M was already separated from his family, due to his voluntary placement in the children's home, but without the order he could have been removed from that safe environment by the applicants. The dissentients (Judges: Ress, Fuhrmann, Pantiru, and Kovler) considered that:

> Before public authorities have recourse to emergency measures in such delicate issues as care orders the imminent danger should be really established. An imminent danger is the precondition for an emergency care order. If it is still possible to hear the parents of the child and to discuss with them the necessity of the measure, there should be no room for an emergency action.
>
> M. was in no imminent danger since he had already been placed in a children's home. The whole procedure gives the impression of a coup de force. A procedure to have normal care orders prepared with the involvement of the parents would have been under the circumstances a reasonable and fully satisfactory way.

The Grand Chamber was united in determining that the normal care orders in respect of both J and M did not violate Article 8.

> 173. In a situation in which, as detailed in the medical and social reports, the mother of the children was seriously mentally ill, there were social problems in the family and the prospects for the healthy development of the children in foster care appeared far more positive than the expected development in the care of their biological parents, the authorities could reasonably base the contested decisions on the assessment that was made of what was in the best interests of the children. As to the procedural guarantee inherent in Article 8, the evidence shows that the applicants were properly involved in the decision-making process leading to the making of the normal care orders and that they were provided with the requisite protection of their interests...

The judgment of the majority in *K and T* discloses a fair balance between the interests of parents and their children. Where leaving children with their parents creates an immediate serious risk to the children's welfare, the authorities are empowered to take unilateral emergency care measures to protect the children. But, the authorities will be obliged to demonstrate that such a severe decision, and the procedures by which it was reached, were compatible with parental rights under Article 8.

12 The nature and extent of the positive obligation upon States to enable contact between a divorced parent and his/her children was outlined in *Glaser v UK* (2000) 33 EHRR 1.

> 65. The Court's case-law has consistently held that Article 8 includes a right for a parent to have measures taken with a view to his or her being reunited with the child, and an obligation for the national authorities to take such measures. This applies not only to cases dealing with the compulsory taking of children into public care and the implementation of care measures (see, *inter alia*, the *Olsson v Sweden (No 2)* judgment of 27 November 1992, Series A No 250, pp 35–6, § 90), but also to cases where contact and residence disputes concerning children arise between parents and/or other members of the children's family (eg the *Hokkanen v Finland* judgment of 23 September 1994, Series A No 299, p 20, § 55).
>
> 66. The obligation of the national authorities to take measures to facilitate contact by a non-custodial parent with children after divorce is not, however, absolute (*mutatis mutandis, Hokkanen* judgment cited above, p 22, § 58). The establishment of contact may not be able to take place immediately and may require preparatory or phased measures. The co-operation and understanding of all concerned will always be an important ingredient. While national authorities must do their utmost to facilitate such co-operation, any obligation to apply coercion in this area must be limited since the interests as well as the rights and freedoms of all concerned must be taken into account, and more particularly the best interests of the child and his or her rights under Article 8 of the Convention. Where contacts with the parent might appear to threaten those interests or

interfere with those rights, it is for the national authorities to strike a fair balance between them (see *Hokkanen v Finland* cited above, § 58; *Olsson v Sweden (No 2)*, cited above, pp 35–6, § 90). The key consideration is whether those authorities have taken all necessary steps to facilitate contact as can reasonably be demanded in the special circumstances of each case (*mutatis mutandis, Hokkanen v Finland*, cited above, § 58). Other important factors in proceedings concerning children are that time takes on a particular significance as there is always a danger that any procedural delay will result in the *de facto* determination of the issue before the court (*H. v UK* judgment of 8 July 1987, Series A No 120, pp 63–4, §§ 89–90), and that the decision-making procedure provides requisite protection of parental interests. [*W v UK* judgment of 8 July 1987, Series A No 121, pp 28–9, §§ 62–4.]

The Court was unanimous in concluding that the English and Scottish authorities had, in respect of a very difficult post-divorce situation, achieved a fair balance between the competing interests of the applicant, his ex-wife, and their children. The judgment also makes clear the limitations of the Court's role in scrutinizing the actions (or inaction) of the national authorities.

64. Where the measures in issue concern parental disputes over their children, however, it is not for the Court to substitute itself for the competent domestic authorities in regulating contact questions, but rather to review under the Convention the decisions that those authorities have taken in the exercise of their power of appreciation. In so doing, it must determine whether the reasons purporting to justify any measures taken with regard to an applicant's enjoyment of his right to respect for family life are relevant and sufficient...

An example of the Court finding a State in breach of the re-unification obligation in the context of the growing problem of international child abduction by a parent occurred in **Ignaccolo-Zenide v Romania**, judgment of 25 January 2000. The applicant was a French national who married a Romanian national (DZ) in 1980. They had two daughters (born in 1981 and 1984). A divorce was granted to the applicant and DZ by a French court in 1989. The court approved an agreement between the former spouses that parental responsibility was given to DZ and the applicant received access and staying rights. During the next year DZ moved to the United States and the applicant complained to the French courts that DZ was denying her access to her daughters. In May 1991 the Metz Court of Appeal gave parental responsibility to both parents and ordered that the children should live with the applicant. She subsequently brought a number of actions in different courts in the United States, but DZ did not comply with those judgments requiring him to return his daughters to the applicant. In 1994 DZ and his daughters went to live in Romania. Both the US and French Governments requested the Romanian Government to return the children to the applicant in accordance with the 1980 Hague Convention on the Civil Aspects of International Child Abduction. The applicant also made an urgent application under Article 2 of the Hague Convention to the Romanian courts for an order requiring DZ to comply with the 1991 judgment of the Metz Court of Appeal. In December 1994 the Bucharest Court of First Instance issued such an order. The applicant subsequently visited Romania eight times for the purpose of meeting her daughters but, despite several attempts by the Romanian authorities to enforce the Bucharest Court order, the applicant was only able to see her daughters once for a few minutes in 1997. The meeting did not go well and the daughters expressed the wish never to see the applicant again. Before the Court the applicant claimed that the Romanian authorities had not taken sufficient steps to facilitate the return of her daughters. In the judgment of the Chamber:

94....As to the State's obligation to take positive measures, the Court has repeatedly held that Article 8 includes a parent's right to the taking of measures with a view to his or her being reunited with his or her child and an obligation on the national authorities to take such action (see, for example, the following judgments: *Eriksson v Sweden*, 22 June 1989, Series A No 156, pp 26–7, ...). However, the national authorities' obligation to take measures to facilitate reunion is not absolute, since the reunion of a parent with children who have lived for some time with the other parent may not be able to take place immediately and may require preparatory measures to be taken. The nature and extent of such preparation will depend on the circumstances of each case, but the understanding and cooperation of all concerned are always an important ingredient. Whilst national authorities must do their utmost to facilitate such cooperation, any obligation to apply coercion in this area must be limited since the interests as well as the rights and freedoms of all concerned must be taken into account, and more particularly the best interests of the child and his or her rights under Article 8 of the Convention. Where contacts with the parent might appear to threaten those interests or interfere with those rights, it is for the national authorities to strike a fair balance between them...

95. Lastly, the Court considers that the positive obligations that Article 8 of the Convention lays on the Contracting States in the matter of reuniting a parent with his or her children must be interpreted in the light of the Hague Convention of 25 October 1980 on the Civil Aspects of International Child Abduction ('the Hague Convention'). This is all the more so in the instant case as the respondent State is also a party to that instrument, Article 7 of which contains a list of measures to be taken by States to secure the prompt return of children.

96. What is decisive in the present case is therefore whether the national authorities did take all steps to facilitate execution of the order of 14 December 1994 that could reasonably be demanded...

An overwhelming majority of the Court, 6 votes to 1, concluded that the Romanian authorities had failed to make 'adequate and effective' efforts to enforce the applicant's right to the return of her daughters. The Court emphasized that in abduction cases '102....the adequacy of a measure is to be judged by the swiftness of its implementation', because of the danger that the passage of time will undermine the relationship between the abducted children and the parent lawfully entitled to their custody. Here there had been several delays in bailiffs visiting DZ's home to look for the children in 1995 and total inaction by the authorities between December 1995 and January 1997. Consequently, these deficiencies meant that there had been a breach of Article 8.

The judgment in *Ignaccolo-Zenide* demonstrated a sensitive awareness of the potentially destructive effect of the lapse of time upon the durability of the relationship between a separated child and his/her parent(s). A rare case of the Grand Chamber finding that the best interests of the child required that a son be allowed to remain with his mother, who had unlawfully removed him from the country of his birth and where his father lived, was *Neulinger and Shuruk v Switzerland*, judgment of 6 July 2010.

13   State regulation of the adoption of children was examined by the Court in *Keegan v Ireland* A.290 (1994). The applicant met his former girlfriend (Miss V) in May 1986 and they started living together in February 1987. Around Christmas 1987 they decided to have a child. On 14 February 1988 they became engaged. A week later it was confirmed that V was pregnant. However, soon afterwards the relationship between the applicant and V broke down and they ceased living together. In September 1988 V gave birth to a daughter (S) of whom the applicant was the father. The applicant saw S when she was one day old, but he was prevented from seeing her again by V (and her parents). In November 1988 V wrote to the applicant informing him that she had made arrangements for S to be adopted. Under Irish

law the applicant had no right to be heard by the statutory Adoption Board, which approved applications from persons to adopt children placed for adoption. The applicant sought to be appointed as S's guardian by the courts in order to challenge her adoption, but he was unsuccessful. S was, subsequently, adopted. The applicant complained to the Commission alleging, *inter alia*, that Irish law failed to respect his right to respect for family life by allowing the adoption of his daughter without his knowledge or consent. A unanimous Commission considered that there had been a breach of Article 8. After citing its previous rulings in *Johnston v Ireland* and *Berrehab v Netherlands* (considered above), the Court stated that:

> In the present case, the relationship between the applicant and the child's mother lasted for two years during one of which they co-habited. Moreover, the conception of their child was the result of a deliberate decision and they had also planned to get married. Their relationship at this time had thus the hallmark of family life for the purposes of Article 8. The fact that it subsequently broke down does not alter this conclusion any more than it would for a couple who were lawfully married and in a similar situation. It follows that from the moment of the child's birth there existed between the applicant and his daughter a bond amounting to family life. [Para 45.]

All the judges went on to find that the interference with the applicant's right to respect for his family life was not 'necessary in a democratic society' as the Irish Government had provided no justification based upon the needs of S. Therefore, it is clear that the Court requires weighty reasons, derived from the needs of the particular child, to justify an adoption as being compatible with Article 8. The Court did not elaborate the procedure to be followed by the adoption process under Article 8, as it went on to find that the applicant's lack of standing in S's adoption and his inability to challenge the decision in the Irish courts violated Article 6(1).

In the later case of *Söderbäck v Sweden*, 1998-VII, the Court, unanimously, found the child's relationship with the adoptive father (which had lasted for over six years) to be sufficiently weighty to justify the adoption despite the objection of her natural father. The applicant had been a friend of KW from 1980, although they did not have a steady relationship. In 1982 KW gave birth to a daughter (M) of whom the applicant was the father. The applicant only saw M on an occasional basis, due to an alcohol problem that he was experiencing. In 1983 KW met MW and they began to cohabit later that year. During 1989 they married. A few months earlier MW had applied to the District Court for permission to adopt M. The District Court heard the applicant's objections to the adoption request, but decided to approve the adoption as the court found that MW had taken part in the care of M since she was eight months old and she saw him as her father. The applicant's complaint alleging a breach of Article 8 was rejected by the European Court of Human Rights:

> 34.... having regard to the assessment of the child's best interests made by the domestic court, as well as to the limited relations that the applicant had with M during the relevant period, the Court is satisfied that the decision fell within the margin of appreciation. Given the aims sought to be achieved by allowing the adoption to go ahead, it cannot be said that the adverse effects it had on the applicant's relations with the child were disproportionate.

Therefore, the Court was recognizing that the ties between a child and the proposed adoptive parent may be of sufficient duration and quality to outweigh those between the child and her/his natural parent.

In respect of a complaint regarding the authorities' refusal to grant permission for a lesbian to adopt a child, the Grand Chamber in *EB v France*, judgment of 22 January 2008, held that, '41.... the provisions of Article 8 do not guarantee either the right to found a family or the right to adopt...'. However, as the applicant had framed her complaint on the basis of alleged discrimination concerning her sexual orientation (relying on Article 14 in conjunction with Article 8) the Grand Chamber stated that:

46. The Court is not therefore called upon to rule whether the right to adopt, having regard, *inter alia*, to developments in the legislation in Europe and the fact that the Convention is a living instrument which must be interpreted in the light of present-day conditions (see, in particular, *Johnston and Others v Ireland*, judgment of 18 December 1986), should or should not fall within the ambit of Article 8 of the Convention alone.

A majority of the Grand Chamber (10 votes to 7) went on to uphold her complaint. The wording of paragraph 46 suggests that in the future the Court might be willing to find an implied right to adopt embodied in Article 8.

Home

Gillow v UK A.109 (1986)
European Court of Human Rights

The applicants, Mr and Mrs Gillow, moved from England to Guernsey in 1956 so that Mr Gillow could take up employment on the island. In 1957, Mr Gillow bought a plot of land on the island and, after obtaining permission, he built a house called 'Whiteknights' on the site. The Gillows occupied the house as their family residence until 1960 when the family left Guernsey, as Mr Gillow had accepted employment overseas. During the ensuing years the house was let to persons who had licences to occupy it granted by the States of Guernsey Housing Authority. By 1979 the house was unoccupied and the Gillows applied for a licence to enable them to occupy Whiteknights as their retirement home. The authorities refused the applicants permission to occupy Whiteknights and successfully prosecuted them when they lived in the property without a licence. The applicants sold Whiteknights in 1980. Subsequently, they complained to the Commission that, *inter alia*, their right to respect for their home under Article 8 had been violated by the Housing Authority's conduct. The Commission was unanimous in finding a breach of that right.

...

A. WAS 'WHITEKNIGHTS' MR AND MRS GILLOW'S 'HOME' WITHIN THE MEANING OF THE CONVENTION?

46. According to the applicants, they had established Whiteknights as their home in 1958. Although they had subsequently left Guernsey, they had retained ownership of the house, to which they always intended to return, and had kept their furniture in it. On their return in 1979, they lived in the property with a view to taking up permanent residence once the negotiations with the Housing Authority about their residential status had been concluded and the necessary repairs had been carried out.

  These statements, the accuracy of which the Court has no cause to doubt, are supported by the fact that in 1956 the applicants had sold their former home in Lancashire and moved with their family and furniture to Guernsey. Furthermore, the Court is satisfied that they had not established any other home elsewhere in the United Kingdom. Although the applicants had been absent from Guernsey for almost nineteen years, they had in the circumstances retained sufficient continuing links with Whiteknights for it to be considered their home, for the purposes of Article 8 of the Convention, at the time of the disputed measures.

B. WAS THERE ANY INTERFERENCE BY A PUBLIC AUTHORITY WITH THE EXERCISE OF THE APPLICANTS' RIGHT TO RESPECT FOR THEIR 'HOME'?

47. Following the enactment of the Housing Law 1969—which was not amended on this point by the Housing Law 1975—, the applicants were obliged to seek a licence to occupy Whiteknights because, as a consequence of the change in the law, they had lost their residence qualifications. In the Court's opinion, the fact that, on pain of prosecution, they were obliged to obtain a licence to live in their own house on their return to Guernsey in 1979, the refusal of the licences applied for, the institution of criminal proceedings against them for unlawful occupation of the property and, in Mr Gillow's case, his conviction and the imposition of a fine constituted interferences with the exercise of the applicants' right to respect for their home.

C. WERE THE INTERFERENCES JUSTIFIED?

48. In order to determine whether these interferences were justified under the terms of paragraph 2 of Article 8, the Court must examine in turn whether they were in accordance with the law, whether they had an aim that was legitimate under that paragraph and whether they were necessary in a democratic society for the aforesaid aim.

...

2. Legitimate aim

54. The Court refers to the statistics supplied both by the Government and by the applicants concerning the population of Guernsey and the number of empty houses. Although the situation could be said to have improved in some respects in the period between 1976 and 1981, this does not alter the fact that the island is very limited in area. It is therefore legitimate for the authorities to try to maintain the population within limits that permit the balanced economic development of the island. It is also legitimate, in this connection, to show a certain preference for persons who have strong attachments to the island or are engaged in an employment essential to the community when considering whether to grant licences to occupy premises let at a modest rent. The relevant legislation was thus designed to promote the economic well-being of the island. The Court does not find it to be established that the legislation pursued any other purpose.

...

3. Necessary in a democratic society

56. ... Whilst recognising the relevance of the facts relied on by the applicants, the Court considers that the Guernsey legislature is better placed than the international judge to assess the effects of any relaxation of the housing controls. Furthermore, when considering whether to grant a licence, the Housing Authority could exercise its discretion so as to avoid any disproportionality in a particular case. It follows that the statutory obligation imposed on the applicants to seek a licence to live in their home cannot be regarded as disproportionate to the legitimate aim pursued.

There has accordingly been no breach of Article 8 as far as the terms of the contested legislation are concerned.

57. There remains, however, the question whether the manner in which the Housing Authority exercised its discretion in the applicants' case—refusal of permanent and temporary licences, and referral of the matter to the Law Officers with a view to prosecution—corresponded to a pressing social need and, in particular, was proportionate to the legitimate aim pursued.

The statistics submitted to the Court show that, during the relevant period—1979 and 1980—the population of the island had been kept within the levels of recent years, having even marginally declined, and the availability of houses for occupation had not suffered any significant deterioration. Against this background, whilst not overlooking the fact that the average population per square mile of the island was still high in comparison with other countries, the Court considers that insufficient weight was given to the applicants' particular circumstances. They had built Whiteknights as a residence for themselves, and their family. At that time, they possessed residence qualifications and continued to do so until the entry into force of the Housing Law 1969, so that during that period they were entitled to occupy the house without a licence. The property was Mr and Mrs Gillow's place of residence for two years before they left Guernsey in 1960. Thereafter, they had retained ownership of the house and left furniture there. By letting it over a period of eighteen years to persons approved by the Housing Authority, they contributed to the Guernsey housing stock. On their return in 1979, they had no other home in the United Kingdom or elsewhere; Whiteknights was vacant and there were no prospective tenants.

As for the refusals of the temporary licences, the decisions of the Housing Authority were, despite the granting of certain periods of grace, even more striking. Whiteknights needed repairs after eighteen years of rented use, with the result that it could not be occupied in the meantime by anyone other than the applicants.

Finally, as regards the referral of the case to the Law Officers with a view to prosecution, the Government stated that the Housing Authority deferred taking this course on several occasions. This, however, in the Court's view did not materially alleviate Mr and Mrs Gillow's already precarious situation.

58. The Court therefore concludes that the decisions by the Housing Authority to refuse the applicants permanent and temporary licences to occupy Whiteknights, as well as the conviction and fining of Mr Gillow, constituted interferences with the exercise of their right to respect for their home which were disproportionate to the legitimate aim pursued.

There has accordingly been a breach of Article 8 of the Convention as far as the application of the legislation in the particular circumstances of the applicants' case was concerned.

. . .

NOTES

1 The Court was unanimous in finding a breach of Article 8 in the way in which the licensing laws had been applied to the Gillows; however their complaints under Articles 6, 14, Protocol 1 and Protocol 4 were rejected. The Court was comprised of President Wiarda and Judges: Ryssdal, Vilhjalmsson, Lagergren, Pettiti, Evans, and Macdonald.

2 The British Government sought to argue that the term 'home' only applied to a residence legally established in accordance with national law (*Buckley v UK*, 1996-II). The applicant was a Gypsy who had bought land and then moved three caravans onto the property and lived there with her family for a number of years. The local planning authority refused her permission to use her land for residential purposes and when she refused to remove her caravans she was subject to criminal proceedings for failing to comply with an enforcement notice. She claimed that the authority's actions infringed her right to respect for her home. The Court, unanimously, rejected the Government's narrow interpretation of 'home'.

Although in the *Gillow* case the applicants' home had initially been established legally, similar considerations apply in the present case. The Court is satisfied that the applicant bought the land to establish her residence there. She has lived there almost continuously since 1988 . . . and it has not been suggested that she has established, or intends to establish, another residence elsewhere. The case therefore concerns the applicant's right to respect for her 'home'. [Para 54.]

Hence, the Court was focusing on the factual realities of the situation, rather than the domestic legal status of the applicant's residence, when determining whether the applicant could assert the existence of a home commanding respect by the national authorities under Article 8(1). But, a majority of the Court (6 to 3) went on to hold that the authorities' treatment of the applicant could be justified under Article 8(2) as being necessary for the economic well-being of the country and for the protection of the health and rights of other (local) persons.

3 In *Niemietz v Germany* A 251B (p 488), the Court interpreted 'home' broadly to include professional/business premises such as a lawyer's office. This was because the equivalent term in the French text of the Convention ('*domicile*') had a wider meaning than the English term. Furthermore, an expansive definition was consistent with Article 8's underlying aim of protecting persons against arbitrary interferences by public authorities. However, the Court expressed the view that States might have a greater right to interfere with professional/business premises, compared with domestic dwellings, provided they could justify their actions under Article 8(2).

A Chamber was unanimous in finding breaches of companies' right to respect for their homes in *Societe Colas Est and Others v France*, judgment of 16 April 2002. The three applicants were major construction companies. Complaints were made, by a trade association, to the French competition authorities that the applicants were engaging in illegal practices concerning the tendering for roadwork projects. The head of the National Investigation Office, exercising powers granted by a 1945 ordinance, authorized coordinated raids by inspectors on the offices of 56 companies, including the applicants', to seize documents concerning the alleged illegal practices. Subsequently, the domestic courts rejected the applicants' challenges to the lawfulness of the inspections and seizure of the documents. The companies were fined between 3 and 6 million Francs each in respect of unlawful practices. Before the Court the applicants contended that there had been a violation of the right to respect for their homes by the inspectors raiding their offices to seize incriminating documents. The Chamber held that:

41. The Court reiterates that the Convention is a living instrument which must be interpreted in the light of present-day conditions (see, *mutatis mutandis*, *Cossey v the United Kingdom*, judgment of 27 September 1990, Series A No 184, p 14, § 35 *in fine*). As regards the rights secured to companies by the Convention, it should be pointed out that the Court has already recognised a company's right under Article 41 to compensation for non-pecuniary damage sustained as a result of a violation of Article 6 § 1 of the Convention (see *Comingersoll v Portugal* [GC], No 35382/97, §§ 33–5, ECHR 2000-IV). Building on its dynamic interpretation of the Convention, the Court considers that the time has come to hold that in certain circumstances the rights guaranteed by Article 8 of the Convention may be construed as including the right to respect for a company's registered office, branches or other business premises (see, *mutatis mutandis*, *Niemietz*, cited above, p 34, § 30).

...

49. ... At the material time—and the Court does not have to express an opinion on the legislative reforms of 1986, whereby inspectors' investigative powers became subject to prior authorisation by a judge—the relevant authorities had very wide powers which, pursuant to the 1945 ordinance, gave them exclusive competence to determine the expediency, number, length and scale of inspections. Moreover, the inspections in issue took place without any prior warrant being issued by a judge and without a senior police officer being present. That being so, even supposing that the entitlement to interfere may be more far-reaching where the business premises of a juristic person are concerned (see, *mutatis mutandis*, *Niemietz*, cited above, p 34, § 31), the Court considers, having

regard to the manner of proceeding outlined above, that the impugned operations in the competition field cannot be regarded as strictly proportionate to the legitimate aims pursued . . .

50. In conclusion, there has been a violation of Article 8 of the Convention.

So the business premises of companies can fall within Article 8's concept of a home. However, the judgment in *Colas* indicated that the Court may be more protective of business premises occupied by non-corporate persons (e.g. the lawyer in *Niemietz*) than those of legal persons. Is this a sensible distinction—what level of protection should small companies, with only a few shareholders, enjoy?

4   Some of the limits on the Court's wide interpretation of 'home' were revealed in *Loizidou v Turkey*, 1996-VI. The applicant grew up in northern Cyprus and owned several plots of land in that part of the island. During 1972 she moved to another part of the island with her husband. Before the Turkish occupation of northern Cyprus, in 1974, she claimed that work had begun on one of her plots to build a block of flats and that her family intended to live in one of the flats as their home. Mrs Loizidou alleged that since the military occupation the Turkish forces in northern Cyprus had prevented her gaining access to her property in breach of her rights to respect for her home under Article 8 and peaceful enjoyment of her property under Article 1 of Protocol 1. The Court, unanimously, rejected her alleged breach of Article 8 because:

. . . the applicant did not have her home on the land in question. In its opinion it would strain the meaning of the notion 'home' in Article 8 to extend it to comprise property on which it is planned to build a house for residential purposes. Nor can that term be interpreted to cover an area of a State where one has grown up and where the family has its roots but where one no longer lives. [Para 66.]

However, a majority (11 to 6) found that there had been a breach of the applicant's property rights under Protocol 1. Again, the Court was concentrating on the factual aspects of the applicant's residential circumstances in determining whether her 'home' had been subject to interference by State authorities. At what stage of construction should a property be deemed to constitute a person's home?

A later Grand Chamber in *Demopoulos and others v Turkey*, decision of 5 March 2010, further elaborated that:

136. The notion of 'home' has been interpreted dynamically by this Court; however care must be taken to respect the intentions of the authors of the Convention as well as common sense . . . Thus, it is not enough for an applicant to claim that a particular place or property is a 'home'; he or she must show that they enjoy concrete and persisting links with the property concerned (see e.g. *Gillow v the United Kingdom*, 24 November 1986, § 46, Series A no. 109). The nature of the ongoing or recent occupation of a particular property is usually the most significant element in the determination of the existence of a 'home' in cases before the Court. However, where 'home' is claimed in respect of property in which there has never been any, or hardly any, occupation by the applicant or where there has been no occupation for some considerable time, it may be that the links to that property are so attenuated as to cease to raise any, or any separate, issue under Article 8 (see, for example, *Andreou Papi v Turkey*, no. 16094/90, § 54, 22 September 2009). Furthermore, while an applicant does not necessarily have to be the owner of the 'home' for the purposes of Article 8, it may nonetheless be relevant in such cases of claims to 'homes' from the past that he or she can make no claim to any legal rights of occupation or that such time has elapsed that there can be no realistic expectation of taking up, or resuming, occupation in the absence of such rights (see, *mutatis mutandis*,

Vrahimi v Turkey, no. 16078/90, § 60, 22 September 2009, where the applicant had never had any 'possession' in the property which had been owned by a company). Nor can the term 'home' be interpreted as synonymous with the notion of 'family roots', which is a vague and emotive concept (e.g. *Loizidou*, judgment on the merits cited above, § 66).

Consequently, a majority of the Grand Chamber determined that a claim of interference with her right to respect for her home by a person who had only lived as a young child in the then family residence and subsequently moved elsewhere (because of the 1974 Turkish military invasion) was manifestly ill-founded.

5   The full-time Court found a second property could be classified as a person's home in **Demades v Turkey**, judgment of 31 July 2003. The applicant contended that he owned a house in Kyrenia (together with his principal home in Nicosia) and that since 1974 he had been denied access to the property by Turkish armed forces.

31. The Court notes that the applicant's house in Kyrenia was a fully furnished and completely equipped house, which he and his family made regular use of and in which they lived for substantial periods of time over the year. The house was treated by the applicant and his family as a home. It served *inter alia* as a holiday home and for providing hospitality and entertainment to relatives, friends and persons associated with the applicant's business activities.

32. The Court notes in this context that it may not always be possible to draw precise distinctions, since a person may divide his time between two houses or form strong emotional ties with a second house, treating it as his home. Therefore, a narrow interpretation of the word 'home' could give rise to the same risk of inequality of treatment as a narrow interpretation of the notion of 'private life', by excluding persons who find themselves in the above situations.

33. The Court recalls that the Convention is a living instrument to be interpreted in the light of societal changes and in line with present-day conditions (see *Cossey v the United Kingdom*, judgment of 27 September 1990, Series A No 184, p. 14, § 35). Furthermore, it notes that in its relevant case-law it has adopted an extensive interpretation of the notion of 'home' (see, *inter alia*, *Société Colas Est and Others v France* No 37971/97, §§ 40–2, ECHR 2002-II; and *Niemietz v Germany*, judgment of 16 December 1992, Series A No 251-B, §§ 29–30).

34. Accordingly, the Court considers that in the circumstances of the present case, the house of the applicant qualified as 'home' within the meaning of Article 8 of the Convention at the time when the acts complained of took place.

35. The Court observes that the present case differs from the *Loizidou* case since, unlike Mrs Loizidou, the applicant actually had a home in Kyrenia, albeit a secondary one.

36. The Court notes that since 1974 the applicant has been unable to gain access to and to use that home. In connection with this the Court recalls that, in its judgment in the case of *Cyprus v Turkey* ([ECHR 2001-IV] §§ 172–5), it concluded that the complete denial of the right of Greek-Cypriot displaced persons to respect for their homes in northern Cyprus since 1974 constituted a continuing violation of Article 8 of the Convention. The Court reasoned as follows:

'172. The Court observes that the official policy of the "TRNC" authorities to deny the right of the displaced persons to return to their homes is reinforced by the very tight restrictions operated by the same authorities on visits to the north by Greek Cypriots living in the south. Accordingly, not only are displaced persons unable to apply to the authorities to reoccupy the homes which they left behind, they are physically prevented from even visiting them.

'173. The Court further notes that the situation impugned by the applicant Government has obtained since the events of 1974 in northern Cyprus. It would appear that it has never been reflected in 'legislation' and is enforced as a matter of policy in furtherance of a bi-zonal arrangement designed, it is claimed, to minimise the risk of conflict which the intermingling of the Greek and Turkish-Cypriot communities in the north might engender. That bi-zonal arrangement is being pursued within the framework of the inter-communal talks sponsored by the United Nations Secretary-General (see paragraph 16 above).

'174. The Court would make the following observations in this connection: firstly, the complete denial of the right of displaced persons to respect for their homes has no basis in law within the meaning of Article 8 § 2 of the Convention (see paragraph 173 above); secondly, the inter-communal talks cannot be invoked in order to legitimate a violation of the Convention; thirdly, the violation at issue has endured as a matter of policy since 1974 and must be considered continuing.

'175. In view of these considerations, the Court concludes that there has been a continuing violation of Article 8 of the Convention by reason of the refusal to allow the return of any Greek-Cypriot displaced persons to their homes in northern Cyprus.'

37. The Court sees no reason in the instant case to depart from the above reasoning and findings in the case of *Cyprus v Turkey (op. cit.)*. Accordingly, it concludes that there has been a continuing violation of Article 8 of the Convention by reason of the complete denial of the right of the applicant to respect for his home.

Judge Gölcüklü, the judge of Turkish nationality, dissented as he believed the status of northern Cyprus should be resolved through international negotiations and bilateral talks between the two communities on Cyprus. The judgment of the Chamber suggests that the more time spent in, and use made of, a second property the stronger the claim will be for it to be classified as a home under Article 8. Given the popularity of second homes (both within national territories and, increasingly, in other member States) the judgment in *Demades* offers the potential for such properties to be brought within the protection of Article 8 with consequent enhanced legal rights for owners (which may be especially reassuring to foreign nationals).

6   States can be held liable under Article 8 for causing, or allowing others to create, severe environmental pollution which interferes with persons' right to respect for their homes. In *Lopez Ostra v Spain* A.303C (1994), the applicant claimed that her family home had been subject to serious pollution (including gas fumes and pestilent smells) from a private sector tannery reprocessing plant, which had been built with a State subsidy on municipal land only 12m from the applicant's flat. The pollution persisted for several years and the applicant's family eventually had to move to accommodation provided by the local authority because their health was being adversely affected by the pollution. The Court held that severe environmental pollution could interfere with the right to respect for a person's home even where it did not seriously endanger the health of the residents. The Spanish authorities sought to justify the operation of the reprocessing plant as being necessary for the economic well-being of the town, however the Court held that '...the State did not succeed in striking a fair balance between the interest of the town's economic well-being–that of having a waste-treatment plant–and the applicant's effective enjoyment of her right to respect for her home and her private and family life' (para 58). Therefore, the Court unanimously found a breach of the applicant's rights under Article 8 and awarded her 4 million pesetas compensation for pecuniary and non-pecuniary damage. This was the first occasion where the Court had upheld an environmental pollution claim brought under Article 8. However, in the earlier case of *Powell and Rayner v UK,* A.172 (1990), the Court implicitly acknowledged that environmental claims could, in appropriate circumstances, be brought within the ambit

of Article 8. There two persons living beneath the flight paths of aircraft using Heathrow airport claimed that the noise generated by the jet engines interfered with their rights to respect for their homes. However, the Commission and the Court concluded that the airport was necessary for the economic well-being of the UK and the relevant authorities had taken sufficient steps (such as providing noise insulation for the worst affected homes) to respect the applicants' rights under Article 8. See p 570 for a discussion of the positive obligations on States to 'respect' persons' rights under Article 8(1).

A Grand Chamber of the Court has developed the principles in *Lopez Ostra* to find a State liable under Article 8 where it failed to warn local residents of the risks they faced from a nearby private chemical factory and the safety procedures that they should observe if there was an accident at the plant: *Guerra v Italy*, 1998-I. The 40 female applicants lived in the town of Manfredonia about 1 km from a chemical factory. They alleged, and it was not disputed by the Italian Government, that the plant had released large quantities of pollutants over many years (including inflammable gases, sulphur dioxide, and nitric oxide). In 1976 there had been an explosion at the factory which released arsenic compounds which resulted in 150 people being admitted to hospital with acute poisoning. The release of other highly toxic chemicals from the separate factory disaster in Seveso prompted the (former) EEC to issue a Directive regarding safety matters at dangerous industrial sites. This Directive was incorporated into Italian law during 1988 and local mayors were, *inter alia*, obliged to inform their residents of hazardous industrial activities in the locality together with the procedures to be followed in an emergency. In 1989 an official panel of experts had made recommendations to the central government about the factory at Manfredonia, however, no safety information had been provided to the local population by the end of 1995. The applicants, therefore, brought a complaint under the ECHR. The Court, unanimously, concluded that there had been a breach of their rights to respect for their private and family lives; because they had waited many years '... for essential information that would have enabled them to assess the risks they and their families might run if they continued to live at Manfredonia, a town particularly exposed to danger in the event of an accident at the factory' (para 60). The Court awarded each applicant non-pecuniary damages of 10 million lire. We can presume that the long history of pollution from this particular factory was a decisive factor in the Court's willingness to find the authorities liable for failing to provide advice to the local population.

There was profound disagreement between a Chamber and a Grand Chamber in respect of the approach to applying Article 8 to the regulation of night flights using Heathrow airport. The eight applicants in *Hatton and Others v UK*, judgment of 2 October 2001, lived near the airport or under flight paths of aircraft using the airport. They complained that the Department of Transport's system of regulating night flights, using noise quotas and numbers of flights, had not been preceded by rigorous investigations into the incidents of sleep disturbance of affected residents or the economic benefits of night flights. A majority of the Chamber, 5 votes to 2, held that:

97. The Court would, however, underline that in striking the required balance, States must have regard to the whole range of material considerations. Further, in the particularly sensitive field of environmental protection, mere reference to the economic well-being of the country is not sufficient to outweigh the rights of others. The Court recalls that in the above-mentioned *Lopez Ostra v Spain* case, and notwithstanding the undoubted economic interest for the national economy of the tanneries concerned, the Court looked in considerable detail at 'whether the national authorities took the measures necessary for protecting the applicant's right to respect for her home and for her private and family life ...' (judgment of 9 December 1994, p 55, § 55). It considers that States are

required to minimise, as far as possible, the interference with these rights, by trying to find alternative solutions and by generally seeking to achieve their aims in the least onerous way as regards human rights. In order to do that, a proper and complete investigation and study with the aim of finding the best possible solution which will, in reality, strike the right balance should precede the relevant project.

The majority went on to conclude that as the British Government had not undertaken adequate inquiries into the costs and benefits of the night flights regime there had been a breach of Article 8. The Government responded by seeking a referral of the case to a Grand Chamber, under Article 43, arguing that the test applied by the Chamber had been inconsistent with the established jurisprudence that accorded States a wide margin of appreciation in environmental/planning decisions which involved complex balancing of competing interests.

In its judgment, **Hatton and Others v UK**, judgment of 8 July 2003, the Grand Chamber began by acknowledging that whilst there was no express right to a clean and quiet environment guaranteed by the Convention, previous jurisprudence, including **Powell and Rayner v UK** and **Lopez Ostra v Spain**, established that:

98. Article 8 may apply in environmental cases whether the pollution is directly caused by the State or whether State responsibility arises from the failure properly to regulate private industry. Whether the case is analysed in terms of a positive duty on the State to take reasonable and appropriate measures to secure the applicants' rights under paragraph 1 of Article 8 or in terms of an interference by a public authority to be justified in accordance with paragraph 2, the applicable principles are broadly similar. In both contexts regard must be had to the fair balance that has to be struck between the competing interests of the individual and of the community as a whole; and in both contexts the State enjoys a certain margin of appreciation in determining the steps to be taken to ensure compliance with the Convention. Furthermore, even in relation to the positive obligations flowing from the first paragraph of Article 8, in striking the required balance the aims mentioned in the second paragraph may be of a certain relevance (see the above-mentioned Powell and Rayner judgment, § 41 and the above-mentioned *López Ostra* judgment, § 51).

But the Grand Chamber acknowledged the democratic legitimation of national authorities and their primary role in evaluating local needs and determining matters of general policy. Therefore, the Court's scrutiny of domestic decisions concerning environmental issues should examine their substantive merits to ensure that they were compatible with Article 8 subject to a 'wide margin of appreciation' being accorded to governments. Additionally, the Court should examine the national decision-making process to ensure that sufficient attention had been given to the interests of the applicant.

In respect of the substantive merits of the Heathrow night flights scheme the Government asserted that hundreds of thousands of London residents were in a similar situation to the applicants, the property market in the region was thriving, and none of the applicants had claimed that they were unable to sell their homes because of noise pollution. Other European hub airports (including Paris Charles de Gaulle, Amsterdam Schiphol, and Frankfurt) had less severe restrictions on night flights and if further restrictions were placed on Heathrow night flights it would be placed at a major competitive disadvantage. Also, the night flights using Heathrow were integral parts of the airlines' networks. The Government contended that it had undertaken detailed studies of the effects of aircraft noise disturbance on residents and public consultations prior to introducing the 1993 night flights regulations.

The applicants supported the judgment of the Chamber and emphasized that even a few aircraft flying at night can cause serious sleep disturbance to individuals. British Airways, reflecting the views of airline trade associations, claimed that night flights at Heathrow play a major role in the transport infrastructure of the UK and contribute significantly to the UK economy and living standards of UK citizens.

The Grand Chamber distinguished the situation in this application from the previous environmental cases of *Lopez Ostra* and *Guerra v Italy*, where the Court had found breaches of Article 8, as the Spanish and Italian authorities had failed to comply with national law whereas the Heathrow night flights scheme was in conformity with British law. A large majority of the Grand Chamber, 12 votes to 5, rejected the Chamber's approach to environmental cases:

> 122. The Court must consider whether the Government can be said to have struck a fair balance between [the economic] interests [of the UK] and the conflicting interests of the persons affected by noise disturbances, including the applicants. Environmental protection should be taken into consideration by Governments in acting within their margin of appreciation and by the Court in its review of that margin, but it would not be appropriate for the Court to adopt a special approach in this respect by reference to a special status of environmental human rights. In this context the Court must revert to the question of the scope of the margin of appreciation available to the State when taking policy decisions of the kind at issue.

> 123. The Court notes that the introduction of the 1993 Scheme for night flights was a general measure not specifically addressed to the applicants in this case, although it had obvious consequences for them and other persons in a similar situation. However, the sleep disturbances relied on by the applicants did not intrude into an aspect of private life in a manner comparable to that of the criminal measures considered in the case of Dudgeon to call for an especially narrow scope for the State's margin of appreciation (see *Dudgeon v the United Kingdom*, [A.45] p 21, § 52 [(1981)]. Rather, the normal rule applicable to general policy decisions would seem to be pertinent here, the more so as this rule can be invoked even in relation to individually addressed measures taken in the framework of a general policy, such as in the above-mentioned *Buckley* [v United Kingdom 1996-IV 74] case. Whilst the State is required to give due consideration to the particular interests the respect for which it is obliged to secure by virtue of Article 8, it must in principle be left a choice between different ways and means of meeting this obligation. The Court's supervisory function being of a subsidiary nature, it is limited to reviewing whether or not the particular solution adopted can be regarded as striking a fair balance.

The majority considered that the Government's decision to adopt a quota-based system (reflecting the noise levels of different types of aircraft) to regulate night flights was not incompatible with Article 8 and it was reasonable to assume that such flights 'contribute at least to a certain extent to the general economy'. Also the majority felt that it was significant that the limited number of persons (2–3 per cent according to the Government's 1992 sleep study) particularly affected by night flights could move elsewhere without financial loss as the housing market in the applicants' area was thriving. Therefore the Grand Chamber did not find that the Government had overstepped their margin of appreciation in making the policy decision concerning the 1993 night flights scheme at Heathrow.

Regarding the procedural aspect of the domestic decision-making process the Grand Chamber held that determinations:

> 128....concerning complex issues of environmental and economic policy such as in the present case must necessarily involve appropriate investigations and studies in order to allow them to strike a fair balance between the various conflicting interests at stake. However, this does not mean that decisions can only be taken if comprehensive and measurable data are available in relation to each and every aspect of the matter to be decided.

The Government had regularly monitored night flights at Heathrow and restrictions, beginning in 1962, were reviewed every five years. Prior to the introduction of the 1993 scheme there had been a number of studies and investigations carried out over many years. The applicants had opportunities to make representations concerning the consultation paper that preceded the 1993 scheme and could have sought judicial review if their views had been ignored. Consequently, the majority did not consider that there had been any fundamental flaws in the procedural aspects of the creation of the 1993 scheme. Therefore, the applicants had not suffered a breach of Article 8.

Five judges (Costa—the President of the Chamber which had originally determined the case, Ress, Turmen, Zupancic, and Steiner) issued a joint dissenting opinion which advocated a much stronger role for the Court in responding to complaints concerning environmental pollution. They began by emphasizing the close connection between human rights protection, health being the most basic human need, and the 'urgent need for decontamination of the environment'. Whilst they acknowledged that the Convention text does not contain a provision on pollution ('yet') the dissenters noted that recent times had witnessed emerging provisions concerning pollution including the European Union's Charter of Fundamental Rights and the Kyoto Protocol. Consequently, they considered that environmental pollution was a matter for international law/jurisdiction. In their opinion the earlier case-law reflected an evolutive interpretation of the Convention such that:

2....In the field of environmental human rights, which was practically unknown in 1950, the Commission and the Court have increasingly taken the view that Article 8 embraces the right to a health environment, and therefore to protection against pollution and nuisances caused by harmful chemicals, offensive smells, agents which precipitate respiratory ailments, noise and so on.

From this perspective, the Grand Chamber's determination that there had been no breach of Article 8:

5....seems to us to deviate from the above developments in the case-law and even to take a step backwards. It gives precedence to economic considerations over basic health conditions...

The dissenters considered that in the context of constant disturbance of persons' sleep at night by aircraft noise there was a positive obligation upon States to 'ensure as far as possible that ordinary people enjoy normal sleeping conditions'. Consequently:

17....The margin of appreciation of the State is narrowed down because of the fundamental nature of the right to sleep, which may be outweighed only by the real, pressing (if not urgent needs) of the State. Incidentally, the Court's own subsidiary role, reflected in the use of the 'margin of appreciation', is itself becoming more and more marginal when it comes to such constellations as the relationship between the protection of the right to sleep as an aspect of privacy and health on the one hand and the very general economic interest on the other hand.

In their assessment, the Government's claims regarding the economic need for night flights were based upon reports produced by the aviation industry and the Government had not made serious attempts to assess the impact of aircraft noise on the applicants' sleep prior to the introduction of the 1993 scheme. Hence the Government had failed to reach a fair balance between the economic well-being of the UK and the protection of the applicants' sleep from the effects of nocturnal aircraft noise.

The Grand Chamber's judgment is significant for establishing the authoritative approach of the full-time Court to cases involving environmental complaints under Article 8. Whilst the majority endorsed the original Court's recognition that serious forms of environmental pollution could result in infringement of persons' rights to respect for their private/family lives and homes, and that States were under both negative duties not to cause such pollution themselves and positive obligations to provide effective regulation of private sector pollution, the Grand Chamber was not willing to apply the Chamber's enhanced level of scrutiny of domestic policy decisions concerning pollution control measures. Although the Grand Chamber judgment referred to 'environmental human rights' for the first time in the Court's jurisprudence, the majority applied the established wide margin of appreciation doctrine to governmental policy decisions concerning environmental protection. The Grand Chamber affirmed the primary role of domestic authorities in determining the fair balance between the interests of local residents affected by a particular source of environmental pollution and the needs of the nation. Environmentalists may be unhappy that the Grand Chamber emphasized its supervisory role, but previous case-law demonstrates that it is not without substance. For example, in *Lopez Ostra* and *Guerra* the original Court found breaches of Article 8 where domestic authorities failed to deal with industrial facilities producing serious forms of environmental pollution. Furthermore, the Grand Chamber's judgment in *Hatton* reveals that the contemporary Court will examine both the substance of the domestic policy decision to assess its compatibility with Article 8 and the procedure followed by the domestic authorities in reaching that decision to ensure that the individual complainants have been afforded an adequate opportunity to participate in the decision-making process.

The Court's methodology of examining both the substantive and procedural aspects of environmental decision-making was applied by a unanimous Chamber in the later case of *Taskin and Others v Turkey*, judgment of 10 November 2004. The ten applicants lived near a site where, in 1992, the Ministry of the Environment granted permission for a company to operate a goldmine. The permit authorized the use of cyanide to extract the gold. The applicants challenged the granting of the permit in the courts, arguing that the cyanidation process created a danger of pollution to the underlying aquifers. In May 1997 the Supreme Administrative Court upheld their challenge finding that the mining permit was not in the general interest due to the risks for the environment and human health. The local Governor ordered the closure of the mine in February 1998. During 1999 the Prime Minister sought a report, from the Turkish Institute of Scientific and Technical Research, on the environmental impact of the use of cyanide at the mine. That report indicated that risks noted in the Supreme Court's judgment had now been eliminated or reduced. Consequently, ministers authorized the resumption of mining. The applicants, again, challenged those decisions in the domestic courts. In 2002 the Turkish Cabinet decided that the mining company should be allowed to continue its extraction of gold. That decision was not made public. Before the European Court the applicants submitted, *inter alia*, that the granting of the permit for extracting gold by the use of cyanide violated their rights under Article 8. The Chamber ruled that in respect of the substantive decision to grant the permit the Supreme Court had found that it was contrary to the public interest, therefore the Chamber did not need to examine that issue further. Regarding the decision-making processes concerning the authorization of mining the Chamber found that the administrative authorities had failed to comply with domestic legislation or court decisions thereby depriving the applicants of effective procedural protection. Consequently, there had been a breach of Article 8. Similar conclusions were reached in *Ockan and Others v Turkey*, judgment of 28 March 2006, where another 315 local residents successfully challenged the authorities' actions regarding the mine.

Another Spanish local authority failed to protect a person's home from severe noise pollution in *Moreno Gomez v Spain*, judgment of 16 November 2004. The applicant began living in a flat located in a residential part of Valencia during 1970. From 1974 the local council licensed over 120 bars, pubs, and discotheques to operate in the vicinity of her home. Despite repeated complaints by the applicant, and other local residents, the local authority failed to reduce the level of noise caused by the licensed establishments (an expert report commissioned by the council in 1993 stated that the night-time noise levels were unacceptable and exceeded permitted limits and in 1995 the police told the council that the nightclubs did not close on time). A unanimous Chamber found a breach of Article 8.

61. Although the Valencia City Council has used its powers in this sphere to adopt measures (such as the bylaw concerning noise and vibrations) which should in principle have been adequate to secure respect for the guaranteed rights, it tolerated, and thus contributed to, the repeated flouting of the rules which it itself had established during the period concerned. Regulations to protect guaranteed rights serve little purpose if they are not duly enforced and the Court must reiterate that the Convention is intended to protect effective rights, not illusory ones. The facts show that the applicant suffered a serious infringement of her right to respect for her home as a result of the authorities' failure to take action to deal with the night-time disturbances.

62. In these circumstances, the Court finds that the respondent State has failed to discharge its positive obligation to guarantee the applicant's right to respect for her home and her private life, in breach of Article 8 of the Convention.

Accordingly, the Chamber ordered Spain to pay the applicant 3,884 euros just satisfaction to cover the cost of double glazing her bedroom (879 euros) and to compensate her for non-pecuniary damage suffered.

A unanimous Chamber found that the domestic authorities had failed adequately to respect the home and private life of a woman who lived in a council flat located within the 'sanitary security zone' designated around Russia's largest iron smelter. The Severstal steel plant at Cherepovets had been built in Soviet times and in 1965 the Government established a 5 km wide zone around the plant to separate it from residential areas. However, thousands of persons lived within that zone (the plant employs approximately 60,000 workers). The applicant in *Fadeyeva v Russia*, judgment of 9 June 2005, has lived in the zone since 1982. The Severstal plan was privatized in 1993. The applicant brought proceedings against the steelworks and the local authority complaining that the pollution from the plant was very severe (dust levels were 1.6–1.9 times higher than the maximum permitted level and there were excessive concentrations of hazardous chemicals discharged into the atmosphere including hydrogen sulphide and ammonia). The outcome of those proceedings resulted in the applicant being placed on the council's waiting list for new housing (she was person number 6,820 on the list; the applicant claimed that the first person on the list had been waiting since 1968 for a new council home). The Government's current programme for reducing the pollution from the Severstal plant aims to achieve safe levels of emissions by 2010–15. The Court found that:

88. In the instant case, however, the very strong combination of indirect evidence and presumptions makes it possible to conclude that the applicant's health deteriorated as a result of her prolonged exposure to the industrial emissions from the Severstal steel-plant. Even assuming that the pollution did not cause any quantifiable harm to her health, it inevitably made the applicant more vulnerable to various diseases. Moreover, there can be no doubt that it adversely affected the quality of life at her home. Therefore, the Court accepts that the actual detriment to the

applicant's health and well-being reached a level sufficient to bring it within the scope of Article 8 of the Convention.

...

132. In sum, the Court finds the following. The State authorised the operation of a polluting enterprise in the middle of a densely populated town. Since the toxic emissions from this enterprise exceeded the safe limits established by the domestic legislation and might endanger the health of those living nearby, the State established that a certain territory around the plant should be free of any dwelling. However, these legislative measures were not implemented in practice.

133. It would be going too far to state that the State or the polluting enterprise were under an obligation to provide the applicant with free housing, and, in any event, it is not the Court's role to dictate precise measures which should be adopted by the States in order to comply with their positive duties under Article 8 of the Convention. In the present case, however, although the situation around the plant called for a special treatment of those living within the zone, the State did not offer the applicant any effective solution to help her move from the dangerous area. Furthermore, although the polluting enterprise at issue operated in breach of domestic environmental standards, there is no information that the State designed or applied effective measures which would take into account the interests of the local population, affected by the pollution, and which would be capable of reducing the industrial pollution to acceptable levels.

134. The Court concludes that, despite the wide margin of appreciation left to the respondent State, it has failed to strike a fair balance between the interests of the community and the applicant's effective enjoyment of her right to respect for her home and her private life. There has accordingly been a violation of Article 8.

The Chamber considered that as the applicant's lengthy exposure to the plant's industrial pollution had caused her 'much inconvenience, mental distress and even a degree of physical suffering' she should be awarded 6,000 euros compensation for non-pecuniary damage (this sum took into account the fact that the Court could not award compensation for damage suffered prior to 1998, the date when Russia became bound by the Convention).

In determining if alleged pollution is sufficiently serious in its effects to fall within Article 8, the Court has had regard to international guidelines. For example, in *Fagerskiold v Sweden*, decision of 28 February 2008, the applicants had complained about alleged noise pollution from a wind turbine located several hundred metres from their holiday home. However, the Chamber considered that:

...even having regard to the applicants' submission that the noise level could be 3 to 5 dB higher than shown by the noise tests, that is roughly between 42 and 45 dB, this does not exceed the level recommended by the WHO [World Health Organization], either outdoors or indoors, and it only slightly exceeds the recommended maximum level in Sweden. It is also significantly inferior to the noise levels measured in the cases cited above (*Moreno Gómez, Hatton and Others*...). Therefore, in the Court's view, the nuisance caused by the wind turbine cannot be found to reach the level of constituting severe environmental pollution. [Page 16.]

Consequently the application was declared manifestly ill-founded.

Where an environmentally dangerous extractive or industrial activity is being undertaken the Court has in recent times held that States' regulation of the activity must be guided by the 'precautionary principle' (that scientific uncertainty about the activity does not justify a failure to introduce effective regulation). Applying this principle a Chamber found a breach of Article 8 where the domestic authorities had failed adequately to protect local residents from pollution caused by a gold mining company using sodium cyanide (as in *Taskin* above): *Tatar v Romania*, judgment of 27 January 2009.

A united Chamber found that the highway authorities had failed to take adequate measures to protect the applicant in his home from suffering excessive noise pollution caused by lorries using the road adjoining his house as a route to avoid paying a motorway toll in *Dees v Hungary*, judgment of 9 November 2010.

Regarding the Court's stance towards environmental pollution Ole W. Pedersen has commented:

> Thus it can be argued that the approach taken by the Court, when ruling that certain environmental harms constitute Convention infringements, may be activist, but it merely is attuned to developments already taking place on the international arena and, most importantly, on the European national level. In other words, the Court's environmental jurisprudence simply echoes that developing in the jurisdictions of the contracting Member States and accusations of judicial activism are not as well-founded as they may appear at first sight. ['The Ties that Bind: The Environment, the European Convention on Human Rights and the Rule of Law' (2010) 16(4) *European Public Law* 571 at 586.]

For an examination of the obligations upon States, under Article 2, to protect persons from lethal pollution disasters see *Oneryildiz v Turkey*, p 126.

7   An extreme example of an interference with peoples' homes was found to have occurred in *Akdivar v Turkey*, 1996-IV, where a Grand Chamber of the Court (by 19 votes to 2) determined that the security forces' deliberate burning of the applicants' homes and contents amounted to a serious interference with their rights to respect for their family lives and homes. The destruction of the homes followed a terrorist attack, by the PKK (Workers' Party of Kurdistan), on a nearby gendarme station in which a soldier was killed. Subsequently, in *Mentes v Turkey*, 1997-VIII, another Grand Chamber (by 16 votes to 5) accepted the Commission's finding of fact that gendarmes had required residents, including the applicants, to leave their homes in the lower neighbourhood of Saggoze village and the soldiers had then set fire to those properties with all the residents' belongings inside (including the clothing and footwear of the residents' children). This action, again, took place in the context of the security forces' campaign in south-east Turkey against the rebel PKK. However, in neither case did the Court consider that the evidence was sufficient to establish the existence of an administrative practice regarding the destruction of villagers' homes by security forces. In *Selcuk and Asker v Turkey*, 1998-II, a Chamber of the Court found, by 8 votes to 1, that the burning of the homes of the applicants (a 54-year-old woman and a man of 60) by the security forces amounted, *inter alia*, to 'grave and unjustified' interferences with the applicants' right to respect for their homes.

8   Another tactic of the Turkish security forces in combating the PKK was found to violate persons' right to respect for their homes in *Dogan and Others v Turkey*, judgment of 29 June 2004. The authorities prevented the 15 applicants from returning to their homes, located in a village in south-east Turkey where widespread terrorist activities were taking place, for nine years. A unanimous Chamber determined that the authorities' refusal to allow the applicants access to their village constituted '159....a serious and unjustified interference with the right to respect for family lives and homes'. The scale of the security forces' strategy was revealed by the fact that approximately 1,500 applications similar to *Dogan* had been registered with the Court by the time of the above judgment (Registrar's press release 29 June 2004). Subsequently, the Turkish Parliament enacted the Law on Compensation

for Losses resulting from Terrorism and the Fight against Terrorism (2004); this statute established Compensation Commissions in 76 provinces to which persons who had suffered damage through acts of terrorism or anti-terrorism measures taken by the authorities could apply for compensation. By early 2006 over 170,000 persons had applied to the Commissions. In *Icyer v Turkey*, decision of 9 February 2006, the applicant complained to the Court regarding his alleged eviction and subsequent exclusion from his home/village in 1994. The Turkish Government responded that there was currently no prohibition on his return to the village and as he had not applied for compensation under the 2004 Law he had failed to exhaust domestic remedies. The Court found that the Law provided a practical remedy for the applicant and that as he had failed to utilize that domestic remedy his application should be declared inadmissible. More generally, the Court observed that the 2004 Law demonstrated that Turkey had addressed the systemic problem identified in *Dogan*. Subsequently, nearly 1,500 similar applications were rejected by the Court for non-exhaustion of domestic remedies.

9 A Grand Chamber majority, of 10, in *Chapman v UK*, judgment of 18 January 2001, stated that:

> 99. It is important to recall that Article 8 does not in terms give a right to be provided with a home. Nor does any of the jurisprudence of the Court acknowledge such a right. While it is clearly desirable that every human being has a place where he or she can live in dignity and which he or she can call home, there are unfortunately in the Contracting States many persons who have no home. Whether the State provides funds to enable everyone to have a home is a matter for political not judicial decision.

However, the minority, of 7, issued a joint dissenting opinion in which they expressed the view that:

> 7. We would also take issue with the relevance or validity of the statement in paragraph 99 of the judgment to the effect that Article 8 does not give a right to be provided with a home....Furthermore, it is not the Court's case-law that a right to be provided with a home is totally outside the ambit of Article 8. The Court has accepted that there may be circumstances where the authorities' refusal to take steps to assist in housing problems could disclose a problem under Article 8—see for example the case of *Marzari v Italy*, where the Court held a refusal of the authorities to provide housing assistance to an individual suffering from a severe disease might in certain circumstances raise an issue because of the impact of such refusal on the private life of the individual (No 3644/97, decision of 4 May 1999)...

The Court was clearly very divided on the issue of whether Article 8 obliges States to provide assistance to persons to establish a home. *Chapman* is examined further at p 586.

10 A unanimous Chamber found the summary powers of a local authority to evict a Gypsy family from a council-owned caravan site violated Article 8 in *Connors v UK*, judgment of 27 May 2004. The applicant and his family led a traditional travelling lifestyle for a number of years. However, they suffered harassment and consequently settled on a Gypsy site run by Leeds City Council in 1984. Thirteen years later the applicant and his family moved off the site as they were adversely affected by anti-social behaviour of others. They were not able to adjust to living in a house and returned to the site in October 1998. The Council provided them with a licence to occupy a specified plot. Clause 18 of the licence provided that, 'no nuisance is to be caused by the occupier, his guests, nor any member of his family to any other person...' In December 1998 the

Council gave the applicant a written warning that continued incidents of anti-social behaviour by his adult sons at the site (they did not live on the site but frequently visited the applicant) could jeopardize his occupation of the site. In January 2000 the Council served a notice to quit on the applicant and his family requiring them to leave the site. No reasons were given for the notice. In subsequent summary legal proceedings the Council made reference to the requirements of clause 18 in the applicant's licence. The County Court granted the Council a possession order in June 2000. The Council undertook not to enforce the order for one month. The applicant did not leave the site voluntarily and in August 2000 he and his family were forcibly evicted. Before the Court the applicant contended that the eviction had interfered with his right to respect for his private life, family life, and home. The Government accepted that contention and the parties agreed that the interference had been in accordance with the law and for a legitimate aim, namely protecting the rights of other occupants of the site and the Council. The issue of dispute between the parties was the necessity of the interference. The applicant complained that the summary possession proceedings did not enable him to challenge the allegations made against his family. The Government contended that judicial review proceedings were available to ensure that local authorities acted in accordance with the principles of reasonableness and procedural propriety.

93. The Court would not under-estimate the difficulties of the task facing the authorities in finding workable accommodation solutions for the gypsy and traveller population and accepts that this is an area in which national authorities enjoy a margin of appreciation in adopting and pursuing their social and housing policies. The complexity of the situation has, if anything, been enhanced by the apparent shift in habit in the gypsy population which remains nomadic in spirit if not in actual or constant practice. The authorities are being required to give special consideration to a sector of the population which is no longer easy to define in terms of the nomadism which is the *raison d'être* of that special treatment.

94. However, even allowing for the margin of appreciation which is to be afforded to the State in such circumstances, the Court is not persuaded that the necessity for a statutory scheme which permitted the summary eviction of the applicant and his family has been sufficiently demonstrated by the Government. The power to evict without the burden of giving reasons liable to be examined as to their merits by an independent tribunal has not been convincingly shown to respond to any specific goal or to provide any specific benefit to members of the gypsy community....It would rather appear that the situation in England as it has developed, for which the authorities must take some responsibility, places considerable obstacles in the way of gypsies pursuing an actively nomadic lifestyle while at the same time excluding from procedural protection those who decide to take up a more settled lifestyle.

95. In conclusion, the Court finds that the eviction of the applicant and his family from the local authority site was not attended by the requisite procedural safeguards, namely the requirement to establish proper justification for the serious interference with his rights and consequently cannot be regarded as justified by a 'pressing social need' or proportionate to the legitimate aim being pursued. There has, accordingly, been a violation of Article 8 of the Convention.

Hence, domestic law provided inadequate protection for Gypsies living on public authority camp sites. Subsequently, the enactment of section 209 of the Housing Act 2004 extended statutory protection to local authority sites occupied by Gypsies.

In the later case of *McCann v UK*, judgment of 13 May 2008, a unanimous Chamber applied *Connors* to the termination of a husband's joint tenancy of a council house by the securing of his (separated) wife signing a notice to quit.

50. The Court is unable to accept the Government's argument that the reasoning in *Connors* was to be confined only to cases involving the eviction of gypsies or cases where the applicant sought to challenge the law itself rather than its application in his particular case. The loss of one's home is a most extreme form of interference with the right to respect for the home. Any person at risk of an interference of this magnitude should in principle be able to have the proportionality of the measure determined by an independent tribunal in the light of the relevant principles under Article 8 of the Convention, notwithstanding that, under domestic law, his right of occupation has come to an end.

Consequently, as the applicant had not had the benefit of such procedural safeguards there had been a breach of Article 8. A similar approach was applied by the Court in *Kay and others v UK*, judgment of 21 September 2010. The UK Supreme Court, sitting in a special nine-member formation, responded by reversing its previous rulings:

49.…if our law is to be compatible with Article 8, where a court is asked to make an order for possession of a person's home at the suit of a local authority, the court must have the power to assess the proportionality of making the order, and, in making that assessment, to resolve any relevant dispute of fact. [*Manchester City Council v Pinnock* [2010] UKSC 45.]

So, eventually, domestic law was extended to meet the requirements of Article 8.

11   The full-time Court affirmed that the term 'home' in Article 8 was an autonomous concept in *Prokopovich v Russia*, judgment of 18 November 2004.

36. The Court recalls the Convention organs' case-law that the concept of 'home' within the meaning of Article 8 is not limited to those which are lawfully occupied or which have been lawfully established. 'Home' is an autonomous concept which does not depend on classification under domestic law. Whether or not a particular habitation constitutes a 'home' which attracts the protection of Article 8 § 1 will depend on the factual circumstances, namely, the existence of sufficient and continuous links with a specific place (see the following authorities: *Buckley v the United Kingdom*, judgment of 25 September 1996, Reports of Judgments and Decisions 1996-IV, §§ 52–4, and Commission's report of 11 January 1995, § 63; *Gillow v the United Kingdom*, judgment of 24 November 1986, Series A No 109, § 46; *Wiggins v the United Kingdom*, No 7456/76, Commission decision of 8 February 1978, Decisions and Reports (DR) 13, p 40).

Accordingly, the Chamber was united in determining that the flat of her deceased male partner, which she had lived in for ten years, was her home. The eviction of the applicant, a few days after the sudden death of her partner, by police officers (one of whom had acquired the tenancy of the flat) breached Article 8 as it was not in conformity with Russian law (evictions had to be ordered by a court).

12   A unanimous Chamber held that the right to respect for a person's home extended to an obligation upon States to undertake effective investigations into complaints regarding alleged unlawful searches of homes by State agents. The applicant in *HM v Turkey*, judgment of 8 August 2006, was a teacher and union official who had complained about alleged police violence and had been acquitted of participating in unlawful protests. He subsequently lodged a complaint with the public prosecutor that his home had been searched by plain clothed persons, who claimed to be police officers, without a search warrant. The prosecutor ended his investigation, after five days, when the police denied any involvement in the alleged search. Having regard to the prosecutor's failure to take statements from the applicant's family members, who asserted that they had witnessed the unlawful search, the

Chamber concluded that there had not been an effective investigation and therefore a breach of Article 8 had occurred.

Correspondence

Kennedy v UK judgment of 18 May 2010
European Court of Human Rights

The applicant had been charged with murder. He claimed that the police had framed him to cover up their misconduct. His subsequent conviction was overturned on appeal. After two retrials he was convicted of manslaughter. After serving his sentence he became active in campaigning against miscarriages of justice. He later believed that his mail, telephone calls, and email communications were being intercepted (by the police/security services). Therefore, he lodged complaints with the Investigatory Powers Tribunal (IPT) established under the Regulation of Investigatory Powers Act 2000 (RIPA). Four years later the IPT notified him that no determination had been made in his favour (meaning either that he had not been subject to interception of his communications or any interception had been lawful).

RIPA provided an extensive legislative system for, *inter alia*, the authorization of interception warrants by the Home Secretary at the request of named agencies (e.g. the police) where specified grounds were satisfied (e.g. as being necessary for preventing or detecting serious crime). A detailed Interception of Communications Code of Practice was published by the Home Office which elaborated further safeguards (e.g. on the storage and destruction of intercepted materials). A Commissioner (who holds/held high judicial office) must be appointed, by the Prime Minister, under RIPA to review the exercise of the interception powers granted by the Act. The members of the IPT must also be senior judges/lawyers.

In his complaint to the Court the applicant alleged that his communications were being intercepted in order to intimidate him and undermine his business in breach of Article 8.

118. It is not disputed that mail, telephone and email communications, including those made in the context of business dealings, are covered by the notions of 'private life' and 'correspondence' in Article 8 § 1.

119. The Court has consistently held in its case-law that its task is not normally to review the relevant law and practice *in abstracto*, but to determine whether the manner in which they were applied to, or affected, the applicant gave rise to a violation of the Convention (see, *inter alia, Klass and Others* [*v Germany* A.28 (1978) . . .). However, in recognition of the particular features of secret surveillance measures and the importance of ensuring effective control and supervision of them, the Court has permitted general challenges to the relevant legislative regime.

120. The Court's approach to assessing whether there has been an interference in cases raising a general complaint about secret surveillance measures was set out in its *Klass and Others* judgment:

'34. . . . The question arises in the present proceedings whether an individual is to be deprived of the opportunity of lodging an application with the Commission because, owing to the secrecy of the measures objected to, he cannot point to any concrete measure specifically affecting him. In the Court's view, the effectiveness (l'effet utile) of the Convention implies in such circumstances some possibility of having access to the Commission. If this were not so, the efficiency of the Convention's enforcement machinery would be materially weakened. The procedural provisions of the Convention must, in view of the fact that the Convention and its institutions were set up to protect the individual, be applied in a manner which serves to make the system of individual applications efficacious.

The Court therefore accepts that an individual may, under certain conditions, claim to be the victim of a violation occasioned by the mere existence of secret measures or of legislation permitting secret measures, without having to allege that such measures were in fact applied to him. The relevant conditions are to be determined in each case according to the Convention right or rights alleged to have been infringed, the secret character of the measures objected to, and the connection between the applicant and those measures.'

...

123. . . . Where actual interception was alleged, the Court has held that in order for there to be an interference, it has to be satisfied that there was a reasonable likelihood that surveillance measures were applied to the applicant . . .

...

125. The Court observes that the present applicant complained of an interference with his communications both on the basis that, given the circumstances of his particular case, he had established a reasonable likelihood of interception and on the basis of the very existence of measures permitting secret surveillance.

126. The applicant has alleged that the fact that calls were not put through to him and that he received hoax calls demonstrates a reasonable likelihood that his communications are being intercepted. The Court disagrees that such allegations are sufficient to support the applicant's contention that his communications have been intercepted. Accordingly, it concludes that the applicant has failed to demonstrate a reasonable likelihood that there was actual interception in his case.

127. Insofar as the applicant complains about the RIPA regime itself, the Court observes, first, that the RIPA provisions allow any individual who alleges interception of his communications to lodge a complaint with an independent tribunal, a possibility which was taken up by the applicant. The IPT concluded that no unlawful, within the meaning of RIPA, interception had taken place.

128. As to whether a particular risk of surveillance arises in the applicant's case, the Court notes that under the provisions of RIPA on internal communications, any person within the United Kingdom may have his communications intercepted if interception is deemed necessary on one or more of the grounds listed in section 5(3). The applicant has alleged that he is at particular risk of having his communications intercepted as a result of his high-profile murder case, in which he made allegations of police impropriety, and his subsequent campaigning against miscarriages of justice. The Court observes that neither of these reasons would appear to fall within the grounds listed in section 5(3) RIPA. However, in light of the applicant's allegations that any interception is taking place without lawful basis in order to intimidate him, the Court considers that it cannot be excluded that secret surveillance measures were applied to him or that he was, at the material time, potentially at risk of being subjected to such measures.

129. In the circumstances, the Court considers that the applicant can complain of an interference with his Article 8 rights. The Government's objection concerning the applicant's lack of victim status is accordingly dismissed.

...

166. . . . The Court considers that the Commissioner's role in ensuring that the provisions of RIPA and the Code are observed and applied correctly is of particular value and his biannual review of a

random selection of specific cases in which interception has been authorised provides an important control of the activities of the intercepting agencies and of the Secretary of State himself.

167. The Court recalls that it has previously indicated that in a field where abuse is potentially so easy in individual cases and could have such harmful consequences for democratic society as a whole, it is in principle desirable to entrust supervisory control to a judge (see *Klass and Others*, cited above, § 56). In the present case, the Court highlights the extensive jurisdiction of the IPT to examine any complaint of unlawful interception. Unlike in many other domestic systems (see, for example, the G 10 Law discussed in the context of *Klass and Others* ...), any person who suspects that his communications have been or are being intercepted may apply to the IPT. The jurisdiction of the IPT does not, therefore, depend on notification to the interception subject that there has been an interception of his communications. The Court emphasises that the IPT is an independent and impartial body, which has adopted its own rules of procedure. The members of the tribunal must hold or have held high judicial office or be experienced lawyers. In undertaking its examination of complaints by individuals, the IPT has access to closed material and has the power to require the Commissioner to provide it with any assistance it thinks fit and the power to order disclosure by those involved in the authorisation and execution of a warrant of all documents it considers relevant. In the event that the IPT finds in the applicant's favour, it can, *inter alia*, quash any interception order, require destruction of intercept material and order compensation to be paid. The publication of the IPT's legal rulings further enhances the level of scrutiny afforded to secret surveillance activities in the United Kingdom.

168. Finally, the Court observes that the reports of the Commissioner scrutinise any errors which have occurred in the operation of the legislation. In his 2007 report, the Commissioner commented that none of the breaches or errors identified were deliberate and that, where interception had, as a consequence of human or technical error, unlawfully taken place, any intercept material was destroyed as soon as the error was discovered. There is therefore no evidence that any deliberate abuse of interception powers is taking place.

169. In the circumstances, the Court considers that the domestic law on interception of internal communications together with the clarifications brought by the publication of the Code indicate with sufficient clarity the procedures for the authorisation and processing of interception warrants as well as the processing, communicating and destruction of intercept material collected. The Court further observes that there is no evidence of any significant shortcomings in the application and operation of the surveillance regime. On the contrary, the various reports of the Commissioner have highlighted the diligence with which the authorities implement RIPA and correct any technical or human errors which accidentally occur. Having regard to the safeguards against abuse in the procedures as well as the more general safeguards offered by the supervision of the Commissioner and the review of the IPT, the impugned surveillance measures, insofar as they may have been applied to the applicant in the circumstances outlined in the present case, are justified under Article 8 § 2.

. . .

FOR THESE REASONS, THE COURT UNANIMOUSLY

. . .

2. *Holds* that there has been no violation of Article 8 ...

NOTES

1 The Chamber was composed of President Garlicki and Judges: Bratza, Bonello, Mijovic, Hirvela, Bianku, and Vucinic.

2 The above judgment confirms the ever-broadening forms of communication that are recognized as falling within the scope of 'correspondence'. It also repeats the well-established distinction between complaints that an applicant's correspondence has been subject to interception that is in breach of Article 8 and allegations that an interception regime violates Article 8.

3 The legality of the interception of postal communications and telephone tapping under the Convention had first been addressed by the Court in *Klass and others v Germany* A.28 (1978). There the Court held that the West German law permitting the interception of postal and telephonic communications in national security cases was consistent with Article 8; although an 'interference by a public authority' with the 'right to respect' for a person's 'private and family life...and his correspondence', it was justified as being necessary in the 'interests of national security' and/or for 'the prevention of disorder or crime'. The Court accepted that some power of interception was permissible to prevent espionage and terrorism and, bearing in mind the 'margin of appreciation' doctrine, concluded that the controls built into the West German system to prevent abuse were sufficient. Under that system, permission to intercept communications was given by a government minister applying certain criteria as to 'reasonable suspicion', etc. An independent Commission, chaired by a person qualified for judicial office, reviewed and could reverse the Minister's decisions. A Board composed of government and opposition members of parliament kept a more general watch on the system. Where national security allowed, a person whose communications had been intercepted must have been informed of this occurrence after the event. Such a person could challenge the legality of the interception in the German courts. Although the Court stated that it was 'in principle desirable to entrust supervisory control to a judge', the above safeguards were sufficient, at least in a national security context.

4 In *Malone v UK* A.82 (1984), the applicant had been prosecuted for allegedly handling stolen property (eventually he was acquitted on certain counts and the jury disagreed on others) and during his trial the prosecution acknowledged that his telephone had been tapped. He challenged the legality of the tapping before the High Court, but it held that the tapping did not violate any of his legal rights recognized by English law (see *Malone v Metropolitan Police Comr (No 2)* [1979] Ch 344). Subsequently, Malone complained to the Commission that the tapping violated his rights under Article 8. The Court ruled that the English practice of the Home Secretary issuing warrants authorizing the police to tap a person's telephone was not 'in accordance with the law', as required by Article 8(2), because:

> 79.... on the evidence before the Court, it cannot be said with any reasonable certainty what elements of the powers to intercept are incorporated in legal rules and what elements remain within the discretion of the executive. In view of the attendant obscurity and uncertainty as to the state of the law in this essential respect, the Court cannot but reach a similar conclusion to that of the Commission. In the opinion of the Court, the law of England and Wales does not indicate with reasonable clarity the scope and manner of exercise of the relevant discretion conferred on the public authorities. To that extent, the minimum degree of legal protection to which citizens are entitled under the rule of law in a democratic society is lacking...

The British Parliament enacted the Interception of Communications Act 1985 so as to comply with the Court's judgment in *Malone*. The Act, *inter alia*, made it a criminal offence intentionally to intercept a postal communication or a communication transmitted by a public telecommunications system. The Home Secretary was given a statutory discretion to issue warrants for the lawful interception of communications in defined circumstances (e.g. for the purpose of detecting serious crime). A Tribunal was also created to determine complaints that communications had been unlawfully intercepted. However, the Court found a breach of Article 8 in *Halford v UK*, judgment of 25 June 1997, as the Act failed to regulate the interception of telecommunications made on internal networks operated by public authorities. Also in the later case of *Liberty and others v UK*, judgment of 1 July 2008, a united Chamber found a violation of Article 8 in respect of the interception of telecommunications between Ireland and the UK during the 1990s. The three applicant non-governmental human rights organizations (based in the UK and Ireland) alleged that a Ministry of Defence facility in Cheshire intercepted public telecommunications between the two countries (including communications between the applicant organizations). In response the British Government submitted that:

47. For security reasons, the Government adopted a general policy of neither confirming nor denying allegations made in respect of surveillance activities. For the purposes of this application, however, they were content for the Court to proceed on the hypothetical basis that the applicants could rightly claim that communications sent to or from their offices were intercepted at the Capenhurst Electronic Test Facility during the relevant period. Indeed, they submitted that, in principle, any person who sent or received any form of telecommunication outside the British Islands during the period in question could have had such a communication physically intercepted under a section 3(2) warrant. However, the Government emphatically denied that any interception was being conducted without the necessary warrants and it was their position that, if interception of the applicants' communications did occur, it would have been lawfully sanctioned by an appropriate warrant under section 3(2) of the 1985 Act.

The Chamber then examined whether the 1985 regulatory system satisfied the requirements of Article 8(2).

69. In conclusion, the Court does not consider that the domestic law at the relevant time indicated with sufficient clarity, so as to provide adequate protection against abuse of power, the scope or manner of exercise of the very wide discretion conferred on the State to intercept and examine external communications. In particular, it did not, as required by the Court's case-law, set out in a form accessible to the public any indication of the procedure to be followed for selecting for examination, sharing, storing and destroying intercepted material. The interference with the applicants' rights under Article 8 was not, therefore, 'in accordance with the law'.

5 The regulation of telephone tapping in France was found not to be 'in accordance with the law', because of uncertainty regarding the scope of the power to order intercepts and the lack of adequate safeguards in *Kruslin v France* A.176-A (1990). An investigating judge had issued a warrant for the police to tap the home telephone of a suspect. Subsequently, Kruslin used that phone and made statements which implicated himself in serious crimes for which he was eventually sentenced to 15 years' imprisonment. Kruslin claimed that the interception violated Article 8. The Court, unanimously, acknowledged that case-law of the French Court of Cassation had interpreted specific articles of the Code of Criminal Procedure as empowering the issuing of warrants to tap telephones. Very significantly, the Court treated this case-law as satisfying the domestic legal basis requirement of 'in accordance with the law' (see p 590):

In relation to paragraph 2 of Article 8 of the Convention and other similar clauses, the Court has always understood the term 'law' in its 'substantive' sense, not its 'formal' one; it has included both enactments of lower rank than statutes...and unwritten law. The *Sunday Times, Dudgeon* and *Chappell* judgments admittedly concerned the United Kingdom, but it would be wrong to exaggerate the distinction between common-law countries and Continental countries as the Government rightly pointed out. Statute law is, of course, also of importance in common-law countries. Conversely, case-law has traditionally played a major role in Continental countries, to such an extent that whole branches of positive law are largely the outcome of decisions by the courts.... Were it to overlook case-law, the Court would undermine the legal system of the Continental States almost as much as the *Sunday Times* judgment would have 'struck at the very roots' of the United Kingdom's legal system if it had excluded the common law from the concept of 'law'. In a sphere covered by the written law, the 'law' is the enactment in force as the competent courts have interpreted it in the light, if necessary, of any new practical developments. [Para 29.]

But the Court did not consider that French law satisfied the Convention requirement of 'sufficient precision':

Tapping and other forms of interception of telephone conversations represent a serious interference with private life and correspondence and must accordingly be based on a 'law' that is particularly precise. It is essential to have clear, detailed rules on the subject, especially as the technology available for use is continually becoming more sophisticated.

...Above all, the system does not for the time being afford adequate safeguards against various possible abuses. For example, the categories of people liable to have their telephones tapped by judicial order and the nature of the offences which may give rise to such an order are nowhere defined. Nothing obliges a judge to set a limit on the duration of telephone tapping. Similarly unspecified are the procedures for drawing up the summary reports containing intercepted conversations...the circumstances in which recordings may or must be erased or the tapes be destroyed, in particular where an accused has been discharged by an investigating judge or acquitted by a court. [Paras 33 and 35.]

Therefore, Kruslin's application was successful. The Court's elaboration of some of the factors that domestic law must address in regulating the interception of telecommunications provides a helpful check-list that can be used to evaluate the compatibility of other legal systems' provisions on tapping with Article 8.

6 The Swiss law and practice of telephone tapping was also found not to be 'in accordance with the law' in ***Kopp v Switzerland***, 1998-III. The applicant was a lawyer whose wife had been a member of the Swiss Federal Government (she had served as Head of the Federal Department of Justice and Police). Accusations had been made that while in office she had provided confidential official information to the applicant for the benefit of one of his clients. The wife resigned and an official inquiry was launched (it eventually reported that the allegations were unfounded). During the course of the inquiry the Federal Court granted an application by the Federal Attorney-General for an order that all the applicant's telephone lines be tapped (this was on the basis that the applicant was a 'third party' who might be in communication with an offender). Swiss law provided for the protection of clients' communications with their lawyers to be legally privileged. The tapping was ended after three weeks and the applicant was subsequently informed that it had occurred and the recordings had been destroyed. He challenged the legality of the interception in the Swiss courts but they upheld the lawfulness of the tapping. The Commission, unanimously, found a violation of Article 8. The Court (also unanimously) applied ***Halford*** to rule that the applicant's professional telephone conversations fell within the ambit of this Article:

In the Court's view, it is clear from its case-law that telephone calls made from or to business premises, such as those of a law firm, may be covered by the notions of 'private life' and 'correspondence' within the meaning of Article 8(1).... [Para 50.]

The main issue for the Court was whether Swiss law provided sufficient foreseeability regarding which of the applicant's intercepted calls were legally privileged and which were not. In the judgment of the Court the domestic law was not sufficiently precise on this matter. Furthermore, the Court found it an 'astonishing' practice that an official within the legal department of the Post Office determined which intercepted calls were legally privileged. The Court favoured an independent judge, not a member of the executive, determining the status of intercepted conversations where questions of legal privilege between lawyers and their clients arose. Consequently, the interference with the applicant's telephone calls did not satisfy the requirements of Article 8(2). As in *Niemietz* (p 488) the Court was maintaining a vigorous attitude towards the sanctity of lawyer/client communications.

The secret interception by the Swiss Federal Public Prosecutor's Office of a telephone call from a woman in the former Soviet Embassy in Berne to a businessman (the caller was seeking to buy a beauty product) was also found to be in breach of Article 8 in *Amann v Switzerland* (see p 506).

7   The Dutch scheme regulating the recording of prisoners' telephone conversations was found to violate Article 8 in *Doerga v The Netherlands*, judgment of 27 April 2004. In early January 1995 the applicant was serving a sentence of imprisonment in Marwei penitentiary. The authorities suspected that he had given the police, via a telephone call, a false tip-off regarding an alleged escape plan by fellow inmates. Therefore, the prison authorities decided to intercept, record, and retain copies of the applicant's telephone conversations made from the prison. In October 1995 an explosive device was detonated in the car of the applicant's ex-girlfriend which seriously injured her son. Subsequently the applicant was convicted of, *inter alia*, causing an explosion and sentenced to a further nine years' imprisonment. Part of the evidence against the applicant was based upon an intercepted telephone conversation in which he warned his sister never to approach the ex-girlfriend's car. The applicant submitted that the interception of his telephone conversations violated Article 8 as it was not based upon clear statutory provisions. The Government contended that the domestic scheme satisfied Article 8(2) as being in accordance with the law as the interception arrangements were based upon a published circular issued by the Deputy Minister of Justice and internal regulations of Marwei penitentiary. The Chamber, unanimously, determined that:

52. The Court finds that the rules at issue in the present case are lacking both in clarity and detail in that neither circular No 1183/379 nor the internal regulations of the Marwei penitentiary give any precise indication as to the circumstances in which prisoners' telephone conversations may be monitored, recorded and retained by penitentiary authorities or the procedures to be observed....

53. Although the Court accepts, having regard to the ordinary and reasonable requirements of imprisonment, that it may be necessary to monitor detainees' contacts with the outside world, including contacts by telephone, it does not find that the rules at issue can be regarded as being sufficiently clear and detailed to afford appropriate protection against arbitrary interference by the authorities with the applicant's right to respect for his private life and correspondence.

54. The interference complained of was not therefore 'in accordance with the law' as required by the second paragraph of Article 8 and there has been a violation of this provision. In these circumstances, an examination of the necessity of the interference is not required.

8 A unanimous Chamber ruled that Moldovan law failed to provide sufficient safeguards against abuse of telephone interceptions by public authorities in *Iordachi and others v Moldova*, judgment of 10 February 2009. The applicants, members of a Moldovan non-governmental organization representing persons bringing complaints against Moldova to the

Court, believed that they were at serious risk of having their communications intercepted. The Supreme Court informed the applicants that 99.2 per cent of governmental requests for interception warrants had been approved in 2007. The Strasbourg Court found that Moldovan law, *inter alia*, failed to define clearly the nature of offences for which interception warrants might be sought, no clear rules existed regulating the screening/storing/destroying of interception data, and the domestic courts had failed to exercise robust scrutiny over requests for interception warrants. Consequently, Article 8 had been breached.

9 The interception of written correspondence has mainly been challenged in the context of communications with and from prisoners. In *Golder v UK* A.18 (1975), the Court found that the refusal to allow a prisoner to write to his solicitor for legal advice, concerning the possibility of suing a prison officer, was an interference with the right to respect for correspondence which could not be said to be 'necessary in a democratic society' (regarding this concept, see p 592). A number of prisoners complained about the stopping, by prison authorities, of letters that they had tried to send to family members, lawyers, and the media in *Silver v UK* A.61 (1983). The Court held that many of the administrative restrictions on prisoners' correspondence developed and applied by the Home Office did not meet the criteria of being 'in accordance with the law' (on this concept, see p 590). By way of contrast in *Schönenberger and Durmaz v Switzerland* A.137 (1988), a lawyer's letter to a potential client being held in custody was retained by the public prosecutor. The Court held that this interference with the lawyer's right to respect for his correspondence was not a proportionate response to the State's legitimate aim of preventing crime and therefore a breach of Article 8 had occurred. In *Campbell v UK* A.233 (1992), the Government admitted that letters from the Commission to prisoners were opened, but not read, to ensure that they genuinely originated from the Strasbourg authorities. The Court, by 8 votes to 1, did not consider that this practice was 'necessary in a democratic society' and therefore amounted to a breach of Article 8.

> For its part, the Court considers that it is of importance to respect the confidentiality of mail from the Commission since it may concern allegations against the prison authorities or prison officials.... The opening of letters from the Commission undoubtedly gives rise to the possibility that they will be read and may also conceivably, on occasions, create the risk of reprisals by the prison staff against the prisoner concerned.
>
> Moreover, there is no compelling reason why such letters from the Commission should be opened. The risk, adverted to by the Government, of Commission stationery being forged in order to smuggle prohibited material or messages into prison, is so negligible that it must be discounted. [Para 62.]

In *Petra v Romania*, 1998-VIII, the applicant (prisoner) complained that he had been obliged to hand over letters he had written to the Commission to the governor of his prison, who sent them to the authorities in Bucharest for eventual forwarding to Strasbourg, and that letters from the Commission to him arrived open and after lengthy delays. The Romanian Government accepted that the applicant had experienced an 'interference by a public authority' with his right to respect for his correspondence. The Court, unanimously, found that these interferences were not 'in accordance with the law' as the relevant legal provisions were too vague and some were not publicly available.

> ...the domestic provisions applicable to the monitoring of prisoners' correspondence...leave the national authorities too much latitude. In particular, they go no further than indicating in a very general way the right of convicted prisoners to receive and send mail and they give prison governors the power to keep any letter or any newspaper, book or magazine 'unsuited to the process of

rehabilitating a prisoner'. Monitoring of correspondence therefore seems to be automatic, independent of any decision by a judicial authority and unappealable.

The implementing regulations have not been published, so that the applicant was unable to acquaint himself with them. [Para 37.]

Requiring a prisoner to submit his correspondence to a medical consultant via the prison doctor and allowing the latter to inspect the consultant's correspondence with the prisoner/patient was found to breach Article 8 in *Szuluk v UK*, judgment of 2 June 2009. The unanimous Chamber ruled that:

53....In light of the severity of the applicant's medical condition, the Court considers that uninhibited correspondence with a medical specialist in the context of a prisoner suffering from a life-threatening condition should be afforded no less protection than the correspondence between a prisoner and an MP.

What about prisoners suffering from less serious health problems who wish to correspond in confidence with external doctors?

10 The Court was unanimous in concluding that a Trustee in Bankruptcy's reading and copying of legal correspondence sent to a bankrupt person was not 'necessary in a democratic society' and, therefore, in breach of Article 8. In *Foxley v UK* (2000) 31 EHRR 637, the applicant had been a former ammunition procurement officer at the Ministry of Defence who was convicted of corruption in 1993. He was sentenced to four years' imprisonment. The court also found that he had benefited from the crimes to the extent of £2 million. Consequently, the court made a confiscation order against Foxley (under the Criminal Justice Act 1988) for £1.5 million, being his total realizable assets. In 1995 enforcement proceedings were begun against him and Ms SD was appointed as Receiver to realize his property. In 1996 Foxley was declared bankrupt, in proceedings begun by the Ministry of Defence, and Ms SD was appointed as his Trustee in Bankruptcy. In September of that year she obtained, *ex parte*, an Order from Reading County Court (made under the Insolvency Act 1986) for the Post Office to redirect Foxley's mail to her for three months. The purpose of the interception of his mail was to enable the Trustee to try and track down Foxley's assets. During that time 71 letters were redirected to the Trustee. This correspondence included two letters from Foxley's legal advisers relating to his application under the Convention, letters from the Legal Aid Board involving civil proceedings to which he was a party, and a letter from the police. Each of these letters was copied by the Trustee and then forwarded to Foxley. After the Order expired the Post Office continued to redirect his mail for a further three weeks and the Trustee copied those items. The applicant complained to Strasbourg that the interception of his correspondence violated Article 8. The Court found a breach in respect of the interference with Foxley's correspondence after the Order expired because:

35....The Government do not dispute the fact that two mail deliveries were re-directed by the Post Office to the Trustee in Bankruptcy after the expiry date. It is to be noted that, regardless of the alleged breakdown in the administrative arrangements for redirecting the applicant's correspondence relied on by the Government, it nevertheless remains the case that the Trustee in Bankruptcy exercised her discretion to open letters and to retain copies of some of them. In the view of the Court, the Trustee in Bankruptcy must be taken to have known that the re-direction Order which she herself applied for and obtained no longer provided her with a legal basis to interfere with the applicant's correspondence. On that account, the actions of the Trustee in Bankruptcy after 27 December 1996 were not in accordance with the law....

As for the interception of Foxley's legal correspondence during the period of the Order:

43. The Court recalls that the notion of necessity implies that the interference corresponds to a pressing social need and, in particular, that it is proportionate to the legitimate aim pursued. In determining whether an interference is 'necessary in a democratic society' regard may be had to the State's margin of appreciation (see the *Campbell v UK* judgment of 25 March 1992, Series A No 233, p 18, § 44). It further observes that in the field under consideration—the concealment of a bankrupt's assets to the detriment of his creditors—the authorities may consider it necessary to have recourse to the interception of a bankrupt's correspondence in order to identify and trace the sources of his income. Nevertheless, the implementation of the measures must be accompanied by adequate and effective safeguards which ensure minimum impairment of the right to respect for his correspondence. This is particularly so where, as in the case at issue, correspondence with the bankrupt's legal advisers may be intercepted. The Court notes in this connection that the law-yer-client relationship is, in principle, privileged and correspondence in that context, whatever its purpose, concerns matters of a private and confidential nature (the above-mentioned *Campbell* judgment, pp 18–19, §§ 46 and 48).

44. Admittedly, as the Government have pointed out, it may be difficult to identify from the envel-ope whether its contents attract legal professional privilege. However, the Government have not challenged the accuracy of the applicant's allegations that letters from his legal advisers, once opened, were read, photocopied and a copy committed to file before being forwarded to him. The Court can see no justification for this procedure and considers that the action taken was not in keep-ing with the principles of confidentiality and professional privilege attaching to relations between a lawyer and his client. It notes in this connection that the Government have not sought to argue that the privileged channel of communication was being abused; nor have they invoked any other exceptional circumstances which would serve to justify the interference with reference to their margin of appreciation.

45. The Court would further observe that the fact that the Trustee in Bankruptcy was also the court-appointed Receiver made it even more compelling to forward, unread, the applicant's correspond-ence from his legal adviser in connection with the receivership proceedings. However, and the Government have not contradicted the applicant's declaration, the Trustee in Bankruptcy retained copies of the relevant letters before transmitting them to the applicant.

46. For the above reasons, the Court finds that there was no pressing social need for the open-ing, reading and copying to file of the applicant's correspondence with his legal advisers and that, accordingly, the interference was not 'necessary in a democratic society' within the meaning of Article 8 § 2. Accordingly, there has been a breach of Article 8 in that respect....

The judgment is significant for the Court's protection of legal correspondence beyond the context of interferences with mail to and from prisoners. In this case the breach of Article 8 took place in the realm of civil proceedings.

Respect for the rights protected under Article 8(1)

....

X and Y v Netherlands A.91 (1985)
European Court of Human Rights

Y was a 16-year-old mentally handicapped girl who had been living in a privately run home for disabled children. One night, the son-in-law of the directress forced Y to have sexual intercourse with him. This action caused Y to experience major mental disturbance. X, who was Y's father, notified the police of the matter. Later the public prosecutor's office decided not to initiate a prosecution against the son-in-law. X appealed against that decision to the Court of Appeal, but that court upheld the prosecutor's decision as complaints by persons over 16 had to be made by them (even thought Y was incapable of making such a complaint because of her disabilities). Mr X complained to the Commission on behalf of Y and himself arguing that the Netherlands had failed, *inter alia*, to respect their rights to respect for their private and family life. The Commission, unanimously, found a breach of Article 8, but concluded that as regards Mr X no separate issue arose concerning his right to respect for family life.

22. There was no dispute as to the applicability of Article 8: the facts underlying the application to the Commission concern a matter of 'private life', a concept which covers the physical and moral integrity of the person, including his or her sexual life.

23. The Court recalls that although the object of Article 8 is essentially that of protecting the individual against arbitrary interference by the public authorities, it does not merely compel the State to abstain from such interference: in addition to this primarily negative undertaking, there may be positive obligations inherent in an effective respect for private or family life. These obligations may involve the adoption of measures designed to secure respect for private life even in the sphere of the relations of individuals between themselves.

1. Necessity for criminal-law provisions

24. The applicants argued that, for a young girl like Miss Y, the requisite degree of protection against the wrongdoing in question would have been provided only by means of the criminal law. In the Government's view, the Convention left it to each State to decide upon the means to be utilised and did not prevent it from opting for civil-law provisions.

The Court, which on this point agrees in substance with the opinion of the Commission, observes that the choice of the means calculated to secure compliance with Article 8 in the sphere of the relations of individuals between themselves is in principle a matter that falls within the Contracting States' margin of appreciation. In this connection, there are different ways of ensuring 'respect for private life', and the nature of the State's obligation will depend on the particular aspect of private life that is at issue. Recourse to the criminal law is not necessarily the only answer.

25. The Government cited the difficulty encountered by the legislature in laying down criminal-law provisions calculated to afford the best possible protection of the physical integrity of the mentally handicapped: to go too far in this direction might lead to unacceptable paternalism and occasion an inadmissible interference by the State with the individual's right to respect for his or her sexual life.

The Government stated that under Article 1401 of the Civil Code, taken together with Article 1407, it would have been possible to bring before or file with the Netherlands courts, on behalf of Miss Y:

— an action for damages against Mr B, for pecuniary or non-pecuniary damage;
— an application for an injunction against Mr B, to prevent repetition of the offence;
— a similar action or application against the directress of the children's home.

The applicants considered that these civil-law remedies were unsuitable. They submitted that, amongst other things, the absence of any criminal investigation made it harder to furnish evidence on the four matters that had to be established under Article 1401, namely a wrongful act, fault, damage and a causal link between the act and the damage. Furthermore, such proceedings were lengthy and involved difficulties of an emotional nature for the victim, since he or she had to play an active part therein.

26. At the hearings, the Commission's Delegate adopted the applicants' submissions in their essentials; he also doubted whether Article 1401 could provide a proper basis for an award of compensation for non-pecuniary damage. He added that the need for protection existed *erga omnes*, whilst an injunction could only be directed to a limited circle of persons. Finally, the civil law lacked the deterrent effect that was inherent in the criminal law.

27. The Court finds that the protection afforded by the civil law in the case of wrongdoing of the kind inflicted on Miss Y is insufficient. This is a case where fundamental values and essential aspects of private life are at stake. Effective deterrence is indispensable in this area and it can be achieved only by criminal-law provisions; indeed, it is by such provisions that the matter is normally regulated.

Moreover, as was pointed out by the Commission, this is in fact an area in which the Netherlands has generally opted for a system of protection based on the criminal law. The only gap, so far as the Commission and the Court have been made aware, is as regards persons in the situation of Miss Y; in such cases, this system meets a procedural obstacle which the Dutch legislature had apparently not foreseen.

28. According to the Government, it was the exceptional nature of the facts of the case which disclosed the gap in the law and it could not be said that there had been any failure on the part of the legislature. The Criminal Code admittedly contained no specific provision to the effect that it was an offence to make sexual advances to the mentally handicapped. However, criminal proceedings could in certain circumstances be instituted on the basis of Article 239(2) of the Criminal Code, with or without a complaint by the victim, against anyone who violated the sexual integrity of a mentally handicapped person. Under this Article, it was an offence to commit an act of indecency 'while another person is present against his will', a phrase which the Supreme Court had interpreted as also covering a person who was the actual victim of an indecent act.

According to the applicants, on the other hand, the current Criminal Code offered insufficient protection.

29. Two provisions of the Criminal Code are relevant to the present case, namely Article 248*ter* and Article 239(2).

Article 248*ter* requires a complaint by the actual victim before criminal proceedings can be instituted against someone who has contravened this provision. [This Article penalises a person who abuses a dominant position in order to deliberately cause a minor to commit indecent acts.] The Arnhem Court of Appeal held that, in the case of an individual like Miss Y, the legal representative could not act on the victim's behalf for this purpose. The Court of Appeal did not feel able to fill this gap in the law by means of a broad interpretation to the detriment of Mr B. It is in no way the task of the European Court of Human Rights to take the place of the competent national courts in the interpretation of domestic law, it regards it as established that in the case in question criminal proceedings could not be instituted on the basis of Article 248*ter*.

As for Article 239(2), this is apparently designed to penalise indecent exposure and not indecent assault, and was not clearly applicable to the present case. Indeed, no one, even the public prosecutor's office, seems to have considered utilising this provision at the time, or even referring to it at the outset of the Strasbourg proceedings.

30. Thus, neither Article 248*ter* nor Article 139(2) of the Criminal Code provided Miss Y with practical and effective protection. It must therefore be concluded, taking account of the nature of the wrongdoing in question, that she was the victim of a violation of Article 8 of the Convention.

...

FOR THESE REASONS, THE COURT UNANIMOUSLY

1. Holds that there has been a violation of Article 8 as regards Miss Y:

...

3. Holds that the respondent State is to pay to Miss Y three thousand (3,000) Dutch guilders under Article 50.

NOTES

1 The Court was composed of President Ryssdal and Judges: Wiarda, Walsh, Evans, Russo, Bernhardt, and Gersing.

2 The first case in which the Court stated that Article 8 involved positive obligations on States to 'respect' people's Article 8(1) rights was *Marckx v Belgium* A.31 (1979) (p 528).

3 Another early case involving the positive aspect of respect was *Airey v Ireland* A.32 (1979). The applicant was a woman from a poor background who had been assaulted by her alcoholic husband. At first she tried to obtain his approval to conclude a separation agreement with her, but after seven years of failure she sought to obtain a decree of judicial separation. However, the legal costs of such an application to the High Court were up to £1,200 and she could not afford them (her weekly wage was £40) and no legal aid was available. She complained to Strasbourg alleging, *inter alia*, a breach of her right to respect for her family life caused by the lack of an accessible legal procedure in family law matters. A majority, 4 votes to 3, of the Court found a violation of Article 8.

The Court does not consider that Ireland can be said to have 'interfered' with Mrs Airey's private or family life: the substance of her complaint is not that the State has acted but that it has failed to act. However, although the object of Article 8 is essentially that of protecting the individual against arbitrary interference by the public authorities, it does not merely compel the State to abstain from such interference: in addition to this primarily negative undertaking, there may be positive obligations inherent in an effective respect for private or family life ...

In Ireland, many aspects of private or family life are regulated by law. As regards marriage, husband and wife are in principle under a duty to cohabit but are entitled, in certain cases, to petition for a decree of judicial separation; this amounts to recognition of the fact that the protection of their private or family life may sometimes necessitate their being relieved from the duty to live together.

Effective respect for private or family life obliges Ireland to make this means of protection effectively accessible, when appropriate, to anyone who may wish to have recourse thereto. However, it was not effectively accessible to the applicant: not having been put in a position in which she could apply to the High Court, she was unable to seek recognition in law of her de facto separation from her husband. She has therefore been the victim of a violation of Article 8. [Paras 32–3.]

This ruling does not create a general right to legal aid in domestic disputes, but obliges States either to simplify judicial proceedings, thereby allowing applications in person, or to provide expert legal help for lay persons. The Court later refused to develop the above reasoning to impose an obligation on States to create a right of divorce in domestic family law. Mr Johnston and his long-term partner (Janice Williams-Johnston) sought to argue that their right to respect for their family life created such an obligation for Ireland in *Johnston v Ireland* A.112 (1986) (and see p 528). However, an overwhelming majority of the Court, 16 votes to 1, held that:

It is true that, on this question, Article 8, with its reference to the somewhat vague notion of 'respect' for family life, might appear to lend itself more readily to an evolutive interpretation than does Article 12. Nevertheless, the Convention must be read as a whole and the Court does not consider that a right to divorce, which it has found to be excluded from Article 12 can, with consistency, be derived from Article 8, a provision of more general purpose and scope. The Court is not oblivious to the plight of the first and second applicants. However, it is of the opinion that, although the protection of private or family life may sometimes necessitate means whereby spouses can be relieved from the duty to live together (see the *Airey* judgment, A.32), the engagements undertaken by Ireland under Article 8 cannot be regarded as extending to an obligation on its part to introduce measures permitting the divorce and the re-marriage which the applicants seek. On this point, there is therefore no failure to respect the family life of the first and second applicants. [Paras 57–8.]

Hence, the scope of other Articles of the Convention can have a direct impact on the meaning of 'respect' in Article 8. In 1995, by a margin of 0.6 per cent of the vote, the Irish electorate voted to remove the constitutional ban on divorce in that country.

4   A united Chamber found a breach of Article 8, invoking *X and Y v Netherlands*, where the domestic courts had prevented the police discovering who had placed a fictitious advertisement concerning a child on a dating website. In *KU v Finland*, judgment of 2 December 2008, when the applicant was 12 years old, someone put the advertisement (with a link to the applicant's webpage) stating that he was looking for an intimate relationship with a boy on the dating site.

49. The Court considers that practical and effective protection of the applicant required that effective steps be taken to identify and prosecute the perpetrator, that is, the person who placed the advertisement. In the instant case such protection was not afforded. An effective investigation could never be launched because of an overriding requirement of confidentiality.

The Chamber considered that Article 8 required national law to provide a mechanism to balance the conflicting interests of the applicant and the person who placed the false advertisement.

In *Jankovic v Croatia*, judgment of 5 March 2009, a different Chamber also applied *X and Y v Netherlands* to find (unanimously) a breach of Article 8 in respect of the authorities' failure to bring/permit appropriate criminal law proceedings against three persons alleged to have physically and verbally assaulted the applicant.

57. The above analysis shows firstly that the relevant State authorities decided not to prosecute the alleged perpetrators of an act of violence against the applicant. Furthermore, the relevant authorities did not allow the applicant's attempts at a private prosecution. Lastly, as to the Government's contention that adequate protection was given to the applicant in the minor-offences proceedings, the Court notes that those proceedings were terminated owing to statutory limitation and were thus concluded without any final decision on the attackers' guilt. In view of these findings, the Court holds the view that the decisions of the national authorities in this case reveal inefficiency and a failure to act on the part of the Croatian judicial authorities.

5   Transsexuals are a group who only relatively recently found it possible to overcome the broad margin of appreciation historically given to States, in respect of their legal and administrative recognition of such persons, by the Court. In *Rees v UK* A.106 (1986), a majority of 12 to 3 judges found that the UK was not failing to respect the right to private life of a post-operative transsexual by refusing to amend its birth registration system to alter the recorded sex of the applicant. A similar decision was reached, by 10 votes to 8, in *Cossey v UK* A.184 (1990). However, in *B v France* A.232-C (1992), the applicant won her case as a majority of the Court (15 votes to 6) held that the refusal of the French authorities to allow the applicant to change her forename to a feminine one, coupled with their refusal to amend the contemporary civil status register, created such difficulties for the applicant in her daily life that the State had not done enough to respect her private life under Article 8. **Sheffield and Horsham v UK**, 1998-V, renewed transsexuals' challenges to their treatment under English law. Kristina Sheffield was a 52-year-old post-operative transsexual who had been registered as a male at birth. After completion of her medical treatment she was given a new passport and driving licence which reflected her new name (which she had changed by deed poll). But, her birth certificate, social security, and police records continued to record her original name and gender. Also when she entered into a motor insurance contract she had to give her sex as male. Rachel Horsham, a British citizen, was also a 52-year-old post-operative transsexual. She had been living in the Netherlands since 1974 and had acquired Dutch citizenship in 1993. After completing gender re-assignment surgery in 1992 she requested a new passport from the British authorities. This was granted after an order from the Dutch courts recognized her new status. Nevertheless, the British authorities would not amend her British birth certificate and they informed her that if she were to marry a man, even abroad, that marriage would not be recognized if she were to become domiciled in the UK. Both applicants claimed, *inter alia*, that the British authorities had failed to respect their right to private lives under Article 8. The Commission found a breach of that right (by 15 votes to 1). Subsequently, Liberty (the human rights NGO) was given permission to submit a written brief on the comparative treatment of transsexuals in member States, to the Court. The majority of the Court, 11 votes to 9, began by reiterating that:

...the notion of 'respect' is not clear-cut, especially as far as the positive obligations inherent in that concept are concerned: having regard to the diversity of the practices followed and the situations obtaining in the Contracting States, the notion's requirements will vary considerably from case to case. In determining whether or not a positive obligation exists, regard must be had to the fair balance that has to be struck between the general interest of the community and the interests of the individual, the search for which balance is inherent in the whole of the Convention (see the...*Rees* judgment, p.15:37; and the...*Cossey* judgment, p.15:37). [Para 52.]

In its view:

...the applicants have not shown that since the date of adoption of its *Cossey* judgment in 1990 there have been any findings in the area of medical science which settle conclusively the doubts concerning the causes of the condition of transsexualism....As to legal developments in this area, the Court has examined the comparative study which has been submitted by Liberty. However, the Court is not fully satisfied that the legislative trends outlined by *amicus* suffice to establish the existence of any common European approach to the problems created by the recognition in law of post-operative gender status. In particular, the survey does not indicate that there is as yet any common approach as to how to address the repercussions which the legal recognition of a change of sex may entail for other areas of law such as marriage, filiation, privacy or data protection, or the circumstances in which a transsexual may be compelled by law to reveal his or her pre-operative gender.

The Court is accordingly not persuaded that it should depart from its *Rees* and *Cossey* decisions and conclude that on the basis of scientific and legal developments alone the respondent State can no longer rely on a margin of appreciation to defend its continuing refusal to recognise in law a transsexual's post-operative gender. For the Court, it continues to be the case that transsexualism raises complex scientific, legal, moral and social issues, in respect of which there is no generally shared approach among the Contracting States (see the *X Y and Z v UK* judgment...).

Nor is the Court persuaded that the applicants' case histories demonstrate that the failure of the authorities to recognise their new gender gives rise to detriment of sufficient seriousness as to override the respondent State's margin of appreciation in this area (cf *B v France*). [Paras 56–9.]

Accordingly, the majority found no breach of Article 8. But, the Court was unimpressed with the British Government's inertia over the legal position of transsexuals.

> ...the Court cannot but note that despite its statements in the *Rees* and *Cossey* cases on the importance of keeping the need for appropriate legal measures in this area under review having regard in particular to scientific and societal developments, it would appear that the respondent State has not taken any steps to do so. [Para 60.]

However, in 2002 a Grand Chamber of the full-time Court was united in finding that the partial recognition by British administrative authorities of post-operative transsexuals' new identities did not satisfy the requirements of Article 8. In **Christine Goodwin v UK**, judgment of 11 July 2002, the applicant had been born a man but underwent gender re-assignment surgery provided by the National Health Service. She had to, *inter alia*, enter into a special arrangement with the Department of Social Security (involving her paying national insurance contributions directly to the Department after her sixtieth birthday) in order to prevent her employer from discovering her original gender, due to the fact that the Department continued to classify her as a male in respect of contributions and pension entitlements. Before the Court she alleged that the British Government, despite warnings from the original Court, had failed to take any further measures to reduce the suffering experienced by her, and other post-operative transsexuals, in their daily lives. The Court endorsed the well-established fair balance test to determine the existence of positive obligations under this Article. Whilst noting the earlier British transsexuals judgments the Grand Chamber emphasized the importance of interpreting Convention rights in a practical and dynamic manner. Furthermore:

> 78....The Court is struck by the fact that nonetheless the gender re-assignment which is lawfully provided is not met with full recognition in law, which might be regarded as the final and culminating step in the long and difficult process of transformation which the transsexual has undergone. The coherence of the administrative and legal practices within the domestic system must be regarded as an important factor in the assessment carried out under Article 8 of the Convention. Where a State has authorised the treatment and surgery alleviating the condition of a transsexual, financed or assisted in financing the operations and indeed permits the artificial insemination of a woman living with a female-to-male transsexual (as demonstrated in the case of *X., Y. and Z. v the United Kingdom* [1997-II 619]), it appears illogical to refuse to recognise the legal implications of the result to which the treatment leads.

The Grand Chamber did not consider that the contemporary state of medical science provided any conclusive argument as to the question of the extent of legal recognition of post-operative transsexuals required by the Convention. Regarding the consensus amongst member States and in the wider international community, the results of a survey, submitted by Liberty, demonstrated a continuing trend towards the legal recognition of the new identities of such persons. Very significantly the Grand Chamber observed that:

> 85....In the later case of *Sheffield and Horsham*, the Court's judgment laid emphasis on the lack of a common European approach as to how to address the repercussions which the legal recognition of a change of sex may entail for other areas of law such as marriage, filiation, privacy or data protection. While this would appear to remain the case, the lack of such a common approach among forty-three Contracting States with widely diverse legal systems and traditions is hardly surprising. In accordance with the principle of subsidiarity, it is indeed primarily for the Contracting States to decide on the measures necessary to secure Convention rights within their jurisdiction

and, in resolving within their domestic legal systems the practical problems created by the legal recognition of post-operative gender status, the Contracting States must enjoy a wide margin of appreciation. The Court accordingly attaches less importance to the lack of evidence of a common European approach to the resolution of the legal and practical problems posed, than to the clear and uncontested evidence of a continuing international trend in favour not only of increased social acceptance of transsexuals but of legal recognition of the new sexual identity of post-operative transsexuals.

At the domestic level the Grand Chamber noted that an Interdepartmental Working Group had produced a report in the spring of 2000 examining options for resolving the difficulties faced by post-operative transsexuals and in *Bellinger v Bellinger* [2001] 3 FCR 1, the Court of Appeal had expressed 'dismay' that no official action had been taken to implement the report. The Grand Chamber held that:

90. . . . In the twenty first century the right of transsexuals to personal development and to physical and moral security in the full sense enjoyed by others in society cannot be regarded as a matter of controversy requiring the lapse of time to cast clearer light on the issues involved. In short, the unsatisfactory situation in which post-operative transsexuals live in an intermediate zone as not quite one gender or the other is no longer sustainable.

93. . . . Having regard to the above considerations, the Court finds that the respondent Government can no longer claim that the matter falls within their margin of appreciation, save as regards the appropriate means of achieving recognition of the right protected under the Convention. Since there are no significant factors of public interest to weigh against the interest of this individual applicant in obtaining legal recognition of her gender re-assignment, it reaches the conclusion that the fair balance that is inherent in the Convention now tilts decisively in favour of the applicant. There has, accordingly, been a failure to respect her right to private life in breach of Article 8 of the Convention.

So, the continuing reluctance of the British authorities to accord full legal recognition to the new personalities of post-operative transsexuals was finally found not to be justifiable in the light of the general international treatment of such persons. The British Government responded, constructively, by securing the enactment of the Gender Recognition Act 2004. The Act entitled transsexual persons who (a) have/had gender dysphoria, (b) have lived in the acquired gender for the preceding two years, and (c) who intend to live in the acquired gender until death, to apply to Gender Recognition Panels (comprising at least one lawyer and one registered medical practitioner/chartered psychologist) for a certificate, which will entitle them to a new birth certificate (reflecting their acquired gender) and to marry someone of the opposite gender to their acquired gender. Under this statutory scheme transsexuals will not be obliged to have undergone surgery in order to be entitled to a certificate. The Act did not apply retrospectively, consequently a male-to-female transsexual who was denied a pension (after the Court's judgment in *Christine Goodwin* and before the Act came into effect in 2005) until she reached the male retirement age was found to have suffered a breach of Article 8 by a unanimous Chamber in *Grant v UK*, judgment of 23 May 2006. However, the Chamber observed that the Government had acted with 'laudable expedition' in securing the passage of the Act.

6   The Court has been gradually recognizing an ever-widening variety of situations where individuals can claim that in order to respect their private and family lives the State must facilitate access to personal information held on them. One such situation is where the State has assumed responsibility for the upbringing of a young person. In *Gaskin v UK* A.160

(1989), the applicant was a man who had been brought up in the voluntary care of a local authority. After he had reached adulthood he sought access to the case records regarding his childhood kept on him by the authority. These records comprised files written by persons such as foster parents, social workers, and medical practitioners. The applicant wished to gain access to his records in order to learn about his past and because he wished to sue the authority for alleged negligence in performing its childcare duties to him. In accordance with the existing national administrative policy the local authority would only allow Gaskin access to those files which the authors were willing to permit him to see (65 documents out of a total of 352). He asserted that the refusal to allow him access to all the files was a breach of his right to respect for his private and family life under Article 8(1). The Commission, on the casting vote of the acting President, found a breach of that right. The Court, by 11 votes to 6, held that:

> In the Court's opinion, persons in the situation of the applicant have a vital interest, protected by the Convention, in receiving the information necessary to know and to understand their childhood and early development. On the other hand, it must be borne in mind that confidentiality of public records is of importance for receiving objective and reliable information, and that such confidentiality can also be necessary for the protection of third persons. Under the latter aspect, a system like the British one, which makes access to records dependent on the consent of the contributor, can in principle be considered to be compatible with the obligations under Article 8, taking into account the State's margin of appreciation. The Court considers, however, that under such a system the interests of the individual seeking access to records relating to his private and family life must be secured when a contributor to the records either is not available or improperly refuses consent. Such a system is only in conformity with the principle of proportionality if it provides that an independent authority finally decides whether access has to be granted in cases where a contributor fails to answer or withholds consent. No such procedure was available to the applicant in the present case.
>
> Accordingly, the procedures followed failed to secure respect for Mr Gaskin's private and family life as required by Article 8 of the Convention. There has therefore been a breach of that provision. [Para 49.]

The full-time Court reached a similar conclusion in the later case of *MG v UK*, judgment of 24 September 2002. The applicant had been in the voluntary care of his local authority during various periods of his childhood in the 1960s. In 1995 he requested access to his social service records. The authority provided him with summaries of that information but would not give him full access. The authority informed him that the Access to Personal Files Act 1987 did not apply to records, like his, created prior to 1989. The Court, unanimously, held that:

> 30. . . . Most importantly, and as in Mr Gaskin's case, he had no appeal against a refusal of access to any independent body. . . .
>
> 31. In such circumstances, the Court concludes that there has been a failure to fulfil the positive obligation to protect the applicant's private and family life in respect of his access to his social service records from April 1995 when the applicant first requested them.

Significantly, the Court noted that the Data Protection Act 1998 had, since March 2000, given the applicant a statutory right of access to his care/personal files (held in both manual and electronic form) irrespective of the date of their creation. Furthermore, the Act granted him enforcement rights before the Data Protection Commissioner and the domestic courts.

A unanimous Chamber held that a patient's right of access to her/his personal medical records included the right to take copies of those records in *KH and others v Slovakia*, judgment of 29 April 2009. The eight female applicants (of Roma ethnicity) feared that unauthorized sterilizations had been performed on them whilst they had received hospital treatment. They authorized lawyers to inspect their medical records and make photocopies of them, with the purpose of determining if they had a legal basis for suing the hospitals. The medical authorities and the domestic courts refused to permit the applicants' lawyers to copy their clients' medical records. The Chamber stated that, '47....such positive obligations should extend, in particular in cases like the present one where personal data are concerned, to the making available to the data subject of copies of his or her data files.' Therefore, a breach of Article 8 had occurred.

Developing the above reasoning in *Gaskin* the Court has also ruled that where a State engages in dangerous actions, which expose persons to special health risks, then the authorities must facilitate access for the affected persons to relevant information concerning those actions. In *McGinley and Egan v UK*, 1998-III, the applicants were former servicemen who had been on official duties at the sites of British atmospheric nuclear weapons tests held in the Pacific Ocean during the late 1950s. Many years after they had left the services they claimed war pensions in respect of illnesses which they asserted had been caused by their exposure to the nuclear tests. The Ministry of Defence disputed their claims arguing that the applicants' medical records did not disclose any links between the tests and their current illnesses. The independent Pensions Appeal Tribunal rejected the applicants' claims. The applicants complained to the Commission that, *inter alia*, they had been denied access to official records of the radiation levels at the test sites in breach of Article 8. A majority of the Commission (23 votes to 3) found a violation of this Article. The Court stated that:

> Where a Government engages in hazardous activities, such as those in issue in the present case, which might have hidden adverse consequences on the health of those involved in such activities, respect for private and family life under Article 8 requires that an effective and accessible procedure be established which enables such persons to seek all relevant and appropriate information. [Para 101.]

A majority of the Court (5 votes to 4) concluded that the statutory disclosure of documents procedure available to appellants before the Pensions Appeal Tribunal satisfied the above Convention requirement, therefore no breach of Article 8 had occurred.

However, in the later case of *Roche v UK*, judgment of 19 October 2005, a unanimous Grand Chamber held that:

> 165. The Court's *McGinley and Egan* judgment did not imply that a disclosure procedure linked to litigation could, as a matter of principle, fulfil the positive obligation of disclosure to an individual, such as the present applicant, who has consistently pursued such disclosure independently of any litigation.

The Grand Chamber concluded that the Government's protracted and limited disclosure of information to the applicant, regarding the poison gas tests that he was subject to at Porton Down in the early 1960s, did not satisfy the requirements of Article 8. Hence, the above cases demonstrate that where public authorities are in a close relationship with vulnerable persons (such as children in care or personnel subject to military discipline) the right to respect under Article 8 can encompass informational rights.

A Grand Chamber was divided in respect of the extent of the authorities' obligation to provide information on her natural parents to a person who had been deliberately abandoned by them in *Odievre v France*, judgment of 13 February 2003. The applicant's natural mother had formally abandoned her daughter to the local Health and Social Services Department, in 1965, with a request that the birth be kept secret. This process of abandonment had a long history in France going back to 1638 and was designed to provide an alternative to illegal abortions or infanticide. The applicant was adopted in 1969. In 1990 the applicant was able to obtain non-identifying information about her natural parents (including their nationality, health, and occupations) from the authorities. However, she was unable to gain information about her two siblings from the authorities due to secrecy surrounding her birth and abandonment. Before the Court she argued that the authorities' failure to disclose to her information in their files about her birth and natural family violated her right to respect for her private life. The French Government responded that it was seeking to protect the identity of the applicant's mother and the circumstances of the applicant's birth in accordance with the express request of the mother. The authorities considered that it was a legitimate aim to have a system which alleviated the distress of mothers who did not have the capacity/will to bring up their children and that the process of formal abandonment was used by about 600 mothers per year in present times. The Court held that:

28. ... Birth, and in particular the circumstances in which a child is born, forms part of a child's, and subsequently the adult's, private life guaranteed by Article 8 of the Convention. That provision is therefore applicable in the instant case.

But the judges were split on the issue of whether the French authorities had complied with their duties under this Article. A majority, of ten, concluded that:

47. The Court reiterates that the choice of the means calculated to secure compliance with Article 8 in the sphere of the relations of individuals between themselves is in principle a matter that falls within the Contracting States' margin of appreciation. In this connection, there are different ways of ensuring 'respect for private life', and the nature of the State's obligation will depend on the particular aspect of private life that is at issue ...

48. The Court observes that most of the Contracting States do not have legislation that is comparable to that applicable in France, at least as regards the child's permanent inability to establish parental ties with the natural mother if she continues to keep her identity secret from the child she has brought into the world. However, it notes that some countries do not impose a duty on natural parents to declare their identities on the birth of their children and that there have been cases of child abandonment in various other countries that have given rise to renewed debate about the right to give birth anonymously. In the light not only of the diversity of practice to be found among the legal systems and traditions but also of the fact that various means are being resorted to for abandoning children, the Court concludes that States must be afforded a margin of appreciation to decide which measures are apt to ensure that the rights guaranteed by the Convention are secured to everyone within their jurisdiction.

48. The Court observes that in the present case the applicant was given access to non-identifying information about her mother and natural family that enabled her to trace some of her roots, while ensuring the protection of third-party interests.

49. In addition, while preserving the principle that mothers may give birth anonymously, the system recently set up in France improves the prospect of their agreeing to waive confidentiality, something which, it will be noted in passing, they have always been able to do even before the adoption of the law of 22 January 2002. The new legislation will facilitate searches for information about a person's biological origins, as a National Council on Access to Information about Personal Origins has been set up. The Council is an independent body composed of members of the national

legal service, representatives of associations having an interest in the subject-matter of the law and professional people with good practical knowledge of the issues. The legislation is already in force and the applicant may use it to request disclosure of her mother's identity, subject to the latter's consent being obtained to ensure that her need for protection and the applicant's legitimate request are fairly reconciled. Indeed, though unlikely, the possibility that the applicant will be able to obtain the information she is seeking through the new Council that has been set up by the legislature cannot be excluded.

The French legislation thus seeks to strike a balance and to ensure sufficient proportion between the competing interests. The Court observes in that connection that the States must be allowed to determine the means which they consider to be best suited to achieve the aim of reconciling those interests. Overall, the Court considers that France has not overstepped the margin of appreciation which it must be afforded in view of the complex and sensitive nature of the issue of access to information about one's origins, an issue that concerns the right to know one's personal history, the choices of the natural parents, the existing family ties and the adoptive parents.

Consequently, there has been no violation of Article 8 of the Convention.

Whereas, a sizeable minority, of seven judges, believed that:

12....the suggestion that the States had to be afforded a margin of appreciation owing to the absence of a common denominator between their domestic laws simply does not tally with the extracts of comparative law on which the Court itself relies. Thus, as the Court notes: 'It is relatively rare for mothers to be entitled to give birth anonymously under European domestic legislation.'...

13. In fact, no other legislative system is so weighted in favour of the protection of maternal anonymity—a birth in secret followed by the abandonment of the child in secret—as that formalised and institutionalised in France...

21. Unlike the majority, we therefore consider that in the instant case the French legislation has not struck a fair balance between the interests concerned (see paragraph 49, *in fine*) and that there has been a violation of Article 8 of the Convention.

Do you consider the Court was unduly deferential to the French system, which prioritized the preservation of maternal identity as a means of securing the welfare of unwanted children through the formal abandonment process, over the wishes of such a child (now an adult) to discover her natural mother/family?

7   In *Botta v Italy*, 1998-I, the applicant was a disabled person who claimed that the Italian authorities had not taken sufficient action to enforce domestic legal provisions requiring private businesses to provide facilities for disabled persons. During 1991 Mr Botta complained to the mayor of a beach resort that none of the private beach contractors had installed facilities for disabled people (e.g. access ramps and specially equipped lavatories) that were required under Italian law. His complaints were rejected and by 1997 some of the relevant private beaches had built access ramps. The council had adopted a plan that all the appropriate facilities were to be constructed by the summer of 1999. The applicant complained to the Commission that the Italian public authorities had failed to 'respect' his 'private life' by their failure to enforce the provision of necessary facilities for disabled people on the private beaches. The Commission (by 24 votes to 6) found no violation of his rights under Article 8. The Court, unanimously, also held that his complaint fell outside the scope of this Article.

...the right asserted by Mr Botta, namely the right to gain access to the beach and the sea at a place distant from his normal place of residence during the holidays, concerns interpersonal relations of such broad and indeterminate scope that there can be no conceivable direct link between the measures the State was urged to take in order to make good the omissions of the private bathing establishments and the applicant's private life. [Para 35.]

Interestingly, the Commission had expressed the view, before the Court, that the social nature of Mr Botta's claim was more appropriate for resolution under the 'flexible protection machinery' of the European Social Charter (see D. J. Harris, *The European Social Charter*, 2nd edn (Ardsley, NY: Transnational Publishers Inc, 2001). The Court's judgment may enable disabled persons to make successful applications under Article 8 if they can show that the action required of the State is of direct importance to the very essence of their 'physical and psychological integrity'; this might include the provision of essential medical or social welfare support.

8 The Court has also expressed the opinion that States are not obliged to make social welfare payments in order comply with their Convention duty to respect a person's family life. In *Petrovic v Austria*, 1998-II, the applicant was the father of a young child who applied to the Austrian authorities for a parental leave allowance so that he could look after his child, while his wife continued to work. The Austrian administration, and later the domestic courts, ruled that only women were eligible for this type of allowance. Petrovic then complained to the Commission alleging a breach of Article 14 (right to non-discriminatory treatment) taken together with Article 8 (right to respect for family life). The Commission (by 25 votes to 5) found a violation. Before the Court, the Austrian Government argued that such an allowance did not come within the scope of Article 8 as that provision did not oblige States to provide financial assistance to families. The Court held that:

In this connection the Court, like the Commission, considers that the refusal to grant Mr Petrovic a parental leave allowance cannot amount to a failure to respect family life, since Article 8 does not impose any positive obligation on States to provide the financial assistance in question. [Para 26.]

However, if States decided to make available such a payment, as Austria had done for mothers, then it fell within the ambit of Article 8. A majority of the Court (7 votes to 2) then held that Austria's refusal to make such an allowance available to fathers did not exceed the State's margin of appreciation when judged by the standards of the time when Petrovic sought an allowance (i.e. the late 1980s). Subsequently, in 1990, the Austrian Parliament had amended its legislation to enable fathers to claim the parental leave allowance. Again, we see the Court adopting a very cautious attitude towards the imposition of financial obligations upon States under the terms of Article 8.

9 A Chamber was unanimous in finding that the German courts had failed adequately to protect the private life of Princess Caroline, the eldest daughter of Prince Rainer III of Monaco, from intrusive media reporting in *Von Hannover v Germany*, judgment of 24 June 2004. The applicant did not perform any functions on behalf of the State of Monaco, though she was the president of various cultural foundations and represented the ruling family at some social events. She lived in the Paris area for most of the time. Since the early 1990s she had sought, frequently via the courts, to prevent the tabloid press in several European countries from publishing photos (taken by 'paparazzi' photographers) of her and her family engaged in everyday activities. In 1993 she sought an injunction from the German courts to prevent the Burda media company further publishing a series of photographs it had printed in its *Bunte* magazine showing her, *inter alios*, with her daughter canoeing, with a man in a restaurant, and shopping with her bodyguard. The Constitutional Court ruled that as she was a figure of contemporary society '*par excellence*' she had to tolerate the publication of photos taken of her in public places as the public had a legitimate interest in knowing how she behaved in public. However, the publication of the photos of her and her children infringed her right to protection of her personality. In a second set of proceedings, begun in 1997, she unsuccessfully sought to persuade the German courts to prevent Burda from republishing further photos showing her skiing, visiting a horse show with her husband (Prince Ernst August von Hannover), and leaving her house.

Before the Court, the applicant contended that German law, in violation of Article 8, provided minimal protection for her private life from the publication by the 'entertainment press' of 'voyeuristic' photos of her engaging in domestic activities. The Government responded that the public had a legitimate interest in knowing how figures of contemporary society behaved in public and the domestic courts had prohibited the publication of photos taken of the applicant in a 'secluded place'. The Association of Editors of German Magazines, in a written submission, submitted that the public had a legitimate interest in being informed about public figures, as well as politicians, and that the boundary between political commentary and entertainment was becoming blurred. The Chamber held that:

50. The Court reiterates that the concept of private life extends to aspects relating to personal identity, such as a person's name (see *Burghartz v Switzerland*, judgment of 22 February 1994, A. 280-B) or a person's picture (see *Schussel v Austria* (dec.) No 42409/98, 21 February 2002).

...

53. In the present case there is no doubt that the publication by various German magazines of photos of the applicant in her daily life either on her own or with other people falls within the scope of her private life.

After acknowledging the well-established existence of positive obligations upon States to provide effective respect for private and family life the Chamber observed that:

59. Although freedom of expression also extends to the publication of photos, this is an area in which the protection of the rights and reputation of others takes on particular importance. The present case does not concern the dissemination of 'ideas', but of images containing very personal or even intimate 'information' about an individual. Furthermore, photos appearing in the tabloid press are often taken in a climate of continual harassment which induces in the person concerned a very strong sense of intrusion into their private life or even of persecution.

60. In the cases in which the Court has had to balance the protection of private life against the freedom of expression it has always stressed the contribution made by photos or articles in the press to a debate of general interest (see, as a recent authority, *News Verlags GmbH & Co KG v Austria*, No 31457/96, § 52 *et seq.*, ECHR 2000-I, and *Krone Verlag GmbH & Co. KG v Austria*, No 34315/96, § 33 *et seq.*, 26 February 2002). The Court thus found, in one case, that the use of certain terms in relation to an individual's private life was not 'justified by considerations of public concern' and that those terms did not '[bear] on a matter of general importance' (see *Tammer* [*v Estonia*, ECHR 2001-I] § 68) and went on to hold that there had not been a violation of Article 10. In another case, however, the Court attached particular importance to the fact that the subject in question was a news item of 'major public concern' and that the published photographs 'did not disclose any details of [the] private life' of the person in question (see *Krone Verlag*, cited above, § 37) and held that there had been a violation of Article 10. Similarly, in a recent case concerning the publication by President Mitterand's former private doctor of a book containing revelations about the President's state of health, the Court held that 'the more time passed the more the public interest in President Mitterand's two seven-year presidential terms prevailed over the requirements of the protection of

his rights with regard to medical confidentiality' (see *Plon (Société) v France*, No 58148/00, 18 May 2004) and held that there had been a breach of Article 10.

...

61. The Court points out at the outset that in the present case the photos of the applicant in the various German magazines show her in scenes from her daily life, thus engaged in activities of a purely private nature such as practising sport, out walking, leaving a restaurant or on holiday. The photos, in which the applicant appears sometimes alone and sometimes in company, illustrate a series of articles with such anodyne titles as 'Pure happiness', 'Caroline . . . a woman returning to life', . . .

63. The Court considers that a fundamental distinction needs to be made between reporting facts—even controversial ones—capable of contributing to a debate in a democratic society relating to politicians in the exercise of their functions, for example, and reporting details of the private life of an individual who, moreover, as in this case, does not exercise official functions. While in the former case the press exercises its vital role of 'watchdog' in a democracy by contributing to 'impart[ing] information and ideas on matters of public interest' (*Observer and Guardian* [v UK, A.216 (1991)) it does not do so in the latter case.

64. Similarly, although the public has a right to be informed, which is an essential right in a democratic society that, in certain special circumstances, can even extend to aspects of the private life of public figures, particularly where politicians are concerned (see *Plon (Société)*, cited above, ibid), this is not the case here. The situation here does not come within the sphere of any political or public debate because the published photos and accompanying commentaries relate exclusively to details of the applicant's private life.

65. As in other similar cases it has examined, the Court considers that the publication of the photos and articles in question, of which the sole purpose was to satisfy the curiosity of a particular readership regarding the details of the applicant's private life, cannot be deemed to contribute to any debate of general interest to society despite the applicant being known to the public (see, *mutatis mutandis*, *Jaime Campmany y Diez de Revenga and Juan Luís Lopez-Galiacho Perona v Spain* (dec.), No 54224/00, 12 December 2000; *Julio Bou Gibert and El Hogar Y La Moda J.A. v Spain* (dec.), No 14929/02, 13 May 2003; and *Prisma Presse* [v France (dec.), Nos 66910/01 and 71612/01, 1 July 2003]).

66. In these conditions freedom of expression calls for a narrower interpretation (see *Prisma Presse*, cited above, and, by converse implication, *Krone Verlag*, cited above, § 37).

67. In that connection the Court also takes account of the resolution of the Parliamentary Assembly of the Council of Europe on the right to privacy, which stresses the 'one-sided interpretation of the right to freedom of expression' by certain media which attempt to justify an infringement of the rights protected by Article 8 of the Convention by claiming that 'their readers are entitled to know everything about public figures'.

68. The Court finds another point to be of importance: even though, strictly speaking, the present application concerns only the publication of the photos and articles by various German magazines, the context in which these photos were taken—without the applicant's knowledge or consent—and the harassment endured by many public figures in their daily lives cannot be fully disregarded (see paragraph 59 above).

In the present case this point is illustrated in particularly striking fashion by the photos taken of the applicant at the Monte Carlo Beach Club tripping over an obstacle and falling down. It appears that these photos were taken secretly at a distance of several hundred metres, probably from a neighbouring house, whereas journalists and photographers' access to the club was strictly regulated.

...

72. The Court has difficulty in agreeing with the domestic courts' interpretation of section 23(1) of the Copyright (Arts Domain) Act, which consists in describing a person as such as a figure of contemporary society 'par excellence'. Since that definition affords the person very limited protection of their private life or the right to control the use of their image, it could conceivably be appropriate for politicians exercising official functions. However, it cannot be justified for a 'private' individual, such as the applicant, in whom the interest of the general public and the press is based solely on her membership of a reigning family whereas she herself does not exercise any official functions.

In any event the Court considers that, in these conditions, the Act has to be interpreted narrowly to ensure that the State complies with its positive obligation under the Convention to protect private life and the right to control the use of one's image.

73. Lastly, the distinction drawn between figures of contemporary society 'par excellence' and 'relatively' public figures has to be clear and obvious so that, in a state governed by the rule of law, the individual has precise indications as to the behaviour he or she should adopt. Above all, they need to know exactly when and where they are in a protected sphere or, on the contrary, in a sphere in which they must expect interference from others, especially the tabloid press.

74. The Court therefore considers that the criteria on which the domestic courts based their decisions were not sufficient to protect the applicant's private life effectively. As a figure of contemporary society 'par excellence' she cannot—in the name of freedom of the press and the public interest—rely on protection of her private life unless she is in a secluded place out of the public eye and, moreover, succeeds in proving it (which can be difficult). Where that is not the case, she has to accept that she might be photographed at almost any time, systematically, and that the photos are then very widely disseminated even if, as was the case here, the photos and accompanying articles relate exclusively to details of her private life.

75. In the Court's view, the criterion of spatial isolation, although apposite in theory, is in reality too vague and difficult for the person concerned to determine in advance. In the present case merely classifying the applicant as a figure of contemporary society 'par excellence' does not suffice to justify such an intrusion into her private life.

(d) Conclusion

76. As the Court has stated above, it considers that the decisive factor in balancing the protection of private life against freedom of expression should lie in the contribution that the published photos and articles make to a debate of general interest. It is clear in the instant case that they made no such contribution since the applicant exercises no official function and the photos and articles related exclusively to details of her private life.

77. Furthermore, the Court considers that the public does not have a legitimate interest in knowing where the applicant is and how she behaves generally in her private life even if she appears in places that cannot always be described as secluded and despite the fact that she is well known to the public.

Even if such a public interest exists, as does a commercial interest of the magazines in publishing these photos and these articles, in the instant case those interests must, in the Court's view, yield to the applicant's right to the effective protection of her private life.

78. Lastly, in the Court's opinion the criteria established by the domestic courts were not sufficient to ensure the effective protection of the applicant's private life and she should, in the circumstances of the case, have had a 'legitimate expectation' of protection of her private life.

79. Having regard to all the foregoing factors, and despite the margin of appreciation afforded to the State in this area, the Court considers that the German courts did not strike a fair balance between the competing interests.

80. There has therefore been a breach of Article 8 of the Convention.

81. Having regard to that finding, the Court does not consider it necessary to rule on the applicant's complaint relating to her right to respect for her family life.

The judgment of the Court determined that a person's picture falls within the Article 8(1) concept of private life and that States are under a positive obligation to protect such pictures from abuse by others. The media will only be able to justify the publication of a person's photo if it makes a contribution to an issue of general interest. The Court did not accept that pictures of the domestic life of a member of a royal family fell into that category. Serious investigative journalism (e.g. exposing political or financial corruption) should not fear the implications of this judgment. However, member States may have to reconsider their domestic arrangements to ensure that the publishers of paparazzi-type photographs can justify their continued publication (e.g. to expose the hypocrisy of public figures caught cheating on their spouses?).

10 The protection of a person's privacy from media revelations does not oblige member States to establish a legal obligation on the media to give prior notification to a person that disclosures about his/her private life are about to be made by a specific media organization. In *Mosley v UK*, judgment of 10 May 2011, the applicant alleged a breach of Article 8 as English law failed to provide him with a legal right to advance notice that the *News of the World* newspaper was going to make sensational (and inaccurate) disclosures regarding his sexual activities. The united Chamber, having noted that the applicant had been unable to identify any jurisdiction where such a legal obligation existed, held that:

132. ... Thus, having regard to the chilling effect to which a pre-notification requirement risks giving rise, to the significant doubts as to the effectiveness of any pre-notification requirement and to the wide margin of appreciation in this area, the Court is of the view that Article 8 does not require a legally binding pre-notification requirement.

Of course the imposition of such an obligation would enable individuals in similar circumstances to the applicant to obtain injunctions to prevent the media disclosing the material about their private lives. Note, the contemporaneous debate in the UK regarding injunctions and 'super injunctions' (court orders preventing the media disclosing even the existence of an injunction) obtained by (allegedly) well-known persons preventing various media organizations publishing pieces about them.

11 The Grand Chamber in *Chapman v UK*, judgment of 18 January 2001, identified an inchoate obligation upon States to facilitate the traditional lifestyles of minorities. The applicant was born a Gypsy and travelled constantly in caravans with her family in search of work. She and her husband, together with their children, stopped in various temporary and unofficial camp sites whilst they were on a waiting list for a permanent site. The police and local authority officials repeatedly moved them from their unofficial camps. This disrupted the education of her children. Consequently, in 1985, the applicant bought a piece of land, in Hertfordshire, with the intention of residing in a mobile home on the plot. She applied for planning permission to use her land for residential purposes but this was refused by the local authority, as the land was within the Green Belt (an area protected from residential development). Subsequently, she was fined several hundred pounds by the magistrates' court for continuing to live on her land without planning permission. The applicant complained to the Commission alleging that the enforcement actions interfered with her rights to respect for her home, private, and family life as a Gypsy with a traditional lifestyle of living in mobile homes, which allowed for travelling, as protected by Article 8. The Commission, by 18 votes to 9, found no breach of that Article.

The majority of the Grand Chamber, ten judges, considered that:

93.... there may be said to be an emerging international consensus amongst the Contracting States of the Council of Europe recognising the special needs of minorities and an obligation to protect their security, identity and lifestyle... not only for the purpose of safeguarding the interests of the minorities themselves but to preserve a cultural diversity of value to the whole community.

94. However, the Court is not persuaded that the consensus is sufficiently concrete for it to derive any guidance as to the conduct or standards which Contracting States consider desirable in any particular situation. The Framework Convention [for the Protection of National Minorities (1995)], for example, sets out general principles and goals but signatory states were unable to agree on means or implementation. This reinforces the Court's view that the complexity and sensitivity of the issues involved in policies balancing the interests of the general population, in particular with regard to environmental protection and the interests of a minority with possibly conflicting requirements, renders the Court's role a strictly supervisory one.

...

95. Nonetheless, although the fact of being a member of a minority with a traditional lifestyle different from that of the majority of a society does not confer an immunity from general laws intended to safeguard assets common to the whole society such as the environment, it may have an incidence on the manner in which such laws are to be implemented. As intimated in the *Buckley* [v UK] judgment, the vulnerable position of gypsies as a minority means that some special consideration should be given to their needs and their different lifestyle both in the relevant regulatory planning framework and in arriving at the decisions in particular cases (*loc cit*, paras 76, 80, 84). To this extent there is thus a positive obligation imposed on the Contracting States by virtue of Article 8 to facilitate the gypsy way of life...

However, the majority were not willing to accept the applicant's contention that because the number of Gypsies in the UK was greater than the number of spaces available in authorized Gypsy sites the actions taken against her were automatically a breach of Article 8. According to the Court:

98.... This would be tantamount to imposing on the United Kingdom, as on all the other Contracting States, an obligation by virtue of Article 8 to make available to the gypsy community an adequate number of suitably equipped sites. The Court is not convinced, despite the undoubted evolution that has taken place in both international law, as evidenced by the Framework Convention, and domestic legislations in regard to protection of minorities, that Article 8 can be interpreted to involve such a far-reaching positive obligation of general social policy being imposed on States (see paragraphs 93–4 above).

Hence the Court's task was to determine whether the respondent State had 'relevant and sufficient' reasons for the measures taken against the applicant. The majority found that test was satisfied having regard to, *inter alia*, the Planning Inspectors' hearing the applicant's submissions and visiting the site, the extension of time given to the applicant to comply with planning requirements, and the applicant's freedom to seek lawful places for her mobile home on authorized sites outside Hertfordshire. Consequently no violation of Article 8 had occurred.

The seven dissentients issued a joint opinion in which they disagreed with the majority's assessment that the planning proceedings taken against the applicant were necessary in a democratic society. In the belief of the dissentients, the developing European consensus 'recognizing the special needs of minorities and an obligation to protect their security, identity and lifestyle', demanded a greater degree of protection for the applicant than that accorded to her by the majority.

> 3. ... This consensus includes a recognition that the protection of the rights of minorities, such as gypsies, requires not only that Contracting States refrain from policies or practices which discriminate against them but that also, where necessary, they should take positive steps to improve their situation through, for example, legislation or specific programmes. We cannot therefore agree with the majority's assertion that the consensus is not sufficiently concrete or with their conclusion that the complexity of the competing interests renders the Court's role a strictly supervisory one (see paragraphs 93–4). This does not reflect in our view the clearly recognised need of gypsies to protection of their effective enjoyment of their rights and perpetuates their vulnerability as a minority with differing needs and values from the general community. The impact of planning and enforcement measures on the enjoyment by a gypsy of the right to respect for home, private and family life therefore has a dimension beyond environmental concerns. Having regard to the potential seriousness of an interference which prohibits a gypsy from pursuing his or her lifestyle at a particular location, we consider that, where the planning authorities have not made any finding that there is available to the gypsy any alternative, lawful site to which he or she can reasonably be expected to move, there must exist compelling reasons for the measures concerned.

Hence the dissentients believed that the European consensus required more practical measures of support for persons like the applicant from States than the majority were willing to require under the Convention. The relatively large size of the group of dissentients in *Chapman* suggests that the Court may in the future demand even greater practical measures of support for minorities from States.

12 A unanimous Chamber has held that inherent in the right to respect for correspondence is a positive obligation upon States to provide writing materials and stamped envelopes to allow a prisoner to correspond with the Court. In *Cotlet v Romania*, judgment of 3 June 2003, the Chamber found that there were no stamped envelopes for overseas correspondence available in the prison where the applicant was being detained and he had not received the two free envelopes a month he was entitled to. Consequently, there had been breach of Article 8.

13 Given the divergent legal approaches amongst member States to assisted suicides a united Chamber ruled that domestic authorities had a wide margin of appreciation to regulate the circumstances in which pharmaceuticals capable of ending a person's life were made available. Consequently, the refusal by the Swiss authorities to supply (without a prescription) a drug (sodium pentobarbital) to a man, suffering from bi-polar affective disorder, who wished to use the drug to commit suicide did not constitute a breach of the State's positive obligations under Article 8: *Haas v Switzerland*, judgment of 20 January 2011.

14 More generally the author has concluded that:

> We have seen that the textual basis for the positive obligations enforced by the Court under Article 8 is the duty upon states to 'respect' the rights elaborated in paragraph one of that provision. Whilst the Court's justification for developing these obligations has been to seek to ensure that the guaranteed rights are effectively safeguarded by states. In the early jurisprudence the Court declared that the notion of respect was ill-defined in the context of positive obligations and therefore states would be accorded a wide margin of appreciation when determining if they had

complied with their Convention responsibilities. However, over time the Court limited the use of the margin of appreciation in deciding whether a specific positive obligation existed. The fair balance test emerged as the common judicial method for determining both the existence of individual positive obligations and compliance with the requirements of an established positive obligation. [A. R. Mowbray, *The Development of Positive Obligations under the ECHR by the European Court of Human Rights* (Oxford: Hart Publishing, 2004), p 186.]

Article 8(2)

Interference by public authorities with the rights protected by Article 8

Generally, applicants must prove that the respondent State has in some way acted in a manner which causes an interference with protected rights (e.g. by a public official withholding the lawyer's letter in **Schonenberger and Durmaz v Switzerland** (p 568)). However, in certain cases involving Article 8 rights the Court has been willing to find that the applicant has been a victim of an interference with protected rights through the existence of a particular statutory regime. In **Norris v Ireland** (p 491), the criminal prohibitions on private consensual homosexual acts were held to amount to an 'interference' with the applicant's right to respect for his private life even though he had never been subject to police questioning or prosecution. The Court held that:

38. It is true that, unlike Mr Dudgeon, Mr Norris was not the subject of any police investigation. However, the Court's finding in the *Dudgeon* case that there was an interference with the applicant's right to respect for his private life was not dependent upon this additional factor. As was held in that case, 'the maintenance in force of the impugned legislation constitutes a continuing interference with the applicant's right to respect for his private life... within the meaning of Article 8(1). In the personal circumstances of the applicant, the very existence of this legislation continuously and directly affects his private life... [Para 41.]

Therefore, where applicants can establish that the existence of legislation infringes important rights under Article 8 and has a deleterious effect on their lives they may be able to bring a successful case under this Article. Also where legislation permits secret measures, such as the interception of telephone calls, applications can successfully argue that the existence of these laws amounts to an interference with their protected rights. In **Klass v Germany** (p 564), the Court held that:

...in the mere existence of the legislation itself, there is involved, for all those to whom the legislation could be applied, a menace of surveillance; this menace necessarily strikes at freedom of communication between users of the postal and telecommunications services and thereby constitutes an 'interference by a public authority' with the applicants' right to respect for private and family life and correspondence. [Para 41.]

This is a helpful broadening, by the Court, of the notion of an 'interference', because if these secret measures are effectively implemented individuals will not normally know, or be able to prove, that they have in fact been subject to them.

In accordance with the law

Silver v UK A.61 (1983)
European Court of Human Rights

The seven applicants (six of whom were prisoners) complained that the stopping and delaying of their mail by the prison authorities amounted, *inter alia*, to a breach of Article 8. The detailed rules governing correspondence to and from prisoners were contained in confidential Standing Orders and Circular Instructions, types of internal administrative guidance, issued by the Home Secretary to prison governors. Members of Parliament had access to these provisions and prisoners were given information about some of the rules via cell cards. The Commission (with one dissentient) found the censorship of most of the applicants' correspondence to be in breach of Article 8.

...

A. WERE THE INTERFERENCES 'IN ACCORDANCE WITH THE LAW'?

1. General principles

85. In its *Sunday Times* judgment [*Sunday Times v UK* A.30 (1979)], the Court examined the meaning of the expression 'prescribed by law', noting in this connection certain differences which exist between the French and English versions of Articles 8, 9, 10 and 11 of the Convention, Article 1 of Protocol No 1 and Article 2 of Protocol No 4.

The Government accepted that the principles enounced in the said judgment concerning the expressing 'prescribed by law/prévues par la loi' in Article 10 were also applicable to the expression 'in accordance with the law/prévue par la loi' in Article 8. Indeed, this must be so, particularly because the two provisions overlap as regards freedom of expression through correspondence and not to give them an identical interpretation could lead to different conclusions in respect of the same interference.

86. A first principle that emerges from the *Sunday Times* judgment is that the interference in question must have some basis in domestic law in the present case, it was common ground between Government, Commission and applicants that a basis for the interferences was to be found in the Prison Act and the Rules, but not in the Orders and Instructions which lacked the force of law...

There was also no dispute that the measures complained of were in conformity with English law.

87. A second principle is that 'the law must be adequately accessible: the citizen must be able to have an indication that is adequate, in the circumstances, of the legal rules applicable to a given case'. Clearly, the Prison Act and the Rules met this criterion, but the Orders and Instructions were not published.

88. A third principle is that 'a norm cannot be regarded as a 'law' unless it is formulated with sufficient precision to enable the citizen to regulate his conduct: he must be able—if need be with appropriate advice—to foresee, to a degree that is reasonable in the circumstances, the consequences which a given action may entail' (ibid).

A law which confers a discretion must indicate the scope of that discretion. However, the Court has already recognised the impossibility of attaining absolute certainty in the framing of laws and the risk that the search for certainty may entail excessive rigidity (ibid). These observations are of particular weight in the 'circumstances' of the present case, involving as it does, in the special context of imprisonment, the screening of approximately 10 million items of correspondence in a year ....It would scarcely be possible to formulate a law to cover every eventuality. Indeed, the applicants themselves did not deny that some discretion should be left to the authorities.

In view of these considerations, the Court points out once more that 'many laws are inevitably couched in terms which, to a greater or lesser extent, are vague and whose interpretation and application are questions of practice' (ibid). And in the present case the operation of the correspondence control system was not merely a question of practice that varied in each individual instance: the Orders and Instructions established a practice which had to be followed save in exceptional circumstances....In these conditions, the Court considers that although those directives did not themselves have the force of law, they may—to the admittedly limited extent to which those concerned were made sufficiently aware of their contents—be taken into account in assessing whether the criterion of foreseeability was satisfied in the application of the Rules.

89. For this reason, the Court cannot accept the applicant's additional contention that the conditions and procedures governing interferences with correspondence—and in particular the directives set out in the Order and Instructions—should be contained in the substantive law itself.

90. The applicants further contended that the law itself must provide safeguards against abuse.

The Government recognised that the correspondence control system must itself be subject to control and the Court finds it evident that some form of safeguards must exist. One of the principles underlying the Convention is the rule of law, which implies that an interference by the authorities with an individual's rights should be subject to effective control. (See inter alia Klass v Germany A.28 (1978).) This is especially so where, as in the present case, the law bestows on the executive wide discretionary powers, the application whereof is a matter of practice which is susceptible to modification but not to any Parliamentary scrutiny (see paragraph 26 above).

However, the Court does not interpret the expression 'in accordance with the law' as meaning that the safeguards must be enshrined in the very text which authorises the imposition of restrictions...

The Court then examined the circumstances surrounding the censorship and delaying of the applicants' mail. The Court concluded that most of the interferences with the applicants' right to respect for their correspondence were not foreseeable and, therefore, were not 'in accordance with the law'.

FOR THESE REASONS, THE COURT UNANIMOUSLY

...

Holds that, with the exception of Mr Silver's letter no 7, Mr Noe's letters nos 10 and 12 and Mr Cooper's letters nos 28 to 31, the stopping or delaying of all the letters written by or addressed to each applicant which are at issue in the present case constituted a violation of Article 8;...

NOTES

1   The Court was composed of President Wiarda and Judges: Thor Vilhjalmsson, Gölcüklü, Matscher, Pettiti, Evans, and Russo.

2   The *Sunday Times* case is examined at p 637.

3   The need for a reasonably precise domestic legal framework regulating the use of hi-tech surveillance devices, such as concealed transmitters, by law enforcement agencies was confirmed by a unanimous Court in *Khan v UK*, 2000-V. The applicant arrived at Manchester airport from Pakistan in September 1992. He was searched by customs officers, but no drugs were found on him. In January 1993, the Chief Constable of South Yorkshire authorized, in accordance with administrative Guidelines issued by the Home Office in

1984, the installation of a listening device on B's premises (the Chief Constable believed that conventional methods of surveillance were unlikely to provide evidence that B was dealing in drugs). The aural surveillance device recorded a conversation in B's house during which Khan admitted involvement in the illegal importation of drugs. Subsequently, the trial judge ruled that the tape recording of Khan's conversation obtained by the use of the surveillance device was admissible. Thereupon Khan pleaded guilty to a charge of being knowingly concerned in the fraudulent evasion of the prohibition on the importation of heroin. He was sentenced to three years' imprisonment. Khan eventually appealed to the House of Lords (**R v Khan (Sultan)** [1996] 3 All ER 289), where Lord Nolan, on behalf of his brethren, gave a speech in which he held that there was no right to privacy in English law and the admission of the recording was not unlawful or unfair. The Court ruled that:

26.... In the context of covert surveillance by public authorities, in this instance the police, domestic law must provide protection against arbitrary interference with an individual's right under Article 8. Moreover, the law must be sufficiently clear in its terms to give individuals an adequate indication as to the circumstances in which and the conditions on which public authorities are entitled to resort to such covert measures (*Malone v UK*...).

27. At the time of the events in the present case, there existed no statutory system to regulate the use of covert listening devices, although the Police Act 1997 now provides such a statutory framework. The Home Office Guidelines at the relevant time were neither legally binding nor were they directly publicly accessible. The Court also notes that Lord Nolan in the House of Lords commented that under English law there is, in general, nothing unlawful about a breach of privacy. There was, therefore, no domestic law regulating the use of covert listening devices at the relevant time.

Consequently, the Court found a breach of Article 8. The judgment is to be welcomed as demonstrating the Court applying its well-established jurisprudence regarding the rule of law requirements of Article 8 to new technological methods of State surveillance. A later, unanimous, Grand Chamber in **Bykov v Russia**, judgment of 21 January 2009, determined that there had been a violation of Article 8 as domestic law in that State had also failed to provide adequate regulation over the use of a concealed radio-transmitter (as part of a covert operation) by the police and the Federal Security Service. In **Uzun v Germany**, judgment of 2 September 2010, a united Chamber found no breach of Article 8 where a senior prosecutor had authorized the police to place a hidden global positioning tracking device in a car used by the applicant (a suspected terrorist). The Chamber considered that such surveillance, regarding a person's movements in public places, was less intrusive than secret visual or audio monitoring, consequently the safeguards against abuse did not have to be as strict. The Code of Criminal Procedure provided a sufficient legal basis for the surveillance.

4   For the application of this concept to a continental civil law jurisdiction see **Kruslin v France** (p 565).

Necessary in a democratic society

1   In **Silver v UK** (above) it was noted that:

On a number of occasions, the Court had stated its understanding of the phrase 'necessary in a democratic society', the nature of its functions in the examination of issues turning on that phrase and the manner in which it will perform those functions. It suffices here to summarise certain principles:

(a) the adjective 'necessary' is not synonymous with 'indispensable', neither has it the flexibility of such expressions as 'admissible', 'ordinary', 'useful', 'reasonable', or 'desirable'. (see *Handyside v UK* A.24 (1976))

(b) the Contracting States enjoy a certain but not unlimited margin of appreciation in the matter of the imposition of restrictions, but it is for the Court to give the final ruling on whether they are compatible with the Convention.

(c) the phrase 'necessary in a democratic society' means that, to be compatible with the Convention, the interference must, *inter alia*, correspond to a 'pressing social need' and be 'proportionate to the legitimate aim pursued'.

(d) those paragraphs of Articles of the Convention which provide for an exception to a right guaranteed are to be narrowly interpreted (see *Klass v Germany* A.28 (1978). [Para 97.]

2 *Handyside* is examined at p 627.

3 Examples of where the Court has found governmental action to be 'necessary' include: the maintenance of a secret register of persons considered to be a threat to national security, see *Leander v Sweden* (p 505) and to allow officials to intercept communications in order to combat espionage and terrorism, see *Klass v Germany* (p 564). The regulation of housing, in *Gillow v UK* (p 543), was considered to be 'necessary' for the economic well-being of the country.

4 A wide 'margin of appreciation' has been accorded by the Court to national authorities in a number of circumstances including: (a) technically complex regulatory processes (e.g. the control of noise pollution in *Powell and Rayner v UK* (p 549); (b) matters of social policy where there are no common European standards (e.g. regulating the use of *in vitro* fertilization treatment, see *Evans v UK* (p 520); and (c) where issues of national security are involved (e.g. *Leander v Sweden*, p 505). More generally on this doctrine, see p 633.

5 The Court found that there was no 'pressing social need' for the maintenance of criminal sanctions against private consensual homosexual activity by adults in *Dudgeon v UK* and *Norris v Ireland* (p 491). In both cases the Court was heavily influenced by the fact that the great majority of Council of Europe member States did not consider it necessary or appropriate to criminalize such behaviour. Also, the British armed forces' investigations into the private lives and subsequent discharge of homosexual personnel were not justifiable under Article 8(2) in *Smith and Grady v UK* (p 492).

6 The issuing and execution of the search warrant against the applicant's law offices in *Niemietz v Germany* (p 488) was held, by the Court, not to be a proportionate interference with the applicant's right to respect for his private life. Although the public prosecutor was concerned with a substantial crime, the warrant issued was drafted in very wide terms and impinged upon professional secrecy. The ability of the French customs service to conduct searches of homes without the need for a judge to issue a search warrant led the Court to find a breach of Article 8 in *Funke v France* A.256-A (1993). Three customs officers and a senior police officer searched the applicant's home for evidence of alleged offences involving foreign financial transactions. The Court held that:

Above all, in the absence of any requirement of a judicial warrant the restrictions and conditions provided for in law, which were emphasised by the Government..., appear too lax and full of loopholes for the interferences with the applicant's rights to have been strictly proportionate to the legitimate aim pursued. [Para 57.]

Again, in *Camenzind v Switzerland*, 1997-VIII, the Court reiterated that where domestic law authorized a search without the need for a judicial warrant, the Court would be particularly vigilant in ensuring that the requirements of Article 8 had been complied with. There the telecommunication authorities had evidence that Mr Camenzind had been using an unauthorized cordless telephone. The director of the Berne telecommunications authority issued a warrant, under the Federal Administrative Criminal Law Act 1974, for the search of the applicant's house with a view to finding and seizing the telephone. A single official executed the warrant, with the applicant's permission, by checking the conformity of every telephone and television set in each room of the applicant's house; no unauthorized equipment was found, but the applicant admitted that he had previously tested such a telephone. No furniture was searched nor were any documents examined. The Court, with one dissent, concluded that the limited scope of the search meant that it was a proportionate response by the authorities towards the legitimate aim of preventing disorder or crime. In *Chappell v UK* A.152 (1989), the Court upheld the concurrent execution of a judicial warrant to search for obscene videos by 11 police officers and an Anton Piller order (issued by the civil courts authorizing plaintiff film companies to enter Chappell's video rental premises with the objective of seizing allegedly illegal copies of their films) by five employees of the film companies and their solicitors. Although the Court was critical of the concurrent nature of the searches and the aggregate number of persons involved in searching Chappell's premises, the Court ruled that they were a proportionate response to the legitimate aims of preventing crime and protecting the rights of the film companies. Marc-Andre Eissen, a former Registrar of the Court, observed that while the term 'proportionality' is not found in the text of the Convention, the Court has discovered its essence contained in the express language of various Articles. In regard to the phrase 'necessary in a democratic society' embodied in paragraph 2 of Articles 8–11, he stated that: 'from "necessity" to proportionality is but a small step, since for a measure to be necessary it must surely correspond to a "pressing social need" both as a matter of principle and regarding its impact, its scale and its compass' (at p 126). More generally, he noted:

> Over the years proportionality has put down solid and lasting roots in the case-law of the European Court of Human Rights, and these roots will in all likelihood go even deeper, continuing to broaden the scope of the principle so as to embrace even more aspects of the Convention. Indeed the extent to which this has already occurred suggests that it has even now acquired the status of a general principle in the Convention system, a status which it already has in numerous legal systems and in community law. ['The Principle of Proportionality in the Case-Law of the European Court of Human Rights' in Macdonald, Matscher, and Petzold (eds), *The European System for the Protection of Human Rights* (Dordrecht: Martinus Nijhoff, 1993), p 146.]

In a later study Dr Yutaka Arai-Takahashi concluded:

> It must be recalled that under the Convention, there exist two types of proportionality evaluation emphasised by the Strasbourg organs. Firstly, they have asserted that a 'fair balance' must be struck between the right of individual applicants and the general interests of the public. A search for such balance is considered as 'inherent' in the whole of the Convention. The second meaning of proportionality is a modified and more specific version of the first and defined as a reasonable relationship between the means employed, including their severity and duration, and the public objective to be sought. This corresponds to the third element of the proportionality test developed by the European Community law and German administrative law. [Y. Arai-Takahashi, *The Margin of Appreciation Doctrine and the Principle of Proportionality in the Jurisprudence of the ECHR* (Antwerp: Intersentia, 2002), p 193.]

My analysis of the case-law led to the final observation that:

> ...the development and use of the fair balance principle by the Court operates symbiotically with the responsibilities of member States under the Convention. As democratic societies subject to the rule of law their national authorities need to balance community interests against the basic human rights of individuals. But if the latter believe that their Convention rights have been unjustifiable infringed, the Convention, subject to the exhaustion of domestic remedies and the other admissibility criteria, enables the Court to reach a determination. [A. Mowbray, 'A Study of the Principle of Fair Balance in the Jurisprudence of the European Court of Human Rights' (2010) 10(2) *Human Rights Law Review* 289 at 317.]

Legitimate aim of interference

1   The final requirement, under Article 8(2), for States which seek to justify an interference with protected Article 8(1) rights is to show that their actions were taken for a legitimate purpose. Only those aims listed in Article 8(2) can be invoked by States, but the aims are couched in broad terms.

2   'National security' has been successfully invoked in a number of cases including *Leander v Sweden* (p 505) and *Klass v Germany* (p 564). However, the Court did not uphold the British armed forces treatment of homosexual personnel in *Smith and Grady v UK* (p 492).

3   'Public safety' was accepted by the Court as one of the justifications for the British planning authorities' refusal to allow Buckley to live in her caravans on her land in the countryside. The authorities had determined that there was a danger to road traffic safety if she were allowed to live on her land and thereby seek access to and from the public highway. See *Buckley v UK* (p 545).

4   The 'economic well-being of the country' was accepted by the Court as the justification for Guernsey's housing control laws in *Gillow v UK* (p 543).

5   In *Malone v UK* (p 564) the Court recognized that a legal regime authorizing the interception of communications, with appropriate safeguards to meet the requirements of Article 8(2), may be justified as being necessary 'for the prevention of disorder or crime'. Also in *McLeod v UK*, 1998-VII, the Court held that the power of the police to enter private premises to prevent a breach of the peace had this legitimate aim. The applicant was involved in lengthy and acrimonious legal proceedings with her ex-husband concerning the former matrimonial home, which she occupied with her frail mother who was in her seventies, and its contents. She had failed to comply with a court order to deliver specified property to her ex-husband and the court granted her seven days to comply or face imprisonment for contempt of court. Her ex-husband offered to collect the listed items from the former matrimonial home at a specified time. His solicitors arranged for two police officers to be present at the house when the ex-husband (together with his brother, sister, and a solicitor's clerk) arrived to collect the specified items. One of the police officers knocked at the door and the applicant's mother informed him that her daughter was not at home. The mother stated that the police officer told her that they had a court order to execute. She, thereupon, let all of them into the house. The police officers did not remove any property, but checked that only the listed items were taken. For most of the time the officers were located on the driveway of the house. During the course of the removal operation the applicant returned to the house and became angry. The police only allowed her to inspect the

contents of the removal van, rather than unload its contents, as they feared there was likely to be a breach of the peace. Subsequently, the applicant successfully sued her ex-husband for trespass, but her similar claim against the police was rejected by the Court of Appeal (see, *McLeod v Metropolitan Police Comr* [1994] 4 All ER 553). That court held that the police officers' actions could be justified under the common law preventive power recognized in *Thomas v Sawkins* [1935] 2 KB 249 and preserved by section 17(6) of the Police and Criminal Evidence Act 1984. The applicant complained to the Commission alleging, *inter alia*, that the entry of the police into her home and the failure of the English courts to grant her protection amounted to a violation of her right to respect for her private life and home under Article 8. By a majority, of 14 to 2, the Commission found no breach of that Article. The Court concluded that the police officers' power of entry to private premises to deal with or prevent a breach of the peace was defined with sufficient clarity for it to be 'in accordance with the law'. However, a majority of the Court, 7 votes to 2, decided that the entry of the officers into the applicant's home was a disproportionate response to the legitimate aim pursued:

> 57....upon being informed that the applicant was not present, the police officers should not have entered her house, as it should have been clear to them that there was little or no risk of disorder or crime occurring.... The fact that an altercation did occur upon her return is, in its opinion, immaterial in ascertaining whether the police officers were justified in entering the property initially.

Judges Freeland and Mifsud Bonnici wrote a partly dissenting opinion in which they concluded that the police had acted in a proportionate manner. They noted:

> 4....as a matter of common knowledge, the intensity and bitterness of domestic disputes tend all too often to escalate into disorder or violence, particularly where the division of property is involved; and it is by no means unusual for British police to be called on to intervene to prevent such escalation.

While the judgment of the Court holds that this controversial power of entry is compatible with Article 8, it reinforces domestic *dicta* that the police must be cautious in their utilization of such an intrusive power.

A unanimous Chamber followed the approach of *McLeod* in a later case where the police mistakenly obtained and executed a search warrant on the wrong premises. In *Keegan v UK*, judgment of 18 July 2006, the complainants were an innocent family whose home was forcibly entered and searched by the police in the erroneous belief that an armed robber was living in the house.

> 33....although the police did not act with malice and indeed with the best of intentions, there was no reasonable basis for their action in breaking down the applicants' door early one morning while they were in bed. Put in Convention terms, there might have been relevant reasons, but, as in the circumstances they were based on a misconception which could, and should, have been avoided with proper precautions, they cannot be regarded as sufficient (see *mutatis mutandis, McLeod*...).

Consequently, although the police had been acting in pursuit of the legitimate aim of preventing disorder and crime the Chamber found a breach of Article 8.

6 The Court upheld the prosecution and conviction of the applicants in *Laskey, Jaggard and Brown v UK* (p 499) as being in pursuit of the legitimate aim of the 'protection of health'.

7 The criminal prohibitions on consensual homosexual conduct successfully challenged in *Dudgeon v UK* (p 491), were accepted by the Court as being for the legitimate aim of the 'protection of…morals'. The Court elaborated upon the scope of this justification by noting that it:

47.…may imply safeguarding the moral ethos or moral standards of a society as a whole, but may also, as the Government pointed out, cover protection of the moral interests and welfare of a particular section of society, for example schoolchildren.

8 The justification of interferences taken for 'the protection of the rights and freedoms of others was successfully invoked in *Chappell v UK* (p 594), where it was acknowledged that the search of Chappell's business premises under the authority of the Anton Piller order was aimed at protecting the intellectual property rights of the film companies against illegal copying/distribution of their films.

11 ARTICLE 9 FREEDOM OF THOUGHT, CONSCIENCE AND RELIGION

An ever-widening range of beliefs have been recognized as falling within this Article, including those of non-believers in religion (*Buscarini*). The Court has held that the right to manifest one's beliefs is more circumscribed than the right to freedom of thought, conscience and religion (*Kalac*). Furthermore, in applying the limitations contained in Article 9(2) the Court has been sensitive to the varied constitutional traditions of member States, for example the Turkish principle of secularism in public institutions as applied to the contentious issue of the wearing of the Islamic headscarf (*Leyla Sahin*). However, the Court has also ruled, in several cases, that States must be cautious when interfering in the internal affairs of religious organizations and observe a neutral stance between competing factions (e.g. in *Hasan and Chaush*).

The Court's general approach

Kokkinakis v Greece A.260-A (1993)
European Court of Human Rights

Mr Kokkinakis was born in 1909 and had converted from the Christian Eastern Orthodox Church to the Jehovah's Witnesses in 1936. Since that time he had been arrested by the Greek authorities more than 60 times for proselytism. This had resulted in him being interned and imprisoned on several occasions. In 1986 Mr Kokkinakis and his wife called at the home of a Mrs Kyriakaki and engaged in a discussion with her. Mr Kyriakaki, who was the cantor at a local Orthodox church, called the police and Mr and Mrs Kokkinakis were arrested. They were charged under Law 1363/1938 which stated that: 'Anyone engaging in proselytism shall be liable to imprisonment and a fine...By proselytism is meant, in particular, any direct or indirect attempt to intrude on the religious beliefs of a person of a different religious persuasion, with the aim of undermining those beliefs, either by any kind of inducement or promise of an inducement or moral support or material assistance, or by fraudulent means or by taking advantage of his inexperience, trust, need, low intellect or naivety.' The criminal court convicted Mr and Mrs Kokkinakis of proselytism on the basis that they took advantage of Orthodox Christians' inexperience, low intellect, and naivety. The court emphasized that the defendants went to Mrs Kyriakaki's house and '…told her that they brought good news; by insisting in a pressing manner, they gained admittance to the house and began to read from a book on the Scriptures which they interpreted with reference to a king of heaven…encouraging [Mrs Kyriakaki] by means of their judicious, skilful explanations…to change her Orthodox Christian beliefs.' The defendants were each sentenced to four months' imprisonment. They appealed to the Crete Court of Appeal which quashed Mrs Kokkinakis's conviction and upheld Mr Kokkinakis's conviction, but reduced his sentence to three months' imprisonment. He then challenged the constitutionality of Law 1363/1938 before the Court of Cassation, but it rejected his contention. Subsequently Mr Kokkinakis applied to the Commission claiming a violation of, *inter alia*, Article 9. The Commission unanimously found a violation of this Article.

…

A. GENERAL PRINCIPLES

31. As enshrined in Article 9, freedom of thought, conscience and religion is one of the foundations of a 'democratic society' within the meaning of the Convention. It is, in its religious dimension, one of the most vital elements that go to make up the identity of believers and their conception of life, but it is also a precious asset for atheists, agnostics, sceptics and the unconcerned. The pluralism indissociable from a democratic society, which has been dearly won over the centuries, depends on it.

While religious freedom is primarily a matter of individual conscience, it also implies, *inter alia*, freedom to 'manifest [one's] religion'. Bearing witness in words and deeds is bound up with the existence of religious convictions.

According to Article 9, freedom to manifest one's religion is not only exercisable in community with others, 'in public' and within the circle of those whose faith one shares, but can also be asserted 'alone' and in private'; furthermore, it includes in principle the right to try to convince one's neighbour, for example through 'teaching', failing which, moreover, 'freedom to change [one's] religion or belief', enshrined in Article 9, would be likely to remain a dead letter.

…

33. The fundamental nature of the rights guaranteed in Article 9 § 1 is also reflected in the wording of the paragraph providing for limitations on them. Unlike the second paragraphs of Articles 8, 10 and 11, which cover all the rights mentioned in the first paragraphs of those articles, that of Article 9 refers only to 'freedom to manifest one's religion or belief'. In so doing, it recognises that in democratic societies, in which several religions coexist within one and the same population, it may be necessary to place restrictions on this freedom in order to reconcile the interests of the various groups and ensure that everyone's beliefs are respected.

…

B. APPLICATION OF THE PRINCIPLES

36. The sentence passed by the Lasithi Criminal Court and subsequently reduced by the Crete Court of Appeal…amounts to an interference with the exercise of Mr Kokkinakis's right to 'freedom to manifest [his] religion or belief'. Such an interference is contrary to Article 9 unless it is 'prescribed by law', directed at one or more of the legitimate aims in paragraph 2 and 'necessary in a democratic society' for achieving them.

1. 'PRESCRIBED BY LAW'

...

40. The Court has already noted that the wording of many statutes is not absolutely precise. The need to avoid excessive rigidity and to keep pace with changing circumstances means that many laws are inevitably couched in terms which, to a greater or lesser extent, are vague (see, for example and *mutatis mutandis*, the *Müller v Switzerland* judgment of 24 May 1988, Series A No 133, p 20, § 29). Criminal-law provisions on proselytism fall within this category. The interpretation and application of such enactments depend on practice.

  In this instance there existed a body of settled national case-law.... This case-law, which had been published and was accessible, supplemented the letter of section 4 and was such as to enable Mr Kokkinakis to regulate his conduct in the matter.

  As to the constitutionality of section 4 of Law no 1363/1938, the Court reiterates that it is, in the first instance, for the national authorities and in particular the courts, to interpret and apply domestic law (see, as the most recent authority, the *Hadjianastassiou v Greece* judgment of 16 December 1992, Series A No 252, p 18, § 42). And the Greek courts that have had to deal with the issue have ruled that there is no incompatibility...

41. The measure complained of was therefore 'prescribed by law' within the meaning of Article 9 § 2 of the Convention.

2. LEGITIMATE AIM

42. The Government contended that a democratic State had to ensure the peaceful enjoyment of the personal freedoms of all those living on its territory. If, in particular, it was not vigilant to protect a person's religious beliefs and dignity from attempts to influence them by immoral and deceitful means, Article 9 § 2 would in practice be rendered wholly nugatory.

43. In the applicant's submission, religion was part of the 'constantly renewable flow of human thought' and it was impossible to conceive of its being excluded from public debate. A fair balance of personal rights made it necessary to accept that others' thought should be subject to a minimum of influence, otherwise the result would be a 'strange society of silent animals that [would] think but...not express themselves, that [would] talk but...not communicate, and that [would] exist but...not coexist'.

44. Having regard to the circumstances of the case and the actual terms of the relevant courts' decisions, the Court considers that the impugned measure was in pursuit of a legitimate aim under Article 9 § 2, namely the protection of the rights and freedoms of others, relied on by the Government.

3. 'NECESSARY IN A DEMOCRATIC SOCIETY'

45. Mr Kokkinakis did not consider it necessary in a democratic society to prohibit a fellow citizen's right to speak when he came to discuss religion with his neighbour. He was curious to know how a discourse delivered with conviction and based on holy books common to all Christians could infringe the rights of others. Mrs Kyriakaki was an experienced adult woman with intellectual abilities; it was not possible, without flouting fundamental human rights, to make it a criminal offence for a Jehovah's Witness to have a conversation with a cantor's wife. Moreover, the Crete Court of Appeal, although the facts before it were precise and absolutely clear, had not managed to determine the direct or indirect nature of the applicant's attempt to intrude on the complainant's religious beliefs; its reasoning showed that it had convicted the applicant 'not for something he had done but for what he was'.

  The Commission accepted this argument in substance.

46. The Government maintained on the contrary, that the Greek courts had based themselves on plain facts which amounted to the offence of proselytism: Mr Kokkinakis's insistence on entering Mrs Kyriakaki's home on a false pretext; the way in which he had approached her in order to gain her trust; and his 'skilful' analysis of the Holy Scriptures calculated to 'delude' the complainant, who did not possess any 'adequate grounding in doctrine' (see paragraphs 9–10 above). They pointed out that if the State remained indifferent to attacks on freedom of religious belief, major unrest would be caused that would probably disturb the social peace.

47. The Court has consistently held that a certain margin of appreciation is to be left to the Contracting States in assessing the existence and extent of the necessity of an interference, but this margin is subject to European supervision, embracing both the legislation and the decisions applying it, even those given by an independent court. The Court's task is to determine whether the measures taken at national level were justified in principle and proportionate.

In order to rule on this latter point, the Court must weigh the requirements of the protection of the rights and liberties of others against the conduct of which the applicant stood accused. In exercising its supervisory jurisdiction, the Court must look at the impugned judicial decisions against the background of the case as a whole (see, *inter alia* and *mutatis mutandis*, the *Barfod v Denmark* judgment of 22 February 1989, Series A No 149, p 12, § 28).

48. First of all, a distinction has to be made between bearing Christian witness and improper proselytism. The former corresponds to true evangelism, which a report drawn up in 1956 under the auspices of the World Council of Churches describes as an essential mission and a responsibility of every Christian and every Church. The latter represents a corruption or deformation of it. It may, according to the same report, take the form of activities offering material or social advantages with a view to gaining new members for a Church or exerting improper pressure on people in distress or in need; it may even entail the use of violence or brainwashing; more generally, it is not compatible with respect for the freedom of thought, conscience and religion of others.

Scrutiny of section 4 of Law no 1363/1938 shows that the relevant criteria adopted by the Greek legislature are reconcilable with the foregoing if and in so far as they are designed only to punish improper proselytism, which the Court does not have to define in the abstract in the present case.

49. The Court notes, however, that in their reasoning the Greek courts established the applicant's liability by merely reproducing the wording of section 4 and did not sufficiently specify in what way the accused had attempted to convince his neighbour by improper means. None of the facts they set out warrants that finding.

That being so, it has not been shown that the applicant's conviction was justified in the circumstances of the case by a pressing social need. The contested measure therefore does not appear to have been proportionate to the legitimate aim pursued or, consequently, 'necessary in a democratic society . . . for the protection of the rights and freedoms of others'.

50. In conclusion, there has been a breach of Article 9 of the Convention.

. . .

FOR THESE REASONS, THE COURT

1. Holds by six votes to three that there has been a breach of Article 9;

. . .

NOTES

1 The majority were comprised of President Ryssdal and Judges: Bernhardt, Pettiti, De Meyer, Martens, and Lopes Rocha.

In his partly concurring judgment Pettiti J emphasized the importance of this case as '…the first real case concerning freedom of religion to have come before the European Court…' (p 25). Therefore, he considered that the majority's reasoning:

> …could also have better reflected the fact that Article 9 applies also to non-religious philosophical beliefs and that the application of it must protect people from abuse by certain sects; but here it is for the States to legislate so that any deviation leading to attempts at brainwashing are regulated by the ordinary law. Non-criminal proselytism remains the main expression of freedom of religion. Attempting to make converts is not in itself an attack on the freedom and beliefs of others or an infringement of their rights. [P 27.]

He concluded that the Greek law on proselytism was in breach of the Convention because; 'the expression "proselytism that is not respectable", which is a criterion used by the Greek courts when applying the Law, is sufficient for the enactment and the case-law applying it to be regarded as contrary to Article 9' (p 25). This was due to the vagueness of the charge and the lack of a clear definition of proselytism in Greek law. For academic support of his view see T. J. Gunn, 'Adjudicating Rights of Conscience Under the ECHR' in J. D. van der Vyver and J. Witte (ed), *Religious Human Rights in Global Perspective* (The Hague: Martinus Nijhoff, 1996).

De Meyer J cited the dictionary definition (from *Le Petit Robert*) of proselytism as 'zeal in spreading the faith'. He determined that Mr Kokkinakis had shown such zeal but had not acted improperly (Mrs Kyriakaki had let him into her house and she had not asked him to leave). Similarly Martens J observed that:

> …what occasioned this debate was a normal and perfectly inoffensive call by two elderly Jehovah's Witnesses (the applicant was 77 at the time) trying to sell some of the sect's booklets to a lady who, instead of closing the door, allowed the old couple entry, either because she was no match for their insistence or because she believed them to be bringing tidings from relatives on the mainland. There is no trace of violence or of anything that could properly be styled coercion; at the worst there was a trivial lie. If resort to criminal proceedings was at all warranted, a prosecution for disturbance of domestic peace would seem the severest possible response. [P 33.]

As a matter of principle he also considered that it was contrary to Article 9 for States to make it a criminal offence for persons to attempt to induce others to change their religion. His research indicated that Greece was the only party to the Convention which made proselytism a criminal offence per se.

Valticos J (the elected judge of Greek nationality) dissented from the majority with regard to both the scope of Article 9 and the assessment of the facts. In his conception Article 9:

> …is designed to ensure religious peace and tolerance, not to permit religious clashes and even wars, particularly at a time when many sects manage to entice simple, naive souls by doubtful means.…I may add that the term 'teaching' in Article 9 undoubtedly refers to religious teaching in school curricular or in religious institutions, and not to personal door-to-door canvassing as in the present case. [P 30.]

As for the Greek definition of criminal proselytism he considered that:

> this definition of, if one may so term it, rape of the belief of others cannot in any way be regarded as contrary to Article 9 of the Convention. On the contrary, it is such as to protect individuals' freedom of religious belief. [P 31.]

His evaluation of the facts was that:

... we have a militant Jehovah's Witness, a hard-bitten adept of proselytism, a specialist in conversion, a martyr of the criminal courts whose earlier convictions have served only to harden him in his militancy, and, on the other hand, the ideal victim, a naive woman, the wife of a cantor in the Orthodox Church (if he manages to convert her, what a triumph!). He swoops on her, trumpets that he has good news for her (the play on words is obvious, but no doubt not to her), manages to get himself let in and, as an experienced commercial traveller and cunning purveyor of a faith he wants to spread, expounds to her his intellectual wares cunningly wrapped up in a mantle of universal peace and radiant happiness. Who, indeed, would not like peace and happiness? But is this the mere exposition of Mr Kokkinakis's beliefs or is it not rather an attempt to beguile the simple soul of the cantor's wife? Does the Convention afford its protection to such undertakings? Certainly not. [P 31.]

Contrast this portrayal of the facts with that of Martens J above. Foighel and Loizou JJ also dissented. Like Valticos J, they held that the Greek definition of unlawful proselytism was in conformity with Article 9. Furthermore:

the term 'teach' entails openness and uprightness and the avoidance of the use of devious or improper means or false pretexts as in this case in order to gain access to a person's home and, once there, by abusing the courtesy and hospitality extended, take advantage of the ignorance or inexperience in theological doctrine of someone who has no specialist training and try to get that person to change his or her religion. ... The persistent efforts of some fanatics to convert others to their own beliefs by using unacceptable psychological techniques on people, which amount in effect to coercion, cannot in our view come within the ambit of the natural meaning of the term 'teach' to be found in paragraph 1 of this Article. [Pp 40–1.]

2 P. W. Edge has observed that:

The majority are compounding two distinct justifications for freedom of religion here–social justifications that religious freedom helps to produce a functioning pluralist society where individuals all feel a part of the State's society; and the personal development argument which sees religious freedom, in a way similar to the right to privacy, as providing scope for personal development and self-definition. ['Current Problems in Article 9 of the ECHR' [1996] *Juridical Review* 42 at 47.]

3 The Court has subsequently applied its approach in *Kokkinakis* to acts of proselytism carried out by Greek military officers of another sect in *Larissis v Greece*, 1998-I. The three applicants were Air Force officers in the same unit who were members of the Pentecostal Church (which held that all members were under a duty to engage in proselytism). Airman A claimed that two of the applicants had engaged him in religious discussions on seven occasions (during which they had claimed that some of their members had the divine power to speak in foreign languages) and they repeatedly asked him if he had visited a Pentecostal church when he returned from various periods of leave. Airman K asserted that the applicants had engaged him in theological discussions on about 80 occasions. Airman NK, who had converted to the Pentecostal church, stated that he had voluntarily sought the religious help of the applicants, but his father claimed that NK was a highly susceptible young person. One of the applicants had been summoned to a fellow believer's house where he had preached a sermon calling upon all the family and their neighbours to join the Pentecostal church. Mrs Z, whose husband had joined the Pentecostal church, visited the applicants' homes where they urged her to convert (she also alleged that the applicants informed her that she and her children were possessed by the devil). She developed mental problems and decided to sever all links with the applicants and their church. The Greek military courts convicted the applicants of proselytism (under the same law as in *Kokkinakis*) in respect of these activities and sentenced each of them to approximately one year's imprisonment (convertible into financial penalties), but suspended the penalties provided the applicants did not commit new offences within three years. The applicants complained to the Commission alleging, *inter alia*, a breach of their rights under Article 9. The Commission found a violation of Article 9 in respect of the convictions involving the civilians (24 votes to 5), but no breach in respect of the convictions involving the junior military personnel. The Court restated the distinction between 'proper' and 'improper' proselytism articulated in *Kokkinakis*. However, different factors applied to the applicants' behaviour towards their subordinates and ordinary civilians. Regarding the former:

> 51....the Court notes that the hierarchical structures which are a feature of life in the armed forces may colour every aspect of the relations between military personnel, making it difficult for a subordinate to rebuff the approaches of an individual of superior rank or to withdraw from a conversation initiated by him. Thus, what would in the civilian world be seen as an innocuous exchange of ideas which the recipient is free to accept or reject, may, within the confines of military life, be viewed as a form of harassment or the application of undue pressure in abuse of power. It must be emphasised that not every discussion about religion or other sensitive matters between individuals of unequal rank will fall within this category. Nonetheless, where the circumstances so require, States may be justified in taking special measures to protect the rights and freedoms of subordinate members of the armed forces.

A majority of the Court (8 to 1 and 7 to 2) found that the convictions of the applicants in respect of their proselytism towards the junior personnel were not in breach of Article 9. However, by 7 votes to 2 the Court concluded that the convictions involving the civilians were in breach of Article 9, as the applicants had not behaved improperly and the civilians were not subject to the same pressures and constraints in responding to the applicants as the junior airmen had been. In his dissent Valticos J (joined by Morenilla J) considered that, '...the prestige of the officers' uniform may have had an effect even on civilians...'. Counsel for the applicants has criticized the decision, in his view '...the Court is often far too conservative and deferential to the existing legislation of the member States' (J. W. Montgomery, 'When is Evangelism Illegal?' (1998) *New Law Journal* 524 at 525). Would the Court's reasoning be applicable to other hierarchical state organizations such as the police service? What about proselytism in the context of unequal professional relationships, for example between medical doctors and their patients or teachers and their pupils?

The limitations that a military career may place on the exercise of Article 9 rights are considered further in the *Kalac* judgment at p 611.

4 The extent to which States and their national legal systems should protect persons' religious beliefs from denigration and ridicule by others has caused difficulties for the Commission and the Court in the field of artistic expression; especially as artists will be trying to argue their right to freedom of expression under Article 10 (see further p 667). In *Choudhury v UK*, decision of 5 March 1991, the applicant complained that English law had failed to protect his right to freedom of religion under Article 9. Mr Choudhury was a Muslim who had been refused permission by the High Court to bring a private prosecution against Salman Rushdie, and his publishers, in respect of his novel *The Satanic Verses*, which the applicant contended was blasphemous in its treatment of leading figures in Islam. The High Court ruled that under English law the offence of blasphemy only applied to publications directed against the Christian religion (see *R v Chief Metropolitan Stipendiary Magistrate, ex p Choudhury* [1991] 1 All ER 306). The Commission unanimously declared the application inadmissible because:

> [Mr Choudhury] does not claim, and it clearly is not the case, that any State authority, or any body for which the United Kingdom Government may be responsible under the Convention, directly interfered in the applicant's freedom to manifest his religion or belief.
>
> The question in the present case is therefore whether the freedom of Article 9 of the Convention may extend to guarantee a right to bring any specific form of proceedings against those who, by authorship or publication, offend the sensitivities of an individual or a group of individuals. The Commission finds no indication in the present case of a link between freedom from interference with the freedoms of Article 9(1) of the Convention and the applicant's complaints.
>
> Accordingly, this part of the application must be declared incompatible *ratione materiae* with the provisions of the Convention within the meaning of Article 27(2).

Likewise, the Commission declared the applicant's complaint under Article 14, of discriminatory treatment of Islam compared to Christianity in the English law on blasphemy, inadmissible because his substantive complaint had been held to fall outside the protection of Article 9. Hence the Commission was not willing to interpret Article 9(1) as providing religious believers with a right to prosecute those who allegedly insulted their beliefs.

However, the Court, in the context of applying Article 10, has stated that in certain circumstances States may be under a Convention obligation to protect believers from extreme attacks upon their beliefs. In *Otto-Preminger Institute v Austria* A.295-A (1994), the applicant organization ran an 'art-house' cinema in Innsbruck. During May 1985 they planned to show a film called *Das Liebeskonzil* (Council in Heaven) which contained a production of the nineteenth-century play, of the same title, written by Oskar Panizza (who had been imprisoned for blasphemy in 1895 by the German courts for publishing his play). According to the Court the film:

> ...portrays the God of the Jewish religion, the Christian religion and the Islamic religion as an apparently senile old man prostrating himself before the devil with whom he exchanges a deep kiss and calling the devil his friend....Other scenes show the Virgin Mary permitting an obscene story to be read to her and the manifestation of a degree of erotic tension between the Virgin Mary and the devil. The adult Jesus Christ is portrayed as a low grade mental defective...[Para 22.]

The applicant informed its 2,700 members of the showings and it also advertised the events to the general public (only persons over 17 years of age would be admitted) via window displays throughout Innsbruck and in a brief announcement in a regional newspaper. The Innsbruck diocese of the Roman Catholic church (87 per cent of Tyrolleans are Roman Catholic believers) requested the Public Prosecutor to bring criminal charges against the applicant in respect of its proposed film performances. The Prosecutor instituted proceedings against the applicant's manager and applied for the seizure of the film under the Media Act. The Regional Court ordered the immediate seizure of the film. Subsequently, the Regional Court approved the forfeiture of the film. The applicant contended that these orders amounted to a violation of its right to freedom of expression under Article 10. The Commission concluded (by 9 votes to 5) that the seizure of the film violated Article 10 and that the forfeiture was a similar violation (by 13 votes to 1). Before the Court, the Austrian Government argued that the court orders were necessary to 'protect the rights of others' in the form of the right to respect for their religious beliefs held by the Tyrolleans and, therefore, could be justified under Article 10(2) (for further elaboration of this provision, see p 721). The majority of the Court agreed with this argument:

> 47. Those who choose to exercise the freedom to manifest their religion, irrespective of whether they do so as members of a religious majority or a minority, cannot reasonably expect to be exempt from all criticism. They must tolerate and accept the denial by others of their religious beliefs and even the propagation by others of doctrines hostile to their faith. However, the manner in which religious beliefs and doctrines are opposed or denied is a matter which may engage the responsibility of the State, notably its responsibility to ensure the peaceful enjoyment of the right guaranteed under Article 9 to the holders of those beliefs and doctrines. Indeed, in extreme cases the effect of particular methods of opposing or denying religious beliefs can be such as to inhibit those who hold such beliefs from exercising their freedom to hold and express them.
>
> In the *Kokkinakis* judgment the Court held, in the context of Article 9, that a State may legitimately consider it necessary to take measures aimed at repressing certain forms of conduct, including the imparting of information and ideas, judged incompatible with the respect for the freedom of thought, conscience and religion of others. The respect for the religious feelings of believers as guaranteed in Article 9 can legitimately thought to have been violated by provocative portrayals of objects of religious veneration; and such portrayals can be regarded as malicious violation of the spirit of tolerance, which must also be a feature of democratic society.

The majority (President Ryssdal and Judges: Gölcüklü, Matscher, Walsh, Macdonald, and Gotchev) then invoked the controversial margin of appreciation doctrine (see p 633) to determine that the seizure/forfeiture of the film 'was necessary in a democratic society' and that no breach of Article 10 had occurred:

> 50. . . . it is not possible to discern throughout Europe a uniform conception of the significance of religion in society, even within a single country such conceptions may vary. For that reason it is not possible to arrive at a comprehensive definition of what constitutes a permissible interference with the exercise of the right to freedom of expression where such expression is directed against the religious feelings of others. A certain margin of appreciation is therefore to be left to the national authorities in assessing the existence and extent of the necessity of such interference.

The three dissentients (Judges Palm, Pekkanen, and Makarczyk) considered that:

> 6. The Convention does not, in terms, guarantee a right to protection of religious feelings. More particularly, such a right cannot be derived from the right to freedom of religion, which in effect includes a right to express views critical of the religious opinions of others.
>
> Nevertheless, it must be accepted that it may be 'legitimate' for the purpose of Article 10 to protect the religious feelings of certain members of society against criticism and abuse to some extent; tolerance works both ways and the democratic character of a society will be affected if violent and abusive attacks on the reputation of a religious group are allowed. Consequently, it must also be accepted that it may be 'necessary in a democratic society' to set limits to the public expression of such criticism or abuse. To this extent, but no further, we can agree with the majority.

However, the dissentients did not consider that the seizure/forfeiture of the film was a proportionate response by the Austrian authorities when considered in the light of the applicant's warnings to prospective viewers of the nature of the film, and the fact that only paying adults would be able to see the film.

In the later case of **Wingrove v UK**, 1996-V, a majority of the Court upheld the lawfulness of the British Board of Film Classification's refusal to grant a classification certificate (thereby preventing its lawful distribution within the UK) to the applicant's 18-minute video work entitled *Visions of Ecstasy*. The video, which had no dialogue, was claimed by the applicant film director to be based upon the life of St Teresa of Avila, a sixteenth-century Carmelite nun, who experienced ecstatic visions of Jesus Christ. The Court described the work as portraying, '...*inter alia*, a female character astride the recumbent body of the crucified Christ engaged in an act of an overtly sexual nature' (para 61). The Board, and later the statutory Video Appeals Committee, concluded that the video was blasphemous and should not therefore be given a certificate. The applicant claimed that these decisions violated his right to freedom of expression under Article 10. The Commission (by 14 votes to 2) found there had been a violation of this Article. The Government relied upon the Court's decision in *Otto-Preminger Institute* to contend that States may restrict the publication of provocative depictions of objects of religious veneration in order to ensure respect for the religious beliefs of followers of the religion concerned. The Court's majority (President Bernhardt and Judges: Thor Vilhjalmsson, Pettiti, Morenilla, Freeland, Mifsud Bonnici, and Gotchev) agreed that States might restrict video works under Article 10(2) in order to protect the right of other citizens not to be offended in their religious feelings.

50. It is true that the English law of blasphemy only extends to the Christian faith. Indeed the anomaly of this state of affairs in a multi-denominational society was recognised by the Divisional Court in *R v Chief Magistrate, ex p Choudhury* [above]. However, it is not for the European Court to rule *in abstracto* as to the compatibility of domestic law with the Convention. The extent to which English law protects other beliefs is not in issue before the Court which must confine its attention to the case before it. The uncontested fact that the law of blasphemy does not treat on an equal footing the different religions practised in the United Kingdom does not detract from the legitimacy of the aim pursued in the present context.

Following the approach in *Otto-Preminger Institute*, the Court then upheld the authorities' refusal to classify the video as being within the State's broad margin of appreciation concerning expression directed at religious beliefs.

58. Whereas there is little scope under Article 10(2) of the Convention for restrictions on political speech or on debate of questions of public interest, a wider margin of appreciation is generally available to the Contracting States when regulating freedom of expression in relation to matters liable to offend intimate personal convictions within the sphere of morals or, especially, religion. Moreover, as in the field of morals, and perhaps to an even greater degree, there is no uniform European conception of the requirements of 'the protection of the rights of others' in relation to attacks on their religious convictions. What is likely to cause substantial offence to persons of a particular religious persuasion will vary significantly from time to time and from place to place, especially in an era characterised by an ever growing array of faiths and denominations. By reason of their direct and continuous contact with the vital forces of their countries, State authorities are in principle in a better position than the international judge to give an opinion on the exact content of these requirements with regard to the rights of others as well as on the 'necessity' of a 'restriction' intended to protect from such material those whose deepest feelings and convictions would be seriously offended.

Judge De Meyer in his dissent expressed the view that in respect of the criminal law of blasphemy, '...the necessity of such laws is very much open to question. I would rather join in Mr Patten's [a former Home Office Minister] remark that for the faithful "the strength of their own belief is the best armour against mockers and blasphemers"' (para 4). The other dissentient, Lohmus J was concerned that:

In cases of prior restraint (censorship) there is interference by the authorities with freedom of expression even though the members of the society whose feelings they seek to protect have not called for such interference. The interference is based on the opinion of the authorities that they understand correctly the feelings they claim to protect. The actual opinion of believers remains unknown. I think that is why we cannot conclude that the interference corresponded to a 'pressing social need'.

The law of blasphemy only protects the Christian religion and, more specifically, the established Church of England. The aim of the interference was therefore to protect the Christian faith alone and not other beliefs. This in itself raises the question whether the interference was 'necessary in a democratic society'. [Paras 3–4.]

Lord Lester has criticized the majority's judgment in *Wingrove* as a 'timorous ruling'. In his opinion:

I do not discern a satisfactory logical, philosophical or jurisprudential basis for protecting political expression and media freedom more strongly than artistic and cultural expression. The distinction sought to be made between them seems arbitrary and unworkable. Many famous works of art, literature and music have been censored because they shock or offend against the political, religious, sexual or aesthetic mores of the prevailing orthodoxy.' ['Universality versus Subsidiarity: A Reply' [1998] *European Human Rights Law Review* 73 at 77.]

Article 9(1)

Freedom of thought, conscience and religion: protected beliefs

1 Pacifism has been recognized as a belief falling within the protection of Article 9(1). In *Arrowsmith v UK* 19 DR 5 (1978), the applicant had been sentenced to 18 months' imprisonment under the Incitement to Disaffection Act 1934 for distributing leaflets, calling upon military personnel to refuse to serve in Northern Ireland, outside an army base in England. She claimed that her conviction and sentence violated her right to manifest her pacifist belief under Article 9(1). The Government accepted her definition of pacifism as being, 'the commitment, in both theory and practice, to the philosophy of securing one's political or other objectives without resort to the threat or use of force against another human being under any circumstances, even in response to the threat or use of force.' The Commission expressed the opinion that:

69. . . . pacifism as a philosophy and, in particular, as defined above, falls within the ambit of the right to freedom of thought and conscience. The attitude of pacifism may therefore be seen as a belief ('conviction') protected by Article 9(1).

Then the Commission considered whether Ms Arrowsmith had been manifesting her belief (for a general examination of this topic, see p 611) by distributing the leaflets:

71. . . . the term 'practice' as employed in Article 9(1) does not cover each act which is motivated or influenced by a religion or a belief. It is true that public declarations proclaiming generally the idea of pacifism and urging the acceptance of a commitment to non-violence may be considered as a normal and recognised manifestation of pacifist belief. However, when the actions of individuals

do not actually express the belief concerned they cannot be considered to be as such protected by Article 9(1) even when they are motivated or influenced by it.

After examining the contents of Arrowsmith's leaflets the Commission concluded that they did not reflect pacifist views, but a policy opposed to British military involvement in Northern Ireland. Consequently, distributing the leaflets was not a manifestation of a protected belief and Arrowsmith's conviction/imprisonment did not violate Article 9. Subsequently, the Committee of Ministers agreed with the Commission's Opinion: Res DH(79)4.

2 *Valsamis v Greece* and *Efstratiou v Greece*, 1996-VI , involved parents requesting that their children be exempted from participating in school parades on the National Day of Greece. The parents' objection was based upon their membership of the Jehovah's Witnesses, whose beliefs forbid any conduct or practice associated with war or violence. In a small number of municipalities the school parades were accompanied by military parades, therefore the applicants asked that their children be exempted from their respective parades (even though there was no military presence at these celebrations). The children's headteachers refused the requests in accordance with a circular issued by the Ministry of Education and Religious Affairs stating that no children should be exempted from national celebrations. The children did not attend the school parades and each child was punished by suspension from school for one day by their headteachers. The parents complained to the Commission alleging, *inter alia*, a breach of their rights under Article 2 of Protocol 1 (States shall respect parents religious and philosophical convictions in matters of education and teaching) and Article 9. The Commission concluded (by 19 votes to 10) that there had been no breach of Protocol 1, as the relevant parades did not have a military character, and (by 17 votes to 12) there had been no breach of Article 9. A majority of the Court (seven judges) concluded that:

31. While it is not for the Court to rule on the Greek State's decisions as regards the setting and planning of the school curriculum, it is surprised that pupils can be required on pain of suspension from school—even if only for a day—to parade outside the school precincts on a holiday. Nevertheless, it can discern nothing, either in the purpose of the parade or in the arrangements for it, which could offend the applicants' pacifist convictions to an extent prohibited by the second sentence of Article 2 of Protocol No 1. Such commemorations of national events serve, in their way, both pacifist objectives and the public interest. The presence of military representatives at some of the parades which take place in Greece on the day in question does not in itself alter the nature of the parades.

Consequently, there was no breach of the Protocol or Article 9. Judges Thor Vilhjalmsson and Jambrek dissented. In their opinion:

Victoria Valsamis stated that the parade she did not participate in had a character and symbolism that were clearly contrary to her neutralist, pacifist and thus religious, beliefs. We are of the opinion that the Court has to accept that and we find no basis for seeing Victoria's participation in this parade as necessary in a democratic society; even if this public event clearly was for most people an expression of national values and unity. [P 32.]

For the dissenters the Greek authorities' actions amounted to a violation of the parents' rights under Protocol 1 and the children's rights under Article 9.

3 However, the conscientious objection to compulsory military service of a member of the Jehovah's Witnesses was upheld in a ground-breaking judgment of the Grand Chamber in *Bayatyan v Armenia*, judgment of 7 July 2011. The applicant had been sentenced to over

two years' imprisonment for refusing to undertake military service. He contended that violated his rights under Article 9. The Armenian Government relied on opinions of the former European Commission that in cases involving compulsory military service Article 9 had to be interpreted with regard to Article 4(3)(b) (that excludes compulsory military, or civilian, service from the prohibition of 'forced or compulsory labour'). A Chamber, subject to one dissent, confirmed that approach. But, the Grand Chamber, with the Armenian judge dissenting, found that there was now a European consensus recognizing the right to conscientious objection in respect of compulsory military service (only Azerbaijan and Turkey did not recognize conscientious objection). Accordingly, the Grand Chamber held that:

109....in line with the 'living instrument' approach, the Court therefore takes the view that it is not possible to confirm the case-law established by the Commission, and that Article 9 should no longer be read in conjunction with Article 4 § 3 (b). Consequently, the applicant's complaint is to be assessed solely under Article 9.

110. In this respect, the Court notes that Article 9 does not explicitly refer to a right to conscientious objection. However, it considers that opposition to military service, where it is motivated by a serious and insurmountable conflict between the obligation to serve in the army and a person's conscience or his deeply and genuinely held religious or other beliefs, constitutes a conviction or belief of sufficient cogency, seriousness, cohesion and importance to attract the guarantees of Article 9... Whether and to what extent objection to military service falls within the ambit of that provision must be assessed in the light of the particular circumstances of the case.

The majority went on to find that the applicant's objection had been based upon his religious beliefs and that his conviction was not necessary in a democratic society given that he had been willing to undertake civilian service (which was not available at that time in Armenia despite the Government's pledge to introduce it). Therefore, Article 9 had been violated. This judgment is yet another powerful example of the Court revising ECHR jurisprudence to reflect contemporary standards.

4 Other non-religious beliefs, such as veganism, have been accepted by the Commission as falling within the protection of Article 9(1). For example, in *H v UK* (1993) 16 EHRR CD 44, the applicant was a convicted prisoner who refused to work in the prison print shop because he contended that some of the dyes were derived from animal products and as a vegan he objected to working with animal products. The prison authorities found him guilty of a disciplinary offence and he lost two days' remission from his sentence and was fined. The Commission expressed the view that, '...vegan convictions with regard to animal products fall within the scope of Article 9(1)...' (p 45). However, the Commission found that the Government could justify their actions under Article 9(2) as a proportionate interference with H's rights taken in the interests of preserving good order in the prison system; therefore, his complaint was found to be manifestly ill-founded.

5 In *Buscarini v San Marino*, 1999-I, the Court expressly stated that Article 9 covers the freedom not to hold religious beliefs or to practise a religion. The applicants had been elected to the parliament of the Republic of San Marino in 1993. However, they were not allowed to take their seats until they swore an oath which included the words 'I...swear on the Holy Gospels ever to be faithful to and obey the Constitution of the Republic...'. The applicants objected to the wording of the oath as they considered that it infringed their freedom of religion and conscience under Article 9. The Commission, unanimously, upheld their complaint. The Court was also unanimous in its interpretation and application of Article 9 to the applicants' case. 'That freedom entails, *inter alia*, freedom to hold or not to hold religious beliefs and to practise or not to practise a religion' (para 34). The Government sought to argue that having regard to the history, traditions, and social fabric of San Marino, requiring parliamentarians to take the oath was necessary to maintain public order. But, the Court did not consider that such an obligation was necessary in a democratic society.

39. It is not in doubt that, in general, San Marinese law guarantees freedom of conscience and religion. In the instant case, however, requiring the applicants to take the oath on the Gospels was tantamount to requiring two elected representatives of the people to swear allegiance to a particular religion, a requirement which is not compatible with Article 9. As the Commission rightly stated in its report, it would be contradictory to make the exercise of a mandate intended to represent different views of society within Parliament subject to a prior declaration of commitment to a particular set of beliefs.

Therefore, the Court found a violation of Article 9.

6   A Grand Chamber held that, '58....supporters of secularism are able to lay claim to views attaining the "level of cogency, seriousness, cohesion and importance" required for them to be considered "convictions" within the meaning of Articles 9 of the Convention and 2 of Protocol No. 1...' in *Lautsi and others v Italy*, judgment of 18 March 2011. However, a large majority, 15 votes to 2, went on to find no breach of those provisions through the display of crucifixes in the classrooms of State schools attended by the first applicant's sons. As there was no consensus amongst the member States regarding the presence of religious symbols in publicly funded schools, the Court held that States were to be accorded a margin of appreciation to determine the issue according to domestic traditions.

The right to manifest a person's religion or belief

Kalac v Turkey 1997-IV
European Court of Human Rights

The applicant had pursued a career as a judge advocate in the Turkish Air Force. In 1990 he held the rank of Group Captain and was serving as the High Command's Director of Legal Affairs. During August 1990 the Supreme Military Council, composed of the Prime Minister, Minister of Defence, Chief of Staff, and 11 generals, ordered the compulsory retirement of three officers (including the applicant) and 28 non-commissioned officers for breaches of discipline and scandalous conduct. The applicant was alleged to have 'adopted unlawful fundamentalist opinions'. Subsequently, the President of the Republic approved the order. The applicant sought to challenge the order before the Supreme Administrative Court of the Armed Forces, but that body ruled that it did not have jurisdiction over the order. Before the Commission the applicant alleged that he had been removed from his post on account of his religious convictions in breach of Article 9. The Commission, unanimously, found a breach of that Article.

...

25. The Government argued that the question whether Mr Kalaç should be allowed to remain a member of the armed forces lay at the heart of the problem submitted to the Court. His compulsory retirement was not an interference with his freedom of conscience, religion or belief but was intended to remove from the military legal service a person who had manifested his lack of loyalty

to the foundation of the Turkish nation, namely secularism, which it was the task of the armed forces to guarantee. The applicant belonged to the Süleyman sect, as a matter of fact, if not formally, and participated in the activities of the Süleyman community, which was known to have unlawful fundamentalist tendencies. Various documents annexed to the memorial to the Court showed that the applicant had given it legal assistance, had taken part in training sessions and had intervened on a number of occasions in the appointment of servicemen who were members of the sect. On the basis of those documents, a committee of five officers drawn from the highest echelons of the military had concluded that by taking and carrying out instructions from the leaders of the sect Group Captain Kalaç had breached military discipline and should accordingly be compulsorily retired pursuant to section 50(c) of the Military Personnel Act. The Supreme Military Council had based its decision on this opinion, which had been approved by the high command and the air force chief of staff.

Lastly, facilities to practise one's religion within the armed forces were provided in Turkey for both Muslims and the adherents of other faiths. However, the protection of Article 9 could not extend, in the case of a serviceman, to membership of a fundamentalist movement, in so far as its members' activities were likely to upset the army's hierarchical equilibrium.

26. The Commission, basing its opinion on the documents submitted to it by the Government, took the view that the applicant's compulsory retirement constituted interference with the right guaranteed by Article 9 § 1 and concluded that there had been a breach of that provision on the ground that the interference in question was not prescribed by law within the meaning of the second paragraph, finding that the relevant provisions did not afford adequate protection against arbitrary decisions. The Delegate observed that, in support of their memorial to the Court, the Government had produced documents which, during the proceedings before the Commission, had been said to be 'secret in the interests of national security'. In any event, these documents did not support the argument that Mr Kalaç had any links with a sect.

27. The Court reiterates that while religious freedom is primarily a matter of individual conscience, it also implies, *inter alia*, freedom to manifest one's religion not only in community with others, in public and within the circle of those whose faith one shares, but also alone and in private (see the *Kokkinakis v Greece* judgment of 25 May 1993, Series A No 260-A, p 17, § 31). Article 9 lists a number of forms which manifestation of one's religion or belief may take, namely worship, teaching, practice and observance. Nevertheless, Article 9 does not protect every act motivated or inspired by a religion or belief. Moreover, in exercising his freedom to manifest his religion, an individual may need to take his specific situation into account.

28. In choosing to pursue a military career Mr Kalaç was accepting of his own accord a system of military discipline that by its very nature implied the possibility of placing on certain of the rights and freedoms of members of the armed forces limitations incapable of being imposed on civilians (see the *Engel and Others v Netherlands* judgment of 8 June 1976, Series A No 22, p 24, § 57). States may adopt for their armies disciplinary regulations forbidding this or that type of conduct, in particular an attitude inimical to an established order reflecting the requirements of military service.

29. It is not contested that the applicant, within the limits imposed by the requirements of military life, was able to fulfil the obligations which constitute the normal forms through which a Muslim practises his religion. For example, he was in particular permitted to pray five times a day and to perform his other religious duties, such as keeping the fast of Ramadan and attending Friday prayers at the mosque.

30. The Supreme Military Council's order was, moreover, not based on Group Captain Kalaç's religious opinions and beliefs or the way he had performed his religious duties but on his conduct and attitude. According to the Turkish authorities, this conduct breached military discipline and infringed the principle of secularism.

31. The Court accordingly concludes that the applicant's compulsory retirement did not amount to an interference with the right guaranteed by Article 9 since it was not prompted by the way the applicant manifested his religion.

There has therefore been no breach of Article 9.

FOR THESE REASONS, THE COURT UNANIMOUSLY

...

Holds that there has been no breach of Article 9 of the Convention.

NOTES

1 The Court was comprised of President Ryssdal and Judges: Gölcüklü, Pettiti, Russo, Spielmann, Foighel, Freeland, Baka, and Gotchev.

2 The Court's judgment indicates that the right to manifest one's religion or belief is more circumscribed than the right to freedom of thought, conscience, and religion. By voluntarily pursuing a chosen career the applicant was held to have accepted the consequent necessary limitations on the right to manifest his religious belief.

3 A similar approach to this right had been articulated by the Commission in the earlier case of *Ahmad v UK*, 22 DR 27 (1981). Mr Ahmad was a devout Muslim who was under a religious duty to attend Friday prayers at a mosque if he was within travelling distance of such an establishment. From 1968 until 1972 he was employed as a full-time teacher by the Inner London Education Authority. During that time Ahmad did not seek permission to attend a mosque for Friday prayers. In 1974 he was moved to another teaching area in London and he chose a school near a mosque. He then asserted the right to attend the mosque for prayers even if this conflicted with his teaching duties on Fridays. His employers refused him permission to attend prayers on Friday afternoons and stated that if he wished to be absent from work at that time he must switch to a part-time contract of employment. He then resigned from his position and claimed constructive dismissal. Eventually the Court of Appeal, by a majority of 2 to 1, rejected his claim: see *Ahmad v ILEA* [1978] 1 All ER 574. The Commission expressed the view that a person, '…may, in the exercise of his freedom to manifest his religion, have to take into account his particular professional or contractual position' (p 133). Relevant factors in Mr Ahmad's case were his voluntary acceptance of his full-time teaching contract in 1968 and his failure to inform his employers for six years that he might need time off on Fridays to attend a mosque. Consequently, the Commission declared his application to be manifestly ill-founded.

4 Likewise, in *Stedman v UK* (1997) 23 EHRR CD 168, the Commission found the applicant's complaints to be inadmissible because of her contractual obligations. She argued that her dismissal from employment by a private sector company for refusing to agree to work on Sundays (on a rota basis) was a violation of, *inter alia*, her freedom to manifest her Christian religion in worship, practice, and observance as guaranteed by Article 9. However the Commission stated that:

…the applicant was dismissed for failing to agree to work certain hours rather than for her religious belief as such and was free to resign and did in effect resign from her employment.

The Commission thus considers that, had the applicant been employed by the State and dismissed in similar circumstances, such dismissal would not have amounted to an interference with her rights under Article 9(1). *A fortiori* the United Kingdom cannot be expected to have legislation that would protect employees against such dismissals by private employers. [Para 1.]

5 The Court found a breach of this right in *Serif v Greece*, judgment of 14 December 1999. The applicant was a Greek citizen who was elected by fellow Muslims in Thrace to be their Mufti (religious leader). However, the President of Greece had appointed another person to that position. Subsequently the applicant was convicted of 'usurping the functions of a minister of a known religion' and fined. The Court was unanimous in holding that:

The facts underlying the applicant's conviction, as they transpire from the relevant domestic court decisions, were issuing a message about the religious significance of a feast, delivering a speech at a religious gathering, issuing another message on the occasion of a religious holiday and appearing in the clothes of a religious leader. In these circumstances, the Court considers that the applicant's conviction amounts to an interference with his right under Article 9(1) of the Convention, 'in community with others and in public, to manifest his religion in worship and teaching'.

...in the Court's view, punishing a person for the mere fact that he acted as the religious leader of a group that willingly followed him can hardly be considered compatible with the demands of religious pluralism in a democratic society.

...Although the Court recognises that it is possible that tension is created in situations where a religious or any other community becomes divided, it considers that this is one of the unavoidable consequences of pluralism. The role of the authorities in such circumstances is not to remove the cause of tension by eliminating pluralism, but to ensure that the competing groups tolerate each other... [Paras 39, 51, and 53.]

Consequently, States must be careful about when and how they intervene in the domestic struggles within particular religious groups.

An analogous breach was found by a unanimous Chamber in the later case of *Agga v Greece*, judgment of 17 October 2002 (note, the same applicant successfully invoked this right in two similar applications: judgments of 13 July 2006).

The full-time Court has found that the Bulgarian Government unlawfully interfered in the organizational arrangements of Bulgarian Muslims. A Grand Chamber, unanimously, found a breach of Article 9 in *Hasan and Chaush v Bulgaria*, 2000-XI. Following the emergence of democracy in Bulgaria some Muslim believers and activists sought to replace the established leadership of their religion in the country, as they believed the leadership had collaborated with the former communist regime. In 1991 a new government (Union of Democratic Forces) was formed after a general election. Early in 1992 the Directorate of Religious Denominations, a governmental body attached to the Council of Ministers, declared the election, in 1988, of the Chief Mufti of Bulgarian Muslims (Mr Gendzhev) null and void and proclaimed his removal from that position. In September 1992 the National Conference of Muslims elected the first applicant as Chief Mufti and approved a new statute to govern their organization. The Directorate of Religious Denominations registered the statute and new leadership in the following month. Mr Gendzhev's supporters elected him the President of the Supreme Holy Council and proclaimed themselves the legitimate representatives of Muslim believers. At the end of 1994 a new government, formed by the Bulgarian Socialist Party, was elected. In February 1995 the Deputy Prime Minister issued a Decree approving the statute of Mr Gendzhev's organization. Later that month the Directorate of Religious Denominations issued a decision registering Mr Gendzhev as the leader of the Bulgarian Muslim community. Thereupon, the new leadership, accompanied by private security guards, entered the premises of the Chief Mufti's Office in Sofia and forcibly evicted the staff. The applicant contended that the police protected the new occupants. Subsequently, the new leader took control of all the assets of Bulgarian Muslim religious organizations. The first applicant challenged the lawfulness of the actions of the Council of Ministers before the Supreme Court, but his appeal was dismissed in July 1995.

Mr Hasan was re-elected Chief Mufti by a conference of his supporters, however, the Council of Ministers did not reply to his request to be registered as the leader. In 1996 the Supreme Court ruled that the Council of Ministers had acted unlawfully by tacitly refusing to register him as Chief Mufti. The Council of Ministers did not grant registration to the applicant. Subsequently, the Union of Democratic Forces formed a new government in 1997 and it encouraged the applicant and his supporters to negotiate an agreement with Mr Gendzhev and his organization. A unification conference was held in October 1997 and it elected a new leadership composed of the first applicant's supporters and others. Later that month the Deputy Prime Minister registered the newly elected leadership. Mr Gendzhev continued to claim he was the Chief Mufti but his position was not recognized by the Bulgarian courts. The applicants asserted that the forced replacement of their leadership in 1995, endorsed by the government, amounted to a violation of their right to manifest their religion. The Grand Chamber held that:

62. The Court recalls that religious communities traditionally and universally exist in the form of organised structures. They abide by rules which are often seen by followers as being of a divine origin. Religious ceremonies have their meaning and sacred value for the believers if they have been conducted by ministers empowered for that purpose in compliance with these rules. The personality of the religious ministers is undoubtedly of importance to every member of the community. Participation in the life of the community is thus a manifestation of one's religion, protected by Article 9 of the Convention.

Where the organisation of the religious community is at issue, Article 9 of the Convention must be interpreted in the light of Article 11, which safeguards associative life against unjustified State interference. Seen in this perspective, the believers' right to freedom of religion encompasses the expectation that the community will be allowed to function peacefully, free from arbitrary State intervention. Indeed, the autonomous existence of religious communities is indispensable for pluralism in a democratic society and is thus an issue at the very heart of the protection which Article 9 affords. It directly concerns not only the organisation of the community as such but also the effective enjoyment of the right to freedom of religion by all its active members. Were the organisational life of the community not protected by Article 9 of the Convention, all other aspects of the individual's freedom of religion would become vulnerable.

...

78. Nevertheless, the Court considers, like the Commission, that facts demonstrating a failure by the authorities to remain neutral in the exercise of their powers in this domain must lead to the conclusion that the State interfered with the believers' freedom to manifest their religion within the meaning of Article 9 of the Convention. It recalls that, but for very exceptional cases, the right to freedom of religion as guaranteed under the Convention excludes any discretion on the part of the State to determine whether religious beliefs or the means used to express such beliefs are legitimate. State action favouring one leader of a divided religious community or undertaken with the purpose of forcing the community to come together under a single leadership against its own wishes would likewise constitute an interference with freedom of religion. In democratic societies the State does not need to take measures to ensure that religious communities are brought under a unified leadership (see *Serif*, cited above, § 52).

...

82. The Court therefore finds, like the Commission, that Decree R-12, the decision of the Directorate of Religious Denominations of 23 February 1995, and the subsequent refusal of the Council of Ministers to recognise the existence of the organisation led by Mr Hasan were more than acts of routine registration or of correcting past irregularities. Their effect was to favour one faction

of the Muslim community, granting it the status of the single official leadership, to the complete exclusion of the hitherto recognised leadership. The acts of the authorities operated, in law and in practice, to deprive the excluded leadership of any possibility of continuing to represent at least part of the Muslim community and of managing its affairs according to the will of that part of the community.

There was therefore an interference with the internal organisation of the Muslim religious community and with the applicants' right to freedom of religion as protected by Article 9 of the Convention.

The Grand Chamber went on to find that the interference was not 'prescribed by law' as it was arbitrary and the repeated failures by the Council of Ministers to comply with the judgments of the Supreme Court concerning the applicants constituted a breach of the rule of law.

Subsequently, the organization headed by Mr Gendzhev challenged the government's activities in organizing the 1997 unification conference in *Supreme Holy Council of the Muslim Community v Bulgaria*, judgment of 16 December 2004. The applicant organization asserted that the authorities had manipulated that conference with the aim of favouring one leadership faction over the other. A united Chamber observed that:

83. The Court considers that the applicant organisation's allegation that the mayors of a number of localities and political figures participated too closely in the selection of delegates to the October 1997 assembly does not appear implausible.

The Chamber went on to hold that:

80. . . . Neutral mediation between groups of believers would not in principle amount to State interference with the believers' rights under Article 9 of the Convention, although the State authorities must be cautious in this particularly delicate area.

. . .

94. In the present case, the relevant law and practice and the authorities' actions in October 1997 had the effect of compelling the divided community to have a single leadership against the will of one of the two rival leaderships.

95. As a result, one of the groups of leaders was favoured and the other excluded and deprived of the possibility of continuing to manage autonomously the affairs and assets of that part of the community which supported it.

. . .

98. In sum, the Court considers that the Bulgarian authorities went beyond the limits of their margin of appreciation under Article 9(2) of the Convention.

99. It follows that the interference with the applicant organisation's rights under Article 9 of the Convention in 1997 was not necessary in a democratic society for the protection of public order or the rights and freedoms of others and was therefore contrary to that provision.

These two cases disclose strong suggestions of political considerations influencing governmental decisions concerning the recognition of religious leaders and their organizations. Two governments, composed of different political parties, were responsible for the unlawful interferences with Muslim organizations in Bulgaria.

The refusal of the Moldovan Government and courts to grant legal recognition to a new religious organization (the first applicant) which had split from the recognized, Orthodox Christian, Metropolitan Church of Moldova was determined to be an unjustifiable interference by a unanimous Chamber in *Metropolitan Church of Bessarabia and Others v Moldova*, 2001-XII. Under Moldovan law an unrecognized religious organization was not able to operate, for example its clergy could not perform religious services and the organization was not entitled to judicial protection of its assets. Consequently, the Court concluded that the authorities' refusal was not a proportionate response to the legitimate aim of protecting public order and safety. Hence, States may be liable for interfering with the organization of religious groups by either withdrawing official recognition (as in *Hasan and Chaush*) or refusing recognition (as in *Metropolitan Church*).

6 The Court has ruled that the ritual slaughter of animals in accordance with religious requirements falls within this aspect of Article 9: *The Jewish Liturgical Association Cha'are Shalom Ve Tsedek v France*, judgment of 27 June 2000. The applicant Association had its origins in the 1980s as an orthodox group which split from the main Central Consistory (Union of Jewish Congregations of France). The French Government had authorized the Central Consistory to designate persons who would conduct the ritual slaughter (involving in part the cutting of the throats of animals which had not been stunned) and certification of meat in conformity with the 'Shulchan Aruch' (prescriptions governing kosher meat). The applicant Association wished the animals to be slaughtered in accordance with even stricter religious requirements than those observed by the Central Consistory's designated slaughterers. Consequently, the Association applied to the authorities for permission to appoint its own certified slaughterers. The Minister of the Interior refused the Association's request because, *inter alia*, the Association was not sufficiently representative within the French Jewish community. The Association brought a complaint at Strasbourg alleging a breach of its right under Article 9 to manifest its religion through observance of the rites of the Jewish religion. The Court held that:

73. The Court next reiterates that Article 9 lists a number of forms which manifestation of one's religion or belief may take, namely worship, teaching, practice and observance (see the *Kalaç v Turkey* judgment of 1 July 1997, Reports 1997-IV, p 1209, § 27). It is not contested that ritual slaughter, as indeed its name indicates, constitutes a rite or 'rite' (the word in the French text of the Convention corresponding to 'observance' in the English), whose purpose is to provide Jews with meat from animals slaughtered in accordance with religious prescriptions, which is an essential aspect of practice of the Jewish religion. The applicant association employs ritual slaughterers and kashrut inspectors [person's who ensure the observance of Jewish food law] who slaughter animals in accordance with its prescriptions on the question, and it is likewise the applicant association which, by certifying as 'glatt' [the strictest form of] kosher the meat sold in its members' butcher's shops, exercises religious supervision of ritual slaughter.

74. It follows that the applicant association can rely on Article 9 of the Convention with regard to the French authorities' refusal to approve it, since ritual slaughter must be considered to be covered by a right guaranteed by the Convention, namely the right to manifest one's religion in observance, within the meaning of Article 9.

A majority of the Court, 12 votes to 5, went on to conclude that there had not been a breach of the Association's right as the organization, and its members, could easily obtain supplies of 'glatt' meat from Belgium or they could seek to reach an agreement with the Central Consistory for the latter body to designate members of the Association as approved slaughterers. Significantly, the Court stated that, '...the right to freedom of religion guaranteed by Article 9 of the Convention cannot extend to the right to take part in person in the performance of ritual slaughter...' (para 81). Furthermore, States can also seek to justify restrictions on the religious slaughter of animals under the exceptions contained in Article 9(2), such as public safety or health.

7 The prohibition of female students wearing the Islamic headscarf, covering their hair and throat, whilst attending classes and examinations at Istanbul University was found not to violate Article 9 by a Chamber and Grand Chamber in *Leyla Sahin v Turkey*, judgment of 10 November 2005. In 1997 the applicant, who had completed four years of medical study at another Turkish medical school, enrolled at the Faculty of Medicine at Istanbul University. During February 1998 the Vice Chancellor of Istanbul University issued a circular, based upon the Constitution and his legal powers, providing that students wearing the Islamic headscarf (or with beards) must not be admitted to classes etc. Consequently, the applicant, who wore such a scarf out of religious conviction, was denied access to lectures and examinations. She challenged the legality of the circular before the administrative courts, but her complaints were rejected. She was subject to a formal disciplinary warning by the Dean of the Faculty of Medicine, in May 1998, for failing to comply with the University rules on dress. In April 1999, after a disciplinary hearing, she was suspended from the University, for one semester, in respect of her participation in an unauthorized demonstration at the University (against the dress rules). Her challenge to that decision was dismissed by the administrative court. Later in 1999 she abandoned her studies in Turkey and registered at Vienna University. She complained to Strasbourg alleging, *inter alia*, a breach of her right to manifest her religion. The Chamber was unanimous in finding no breach of the Convention. She then sought a re-hearing before the Grand Chamber. The latter found that the applicant's decision to wear the headscarf was motivated by a religion or belief (the Court did not decide whether the wearing of the scarf was a religious duty) and the University's decision to place restrictions on the wearing of the scarf was an interference with her right to manifest her religion. However, the restrictions were prescribed by law and for the legitimate aims of protecting the rights and freedoms of others and of protecting public order. The Grand Chamber found that the well-established Turkish constitutional principle of secularism was the:

116....paramount consideration underlying the ban on the wearing of religious symbols in universities. In such a context, where the values of pluralism, respect for the rights of others and, in particular, equality before the law of men and women are being taught and applied in practice, it is understandable that the relevant authorities should wish to preserve the secular nature of the institution concerned and so consider it contrary to such values to allow religious attire, including, as in the present case, the Islamic headscarf, to be worn.

117. The Court must now determine whether in the instant case there was a reasonable relationship of proportionality between the means employed and the legitimate objectives pursued by the interference.

118. Like the Chamber (see paragraph 111 of its judgment), the Grand Chamber notes at the outset that it is common ground that practising Muslim students in Turkish universities are free, within the limits imposed by educational organisational constraints, to manifest their religion in accordance with habitual forms of Muslim observance. In addition, the resolution adopted by Istanbul University on 9 July 1998 shows that various other forms of religious attire are also forbidden on the university premises [prohibiting students from wearing clothes manifesting any religion, faith, race or political/ideological persuasion].

119. It should also be noted that when the issue of whether students should be allowed to wear the Islamic headscarf surfaced at Istanbul University in 1994 in relation to the medical courses, the Vice Chancellor reminded them of the reasons for the rules on dress. Arguing that calls for permission to wear the Islamic headscarf in all parts of the university premises were misconceived and pointing to the public-order constraints applicable to medical courses, he asked the students to abide by the rules, which were consistent with both the legislation and the case-law of the higher courts.

120. Furthermore, the process whereby the regulations that led to the decision of 9 July 1998 were implemented took several years and was accompanied by a wide debate within Turkish society and the teaching profession. The two highest courts, the Supreme Administrative Court and the Constitutional Court, have managed to establish settled case-law on this issue. It is quite clear that throughout that decision-making process the university authorities sought to adapt to the evolving situation in a way that would not bar access to the university to students wearing the veil, through continued dialogue with those concerned, while at the same time ensuring that order was maintained and in particular that the requirements imposed by the nature of the course in question were complied with.

121. In that connection, the Court does not accept the applicant's submission that the fact that there were no disciplinary penalties for failing to comply with the dress code effectively meant that no rules existed. As to how compliance with the internal rules should have been secured, it is not for the Court to substitute its view for that of the university authorities. By reason of their direct and continuous contact with the education community, the university authorities are in principle better placed than an international court to evaluate local needs and conditions or the requirements of a particular course (see, *mutatis mutandis*, *Valsamis v Greece*, judgment of 18 December 1996, Reports 1996-VI, p 2325, § 32). Besides, having found that the regulations pursued a legitimate aim, it is not open to the Court to apply the criterion of proportionality in a way that would make the notion of an institution's 'internal rules' devoid of purpose. Article 9 does not always guarantee the right to behave in a manner governed by a religious belief (*Pichon and Sajous v France* (dec.), No 49853/99, ECHR 2001-X) and does not confer on people who do so the right to disregard rules that have proved to be justified (see the opinion of the Commission, § 51, contained in its report of 6 July 1995 appended to the *Valsamis* judgment cited above, p 2337).

122. In the light of the foregoing and having regard to the Contracting States' margin of appreciation in this sphere, the Court finds that the interference in issue was justified in principle and proportionate to the aim pursued.

123. Consequently, there has been no breach of Article 9 of the Convention.

Judge Tulkens dissented. She did not believe that the reasons underlying the restriction on the applicant's freedom to wear the Islamic headscarf at the University were relevant and sufficient.

10. ... While everyone agrees on the need to prevent radical Islamism, a serious objection may nevertheless be made to such reasoning. Merely wearing the headscarf cannot be associated with fundamentalism and it is vital to distinguish between those who wear the headscarf and 'extremists' who seek to impose the headscarf as they do other religious symbols. Not all women who wear the headscarf are fundamentalists and there is nothing to suggest that the applicant held fundamentalist views. She is a young adult woman and a university student and might reasonably be expected to have a heightened capacity to resist pressure, it being noted in this connection that the judgment fails to provide any concrete example of the type of pressure concerned. The applicant's personal interest in exercising the right to freedom of religion and to manifest her religion by an external symbol cannot be wholly absorbed by the public interest in fighting extremism.

...

12....The applicant, a young adult university student, said—and there is nothing to suggest that she was not telling the truth—that she wore the headscarf of her own free will. In this connection, I fail to see how the principle of sexual equality can justify prohibiting a woman from following a practice which, in the absence of proof to the contrary, she must be taken to have freely adopted. Equality and non-discrimination are subjective rights which must remain under the control of those who are entitled to benefit from them. 'Paternalism' of this sort runs counter to the case-law of the Court, which has developed a real right to personal autonomy on the basis of Article 8 (*Keenan v the United Kingdom*, judgment 3 April 2001, § 92; *Pretty v the United Kingdom*, judgment of 29 April 2002, §§ 65–7; *Christine Goodwin v the United Kingdom*, judgment of 11 July 2002, § 90). Finally, if wearing the headscarf really was contrary to the principle of the equality of men and women in any event, the State would have a positive obligation to prohibit it in all places, whether public or private.

We have also seen the successful invocation of the need to protect the constitutional principle of secularism by Turkey in **Kalac**, above, and the principle was also central to the dissolution of the party in **Refah Partisi**, see p 741.

8 The refusal of the authorities to provide a Buddhist prisoner with a vegetarian diet, as elaborated in the teaching of his faith, was found to violate this aspect of Article 9 by a unanimous Chamber in **Jakobski v Poland**, judgment of 7 December 2010.

52. According to the applicant's religion he was supposed to have a simple meat-free diet. He merely asked to be granted a vegetarian diet, excluding meat products. The Court notes that his meals did not have to be prepared, cooked and served in a prescribed manner, nor did he require any special products (see, *mutatis mutandis, D and E.S. v United Kingdom*, no. 13669/88, Commission decision of 7 March 1990, Decisions and Reports (DR) 65, p. 245; *X v United Kingdom*, no. 5947/72, Commission decision of 5 March 1976, Decisions and Reports (DR) 5, p. 8). Unlike in the latter case, he was not offered any alternative diet, nor was the Buddhist Mission consulted on the issue of the appropriate diet. The Court is not persuaded that the provision of a vegetarian diet to the applicant would have entailed any disruption to the management of the prison or to any decline in the standards of meals served to other prisoners.

53. In this respect the Court points out that the recommendation of the Committee of Ministers to the member States, namely Recommendation (Rec 92006)2) on the European Prison Rules recommend that prisoners should be provided with food that takes into account their religion. In recent judgments the Court has drawn the authorities' attention to the importance of this recommendation, notwithstanding its non-binding nature (see *Sławomir Musiał v Poland*, no. 28300/06, § 96, ECHR 2009-...(extracts)).

54. Having regard to all the foregoing factors, and despite the margin of appreciation left to the respondent State, the Court finds that the authorities failed to strike a fair balance between the interests of the prison authorities and those of the applicant, namely the right to manifest his religion through observance of the rules of the Buddhist religion.

Clearly a key factor in the Court's assessment was the limited burden involved in satisfying the applicant's religious practices.

Article 9(2)

Express limitations on the right to manifest a person's religion or belief

....

Manoussakis v Greece 1996-IV
European Court of Human Rights

The applicants were Jehovah's Witnesses living in Crete who rented a private room in a building for the purpose of holding religious and other meetings. In June 1983 they lodged, with the Minister of Education and Religious Affairs, an application for permission to use the room as a place of worship. Law No 1363/1938 provided that the construction and operation of temples (defined as any type of building open to the public for the purpose of divine worship) required the authorization of the recognized ecclesiastical authorities and the Ministry of Education and Religious Affairs. Failure to obtain authorization was made a criminal offence punishable with closure of the place of worship and imprisonment for persons operating the temple. A Royal Decree in 1939 provided that it was for the Minister of Education and Religious Affairs to determine whether there were essential reasons for granting an application. In July 1983 a local Orthodox parish church notified the police that the applicants' room was being used as an unauthorized place of worship and requested the taking of punitive action against those persons responsible for the room. During the subsequent two years the Ministry informed the applicants that it was not in a position to make a determination of their application. In 1986 the public prosecutor began criminal proceedings against the applicants under the 1938 Law. The first instance criminal court acquitted the applicants, but on appeal they were convicted and sentenced to three months' imprisonment (convertible to a fine). The applicants complained to the Commission that, *inter alia*, their rights under Article 9 had been violated. A unanimous Commission subsequently upheld the applicants' claim under this Article.

...

II. ALLEGED VIOLATION OF ARTICLE 9 OF THE CONVENTION

A. WHETHER THERE WAS AN INTERFERENCE

36. The validity of the private agreement concluded by the applicants on 30 March 1983 is not in dispute.

The applicants' conviction by the Heraklion Criminal Court sitting on appeal for having used the premises in question without the prior authorisation required under Law No 1363/1938 was therefore an interference with the exercise of their 'freedom...to manifest [their] religion..., in worship...and observance'. Such interference breaches Article 9 unless it was 'prescribed by law', pursued one or more of the legitimate aims referred to in paragraph 2 and was 'necessary in a democratic society' to attain such aim or aims.

B. JUSTIFICATION OF THE INTERFERENCE

1. 'Prescribed by law'

37. In the applicants' submission, Law No 1363/1938 and its implementing Decree of 20 May/2 June 1939 lay down a general and permanent prohibition on the establishment of a church or a place of worship of any religion—the law uses the term 'faith'—other than the orthodox religion. They maintained that this prohibition could only be lifted by a formal decision or a specific discretionary measure.

This discretionary power was, in their view, clearly derived from section 1 of Law No 1363/1938, which empowers the Government to grant or to refuse the authorisation, or to remain silent in response to an application duly submitted, without setting any limit as to time or establishing any substantive condition.

They argued that a law which made the practice of a religion subject to the prior grant of an authorisation, whose absence incurred liability to a criminal sanction, constituted an 'impediment' to that religion and could not be regarded as a law designed to protect freedom of religion within the meaning of Article 13 of the Constitution. As regards freedom of religion and worship, the Constitution purported to be more, or at least not less, protective than the Convention because the only grounds on which it permitted restrictions to be placed on the practice of any 'known religion' were 'public order' and 'public morals'.

In addition, the applicants pointed to the unusual character, as regards Greek public and administrative law, of the procedure established by Law No 1363/1938 for the construction or the operation of a place of worship. It was the only procedure in respect of which provision was made for the intervention of two authorities, administrative and religious. They criticised the manner in which the Supreme Administrative Court interpreted this Law, namely in the context of the restrictions, suggestions and directives of the Constitution, and the importance attached by that court to compliance with the conditions laid down by Royal Decree of 20 May/2 June 1939 for submitting in due form applications for authorisation together with all that those conditions entailed in terms of inquisitorial process and the difficulty in obtaining such authorisation. The wording of this decree conferred a number of different discretionary powers, each of which was sufficient basis for a negative response to the application.

38. The Court notes that the applicants' complaint is directed less against the treatment of which they themselves had been the victims than the general policy of obstruction pursued in relation to Jehovah's Witnesses when they wished to set up a church or a place of worship. They are therefore in substance challenging the provisions of the relevant domestic law.

However, the Court does not consider it necessary to rule on the question whether the interference in issue was 'prescribed by law' in this instance because, in any event, it was incompatible with Article 9 of the Convention on other grounds.

2. Legitimate aim

39. According to the Government, the penalty imposed on the applicants served to protect public order and the rights and freedoms of others. In the first place, although the notion of public order had features that were common to the democratic societies in Europe, its substance varied on account of national characteristics. In Greece virtually the entire population was of the Christian Orthodox faith, which was closely associated with important moments in the history of the Greek nation. The Orthodox Church had kept alive the national conscience and Greek patriotism during the periods of foreign occupation. Secondly, various sects sought to manifest their ideas and doctrines using all sorts of 'unlawful and dishonest' means. The intervention of the State to regulate this area with a view to protecting those whose rights and freedoms were affected by the activities of socially dangerous sects was indispensable to maintain public order on Greek territory.

40. Like the applicants, the Court recognises that the States are entitled to verify whether a movement or association carries on, ostensibly in pursuit of religious aims, the activities which are harmful to the population. Nevertheless, it recalls that Jehovah's Witnesses come within the definition of 'known religion' as provided for under Greek law. (See *Kokkinakis v Greece*.) This was moreover conceded by the Government.

However, having regard to the circumstances of the case and taking the same view as the Commission, the Court considers that the impugned measure pursued a legitimate aim for the purposes of Article 9(2) of the Convention, namely the protection of public order.

3. 'Necessary in a democratic society'

41. The main thrust of the applicants' complaint is that the restrictions imposed on Jehovah's Witnesses by the Greek Government effectively prevent them from exercising their right to freedom of religion. In terms of the legislation and administrative practice, their religion did not, so they claimed, enjoy in Greece the safeguards guaranteed to it in all the other Member States of the Council of Europe. The 'pluralism, tolerance and broadmindedness without which there is no democratic society' was therefore seriously jeopardised in Greece.

They contended that the Jehovah's Witnesses' movement should be presumed—even if the presumption was a rebuttable one—to respect certain moral rules and not in itself to prejudice public order. Its doctrines and its rites abided by and extolled social order and individual morality. Accordingly, the political authorities should intervene only in the event of abuse or perversion of such doctrines and rites, and should do so punitively rather than preventively.

More particularly, their conviction had been persecutory, unjustified and not necessary in a democratic society as it had been 'manufactured' by the State. The State had compelled the applicants to commit an offence and to bear the consequences solely because of their religious beliefs. The apparently innocent requirement of an authorisation to operate a place of worship had been transformed from a mere formality into a lethal weapon against the right to freedom of religion. The term 'dilatory' used by the Commission to describe the conduct of the Minister of Education and Religious Affairs in relation to their application for an authorisation was euphemistic.

The struggle for survival by certain religious communities outside the Eastern Orthodox Church, and specifically by Jehovah's Witnesses, was carried on in a climate of interference and oppression by the State and the dominant church as a result of which Article 9 of the Convention had become a dead letter. The Article was the object of frequent and blatant violations aimed at eliminating freedom of religion. The applicants cited current practice in Greece in support of their contentions, giving numerous examples. They requested the Court to examine their complaints in the context of these other cases.

42. According to the Government, in order to resolve the question of the necessity of the applicants' conviction, the Court should first examine the necessity of the requirement of prior authorisation, which owed its existence to historical considerations. In their view, the former presupposed the latter. The applicants' true aim was not to complain about their conviction but to fight for the abolition of that requirement.

There were essential public order grounds to justify making the setting up of a place of worship subject to approval by the State. In Greece this control applied to all faiths; otherwise it would be both unconstitutional and contrary to the Convention. Jehovah's Witnesses were not exempt from the requirements of legislation which concerned the whole population. The setting up of a church or a place of worship in Greece was, so the Government affirmed, often used as a means of proselytism, in particular by Jehovah's Witnesses who engaged in intensive proselytism, thereby infringing the law that the Court had itself found to be in conformity with the Convention. (See *Kokkinakis v Greece*.)

The sanction imposed on the applicants had been light and had been motivated not by the manifestation by them of their religion but by their disobedience to the law and their failure to comply with an administrative procedure. It was the result of the applicants' culpable neglect to have recourse to the remedy available under the Greek legal system.

Finally, the Government referred to the fact that various States parties to the Convention had legislation containing restrictions similar to those enacted in Greece in this field.

43. The Commission considered that the authorisation requirement introduced by Law No 1363/1938 might appear open to criticism. In the first place, the intervention of the Greek Orthodox Church in the procedure raised a complex question under paragraph 2 of Article 9. Secondly, classifying as a criminal offence the operation of a place of worship without the authorities' prior authorisation was disproportionate to the legitimate aim pursued, especially when, as in this case, the underlying cause of the applicants' conviction lay in the dilatory attitude of the relevant authorities.

44. As a matter of case law, the Court has consistently left the Contracting States a certain margin of appreciation in assessing the existence and extent of the necessity of an interference, but this margin is subject to European supervision, embracing both the legislation and the decisions applying it. The Court's task is to determine whether the measures taken at national level were justified in principle and proportionate.

In delimiting the extent of the margin of appreciation in the present case the Court must have regard to what is at stake, namely the need to secure true religious pluralism, an inherent feature of the notion of a democratic society. Further, considerable weight has to be attached to that need when it comes to determining, pursuant to paragraph 2 of Article 9, whether the restriction was proportionate to the legitimate aim pursued. The restrictions imposed on the freedom to manifest religion by the provisions of Law No 1363/1938 and of the Decree of 20 May/2 June 1939 call for very strict scrutiny by the Court.

45. The Court notes in the first place that Law No 1363/1938 and the Decree of 20 May/2 June 1939—which concerns churches and places of worship that are not part of the Greek Orthodox Church—allow far-reaching interferences by the political, administrative and ecclesiastical authorities with the exercise of religious freedom. In addition to the numerous formal conditions prescribed in section 1(1) and (3) of the decree, some of which confer a very wide discretion on the police, mayor or chairman of the district council, there exists in practice the possibility for the Minister of Education and Religious Affairs to defer his reply indefinitely—the decree does not lay down any time-limit—or to refuse his authorisation without explanation or without giving a valid reason. In this respect, the Court observes that the decree empowers the Minister—in particular when determining whether the number of those requesting an authorisation corresponds to that mentioned in the decree—to assess whether there is a 'real need' for the religious community in question to set up a church. This criterion may in itself constitute grounds for refusal, without reference to the conditions laid down in Article 13(2) of the Constitution.

46. The Government maintained that the power of the Minister of Education and Religious Affairs to grant or refuse the authorisation requested was not discretionary. He was under a duty to grant the authorisation if he found that the three conditions set down in Article 13(2) of the Constitution were satisfied, namely that it must be in respect of a known religion, that there must be no risk of prejudicing public order or public morals and that there is no danger of proselytism.

47. The Court observes that, in reviewing the lawfulness of refusals to grant the authorisation, the Supreme Administrative Court has developed case law limiting the Minister's power in this matter and according the local ecclesiastical authority a purely consultative role.

The right to freedom of religion as guaranteed under the Convention excludes any discretion on the part of the State to determine whether religious beliefs or the means used to express such beliefs are legitimate. Accordingly, the Court takes the view that the authorisation requirement under Law No 1363/1938 and the Decree of 20 May/2 June 1939 is consistent with Article 9 of the

Convention only in so far as it is intended to allow the Minister to verify whether the formal conditions laid down in those enactments are satisfied.

48. It appears from the evidence and from the numerous other cases cited by the applicants and not contested by the Government that the State has tended to use the possibilities afforded by the above-mentioned provisions to impose rigid, or indeed prohibitive, conditions on practice of religious beliefs by certain non-orthodox movements, in particular Jehovah's Witnesses. Admittedly the Supreme Administrative Court quashes for lack of reasons any unjustified refusal to grant an authorisation, but the extensive case law in this field seems to show a clear tendency on the part of the administrative and ecclesiastical authorities to use these provisions to restrict the activities of faiths outside the Orthodox church.

49. In the instant case the applicants were prosecuted and convicted for having operated a place of worship without first obtaining the authorisations required by law.

50. In their memorial the Government maintained that under section 1(1) of the Decree of 20 May/2 June 1939 an authorisation from the local bishop was necessary only for the construction and operation of a church and not for a place of worship as in the present case. An application to the Minister of Education and Religious Affairs, indeed one such as that submitted by the applicants, was sufficient.

51. The Court notes, nevertheless, that both the Heraklion public prosecutor's office, when it was bringing proceedings against the applicants, and the Heraklion Criminal Court sitting on appeal, in its judgment of 15 February 1990, relied expressly on the lack of the bishop's authorisation as well as the lack of an authorisation from the Minister of Education and Religious Affairs. The latter, in response to five requests made by the applicants between 25 October 1983 and 10 December 1984, replied that he was examining their file. To date, as far as the Court is aware, the applicants have not received an express decision. Moreover, at the hearing a representative of the Government himself described the Minister's conduct as unfair and attributed it to the difficulty that the latter might have had in giving legally valid reasons for an express decision refusing the authorisation or to his fear that he might provide the applicants with grounds for appealing to the Supreme Administrative Court to challenge an express administrative decision.

52. In these circumstances the Court considers that the Government cannot rely on the applicants' failure to comply with a legal formality to justify their conviction. The degree of severity of the sanction is immaterial.

53. Like the Commission, the Court is of the opinion that the impugned conviction had such a direct effect on the applicants' freedom of religion that it cannot be regarded as proportionate to the legitimate aim pursued, nor, accordingly, as necessary in a democratic society.

In conclusion, there has been a violation of Article 9.

...

FOR THESE REASONS, THE COURT UNANIMOUSLY

...

Holds that there has been a breach of Article 9 of the Convention;

...

NOTES

1 The Court was composed of President Bernhardt and Judges: Macdonald, Valticos, Martens, Loizou, Freeland, Wildhaber, Gotchev, and Kuris. Martens J issued a separate concurring opinion in which he expressed the view that Law No 1363/1938 was in breach of

Article 9 for containing too many discretionary elements (such as the 'advisory' role of the established clerical authorities) to satisfy the Convention's 'prescribed by law' requirements (for an examination of these in the context of Article 8, see p 590).

2 The above judgment makes clear that States may operate a prior registration/approval scheme for places of worship. However, the Court will closely examine whether the application of a national scheme to a particular group of worshippers complies with the conditions laid down in Article 9(2).

3 In *Pentidis v Greece*, 1997-III, the applicants, who were Jehovah's Witnesses, had been convicted under Law No 1363/1938 for establishing a place of worship (a rented room) without authorization by the competent authorities. The Commission found a breach of Article 9. Before the Court, the applicants stated that they had applied, in February 1997, to the Minister for permission to operate their place of worship. By early May 1997 the Minister had granted them permission and they requested the Court to strike out their case. The Court agreed to their request.

4 In *Martins Casimiro and Cerveira Ferreira v Luxembourg*, decision of 27 April 1999, the applicants and their son, F, were Seventh-day Adventists (this religious group believed Saturday should be a day of total rest). They sought permission from the domestic courts for their son to be exempted from the legal duty of attending school on Saturdays. When their request was refused the applicants complained to the Court alleging a breach of their right freely to manifest their religion. The Court declared their application inadmissible because:

The dispensation requested by the applicants would have had the effect of excluding the child from the normal school timetable as Saturday was one of the days of the school week. The court of first instance had stated that dispensation of that sort would have infringed the rights of the other pupils, too, as it was potentially disruptive of the school system. States had a duty to ensure that children were able to exercise their right to education. Furthermore, where the parents' right to respect for their religious convictions, rather than enhancing the child's right to education, came into conflict with it, the interests of the child prevailed. Under the circumstances, the Court held that the statutory provision that precluded the applicants from being granted general dispensation from the obligation to ensure that their son, a minor, attended school on Saturdays was justified for the protection of the rights and freedoms of others, notably the right to education...

12 ARTICLE 10 FREEDOM OF EXPRESSION

There is an extensive body of jurisprudence concerning Article 10 in which the Court has distinguished between three categories of expression. The most protected class of expression has been political expression as the Court considers that such expression is essential for the creation and effective operation of pluralistic democracies, which are necessary to ensure respect for fundamental human rights (*Lingens*). Political expression has been continually expanded to encompass, *inter alia*, media comment on political figures (*Oberschlick v Austria No 2*), criticism of the government and its institutions (*Castells*), political advertising (*TV Vest*), and wider matters of public interest such as the freedom of academic opinion (*Boldea*). Artistic expression ranges from paintings (*Muller*) to poetry (*Karata*). Generally, the Court has granted States a wide margin of appreciation to restrict forms of artistic expression that national authorities consider obscene (*Muller*) or blasphemous (*Otto Preminger Institute*). But in recent judgments there are indications that the Court is becoming more willing to subject domestic interferences to greater scrutiny where they involve satirical works of art having a social commentary (*Vereinigung Bildener Kunstler*) or established pieces of literature (*Akdas*). The final category of expression involves matters of commercial interest, including advertising by companies (*Krone Verlag*).

The constant evolution of media technology has presented the Court with new contexts in which to apply this Article, from the emergence of satellite broadcasting in the early 1990s (*Autronic*) to the creation of internet archives (*Times Newspapers Ltd (Nos 1 and 2)*).

The Court has also slowly begun to develop a positive obligations aspect to States' duties under Article 10 (for example to secure impartial and accurate coverage of political affairs in the audio-visual media (*Manole*)).

The Court's general approach

Handyside v UK A.24 (1976)
European Court of Human Rights

The applicant was a publisher who secured the British rights to a book called *The Little Red Schoolbook* which was originally written and published in Denmark. After translations it had also been published by others in a number of member States including Belgium, France, Germany, Greece, Italy, and Sweden. The applicant arranged an English translation and then prepared an edition for the UK with the help of various children and teachers. This was to be a reference book of 208 pages and costing 30p. It included chapters on, *inter alia*,

'Education', 'Teachers', and 'Pupils'; the latter chapter contained 26 pages of information on matters concerning sex (topics included abortion, homosexuality, intercourse, and masturbation). After printing, the applicant sent out several hundred review copies and placed a number of advertisements in the specialist educational/publishing press. Subsequently, the book was subject to widespread comment, both favourable and critical, in popular newspapers. A number of complaints were made to the Director of Public Prosecutions about the book and he asked the Metropolitan Police to investigate the matter. They obtained a search warrant, granted by the judicial authorities under the Obscene Publications Act 1959, authorizing a search of the applicant's business premises. A number of copies of the book were seized during the search. Soon afterwards the applicant was charged with having in his possession several hundred copies of an obscene publication (*The Schoolbook*) for gain; contrary to the 1959 Act. The Magistrates' Court found him guilty and fined him £50 and made a forfeiture order for the destruction of the books that had been seized. The applicant appealed to the Inner London Quarter Sessions, but that court upheld the magistrates' decisions and the books were destroyed. Several thousand copies of the book had been sold throughout the UK before the applicant had been prosecuted. No proceedings were brought in Northern Ireland, the Channel Islands, or the Isle of Man, but unsuccessful prosecutions were brought in Scotland. Later the applicant published a revised edition of the book taking account of the prosecution's criticisms of the original text; no legal action was taken against the amended version. The applicant complained to the Commission alleging a breach of a number of his Convention rights, including his right to freedom of expression under Article 10. By a majority (8 votes to 5, with 1 abstention) the Commission found no violation of Article 10.

I. ON THE ALLEGED VIOLATION OF ARTICLE 10 OF THE CONVENTION

...

43. The various measures challenged—the applicant's criminal conviction, the seizure and subsequent forfeiture and destruction of the matrix and of hundreds of copies of the *Schoolbook*—were without any doubt, and the Government did not deny it, 'interferences by public authority' in the exercise of his freedom of expression which is guaranteed by paragraph I of the text cited above. Such interferences entail a 'violation' of Article 10 if they do not fall within one of the exceptions provided for in paragraph 2, which is accordingly of decisive importance in this case.

44. If the 'restrictions' and 'penalties' complained of by Mr Handyside are not to infringe Article 10, they must, according to paragraph 2, in the first place have been 'prescribed by law'. The Court finds that this was the case. In the United Kingdom legal system, the basis in law for the measures in question was the 1959/1964 Acts . . . Besides, this was not contested by the applicant who further admitted that the competent authorities had correctly applied those Acts.

45. Having thus ascertained that the interferences complained of satisfied the first of the conditions in paragraph 2 of Article 10, the Court then investigated whether they also complied with the others. According to the Government and the majority of the Commission, the interferences were 'necessary in a democratic society', 'for the protection of . . . morals'.

46. Sharing the view of the Government and the unanimous opinion of the Commission, the Court first finds that the 1959/1964 Acts have an aim that is legitimate under Article 10 § 2, namely, the protection of morals in a democratic society . . .

47. The Court must also investigate whether the protection of morals in a democratic society necessitated the various measures taken against the applicant and the *Schoolbook* under the 1959/1964 Acts. . . .

The Commission's report and the subsequent hearings before the Court in June 1976 brought to light clear-cut differences of opinion on a crucial problem, namely, how to determine whether the actual 'restrictions' and 'penalties' complained of by the applicant were 'necessary in a democratic society', 'for the protection of morals'. According to the Government and the majority of the Commission, the Court has only to ensure that the English courts acted reasonably, in good faith and within the limits of the margin of appreciation left to the Contracting States by Article 10 § 2. On the other hand the minority of the Commission sees the Court's task as being not to review the Inner London Quarter Sessions judgment but to examine the *Schoolbook* directly in the light of the Convention and of nothing but the Convention.

48. The Court points out that the machinery of protection established by the Convention is subsidiary to the national systems safeguarding human rights (judgment of 23 July 1968 on the merits of the *'Belgian Linguistic'* case, Series A No 6, p 35, § 10 *in fine*). The Convention leaves to each Contracting State, in the first place, the task of securing the rights and freedoms it enshrines. The institutions created by it make 'their own contribution to this task but they become involved only through contentious proceedings and once all domestic remedies have been exhausted' (Article 26).

These observations apply, notably, to Article 10 § 2. In particular, it is not possible to find in the domestic law of the various Contracting States a uniform European conception of morals. The view taken by their respective laws of the requirements of morals varies from time to time and from place to place, especially in our era which is characterised by a rapid and far-reaching evolution of opinions on the subject. By reason of their direct and continuous contact with the vital forces of their countries. State authorities are in principle in a better position than the international judge to give an opinion on the exact content of these requirements as well as on the 'necessity' of a 'restriction' or 'penalty' intended to meet them. The Court notes at this juncture that, whilst the adjective 'necessary', within the meaning of Article 10 § 2, is not synonymous with 'indispensable' (cf, in Articles 2 § 2 and 6 § 1, the words 'absolutely necessary' and 'strictly necessary' and, in Article 15 § 1, the phrase 'to the extent strictly required by the exigencies of the situation'), neither has it the flexibility of such expressions as 'admissible', 'ordinary' (cf Article 4 § 3), 'useful' (cf the French text of the first paragraph of Article 1 of Protocol No 1), 'reasonable' (cf Articles 5 § 3 and 6 § 1) or 'desirable'. Nevertheless, it is for the national authorities to make the initial assessment of the reality of the pressing social need implied by the notion of 'necessity' in this context.

Consequently, Article 10 § 2 leaves to the Contracting States a margin of appreciation. This margin is given both to the domestic legislator ('prescribed by law') and to the bodies, judicial amongst others, that are called upon to interpret and apply the laws in force (*Engel and Others* judgment of 8 June 1976, Series A No 22, pp 41–2, § 100; cf, for Article 8 § 2, *De Wilde, Ooms and Versyp* judgment of 18 June 1971, Series A No 12, pp 45–6, § 93, and the *Golder* judgment of 21 February 1975, Series A No 18, pp 21–2, § 45).

49. Nevertheless, Article 10 § 2 does not give the Contracting States an unlimited power of appreciation. The Court, which, with the Commission, is responsible for ensuring the observance of those States engagements (Article 19), is empowered to give the final ruling on whether a 'restriction' or 'penalty' is reconcilable with freedom of expression as protected by Article 10. The domestic margin of appreciation thus goes hand in hand with a European supervision. Such supervision concerns both the aim of the measure challenged and its 'necessity'; it covers not only the basic legislation but also the decision applying it, even one given by an independent court. In this respect, the Court refers to Article 50 of the Convention ('decision or . . . measure taken by a legal authority or any other authority') as well as to its own case-law (*Engel and Others* judgment of 8 June 1976, Series A No 22, pp 41–2, § 100).

The Court's supervisory functions oblige it to pay the utmost attention to the principles characterising a 'democratic society'. Freedom of expression constitutes one of the essential foundations of such a society, one of the basic conditions for its progress and for the development of every man. Subject to paragraph 2 of Article 10, it is applicable not only to 'information' or 'ideas' that are favourably received or regarded as inoffensive or as a matter of indifference, but also to those that offend, shock or disturb the State or any sector of the population. Such are the demands of that pluralism, tolerance and broadmindedness without which there is no 'democratic society'. This means, amongst other things, that every 'formality', 'condition', 'restriction' or 'penalty' imposed in this sphere must be proportionate to the legitimate aim pursued.

From another standpoint, whoever exercises his freedom of expression undertakes 'duties and responsibilities' the scope of which depends on his situation and the technical means he uses. The Court cannot overlook such a person's 'duties' and 'responsibilities' when it enquires, as in this case, whether 'restrictions' or 'penalties' were conducive to the 'protection of morals' which made them 'necessary' in a 'democratic society'.

50. It follows from this that it is in no way the Court's task to take the place of the competent national courts but rather to review under Article 10 the decisions they delivered in the exercise of their power of appreciation.

However, the Court's supervision would generally prove illusory if it did no more than examine these decisions in isolation; it must view them in the light of the case as a whole, including the publication in question and the arguments and evidence adduced by the applicant in the domestic legal system and then at the international level. The Court must decide, on the basis of the different data available to it, whether the reasons given by the national authorities to justify the actual measures of 'interference' they take are relevant and sufficient under Article 10 § 2 (cf, for Article 5 § 3, the *Wemhoff* judgment of 27 June 1968, Series A No 7, pp 24–5, § 12, the *Neumeister* judgment of 27 June 1968, Series A No 8, p 37, § 5, the *Stögmüller* judgment of 10 November 1969, Series A No; 9, p 39, § 3, the *Mattznetter* judgment of 10 November 1969, Series A No 10, p 31, § 3, and the *Ringeisen* judgment of 16 July 1971, Series A No 13, p 42, § 104.

51. Following the method set out above, the Court scrutinized under Article 10 § 2 the individual decisions complained of, in particular, the judgment of the Inner London Quarter Sessions. . . .

52. The Court attaches particular importance to a factor to which the judgment of 29 October 1971 did not fail to draw attention, that is, the intended readership of the *Schoolbook*. It was aimed above all at children and adolescents aged from twelve to eighteen. Being direct, factual and reduced to essentials in style, it was easily within the comprehension of even the youngest of such readers. The applicant had made it clear that he planned a wide-spread circulation. . . .

Basically the book contained purely factual information that was generally correct and often useful, as the Quarter Sessions recognised. However, it also included, above all in the section on sex and in the passage headed 'Be yourself' in the chapter on pupils . . . sentences or paragraphs that young people at a critical stage of their development could have interpreted as an encouragement to indulge in precocious activities harmful for them or even to commit certain criminal offences. In these circumstances, despite the variety and the constant evolution in the United Kingdom of views on ethics and education, the competent English judges were entitled, in the exercise of their discretion, to think at the relevant time that the *Schoolbook* would have pernicious effects on the morals of many of the children and adolescents who would read it.

However, the applicant maintained, in substance, that the demands of the 'protection of morals' or, to use the wording of the 1959/1964 Acts, of the war against publications likely to 'deprave and corrupt', were but a pretext in his case. The truth of the matter, he alleged, was that an attempt had been made to muzzle a small-scale publisher whose political leanings met with the disapproval of a fragment of public opinion. Proceedings were set in motion, said he, in an atmosphere little short of 'hysteria', stirred up and kept alive by ultra-conservative elements. . . .

For its part the Court finds that the anti-authoritarian aspects of the *Schoolbook* as such were not held in the judgment of 29 October 1971 to fall foul of the 1959/1964 Acts. Those aspects were taken into account only insofar as the appeal court considered that, by undermining the moderating influence of parents, teachers, the Churches and youth organisations, they aggravated the tendency to 'deprave and corrupt' which in its opinion resulted from other parts of the work. It should be added that the revised edition was allowed to circulate freely by the British authorities despite the fact that the anti-authoritarian passages again appeared there in full and even, in some cases, in stronger terms.

As the Government noted, this is hard to reconcile with the theory of a political intrigue.

The Court thus allows that the fundamental aim of the judgment of 29 October 1971, applying the 1959/1964 Acts, was the protection of the morals of the young, a legitimate purpose under Article 10 § 2. Consequently the seizures effected on 31 March and 1 April 1971, pending the outcome of the proceedings that were about to open, also had this aim.

53. It remains to examine the 'necessity' of the measures in dispute, beginning with the said seizures. . . .

54. A series of arguments which merit reflection was advanced by the applicant and the minority of the Commission concerning the 'necessity' of the sentence and the forfeiture at issue.

Firstly, they drew attention to the fact that the original edition of the *Schoolbook* was the object of no proceedings in Northern Ireland, the Isle of Man and the Channel Islands and of no conviction in Scotland and that, even in England and Wales, thousands of copies circulated without impediment despite the judgment of 29 October 1971. . . . The competent authorities in Northern Ireland, the Isle of Man and the Channel Islands may, in the light of local conditions, have had plausible reasons for not taking action against the book and its publisher. . . . Their failure to act—into which the Court does not have to enquire and which did not prevent the measures taken in England from leading to revision of the *Schoolbook*—does not prove that the judgment of 29 October 1971 was not a response to a real necessity, bearing in mind the national authorities' margin of appreciation.

These remarks also apply, *mutatis mutandis*, to the circulation of many copies in England and Wales.

. . .

57. The applicant and the minority of the Commission laid stress on the further point that, in addition to the original Danish edition, translations of the '*Little Book*' appeared and circulated freely in the majority of the member States of the Council of Europe.

Here again, the national margin of appreciation and the optional nature of the 'restrictions' and 'penalties' referred to in Article 10 § 2 prevent the Court from accepting the argument. The Contracting States have each fashioned their approach in the light of the situation obtaining in their respective territories; they have had regard, *inter alia*, to the different views prevailing there about the demands of the protection of morals in a democratic society. The fact that most of them decided to allow the work to be distributed does not mean that the contrary decision of the Inner London Quarter Sessions was a breach of Article 10. Besides, some of the editions published outside the United Kingdom do not include the passages, or at least not all the passages, cited in the judgment of 29 October 1971 as striking examples of a tendency to 'deprave and corrupt'.

. . .

59. On the strength of the data before it, the Court thus reaches the conclusion that no breach of the requirements of Article 10 has been established in the circumstances of the present case.

. . .

FOR THESE REASONS, THE COURT

Holds by thirteen votes to one that there has been no breach of Article 10 of the Convention;

. . .

NOTES

1 The Court was composed of President Balladore Pallieri and Judges: Zekia, Wiarda, Pedersen, Thor Vilhjalmsson, Petren, Ryssdal, Bozer, Ganshof van der Meersch, Fitzmaurice, Bindschedler-Robert, Evrignis, and Delvaux. Judge Mosler dissented on the ground that he had a different conception of the meaning to be given to the term 'necessary' in Article 10(2). For him this expression meant that the measures taken by the national authorities had to be 'appropriate for achieving the [legitimate] aim' under Article 10(2). He did not believe that the English measures were appropriate to achieve their aim of protecting schoolchildren from gaining access to the book as (a) many copies had already been distributed before the prosecution of Handyside and (b) he could not understand why legal action against the publication of the book had not been taken in other parts of the UK if the authorities considered that it presented such a danger to the moral welfare of youngsters.

2 The majority's elaboration of the concept of 'necessary in a democratic society' as involving the existence of a 'pressing social need' has been accepted in subsequent cases as the authoritative interpretation.

3 When studying the cases involving Article 10 do you think that the Court's judgments exhibit the values of 'pluralism, tolerance and broadmindedness' when confronted with those who express views that 'offend, shock or disturb the State or any sector of the population'?

4 The Court has ruled that in certain circumstances Article 10, as with a number of other substantive rights enshrined in the Convention, imposes positive obligations upon member States. In *Ozgur Gundem v Turkey*, judgment of 16 March 2000, the applicant newspaper was represented by its editor and owners. The paper had been published between 1992 and 1994. During that time the paper alleged that it had been subject to serious attacks and harassment, for which the Turkish authorities were directly or indirectly responsible, and that despite repeated requests the Government had done little to protect the paper and its staff. It was not disputed that seven persons connected with the paper (including journalists) had been killed by 'unknown perpetrators', armed attacks on newsagents selling the paper had occurred, and two bombs had exploded at offices of the paper. The paper argued, *inter alia*, that the State's failure to protect the paper and its personnel violated Article 10. In a unanimous judgment:

> The Court recalls the key importance of freedom of expression as one of the preconditions for a functioning democracy. Genuine, effective exercise of this freedom does not depend merely on the State's duty not to interfere, but may require positive measures of protection, even in the sphere of relations between individuals (*mutatis mutandis*, the *X and Y v The Netherlands*, A.91 (1985)). In determining whether or not a positive obligation exists, regard must be had to the fair balance that has to be struck between the general interest of the community and the interests of the individual, the search for which is called for throughout the Convention. The scope of this obligation will inevitably vary, having regard to the diversity of situations obtaining in Contracting States, the difficulties involved in policing modern societies and the choices which must be made in terms of priorities and resources. Nor must such an obligation be interpreted in such a way as to impose an impossible or disproportionate burden on the authorities (see, *Rees v UK*, A.106 (1986) and *Osman v UK*, Reports 1998-VIII).
>
> In the present case, the authorities were aware that Ozgur Gundem, and persons associated with it, had been subject to a series of violent acts and that the applicants feared that they were being targeted deliberately in efforts to prevent publication and distribution of the newspaper. No

response however was given to almost all petitions and requests for protection submitted by the newspaper or its staff. The Government have only been able to identify one protective measure concerning the distribution of the newspaper which was taken while the newspaper was still in existence....

The Court has noted the Government's submissions concerning its strongly-held conviction that Ozgur Gundem and its staff supported the PKK and acted as its propaganda tool. This does not, even if true, provide a justification for failing to take steps effectively to investigate and, where necessary, provide protection against unlawful acts involving violence.

The Court concludes that the Government have failed, in the circumstances, to comply with their positive obligation to protect Ozgur Gundem in the exercise of its freedom of expression. [Paras 43–6.]

In another later Turkish case a unanimous Chamber found a breach of the positive obligation to protect the freedom of expression of a journalist who was murdered, by extreme nationalists, after he published controversial articles reflecting on the identity of Turkish citizens with Armenian ancestry: *Dink v Turkey*, judgment of 14 September 2010.

A large majority (11 votes to 7) of a Grand Chamber determined that Switzerland had failed to comply with its positive obligation to protect political expression in *Verein Gegen Tierfabriken Schweiz (VgT) v Switzerland (no 2)*, judgment of 30 June 2009. This was a second complaint, see p 663 for the original case, by a campaigning association that the Swiss authorities had (again) refused to permit the broadcasting of the association's television advertisement criticizing the intensive rearing of pigs. Taking account of the importance of expression concerning topics of public interest, the Court's earlier judgment upholding a breach of Article 10 and the formalistic rejection of the Association's subsequent litigation by the Swiss Federal Court, the Grand Chamber ruled that (another) violation of Article 10 had occurred. The fact that the Association had to bring a second complaint to Strasbourg disclosed serious weaknesses in the execution of the first judgment.

A government's extensive interference with the main national television channel's coverage of political and public interest topics breached the State's positive obligation to safeguard impartial coverage of these matters according to the united Chamber in *Manole and others v Moldova*, judgment of 17 September 2009.

107....a positive obligation arises under Article 10. The State, as the ultimate guarantor of pluralism, must ensure, through its law and practice, that the public has access through television and radio to impartial and accurate information and a range of opinion and comment, reflecting *inter alia* the diversity of political outlook within the country and that journalists and other professionals working in the audiovisual media are not prevented from imparting this information and comment.

As the communist government had ordered that two-thirds of news coverage should be of pro-government reports, opposition politicians and critics of the government were banned from appearing on television and only selected television reporters were allowed to interview members of the government, the Chamber ruled that Article 10 had been violated. The government's abuse of its power over the mass media was met with an affirmation of an overriding positive obligation under this Article.

The margin of appreciation

Another important aspect of the Court's judgment in *Handyside* is its articulation of the idea of the 'margin of appreciation'. This variable discretion is granted to national authorities by the Court when it examines whether a State has violated an applicant's Convention rights under Articles 8–11. It has also been applied, less frequently, in cases involving other rights including, Article 5 (*Winterwerp v Netherlands* A.33 (1979)), Article 1 of the First Protocol (*James v UK* A.98 (1986)), and Article 3 of the First Protocol (*Mathieu-Mohin and Clerfayt v Belgium* A.113 (1987)). The creation and use of this concept by the Court has been controversial with different judges taking opposing stances on the concept (e.g. see below the majority and dissenting judgments in *The Sunday Times v UK*) and academic writers supporting or criticizing the doctrine.

1   In a major study examining the Court's utilization of the concept across the range of Convention rights Howard Yourow describes the construct in the following terms:

> ...the margin doctrine is a technique for weighing and balancing claims and state defenses, especially in the determination of necessity for state action under the Article 8–11 limitation clauses. It is a method of determining aberrant state action, in conjunction with the consensus standard. It is also a more formal standard for the determination of deference to state discretion in several different but interrelated categories within the vertical division of power between Strasbourg and the State Parties: deference to the will of the democratic legislature, to state executive and judicial fact-finding in the individual cases, to state interpretation of the Convention, and to choice of means in carrying out responsibility for enforcement under the subsidiarity principle. [H. C. Yourow, *The Margin of Appreciation Doctrine in the Dynamics of European Human Rights Jurisprudence* (Dordrecht: Martinus Nijhoff, 1996), pp 195–6.]

2   During an early analysis of the case-law Thomas O'Donnell explained that the phrase 'the margin of appreciation' was a translation of the French concept of *marge d'appreciation*, which was a method of judicial review devised by the Conseil d'Etat. He deduced three standards used by the European Court of Human Rights when applying the doctrine to Convention rights. First, the consensus standard where the existence of a common practice among member States (e.g. regarding the legal status of illegitimate children as in the *Marckx* case (p 528)) led the Court to adopt a narrow margin of appreciation when judging the legality of respondent States' conduct. Secondly, the protection of fundamental rights whereby the Court categorized specific rights as essential for the maintenance of a democratic political system (e.g. freedom of the press in *The Sunday Times* case (below)) with the consequence that the Court accorded States a narrow margin of appreciation to interfere with these basic liberties. Thirdly, the use of textual analysis of the relevant Convention provisions to determine the breadth of the margin in different cases (e.g. the terms of Article 10(2) encouraged a wide discretion being accorded to the British authorities in *Handyside* (above)). He was generally supportive of the device:

> The margin of appreciation doctrine is an important and probably enduring concept in the jurisprudence of the Court....The margin of appreciation continues to allow governments some flexibility in meeting their obligations. But it also allows the Court some flexibility. Subject to the Court's establishment of clear and principled standards for its use, the doctrine of margin of appreciation can become the necessary jurisprudential grease in the enforcement mechanisms provided by the Convention. [T. A. O'Donnell, 'The Margin of Appreciation Doctrine: Standards in the Jurisprudence of the European Court of Human Rights' (1982) 4 *Human Rights Quarterly* 474 at 496.]

3   A similar view of the significance of the doctrine as a mechanism for demarcating the roles of national governments and the Strasbourg institutions regarding the protection of fundamental liberties was expounded by a former President of the Commission and the Court.

…many of the rights and freedoms are defined in the Convention in too general terms to be fully 'self-executing', while the evolution of social and moral concepts may add a further element of uncertainty as to the scope or implications of those rights and freedoms. The so-called 'supervisory function', therefore, has in it a creative, legislative element comparable to that of the judiciary in common law countries; so that in certain cases its exercise might strain the enthusiasm of the Member States for the Convention. The doctrine of the 'margin of appreciation', as I see it, is one of the more important safeguards developed by the Commission and the Court to reconcile the effective operation of the Convention with the sovereign powers and responsibilities of governments in a democracy. With the doctrine, moreover, goes the principle applied by the Commission and the Court in certain cases that a balance must be sought between the exercise by the individual of the right guaranteed to him and the protection of the public interest. A striking example is the *Klass* case where, in appreciating whether the surveillance of certain individuals was a legitimate interference with their freedom of correspondence under Article 8, the Court took judicial notice of the evolution in democratic societies of concepts regarding the treatment of terrorism in Europe. [Sir Humphrey Waldock, 'The Effectiveness of the System set up by the European Convention on Human Rights' (1980) 1 *Human Rights Law Journal* 1 at 9.]

Professor J. G. Merrills also echoes this positive view of the concept:

…the margin of appreciation is a way of recognising that the international protection of human rights and sovereign freedom of action are not contradictory but complementary. Where the one ends, the other begins. In helping the international judge to decide how and where the boundary is to be located, the concept of the margin of appreciation has a vital part to play. [*The Development of International Law by the European Court of Human Rights*, 2nd edn (Manchester: Manchester University Press, 1993), pp 174–5.]

4   Timothy Jones, however, is critical of the Court's use of this 'imprecise legal doctrine'. He considers that:

Although the Court has often repeated that the limitations to Convention rights must be narrowly interpreted, the general effect of permitting national authorities a margin of appreciation can only be to devalue Convention rights and freedoms at the expense of the limitations. [Timothy H. Jones, 'The Devaluation of Human Rights Under the European Convention' (1995) *Public Law* 430 at 449.]

5   Judge Macdonald expressed scepticism regarding the pragmatic justification that the doctrine is necessary to avoid damaging conflicts between States and the Court in the era leading up to a truly uniform system of European human rights protection.

The argument assumes that there is still a need for some pragmatic device which can accommodate the sovereignty concerns of the Contracting States. But perhaps the Convention system is now sufficiently mature to be able to move beyond the margin of appreciation and grapple more openly with the questions of appropriateness which that device obscures.…The margin of appreciation should not permit the Court's evasion of its responsibility to articulate the reasons why its intervention in particular cases may or may not be appropriate. Until this responsibility is taken more seriously, the principled reasons which both justify and limit the Court's role will remain buried beneath the pragmatism of the margin of appreciation, and the emergence of a theoretical vision of its role in the European legal order will continue to be limited. [R. St J. Macdonald, 'The Margin of Appreciation' in Macdonald, Matscher, and Petzold (eds), *The European System for the Protection of Human Rights* (Dordrecht: Martinus Nijhoff, 1993), p 124.]

6   Paul Mahoney, subsequently Registrar of the Court, believes that the doctrine is a 'legitimate principle of interpretation of the Convention'. In his opinion the origins of the concept are found in the basic philosophical values embodied in the Convention system. Such values include (a) evolutive interpretation, as the Court is required to interpret the general textual language of the Convention, (b) subsidiarity, as Article 1 locates primary responsibility for safeguarding Convention rights with the member States, (c) democracy, as the Convention system recognizes that member States' parliaments have the major responsibility for regulating changes in matters of social, economic, and political controversy, and (d) cultural diversity, due to the fact that member States reflect a great variety of cultural and ideological beliefs. Consequently:

> ...the international enforcement bodies which operate under the Convention must in their turn pay a degree of deference, through the doctrine of the margin of appreciation, to the sovereignty of the Contracting States. 'Sovereignty' not so much in the sense of the exercise of imperium, that is the State being supreme or not being accountable; but rather in the sense of the freedom of different societies to disagree, to choose different solutions according to their own notions and needs (perhaps even from one region of the country to another), in relation to the regulation of the vast range of human activity covered by the Convention. [P 3.]

Factors which he identifies as influencing the scope of the margin of appreciation are (a) the existence of common ground among member States regarding a right under the Convention will generally result in the Court granting a narrow margin to deviant States, (b) the nature of the right (e.g. a wide margin is accorded in respect of State actions interfering with the right to property), (c) the nature of the duty incumbent on the State (is it a positive or negative one), (d) the nature of the legitimate aim pursued by the State when interfering with the right (e.g. the protection of morals enables States to claim a wider margin because of cultural diversity), (e) the nature of the activity being regulated (e.g. the importance for the individual and the implications for society as a whole), (f) the circumstances surrounding the case (e.g. if the State is experiencing a state of emergency a greater margin will be allowed), and (g) the actual wording of the Convention (e.g. the limitations on the right to liberty in Article 5 are exhaustively defined, therefore there is little discretion for States). In conclusion he does not feel that the doctrine deserves some of the criticisms to which it has been subject. ('Marvellous Richness of Diversity or Invidious Cultural Relativism?' (1998) 19 *Human Rights Law Journal* 1.)

Applying the above analysis Mahoney has argued that the principle of subsidiarity requires the Court to apply differing margins of appreciation to the various types of expression falling within Article 10.

> ...that logic gives priority to the universality of the standard of freedom of expression laid down in Article 10 in regard to political and public-concern speech, but much more scope for subsidiarity— that is the exercise of democratic discretion at local level—in regard to cultural or artistic speech.... Between those two clear poles exists a vast territory of human expression-public, private, collective, professional, commercial, social, scientific, etc—blending a multitude of interests. Whether the pull is in the direction of universality or the direction of subsidiarity will depend on the context and on the mix of interests at stake. The tension between universality and subsidiarity will always be present, to a varying degree, in all free speech cases. ['Universality versus Subsidiarity in the Strasbourg Case Law on Free Speech: Explaining Some Recent Judgments' [1997] *European Human Rights Law Review* 364 at 379.]

Lord Lester criticized this differential application of the margin doctrine to various forms of expression (see p 608).

7 Jeroen Schokkenbroek identified three categories of cases where the Court utilizes the margin doctrine. First, where the relevant Convention provision involves a balancing of interests (e.g. paragraph 2 of Articles 8–11). Secondly, where the Article in question contains vague expressions (e.g. the phrase 'public emergency threatening the life of the nation' in Article 15(1)). Thirdly, where the Court has to determine whether a State has failed to comply with a positive obligation to protect a Convention right (e.g. the right of access to a court under Article 6(1)). His main criticism of the Court's application of the doctrine is that the concept has not always been applied consistently. This may be due to the different composition of Chambers of the Court. Therefore, '…it would be highly desirable if the Court were to adopt a more coherent approach, stating clearly in its judgments the principles which govern the decision to have recourse to the margin of appreciation and the width of the margin.' ('The Basis, Nature and Application of the Margin of Appreciation Doctrine in the Case-Law of the European Court of Human Rights' (1998) 19 *Human Rights Law Journal* 30 at 36.)

8 After a detailed analysis of the case-law, Dr Yutaka Arai-Takahashi concluded that:

Even in the increasingly harmonised constitutional dimension, however, the diversity of values embraced by member States makes it hardly conceivable for the Strasbourg organs to establish an 'autonomous' meaning for such elusive notions as 'morals' or 'public interest'. Nor is it desirable to enforce uniform standards of the Convention at the expense of regional legitimacy and of richness in cultural values and traditions amongst member States. The margin of appreciation must be understood as an essential constitutional device designed to preserve the fundamental prerequisite and virtue of a liberal democratic society: value pluralism. The doctrine's only defensible rationale during and after the process of integration is to enable the Strasbourg Court to provide endorsement of the maintenance of cultural diversity, ensuring to the citizens of Europe the means to articulate and practice their preferred values within a multi-cultural democracy. [Y. Arai-Takahashi, *The Margin of Appreciation Doctrine and the Principle of Proportionality in the Jurisprudence of the ECHR* (Antwerp: Intersentia, 2002), p 249.]

9 Professor Gerards has identified three main factors considered by the Court when applying the doctrine. First, whether there is a European consensus on the matter being challenged; secondly, whether the issue is best left for resolution by domestic authorities; and, thirdly, the importance of the right invoked by the applicant (J. Gerards, 'Pluralism, Deference and the Margin of Appreciation Doctrine' (2011) 17(1) *European Law Journal* 80).

....

Sunday Times v UK A.30 (1979)
European Court of Human Rights

During the late 1950s the Distillers drugs company began selling a sedative which contained the drug thalidomide. By the early 1960s it was discovered that the taking of thalidomide by women during certain stages of pregnancy could cause severe deformities in their babies. The company then withdrew the drug. Subsequently, civil actions for alleged negligence were brought against the company on behalf of the disabled children. A settlement, involving 70 cases, was reached in 1968. Several hundred other actions were subject to continuing negotiations between the plaintiffs' lawyers and the company. In 1972 the *Sunday Times* newspaper published an article criticizing the law relating to the liability of drug companies and calling upon Distillers to 'think again' about the level of their current offer of compensation to the thalidomide victims. Distillers asked the Attorney General to bring proceedings for contempt of court against the newspaper, but he declined to do so. The editor then sent the Attorney General a draft of another article which he proposed to publish. This piece contained evidence and argument to suggest that Distillers had not exercised due care in testing the safety of thalidomide before marketing it. Thereupon, the Attorney General sought an injunction, under the law of contempt of court, to prevent the newspaper publishing the article. The Divisional Court ([1972] 3 All ER 1136) granted the injunction, but the Court of Appeal ([1973] 1 All ER 815) discharged it. On appeal, the House of Lords ([1973] 3 All ER 54) renewed the injunction. The publisher, editor, and a group of journalists then complained to the Commission of, *inter alia*, a breach of their rights under Article 10. The Commission (by 8 votes to 5) found that the injunction was a violation of the applicants' rights to freedom of expression.

...

I. ON ARTICLE 10

...

44. Originally, the injunction in question was granted by the Divisional Court and concerned only the draft *Sunday Times* article... It was discharged by the Court of Appeal... but the House of Lords restored it and considerably widened its scope by directing the Divisional Court to order

> 'That... Times Newspapers Ltd, by themselves, their servants, agents or otherwise, be restrained from publishing, or causing or authorising or procuring to be published or printed, any article or matter which prejudges the issues of negligence, breach of contract or breach of duty, or deals with the evidence relating to any of the said issues arising on any actions pending or imminent against Distillers... in respect of the development, distribution or use of the drug "thalidomide".'

45. It is clear that there was an 'interference by public authority' in the exercise of the applicants' freedom of expression which is guaranteed by paragraph 1 of Article 10. Such an interference entails a 'violation' of Article 10 if it does not fall within one of the exceptions provided for in paragraph 2 (*Handyside* judgment of 7 December 1976, Series A No 24, p 21, § 43). The Court therefore has to examine in turn whether the interference in the present case was 'prescribed by law', whether it had an aim or aims that is or are legitimate under Article 10 § 2 and whether it was 'necessary in a democratic society' for the aforesaid aim or aims.

A. WAS THE INTERFERENCE 'PRESCRIBED BY LAW'?

...

47. The Court observes that the word 'law' in the expression 'prescribed by law' covers not only statute but also unwritten law. Accordingly, the Court does not attach importance here to the fact that contempt of court is a creature of the common law and not of legislation. It would clearly be contrary to the intention of the drafters of the Convention to hold that a restriction imposed by virtue of the common law is not 'prescribed by law' on the sole ground that it is not enunciated in legislation: this would deprive a common-law State which is Party to the Convention of the protection of Article 10 § 2 and strike at the very roots of that State's legal system.

...

48. The expression 'prescribed by law' appears in paragraph 2 of Articles 9, 10 and 11 of the Convention, the equivalent in the French text being in each case 'prévues par la loi'. However, when the same French expression appears in Article 8 § 2 of the Convention, in article 1 of Protocol No 1

and in Article 2 of Protocol No 4, it is rendered in the English text as 'in accordance with the law', 'provided for by law' and 'in accordance with law', respectively. Thus confronted with versions of a law-making treaty which are equally authentic but not exactly the same, the Court must interpret them in a way that reconciles them as far as possible and is most appropriate in order to realise the aim and achieve the object of the treaty (see the *Wemhoff* judgment of 27 June 1968, Series A No 7, p 23, § 8, and Article 33 § 4 of the Vienna Convention of 23 May 1969 on the Law of Treaties).

49. In the Court's opinion, the following are two of the requirements that flow from the expression 'prescribed by law'. Firstly, the law must be adequately accessible: the citizen must be able to have an indication that is adequate in the circumstances of the legal rules applicable to a given case. Secondly, a norm cannot be regarded as a 'law' unless it is formulated with sufficient precision to enable the citizen to regulate his conduct: he must be able—if need be with appropriate advice—to foresee, to a degree that is reasonable in the circumstances, the consequences which a given action may entail. Those consequences need not be foreseeable with absolute certainty: experience shows this to be unattainable. Again, whilst certainty is highly desirable, it may bring in its train excessive rigidity and the law must be able to keep pace with changing circumstances. Accordingly, many laws are inevitably couched in terms which, to a greater or lesser extent, are vague and whose interpretation and application are questions of practice.

50. In the present case, the question whether these requirements of accessibility and foreseeability were satisfied is complicated by the fact that different principles were relied on by the various Law Lords concerned. The Divisional Court had applied the principle that a deliberate attempt to influence the settlement of pending proceedings by bringing public pressure to bear on a party constitutes contempt of court (the 'pressure principle' . . .). Certain members of the House of Lords also alluded to this principle whereas others preferred the principle that it is contempt of court to publish material which prejudges, or is likely to cause public prejudgment of, the issues raised in pending litigation (the 'prejudgment principle' . . .).

51. The applicants do not claim to have been without an indication that was adequate in the circumstances of the 'pressure principle'. . . .

The Court also considers that there can be no doubt that the 'pressure principle' was formulated with sufficient precision to enable the applicants to foresee to the appropriate degree the consequences which publication of the draft article might entail. . . .

52. The applicants contend, on the other hand, that the prejudgment principle was novel and that they therefore could not have had an adequate indication of its existence. . . .

As regards the formulation of the 'prejudgment principle', the Court notes that reference was made in the House of Lords to various authorities . . .

To sum up, the Court does not consider that the applicants were without an indication that was adequate in the circumstances of the existence of the 'prejudgment principle'. Even if the Court does have certain doubts concerning the precision with which that principle was formulated at the relevant time, it considers that the applicants were able to foresee, to a degree that was reasonable in the circumstances, a risk that publication of the draft article might fall foul of the principle.

53. The interference with the applicants' freedom of expression was thus 'prescribed by law' within the meaning of Article 10 § 2.

B. DID THE INTERFERENCE HAVE AIMS THAT ARE LEGITIMATE UNDER ARTICLE 10 § 2?

54. In the view of the applicants, the Government and the minority of the Commission, the law of contempt of court serves the purpose of safeguarding not only the impartiality and authority of the judiciary but also the rights and interests of litigants.

The majority of the Commission, on the other hand, whilst accepting that the law of contempt has the general aim of securing the fair administration of justice and that it thereby seeks to achieve purposes similar to those envisaged in Article 10 § 2 where it speaks of maintaining the authority and impartiality of the judiciary, considered that it was not called upon to examine separately whether that law has the further purpose of protecting the rights of others.

55. The Court first emphasises that the expression 'authority and impartiality of the judiciary' has to be understood 'within the meaning of the Convention' (see, *mutatis mutandis*, the *König* judgment of 28 June 1978, Series A No 27, pp 29–30, § 88). For this purpose, account must be taken of the central position occupied in this context by Article 6 which reflects the fundamental principle of the rule of law (see, for example, the *Golder* judgment of 21 February 1975, Series A No 18, p 17, § 34).

The term 'judiciary' ('pouvoir judiciaire') comprises the machinery of justice or the judicial branch of government as well as the judges in their official capacity. The phrase 'authority of the judiciary' includes, in particular, the notion that the courts are, and are accepted by the public at large as being, the proper forum for the ascertainment of legal rights and obligations and the settlement of disputes relative thereto; further, that the public at large have respect for and confidence in the courts' capacity to fulfil that function.

56. In the present case, the Court shares the view of the majority of the Commission that, insofar as the law of contempt may serve to protect the rights of litigants, this purpose is already included in the phrase 'maintaining the authority and impartiality of the judiciary': the rights so protected are the rights of individuals in their capacity as litigants, that is as persons involved in the machinery of justice, and the authority of that machinery will not be maintained unless protection is afforded to all those involved in or having recourse to it. It is therefore not necessary to consider as a separate issue whether the law of contempt has the further purpose of safeguarding 'the rights of others'.

57. It remains to be examined whether the aim of the interference with the applicants' freedom of expression was the maintenance of the authority and impartiality of the judiciary.

The reasons why the draft article was regarded as objectionable by the House of Lords...may be briefly summarised as follows:

— by 'prejudging' the issue of negligence, it would have led to disrespect for the processes of the law or interfered with the administration of justice;

— it was of a kind that would expose Distillers to public and prejudicial discussion of the merits of their case, such exposure being objectionable as it inhibits suitors generally from having recourse to the courts;

— it would subject Distillers to pressure and to the prejudices of prejudgment of the issues in the litigation and the law of contempt was designed to prevent interference with recourse to the courts;

— prejudgment by the press would have led inevitably in this case to replies by the parties, thereby creating the danger of a 'trial by newspaper' incompatible with the proper administration of justice;

— the courts owe it to the parties to protect them from the prejudices of prejudgment which involves their having to participate in the flurries of pre-trial publicity.

The Court regards all these various reasons as falling within the aim of maintaining the 'authority...of the judiciary' as interpreted by the Court in the second sub-paragraph of paragraph 55 above.

Accordingly, the interference with the applicants' freedom of expression had an aim that is legitimate under Article 10 § 2.

C. WAS THE INTERFERENCE 'NECESSARY IN A DEMOCRATIC SOCIETY' FOR MAINTAINING THE AUTHORITY OF THE JUDICIARY?

...

59. The Court has already had the occasion in its above-mentioned *Handyside* judgement to state its understanding of the phrase 'necessary in a democratic society', the nature of its functions in the examination of issues turning on that phrase and the manner in which it will perform those functions....

This does not mean that the Court's supervision is limited to ascertaining whether a respondent State exercised its discretion reasonably, carefully and in good faith. Even a Contracting State so acting remains subject to the Court's control as regards the compatibility of its conduct with the engagements it has undertaken under the Convention...

Again, the scope of the domestic power of appreciation is not identical as regards each of the aims listed in Article 10 § 2. The *Handyside* case concerned the 'protection of morals'. The view taken by the Contracting States of the 'requirements of morals', observed the Court, 'varies from time to time and from place to place, especially in our era', and 'State authorities are in principle in a better position than the international judge to give an opinion on the exact content of these requirements' (p 22, § 48). Precisely the same cannot be said of the far more objective notion of the 'authority' of the judiciary. The domestic law and practice of the Contracting States reveal a fairly substantial measure of common ground in this area. This is reflected in a number of provisions of the Convention, including Article 6, which have no equivalent as far as 'morals' are concerned. Accordingly, here a more extensive European supervision corresponds to a less discretionary power of appreciation....

60. Both the minority of the Commission and the Government attach importance to the fact that the institution of contempt of court is peculiar to common-law countries and suggest that the concluding words of Article 10 § 2 were designed to cover this institution which has no equivalent in many other member States of the Council of Europe.

However, even if this were so, the Court considers that the reason for the insertion of those words would have been to ensure that the general aims of the law of contempt of court should be considered legitimate aims under Article 10 § 2 but not to make that law the standard by which to assess whether a given measure was 'necessary'. If and to the extent that Article 10 § 2 was prompted by the notions underlying either the English law of contempt of court or any other similar domestic institution, it cannot have adopted them as they stood: it transposed them into an autonomous context. It is 'necessity' in terms of the Convention which the Court has to assess, its role being to review the conformity of national acts with the standards of that instrument....

61. Again, the Court cannot hold that the injunction was not 'necessary' simply because it could or would not have been granted under a different legal system. As noted in the judgment of 9 February 1967 in the *'Belgian Linguistic'* case, the main purpose of the Convention is 'to lay down certain international standards to be observed by the Contracting States in their relations with persons under their jurisdiction' (Series A No 5, p 19). This does not mean that absolute uniformity is required and, indeed, since the Contracting States remain free to choose the measures which they consider appropriate, the Court cannot be oblivious of the substantive or procedural features of their respective domestic laws (see, *mutatis mutandis*, judgment of 23 July 1968 in the *'Belgian Linguistic'* case, Series A No 6, pp 34–5).

62. It must now be decided whether the 'interference' complained of corresponded to a 'pressing social need', whether it was 'proportionate to the legitimate aim pursued' whether the reasons given by the national authorities to justify it are 'relevant and sufficient under Article 10 § 2' (above-mentioned *Handyside* judgment, pp 22–4, §§ 48–50).

...

Nevertheless, the proposed *Sunday Times* article was couched in moderate terms and did not present just one side of the evidence or claim that there was only one possible result at which a court could arrive; although it analysed in detail evidence against Distillers, it also summarised arguments in their favour and closed with the words 'There appears to be no neat set of answers...'. In the Court's opinion, the effect of the article, if published, would therefore have varied from reader to reader. Accordingly, even to the extent that the article might have led some readers to form an opinion on the negligence issue, this would not have had adverse consequences for the 'authority of the judiciary', especially since, as noted above, there had been a nationwide campaign in the meantime.

...

As the Court remarked in its *Handyside* judgment, freedom of expression constitutes one of the essential foundations of a democratic society; subject to paragraph 2 of Article 10, it is applicable not only to information or ideas that are favourably received or regarded as inoffensive or as a matter of indifference, but also to those that offend, shock or disturb the State or any sector of the population (p 23, § 49).

These principles are of particular importance as far as the press is concerned. They are equally applicable to the field of the administration of justice, which serves the interests of the community at large and requires the co-operation of an enlightened public. There is general recognition of the fact that the courts cannot operate in a vacuum. Whilst they are the forum for the settlement of disputes, this does not mean that there can be no prior discussion of disputes elsewhere, be it in specialised journals, in the general press or amongst the public at large. Furthermore, whilst the mass media must not overstep the bounds imposed in the interests of the proper administration of justice, it is incumbent on them to impart information and ideas concerning matters that come before the courts just as in other areas of public interest. Not only do the media have the task of imparting such information and ideas: the public also has a right to receive them (see, *mutatis mutandis*, the *Kjeldsen, Busk Madsen and Pedersen* judgment of 7 December 1976, Series A No 23, p 26, § 52).

To assess whether the interference complained of was based on 'sufficient' reasons which rendered it 'necessary in a democratic society', account must thus be taken of any public interest aspect of the case. The Court observes in this connection that, following a balancing of the conflicting interests involved, an absolute rule was formulated by certain of the Law Lords to the effect that it was not permissible to prejudge issues in pending cases: ...the Court points out that it has to take a different approach. The Court is faced not with a choice between two conflicting principles but with a principle of freedom of expression that is subject to a number of exceptions which must be narrowly interpreted (see, *mutatis mutandis*, the *Klass* judgment of 6 September 1978, Series A No 28, p 21, § 42). ...It is not sufficient that the interference involved belongs to that class of the exceptions listed in article 10 § 2 which has been invoked; neither is it sufficient that the interference was imposed because its subject-matter fell within a particular category or was caught by a legal rule formulated in general or absolute terms: the Court has to be satisfied that the interference was necessary having regard to the facts and circumstances prevailing in the specific case before it.

66. The thalidomide disaster was a matter of undisputed public concern. It posed the question whether the powerful company which had marketed the drug bore legal or moral responsibility towards hundreds of individuals experiencing an appalling personal tragedy or whether the victims could demand or hope for indemnification only from the community as a whole; fundamental issues concerning protection against the compensation for injuries resulting from scientific developments were raised and many facets of the existing law on these subjects were called in question.

As the Court has already observed, Article 10 guarantees not only the freedom of the press to inform the public but also the right of the public to be properly informed.

In the present case, the families of numerous victims of the tragedy, who were unaware of the legal difficulties involved, had a vital interest in knowing all the underlying facts and the various possible solutions. They could be deprived of this information, which was crucially important for them, only if it appeared absolutely certain that its diffusion would have presented a threat to the 'authority of the judiciary'.

…

It is true that, if the *Sunday Times* article had appeared at the intended time, Distillers might have felt obliged to develop in public, and in advance of any trial, their arguments on the facts of the case …; however, those facts did not cease to be a matter of public interest merely because they formed the background to pending litigation. By bringing to light certain facts, the article might have served as a brake on speculative and unenlightened discussion.

67. Having regard to all the circumstances of the case and on the basis of the approach described … above, the Court concludes that the interference complained of did not correspond to a social need sufficiently pressing to outweigh the public interest in freedom of expressing within the meaning of the Convention. The Court therefore finds the reasons for the restraint imposed on the applicants not to be sufficient under Article 10 § 2. That restraint proves not to be proportionate to the legitimate aim pursued; it was not necessary in a democratic society for maintaining the authority of the judiciary.

68. There has accordingly been a violation of Article 10.

FOR THESE REASONS, THE COURT

Holds by eleven votes to nine that there has been a breach of Article 10 of the Convention: …

NOTES

1 The majority was comprised of President Balladore Pallieri and Judges: Mosler, Zekia, O'Donoghue, Pedersen, Evrigenis, Teitgen, Lagergren, Gölcüklü, Pinheiro Farinha, and Garcia De Enterria. The dissentients were Judges: Wiarda, Cremona, Thor Vilhjalmsson, Ryssdal, Ganshof van der Meersch, Fitzmaurice, Bindschedler-Robert, Liesch, and Matscher. In their joint dissent the minority disagreed with the majority regarding (a) the extent of the margin of appreciation to be given to the UK in respect of the law of contempt of court and (b) the necessity of the interference with the applicants' freedom of expression. The dissentients did not believe that the national margin of appreciation was narrower in cases involving the maintenance of the authority of the judiciary than in disputes concerning the protection of morals.

Even though there might exist a fairly broad measure of common ground between the Contracting States as to the substance of Article 6, it nevertheless remains the fact that the judicial institutions and the procedures can vary considerably from one country to another. Thus, contrary to what the majority of the Court holds, the notion of the authority of the judiciary is by no means divorced from national circumstances and cannot be determined in a uniform way. [Pp 51–2.]

The dissentients were also satisfied that the House of Lords was entitled to consider that it was necessary to restore the injunction, in order to prevent the applicants prejudicing the administration of justice in the civil action against Distillers.

2 The Court's judgment contains several very important rulings. These include the relationship between the rights granted by Article 10(1) and the limitations permitted under Article 10(2). According to the Court, the former have precedence and the latter must be

interpreted narrowly. Also, the Court was willing to accept that common law jurisprudence could, if it was sufficiently accessible and precise, satisfy the requirements of Article 10(2) as being 'prescribed by law'. For the Court's acceptance of case-law in civil law States as meeting the analogous requirements of being 'in accordance with the law' under Article 8(2), see *Kruslin v France*, p 565.

3   The *Sunday Times* case was a significant factor in the British Government's decision to seek statutory reform of parts of the common law in the Contempt of Court Act 1981. Aspects of that legislation have been considered by the Court in *Goodwin v UK*, Reports of Judgments and Decisions, 1996-II, see p 726.

Article 10(1)

The scope of freedom of expression

(i) POLITICAL EXPRESSION

Lingens v Austria A.103 (1986)
European Court of Human Rights

The applicant was the editor of a magazine (*Profil*) published in Austria. Shortly after the Austrian general election in 1975, Simon Wiesenthal (President of the Jewish Documentation Centre) accused the leader of the Austrian Liberal Party (Friedrich Peter) of having served in the SS infantry during the Second World War. Mr Peter admitted that fact but denied any personal involvement in the massacre of civilians by his brigade. The next day Mr Peter had a meeting with the Austrian Chancellor (Bruno Kreisky) about the formation of a new government. Subsequently, Mr Kreisky gave a television interview during which he supported Mr Peter and criticized Mr Wiesenthal's organization as a 'political mafia'. Soon afterwards the applicant published two articles that contained strong criticism of Mr Kreisky, including the terms 'basest opportunism', 'immoral', and 'undignified'. Mr Kreisky then brought a private prosecution against Lingens for alleged criminal defamation. The Vienna Regional Court accepted that Lingens had published his articles in good faith, but as he had not been able to prove the truth of his statements (as required by the Austrian Criminal Code) he was found guilty. The court fined Lingens 20,000 schillings and ordered the confiscation of copies of the offending articles. The Vienna Court of Appeal upheld the conviction, but reduced the fine to 15,000 schillings. Lingens complained to the Commission that his conviction violated his rights under Article 10. The Commission unanimously found a violation of that Article.

I. ALLEGED VIOLATION OF ARTICLE 10

...

36. ...the Court agrees with the Commission and the Government that the conviction in question was indisputably based on Article 111 of the Austrian Criminal Code (see paragraph 21 above); it was moreover designed to protect 'the reputation or rights of others' and there is no reason to suppose

that it had any other purpose (see Article 18 of the Convention). The conviction was accordingly 'prescribed by law' and had a legitimate aim under Article 10 § 2 of the Convention.

37. In their respective submissions the Commission, the Government and the applicant concentrated on the question whether the interference was 'necessary in a democratic society' for achieving the above-mentioned aim....

41. In this connection, the Court has to recall that freedom of expression, as secured in paragraph 1 of Article 10, constitutes one of the essential foundations of a democratic society and one of the basic conditions for its progress and for each individual's self-fulfilment. Subject to paragraph 2, it is applicable not only to 'information' or 'ideas' that are favourably received or regarded as inoffensive or as a matter of indifference, but also to those that offend, shock or disturb. Such as the demands of that pluralism, tolerance and broadmindedness without which there is no 'democratic society' (see the above-mentioned *Handyside* judgment, Series A No 24, p 23, § 49).

These principles are of particular importance as far as the press is concerned. Whilst the press must not overstep the bounds set, *inter alia*, for the 'protection of the reputation of others', it is nevertheless incumbent on it to impart information and ideas on political issues just as on those in other areas of public interest. Not only does the press have the task of imparting such information and ideas: the public also has a right to receive them (see, *mutatis mutandis*, the above-mentioned *Sunday Times* judgment, Series A No 30, p 40, § 65). In this connection, the Court cannot accept the opinion, expressed in the judgment of the Vienna Court of Appeal, to the effect that the task of the press was to impart information, the interpretation of which had to be left primarily to the reader.

42. Freedom of the press furthermore affords the public one of the best means of discovering and forming an opinion of the ideas and attitudes of political leaders. More generally, freedom of political debate is at the very core of the concept of a democratic society which prevails throughout the Convention.

The limits of acceptable criticism are accordingly wider as regards a politician as such than as regards a private individual. Unlike the latter, the former inevitably and knowingly lays himself open to close scrutiny of his every word and deed by both journalists and the public at large, and he must consequently display a greater degree of tolerance. No doubt Article 10 § 2 enables the reputation of others—that is to say, of all individuals—to be protected, and this protection extends to politicians too, even when they are not acting in their private capacity; but in such cases the requirements of such protection have to be weighed in relation to the interests of open discussion of political issues.

43. The applicant was convicted because he had used certain expressions ('basest opportunism', 'immoral' and 'undignified') *apropos* of Mr Kreisky, who was Federal Chancellor at the time, in two articles published in the Viennese magazine *Profil* on 14 and 21 October 1975. The articles dealt with political issues of public interest in Austria which had given rise to many heated discussions concerning the attitude of Austrians in general—and the Chancellor in particular—to National Socialism and to the participation of former Nazis in the governance of the country. The content and tone of the articles were on the whole fairly balanced but the use of the aforementioned expressions in particular appeared likely to harm Mr Kreisky's reputation.

However, since the case concerned Mr Kreisky in his capacity as a politician, regard must be had to the background against which these articles were written. They had appeared shortly after the general election of October 1975. Many Austrians had thought beforehand that Mr Kreisky's party would lose its absolute majority and, in order to be able to govern, would have to form a coalition with Mr Peter's party. When, after the elections, Mr Wiesenthal made a number of revelations about Mr Peter's Nazi past, the Chancellor defended Mr Peter and attacked his detractor, whose activities he described as 'mafia methods'; hence Mr Lingens' sharp reaction...

What was at issue was not his right to disseminate information but his freedom of opinion and his right to impart ideas; the restrictions authorised in paragraph 2 of Article 10 nevertheless remained applicable....

In the Court's view, a careful distinction needs to be made between facts and value-judgments. The existence of facts can be demonstrated, whereas the truth of value-judgments is not susceptible of proof. The Court notes in this connection that the facts on which Mr Lingens founded his value-judgment were undisputed, as was also his good faith.

Under paragraph 3 of Article 111 of the Criminal Code, read in conjunction with paragraph 2, journalists in a case such as this cannot escape conviction for the matters specified in paragraph 1 unless they can prove the truth of their statements.

As regards value-judgments this requirement is impossible of fulfilment and it infringes freedom of opinion itself, which is a fundamental part of the right secured by Article 10 of the Convention....

47. From the various foregoing considerations it appears that the interference with Mr Lingens' exercise of the freedom of expression was not 'necessary in a democratic society . . . for the protection of the reputation . . . of others'; it was disproportionate to the legitimate aim pursued. There was accordingly a breach of Article 10 of the Convention.

...

FOR THESE REASONS, THE COURT UNANIMOUSLY

Holds that there has been a breach of Article 10 of the Convention;

...

NOTES

1 The Court was composed of President Ryssdal and Judges: Ganshof van der Meersch, Cremona, Wiarda, Thor Vilhjalmsson, Bindschedler-Robert, Lagergren, Gölcüklü, Matscher, Pinheiro Farina, Pettiti, Walsh, Evans, Macdonald, Russo, Bernhardt, Gersing, and Spielmann.

2 The above judgment is notable for the vigorous protection given to media comment on political ideas and politicians by the Court. It is especially important in preventing States from requiring the media to prove the truthfulness of their good faith value judgements regarding political figures.

3 The same principles were applied by the Court in *Oberschlick v Austria* A.204 (1991), where another magazine editor published the details of criminal information, which he had lodged with the authorities, alleging that the Secretary General of the Austrian Liberal Party had unlawfully espoused views similar to Nazi policy. Furthermore, the magazine article elaborated upon the nature of the criminal charges. Oberschlick was convicted by the Austrian courts under the same defamation law as *Lingens*. A majority of the Court (16 votes to 3) concluded that there had been a violation of the applicant's rights under Article 10, because the Austrian courts had required him to prove the truth of parts of the article which were value judgements. In a subsequent case he also successfully challenged an Austrian conviction for publishing an article in which he called a leading politician an 'idiot': *Oberschlick v Austria (No 2)*, Reports of Judgments and Decisions, 1997-IV. Jorg Haider, the leader of the Austrian Freedom Party and Governor of Carinthia, had given a speech in which he claimed that all soldiers who served in the Second World War (irrespective of which side they were on) had fought for peace and freedom and that they were the only people entitled to freedom of expression in modern times. Oberschlick published the speech together with his criticisms under the title 'PS: Idiot instead of Nazi'. The Austrian

courts upheld Haider's claim of defamation against the applicant. The Commission (by 14 votes to 1) found a breach of Article 10. A majority of the Court (7 votes to 2) also held that the applicant's conviction violated his rights under that provision.

In the Court's view, the applicant's article, and in particular the word 'Idiot', may certainly be considered polemical, but they did not on that account constitute a gratuitous personal attack, as the author provided an objectively understandable explanation for them derived from Mr Haider's speech-which was itself provocative. As such, they were part of the political discussion provoked by Mr Haider's speech and amounted to an opinion, whose truth is not susceptible of proof. Such an opinion may, however, be excessive, in particular in the absence of any factual basis, but...that was not so in this instance. It is true that calling a politician [an Idiot] in public may offend him. In the instant case, however, the word does not seem disproportionate to the indignation knowingly aroused by Mr Haider. [Paras 33–4.]

Therefore, the Court did not consider that it was necessary for the Austrian courts to have convicted the applicant of defamation in order to protect the reputation or rights of Haider. Matscher and Thor Vilhjalmsson JJ dissented on the basis that they considered 'an insult can never be a value judgment' deserving protection under Article 10. However, it is clear that the majority of the Court was willing to safeguard political commentators' use of highly pejorative language where it was part of a reasoned critique. J. McBride has observed that: 'the recognition that insults can be protected is undoubtedly important but determining whether the use of one was justified is often likely to be problematic' ('Judges, Politicians and the Limits to Critical Comment' (1998) 23 *European Law Review* 77 at 88).

On the latter point see **Wabl**, Note 10.

In the later case of **Wirtschafts-Trend Zeitschriften-Verlags GMBH v Austria**, judgment of 27 October 2005, the publishers of *Profil* (see above **Lingens**) successful claimed a breach of Article 10 in respect of their civil liability for a book review which criticized Jorg Haider's reference to (Nazi) concentration camps as 'punishment camps'. The unanimous Chamber found the fact that Haider had used that description was a sufficient basis for the magazine's value judgements.

4   A large majority (6 votes to 1) of a Chamber found that a journalist's reference to a right-wing politician as a 'closet Nazi' was a value judgement which could be justified in *Scharsach and News Verlagsgesellschaft mbH v Austria*, judgment of 13 November 2003. The named politician had, *inter alia*, publicly criticized legislation which banned National Socialist activities. Therefore, the Chamber did not think that the journalist's article on a matter of public interest exceeded fair comment and his conviction for defamation (accompanied by a fine of 4,360 euros) constituted a breach of Article 10.

5   The acceptable limits of media commentary on a political figure were found to have been breached in *Tammer v Estonia*, judgment of 6 February 2001. The applicant was a journalist who published an article in which he described the lover of a former Prime Minister (she had given birth to the latter's child whilst he was married to another person) and who had then served as one of his officials whilst being active in his political party, as being a person who broke up another's marriage and an unfit and careless mother (using offensive Estonian words). The woman brought a private prosecution against the applicant for having insulted her. The domestic courts found him guilty and fined him. The Court was unanimous in rejecting the applicant's claim that he had suffered a violation of Article 10.

68....it observes that Ms Laanaru resigned from her governmental position in October 1995...Despite her continued involvement in the political party the Court does not find it established that the use of the impugned terms in relation to Ms Laanaru's private life was justified by considerations of public concern or that they bore on a matter of general importance. In particular, it has not been substantiated that her private life was among the issues that affected the public in April 1996 [when the article was published]. The applicant's remarks could therefore scarcely be regarded as serving the public interest.

Hence, the use of insulting terminology to describe aspects of the private life of a political figure did not come within the boundaries of protected political expression. In contrast, the conviction of a newspaper editor and the publisher for infringing the privacy of a senior parliamentarian, by reporting the conviction of her husband for drunkenness and assaulting a police officer, was found to have breached Article 10 in *Karhuvaara and Iltalehti v Finland*, judgment of 16 November 2004. The Court acknowledged that the applicants' factual references to the parliamentarian in the coverage of the husband's conviction had a degree of legitimate public interest.

45. On the other hand, it is to be noted that the subject matter of the contested reporting did not have any express bearing on political issues or any direct links with the person of Mrs A. as a politician. Consequently, the articles in question did not pertain to any matter of great public interest as far as Mrs A.'s involvement was concerned. However, the public has the right to be informed, which is an essential right in a democratic society that, in certain special circumstances, may even extend to aspects of the private life of public figures, particularly where politicians are concerned (see *Von Hannover v Germany*, [ECHR 2004] § 64). In this connection the Court notes the District Court's opinion, according to which the conviction of the spouse of a politician could affect people's voting decisions. In the Court's opinion this indicates that, at least to some degree, a matter of public interest was involved in the reporting.

It is significant that the newspaper articles in this case did not contain any criticism of the politician.

6 The Court has ruled that the freedom of political expression is even wider when it is directed at the institutions of government, rather than against specific politicians. In *Castells v Spain* A.236 (1992), the applicant was a Spanish Senator representing a party which supported independence for the Basque country. He wrote an article in 1979 for a magazine, circulating in the Basque region, which accused the State of a number of murders. In his words: 'Behind these acts there can only be the Government…We know that they are increasingly going to use as a political instrument the ruthless hunting down of Basque dissidents and their political elimination.' Subsequently, Castells was convicted of insulting the Government after the Supreme Court held that defence of truth was not available in respect of this offence. Castells then complained to the Strasbourg authorities. The Court, unanimously, stated that:

While freedom of expression is important for everybody, it is especially so for an elected representative of the people. He represents his electorate, draws attention to their preoccupations and defends their interests. Accordingly, interferences with the freedom of expression of an opposition Member of Parliament, like the applicant call for the closest scrutiny on the part of the Court…The limits of permissible criticism are wider with regard to the Government than in relation to a private citizen, or even a politician. In the democratic system the actions or omissions of the Government must be subject to the close scrutiny not only of the legislative and judicial authorities but also of the press and public opinion. Furthermore, the dominant position which the Government occupies makes it necessary for it to display restraint in resorting to criminal proceedings, particularly where other means are available for replying to the unjustified attacks and criticisms of its adversaries or the media. [Paras 42–6.]

The Court concluded that as the Spanish courts had prevented Castells from pleading the truthfulness of his statements, as he had wished to do, there had been a violation of his rights under Article 10(1).

The combined effects of the judgments in *Lingens* and *Castells* has been the creation by the Court of complimentary European defences, under Article 10, of fair comment for good faith media commentaries upon politicians and the truthfulness of factual statements about public bodies.

Subsequently, the full-time Court criticized Ukrainian defamation law for failing to distinguish between value judgements and statements of fact in *Ukrainian Media Group v Ukraine*, judgment of 29 March 2005.

7   A Grand Chamber of the Court has applied *Castells* to protect vitriolic criticism of government policy by an opposition politician in *Incal v Turkey*, 1998-IV. The applicant, a lawyer by profession, was a member of the executive committee of the Izmir section of the People's Labour Party ('the HEP'). That committee decided to distribute a leaflet which was highly critical of the measures being taken by local authorities against illegal traders and squatters (most of whom were Kurds). The committee sent a copy of the leaflet to the Izmir prefecture and asked for permission to distribute it. The leaflet was referred to the security police who considered that it contained illegal separatist propaganda and, therefore, they sent it to the public prosecutor. At the request of the public prosecutor the National Security Court issued an injunction ordering the seizure of the leaflet. Subsequently, all 10,000 copies of the leaflet were seized and the applicant was convicted of non-public incitement to commit an offence for which he was sentenced to six months' imprisonment and banned from driving for 15 days (also conviction of this offence meant that the applicant was debarred from the civil service and forbidden to take part in a number of activities within political organizations and trade unions). The applicant complained to the Commission alleging a breach of, *inter alia*, Article 10. A unanimous Commission upheld that claim. The Court accepted that the applicant's conviction had the legitimate aim of preventing disorder. In the Court's opinion:

The leaflet began by complaining of an atmosphere of hostility towards citizens of Kurdish origin in Izmir and suggested that the measures concerned were directed against them in particular, to force them to leave the city. The text contained a number of virulent remarks about the policy of the Turkish Government and made serious accusations, holding them responsible for the situation. Appealing to 'all democratic patriots', it described the authorities' actions as 'terror and as part of a 'special war' being conducted 'in the country' against 'the Kurdish people'. It called on citizens to 'oppose' this situation, in particular by means of 'neighbourhood committees'. The Court certainly sees in these phrases appeals to, among others, the population of Kurdish origin, urging them to band together to raise certain political demands. Although the reference to 'neighbourhood committees' appears unclear, those appeals cannot, however, if read in context, be taken as incitement to the use of violence, hostility or hatred between citizens. [Para 50.]

While the Court was willing to take into account the problems of preventing terrorism when evaluating the leaflet it did, '…not discern anything which would warrant the conclusion that Mr Incal was in any way responsible for the problems of terrorism in Turkey, and more specifically in Izmir' (para 58). Therefore, the Court, unanimously, held that the applicant's conviction was disproportionate to the aim pursued and consequently in breach of Article 10.

Hence the Court is willing to safeguard the outspoken criticisms voiced by opposition politicians provided they respect the democratic process by refraining from inciting violence against the State or other citizens: see further, A. Mowbray, 'The Role of the European Court of Human Rights in the Promotion of Democracy' (1999) *Public Law* 703.

Should the advocacy of violence be accorded protection under Article 10? Is it relevant that a number of European States have experienced terrorist campaigns by various groups claiming political (and recently religious) motivation? What if a State is responding to a perceived terrorist campaign by the use of military and security forces in ways which violate Convention rights—does this justify critics' encouragement of violent opposition? A majority of the Court was not willing to find a breach of Article 10 where an opposition politician was punished for appearing to express support for a 'terrorist organization'. In *Zana v Turkey*, 1997-VII, the applicant (a former mayor of Diyarbakir) while serving a prison sentence during 1987 gave an interview to journalists in which he said: 'I support the PKK [Workers' Party of Kurdistan] national liberation movement; on the other hand, I am not in favour of massacres. Anyone can make mistakes, and the PKK kill women and children by mistake...' The interview was subsequently published in a national newspaper. Later, the Diyarbakir National Security Court convicted the applicant of 'defending an act punishable by law as a serious crime' and sentenced him to 12 months' imprisonment for his statement. The Commission, with the President's casting vote, rejected the applicant's complaint under Article 10. The Court found that the interference with the applicant's freedom of expression was 'prescribed by law' and for the legitimate aims of maintaining national security and public safety, preventing crime, and preserving territorial integrity (according to the Turkish Government, since 1985, the confrontation between the PKK and security forces had resulted in 4,036 civilian and 3,884 security forces deaths). Furthermore, the Court (by 12 votes to 8) held that the applicant's conviction was 'necessary in a democratic society' because:

> Those words [he spoke in his interview] could be interpreted in several ways but, at all events, they are both contradictory and ambiguous. They are contradictory because it would seem difficult simultaneously to support the PKK, a terrorist organisation which resorts to violence to achieve its ends, and to declare oneself opposed to massacres; they are ambiguous because Mr Zana disapproves of the massacres of women and children, he at the same time describes them as 'mistakes' that anybody could make. The statement cannot, however, be looked at in isolation. It had a special significance in the circumstances of the case, as the applicant must have realised...the interview coincided with murderous attacks carried out by the PKK on civilians in south-east Turkey, where there was extreme tension at the material time. In those circumstances the support given to the PKK—described as a 'national liberation movement'—by the former mayor of Diyarbakir, the most important city in south-east Turkey, in an interview published in a major national daily newspaper, had to be regarded as likely to exacerbate an already explosive situation in that region. [Paras 58–60.]

For a further consideration of expression involving the alleged endorsement of violence, see *Karata v Turkey* (p 671) and *Erdogdu and Ince v Turkey* (p 694).

8 A unanimous Chamber doubted whether a speech by an opposition politician in which he described the country's President as a liar and slanderer could be classified as the expression of an opinion in a political debate. The Chamber in *Pakdemirli v Turkey*, judgment of 22 February 2005, considered that the comments amounted to a hail of insults, albeit in the context of a lengthy relationship of political antagonism between the two politicians. Therefore, the domestic courts' determination that the applicant's comments amounted to defamation could be justified under Article 10(2) as being for the protection of the reputation/rights of the President. However, the Chamber concluded that the amount of damages that the applicant had been ordered to pay (approximately 60,000 euros, the highest amount ever awarded by a Turkish court) was not a proportionate sum and resulted in the applicant having suffered a breach of Article 10.

9 The Court has stated that special protection should be afforded to political expression taking place within public representative democratic institutions. The applicant in *Jerusalem v Austria*, judgment of 27 February 2001, was a member of the Vienna Municipal Council (which also acted as the Regional Parliament). During a debate on sects she expressed the view that a specified organization was a sect. Later, that organization obtained an injunction preventing her from repeating the statement. When examining her complaint that the injunction violated her freedom of expression under Article 8 the Court, unanimously, held that:

40. As regards the impugned statements of the applicant, the Court observes that they were made in the course of a political debate within the Vienna Municipal Council. It is not decisive that this debate occurred before the Vienna Municipal Council sitting as the local council and not as the Land Parliament. Irrespective of whether the applicant's statements were covered by parliamentary immunity, the Court finds that they were made in a forum which was at least comparable to Parliament as concerns the public interest in protecting the participants' freedom of public expression. In a democracy, Parliament or such comparable bodies are the essential fora for political debate. Very weighty reasons must be advanced to justify interfering with the freedom of expression exercised therein.

The Court went on to find that as the Austrian courts had required the applicant to prove the truth of her statements and, at the same time, denied her the opportunity to produce evidence to support her words she had suffered a breach of Article 10. How far down the domestic hierarchy of representative bodies (national and regional parliaments, city councils, etc) should this principle be applied? For the Court's evaluation of the compatibility of parliamentary immunity with a member of the public's right to defend her reputation via defamation proceedings see *A v UK*, p 398.

10 The limits of a politician's ability to counter-attack defamatory media comments about him/herself were revealed in *Wabl v Austria*, judgment of 21 March 2000. The applicant was a Green member of the Austrian Parliament who had participated in a protest campaign against the stationing of fighter planes near Graz airport. During the protests a police officer accused the applicant of scratching his arm (proceedings were later dropped against the applicant). A local newspaper published an article with the headline 'Police Officer claims: AIDS test for Wabl!'. In the text the officer argued that the applicant should have an AIDS test in order to discover if he had the disease (and might thereby have passed it on to the officer). The applicant asked the newspaper to publish a rectification and it did so a few days later stating '…we wish to apologise for any gross claims which were not appropriate to our standards of fairness…' The same edition of the paper also included a report from the local public health expert who reassured the public that AIDS could not be caught from scratches. On the same day as the paper published its rectification the applicant gave a press conference in which he stated that the newspaper's coverage was 'Nazi-journalism'. The newspaper publishers sought an injunction to prevent the applicant repeating his comment that they were responsible for Nazi journalism. Eventually, the Supreme Court granted the injunction because the applicant's right to freedom of expression could not justify such a serious attack on the paper's reputation. The applicant also successfully sued the publishers for defamation in respect of their original article. He then complained to the Commission alleging that the Supreme Court's injunction violated his rights under Article 10. The Commission found no breach. A majority of the Court (6 votes to 1) concluded that, '...the Supreme Court was entitled to consider that the injunction was "necessary in a democratic society" for the protection of the reputation and rights of others' (para 45). In finding no violation, the majority was particularly influenced by the 'not only polemical but particularly offensive' nature of the applicant's remark.

In her dissent Judge Greve expressed the belief that, 'a democratic political debate requires that where a politician is attacked, not for his political views but on a purely personal level, he should not be in a more disadvantageous position than the press, and that he should be allowed sufficient latitude to reply to press attacks.'

The Court's repugnance towards Nazi ideology is examined below in *Lehideux*. The judgment in *Wabl* cautions politicians to exercise restraint in attacking the media and not to allow themselves to be provoked into making hasty counter-blasts to scurrilous journalism.

11 The Court has not allowed the same wide limits of acceptable criticism in respect of civil servants, acting in their official capacity, as it has of politicians. In *Janowski v Poland*, 1999-I, the applicant was a journalist who encountered two municipal guards ordering street vendors to leave a square in a Polish town. He formed the view that the guards were acting unlawfully, because the council had not passed a resolution to clear the square. A verbal exchange ensued between him and the guards in which he called them 'oafs' and 'dumb'. Janowski was subsequently convicted of 'insulting a civil servant...during and in connection with carrying out his official duties' and fined 1,500,000 zlotys. He complained to the Commission which, by 8 votes to 7, found a breach of Article 10. The Court held that:

> 33....those limits may in some circumstances be wider with regard to civil servants exercising their powers than in relation to private individuals. However, it cannot be said that civil servants knowingly lay themselves open to close scrutiny of their every word and deed to the extent to which politicians do and should therefore be treated on an equal footing with the latter when it comes to the criticism of their actions (cf *Oberschlick v Austria (No 2)* 1997, para 29).
>
> What is more, civil servants must enjoy public confidence in conditions free of undue perturbation if they are to be successful in performing their tasks and it may therefore prove necessary to protect them from offensive and abusive verbal attacks when on duty.

A majority of the Court, 12 votes to 5, went on to find that the applicant's conviction was a proportionate response to the legitimate aim of preventing disorder and did not breach Article 10. Significantly, a number of senior members of the Court, including the President, a Vice-President, and a Chamber President, dissented. President Wildhaber found no 'pressing need' for the applicant's conviction; 'since the applicant used only two moderately insulting words, in a spontaneous and lively discussion, to defend a position which was legally correct and in which he had no immediate personal interest.' Judges Bratza and Rozakis considered that the applicant's comments fell within the protected category of matters of public concern as he perceived the officials to be acting in excess of their authority. Likewise Judge Bonello concluded that: 'I fail to discern any urgent social exigency in condemning those who attempt to prevent abuses, even through immoderate disapproval. The state has a greater necessity to silence those who usurp power than those who raise their voices when power is usurped.' The majority's decision on the facts of this case certainly seems unduly protective of officials in the light of these powerful dissents.

In the later case of *Yankov v Bulgaria*, see p 213, a unanimous Chamber, presided over by Judge Rozakis, distinguished *Janowski* in respect of the applicant's criticism of officials in a manuscript.

136. The applicant also made remarks such as 'well-fed idlers' and 'simple villagers' (about the prison warders), 'a provincial parvenu' (about a police officer whose name was also stated) and 'powerful unscrupulous people' (apparently about prosecutors and investigators generally).

137. While the above statements were undoubtedly insulting, they were far from being grossly offensive. The Court also notes that they were made in a manuscript in which the applicant, in a language and style characteristic of personal memoirs or a similar literary form, recounted his arrest and detention. It was a narrative in which the applicant described moments of his life as a detainee and explained his opinion about the criminal proceedings against him, taking a critical stand as regards allegedly unlawful acts by State officials (distinguish, *Janowski v Poland*, § 32).

138. The Court considers that since the offensive remarks were written in the context of substantive criticism of the administration of justice and officials involved in it, made in a literary form, the State authorities should have shown restraint in their reaction.

139. What is more, the Court is struck by the fact that the applicant was punished for having written down his own thoughts in a private manuscript which, apparently, he had not shown to anyone at the time it was seized. He had neither 'uttered' nor 'disseminated' any offensive or defamatory statements. In particular, there was no allegation that the applicant had circulated the text among the other detainees.

140. To that extent, the case may raise issues relating to the applicant's freedom of thought under Article 9 of the Convention or his right to respect for his private life under Article 8. However, in so far as the manuscript was seized when the applicant was about to hand it over to his lawyer and thus to 'impart' its content and make it available to others, the Court does not need to decide whether it would be more appropriate to consider the case from the standpoint of those provisions.

141. Nonetheless, the fact that the applicant's remarks were never made public is relevant to the assessment of the proportionality of the interference under Article 10 of the Convention. The Court notes in this respect, in addition, that the manuscript was not in a form ready for publication and that there was no immediate danger of its dissemination, even if it had been taken out of the prison.

142. While the members of the prison administration who saw the applicant's manuscript after its seizure must have felt personally insulted by certain remarks which concerned them, it is difficult to accept that that was a sufficient reason to punish the applicant in response. Civil servants have a duty to exercise their powers by reference to professional considerations only, without being unduly influenced by personal feelings. The need to ensure that civil servants enjoy public confidence in conditions free of undue perturbation can justify an interference with the freedom of expression only where there is a real threat in this respect. The applicant's manuscript obviously did not pose such a threat.

143. Having regard to all the relevant circumstances, it cannot be accepted that a fair balance was struck between the competing rights and interests: the applicant's right to freedom of expression on the one hand and the need to maintain the authority of the judiciary and to protect the reputation of civil servants. By punishing the applicant, a prisoner, with seven days' confinement in a disciplinary cell for having included moderately offensive remarks in a private manuscript critical of the justice system, which had not been circulated among the detainees, the authorities overstepped their margin of appreciation.

144. The Court finds, therefore, that the interference with the applicant's freedom of expression was not necessary in a democratic society within the meaning of Article 10 § 2 of the Convention.

145. There has therefore been a violation of Article 10 of the Convention.

The Chamber's requirement that insulting comments must create a 'real threat' (paragraph 142) to public confidence in civil servants if they are to be lawfully punished under Article 10 is a welcome strengthening of the protection of freedom of expression concerning public officials.

12 In *Thorgeirson v Iceland* A.239 (1992), the respondent government sought to draw a distinction between political expression and the discussion of other matters of public interest. In the Icelandic Government's opinion Article 10 did not accord the second category of expression the same breadth of protection as the former. The applicant was a journalist who wrote two articles in a daily newspaper about allegations of police brutality. Describing the 'Reykjavik night-life jungle' he wrote that 'the beasts in uniform in the aforementioned jungle attacked [a named fellow journalist]' and of 'those wild beasts in uniform that creep around'. At the instigation of the Reykjavik Police Association, the public prosecutor charged Thorgeirson with criminal defamation of unspecified members of the Reykjavik police force. He was convicted and fined 10,000 crowns. The European Court, by 8 votes to 1, rejected the Government's purported distinction: '...there is no warrant in [the Court's] case-law for distinguishing, in the manner suggested by the Government, between political discussion and discussion of other matters of public concern' (para 64).

The Court concluded that the applicant's articles were directed at a matter of serious public interest and that placed in their context the language used was not excessive. Therefore, his conviction was not a proportionate response and violated Article 10. This judgment reinforces the protection given to the media by the Court when journalists are seeking to draw popular attention to matters of legitimate public concern. The Court applied this reasoning to a satirical newspaper's publication of the tax affairs of a senior businessman in *Fressoz and Roire v France*, 1999-I. The applicants were the publishing director and a journalist on the French weekly *Le Canard enchaine*. During 1989 there was industrial unrest over pay levels in the Peugeot motor company and the chairman/managing director of the company, Mr Jacques Calvert, refused to award the increase being sought by the workers. The applicants then published an article which disclosed that Mr Calvert had received pay increases totalling 46 per cent in recent years. The article also contained extracts derived from Mr Calvert's tax forms which had been sent anonymously to the newspaper. Eventually, the applicants were convicted of handling photocopies of the tax returns obtained through a breach of professional confidence by an unidentified tax official and fined 15,000 francs. The applicants complained to the Commission alleging, *inter alia*, a breach of Article 10. The Commission, by 21 votes to 11, upheld that complaint. A unanimous Court held that the newspaper article dealt with a matter of general interest.

The article was published during an industrial dispute—widely reported in the press—at one of the major French car manufacturers. The workers were seeking a pay rise which the management were refusing. The article showed that the company chairman had received large pay increases during the period under consideration while at the same time opposing his employees' claims for a rise. By making such a comparison against that background, the article contributed to a public debate on a matter of general interest. It was not intended to damage Mr Calvert's reputation but to contribute to the more general debate on a topic that interested the public...[Para 50.]

As local taxpayers had access to official lists of the taxable income of fellow residents in France, financial reviews frequently published the remuneration of senior business executives, and the applicants had published the article in good faith, the Court concluded that the conviction of the applicants was a disproportionate interference with their freedom of expression which violated Article 10. This ruling further expands the scope of protected expression involving matters of general interest to cover not only comments upon the behaviour of State officials but also the financial rewards received by the senior personnel of major (private sector) companies. Because of the economic and social power exercised by such persons their remuneration can be seen as being of legitimate concern to the public (whether as employees, shareholders, or consumers). Compare the discussion of the pay and bonuses paid to bankers in the light of the financial crisis of 2008 and its aftermath.

13 A majority of a Grand Chamber has also accorded Article 10 protection to a television journalist who produced a programme in which other persons expressed unlawful racist views: *Jersild v Denmark* A.298 (1994). The applicant worked for the Danish Broadcasting Company on its Sunday News Magazine (a serious programme dealing with a wide range of social and political issues aimed at a well-informed audience). The programme editors decided to produce a segment on a group of young people, called 'the Greenjackets', who had been featured in the newspapers because of their racist comments. The applicant recorded several hours of interviews with members of the Greenjackets and then edited these recordings to produce a programme segment lasting a few minutes. This piece was then broadcast as part of one edition of the programme. The segment contained a number of racist comments made by members of the Greenjackets, including the statement by one interviewee that 'a nigger is not a human being, it's an animal, that goes for all the other foreign workers as well, Turks, Yugoslavs and whatever they are called.' Subsequently, the public prosecutor brought criminal proceedings against the Greenjacket members for making unlawful racist comments and against the applicant for aiding and abetting the expression of such unlawful speech. The applicant was convicted and fined 1,000 kroner (the Greenjackets were also found guilty). The Commission (by 12 votes to 4) considered that the applicant's conviction violated Article 10. The Court emphasized '...the vital importance of combating racial discrimination in all its forms and manifestations' (para 30). Indeed, it felt that, 'there can be no doubt that the remarks in respect of which the Greenjackets were convicted were more than insulting to members of the targeted groups and did not enjoy the protection of Article 10' (para 35). However:

> News reporting based on interviews, whether edited or not, constitutes one of the most important means whereby the press is able to play its vital role of 'public watchdog'...The punishment of a journalist for assisting in the dissemination of statements made by another person in an interview would seriously hamper the contribution of the press to discussion of matters of public interest and should not be envisaged unless there are particularly strong reasons for doing so. [Para 35.]

As the applicant did not have a racist purpose when compiling his report and taken as a whole his segment could not objectively be viewed as having such a purpose, his conviction was not necessary in a democratic society. The dissentients considered that (a) the majority did not accord sufficient protection to those persons who have to suffer from racist hatred and (b) they did not believe that the applicant had done enough to counterbalance/challenge the racist views expressed in his broadcast. The common ground between all members of the Court was that the intentional promotion of racist opinions would not be granted the protection of Article 10. In the later case of *Lehideux and Isorni v France*, 1998-VII, the

Court developed this approach by stating that support for a pro-Nazi policy would not enjoy the protection of this Article. The two applicants, who died before the Court pronounced its judgment, published an advertisement in the French newspaper *Le Monde* during 1984 which was headed 'People Of France, You Have Short Memories'. The advertisement went on to defend the actions of Marshall Philippe Petain (the leader of the Vichy Government in France during the Second World War who was subsequently sentenced to death by the French courts for collaboration with the Nazis). The text claimed, *inter alia*: 'That in the thick of difficulties which no French Head of State had ever known, Nazi atrocities and persecutions, he protected them against German omnipotence and barbarism, thus ensuring that two million prisoners of war were saved.' An association of former resistance members filed a criminal complaint and civil suit against the applicants for publicly defending the crimes of collaboration with the enemy. Eventually, the Paris Court of Appeal found the applicants guilty and awarded civil damages of one franc against them. They then complained to the Commission alleging a breach of, *inter alia*, Article 10. By 23 votes to 8 the Commission expressed the opinion that there had been a breach of that Article. The Court found that there had been an interference with the applicants' right to freedom of expression and that it had the legitimate aims of protecting the reputations of others and preventing disorder or crime. However, the Court was divided on whether the interference was 'necessary in a democratic society'. A majority of 15 considered that it was not. The majority distinguished debate over the aims and policies of Petain from, '…the category of clearly established historical facts—such as the Holocaust—whose negation or revision would be removed from the protection of Article 10 by Article 17' (para 47). Furthermore:

There is no doubt that, like any other remark directed against the Convention's underlying values (see, *mutatis mutandis*, the *Jersild v Denmark* judgment…), the justification of a pro-Nazi policy could not be allowed to enjoy the protection afforded by Article 10. In the present case, however, the applicants explicitly stated their disapproval of 'Nazi atrocities and persecution' and of 'German omnipotence and barbarism'. Thus they were not so much praising a policy as a man, and doing so for a purpose-namely securing revision of Philippe Petain's conviction- whose pertinence and legitimacy at least, if not the means employed to achieve it, were recognised by the Court of Appeal. [Para 53.]

Therefore, having regard to the fact that the events referred to in the advertisement had occurred more than 40 years ago, the majority held that the applicants' conviction violated their rights under Article 10. The six dissenters emphasized that the French authorities should have been accorded a wider margin of appreciation in this case. In the opinion of Judges Foighel, Loizou, and Freeland:

In cases involving the right to freedom of expression the Court has generally been particularly restrictive in its approach to the margin of appreciation, although it has been prepared to accept a wider margin in relation to issues likely to offend personal convictions in the religious or moral domain. The latter category, based as it is on the principle that the margin of appreciation is wider where the aim pursued cannot be objectively defined on the European scale, is in our view not to be regarded as confined to those particular issues. It may include an issue such as that in question in the present case, where the aim pursued arose out of historical circumstances peculiar to France and where the French authorities were uniquely well placed, by virtue of their direct and continuous contact with the vital forces of their country, to assess the consequences for the protection of the rights of other groups, such as the associations of former resistance fighters and of deportees who were civil parties to the domestic proceedings, and more generally for the process of healing the wounds and divisions in French society resulting from the events of the 1940s. [Para 4.]

This case reinforces the judgment in *Jersild* by elaborating upon the types of expression that will be denied protection under Article 10. These now include: intentionally racist statements, expression supporting Nazi ideology, and revisionist views seeking to deny historical facts concerning major human rights abuses such as the Holocaust (defamatory statements are similarly excluded, see *Tolstoy Miloslavsky v UK*, p 701).

14 British restrictions on the ability of a pressure group to inform electors of the beliefs of parliamentary candidates were found to be in breach of Article 10 by a majority of a Grand Chamber, in *Bowman v UK*, 1998-I. The applicant was the executive director of the Society for the Protection of the Unborn Child, an organization of 50,000 persons which is opposed to, *inter alia*, abortion and campaigns for a change in the current law regarding abortion in the UK. The major political parties in the UK do not have official policies regarding abortion, but leave it to the conscience of their individual Members of Parliament. The Society, therefore, took the view that if electors were to be able to change the law governing abortion by their choice of MPs they needed to know the local candidates' views on abortion. Consequently, just before the general election in 1992, the applicant arranged the distribution of 1.5 million leaflets containing this information on individual candidates; 25,000 of these leaflets were distributed in Halifax. In 1993, the applicant was charged with contravening section 75 of the Representation of the People Act 1983, which prohibits, during the election period, unauthorized persons expending more than £5 in publishing materials with the view to promoting (or preventing) the election of a candidate. Conviction may be punished with imprisonment for up to one year and/or a fine of up to £5,000 and/or disqualification from voting/election for up to five years. The court directed the acquittal of the applicant because the summons against her had been issued out of time. However, she had been convicted of a similar offence in 1979. She complained to the Commission of an alleged violation of her right to freedom of expression under Article 10 and a majority (28 votes to 1) found a breach. The Court determined that section 75 amounted to a restriction on her freedom of expression by limiting the amount of money she could spend on promotional leaflets for the Society during election campaigns. All the parties accepted that this restriction was 'prescribed by law' and the Court concluded that it was for the legitimate aim of 'protecting the rights of others' (i.e. those of the candidates and electors in Halifax). Therefore, the main issue for the Court was whether section 75 was 'necessary in a democratic society'. The majority (14 judges) noted that under Article 3 of Protocol 1 to the Convention, States had undertaken to hold 'free elections'.

Free elections and freedom of expression, particularly freedom of political debate, together form the bedrock of any democratic system... The two rights are inter-related and operate to reinforce each other... For this reason, it is particularly important in the period preceding an election that opinions and information of all kinds are permitted to circulate freely. Nevertheless, in certain circumstances the two rights may come into conflict and it may be considered necessary, in the period preceding or during an election, to place certain restrictions, of a type which would not usually be acceptable, on freedom of expression, in order to secure the 'free expression of the opinion of the people in the choice of the legislature'. [note, this is the wording of Article 3 of the First Protocol] The Court recognises that, in striking the balance between these two rights, the Contracting States have a margin of appreciation... [Paras 42–3.]

The Court then examined the proportionality of the restrictions imposed on the applicant's dissemination of promotional materials:

> ...s.75 of the 1983 Act operated, for all practical purposes, as a total barrier to Mrs Bowman's publishing information with a view to influencing the voters of Halifax in favour of an anti-abortion candidate. It is not satisfied that it was necessary thus to limit her expenditure to £5 in order to achieve the legitimate aim of securing equality between candidates, particularly in view of the fact that there were no restrictions placed upon the freedom of the press to support or oppose the election of any particular candidate or upon political parties and their supporters to adver-tise at national or regional level, provided that such advertisements were not intended to promote or prejudice the electoral prospects of any particular candidate in any particular constituency. It accordingly concludes that the restriction in question was disproportionate to the aim pursued. [Para 47.]

The six dissentients did not consider that the restrictions imposed on election publications by the 1983 Act were in breach of Article 10. Valticos J thought that, 'there is something slightly ridiculous in seeking to give the British Government lessons in how to hold elections and run a democracy...' Loizou, Baka, and Jambrek JJ believed that the restrictions fell within the UK's margin of appreciation and that they were part of a 'balanced democratic electoral system'. Freeland and Levits JJ perceived section 75 as promoting fairness between candidates.

The low level of permitted expenditure (£5 or less) under section 75 seems to have been a decisive factor in the Court's assessment of the proportionality of the restrictions governing the applicant (and other campaigners/pressure groups). Section 131 of the Political Parties, Elections and Referendums Act 2000, increased the permitted level of expenditure to £500 in respect of each parliamentary candidate.

15 The prohibition on certain groups of local government officers from engaging in party political activities was upheld by a majority of the Court in *Ahmed v UK*, 1998-VI. The former (Conservative) Government had established a Committee, chaired by Sir David Widdicombe an eminent QC, to examine the roles of councillors and officers in local gov-ernment. In its report the Committee noted that the tradition of local government service in the UK had been one of politically neutral officers serving whichever party was in con-trol. To maintain that impartiality the Committee recommended that either the terms and conditions of officers or legislation should prohibit senior officers from engaging in defined party political activities. This proposal was accepted by the Government which secured the passage of the Local Government and Housing Act 1989. Under the Act, the Secretary of State for the Environment was empowered to make Regulations limiting the political activ-ities of local government officers. Regulations were issued in 1990 which applied to three groups of officers: (a) the most senior officers in local government (e.g. chief executives and heads of departments; totalling about 12,000 officers), (b) officers whose salary exceeds approximately £26,000 per annum and whose posts have not been exempted by their local authorities (about 28,000 officers in total), and (c) officers on lower salaries whose duties involve them in, *inter alia*, giving regular advice to local authority committees or speaking on behalf of their authorities to the media on a regular basis (approximately 7,000 officers in total). Officers falling within these groups were prohibited from, *inter alia*, (i) standing as a candidate or canvassing in elections for the House of Commons, European Parliament, or any local authority, (ii) holding an office within any political party, and (iii) publishing any written or artistic work with the intention of affecting public support for a political party. However, officers holding such 'politically restricted posts' were not prevented from being members of political parties. Politically restricted officers could apply for exemption from the Regulations to an independent adjudicator. The applicants were four local government officers who held politically restricted posts which prevented them from engaging in party political activities. They, together with their trade union, challenged the Regulations by way of judicial review proceedings. The High Court and the Court of Appeal dismissed the challenges. Thereupon, the applicants applied to the Commission arguing that the Regulations violated their rights under several Articles including freedom of expression. The Commission, by 13 votes to 4, expressed the opinion that there had been a breach of Article 10. Before the Court, the (new Labour) Government did not deny that the Regulations interfered with the applicants' freedom of expression under Article 10(1), but it sought to claim that the interference was justified under Article 10(2). The Court found the Regulations were 'prescribed by law' and had the legitimate aim of protecting the rights of others, both councillors and the electorate, to effective democracy at the local level. According to the Court the aim of protecting effective political democracy was not restricted to situations where the constitutional order was threatened by a political party (e.g. as in *Vogt v Germany*, p 683).

To limit this notion to that context would be to overlook both the interests served by democratic institutions such as local authorities and the need to make provision to secure their proper functioning where this is considered necessary to safeguard those interests. The Court recalls in this respect that democracy is a fundamental feature of the European public order....For the Court this notion of effective political democracy is just as applicable to the local level as it is to the national level bearing in mind the extent of decision-making entrusted to local authorities and the proximity of the local electorate to the policies which their local politicians adopt. [Para 52.]

A majority of the Court, 6 votes to 3, held that the Regulations (as applied to the applicants) were 'necessary in a democratic society'. In its view the Widdicombe Report had identified the 'pressing social need' for action to preserve the political impartiality of relevant local government officers. Furthermore, the Regulations were a proportionate response as they only applied to approximately 2 per cent of local government officers and the holders of politically restricted posts were able to join political parties and make political comments, provided the latter were not partisan. Therefore, the Court found no breach of the applicants' rights under Article 10 (or other provisions in the Convention). The dissentients did not consider the restrictions placed on the applicants were either required by a pressing social need ('other democratic societies appear to function without such general and far-reaching restrictions', para 5) or proportional (e.g. restricted officers had to resign before they were able to stand for election to Parliament or the European Parliament ('This particular interference can hardly be deemed instrumental in strengthening democracy, since a healthy democracy has need of the best and most experienced parliamentarians', para 6). Professor Morris has also expressed criticism of the Court's judgment:

Its broad-brush approach towards the question of proportionality stood in marked contrast to that of the Commission, which had emphasised, *inter alia*, the large class of employees embraced by the Regulations and the limited possibilities of exemption. The Court did not address points raised by the applicants relating to the discretion accorded to employers in defining employees' duties; the potential gap between contractual duties and the frequency with which they were performed in practice; and the application of the restrictions to those whose duties were purely of a professional or technical nature. [Gillian S. Morris, 'The Political Activities of Local Government Workers and the ECHR' [1999] *Public Law* 211 at 216.]

16 The Court adopted a similar stance in respect of restrictions on the political activities of police officers in **Rekvényi v Hungary**, judgment of 20 May 1999. The Hungarian Constitution was amended in 1993 to prohibit career members of the police (and members of the armed forces and civil national security services) from engaging 'in any political activity' or joining any political party. Regulations elaborated what forms of political conduct were permitted, for example officers could stand for election to Parliament if their membership of the police service was suspended for the 60 days preceding the election. The applicant, a police officer and the Secretary General of the Police Independent Trade Union, complained that these restrictions violated, *inter alia*, his right to freedom of expression. The Commission, by 21 votes to 9, found a violation of Article 10. The Court, unanimously, found that there had been an interference with the applicant's freedom of political expression, but that it could be justified under Article 10(2). The historical situation during the Communist period in Hungary, when the police force was a 'tool' of the ruling political party, was invoked by the Government to explain the Constitutional ban.

> The Court notes that Hungary is not alone, in that a number of Contracting States restrict certain political activities on the part of their police.... Ultimately the police force is at the service of the State. Members of the public are therefore entitled to expect that in their dealings with the police they are confronted with politically-neutral officers who are detached from the political fray... In the Court's view, the desire to ensure that the crucial role of the police in society is not compromised through the corrosion of the political neutrality of its officers is one that is compatible with democratic principles.
>
> This objective takes on a special historical significance in Hungary because of that country's experience of a totalitarian regime which relied to a great extent on its police's direct commitment to the ruling party.
>
> Accordingly, the Court concludes that the restriction in question pursued legitimate aims within the meaning of paragraph 2 of Article 10, namely the protection of national security and public safety and the prevention of disorder. [Para 41.]

As the Regulations allowed the police to engage in a number of forms of political expression the Court held that the restrictions were a proportionate response to a pressing social need. Would the Court have reached the same conclusion if the constitutional ban on political activity had not been subject to limitations and exceptions?

The Court has also considered restrictions on the freedom of expression of civil servants (teachers) in **Vogt v Germany** (p 683) and military personnel (p 711).

17 The academic views, on a contentious issue of constitutional law, of a senior judge expressed in a public lecture were infringed under Article 10 by the adverse reactions of a Head of State in **Wille v Liechtenstein**, judgment of 28 October 1999. The applicant had been a member of the Government of Liechtenstein in 1992 when there had been conflict between Prince Hans-Adam II, the Head of State, and the Government over a matter of political competence concerning a plebiscite. The applicant did not stand for re-election to parliament and in 1993 the Diet nominated him to be President of the Liechtenstein Administrative Court. The Prince formally appointed the applicant to that position for a fixed term. During February 1995 the applicant gave a lecture at the Liechtenstein-Institut, a research body, on the 'Nature and Functions of the Liechtenstein Constitutional Court'. In the course of that lecture the applicant expressed his belief that the Constitutional Court was competent to rule on the interpretation of the constitution in cases of disagreement between the Prince and the Diet. The applicant's lecture was reported in the national newspaper. Ten days later the Prince wrote (on heraldic notepaper) to the applicant at his home address stating '...in my eyes your attitude, Dr Wille, makes you unsuitable for public office. I do not intend to get involved in a long public or private debate with you, but I should like to inform you in good time that I shall not appoint you again to a public office should you be proposed by the Diet or any other body....' Subsequently the Diet, unanimously, concluded that the applicant's lecture had not called into question his judicial office. There was also a public exchange of correspondence between the applicant and the Prince. In 1997 the Diet proposed the applicant's re-appointment to the Presidency of the Administrative Court, as his original term of office had expired. The Prince refused to accept the proposed appointment. Later the applicant complained to the Commission alleging, *inter alia*, a breach of Article 10. By 15 votes to 4 the Commission upheld the complaint. The Court rejected the Government's argument that the Prince's letter was merely an item of private correspondence. Furthermore:

46. The Court reiterates in this connection that the responsibility of a State under the Convention may arise for acts of all its organs, agents and servants. As is the case in international law generally, their rank is immaterial since the acts by persons accomplished in an official capacity are imputed to the State in any case. In particular, the obligations of a Contracting Party under the Convention can be violated by any person exercising an official function vested in him (see *Ireland v UK*, Comm Report 25.1.76, Yearbook 19, p 512, at p 758)....

50. Considering the contents of this letter the Court finds that there has been an interference by a State authority with the applicant's freedom of expression. The measure complained of occurred in the middle of the applicant's term of office as President of the Administrative Court; it was unconnected with any concrete recruitment procedures involving an appraisal of personal qualifications. From the terms of the letter of 27 February 1995 it appears that the Prince had come to a resolution regarding his future conduct towards the applicant, which related to the exercise of one of his sovereign powers, ie his power to appoint State officials. Moreover, the said letter was expressly addressed to the applicant as the President of the Administrative Court, though sent to his place of residence. Thus, the measure complained of was taken by an organ which was competent to act in the manner it did and whose acts engage the responsibility of Liechtenstein as a State under the Convention. The right of the applicant to exercise his freedom of expression was interfered with once the Prince, criticising the contents of the applicant's speech, announced the intention to sanction the applicant because he had freely expressed his opinion. The announcement by the Prince of his intention not to reappoint the applicant to a public post constituted a reprimand for the previous exercise by the applicant of his right to freedom of expression and, moreover, had a chilling effect on the exercise by the applicant of his freedom of expression, as it was likely to discourage him from making statements of that kind in the future.

51. It follows that there was an interference with the exercise of the applicant's right to freedom of expression, as secured in Article 10 § 1.

The Court then examined whether the Prince's interference was 'necessary in a democratic society'. A majority, 16 votes to 1, concluded that it was not.

64. ... Since the applicant was a high-ranking judge at that time, the Court must bear in mind that, whenever the right of freedom of expression of persons in such a position is at issue, the 'duties and responsibilities' referred to in Article 10 § 2 assume a special significance since it can be expected of public officials serving in the judiciary that they should show restraint in exercising their freedom of expression in all cases where the authority and impartiality of judiciary are likely to be called in question. Nevertheless the Court finds that an interference with the freedom of expression of a judge in a position such as the applicant's calls for close scrutiny on the part of the Court.

65. As regards the applicant's lecture on 16 February 1995, the Court observes that this lecture formed part of a series of academic lectures at a Liechtenstein research institute on questions of constitutional jurisdiction and fundamental rights ... The applicant's discourse included a statement on the competences of the Constitutional Court under Article 112 of the Liechtenstein Constitution. It was the applicant's view that the term 'Government' used in this provision included the Prince, an opinion allegedly in conflict with the principle of the Prince's immunity from the jurisdiction of the Liechtenstein judiciary ...

66. In the applicant's view this statement was an academic comment on the interpretation of Article 112 of the Constitution. The Government, on the other hand, maintained that although it was being made in the guise of a legally aseptic statement, it constituted, in essence, a highly political statement involving an attack on the existing constitutional order and not reconcilable with the public office held by the applicant at the time.

67. The Court accepts that the applicant's lecture, since it dealt with matters of constitutional law and more specifically with the issue of whether one of the sovereigns of the State was subject to the jurisdiction of a constitutional court, inevitably had political implications. It holds that questions of constitutional law, by their very nature, have political implications. It cannot find, however, that this element alone should have prevented the applicant from making any statement on this matter. The Court further observes that in the context of introducing a bill amending the Constitutional Court Act in 1991, the Liechtenstein Government had, in its accompanying comments, held a similar view, which had been opposed by the Prince but had found agreement in the Liechtenstein Diet, albeit only by a majority ... The opinion expressed by the applicant cannot be regarded as an untenable proposition since it was shared by a considerable number of persons in Liechtenstein. Moreover, there is no evidence to conclude that the applicant's lecture contained any remarks on pending cases, severe criticism of persons or public institutions or insults of high officials or the Prince.

68. Turning to the Prince's reaction, the Court observes that he announced his intention not to appoint the applicant to public office again, should the applicant be proposed by the Diet or any other body. The Prince considered that the above-mentioned statement by the applicant clearly infringed the Liechtenstein Constitution. In this context, he also made reference to a political controversy with the Liechtenstein Government in October 1992 and, in conclusion, he reproached the applicant, who had been a member of Government at that time and President of the Liechtenstein Administrative Court since 1993, with regarding himself as not being bound by the Constitution. In the Prince's view, the applicant's attitude towards the Constitution made him unsuitable for public office.

69. The Prince's reaction was based on general inferences drawn from the applicant's previous conduct in his position as a member of Government, in particular on the occasion of the political controversy in 1992, and his brief statement, as reported in the press, on a particular, though controversial, constitutional issue of judicial competence. No reference was made to any incident suggesting that the applicant's view, as expressed at the lecture in question, had a bearing on his performance as President of the Administrative Court or on any other pending or imminent proceedings. Also the Government did not refer to any instance where the applicant, in the pursuit of his judicial duties or otherwise, had acted in an objectionable way.

70. On the facts of the present case, the Court finds that, while relevant, the reasons relied on by the Government in order to justify the interference with the applicant's right to freedom of expression are not sufficient to show that the interference complained of was 'necessary in a democratic society'. Even allowing for a certain margin of appreciation, the Prince's action appears disproportionate to the aim pursued. Accordingly the Court holds that there has been a violation of Article 10 of the Convention.

The Court awarded the applicant 10,000 Swiss Francs non-pecuniary damage for the distress that he had suffered. The Court's judgment emphasizes the close connection between matters of constitutional law and political discourse. It is also significant for the Court's ruling that States are potentially liable under the Convention for the actions of all their organs, including those of the Head of State when acting in an official capacity. This European legal accountability is of value to individuals as under domestic law such office-holders may not be amenable to normal legal actions (e.g. the personal prerogative immunity of the British sovereign from criminal or civil proceedings in domestic courts).

The imposition of an administrative fine/costs (totalling about 100 euros) on a university lecturer for alleging, at a faculty meeting, that academic colleagues had been guilty of plagiarism was found to breach Article 10 by a united Chamber in *Boldea v Romania*, judgment of 15 February 2007. The Chamber noted that the alleged plagiarists, who had brought the proceedings against the applicant, had been subject to a verbal warning about their academic behaviour by the university and the applicant had been expressing his professional judgement about colleagues' work (not their private lives).

18 The Court addressed the issue of political advertising in *VGT Verein Gegen Tierfabriken v Switzerland*, judgment of 28 June 2001. The applicant association had the aim of protecting animals. In response to television commercials broadcast on Swiss television by the meat industry, the applicant produced a commercial of just under one minute in length. The applicant's commercial showed a sow building a nest in the forest for her piglets and then inside a large building with pigs kept in small pens. The commercial ended with the words, 'eat less meat, for the sake of your health, the animals and the environment!'. The company responsible for advertisements on Swiss national television refused to accept the applicant's commercial as it considered the advertisement to be of a political character. Subsequently, the Federal Court upheld the decision not to broadcast the commercial as Swiss legislation prohibited political advertising. The applicant contended that the refusal to broadcast the advertisement violated its freedom of expression. A unanimous Chamber endorsed the domestic courts' view that the commercial had a political character.

57. In the Court's opinion the commercial indubitably fell outside the regular commercial context in the sense of inciting the public to purchase a particular product. Rather, with its concern for the protection of animals, expressed partly in drastic pictures, and its exhortation to reduce meat consumption, the commercial reflected controversial opinions pertaining to modern society in general and also lying at the heart of various political debates.

The Court found that the ban on political advertisements had a basis in Swiss law and was for the legitimate aim, under Article 10(2), of preventing wealthy groups from obtaining a competitive advantage in politics. As to whether the ban on the applicant's advertisement was 'necessary in a democratic society' the Chamber held that:

69. It follows that the Swiss authorities had a certain margin of appreciation to decide whether there was a 'pressing social need' to refuse the broadcasting of the commercial. Such a margin of appreciation is particularly essential in commercial matters, especially in an area as complex and fluctuating as that of advertising (see *markt intern Verlag GmbH and Klaus Beermann v Germany*, judgment of 20 November 1989, Series A No 165, pp 19–20, § 33, and *Jacubowski v Germany*, judgment of 23 June 1994, Series A No 291-A, p 14, § 26).

70. However, the Court has found above that the applicant association's film fell outside the regular commercial context inciting the public to purchase a particular product. Rather, it reflected controversial opinions pertaining to modern society in general (see paragraph 57 above). The Swiss

authorities themselves regarded the content of the applicant association's commercial as being 'political' within the meaning of section 18(5) of the Federal Radio and Television Act. Indeed, it cannot be denied that in many European societies there was, and is, an ongoing general debate on the protection of animals and the manner in which they are reared.

71. As a result, in the present case the extent of the margin of appreciation is reduced, since what is at stake is not a given individual's purely 'commercial' interests, but his participation in a debate affecting the general interest (see *Hertel* [*v Switzerland* 1998-VI]).

72. The Court will consequently examine carefully whether the measure in issue was proportionate to the aim pursued. In that regard, it must balance the applicant association's freedom of expression, on the one hand, with the reasons adduced by the Swiss authorities for the prohibition of political advertising, on the other, namely to protect public opinion from the pressures of powerful financial groups and from undue commercial influence; to provide for a certain equality of opportunity among the different forces of society; to ensure the independence of broadcasters in editorial matters from powerful sponsors; and to support the press.

73. It is true that powerful financial groups can obtain competitive advantages in the area of commercial advertising and may thereby exercise pressure on, and eventually curtail the freedom of, the radio and television stations broadcasting the commercials. Such situations undermine the fundamental role of freedom of expression in a democratic society as enshrined in Article 10 of the Convention, in particular where it serves to impart information and ideas of general interest, which the public is moreover entitled to receive. Such an undertaking cannot be successfully accomplished unless it is grounded in the principle of pluralism of which the State is the ultimate guarantor. This observation is especially valid in relation to audio-visual media, whose programmes are often broadcast very widely (see *Informationsverein Lentia and Others v Austria (no. 1)*, judgment of 24 November 1993, Series A No 276, p 16, § 38).

74. In the present case, the contested measure, namely the prohibition of political advertising as provided in section 18(5) of the Federal Radio and Television Act, was applied only to radio and television broadcasts, and not to other media such as the press. The Federal Court explained in this respect in its judgment of 20 August 1997 that television had a stronger effect on the public on account of its dissemination and immediacy. In the Court's opinion, however, while the domestic authorities may have had valid reasons for this differential treatment, a prohibition of political advertising which applies only to certain media, and not to others, does not appear to be of a particularly pressing nature.

75. Moreover, it has not been argued that the applicant association itself constituted a powerful financial group which, with its proposed commercial, aimed at endangering the independence of the broadcaster; at unduly influencing public opinion or at endangering equality of opportunity among the different forces of society. Indeed, rather than abusing a competitive advantage, all the applicant association intended to do with its commercial was to participate in an ongoing general debate on animal protection and the rearing of animals. The Court cannot exclude that a prohibition of 'political advertising' may be compatible with the requirements of Article 10 of the Convention in certain situations. Nevertheless, the reasons must be 'relevant' and 'sufficient' in respect of the particular interference with the rights under Article 10. In the present case, the Federal Court, in its judgment of 20 August 1997, discussed at length the general reasons which justified a prohibition of 'political advertising'. In the Court's opinion, however, the domestic authorities have not demonstrated in a 'relevant and sufficient' manner why the grounds generally advanced in support of the prohibition of political advertising also served to justify the interference in the particular circumstances of the applicant association's case.

76. The domestic authorities did not adduce the disturbing nature of any particular sequence, or of any particular words, of the commercial as a ground for refusing to broadcast it. It therefore

mattered little that the pictures and words employed in the commercial at issue may have appeared provocative or even disagreeable.

77. In so far as the Government pointed out that there were various other possibilities to broadcast the information at issue, the Court observes that the applicant association, aiming at reaching the entire Swiss public, had no other means than the national television programmes of the Swiss Radio and Television Company at its disposal, since these programmes were the only ones broadcast throughout Switzerland. The Commercial Television Company was the sole instance responsible for the broadcasting of commercials within these national programmes. Private regional television channels and foreign television stations cannot be received throughout Switzerland.

78. The Government have also submitted that admitting the applicant association's claim would be to accept a 'right to broadcast' which in turn would substantially interfere with the rights of the Commercial Television Company to communicate information. Reference was further made to the danger of untimely interruptions in television programmes by means of commercials. The Court recalls that its judgment is essentially declaratory. Its task is to determine whether the Contracting States have achieved the result called for by the Convention. Various possibilities are conceivable as regards the organisation of broadcasting television commercials; the Swiss authorities have entrusted the responsibility in respect of national programmes to one sole private company. It is not the Court's task to indicate which means a State should utilise in order to perform its obligations under the Convention (see *De Cubber v Belgium*, judgment of 26 October 1984, Series A No 86, p 20, § 35).

79. In the light of the foregoing, the measure in issue cannot be considered as 'necessary in a democratic society'. Consequently, there has been a violation of Article 10 of the Convention.

The above judgment reveals that the Court will accord States a narrower margin of appreciation to restrict advertisements of a political nature compared to those concerned with purely business/commercial interests (on the latter see **Krone Verlag**, p 680). Paragraph 75 also left open the possibility that in unspecified circumstances States might be able to justify a ban on political advertising under Article 10(2); see further **TV Vest** (below).

In the subsequent case of **Murphy v Ireland**, judgment of 10 July 2003, another Chamber ruled that States should be granted a wider margin of appreciation when regulating advertisements of a religious nature. The applicant, a pastor, had sought to have a radio advertisement, inviting listeners to attend a video presentation about Christ at his faith centre, broadcast on a local commercial radio station. The station was willing to broadcast the advertisement, but the Independent Radio and Television Commission prevented the broadcast as legislation prohibited advertisements 'directed towards any religious…end…' on Irish radio and television stations. The Irish Government sought to justify the ban, before the Court, on the ground, *inter alia*, of religious sensitivities in Ireland as there had been a long history of religious division. The Court, unanimously, held that:

67. In this latter respect, there is little scope under Article 10 § 2 of the Convention for restrictions on political speech or on debate of questions of public interest (see, *mutatis mutandis*, among many other authorities, *Lingens v Austria*, judgment of 8 July 1986, Series A No 103, § 42; *Castells v Spain*, judgment of 23 April 1992, Series A No 236, § 43; and *Thorgeir Thorgeirson v Iceland*, judgment of 25 June 1992, Series A No 239, § 63). However, a wider margin of appreciation is generally available to the Contracting States when regulating freedom of expression in relation to matters liable to offend intimate personal convictions within the sphere of morals or, especially, religion. Moreover, as in the field of morals, and perhaps to an even greater degree, there is no uniform European conception of the requirements of 'the protection of the rights of others' in relation to

attacks on their religious convictions. What is likely to cause substantial offence to persons of a particular religious persuasion will vary significantly from time to time and from place to place, especially in an era characterised by an ever growing array of faiths and denominations. By reason of their direct and continuous contact with the vital forces of their countries, State authorities are in principle in a better position than the international judge to give an opinion on the exact content of these requirements with regard to the rights of others as well as on the 'necessity' of a 'restriction' intended to protect from such material those whose deepest feelings and convictions would be seriously offended (the *Wingrove* [*v UK* 1996-V] judgment, at § 58).

The Court therefore observes that it is this margin of appreciation which distinguishes the present case from the above-cited case of *Vgt Verein gegen Tierfabriken v Switzerland*. In the latter case, the Court considered that the advertisement prohibited concerned a matter of public interest to which a reduced margin of appreciation applied.

...

81. ... the Court observes that there appears to be no clear consensus between the Contracting States as to the manner in which to legislate for the broadcasting of religious advertisements. Certain States have similar prohibitions (for example, Greece, Switzerland and Portugal), certain prohibit religious advertisements considered offensive (for example, Spain and see also Council Directive 89/552/EEC) and certain have no legislative restriction (the Netherlands). There appears to be no 'uniform conception of the requirements of the protection of the rights of others' in the context of the legislative regulation of the broadcasting of religious advertising (see paragraph 67 above).

82. In the circumstances, and given the margin of appreciation accorded to the State in such matters, the Court considers that the State has demonstrated that there were 'relevant and sufficient' reasons justifying the interference with the applicant's freedom of expression within the meaning of Article 10 of the Convention.

In consequence, it concludes that there has been no violation of the Convention.

More generally on the topic of freedom of expression concerning religious beliefs, see p 604.

The imposition of a fine on a television company for broadcasting campaigning advertisements by a small political party breached Article 10 in the opinion of the united Chamber in *TV Vest AS and Rogaland Pensjonistparti v Norway*, judgment of 11 December 2008. Norwegian legislation prohibited all political advertising on television, but the first applicant broadcast several commercials paid for by the second applicant political party during a local/regional election campaign. The Chamber noted that there was no consensus amongst the member States as to whether television advertisements by political parties were banned or permitted. Accordingly:

67. ... In so far as this absence of European consensus could be viewed as emanating from different perceptions regarding what is 'necessary' for the proper functioning of the 'democratic' system in the respective States, the Court is prepared to accept that it speaks in favour of allowing a somewhat wider margin of appreciation than that normally accorded with respect to restrictions on political speech in relation to Article 10 of the Convention.

However, the Chamber did not accept the Supreme Court's view that the fine/ban could be justified as necessary to protect against the financially powerful being able to dominate the television campaign or prevent the devaluation of the political debate. The Chamber found nothing in the second applicant's advertisements that lowered the nature of the election campaign nor were they a wealthy/powerful organization. Do you think it is significant that Norway, unlike the UK, did not provide for free television election broadcasts by political parties?

(II) ARTISTIC EXPRESSION

Müller v Switzerland A.133 (1988)
European Court of Human Rights

Josef Muller is a painter who has exhibited his works on many occasions in private galleries and museums in Switzerland and other countries. In 1981 he was invited by the organizers (who subsequently became his fellow applicants in this case) of a contemporary art exhibition, 'Fri-Art 81' marking the 500th anniversary of the Canton of Fribourg's entry into the Swiss Confederation, to produce and exhibit works in their event. He produced three large paintings which were on show when the exhibition began. The exhibition had been advertised in the press and on posters, and free access was available to everyone. A juvenile reacted violently to Muller's paintings and her father complained to the local public prosecutor. The prosecutor informed an investigating judge that the paintings appeared to fall within the scope of Article 204 of the Criminal Code, which prohibited obscene publications. The judge went to the exhibition and then had the pictures removed and seized by the police. In 1982 the Sarine District Criminal Court convicted the applicants of publishing obscene material, each of them was fined 300 Swiss francs and the confiscated paintings were ordered to be deposited with the cantonal art museum for safekeeping. The Cantonal Court dismissed the applicants' appeals noting that: 'these are not works which, in treating a particular subject or scene, allude to sexual activity more or less discreetly. They place it in the foreground, depicting it not in the embrace of man and woman but in vulgar images of sodomy, fellatio between males, bestiality, erect penises and masturbation.' The Federal Court also dismissed their further appeals. In 1988 the Sarine District Criminal Court granted Muller's application to have the paintings returned to him. The applicants complained of a violation of their rights under Article 10. The Commission expressed the opinion that there had been a violation of this Article in respect of the confiscation of the paintings (11 votes to 3) but there had been no breach of the Convention in respect of the convictions (unanimously).

AS TO THE LAW

...

27. The applicants indisputably exercised their right to freedom of expression—the first applicant by painting and then exhibiting the works in question, and the nine others by giving him the opportunity to show them in public at the 'Fri-Art 81' exhibition they had mounted.

Admittedly, Article 10 does not specify that freedom of artistic expression, in issue here, comes within its ambit; but neither, on the other hand, does it distinguish between the various forms of expression. As those appearing before the Court all acknowledged, it includes freedom of artistic expression—notably within freedom to receive and impart information and ideas—which affords the opportunity to take part in the public exchange of cultural, political and social information and ideas of all kinds. Confirmation, if any were needed, that this interpretation is correct, is provided by the second sentence of paragraph 1 of Article 10, which refers to 'broadcasting, television or cinema enterprises', media whose activities extend to the field of art. Confirmation that the concept of freedom of expression is such as to include artistic expression is also to be found in article 19 § 2 of the International Covenant on Civil and Political Rights, which specifically includes within the right of freedom of expression information and ideas 'in the form of art'.

28. The applicants clearly suffered 'interference by public authority' with the exercise of their freedom of expression—firstly, by reason of their conviction by the Sarine District Criminal Court on 24 February 1982, which was confirmed by the Fribourg Cantonal Court on 26 April 1982 and then by

the Federal Court on 26 January 1983 . . . and secondly on account of the confiscation of the paintings, which was ordered at the same time but subsequently lifted . . .

I. THE APPLICANTS' CONVICTION

1. 'Prescribed by law'

29. In the applicants' view, the terms of Article 204 § 1 of the Swiss Criminal Code, in particular the word 'obscene', were too vague to enable the individual to regulate his conduct and consequently neither the artist nor the organisers of the exhibition could foresee that they would be committing an offence. This view was not shared by the Government and the Commission.

According to the Court's case-law, 'foreseeability' is one of the requirements inherent in the phrase 'prescribed by law' in Article 10 § 2 of the Convention. A norm cannot be regarded as a 'law' unless it is formulated with sufficient precision to enable the citizen—if need be, with appropriate advice—to foresee, to a degree that is reasonable in the circumstances, the consequences which a given action may entail . . .

In the present instance, it is also relevant to note that there were a number of consistent decisions by the Federal Court on the 'publication' of 'obscene' items. . . . These decisions, which were accessible because they had been published and which were followed by the lower courts, supplemented the letter of Article 204 § 1 of the Criminal Code. The applicants' conviction was therefore 'prescribed by law' within the meaning of Article 10 § 2 of the Convention.

2. The legitimacy of the aim pursued

30. The Government contended that the aim of the interference complained of was to protect morals and the rights of others. On the latter point, they relied above all on the reaction of a man and his daughter who visited the 'Fri-Art 81' exhibition . . .

The applicants' conviction consequently had a legitimate aim under Article 10 § 2.

3. 'Necessary in a democratic society'

31. The submissions of those appearing before the Court focused on the question whether the disputed interference was 'necessary in a democratic society' for achieving the aforementioned aim.

In the applicants' view, freedom of artistic expression was of such fundamental importance that banning a work or convicting the artist of an offence struck at the very essence of the right guaranteed in Article 10 and had damaging consequences for a democratic society. No doubt the impugned paintings reflected a conception of sexuality that was at odds with the currently prevailing social morality, but, the applicants argued, their symbolical meaning had to be considered, since these were works of art. Freedom of artistic expression would become devoid of substance if paintings like those of Josef Felix Müller could not be shown to people interested in the arts as part of an exhibition of experimental contemporary art.

In the Government's submission, on the other hand, the interference was necessary, having regard in particular to the subject-matter of the paintings and to the particular circumstances in which they were exhibited.

For similar reasons and irrespective of any assessment of artistic or symbolical merit, the Commission considered that the Swiss courts could reasonably hold that the paintings were obscene and were entitled to find the applicants guilty of an offence under Article 204 of the Criminal Code.

32. The Court has consistently held that in Article 10 § 2 the adjective 'necessary' implies the existence of a 'pressing social need' (see, as the most recent authority, the *Lingens* judgment of 8 July 1986, Series A No 103, p 25, § 39). The Contracting States have a certain margin of appreciation in assessing whether such a need exists, but this goes hand in hand with a European supervision, embracing both the legislation and the decisions applying it . . .

In exercising its supervisory jurisdiction, the Court cannot confine itself to considering the impugned court decisions in isolation; it must look at them in the light of the case as a whole, including the paintings in question and the context in which they were exhibited. The Court must determine whether the interference at issue was 'proportionate to the legitimate aim pursued' and whether the reasons adduced by the Swiss courts to justify it are 'relevant and sufficient' (see the same judgment, p 26, § 40).

... Those who create, perform, distribute or exhibit works of art contribute to the exchange of ideas and opinions which is essential for a democratic society. Hence the obligation on the State not to encroach unduly on their freedom of expression.

34. Artists and those who promote their work are certainly not immune from the possibility of limitations as provided for in paragraph 2 of Article 10. Whoever exercises his freedom of expression undertakes, in accordance with the express terms of the paragraph, 'duties and responsibilities'; their scope will depend on his situation and the means he uses (see, *mutatis mutandis*, the *Handyside* judgment previously cited, p 23, § 49). In considering whether the penalty was 'necessary in a democratic society', the Court cannot overlook this aspect of the matter.

33. The applicants' conviction on the basis of Article 204 of the Swiss Criminal Code was intended to protect morals. Today, as at the time of the *Handyside* judgment (previously, cited, p 22, § 48), it is not possible to find in the legal and social orders of the Contracting States a uniform European conception of morals. The view taken of the requirements of morals varies from time to time and from place to place, especially in our era, characterised as it is by a far-reaching evolution of opinions on the subject. By reason of their direct and continuous contact with the vital forces of their countries, State authorities are in principle in a better position than the international judge to give an opinion on the exact content of these requirements as well as on the 'necessity' of a 'restriction' or 'penalty' intended to meet them.

36. In the instant case, it must be emphasised that—as the Swiss courts found both at the cantonal level at first instance and on appeal and at the federal level—the paintings in question depict in a crude manner sexual relations, particularly between men and animals ... They were painted on the spot—in accordance with the aims of the exhibition, which was meant to be spontaneous—and the general public had free access to them, as the organisers had not imposed any admission charge or any age-limit. Indeed, the paintings were displayed in an exhibition which was unrestrictedly open to—and sought to attract—the public at large.

The Court recognises, as did the Swiss courts, that conceptions of sexual morality have changed in recent years. Nevertheless, having inspected the original paintings, the Court does not find unreasonable the view taken by the Swiss courts that those paintings, with their emphasis on sexuality in some of its crudest forms, were 'liable grossly to offend the sense of sexual propriety of persons of ordinary sensitivity'. Note, this is the Swiss definition of obscenity.... In the circumstances, having regard to the margin of appreciation left to them under Article 10 § 2, the Swiss courts were entitled to consider it 'necessary' for the protection of morals to impose a fine on the applicants for publishing obscene material.

The applicants claimed that the exhibition of the pictures had not given rise to any public outcry and indeed that the press on the whole was on their side. It may also be true that Josef Felix Müller has been able to exhibit works in a similar vein in other parts of Switzerland and abroad, both before and after the 'Fri-Art 81' exhibition. It does not, however, follow that the applicants' conviction in Fribourg did not, in all the circumstances of the case, respond to a genuine social need, as was affirmed in substance by all three of the Swiss courts which dealt with the case.

37. In conclusion, the disputed measure did not infringe Article 10 of the Convention.

II. THE CONFISCATION OF THE PAINTINGS

...

3. 'Necessary in a democratic society'

40. Here again, those appearing before the Court concentrated their submissions on the 'necessity' of the interference.

The applicants considered the confiscation to be disproportionate in relation to the aim pursued. In their view, the relevant courts could have chosen a less Draconian measure or, in the interests of protecting human rights, could have decided to take no action at all. They claimed that by confiscating the paintings the Fribourg authorities in reality imposed their view of morals on the country as a whole and that this was unacceptable, contradictory and contrary to the Convention, having regard to the well-known diversity of opinions on the subject.

The Government rejected these contentions. In declining to take the drastic measure of destroying the paintings, the Swiss courts took the minimum action necessary. The discharge of the confiscation order on 20 January 1988, which the first applicant could have applied for earlier, clearly showed that the confiscation had not offended the proportionality principle; indeed, it represented an application of it.

The Commission considered the confiscation of the paintings to be disproportionate to the legitimate aim pursued. In its view, the judicial authorities had no power to weigh the conflicting interests involved and order measures less severe than confiscation for an indefinite period.

...

42. A principle of law which is common to the Contracting States allows confiscation of 'items whose use has been lawfully adjudged illicit and dangerous to the general interest' (see, *mutatis mutandis*, the *Handyside* judgment previously cited, Series A No 24, p 30, § 63). In the instant case, the purpose was to protect the public from any repetition of the offence.

43. The applicants' conviction responded to a genuine social need under Article 10 § 2 of the Convention (see paragraph 36 above). The same reasons which justified that measure also apply in the view of the Court to the confiscation order made at the same time.

Undoubtedly, as the applicants and the Commission rightly emphasised, a special problem arises where, as in the instant case, the item confiscated is an original painting: on account of the measure taken, the artist can no longer make use of his work in whatever way he might wish.

Thus Josef Felix Müller lost, in particular, the opportunity of showing his paintings in places where the demands made by the protection of morals are considered to be less strict than in Fribourg.

It must be pointed out, however ... it is open to the owner of a confiscated work to apply to the relevant cantonal court to have the confiscation order discharged or varied if the item in question no longer presents any danger or if some other, more lenient, measure would suffice to protect the interests of public morals. In its decision of 20 January 1988, the Sarine District Criminal Court stated that the original confiscation 'was not absolute but merely of indeterminate duration, which left room to apply for a reconsideration' ... It granted Mr Müller's application because 'the preventive measure [had] fullfilled its function, namely to ensure that such paintings [were] not exhibited in public again without any precautions' (ibid).

Admittedly, the first applicant was deprived of his works for nearly eight years, but there was nothing to prevent him from applying earlier to have them returned; the relevant case-law of the Basle Court of Appeal was public and accessible, and, what is more, the Agent of the Government himself drew his attention to it during the Commission's hearing on 6 December 1985; there is no evidence before the Court to show that such an application would have failed.

That being so, and having regard to their margin of appreciation, the Swiss courts were entitled to hold that confiscation of the paintings in issue was 'necessary' for the protection of morals.

44. In conclusion, the disputed measure did not infringe Article 10 of the Convention.

FOR THESE REASONS, THE COURT

Holds by six votes to one that the applicants' conviction did not infringe Article 10 of the Convention;

Holds by five votes to two that the confiscation of the paintings did not infringe Article 10 of the Convention.

NOTES

1 The majority was comprised of President Ryssdal and Judges: Cremona, Bindschedler-Robert, Evans, and Bernhardt. Spielmann J dissented as he believed that the applicants' convictions and the confiscation of Muller's paintings should be considered together. In his opinion 'freedom of expression is the rule and interferences by the State, properly justified, must remain the exception'. As the paintings had been returned to Muller in 1988, he did not consider that it was 'necessary' to seize them in 1981 or convict the applicants. De Meyer J partly dissented on the ground that in the context of the exhibition of the paintings in 1981 he did not consider that it was necessary for them to be confiscated.

2 Restricting access to works of art, so that only certain sections of the public can view them, may not of itself prevent States successfully invoking Article 10(2) as a justification for convicting the artists/organizers or confiscating the works of art. For example, in *Otto Preminger Institute v Austria* A.295-A (1994) (discussed at p 605) only paying viewers over 17 years of age would have been admitted to the cinema, but the majority of the Court still found the Austrian authorities' actions (including the seizure/forfeiture of the film) to be lawful under Article 10(2) as being 'necessary' to protect the religious feelings of the local Catholic population.

3 See also *Wingrove v UK*, Reports of Decisions and Judgments, 1996-V (p 606), for another unsuccessful claim that distribution of a video work had been prevented in breach of Article 10.

4 Artistic expression may contain a significant political statement or message and the application of Article 10 to this hybrid form of expression was examined by the Court in *Karata v Turkey*, judgment of 8 July 1999. The applicant, a Turk of Kurdish origin, published a collection of his own poems (entitled 'The song of a rebellion—Dersim'; the latter being the name of a former region where there had been many riots between Kurdish clans and government forces between 1847 and 1938) in 1991. The poems contained verses which included:

> ... thousands of years
> of disasters have not altered our lives
> for our Kurdistan
> for our Dersim
> we will sacrifice our heads, drunk on the fire of rebellion
>
> ...
>
> the whelps of the Ottoman whore
> repeatedly pound our mountains
> the waters that run
> our springtime
>
> ...
>
> they are preparing genocide
> like those who know no bounds.

Subsequently, the Istanbul National Security Court convicted the applicant of disseminating propaganda against the 'indivisible unity of the State' and sentenced him to one year, eight months' imprisonment and a fine of 41 million Turkish Lira. The Court found that the interference with the applicant's freedom of expression was 'prescribed by law' and had legitimate aims (protection of national security and territorial integrity and the prevention of disorder and crime). However, a majority of the Court (12 votes to 5) did not consider that his conviction and sentence was a proportionate response.

> The work in issue contained poems which, through the frequent use of pathos and metaphors, called for self-sacrifice for 'Kurdistan' and included some particularly aggressive passages directed at the Turkish authorities. Taken literally, the poems may be construed as inciting readers to hatred, revolt and the use of violence. In deciding whether they in fact did so, it must nevertheless be borne in mind that the medium used by the applicant was poetry, a form of artistic expression that appeals to only a minority of readers....
>
> In the instant case, the poems had an obvious political dimension. Using colourful imagery, they expressed deep-rooted discontent with the lot of the population of Kurdish origin in Turkey. In that connection, the Court recalls that there is little scope under Article 10(2) of the Convention for restrictions on political speech or on debate on matters of public interest...
>
> The Court observes, however, that the applicant is a private individual who expressed his views through poetry—which by definition is addressed to a very small audience-rather than through the mass media, a fact which limited their potential impact on 'national security', '[public] order' and 'territorial integrity' to a substantial degree. Thus, even though some of the passages from the poems seem very aggressive in tone and to call for the use of violence, the Court considers that the fact that they were artistic in nature and of limited impact made them less a call to an uprising than an expression of deep distress in the face of a difficult political situation. [Paras 49–52.]

Hence the Court was according greater latitude to political expression by artists working in minority (elite?) forms of art. But four dissentients, led by the President of the Court, considered that the crucial factor was the content of the work—not its form.

> The majority of the Court says that poetry is a form of artistic expression that 'appeals only to a minority of readers' and is 'of limited impact'. We disagree with this assessment. It seems to us that the Court saw the poetic form as being more important than the substance, that is to say the tone and content. We consider that the Court should be wary of adopting an ivory tower approach. One only has to think of words of the 'Marseillaise' as an example of a poetic call to arms. [Joint Partly Dissenting Opinion of Judges Wildhaber, Pastor Ridruejo, Costa, and Baka.]

Yet, in the later case of *Alinak v Turkey*, judgment of 29 March 2005, a unanimous Chamber (presided over by Judge Costa) took account of the fact that the form of publication was a novel, when assessing whether it was necessary in a democratic society for the author's words to be censored. The applicant, a former MP, wrote a novel, using fictional characters, based on real events concerning the ill-treatment of residents of an actual village by members of the Turkish security forces. Passages in the book were very emotive and critical of the authorities. For example:

> You cannot terminate it by killing them. There are too many to kill. Whomsoever you want to kill is only the cog of the machine. Even if you break the cog of the machine there are too many degenerated people out there waiting to become the cog! When you are struggling with the first ones, the same old tyrannising machinery continues to function, and this goes on forever. We have to stop this machinery!

A few weeks after the novel was published the State Security Court ordered the seizure of copies of the book. The Chamber determined that:

> 41. The Court notes that the book contains passages in which graphic details are given of fictional ill-treatment and atrocities committed against villagers, which no doubt creates in the mind of the reader a powerful hostility towards the injustice to which the villagers were subjected in the tale. Taken literally, certain passages might be construed as inciting readers to hatred, revolt and the use of violence. In deciding whether they in fact did so, it must nevertheless be borne in mind that the medium used by the applicant was a novel, a form of artistic expression that appeals to a relatively narrow public compared to, for example, the mass media.
>
> . . .
>
> 45. . . . Thus, even though some of the passages from the book seem very hostile in tone, the Court considers that their artistic nature and limited impact reduce them to an expression of deep distress in the face of tragic events, rather than a call to violence.

The Chamber went on to conclude that the seizure of the book was a disproportionate response and amounted to a violation of Article 10. For a novel with a strong political theme that did not satisfy Article 10(2) see *Lindon et al* (p 721).

5   Artistic satire deeply divided a Chamber in *Vereinigung Bildender Künstler v Austria*, judgment of 25 January 2007. The applicant association of artists ran one of Austria's most famous galleries of contemporary art. In 1998 the association held an exhibition entitled 'The Century of Artistic Freedom' which contained a work ('Apocalypse') by the Austrian artist Otto Mühl. The piece comprised paintings of the naked bodies of 34 famous persons (including Mother Teresa) engaged in sexual activity with their heads produced from newspaper photographs (the eyes of some persons being covered by black bands). One person depicted was an Austrian MP. He brought proceedings, under the Copyright Act, against the association claiming that the work debased his public standing. The courts granted an injunction preventing the association from exhibiting the work and ordered the payment of approximately 1,500 euros compensation/costs to him. A narrow majority of the Chamber (4 votes to 3) held that:

> 33. . . . It was common ground in the understanding of the domestic courts at all levels that the painting obviously did not aim to reflect or even to suggest reality; the Government, in their submissions, have not alleged otherwise. The Court finds that such portrayal amounted to a caricature of the persons concerned using satirical elements. It notes that satire is a form of artistic expression and social commentary and, by its inherent features of exaggeration and distortion of reality, naturally aims to provoke and agitate. Accordingly, any interference with an artist's right to such expression must be examined with particular care.

The respondent State could seek to justify the interference with the applicant's freedom of expression as being for the legitimate aim of protecting the reputation of the MP. However, the permanent injunction was a disproportionate measure (especially since a vandal had thrown red paint over the work and partially covered the depiction of the MP). The dissentients, *inter alia*, considered that the injunction was justified to protect the dignity of the MP. It is interesting to speculate whether the Chamber would have been more unified if the domestic courts had sought to grant the injunction on the basis of protecting public morals.

(III) COMMERCIAL EXPRESSION

....

Markt intern Verlag GmbH and Klaus Beermann v Germany A.165 (1989)
European Court of Human Rights

The applicant publishing company was founded to defend the interests of small and medium-sized retail companies against the competition of large supermarkets and mail order enterprises. Mr Beermann was the editor-in-chief. The company published a weekly bulletin which provided information on the commercial activities of the large firms in the beauty products industry and this was sold to subscribers. In 1975 Beermann published an article in the bulletin about an English mail order company ('Cosmetic Club International') which retold the allegations of a German chemist about her claimed failure to obtain a refund from the English company. The article noted that the mail order company denied any knowledge of the complaint and promised a swift investigation of the matter. The bulletin had published previous articles on the mail order company advising retailers to be cautious in their dealings with the firm. The mail order company instituted proceedings in the Hamburg Regional Court against the applicants and the court granted an injunction preventing the bulletin repeating the 1975 statements. The applicants appealed and the Hanseatic Court of Appeal found in their favour. The company appealed to the Federal Court of Justice which ordered the applicants to refrain from republishing the 1975 statements (with a fine of up to 500,000 DM or imprisonment for up to six months for breach of the order) under the terms of the Unfair Competition Act 1909 (this stated that 'Any person who in the course of business commits, for purposes of competition, acts contrary to honest practices may be enjoined from further engaging in those acts and held liable in damages'). The Federal Constitutional Court declined to review the judgment. The applicants petitioned the Commission which (by 12 votes to 1) found a violation of Article 10.

...

AS TO THE LAW

24. The applicants claimed that the prohibition imposed on them by the German courts under section 1 of the 1909 Act and the broad interpretation which those courts gave to that provision had infringed Article 10 of the Convention...

A. APPLICABILITY OF ARTICLE 10

25. The Government primarily disputed the applicability of Article 10. Before the Court they argued that if the case were examined under that provision, it would fall, by reason of the contents of the publication of 20 November 1975 and the nature of markt intern's activities, at the extreme limit of Article 10s field of application. The wording and the aims of the information bulletin in question showed that it was not intended to influence or mobilise public opinion, but to promote the economic interests of a given group of undertakings. In the Government's view, such action fell within the scope of the freedom to conduct business and engage in competition, which is not protected by the Convention.

The applicants did not deny that they defended the interests of the specialised retail trade. However, they asserted that markt intern did not intervene directly in the process of supply and demand. The undertaking depended exclusively on its subscribers and made every effort, as was proper, to satisfy the requirements of its readers, whose preoccupations the mainstream press neglected. To restrict the freedom of expression to news items of a political or cultural nature would result in depriving a large proportion of the press of any protection. . . .

It is clear that the contested article was addressed to a limited circle of tradespeople and did not directly concern the public as a whole; however, it conveyed information of a commercial nature. Such information cannot be excluded from the scope of Article 10 § 1 which does not apply solely to certain types of information or ideas or forms of expression (see, *mutatis mutandis*, the *Müller* judgment of 24 May 1988, Series A No 133, p 19, § 27).

B. COMPLIANCE WITH ARTICLE 10

27. In the Court's view, the applicants clearly suffered an 'interference by public authority' in the exercise of the right protected under Article 10, in the form of the injunction issued by the Federal Court of Justice restraining them from repeating the statements appearing in the information bulletin of 20 November 1975. . . .

1. 'Prescribed by law'

. . .

29. The applicants argued that the disputed interference was not 'prescribed by law', because it was not foreseeable. The relevant German legislation did not indicate the dividing line between freedom of the press and unfair competition. . . .

The Government maintained, on the other hand, that, because of their considerable experience of litigation, the applicants had been familiar with the text and the interpretation of the 1909 Act long before the contested article was published. On this question the Commission shared the Government's view. . . .

30. The Court has already acknowledged the fact that frequently laws are framed in a manner that is not absolutely precise. This is so in spheres such as that of competition, in which the situation is constantly changing in accordance with developments in the market and in the field of communication . . .

In this instance, there was consistent case-law on the matter from the Federal Court of Justice . . .

This case-law which was clear and abundant and had been the subject of extensive commentary, was such as to enable commercial operators and their advisers to regulate their conduct in the relevant sphere.

2. Legitimate aim

. . .

According to the actual wording of the judgment of 16 January 1980, the contested article was liable to raise unjustified suspicions concerning the commercial policy of the Club and thus damage its business. The Court finds that the interference was intended to protect the reputation and the rights of others, legitimate aims under paragraph 2 of Article 10.

3. 'Necessary in a democratic society'

32. The applicants argued that the injunction in question could not be regarded as 'necessary in a democratic society'. The Commission agreed with this view.

The Government, however, disputed it. In their view, the article published on 20 November 1975 did not contribute to a debate of interest to the general public, but was part of an unlawful competitive strategy aimed at ridding the beauty products market of an awkward competitor for specialist retailers. . . .

33. The Court has consistently held that the Contracting States have a certain margin of appreciation in assessing the existence and extent of the necessity of an interference, but this margin is subject to a European supervision as regards both the legislation and the decisions applying it, even those given by an independent court…

Such a margin of appreciation is essential in commercial matters and, in particular, in an area as complex and fluctuating as that of unfair competition. Otherwise, the European Court of Human Rights would have to undertake a re-examination of the facts and all the circumstances of each case. The Court must confine its review to the question whether the measures taken on the national level are justifiable in principle and proportionate…

34. In this case, in order to establish whether the interference was proportionate it is necessary to weigh the requirements of the protection of the reputation and the rights of others against the publication of the information in question. In exercising its power of review, the Court must look at the impugned court decision in the light of the case as a whole…

Markt intern published several articles on the Club criticising its business practices and these articles, including that of 20 November 1975, were not without a certain effect…On the other hand, the Club honoured its promises to reimburse dissatisfied customers and, in 1975, 11,870 of them were reimbursed…

The national courts did weigh the competing interests at stake…

The Federal Court of Justice based its judgment of 16 January 1980 on the premature nature of the disputed publication and on the lack of sufficient grounds for publicising in the information bulletin an isolated incident and, in doing so, took into consideration the rights and legal interests meriting protection…

35. In a market economy an undertaking which seeks to set up a business inevitably exposes itself to close scrutiny of its practices by its competitors. Its commercial strategy and the manner in which it honours its commitments may give rise to criticism on the part of consumers and the specialised press. In order to carry out this task, the specialised press must be able to disclose facts which could be of interest to its readers and thereby contribute to the openness of business activities.

However, even the publication of items which are true and describe real events may under certain circumstances be prohibited: the obligation to respect the privacy of others or the duty to respect the confidentiality of certain commercial information are examples. In addition, a correct statement can be and often is qualified by additional remarks, by value judgments, by suppositions or even insinuations. It must also be recognised that an isolated incident may deserve closer scrutiny before being made public; otherwise an accurate description of one such incident can give the false impression that the incident is evidence of a general practice. All these factors can legitimately contribute to the assessment of statements made in a commercial context, and it is primarily for the national courts to decide which statements are permissible and which are not.

36. In the present case, the article was written in a commercial context; markt intern was not itself a competitor in relation to the Club but it intended—legitimately—to protect the interests of chemists and beauty product retailers. The article itself undoubtedly contained some true statements, but it also expressed doubts about the reliability of the Club, and it asked the readers to report 'similar experiences' at a moment when the Club had promised to carry out a prompt investigation of the one reported case.

According to the Federal Court of Justice…there was not sufficient cause to report the incident at the time of the publication. The Club had agreed to undertake an immediate investigation in order to clarify the position. Furthermore, the applicants had been aware that criticisms of the Club could not be fully justified before further clarification had been sought, as they themselves had described the reply of the Club as a provisional answer. In the opinion of the Federal Court they should therefore have taken into consideration that any such premature publication of the incident was bound to have adverse effects on the Club's business because it gave the specialised retailers an effective argument capable of being used against the Club with their customers, and one which could be used even if the incident should turn out to be an isolated mishap from which no conclusion could be drawn as to the Club's business policy.

37. In the light of these findings and having regard to the duties and responsibilities attaching to the freedoms guaranteed by Article 10, it cannot be said that the final decision of the Federal Court of Justice—confirmed from the constitutional point of view by the Federal Constitution Court—went beyond the margin of appreciation left to the national authorities. It is obvious that opinions may differ as to whether the Federal Court's reaction was appropriate or whether the statements made in the specific case by markt intern should be permitted or tolerated. However, the European Court of Human Rights should not substitute its own evaluation for that of the national courts in the instant case, where those courts, on reasonable grounds, had considered the restrictions to be necessary.

38. Having regard to the foregoing, the Court reaches the conclusion that no breach of Article 10 has been established in the circumstances of the present case.

FOR THESE REASONS, THE COURT

Holds, by nine votes to nine, with the casting vote of the President (Rule 20 § 3 of the Rules of Court), that there has been no violation of Article 10 of the Convention.

JOINT DISSENTING OPINION OF JUDGES GÖLCÜKLÜ, PETTITI, RUSSO, SPIELMANN, DE MEYER, CARRILLO, SALCEDO AND VALTICOS

...

It is just as important to guarantee the freedom of expression in relation to the practices of a commercial undertaking as it is in relation to the conduct of a head of government, which was at issue in the Lingens case....

The fact that a person defends a given interest, whether it is an economic interest or any other interest, does not, moreover, deprive him of the benefit of freedom of expression.

In order to ensure the openness of business activities, it must be possible to disseminate freely information and ideas concerning the products and services proposed to consumers. Consumers, who are exposed to highly effective distribution techniques and to advertising which is frequently less than objective, deserve, for their part too, to be protected, as indeed do retailers.

In this case, the applicants had related an incident which in fact occurred, as has not been contested, and requested retailers to supply them with additional information.

They had exercised in an entirely normal manner their basic right to freedom of expression.

This right was, therefore, violated in their regard by the contested measures.

Having said this, we consider it necessary to make three further observations in relation to the present judgment.

We find the reasoning set out therein with regard to the 'margin of appreciation' of States a cause for serious concern. As is shown by the result to which it leads in this case, it has the effect in practice of considerably restricting the freedom of expression in commercial matters.

By claiming that it does not wish to undertake a re-examination of the facts and all the circumstances of the case, the Court is in fact eschewing the task, which falls to it under the Convention, of carrying out 'European supervision' as to the conformity of the contested 'measures' 'with the requirements' of that instrument.

On the question of the need to 'weigh the competing interests at stake', it is sufficient to note that in this case the interests which the applicants sought 'legitimately' to protect were not taken into consideration at all.

NOTES

1 The majority was comprised of President Ryssdal and Judges: Cremona, Thor Vilhjalmsson, Matscher, Walsh, Evans, Bernhardt, Palm, and Foighel. Martens J (with the approval of Macdonald J) issued a separate dissenting opinion. They expressed the view that, 'the socio-economic press is just as important as the political and cultural press for the progress of our modern societies and for the development of every man.' They were also critical of the German legal regime because, '...a rule extending the scope of the law on unfair competition to the detriment of freedom of the press is unknown in the other Member States of the Council of Europe, and rightly so because, in certain respects, all newspapers may be regarded as partisan, having espoused the cause of certain specific interests.'

2 The majority was not willing to accord the same degree of protection under Article 10 to publications concerned with commercial/business matters, even when they contained true statements of fact, that they were to political and artistic expression. Of course, much of the contemporary media is owned by private sector companies which have as one of their dominant aims the creation of profits for their owners. Therefore, the expression of matters of political or public interest and the creation of artistic works may be underpinned by commercial factors.

3 The Hanseatic Court of Appeal had previously granted an injunction, under the 1909 Act, preventing a vet from giving further statements to the general press criticizing his fellow vets for failing to provide adequate emergency care during the night-time. In *Barthold v Germany* A.90 (1985), the Court (by 5 votes to 2) held that the ruling violated the applicant's rights under Article 10. The Court felt that the approach of the Court of Appeal, '...risks discouraging members of the liberal professions from contributing to public debate on topics affecting the life of the community if ever there is the slightest likelihood of their utterances being treated as entailing, to some degree, an advertising effect' (para 58). Such a response was not a proportionate response and consequently not 'necessary in a democratic society'. This case can, therefore, be distinguished from *markt intern* as (a) the publication was in an ordinary newspaper and (b) the article was concerned with a matter of general public interest. In the later case of *Hertel v Switzerland*, 1998-VI, a majority of the Court (6 votes to 3) held that a State's margin of appreciation should be reduced when commercial speech also encompassed matters of public interest.

Such a margin of appreciation is particularly essential in commercial matters, especially in an area as complex and fluctuating as that of unfair competition...It is however necessary to reduce the extent of the margin of appreciation when what is at stake is not a given individual's purely 'commercial' statements, but his participation in a debate affecting the general interest, for example, over public health; in the instant case, it cannot be denied that such a debate existed. It concerned the effects of microwaves on human health...In that respect, the present case is substantially different from the *markt intern* and *Jacubowski* cases...[Para 47.]

Therefore, the majority found that the injunction granted by the Swiss courts against the applicant (an independent researcher), at the request of an association representing electrical manufacturers, which prohibited him from restating his view that food prepared in a microwave oven is a danger to health, was not 'necessary in a democratic society'. In the opinion of the Court:

The effect of the injunction was thus partly to censor the applicant's work and substantially to reduce his ability to put forward in public views which have their place in a public debate whose existence cannot be denied. It matters little that his opinion is a minority one and may appear to be devoid of merit since, in a sphere in which it is unlikely that any certainty exists, it would be particularly unreasonable to restrict freedom of expression only to generally accepted ideas. [Para 50.]

Hence the Court was seeking to protect the ability of controversial, but bona fide, contributors to participate in public debates about matters of general interest.

4 The 1909 Act was also central to the case of *Jacubowski v Germany* A.291-A (1994). The applicant was a journalist who had been the editor-in-chief of a news agency run by a commercial company. The owners of the agency dismissed him in July 1984. Within a few weeks the agency issued a press release explaining its own reorganization and criticizing the applicant's management (in October 1984 the applicant secured a court order requiring the agency to publish another press release in which he was able to state his response to the criticisms). In September 1984 the applicant sent a collection of newspaper articles critical of the news agency together with a circular letter stating his wish to discuss future developments to 40 clients of the news agency. Several months later the applicant established his own public relations agency. Jacubowski's former employers initiated proceedings under the 1909 Act against him. The Dusseldorf Court of Appeal granted an injunction against Jacubowski preventing him from issuing further similar mailings. The Federal Constitutional Court declined to intervene. The applicant then complained to Strasbourg alleging a violation of Article 10. The Commission unanimously found a breach, but the Court (by 6 votes to 3) dismissed his claims. The Court held that the German courts had not exceeded the national margin of appreciation in commercial matters. In particular the Court gave emphasis to the fact that all the German courts had concluded that Jacubowski's actions, in publishing his own circular to former clients, had been unfair competition in breach of 'accepted moral standards' designed to attract them to his new business. Also, he was able to voice his opinions and defend himself by other means. Therefore, the Court decided that the injunction was not a disproportionate interference with the applicant's freedom of expression.

5 The Court has unanimously held that advertising by a lawyer falls within the scope of Article 10 in *Casado Coca v Spain* A.285 (1994). The applicant was a lawyer practising in Barcelona who published advertisements in a local property owners' newsletter which gave his name, his status as a lawyer, and his office address/telephone number. The Barcelona Bar Council brought disciplinary proceedings against him—at that time advertising by members of the Bar was prohibited unless it related to changes in the details of a practice—and he received a written warning for disregarding the ban on professional advertising. He challenged this penalty before the domestic courts, but the Constitutional Court found no breach of his fundamental rights. The Commission (on the casting vote of the President) found a breach of Article 10. Before the Court, the Spanish Government argued that advertising did not fall within the ambit of Article 10. This bold contention was rejected:

The Court would first point out that Article 10 guarantees freedom of expression to 'everyone'. No distinction is made in it according to whether the type of aim pursued is profit-making or not...In its *Barthold v Germany* judgment (above) the Court left open the question whether commercial advertising as such came within the scope of the guarantees under Article 10, but its later case-law provides guidance on this matter. Article 10 does not apply solely to certain types of information or ideas or forms of expression (see the *markt intern Verlag GmbH and Klaus Beermann v Germany* judgment (above)), in particular those of a political nature; it also encompasses artistic expression (see the *Muller v Switzerland* judgment (above)), information of a commercial nature (see *markt intern Verlag*)—as the Commission rightly pointed out—and even light music and commercials transmitted by cables (see the *Groppera Radio AG v Switzerland* judgment (1990) A.173). In the instant case the impugned notices merely gave the applicant's name, profession, address and telephone number. They were clearly published with the aim of advertising, but they provided persons requiring legal assistance with information that was of definite use and likely to facilitate their access to justice. Article 10 is therefore applicable. [Paras 35–7.]

The Court found that the restrictions on Bar advertisements were 'prescribed by law' and had the legitimate aim of protecting the interests of the public and ensuring respect for members of the Bar. 'In this connection, the special nature of the profession practised by members of the Bar must be considered; in their capacity as officers of the court they benefit from an exclusive right of audience and immunity from legal process in respect of their oral presentation of cases in court, but their conduct must be discreet, honest and dignified' (para 46). Furthermore, a majority of the judges (7 votes to 2) considered that the limitations placed upon the applicant's freedom to advertise his services were 'necessary in a democratic society'. The majority emphasized that the margin of appreciation to be given to States' regulation of advertising was 'particularly essential' and:

The wide range of regulations and the different rates of change in the Council of Europe's member States indicate the complexity of the issue. Because of their direct, continuous contact with their members, the Bar authorities and the country's courts are in a better position than an international court to determine how, at a given time, the right balance can be struck between the various interests involved, namely the requirements of the proper administration of justice, the dignity of the profession, the right of everyone to receive information about legal assistance and affording members of the Bar the possibility of advertising their practices. [Para 55.]

The majority noted that the penalty imposed on the applicant was 'almost a token one in nature', therefore the authorities' actions had been a proportionate interference which could be justified under Article 10(2).

A unanimous Chamber of the full-time Court refused to grant a State a 'wide' margin of appreciation to regulate newspaper advertising in ***Krone Verlag GmbH & Co KG (No 3) v Austria***, judgment of 11 December 2003. The applicant company was the publisher of a daily newspaper. In December 1994 the Salzburg edition of its paper published several advertisements comparing its subscription price to that of another (identified) local paper. The other paper responded by applying to the courts, under the Unfair Competition Act, for an injunction to prevent the applicant from re-printing its advertisement. Eventually the Austrian courts granted an injunction preventing the applicant from publishing advertisements comparing its price with that of the other paper unless the advertisements detailed, *inter alia*, the different coverage of foreign/domestic politics, economic, and cultural issues in the two newspapers. The applicant complained that the injunction violated its freedom of expression guaranteed by Article 10. The Strasbourg judgment held that:

30. The Court reiterates that under its case-law the States parties to the Convention have a certain margin of appreciation in assessing the necessity of an interference, but this margin is subject to European supervision as regards both the relevant rules and the decisions applying them (see *markt intern Verlag GmbH and Klaus Beermann*, § 33). Such a margin of appreciation is particularly essential in the complex and fluctuating area of unfair competition. The same applies to advertising. The Court's task is therefore confined to ascertaining whether the measures taken at national level are justifiable in principle and proportionate (see *Casado Coca v Spain*, judgment of

24 February 1994, Series A No 285-A, p 28, § 50; and *Jacubowski v Germany*, judgment of 26 May 1994, No 15088/89, § 26).

31. For the public, advertising is a means of discovering the characteristics of services and goods offered to them. Nevertheless, it may sometimes be restricted, especially to prevent unfair competition and untruthful or misleading advertising. In some contexts, the publication of even objective, truthful advertisements might be restricted in order to ensure respect for the rights of others or owing to the special circumstances of particular business activities and professions. Any such restrictions must, however, be closely scrutinised by the Court, which must weigh the requirements of those particular features against the advertising in question; to this end, the Court must look at the impugned penalty in the light of the case as a whole (see *Casado Coca*, cited above, § 51).

32. Turning to the circumstances of the present case, the Court considers that the domestic courts based their decision first and foremost on the assumption that the two newspapers were not of comparable quality and that a comparison of their prices would therefore be misleading. On the other hand, the courts also stated that the two newspapers were competitors in the same market and for the same circle of readers. The Court finds these two statements rather inconsistent.

33. In looking further at the impact of the impugned injunction on the applicant company, the Court observes that no penalty was imposed. However, the measure at issue has quite far-reaching consequences as regards future advertising involving price comparison: the applicant company will also need to provide information on how its reporting style differs on matters of foreign or domestic politics, economy, culture, science, health, environmental issues and law. The Court considers the injunction to be far too broad, impairing the very essence of price comparison. Moreover, its practical implementation—though not impossible in general—appears to be highly difficult for the applicant company. Furthermore, the applicant company risks the imposition of fines for non-compliance with this order.

34. The Court notes that the domestic courts have given priority to the protection of the reputation of the other competitor and the rights of the consumers against misleading advertising in the instant case. However, when balancing the conflicting interests involved and taking account of the impact of the injunction on the applicant company's possibilities in future for advertising involving price comparison, the Court considers that the Austrian courts have overstepped their margin of appreciation in the present case, and that the measure at issue is disproportionate, and therefore not 'necessary in a democratic society' within the meaning of Article 10 § 2 of the Convention.

35. Accordingly, there has been a violation of Article 10 of the Convention.

Here, the Court considered that the extent of the restrictions placed on the applicant's freedom to advertise the comparative price of its newspaper were too onerous even though the domestic authorities were accorded a 'certain' margin of appreciation.

6 The full-time Court has held that States may be required to provide legal aid to impecunious defendants subject to defamation actions brought against them by economically powerful companies. In *Steel and Morris v UK*, see p 411, the Chamber held that:

94. The Court further does not consider that the fact that the plaintiff in the present case was a large multinational company should in principle deprive it of a right to defend itself against defamatory allegations or entail that the applicants should not have been required to prove the truth of the statements made. It is true that large public companies inevitably and knowingly lay themselves open to close scrutiny of their acts and, as in the case of the businessmen and women who manage them, the limits of acceptable criticism are wider in the case of such companies (see *Fayed v the United Kingdom*, judgment of 21 September 1994, Series A No 294-B, § 75). However, in addition

to the public interest in open debate about business practices, there is a competing interest in protecting the commercial success and viability of companies, for the benefit of shareholders and employees, but also for the wider economic good. The State therefore enjoys a margin of appreciation as to the means it provides under domestic law to enable a company to challenge the truth, and limit the damage, of allegations which risk harming its reputation (see *markt intern Verlag GmbH and Beerman v Germany*, judgment of 20 November 1989, Series A No 165, §§ 33–38).

95. If, however, a State decides to provide such a remedy to a corporate body, it is essential, in order to safeguard the countervailing interests in free expression and open debate, that a measure of procedural fairness and equality of arms is provided for. The Court has already found that the lack of legal aid rendered the defamation proceedings unfair, in breach of Article 6 § 1. The inequality of arms and the difficulties under which the applicants laboured are also significant in assessing the proportionality of the interference under Article 10. As a result of the law as it stood in England and Wales, the applicants had the choice either to withdraw the leaflet and apologise to McDonald's, or bear the burden of proving, without legal aid, the truth of the allegations contained in it. Given the enormity and complexity of that undertaking, the Court does not consider that the correct balance was struck between the need to protect the applicants' rights to freedom of expression and the need to protect McDonald's rights and reputation. The more general interest in promoting the free circulation of information and ideas about the activities of powerful commercial entities, and the possible 'chilling' effect on others are also important factors to be considered in this context, bearing in mind the legitimate and important role that campaign groups can play in stimulating public discussion (see, for example, *Lingens v Austria*, judgment of 8 July 1986, Series A No 103, § 44, *Bladet Tromsø* § 64, *Thorgeir Thorgeirson* § 68). The lack of procedural fairness and equality therefore gave rise to a breach of Article 10 in the present case.

7   Professor Munro has commented:

The recognition of a category of commercial speech may be traced back earlier than the European Convention, to First Amendment case law in the United States. Indeed, it may not go too far to say that the categorisation approach to issues of freedom of expression may itself be attributed broadly to American origins....

   Granting acceptance of a market economy, there is a general acceptance that advertising necessarily has a place in it. More positively, it is reasonable to contend that advertising performs useful social and educational functions. Speaking for the majority of the United States Supreme Court in *Virginia State Board of Pharmacy v Virginia Citizens Consumer Council*, Blackmun J. said:

   'So long as we preserve a predominantly free enterprise economy, the allocation of our resources in large measure will be made through numerous private economic decisions. It is a matter of public interest that those decisions, in the aggregate, be intelligent and well informed. To this end the free flow of commercial information is indispensable...

   'As to the particular consumer's interest in the free flow of commercial information, that interest may be as keen, if not keener by far, than his interest in the day's most urgent political debate. [425 U.S. 748, 763 (1976)]...'

When advertising represents the artistic creations of individuals, there is also justification by the same arguments for self-expression as apply to other artistic works. There could even be constructed an argument that businesses have rights to self-expression, given that expression has economic as well as personal and political applications.

   If advertising may be justified on the basis of its social utility, there should be no difficulty in defending other types of commercial speech such as corporate communications. The activities of business and commerce are, in general, in the public interest, so commercial speech scarcely deserves to be treated as 'low value' speech as if it involved criminality.... [Colin R. Munro, 'The Value of Commercial Speech' (2003) 62(1) *Cambridge Law Journal* 134 at 135 and 156–7.]

Freedom to hold opinions

The dismissal of a State employee because of her political opinions and activities has been adjudged to amount to an interference with her rights under Article 10(1). In **Vogt v Germany** A.323 (1995), the applicant had been a secondary school language teacher employed by the Government of Lower Saxony. During her time as a student in the early 1970s she had joined the German Communist Party and she continued her membership throughout her training as a probationary teacher. In 1979, before the end of her probationary period, she was appointed a permanent civil servant (the formal status of teachers in State schools in Germany). Her assessment report for 1981 described her work as entirely satisfactory and stated that she was held in high regard by her pupils and their parents and by colleagues. However, in 1982 the regional council began disciplinary proceedings against her for allegedly failing to comply with the duty of loyalty to the constitution which all German civil servants were under a statutory duty to respect. The basis of the case against her was that she had engaged in political activities on behalf of the Communist Party, such as distributing its literature and standing as a candidate for the party in federal elections (in a series of cases the Federal Administrative Court had ruled that civil servants who played an active role in the Communist Party were in breach of their duty of loyalty, because they were necessarily identifying with the party's anti-constitutional aims). In 1987 the local Administrative Court found that she had breached her duty of loyalty and ordered her dismissal. Despite her claims that in her opinion membership of the Communist Party was not in breach of her duty of loyalty, the German appellate courts upheld her dismissal. The Commission (by 13 votes to 1) considered that there had been a breach of, *inter alia*, Article 10. The Court (by 17 votes to 2) held that the applicant fell within Article 10:

> The Court reiterates that the right of recruitment to the civil service was deliberately omitted from the Convention. Consequently, the refusal to appoint a person as a civil servant cannot as such provide the basis for a complaint under the Convention. This does not mean, however, that a person who has been appointed as a civil servant cannot complain on being dismissed if that dismissal violates one of his or her rights under the Convention. Civil servants do not fall outside the scope of the Convention.... According to the authorities, she had by her activities on behalf of the [German Communist Party] and by her refusal to dissociate herself from that party expressed views inimical to the above-mentioned system. It follows that there was indeed an interference with the exercise of the right protected by Article 10 of the Convention. [Paras 43–4.]

The Court found that the authorities' actions were 'prescribed by law' and had the legitimate aims of protecting national security, preventing disorder, and protecting the rights of others.

> The Court notes that a number of Contracting States impose a duty of discretion on their civil servants.... This notion has a special importance in Germany because of that country's experience under the Weimar Republic, which, when the Federal Republic was founded after the nightmare of Nazism, led to its constitution being based on the principle of a 'democracy capable of defending itself'. [Para 50.]

However, a bare majority of the Court (10 votes to 9) considered that it was not 'necessary in a democratic society' for Mrs Vogt to have been dismissed. The majority felt that the punishment was disproportionate having regard to: (a) the virtual impossibility of such persons finding employment as teachers elsewhere in Germany, (b) that her position did not involve security risks, (c) that her work at school had been wholly satisfactory, (d) '...not even the prolonged investigations lasting several years were apparently capable of yielding any instance where Mrs Vogt had actually made specific pronouncements belying her emphatic assertion that she upheld the values of the German constitutional order' (para 60), and (e) the Communist Party had not been banned in Germany and, therefore, the applicant's activities on its behalf were lawful.

The dissentients believed that the dismissal of the applicant was a proportionate response in the light of: (a) the fact that her activities on behalf of the Communist Party had intensified after she had been appointed as a civil servant, (b) the 'special history' of Germany's constitutional order, and (c) '...at the relevant time the East-West confrontation and the antagonism between the communist regime on the one side and the West German democratic order on the other made it necessary to strengthen the democratic order and not to allow it to be undermined.'

The judgments in this case provide a fascinating illustration of the breadth of factors, including constitutional history and geo-political relationships, that the Court is willing to examine when applying Article 10.

Right to receive and impart information and ideas

Autronic AG v Switzerland A.178 (1990)
European Court of Human Rights

The applicant was a limited company incorporated in Switzerland which specialized in electronics. During the early 1980s it sold 90 cm dish aerials for the domestic reception of television programmes broadcast by satellites. At that time the only programmes capable of being received by persons using the aerial in Switzerland were programmes broadcast by a Soviet Union telecommunications satellite (G-Horizont). The applicant applied to the Head Office of the Swiss national Post and Telecommunications Authority (PTT) in the spring of 1982 for permission to give a showing, at the Basle Trade Fair, of the Soviet television programmes which could be received by its aerial. The PTT wrote to the Soviet Union's Embassy in Berne which granted permission for the duration of the fair. In the summer of 1982 the applicant made a similar application to the PTT in respect of another trade exhibition. The request was passed on to the Soviet Union's Embassy, but they did not reply. Therefore, the PTT informed the applicant that it could not grant permission and that an unauthorized reception of the Soviet broadcasts would be contrary to the Swiss Radio Regulations. Some months later the applicant applied to the PTT for a declaratory ruling that the reception for private use of uncoded television programmes broadcast by foreign satellites did not require the consent of the broadcasting State's authorities. In 1983 the PTT ruled that it could only grant a receiving licence with the consent of the broadcasting State's authorities. The applicant sought to challenge that ruling in the Swiss court, but the Federal Court decided that the applicant did not have an interest worthy of protection as only 'eccentrics' would be inclined to buy its equipment. The applicant complained to the Commission of an alleged interference with its right to receive information, namely foreign satellite television programmes, contained in Article 10. A majority (11 votes to 2, with 1 abstention) found a violation.

...

A. APPLICABILITY OF ARTICLE 10

44. In the Government's submission, the right to freedom of expression was not relevant to the applicant company's complaint in the present case....Freedom of expression that was exercised as in the present case, exclusively for pecuniary gain came under the head of economic freedom, which was outside the scope of the Convention. The 'information' in question was therefore not protected by Article 10.

...

47. In the Court's view, neither Autronic AG's legal status as a limited company nor the fact that its activities were commercial nor the intrinsic nature of freedom of expression can deprive Autronic AG of the protection of Article 10. The Article applies to 'everyone', whether natural or legal persons. The Court has, moreover, already held on three occasions that it is applicable to profit-making corporate bodies (see the *Sunday Times* judgment of 26 April 1979, Series A No 30, the *Markt Intern Verlag GmbH and Klaus Beermann* judgment of 20 November 1989, Series A No 165, and the *Groppera Radio AG* judgment of 28 March 1990, Series A No 173). Furthermore, Article 10 applies not only to the content of information but also to the means of transmission or reception since any restriction imposed on the means necessarily interferes with the right to receive and impart information. Indeed the Article expressly mentions in the last sentence of its first paragraph certain enterprises essentially concerned with the means of transmission.

Before the Convention institutions the applicant company complained of an interference with its freedom to receive information and ideas regardless of frontiers, and not with its freedom to impart them. Like the Commission, the Court is of the view that the reception of television programmes by means of a dish or other aerial comes within the right laid down in the first two sentences of Article 10 § 1, without it being necessary to ascertain the reason and purpose for which the right is to be exercised. As the administrative and judicial decisions complained of...prevented Autronic AG from lawfully receiving G-Horizont's transmissions, they therefore amounted to 'interference by public authority' with the exercise of freedom of expression.

...

B. COMPLIANCE WITH ARTICLE 10

...

2. Paragraph 2 of Article 10

53. It must be determined whether the interference complained of was 'prescribed by law', was in pursuance of one or more of the legitimate aims listed in paragraph 2 and was 'necessary in a democratic society' in order to achieve them.

(a) 'Prescribed by law'

It does not appear necessary to decide the question, since even supposing that the 'prescribed by law' condition is satisfied, the court comes to the conclusion that the interference was not justified (see paragraphs 60–3 below).

(b) Legitimate aim

58. The Government contended that the impugned interference was in pursuance of two aims recognised in the Convention.

The first of these was the 'prevention of disorder' in telecommunications. It was important to have regard to the limited number of frequencies available, to prevent the anarchy that might be caused by unlimited international circulation of information and to ensure cultural and political pluralism.

Secondly, the interference was, the Government maintained, aimed at 'preventing the disclosure of information received in confidence': the secrecy of telecommunications, which covered the television transmissions in question and was guaranteed in Article 22 of the International Telecommunications Convention, had to be protected....

59. The Court finds that the interference was in pursuance of the two aims cited by the Government, which were fully compatible with the Convention—the prevention of disorder in telecommunications and the need to prevent the disclosure of confidential information.

(c) 'Necessary in a democratic society'

60. The applicant company submitted that the refusal to give it permission did not correspond to any pressing social need; it was not necessary in order to prevent the disclosure of confidential information, since broadcasters anxious to restrict their broadcasts to a particular audience would encode them....

61. The Court has consistently held that the Contracting States enjoy a certain margin of appreciation in assessing the need for an interference, but this margin goes hand in hand with European supervision, whose extent will vary according to the case. Where, as in the instant case, there has been an interference with the exercise of the rights and freedoms guaranteed in paragraph 1 of Article 10, the supervision must be strict, because of the importance of the rights in question; the importance of these rights has been stressed by the Court many times....

62. The Government maintained that the Court, in carrying out its review, should look at matters as they stood at the material time and, in particular, should ignore the legal and technical developments that had taken place since....

The Court observes that later developments can be taken into account in so far as they contribute to a proper understanding and interpretation of the relevant rules.

In the technical field, several other telecommunications satellites broadcasting television programmes have come into service. In the legal field, developments have included, at international level, the signature within the Council of Europe on 5 May 1989 of the European Convention on Transfrontier Television and, at national level, the fact that several member States allow reception of uncoded television broadcasts from telecommunications satellites without requiring the consent of the authorities of the country in which the station transmitting to the satellite is situated.

The latter circumstance is not without relevance, since the other States signatories to the International Telecommunications Convention and the international authorities do not appear to have protested at the interpretation of Article 22 of this Convention and the provisions of the Radio Regulations that it implies. The contrary interpretation of these provisions, which was relied on by the Swiss Government in support of the interference, is consequently not convincing....

63. That being so, the Government's submission based on the special characteristics of telecommunications satellites cannot justify the interference. The nature of the broadcasts in issue, that is to say uncoded broadcasts intended for television views in the Soviet Union, in itself precludes describing them as 'not intended for the general use of the public' within the meaning of numbers 1992–1994 of the Radio Regulations. Leaving aside the international rules discussed above, there was therefore no need to prohibit reception of these broadcasts.

Before the Court the Swiss Government also argued that a total ban on unauthorised reception of transmissions from telecommunications satellites was the only way of ensuring 'the secrecy of international correspondence', because there was no means of distinguishing signals conveying such correspondence from signals intended for the general use of the public. That submission is unpersuasive, since the Government had already conceded before the Commission that there was no risk of obtaining secret information by means of dish aerials receiving broadcasts from telecommunications satellites.

The Court concludes that the interference in question was not 'necessary in a democratic society' and that there has accordingly been a breach of Article 10.

…

FOR THESE REASONS, THE COURT

Holds by sixteen votes to two that Article 10 applied and that there has been a breach of it;

NOTES

1 The majority was comprised of President Ryssdal and Judges: Cremona, Thor Vilhjalmsson, Gölcüklü, Pettiti, Walsh, Evans, Macdonald, Russo, Bernhardt, Spielmann, De Meyer, Carrillo Salcedo, Martens, Palm, and Foighel. Bindschedler-Robert and Matscher JJ issued a dissenting opinion in which they expressed the view that:

…Article 10 presupposes a minimum of identification between the person claiming to rely on the right protected by that Article and the 'information' transmitted or received. In the instant case, however, the content of the information—by pure chance Soviet programmes in Russian—was a matter of complete indifference to the company and to the visitors to the trade fair who were likely to see the programmes; the sole purpose was to give a demonstration of the technical characteristics of the dish aerial in order to promote sales of it. That being so, we consider it an abuse of process on the part of the company to invoke freedom of information, and Article 10 is accordingly not, in our opinion, applicable in the instant case. [Para 1.]

They also considered that the Swiss response was reasonable in the light of the conventions governing international broadcasting and the practice of the majority of States regarding the receipt of foreign satellite broadcasts.

2 During the 1990s the use of satellites to broadcast television, and radio, programmes directly to people's homes became a major commercial activity with large media companies investing billions of pounds in the hardware (and software) to broadcast encrypted programmes to subscribers. By 2010, BSkyB had ten million customers in the UK and sister companies broadcast to other European States.

3 The Court has interpreted the right to impart information and ideas as encompassing the retransmission of commercial radio programmes, including light music, by a local cable operator. In *Groppera Radio AG v Switzerland* A.173 (1990), extracts below, the judgment stated that:

55.…the Court does not consider it necessary to give on this occasion a precise definition of what is meant by 'information' and 'ideas'. 'Broadcasting' is mentioned in the Convention precisely in relation to freedom of expression. Like the Commission, the Court considers that both broadcasting of programmes over the air and cable retransmission of such programmes are covered by the right enshrined in the first two sentences of Article 10(1), without there being any need to make distinctions according to the content of the programmes.

Obviously, the substance of broadcasts may be highly significant in determining whether a State can justify interfering with them lawfully under Article 10(2).

4 The Grand Chamber has been unwilling to construe the right to receive information in Article 10(1) as creating any general positive duties on governmental bodies in member

States to foster public awareness of important matters, such as local environmental hazards. In *Guerra v Italy*, 1998-I, discussed at p 550:

> The Court reiterates that freedom to receive information, referred to in paragraph [1] of Article 10 of the Convention, 'basically prohibits a government from restricting a person from receiving information that others wish or may be willing to impart to him' (see the *Leander v Sweden* judgment (1987) A.116). That freedom cannot be construed as imposing on a State, in circumstances such as those of the present case, positive obligations to collect and disseminate information of its own motion. [Para 53.]

This ruling makes it very difficult for applicants to assert any general right to freedom of information against State bodies under the terms of Article 10(1).

Another Grand Chamber, unanimously, adopted the above approach in *Roche v UK*, judgment of 19 October 2005.

The licensing of broadcasting, television, or cinema

Groppera Radio AG v Switzerland A.173 (1990)
European Court of Human Rights

The applicants were a company incorporated under Swiss law which produced radio programmes, the owner of that company, and two journalists who worked for the company. In 1979 a private Italian company built a radio station on the Pizzo Groppera, an Italian mountain 6 km from the Swiss border. The station had the most powerful FM radio transmitter in Europe and was, therefore, able to broadcast over a distance of 200 km to the north-west thereby reaching nearly one-third of the Swiss population (especially in the Zurich area). The owner of the radio station was a man who used the transmitter as a means of evading the State broadcasting monopoly in Switzerland. Throughout the early 1980s the station broadcast programmes which were wholly financed by Swiss advertisers. In 1982 the Swiss federal government altered the law to allow local radio stations to be established within the country, thereby ending the monopoly of the Swiss Radio Broadcasting Company. The owner of the Groppera station was granted one of the new Swiss local licences on condition that his company ceased broadcasting from the Italian mountain. He then sold the Groppera station to the applicant company and its current owner. The applicant company continued broadcasting to the Zurich area from the Groppera station using the name 'Sound Radio'; its programmes contained light music, information bulletins, and commercials. In 1983 the Swiss federal government issued an Ordinance which allowed the licensing of community-antenna installations. Such licence holders were able to operate a local distribution network through which they could rebroadcast radio programmes to their subscribers provided that the programmes originated from transmitters which complied with the International Telecommunications Convention. Several of the licensed local community networks in Switzerland rebroadcast the programmes transmitted by the applicant company. However, in 1984 they were warned by the Swiss Post and Telecommunications Authority that as the applicant company's broadcasts did not comply with the international rules (e.g. the Groppera station had never been granted a broadcasting licence by the Italian authorities) they were acting contrary to their community licences (and committing a criminal offence) by rebroadcasting the applicant's programmes. One licence holder, the Maur cooperative, challenged the PTT's decision in an administrative law appeal. However, before the appeal was heard the Groppera transmitter was damaged by lightning (and never resumed transmitting), therefore the Swiss Federal Court ruled that it was not necessary to examine the merits of the appeal. The applicants complained to the Commission that the Swiss authorities' ban on the retransmission of their broadcasts by local cable operators infringed their right to impart information and ideas regardless of frontiers under Article 10(1). The Commission (by 7 votes to 6) found a violation of Article 10.

II. ALLEGED VIOLATION OF ARTICLE 10

A. WHETHER THERE WAS AN INTERFERENCE

...the Court does not consider it necessary to give on this occasion a precise definition of what is meant by 'information' and 'ideas'. 'Broadcasting' is mentioned in the Convention precisely in relation to freedom of expression. Like the Commission, the Court considers that both broadcasting of programmes over the air and cable retransmission of such programmes are covered by the right enshrined in the first two sentences of Article 10 § 1, without there being any need to make distinctions according to the content of the programmes. The disputed administrative decisions certainly interfered with the cable retransmission of Sound Radio's programmes and prevented the subscribers in the Maur area from receiving them by that means; they therefore amounted to 'interference by public authority' with the exercise of the aforesaid freedom.

B. WHETHER THE INTERFERENCE WAS JUSTIFIED

56. The Government submitted, in the alternative, that the interference was in keeping with paragraph 1 *in fine*, according to which Article 10 'shall not prevent States from requiring the licensing of broadcasting...enterprises'; in the further alternative, they argued that it was justified under paragraph 2.

1. Paragraph I, third sentence, of Article 10

...

59. The Court agrees with the Government that the third sentence of Article 10 § 1 is applicable in the present case. What has to be determined is the scope of its application.

60. The insertion of the sentence in issue, at the advanced stage of the preparatory work on the Convention, was clearly due to technical or practical considerations such as the limited number of available frequencies and the major capital investment required for building transmitters. It also reflected a political concern on the part of several States, namely that broadcasting should be the preserve of the State. Since then, changed views and technical progress, particularly the appearance of cable transmission, have resulted in the abolition of State monopolies in many European countries and the establishment of private radio stations—often local ones—in addition to the public services. Furthermore, national licensing systems are required not only for the orderly regulation of broadcasting enterprises at the national level but also in large part to give effect to international rules....

61. The object and purpose of the third sentence of Article 10 § 1 and the scope of its application must however be considered in the context of the Article as a whole and in particular in relation to the requirements of paragraph 2.

There is no equivalent of the sentence under consideration in the first paragraph of Articles 8, 9 and 11, although their structure is in general very similar to that of Article 10. Its wording is not unlike that of the last sentence of Article 11 § 2. In this respect, however, the two Articles differ in their structure. Article 10 sets out some of the permitted restrictions even in paragraph 1. Article 11, on the other hand, provides only in paragraph 2 for the possibility of special restrictions on the exercise of the freedom of association by members of the armed forces, the police and the administration of the State, and it could be inferred from this that those restrictions are not covered by the requirements in the first sentence of paragraph 2, except for that of lawfulness ('lawful'/'légitimes'). A comparison of the two Articles thus indicates that the third sentence of Article 10 § 1, in so far as it amounts to an exception to the principle set forth in the first and second sentences, is of limited scope....

This supports the conclusion that the purpose of the third sentence of Article 10 § 1 of the Convention is to make it clear that States are permitted to control by a licensing system the way in which broadcasting is organised in their territories, particularly in its technical aspects. It does not, however, provide that licensing measures shall not otherwise be subject to the requirements of paragraph 2, for that would lead to a result contrary to the object and purpose of Article 10 taken as a whole.

62. The sentence in question accordingly applies in the instant case inasmuch as it permits the orderly control of broadcasting in Switzerland.

...

64. In sum, the interference was in accordance with the third sentence of paragraph 1; it remains to be determined whether it also satisfied the conditions in paragraph 2, that is to say whether it was 'prescribed by law' had a legitimate aim or aims and was 'necessary in a democratic society' in order to achieve them.

2. Paragraph 2 of Article 10

(a) 'Prescribed by law'

...In short, the rules in issue were such as to enable the applicants and their advisers to regulate their conduct in the matter.

(b) Legitimate aim

69. The Government contended that the impugned interference pursued two aims recognised by the Convention.

The first of these was the 'prevention of disorder' in telecommunications, the order in question being laid down in the International Telecommunication Convention and the Radio Regulations and being universally binding. Sound Radio had disregarded three basic principles of the international frequency order:

(a) the licensing principle, whereby the establishment or operation of a broadcasting station by a private person or by an enterprise was subject to the issue of a licence (number 2020 of the Radio Regulations), as Sound Radio had never received a licence from the Italian authorities;

(b) the co-ordination principle, which required special agreements to be concluded between States where the frequency used was between 100 and 108 MHz (number 584 of the Radio Regulations), because there was no such agreement between Switzerland and Italy;

(c) the principle of economic use of the frequency spectrum (Article 33 of the International Telecommunication Convention and number 2666 of the Radio Regulations), because the Pizzo Groppera had the most powerful VHF transmitter in Europe.

The Government submitted, secondly, that the interference complained of was for the 'protection of the... rights of others', as it was designed to ensure pluralism, in particular of information, by allowing a fair allocation of frequencies internationally and nationally.

...

70. The Court finds that the interference in issue pursued both the aims relied on, which were fully compatible with the Convention, namely the protection of the international telecommunications order and the protection of the rights of others.

(c) 'Necessary in a democratic society'

71. The applicants submitted that the ban affecting them did not answer a pressing social need; in particular, it went beyond the requirements of the aims being pursued. It was tantamount to censorship or jamming.

The Government stated that they had had no other recourse seeing that their representations to the Italian authorities continued to be fruitless....

72. According to the Court's settled case-law, the Contracting States enjoy a certain margin of appreciation in assessing whether and to what extent an interference is necessary, but this margin goes hand in hand with European supervision covering both the legislation and the decisions applying it; when carrying out that supervision, the Court must ascertain whether the measures taken at national level are justifiable in principle and proportionate (see, as the most recent authority, the *Markt Intern Verlag GmbH and Klaus Beermann* judgment of 20 November 1989, Series A No 165, pp 19–20, § 33).

73. In order to verify that the interference was not excessive in the instant case, the requirements of protecting the international telecommunications order as well as the rights of others must be weighed against the interest of the applicants and others in the retransmission of Sound Radio's programmes by cable.

The Court reiterates, firstly, that once the 1983 Ordinance had come into force, most Swiss cable companies ceased retransmitting the programmes in question.... Moreover, the Swiss authorities never jammed the broadcasts from the Pizzo Groppera, although they made approaches to Italy and the International Telecommunication Union.... Thirdly, the impugned ban was imposed on a company incorporated under Swiss law—the Maur co-operative—whose subscribers all lived on Swiss territory and continued to receive the programmes of several other stations. Lastly and above all, the procedure chosen could well appear necessary in order to prevent evasion of the law; it was not a form of censorship directed against the content or tendencies of the programmes concerned, but a measure taken against a station which the authorities of the respondent State could reasonably hold to be in reality a Swiss station operating from the other side of the border in order to circumvent the statutory telecommunications system in force in Switzerland.

The national authorities accordingly did not in the instant case overstep the margin of appreciation left to them under the Convention.

C. CONCLUSION

74. In conclusion, no breach of Article 10 is made out, as the disputed measure was in accordance with paragraph 1 *in fine* and satisfied the requirements of paragraph 2.

...

FOR THESE REASONS, THE COURT

...

Holds by sixteen votes to three that there has been no breach of Article 10;

NOTES

1 The plenary court was composed of President Ryssdal and Judges: Cremona, Thor Vilhjalmsson, Bindschedler-Robert, Gölcüklü, Matscher, Pinheiro Farina, Walsh, Evans, Macdonald, Russo, Spielmann, Valticos, Martens, Palm, and Foighel. In his dissent Pettiti J

observed that: 'freedom of expression; which is a fundamental right including the right to receive a communication, is even more necessary in the field of telecommunications. The countries of Eastern Europe have been encouraged on the path to democracy thanks to broadcasts across frontiers...'. Likewise, Bernhardt J in his dissent expressed the view that: 'this freedom of cross-boundary communication is an essential element of present-day democracy and must be taken into account when interpreting the other provisions in Article 10.' De Meyer J did not consider that the Swiss authorities were justified in banning the retransmission of the applicants' broadcasts as it was not certain that they were unlawful under international law.

2   The Court's interpretation in *Groppera* of the licensing power enshrined in Article 10(1) is very important as it makes clear that while States can avail themselves of this power to regulate broadcasting within their territories, these regulatory systems must comply with the conditions laid out in Article 10(2). Consequently, States cannot simply justify their interference with broadcasters by reference to the licensing power under Article 10(1), they must also show that the particular interference was lawful under Article 10(2). Furthermore, broadcasting technology is having a profound effect upon national and international systems of regulation. As we have already noted, by the 1990s extraterritorial broadcasts were being beamed down from satellites with large reception areas, rather than from land-based transmitters with limited foreign coverage. Additionally, digital broadcast technology is expanding the number of television and radio channels that can be broadcast on the available frequencies; therefore, States will find it increasingly difficult to argue that a scarcity of broadcasting capacity entitles them to a dominant occupancy of the available channels (see below the *Lentia* judgment).

3   A Chamber of the Court subsequently refined the plenary Court's above interpretation of the licensing power in *Informationsverein Lentia v Austria* A.276 (1993). There a number of persons, organizations, and a private company sought unsuccessfully to establish radio and television stations in Austria. However, they were unable to do so because Austrian constitutional and federal legislation provided that broadcasting was a public service monopoly through the radio and television programmes produced by the Austrian Broadcasting Corporation. The applicants complained to the Commission that the impossibility of obtaining operating licences infringed their right to communicate information under Article 10(1). The Commission (unanimously in respect of one applicant and by 14 votes to 1 in respect of the other applicants) found a breach of Article 10. The Court (unanimously) accepted the Austrian Government's contention that the licensing power, contained in Article 10(1), enabled national authorities to take account of matters going beyond purely technical considerations when exercising that prerogative.

Technical aspects are undeniably important, but the grant or refusal of a licence may also be made conditional on other considerations, including such matters as the nature and objectives of a proposed station, its potential audience at national, regional or local level, the rights and needs of a specific audience and the obligations deriving from international legal instruments.

This may lead to interferences whose aims will be legitimate under the third sentence of paragraph 1, even though they do not correspond to any of the aims set out in paragraph 2. The compatibility of such interferences with the Convention must nevertheless be assessed in the light of the other requirements of paragraph 2. [Para 32.]

As the public monopoly of broadcasting in Austria was capable of contributing to the quality and balance of programmes, the Court held that such a licensing system was consistent with the State's licensing power. However, it was then necessary to examine whether it satisfied the conditions of Article 10(2). The Government emphasized the political dimension of the audio-visual media and the importance of ensuring that programmes were objective, impartial, diverse, and balanced in their coverage.

The Court has frequently stressed the fundamental role of freedom of expression in a democratic society.... Such an undertaking cannot be successfully accomplished unless it is grounded in the principle of pluralism, of which the State is the ultimate guarantor. This observation is especially valid in relation to audio-visual media, whose programmes are often broadcast very widely.

Of all the means of ensuring that these values are respected, a public monopoly is the one which imposes the greatest restrictions on the freedom of expression.... The far-reaching character of such restrictions means that they can only be justified where they correspond to a pressing social need.

As a result of the technical progress made over the last decades, justification for these restrictions can no longer today be found in considerations relating to the number of frequencies and channels available; the Government accepted this. Secondly, for the purposes of the present case they have lost much of their raison d'être in view of the multiplication of foreign programmes aimed at Austrian audiences.... Finally and above all, it cannot be argued that there are no equivalent less restrictive solutions; it is sufficient by way of example to cite the practice of certain countries which either issue licences subject to specified conditions of variable content or make provision for forms of private participation in the activities of the national corporation. [Paras 38–9.]

Also, the Government's argument that the small size of the Austrian broadcasting market meant that it could not sustain a number of private broadcasters and economic forces would lead to the creation of private monopolies was rejected by the Court.

Their assertions are contradicted by the experience of several European States, of a comparable size to Austria, in which the coexistence of private and public stations, according to rules which vary from country to country and accompanied by measures preventing the development of private monopolies, shows the fears expressed to be groundless. [Para 42.]

Therefore, the Court ruled that the interferences with the applicants' rights were disproportionate to the aim pursued and accordingly were not necessary in a democratic society. Hence there had been a violation of Article 10. This was a highly significant judgment which may have pleased States in clarifying the breadth of their licensing power, but balanced that authority by continuing to emphasize the need for licensing decisions to be compatible with the requirements of Article 10(2). Furthermore, the Court's analysis, especially its emphasis on pluralism in the media, makes it virtually impossible for States to defend a state monopoly of audio-visual broadcasting as being compatible with Article 10 in contemporary times.

Austria's subsequent attempt to liberalize the holding of broadcasting licences by non-state groups was held by a unanimous Court to have violated Article 10 in the case of *Radio ABC v Austria*, 1997-VI. The applicant non-profit-making association had applied unsuccessfully for a licence to operate a radio station in the Vienna area on several occasions since 1989. However, the Court noted with satisfaction that in 1997 Austria had introduced new legislation designed to satisfy its broadcasting obligations under the Convention.

Article 10(2)

Duties and responsibilities

1 The subject matter of a piece of 'expression' falling within Article 10(1) will have a direct effect upon the nature of the author/publisher's duties and responsibilities under Article 10(2). In *Otto-Preminger Institute v Austria* (discussed at p 605), the Court stated that:

> 49. However, as is borne out by the wording itself of Article 10(2), whoever exercises the rights and freedoms enshrined in the first paragraph of that Article undertakes 'duties and responsibilities'. Among them—in the context of religious opinions and beliefs—may legitimately be included an obligation to avoid as far as possible expressions that are gratuitously offensive to others and thus an infringement of their rights, and which therefore do not contribute to any form of public debate capable of furthering progress in human affairs.

2 The broader political and social context in which a publication takes place is also relevant when assessing the nature of these obligations. In *Erdogdu and Ince v Turkey*, judgment of 8 July 1999, the applicants were the editor and a journalist of a monthly review (*Democratic Opposition*) published in Istanbul. During 1992 the review published an interview, conducted by Mr Ince, with a Turkish sociologist regarding the Kurdish issue. In the interview the sociologist expressed his analysis of Kurdish society and expressed the view that in some regions the formation of a Kurdish State could be detected. Subsequently, the Istanbul National Security Court found the applicants guilty of disseminating propaganda against the indivisibility of the State. The Commission, by 31 votes to 1, found a breach of Article 10. A unanimous Court upheld that opinion. It found that the published interview did not incite violence. However, the Court stressed that:

> ...the 'duties and responsibilities' which accompany the exercise of the right to freedom of expression by media professionals assume special significance in situations of conflict and tension. Particular caution is called for when consideration is being given to the publication of the views of representatives of organisations which resort to violence against the State lest the media become a vehicle for the dissemination of hate speech and the promotion of violence. At the same time, where such views cannot be categorised as such, Contracting States cannot with reference to the protection of territorial integrity or national security or the prevention of crime or disorder restrict the right of the public to be informed of them by bringing the weight of the criminal law to bear on the media. [Para 54.]

Consequently, where there is civil strife in a society the media must be careful not to encourage further acts of violence.

3 The Court has also interpreted this phrase as imposing obligations upon the manner in which journalists research their articles. In *Bladet Tromso and Stensaas v Norway*, judgment of 20 May 1999, the applicant local newspaper and its editor had been found liable, and ordered to pay damages, for publishing defamatory statements in respect of the crew of a seal-hunting vessel. The applicants had published a number of articles concerning the behaviour of seal hunters. The major source of these articles was a Mr Lindberg who was a freelance journalist. In March 1988 he was appointed as an unpaid seal-hunting inspector by the Ministry of Fisheries. After serving onboard a seal-hunting ship, for one month, he gave an interview to the applicants in which he alleged that some hunters were killing seals unlawfully. The applicants then published those allegations and denials of them by some crew members from the ship on which Lindberg had served. Two months later Lindberg sent his official report on the expedition to the Ministry. In it he alleged a series of breaches of the regulations governing seal hunting and he identified five named crew members as responsible for this alleged misconduct. The Norwegian Government decided to withhold publication of the report as it contained allegations of criminal behaviour. However, the applicants had received a copy of the report and they published extracts from it and then a few days later they published the whole report, but they deleted the names of the crew members identified by Lindberg. Further denials by the crew of the ship were also published. In February 1989 Lindberg produced a film, containing footage shot during his service as an inspector, which showed breaches of the regulations by seal hunters. The film gained coverage on national and international television programmes and the Norwegian Government responded by establishing a Commission of Inquiry. The latter body reported in 1990 and found that most of Lindberg's allegations against named hunters were not proven, but that several breaches of hunting regulations had occurred. Subsequently, the crew successfully sued Lindberg and the applicants for defamation. The Commission found, by 24 votes to 7, that the Norwegian courts had violated the applicants' rights under Article 10. Before the Court it was accepted that there had been an infringement of the applicants' freedom of expression and that it had been 'prescribed by law' and was for the legitimate aim of protecting the 'reputation or rights' of the seal hunters. The contentious issue was whether the other conditions in Article 10(2) had been satisfied. The Court held that:

> By reason of the 'duties and responsibilities' inherent in the exercise of the freedom of expression, the safeguard afforded by Article 10 to journalists in relation to reporting on issues of general interest is subject to the proviso that they are acting in good faith in order to provide accurate and reliable information in accordance with the ethics of journalism...
>
> The Court notes that the expressions in question consisted of factual statements, not value-judgments (cf *Lingens v Austria* A.103 (1986)). They did not emanate from the newspaper itself but were based on or were directly quoting from the Lindberg report, which the newspaper had not verified by independent research...It must therefore be examined whether there were any special grounds in the present case for dispensing the newspaper from its ordinary obligation to verify factual statements that were defamatory of private individuals. In the Court's view, this depends in particular on the nature and degree of the defamation at hand and the extent to which the newspaper could reasonably regard the Lindberg report as reliable with respect to the allegations in question. [Paras 65–6.]

The majority of the Court, 13 votes, considered that while some of the accusations were relatively serious their adverse effects were reduced as the applicants had not named individual seal hunters.

> As regards the second issue, the trustworthiness of the Lindberg report, it should be observed that the report had been drawn up by Mr Lindberg in an official capacity as an inspector appointed by the Ministry of Fisheries to monitor the seal hunt...In the view of the Court, the press should normally be entitled, when contributing to public debate on matters of legitimate concern, to rely on the contents of official reports without having to undertake independent research. Otherwise, the vital public-watchdog role of the press may be undermined... [Para 68.]

Consequently, the applicants were entitled to have relied upon the accuracy of the contents of the Lindberg report and the domestic judgment of defamation against them was a disproportionate action which violated Article 10. Whereas according to the dissentients:

Few stories can be so important in a democratic society or deserving of protection under Article 10 of the Convention, that the basic ethics of journalism—which require *inter alia* journalists to check their facts before going to press with a story in circumstances such as the present—can be sacrificed for the commercial gratification of an immediate scoop.

Hence the Court generally requires journalists to check the accuracy of their factual assertions before publication, if the journalists are to satisfy this element of Article 10(2). However, a large majority of the judges is willing to allow journalists to rely on the content of official reports, even unpublished ones, as the factual basis for their articles. To what extent do you think the Court's decision in the above case was influenced by the applicants' publication of the whole of the Lindberg report and their reporting of individual hunters' denials of unlawful behaviour?

In the later case of **Selisto v Finland**, judgment of 16 November 2004, the Chamber, 6 votes to 1, found that the criminal conviction of the applicant journalist for defamation in writing a series of articles dealing with surgery undertaken by an unnamed doctor, who allegedly had an alcohol abuse problem, violated Article 10. The Chamber noted that the factual basis of the applicant's articles had not been disputed.

60. . . . It is also of importance that the depicted events and quotations in the article of 27 February 1996 were derived from the police's pre-trial record, which was a public document. In the Court's opinion no general duty to verify the veracity of statements contained in such documents can be imposed on reporters and other members of the media, who must be free to report on events based on information gathered from official sources. If this were not the case the efficacy of Article 10 of the Convention would to a large degree be lost.

4 The Court has accorded protection, under Article 10, to journalists who quote from the work of other media persons. In **Thoma v Luxembourg**, judgment of 29 March 2001, the applicant was a radio broadcaster who presented a weekly programme dealing with environmental issues. In one broadcast he quoted extensively from a newspaper article written by another journalist (Josy Braun) in which the latter accused many forestry officials of corruption. Subsequently, 63 officials successfully sued the applicant for damaging their reputations. The Court held that:

64. . . . A general requirement for journalists systematically and formally to distance themselves from the content of a quotation that might insult or provoke others or damage their reputation is not reconcilable with the press's role of providing information on current events, opinions and ideas. In the instant case, the résumé of the programme shows that in any event the applicant consistently took the precaution of mentioning that he was beginning a quotation and of citing the author, and that, in addition, he described the entire article by his fellow journalist as 'strongly worded' when commenting on it. He had also asked a third party, a woodlands owner, whether he thought that what Josy Braun had written in his article was true.

Therefore, the Court found that the civil judgments against the applicant were not 'necessary in a democratic society' and had violated his right to freedom of expression.

5 A unanimous Chamber ruled that the principles of responsible journalism encompassed the obligation to ensure the accuracy of historical information contained in an internet archive of previous issues of a newspaper. In *Times Newspapers Ltd (Nos 1 and 2) v UK*, judgment of 10 March 2009, the applicant publisher contended that its continuing liability, under common law defamation ('the internet publication rule'), in respect of each accessing of an article contained in its internet archive of previous editions amounted to an infringement of its freedom of expression. But, the Chamber found no breach of Article 10 as the judges considered the requirement to amend the internet archive to note that an article was the subject of defamation proceedings was not unduly burdensome.

6 Another factor influencing the scope of the author/publisher's duties and responsibilities is the type of media involved. In *Jersild v Denmark* (discussed at p 655), the Court observed that:

> In considering the 'duties and responsibilities' of a journalist, the potential impact of the medium concerned is an important factor and it is commonly acknowledged that the audio-visual media often have a much more immediate and powerful effect than the print media ... [Para 31.]

7 The occupation of a person may also affect the extent of such duties and responsibilities. A majority of the Court in *Ahmed v UK* (p 658) adopted a more tolerant attitude towards restrictions on the freedom of expression of local government officers because:

> ... whenever the right to freedom of expression of public servants such as the applicants is in issue the 'duties and responsibilities' referred to in Article 10(2) assume a special significance, which justifies leaving to the authorities of the respondent State a certain margin of appreciation in determining whether the impugned interference is proportionate to the aim as stated. [Para 61.]

Similarly the Court has required 'restraint' in the exercise of freedom of expression of serving judges when making extra-judicial public comments: see *Wille v Liechtenstein* (p 660). However, a unanimous Grand Chamber later gave protection, under Article 10, to a public servant 'whistleblower' who divulged internal correspondence so as to alert the media to the dangers of official corruption. The applicant in *Guja v Moldova*, judgment of 12 February 2008, had been the head of the press department of the Prosecutor General's Office. In 2003 the President of Moldova gave a speech in which he called upon public officials to fight corruption. A few days later the applicant sent copies of two letters, written by the Deputy Speaker of Parliament and a Deputy Minister to prosecutors about pending criminal proceedings against named police officers, to a newspaper. The newspaper subsequently published an article accusing the Deputy Speaker of intimidating prosecutors. Pictures of the two letters were attached to the article. Following investigations into who had leaked the letters, the applicant acknowledged that he had done so in support of the President's call. The applicant was dismissed. After citing *Ahmed*, the Grand Chamber held that:

> 72. ... a civil servant, in the course of his work, may become aware of in-house information, including secret information, whose divulgation or publication corresponds to a strong public interest. The Court thus considers that the signalling by a civil servant or an employee in the public sector of illegal conduct or wrongdoing in the workplace should, in certain circumstances, enjoy protection. This may be called for where the employee or civil servant concerned is the only person, or part of a small category of persons, aware of what is happening at work and is thus best placed to act in the public interest by alerting the employer or the public at large. ...

> 73. In the light of the duty of discretion referred to above, disclosure should be made in the first place to the person's superior or other competent authority or body. It is only where this is clearly impracticable that the information could, as a last resort, be disclosed to the public ...

Having regard to the absence of any Moldovan legislation or administrative procedures regulating whistleblowing, the public interest in the material disclosed by the applicant and his good faith, combined with the severity of the penalty imposed upon him, the Grand Chamber concluded that he had suffered a breach of Article 10. The judgment in *Guja* places onerous obligations on public servants who seek to rely upon this Article to justify their whistleblowing to the media.

Formalities, conditions, restrictions, or penalties

1 The majority of a Grand Chamber of the original Court stated that the prevention of the media from publishing a contentious article (often termed prior restraint) by State authorities can be justified as being in accordance with the Convention depending upon the circumstances of the case. In *Observer and Guardian v UK* (see p 707):

60. For the avoidance of doubt...the Court would only add to the foregoing that Article 10 of the Convention does not in terms prohibit the imposition of prior restraints on publication, as such. This is evidenced not only by the words 'conditions', 'restrictions', 'preventing' and 'prevention' which appear in that provision, but also by the Court's *Sunday Times* judgment (1979) and its *markt intern Verlag GmbH and Klaus Beermann* judgment (1989). On the other hand, the dangers inherent in prior restraints are such that they call for the most careful scrutiny on the part of the Court. This is especially so as far as the press is concerned, for news is a perishable commodity and to delay its publication, even for a short period, may well deprive it of all its value and interest.

2 The full-time Court has held that domestic law authorizing prior restraints on publications must be sufficiently precise to enable the media to know when they may be prevented from exercising freedom of expression. In *Gaweda v Poland*, judgment of 14 March 2002, the applicant had applied to the Polish courts, in 1993 and 1994, for the registration of the titles of two periodicals that he wished to publish. The proposed titles were *The Social and Political Monthly—A European Moral Tribunal* and *Germany—A Thousand-year-old Enemy of Poland*. The domestic courts refused to register the titles as the courts considered that they were untruthful and so contrary to the Press Act 1984. A united Chamber of the European Court stated that:

40. The Court considers that, although Article 10 of the Convention does not in terms prohibit the imposition of prior restraints on publications...the relevant law must provide a clear indication of the circumstances when such restraints are permissible and, a fortiori, when the consequences of the restraint are to block publication of a periodical completely, as in the present case. This is so because of the potential threat that such prior restraints, by their very nature, pose to the freedom of expression guaranteed by Article 10.

41. In the present case, the system for the registration of periodicals is governed by the Press Act of 1984. Under section 20 of that Act, a court can refuse registration only if it establishes that the request for registration does not contain various information concerning the prospective periodical or if it finds that it would infringe the right to protection of the titles of any existing periodicals. Section 5 of the Ordinance on the registration of periodicals, as applicable at the material time, provided that registration was not permissible if it would be inconsistent with the regulations in force or 'with the real state of affairs'.

42. The courts, when refusing the applicant's request to have the two periodicals registered, relied essentially on section 5 of the ordinance in so far as it required that the registration be

refused if it would be 'inconsistent with the real state of affairs'. In its decision of 9 September 1993 the Bielsko-Bial a Regional Court refused registration considering that the proposed title would suggest that a European institution had been established in Kęty, which was clearly not true. On 17 February 1994, in its further decision under scrutiny in the present case, the court considered that the registration of a periodical entitled *Germany—A thousand-year-old enemy of Poland* would be inconsistent with the real state of affairs in that it unduly concentrated on negative aspects of Polish-German relations and thus gave an unbalanced picture of the facts.

43. As is clear from the above, the courts in the present case inferred from the notion 'inconsistent with the real state of affairs' contained in section 5 of the ordinance a power to refuse registration where they considered that a title did not satisfy the test of truth, i.e. that the proposed titles of the periodicals conveyed an essentially false picture. While the terms used in this limb were ambiguous and lacked the clarity that one would expect in a legal provision of this nature, they suggested at most that registration could be refused where the request for registration did not conform to the technical details specified by section 20 of the Press Act. To go further, as the courts did in the present case, and require of the title of a magazine that it embody truthful information, is, firstly, inappropriate from the standpoint of freedom of the press. The title of a periodical is not a statement as such, since its function is essentially to identify the given periodical on the press market for its actual and prospective readers. Secondly, such interpretation would require a legislative provision which clearly authorised it. In short, the interpretation given by the courts introduced new criteria, which could not be foreseen on the basis of the text specifying situations in which the registration of a title could be refused.

...

47. The Court acknowledges that the judicial character of the system of registration is a valuable safeguard of freedom of the press. However, the decisions given by the national courts in this area must also conform to the principles of Article 10. The Court observes that in the present case this in itself did not prevent the courts from imposing a prior restraint on the printed media which entailed a ban on publication of entire periodicals on the basis of their titles.

48. The Court concludes that the law applicable in the present case was not formulated with sufficient precision to enable the applicant to regulate his conduct. Therefore, the manner in which restrictions were imposed on the applicant's exercise of his freedom of expression was not 'prescribed by law' within the meaning of Article 10 § 2 of the Convention.

49. In the light of the above considerations the Court does not consider it necessary to examine whether the other requirements laid down by paragraph 2 of Article 10 of the Convention were satisfied. The Court also notes in this respect that, in any event, the Government did not develop their arguments in support of their conclusion that in the present case these requirements had been met.

50. Accordingly, the Court concludes that there has been a violation of Article 10 of the Convention.

3   In the later case of *Cumpana and Mazare v Romania*, judgment of 17 December 2004, a united Grand Chamber treated a judicial order banning two journalists from working in that profession for one year, as a penalty for defamation of two public officials, fell within the concept of prior restraints.

118. As regards the order prohibiting the applicants from working as journalists for one year, which, moreover, was not remitted, the Court reiterates that prior restraints on the activities of

journalists call for the most careful scrutiny on its part and are justified only in exceptional circumstances...The Court considers that, although it would not appear from the circumstances of the case that the sanction in question had any significant practical consequences for the applicants, it was particularly severe and could not in any circumstances have been justified by the mere risk of the applicants' reoffending.

119. The Court considers that by prohibiting the applicants from working as journalists as a preventive measure of general scope, albeit subject to a time-limit, the domestic courts contravened the principle that the press must be able to perform the role of a public watchdog in a democratic society.

The Court went on to find a breach of Article 10 (see p 707).

4   Belgian legislation and case-law empowering judges to grant prior restraints on the media were found to be lacking clarity and consistency by a unanimous Chamber in *RTBF v Belgium*, judgment of 29 March 2011. Therefore, an injunction preventing the applicant from broadcasting a television programme about the rights of patients, issued by a judge at the request of a doctor, was found to have breached Article 10.

5   In *Mosley v UK* (see p 586), the Chamber observed that:

117....prior restraints may be more readily justified in cases which demonstrate no pressing need for immediate publication and in which there is no obvious contribution to a debate of general public interest.

This may give some comfort to celebrities concerned about media disclosures regarding their personal behaviour.

Prescribed by law

The Court's elaboration of the meaning to be given to this phrase has been examined above in the *Sunday Times* case (p 637). As the judgment in *Tolstoy Miloslavsky* (below) reveals in particular contexts, such as the calculation of the quantum of damages to be awarded by a jury, the domestic legal provisions may be very generalized and yet satisfy this provision of the Convention. In *Rekvényi v Hungary* (p 660) the Court stated that:

The level of precision required of domestic legislation—which cannot in any case provide for every eventuality—depends to a considerable degree on the content of the instrument in question, the field it is designed to cover and the number and status of those to whom it is addressed...Because of the general nature of constitutional provisions, the level of precision required of them may be lower than for other legislation. [Para 34.]

In the context of judicial orders backed by penal sanctions the Court, by 16 votes to 1, found that magistrates' orders binding over two hunt saboteurs to keep the peace and not to behave *contra bonos mores* did not comply with the level of precision required by this element of Article 10(2): *Hashman and Harrup v UK*, 1999-VIII. The two applicants had blown a hunting horn and shouted ('hallooing') while driving in a car on a road near a fox hunt. Their purpose was to distract the hounds and prevent the killing of foxes. On the relevant day one hound left the pack and was run over and killed by a lorry, however the applicants stated that they were nowhere near the location where the hound was killed. A complaint was made to the local magistrates and they bound over the applicants to keep the peace and be of good behaviour in the sum of £100 for 12 months. The applicants appealed to the Crown Court. The court found, *inter alia*, that the applicants' actions were unlawful, but as no violence had been involved it could not be said that they had committed a breach of the peace. However, their conduct was *contra bonos mores* (defined as behaviour which is 'wrong rather than right in the judgment of the majority of contemporary fellow citizens') and their appeal should be rejected. The applicants complained to the Commission alleging, *inter alia*, a breach of Article 10. By 25 votes to 4 the Commission found a breach of that provision. The Court noted that the applicants had not been found to have committed a breach of the peace and therefore the binding over order had prospective effect (unlike the order in *Steel*, below). Furthermore, 'with specific reference to the facts of the present case, the Court does not accept that it must have been evident to the applicants what they were being ordered not [to] do for the period of their binding over' (para 40). Therefore, the order did not comply with Article 10(2). It is highly desirable for the Court to demand greater precision in domestic penal provisions and orders, compared with civil law obligations, under this element of Article 10(2). Indeed, in 1994 the English Law Commission had recommended abolition of the power to bind over, 'because an order binding someone to be of good behaviour is made in such wide terms, it fails to give sufficient indication to the person bound over of the conduct which he or she must avoid in order to be safe from coercive sanctions...' ('Binding Over', para 4.34).

If the actions of public officials, such as police officers, were not in conformity with national law then the Court will hold that those actions were not 'prescribed by law'; see the Court's judgment regarding Needham, Polden, and Cole in *Steel v UK* (p 713).

The failure of Dutch law to provide for the determination by a judge of the issue whether a publisher should be required to disclose, to the police, source materials obtained in confidence was found to breach this element of Article 10 by a united Grand Chamber in *Sanoma Uitgevers BV v Netherlands*, judgment of 14 September 2010. See *Goodwin*, p 726, for the original Court's protection of journalists' sources.

Necessary in a democratic society

The Court's interpretation of this provision as involving the obligation on a respondent State to show that its actions were motivated by the existence of 'a pressing social need' has been noted above in the *Handyside* case (p 627). In addition, the Court also considers whether the respondent State's conduct was a proportional response in respect of the legitimate aim being pursued.

Tolstoy Miloslavsky v UK A.316 (1995)
European Court of Human Rights

The applicant, Count Nikolai Tolstoy Miloslavsky (a descendant of the famous Russian author), is a British citizen and historian. He wrote a pamphlet entitled 'War Crimes and the Wardenship of Winchester College', in which he claimed that the Warden of the College (Lord Aldington) was a '...major war criminal, whose activities merit comparison with those of the worst butchers of Nazi Germany or Soviet Russia...'. The allegations concerned Lord Aldington's alleged role as a senior military officer in Austria during the summer of 1945 when many thousands of Cossack and Yugoslav prisoners of war and refugees were handed over to Soviet and Titoist communist forces. Another person who bore a grievance against Lord Aldington circulated the pamphlet to parents, boys, staff, and former members of Winchester College (a well-known public school), parliamentarians and the press in 1987. Lord Aldington began proceedings against that person for libel and the applicant joined those proceedings at his own request. The defendants pleaded the defences of 'justification' (i.e. the substantial truth of their publication) and 'fair comment'. Lord Aldington asked for trial by a single judge, but the applicant exercised his right to trial by jury. The trial lasted for nearly two months during which both Lord Aldington and the applicant gave evidence and were cross-examined. In his summing-up the trial judge informed the jury that if they found for Lord Aldington they should award a sum of damages which would compensate him for the wrong that had been done to him by the applicant's publication. The jury, unanimously, found in favour of Lord Aldington (and rejected the defences raised by the applicant), and awarded him £1,500,000 damages (an amount three times larger than the previous highest English libel jury award). The trial judge, at the request of Lord Aldington, also granted an injunction restraining the defendants from publishing the words contained in the pamphlet or allegations to a similar effect. Lord Aldington offered not to enforce £1,200,000 of the damages awarded, but the applicant declined the offer claiming that the trial had been a travesty of justice. The Court of Appeal refused to grant the applicant leave to appeal unless he provided £125,000 security for Lord Aldington's costs in respect of the appeal. The applicant was unable to provide such a sum and his appeal was dismissed. Neither did he pay any part of the damages or costs awarded to Lord Aldington.

At the time of the applicant's trial the Court of Appeal could only set aside a jury's award of damages where it was capricious, unconscionable, or irrational. However, in the later case of **Rantzen v Mirror Group Newspapers (1986) Ltd** [1993] 4 All ER 975, the Court of Appeal had regard to Article 10 of the Convention and ruled that a libel jury's almost limitless power to award damages was not compatible with Article 10(2). Therefore, trial judges should guide such juries by referring them to awards made by the Court of Appeal. Also, the Court of Appeal should subject jury awards of large sums to more searching scrutiny to ensure that they were necessary to compensate the plaintiff.

Subsequently the applicant complained to the Commission alleging a violation of several Convention rights. However, the Commission only upheld his claim under Article 10 (unanimously).

I. ALLEGED VIOLATION OF ARTICLE 10 OF THE CONVENTION

33. The applicant alleged a violation of Article 10 of the Convention...
   He maintained that the quantum of the damages awarded against him could not be considered to have been 'prescribed by law'. In addition, the size of the award and the breadth of the injunction had been disproportionate to the aim of protecting Lord Aldington's 'reputation or rights' and had thus not been 'necessary in a democratic society'.

34. The Government disputed these contentions. The Commission shared the applicant's view that the award was disproportionate but did not state any opinion on his other complaints.

35. The Court observes in the first place that the case before it is limited solely to a complaint concerning the amount of damages awarded and the court injunction. In this regard it is unlike the defamation cases it has examined hitherto (see, for instance, the *Lingens v Austria* judgment of 8 July 1986...), which have concerned either the decision determining liability alone or both that and the sanction.
   Both the award of damages and the injunction clearly constituted an interference with the exercise by the applicant of his right to freedom of expression, as guaranteed by paragraph 1 of Article 10

and this was not disputed before the Court. Such an interference entails a violation of Article 10 unless it was 'prescribed by law', pursued an aim or aims that is or are legitimate under Article 10 § 2 and was 'necessary in a democratic society' to attain the aforesaid aim or aims.

A. WAS THE AWARD 'PRESCRIBED BY LAW'?

36. As regards the amount of damages awarded, the applicant complained that it was not 'prescribed by law'.

I. General principles

37. The expression 'prescribed by law' in Article 10 § 2 must be interpreted in the light of the general principles concerning the corresponding words 'in accordance with the law' in Article 8 § 2 (see the *Sunday Times v UK (No 1)* judgment of 26 April 1979...), as follows:

'...the expression...requires first that the impugned measures should have a basis in domestic law. It also refers to the quality of the law in question, requiring that it be accessible to the persons concerned and formulated with sufficient precision to enable them—if need be, with appropriate legal advice—to foresee, to a degree that is reasonable in the circumstances, the consequences which a given action may entail. A law which confers a discretion is not in itself inconsistent with this requirement, provided that the scope of the discretion and the manner of its exercise are indicated with sufficient clarity, having regard to the legitimate aim in question, to give the individual adequate protection against arbitrary interference'.

The Court further reiterates that the word 'law' covers not only statute but also common law (see the above-mentioned *Sunday Times* judgment, p 30, § 47).

2. Application of the above principles

38. The applicant did not deny that the award had a basis in domestic law. However, he complained that the law in question did not enable him to foresee to a reasonable degree that the amount would be as high as £1.5 million.

At English common law there was no upper or lower limit on the amount of damages. The extent to which a judge could give guidance was strictly circumscribed. No specific figures could be suggested and awards of damages in other libel cases or even in personal injury cases had to be disregarded for the purposes of comparison. Guidance could only be given to help the jury to appreciate the real value of large sums of money, for instance by inviting them to reflect on the value of a house... At the material time, there had been no principle recognised in English law that required the award to be proportionate to the aim of repairing the damage to the plaintiff's reputation. The jury gave no reasons for its decision and the award could be overturned by the Court of Appeal only if it was so unreasonable that it could not have been made by sensible people but must have been arrived at capriciously, unconscionably or irrationally...

The applicant pointed out that, as a result of the above, in his case the trial judge had not directed the jury to ensure that the award was proportionate to the damage that Lord Aldington had suffered. The jury had, on the contrary, been encouraged to consider 'enormous damages' and had been informed by the judge that 'there is no league of damages in defamation cases'. The award made, although it had supposedly not included any punitive damages, had been three times the largest amount previously awarded by an English libel jury and had been substantially greater than the sum that would be awarded to a plaintiff suffering permanent and extremely severe physical or mental disablement in a personal injury action. It would have been impossible for the applicant's legal advisers to predict that an award of the magnitude in question would be made.

39. The Government argued that a remedy such as the libel award made in the applicant's case needed to be flexible to accommodate the facts of each individual case, especially the facts of so

exceptional a case as the present one. Only by maintaining such flexibility could the law achieve the purpose of compensation under the law of libel, namely to empower the jury to award, in the light of the relevant criteria at common law . . . , the sum that it considered to be appropriate in the circumstances. In any event, it was not for the Court to assess English libel law in the abstract.

40. The Court notes in the first place that the libel as found by the jury was of an exceptionally serious nature. Indeed, during the hearing at the High Court, counsel for the applicant and the applicant himself had accepted that, if libel were to be established, the jury would have to award a very substantial sum in damages (see paragraph 11 above).

41. The Court accepts that national laws concerning the calculation of damages for injury to reputation must make allowance for an open-ended variety of factual situations. A considerable degree of flexibility may be called for to enable juries to assess damages tailored to the facts of the particular case. Indeed, this is reflected in the trial judge's summing-up to the jury in the present case. . . . It follows that the absence of specific guidelines in the legal rules governing the assessment of damages must be seen as an inherent feature of the law of damages in this area.

Accordingly, it cannot be a requirement of the notion of 'prescribed by law' in Article 10 of the Convention that the applicant, even with appropriate legal advice, could anticipate with any degree of certainty the quantum of damages that could be awarded in his particular case.

42. It is further observed that the discretion enjoyed by the jury in the assessment of damages was not unfettered. A jury was bound to take into account such factors as injury to feelings, the anxiety and uncertainty undergone in the litigation, the absence of apology, the reaffirmation of the truth of the matters complained of, vindication of the plaintiff's reputation. . . . It was for the trial judge to direct the jury on the law. In addition, the Court of Appeal had power to set aside an award, *inter alia* on the ground of irrationality and to order a new trial. It therefore appears that, although the principle of proportionality as such may not have been recognised under the relevant national law, decisions on awards were subject to a number of limitations and safeguards.

43. In jury trials, the lack of reasoning for awards of damages is the norm and is to a large extent unavoidable. The applicant's submission to the effect that the absence of reasons affected the foreseeability of a particularly high award being made in his case is thus not persuasive. Moreover, the argument could apply to any award whatever the magnitude and concerns less the size of the award than the very nature of the jury system itself.

44. Having regard to the fact that a high degree of flexibility may be justified in this area . . . , the various criteria to be taken into account by juries in the assessment of damages as well as the review exercised by the Court of Appeal, the Court reaches the conclusion that the relevant legal rules concerning damages for libel were formulated with sufficient precision. In short, the award was 'prescribed by law'.

B. DID THE AWARD AND THE INJUNCTION PURSUE A LEGITIMATE AIM?

45. The award and the injunction clearly pursued the legitimate aim of protecting the 'reputation or rights of others'. This was not disputed.

C. WERE THE AWARD AND THE INJUNCTION 'NECESSARY IN A DEMOCRATIC SOCIETY'?

1. The award

46. The applicant and the Commission were of the view that the amount of damages awarded—£1.5 million—was disproportionate to the legitimate aim of protecting Lord Aldington's reputation or rights . . .

47. The Government maintained that there was a reasonable relationship of proportionality between the amount of the award and the aim of compensating the damage done to Lord Aldington and restoring his reputation. They pointed out that Article 10 imposed 'duties and responsibilities'. The applicant's pamphlet had been false and unfair and had been expressly designed to provoke a libel action....

48. The Court recalls at the outset that its review is confined to the award as it was assessed by the jury, in the circumstances of judicial control existing at the time, and does not extend to the jury's finding of libel. It follows that its assessment of the facts is even more circumscribed than would have been the case had the complaint also concerned the latter.

In this connection, it should also be observed that perceptions as to what would be an appropriate response by society to speech which does not or is not claimed to enjoy the protection of Article 10 of the Convention may differ greatly from one Contracting State to another. The competent national authorities are better placed than the European Court to assess the matter and should therefore enjoy a wide margin of appreciation in this respect.

49.... However, the Court takes note of the fact that the applicant himself and his counsel accepted that if the jury were to find libel, it would have to make a very substantial award of damages... While this is an important element to be borne in mind it does not mean that the jury was free to make any award it saw fit since, under the Convention, an award of damages for defamation must bear a reasonable relationship of proportionality to the injury to reputation suffered.

The jury had been directed not to punish the applicant but only to award an amount that would compensate the non-pecuniary damage to Lord Aldington.... The sum awarded was three times the size of the highest libel award previously made in England... and no comparable award has been made since. An award of the present size must be particularly open to question where the substantive national law applicable at the time fails itself to provide a requirement of proportionality.

50. In this regard it should be noted that, at the material time, the national law allowed a great latitude to the jury. The Court of Appeal could not set aside an award simply on the grounds that it was excessive but only if the award was so unreasonable that it could not have been made by sensible people and must have been arrived at capriciously, unconscionably or irrationally.... In a more recent case, *Rantzen v Mirror Group Newspapers Ltd*, the Court of Appeal itself observed that to grant an almost limitless discretion to a jury failed to provide a satisfactory measurement for deciding what was 'necessary in a democratic society' for the purposes of Article 10 of the Convention. It noted that the common law—if properly understood—required the courts to subject large awards of damages to a more searching scrutiny than had been customary.

As to what guidance the judge could give to the jury, the Court of Appeal stated that it was to be hoped that in the course of time a series of decisions of the Court of Appeal... would establish some standards as to what would be 'proper' awards. In the meantime the jury should be invited to consider the purchasing power of any award which they might make and to ensure that any award they made was proportionate to the damage which the plaintiff had suffered and was a sum which it was necessary to award him to provide adequate compensation and to re-establish his reputation...

The Court cannot but endorse the above observations by the Court of Appeal to the effect that the scope of judicial control, at the trial and on appeal, at the time of the applicant's case did not offer adequate and effective safeguards against a disproportionately large award.

51. Accordingly, having regard to the size of the award in the applicant's case in conjunction with the lack of adequate and effective safeguards at the relevant time against a disproportionately large award, the Court finds that there has been a violation of the applicant's rights under Article 10 of the Convention.

2. The injunction

52. The applicant further alleged that the injunction…was disproportionate to the aim of protecting Lord Aldington's reputation or rights. It was sweepingly broad and was ordered as a consequence of a verdict of the jury for which no reasons were given and which the judge had interpreted in the widest possible way. It prevented any comment on the role of Lord Aldington in relation to the handover of Cossacks and Yugoslavs…

At any rate, the injunction was disproportionate if considered together with the award, as the measures served in part the same function. The jury was not aware when it made the award that the judge would order an injunction. It was thus very likely that the award was intended not only to compensate Lord Aldington but also to deter the applicant from publishing in the future.

53. The Government contested these allegations. They maintained that in the light of the jury's verdict the judge had been entitled to prevent future repetition of the libel by the applicant and this had been the purpose of the injunction…

D. RECAPITULATION

55. In sum, the Court concludes that the award was 'prescribed by law' but was not 'necessary in a democratic society' as there was not, having regard to its size in conjunction with the state of national law at the relevant time, the assurance of a reasonable relationship of proportionality to the legitimate aim pursued. Accordingly, on the latter point, there has been a violation of Article 10. On the other hand, the injunction, either taken alone or together with the award, did not give rise to any breach of that Article.

…

FOR THESE REASONS, THE COURT

Holds unanimously that the award was 'prescribed by law' within the meaning of Article 10 of the Convention;

Holds unanimously that the award, having regard to its size taken in conjunction with the state of national law at the relevant time was not 'necessary in a democratic society' and thus constituted a violation of the applicant's rights under Article 10;

Holds unanimously that the injunction, either taken alone or together with the award, did not give rise to a breach of Article 10;

NOTES

1   The Court was composed of President Ryssdal and Judges: Walsh, Russo, Palm, Foighel, Pekkanen, Freeland, Repik, and Jambrek.

2   *Dicta* in paragraph 48 of the judgment above indicates that the Court does not consider that defamatory statements fall within the protection of Article 10. Hence their status under the Convention is analogous to that of intentionally racist expression: see *Jersild* (p 655).

3   The liability of a newspaper, found in civil proceedings to have infringed the privacy of the model Naomi Campbell, to pay her lawyers a 'success fee' of £365,000 in addition to approximately £500,000 of actually incurred legal costs was determined to be disproportionate and a breach of Article 10 by a united Chamber in *MGN Ltd v UK*, judgment of 18 January 2011. An official report into costs in English civil cases had concluded that the rules governing defamation and related claims created 'the most bizarre and expensive system that it is possible to devise'!

4   A unanimous Grand Chamber of the full-time Court considered the imposition of sentences of seven months' imprisonment on two journalists for defaming a deputy mayor and judge in *Cumpana and Mazare v Romania*, judgment of 17 December 2004. The Grand Chamber held that:

> 115. Although sentencing is in principle a matter for the national courts, the Court considers that the imposition of a prison sentence for a press offence will be compatible with journalists' freedom of expression as guaranteed by Article 10 of the Convention only in exceptional circumstances, notably where other fundamental rights have been seriously impaired, as, for example, in the case of hate speech or incitement to violence (see, *mutatis mutandis*, *Feridun Yazar v Turkey*, No 42713/98, § 27, 23 September 2004, and *Sürek and Özdemir* v Turkey [GC], Nos 23927/94 and 24277/94, § 63, 8 July 1999). In this connection, the Court notes the recent legislative initiatives by the Romanian authorities, leading to the removal of the offence of insult from the Criminal Code and the abolition of prison sentences for defamation.
>
> 116. The circumstances of the present case—a classic case of defamation of an individual in the context of a debate on a matter of legitimate public interest—present no justification whatsoever for the imposition of a prison sentence. Such a sanction, by its very nature, will inevitably have a chilling effect, and the fact that the applicants did not serve their prison sentence does not alter that conclusion, seeing that the individual pardons they received are measures subject to the discretionary power of the President of Romania; furthermore, while such an act of clemency dispenses convicted persons from having to serve their sentence, it does not expunge their conviction.

Therefore, the prison sentences combined with the added penalties of disqualification from exercising their civil rights for the period of imprisonment and prohibition from working as journalists for one year were 'manifestly disproportionate' in the judgment of the Court and constituted a breach of Article 10. This approach by the Court to the imprisonment of journalists for defamatory comments is a welcome enhancement of the protection of media persons seeking to expose alleged corruption by public officials. Subsequently, the Parliamentary Assembly, in Resolution 1577 (2007), called upon all member States to abolish imprisonment as a punishment for defamation.

Legitimate aims of interferences with freedom of expression

(I) NATIONAL SECURITY

1   In *Observer and Guardian v UK* A.216 (1991), the publishers, editors, and journalists of two newspapers complained about injunctions issued by the English courts preventing them publishing claims of official misconduct made by Peter Wright in his infamous book *Spycatcher*. Wright had been employed by the British Security Service for many years until he retired to Australia in 1976. Then he wrote the book containing his memoirs, which, *inter alia*, alleged that the Security Service had conducted illegal activities to try and undermine the 1974–9 British Labour Government and that a former head of the Service had been a Soviet agent. In 1985, the UK Government began proceedings in the Australian courts to restrain the publication of *Spycatcher* claiming that the disclosure of information gained by Wright during his employment by the Service would be a breach of his duty of confidence derived from his former position. While the Australian proceedings were still pending, the applicants published articles based on the manuscript of the book. Thereupon, the Attorney General began proceedings against the applicant newspaper publishers in the English courts, relying on the breach of confidence principle, for injunctions to prevent them publishing any further articles based on *Spycatcher* material. The evidential basis of the Attorney General's claim was two affidavits sworn by the Cabinet Secretary (Sir Robert Armstrong) in which he asserted that any publication of information coming from Wright would cause unquantifiable damage to the Service and undermine the confidence of friendly countries in the Service. The High Court granted interim injunctions (pending the full hearing of the action) against the applicants in June 1986. Those injunctions were subsequently upheld by the Court of Appeal (July 1986) and by a majority of the House of Lords (30 July 1987). However, on 14 July 1987, *Spycatcher* was published in the USA and became a best-seller. The British Government did not prevent personal imports of the book into the UK, but did take steps to prevent the book being available in public libraries and British booksellers. In June 1988, the High Court of Australia refused to prevent publication of the book in Australia, on the ground that under international law the British Government's interests in its security services was unenforceable in the Australian courts. In October 1988, the House of Lords held, in the substantive proceedings against the applicants, that no injunction should be granted against the applicants as the worldwide publication of *Spycatcher* had destroyed any secrecy as to its contents. However, members and former members of the Security Service owed a lifelong duty of confidence to the Crown: see *A-G v Guardian Newspapers Ltd (No 2)* [1988] 3 All ER 545.

The Commission found a violation, by 6 votes to 5, of Article 10 in respect of interim injunctions issued against the applicants between July 1986 and 30 July 1987. A unanimous Commission also found a breach of Article 10 in respect of the injunctions between 30 July 1987 and October 1988. Before the Court, the Government argued that all the injunctions were, *inter alia*, necessary for the protection of national security. The Court accepted that the injunctions had aims that were legitimate under Article 10(2). However, the Court was divided on the issue whether the injunctions were necessary between July 1986 and July 1987. A majority (14 votes to 10) held that they were necessary, because, having regard to the margin of appreciation to be accorded to national courts in this context, '...'it was not unreasonable to suppose that where a former senior employee of a security service—an "insider", such as Mr Wright—proposed to publish, without authorisation, his memoirs, there was at least a risk they would comprise material the disclosure of which might be detrimental to that service...' (para 61). As for the injunctions between 30 July 1987 and October 1988, the Court was unanimously of the view that they were not necessary in a democratic society.

> As regards the interests of national security relied on, the Court observes that in this respect the Attorney General's case underwent, to adopt the words of Scott J, 'a curious metamorphosis'...As emerges from Sir Robert Armstrong's evidence...injunctions were sought at the outset, *inter alia*, to preserve the secret character of information that ought to be kept secret. By 30 July 1987, however, the information had lost that character...By then, the purpose of the injunctions had thus become confined to the promotion of the efficiency and reputation of the Security Service, notably by: preserving confidence in that Service on the part of third parties; making it clear that the unauthorised publication of memoirs by its former members would not be countenanced; and deterring others who might be tempted to follow in Mr Wright's footsteps.
>
> The Court does not regard these objectives as sufficient to justify the continuation of the interference complained of. It is, in the first place, open to question whether the actions against Observer and Guardian could have served to advance the attainment of these objectives any further than had already been achieved by the steps taken against Mr Wright himself.... Above all, continuation of the restrictions after July 1987 prevented newspapers from exercising their right and duty to purvey information, already available, on a matter of legitimate public concern. [Para 69.]

The Court's judgment is significant in that it demonstrates the exercise of the Strasbourg 'European supervision' to rule that a government's claim of national security interests was not fully justified under Article 10(2). The domestic proceedings are commented upon by E. Barendt in 'Spycatcher and Freedom of Speech' [1989] *Public Law* 204 and the European dimension by I. Leigh in 'Spycatcher in Strasbourg' [1992] *Public Law* 200.

2   The Court applied a similar analysis in *Sunday Times v UK (No 2)* A.217 (1991), holding (unanimously) that it was not necessary for the English courts to grant injunctions preventing this newspaper publishing serial extracts from *Spycatcher* once the book had been published in the USA.

3   The government responded to the *Spycatcher* saga by securing the passage of the Official Secrets Act 1989. Under section 1 it was made a criminal offence for a current or former member of the Security or Intelligence Services to disclose any information relating to security or intelligence matters which he has acquired through his membership of those organizations, unless the disclosure is made in accordance with his official duty. In 1997 Richard Tomlinson, a former member of the Intelligence Service (MI6), was convicted of breaching this provision in regard to plans to publish his memoirs outside the UK (he served nine months' imprisonment).

4   The Court has also rejected another government's claim that national security interests should prevail over freedom of expression in the analogous case of *Vereniging Weekblad Bluf! v Netherlands* A.306-A (1995). The applicant was a left-wing association which published a weekly journal called *Bluf!*. In the spring of 1987 the staff of *Bluf!* gained possession of a 1981 quarterly report produced, for internal readership, by the Dutch internal security service (the BVD). The report showed that the BVD was interested in the activities of the Dutch Communist Party and the anti-nuclear movement. The editor of *Bluf!* decided to publish the report as a supplement to an issue of the journal. However, before the issue was distributed an investigating judge ordered the seizure of the entire print run. Nevertheless, the applicant was able to reprint the issue and sell 2,500 copies on the streets of Amsterdam the next day. To prevent public disorder the authorities did not seek to stop the sale of the issue on the streets. Subsequently, the public prosecutor secured an order from the courts requiring the withdrawal of the issue from circulation. The applicant complained to the Commission that the seizure and withdrawal orders violated Article 10. By 16 votes to 2 the Commission found a violation. Before the Court, the applicant contended that it was contrary to the concept of the rule of law, embodied in the 'prescribed by law' element of Article 10(2), for States to seize/withdraw publications unless those orders were made in the context of criminal proceedings. The judges, unanimously, rejected that contention:

> The Court cannot accept the argument that Article 10 precludes ordering the seizure and withdrawal from circulation of printed matter other than in criminal proceedings. National authorities must be able to take such measures solely in order to prevent punishable disclosure of a secret without taking criminal proceedings against the party concerned, provided that national law affords that party sufficient procedural safeguards. Netherlands law satisfies that condition.... [Para 32.]

Hence, the orders were 'prescribed by law' and they had the legitimate aim of protecting national security because:

> The Court recognises that the proper functioning of a democratic society based on the rule of law may call for institutions like the BVD which, in order to be effective, must operate in secret and be afforded the necessary protection. In this way a State may protect itself against the activities of

individuals and groups attempting to undermine the basic values of a democratic society. In view of the particular circumstances of the case . . . the interferences were unquestionably designed to protect national security . . . [Paras 35–6.]

However, the Court doubted whether the information contained in the six-year-old BVD report was sufficiently sensitive to justify the Dutch authorities prohibiting its distribution. In the light of the earlier judgments in *The Guardian and Observer* and *The Sunday Times (No 2)*, the Court also noted that it had ruled that it was not necessary to prevent the disclosure of information that had already been made public.

Admittedly, in the instant case the extent of publicity was different. However, the information in question was made accessible to a large number of people, who were able in their turn to communicate it to others. Furthermore, the events were commented on by the media. That being so, the protection of the information as a State secret was no longer justified and the withdrawal of issue No 267 of *Bluf!* no longer appeared necessary to achieve the legitimate aim pursued. It would have been quite possible, however, to prosecute the offenders. [Para 45.]

Therefore, the Court found the Dutch authorities' actions had violated the applicant's freedom of expression under Article 10.

The judgment reveals the Court again making its own assessment of whether national security interests, even in the sensitive field of security service operations, require the limitation of freedom of expression concerning such activities. Clearly, the more historic that information is and/or the wider the existing dissemination of that information, the less likely the Court will be to uphold the necessity of further restrictions on publication.

Territorial integrity or public safety

The aim of preserving territorial integrity was recognized by the Court in *Zana v Turkey* (p 650) and the objective of protecting public safety was upheld by the Court in *Grigoriades v Greece* (p 712).

For the prevention of disorder or crime

1   This phrase encompasses two separate aims and the notion of 'disorder' is sufficiently flexible to include the prevention of disorder within discrete groups in society (such as the military): see *Engel v Netherlands* A.22 (1976) (other aspects of this case are examined at p 368). Two of the applicants, Dona and Schul (who were military conscripts), had been sentenced to three and four months' detention in a disciplinary unit for having published and distributed an edition of a journal, entitled *Alarm*, to other soldiers. The specific edition contained the statement:

. . . in addition to ordinary punishments, the army bosses have at their disposal a complete series of other measures-of which transfer is only one-to suppress the soldiers. . . . That only comes to an end when these people, who can only prove their authority by punishment and intimidation, have to look for a normal job.

The military disciplinary authorities found the applicants guilty of publishing a writing tending to undermine discipline. Before the Court, the Dutch Government argued that the interference with the applicants' freedom of expression was justified to prevent disorder within the army. The Court, unanimously, held that:

> 98. . . . the concept of 'order' as envisaged by this provision, refers not only to public order or 'ordre public' within the meaning of Articles 6(1) and 9(2) of the Convention and Article 2(3) of Protocol No 4: it also covers the order that must prevail within the confines of a specific social group. This is so, for example, when, as in the case of the armed forces, disorder in that group can have repercussions on order in society as a whole. It follows that the disputed penalties met this condition if and to the extent that their purpose was the prevention of disorder within the Netherlands armed forces.
>
> Mr Dona and Mr Schul admittedly maintain that Article 10(2) takes account of the 'prevention of disorder' only in combination with the 'prevention of crime'. The Court does not share this view. While the French version uses the conjunctive 'et', the English employs the disjunctive 'or'. Having regard to the context and the general system of Article 10, the English version provides a surer guide on this point.

The Court went on to find that the Dutch military authorities had well-founded reasons for finding that the applicants had attempted to undermine military disciple by publishing the edition of *Alarm* and that the punishments were necessary to prevent disorder. Indeed, the Court ruled that, 'there was thus no question of depriving them of their freedom of expression but only of punishing the abusive exercise of that freedom on their part' (para 101). Therefore, the applicants' claims under Article 10 were rejected.

2   In the later case of *Vereinigung Demokratischer Soldaten Osterreichs and Gubi v Austria* A.302 (1994), the Court adopted a more tolerant and protective attitude towards the distribution of critical publications to military personnel. The applicant association published a monthly magazine (*The Hedgehog*) aimed at soldiers in the Austrian army. However, the Federal Minister of Defence refused to allow the magazine to be distributed at the barracks in the same way (at public expense) as the other two military magazines published in Austria. Gubi was a conscript soldier who was caught distributing an issue of *The Hedgehog* in his barracks. He was sentenced to three days' custody, by his commanding officer, for distributing the magazine. The applicants complained that the authorities' decisions violated Article 10. The Commission (by 12 votes to 9) found a breach of that Article. The Court accepted that the authorities had acted for the legitimate purpose of preventing disorder in the military. But the majority (6 votes to 3) did not consider that the Austrian Government had acted proportionately in refusing to distribute the magazine.

> 38. None of the issues of *The Hedgehog* submitted in evidence recommended disobedience or violence, or even questioned the usefulness of the army. Admittedly, most of the issues set out complaints, put forward proposals for reforms or encourage the readers to institute legal complaints or appeals proceedings. However, despite their often polemical tenor, it does not appear that they overstepped the bounds of what is permissible in the context of a mere discussion of ideas, which must be tolerated in the army of a democratic State just as it must be in the society that such an army serves.

Likewise a larger majority of the Court (8 votes to 1) held that the action against Gubi was a disproportionate response having regard to the contents of the magazine he was caught distributing.

Hence, it now seems that the Court will safeguard the distribution of critical publications within the armed forces of member States provided such journals do not seek to undermine the existence or operational effectiveness of the military services. Such an approach is to be welcomed as a safeguard against the dangers of insularity, complacency, and authoritarianism occurring within these powerful organizations. Indeed in **Grigoriades v Greece**, 1997-VII, the majority of a Grand Chamber found a breach where a conscript officer had been punished for sending a letter criticizing the army to his commanding officer. In his letter the applicant wrote that, 'the army remains a criminal and terrorist apparatus which, by creating an atmosphere of intimidation and reducing to tatters the spiritual welfare of the radical youth, clearly aims at transforming people to mere parts of an apparatus of domination which ruins human nature and transforms human relations from relations of friendship and love to relations of dependence...'. The military courts found the applicant guilty of insulting the army and sentenced him to three months' imprisonment. He complained to the Commission which expressed the opinion that there had been a breach of Article 10 (by 28 votes to 1). The Court accepted that the applicant's conviction had the objective of seeking to maintain an effective military defence (which on this occasion was classified as falling within the legitimate aim of 'protecting national security and public safety'). In considering if the conviction was 'necessary in a democratic society' the Court held:

Article 10 does not stop at the gates of army barracks. It applies to military personnel as to all other persons within the jurisdiction of the Contracting States.... It is true that the contents of the letter included certain strong and intemperate remarks concerning the armed forces in Greece. However, the Court notes that those remarks were made in the context of a general and lengthy discourse critical of army life and the army as an institution. The letter was not published by the applicant or disseminated by him to a wider audience.... Nor did it contain any insults directed against either the recipient of the letter or any other person. Against such a background the Court considers the objective impact on military discipline to have been insignificant. [Paras 45–7.]

Consequently, by 12 votes to 8, the Court determined that the applicant's conviction was a breach of Article 10.

3 The Court applied the prevention of disorder aim to a public protest situation in **Chorherr v Austria** A.266-B (1993). During October 1985 a military ceremony was held in Vienna's Rathausplatz to celebrate the thirtieth anniversary of Austrian neutrality and the fortieth anniversary of the end of the Second World War. About 50,000 people attended. While the ceremony was being held the applicant, and a friend, walked among the spectators distributing copies of a leaflet which called for a referendum on the purchase of fighter aircraft by the Austrian armed forces. The applicant wore a rucksack with an enlargement of the leaflet on the back which projected about 50 cm above his head (this contained the slogan 'Austria does not need any interceptor fighter planes'). The applicant's actions caused a commotion among some of the spectators whose views were blocked and two police officers informed him that he was disturbing public order and that he should cease his demonstration. The applicant refused, asserting his right to freedom of expression, and he was arrested. At the police station administrative criminal proceedings were instituted against him and he was released later that day (one-and-a-half hours after the military ceremony had ended). Chorherr challenged the conduct of the police before the Constitutional Court, but it dismissed his claim. Eventually he was fined 700 schillings for breach of the peace. The applicant complained to the Commission alleging, *inter alia*, a breach of his rights under Article 10. The Commission, on the casting vote of the acting president, found a violation of that provision. All the participants to the proceedings before the Court accepted that the measures taken against Chorherr interfered with his right to freedom of expression under Article 10(1). However, a majority of the Court, 6 votes to 3, found the interference to be justified under Article 10(2). The majority considered the measures were 'prescribed by law' and had the legitimate aim of preventing disorder at the military ceremony. In its opinion the police response to Chorherr's behaviour was within the State's margin of appreciation and proportionate because:

> 33....when he chose this event for his demonstration against the Austrian armed forces, Mr Chorherr must have realised that it might lead to a disturbance requiring measures of restraint, which in this instance, moreover, were not excessive.

Hence, the venue of a public protest is a major factor in determining the lawfulness of State restrictions on the conduct of the protestors under Article 10(2).

4 The reasoning in *Chorherr* was developed by the Court in *Steel v UK*, 1998-VII. The case was brought by a number of persons who had engaged in various forms of public protest. Ms Steel, together with 60 others, had attempted to obstruct and disrupt a grouse shoot in Yorkshire. She walked in front of a member of the shoot as he lifted his shotgun to fire, thereby preventing the shooting of grouse. The police warned the protesters to stop their protest and when the warning was ignored the police arrested 13 demonstrators (including the applicant). She was detained for 44 hours by the police and subsequently the Crown Court upheld a complaint of breach of the peace against her. The court ordered that she agree to be bound over to keep the peace for 12 months in the sum of £100 (if a person breaches such an order they are liable to forfeit the specified sum of money). Steel refused to be bound over and was committed to prison for 28 days. Ms Lush, the second applicant (together with about 25 other protesters), broke into a construction site that was part of the M11 motorway extension in East London. The protesters climbed up trees that were to be felled and climbed onto machinery. The protesters were removed on several occasions by security guards and the former did not use any violence nor did they damage any machinery. Finally the applicant was arrested, while standing under the bucket of a mechanical digger, for conduct likely to provoke a disturbance of the peace. She was detained by the police for 17 hours and later the magistrates' court found the complaint against her made out. The court ordered her to agree to be bound over for 12 months to keep the peace in the sum of £100. When Lush refused she was committed to prison for seven days. The remaining applicants, Ms Needham, Mr Polden, and Mr Cole, held a protest outside a London conference centre where the 'Fighter Helicopter II' conference was being held. The applicants distributed leaflets and held up banners saying 'Work for Peace not War'. They were arrested by the police for alleged breach of the peace. After seven hours' detention they were released. In subsequent proceedings the prosecution decided not to call any evidence and the magistrates dismissed the case against the applicants. All the various applicants complained to the Commission alleging, *inter alia*, a breach of their right to freedom of expression under Article 10. A unanimous Commission found that there had been no breach of this Article in respect of Steel and Lush, but there had been a violation in regard to the other applicants. Before the Court, the British Government sought to argue that Article 10 was not applicable to Steel and Lush as their protests had not been peaceful. This argument was rejected:

> 92. The Court recalls that the first and second applicants were arrested while protesting against a grouse shoot and the extension of a motorway respectively. It is true that these protests took the form of physically impeding the activities of which the applicants disapproved, but the Court considers nonetheless that they constituted expressions of opinion within the meaning of Article 10 (see, for example, *Chorherr v Austria*...). The measures taken against the applicants were, therefore, interferences with their right to freedom of expression.

The Court went on to find that the arrests and detention of Steel and Lush were 'prescribed by law' and for the legitimate aims of preventing disorder and protecting the rights of others. However, the judges were divided on the question of whether the authorities' actions were 'necessary in a democratic society'. The Court stated that:

101. It is true that States enjoy a certain margin of appreciation in assessing whether and to what extent any interference with the exercise of freedom of expression is necessary, particularly as regards the choice of reasonable and appropriate means to be used to ensure that lawful activities can take place peacefully (see the above mentioned *Chorherr* judgment...).

In respect of Ms Steel a bare majority of the Court (5 votes to 4) decided that there was no breach of Article 10:

105. Forty-four hours is undoubtedly a long period of detention in such a case. However, the Court recalls that Ms Steel's behaviour prior to her arrest had created a danger of serious physical injury to herself and others and had formed part of a protest against grouse shooting which risked culminating in disorder and violence. Particularly given the risk of an early resumption by her, if released, of her protest activities against field sports, and the possible consequences of this eventuality, both of which the police were best placed to assess, the Court does not consider that this detention was disproportionate.

However, in their joint partly dissenting opinion Judges Valticos and Makarczyk wrote that:

What is not in any event debatable is that to detain for 44 hours and then sentence to twenty-eight days' imprisonment a person who, albeit in an extreme manner, jumped up and down in front of a member of the shoot to prevent him from killing a feathered friend is so manifestly extreme, particularly in a country known for its fondness for animals, that it amounted, in our view, to a violation of the Convention.

Although the Court recognized that Ms Lush's conduct was arguably less serious than Steel's, all the judges agreed that her arrest and detention was not a disproportionate response by the State. As for the other three applicants, the Court, unanimously, ruled that:

...the measures taken against Ms Needham, Mr Polden and Mr Cole were not 'lawful' or 'prescribed by law', since it is not satisfied that the police had grounds reasonably to apprehend that the applicants' peaceful protest would cause a breach of the peace. For similar reasons...it considers that the interference with the exercise by the applicants of their right to freedom of expression was also disproportionate to the aims of preventing disorder and protecting the rights of others, and was not, therefore, 'necessary in a democratic society. [Para 110.]

Therefore, the Court found a breach of Article 10 in respect of these applicants. One positive aspect of this decision was the Court's willingness to treat physical behaviour, especially that of a symbolic nature, as a form of expression falling within Article 10(1). Nevertheless, where such conduct creates a threat to public order the Court allows the national authorities considerable latitude in restricting or terminating the exercise of this type of expression.

The conviction of a vice-president of a lawful political party for wearing a 'totalitarian symbol' (a five-pointed red star) during an authorized demonstration was determined to breach Article 10 in **Vajnai v Hungary**, judgment of 8 July 2008. The united Chamber considered that the Hungarian ban was too broad as the red star symbol had multiple associations (including use by lawful political parties in other member States as well as links with previous communist regimes that had committed mass violations of human rights). Furthermore, the Hungarian Government had not been able to provide any examples of where disorder had occurred in Hungary caused by the wearing of the red star symbol.

In the later case of *Women on Waves and others v Portugal*, judgment of 3 February 2009, a unanimous Chamber emphasized that freedom of expression entitled persons to select the form in which their ideas were expressed, particularly where symbolic protest activities were undertaken, without unreasonable interference by public authorities. The first applicant, a Dutch foundation, had chartered a ship to visit Portugal to promote the decriminalization of abortion. The Portuguese Government deployed a warship to block the chartered ship from entering Portuguese waters. The Chamber determined that was a disproportionate means of seeking, *inter alia*, to prevent disorder and consequently a breach of Article 10 had occurred.

5   The British Government sought to justify the disclosure order and contempt of court proceedings brought against the applicant journalist in *Goodwin v UK* (p 726) as being necessary 'for the prevention of crime'. However, the Court ruled that it did not have to decide if this aim was relevant in that case as the interferences had the undisputed aim of protecting the rights of others.

For the protection of health or morals

Open Door and Dublin Well Woman v Ireland A.246 (1992)
European Court of Human Rights

The applicants were (a) Open Door Counselling, a non-profit-making company engaged in counselling pregnant women in Ireland, (b) Dublin Well Woman Centre, a non-profit-making company providing medical and counselling services to women in Dublin, (c) two individual counsellors working for Dublin Well Woman, and (d) two Irish women of child-bearing age. In 1983, after a referendum, the Irish Constitution was amended to include Article 40.3.3 which read: 'The State acknowledges the right to life of the unborn and, with due regard to the equal right to life of the mother, guarantees in its laws to respect, and, as far as practicable, by its laws to defend and vindicate that right.' In 1985 the Society for the Protection of Unborn Children (Ireland) brought a private action against the applicant companies claiming that they were acting unlawfully in respect of Article 40.3.3 by counselling women to seek abortions outside Ireland. It was accepted by the applicant companies that they, *inter alia*, discussed abortion as one option with pregnant women and made arrangements (if such a woman so requested) for her to be referred to a clinic in Great Britain. The High Court found that the applicant companies' activities violated Article 40.3.3 and granted an injunction perpetually restraining them from undertaking such conduct. On appeal, the Supreme Court rejected the applicants' arguments but amended the injunction to require, '...the defendants and each of them, their servants or agents be perpetually restrained from assisting pregnant women within the jurisdiction to travel abroad to obtain abortions by referral to a clinic, by the making for them of travel arrangements, or by informing them of the identity and location of and the method of communicating with a specified clinic...'. Costs were awarded against the applicant companies as a result of which Open Door had no assets and ceased its activities. The applicants complained to the Commission that the injunction violated, *inter alia*, their rights to impart or receive information contrary to Article 10 of the Convention. The Commission found a breach in respect of the applicant companies and their counsellors, by 8 votes to 5, and in regard to the women applicants, by 7 votes to 6.

In separate proceedings the European Court of Justice held that the medical termination of pregnancy, performed in accordance with the law of the State in which it was carried out, was a service within the meaning of Article 60 of the Treaty of Rome. However, the provision of information by Irish student associations to their members, about abortion facilities in other member States of the European Community, was too remote from the performance of medical terminations for Irish judicial restrictions on the distribution of such information to be in breach of the Treaty: *Society for the Protection of Unborn Children (Ireland) Ltd v Stephen Grogan* [1991] ECR I-4685. Also, the Irish courts gave judgment in the notorious case of *A-G v X* [1992] 1 IR 1, where the Attorney General had sought an injunction to prevent a 14-year-old girl (who claimed that she had been raped) from leaving Ireland to have an abortion. The Supreme Court ruled that the termination of pregnancy was lawful under Article 40.3.3 where there was a substantial risk to the life of the mother if the pregnancy was not ended. In the circumstances, the girl had expressed the desire to commit suicide, the Supreme Court discharged the injunction preventing her from leaving the country. As a result of these legal developments the Irish Government made the following statement, during the oral hearing before the European Court of Human Rights: '…persons who are deemed to be entitled under Irish law to avail themselves of termination of pregnancy in these circumstances must be regarded as being entitled to have appropriate access to information in relation to the facilities for such operations, either in Ireland or abroad.'

…

III. ALLEGED VIOLATION OF ARTICLE 10

53. The applicants alleged that the Supreme Court injunction, restraining them from assisting pregnant women to travel abroad to obtain abortions, infringed the rights of the corporate applicants and the two counsellors to impart information, as well as the rights of Mrs X and Ms Geraghty to receive information. They confined their complaint to that part of the injunction which concerned the provision of information to pregnant women as opposed to the making of travel arrangements or referral to clinics (see paragraph 20 above)…

A. WAS THERE AN INTERFERENCE WITH THE APPLICANTS' RIGHTS?

55. The Court notes that the Government accepted that the injunction interfered with the freedom of the corporate applicants to impart information. Having regard to the scope of the injunction which also restrains the 'servants or agents' of the corporate applicants from assisting 'pregnant women'…there can be no doubt that there was also an interference with the rights of the applicant counsellors to impart information and with the rights of Mrs X and Ms Geraghty to receive information in the event of being pregnant.…

B. WAS THE RESTRICTION 'PRESCRIBED BY LAW'?

60. Taking into consideration the high threshold of protection of the unborn provided under Irish law generally and the manner in which the courts have interpreted their role as the guarantors of constitutional rights, the possibility that action might be taken against the corporate applicants must have been, with appropriate legal advice, reasonably foreseeable (See the *Sunday Times v UK* judgment of 26 April 1979, Series A No 30, p 31, § 49). This conclusion is reinforced by the legal advice that was actually given to Dublin Well Woman that, in the light of Article 40.3.3°, an injunction could be sought against its counselling activities…

The restriction was accordingly 'prescribed by law'.

C. DID THE RESTRICTION HAVE AIMS THAT WERE LEGITIMATE UNDER ARTICLE 10 § 2?

61. The Government submitted that the relevant provisions of Irish law are intended for the protection of the rights of others—in this instance the unborn—, for the protection of morals and, where appropriate, for the prevention of crime.

62. The applicants disagreed, contending *inter alia* that, in view of the use of the term 'everyone' in Article 10 § 1 and throughout the Convention, it would be illogical to interpret the 'rights of others' in Article 10 § 2 as encompassing the unborn.

63. The Court cannot accept that the restrictions at issue pursued the aim of the prevention of crime since, as noted above neither the provision of the information in question nor the obtaining of an abortion outside the jurisdiction involved any criminal offence. However, it is evident that the protection afforded under Irish law to the right to life of the unborn is based on profound moral values concerning the nature of life which were reflected in the stance of the majority of the Irish people against abortion as expressed in the 1983 referendum. . . . The restriction thus pursued the legitimate aim of the protection of morals of which the protection in Ireland of the right to life of the unborn is one aspect. It is not necessary in the light of this conclusion to decide whether the term 'others' under Article 10 § 2 extends to the unborn.

D. WAS THE RESTRICTION NECESSARY IN A DEMOCRATIC SOCIETY?

64. The Government submitted that the Court's approach to the assessment of the 'necessity' of the restraint should be guided by the fact that the protection of the rights of the unborn in Ireland could be derived from Articles 2, 17 and 60 of the Convention. They further contended that the 'proportionality' test was inadequate where the rights of the unborn were at issue. The Court will examine these issues in turn.

1. Article 2

65. The Government maintained that the injunction was necessary in a democratic society for the protection of the right to life of the unborn and that Article 10 should be interpreted *inter alia* against the background of Article 2 of the Convention which, they argued, also protected unborn life. The view that abortion was morally wrong was the deeply held view of the majority of the people in Ireland and it was not the proper function of the Court to seek to impose a different viewpoint.

66. The Court observes at the outset that in the present case it is not called upon to examine whether a right to abortion is guaranteed under the Convention or whether the foetus is encompassed by the right to life as contained in Article 2. The applicants have not claimed that the Convention contains a right to abortion, as such, their complaint being limited to that part of the injunction which restricts their freedom to impart and receive information concerning abortion abroad.

Thus the only issue to be addressed is whether the restrictions on the freedom to impart and receive information contained in the relevant part of the injunction are necessary in a democratic society for the legitimate aim of the protection of morals as explained above (see paragraph 63). It follows from this approach that the Government's argument based on Article 2 of the Convention does not fall to be examined in the present case. On the other hand, the arguments based on Articles 17 and 60 fall to be considered below (see paragraphs 78 and 79).

2. Proportionality

67. The Government stressed the limited nature of the Supreme Court's injunction which only restrained the provision of certain information. . . . There was no limitation on discussion in Ireland

about abortion generally or the right of women to travel abroad to obtain one. They further contended that the Convention test as regards the proportionality of the restriction was inadequate where a question concerning the extinction of life was at stake. The right to life could not, like other rights, be measured according to a graduated scale. It was either respected or it was not. Accordingly, the traditional approach of weighing competing rights and interests in the balance was inappropriate where the destruction of unborn life was concerned. Since life was a primary value which was antecedent to and a prerequisite for the enjoyment of every other right, its protection might involve the infringement of other rights such as freedom of expression in a manner which might not be acceptable in the defence of rights of a lesser nature.

The Government also emphasised that, in granting the injunction, the Supreme Court was merely sustaining the logic of Article 40.3.3° of the Constitution. The determination by the Irish courts that the provision of information by the relevant applicants assisted in the destruction of unborn life was not open to review by the Convention institutions.

68. The Court cannot agree that the State's discretion in the field of the protection of morals is unfettered and unreviewable (see, *mutatis mutandis*, for a similar argument, the *Norris v Ireland* judgment of 26 October 1988, Series A No 142, p 20, § 45).

It acknowledges that the national authorities enjoy a wide margin of appreciation in matters of morals, particularly in an area such as the present which touches on matters of belief concerning the nature of human life. . . .

However this power of appreciation is not unlimited. It is for the Court, in this field also, to supervise whether a restriction is compatible with the Convention.

69. As regards the application of the 'proportionality' test, the logical consequence of the Government's argument is that measures taken by the national authorities to protect the right to life of the unborn or to uphold the constitutional guarantee on the subject would be automatically justified under the Convention where infringement of a right of a lesser stature was alleged. It is, in principle, open to the national authorities to take such action as they consider necessary to respect the rule of law or to give effect to constitutional rights. However, they must do so in a manner which is compatible with their obligations under the Convention and subject to review by the Convention institutions. To accept the Government's pleading on this point would amount to an abdication of the Court's responsibility under Article 19 'to ensure the observance of the engagements undertaken by the High Contracting Parties . . .'.

70. Accordingly, the Court must examine the question of 'necessity' in the light of the principles developed in its case-law (see, *inter alia*, the *Observer and Guardian v UK* judgment of 26 November 1991, Series A No 216, pp 29–30, § 59). It must determine whether there existed a pressing social need for the measures in question and, in particular, whether the restriction complained of was 'proportionate to the legitimate aim pursued' (ibid). . . .

72. While the relevant restriction, as observed by the Government, is limited to the provision of information, it is recalled that it is not a criminal offence under Irish law for a pregnant woman to travel abroad in order to have an abortion. Furthermore, the injunction limited the freedom to receive and impart information with respect to services which are lawful in other Convention countries and may be crucial to a woman's health and well-being. Limitations on information concerning activities which, notwithstanding their moral implications, have been and continue to be tolerated by national authorities, call for careful scrutiny by the Convention institutions as to their conformity with the tenets of a democratic society.

73. The Court is first struck by the absolute nature of the Supreme Court injunction which imposed a 'perpetual' restraint on the provision of information to pregnant women concerning abortion facilities abroad, regardless of age or state of health or their reasons for seeking counselling on the termination of pregnancy. The sweeping nature of this restriction has since been highlighted

by the case of *A-G v X* and by the concession made by the Government at the oral hearing that the injunction no longer applied to women who, in the circumstances as defined in the Supreme Court's judgment in that case, were not free to have an abortion in Ireland or abroad...

74. On that ground alone the restriction appears over broad and disproportionate. Moreover, this assessment is confirmed by other factors.

75. In the first place, it is to be noted that the corporate applicants were engaged in the counselling of pregnant women in the course of which counsellors neither advocated nor encouraged abortion, but confined themselves to an explanation of the available options....The decision as to whether or not to act on the information so provided was that of the woman concerned. There can be little doubt that following such counselling there were women who decided against a termination of pregnancy. Accordingly, the link between the provision of information and the destruction of unborn life is not as definite as contended. Such counselling had in fact been tolerated by the State authorities even after the passing of the Eighth Amendment in 1983 until the Supreme Court's judgment in the present case. Furthermore, the information that was provided by the relevant applicants concerning abortion facilities abroad was not made available to the public at large.

76. It has not been seriously contested by the Government that information concerning abortion facilities abroad can be obtained from other sources in Ireland such as magazines and telephone directories...or by persons with contacts in Great Britain. Accordingly, information that the injunction sought to restrict was already available elsewhere although in a manner which was not supervised by qualified personnel and thus less protective of women's health. Furthermore, the injunction appears to have been largely ineffective in protecting the right to life of the unborn since it did not prevent large numbers of Irish women from continuing to obtain abortions in Great Britain.

77. In addition, the available evidence, which has not been disputed by the Government, suggests that the injunction has created a risk to the health of those women who are now seeking abortions at a later stage in their pregnancy, due to lack of proper counselling, and who are not availing themselves of customary medical supervision after the abortion has taken place....Moreover, the injunction may have had more adverse effects on women who were not sufficiently resourceful or had not the necessary level of education to have access to alternative sources of information....These are certainly legitimate factors to take into consideration in assessing the proportionality of the restriction.

3. Articles 17 and 60

78. The Government, invoking Articles 17 and 60 of the Convention, have submitted that Article 10 should not be interpreted in such a manner as to limit, destroy or derogate from the right to life of the unborn which enjoys special protection under Irish law.

79. Without calling into question under the Convention the regime of protection of unborn life that exists under Irish law, the Court recalls that the injunction did not prevent Irish women from having abortions abroad and that the information it sought to restrain was available from other sources (see paragraph 76 above). Accordingly, it is not the interpretation of Article 10 but the position in Ireland as regards the implementation of the law that makes possible the continuance of the current level of abortions obtained by Irish women abroad.

4. Conclusion

80. In the light of the above, the Court concludes that the restraint imposed on the applicants from receiving or imparting information was disproportionate to the aims pursued. Accordingly there has been a breach of Article 10.

...

FOR THESE REASONS, THE COURT

...

Holds by fifteen votes to eight that there has been a violation of Article 10; ...

NOTES

1 The majority of the plenary Court was comprised of President Ryssdal and Judges: Thor Vilhjalmsson, Gölcüklü, Macdonald, Bernhardt, Spielmann, De Meyer, Valticos, Martens, Palm, Foighel, Pekkanen, Loizou, Morenilla, and Freeland. Cremona J emphasized the paramount place accorded to the protection of unborn life in the fabric of Irish public policy (endorsed by the electorate in the constitutional referendum which preceded Article 40.3.3) as the basis for his dissent. A similar view was expressed by Matscher J. In their combined dissenting opinion Pettiti, Russo, Lopes Rocha, and Bigi JJ wrote:

In our view, the restrictions were justified and, in any event, did not overstep the bounds of what was permissible. It was by any standards a minimal interference with the right to freedom of expression—concerning the aspect of that freedom relating to the communication and receipt of information—aimed at securing the primacy of values such as the right to life of the unborn child in accordance with the principle of the Irish legal system, which cannot be criticised on the basis of different principles applied in other legal systems.

De Meyer J agreed with the decision of the majority, but on the separate reasoning that he did not believe that prior restraints, such as the Supreme Court's injunction, were permissible under Article 10 (see his dissent in *The Observer and Guardian*, p 707). Baka J considered the injunction to be a proportionate response having regard to the constitutional rights of the unborn in Ireland. Likewise, Blayney J (the *ad hoc* Irish judge appointed because Walsh J had been a member of the Supreme Court which issued the injunction) considered that the injunction was the only measure possible to uphold Article 40.3.3.

2 The Court made clear that it was not going to express a view on the controversial question of whether the Convention provides a right to abortion in the above judgment, even though that issue was highly pertinent to the constitutional provisions in Ireland.

3 After the above ruling the Irish Government proposed three constitutional amendments. Sixty per cent of the voters in a referendum approved an amendment to Article 40 which provides: 'Subsection 3 of this section shall not limit freedom to obtain or make available, in the State, subject to such conditions as may be laid down by law, information relating to services lawfully available in another State' (Article 40.3.5). See L. Flynn, 'Ireland' in C. A. Gearty (ed), *European Civil Liberties and the ECHR* (The Hague: Martinus Nijhoff, 1997), ch 5. For a consideration of the EC dimension to the saga see B. Wilkinson, 'Abortion, the Irish Constitution and the EEC' [1992] *Public Law* 20. Despite this reform Ireland was found to have breached the right to respect for her private life of a woman who claimed that she had to leave Ireland to obtain an abortion in *A, B and C v Ireland*, judgment of 16 December 2010 (see p 501).

4 The British Government successfully invoked the aim of protecting morals to justify the conviction of the publisher and destruction of copies of his book in *Handyside v UK* (p 627). However, a united Chamber in *Akdas v Turkey*, judgment of 16 February 2010, held that whilst the requirements of morals still varied between, and within, member States, that was not sufficient to justify denying public access to a novel belonging to the European literary heritage. The applicant had published a Turkish translation of Guillaume Apollinaire's erotic novel *Les Onze Mille Verges* (The Eleven Thousand Rods), originally published in France during 1907. The Turkish courts ordered the seizure of all copies of the book and fined the applicant for publishing obscene material. The Chamber found that as the novel had been published in many languages in different countries and had been accorded recognition during the century of its existence, the actions taken against the applicant breached Article 10.

For the protection of the reputation or rights of others

1   This aim has commonly been invoked by States when they seek to defend national court judgments in defamation cases before the Court. A Grand Chamber, by 13 votes to 4, applied this restriction to find no breach of Article 10 regarding the conviction for defamation of the author and publisher of a novel (partly based on actual murders) in which Jean-Marie Le Pen (the leader of the National Front in France) was described as the 'chief of a gang of killers' and as 'a vampire who thrives on the bitterness of his electorate, but sometimes also on their blood'. In *Lindon, Otchakovsky-Laurens and July v France*, judgment of 22 October 2007, the Grand Chamber held that, '57. . . . the reputation of a politician, even a controversial one, must benefit from the protection afforded by the Convention.'

2   The Court has determined a series of cases where the media published criticisms of domestic judges and were then subject to legal sanctions. In *Barfod v Denmark* A.149 (1989), the Greenland Local Government had introduced a controversial new tax which had been challenged by a number of persons. The Greenland High Court, composed of a professional judge and two lay judges (both of whom were local government employees) upheld the legality of the tax. Subsequently, the applicant, who was not a journalist, wrote a critical article for a magazine in which he stated that the lay judges 'did their duty'. The professional judge considered that this comment might damage the lay judges' reputations in the eyes of the public and impair confidence in the legal system; therefore he asked for a criminal investigation to be commenced. Later, the applicant was charged with defamation of character. The District Court found him guilty and fined him 2,000 Danish Crowns. On appeal the High Court agreed with the applicant that the two lay judges should have refrained from participating in the case because of their employment, but it upheld the applicant's conviction as he had made serious accusations against them without adducing any proof. The Commission, by 14 votes to 1, found a violation of Article 10. Before the Court, the applicant accepted the Government's argument that his conviction had the aims of protecting the reputation of others (the lay judges) and, indirectly, maintaining the authority of the judiciary. The Court's judgment concentrated upon whether the interference with the applicant's freedom of expression was necessary in a democratic society.

The Court noted that the Greenland High Court had affirmed the applicant's right to criticize the composition of the court which determined the tax case. However:

The High Court's finding that there was no proof of the accusations against the lay judges remains unchallenged; the applicant must accordingly be considered to have based his accusations on the mere fact that the lay judges were employed by the Local Government . . . it was certainly not proof of actual bias and the applicant cannot reasonably have been unaware of that.

The State's legitimate interest in protecting the reputation of the two lay judges was accordingly not in conflict with the applicant's interest in being able to participate in free public debate on the question of the structural impartiality of the High Court. [Paras 33–4.]

Therefore, a majority of the Court, 6 votes to 1, concluded that the applicant's conviction had not violated Article 10.

In **Prager and Oberschlick v Austria** A.313 (1995), the first applicant was a journalist and the second applicant a publisher of the Austrian journal *Forum* (for other cases brought by this applicant, see p 646). During 1987 the journal published a 13-page article entitled 'Danger! Harsh Judges!' written by Prager. After a short summary of the main conclusions the article described in detail the attitudes of nine members of the Vienna Regional Criminal Court. Passages of the article included the following: 'They treat each accused at the outset as if he had already been convicted'; 'Some Austrian criminal court judges are capable of anything'; 'Nothing was comparable to . . . Judge [J]'s arrogant bullying'; 'Type: rabid . . . [J]'. Judge J brought a prosecution against the applicants for defamation. The Eisenstadt Regional Court found Prager guilty and sentenced him to 120-day fines at the rate of 30 Austrian schillings per day. Oberschlick was ordered to pay Judge J damages of 30,000 schillings and the remaining stocks of the relevant issue of the journal were confiscated. The Vienna Court of Appeal upheld the judgment, but reduced the damages to 20,000 schillings. The Commission, by 15 votes to 12, rejected the applicants' contention that there had been a breach of Article 10. The Court accepted that the aim of the interferences was to protect the Viennese judges' reputations and to maintain the authority of the judiciary. After restating its established view that the media has the role of informing the people about matters of public interest, the Court held that:

> This undoubtedly includes questions concerning the functioning of the system of justice, an institution that is essential for any democratic society. The press is one of the means by which politicians and public opinion can verify that judges are discharging their heavy responsibilities in a manner that is in conformity with the aim which is the basis of the task entrusted to them.
>
> Regard must, however, be had to the special role of the judiciary in society. As the guarantor of justice, a fundamental value in a law-governed State, it must enjoy public confidence if it is to be successful in carrying out its duties. It may therefore prove necessary to protect such confidence against destructive attacks that are essentially unfounded, especially in view of the fact that judges who have been criticised are subject to a duty of discretion that precludes them from replying. [Para 34.]

Even allowing that '. . . journalistic freedom also covers possible recourse to a degree of exaggeration, or even provocation' (para 37), a bare majority of the Court (5 votes to 4) concluded that the interferences with the applicants' freedom of expression were proportionate responses. This was because the majority considered that the applicants had not established a sufficient factual basis for their excessively wide accusations against the Viennese judges.

> Nor, in the Court's view, could Mr Prager invoke his good faith or compliance with the ethics of journalism. The research that he had undertaken does not appear adequate to substantiate such serious allegations. In this connection it suffices to note that, on his own admission, the applicant had not attended a single criminal trial before Judge J. Furthermore he had not given the judge any opportunity to comment on the accusations leveled against him. [Para 37.]

The four dissenting judges took an entirely opposing view of the research undertaken by the author:

> . . . Mr Prager after his curiosity had been aroused by academic literature, not only spent a lot of time [six months, during which he visited the court on a daily basis for three and a half months] and energy in verifying on the spot the reasons for the phenomena described by sociologists, but was honestly shocked by what he found. [Para 2.]

Also, they felt that the Austrian courts had only taken into account the specified isolated passages and not the context of the whole article. For the dissentients, the applicants' conviction was not necessary in a democratic society.

In *De Haes and Gijsels v Belgium*, 1997-I, the first applicant was a journalist and the second applicant a publisher of the weekly magazine *Humo*. The applicants published five lengthy articles, over a period of several months during 1986, criticizing the judges of the Antwerp Court of Appeal for their determination of a controversial divorce and child custody case. The case concerned a Belgian notary who was granted custody of his children despite unproven allegations of child abuse having been made against him by his ex-wife/parents-in-law. The applicants claimed that the notary had received favourable treatment in the courts because of his family and political connections. In one article they stated: 'Most of the judges of the Third Division of the Court of Appeal, who awarded custody to the notary, also belong to extreme-right-wing circles. Judge [YB] is the son of a bigwig in the gendarmerie who was convicted in 1948 of collaboration...' Subsequently, that judge, together with two fellow judges and an advocate-general (who had all been criticized by name in *Humo*), began proceedings against the applicants seeking damages for the allegedly defamatory criticisms published in the magazine. The Brussels tribunal de premiere instance upheld the action and ordered the applicants to pay each of the plaintiffs one franc in respect of non-pecuniary damage and publish the whole of its judgment in the magazine (and in six daily newspapers at the applicants' expense). The Brussels Court of Appeal and the Court of Cassation rejected the applicants' appeals. The applicants petitioned the Commission and that body found, *inter alia*, a breach of Article 10 (by 6 votes to 3). Before the Court it was accepted that the interferences with the applicants' freedom of expression had the legitimate aim of protecting the reputation or rights of the named judges/advocate-general. The Court, therefore, concentrated upon the issue of whether the defamation judgments were 'necessary in a democratic society'. It was noted that the applicants' articles, '...contain a mass of detailed information about the circumstances in which the decisions on the custody of Mr X's children were taken. That information was based on thorough research into the allegations against Mr X and on the opinions of several experts who were said to have advised the applicants to disclose them in the interests of the children' (para 39). However, the Court was unwilling to afford Article 10 protection to a part of the applicants' criticisms:

One of the allusions to the alleged political sympathies was inadmissible-the one concerning the past history of the father of one of the judges criticised. It is unacceptable that someone should be exposed to opprobrium because of matters concerning a member of his family. A penalty was justifiable on account of that allusion by itself. [Para 45.]

But, as for the other parts, the majority of the Court (7 votes to 2) considered that:

Looked at against the background of the case, the accusations in question amount to an opinion, whose truth, by definition, is not susceptible of proof. Such an opinion may, however, be excessive, in particular in the absence of any factual basis, but it was not so in this instance; in that respect the present case differs from the *Prager and Oberschlick* case.

Although Mr De Haes and Mr Gijsels' comments were without doubt severely critical, they nevertheless appear proportionate to the stir and indignation caused by the matters alleged in their articles. As to the journalists' polemical and even aggressive tone, which the Court should not be taken to approve, it must be remembered that Article 10 protects not only the substance of the ideas and information expressed but also the form in which they are conveyed.

In conclusion, the Court considers that, regard being had to the seriousness of the circumstances of the case and of the issues at stake, the necessity of the interference with the exercise of the applicants' freedom of expression has not been shown, except as regards the allusion to the past history of the father of one of the judges in question. [Paras 47–9.]

From the above judgments it is clear that the Court will only accord the protection of Article 10 to media criticisms of domestic judges where the commentators can establish a factual basis for their accusations. The more vitriolic the criticism, the greater the need to show an evidential basis for the views expressed. Critical commentary on institutional factors affecting the judiciary, rather than personal attacks on named judges, and on judicial decisions which have general social/political implications appear easier to justify before the Court. However, the majority's approach in *Prager and Oberschlick* places an excessively high evidential/research burden upon journalists.

Where a judge is also a political figure then the Court is willing to accord the media wider freedom to make critical value judgements about such a person. In *Hirco v Slovakia*, judgment of 20 July 2004, the applicant was the publisher of a weekly journal. In 1994 he published several articles expressing criticism of the domestic courts' rulings in a civil case between a Minister and a poet (these proceedings were later found to have infringed Article 10 by the Court in *Feldek v Slovakia*, judgment of 12 July 2001). One of the articles included an interview with the poet's lawyer in which the latter noted that a named Supreme Court judge who had participated in the proceedings was an election candidate for a political party which had strong views on the topic of the proceedings. The lawyer expressed the view that the judge's political links had influenced his decision in the proceedings. Subsequently, the judge won damages against the applicant for interfering with his civil and professional honour. The Court held that, '46.... the limits of acceptable criticism are wider in respect of a judge who enters political life.' Taking account of the facts that the critical articles were not published in bad faith and the domestic proceedings were related to an important issue subject to political debate the Court, unanimously, found a breach of Article 10. For an examination of the lawfulness under Article 6(1) of a politician sitting as a judge see *Pabla Ky v Finland*, p 436.

3 The Court has accorded States a narrower margin of appreciation to restrict and punish lawyers' criticisms of the administration of justice. In *Nikula v Finland*, judgment of 21 March 2002, the Court was faced with the unusual situation where a defence lawyer had been convicted of defamation in respect of her criticisms, during court proceedings, of the conduct of the prosecutor. The applicant had represented a businessman charged with fraud. The prosecutor decided not to bring charges against the defendant's brother, who had been involved in the same business, but to summon him as a prosecution witness. The applicant objected to the brother being called as a witness and she read out in court a memorandum entitled 'Role manipulation and unlawful presentation of evidence'. In the document she accused the prosecutor of '...procedural tactics, to make a witness out of a co-accused so as to support the indictment...deliberate abuse of discretion...committing role manipulation, thereby breaching his official duties and jeopardising legal security...' After the conclusion of the trial, the defendant having been convicted, the prosecutor initiated a private prosecution against the applicant. Subsequently, the Court of Appeal convicted her of negligent defamation and fined her 716 euros together with 505 euros damages to be paid to the prosecutor. On appeal the Supreme Court upheld her conviction, but waived the fine due to the minor nature of the offence. Before the Strasbourg Court, the applicant complained that her right to express herself freely as a defence lawyer had been violated, in breach of Article 10, by the defamation conviction. Applying Article 10(2) the Court found that her conviction was 'prescribed by law' and served the legitimate aim of protecting the prosecutor's reputation and rights. Therefore, the contentious issue was whether the conviction was 'necessary in a democratic society'. The Court observed that lawyers play a central role in the administration of justice, as intermediaries between the public and the courts, consequently they must contribute to the maintenance of public confidence in that system.

46.... While lawyers too are certainly entitled to comment in public on the administration of justice, their criticism must not overstep certain bounds. In that connection, account must be taken of the need to strike the right balance between the various interests involved, which include the public's right to receive information about questions arising from judicial decisions, the requirements of the proper administration of justice and the dignity of the legal profession. The national authorities have a certain margin of appreciation in assessing the necessity of an interference, but this margin is subject to European supervision as regards both the relevant rules and the decisions applying them... However, in the field under consideration in the present case there are no particular circumstances—such as a clear lack of common ground among, member States regarding the principles at issue or a need to make allowance for the diversity of moral conceptions—which would justify granting the national authorities a wide margin of appreciation (cf, for example, the *Sunday Times v the United Kingdom* judgment of 26 April 1979, Series A No 30, pp 35–7, § 59, with further reference to the *Handyside v the United Kingdom* judgment of 7 December 1976, Series A No 24).

The Court considered that although some of the applicant's comments were 'inappropriate', they were made in the courtroom and related to the prosecutor's conduct of the case. According to the Court, '51.... in that procedural context [the prosecutor] had to tolerate very considerable criticism by the applicant in her capacity as defence counsel.' In the view of the Court:

55. It is therefore only in exceptional cases that restriction—even by way of a lenient criminal sanction—of defence counsel's freedom of expression can be accepted as necessary in a democratic society.

Consequently, a large majority of the Court, 5 votes to 2, concluded that the conviction of the applicant was not 'necessary in a democratic society'.

Judges Caflisch and Pastor Ridruejo issued a dissenting opinion in which they expressed the belief that:

56. Clearly the accusations made by the applicant in open court were of some gravity. They amounted to stating, not only that prosecutor T. had acted wrongly—which, in and of itself, was legitimate—, but also that he had abused his functions and acted dishonestly. This is one of the worst things to say about a public official, magistrate or not. Not only does it mean that the magistrate is unfit to discharge his/her duties and, possibly, to fill other posts; it also taints the reputation of the judiciary. In other words, the interests protected by the measure are of considerable importance.

Taking account of the waiving of the applicant's fine by the Supreme Court and the absence of a criminal record in respect of her conviction, they considered that the measures taken against her were proportional and fell within Article 10(2).

The judgment of the Court is to be strongly endorsed compared to that of the dissentients. The latter minority appear to have conflated the separate positions of prosecutors and judges. As the Court correctly explained, these are different functions and defence counsel should have greater freedom to criticize prosecutors, *qua* their institutional opponents, compared to their latitude to censure judges (who must be independent and impartial in order to satisfy the demands of Article 6). The refusal of the Court to accord national authorities a wide margin of appreciation in restricting the freedom of expression of defence counsel is also very important in safeguarding the ability of such lawyers properly to represent their clients' interests.

4 The 'rights of others' includes legal rights, such as proprietary and contractual rights. In **Goodwin v UK**, 1996-II, the applicant had been employed as a trainee journalist by the publisher of a specialist journal (*The Engineer*). A few months after he began working for the journal a source rang him to provide information, on an unattributable basis, regarding the financial problems of a company (Tetra Ltd). Goodwin telephoned Tetra to confirm the information and obtain their comments. The information derived from a draft of Tetra's confidential business plan and, therefore, the next day Tetra applied (*ex parte*) to the High Court for an injunction to prevent the publishers of *The Engineer* from publishing any information derived from the plan. The court granted the injunction and Tetra notified all the national newspapers and relevant journals of the order (thereby preventing them from disclosing details of the plan). Subsequently, the High Court ordered Goodwin and his employer/publisher to disclose his notes of the telephone conversation with his source (which identified that person) so that Tetra could take further action against that person. The order was made under section 10 of the Contempt of Court Act 1981 which states that, 'No court may require a person to disclose . . . the source of information contained in a publication for which he is responsible, unless it be established to the satisfaction of the court that disclosure is necessary in the interests of justice . . . '. Goodwin and his employer/publisher refused to comply and appealed. Both the Court of Appeal and the House of Lords confirmed the disclosure order (**X Ltd v Morgan-Grampian (Publishers) Ltd** [1990] 2 All ER 1). Goodwin continued to refuse to disclose his notes and was found guilty of contempt of court and fined £5,000. He complained to the Commission that the disclosure order and fine constituted a violation of his rights under Article 10. By 11 votes to 6 the Commission found a breach. It was not disputed before the Court that these measures had the aim of protecting Tetra's rights. The Court held, however, that the:

> 39. Protection of journalistic sources is one of the basic conditions for press freedom, as is reflected in the laws and the professional codes of conduct in a number of Contracting States and is affirmed in several international instruments on journalistic freedoms . . . Without such protection, sources may be deterred from assisting the press in informing the public on matters of public interest. As a result the vital public-watchdog role of the press may be undermined and the ability of the press to provide accurate and reliable information may be adversely affected. Having regard to the importance of the protection of journalistic sources for press freedom in a democratic society and the potentially chilling effect an order of source disclosure has on the exercise of that freedom, such a measure cannot be compatible with Article 10 of the Convention unless it is justified by an overriding requirement in the public interest.

The majority of the Court (11 votes to 7) felt that the High Court injunction protected Tetra from having its confidential financial information published by the media. Therefore, the issue was whether it was also necessary to require the applicant to disclose his source. The majority acknowledged that the company had legitimate reasons in unmasking a disloyal employee and seeking to prevent future unauthorized disclosures, but these were not sufficient to amount to an overriding public interest. Consequently, the disclosure order and fine imposed on the applicant were in breach of Article 10. The dissentients felt that the majority accorded insufficient weight to the interests of Tetra and the domestic courts were in a better position to balance those interests against the rights of the applicant and the public.

This is a very important judgment for the media as it demonstrates the Court protecting one of the basic means by which the media obtain their information. Hence, Article 10 encompasses news-gathering techniques as well as the distribution of acquired information. For a discussion of this case, see S. Tierney, 'Press Freedom and Public Interest: The Developing Jurisprudence of the European Court of Human Rights' [1998] *European Human Rights Law Review* 419.

In *Roemen and Schmit v Luxembourg*, judgment of 25 February 2003, a unanimous Chamber of the full-time Court rigorously applied *Goodwin* to the searches of a journalist's home and office, ordered by an investigating judge, seeking to discover who had supplied him with information. The first applicant had published an article in a daily newspaper disclosing that a Minister had been given a fiscal fine for value-added tax fraud. The Chamber stated:

> 57. ... The Court considers that, even if unproductive, a search conducted with a view to uncover a journalist's source is a more drastic measure than an order to divulge the source's identity. This is because investigators who raid a journalist's workplace unannounced and armed with search warrants have very wide investigative powers, as, by definition, they have access to all the documentation held by the journalist. The Court reiterates that 'limitations on the confidentiality of journalistic sources call for the most careful scrutiny by the Court' (see *Goodwin*, cited above, pp 500–1, § 40). It thus considers that the searches of the first applicant's home and workplace undermined the protection of sources to an even greater extent than the measures in issue in *Goodwin*.

The Chamber concluded that the searches were a disproportionate interference with the applicant's freedom of expression and breached Article 10.

5   A person's right to respect for his/her religious beliefs and feelings, as guaranteed by Article 9, also falls within the aim of protecting the 'rights of others'; see *Otto-Preminger-Institute v Austria* (p 605).

For preventing the disclosure of information received in confidence

This exception was invoked by the respondent State in *Stoll v Switzerland*, judgment of 10 December 2007, to justify the imposition of a criminal fine (equivalent to 476 euros) on the applicant journalist for publishing secret official deliberations. The applicant had obtained, from an unknown person, a copy of a secret strategy paper written by the Swiss Ambassador to the USA advising his foreign ministry on the sensitive topic of negotiations regarding the compensation due to Holocaust victims in respect of unclaimed assets held in Swiss bank accounts. The applicant then wrote two articles, based on the secret paper, that were very critical of the ambassador. The Grand Chamber held that:

> 126. The Court agrees with the Government and the third-party interveners that it is vital to diplomatic services and the smooth functioning of international relations for diplomats to be able to exchange confidential or secret information ...
>
> 128. ... As exceptions to the exercise of freedom of expression, [the grounds listed in Article 10(2)] must be subjected to close and careful scrutiny by the Court. In other words, while the confidentiality of diplomatic reports is justified in principle, it cannot be protected at any price.

A majority of the Grand Chamber (12 votes to 5) determined that the sensationalist headings and content of the articles disclosed that the applicant's intention had been to scandalize the ambassador, rather than to inform the public about a matter of general interest, with the consequence that there had been no breach of Article 10. So the nature of the disclosure of official secrets will have a profound effect on the ability of governments to rely upon this exception.

For maintaining the authority and impartiality of the judiciary

1   The Court has interpreted this aim broadly to encompass the protection of individual judges from unjustified criticism by the media (see p 721, Note 2) and more generally the maintenance of public confidence in the machinery of justice (see *The Sunday Times*, p 637).

2   A unanimous Court found a breach of Article 10 in *Weber v Switzerland* A.177 (1990). The applicant was a well-known Swiss ecologist and journalist. During 1980 a newspaper published a vitriolic letter attacking the applicant's integrity. Weber responded by lodging a complaint of defamation against the author of the letter. The investigating judge ordered the disclosure of the accounts of the applicant's environmental association. Weber became dissatisfied with the conduct of the investigating judge and on 1 March 1982 he lodged a criminal complaint alleging misuse of judicial authority and coercion against the judge. The next day Weber held a press conference at which he stated, *inter alia*, that he had lodged the criminal complaint against the judge. Subsequently, Weber was fined 300 Swiss francs for breaching the confidentiality of a judicial investigation by holding his press conference. The Commission, unanimously, found that the fine violated Weber's rights under Article 10. Before the Court it was accepted that the fine infringed Weber's right to freedom of expression and that the interference was prescribed by law. The Court found that the interference had the legitimate aim of seeking to ensure the proper conduct of the judicial investigation and therefore it fell within Article 10(2) as being designed to protect the 'authority and impartiality of the judiciary'. However, the Court did not accept that the interference was 'necessary in a democratic society'.

> As to the submission that the impugned statements by Mr Weber on 2 March 1982 could be interpreted as an attempt to bring pressure to bear on the investigating judge and could therefore have been prejudicial to the proper conduct of the investigation, the Court notes that by that time the investigation was practically complete, because on the previous day the judge had committed [the letter writer] for trial, and that from then on any attempt of that kind would have been belated and thus devoid of effect.... It was accordingly not necessary to impose a penalty on the applicant from this point of view ... [Para 51.]

While the applicant succeeded on the facts of his case, it is clear that the Court interprets this legitimate aim as encompassing the prohibition on parties to legal proceedings bringing improper media pressure on judges hearing their cases.

3   In *Worm v Austria*, 1997-V, the applicant was a journalist who had an article published in the Austrian magazine *Profil* (this journal also published the article that was the basis of the *Lingens* judgment, p 644). The article was concerned with the ongoing criminal trial of a former Minister of Finance (Androsch) for alleged tax evasion. In the piece, Worm

wrote that the defendant's activities 'permits no other interpretation than that Androsch was evading taxes'. A few months later the court (composed of two professional judges and two lay judges) convicted Androsch of tax evasion and fined him 1.8 million Austrian schillings. Thereupon Worm was charged with the offence of having exercised prohibited influence on criminal proceedings. The Vienna Regional Criminal Court acquitted him, but the public prosecutor appealed and the Vienna Court of Appeal found Worm guilty and fined him 48,000 schillings (and made the magazine's publisher jointly liable for the fine). The applicant complained to the Commission which, by 18 votes to 11, expressed the opinion that there had been a breach of Article 10. The Court found that the applicant's conviction pursued the aim of 'maintaining the authority and impartiality of the judiciary'.

40. The phrase 'authority of the judiciary' includes, in particular, the notion that the courts are, and are accepted by the public at large as being, the proper forum for the settlement of legal disputes and for the determination of a person's guilt or innocence on a criminal charge; further, that the public at large have respect for and confidence in the court's capacity to fulfil that function...

'Impartiality' normally denotes lack of prejudice or bias (see the *Piersack v Belgium* judgment (1982) A.53). However, the Court has repeatedly held that what is at stake in maintaining the impartiality of the judiciary is the confidence which the courts in a democratic society must inspire in the accused, as far as criminal proceedings are concerned, and also in the public at large...

It follows that, in seeking to maintain the 'authority and impartiality of the judiciary', the Contracting States are entitled to take account of considerations going—beyond the concrete case—to the protection of the fundamental role of courts in a democratic society.

In considering whether the applicant's conviction was 'necessary in a democratic society' the Court stated:

50. Restrictions on freedom of expression permitted by the second paragraph of Article 10 'for maintaining the authority and impartiality of the judiciary' do not entitle States to restrict all forms of public discussion on matters pending before the courts. There is general recognition of the fact that the courts cannot operate in a vacuum. While the courts are the forum for the determination of a person's guilt or innocence on a criminal charge, this does not mean that there can be no prior or contemporaneous discussion of the subject matter of criminal trials elsewhere, be it in specialised journals, in the general press or among the public at large (see *The Sunday Times (No 1)* judgment). Provided that it does not overstep the bounds imposed in the interests of the proper administration of justice, reporting, including comment, on court proceedings contributes to their publicity and is thus perfectly consonant with the requirement under Article 6(1) of the Convention that hearings be public. Not only do the media have the task of imparting such information and ideas: the public also has a right to receive them. This is all the more so where a public figure is involved, such as, in the present case, a former member of the Government....

However, public figures are entitled to the enjoyment of the guarantees of a fair trial set out in Article 6, which in criminal proceedings include the right to an impartial tribunal, on the same basis as every other person. This must be borne in mind by journalists when commenting on pending criminal proceedings since the limits of permissible comment may not extend to statements which are likely to prejudice, whether intentionally or not, the chances of a person receiving a fair trial or to undermine the confidence of the public in the role of the courts in the administration of criminal justice.

A majority of the Court (7 votes to 2) concluded that the Vienna Court of Appeal's conviction of the applicant had not exceeded the national margin of appreciation and, therefore, Article 10 had not been breached.

This case complements the *Sunday Times (No 1)* judgment (where there were press comments on a pending civil action) by demonstrating how the Court applies Article 10 to media discussion of a continuing criminal trial. The Court's analysis in *Worm* indicates that journalists must be very cautious in their commentary, as compared with their objective factual reporting, on such proceedings. Significantly, the Court considered that it was permissible under Article 10 for the Vienna Court of Appeal to have regard to the susceptibility of the lay judges in the Androsch trial to media comments upon the case. Therefore, the media may have to be even more circumspect in its comments on trials being determined by lay persons.

4 A unanimous Grand Chamber of the full-time Court concluded that the imprisonment, for five days, of a defence lawyer for his 'discourteous' comments to the judges presiding over the criminal trial was a disproportionate sentence which failed to achieve the right balance between the need to protect the authority of the judiciary and the applicant's right to freedom of expression in *Kyprianou v Cyprus*, judgment of 15 December 2005 (see p 442). This finding of a breach of Article 10 reflects the contemporary Court's recognition of the importance, for the proper administration of justice, of safeguarding the freedom of expression of lawyers to defend their clients (see also *Nikula*, p 724).

13 ARTICLE 11 FREEDOM OF ASSEMBLY AND ASSOCIATION

The Court has been highly protective of the rights of political parties and organizations under this Article, reflecting the symbiotic relationship with freedom of political expression analysed in the previous chapter (*United Communist Party of Turkey*). Whilst the limitations permitted by Article 11(2) are construed narrowly when applied to such bodies, judgments demonstrate that States can dissolve political parties that seek to promulgate policies contrary to Convention values, for example Islamic fundamentalism (*Refah Partisi*) or terrorist violence (*Herri Batasuna*). Alongside not restricting peaceful assemblies (interpreted to cover both static assemblies and moving processions), unless the Article 11(2) conditions are satisfied, States have been required to undertake positive obligations to secure the effective right of peaceful protest (*Plattform 'Arzte fur das Leben'*).

Trade unionists may have been unhappy that the Court developed a negative right of association within Article 11, that applied to both pre-entry (*Sorensen*) and post-entry closed shops (*Young, James and Webster*). But in recent years the Court has revised its early jurisprudence to become more protective of the rights to form trade unions and for those organizations effectively to represent their members' interests, for example through collective bargaining (*Demir and Baykara*).

The Court's general approach

United Communist Party of Turkey v Turkey 1998-I
European Court of Human Rights

The first applicant ('the TBKP') was a (dissolved) political party and the other applicants were Mr Sargin, Chairman of the Party, and Mr Yagci, General Secretary of the Party. The Party was formed in June 1990 and on the day of its formation the constitution and programme of the Party were sent to the Principal State Counsel at the Court of Cassation for assessment of their compatibility with the Constitution and Law No 2820 on the regulation of political parties. A few days later, while the Party was preparing to participate in a general election, the Counsel applied to the Constitutional Court for an order dissolving the TBKP. The Counsel specified a number of grounds for the order (based particularly on the Party's programme towards a peaceful and democratic solution of the 'Kurdish problem'). In July 1991 the Constitutional Court made an order dissolving the Party. The effect of this order was the liquidation of the Party and the transfer of its assets to the Treasury. Also the individual applicants, together with other founders and managers of the Party, were banned from holding similar office in any other political body. The Constitutional Court based its order on the fact that the TBKP used the word 'communist' in its name contrary to Law No 2820, and that the Party's constitution and programme contained statements likely to undermine the territorial integrity of the State and the unity of the nation in violation of the national Constitution. The applicants complained to the Commission alleging, *inter alia*, that the dissolution of the TBKP amounted to a breach of Article 11. The Commission, unanimously, found a violation of that Article.

...

AS TO THE LAW

I. ALLEGED VIOLATION OF ARTICLE 11 OF THE CONVENTION

18. The applicants maintained that the fact that the United Communist Party of Turkey ('the *TBKP*') had been dissolved and its leaders—including Mr Sargin and Mr Yagci—banned from holding similar office in any other political party had infringed their right to freedom of association, as guaranteed by Article 11 of the Convention . . .

A. APPLICABILITY OF ARTICLE 11

1. Submissions of those appearing before the Court

(a) The Government

19. The Government submitted that Article 11 did not in any event apply to political parties. Where in its constitution or programme a party attacked a State's constitutional order, the Court should declare the Convention to be inapplicable *ratione materiae* or apply Article 17, rather than apply Article 11.

Even a cursory examination of the Convention showed that neither Article 11 nor any other Article made any mention of political parties or referred to the States' constitutional structures. It was significant that the only Article containing a reference to political institutions was in Protocol No 1 (Article 3) and did not confer any right on individuals as it was worded so as to create an obligation on the States . . .

20. The constitution and programme of the *TBKP* were clearly incompatible with Turkey's fundamental constitutional principles. By choosing to call itself 'communist', the *TBKP* perforce referred to a subversive doctrine and a totalitarian political goal that undermined Turkey's political and territorial unity and jeopardised the fundamental principles of its public law, such as secularism. 'Communism' invariably presupposed seizing power and aimed to establish a political order that would be unacceptable, not just in Turkey but also in the other member States of the Council of Europe. Further, the use of certain names was also proscribed in other legal systems in the West. In that respect, the Government referred to the German, Polish and Portuguese constitutions. In any event, whatever the intentions of the *TBKP* and its leaders in choosing the name 'communist' in 1990 (after the fall of the Berlin Wall) may have been, that name could not, in the Government's view, be considered devoid of political meaning.

. . . In the Government's submission, the States Parties to the Convention had at no stage intended to submit their constitutional institutions, and in particular the principles they considered to be the essential conditions of their existence, to review by the Strasbourg institutions. For that reason, where a political party such as the *TBKP* had called those institutions or principles into question, it could not seek application of the Convention or its Protocols.

...

(b) The applicants

22. The applicants maintained that there was no doubt that political parties came within the ambit of Article 11. They pointed out that the scope of the Convention could not be restricted by relying on the Turkish Constitution. Domestic law had to be construed in the light of the Convention, not the other way round.

(c) The Commission

23. The Commission expressed the opinion that there was nothing in the wording of Article 11 to limit its scope to a particular form of association or group or suggest that it did not apply to political parties. On the contrary, if Article 11 was considered to be a legal safeguard that ensured the proper functioning of democracy, political parties were one of the most important forms of association it protected. In that connection, the Commission referred to a number of decisions in which it had examined, under Article 11, various restrictions on the activities of political parties and even the dissolution of such parties, thereby implicitly accepting that Article 11 applied to that type of association (see the *German Communist Party* case, application no 250/57, Yearbook 1, P 225; the *Greek* case, Yearbook, 1969, p 170 § 392; the *France, Norway, Denmark, Sweden and the Netherlands v Turkey* case, applications Nos 9940–9944/82, DR 35, p 143).

At the hearing before the Court the Delegate of the Commission also said that it was unnecessary to apply Article 17 of the Convention since the present case was clearly distinguishable from the rare cases in which the Commission had had recourse to that provision. In such cases the aim of the offending actions of the applicants concerned had been to spread violence (see the German Communist Party case cited above) or hatred (see the Remer case cited above). Conversely, there was nothing in the *TBKP*'s constitution or programme to suggest that it was not a democratic party, or that it resorted to illegal or undemocratic methods, encouraged the use of violence, aimed to undermine Turkey's democratic and pluralist political system or pursued objectives that were racist or likely to destroy the rights and freedoms of others.

2. The Court's assessment

24. The Court considers that the wording of Article 11 provides an initial indication as to whether political parties may rely on that provision. It notes that although Article 11 refers to 'freedom of association with others, including the right to form…trade unions…;' the conjunction 'including' clearly shows that trade unions are but one example among others of the form in which the right to freedom of association may be exercised. It is therefore not possible to conclude, as the Government did, that by referring to trade unions—for reasons related mainly to issues that were current at the time—those who drafted the Convention intended to exclude political parties from the scope of Article 11.

25. However, even more persuasive than the wording of Article 11, in the Court's view, is the fact that political parties are a form of association essential to the proper functioning of democracy. In view of the importance of democracy in the Convention system (see paragraph 45 below), there can be no doubt that political parties come within the scope of Article 11.

27. The Court notes on the other hand that an association, including a political party, is not excluded from the protection afforded by the Convention simply because its activities are regarded by the national authorities as undermining the constitutional structures of the State and calling for the imposition of restrictions. As the Court has said in the past, while it is in principle open to the national authorities to take such action as they consider necessary to respect the rule of law or to give effect to constitutional rights, they must do so in a manner which is compatible with their obligations under the Convention and subject to review by the Convention institutions (see the *Open Door and Dublin Well Woman v Ireland* judgment of 29 October 1992, Series A No 246-A, p 29, § 69).

28. The Preamble to the Convention refers to the 'common heritage of political traditions, ideals, freedom and the rule of law' (see paragraph 45 below), of which national constitutions are in fact often the first embodiment. Through its system of collective enforcement of the rights it establishes (see the *Loizidou v Turkey (Preliminary Objections)* judgment of 23 March 1995, Series A No 310, p 26, § 70), the Convention reinforces, in accordance with the principle of subsidiarity, the protection afforded at national level, but never limits it (Article 60 of the Convention).

29. The Court points out, moreover, that Article 1 requires the States Parties to 'secure to everyone within their jurisdiction the rights and freedoms defined in Section 1 of th[e] Convention'. That provision, together with Articles 14, 2 to 13 and 63, demarcates the scope of the Convention *ratione personae, materiae* and *loci* (see the *Ireland v UK* judgment of 18 January 1978, Series A No 25, p 90, § 238). It makes no distinction as to the type of rule or measure concerned and does not exclude any part of the member States' jurisdiction from scrutiny under the Convention. It is, therefore, with respect to their jurisdiction as a whole—which is often exercised in the first place through the Constitution—that the States Parties are called on to show compliance with the Convention.

30. The political and institutional organisation of the member States must accordingly respect the rights and principles enshrined in the Convention. It matters little in this context whether the provisions in issue are constitutional (see, for example, the *Gitonas v Greece* judgment of 1 July 1997, Reports of Judgments and Decisions 1997-V) or merely legislative (see, for example, the *Mattieu-Mohin and Clerfayt v Belgium* judgment of 2 March 1987, Series A No 113). From the moment that such provisions are the means by which the State concerned exercises its jurisdiction, they are subject to review under the Convention.

31. Moreover, it may on occasion prove difficult, even artificial, in proceedings before the Court, to attempt to distinguish between what forms part of a State's institutional structures and what relates to fundamental rights in the strict sense. That is particularly true of an order for dissolution of the kind in issue in the present case. In view of the role played by political parties (see paragraph 25 above), such measures affect both freedom of association and, consequently, democracy in the State concerned.

32. It does not, however, follow that the authorities of a State in which an association, through its activities, jeopardises that State's institutions are deprived of the right to protect those institutions. In this connection, the Court points out that it has previously held that some compromise between the requirements of defending democratic society and individual rights is inherent in the system of the Convention (see, *mutatis mutandis*, the *Klass v Germany* judgment of 6 September 1978, Series A No 28, p 28, § 59). For there to be a compromise of that sort any intervention by the authorities must be in accordance with paragraph 2 of Article 11, which the Court considers below (see paragraphs 37 *et seq*). Only when that review is complete will the Court be in a position to decide, in the light of all the circumstances of the case, whether Article 17 of the Convention should be applied.

33. Before the Commission the Government also submitted, in the alternative, that while Article 11 guaranteed freedom to form an association, it did not on that account prevent one from being dissolved.

The Commission took the view that freedom of association not only concerned the right to form a political party but also guaranteed the right of such a party, once formed, to carry on its political activities freely.

The Court reiterates that the Convention is intended to guarantee rights that are not theoretical or illusory, but practical and effective (see, among other authorities, the *Artico v Italy* judgment of 13 May 1980, Series A No 37, p 16, § 33, and the *Loizidou* judgment cited above, p 27, § 72). The right guaranteed by Article 11 would be largely theoretical and illusory if it were limited to the founding of an association, since the national authorities could immediately disband the association without having to comply with the Convention. It follows that the protection afforded by article 11 lasts for an association's entire life and that dissolution of an association by a country's authorities must accordingly satisfy the requirements of paragraph 2 of that provision (see paragraphs 35–47 below).

34. In conclusion Article 11 is applicable to the facts of the case.

B. COMPLIANCE WITH ARTICLE 11

1. Whether there has been an interference

...

35. Before the Commission, the Government submitted that the dissolution of the *TBKP* had not constituted an interference with Mr Sargin and Mr Yagci's right to freedom of association. However, it did not reiterate that argument before the Court.

36. Like the Commission, the Court concludes that there has been an interference with that right in respect of all three applicants, having regard (in the case of Mr Sargin and Mr Yagci) to their role as founders and leaders of the party and to the ban which prevented them from discharging similar responsibilities in any other political grouping...

2. Whether the interference was justified

37. Such an interference will constitute a breach of Article 11 unless it was 'prescribed by law', pursued one or more legitimate aims under paragraph 2 and was 'necessary in a democratic society' for the achievement of those aims.

(a) 'Prescribed by law'

38. It was common ground that the interference was 'prescribed by law', as the measures ordered by the Constitutional Court were based on Articles 2, 3 § 1, 6, 10 § 1 and 14 § 1, and former Article 68 of the Constitution and sections 78, 81 and 96(3) of Law No 2820 on the regulation of political parties...

(b) Legitimate aim

39. The Government maintained that the interference pursued a number of legitimate aims: ensuring national security, public safety and territorial integrity and protecting the rights and freedom of others...

40. The Commission distinguished between the different grounds relied on by the Constitutional Court for dissolving the *TBKP*. Inasmuch as the interference was based on the use of the word 'communist' in the party's name, it could not, in the Commission's view, be said to be justified by any of the legitimate aims referred to in Article 11. Indeed, the Constitutional Court had recognised that there was nothing to suggest that the *TBKP* would not respect democratic institutions or that it intended to establish a dictatorship...

On the other hand, inasmuch as the dissolution was based on a distinction drawn in the *TBKP*'s programme between Turks and Kurds, it could, in the Commission's view, be said to have been ordered with the aim of protecting territorial integrity and thus 'national security'. It was not that the *TBKP* was a terrorist organisation or one sponsoring terrorism, but it could be regarded as openly pursuing the creating of a separate Kurdish nation and consequently a redistribution of the territory of the Turkish State.

41. Like the Commission, the Court considers that the dissolution of the *TBKP* pursued at least one of the 'legitimate aims' set out in Article 11: the protection of 'national security'.

(c) 'Necessary in a democratic society'

(i) General principles

42. The Court reiterates that notwithstanding its autonomous role and particular sphere of application, Article 11 must, in the present case, also be considered in the light of Article 10. The protection of opinions and the freedom to express them is one of the objectives of the freedoms of assembly and association as enshrined in Article 11 (see, among other authorities, the *Young, James and Webster v UK* judgment of 13 August 1981, Series A, No 44, p 23, § 57, and the *Vogt v Germany* judgment of 26 September 1995, Series A No 323, p 30, § 64).

43. That applies all the more in relation to political parties in view of their essential role in ensuring pluralism and the proper functioning of democracy (see paragraph 25 above).

As the Court has said many times, there can be no democracy without pluralism. It is for that reason that freedom of expression as enshrined in Article 10 is applicable, subject to paragraph 2, not only to 'information' or 'ideas' that are favourably received or regarded as inoffensive or as a matter of indifference, but also to those that offend, shock or disturb (see, among many other authorities, the *Vogt* judgment cited above, p 25, § 52). The fact that their activities form part of a collective exercise of freedom of expression in itself entitles political parties to seek the protection of Articles 10 and 11 of the Convention.

44. In the *Informationsverein Lentia v Austria* judgment the Court described the State as the ultimate guarantor of the principle of pluralism (see the judgment of 24 November 1993, Series A No 276, p 16, § 38). In the political sphere that responsibility means that the State is under the obligation, among others, to hold, in accordance with Article 3 of Protocol No 1, free elections at reasonable intervals by secret ballot under conditions which will ensure the free expression of the opinion of the people in the choice of the legislature. Such expression is inconceivable without the participation of a plurality of political parties representing the different shades of opinion to be found within a country's population. By relaying this range of opinion, not only within political institutions but also—with the help of the media—at all levels of social life, political parties make an irreplaceable contribution to political debate, which is at the very core of the concept of a democratic society (see the *Lingens v Austria* judgment of 8 July 1986, Series A No 103, p 26, § 42, and the *Castells v Spain* judgment of 23 April 1992, Series A No 236, p 23, § 43).

45. Democracy is without doubt a fundamental feature of the European public order (see the *Loizidou* judgment cited above, p 27, § 75).

That is apparent, firstly, from the Preamble to the Convention, which establishes a very clear connection between the Convention and democracy by stating that the maintenance and further realisation of human rights and fundamental freedoms are best ensured on the one hand by an effective political democracy and on the other by a common understanding and observance of human rights (see the *Klass* judgment cited above, p 28, § 59). The Preamble goes on to affirm that European countries have a common heritage of political tradition, ideals, freedom and the rule of law. The Court has observed that in that common heritage are to be found the underlying values of the Convention (see the *Soering v UK* judgment of 7 July 1989, Series A No 161, p 35, § 88); it has pointed out several times that the Convention was designed to maintain and promote the ideals and values of a democratic society (see the *Kjeldsen, Busk Madsen and Pedersen v Denmark* judgment of 7 December 1976, Series A No 23, p 27, § 53, and the *Soering* judgment cited above, p 34, § 87).

In addition, Articles 8, 9, 10 and 11 of the Convention require that interference with the exercise of the rights they enshrine must be assessed by the yardstick of what is 'necessary in a democratic society'. The only type of necessity capable of justifying an interference with any of those rights is, therefore, one which may claim to spring from 'democratic society'. Democracy thus appears to be the only political model contemplated by the Convention and, accordingly, the only one compatible with it.

The Court has identified certain provisions of the Convention as being characteristic of democratic society. Thus in its very first judgment it held that in a 'democratic society within the meaning of the Preamble and the other clauses of the Convention', proceedings before the judiciary should be conducted in the presence of the parties and in public and that that fundamental principle was upheld in Article 6 of the Convention (see the *Lawless v Ireland* judgment of 14 November 1960 (preliminary objections and questions of procedure), Series A No 1, p 13). In a field closer to the one concerned in the instant case, the Court has on many occasions stated, for example, that freedom of expression constitutes one of the essential foundations of a democratic society and one of the basic conditions for its progress and each individual's self-fulfilment (see, among other authorities, the *Vogt* judgment cited above, p 25, § 52), whereas in the *Mattieu-Mohin and Clerfayt* judgment cited above, it noted the prime importance of Article 3 of Protocol No 1, which enshrines a characteristic principle of an effective political democracy (p 22, § 47).

46. Consequently, the exceptions set out in Article 11 are, where political parties are concerned, to be construed strictly; only convincing and compelling reasons can justify restrictions on such parties' freedom of association. In determining whether a necessity within the meaning of Article 11 § 2 exists, the Contracting States possess only a limited margin of appreciation, which goes hand in hand with rigorous European supervision embracing both the law and the decisions applying it, including those given by independent courts. The Court has already held that such scrutiny was necessary in a case concerning a Member of Parliament who had been convicted of proferring insults (see the *Castells* judgment cited above, pp 22–3, § 42); such scrutiny is all the more necessary where an entire political party is dissolved and its leaders banned from carrying on any similar activity in the future.

47. When the Court carries out its scrutiny, its task is not to substitute its own view for that of the relevant national authorities but rather to review under Article 11 the decisions they delivered in the exercise of their discretion. This does not mean that it has to confine itself to ascertaining whether the respondent State exercised its discretion reasonably, carefully and in good faith; it must look at the interference complained of in the light of the case as a whole and determine whether it was 'proportionate to the legitimate aim pursued' and whether the reasons adduced by the national authorities to justify it are 'relevant and sufficient'. In so doing, the Court has to satisfy itself that the national authorities applied standards which were in conformity with the principles embodied in Article 11 and, moreover, that they based their decisions on an acceptable assessment of the relevant facts (see, *mutatis mutandis*, the *Jersild v Denmark* judgment of 23 September 1994, Series A No 298, p 26, § 31).

(ii) Application of the principles to the present case

...

(ii) The Court's assessment

51. The Court notes at the outset that the *TBKP* was dissolved even before it had been able to start its activities and that the dissolution was therefore ordered solely on the basis of the *TBKP*'s constitution and programme, which however—as is for that matter apparent from the Constitutional Court's decision—contain nothing to suggest that they did not reflect the party's true objectives and its leaders' true intentions (see paragraph 58 below)....

The Court can therefore confine its review to the other two grounds, which were upheld by the Constitutional Court.

53. In the first of these it was alleged that the *TBKP* had included the word 'communist' in its name, contrary to section 96(3) of Law no 2820.... The Constitutional Court held, in particular, that that provision prohibited the formation of political parties on a purely formal ground: the mere fact of using a name proscribed in that section sufficed to trigger its application and consequently to entail the dissolution of any political party that, like the *TBKP*, had contravened it....

54. The Court considers that a political party's choice of name cannot in principle justify a measure as drastic as dissolution, in the absence of other relevant and sufficient circumstances.... The Court also attaches much weight to the Constitutional Court's finding that the *TBKP* was not seeking, in spite of its name, to establish the domination of one social class over the others, and that, on the contrary, it satisfied the requirements of democracy, including political pluralism, universal suffrage and freedom to take part in politics....

Accordingly, in the absence of any concrete evidence to show that in choosing to call itself 'communist', the *TBKP* had opted for a policy that represented a real threat to Turkish society or the Turkish State, the Court cannot accept that the submission based on the party's name may, by itself, entail the party's dissolution.

55. The second submission accepted by the Constitutional Court was that the *TBKP* sought to promote separatism and the division of the Turkish nation....

56. The Court notes that although the *TBKP* refers in its programme...to the Kurdish 'people' and 'nation' and Kurdish 'citizens', it neither describes them as a 'minority' nor makes any claim—other than for recognition of their existence—for them to enjoy special treatment or rights, still less a right to secede from the rest of the Turkish population. On the contrary, the programme states: 'The *TBKP* will strive for a peaceful, democratic and fair solution of the Kurdish problem, so that the Kurdish and Turkish peoples may live together of their free will within the borders of the Turkish Republic, on the basis of equal rights and with a view to democratic restructuring founded on their common interests....

The *TBKP* also said in its programme: 'A solution to the Kurdish problem will only be found if the parties concerned are able to express their opinions freely, if they agree not to resort to violence in any form in order to resolve the problem and if they are able to take part in politics with their own national identity.'

57. The Court considers one of the principal characteristics of democracy to be the possibility it offers of resolving a country's problems through dialogue, without recourse to violence, even when they are irksome. Democracy thrives on freedom of expression. From that point of view, there can be no justification for hindering a political group solely because it seeks to debate in public the situation of part of the State's population and to take part in the nation's political life in order to find, according to democratic rules, solutions capable of satisfying everyone concerned. To judge by its programme, that was indeed the *TBKP*'s objective in this area. That distinguishes the present case from those referred to by the Government....

58. Admittedly, it cannot be ruled out that a party's political programme may conceal objectives and intentions different from the ones it proclaims. To verify that it does not, the content of the programme must be compared with the party's actions and the positions it defends. In the present case, the *TBKP*'s programme could hardly have been belied by any practical action it took since it was dissolved immediately after being formed and accordingly did not even have time to take any action. It was thus penalised for conduct relating solely to the exercise of freedom of expression.

59. The Court is also prepared to take into account the background of cases before it, in particular the difficulties associated with the fight against terrorism (see, among other authorities, the *Ireland v UK* judgment cited above, pp 9 *et seq*, §§ 11 *et seq*, and the *Aksoy v Turkey* judgment of 18 December 1996, Reports 1996-VI, p..., §§ 70 and 84). In the present case, however, it finds no evidence to enable it to conclude, in the absence of any activity by the *TBKP*, that the party bore any responsibility for the problems which terrorism poses in Turkey.

60. Nor is there any need to bring Article 17 into play as nothing in the constitution and programme of the *TBKP* warrants the conclusion that it relied on the Convention to engage in activity or perform acts aimed at the destruction of any of the rights and freedoms set forth in it (see, *mutatis mutandis*, the *Lawless v Ireland* judgment of 1 July 1961 (merits) Series A No 3, pp 45–46, § 7).

61. Regard being had to all the above, a measure as drastic as the immediate and permanent dissolution of the *TBKP*, ordered before its activities had even started and coupled with a ban barring its leaders from discharging any other political responsibility, is disproportionate to the aim infringed Article 11 of the Convention.

...

FOR THESE REASONS, THE COURT UNANIMOUSLY
Holds that there has been a violation of Article 11 of the Convention;

...

NOTES

1 The Grand Chamber was composed of President Bernhardt and Judges: Gölcüklü, Matscher, Macdonald, Russo, Valticos, Palm, Foighel, Pekkanen, Loizou, Morenilla, Freeland, Baka, Lopes Rocha, Wildhaber, Makarczyk, Kuris, Lohmus, and Van Dijk.

2 The judgment clearly demonstrates that the Court follows the same analytical framework in applying Article 11 as it does in cases invoking Articles 8, 9, and 10 (see previous chapters). This method involves examining whether there has been an 'interference' with the applicant's rights granted by paragraph 1 of the Article and, if that is so, then considering whether the interference was 'justified' under paragraph 2 of the Article (i.e. was it 'prescribed by law', did it have a 'legitimate aim', and was it 'necessary in a democratic society'): see paragraphs 35 and 37 in the judgment above.

3 The Court was also willing to interpret the right to freedom of association broadly so as to include political parties (even where the State fears that a specific party may undermine the prevailing constitutional arrangements, although the State can take action to protect its institutions from that party provided its actions satisfy the conditions of Article 11(2)). However, the limitations contained within Article 11 are construed strictly when applied to political parties, because of the latter's fundamental role in the maintenance of democratic societies. Hence, the Court will only allow States a limited margin of appreciation when determining if an interference with a political party's Article 11(1) rights was necessary under Article 11(2).

4 In its judgment the Court held that the right to freedom of association is not restricted to the initial right to form an association but also continues throughout the lifetime of the organization. If state authorities wish to dissolve a particular association they must comply with the conditions laid down in Article 11(2).

5 Earlier the two individual applicants in the above case had succeeded in another action they had brought under the Convention against Turkey. In *Yagci and Sargin v Turkey* A.319 (1995), they challenged the authorities' conduct leading up to the establishment of the United Communist Party of Turkey. During 1987 the applicants held a press conference in Brussels at which they announced their intention of returning to Turkey in order to form the party. As soon as they alighted from the plane in Ankara (on 16 November 1987) the police arrested them. They were charged with leading an organization which, *inter alia*, had the unlawful aim of establishing the domination of one social class. The National Security Court ordered that they be held in custody pending trial. Eventually the applicants were released from custody in May 1990 (and, as we know from the above case, they established the party the following month). The Turkish courts finally acquitted the applicants in January 1992. Subsequently, the European Court of Human Rights held, by 8 votes to 1, that the above treatment violated the applicants' rights under Article 5(3) and Article 6(1).

6   Another Grand Chamber applied the principles articulated in the **United Communist Party** judgment in the later case of **Socialist Party v Turkey**, 1998-III. The applicants in this case were another Turkish political party and two Chairmen of the Party. In 1988, when the Socialist Party was preparing to take part in a general election, State Counsel applied to the Constitutional Court for an order dissolving the Party. The Constitutional Court dismissed the application as unfounded. However, criminal proceedings were then brought against the leaders of the Party (including one of the applicants) in the National Security Courts for allegedly disseminating harmful propaganda. All the accused were acquitted following a repeal of the relevant legislation. In 1991 the Party was formally allowed by the authorities to participate in the general election. However, a few months later State Counsel made a second application for the Party to be dissolved on the grounds that it had engaged in activities likely to undermine the territorial integrity and unity of the nation contrary to the Constitution. Counsel particularly relied upon election publications from the Party and speeches made by the Chairman. In July 1992 the Constitutional Court ordered the dissolution of the Party as it had argued for the creation of an independent federated State (comprising separate States for Turks and Kurds). The applicants complained to the Commission which, unanimously, found a breach of Article 11. Before the Court, the Turkish Government sought to distinguish the **United Communist Party** case on the basis that in the present action the dissolution of the Party was based upon its activities after its formation (and not simply on its constitution and programme). The Court, unanimously, found that there had been an interference with the applicants' right to freedom of association and that it was 'prescribed by law' and had the 'legitimate aim' of protecting national security (on the same basis as in **United Communist Party**). Therefore, the major question was whether the dissolution was 'necessary in a democratic society'. The Court noted:

> Having analysed [the Chairman's] statements, the Court finds nothing in them that can be considered a call for the use of violence, an uprising or any other form of rejection of democratic principles. On the contrary, he stressed on a number of occasions the need to achieve the proposed political reform in accordance with democratic rules, through the ballot box and by holding referenda. At the same time, he spoke out against 'the former culture idolising violence...
>
> At the hearing the Agent for the Government stated that [the Chairman] had 'justified the use of violent and terrorist methods' by saying in particular 'The Kurd has proved himself through the fight of impoverished peasants by linking its destiny [to theirs]'... Furthermore, by calling on those present to 'sow courage, rather than watermelons', [the Chairman] had, in the Government's submission, 'exhorted them to stop all activities other than the destruction of order'. Lastly, by using the phrase 'The Kurdish people are standing up' he had called upon them to revolt.
>
> While the Court accepts that these phrases were directed at citizens of Kurdish origin and constituted an invitation to them to rally together and assert certain political claims, it finds no trace of any incitement to use violence or infringe the rules of democracy. In that regard, the relevant statements were scarcely any different from those made by other political groups that were active in other countries of the Council of Europe....
>
> In the Court's view, the fact that such a political programme is considered incompatible with the current principles and structures of the Turkish State does not make it incompatible with the rules of democracy. It is of the essence of democracy to allow diverse political programmes to be proposed and debated, even those that call into question the way a State is currently organised, provided that they do not harm democracy itself. [Paras 46–7.]

Therefore, the Court held that the dissolution of the Party had been a disproportionate action that was in breach of Article 11. The effect of this judgment is to safeguard the right of political parties to continue non-violent campaigns for political manifestos which challenge the basic ideologies and constitutional structures of their States, so long as the parties adhere to the Convention's idea of political democracy. In **United Communist Party** the Court identified a number of the elements which constitute this form of society including: the free expression of the people (by secret ballot) in the choice of the legislature, the plurality of political parties contesting such elections, respect for human rights (especially freedom of expression), and the rule of law: see further A. Mowbray, 'The Role of the European Court of Human Rights in the Promotion of Democracy' [1999] *Public Law* 703.

7 A unanimous Grand Chamber found no breach of Article 11 in respect of the dissolution of a political party supporting fundamentalist Islamic views in **Refah Partisi (The Welfare Party) and Others v Turkey**, judgment of 13 February 2003. The applicant political party and three of its leading members alleged a breach of their right to freedom of association. After the Turkish general election of 1995, Refah was the largest political party in the national parliament (with 158 members out of a total of 450). Refah formed a coalition government with another party. In May 1997, Principal State Counsel applied to the Constitutional Court seeking the dissolution of Refah on the ground that it had become a centre of activities contrary to the principles of secularism. State Counsel relied on a number of statements made by leading figures in Refah advocating, *inter alia*, the abolition of secularism in Turkey, establishing the supremacy of the Koran through holy war (jihad), and the introduction of Islamic law (sharia) in Turkey. In January 1998, the Constitutional Court dissolved Refah, ordered the transfer of the Party's assets to the Treasury, and terminated the applicants' office as MPs/banned them from becoming members or leaders of any other political party for five years. A Chamber of the European Court, by 5 votes to 4, found no breach of the applicants' rights under Article 11. Thereupon, the applicants obtained the permission of the Grand Chamber for a re-hearing under Article 43. The Grand Chamber found that the domestic judgment against the applicants was 'prescribed by law' and had the legitimate aims, under Article 11(2), of protecting national security and public safety, preventing disorder or crime, and protecting the rights and freedoms of others. As to whether it was 'necessary in a democratic society' the Grand Chamber held that:

98. On that point, the Court considers that a political party may promote a change in the law or the legal and constitutional structures of the State on two conditions: firstly, the means used to that end must be legal and democratic; secondly, the change proposed must itself be compatible with fundamental democratic principles. It necessarily follows that a political party whose leaders incite to violence or put forward a policy which fails to respect democracy or which is aimed at the destruction of democracy and the flouting of the rights and freedoms recognised in a democracy cannot lay claim to the Convention's protection against penalties imposed on those grounds (see *Yazar and Others v Turkey*, Nos 22723/93, 22724/93, and 22725/93, § 49, ECHR 2002-II, and, *mutatis mutandis*, the following judgments: *Stankov and the United Macedonian Organisation Ilinden v Bulgaria*, Nos 29221/95 and 29225/95, § 97, ECHR 2001-IX, and *Socialist Party and Others v Turkey*, judgment of 25 May 1998, Reports 1998-III, pp 1256–7, §§ 46–7).

99. The possibility cannot be excluded that a political party, in pleading the rights enshrined in Article 11 and also in Articles 9 and 10 of the Convention, might attempt to derive therefrom the right to conduct what amounts in practice to activities intended to destroy the rights or freedoms set forth in the Convention and thus bring about the destruction of democracy (see *Communist Party (KPD) v Germany*, No 250/57, Commission decision of 20 July 1957, Yearbook 1, p 222). In view of the very clear link between the Convention and democracy (see paragraphs 86–9 above), no one must be authorised to rely on the Convention's provisions in order to weaken or destroy the ideals and values of a democratic society. Pluralism and democracy are based on a compromise that

requires various concessions by individuals or groups of individuals, who must sometimes agree to limit some of the freedoms they enjoy in order to guarantee greater stability of the country as a whole (see, *mutatis mutandis, Petersen v Germany* (dec.), No 39793/98, ECHR 2001-XII).

In that context, the Court considers that it is not at all improbable that totalitarian movements, organised in the form of political parties, might do away with democracy, after prospering under the democratic regime, there being examples of this in modern European history.

100. The Court reiterates, however, that the exceptions set out in Article 11 are, where political parties are concerned, to be construed strictly; only convincing and compelling reasons can justify restrictions on such parties' freedom of association. In determining whether a necessity within the meaning of Article 11 § 2 exists, the Contracting States have only a limited margin of appreciation. Although it is not for the Court to take the place of the national authorities, which are better placed than an international court to decide, for example, the appropriate timing for interference, it must exercise rigorous supervision embracing both the law and the decisions applying it, including those given by independent courts. Drastic measures, such as the dissolution of an entire political party and a disability barring its leaders from carrying on any similar activity for a specified period, may be taken only in the most serious cases (see the following judgments: *United Communist Party of Turkey and Others*, cited above, p 22, § 46; *Socialist Party and Others*, cited above, p 1258, § 50; and *Freedom and Democracy Party (ÖZDEP) v Turkey* [GC], No 23885/94, § 45, ECHR 1999-VIII). Provided that it satisfies the conditions set out in paragraph 98 above, a political party animated by the moral values imposed by a religion cannot be regarded as intrinsically inimical to the fundamental principles of democracy, as set forth in the Convention.

(d) Imputability to a political party of the acts and speeches of its members

101. The Court further considers that the constitution and programme of a political party cannot be taken into account as the sole criterion for determining its objectives and intentions. The political experience of the Contracting States has shown that in the past political parties with aims contrary to the fundamental principles of democracy have not revealed such aims in their official publications until after taking power. That is why the Court has always pointed out that a party's political programme may conceal objectives and intentions different from the ones it proclaims. To verify that it does not, the content of the programme must be compared with the actions of the party's leaders and the positions they defend. Taken together, these acts and stances may be relevant in proceedings for the dissolution of a political party, provided that as a whole they disclose its aims and intentions (see *United Communist Party of Turkey and Others*, cited above, p 27, § 58, and *Socialist Party and Others*, cited above, pp 1257–8, § 48).

(e) The appropriate timing for dissolution

102. In addition, the Court considers that a State cannot be required to wait, before intervening, until a political party has seized power and begun to take concrete steps to implement a policy incompatible with the standards of the Convention and democracy, even though the danger of that policy for democracy is sufficiently established and imminent. The Court accepts that where the presence of such a danger has been established by the national courts, after detailed scrutiny subjected to rigorous European supervision, a State may 'reasonably forestall the execution of such a policy, which is incompatible with the Convention's provisions, before an attempt is made to implement it through concrete steps that might prejudice civil peace and the country's democratic regime' (see the *Chamber's* judgment, § 81).

103. The Court takes the view that such a power of preventive intervention on the State's part is also consistent with Contracting Parties' positive obligations under Article 1 of the Convention to secure the rights and freedoms of persons within their jurisdiction. Those obligations relate not only to any interference that may result from acts or omissions imputable to agents of the State or occurring in public establishments but also to interference imputable to private individuals within non-State entities (see, for example, with regard to the State's obligation to make private hospitals

adopt appropriate measures to protect life, *Calvelli and Ciglio v Italy* [GC], No 32967/96, § 49, ECHR 2002-I). A Contracting State may be justified under its positive obligations in imposing on political parties, which are bodies whose raison d'être is to accede to power and direct the work of a considerable portion of the State apparatus, the duty to respect and safeguard the rights and freedoms guaranteed by the Convention and the obligation not to put forward a political programme in contradiction with the fundamental principles of democracy.

...

110. While it can be considered, in the present case, that Refah's policies were dangerous for the rights and freedoms guaranteed by the Convention, the real chances that Refah would implement its programme after gaining power made that danger more tangible and more immediate. That being the case, the Court cannot criticise the national courts for not acting earlier, at the risk of intervening prematurely and before the danger concerned had taken shape and become real. Nor can it criticise them for not waiting, at the risk of putting the political regime and civil peace in jeopardy, for Refah to seize power and swing into action, for example by tabling bills in Parliament, in order to implement its plans.

In short, the Court considers that in electing to intervene at the time when they did in the present case the national authorities did not go beyond the margin of appreciation left to them under the Convention.

The Grand Chamber found that the statements of the individual applicants, and other identified members of Refah, could be imputed to the Party as it had not taken any disciplinary action against them.

119. The Court sees no reason to depart from the Chamber's conclusion that a plurality of legal systems, as proposed by Refah, cannot be considered to be compatible with the Convention system. In its judgment, the Chamber gave the following reasoning:

'70. . . . the Court considers that Refah's proposal that there should be a plurality of legal systems would introduce into all legal relationships a distinction between individuals grounded on religion, would categorise everyone according to his religious beliefs and would allow him rights and freedoms not as an individual but according to his allegiance to a religious movement.

'The Court takes the view that such a societal model cannot be considered compatible with the Convention system, for two reasons.

'Firstly, it would do away with the State's role as the guarantor of individual rights and freedoms and the impartial organiser of the practice of the various beliefs and religions in a democratic society, since it would oblige individuals to obey, not rules laid down by the State in the exercise of its above-mentioned functions, but static rules of law imposed by the religion concerned. But the State has a positive obligation to ensure that everyone within its jurisdiction enjoys in full, and without being able to waive them, the rights and freedoms guaranteed by the Convention (see, *mutatis mutandis*, *Airey v Ireland*, judgment of 9 October 1979, Series A No 32, p. 14, § 25).

'Secondly, such a system would undeniably infringe the principle of non-discrimination between individuals as regards their enjoyment of public freedoms, which is one of the fundamental principles of democracy. A difference in treatment between individuals in all fields of public and private law according to their religion or beliefs manifestly cannot be justified under the Convention, and more particularly Article 14 thereof, which prohibits discrimination. Such a difference in treatment cannot maintain a fair balance between, on the one hand, the claims of certain religious groups who wish to be governed by their own rules and on the other the interest of society as a whole, which must be based on peace and on tolerance between the various religions and beliefs (see, *mutatis mutandis*, the judgment of 23 July 1968 in the *"Belgian linguistic"* case, Series A No 6, pp. 33–5, §§ 9 and 10, and *Abdulaziz, Cabales and Balkandali v the United Kingdom*, judgment of 28 May 1985, Series A No 94, pp. 35–6, § 72).'

...

123. The Court concurs in the Chamber's view that sharia is incompatible with the fundamental principles of democracy, as set forth in the Convention:

> '72. Like the Constitutional Court, the Court considers that sharia, which faithfully reflects the dogmas and divine rules laid down by religion, is stable and invariable. Principles such as pluralism in the political sphere or the constant evolution of public freedoms have no place in it. The Court notes that, when read together, the offending statements, which contain explicit references to the introduction of sharia, are difficult to reconcile with the fundamental principles of democracy, as conceived in the Convention taken as a whole. It is difficult to declare one's respect for democracy and human rights while at the same time supporting a regime based on sharia, which clearly diverges from Convention values, particularly with regard to its criminal law and criminal procedure, its rules on the legal status of women and the way it intervenes in all spheres of private and public life in accordance with religious precepts.... In the Court's view, a political party whose actions seem to be aimed at introducing sharia in a State party to the Convention can hardly be regarded as an association complying with the democratic ideal that underlies the whole of the Convention.'

124. The Court must not lose sight of the fact that in the past political movements based on religious fundamentalism have been able to seize political power in certain States and have had the opportunity to set up the model of society which they had in mind. It considers that, in accordance with the Convention's provisions, each Contracting State may oppose such political movements in the light of its historical experience.

125. The Court further observes that there was already an Islamic theocratic regime under Ottoman law. When the former theocratic regime was dismantled and the republican regime was being set up, Turkey opted for a form of secularism which confined Islam and other religions to the sphere of private religious practice. Mindful of the importance for survival of the democratic regime of ensuring respect for the principle of secularism in Turkey, the Court considers that the Constitutional Court was justified in holding that Refah's policy of establishing sharia was incompatible with democracy...

...

130. The Court considers that, whatever meaning is ascribed to the term 'jihad' used in most of the speeches mentioned above (whose primary meaning is holy war and the struggle to be waged until the total domination of Islam in society is achieved), there was ambiguity in the terminology used to refer to the method to be employed to gain political power. In all of these speeches the possibility was mentioned of resorting 'legitimately' to force in order to overcome various obstacles Refah expected to meet in the political route by which it intended to gain and retain power.

131. Furthermore, the Court endorses the following finding of the Chamber:

> '74. ...

> 'While it is true that [Refah's] leaders did not, in government documents, call for the use of force and violence as a political weapon, they did not take prompt practical steps to distance themselves from those members of [Refah] who had publicly referred with approval to the possibility of using force against politicians who opposed them. Consequently, Refah's leaders did not dispel the ambiguity of these statements about the possibility of having recourse to violent methods in order to gain power and retain it (see, *mutatis mutandis*, *Zana v Turkey*, judgment of 25 November 1997, Reports 1997-VII, p. 2549, § 58).'

(a) Overall examination of 'pressing social need'

132. In making an overall assessment of the points it has just listed above in connection with its examination of the question whether there was a pressing social need for the interference in issue in the present case, the Court finds that the acts and speeches of Refah's members and leaders cited by the Constitutional Court were imputable to the whole of the party, that those acts and speeches revealed Refah's long-term policy of setting up a regime based on sharia within the framework of a plurality of legal systems and that Refah did not exclude recourse to force in order to implement its policy and keep the system it envisaged in place. In view of the fact that these plans were incompatible with the concept of a 'democratic society' and that the real opportunities Refah had to put them into practice made the danger to democracy more tangible and more immediate, the penalty imposed on the applicants by the Constitutional Court, even in the context of the restricted margin of appreciation left to Contracting States, may reasonably be considered to have met a 'pressing social need'.

(b) Proportionality of the measure complained of

133. After considering the parties' arguments, the Court sees no good reason to depart from the following considerations in the Chamber's judgment:

> '82.... The Court has previously held that the dissolution of a political party accompanied by a temporary ban prohibiting its leaders from exercising political responsibilities was a drastic measure and that measures of such severity might be applied only in the most serious cases (see the previously cited *Socialist Party and Others v Turkey* judgment, p 1258, § 51). In the present case it has just found that the interference in question met a 'pressing social need'. It should also be noted that after [Refah's] dissolution only five of its MPs (including the applicants) temporarily forfeited their parliamentary office and their role as leaders of a political party. The 152 remaining MPs continued to sit in Parliament and pursued their political careers normally.... The Court considers in that connection that the nature and severity of the interference are also factors to be taken into account when assessing its proportionality (see, for example, *Sürek v Turkey (No 1)* [GC], No 26682/95, § 64, ECHR 1999-IV).'

134. The Court also notes that the pecuniary damage alleged by the applicants was made up largely of a loss of earnings and is speculative in nature. In view of the low value of Refah's assets, their transfer to the Treasury can have no bearing on the proportionality of the interference in issue. Moreover, the Court observes that the prohibition barring three of the applicants, Mr Necmettin Erbakan, Mr Şevket Kazan and Mr Ahmet Tekdal, from engaging in certain types of political activity for a period of five years was temporary, and that, through their speeches and the stances they adopted in their capacity as the chairman and vice-chairmen of the party, they bear the main responsibility for Refah's dissolution.

It follows that the interference in issue in the present case cannot be regarded as disproportionate in relation to the aims pursued.

4. The Court's conclusion regarding Article 11 of the Convention

135. Consequently, following a rigorous review to verify that there were convincing and compelling reasons justifying Refah's dissolution and the temporary forfeiture of certain political rights imposed on the other applicants, the Court considers that those interferences met a 'pressing social need' and were 'proportionate to the aims pursued'. It follows that Refah's dissolution may be regarded as 'necessary in a democratic society' within the meaning of Article 11 § 2.

136. Accordingly, there has been no violation of Article 11 of the Convention.

Clearly, the frequent expression of extreme views contrary to recognized Convention values, including religious and political pluralism and the prohibition on the use of violence to effect political change, by leading members of Refah led the Grand Chamber to conclude that the dissolution of the party was compatible with Article 11(2). On the importance of the principle of secularism for Turkey see **Leyla Sahin** above, p 618. Commenting on **Refah**, D. McGoldrick has observed that, '... it must be admitted that there can be some severe tensions between Islamic beliefs and the organisation of modern democratic states' ('Multiculturalism and its Discontents' (2005) 5(1) *Human Rights Law Review* 27 at 48).

8 The dissolution of political parties connected with the Basque terrorist organization ETA, by order of the domestic courts, was determined to be lawful under Article 11(2) by a united Chamber in **Herri Batasuna and Batasuna v Spain**, judgment of 30 June 2009. The Chamber found that the views and actions of the applicant political parties posed a serious threat to Spanish democracy, therefore the dissolution orders were proportional measures.

9 A unanimous Chamber extended the Court's generally protective stance towards political parties to non-governmental organizations in **Tebieti Muhafize Cemiyyeti & Israfilov v Azerbaijan**, judgment of 8 October 2009. The Chamber found that the dissolution of the applicant (environmental campaigning) association for breaches of the association's constitution and unproven allegations of misconduct was disproportionate and arbitrary, therefore a violation of Article 11 had occurred. By applying an analogous form of analysis to the dissolution of a non-governmental organization as it had previously utilized in respect of political parties, the Court accorded significant protection to organizations working to enhance civic society in member States.

Article 11(1)

The right to freedom of peaceful assembly

Ezelin v France A.202 (1991)
European Court of Human Rights

The applicant was a lawyer (*avocat*) who practised in Basse-Terre (Guadeloupe). In 1983 he was the Vice-Chairman of the Trade Union of the Guadeloupe Bar. During February of that year a number of Guadeloupe independence movements and trade unions held a public demonstration in Basse-Terre to protest against the conviction of three militants for criminal damage to public buildings. Prior notice of the demonstration had been given and the authorities had not prohibited it. According to the police about 1,000 demonstrators took part in the march and during its course the crowd chanted abuse against a named police officer (saying 'one day you will pay'). Outside the law courts the demonstrators also shouted abuse at the judges and unknown persons painted graffiti on the walls of the administrative building (calling the judges 'pimps'). The applicant carried a placard during the demonstration which read 'Trade Union of the Guadeloupe Bar against the Security and Freedom Act'. A subsequent judicial investigation was unable to identify which of the demonstrators had been responsible for uttering the insulting/threatening words or painting the graffiti. However, the Principal Public Prosecutor asked the Chairman of the Guadeloupe Bar to bring disciplinary proceedings against the applicant for allegedly having infringed Article 106 of the Decree regulating the profession of *avocat* (which, *inter alia*, made such persons liable to disciplinary sanction for 'breach of integrity honour or discretion, even relating to non-professional matters'). The Bar Council decided not to impose any disciplinary sanction on the applicant as the earlier judicial investigation had not revealed any evidence that he had committed acts in breach of Article 106. The Prosecutor appealed against that ruling to the Basse-Terre Court of Appeal which found the applicant guilty and sentenced him to a formal reprimand. The Court of Appeal's judgment stated that: '...it is not alleged that Mr Ezelin took part in this demonstration any more actively than by his constant presence and by carrying a placard....He was there in his capacity as an *avocat*, since he carried a placard announcing his profession, and at no time did he dissociate himself from the demonstrators' offensive and insulting acts or leave the procession. Such misconduct on the part of a member of the Bar publicly proclaiming his profession cannot be justified...'. The Court of Cassation dismissed the applicant's appeal and he then complained to the Commission. The latter body, by 15 votes to 6, found a breach of Article 11.

...

II. ALLEGED VIOLATION OF ARTICLE 11

...

37. Notwithstanding its autonomous role and particular sphere of application, Article 11 must, in the present case, also be considered in the light of Article 10 (see the *Young, James and Webster* judgment of 13 August 1981, Series A No 44, p 23, § 57). The protection of personal opinions, secured by Article 10, is one of the objectives of freedom of peaceful assembly as enshrined in Article 11.

A. WHETHER THERE WAS AN INTERFERENCE WITH THE EXERCISE OF THE FREEDOM OF PEACEFUL ASSEMBLY

38. In the Government's submission, Mr Ezelin had not suffered any interference with the exercise of his freedom of peaceful assembly and freedom of expression: he had been able to take part in the procession of 12 February 1983 unhindered and to express his convictions publicly, in his professional capacity and as he wished; he was reprimanded only after the event and on account of personal conduct deemed to be inconsistent with the obligations of his profession.

39. The Court does not accept this submission. The term 'restrictions' in paragraph 2 of Article 11—and of Article 10—cannot be interpreted as not including measures—such as punitive measures—taken not before or during but after a meeting (cf in particular, as regards Article 10, the *Handyside* judgment of 7 December 1976, Series A No 24, p 21, § 43, and the *Müller* judgment of 24 May 1988, Series A No 133, p 19, § 28).

40. In the second place, the Government maintained that despite the peaceful nature of Mr Ezelin's own intentions and behaviour, the sanction of which he complained had in no way infringed his freedom of peaceful assembly seeing that the demonstration had got out of hand.

In the Commission's opinion, no intentions that were not peaceful could be imputed to the applicant.

41. The Court points out that prior notice had been given of the demonstration in question and that it was not prohibited. In joining it, the applicant availed himself of his freedom of peaceful assembly. Moreover, neither the report made by the Chief Superintendent of the Basse-Terre police nor any other evidence shows that Mr Ezelin himself made threats or daubed graffiti.

The Court of Appeal found the charge of not having 'dissociate[d] himself from the demonstrators' offensive and insulting acts or [left] the procession'...proven. The Court of Cassation noted that at no time did he 'express his disapproval of these excesses or leave the procession in order to dissociate himself from these criminal acts' . . .

The Court accordingly finds that there was in this instance an interference with the exercise of the applicant's freedom of peaceful assembly.

B. WHETHER THE INTERFERENCE WAS JUSTIFIED

42. It must therefore be determined whether the sanction complained of was 'prescribed by law', prompted by one or more of the legitimate aims set out in paragraph 2 and 'necessary in a democratic society' for achieving them.

1. 'Prescribed by law'

. . .

In the instant case the legal basis of the sanction complained of lay solely in the special rules governing the profession of avocat. Article 106 of the relevant Decree of 9 June 1972 provides unequivocally that any avocat, even in his non-professional activities, has special obligations . . . ; and the Court of Cassation has held that these include the respect due to the judicial authorities . . .

That being so, the interference was 'prescribed by law'.

2. Legitimate aim

. . .

47. It is apparent from the evidence that Mr Ezelin incurred the punishment because he had not dissociated himself from the unruly incidents which occurred during the demonstration. As the Commission noted, the authorities took the view that such an attitude was a reflection of the fact that the applicant, as an avocat, endorsed and actively supported such excesses. The interference was therefore in pursuit of a legitimate aim, the 'prevention of disorder'.

3. Necessity in a democratic society

48. In the applicant's submission, the interference of which he was complaining was not 'necessary in a democratic society'. To claim that he should have left the procession in order to express his disapproval of acts committed by other demonstrators was, he said, to deny his right to freedom of peaceful assembly.

49. The Government, on the other hand, submitted that the disputed measure did indeed answer a 'pressing social need', having regard in particular to Mr Ezelin's position as an avocat and to the local background. By not disavowing the unruly incidents that had occurred during the demonstration, the applicant had *ipso facto* approved them. . . .

50. The Commission contended that a disciplinary penalty based on an impression to which Mr Ezelin's behaviour might give rise was not compatible with the strict requirement of a 'pressing social need' and therefore could not be regarded as 'necessary in a democratic society'.

51. The Court has examined the disciplinary sanction in question in the light of the case as a whole in order to determine in particular whether it was proportionate to the legitimate aim pursued, having regard to the special importance of freedom of peaceful assembly and freedom of expression, which are closely linked in this instance.

52. The proportionality principle demands that a balance be struck between the requirements of the purposes listed in Article 11 § 2 and those of the free expression of opinions by word, gesture or even silence by persons assembled on the streets or in other public places. The pursuit of a just balance must not result in avocats being discouraged, for fear of disciplinary sanctions, from making clear their beliefs on such occasions.

53. Admittedly, the penalty imposed on Mr Ezelin was at the lower end of the scale of disciplinary penalties given in Article 107 of the Degree of 9 June 1972...; it had mainly moral force, since it did not entail any ban, even a temporary one, on practising the profession or on sitting as a member of the Bar Council. The Court considers, however, that the freedom to take part in a peaceful assembly—in this instance a demonstration that had not been prohibited—is of such importance that it cannot be restricted in any way, even for an avocat, so long as the person concerned does not himself commit any reprehensible act on such an occasion.

In short, the sanction complained of, however, minimal, does not appear to have been 'necessary in a democratic society'. It accordingly contravened Article 11.

...

FOR THESE REASONS, THE COURT

...

Holds by six votes to three that there has been a violation of Article 11;...

NOTES

1 The Court was comprised of Judges: Cremona, Gölcüklü, Walsh, Spielmann, De Meyer, and Pekkanen. President Ryssdal dissented as he believed that the authorities' punishment of Ezelin did not exceed the margin of appreciation to be accorded to national regulation of professional (i.e. lawyers') behaviour. Similarly, Matscher J thought that there was 'not the slightest doubt' that Ezelin was in serious breach of his ethical duty of 'discretion' and, therefore, the minimal punishment imposed on him was proportionate. Pettiti J also felt the punishment was within France's margin of appreciation. He also observed that 'the Court, in its majority, like the Commission, showed the importance which it attached to the right to demonstrate, but did the case under examination provide an appropriate occasion for expressing this principle?'

2 This was the first case in which the Court found a breach of the right of peaceful assembly. The judgment does not distinguish between the freedom to assemble peacefully for static meetings or moving processions. The Court also accorded a broad scope to the right by interpreting it as being infringed through the imposition of subsequent punishments. Individuals seeking to assert the right must, however, ensure that they do not commit any 'reprehensible' acts on the occasion of the assembly. Although the Court did not elaborate upon the meaning of that term it will presumably include actions which are not compatible with peaceful forms of protest (e.g. acts of violence directed at opponents or police officers seeking lawfully to control assemblies in accordance with Article 11(2)).

3 The Court had provided an insight into its approach to this right in the earlier case of *Plattform 'Arzte fur das Leben' v Austria* A.139 (1988), which directly concerned Article 13 (the right to an effective domestic remedy for violation of Convention rights). The applicant association was a group of doctors who campaigned against abortion. In 1980 they notified the police that they intended to hold a religious service at Stadl-Paura Church, in Upper Austria, and then march to the surgery of a doctor who performed abortions. The police did not object and gave permission for the use of the highway. Subsequently, two counter-demonstrations were banned by the police. Shortly before the march began the organizers feared that incidents might occur so they changed the route to process to an alter on a nearby hillside (rather than march to the doctor's surgery). The police did not object, but warned that it would be impossible to prevent counter-demonstrators throwing objects at the marchers. About 500 counter-demonstrators tried to disrupt the association's service and march by shouting at them and throwing eggs and clumps of grass at the participants. Eventually, when physical violence was about to occur, special riot-control police formed a cordon between the protestors and the counter-demonstrators. Later the association made a disciplinary complaint against the police alleging that they had failed to provide sufficient protection for its members. The Upper Austrian Safety Authority rejected the complaint. The association lodged an appeal with the Constitutional Court but it ruled that the Court had no jurisdiction. In 1982 the association obtained permission for a second demonstration against abortion to be held in the cathedral square in Salzburg. About 350 counter-demonstrators gathered in the square and the police formed a cordon between them and the association's members. Eventually, the police cleared the square. The association complained to the Commission about the alleged failings of the Austrian police and other State authorities to protect the Convention rights of the association and its members. The Commission unanimously found a breach of Article 13. Before the Court, the Austrian Government argued that Article 11 did not impose any positive obligations on States to protect demonstrations, therefore it was not possible for the association to argue that any of its substantive Convention rights had been violated. The Court, unanimously, stated:

A demonstration may annoy or give offence to persons opposed to the ideas or claims that it is seeking to promote. The participants must, however, be able to hold the demonstration without having to fear that they will be subjected to physical violence by their opponents; such a fear would be liable to deter associations or other groups supporting common ideas or interests from openly expressing their opinions on highly controversial issues affecting the community. In a democracy the right to counter-demonstrate cannot extend to inhibiting the exercise of the right to demonstrate.

Genuine, effective freedom of peaceful assembly cannot, therefore, be reduced to a mere duty on the part of the State not to interfere: a purely negative conception would not be compatible with the object and purpose of Article 11. Like Article 8, Article 11 sometimes requires positive measures to be taken, even in the sphere of relations between individuals, if need be (see, *mutatis mutandis, X and Y v Netherlands* (1985) A.91).

While it is the duty of Contracting States to take reasonable and appropriate measures to enable lawful demonstrations to proceed peacefully, they cannot guarantee this absolutely and they have a wide discretion in the choice of the means to be used . . . In this area the obligation they enter into under Article 11 of the Convention is an obligation as to measures to be taken and not as to results to be achieved. [Paras 32 and 34.]

Having regard to the fact that large numbers of police, including riot-control units, were deployed at the 1980 demonstration and one hundred officers separated the association's members from the counter-demonstrators in Salzburg, the Court concluded 'it thus clearly appears that the Austrian authorities did not fail to take reasonable and appropriate measures' (para 39). Hence, as the association had no arguable claim that Article 11 had been violated, Article 13 did not apply in the present case. While the applicant association lost their action, the judgment of the Court revealed an interpretation of Article 11 which was favourable to the rights of peaceful protestors by subjecting States to both negative and positive duties in regard to such persons. However, as we have seen in relation to the positive duty of respect under Article 8, the Court accords States a broad latitude in fulfilling such positive obligations. Clearly, applicants cannot expect the Court to reject contemporaneous police decisions which involve 'reasonable and appropriate measures' to safeguard the Article 11 rights of peaceful protestors.

4 A Chamber of the full-time Court found a breach of the right to peaceful assembly in *Djavit An v Turkey*, judgment of 20 February 2003. The applicant was a Cypriot national of Turkish origin living in the northern part of Cyprus. He was an opponent of the Turkish-Cypriot authorities and the Turkish military presence in northern Cyprus. The applicant held the position of Turkish-Cypriot coordinator of the 'Movement for an Independent and Federal Cyprus', an unregistered association of Turkish and Greek Cypriots founded to develop close relations between the two communities. Between 1992 and 1998 the Turkish-Cypriot authorities refused the applicant permission to cross the 'green line', separating the Turkish and Greek communities, 46 times (and granted him permission on six occasions) when he wished to attend bi-communal events and meetings in the Greek-Cypriot community. The Chamber, subject to the dissent of the Turkish *ad hoc* Judge, found that there were no laws in the 'Turkish Republic of Northern Cyprus' regulating the issuing of permits to person wishing to cross the green line. Consequently, the interferences with the applicant's freedom of peaceful assembly were not 'prescribed by law' as required by Article 11(2). More generally, the Court affirmed the views of the Commission in *Rassemblement Jurassien and Unite Jurassienne v Switzerland* (1979) 17 DR 93 that:

> 56. . . . this right covers both private meetings and meetings in public thoroughfares as well as static meetings and public processions; in addition it can be exercised by individuals and those organising the assembly . . . the Court considers that, although the essential object of Article 11 is to protect the individual against arbitrary interference by public authorities with the exercise of the rights protected, there may in addition be positive obligations to secure the effective enjoyment of these rights.

5 The full-time Court has found Bulgaria to be in breach of this provision in two cases involving the same organization representing minority Macedonian interests. In *Stankov and the United Macedonian Organisation Ilinden v Bulgaria*, judgment of 2 October 2001, a Chamber, by 6 votes to 1, determined that the authorities' repeated prohibition of commemorative meetings arranged by the applicant organization between 1994 and 1997 could not be justified as being necessary in a democratic society. The Chamber found that no public disorder had occurred at previous meetings held by the applicant organization and it advocated non-violent political change on behalf of a small minority of people. Four years later in *United Macedonian Organisation Ilinden and Ivanov v Bulgaria*, judgment of 20 October 2005, a unanimous Chamber concluded that the applicants' right to freedom of assembly had been violated in respect of 12 events between 1998 and 2003. The Chamber also found that on one occasion where the applicant organization was able to hold a meeting the authorities did not do all they reasonably could to protect its members from physical violence by counter-demonstrators. The Chamber delivered a separate judgment in *United Macedonian Organisation-PIRIN and Others v Bulgaria*, judgment of 20 October 2005, which concluded that the Bulgarian Constitutional Court's dissolution of the applicant political party in 2000 breached Article 11. In the unanimous judgment of the Chamber, the Party's peaceful advocacy of autonomy or secession for the region of Pirin Macedonia was not sufficient to justify the dissolving of the organization. Later, the Court, by 5 votes to 2, found another breach of the right to peaceful assembly in respect of bans imposed on two public rallies which PIRIN sought to hold during 1998 in Sofia. The Court concluded that the authorities' belief that separatist views would be expressed at the rallies did not justify the imposition of bans: *Ivanov and Others v Bulgaria*, judgment of 24 November 2005 (note, this was a different Mr Ivanov from the applicant in the earlier case). Another complaint brought by the **United Macedonian Organisation Ilinden v Bulgaria**, judgment of 19 January 2006, involving the refusal of the authorities to register the association during the late 1990s was found, by 6 votes to 1, to amount to a breach of the right to freedom of association. The Chamber considered that as the organization only had about 3,000 supporters and its public influence was minimal the State's argument that it had been necessary to refuse to register the association in order to protect the majority of the population in the Pirin region was not a proportionate justification. These cases disclose serious and repeated failings in the Bulgarian authorities' conduct towards this section of its population.

6   The domestic authorities' banning of a silent protest, organized by a Green MP, at a cemetery where SS veterans were gathering to mark the deaths of SS soldiers in the Second World War was found to breach the MP's right to freedom of assembly by a large majority (6 votes to 1) of the Chamber in **Ollinger v Austria**, judgment of 29 June 2006. The Austrian Constitutional Court had concluded that the ban on the applicant's protest was justified in order to protect members of the public who would be visiting the graves of their relatives. However, the Chamber determined that the ban was a disproportionate measure as the applicant's assembly had been planned as a silent protest and was not directed at the beliefs of the cemetery users. The judgment reveals that domestic authorities may have to engage in a tripartite balancing of interests involving protestors, counter-protestors, and affected members of the public when evaluating how to regulate peaceful assemblies.

7   Whilst the right has mainly been invoked in the context of assemblies concerned with matters of politics/public interest, a unanimous Chamber expressed the view that it could be extended to social gatherings. In the joined cases of **Friend** and **The Countryside Alliance and others v UK**, decision of 24 November 2009, the applicants who were involved in or supported hunting challenged legislation banning the hunting of mammals with dogs in Scotland and England/Wales. The first applicant contended that the bans violated the essence of his right to peacefully assemble with fellow hunters. The Chamber held that it was willing:

> 50. . . . to assume that Article 11 may extend to the protection of an assembly of an essentially social character, it notes that the hunting bans in Scotland, England and Wales as they apply to the first applicant do not prevent or restrict his right to assemble with other huntsmen and thus do not interfere with his right of assembly *per se*. The hunting bans only prevent a hunt from gathering for the particular purpose of killing a wild mammal with hounds; as such, the hunting bans restrict not the right of assembly but a particular activity for which huntsmen assemble. The hunt remains free to engage in any one of a number of alternatives to hunting such as drag or trail hunting . . . It is also of some relevance that the wider public or social dimensions to a traditional hunt have also been preserved in drag or trail hunting. In the Court's view the mere fact that, prior to the bans, hunting culminated in the killing of a wild mammal by hounds is not sufficient for it to find that the bans struck at the very essence of the right of assembly

Furthermore, even if the applicant's right under Article 11(1) had been infringed the legislative bans could be justified under Article 11(2). The Chamber determined that the bans pursued the legitimate aim of the 'protection of morals' as they were '50. . . . designed to eliminate the hunting and killing of animals for sport in a manner which the legislature judged to cause suffering and to be morally and ethically objectionable.' Regarding the proportionality of the bans:

> 50. . . . a wider margin of appreciation must be accorded to State authorities in regulating a particular assembly the further that assembly moves from one of a political character to one of a

purely social character. The Court notes that the legislative measures in question in the present case were very recently introduced after extensive debate by the democratically–elected representatives of the State on the social and ethical issues raised by the method of hunting in question. Having regard to the nature and limited scope of any interference with the rights guaranteed by Article 11, the Court finds that the measures may be regarded as falling within the margin of appreciation enjoyed by the State and as being proportionate to the legitimate aim served thereby.

Consequently, the Chamber declared the complaints inadmissible.

The right to freedom of association with others

1   The plenary Court has ruled that public law associations fall outside the scope of Article 11. In *Le Compte, Van Leuven and De Meyere v Belgium* A.43 (1981), the applicants were medical doctors who had been subject to disciplinary proceedings and punishments by the Belgian Ordre des medecins. The Ordre had been established by an Act of the Belgian Parliament and its disciplinary functions were defined in a Royal Decree. The latter instrument required all doctors practising in Belgium to be registered with the Ordre. Other private associations of doctors also existed in Belgium to protect their professional interests. The applicants complained to the Commission that, *inter alia*, the obligation to join the Ordre inhibited their freedom of association and the mere existence of the Ordre had the effect of eliminating freedom of association. The Commission, unanimously, found no breach of Article 11(1) as the Ordre did not constitute an association within the meaning of that provision. The Court likewise, unanimously, found no breach of that Article.

The Court notes firstly that the Belgian Ordre des medecins is a public-law institution. It was founded not by individuals but by the legislature; it remains integrated within the structures of the State and judges are appointed to most of its organs by the Crown. It pursues an aim which is in the general interest, namely the protection of health, by exercising under the relevant legislation a form of control over the practice of medicine. Within the context of this latter function, the Ordre is required in particular to keep the register of medical practitioners. For the performance of the tasks conferred on it by the Belgian State, it is legally invested with administrative as well as rule-making and disciplinary prerogatives out of the orbit of the ordinary law ... and, in this capacity, employs processes of a public authority ...

Having regard to these various factors taken together, the Ordre cannot be considered as an association within the meaning of Article 11. However, there is a further requirement: if there is not to be a violation, the setting up of the Ordre by the Belgian State must not prevent practitioners from forming together or joining professional associations. Totalitarian regimes have resorted—and resort—to the compulsory-regimentation of the professions by means of closed and exclusive organisations taking the place of the professional associations and the traditional trade unions. The authors of the Convention intended to prevent such abuses ...

The Court notes that in Belgium there are several associations formed to protect the professional interests of medical practitioners and which they are completely free to join or not ... In these circumstances the existence of the Ordre and its attendant consequence- that is to say, the obligation on practitioners to be entered on the register of the Ordre and to be subject to the authority of its organs- clearly have neither the object nor the effect of limiting, even less suppressing, the right guaranteed by Article 11(1). [Paras 64–5.]

Hence the Court wished to uphold the legitimacy of State-supported regulatory organizations for the liberal professions, such as medicine. However, it imposed the correlative duty on States to ensure that such public law associations are not monopolistic and that practitioners can create and join their own supplementary professional associations if they so desire.

In the later case of *Sigurdur A Sigurjonsson v Iceland* (examined at p 775), the Government argued that the Frami association of taxicab drivers was a professional organization of a public law character that fell outside the scope of Article 11. Although the association had been formed by taxicab drivers to protect their professional interests, it also performed functions which served the public interest, such as approving the suitability of vehicles for use as taxicabs and fixing the rates for taxicabs. This submission was rejected:

> The Court agrees with the applicant and the Commission that the above-mentioned elements are not sufficient for Frami to be regarded as a public-law association outside the ambit of Article 11. Admittedly, Frami performed certain functions which were to some extent provided for in the applicable legislation and which served not only its members but also the public at large. However, the role of supervision of the implementation of the relevant rules was entrusted primarily to another institution…Frami was established under private law and enjoyed full autonomy in determining its own aims, organisation and procedure.…Frami was therefore predominantly a private law–organisation and must thus be considered an 'association' for the purposes of Article 11. [Para 31.]

The key criteria adopted by the Court to distinguish public law associations are: (a) the form of law under which the organisations are constituted (b) the degree of State control and influence over the organizations and (c) the extent to which the organizations perform public functions, as opposed to the private aims of their members.

In *Chassagnou v France* (examined at p 778), the Court stated that:

> If Contracting States were able, at their discretion, by classifying an association as 'public' or 'para-administrative', to remove it from the scope of Article 11, that would give them such latitude that it might lead to results incompatible with the object and purpose of the Convention…The term 'association' therefore possesses an autonomous meaning; the classification in national law has only relative value and constitutes no more than a starting-point. [Para 100.]

Having regard to the facts that the statutory hunting associations were composed of private individuals, were not integrated within the structures of the State, and did not enjoy prerogatives outside the scope of the ordinary law, the Court concluded that they were 'associations' which fell within the ambit of Article 11. However, German statutory hunting associations were classified as public law associations in the later case of *Herrmann v Germany*, judgment of 20 January 2011. The Chamber found that they enjoyed public law privileges including being empowered to issue costs orders enforced by the public exchequer. Consequently, the applicant landowner who had ethical objections to being required to belong to a hunting association and permit hunting on his land had his complaint under Article 11 declared inadmissible. But, in June 2011 the Grand Chamber agreed to reconsider the case under Article 43.

2   For the application of this right to political parties see the *United Communist Party of Turkey* and *The Socialist Party* cases at p 731. In *Ahmed v UK* (p 658), the applicants also alleged that the Regulations prevented them being active in an organizational/administrative capacity and holding offices within political parties were contrary to Article 11. The Court did not directly rule on whether Article 11(1) provides these specific rights.

> The Court notes that it has found the interferences with the applicants' rights under Article 10 to be justified from the standpoint of the requirements of the second paragraph of that Article.

Notwithstanding its autonomous role and particular sphere of application, Article 11 must in the present case also be considered in the light of Article 10 having regard to the fact that the freedom to hold opinions and to receive and impart information and ideas is one of the objectives of freedom of assembly and association as enshrined in Article 11 ... In the Court's view, the conclusions which it reached regarding the foreseeability of the impugned measures, the legitimacy of the aim pursued by them and their necessity hold true for the purposes of the requirements of the second paragraph of Article 11. It would also reiterate that [the relevant part of the Regulations] is limited to restricting the extent of the applicants' participation in an administrative and representative capacity in a political party of which they are members. The Regulations do not restrict the applicants' rights to join any political party of their choosing.

The Court finds accordingly that there has been no violation of the applicants' rights under Article 11 of the Convention. [Paras 70–1.]

3 The Court has stated that:

...the right to form an association is an inherent part of the right set forth in Article 11, even if that Article only makes express reference to the right to form trade unions. That citizens should be able to form a legal entity in order to act collectively in a field of mutual interest is one of the most important aspects of the right to freedom of association, without which that right would be deprived of any meaning. The way in which national legislation enshrines this freedom and its practical application by the authorities reveal the state of democracy in the country concerned. Certainly States have a right to satisfy themselves that an association's aim and activities are in conformity with the rules laid down in legislation, but they must do so in a manner compatible with their obligations under the Convention and subject to review by the Convention institutions. [*Sidiropoulos v Greece*, 1998-IV, at para 40.]

In a unanimous judgment the Court went on to find a breach of Article 11, as the Greek courts' refusal to register the applicants' proposed cultural association ('Home of Macedonian Civilisation') was a disproportionate response to the legitimate aims of protecting national security and preventing disorder. Although some Greek newspapers had accused the applicants of seeking to undermine the territorial integrity of Greece in favour of the neighbouring 'Former Yugoslav Republic of Macedonia', the Court concluded that there was nothing illegitimate in the aims of the proposed association. However, if the association were to engage in other, unlawful, activities at a later time then the Greek authorities had powers to dissolve the association.

4 Later examples of States violating Article 11 through their refusals to register political parties include *Presidential Party of Mordovia v Russia*, judgment of 5 October 2004, where the authorities' refusal to re-register the applicant political association was contrary to domestic law and therefore not 'prescribed by law' and *Partidul Comunistilor (Nepeceristi) and Ungureanu v Romania*, judgment of 3 February 2005. In the latter case the Court found that the refusal of the Romanian courts to register the applicant communist political party was a disproportionate measure having regard to the fact that the applicant's constitution and political programme did not contain anything contrary to democratic principles. Furthermore, whilst the Court was sensitive to the history of totalitarian communism in Romania prior to 1989, it noted that political parties advocating Marxist ideology were present in a number of member States.

5 The Court has upheld the discretion of national authorities to refuse to register associations which have adopted misleading (and potentially defamatory) names. In *APEH Uldozotteinek Szovetsege, Ivanyi, Roth and Szerdahelyi v Hungary*, decision of 31 August

1999, the first applicant was an unregistered association formed with the name 'Alliance of APEH's persecutees' by the other applicants. APEH is the abbreviated name of the Hungarian national tax authority. The Supreme Court refused to register the association because, *inter alia*, its name was misleading in that it suggested the association was linked to the tax authority and the name was defamatory. The Court found that the applicants could have founded and registered an association to promote the interests of taxpayers if they had chosen another name. Therefore, the interference with their right to freedom of association was not severe and it was legitimate for the authorities to refuse to register an association with a misleading nomenclature. Consequently, the application was declared manifestly ill-founded. Hence Article 11 does not give persons an unqualified right to form associations under any name of their own choice.

6　A unanimous Grand Chamber found no breach of Article 11 in respect of the authorities' refusal to register an association called the 'Union of People of Silesian Nationality' in *Gorzelik and Others v Poland*, judgment of 17 February 2004. The domestic refusal was based on the name of the association and provisions within the organization's memorandum of association which characterized Silesians as a 'national minority'. If the association had been registered the effect would have been to confer electoral privileges on the organization as a representative of a 'national minority'. The Grand Chamber accepted that there was a 'pressing social need' for the Polish authorities to regulate the ability of associations to describe themselves as organizations of a 'national minority' and thereby claim electoral privileges. Furthermore, the authorities' refusal of registration under the chosen name was a proportional response as the applicants could have established a registered association to carry out their cultural activities under another name which did not assert that the members were a national minority.

7　A unanimous Chamber of the full-time Court determined that a regional law prohibiting Freemasons from being nominated/appointed to specified public offices (including universities, leisure and cultural organizations) violated the right to freedom of association of a Masonic association in *Grande Oriente D'Italia Di Palazzo Giustiniani v Italy*, judgment of 2 August 2001. The applicant association had been created in 1805 and was, under Italian law, an unrecognized private law association which grouped together several Masonic Lodges (having approximately 12,500 members). In 1996 the Marches Region passed a Regional Law requiring applicants for specified public offices to declare, *inter alia*, that they were not members of a Masonic Lodge. The applicant contended that such a restriction interfered with its freedom of association under Article 11 by depriving its members of access to numerous regional public offices and that the Regional Law also created a negative image of the association. The Chamber considered that the applicant fell within the scope of Article 11 because it was:

15. . . . not suspected of undermining the constitutional structures. Additionally, and above all, the Court accepts that the measure in question may cause the applicant association-as it submits-damage in terms of loss of members and prestige.

In the view of the Chamber, the interference was 'prescribed by law' and, given the recent controversy about the activities of certain Freemasons in Italian public life, the Regional Law fell within the legitimate aims of protecting national security and preventing disorder under Article 11(2). As to whether the restriction was 'necessary in a democratic society':

24. The Court has examined the impugned measure in the light of the case as a whole in order to determine, in particular, whether it was proportionate to the legitimate aim pursued.

25. The proportionality principle demands that a balance be struck between the requirements of the purposes listed in Article 11 § 2 of the Convention and those of the free exercise of freedom of association. The pursuit of a just balance must not result in individuals being discouraged, for fear of having their applications for office rejected, from exercising their right of association on such occasions.

26. Compared with the total number of members of the applicant association, the number of actual or potential members of the association who may be confronted with the dilemma of choosing between being Freemasons and competing for the public offices referred to in section 5 of the 1996 Law cannot be said to be large. Consequently, the damage which the applicant association may suffer is likewise limited. The Court considers, however, that freedom of association is of such importance that it cannot be restricted in any way, even in respect of a candidate for public office, so long as the person concerned does not himself commit any reprehensible act by reason of his membership of the association. It is also clear that the association will suffer the consequences of its members' decisions. In short, the prohibition complained of, however minimal it might be for the applicant association, does not appear 'necessary in a democratic society'.

Therefore, the Chamber found a breach of Article 11. Paragraph 26 of the judgment is a very robust application of the right to freedom of association by the Court. In assessing the proportionality of the Marches' restriction on Freemasons it is relevant to note that it was the most severe response of a regional legislature in Italy (others had required applicants/nominees for public offices to declare any associations to which they belonged or prohibited such persons from being members of secret associations).

8 On the same day as the judgment in *Grande Oriente*, another Chamber found a violation of the right to freedom of association of a judge who was disciplined for having been a member of a Masonic Lodge forming part of the Grande Oriente D'Italia di Palazzo Giustiniani in *NF v Italy*, judgment of 2 August 2001. In 1990 guidelines passed by the National Council of the Judiciary stated that a judge's membership of lawful associations, which were governed by specific rules of conduct (e.g. the Freemasons), could be problematic. Nevertheless, in 1991 the applicant became a member of the Adriano Lemmi Lodge in Milan. During the summer of 1992 the applicant became aware, via press reports, that prosecutors had begun investigations into some of the Lodges associated with the Grande Oriente. Therefore, in October 1992 the applicant asked to distance himself from the association and in the following month he was made a 'dormant member'. In 1994 he was summoned before a disciplinary section of the National Council of the Judiciary and accused of having undermined the prestige of the judiciary by committing a serious breach of his duties through his membership of the Freemasons. Despite the applicant's contention that the National Council of the Judiciary had only issued revised guidelines stating that judicial office was incompatible with membership of the Freemasons in 1993, the disciplinary section found he had breached Article 18 of the Royal Legislative Decree No 511 of 1946 (which provided that a disciplinary sanction would be imposed on any judge who 'fails to fulfil his duties or behaves, in or outside the office, in a manner unworthy of the trust and consideration which he must enjoy'). The disciplinary section issued a warning to the applicant. Subsequently, the National Council of the Judiciary opposed the promotion of the applicant on two occasions in the light of the disciplinary warning that had been issued to him. The major issue for the Court was whether the disciplinary sanction imposed on the applicant had been 'prescribed by law'. He contended that at the time he joined the Freemasons it was not foreseeable that membership would be deemed to be contrary to judicial duties under the 1946 Decree.

29. With regard to the requirement of foreseeability, the Court reiterates that a law is 'foreseeable' if it is formulated with sufficient precision to enable the individual—if need be with appropriate advice—to regulate his conduct (see *Hasan and Chaush v Bulgaria* [GC], No 30985/96, § 84, ECHR 2000-XI).

30. It therefore needs to be determined in particular whether domestic law laid down with sufficient precision the conditions in which a judge should refrain from joining the Freemasons.

31. The Court notes first that Article 18 of the 1946 decree does not define whether and how a judge can exercise his or her right of association. Furthermore, the Constitutional Court noted that this provision was of a general nature. That said, the guidelines passed by the National Council of the Judiciary in 1990 had stated that a judge's membership of lawful associations which, like the Freemasons, were governed by specific rules of conduct could be problematical for him or her. The Court must therefore determine whether Article 18, combined with the above-mentioned guidelines support the proposition that the sanction in question was foreseeable. In that connection the Court notes that these guidelines had been passed in the context of an examination of the specific question of judges' membership of the Freemasons and that the National Council of the Judiciary, the body responsible for supervising the discipline and independence of judges, had the power to enact such provisions. However, even if the guidelines had primarily been concerned with membership of the Freemasons, the wording used to refer to it ('membership...raises delicate problems') was ambiguous and could give the impression that not all Masonic lodges were being taken into consideration, especially as these guidelines were passed after the big debate in Italy on the illegality of the secret lodge, P2; indeed, the guidelines merely stated that 'naturally, members of the judiciary are prohibited by law from joining the associations proscribed by Law No 17 of 1982'. With regard to other associations, they contained the following passage: 'the [National] Council [of the Judiciary] considers it necessary to suggest to the Minister of Pardons and Justice that it might be advisable to consider including among the restrictions on judges' rights of association reference to all associations which—for their organisation and purposes—impose particularly strong bonds of hierarchy and solidarity on their members.'

Accordingly, the wording of the guidelines of 22 March 1990 was not sufficiently clear to enable the users, who, being judges, were nonetheless informed and well-versed in the law, to realise—even in the light of the preceding debate—that their membership of an official Masonic lodge could lead to sanctions being imposed on them.

The Court's assessment is confirmed by the fact that the National Council of the Judiciary itself felt the need to come back to the issue on 14 July 1993 and state in clear terms that the exercise of judicial functions was incompatible with membership of the Freemasons.

32. In these conditions the Court concludes that the condition of foreseeability was not satisfied and that, accordingly, the interference was not prescribed by law.

33. Having reached that conclusion, the Court does not need to satisfy itself that the other requirements (legitimate aim, necessity of the interference and special limits for certain categories) required by the first and second sentences of paragraph 2 of Article 11 have been complied with.

34. Accordingly, there has been a violation of Article 11 of the Convention.

Three members of the Court dissented as they considered that a 'highly trained' judge knowing the legal background to the statutory dissolution of the P2 Lodge in the early 1980s should have foreseen that membership of the Freemasons was incompatible with judicial office in Italy. According to Judge Bonello, '20.... It is risible, in my view, to hold that he could have believed in good faith that an Italian judge could embrace Freemasonry with the blessing of the law.'

9 A Grand Chamber reached a similar conclusion to that in *NF* during the later case of *Maestri v Italy*, judgment of 17 February 2004. The applicant was a judge who had been a member of a Masonic Lodge affiliated to the Grande Oriente D'Italia di Palazzo Giustiniani from 1981 until March 1993. In 1995, the National Council of the Judiciary found that his former membership of the Freemasons breached Article 18 of the 1946 Royal Legislative Decree and he was given a reprimand. The applicant contended that this sanction had resulted in his career being stalled. Once again the basic issue for the Court was the question whether the prohibition on membership of the Freemasons by Italian judges was sufficiently foreseeable at the time of the applicant's membership. The Grand Chamber held that:

40. Lastly, the Court considers it important to emphasise that the debate of 22 March 1990 did not take place in the context of disciplinary supervision of judges, as was the case for the directive of 14 July 1993, but in the context of their career progression. It is therefore clear from an overall examination of the debate that the National Council of the Judiciary was questioning whether it was advisable for a judge to be a Freemason, but there was no indication in the debate that membership of the Freemasons could constitute a disciplinary offence in every case.

41. Accordingly, the wording of the directive of 22 March 1990 was not sufficiently clear to enable the applicant, who, being a judge, was nonetheless informed and well-versed in the law, to realise—even in the light of the preceding debate and of developments since 1982—that his membership of a Masonic lodge could lead to sanctions being imposed on him.

The Court's assessment is confirmed by the fact that the National Council of the Judiciary itself felt the need to come back to the issue on 14 July 1993 and state in clear terms that the exercise of judicial functions was incompatible with membership of the Freemasons.

42. That being so, the Court concludes that the condition of foreseeability was not satisfied in respect of the period after March 1990 either and that, accordingly, the interference was not prescribed by law. There has therefore been a violation of Article 11 of the Convention.

Six judges dissented and in a joint dissenting opinion Judges Bonello, Straznicka, Birsan, Jungwiert, and Del Tufo stated:

10. In our view it is important from the outset to recall very briefly some facts that deeply affected Italian Freemasonry from the 1970s onwards: the detection of P2, a secret and deviant Masonic lodge...the suspicion that some Masonic lodges were implicated in subversive plots to overthrow Italian democracy...and indications that part of Italian Freemasonry had close links with the Mafia, terrorism and organised crime. The report by the Parliamentary Commission of Inquiry on the P2 lodge, transmitted by President Tina Anselmi in 1984, should be kept in mind, too, as should, *inter alia*, the fact that a Grand Master of the Grande Oriente of Italy left the association and founded a new observance in consequence of the disreputable situation Italian Freemasonry was in, and the fact that, for the same reasons, British Freemasonry formally decided to withhold recognition of the Grande Oriente (the official Masonic association) of Italy and banned its affiliates from having connections with their Italian brothers.

> It is against this social and historical background that the events at issue took place, and that the applicant remained affiliated to the Freemasons.

The dissentients considered that it was 'bewildering' that the 'emphatic, public and reiterated proscription of Freemasonry for Italian judges' was not considered to be sufficiently foreseeable by the majority.

It is important to appreciate that both NF and Maestri won their cases on the ground that domestic law governing judicial membership of the Freemasons was imprecise. These judgments are not authority for a general principle that prohibitions on judicial membership of the Freemasons are always incompatible with Article 11.

10   A Chamber has held that member States are under a positive obligation effectively to investigate interferences by individuals with the freedom of association of others. In ***Ouranio Toxo and Others v Greece***, judgment of 20 October 2005, the applicant organization was a political party founded to defend the interests of the Macedonian minority living in Greece. It hung a sign outside its headquarters with its name in Greek and Macedonian. The local priests called on their followers to protest against the 'enemies of Greece' and the town council passed a resolution to organize protests against the applicant Party. After the police removed the sign it was replaced and protestors, including the mayor and councillors, gather outside the headquarters. A number of people attacked the headquarters and the staff inside. Despite telephone calls to the local police station (500 metres away) no police were deployed to protect the applicant's staff. Subsequently, the public prosecutor charged the individual applicants (members of the Party's secretariat) with inciting discord, but none of the protestors who attacked the headquarters/staff were charged. The Chamber found that the Greek Government had not provided any explanation as to why no police were available to protect the applicants from foreseeable harm. Consequently, the acts and omissions of the authorities amounted to a breach of the applicants' freedom of association.

11   A unanimous Chamber held that the dissolution of a public sector trade union (having 40,000 members working in the post office and telecommunications service) constituted a breach of Article 11 in ***Tum Haber Sen and Cinar v Turkey***, judgment of 21 February 2006. The Chamber found that the dissolution of the trade union had occurred simply because its members were civil servants. However, the Government had provided no explanation why such a measure was required in order to satisfy a 'pressing social need'.

12   Professor Alkema has noted that the inclination to associate is inherent in human nature, and that association is fundamental for the development of the personalities of individual human beings and for society as a whole. In terms of the legal right he believes that:

> It is desirable to extend the general notion of the freedom of association laid down in Article 11 of the ECHR into two directions. It should be broad and comprise all organisational and legal forms of co-operation between individuals irrespective of a profit motive. It should also go in depth and deal with the legal details of the organisations and cover the diverse aspects of membership, structure and formalities. Article 11 thus offers a comprehensive framework within which any interference can be tested on legality and necessity. [E. Alkema, 'Freedom of Association and Civil Society', 34A *Yearbook of the European Convention on Human Rights* (Dordrecht: Martinus Nijhoff, 1994), p 52 at p 82.]

How far does this conception of Article 11 exceed the current jurisprudence?

The right to form and to join trade unions for the protection of his interests

Demir and Baykara v Turkey judgment of 12 November 2008
European Court of Human Rights

The applicants were a member of and the president of a trade union (Tum Bel Sen) formed in 1990 by civil servants employed by various municipalities. The union's constitution provided for the organization to promote democratic trade unionism and assist its members. In 1993 the trade union entered into a collective agreement with Gaziantep Municipal Council extending over two years. The agreement covered all aspects of the working conditions of the Council's employees (e.g. salaries). However, within a few months the Council failed to meet its obligations under the collective agreement so the second applicant, in her capacity as union president, brought civil proceedings against the Council. In June 1994 the Gaziantep District Court found in favour of the union. However, the Court of Cassation, in December 1994, quashed the District Court's decision holding that the union had no legal authority to enter into collective agreements. The District Court, in March 1995, re-affirmed its original judgment ruling that the lacuna in domestic trade union law should be filled by reference to international treaties concerning these matters and ratified by Turkey. The Court of Cassation subsequently quashed that judgment on the basis that the freedom to join a trade union and to bargain collectively could only be exercised if specific legislation had been enacted and current legislation did not permit civil servants to form trade unions. Following the Court of Cassation's final ruling accountants from the Audit Court brought proceedings against Council officials and members of the union for the repayment of monies paid under the collective agreement.

The applicants complained to Strasbourg alleging that the domestic courts had breached Article 11 by denying them the right to form a trade union and to enter into collective agreements. A unanimous Chamber, judgment of 21 November 2006, held that there had been violations of that Article as the domestic courts had failed to recognize the legal personality of the trade union and had determined the collective agreement between the union and the Council to be null and void. The Turkish Government then successfully sought a referral to the Grand Chamber.

96. The Court must now deal with the Government's objection that the application is incompatible *ratione materiae* with the provisions of the Convention on the ground that Article 11 of the Convention is not applicable to 'members . . . of the administration of the State'.

It is true that paragraph 2 *in fine* of this provision clearly indicates that the State is bound to respect the freedom of association of its employees, subject to the possible imposition of lawful restrictions on the exercise by members of its armed forces, police or administration of the rights protected in that Article (see *Swedish Engine Drivers' Union v Sweden*, § 37, Series A no. 20).

97. In this connection, the Court considers that the restrictions imposed on the three groups mentioned in Article 11 are to be construed strictly and should therefore be confined to the 'exercise' of the rights in question. These restrictions must not impair the very essence of the right to organise. On this point the Court does not share the view of the Commission that the term 'lawful' in the second sentence of Article 11 § 2 requires no more than that the restriction in question should have a basis in national law, and not be arbitrary and that it does not entail any requirement of

proportionality (see *Council of Civil Service Unions and Others v the United Kingdom*, no. 11603/85, Commission decision of 20 January 1987, Decisions and Reports 50, p. 241). Moreover, in the Court's view, it is incumbent on the State concerned to show the legitimacy of any restrictions to such persons' right to organise. The Court further considers that municipal civil servants, who are not engaged in the administration of the State as such, cannot in principle be treated as 'members of the administration of the State' and, accordingly, be subjected on that basis to a limitation of their right to organise and to form trade unions (see, *mutatis mutandis, Tüm Haber Sen and Çınar* [v *Turkey*, ECHR 2006], §§ 35–40 and 50).

98. The Court observes that these considerations find support in the majority of the relevant international instruments and in the practice of European States.

...

106. As to European practice, the Court reiterates that the right of public servants to join trade unions is now recognised by all Contracting States. This right applies to public servants under a career or contractual system and to employees of publicly owned industrial or commercial enterprises, whether national or municipal. Civil servants, whether they work for central government or a local authority, are generally entitled to join the trade union of their choosing. The Court also takes note of the fact that the density of trade-union membership is generally higher in the public sector than in the private sector, which constitutes a manifest indication of a favourable legal and administrative environment created by member States. In the majority of member States, the few restrictions that can be found are limited to judicial offices, to the police and to the fire services, with the most stringent restrictions, culminating in the prohibition of union membership, being reserved for members of the armed forces.

107. The Court concludes from this that 'members of the administration of the State' cannot be excluded from the scope of Article 11. At most the national authorities are entitled to impose 'lawful restrictions' on those members, in accordance with Article 11 § 2. In the present case, however, the Government have failed to show how the nature of the duties performed by the applicants, as municipal civil servants, requires them to be regarded as 'members of the administration of the State' subject to such restrictions. Accordingly, the applicants may legitimately rely on Article 11 of the Convention and any interference with the exercise of the right concerned must satisfy the requirements of paragraph 2 of that Article.

...

109. The Court reiterates that Article 11 § 1 presents trade-union freedom as one form or a special aspect of freedom of association (see *National Union of Belgian Police v Belgium*, 27 October 1975, § 38, Series A no. 19; and *Swedish Engine Drivers' Union*, cited above, § 39). The Convention makes no distinction between the functions of a Contracting State as holder of public power and its responsibilities as employer. Article 11 is no exception to that rule. On the contrary, paragraph 2 *in fine* of this provision clearly indicates that the State is bound to respect freedom of assembly and association, subject to the possible imposition of 'lawful restrictions' in the case of members of its armed forces, police or administration (see *Tüm Haber Sen and Çınar*, cited above, § 29). Article 11 is accordingly binding upon the 'State as employer', whether the latter's relations with its employees are governed by public or private law (see *Swedish Engine Drivers' Union* [v *Sweden*, A.20 (1976)], § 37).

110. The Court further reiterates that, although the essential object of Article 11 is to protect the individual against arbitrary interference by public authorities with the exercise of the rights protected, there may in addition be positive obligations on the State to secure the effective enjoyment of such rights. In the specific context of the present case, the responsibility of Turkey would be engaged if the facts complained of by the applicants—that is to say, principally, the non-recognition of their union by the State at the material time—resulted from a failure on its part to secure to

the applicants under domestic law the rights set forth in Article 11 of the Convention (see *Wilson, National Union of Journalists and Others v the United Kingdom*, nos. 30668/96, 30671/96 and 30678/96, § 41, ECHR 2002-V; and *Gustafsson v Sweden*, 25 April 1996, § 45, Reports 1996-II).

...

112. The Court must ascertain in the first place whether the Government's argument that the cassation judgment of 6 December 1995 had no effects on the union activities of Tüm Bel Sen is confirmed by the facts of the case.

113. It observes in this connection that the said judgment, to the extent that it was found therein that the applicant trade union had not acquired legal personality when it was created and, accordingly, that it was not entitled to take or defend legal proceedings, had two effects on the union's activities, one retrospective, the other prospective.

114. The judgment in question had the retrospective effect of rendering null and void *ab initio* all the activities and actions that Tüm Bel Sen had undertaken between 1991 and 1993 in relation to the Gaziantep Municipal Council for the purpose of protecting its members' interests, including the collective agreement involved in the present case. That effect was compounded by the decisions of the Audit Court requiring the reimbursement of the advantages obtained by members of the trade union as a result of negotiations with the employing authority.

115. As to the prospective effect of the cassation judgment in question, the Court regards as credible the applicants' argument that the trade union Tüm Bel Sen had seen its activities considerably restricted as a result of the reluctance on the part of the heads of local authorities to enter into negotiations with it. It can be seen from the case file, firstly, that heads of municipal authorities who had agreed to grant advantages to civil servants under collective agreements had faced administrative, financial and judicial proceedings prior to the enactment of Law no. 4688 on 25 June 2001, and, secondly, that even after that date they were themselves obliged to reimburse to the State any additional sums that had been paid at the material time and then in turn bring proceedings against the civil servants who had received them.

...

126. The Court thus considers that the combined effect of the restrictive interpretation by the Court of Cassation and the legislature's inactivity between 1993 and 2001 prevented the State from fulfilling its obligation to secure to the applicants the enjoyment of their trade-union rights and cannot be justified as 'necessary in a democratic society' within the meaning of Article 11 § 2 of the Convention.

127. Accordingly, there has been a violation of Article 11 of the Convention on account of the failure to recognise the right of the applicants, as municipal civil servants, to form a trade union.

...

132. The parties agreed that the Grand Chamber had to examine the complaint concerning the annulment of the collective agreement separately from the complaint concerning the applicants' right to form trade unions.

...

140. The development of the Court's case-law concerning the constituent elements of the right of association can be summarised as follows: the Court has always considered that Article 11 of the Convention safeguards freedom to protect the occupational interests of trade-union members by the union's collective action, the conduct and development of which the Contracting States must both permit and make possible (see *National Union of Belgian Police*, cited above, § 39; *Swedish Engine Drivers' Union*, cited above, § 40; and *Schmidt and Dahlström v Sweden*, 6 February 1976, § 36, Series A no. 21).

141. As to the substance of the right of association enshrined in Article 11 of the Convention, the Court has taken the view that paragraph 1 of that Article affords members of a trade union a right, in order to protect their interests, that the trade union should be heard, but has left each State a free choice of the means to be used towards this end. What the Convention requires, in the Court's view, is that under national law trade unions should be enabled, in conditions not at variance with Article 11, to strive for the protection of their members' interests (see *National Union of Belgian Police*, cited above, § 39; *Swedish Engine Drivers' Union*, cited above, § 40; and *Schmidt and Dahlström*, cited above, § 36).

142. As regards the right to enter into collective agreements, the Court initially considered that Article 11 did not secure any particular treatment of trade unions, such as a right for them to enter into collective agreements (see *Swedish Engine Drivers' Union*, cited above, § 39). It further stated that this right in no way constituted an element necessarily inherent in a right guaranteed by the Convention (see *Schmidt and Dahlström*, cited above, § 34).

143. Subsequently, in the case of *Wilson, National Union of Journalists and Others*, the Court considered that even if collective bargaining was not indispensable for the effective enjoyment of trade-union freedom, it might be one of the ways by which trade unions could be enabled to protect their members' interests. The union had to be free, in one way or another, to seek to persuade the employer to listen to what it had to say on behalf of its members (*Wilson, National Union of Journalists and Others*, cited above, § 44).

144. As a result of the foregoing, the evolution of case-law as to the substance of the right of association enshrined in Article 11 is marked by two guiding principles: firstly, the Court takes into consideration the totality of the measures taken by the State concerned in order to secure trade-union freedom, subject to its margin of appreciation; secondly, the Court does not accept restrictions that affect the essential elements of trade-union freedom, without which that freedom would become devoid of substance. These two principles are not contradictory but are correlated. This correlation implies that the Contracting State in question, whilst in principle being free to decide what measures it wishes to take in order to ensure compliance with Article 11, is under an obligation to take account of the elements regarded as essential by the Court's case-law.

145. From the Court's case-law as it stands, the following essential elements of the right of association can be established: the right to form and join a trade union (see, as a recent authority, *Tüm Haber Sen and Çınar*, cited above), the prohibition of closed-shop agreements (see, for example, *Sørensen and Rasmussen* [v Denmark, ECHR 2006]) and the right for a trade union to seek to persuade the employer to hear what it has to say on behalf of its members (*Wilson, National Union of Journalists and Others*, cited above, § 44).

146. This list is not finite. On the contrary, it is subject to evolution depending on particular developments in labour relations. In this connection it is appropriate to remember that the Convention is a living instrument which must be interpreted in the light of present-day conditions, and in accordance with developments in international law, so as to reflect the increasingly high standard being required in the area of the protection of human rights, thus necessitating greater firmness in assessing breaches of the fundamental values of democratic societies. In other words, limitations to rights must be construed restrictively, in a manner which gives practical and effective protection to human rights (see, *mutatis mutandis*, *Refah Partisi (the Welfare Party) and Others v Turkey* [GC], nos. 41340/98, 41342/98, 41343/98 and 41344/98, § 100, ECHR 2003-II; and *Selmouni v France* [GC], no. 25803/94, § 101, ECHR 1999-V).

(ii) The right to bargain collectively

147. The Court observes that in international law, the right to bargain collectively is protected by ILO Convention No. 98 concerning the Right to Organise and to Bargain Collectively. Adopted in 1949, this text, which is one of the fundamental instruments concerning international labour standards,

was ratified by Turkey in 1952. It states in Article 6 that it does not deal with the position of 'public servants engaged in the administration of the State'. However, the ILO's Committee of Experts interpreted this provision as excluding only those officials whose activities were specific to the administration of the State. With that exception, all other persons employed by government, by public enterprises or by autonomous public institutions should benefit, according to the Committee, from the guarantees provided for in Convention No. 98 in the same manner as other employees, and consequently should be able to engage in collective bargaining in respect of their conditions of employment, including wages.

148. The Court further notes that ILO Convention No. 151 (which was adopted in 1978, entered into force in 1981 and has been ratified by Turkey) on labour relations in the public service ('Convention concerning Protection of the Right to Organise and Procedures for Determining Conditions of Employment in the Public Service') leaves States free to choose whether or not members of the armed forces or of the police should be accorded the right to take part in the determination of working conditions, but provides that this right applies everywhere else in the public service, if need be under specific conditions. In addition, the provisions of Convention No. 151, under its Article 1 § 1, cannot be used to reduce the extent of the guarantees provided for in Convention No. 98.

149. As to European instruments, the Court finds that the European Social Charter, in its Article 6 § 2 (which Turkey has not ratified), affords to all workers, and to all unions, the right to bargain collectively, thus imposing on the public authorities the corresponding obligation to promote actively a culture of dialogue and negotiation in the economy, so as to ensure broad coverage for collective agreements. The Court observes, however, that this obligation does not oblige authorities to enter into collective agreements. According to the meaning attributed by the European Committee of Social Rights (ECSR) to Article 6 § 2 of the Charter, which in fact fully applies to public officials, States which impose restrictions on collective bargaining in the public sector have an obligation, in order to comply with this provision, to arrange for the involvement of staff representatives in the drafting of the applicable employment regulations.

150. As to the European Union's Charter of Fundamental Rights, which is one of the most recent European instruments, it provides in Article 28 that workers and employers, or their respective organisations, have, in accordance with Community law and national laws and practices, the right to negotiate and conclude collective agreements at the appropriate levels.

151. As to the practice of European States, the Court reiterates that, in the vast majority of them, the right of civil servants to bargain collectively with the authorities has been recognised, subject to various exceptions so as to exclude certain areas regarded as sensitive or certain categories of civil servants who hold exclusive powers of the State. In particular, the right of public servants employed by local authorities and not holding State powers to engage in collective bargaining in order to determine their wages and working conditions has been recognised in the majority of Contracting States. The remaining exceptions can be justified only by particular circumstances.

152. It is also appropriate to take into account the evolution in the Turkish situation since the application was lodged. Following its ratification of Convention No. 87 on freedom of association and the protection of the right to organise, Turkey amended, in 1995, Article 53 of its Constitution by inserting a paragraph providing for the right of unions formed by public officials to take or defend court proceedings and to engage in collective bargaining with authorities. Later on, Law no. 4688 of 25 June 2001 laid down the terms governing the exercise by civil servants of their right to bargain collectively.

153. In the light of these developments, the Court considers that its case-law to the effect that the right to bargain collectively and to enter into collective agreements does not constitute an inherent element of Article 11 (*Swedish Engine Drivers' Union*, cited above, § 39, and *Schmidt and Dahlström*, cited above, § 34) should be reconsidered, so as to take account of the perceptible evolution in such

matters, in both international law and domestic legal systems. While it is in the interests of legal certainty, foreseeability and equality before the law that the Court should not depart, without good reason, from precedents established in previous cases, a failure by the Court to maintain a dynamic and evolutive approach would risk rendering it a bar to reform or improvement...

154. Consequently, the Court considers that, having regard to the developments in labour law, both international and national, and to the practice of Contracting States in such matters, the right to bargain collectively with the employer has, in principle, become one of the essential elements of the 'right to form and to join trade unions for the protection of [one's] interests' set forth in Article 11 of the Convention, it being understood that States remain free to organise their system so as, if appropriate, to grant special status to representative trade unions. Like other workers, civil servants, except in very specific cases, should enjoy such rights, but without prejudice to the effects of any 'lawful restrictions' that may have to be imposed on 'members of the administration of the State' within the meaning of Article 11 § 2—a category to which the applicants in the present case do not, however, belong.

...

168. Moreover, the Grand Chamber observes that the Government failed to adduce evidence of any specific circumstances that could have justified the exclusion of the applicants, as municipal civil servants, from the right, inherent in their trade-union freedom, to bargain collectively in order to enter into the agreement in question. The explanation that civil servants, without distinction, enjoy a privileged position in relation to other workers is not sufficient in this context.

169. The Court thus finds that the impugned interference, namely the annulment *ex tunc* of the collective agreement entered into by the applicants' union following collective bargaining with the authority was not 'necessary in a democratic society', within the meaning of Article 11 § 2 of the Convention.

170. There has therefore been a violation of Article 11 of the Convention on this point also, in respect of both the applicants' trade union and the applicants themselves.

...

FOR THESE REASONS, THE COURT UNANIMOUSLY

...

2. *Holds* that there has been a violation of Article 11 of the Convention on account of the interference with the right of the applicants, as municipal civil servants, to form a trade union;

3. *Holds* that there has been a violation of Article 11 of the Convention on account of the annulment *ex tunc* of the collective agreement entered into by the trade union Tüm Bel Sen following collective bargaining with the employing authority;

NOTES

1   The Grand Chamber was composed of President Rozakis and Judges: Bratza, Tulkens, Casadevall, Bonello, Turmen, Traja, Zupancic, Zagrebelsky, Pavlovschi, Garlicki, Gyulumyan, Mijovic, Spielmann, Sikuta, Villiger, and Hirvela.

2   The judgment in **Demir and Baykara** represented a significant expansion of the rights of trade unions and their members from those elaborated in the early jurisprudence of the original Court (see pp 751–5 of the second edition of this work). As two labour law experts have commented:

...it is a decision in which social and economic rights have been fused permanently with civil and political rights, in a process that is potentially nothing less than a socialisation of civil and political rights. And perhaps even more importantly still, it is a decision in which human rights have established their superiority over economic irrationalism and 'competitiveness' in the battle for the soul of labour law, and in which public law has triumphed over private law and public lawyers over private lawyers. [K. D. Ewing and J. Hendy, 'The Dramatic Implications of *Demir and Baykara*' (2010) 39(1) *Industrial Law Journal* 1 at 48.]

3 Professor Hepple considered that the specific reference to trade unions in Article 11 was designed to ensure that they were treated as 'associations' under the Convention, irrespective of their categorization and status under the domestic law of member States: B. Hepple, 'Freedom to form and join or not to join trade unions', 34A *Yearbook of the European Convention on Human Rights* (Dordrecht: Martinus Nijhoff, 1994), p 162 at p 168.

4 In the joined cases of *Wilson and The National Union of Journalist, Palmer, Wyeth and The National Union of Rail, Maritime and Transport Workers, Doolan and Others v United Kingdom*, judgment of 2 July 2002, referred to in the above extracts, a unanimous Chamber found that Britain had failed adequately to safeguard the Article 11 rights of trade unions and their members. During the early 1990s two employers, the publisher of the *Daily Mail* newspaper and a dock company, sought to terminate collective bargaining arrangements with the applicant trade unions. The employers offered financial incentives, including higher rates of pay, to their employees who signed new personal contracts of employment relinquishing trade union rights. The individual applicants refused the new contracts and sought to challenge the legality of the employers' actions. Ultimately, the House of Lords found in favour of the employers. In addition the (Conservative) Government sought changes to employment law which prevented employees from challenging action taken by employers to alter their relationship with all/any class of their employees unless the employer had acted in a manner which no reasonable employer would take. Parliament approved that amendment in section 13 of the Trade Union Reform and Employment Rights Act 1993. The applicants contended, before the Court, that the domestic law at the relevant time failed to protect their rights under Article 11. The incumbent (Labour) Government sought to defend the case by emphasizing the voluntary nature of the system of collective bargaining and recognition operating in the UK. The Court held that:

46.... Furthermore, it is of the essence of the right to join a trade union for the protection of their interests that employees should be free to instruct or permit the union to make representations to their employer or to take action in support of their interests on their behalf. If workers are prevented from so doing, their freedom to belong to a trade union, for the protection of their interests, becomes illusory. It is the role of the State to ensure that trade union members are not prevented or restrained from using their union to represent them in attempts to regulate their relations with their employers.

...

48. Under United Kingdom law at the relevant time it was, therefore, possible for an employer effectively to undermine or frustrate a trade union's ability to strive for the protection of its members' interests. The Court notes that this aspect of domestic law has been the subject of criticism by [the] Social Charter's Committee of Independent Experts and the ILO's Committee on Freedom of Association. It considers that, by permitting employers to use financial incentives to induce employees to surrender important union rights, the respondent State failed in its positive obligation to secure the enjoyment of the rights under Article 11 of the Convention. This failure amounted to a violation of Article 11, as regards both the applicant unions and the individual applicants.

Whilst the above judgment did not accord the trade unions all the protection that they sought, for example the Court declined to find a duty upon employers to recognize particular trade unions within Article 11, it demonstrated that the full-time Court was responsive to the needs of a healthy trade union system within a free-market economy. Significantly, even allowing for the 'wide' margin of appreciation accorded to States in securing the Article 11 rights of trade unions, the Court was united in determining that the Government had failed to comply with its positive obligations under that Article. Indeed, by securing the passage of legislation undermining the ability of trade unions to represent their members the previous Government could be viewed as having unduly favoured one side in the delicate balance of collective bargaining within the UK. The Court's willingness to find in favour of the applicants may also have been bolstered by the condemnation of the relevant domestic legal provisions by other international bodies.

5 The freedom of trade unions to determine who would be permitted to join/remain a member was upheld by a unanimous Chamber in *Associated Society of Locomotive Engineers & Firemen (ASLEF) v UK*, judgment of 27 February 2007. The applicant trade union had about 18,000 members working for railway companies in the UK (most train drivers were members of the union, but unlike the past era of *Young, James & Webster* (below) there was no longer a closed shop). The union had a long-standing policy of opposing fascist groups. In 2002 a Mr Lee joined the union, but a few months later the union discovered that he was an active member of the far-right British National Party. Thereupon the union instituted disciplinary proceedings against Lee which eventually resulted in his expulsion. He then successfully brought legal proceedings against the union based on 1992 legislation which prevented unions from excluding/expelling a person because of their membership of a political party. The union was obliged to re-admit Lee to membership of the union. Subsequently the union brought the case at Strasbourg arguing that there had been a breach of Article 11(1) through an interference with the union's right to determine its membership. The Government sought to justify the interference as being necessary to protect the freedom of association/expression of trade union members/potential members. The Chamber held that:

39. As an employee or worker should be free to join, or not join a trade union without being sanctioned or subject to disincentives (e.g. *Young, James and Webster v the United Kingdom*, judgment of 13 August 1981 . . .), so should the trade union be equally free to choose its members. Article 11 cannot be interpreted as imposing an obligation on associations or organisations to admit whosoever wishes to join. Where associations are formed by people, who, espousing particular values or ideals, intend to pursue common goals, it would run counter to the very effectiveness of the freedom at stake if they had no control over their membership. By way of example, it is uncontroversial that religious bodies and political parties can generally regulate their membership to include only those who share their beliefs and ideals. Similarly, the right to join a union 'for the protection of his interests' cannot be interpreted as conferring a general right to join the union of one's choice irrespective of the rules of the union: in the exercise of their rights under Article 11 § 1 unions must remain free to decide, in accordance with union rules, questions concerning admission to and expulsion from the union . . .

. . .

52. Accordingly, in the absence of any identifiable hardship suffered by Mr Lee or any abusive and unreasonable conduct by the applicant, the Court concludes that the balance has not been properly struck and that the case falls outside any acceptable margin of appreciation.

53. There has, accordingly, been a violation of Article 11 of the Convention.

The European Committee of Social Rights had criticized the relevant UK legislation on several occasions. During 2004 Parliament amended the law to permit unions to exclude/expel persons on the basis of *inter alia* the latter's activities as a member of a political party.

6 In the post-*Demir* era a united Chamber upheld a complaint of discriminatory treatment (breach of Article 14 in conjunction with Article 11) suffered by trade union members in *Danilenkov and others v Russia*, judgment of 30 July 2009. The applicants were members of the Dockers' Union of Russia who had participated in an unsuccessful strike against a private employer in Kaliningrad. Subsequently, the company transferred the applicants to part-time positions or dismissed them. They brought civil claims of discriminatory treatment in the local courts, but the latter ruled that complaints of discrimination could only be dealt with by criminal proceedings (and the prosecution office refused to open such an investigation). The Court held that workers should be free to join (or not join) trade unions without suffering sanctions. Furthermore, individuals affected by discrimination should have effective remedies to challenge their treatment. The criminal remedy in Kaliningrad was not adequate as it required proof beyond reasonable doubt of intent by the employer's senior managers to discriminate against the trade unionists.

The negative right to freedom of association

....

Young, James and Webster v UK A.44 (1981)
European Court of Human Rights

The existence of closed shops (defined by the Court as 'an undertaking or workplace in which, as a result of an agreement or arrangement between one or more trade unions and one or more employers or employers' associations, employees of a certain class are in practice required to be or become members of a specified union' (para 13) have a long history in the UK. There have been both 'pre-entry' closed shops, where an employee must join the union before being engaged, and 'post-entry' closed shops, where an employee must join the union after being engaged. In 1968 a majority of the Royal Commission on Trade Unions and Employer' Associations recommended greater legal protection should be given to existing employees who were dismissed for refusing to join a union following the introduction of a closed shop. The Industrial Relations Act 1971, introduced by Mr Heath's Conservative Government, gave workers the right to be a member of no union or to refuse to be a member of a particular union. When the Labour Party returned to power in 1974 it secured the passage of the Trade Union and Labour Relations Act 1974, which repealed the 1971 legislation and stated that it was only 'unfair' to dismiss an employee for refusing to join a union in a closed shop workplace where (a) the employee objected to being a member of any union on religious grounds or (b) the employee on any reasonable ground objected to being a member of a particular union. Subsequently an amending Act removed the latter ground in 1976. In 1975 British Rail (BR) concluded an agreement with three trade unions, the National Union of Railwaymen (NUR), the Transport Salaried Staffs' Association (TSSA), and the Associated Society of Locomotive Engineers and Firemen (ASLEF), providing that membership of one of those unions was a condition of employment for designated categories of staff. Prior to the agreement about 7,000 employees (out of 250,000) were not members of the specified unions. Eventually 54 employees were dismissed for refusing to join one of the unions. The three applicants were among that group. Mr Young, a clerical officer, had been employed by BR since 1972. He refused to join either of the unions of which he was eligible for membership, as he objected to their political views (the NUR had as one of its aims 'to work for the supersession of the capitalist system by a Socialistic order of society' and the TSSA only gave political donations to the Labour Party). Mr James, a shunter, had been employed by BR since 1974 (although he had also worked for BR during an earlier time in his life). He refused to join the NUR (the only union he was eligible for) as he did not believe that it properly looked after its members' interests. Mr Webster, a clerical officer, had been employed by BR since 1958. He refused to join either the NUR or TSSA as he was opposed to the trade union movement as it then operated. The applicants complained to the Commission alleging that their lawful dismissals, under the prevailing legislation, for refusing to join a designated union amounted to, *inter alia*, a breach of their rights to freedom of thought, conscience, expression, and association under Articles 9, 10, and 11. The Commission, by 14 votes to 3, expressed the opinion that there had been a violation of Article 11, and that it was not necessary to examine the complaints under Articles 9 and 10.

AS TO THE LAW

I. PRELIMINARY: RESPONSIBILITY OF THE RESPONDENT STATE

48. ... Before the substance of the matter is examined, it must be considered whether responsibility can be attributed to the respondent State, the United Kingdom.

The Government conceded that, should the Court find that the termination of the applicants' contracts of employment constituted a relevant interference with their rights under Article II and that that interference could properly be regarded as a direct consequence of TULRA and the Amendment Act, the responsibility of the respondent State would be engaged by virtue of the enactment of that legislation.

A similar approach was adopted by the Commission in its report.

49. Under Article I of the Convention, each Contracting State 'shall secure to everyone within [its] jurisdiction the rights and freedoms defined in...[the] Convention'; hence, if a violation of one of those rights and freedoms is the result of non-observance of that obligation in the enactment of domestic legislation, the responsibility of the State for that violation is engaged. Although the proximate cause of the events giving rise to this case was the 1975 agreement between British Rail and the railway unions, it was the domestic law in force at the relevant time that made lawful the treatment of which the applicants complained. The responsibility of the respondent State for any resultant breach of the Convention is thus engaged on this basis. Accordingly, there is no call to examine whether, as the applicants argued, the State might also be responsible on the ground that it should be regarded as employer or that British Rail was under its control.

II. THE ALLEGED VIOLATION OF ARTICLE II

...

1. The existence of an interference with an Article II right

51. A substantial part of the pleadings before the Court was devoted to the question whether Article II guarantees not only freedom of association, including the right to form and to join trade unions, in the positive sense, but also, by implication, a 'negative right' not to be compelled to join an association or a union.

Whilst the majority of the Commission stated that it was not necessary to determine this issue, the applicants maintained that a 'negative right' was clearly implied in the text. The Government, which saw the Commission's conclusion also as in fact recognising at least a limited negative right, submitted that Article II did not confer or guarantee any right not to be compelled to join an association.

They contended that this right had been deliberately excluded from the Convention and that this was demonstrated by the following passage in the *travaux préparatoires*:

'On account of the difficulties raised by the "closed-shop system" in certain countries, the Conference in this connection considered that it was undesirable to introduce into the Convention a rule under which "no one may be compelled to belong to an association" which features in [Article 20 § 2 of] the United Nations Universal Declaration' (Report of 19 June 1950 of the Conference of Senior Officials, *Collected Edition of the 'Travaux Préparatoires'*, vol IV, p 262).

52. The Court does not consider it necessary to answer this question on this occasion.

The Court recalls, however, that the right to form and to join trade unions is a special aspect of freedom of association (see the *National Union of Belgian Police* judgment of 27 October 1975, Series A No 19, p 17, § 38); it adds that the notion of a freedom implies some measure of freedom of choice as to its exercise.

Assuming for the sake of argument that, for the reasons given in the above-cited passage from the *travaux préparatoires*, a general rule such as that in Article 20 § 2 of the Universal Declaration of Human Rights was deliberately omitted from, and so cannot be regarded as itself enshrined in, the Convention, it does not follow that the negative aspect of a person's freedom of association falls completely outside the ambit of Article II and that each and every compulsion to join a particular trade union is compatible with the intention of that provision. To construe Article II as permitting every kind of compulsion in the field of trade union membership would strike at the very substance of the freedom it is designed to guarantee...

53. The Court emphasises once again that, in proceedings originating in an individual application, it has, without losing sight of the general context, to confine its attention as far as possible to the issues raised by the concrete case before it (see, *inter alia*, the *Guzzardi* judgment of 6 November 1980, Series A No 39, pp 31–2, § 88). Accordingly, in the present case, it is not called upon to review the closed shop system as such in relation to the Convention or to express an opinion on every consequence or form of compulsion which it may engender; it will limit its examination to the effects of that system on the applicants.

54. As a consequence of the agreement concluded in 1975...the applicants were faced with the dilemma either of joining NUR (in the case of Mr James) or TSSA or NUR (in the cases of Mr Young and Mr Webster) or of losing jobs for which union membership had not been a requirement when they were first engaged and which two of them had held for several years. Each applicant regarded the membership condition introduced by that agreement as an interference with the freedom of association to which he considered that he was entitled; in addition, Mr Young and Mr Webster had objections to trade union policies and activities coupled, in the case of Mr Young, with objections to the political affiliations of the specified unions...

As a result of their refusal to yield to what they considered to be unjustified pressure, they received notices terminating their employment. Under the legislation in force at the time...their dismissal was 'fair' and, hence, could not found a claim for compensation, let alone reinstatement or re-engagement.

55. The situation facing the applicants clearly runs counter to the concept of freedom of association in its negative sense.

Assuming that Article II does not guarantee the negative aspect of that freedom on the same footing as the positive aspect, compulsion to join a particular trade union may not always be contrary to the Convention.

However, a threat of dismissal involving loss of livelihood is a most serious form of compulsion and, in the present instance, it was directed against persons engaged by British Rail before the introduction of any obligation to join a particular trade union.

In the Court's opinion, such a form of compulsion, in the circumstances of the case, strikes at the very substance of the freedom guaranteed by Article II. For this reason alone, there has been an interference with that freedom as regards each of the three applicants.

56. Another facet of this case concerns the restriction of the applicants' choice as regards the trade unions which they could join of their own volition. An individual does not enjoy the right to freedom of association if in reality the freedom of action or choice which remains available to him is either non-existent or so reduced as to be of no practical value…such freedom of action or choice as might have been left to the applicants in this respect would not in any way have altered the compulsion to which they were subjected since they would in any event have been dismissed if they had not become members of one of the specified unions.

57. Moreover, notwithstanding its autonomous role and particular sphere of application, Article II must, in the present case, also be considered in the light of Articles 9 and 10 (see, *mutatis mutandis*, the *Kjeldsen, Busk Madsen and Pedersen* judgment of 7 December 1976, Series A No 23, p 26, § 52).

Mr Young and Mr Webster had objections to trade union policies and activities, coupled, in the case of Mr Young, with objections to the political affiliations of TSSA and NUR…Mr James' objections were of a different nature, but he too attached importance to freedom of choice and he had reached the conclusion that membership of NUR would be of no advantage to him…

The protection of personal opinion afforded by Articles 9 and 10 in the shape of freedom of thought, conscience and religion and of freedom of expression is also one of the purposes of freedom of association as guaranteed by Article II. Accordingly, it strikes at the very substance of this Article to exert pressure, of the kind applied to the applicants, in order to compel someone to join an association contrary to his convictions.

In this further respect, the treatment complained of—in any event as regards Mr Young and Mr Webster—constituted an interference with their Article II rights.

2. The existence of a justification for the interference found by the Court

58. The Government expressly stated that, should the Court find an interference with a right guaranteed by paragraph 1 of Articles 9, 10 or II, they would not seek to argue that such interference was justified under paragraph 2.

The Court has nevertheless decided that it should examine this issue of its own motion, certain considerations of relevance in this area being contained in the documents and information with which it has been furnished.

59. An interference with the exercise of an Article II right will not be compatible with paragraph 2 unless it was 'prescribed by law', had an aim or aims that is or are legitimate under that paragraph and was 'necessary in a democratic society' for the aforesaid aim or aims (see, *mutatis mutandis*, the *Sunday Times* judgment of 26 April 1979, Series A No 30, p 29, § 45).

60. The applicants argued that the restrictions of which they complained met none of these three conditions.

The Court does not find it indispensable to determine whether the first two conditions were satisfied, these being issues which were not fully argued before it. It will assume that the interference was 'prescribed by law', within the meaning of the Convention (see the above-mentioned *Sunday Times* judgment, pp 30–1, §§46–9), and had the aim, amongst other things, of protecting the 'rights and freedoms of others', this being the only one of the aims listed in paragraph 2 that might be relevant.

61. In connection with the last point, the Court's attention has been drawn to a number of advantages said to flow from the closed shop system in general, such as the fostering of orderly collective bargaining, leading to greater stability in industrial relations; the avoidance of a proliferation

of unions and the resultant trade union anarchy; the counteracting of inequality of bargaining power; meeting the need of some employers to negotiate with a body fully representative of the workforce; satisfying the wish of some trade unionists not to work alongside non-union employees; ensuring that trade union activities do not enure to the benefit of those who make no financial contribution thereto.

Any comment on these arguments would be out of place in the present case since the closed shop system as such is not under review (see paragraph 53 above).

62. On the other hand, what has to be determined is the 'necessity' for the interference complained of: in order to achieve the aims of the unions party to the 1975 agreement with British Rail, was it 'necessary in a democratic society' to make lawful the dismissal of the applicants, who were engaged at a time when union membership was not a condition of employment?

63. A number of principles relevant to the assessment of the 'necessity' of a given measure have been stated by the Court in its *Handyside* judgment of 7 December 1976 (Series A No 24).

Firstly, 'necessary' in this context does not have the flexibility of such expressions as 'useful' or 'desirable' (p 22, § 48). The fact that British Rail's closed shop agreement may in a general way have produced certain advantages is therefore not of itself conclusive as to the necessity of the interference complained of.

Secondly, pluralism, tolerance and broadmindedness are hall-marks of a 'democratic society' (p 23, § 49). Although individual interests must on occasion be subordinated to those of a group, democracy does not simply mean that the views of a majority must always prevail: a balance must be achieved which ensures the fair and proper treatment of minorities and avoids any abuse of a dominant position. Accordingly, the mere fact that the applicants' standpoint was adopted by very few of their colleagues is again not conclusive of the issue now before the Court.

Thirdly, any restriction imposed on a Convention right must be proportionate to the legitimate aim pursued (p 23, § 49).

64. The Court has noted in this connection that a majority of the Royal Commission on Trade Unions and Employers' Associations, which reported in 1968, considered that the position of existing employees in a newly-introduced closed shop was one area in which special safeguards were desirable... Again, recent surveys suggest that, even prior to the entry into force of the Employment Act 1980... many closed shop arrangements did not require existing non-union employees to join a specified union (see paragraph 13 above); the Court has not been informed of any special reasons justifying the imposition of such a requirement in the case of British Rail. Besides, according to statistics furnished by the applicants, which were not contested, a substantial majority even of union members themselves disagreed with the proposition that persons refusing to join a union for strong reasons should be dismissed from employment. Finally, in 1975 more than 95 per cent of British Rail employees were already members of NUR, TSSA or ASLEF...

All these factors suggest that the railway unions would in no way have been prevented from striving for the protection of their members' interests (see the above-mentioned *National Union of Belgian Police* judgment, p 18, § 39) through the operation of the agreement with British Rail even if the legislation in force had not made it permissible to compel non-union employees having objections like the applicants to join a specified union.

65. Having regard to all the circumstances of the case, the detriment suffered by Mr Young, Mr James and Mr Webster went further than was required to achieve a proper balance between the conflicting interests of those involved and cannot be regarded as proportionate to the aims being pursued. Even making due allowance for a State's 'margin of appreciation' (see, *inter alia*, the above-mentioned *Sunday Times* judgment, p 36, § 59), the Court thus finds that the restrictions complained of were not 'necessary in a democratic society', as required by paragraph 2 of Article II.

There has accordingly been a violation of Article II.

...

FOR THESE REASONS, THE COURT

Holds by eighteen votes to three that there has been a breach of Article II of the Convention; . . .

NOTES

1 The plenary Court was composed of President Wiarda and Judges: Ryssdal, Zekia, Cremona, Ganshof van der Meersch, Bindschedler-Robert, Evrigenis, Liesch, Gölcüklü, Matscher, Pinheiro Farinha, Garcia de Enterria, Pettiti, Walsh, Evans, Macdonald, Russo, and Bernhardt. The Court ruled, unanimously, that it was not necessary to examine Articles 9 and 10 separately, as they had been taken account of in the application of Article 11. Judges Ganshof van der Meersch, Bindschedler-Robert, Liesch, Gölcüklü, Matscher, Pinheiro Farinha, and Pettiti issued a concurring opinion in which they strongly supported the negative aspect of the right.

. . . Protection of freedom of association would be incomplete if it extended to no more than the positive aspect. It is one and the same right that is involved. The 'travaux préparatoires' of the Convention—which anyway are not conclusive—speak only of 'undesirability' and so do not enable one to conclude that the negative aspect of trade union freedom was intended to be excluded from the ambit of Article 11. . . .

We should like to point out that it is not necessary, for there to be a violation of Article 11, that the refusal to join an association was justified by considerations connected with freedom of thought, of conscience or of religion, or with freedom of expression. In our view, the mere fact of being obliged to give the reasons for one's refusal constitutes a violation of freedom of association.

Trade union freedom, a form of freedom of association, involves freedom of choice: it implies that a person has a choice as to whether he will belong to an association or not and that, in the former case, he is able to choose the association. However, the possibility of choice, an indispensable component of freedom of association, is in reality non-existent where there is a trade union monopoly of the kind encountered in the present case. [P 28.]

In direct contrast, Judge Sorensen (joined by Thor Vilhjalmsson and Lagergren JJ) produced a dissenting opinion which articulated an entirely different conception of the negative freedom of association.

. . . It clearly emerges from . . . the drafting history that the State Parties to the Convention could not agree to assume any international obligation in the matter, but found that it should be subject to national regulation only.

. . . no cannon of interpretation can be adduced in support of extending the scope of the Article to a matter which deliberately has been left out and reserved for regulation according to national law and traditions of each State Party to the Convention. . . .

The so-called positive and negative freedom of association are not simply two sides of the same coin or, as the Court puts it, two aspects of the same freedom. There is no logical link between the two.

The positive freedom of association safeguards the possibility of individuals, if they so wish, to associate with each other for the purpose of protecting common interests and pursuing common goals, whether of an economic, professional, political, cultural, recreational or other character, and the protection consists in preventing public authorities from intervening to frustrate such common action. It concerns the individual as an active participant in social activities, and it is in a sense a collective right in so far as it can only be exercised jointly by a plurality of individuals. The negative freedom of association, by contrast, aims at protecting the individual against being grouped together with other individuals with whom he does not agree or for purposes which he does not approve....However strongly such protection of the individual may sometimes be needed, it is neither in logic nor by necessary implication part of the positive freedom of association. [Paras 2, 5, and 6.]

Which view do you think reflects the proper interpretation of Article 11? Was the majority in effect creating a new right?

2   Ironically it was the incoming Conservative Government, led by Mrs Thatcher, that had to represent the British interests before the Court. Her Government's ideological sympathy with the applicants no doubt explains why it did not seek to try and justify their dismissals under Article 11(2). Indeed, a year before the Court gave judgment, the Conservative Government secured a change in legislation (the Employment Act 1980) which provided that, *inter alia*, henceforth in a closed shop situation it was 'unfair' to dismiss an employee where he/she objected on grounds of conscience or other deeply held personal conviction to being a member of any or a particular trade union.

3   In *Sigurdur A Sigurjonsson v Iceland* A.264 (1993), the Court strengthened the jurisprudential basis of the negative element of freedom of association. Under Regulations passed in 1983 taxi drivers working in Reykjavik had to be members of the Frami Automobile Association. This professional association had been formed in 1936 by taxi drivers to protect their interests by, *inter alia*, negotiating their working hours and wage rates, promoting solidarity among taxi drivers, and seeking to maintain limitations on the numbers of taxicabs. The applicant was granted a taxicab licence by the relevant State committee in 1984 and at the same time he joined Frami. In 1985 he stopped paying his Frami membership fees and informed them that he no longer wished to be a member. Frami requested the committee to revoke the applicant's licence which it did. Sigurjonsson then challenged that decision in the Icelandic courts. The Supreme Court eventually ruled that the Regulation imposing an obligation to join Frami lacked a statutory basis. Thereupon, the Government secured a new Act (the Motor Vehicles for Public Hire Law 1989) which made taxicab licences conditional on trade union membership. New Regulations (no 308/1989) were issued under the 1989 Act which gave Frami various public interest powers, such as approving the suitability of vehicles for use as taxicabs. The applicant rejoined Frami but expressed the view that membership was contrary to his own wishes and interests. He also complained to the Commission alleging a violation of his rights under, *inter alia*, Articles 11, 9, and 10. The Commission, by 17 votes to 1, found a violation of Article 11 (and unanimously considered that it was not necessary to examine Articles 9 and 10). Before the Court, the Government argued that the negative aspect of Article 11 should be construed restrictively, having regard to the *travaux préparatoires*. In response the Court observed that the earlier judgment in *Young, James and Webster* 'did not attach decisive importance to them' (para 35). Furthermore, the Court considered that since that decision a new common ground was emerging at the international level. Eleven members of the EC had adopted the Community Charter of the Fundamental Social Rights of Workers in 1989 (which provided workers/employers shall have the freedom to join/not join trade unions/professional organizations). The Committee of Independent Experts under the European Social Charter (1961) considered that the Charter contained an implicit negative right and the International Labour Organization believed that compulsory union membership violated their Convention nos 87 and 98. Therefore a majority of the Court, 8 votes to 1, held that:

...it should be recalled that the Convention is a living instrument which must be interpreted in the light of present-day conditions (see, *Soering v UK* (1989) A.161). Accordingly, Article 11 must be viewed as encompassing a negative right of association. It is not necessary for the Court to determine in this instance whether this right is to be considered on an equal footing with the positive right. [Para 35.]

The Court ruled that the compulsion (by the 1989 Act) for the applicant to join Frami, against his wishes, violated his right to freedom of association under Article 11(1). Consequently it was necessary to examine whether the interference was justified under Article 11(2). The 1989 Act provided the basis for the interference being 'prescribed by law' and it had the legitimate aim of protecting the 'rights and freedoms of others'. The contentious issue, therefore, was whether the interference was 'necessary in a democratic society'. While the Court acknowledged that Frami had a public service role, it did not consider that compulsory membership of the association was required in order to perform those functions. This was because the major responsibility for supervising the law on taxicabs fell to the State licensing committee. Overall:

...the reasons adduced by the Government, although they can be considered relevant, are not sufficient to show that it was 'necessary' to compel the applicant to be a member of Frami, on pain of losing his licence and contrary to his own opinions. In particular, notwithstanding Iceland's margin of appreciation, the measures complained of were disproportionate to the legitimate aim pursued. Consequently, there has been a violation of Article 11. [Para 41.]

Additionally the Court, unanimously, determined that it was not necessary to examine the applicant's complaints under Articles 9 and 10. Thor Vilhjalmsson J dissented on the ground, which he had expressed in the minority opinion in *Young, James and Webster*, that the drafters had never intended to include a negative right within Article 11(1). 'I think that the negative freedom is so special and so clearly distinguishable from the positive freedom of association, that a legal interpretation of the Article cannot result in the inclusion of the negative freedom within its sphere of application.' The judgment of the majority in this case recognizes a maturation of the 'negative aspect' of freedom of association, as it was described in *Young, James and Webster*, into a 'negative right', primarily because of the emergence of a similar right in various parallel international agreements. It may also be pertinent to note that the 1980s witnessed a shift towards an individualistic perspective on political, economic, and social issues by many European societies. However, the Court was cautious not to rule on the status of this right vis-à-vis the positive right which is expressly incorporated in Article 11.

4   The Court has been willing to hold that States may in principle be under a positive duty to intervene in economic relationships between private persons and associations in order to safeguard the formers' negative right to freedom of association. In *Gustafsson v Sweden*, 1996-II, the applicant was a businessman who owned a summer restaurant and youth hostel on the island of Gotland. He did not belong to either of the restaurant employers' associations, which meant that he was not a party to the collective labour agreement between those associations and the Hotel and Restaurant Workers' Union (HRF), nor would he sign an agreement with that union. Gustafsson objected in principle to collective bargaining and claimed that he paid his workers more than the collective agreement rate. In 1987, because of his refusal to sign an agreement with the HRF it placed his restaurant under a 'blockade' and declared a boycott against it. During the next summer other unions introduced sympathy action against Gustafsson with the consequence that deliveries to the restaurant were stopped. He requested the Swedish Government to intervene, to prevent the unions' blockade and sympathy action, but the authorities refused stating that it was a dispute between

private subjects. The Supreme Administrative Court dismissed Gustafsson's challenge of the Government's decision. In 1991, the applicant sold the restaurant due to the difficulties he had in running it with the unions' continuing industrial action. He complained to the Commission that the lack of State protection against the unions' actions amounted to a violation of, *inter alia*, his negative right to freedom of association. By a majority, of 13 to 4, the Commission concluded that there had been a violation of Article 11. The Court began by considering the principles of State liability under Article 11.

45. The matters complained of by the applicant, although they were made possible by national law, did not involve a direct intervention by the State. The responsibility of Sweden would nevertheless be engaged if those matters resulted from a failure on its part to secure to him under domestic law the rights set forth in Article 11 of the Convention (*Sibson v UK* (1994) A.258-A). Although the essential object of Article 11 is to protect the individual against arbitrary interferences by the public authorities with his or her exercise of the rights protected, there may in addition be positive obligations to secure the effective enjoyment of these rights.... It follows that the national authorities may, in certain circumstances, be obliged to intervene in the relationships between private individuals by taking reasonable and appropriate measures to secure the effective enjoyment of the negative right to freedom of association (see, *mutatis mutandis*, *Plattform 'Arzte Fur Das Leben' v Austria* (1991) A.139).

However, the Court recognized that Article 11(1) also safeguards the freedom of trade union members to protect their occupational interests by means of trade union action. Therefore:

In view of the sensitive character of the social and political issues involved in achieving a proper balance between the competing interests and, in particular, in assessing the appropriateness of State intervention to restrict union action aimed at extending a system of collective bargaining, and the wide degree of divergence between the domestic systems in the particular area under consideration, the Contracting States should enjoy a wide margin of appreciation in their choice of the means to be employed. [Para 46.]

The Government, relying on information provided by the HRF, sought to dispute whether the applicant provided better terms and conditions of employment for his workers than those laid down in the applicable collective agreements. Furthermore, the applicant was in effect challenging the essential basis of the Swedish industrial relations system which had been in existence for 60 years. A majority of the Court, 12 votes to 7, concluded that the applicant's principal objection was:

... of a political nature, namely his disagreement with the collective bargaining system in Sweden. However, Article 11 of the Convention does not as such guarantee a right not to enter into a collective agreement (cf *Swedish Engine Drivers' Union v Sweden* (1976) A.20). The positive obligation incumbent on the State under Article 11, including the aspect of protection of personal opinion, may well extend to treatment connected with the operation of a collective bargaining system, but only where such treatment impinges on freedom of association. Compulsion which, as here, does not significantly affect the enjoyment of that freedom, even if it causes economic damage, cannot give rise to any positive obligation under Article 11.

Furthermore, the applicant has not substantiated his submission to the effect that the terms of employment which he offered were more favourable than those required under a collective agreement. Bearing in mind the special role and importance of collective agreements in the regulation of labour relations in Sweden, the Court sees no reason to doubt that the union action pursued legitimate interests consistent with Article 11 of the Convention....

In the light of the foregoing, having regard to the margin of appreciation to be accorded to the respondent State in the area under consideration, the Court does not find that Sweden failed to secure the applicant's rights under Article 11 of the Convention. [Paras 52–4.]

The combination of the uncertain status of the negative right of freedom of association, the ambiguous nature of States' positive duties under Article 11, and the countervailing legitimate interests of trade unions may explain the Court's unwillingness to find a breach of the Convention in this case. In a partly dissenting opinion President Ryssdal and Judges Spielmann, Palm, Foighel, Pekkanen, Loizou, Makarczyk, and Repik expressed the view: 'It is apparent, however, from the Court's case-law that Article 11 is not a vehicle for regulating industrial relations in general or for generally protecting against prejudice suffered as a result of industrial action taken by one of the actors in the labour market against another.' During July 1998 the Court, by 16 votes to 1, dismissed Gustafsson's request for a revision of the judgment (based in part on further evidence regarding the terms on which he had employed his restaurant workers). The Court stated that this further evidence would not have had a decisive influence on the original determination, because that was based upon the 'special role and importance of collective agreements in the regulation of labour relations in Sweden' (para 32).

5   The full-time Court has recognized that Article 11 contains a 'negative' freedom of association in *Chassagnou v France*, 1999-III. There the applicants were landowners who owned small plots of land that were subject to the 'Loi Verdeille' of 1964. This law required them to become members of municipal hunters' associations and allow members of those associations to hunt on their land. Despite the applicants' ethical objections to hunting, the French courts held that they were subject to the requirements of the 1964 law. The applicants then complained to the Commission alleging, *inter alia*, a breach of their freedom under Article 11 not to be forced to join an association against their wishes. The Commission upheld the claim by 24 votes to 8. Before the Court it was accepted that the statutory obligation requiring the applicants to join a hunting association violated their negative freedom of association. However, the French Government sought to justify the obligation under Article 11(2) as being for the legitimate aim of protecting the rights and freedoms of others; that is, to secure democratic participation in the leisure activity of hunting for as many people as possible. A large majority of the Court, 12 votes to 5, held that the statutory obligations were not 'necessary in a democratic society' and consequently there had been a breach of Article 11.

To compel a person by law to join an association such that it is fundamentally contrary to his own convictions to be a member of it, and to oblige him, on account of his membership of that association, to transfer his rights over the land he owns so that the association in question can attain objectives of which he disapproves, goes beyond what is necessary to ensure that a fair balance is struck between conflicting interests and cannot be considered proportionate to the aim pursued. [Para 117.]

6   A Grand Chamber found Danish pre-entry closed shop arrangements to be in breach of 'the negative right to trade union freedom' in the cases of *Sorensen v Denmark* and *Rasmussen v Denmark*, judgment of 11 January 2006. The first applicant was offered a temporary job, prior to going to university, by a company (part of the Danish consumer COOP) to work between May and August 1996. The offer of employment was subject to an obligation to become a member of a designated trade union (the company had a collective agreement with that union governing the terms of employment of the company's employees). When he received his initial payslip he discovered that he had been registered as a

member of that union and a subscription had been deducted. He objected to his employer, as he had applied for membership of another trade union. The company then dismissed him. His legal challenges were rejected by the Danish courts as they ruled that the Act on Protection against Dismissal due to Association Membership 1982 (passed as a result of the Court's judgment in **Young, James and Webster**) permitted dismissal of employees where the latter knew, prior to their employment, that membership of a specified association was a condition of employment (i.e. a pre-entry closed shop scheme). The second applicant, a gardener, became a member of a specific union in the 1980s. But he became unable to support its political affiliations and he joined another union. After a period of unemployment he was offered a job as a gardener by a company on condition that he join the first trade union. He joined that union, despite his opposition to its political views, in order to secure the job. Before the Court both applicants contended, *inter alia*, that the negative right to freedom of association was of equal status to the positive right and that closed shop agreements could no longer be justified in democratic societies. The Danish Government disputed that the negative element was on an equal footing to the positive right and that, given the sensitive social/political issues involved, a wide margin of appreciation should be left to States to regulate closed shop arrangements. In third party written comments the Danish Confederation of Trade Unions contended that closed shop arrangements were of crucial importance in securing fair competition and combating illegal work. The Confederation feared that a judgment in favour of the applicants might result in the destruction of the Danish model of employment relations which had had wide political support for over a century.

55. The parties have discussed at length whether in the area of trade-union membership the negative aspect of the freedom of association should be considered on an equal footing with the positive right. The Court notes that hitherto it has not taken any definite stand on that point (see *Young, James and Webster, Sigurdur Sigurjónsson*, and (in a different context) *Chassagnou and Others*, all cited above).

56. The Court does not in principle exclude that the negative and the positive aspects of the Article 11 right should be afforded the same level of protection in the area under consideration. However, it is difficult to decide this issue in the abstract since it is a matter that can only be properly addressed in the circumstances of a given case. At the same time, an individual cannot be considered to have renounced his negative right to freedom of association in situations where, in the knowledge that trade-union membership is a pre-condition of securing a job, he accepts an offer of employment notwithstanding his opposition to the condition imposed. Accordingly, the distinction made between pre-entry closed-shop agreements and post-entry closed-shop agreements in terms of the scope of the protection guaranteed by Article 11 is not tenable. At most this distinction is to be seen as a consideration which will form part of the Court's assessment of the surrounding circumstances and the issue of their Convention-compatibility.

56.... In the present case, the matters about which the applicants complain did not involve direct intervention by the State. However, Denmark's responsibility would be engaged if these matters resulted from a failure on its part to secure to the applicants under domestic law their negative right to freedom of association.

58. The boundaries between the State's positive and negative obligations under Article 11 of the Convention do not lend themselves to precise definition. The applicable principles are nonetheless similar. Whether the case is analysed in terms of a positive duty on the State or in terms of interference by a public authority which requires to be justified, the criteria to be applied do not differ in substance. In both contexts regard must be had to the fair balance to be struck between the competing interests of the individual and of the community as a whole (see, *mutatis mutandis*,

Broniowski v Poland [GC], No 31443/96, § 144, ECHR 2004-V, and *Hatton and Others v the United Kingdom* [GC], No 36022/97, §§ 98 *et seq.*, ECHR 2003-VIII).

In the area of trade-union freedom and in view of the sensitive character of the social and political issues involved in achieving a proper balance between the respective interests of labour and management, and given the wide degree of divergence between the domestic systems in this field, the Contracting States enjoy a wide margin of appreciation as to how the freedom of trade unions to protect the occupational interests of their members may be secured (see *Swedish Engine Drivers' Union v Sweden*, judgment of 6 February 1976, Series A No 20, pp 14–15, § 39; *Gustafsson*, cited above, pp 652–3, § 45; and *Schettini and Others v Italy* (dec.), No 29529/95, 9 November 2000; *Wilson & the National Union of Journalists and Others*, cited above, § 44). Thus, the Court has so far not found fault with a Contracting State's failure to impose on an employer an obligation to recognise a trade union or to provide for a system of compulsory collective bargaining (see *Wilson & the National Union of Journalists and Others*, § 44 and cases cited therein).

However, where the domestic law of a Contracting State permits the conclusion of closed-shop agreements between unions and employers which run counter to the freedom of choice of the individual inherent in Article 11, the margin of appreciation must be considered reduced. The Court recalls in this connection that although individual interests must on occasion be subordinated to those of a group, democracy does not simply mean that the views of a majority must always prevail: a balance must be achieved which ensures the fair and proper treatment of minorities and avoids any abuse of a dominant position (see *Young, James and Webster*, cited above, § 63, and *Chassagnou and Others*, cited above, §§ 112 and 113). In assessing whether a Contracting State has remained within its margin of appreciation in tolerating the existence of closed-shop agreements, particular weight must be attached to the justifications advanced by the authorities for them and, in any given case, the extent to which they impinge on the rights and interests protected by Article 11. Account must also be taken of changing perceptions of the relevance of closed-shop agreements for securing the effective enjoyment of trade-union freedom.

The Court sees no reason not to extend these considerations to both pre- and post-entry closed-shop agreements.

...

63. As to whether the applicants' personal views and opinions were compromised, it is to be noted that both applicants objected to membership of SID [the trade union they were required to join] because they could not subscribe to the political views of that trade union (and those of the other trade unions affiliated to the Danish Confederation of Trade Unions (LO). Instead, the applicant Sørensen joined the Danish Free Trade Union, and the applicant Rasmussen wishes to re-join the Christian Trade Union. The Government have pointed out that the applicants had the possibility of subscribing to a form of 'non-political membership' of SID or of any other trade union pursuant to the Act on Private Contributions to Political Parties and Disclosure of the Accounts of Political Parties. However, it is to be observed that such 'non-political membership' does not entail any reduction in the payment of the membership fee to the specific trade union. In any event, there is no guarantee that 'non-political membership' will not give rise to some form of indirect support for the political parties to which the specific trade union contributes financially.

64. In these circumstances the court concludes that both applicants were compelled to join SID and that this compulsion struck at the very substance of the freedom of association guaranteed by Article 11.

65. It remains to be determined whether the respondent Government, in authorising the use of the closed-shop agreements at issue, failed in the circumstances to secure the applicants' effective enjoyment of their negative right to freedom of association and thereby violated Article 11 of the Convention. The Court's assessment must be focused on whether a fair balance has been struck

between the applicants' interests and the need to ensure that trade unions are enabled to strive for the protection of their members' interest (see paragraph 58 above).

66. The Court notes the special features of the Danish labour market, in particular the fact that the relationship between employers and employees is governed by a combination of agreements (collective and individual), labour-law principles, general statutes and statutory rules. Moreover, the institution of closed-shop agreements is a long-standing practice in Denmark, although they are unlawful in the public-sector labour market and are not concluded in the part of the private-sector labour market covered by the general agreement between DA [Confederation of Danish Employers] and LO. Closed-shop agreements thus presently affect only approximately 220,000 wage-earners, which is equivalent to less than 10 per cent of all Danish employees on the labour market.

...

68. In January 2003 and again in January 2005 the Minister of Employment presented a Bill to Parliament to amend the Danish Act on Protection against Dismissal due to Association Membership, which aimed at ensuring, among other things, that in the future no agreements could be lawfully concluded which imposed a duty on an employer to employ exclusively or to give preference to persons who were members of an association or a specific association. In the Explanatory Memorandum to the Bill the Government stated among other things that they 'consider that there should be freedom for an employee to decide whether to become a member of an association—just as there should be freedom to choose not to become a member of an association—without this leading to a risk of not being recruited or of being dismissed' and that they 'find it unreasonable that a clause in a collective agreement may prevent an employee who does not wish to be a member of an association or a specific association from obtaining or keeping employment with an employer or may prevent an employer from considering the candidate's qualifications alone'.

69. In the beginning of May 2003 it became clear that the Bill had failed to secure the necessary majority in Parliament and was withdrawn. Nevertheless, it was tabled anew in December 2004 and discussed by Parliament in January 2005. However, once again a majority in favour of changing the law could not be secured.

70. It is to be observed that these legislative attempts to eliminate entirely the use of closed-shop agreements in Denmark would appear to reflect the trend which has emerged in the Contracting Parties, namely that such agreements are not an essential means for securing the interests of trade unions and their members and that due weight must be given to the right of individuals to join a union of their own choosing without fear of prejudice to their livelihood. In fact, only a very limited number of Contracting States including Denmark and Iceland continue to permit the conclusion of closed-shop agreements.

71. It is true that in the context of the Danish debate on this topic LO has voiced its opposition to the attempts to eliminate the remaining areas where pre-entry closed-shop agreements continue to be applied. LO has pointed to the severe consequences which the prohibition of closed-shop clauses would entail, and in particular its view that it would become difficult or impossible to enforce collective agreements vis-à-vis small non-affiliated employers. However, the Court considers that these concerns have been adequately addressed by the Minister for Employment in his reply to question no. 7 put by the Parliamentary Committee, namely that an annulment of a closed-shop provision in a collective-bargaining agreement with a non-organised employer would not change the fact that the collective-bargaining agreement is still valid and must be complied with. Furthermore, the Court has not been informed that the concerns expressed by LO have materialised in any of the very many Contracting Parties which have abolished closed-shop agreements entirely.

72. The Court also observes that the wish of the Danish legislature to bring an end to the use of closed-shop agreements in the private sector is consistent with the manner in which the 1961 Social

Charter has been applied to the issue of pre-entry closed-shop agreements. In its Conclusions XIV-1, XV-1 and XVI-1 the European Committee of Social Rights found that the Danish Act on Protection against Dismissal due to Association Membership infringed Article 5 of the Social Charter and accordingly the Governmental Committee proposed that a recommendation be addressed to Denmark. Admittedly, at the 740th meeting of the Ministers' Deputies in February 2001 the required majority was not obtained. However, shortly thereafter, in September 2002, the Danish Government informed the Governmental Committee of the European Social Charter of their intention to introduce a bill prohibiting closed-shop agreements and the latter therefore decided to await the next assessment by the European Committee of Social Rights. Subsequently, when it had become clear that the bill had failed to secure the necessary majority in Parliament and was withdrawn, in its Conclusions XVII-1 of March 2004 the European Committee of Social Rights maintained that the Danish Act on Protection against Dismissal due to Association Membership infringed Article 5 of the Social Charter, in response to which the Government stated that once the parliamentary situation was more favourable they would resubmit the draft legislation.

73. Reference should also be made to the Community Charter of the Fundamental Social Rights of Workers, adopted by the Heads of State or Government of eleven member States of the European Communities on 9 December 1989. This text provides that every employer and every worker shall have the freedom to join or not to join professional organisations or trade unions without any personal or occupational damage being thereby suffered by them.

74. Article 12 of the Charter of Fundamental Rights of the European Union, proclaimed in Nice on 7 December 2000 (2000/C 364/01), is devoted to freedom of assembly and association. The above-mentioned provisions of the Community Charter of the Fundamental Social Rights of Workers are of obvious relevance for the interpretation of the scope of Article 12. It will be recalled in this connection that Article 53 of the Nice Charter states that nothing therein shall be interpreted as restricting or adversely affecting human rights and fundamental freedoms as recognised, in their respective fields of application, by Union law and international law and by international agreements to which the Union, the Community or all the Member States are party, including the European Convention for the Protection of Human Rights and Fundamental Freedoms, and by the Member States' constitutions.

75. In view of the above it appears that there is little support in the Contracting States for the maintenance of closed-shop agreements and that the European instruments referred to above clearly indicate that their use in the labour market is not an indispensable tool for the effective enjoyment of trade-union freedoms.

76. In conclusion, taking all the circumstances of the case into account and balancing the competing interests at issue, the Court finds that the respondent State has failed to protect the applicants' negative right to trade union freedom.

77. Accordingly, there has been a violation of Article 11 of the Convention in respect of both applicants.

Judges Rozakis, Bratza, and Vajic issued a joint partly dissenting opinion in which they expressed the view that there was 'a very clear distinction in the degree of compulsion' to which the two applicants had been subject. Whilst they agreed with the majority that the threat of dismissal and the potential loss of livelihood was a serious form of compulsion regarding Mr Rasmussen, there was much less compulsion in the case of Mr Sorensen (his employment would have lasted only for ten weeks and he faced no difficulties in obtaining other short-term employment). Therefore, they did not consider that the latter had suffered a breach of Article 11.

Judge Lorenzen, the judge of Danish nationality, with the agreement of Judge Zupancic, dissented as he considered that neither applicant had been 'substantially' affected by the closed shop agreements (in his opinion Mr Rasmussen had not established that the closed shop arrangements had limited his employment opportunities).

It is significant that the Grand Chamber was still not prepared to state unequivocally that the negative aspect/right of freedom of association had the same status as the positive aspect/right. However, the judgment makes it clear that the Court will not accord a wide margin of appreciation to those States (very few) that authorize the creation of closed shops. Do you think it would have made any difference to the Grand Chamber's conclusions if Danish law had given greater protection to workers' political beliefs?

7   The 'negative right of association' (para 45) was applied to an employer, for the first time, who objected to a statutory obligation to pay a levy to a private industrial association (whose policies he disagreed with) in *Vordur Olafsson v Iceland*, judgment of 27 April 2010. The unanimous Chamber found a breach of Article 11 as the State had not achieved a fair balance between the applicant's freedom of association and the public interest in developing Icelandic industries. So here an employer was in an analogous position to employees forced to belong to a trade union they disagreed with on ideological grounds.

Article 11(2)

The restrictions contained in the first sentence

1   Many of the elements in this sentence are similar to those found in Article 10(2). The Court has stated that an interference with the rights guaranteed by Article 11(1), '…constitutes a breach of Article 11 unless it satisfies the requirements of paragraph 2 which are identical to those laid down in paragraph 2 of Article 10, the only exception being where the last sentence of paragraph 2 of Article 11 is applicable': *Vogt v Germany* A.323 (1995), para 66.

2   The Chamber in *Friend v UK*, at p 752, found the legislative bans on hunting mammals with dogs to be compatible with Article 11(2).

3   The Court has given a broad scope to the legitimate aim of protecting 'national security' by recognizing its applicability to governmental measures designed to maintain the territorial integrity of a State: *United Communist Party of Turkey v Turkey*, p 731.

4   A unanimous Chamber applied the legitimate aim of preventing disorder to find no breach of the right to peaceful assembly in *Barraco v France*, judgment of 5 March 2009. The applicant was a lorry driver who participated in a day of protest organized by a trade union. He and other hauliers drove their cars at 10 kph along a motorway obstructing other motorists. After being warned by the police he was arrested and subsequently convicted of obstructing traffic on the highway. The Court found that the authorities had achieved a fair balance between the applicant's method of protest and the prevention of disorder.

5   The Court has explained its approach to applying the legitimate aim of the 'protection of the rights and freedoms of others' in *Chassagnou v France*, p 778.

113. Where these 'rights and freedoms' are themselves among those guaranteed by the Convention or its Protocols, it must be accepted that the need to protect them may lead States to restrict other

rights or freedoms likewise set forth in the Convention. It is precisely this constant search for a balance between the fundamental rights of each individual which constitutes the foundation of a 'democratic society'. The balancing of individual interests that may well be contradictory is a difficult matter, and Contracting States must have a broad margin of appreciation in this respect, since the national authorities are in principle better placed than the European Court to assess whether or not there is a 'pressing social need' capable of justifying interference with one of the rights guaranteed by the Convention.

It is a different matter where restrictions are imposed on a right or freedom guaranteed by the Convention in order to protect 'rights and freedoms' not, as such, enunciated therein. In such a case only indisputable imperatives can justify interference with enjoyment of a Convention right.

Hence the legal source and nature of the particular 'rights and freedoms of others' at issue will determine the extent of the Court's deference towards the State authorities' balancing of conflicting rights and the Court's willingness to uphold restrictions on applicants' Article 11(1) rights.

6   A unanimous Chamber determined that domestic authorities do not have a wide margin of appreciation to prohibit sexual minorities peacefully assembling to campaign in *Alekseyev v Russia*, judgment of 21 October 2010. The applicant was a gay rights activist who notified the mayor of Moscow that he intended to hold marches and assemblies similar to Gay Pride gatherings in other member States. During a period of three years the Moscow city authorities refused permission for over 100 such events. The mayor declared that he would never allow these gatherings in Moscow. Before the Court the Russian Government submitted, *inter alia*, that the domestic authorities should be accorded a wide margin of appreciation regarding the extent of the civil rights to be accorded to gays and lesbians. However, the Court rejected the claim noting that:

84....There is no ambiguity about the other member States' recognition of the right of individuals to openly identify themselves as gay, lesbian or any other sexual minority, and to promote their rights and freedoms, in particular by exercising their freedom of assembly....

85. The Court is therefore unable to accept the Government's claim to a wide margin of appreciation in the present case.

The Court went on to find a breach of Article 11 and a separate breach of Article 14 in conjunction with Article 11 (as the comments of the mayor disclosed discrimination against the applicant's sexual orientation).

More generally, a few days after the above judgment, the Council of Europe's Commissioner for Human Rights issued a press release (786(2010)) expressing concern about restrictions on other groups that had sought to hold peaceful assemblies in several Russian cities.

The restrictions contained in the second sentence

The contemporary approach of the Court was outlined in *Demir and Baykara* at paragraphs 96–107 (p 761). The Grand Chamber took a much tougher approach to the application of these restrictions than the former Commission. Also, whilst not providing a definition of the phrase 'members of the administration of the State', the Grand Chamber concluded that it did not generally include municipal civil servants. Therefore, the burden will be on States to demonstrate that particular officials fall within this limited class and then justify the restrictions imposed upon them. In safeguarding the trade union rights of public servants the Grand Chamber was echoing its increasing protection of such persons' right to litigate their disputes with their employer under Article 6(1) (see p 359).

14 ARTICLE 12   RIGHT TO MARRY

Whilst numerically there has not been a significant amount of case-law involving Article 12, the Court has been confronted with important aspects of the extensive social changes occurring in human relationships throughout member States (paralleling developments we have examined in the jurisprudence concerning respect for private and family life under Article 8). The narrow text of Article 12 coupled with its drafting history prevented the Court finding an implied right to divorce (*Johnston*). However, when confronted with both social and scientific developments, the Court recognized the right of post-operative transsexuals to marry persons of the opposite gender (*Christine Goodwin*). But, the Court has yet unequivocally to accord such a right to same-sex couples (*Schalk and Kopf*).

....

F v Switzerland A.128 (1987)
European Court of Human Rights

The applicant was a Swiss national born in 1943. In 1963 he married Miss G and then divorced her in 1964. In 1966 he married a divorcee. During 1978 he began cohabiting with another woman and in 1981 his wife obtained a divorce. The court issued an order prohibiting F from remarrying within one year (under Article 150 of the Swiss Civil Code a court granting a divorce shall fix a period of between one to three years during which the party at fault shall not be entitled to remarry). In January 1983 Miss N responded to the applicant's advertisement for a secretary. Within four days they were cohabiting and in February 1983 the couple married. Two weeks later F began divorce proceedings. At the beginning of April his wife left the matrimonial home after F renewed a relationship with a former mistress. In October of that year the Civil Court gave judgment in favour of the wife, approved a payment of compensation by F, of 17,000 Swiss francs, to his (former) wife for non-pecuniary damage and imposed a three-year prohibition on F remarrying (because his unacceptable attitude made him solely responsible for the breakdown of the marriage). F's domestic appeals were dismissed. In March 1986, F and his cohabitee stated that they wished to marry; however, the authorities refused to permit the marriage as F's ban was still in force. The couple married in January 1987, when the ban had expired, and their child was born in February 1987. F complained to the Commission alleging that the three-year prohibition on remarriage was incompatible with his right to marry guaranteed by Article 12. By 10 votes to 7, the Commission found a breach of that Article.

32. Article 12 (art 12) secures the fundamental right of a man and a woman to marry and to found a family. The exercise of this right gives rise to personal, social and legal consequences. It is 'subject to the national laws of the Contracting States', but 'the limitations thereby introduced must not restrict or reduce the right in such a way or to such an extent that the very essence of the right is impaired' (see the *Rees* judgment of 17 October 1986, Series A No 106, p 19, para 50).

In all the Council of Europe's member States, these 'limitations' appear as conditions and are embodied in procedural or substantive rules. The former relate mainly to publicity and the solemnisation of marriage, while the latter relate primarily to capacity, consent and certain impediments.

33. The prohibition imposed on F was applied under rules governing the exercise of the right to marry, as Article 12 (art 12) does not distinguish between marriage and remarriage.

The Court notes that a waiting period no longer exists under the laws of other Contracting States, the Federal Republic of Germany having abolished it in 1976, and Austria in 1983. In this connection, it recalls its case-law according to which the Convention must be interpreted in the light of present-day conditions (see the *Airey* judgment of 9 October 1979, Series A No 32, para 26). However, the fact that, at the end of a gradual evolution, a country finds itself in an isolated position as regards one aspect of its legislation does not necessarily imply that that aspect offends the Convention, particularly in a field—matrimony—which is so closely bound up with the cultural and historical traditions of each society and its deep-rooted ideas about the family unit.

34. The measure complained of ultimately amounts to a civil sanction. According to the Federal Court's case-law, it is an order consequent upon a fault of exceptional gravity that has played a decisive role in the breakdown of a marriage...

Although automatically applicable because mandatory as a matter of public policy, Article 150 of the Civil Code nonetheless allows the courts some degree of discretion: the prohibition period to be imposed on the party at fault in the event of divorce granted on the ground of adultery may range from one to three years... In the instant case the Lausanne District Civil Court chose the maximum period, holding that F's unacceptable attitude rendered him solely responsible for the breakdown of the marriage...

The divorce court therefore did not confine itself to appraising the consequences of the break-down of marriage, by approving the agreement made between the couple on 16 May 1983, which provided for payment of compensation for non-pecuniary damage...it also assessed the appli-cant's past conduct in order to draw conclusions about his right to remarry.

35. The Government contended firstly that the application of Article 150 in the instant case was neither unreasonable nor arbitrary nor disproportionate. The sanction complained of undoubtedly did amount to an interference with the exercise of the right to marry, but it did not impair that right's very essence. As part of the Swiss conception of divorce based on matrimonial fault, the system of temporarily prohibiting remarriage was explained by the legislature's determination to protect not only the institution of marriage but also the rights of others and even the person affected by the prohibition.

36. The Court recognises that the stability of marriage is a legitimate aim which is in the public interest. It doubts, however, whether the particular means used were appropriate for achieving that aim. In Switzerland itself, the Study Group on the partial reform of family law and subsequently the Committee of Experts on Family Law Reform would seem to have had similar doubts, since they recommended the repeal of Article 150 of the Civil Code...

In any event, the Court cannot accept the argument that the temporary prohibition of remar-riage is designed to preserve the rights of others, namely those of the future spouse of the divorced person.

On 22 May 1986, the woman with whom F was cohabiting obtained a reduction of the waiting time following her own divorce, which had become absolute a month earlier... The prohibition on F expired on 21 December 1986, after which the registrar was able to carry out the necessary formal-ities...The marriage accordingly took place on 23 January 1987. During the intervening period—of some seven or eight months—the applicant's future wife could consider that she was personally and directly wronged by the measure affecting F. Given that she was neither under age nor insane, her rights were in no way protected by the measure in question.

An unborn child may also be adversely affected by such a prohibition. Admittedly the concept of an 'illegitimate child' no longer exists in Swiss law, under which children born out of wedlock now have almost the same status and the same rights as children born in wedlock. Children born out of wedlock may nonetheless suffer on account of certain prejudices and thus be socially handicapped. While in the instant case the applicant's child was born one month after his parents' marriage...the death of one of the parents or even a delay in completing the legal formalities would have been enough to cause the child to be born out of wedlock.

37. The Government further considered that compelling the person concerned to take time for reflection also helped to protect him from himself. In the Court's view, this argument is not of sufficient weight to justify the impugned interference in the case of a person of full age in possession of his mental faculties.

38. The Government relied in addition on the Johnston judgment of 18 December 1986, according to which 'the prohibition on divorce [cannot], in a society adhering to the principle of monogamy,...be regarded as injuring the substance of the right guaranteed by Article 12 (art 12)' (Series A No 112, p 24, para 52). In the Government's submission, the same applied a fortiori to a mere temporary prohibition on remarriage. No right to remarry could be recognised given that the exercise of it necessarily depended on another right—the right to divorce—which did not flow from the Convention; in short, remarriage subsequent to a divorce could not be equated with a first marriage.

...F's situation is quite distinct from Mr Johnston's, since what was at issue in the case of the latter was the right of a man who was still married to have his marriage dissolved. If national legislation allows divorce, which is not a requirement of the Convention, Article 12 (art 12) secures for divorced persons the right to remarry without unreasonable restrictions.

39. There remains the Government's argument that judicial separation, the waiting period required before divorce can be granted or an innocent spouse's right to oppose divorce have consequences for those concerned which are identical with those of a temporary prohibition on remarriage. The Court considers that such situations are different and that in any case they occur prior to any decree of divorce.

40. In conclusion, the disputed measure, which affected the very essence of the right to marry, was disproportionate to the legitimate aim pursued. There was, therefore, a violation of Article 12 (art 12).

...FOR THESE REASONS, THE COURT

1. Holds by nine votes to eight that there has been a breach of Article 12...

NOTES

1 The Court was composed of President Ryssdal and Judges: Lagergren, Pettiti, Evans, Macdonald, Russo, Bernhardt, Spielmann, and Carrillo Salcedo.

2 Judges Thor Vilhjalmsson, Bindschedler-Robert, Gölcüklü, Matscher, Pinheiro Farina, Walsh, De Meyer, and Valticos issued a joint dissenting opinion in which they expressed the view that:

In our opinion, the facts of the case disclose no violation of the applicant's fundamental rights.

The circumstances in which, after two previous divorces, the third marriage of the person concerned was dissolved were such that the Lausanne Civil Court was entitled to impose on him, when it granted the third divorce, the waiting period of three years provided for in Article 150 of the Swiss Civil Code.

The restriction thus placed on the exercise by the applicant of his right to marry and found a family did not affect the substance of that right. It was merely temporary. It was neither arbitrary nor unreasonable. It was based on legitimate reasons and could be considered to be commensurate with their gravity. It did not go beyond the powers of the competent national authorities.

Those authorities—both the judiciary and the legislature—were entitled to consider, in the exercise of their discretion in the matter, that the restriction in question was justified in order to protect not only the institution of marriage but also the future spouses of a person who, as the Swiss courts had established, had grossly violated fundamental conjugal rights.

With regard to marriage, the State has more extensive powers than in some other fields. This is particularly apparent when one compares the very brief and non-exhaustive reference to 'national laws' in Article 12 (art 12) of the Convention with the more circumscribed and restrictive wording of the second paragraph of each of Articles 8, 9, 10 and 11 (art 8-2, art 9-2, art 10-2, art 11-2).

In this context, such doubts as may be felt as to whether a certain legal rule is appropriate or opportune or should be applied in a given case do not suffice to found a breach of the right secured by Article 12 (art 12) of the Convention. In order for it to be concluded that there has been a breach of this right, it must be shown that the State has impaired the essence of the right or that it has restricted the exercise thereof in an arbitrary or unreasonable manner. That has not been shown in this case.

The dissentients emphasized the wide discretion accorded to States, by the distinct language of Article 12, to regulate the institution of marriage in their own domestic legal and social environments. We have already seen in previous chapters how the common language of the second paragraphs to Articles 8–11 has been interpreted much more restrictively by the Court. Key elements in the Court's judgment were the application of a proportionality test to evaluate whether specific restrictions on a person's right to marry were compatible with the right enshrined in Article 12 and the recognition that where national law allows divorce Article 12 guarantees divorced persons the right to remarry, subject to reasonable restrictions.

3   A unanimous Grand Chamber of the full-time Court found a violation of the right to marry of a post-operative transsexual in ***Christine Goodwin v UK***, judgment of 11 July 2002 (see p 576).

97. The Court recalls that in the cases of *Rees* [v UK A.106 (1986)], *Cossey* [v UK A.184 (1990)] and *Sheffield and Horsham* [v UK 1998-V] the inability of the transsexuals in those cases to marry a person of the sex opposite to their re-assigned gender was not found in breach of Article 12 of the Convention. These findings were based variously on the reasoning that the right to marry referred to traditional marriage between persons of opposite biological sex (the *Rees* judgment, p 19, § 49), the view that continued adoption of biological criteria in domestic law for determining a person's sex for the purpose of marriage was encompassed within the power of Contracting States to regulate by national law the exercise of the right to marry and the conclusion that national laws in that respect could not be regarded as restricting or reducing the right of a transsexual to marry in such a way or to such an extent that the very essence of the right was impaired (the *Cossey* judgment, p 18, §§ 44–6, the *Sheffield and Horsham* judgment, p 2030, §§ 66–7). Reference was also made to the wording of Article 12 as protecting marriage as the basis of the family (*Rees, loc cit*).

98. Reviewing the situation in 2002, the Court observes that Article 12 secures the fundamental right of a man and woman to marry and to found a family. The second aspect is not however a condition of the first and the inability of any couple to conceive or parent a child cannot be regarded as per se removing their right to enjoy the first limb of this provision.

99. The exercise of the right to marry gives rise to social, personal and legal consequences. It is subject to the national laws of the Contracting States but the limitations thereby introduced must not restrict or reduce the right in such a way or to such an extent that the very essence of the right is impaired (see the *Rees* judgment, p 19, § 50; the *F. v Switzerland* judgment of 18 December 1987, Series A No 128, § 32).

100. It is true that the first sentence refers in express terms to the right of a man and woman to marry. The Court is not persuaded that at the date of this case it can still be assumed that these terms must refer to a determination of gender by purely biological criteria (as held by Ormrod J. in the case of *Corbett v Corbett* [1971] PR 83). There have been major social changes in the institution of marriage since the adoption of the Convention as well as dramatic changes brought about by developments in medicine and science in the field of transsexuality. The Court has found above, under Article 8 of the Convention, that a test of congruent biological factors can no longer be decisive in denying legal recognition to the change of gender of a post-operative transsexual. There are other important factors—the acceptance of the condition of gender identity disorder by the medical professions and health authorities within Contracting States, the provision of treatment including surgery to assimilate the individual as closely as possible to the gender in which they perceive that they properly belong and the assumption by the transsexual of the social role of the assigned gender. The Court would also note that Article 9 of the recently adopted Charter of Fundamental Rights of the European Union departs, no doubt deliberately, from the wording of Article 12 of the Convention in removing the reference to men and women.

101. The right under Article 8 to respect for private life does not however subsume all the issues under Article 12, where conditions imposed by national laws are accorded a specific mention. The Court has therefore considered whether the allocation of sex in national law to that registered at birth is a limitation impairing the very essence of the right to marry in this case. In that regard, it finds that it is artificial to assert that post-operative transsexuals have not been deprived of the right to marry as, according to law, they remain able to marry a person of their former opposite sex. The applicant in this case lives as a woman, is in a relationship with a man and would only wish to marry a man. She has no possibility of doing so. In the Court's view, she may therefore claim that the very essence of her right to marry has been infringed.

102. The Court has not identified any other reason which would prevent it from reaching this conclusion. The Government have argued that in this sensitive area eligibility for marriage under national law should be left to the domestic courts within the State's margin of appreciation, adverting to the potential impact on already existing marriages in which a transsexual is a partner. It appears however from the opinions of the majority of the Court of Appeal judgment in *Bellinger v Bellinger* ([2001] 3 FCR 1) that the domestic courts tend to the view that the matter is best handled by the legislature, while the Government have no present intention to introduce legislation.

103. It may be noted from the materials submitted by Liberty that though there is widespread acceptance of the marriage of transsexuals, fewer countries permit the marriage of transsexuals in their assigned gender than recognise the change of gender itself. The Court is not persuaded however that this supports an argument for leaving the matter entirely to the Contracting States as being within their margin of appreciation. This would be tantamount to finding that the range of options open to a Contracting State included an effective bar on any exercise of the right to marry. The margin of appreciation cannot extend so far. While it is for the Contracting State to determine *inter alia* the conditions under which a person claiming legal recognition as a transsexual establishes that gender re-assignment has been properly effected or under which past marriages cease to be valid and the formalities applicable to future marriages (including, for example, the information to be furnished to intended spouses), the Court finds no justification for barring the transsexual from enjoying the right to marry under any circumstances.

104. The Court concludes that there has been a breach of Article 12 of the Convention in the present case.

The above judgment accords States much less freedom to restrict the right to marry of transsexuals than the previous rulings of the original Court. Article 9 of the Charter of Fundamental Rights of the European Union, signed on 7 December 2000, referred to in paragraph 100 above, stipulates: 'The right to marry and the right to found a family shall be guaranteed in accordance with the national laws governing the exercise of these rights.'

4   The Court refused to interpret Article 12 as embodying a right to divorce in *Johnston v Ireland* A.112 (1986). The background to this case has already been explained (p 528).

51. In order to determine whether the applicants can derive a right to divorce from Article 12 (art 12), the Court will seek to ascertain the ordinary meaning to be given to the terms of this provision in their context and in the light of its object and purpose (see the *Golder* judgment of 21 February 1975, Series A No 18, p 14, § 29, and Article 31 § 1 of the Vienna Convention of 23 May 1969 on the Law of Treaties).

52. The Court agrees with the Commission that the ordinary meaning of the words 'right to marry' is clear, in the sense that they cover the formation of marital relationships but not their dissolution. Furthermore, these words are found in a context that includes an express reference to 'national laws'; even if, as the applicants would have it, the prohibition on divorce is to be seen as a restriction on capacity to marry, the Court does not consider that, in a society adhering to the principle of monogamy, such a restriction can be regarded as injuring the substance of the right guaranteed by Article 12 (art 12).

   Moreover, the foregoing interpretation of Article 12 (art 12) is consistent with its object and purpose as revealed by the travaux préparatoires. The text of Article 12 (art 12) was based on that of Article 16 of the Universal Declaration of Human Rights, paragraph 1 of which reads:

> 'Men and women of full age, without any limitation due to race, nationality or religion, have the right to marry and to found a family. They are entitled to equal rights as to marriage, during marriage and at its dissolution.'

In explaining to the Consultative Assembly why the draft of the future Article 12 (art 12) did not include the words found in the last sentence of the above-cited paragraph, Mr Teitgen, Rapporteur of the Committee on Legal and Administrative Questions, said:

> 'In mentioning the particular Article of the Universal Declaration, we have used only that part of the paragraph of the Article which affirms the right to marry and to found a family, but not the subsequent provisions of the Article concerning equal rights after marriage, since we only guarantee the right to marry.' (*Collected Edition of the Travaux préparatoires*, vol 1, p 268)

In the Court's view, the *travaux préparatoires* disclose no intention to include in Article 12 (art 12) any guarantee of a right to have the ties of marriage dissolved by divorce.

53. The applicants set considerable store on the social developments that have occurred since the Convention was drafted, notably an alleged substantial increase in marriage breakdown.

   It is true that the Convention and its Protocols must be interpreted in the light of present-day conditions (see, among several authorities, the above-mentioned *Marckx* judgment, Series A No 31, p 26, § 58). However, the Court cannot, by means of an evolutive interpretation, derive from these instruments a right that was not included therein at the outset. This is particularly so here, where the omission was deliberate....

54. The Court thus concludes that the applicants cannot derive a right to divorce from Article 12 (art 12).

The Court's reasoning is also of general significance as it reveals (in paragraph 53) some of the limitations on the Court's dynamic approach to the interpretation of Convention rights.

5   However, a Chamber of the full-time Court was more amenable to social and conse-quent European legal evolution when considering the sensitive issue of whether same-sex couples could assert a right to marry under Article 12. In **Schalk and Kopf v Austria** (see p 530) the Court observed that whilst the language and historical context of Article 12 clearly restricted its application to men and women, Article 9 of the EU Charter of Fundamental Rights had deliberately omitted reference to men and women in its comparable provision.

61. Regard being had to Article 9 of the Charter, therefore, the Court would no longer consider that the right to marry enshrined in Article 12 must in all circumstances be limited to marriage between two persons of the opposite sex. Consequently, it cannot be said that Article 12 is inapplicable to the applicants' complaint. However, as matters stand, the question whether or not to allow same-sex marriage is left to regulation by the national law of the Contracting State.

62. In that connection the Court observes that marriage has deep-rooted social and cultural con-notations which may differ largely from one society to another. The Court reiterates that it must not rush to substitute its own judgment in place of that of the national authorities, who are best placed to assess and respond to the needs of society . . .

63. In conclusion, the Court finds that Article 12 of the Convention does not impose an obligation on the respondent Government to grant a same-sex couple like the applicants access to marriage.

64. Consequently, there has been no violation of Article 12 of the Convention.

Judge Malinverni, joined by Judge Kovler, issued a concurring opinion in which, relying on the Vienna Convention on the Law of Treaties, he concluded that Article 12 did not apply to same-sex couples. Furthermore, 'no inferences' could be drawn from Article 9 of the EU Charter when interpreting Article 12 of the ECHR.

6   In respect of prisoners claiming the right to conjugal visits a Grand Chamber expressed the *obiter dictum* view, in **Dickson v UK**, judgment of 4 December 2007, that:

81. . . . more than half of the Contracting States allow for conjugal visits for prisoners (subject to a variety of different restrictions), a measure which could be seen as obviating the need for the authorities to provide additional facilities for artificial insemination. However, while the Court has expressed its approval for the evolution in several European countries towards conjugal visits, it has not yet interpreted the Convention as requiring Contracting States to make provision for such visits . . .

For the applicants' invocation of Article 8 as a basis for challenging the prison authorities' refusal to provide artificial insemination facilities for them, see p 520.

7   A unanimous Chamber held that prisoners can invoke the right to marry and States have to justify (e.g. because of security needs) the refusal of permission for a specific prisoner to marry. In **Frasik v Poland**, judgment of 5 January 2010, the applicant prisoner had been held on remand whilst facing charges involving the rape of his partner. She and the appli-cant became reconciled and the latter asked the supervising judge for permission to marry the former in prison. The judge refused, because, *inter alia*, she doubted the sincerity of the

relationship of the applicant and the partner/victim and prison was not a suitable venue for a wedding in the eyes of the judge. Before the Court, the Polish Government did not dispute the application of Article 12, but they observed that the applicant had not in fact married his partner during the seven years since his subsequent release from prison. The Chamber held that:

> 93. . . . there is no question that detained persons forfeit their right guaranteed by Article 12 merely because of their status. Nor is there any place under the Convention system, where tolerance and broadmindedness are the acknowledged hallmarks of democratic society, for any automatic interference with prisoners' rights, including their right to establish a marital relationship with the person of their choice based purely on such arguments as what—in the authorities' view—might be acceptable to or what might offend public opinion . . .

Consequently, the Chamber found a breach of Article 12.

8 The general legislative ban on a father-in-law marrying his daughter-in-law was found to violate Article 12 by a unanimous Chamber in *B and L v UK*, judgment of 13 September 2005. B's marriage to A ended in divorce in 1987. They had a son C. L married C and they had a son W. B and L developed a relationship in 1995 (after C had left the matrimonial home). B and L have been cohabiting since 1996. L and C divorced in 1997. W lives with B and L and calls the former 'Dad'. In 2002 B enquired as to whether he and L could marry. The local Superintendent Registrar of Deaths and Marriages informed B that, under the Marriage Act 1946 as amended, B and L could only marry if A and C were deceased. The applicants complained to the Court alleging a breach of Article 12. In response the Government submitted that, *inter alia*, the ban on B and L marrying was not absolute as they could marry if their former spouses were dead or by obtaining permission through a personal Act of Parliament. Furthermore, the Government observed that 21 member States imposed an absolute or conditional ban on such marriages and the national authorities were in the best position to determine whether such marriages should be permitted.

> 37. The Court must however examine the facts of the case in the context pertaining in the United Kingdom. It observes that this bar on marriage is aimed at protecting the integrity of the family (preventing sexual rivalry between parents and children) and preventing harm to children who may be affected by the changing relationships of the adults around them. These are, without doubt, legitimate aims.
>
> 38. Nonetheless, the bar on marriage does not prevent the relationships occurring. This case shows that. There are no incest, or other criminal law, provisions to prevent extra-marital relationships between parents-in-law and children-in-law being established notwithstanding that children may live in these homes. It cannot therefore be said that in the present case the ban on the applicants' marriage prevents any alleged confusion or emotional insecurity to the second applicant's son.
>
> 39. As regards the need to protect the family from deleterious influences, the Court notes that the majority of the Group in the House of Lords reporting on the possible amendments to the law had taken the view that the bar should be lifted as it was based on tradition and no justification had been shown to exist. That the view of the minority, who considered that the bar remained necessary to prevent unhealthy internal family dynamics, prevailed shows that opinions in this area are divided. Further, the significance that the Court would otherwise attach to the legislature's consideration of the matter is outweighed by one important factor.
>
> 40. Under United Kingdom law the bar on a marriage of this degree of affinity is not subject to an absolute prohibition. Marriages can take place, pursuant to a personal Act of Parliament. From the information before the Court, it transpires that individuals in a similar situation to these applicants

have been permitted to marry: in the *Monk* case [Valerie Mary Hill and Alan Monk (Marriage Enabling) Act 1985, a personal Act permitting the marriage of a mother-in-law and her son-in-law], where there were also children in the household, it was declared that the impediment placed on the marriage served no useful purpose of public policy. The inconsistency between the stated aims of the incapacity and the waiver applied in some cases undermines the rationality and logic of the measure. The Government have argued that the general rule remains valid as the Parliamentary procedure provides a means of ensuring that exceptions are only made where no harm will ensue. The Court would only comment that there is no indication of any detailed investigation into family circumstances in the Parliamentary procedure and that in any event a cumbersome and expensive vetting process of this kind would not appear to offer a practically accessible or effective mechanism for individuals to vindicate their rights. It would also view with reservation a system that would require a person of full age in possession of his or her mental faculties to submit to a potentially intrusive investigation to ascertain whether it is suitable for them to marry (see, *mutatis mutandis*, *F. v Switzerland*, §§ 35–7).

41. The Court concludes that there has been, in the circumstances of this case, a violation of Article 12 of the Convention.

So, the key to the Chamber's unwillingness to defer to the national legislature's view of permissible marital relationships was that exceptions could be secured by an expensive *ad hoc* personal Act procedure.

9   Stringent restrictions on the ability of persons subject to immigration control to marry within the UK were found, *inter alia*, to violate Article 12 by a unanimous Chamber in ***O'Donoghue and others v UK***, judgment of 14 December 2010. The Home Secretary introduced a Certificate of Approval Scheme in 2005 with the objective of preventing non-nationals securing residency rights in the UK via the contracting of sham/bogus marriages. The Scheme did not apply to marriages conducted by the Church of England. However, if affected non-nationals wished to marry in other churches/civic ceremonies they had to obtain a certificate of approval from the government and pay a fee of £295 (after successful domestic litigation the Scheme went through several modifications). The applicants (including a British/Irish national, a Nigerian national, and their son) wished to marry in a Roman Catholic church, but they could not afford to pay the approval scheme fee (until friends provided them with the money for the fee). The Chamber held that:

83. . . . In the context of immigration laws and for justified reasons, the States may be entitled to prevent marriages of convenience, entered solely for the purpose of securing an immigration advantage. However, the relevant laws—which must also meet the standards of accessibility and clarity required by the Convention—may not otherwise deprive a person or a category of persons of full legal capacity of the right to marry with the partners of their choice . . .

The judges concluded that the Scheme impaired the essence of the adult applicants' right to marry due to the level of the fee charged and other aspects of the Scheme, including blanket prohibitions on marriages of specified categories of non-nationals. The Government also accepted that the Scheme breached Article 14 in conjunction with Article 9 as the applicants would not have been subject to restrictions if they had wished to marry under the rites of the Church of England.

During the Strasbourg proceedings the Government informed the Court that it intended to abolish the Scheme. Given the exemption of weddings undertaken by the Church of England from the original Scheme, it is somewhat ironic that in July 2010 a vicar from that church was convicted of conspiracy to facilitate illegal immigration (BBC News online, 29

July 2010). Of 383 weddings conducted by the Rev Alex Brown, in East Sussex, between 2005–9, 360 were bogus ones. Two co-defendants, a solicitor (who was also a pastor) and a Ukrainian national living illegally in the UK were also convicted. The latter 'cajoled' East Europeans living in the UK to contract marriages with hundreds of African men at Brown's church. The women were paid up to £3,000 to undertake the marriages. All three defendants were sentenced to four years' imprisonment. In a later linked prosecution a woman admitted supplying false information for a marriage register (she was given a 12-month conditional discharge). These prosecutions dramatically reveal the abuse of marriage as a means of attempting to circumvent immigration controls.

15 ARTICLE 13 RIGHT TO AN EFFECTIVE REMEDY

The Court has sought to tread a cautious path between ensuring that domestic remedies are effective and respecting varied domestic remedial mechanisms (*Silver*). However, after being confronted with an increasing torrent of complaints regarding delays in judicial proceedings in several member States, the Court adopted a new approach to Article 13 in such cases (*Kudla*). Paralleling developments in the case-law regarding a number of substantive Articles (including Articles 2, 3, and 5), the Court has also created effective investigation obligations upon member States under Article 13 (*Kurt*).

....

Silver v UK A.61 (1983)
European Court of Human Rights

The background to this case has already been outlined (p 590).

B. ARTICLE 13 TAKEN IN CONJUNCTION WITH ARTICLE 8 (ART 13+8)

111. . . . The Commission, having examined various possible channels of complaint, came to the conclusion that there was no effective domestic remedy and, hence, a violation of Article 13 (art 13). The Government requested the Court to hold that the facts of the case disclosed no breach of that provision or, alternatively, that they would disclose no such breach after the coming into effect of the revised Orders [regulating correspondence to and from prisoners].

112. Having held that the scope of the present case does not extend to the correspondence control system in force since December 1981 . . . the Court is unable to examine the Government's alternative plea.

113. The principles that emerge from the Court's jurisprudence on the interpretation of Article 13 (art 13) include the following:

(a) 'where an individual has an arguable claim to be the victim of a violation of the rights set forth in the Convention, he should have a remedy before a national authority in order both to have his claim decided and, if appropriate, to obtain redress (see the above-mentioned *Klass* judgment, Series A No 28, p 29, § 64);

(b) the authority referred to in Article 13 (art 13) may not necessarily be a judicial authority but, if it is not, its powers and the guarantees which it affords are relevant in determining whether the remedy before it is effective (ibid, p 30, § 67);

(c) although no single remedy may itself entirely satisfy the requirements of Article 13 (art 13), the aggregate of remedies provided for under domestic law may do so (see, *mutatis mutandis*, the above-mentioned *X v UK* judgment, Series A No 46, p 26, § 60, and the *Van Droogenbroeck* judgment of 24 June 1982, Series A No 50, p 32, § 56);

(d) neither Article 13 (art 13) nor the Convention in general lays down for the Contracting States any given manner for ensuring within their internal law the effective implementation of any of the provisions of the Convention—for example, by incorporating the Convention into domestic law (see the *Swedish Engine Drivers' Union* judgment of 6 February 1976, Series A No 20, p 18, § 50).

It follows from the last-mentioned principle that the application of Article 13 (art 13) in a given case will depend upon the manner in which the Contracting State concerned has chosen to discharge its obligation under Article 1 (art 1) directly to secure to anyone within its jurisdiction the rights and freedoms set out in section I (see the above-mentioned *Ireland v UK* judgment, Series A No 25, p 91, § 239).

114. In the present case, it was not suggested that any remedies were available to the applicants other than the four channels of complaint examined by the Commission, namely an application to the Board of Visitors, an application to the Parliamentary Commissioner for Administration [the Parliamentary Ombudsman], a petition to the Home Secretary and the institution of proceedings before the English courts.

115. As regards the first two channels, the Court, like the Commission, considers that they do not constitute an 'effective remedy' for the present purposes.

The Board of Visitors cannot enforce its conclusions...nor can it entertain applications from individuals like Mrs. Colne who are not in prison.

As regards the Parliamentary Commissioner, it suffices to note that he has himself no power to render a binding decision granting redress...

116. As for the Home Secretary, if there were a complaint to him as to the validity of an Order or Instruction under which a measure of control over correspondence had been carried out, he could not be considered to have a sufficiently independent standpoint to satisfy the requirements of Article 13 (art 13) (see, *mutatis mutandis*, the above-mentioned *Klass* judgment, Series A No 28, p 26, § 56): as the author of the directives in question, he would in reality be judge in his own cause. The position, however, would be otherwise if the complainant alleged that a measure of control resulted from a misapplication of one of those directives. The Court is satisfied that in such cases a petition to the Home Secretary would in general be effective to secure compliance with the directive, if the complaint was well-founded. The Court notes, however, that even in these cases, at least prior to 1 December 1981, the conditions for the submission of such petitions imposed limitations on the availability of this remedy in some circumstances...

117. The English courts, for their part, are endowed with a certain supervisory jurisdiction over the exercise of the powers conferred on the Home Secretary and the prison authorities by the Prison Act and the Rules...However, their jurisdiction is limited to determining whether or not those powers have been exercised arbitrarily, in bad faith, for an improper motive or in an *ultra vires* manner.

In this connection, the applicants stressed that the Convention, not being incorporated into domestic law, could not be directly invoked before the English courts; however, they acknowledged that it was relevant for the interpretation of ambiguous legislation, according to the presumption of the latter's conformity with the treaty obligations of the UK.

118. The applicants made no allegation that the interferences with their correspondence were contrary to English law...Like the Commission, the Court has found that the majority of the measures complained of in the present proceedings were incompatible with the Convention...In most of the cases, the Government did not contest the Commission's findings. Neither did they maintain that the English courts could have found the measures to have been taken arbitrarily, in bad faith, for an improper motive or in an *ultra vires* manner.

In the Court's view, to the extent that the applicable norms, whether contained in the Rules or in the relevant Orders or Instructions, were incompatible with the Convention there could be no effective remedy as required by Article 13 (art 13) and consequently there has been a violation of that Article (art 13).

To the extent, however, that the said norms were compatible with Article 8 (art 8), the aggregate of the remedies available satisfied the requirements of Article 13 (art 13), at least in those cases in which it was possible for a petition to be submitted to the Home Secretary...a petition to the Home Secretary was available to secure compliance with the directives issued by him and, as regards compliance with the Rules, the English courts had the supervisory jurisdiction described in paragraph 117 above.

119. To sum up, in those instances where the norms in question were incompatible with the Convention and where the Court has found a violation of Article 8 (art 8) to have occurred there was no effective remedy and Article 13 (art 13) has therefore also been violated. In the remaining cases, there is no reason to assume that the applicants' complaints could not have been duly examined by the Home Secretary and/or the English courts and Article 13 (art 13) has therefore not been violated...

FOR THESE REASONS, THE COURT UNANIMOUSLY

...

Holds that there has been a violation of Article 13 to the extent specified in paragraph 119 of the judgment;

...

NOTES

1 The Court was composed of President Wiarda and Judges: Thor Vilhjalmsson, Gölcüklü, Matscher, Pettiti, Evans, and Russo.

2 Even where the Court has found no breach of a substantive Convention right applicants may be able to establish that they had/have an 'arguable claim' of a violation which necessitated States providing them with an 'effective remedy' that satisfied the requirements of Article 13. For example, in *Leander v Sweden* A.116 (1987), as we have already noted (p 505) the respondent State had been able to justify, under Article 8(2), the secret files kept on the applicant. However, the Court went on to consider if there had been a breach of Article 13.

78....For the purposes of the present proceedings, an 'effective remedy' under Article 13 (art 13) must mean a remedy that is as effective as can be having regard to the restricted scope for recourse inherent in any system of secret checks on candidates for employment in posts of importance from a national security point of view. It therefore remains to examine the various remedies available to the applicant under Swedish law in order to see whether they were 'effective' in this limited sense (ibid, p 31, § 69).

79. There can be no doubt that the applicant's complaints have raised arguable claims under the Convention at least in so far as Article 8 (art 8) is concerned and that, accordingly, he was entitled to an effective remedy in order to enforce his rights under that Article as they were protected under Swedish law...

The Court has found the Swedish personnel control system as such to be compatible with Article 8 (art 8). In such a situation, the requirements of Article 13 (art 13) will be satisfied if there exists domestic machinery whereby, subject to the inherent limitations of the context, the individual can secure compliance with the relevant laws...

80. The Government argued that Swedish law offered sufficient remedies for the purposes of Article 13 (art 13), namely

(i) a formal application for the post, and, if unsuccessful, an appeal to the Government;

(ii) a request to the National Police Board for access to the secret police-register on the basis of the Freedom of the Press Act, and, if refused, an appeal to the administrative courts;

(iii) a complaint to the Chancellor of Justice [an office established under the constitution responsible for supervising public authorities];

(iv) a complaint to the Parliamentary Ombudsman.

The majority of the Commission found that these four remedies, taken in the aggregate, met the requirements of Article 13 (art 13), although none of them did so taken alone.

81. The Court notes first that both the Chancellor of Justice and the Parliamentary Ombudsman have the competence to receive individual complaints and that they have the duty to investigate such complaints in order to ensure that the relevant laws have been properly applied by the National Police Board ... In the performance of these duties, both officials have access to all the information contained in the secret police-register ... Several decisions from the Parliamentary Ombudsman evidence that these powers are also used in relation to complaints regarding the operation of the personnel control system ... Furthermore, both officials must, in the present context, be considered independent of the Government. This is quite clear in respect of the Parliamentary Ombudsman. As far as the Chancellor of Justice is concerned, he may likewise be regarded as being, at least in practice, independent of the Government when performing his supervisory functions in relation to the working of the personnel control system ...

82. The main weakness in the control afforded by the Ombudsman and the Chancellor of Justice is that both officials, apart from their competence to institute criminal and disciplinary proceedings ... lack the power to render a legally binding decision. On this point, the Court, however, recalls the necessarily limited effectiveness that can be required of any remedy available to the individual concerned in a system of secret security checks. The opinions of the Parliamentary Ombudsman and the Chancellor of Justice command by tradition great respect in Swedish society and in practice are usually followed ... It is also material—although this does not constitute a remedy that the individual can exercise of his own accord—that a special feature of the Swedish personnel control system is the substantial parliamentary supervision to which it is subject, in particular through the parliamentarians on the National Police Board who consider each case where release of information is requested ...

83. To these remedies, which were never exercised by Mr Leander, must be added the remedy to which he actually had recourse when he complained, in a letter of 5 February 1980 to the Government, that the National Police Board, contrary to the provisions of section 13 of the Personnel Control Ordinance, had omitted to invite him to comment, in writing or orally, on the information contained in the register ... The Government requested the opinion of the Board in this connection; whereupon Mr Leander was given the opportunity to reply, which he did in a letter of 11 March 1980. In its decision of 14 May 1980, which covered also Mr Leander's complaints of 22 October and 4 December 1979, the Government, that is the entire Cabinet, dismissed Mr Leander's various complaints ...

The Court recalls that the authority referred to in Article 13 (art 13) need not necessarily be a judicial authority in the strict sense, but that the powers and procedural guarantees an authority possesses are relevant in determining whether the remedy is effective. There can be no question about the power of the Government to deliver a decision binding on the Board ...

84. It should also be borne in mind that for the purposes of the present proceedings, an effective remedy under Article 13 (art 13) must mean a remedy that is as effective as can be, having regard to the restricted scope for recourse inherent in any system of secret surveillance for the protection of national security (see paragraphs 78–9 above).

Even if, taken on its own, the complaint to the Government were not considered sufficient to ensure compliance with Article 13 (art 13), the Court finds that the aggregate of the remedies set out above (see paragraphs 81–3) satisfies the conditions of Article 13 (art 13) in the particular circumstances of the instant case (see, *mutatis mutandis*, the above-mentioned *Klass* judgment, Series A No 28, p 32, § 72).

Accordingly, the Court concludes that there was no violation of Article 13 (art 13).

Three judges dissented as they did not consider that Sweden had provided the applicant with an effective remedy, the dissenters were particularly concerned that neither the Chancellor of Justice nor the Parliamentary Ombudsman issued legally binding decisions. In subsequent cases, see Note 3, the Court has become more rigorous in assessing whether domestic remedies applying to decisions involving issues of national security met the demands of Article 13.

3 A number of cases have involved the question whether the process of judicial review in English law amounts to an 'effective remedy' for the purposes of Article 13. In *Soering v UK* (see p 192), the Court was unanimous in concluding that it did.

116. . . . In [the applicant's] submission, he had no effective remedy in the United Kingdom in respect of his complaint under Article 3 (art 3). The majority of the Commission arrived at the same conclusion. The United Kingdom Government however disagreed, arguing that Article 13 (art 13) had no application in the circumstances of the present case or, in the alternative, that the aggregate of remedies provided for under domestic law was adequate.

117. In view of the Court's finding regarding Article 3 (art 3) . . . the applicant's claim under that Article (art 3) cannot be regarded either as incompatible with the provisions of the Convention or as not 'arguable' on its merits . . .

118. The United Kingdom Government relied on the aggregate of remedies provided by the Magistrates' Court proceedings, an application for habeas corpus and an application for judicial review . . .

119. The Court will commence its examination with judicial review proceedings since they constitute the principal means for challenging a decision to extradite once it has been taken.

Both the applicant and the Commission were of the opinion that the scope of judicial review was too narrow to allow the courts to consider the subject matter of the complaint which the applicant has made in the context of Article 3 (art 3). The applicant further contended that the courts' lack of jurisdiction to issue interim injunctions against the Crown was an additional reason rendering judicial review an ineffective remedy.

120. Article 13 (art 13) guarantees the availability of a remedy at national level to enforce the substance of the Convention rights and freedoms in whatever form they may happen to be secured in the domestic legal order . . . The effect of Article 13 (art 13) is thus to require the provision of a domestic remedy allowing the competent 'national authority' both to deal with the substance of the relevant Convention complaint and to grant appropriate relief (see, *inter alia*, the *Silver* judgment of 25 March 1983, Series A No 61, p 42, § 113 (a)).

121. In judicial review proceedings the court may rule the exercise of executive discretion unlawful on the ground that it is tainted with illegality, irrationality or procedural impropriety . . . In an extradition case the test of 'irrationality', on the basis of the so-called '*Wednesbury* principles', would be that no reasonable Secretary of State could have made an order for surrender in the circumstances (ibid). According to the United Kingdom Government, a court would have jurisdiction to quash a challenged decision to send a fugitive to a country where it was established that there was a serious risk of inhuman or degrading treatment, on the ground that in all the circumstances of the case the decision was one that no reasonable Secretary of State could take. Although the Convention is not considered to be part of United Kingdom law (ibid), the Court is satisfied that the English courts can review the 'reasonableness' of an extradition decision in the light of the kind of factors relied on by Mr Soering before the Convention institutions in the context of Article 3 (art 3).

122. Mr Soering did admittedly make an application for judicial review together with his application for habeas corpus and was met with an unfavourable response from Lord Justice Lloyd on the issue of 'irrationality'... However, as Lord Justice Lloyd explained, the claim failed because it was premature, the courts only having jurisdiction once the Minister has actually taken his decision (ibid). Furthermore, the arguments adduced by Mr Soering were by no means the same as those relied on when justifying his complaint under Article 3 (art 3) before the Convention institutions. His counsel before the Divisional Court limited himself to submitting that the assurance by the United States authorities was so worthless that no reasonable Secretary of State could regard it as satisfactory under the Treaty. This is an argument going to the likelihood of the death penalty being imposed but says nothing about the quality of the treatment awaiting Mr Soering after sentence to death, this being the substance of his allegation of inhuman and degrading treatment.

There was nothing to have stopped Mr Soering bringing an application for judicial review at the appropriate moment and arguing 'Wednesbury unreasonableness' on the basis of much the same material that he adduced before the Convention institutions in relation to the 'death row phenomenon'. Such a claim would have been given 'the most anxious scrutiny' in view of the fundamental nature of the human right at stake... The effectiveness of the remedy, for the purposes of Article 13 (art 13), does not depend on the certainty of a favourable outcome for Mr Soering (see the *Swedish Engine Drivers' Union* judgment of 6 February 1976, Series A No 20, p 18, § 50), and in any event it is not for this Court to speculate as to what would have been the decision of the English courts.

123. The English courts' lack of jurisdiction to grant interim injunctions against the Crown...does not, in the Court's opinion, detract from the effectiveness of judicial review in the present connection, since there is no suggestion that in practice a fugitive would ever be surrendered before his application to the Divisional Court and any eventual appeal therefrom had been determined.

124. The Court concludes that Mr Soering did have available to him under English law an effective remedy in relation to his complaint under Article 3 (art 3). This being so, there is no need to inquire into the other two remedies referred to by the United Kingdom Government.

There is accordingly no breach of Article 13 (art 13).

The ability of domestic courts to grant injunctions (including interim ones) against the Crown, when applying English law, was greatly extended by the House of Lords' landmark ruling in *M v Home Office* [1993] 3 All ER 537.

However, in the later case of *Chahal v UK* (see p 204) the Court was united in finding a breach of Article 13.

141. The applicants maintained that the only remedy available to them in respect of their claims under Articles 3, 5 and 8 of the Convention (art 3, art 5, art 8) was judicial review, the advisory panel procedure...being neither a 'remedy' nor 'effective'.

They submitted, first, that the powers of the English courts to put aside an executive decision were inadequate in all Article 3 (art 3) asylum cases, since the courts could not scrutinise the facts to determine whether substantial grounds had been shown for belief in the existence of a real risk of ill-treatment in the receiving State, but could only determine whether the Secretary of State's decision as to the existence of such a risk was reasonable according to the 'Wednesbury' principles...

This contention had particular weight in cases where the executive relied upon arguments of national security. In the instant case, the assertion that Mr Chahal's deportation was necessary in the interests of national security entailed that there could be no effective judicial evaluation of the risk to him of ill-treatment in India or of the issues under Article 8 (art 8). That assertion likewise prevented any effective judicial control on the question whether the applicant's continued detention was justified.

142. The Government accepted that the scope of judicial review was more limited where deportation was ordered on national security grounds. However, the Court had held in the past that, where

questions of national security were in issue, an 'effective remedy' under Article 13 (art 13) must mean 'a remedy that is effective as can be', given the necessity of relying upon secret sources of information (see the *Klass v Germany* judgment of 6 September 1978, Series A No 28, p 31, para 69, and the *Leander v Sweden* judgment of 26 March 1987, Series A No 116, p 32, para 84).

Furthermore, it had to be borne in mind that all the relevant material, including the sensitive material, was examined by the advisory panel whose members included two senior judicial figures—a Court of Appeal judge and a former president of the Immigration Appeal Tribunal...The procedure before the panel was designed, on the one hand, to satisfy the need for an independent review of the totality of the material on which the perceived threat to national security was based and, on the other hand, to ensure that secret information would not be publicly disclosed. It thus provided a form of independent, quasi-judicial scrutiny.

143. For the Commission, the present case could be distinguished from that of *Vilvarajah* [A.215 (1991)]...where the Court held that judicial review in the English courts amounted to an effective remedy in respect of the applicants' Article 3 (art 3) claims. Because the Secretary of State invoked national security considerations as grounds for his decisions to deport Mr Chahal and to detain him pending deportation, the English courts' powers of review were limited. They could not themselves consider the evidence on which the Secretary of State had based his decision that the applicant constituted a danger to national security or undertake any evaluation of the Article 3 (art 3) risks. Instead, they had to confine themselves to examining whether the evidence showed that the Secretary of State had carried out the balancing exercise required by the domestic law...

144. The intervenors [including Amnesty International and Liberty] were all of the view that judicial review did not constitute an effective remedy in cases involving national security. Article 13 (art 13) required at least that some independent body should be appraised of all the facts and evidence and entitled to reach a decision which would be binding on the Secretary of State....

145. The Court observes that Article 13 (art 13) guarantees the availability at national level of a remedy to enforce the substance of the Convention rights and freedoms in whatever form they might happen to be secured in the domestic legal order. The effect of this Article (art 13) is thus to require the provision of a domestic remedy allowing the competent national authority both to deal with the substance of the relevant Convention complaint and to grant appropriate relief, although Contracting States are afforded some discretion as to the manner in which they conform to their obligations under this provision (art 13) (see the *Vilvarajah* judgment cited at paragraph 73 above, p 39, para 122).

Moreover, it is recalled that in certain circumstances the aggregate of remedies provided by national law may satisfy the requirements of Article 13 (art 13) (see, *inter alia*, the above-mentioned *Leander* judgment, p 30, para 77).

146. The Court does not have to examine the allegation of a breach of Article 13 taken in conjunction with Article 5 para 1 (art 13+5-1), in view of its finding of a violation of Article 5 para 4 (art 5-4)...Nor is it necessary for it to examine the complaint under Article 13 in conjunction with Article 8 (art 13+8), in view of its finding concerning the hypothetical nature of the complaint under the latter provision (art 8)...

147. This leaves only the first applicant's claim under Article 3 combined with Article 13 (art 13+3). It was not disputed that the Article 3 (art 3) complaint was arguable on the merits and the Court accordingly finds that Article 13 (art 13) is applicable (see the above-mentioned *Vilvarajah* judgment, p 38, para 121).

148. The Court recalls that in its *Vilvarajah* judgment (ibid, p 39, paras 122–6), it found judicial review proceedings to be an effective remedy in relation to the applicants' complaints under Article 3 (art 3). It was satisfied that the English courts could review a decision by the Secretary of State to refuse asylum and could rule it unlawful on the grounds that it was tainted with illegality irrationality or procedural impropriety...In particular, it was accepted that a court would have

jurisdiction to quash a challenged decision to send a fugitive to a country where it was established that there was a serious risk of inhuman or degrading treatment, on the ground that in all the circumstances of the case the decision was one that no reasonable Secretary of State could take...

149. The Court further recalls that in assessing whether there exists a real risk of treatment in breach of Article 3 (art 3) in expulsion cases such as the present, the fact that the person is perceived as a danger to the national security of the respondent State is not a material consideration...

150. It is true, as the Government have pointed out, that in the cases of *Klass* and *Leander*...the Court held that Article 13 (art 13) only required a remedy that was 'as effective as can be' in circumstances where national security considerations did not permit the divulging of certain sensitive information. However, it must be borne in mind that these cases concerned complaints under Articles 8 and 10 of the Convention (art 8, art 10) and that their examination required the Court to have regard to the national security claims which had been advanced by the Government. The requirement of a remedy which is 'as effective as can be' is not appropriate in respect of a complaint that a person's deportation will expose him or her to a real risk of treatment in breach of Article 3 (art 3), where the issues concerning national security are immaterial.

151. In such cases, given the irreversible nature of the harm that might occur if the risk of ill-treatment materialised and the importance the Court attaches to Article 3 (art 3), the notion of an effective remedy under Article 13 (art 13) requires independent scrutiny of the claim that there exist substantial grounds for fearing a real risk of treatment contrary to Article 3 (art 3). This scrutiny must be carried out without regard to what the person may have done to warrant expulsion or to any perceived threat to the national security of the expelling State.

152. Such scrutiny need not be provided by a judicial authority but, if it is not, the powers and guarantees which it affords are relevant in determining whether the remedy before it is effective (see the above-mentioned *Leander* judgment, p 29, para 77).

153. In the present case, neither the advisory panel nor the courts could review the decision of the Home Secretary to deport Mr Chahal to India with reference solely to the question of risk, leaving aside national security considerations. On the contrary, the courts' approach was one of satisfying themselves that the Home Secretary had balanced the risk to Mr Chahal against the danger to national security...It follows from the above considerations that these cannot be considered effective remedies in respect of Mr Chahal's Article 3 (art 3) complaint for the purposes of Article 13 of the Convention (art 13).

154. Moreover, the Court notes that in the proceedings before the advisory panel the applicant was not entitled, *inter alia*, to legal representation, that he was only given an outline of the grounds for the notice of intention to deport, that the panel had no power of decision and that its advice to the Home Secretary was not binding and was not disclosed...In these circumstances, the advisory panel could not be considered to offer sufficient procedural safeguards for the purposes of Article 13 (art 13).

155. Having regard to the extent of the deficiencies of both the judicial review proceedings and the advisory panel, the Court cannot consider that the remedies taken together satisfy the requirements of Article 13 in conjunction with Article 3 (art 13+3).

Accordingly, there has been a violation of Article 13 (art 13).

The decisive factor in **Chahal** was the limited powers of review possessed by English courts when confronted with a government assertion that the decision being challenged had been taken in the interests of national security. Significantly, the Court also held that its less onerous **Leander** standard of a remedy that was 'as effective as can be', having regard to national security considerations, did not apply to Article 13 cases based upon an arguable violation of Article 3 as the latter provision did not permit States to invoke issues of national security as a relevant factor. In *Smith and Grady v UK* (see p 492), a unanimous Court also found a breach of Article 13 in respect of claims under Article 8.

131. The applicants submitted that Article 13 contained two minimum requirements. First, the relevant national authority had to have jurisdiction to examine the substance of an individual's complaint by reference to the Convention or other corresponding provisions of national law and, secondly, that authority had to have jurisdiction to grant a remedy if it accepted that the individual's complaint was well-founded. Moreover, the precise scope of the obligations under Article 13 would depend on the nature of the individual's complaint. The context of the present case was the application of a blanket policy which interfered with the Article 8 rights of a minority group and not an assessment of an individual extradition or expulsion in the context of Article 3 as in the *Soering* and *Vilvarajah* cases...

132. In the applicants' view, the judicial review remedy did not meet the first of these requirements of Article 13 for two connected reasons. Since the Ministry of Defence policy was a blanket policy admitting of no exceptions, it was impossible for the domestic courts to consider the merits of the applicants' individual complaints. However, the impact of the policy on them varied from case to case. In contrast, the domestic courts could and indeed were bound to apply the 'most anxious scrutiny' to the individual facts in the above-mentioned extradition and expulsion cases of *Soering* and *Vilvarajah*. Secondly, the domestic courts could not ask themselves whether a fair balance had been struck between the general interest and the applicants' rights. The domestic courts were confined to asking themselves whether it had been shown that the policy as a whole was irrational or perverse and the burden of proving irrationality was on the applicants. They were required to show that the policy-maker had 'taken leave of his senses' and the applicants had to show that this high threshold had been crossed before the domestic courts could intervene. Moreover, the applicants pointed to the comments of the High Court and of the Court of Appeal as the best evidence that those courts lacked jurisdiction to deal with the substance of the applicants' Convention complaints. In this context, the *Soering* and *Vilvarajah* cases cited above could be distinguished because the test applied in judicial review proceedings concerning proposed extraditions and expulsions happened to coincide with the Convention test.

133. The applicants further contended that their judicial review proceedings did not comply with the second requirement of Article 13 because the domestic courts were not able to grant a remedy even though four out of the five judges who examined the applicants' case considered that the policy was not justified.

134. Although the applicants invoked Article 13 of the Convention in relation to all of their complaints, the Court recalls that it is the applicants' right to respect for their private lives which is principally at issue in the present case... In such circumstances, it is of the view that the applicants' complaints under Article 13 of the Convention are more appropriately considered in conjunction with Article 8.

135. The Court recalls that Article 13 guarantees the availability of a remedy at national level to enforce the substance of Convention rights and freedoms in whatever form they may happen to be secured in the domestic legal order. Thus, its effect is to require the provision of a domestic remedy allowing the competent national authority both to deal with the substance of the relevant Convention complaint and to grant appropriate relief. However, Article 13 does not go so far as to require incorporation of the Convention or a particular form of remedy, Contracting States being afforded a margin of appreciation in conforming with their obligations under this provision. Nor does the effectiveness of a remedy for the purposes of Article 13 depend on the certainty of a favourable outcome for the applicant (see the *Vilvarajah* judgment...p 39, § 122).

136. The Court has found that the applicants' right to respect for their private lives... was violated by the investigations conducted and by the discharge of the applicants pursuant to the policy of

the Ministry of Defence against homosexuals in the armed forces. As was made clear by the High Court and the Court of Appeal in the judicial review proceedings, since the Convention did not form part of English law, questions as to whether the application of the policy violated the applicants' rights under Article 8 and, in particular, as to whether the policy had been shown by the authorities to respond to a pressing social need or to be proportionate to any legitimate aim served, were not questions to which answers could properly be offered. The sole issue before the domestic courts was whether the policy could be said to be 'irrational'.

137. The test of 'irrationality' applied in the present case was that explained in the judgment of Sir Thomas Bingham MR: a court was not entitled to interfere with the exercise of an administrative discretion on substantive grounds save where the court was satisfied that the decision was unreasonable in the sense that it was beyond the range of responses open to a reasonable decision-maker. In judging whether the decision-maker had exceeded this margin of appreciation, the human rights context was important, so that the more substantial the interference with human rights, the more the Court would require by way of justification before it was satisfied that the decision was reasonable. It was, however, further emphasised that, notwithstanding any human rights context, the threshold of irrationality which an applicant was required to surmount was a high one. This is, in the view of the Court, confirmed by the judgments of the High Court and the Court of Appeal themselves. The Court notes that the main judgments in both courts commented favourably on the applicants' submissions challenging the reasons advanced by the Government in justification of the policy. Simon Brown LJ considered that the balance of argument lay with the applicants and that their arguments in favour of a conduct-based code were powerful...Sir Thomas Bingham MR found that those submissions of the applicants were of 'very considerable cogency' and that they fell to be considered in depth with particular reference to the potential effectiveness of a conduct-based code...Furthermore, while offering no conclusive views on the Convention issues raised by the case, Simon Brown LJ expressed the opinion that 'the days of the policy were numbered' in light of the United Kingdom's Convention obligations...and Sir Thomas Bingham MR observed that the investigations and the discharge of the applicants did not appear to show respect for their private lives. He considered that there might be room for argument as to whether there had been a disproportionate interference with their rights under Article 8 of the Convention...Nevertheless, both courts concluded that the policy could not be said to be beyond the range of responses open to a reasonable decision-maker and, accordingly, could not be considered to be 'irrational'.

138. In such circumstances, the Court considers it clear that, even assuming that the essential complaints of the applicants before this Court were before and considered by the domestic courts, the threshold at which the High Court and the Court of Appeal could find the Ministry of Defence policy irrational was placed so high that it effectively excluded any consideration by the domestic courts of the question of whether the interference with the applicants' rights answered a pressing social need or was proportionate to the national security and public order aims pursued, principles which lie at the heart of the Court's analysis of complaints under Article 8 of the Convention. The present applications can be contrasted with the cases of *Soering* and *Vilvarajah* cited above. In those cases, the Court found that the test applied by the domestic courts in applications for judicial review of decisions by the Secretary of State in extradition and expulsion matters coincided with the Court's own approach under Article 3 of the Convention.

139. In such circumstances, the Court finds that the applicants had no effective remedy in relation to the violation of their right to respect for their private lives guaranteed by Article 8 of the Convention. Accordingly, there has been a violation of Article 13 of the Convention.

Thus the answer to the question whether English judicial review satisfies the requirements of Article 13 depends upon the context and substance of the particular application. The traditional deference of the domestic judiciary to the government in cases involving considerations of national security meant that the process of judicial review did not meet the minimum requirements of Article 13 for such cases in the judgment of the Court (*Chahal* and *Smith and Grady*). Whereas, in respect of other areas of governmental decision-making, such as 'ordinary' extradition and deportation decisions (e.g. *Soering* and *Vilvarajah*), judicial review was capable of fulfilling the demands of Article 13.

4   The Court elaborated upon the procedural requirements of an effective domestic remedy concerning the lawfulness of decisions to deport foreigners on national security grounds in *Al-Nashif v Bulgaria*, judgment of 20 June 2002. The applicant was a stateless person of Palestinian origin who had been living lawfully in Bulgaria since 1992. In 1999 the authorities revoked his permanent residence permit and ordered his deportation as he had been teaching religious classes. The applicant sought judicial review of the decision to deport him and the Passport Department responded by certifying that his deportation was ordered because he had undertaken acts contrary to national security. The effect of such certification was to prevent the Sofia District Court from subjecting the deportation decision to judicial review. Thereupon, the applicant was deported to Syria. The Chamber held that:

137. ... Even where an allegation of a threat to national security is made, the guarantee of an effective remedy requires as a minimum that the competent independent appeals authority must be informed of the reasons grounding the deportation decision, even if such reasons are not publicly available. The authority must be competent to reject the executive's assertion that there is a threat to national security where it finds it arbitrary or unreasonable. There must be some form of adversarial proceedings, if need be through a special representative after a security clearance. Furthermore, the question whether the impugned measure would interfere with the individual's right to respect for family life and, if so, whether a fair balance is struck between the public interest involved and the individual's rights must be examined.

As such a remedy had not been available to the applicant the Chamber found a violation of Article 13 (three judges dissented as they considered that the applicant had no arguable claim of a violation of Article 8 and therefore Article 13 was not applicable).

5   The full-time Court has also become increasingly stringent in assessing the adequacy of an aggregation of individual domestic remedies in satisfying Article 13. For example, in *Paul and Audrey Edwards v UK*, judgment of 14 March 2002 and see p 123, the Government submitted that an inquiry into the killing of the applicant's son and the option for the applicants to sue the prison authorities for alleged negligence in the care of their son cumulatively met the requirements of Article 13. The Chamber, unanimously, found procedural defects in the inquiry (e.g. the applicants were not able to participate fully in its hearings) and the inability of the applicants to obtain compensation for the non-pecuniary damage their son and they had suffered meant that:

101. Notwithstanding the aggregate of remedies referred to by the Government, the Court finds that in this case the applicants did not have available to them an appropriate means of obtaining a determination of their allegations that the authorities failed to protect their son's right to life and the possibility of obtaining an enforceable award of compensation for the damage suffered thereby. In the Court's view, this is an essential element of a remedy under Article 13 for a bereaved parent.

102. Accordingly, there has been a breach of Article 13 of the Convention.

6   The Court has developed an extensive body of jurisprudence interpreting Article 13 as requiring States to undertake effective investigations into arguable claims that substantive Convention rights have been violated. Where relatives/friends alleged that a person had been unlawfully killed by State personnel, contrary to Article 2, the Court has ruled that

such an investigation is necessary to satisfy Article 13. For example, in *Kaya v Turkey*, 1998-I, the applicant contended that his brother had been deliberately shot dead by the security forces. The Chamber, by 8 votes to 1, held that:

107. In the instant case the applicant is complaining that he and the next-of-kin have been denied an 'effective' remedy which would have brought to light the true circumstances surrounding the killing of Abdülmenaf Kaya. In the view of the Court the nature of the right which the authorities are alleged to have violated in the instant case, one of the most fundamental in the scheme of the Convention, must have implications for the nature of the remedies which must be guaranteed for the benefit of the relatives of the victim. In particular, where those relatives have an arguable claim that the victim has been unlawfully killed by agents of the State, the notion of an effective remedy for the purposes of Article 13 entails, in addition to the payment of compensation where appropriate, a thorough and effective investigation capable of leading to the identification and punishment of those responsible and including effective access for the relatives to the investigatory procedure ... Seen in these terms the requirements of Article 13 are broader than a Contracting State's procedural obligation under Article 2 to conduct an effective investigation.

The Chamber went on to find a breach of Article 13 as the domestic inquiry into the death of the applicant's brother had been seriously deficient (e.g. the authorities had unquestioningly assumed that the deceased was a terrorist killed during a clash with members of the security forces). Similarly, a unanimous Grand Chamber held in *Ilhan v Turkey*, judgment of 27 June 2000 and see p 114, that '97. [w]here an individual has an arguable claim that he has been tortured or subjected to serious ill-treatment by the State ...' an effective investigation was mandated by Article 13. As there had been significant defects in the domestic inquiry, including the prosecutor failing to interview key witnesses:

103. For these reasons, no effective criminal investigation can be considered to have been conducted in accordance with Article 13. The Court finds therefore that no effective remedy has been provided in respect of Abdullatif Ilhan's injuries and thereby access to any other available remedies, including a claim for compensation has also been denied.
   Consequently, there has been a violation of Article 13 of the Convention.

The above judgment is also important for linking a failure to provide an effective domestic investigation and the consequent inability of the applicant to secure other forms of domestic redress, such as compensation, as key elements in the Court's finding of a breach of Article 13. The Court has also applied Article 13 to applications concerning alleged forced disappearances of persons by State agents in breach of Article 5. For example, in *Kurt v Turkey*, 1998-III and see p 176:

140. ... In the view of the Court, where the relatives of a person have an arguable claim that the latter has disappeared at the hands of the authorities, the notion of an effective remedy for the purposes of Article 13 entails, in addition to the payment of compensation where appropriate, a thorough and effective investigation capable of leading to the identification and punishment of those responsible and including effective access for the relatives to the investigatory procedure (see, *mutatis mutandis*, the ... Aksoy, Aydin and Kaya judgments ...). Seen in these terms, the requirements of Article 13 are broader than a Contracting State's obligation under Article 5 to conduct an effective investigation into the disappearance of a person who has been shown to be under their control and for whose welfare they are accordingly responsible.

A large majority of the Court, 7 votes to 2, determined that there had been a breach of Article 13 as there had been no genuine investigation by the public prosecutor into the applicant's petitions concerning the whereabouts of her son.

For a detailed analysis of the effective investigation duties under Article 13 see A. Mowbray, *The Development of Positive Obligations under the European Convention on Human Rights by the European Court of Human Rights* (Oxford: Hart Publishing, 2004), pp 211–20.

7   A Grand Chamber of the full-time Court pronounced a major expansion of the scope of Article 13 to encompass an obligation upon the legal systems of member States to provide an effective remedy in respect of complaints of unreasonable delays in the determination of persons' civil rights or criminal charges against them (contrary to Article 6(1)) in **Kudla v Poland**, judgment of 26 October 2000. The applicant complained that fraud charges against him had not been conclusively determined by the Polish courts after nine years. The Court held that:

146. In many previous cases in which the Court has found a violation of Article 6 § 1 it did not consider it necessary also to rule on an accompanying complaint made under Article 13. More often than not this was because in the circumstances Article 6 § 1 was deemed to constitute a lex specialis in relation to Article 13.

Thus, where the Convention right asserted by the individual is a 'civil right' recognised under domestic law—such as the right of property—the protection afforded by Article 6 § 1 will also be available (see, for example, the *Sporrong and Lönnroth v Sweden* judgment of 23 September 1982, Series A No 52, pp 31–2, § 88). In such circumstances the safeguards of Article 6 § 1, implying the full panoply of a judicial procedure, are stricter than, and absorb, those of Article 13 (see, for example, the *Brualla Gómez de la Torre* [*v Spain* 1997-VIII] judgment, p 2957, § 41).

The Court has applied a similar logic in cases where the applicant's grievance has been directed at the adequacy of an existing appellate or cassation procedure coming within the ambit of both Article 6 § 1 under its 'criminal' head and Article 13 (see the *Kamasinski v Austria* judgment of 19 December 1989, Series A No 168, pp. 45–6, § 110—in relation to nullity proceedings before the Supreme Court).

In such cases there is no legal interest in re-examining the same subject-matter of complaint under the less stringent requirements of Article 13.

147. There is, however, no overlap and hence no absorption where, as in the present case, the alleged Convention violation that the individual wishes to bring before a 'national authority' is a violation of the right to trial within a reasonable time, contrary to Article 6 § 1. The question of whether the applicant in a given case did benefit from trial within a reasonable time in the determination of civil rights and obligations or a criminal charge is a separate legal issue from that of whether there was available to the applicant under domestic law an effective remedy to ventilate a complaint on that ground. In the present case the issue to be determined before the Article 6 § 1 'tribunals' was the criminal charges brought against the applicant, whereas the complaint that he wanted to have examined by a 'national authority' for the purposes of Article 13 was the separate one of the unreasonable length of the proceedings.

In comparable cases in the past, the Court has nonetheless declined to rule on an accompanying complaint of the absence of an effective remedy as guaranteed by Article 13, considering it unnecessary in view of its prior finding of a breach of the 'reasonable time' requirement laid down in Article 6 § 1 (see, among other examples, . . . *Pizzetti* [*v Italy* A.257-C (1993)]).

148. In the Court's view, the time has come to review its case-law in the light of the continuing accumulation of applications before it in which the only, or principal, allegation is that of a failure to ensure a hearing within a reasonable time in breach of Article 6 § 1.

The growing frequency with which violations in this regard are being found has recently led the Court to draw attention to 'the important danger' that exists for the rule of law within national legal orders when 'excessive delays in the administration of justice' occur 'in respect of which litigants have no domestic remedy' (see, for example, *Bottazzi v Italy* [GC], No 34884/97, § 22, ECHR 1999-V;

Di Mauro v Italy [GC], No 34256/96, § 23, ECHR 1999-V; *A.P. v Italy* [GC], No 35265/97, § 18, 28 July 1999, unreported; and *Ferrari v Italy* [GC], No 33440/96, § 21, 28 July 1999, unreported).

149. Against this background, the Court does now perceive the need to examine the applicant's complaint under Article 13 taken separately, in addition to its earlier finding of a violation of Article 6 § 1 for failure to try him within a reasonable time.

...

152. On the contrary, the place of Article 13 in the scheme of human rights protection set up by the Convention would argue in favour of implied restrictions of Article 13 being kept to a minimum.

By virtue of Article 1 (which provides: 'The High Contracting Parties shall secure to everyone within their jurisdiction the rights and freedoms defined in Section I of this Convention'), the primary responsibility for implementing and enforcing the guaranteed rights and freedoms is laid on the national authorities. The machinery of complaint to the Court is thus subsidiary to national systems safeguarding human rights. This subsidiary character is articulated in Articles 13 and 35 § 1 of the Convention.

The purpose of Article 35 § 1, which sets out the rule on exhaustion of domestic remedies, is to afford the Contracting States the opportunity of preventing or putting right the violations alleged against them before those allegations are submitted to the Court (see, as a recent authority, *Selmouni v France* [GC], No 25803/94, § 74, ECHR 1999-V). The rule in Article 35 § 1 is based on the assumption, reflected in Article 13 (with which it has a close affinity), that there is an effective domestic remedy available in respect of the alleged breach of an individual's Convention rights (ibid).

In that way, Article 13, giving direct expression to the States' obligation to protect human rights first and foremost within their own legal system, establishes an additional guarantee for an individual in order to ensure that he or she effectively enjoys those rights. The object of Article 13, as emerges from the travaux préparatoires (see the *Collected Edition of the 'Travaux Préparatoires' of the European Convention on Human Rights*, vol. II, pp 485 and 490, and vol III, p 651), is to provide a means whereby individuals can obtain relief at national level for violations of their Convention rights before having to set in motion the international machinery of complaint before the Court. From this perspective, the right of an individual to trial within a reasonable time will be less effective if there exists no opportunity to submit the Convention claim first to a national authority; and the requirements of Article 13 are to be seen as reinforcing those of Article 6 § 1, rather than being absorbed by the general obligation imposed by that Article not to subject individuals to inordinate delays in legal proceedings.

153. The Government, however, argued that requiring a remedy for inordinate length of proceedings under Article 13 is tantamount to imposing on States a new obligation to establish a 'right of appeal', in particular a right to appeal on the merits, which, as such, is guaranteed only in criminal matters under Article 2 of Protocol No. 7 to the Convention; and that in practice the exercise of such a remedy could only prolong proceedings in domestic courts...

154. The Court does not accept the Government's submissions.

A remedy for complaining about unreasonable length of proceedings does not as such involve an appeal against the 'determination' of any criminal charge or of civil rights and obligations. In any event, subject to compliance with the requirements of the Convention, the Contracting States—as the Court has held on many previous occasions—are afforded some discretion as to the manner in which they provide the relief required by Article 13 and conform to their Convention obligation under that provision (see, for example, the *Kaya v Turkey* judgment of 19 February 1998, Reports 1998-I, pp 329–30, § 106).

As to the suggestion that requiring yet a further remedy would result in domestic proceedings' being made even more cumbersome, the Court would observe that even though at present there is no prevailing pattern in the legal orders of the Contracting States in respect of remedies for excessive length of proceedings, there are examples emerging from the Court's own case-law on the rule on exhaustion of domestic remedies which demonstrate that it is not impossible to create such remedies and operate them effectively (see, for instance, *Gonzalez Marin v Spain* (dec), No 39521/98, ECHR 1999-VII, and *Tomé Mota v Portugal* (dec.), No 32082/96, ECHR 1999-IX).

155. If Article 13 is, as the Government argued, to be interpreted as having no application to the right to a hearing within a reasonable time as safeguarded by Article 6 § 1, individuals will systematically be forced to refer to the Court in Strasbourg complaints that would otherwise, and in the Court's opinion more appropriately, have to be addressed in the first place within the national legal system. In the long term the effective functioning, on both the national and international level, of the scheme of human rights protection set up by the Convention is liable to be weakened.

156. In view of the foregoing considerations, the Court considers that the correct interpretation of Article 13 is that that provision guarantees an effective remedy before a national authority for an alleged breach of the requirement under Article 6 § 1 to hear a case within a reasonable time.

As such a remedy was not provided by the Polish courts the applicant had suffered a violation of Article 13 (in addition to the separate breach of his right to the determination of the criminal charges against him within a reasonable time under Article 6(1)). Judge Casadevall dissented because:

3....there have been more and more findings of violations based solely or principally on the excessive length of proceedings in a good many member States. But by the terms of the Convention, the Court has a duty to consider and try applications as submitted to it by litigants. To state, as the Court does in paragraph 149, that the time has now come, on account of the number of applications relating to length of proceedings, to examine the complaint under Article 13 taken separately smacks, in my view, more of expediency than of law.

4. Moreover, it is not certain that the level of judicial protection afforded at European level by the Convention will be strengthened merely because the Court will now be able to find a double violation—firstly on account of the excessive length of the proceedings and secondly on account of the lack of any effective remedy to complain of it. The finding of an additional violation of Article 13 is not in itself such as to overcome the endemic structural problems besetting the judicial systems of certain member States, any more than the finding that there is a practice incompatible with the Convention has been. It will not make it easier to reduce the Court's case-load, at least not in the medium term.

5. The aim of this finding of a violation of Article 13 is to confront the States with their responsibilities, in accordance with the subsidiarity principle, and to encourage them to establish in their domestic legal systems an effective remedy that will enable litigants to complain of excessive length of proceedings. Supposing such a remedy is instituted, I can hardly see how the structural problem of the unreasonable length of proceedings could be remedied by the obligation to first exhaust, as required by Article 35 of the Convention, an additional remedy designed to make it possible to complain of the length of proceedings.

There is nothing to warrant an assumption that such an action would be heard within a more reasonable time than the main proceedings. Nor does anything warrant an assumption that the main proceedings would be speeded up as a result of bringing such an action. Ultimately only the litigant would suffer the consequences of this situation.

The judgment in **Kudla** reveals that the large numbers of applications to the Court alleging a breach of the reasonable time guarantee in Article 6(1), see p 431, was a major factor influencing the Grand Chamber to adopt the new interpretation of Article 13. Subsequently, Chambers applied **Kudla** to find breaches of Article 13 in cases against various States that had failed to provide an effective domestic remedy in respect of unreasonable delay complaints including: *Nuvoli v Italy*, judgment of 16 May 2002, *Rados and others v Croatia*, judgment of 7 November 2002, and *Rumpf v Germany*, judgment of 2 September 2010.

On 17 September 2004, the Polish Parliament enacted legislation in response to *Kudla* enabling persons to complain to the appellate courts about unreasonable delays in the lower courts' determination of their cases. The appellate courts were empowered to instruct the lower courts to accelerate proceedings and award compensation to the complainants. On 30 September 2004, the European Court announced that it was giving priority to the determination of four leading cases concerning complaints about the length of proceedings in Polish trials. At the same time, the Court was adjourning its consideration of approximately 700 similar complaints against Poland. On 9 March 2005, the Court ruled in two of the test cases that the applications were inadmissible as the complainants had failed to exhaust domestic remedies by not making applications to the Polish appellate courts under the terms of the 2004 Act. A few months later the Court, unanimously, found that the ability of litigants to seek damages against the Government, under the 2004 Act, in respect of complaints that their cases had not been determined within a reasonable time by the Polish courts was an effective remedy under Article 13. In *Krasuski v Poland*, judgment of 14 June 2005, the Chamber ruled that:

66. The means available to an applicant in domestic law for raising a complaint about the length of the proceedings are 'effective', within the meaning of Article 13 of the Convention, if they 'prevent the alleged violation or its continuation, or provid[e] adequate redress for any violation that has already occurred'. Article 13 thus offers an alternative: a remedy is 'effective' if it can be used either to expedite a decision by the courts dealing with the case or to provide the litigant with adequate redress for delays that have already occurred. The fact that a given remedy is of a purely compensatory nature is not decisive, regardless of whether the proceedings in question have been terminated or are still pending (see *Kudla*, cited above, §§ 158–9; *Caldas Ramirez de Arrellano v Spain* (dec.), No 68874/01, ECHR 2003-I; *Mifsud v France* (dec.) [GC], No 57220/00, ECHR 2002-VIII; and *Paulino Tomás v Portugal* (dec.), No 58698/00, ECHR 2003-VIII).

2. Application of the above principles to the present case

(a) Applicability of Article 13

67. There has been no dispute over the applicability of Article 13 in the present case. The parties agreed that the applicant's complaint under Article 6 § 1, declared admissible by the Court, satisfied the test of 'arguability' for the purposes of Article 13.

(b) Compliance with Article 13

68. In previous similar cases before the Court the Polish Government have been unsuccessful in their pleading that a civil action under Article 417 of the Civil Code created an effective remedy in length of proceedings cases. In particular, their arguments were rejected as being unsupported by any documentary evidence but merely based on the Polish Constitutional Court's *obiter dictum* interpretation of that provision in the judgment of 4 December 2001 and not on any relevant judicial practice (see, for instance, *Malasiewicz v Poland*, No 22072/02, § 32).

69. However, in view of the recent developments at domestic level, most notably the entry into force of the 2004 Act, the Court finds good reasons to reconsider its previous position.

To begin with, the Court finds that section 16 of the 2004 Act created a completely new legal situation in comparison to that subsisting previously. In contrast to the past, the possibility of seeking damages under Article 417 of the Civil Code for the protracted length of judicial proceedings which have terminated now has an explicit legal basis. Also, on a plain reading of section 16, it is clear that the hitherto existing ambiguity as to the application of Article 417 to cases involving compensation for a breach of the right to a hearing within a reasonable time has been removed.

70. The Court does not find any prima facie evidence in support of the applicant's argument that the remedy in question would be 'unrealistic' in this case. Thus, the applicant has not contested the availability of that remedy but confined himself to a bare statement that the remedy would not be effective, without substantiating his assertion in any way. Given that the 2004 Act entered into force on 17 September 2004, the absence of the established judicial practice in respect of Article 417 is not decisive (see, *mutatis mutandis*, *Charzyński v Poland* (dec.) No 15212/03, § 41, ECHR 2004-...). Nor does the fact that he cannot base his action on—in his view—the more favourable, amended provisions of Article 417 make his possible attempt to seek damages futile or purposeless.

71. It is true that the effectiveness of the remedy depends on the Polish civil courts' ability to handle such actions with special diligence and attention, especially in terms of the length of time taken for their determination. It is also true that the level of compensation awarded at domestic level may constitute an important element for the assessment of the adequacy of the remedy (see, *mutatis mutandis*, *Paulino Tomás v Portugal* (dec.) cited above). However, mere doubts as to the effective functioning of a newly created statutory remedy does not absolve the applicant from having recourse to it. It cannot be assumed by the Court that the Polish courts will not give proper effect to the new provision.

72. Having regard to the foregoing, the Court considers that from 17 September 2004, the date on which the 2004 Act entered into force, an action for damages based on Article 417 of the Civil Code acquired a sufficient level of certainty to become an 'effective remedy' within the meaning of Article 13 of the Convention for an applicant alleging a violation of the right to a hearing within a reasonable time in judicial proceedings in Poland.

73. There has accordingly been no violation of Article 13 in the present case.

In **Surmeli v Germany**, judgment of 8 June 2006, a unanimous Grand Chamber found a breach of Article 13 as German law failed to provide an effective remedy to enable the applicant to expedite civil proceedings, in which he was the complainant, or obtain compensation for the delays he had suffered. Whilst in the later case of **McFarlane v Ireland**, judgment of 10 September 2010, a large majority (12 votes to 5) of another Grand Chamber determined that Irish law had not provided the complainant with an effective remedy to deal with the delays in the criminal proceedings against him, which had taken ten-and-a-half years.

8   The full-time Court has interpreted Article 13 as requiring member States to provide a domestic remedy capable of preventing the execution of measures that are contrary to the Convention and whose effects are potentially irreversible. In **Conka v Belgium**, judgment of 5 February 2002, the applicants were Slovakian nationals who complained that their deportation from Belgium violated, *inter alia*, Article 13 in that they did not have such a remedy available to them. Under Belgian law they could have made an application to the Conseil d'Etat using a special extremely urgent procedure to challenge the lawfulness of the deportation orders made against them. However, the applicants contended that this procedure did not meet the requirements of Article 13 as making such an application did not automatically stay the deportation process until the Conseil d'Etat had reached a decision. The Chamber held that:

79. The Court considers that the notion of an effective remedy under Article 13 requires that the remedy may prevent the execution of measures that are contrary to the Convention and whose effects are potentially irreversible (see, *mutatis mutandis*, *Jabari* [v Turkey, 2000-VIII] § 50). Consequently, it is inconsistent with Article 13 for such measures to be executed before the national authorities have examined whether they are compatible with the Convention, although

Contracting States are afforded some discretion as to the manner in which they conform to their obligations under this provision (see *Chahal* [v UK, 1996-V] § 145).

...

81. An application for a stay of execution under the extremely urgent procedure is not suspensive either. The Government stressed, however, that the president of the division may at any time—even on bank holidays and on a few hours' notice, as frequently occurred in deportation cases—summon the parties to attend so that the application can be considered and, if appropriate, an order made for a stay of the deportation order before its execution. It will be noted that the authorities are not legally bound to await the Conseil d'Etat's decision before executing a deportation order. It is for that reason that the Conseil d'Etat has, for example, issued a practice direction directing that on an application for a stay under the extremely urgent procedure the registrar shall, at the request of the judge, contact the Aliens Office to establish the date scheduled for the repatriation and to make arrangements regarding the procedure to be followed as a consequence. Two remarks need to be made about that system.

82. Firstly, it is not possible to exclude the risk that in a system where stays of execution must be applied for and are discretionary they may be refused wrongly, in particular if it was subsequently to transpire that the court ruling on the merits has nonetheless to quash a deportation order for failure to comply with the Convention, for instance, if the applicant would be subjected to ill-treatment in the country of destination or be part of a collective expulsion. In such cases, the remedy exercised by the applicant would not be sufficiently effective for the purposes of Article 13.

83. Secondly, even if the risk of error is in practice negligible—a point which the Court is unable to verify, in the absence of any reliable evidence—it should be noted that the requirements of Article 13, and of the other provisions of the Convention, take the form of a guarantee and not of a mere statement of intent or a practical arrangement. That is one of the consequences of the rule of law, one of the fundamental principles of a democratic society, which is inherent in all the Articles of the Convention (see, *mutatis mutandis*, *Iatridis v Greece* [GC], No 31107/96, § 58, ECHR 1999-II).

However, it appears that the authorities are not required to defer execution of the deportation order while an application under the extremely urgent procedure is pending, not even for a minimum reasonable period to enable the Conseil d'Etat to decide the application. Furthermore, the onus is in practice on the Conseil d'Etat to ascertain the authorities' intentions regarding the proposed expulsions and to act accordingly, but there does not appear to be any obligation on it to do so. Lastly, it is merely on the basis of internal directions that the registrar of the Conseil d'Etat, acting on the instructions of a judge, contacts the authorities for that purpose, and there is no indication of what the consequences might be should he omit to do so. Ultimately, the alien has no guarantee that the Conseil d'Etat and the authorities will comply in every case with that practice, that the Conseil d'Etat will deliver its decision, or even hear the case, before his expulsion, or that the authorities will allow a minimum reasonable period of grace.

Each of those factors makes the implementation of the remedy too uncertain to enable the requirements of Article 13 to be satisfied.

...

85. In conclusion, the applicants did not have a remedy available that satisfied the requirements of Article 13 to air their complaint under Article 4 of Protocol No. 4. Accordingly, there has been a violation of Article 13 of the Convention...

Three judges dissented as they considered that applications under the extremely urgent procedure in practice had suspensive effect. The judgment in **Conka** was endorsed by the Grand Chamber in that later case of **Mamatkulov and Askarov v Turkey**, judgment of 4 February 2005.

9   Both the original and full-time Court have held that Article 13 does not require member States to establish a domestic remedy which enables persons to challenge the lawfulness of national laws for allegedly violating Convention rights (e.g. judicial review of primary legislation): see *Greens and MT v UK*, judgment of 23 November 2010 (p 56).

10   A unanimous Grand Chamber found a breach of Article 13 in conjunction with Article 3 regarding deficiencies in the Greek authorities' consideration of a claim for asylum: *MSS v Belgium and Greece*, judgment of 21 January 2011 (see p 210). The Court noted general defects in the domestic asylum process including the lack of information given to asylum seekers about the decision-making procedure, shortage of interpreters, lack of legal aid, and excessive delays in reaching determinations.

16 ARTICLE 14 PROHIBITION OF DISCRIMINATION

Whilst Article 14 can only be invoked in combination with another right or freedom contained in the Convention and its Protocols, the Court has from the beginning held that there can be a discriminatory breach of Article 14 even where the substantive Article has not been infringed (*Belgian Linguistic*). Furthermore, the Court over the years has identified an ever-growing catalogue of forms of differential treatment which States face heavy burdens in justifying under Article 14; including on the grounds of gender (*Abdulaziz*), illegitimacy (*Inze*), nationality (*Gaygusuz*), and sexual orientation (*Karner*). States are also required to treat persons in distinct circumstances differently when respecting their Convention rights (*Thlimmenos*). A recent major innovation by the Court has been to allow complainants alleging indirect discrimination to use statistical data to support their claims (*DH and others v Czech Republic*).

'Belgian Linguistic' case (No 2) A.6 (1968)
European Court of Human Rights

When Belgium gained independence in 1830 it was in practice composed of two areas, the Flemish (where the inhabitants generally spoke Dutch) and the Walloon (where the population generally spoke French). Many of the activities of government were conducted in French (e.g. judicial proceedings). Education was also dominated by the French language. Between 1900 and 1930 a Flemish separatist movement gained popularity and as a result legislation was passed, in 1932, to place the Dutch and French languages on an equal footing. During 1963 new legislation was enacted which divided the national territory into four linguistic regions: the Flemish, French, German, and the Brussels conurbation. In the first three regions the legislation required the exclusive use of the Flemish, French, and German languages in each of those regions for official purposes. Special arrangements were made for the bilingual communes on the edges of Brussels. The legislation provided that generally State-funded schools would only teach in the designated official language of their region and public funds would not be provided to private schools which did not also teach in the relevant official language. Six applications were made to the Commission challenging different aspects of the above legislation by French-speaking parents (of over 800 children) residing in Dutch-speaking areas of Belgium. The applicants alleged breaches of Article 2 of Protocol 1 (P1-2) right to education, Article 14, and Article 8. The Commission reported that the legislation was not in breach of the first sentence of P1–2 (9 votes to 3) or the second sentence of that Article (unanimously). But, *inter alia*, parts of the legislation applying to Louvain and communes on the periphery of Brussels which prevented certain children from attending French language schools, purely on the basis of their parents' place of residence, breached the first sentence of P1-2 read with Article 14.

8. According to Article 14 (art 14) of the Convention, the enjoyment of the rights and freedoms set forth therein shall be secured without discrimination ('sans distinction aucune') on the ground, *inter alia*, of language; and by the terms of Article 5 of the Protocol (P1-5), this same guarantee applies equally to the rights and freedoms set forth in this instrument. It follows that both Article 2 of the Protocol (P1-2) and Article 8 (art 8) of the Convention must be interpreted and applied by the Court not only in isolation but also having regard to the guarantee laid down in Article 14 (art 14+P1-2, art 14+8).

9. While it is true that this guarantee has no independent existence in the sense that under the terms of Article 14 (art 14) it relates solely to 'rights and freedoms set forth in the Convention', a measure which in itself is in conformity with the requirements of the Article enshrining the right or freedom in question may however infringe this Article when read in conjunction with Article 14 (art 14) for the reason that it is of a discriminatory nature.

Thus, persons subject to the jurisdiction of a Contracting State cannot draw from Article 2 of the Protocol (P1-2) the right to obtain from the public authorities the creation of a particular kind of educational establishment; nevertheless, a State which had set up such an establishment could not, in laying down entrance requirements, take discriminatory measures within the meaning of Article 14 (art 14).

To recall a further example, cited in the course of the proceedings, Article 6 (art 6) of the Convention does not compel States to institute a system of appeal courts. A State which does set up such courts consequently goes beyond its obligations under Article 6 (art 6). However it would violate that Article, read in conjunction with Article 14 (art 14+6), were it to debar certain persons from these remedies without a legitimate reason while making them available to others in respect of the same type of actions.

In such cases there would be a violation of a guaranteed right or freedom as it is proclaimed by the relevant Article read in conjunction with Article 14 (art 14). It is as though the latter formed an integral part of each of the Articles laying down rights and freedoms. No distinctions should be made in this respect according to the nature of these rights and freedoms and of their correlative obligations, and for instance as to whether the respect due to the right concerned implies positive action or mere abstention. This is, moreover, clearly shown by the very general nature of the terms employed in Article 14 (art 14): 'the enjoyment of the rights and freedoms set forth in this Convention shall be secured'.

10. In spite of the very general wording of the French version ('sans distinction aucune'), Article 14 (art 14) does not forbid every difference in treatment in the exercise of the rights and freedoms recognised. This version must be read in the light of the more restrictive text of the English version ('without discrimination'). In addition, and in particular, one would reach absurd results were one to give Article 14 (art 14) an interpretation as wide as that which the French version seems to imply. One would, in effect, be led to judge as contrary to the Convention every one of the many legal or administrative provisions which do not secure to everyone complete equality of treatment in the enjoyment of the rights and freedoms recognised. The competent national authorities are frequently confronted with situations and problems which, on account of differences inherent therein, call for different legal solutions; moreover, certain legal inequalities tend only to correct factual inequalities. The extensive interpretation mentioned above cannot consequently be accepted.

It is important, then, to look for the criteria which enable a determination to be made as to whether or not a given difference in treatment, concerning of course the exercise of one of the rights and freedoms set forth, contravenes Article 14 (art 14). On this question the Court, following the principles which may be extracted from the legal practice of a large number of democratic States, holds that the principle of equality of treatment is violated if the distinction has no objective and reasonable justification. The existence of such a justification must be assessed in relation to the aim and effects of the measure under consideration, regard being had to the principles which normally prevail in democratic societies. A difference of treatment in the exercise of a right laid down in the Convention must not only pursue a legitimate aim: Article 14 (art 14) is likewise violated when it is clearly established that there is no reasonable relationship of proportionality between the means employed and the aim sought to be realised.

In attempting to find out in a given case, whether or not there has been an arbitrary distinction, the Court cannot disregard those legal and factual features which characterise the life of the society in the State which, as a Contracting Party, has to answer for the measure in dispute. In so doing it cannot assume the rôle of the competent national authorities, for it would thereby lose sight of the subsidiary nature of the international machinery of collective enforcement established by the Convention. The national authorities remain free to choose the measures which they consider appropriate in those matters which are governed by the Convention. Review by the Court concerns only the conformity of these measures with the requirements of the Convention.

11. In the present case the Court notes that Article 14, even when read in conjunction with Article 2 of the Protocol (art 14+P1-2), does not have the effect of guaranteeing to a child or to his parent the right to obtain instruction in a language of his choice. The object of these two Articles (art 14+P1-2), read in conjunction, is more limited: it is to ensure that the right to education shall be secured by each Contracting Party to everyone within its jurisdiction without discrimination on the ground, for instance, of language.

This is the natural and ordinary meaning of Article 14 read in conjunction with Article 2 (art 14+P1-2). Furthermore, to interpret the two provisions as conferring on everyone within the jurisdiction of a State a right to obtain education in the language of his own choice would lead to absurd results, for it would be open to anyone to claim any language of instruction in any of the territories of the Contracting Parties.

The Court notes that, where the Contracting Parties intended to confer upon everyone within their jurisdiction specific rights with respect to the use or understanding of a language, as in Article 5 (2) and Article 6 (3) (a) and (e) (art 5-2, art 6-3-a, art 6-3-e) of the Convention, they did so in clear terms. It must be concluded that if they had intended to create for everyone within their jurisdiction a specific right with respect to the language of instruction, they would have done so in express terms in Article 2 of the Protocol (P1-2). For this reason also, the Court cannot attribute to Article 14, when read in conjunction with Article 2 of the Protocol (art 14+P1-2), a meaning which would secure to everyone within the jurisdiction of a Contracting Party a right to education conducted in the language of his own choice.

It remains true that, by virtue of Article 14 (art 14), the enjoyment of the right to education and the right to respect of family life, guaranteed respectively by Article 2 of the Protocol (P1-2) and Article 8 (art 8) of the Convention, are to be secured to everyone without discrimination on the ground, *inter alia*, of language.

12. In order to determine the questions referred to it, the Court will therefore examine whether or not there exist in the present case unjustified distinctions, that is to say discriminations, which affect the exercise of the rights enshrined in Article 2 of the Protocol and Article 8 of the Convention, read in conjunction with Article 14 (art 14+P1-2, art 14+8). In this examination, the Court will take into account the factual and legal features that characterise the situation in Belgium, which is a plurilingual State comprising several linguistic areas.

. . .

FOR THESE REASONS, THE COURT,

1. Holds, by eight votes to seven, that Section 7 (3) of the Act of 2nd August 1963 does not comply with the requirements of Article 14 of the Convention read in conjunction with the first sentence of Article 2 of the Protocol (art 14+P1-2), in so far as it prevents certain children, solely on the basis of the residence of their parents, from having access to the French-language schools existing in the six communes on the periphery of Brussels invested with a special status, of which Kraainem is one;

Reserves for the Applicants concerned the right, should the occasion arise, to apply for just satisfaction in regard to this particular point;

2. Holds, unanimously, with regard to the other points at issue, that there has been and there is no breach of any of the Articles of the Convention (art 8, art 14) and the Protocol (P1-2) invoked by the Applicants.

NOTES

1 The Court was composed of President Cassin and Judges: Verdross, Balladore Pallieri, Mosler, Zekia, Favre, Cremona, and Waldock. Judges Holmback, Maridakis, Rodenbourg, Ross, Wold, Wiarda, and Mast issued dissenting opinions in which they expressed the view that, *inter alia*, the special educational arrangements for the communes around Brussels did not place a disproportionate burden on the applicants and were not therefore in breach of the Convention.

2 The judgment reveals the symbiotic nature of the relationship between the prohibition on discrimination contained in Article 14 and the substantive rights/freedoms enshrined in other Articles of the Convention (and its Protocols). In determining if a difference in treatment with respect to Convention rights infringes Article 14 the Court will examine whether the distinction (a) pursues a legitimate aim and (b) if it is a proportionate measure.

3 The Court's interpretation of Article 14 in the above case makes it clear that there can be a breach of the prohibition on discrimination in circumstances where there is no violation of the related substantive Convention right. A dramatic example of this occurred in **Abdulaziz, Cabales and Balkandali v UK** A.94 (1985). The applicants were aliens lawfully settled in the UK. They complained that under the existing Immigration Rules their (alien) husbands were refused permission to enter and settle in the UK with them. The Court did not find a breach of the applicants' right to respect for their family life under Article 8 (see p 530). However, the applicants also contended that there had been discriminatory treatment which violated Article 14.

II. ALLEGED VIOLATION OF ARTICLE 14 TAKEN TOGETHER WITH ARTICLE 8 (ART 14+8)

A. INTRODUCTION

70. The applicants claimed that, as a result of unjustified differences of treatment in securing the right to respect for their family life, based on sex, race and also—in the case of Mrs Balkandali—birth, they had been victims of a violation of Article 14 of the Convention, taken together with Article 8 (art 14+8). The former Article (art 14) reads as follows:

'The enjoyment of the rights and freedoms set forth in [the] Convention shall be secured without discrimination on any ground such as sex, race, colour, language, religion, political or other opinion, national or social origin, association with a national minority, property, birth or other status.'

In the event that the Court should find Article 8 (art 8) to be applicable in the present case, the Government denied that there was any difference of treatment on the ground of race and submitted that since the differences of treatment on the ground of sex and of birth had objective and reasonable justifications and were proportionate to the aims pursued, they were compatible with Article 14 (art 14).

71. According to the Court's established case-law, Article 14 (art 14) complements the other substantive provisions of the Convention and the Protocols. It has no independent existence since it has effect solely in relation to 'the enjoyment of the rights and freedoms' safeguarded

by those provisions. Although the application of Article 14 (art 14) does not necessarily presuppose a breach of those provisions—and to this extent it is autonomous—there can be no room for its application unless the facts at issue fall within the ambit of one or more of the latter (see...*Rasmussen* judgment, Series A No 87, p 12, para 29).

The Court has found Article 8 (art 8) to be applicable...Although the United Kingdom was not obliged to accept Mr Abdulaziz, Mr Cabales and Mr Balkandali for settlement and the Court therefore did not find a violation of Article 8 (art 8) taken alone...the facts at issue nevertheless fall within the ambit of that Article (art 8)...

Article 14 (art 14) also is therefore applicable.

72. For the purposes of Article 14 (art 14), a difference of treatment is discriminatory if it 'has no objective and reasonable justification', that is, if it does not pursue a 'legitimate aim' or if there is not a 'reasonable relationship of proportionality between the means employed and the aim sought to be realised' (see, *inter alia*, the '*Belgian Linguistic*' judgment...)

The Contracting States enjoy a certain margin of appreciation in assessing whether and to what extent differences in otherwise similar situations justify a different treatment in law (see the above-mentioned *Rasmussen* judgment, ibid, p 15, para 40), but it is for the Court to give the final ruling in this respect.

73. In the particular circumstances of the case, the Court considers that it must examine in turn the three grounds on which it was alleged that a discriminatory difference of treatment was based.

B. ALLEGED DISCRIMINATION ON THE GROUND OF SEX

74. As regards the alleged discrimination on the ground of sex, it was not disputed that under the 1980 Rules it was easier for a man settled in the United Kingdom than for a woman so settled to obtain permission for his or her non-national spouse to enter or remain in the country for settlement....Argument centred on the question whether this difference had an objective and reasonable justification.

75. According to the Government, the difference of treatment complained of had the aim of limiting 'primary immigration'...and was justified by the need to protect the domestic labour market at a time of high unemployment. They placed strong reliance on the margin of appreciation enjoyed by the Contracting States in this area and laid particular stress on what they described as a statistical fact: men were more likely to seek work than women, with the result that male immigrants would have a greater impact than female immigrants on the said market. Furthermore, the reduction, attributed by the Government to the 1980 Rules, of approximately 5,700 per annum in the number of husbands accepted for settlement in the United Kingdom...was claimed to be significant. This was said to be so especially when the reduction was viewed in relation to its cumulative effect over the years and to the total number of acceptances for settlement.

This view was contested by the applicants. For them, the Government's plea ignored the modern role of women and the fact that men may be self-employed and also, as was exemplified by the case of Mr Balkandali...create rather than seek jobs. Furthermore, the Government's figure of 5,700 was said to be insignificant and, for a number of reasons, in any event unreliable...

76. The Government further contended that the measures in question were justified by the need to maintain effective immigration control, which benefited settled immigrants as well as the indigenous population. Immigration caused strains on society; the Government's aim was to advance public tranquillity, and a firm and fair control secured good relations between the different communities living in the United Kingdom.

To this, the applicants replied that the racial prejudice of the United Kingdom population could not be advanced as a justification for the measures.

77. In its report, the Commission considered that, when seen in the context of the immigration of other groups, annual emigration and unemployment and economic activity rates, the impact on the domestic labour market of an annual reduction of 2,000 (as then estimated by the Government) in the number of husbands accepted for settlement in the United Kingdom . . . was not of a size or importance to justify a difference of treatment on the ground of sex and the detrimental consequences thereof on the family life of the women concerned. Furthermore, the long-standing commitment to the reunification of the families of male immigrants, to which the Government had referred as a reason for accepting wives while excluding husbands, no longer corresponded to modern requirements as to the equal treatment of the sexes. Neither was it established that race relations or immigration controls were enhanced by the rules: they might create resentment in part of the immigrant population and it had not been shown that it was more difficult to limit abuses by non-national husbands than by other immigrant groups. The Commission unanimously concluded that there had been discrimination on the ground of sex, contrary to Article 14 (art 14), in securing the applicants' right to respect for family life, the application of the relevant rules being disproportionate to the purported aims.

At the hearings before the Court, the Commission's Delegate stated that this conclusion was not affected by the Government's revised figure (about 5,700) for the annual reduction in the number of husbands accepted for settlement.

78. The Court accepts that the 1980 Rules had the aim of protecting the domestic labour market. The fact that, as was suggested by the applicants, this aim might have been further advanced by the abolition of the 'United Kingdom ancestry' and the 'working holiday' rules . . . in no way alters this finding. Neither does the Court perceive any conclusive evidence to contradict it in the Parliamentary debates, on which the applicants also relied. It is true, as they pointed out, that unemployment in the United Kingdom in 1980 was lower than in subsequent years, but it had nevertheless already attained a significant level and there was a considerable increase as compared with previous years . . .

While the aforesaid aim was without doubt legitimate, this does not in itself establish the legitimacy of the difference made in the 1980 Rules as to the possibility for male and female immigrants settled in the United Kingdom to obtain permission for, on the one hand, their non-national wives or fiancées and, on the other hand, their non-national husbands or fiancés to enter or remain in the country.

Although the Contracting States enjoy a certain 'margin of appreciation' in assessing whether and to what extent differences in otherwise similar situations justify a different treatment, the scope of this margin will vary according to the circumstances, the subject-matter and its background (see the above-mentioned *Rasmussen* judgment, Series A No 87, p 15, para 40).

As to the present matter, it can be said that the advancement of the equality of the sexes is today a major goal in the member States of the Council of Europe. This means that very weighty reasons would have to be advanced before a difference of treatment on the ground of sex could be regarded as compatible with the Convention.

79. In the Court's opinion, the Government's arguments summarised in paragraph 75 above are not convincing.

It may be correct that on average there is a greater percentage of men of working age than of women of working age who are 'economically active' (for Great Britain 90 per cent of the men and 63 per cent of the women) and that comparable figures hold good for immigrants (according to the statistics, 86 per cent for men and 41 per cent for women for immigrants from the Indian sub-continent and 90 per cent for men and 70 per cent for women for immigrants from the West Indies and Guyana) . . .

Nevertheless, this does not show that similar differences in fact exist—or would but for the effect of the 1980 Rules have existed—as regards the respective impact on the United Kingdom labour market of immigrant wives and of immigrant husbands. In this connection, other factors must also be taken into account. Being 'economically active' does not always mean that one is seeking to be employed by someone else. Moreover, although a greater number of men than of women may be inclined to seek employment, immigrant husbands were already by far outnumbered, before the introduction of the 1980 Rules, by immigrant wives...many of whom were also 'economically active'. While a considerable proportion of those wives, in so far as they were 'economically active', were engaged in part-time work, the impact on the domestic labour market of women immigrants as compared with men ought not to be underestimated.

In any event, the Court is not convinced that the difference that may nevertheless exist between the respective impact of men and of women on the domestic labour market is sufficiently important to justify the difference of treatment, complained of by the applicants, as to the possibility for a person settled in the United Kingdom to be joined by, as the case may be, his wife or her husband.

80. In this context the Government stressed the importance of the effect on the immigration of husbands of the restrictions contained in the 1980 Rules, which had led, according to their estimate, to an annual reduction of 5,700 (rather than 2,000, as mentioned in the Commission's report) in the number of husbands accepted for settlement.

Without expressing a conclusion on the correctness of the figure of 5,700, the Court notes that in point of time the claimed reduction coincided with a significant increase in unemployment in the United Kingdom and that the Government accepted that some part of the reduction was due to economic conditions rather than to the 1980 Rules themselves...

In any event, for the reasons stated in paragraph 79 above, the reduction achieved does not justify the difference in treatment between men and women.

81. The Court accepts that the 1980 Rules also had, as the Government stated, the aim of advancing public tranquillity. However, it is not persuaded that this aim was served by the distinction drawn in those rules between husbands and wives.

82. There remains a more general argument advanced by the Government, namely that the United Kingdom was not in violation of Article 14 (art 14) by reason of the fact that it acted more generously in some respects—that is, as regards the admission of non-national wives and fiancées of men settled in the country—than the Convention required.

The Court cannot accept this argument. It would point out that Article 14 (art 14) is concerned with the avoidance of discrimination in the enjoyment of the Convention rights in so far as the requirements of the Convention as to those rights can be complied with in different ways. The notion of discrimination within the meaning of Article 14 (art 14) includes in general cases where a person or group is treated, without proper justification, less favourably than another, even though the more favourable treatment is not called for by the Convention.

83. The Court thus concludes that the applicants have been victims of discrimination on the ground of sex, in violation of Article 14 taken together with Article 8 (art 14+8).

C. ALLEGED DISCRIMINATION ON THE GROUND OF RACE

84. As regards the alleged discrimination on the ground of race, the applicants relied on the opinion of a minority of the Commission. They referred, inter alia, to the whole history of and background to the United Kingdom immigration legislation...and to the Parliamentary debates on the immigration rules.

In contesting this claim, the Government submitted that the 1980 Rules were not racially motivated, their aim being to limit 'primary immigration'...

A majority of the Commission concluded that there had been no violation of Article 14 (art 14) under this head. Most immigration policies—restricting, as they do, free entry—differentiated on the basis of people's nationality, and indirectly their race, ethnic origin and possibly their colour. While a Contracting State could not implement 'policies of a purely racist nature', to give preferential treatment to its nationals or to persons from countries with which it had the closest links did not constitute 'racial discrimination'. The effect in practice of the United Kingdom rules did not mean that they were abhorrent on the grounds of racial discrimination, there being no evidence of an actual difference of treatment on grounds of race.

A minority of the Commission, on the other hand, noted that the main effect of the rules was to prevent immigration from the New Commonwealth and Pakistan. This was not coincidental: the legislative history showed that the intention was to 'lower the number of coloured immigrants'. By their effect and purpose, the rules were indirectly racist and there had thus been a violation of Article 14 (art 14) under this head in the cases of Mrs Abdulaziz and Mrs Cabales.

85. The Court agrees in this respect with the majority of the Commission.

The 1980 Rules, which were applicable in general to all 'non-patrials' wanting to enter and settle in the United Kingdom, did not contain regulations differentiating between persons or groups on the ground of their race or ethnic origin. The rules included in paragraph 2 a specific instruction to immigration officers to carry out their duties without regard to the race, colour or religion of the intending entrant...and they were applicable across the board to intending immigrants from all parts of the world, irrespective of their race or origin.

As the Court has already accepted, the main and essential purpose of the 1980 Rules was to curtail 'primary immigration' in order to protect the labour market at a time of high unemployment. This means that their reinforcement of the restrictions on immigration was grounded not on objections regarding the origin of the non-nationals wanting to enter the country but on the need to stem the flow of immigrants at the relevant time.

That the mass immigration against which the rules were directed consisted mainly of would-be immigrants from the New Commonwealth and Pakistan, and that as a result they affected at the material time fewer white people than others, is not a sufficient reason to consider them as racist in character: it is an effect which derives not from the content of the 1980 Rules but from the fact that, among those wishing to immigrate, some ethnic groups outnumbered others.

The Court concludes from the foregoing that the 1980 Rules made no distinction on the ground of race and were therefore not discriminatory on that account....

86. The Court accordingly holds that the applicants have not been victims of discrimination on the ground of race.

D. ALLEGED DISCRIMINATION ON THE GROUND OF BIRTH

87. Mrs Balkandali claimed that she had also been the victim of discrimination on the ground of birth, in that, as between women citizens of the United Kingdom and Colonies settled in the United Kingdom, only those born or having a parent born in that country could, under the 1980 Rules, have their non-national husband accepted for settlement there...

It was not disputed that the 1980 Rules established a difference of treatment on the ground of birth, argument being centred on the question whether it had an objective and reasonable justification.

In addition to relying on the Commission's report, Mrs Balkandali submitted that the elimination of this distinction from subsequent immigration rules...demonstrated that it was not previously justified.

The Government maintained that the difference in question was justified by the concern to avoid the hardship which women having close ties to the United Kingdom would encounter if, on marriage, they were obliged to move abroad in order to remain with their husbands.

The Commission considered that, notwithstanding the subsequent elimination of this difference, the general interest and the possibly temporary nature of immigration rules required it to express an opinion. It took the view that a difference of treatment based on the mere accident of birth, without regard to the individual's personal circumstances or merits, constituted discrimination in violation of Article 14 (art 14).

88. The Court is unable to share the Commission's opinion. The aim cited by the Government is unquestionably legitimate, for the purposes of Article 14 (art 14). It is true that a person who, like Mrs Balkandali, has been settled in a country for several years may also have formed close ties with it, even if he or she was not born there. Nevertheless, there are in general persuasive social reasons for giving special treatment to those whose link with a country stems from birth within it. The difference of treatment must therefore be regarded as having had an objective and reasonable justification and, in particular, its results have not been shown to transgress the principle of proportionality. This conclusion is not altered by the fact that the immigration rules were subsequently amended on this point.

89. The Court thus holds that Mrs Balkandali was not the victim of discrimination on the ground of birth.

...

FOR THESE REASONS, THE COURT UNANIMOUSLY

Holds that Article 8 was applicable in the present case but that, taken alone, it has not been violated;

Holds that Article 14 was applicable in the present case;

Holds that Article 14 taken together with Article 8 has been violated by reason of discrimination against each of the applicants on the ground of sex; ...

The judgment is very important for its ruling on the Court's attitude towards differences of treatment based solely on the gender of persons. Paragraph 78 of the report indicates that States face a heavy burden in justifying such differences under the requirements of Article 14.

4   In *Schmidt v Germany* A.291-B (1994), a man challenged the legal duty imposed on men living in Baden-Wurttemberg to serve in the local fire brigade or pay a financial contribution in lieu of service. He claimed that the imposition of such burdens on men (women living in the *Land* were not obliged to serve in the fire brigade or pay the levy) amounted to a violation of his rights under, *inter alia*, Article 14 taken together with Article 4(3)(d) (this provision allows States to require persons to undertake 'any work or service which forms part of normal civic obligations'). The Court, by 6 votes to 3, upheld the applicant's assertion of unlawful discrimination.

25. According to the applicant, the Contracting States do not enjoy any margin of appreciation as regards equality of the sexes. He argued that service in the fire brigade was comparable for men and for women and that account could be taken of the biological differences between the two sexes by a sensible division of the various tasks. The concern to protect women could not in itself justify a difference of treatment in this context. As at 31 December 1991, 68,612 women had served in fire brigades in Germany and even in Baden-Württemberg the fire brigades had accepted women since 1978. The financial contribution was of a purely fiscal nature, as in Baden-Württemberg no man had ever been called upon to serve. There was in any case discrimination since women were just as capable as men of paying the levy in question.

26. The Commission in substance accepted the applicant's argument.

27. In the Government's view, on the other hand, the difference of treatment is based on objective and reasonable grounds. Fire brigade duty is a traditional civic obligation in Baden-Württemberg, defined by the Federal Constitutional Court as a 'genuine and potential obligation to perform a public duty'. The Government maintained that, in making this duty compulsory solely for the male sex, the legislature had taken account of the specific requirements of service in the fire brigade and the physical and mental characteristics of women. The sole aim which it had pursued in this

respect was the protection of women. The financial contribution was purely compensatory in nature.

28. The Court notes that some German Länder do not impose different obligations for the two sexes in this field and that even in Baden-Württemberg women are accepted for voluntary service in the fire brigade.

Irrespective of whether or not there can nowadays exist any justification for treating men and women differently as regards compulsory service in the fire brigade, what is finally decisive in the present case is that the obligation to perform such service is exclusively one of law and theory. In view of the continuing existence of a sufficient number of volunteers, no male person is in practice obliged to serve in a fire brigade. The financial contribution has—not in law but in fact—lost its compensatory character and has become the only effective duty. In the imposition of a financial burden such as this, a difference of treatment on the ground of sex can hardly be justified.

29. There has accordingly been a violation of Article 14 taken in conjunction with Article 4 para 3 (d) (art 1414(3)(d)) of the Convention....

An example of the full-time Court finding that a man had suffered gender discrimination contrary to Article 14 occurred in *Willis v UK*, judgment of 11 June 2002. The applicant and his wife had two children and for most of their married life the wife was the major income earner for the family. During her employment she paid full social security contributions. Sadly, the wife developed cancer and in November 1995 the applicant gave up his work to care for her. In June 1996 the wife died. The applicant then applied to the Benefits Agency for the payment of financial benefits equivalent to those that would have been paid to a widow who had a family to bring up (these included a widow's lump sum payment of £1,000 and a widowed mother's allowance of £72.50 per week plus sums for each child). The Agency informed the applicant that such benefits did not exist for widowers. He complained to the Court alleging a breach of Article 14 in conjunction with Article 1 of Protocol 1. The Chamber, unanimously, determined that the widow's benefits were pecuniary rights that fell within the ambit of Article 1. As to the application of Article 14:

40. The Court notes that the applicant's wife worked throughout the best part of her marriage to the applicant and during that time paid full social-security contributions as an employed earner in exactly the same way as a man in her position would have done. It notes also that the applicant gave up work to nurse his wife and care for their children on 3 November 1995 and that, being a relatively low earner, it proved uneconomic for him to return to work on a part-time basis following his wife's death. Despite all this, the applicant was entitled to significantly fewer financial benefits upon his wife's death than he would have been if he were a woman and she had been a man.

41. The Court observes also that the authorities' refusal to grant the applicant a widow's payment and a widowed mother's allowance was based exclusively on the fact that he was a man. It has not been argued that the applicant failed to satisfy any of the other statutory conditions for the award of those benefits and he was accordingly in a like situation to women as regards his entitlement to them.

42. The Court considers that the difference in treatment between men and women as regards entitlement to the widow's payment and widowed mother's allowance, of which the applicant was a victim, was not based on any 'objective and reasonable justification'.

43. There has accordingly been a violation of Article 14 of the Convention taken in conjunction with Article 1 of Protocol No 1.

The Welfare Reform and Pensions Act 1999 replaced the widow's payment with a bereavement payment and the widowed mother's allowance with the widowed parent's allowance. Both the new benefits were payable to men and women who met the qualifying conditions.

5 The Court has taken a similar stance in regard to discriminatory treatment based on the legitimacy of a person's birth. For example, in ***Inze v Austria*** A.126 (1987), the applicant had been born out of wedlock and the Carinthian Hereditary Farms Act 1903 provided that precedence should be given to legitimate children over illegitimate ones when determining the order of succession to such properties. Applying the above legislation the Austrian courts refused to recognize the applicant's claim to his deceased mother's farm (the farm passed to the applicant's legitimate younger half-brother). The applicant complained to the Commission alleging a breach of Article 14 taken in conjunction with Article 1 of Protocol 1 (the right to property). By a majority, 6 votes to 4, the Commission found a violation. The Court was unanimous in holding that:

41....the Convention is a living instrument, to be interpreted in the light of present-day conditions (see, among various authorities, the *Johnston* judgment of 18 December 1986, Series A No 112, p 25, § 53). The question of equality between children born in and children born out of wedlock as regards their civil rights is today given importance in the member States of the Council of Europe. This is shown by the 1975 European Convention on the Legal Status of Children born out of Wedlock, which is presently in force in respect of nine member States of the Council of Europe. It was ratified by the Republic of Austria on 28 May 1980, with a reservation...which is not relevant to the facts of the present case. Very weighty reasons would accordingly have to be advanced before a difference of treatment on the ground of birth out of wedlock could be regarded as compatible with the Convention (see, *mutatis mutandis*, the *Abdulaziz, Cabales and Balkandali* judgment, Series A no 94, p 38, § 78).

42. The Government advanced the following arguments. The criteria for selecting the principal heir were a consequence of the fact that only one heir was entitled to take over a hereditary farm. Furthermore, those criteria were based on objective reasons; in particular, the precedence given to legitimate children corresponded to what could be presumed to be the deceased's intentions. In any event, the provisions of section 7(2) of the Provincial Act only applied to intestate succession and an owner who objected thereto could always make a will.

In addition, the birth criterion reflected the convictions of the rural population and the social and economic condition of farmers. Again, illegitimate children, unlike legitimate children, were usually not brought up on their parents' farm and did not have close links with it.

Finally, one had to bear in mind the special treatment reserved to the surviving spouse, who was normally entitled to stay on the farm and to be maintained by the principal heir.

43. Like the Commission, the Court is not persuaded by the Government's arguments. Most of them are based on general and abstract considerations—concerning such matters as the deceased's intentions, the place where illegitimate children are brought up and the surviving spouse's relations with his or her legitimate children—which may sometimes not reflect the real situation. For instance, Mr Inze was brought up and had worked on the farm in question until the age of 23...Those considerations cannot justify a rule of this kind.

While it is true that the applicant's mother could have made a will in his favour, this does not alter the fact that, in the instant case, he was deprived by law of the possibility of taking over the farm on her death intestate.

44. The Court also considers that the argument relating to the convictions of the rural population merely reflects the traditional outlook. The Government themselves have recognised the ongoing developments in rural society and have accordingly prepared a Bill which takes them into account. In future, the attribution of a hereditary farm is to be based on objective circumstances, notably training for running farms and the fact of having been brought up on the particular property...

The Court wishes to make it clear that these proposed amendments cannot in themselves be taken as demonstrating that the previous rules were contrary to the Convention. They do however show that the aim of the legislation in question could also have been achieved by applying criteria other than that based on birth in or out of wedlock.

45. The Court therefore concludes that there was a breach of Article 14 of the Convention, taken together with Article 1 of Protocol No 1 (art 14+P1-1). . . .

Therefore, the Court is very suspicious of any differential application of Convention rights based upon illegitimacy.

6   The Court has also adopted an identical approach in respect of differential treatment affecting Convention rights based upon a person's nationality. For example, in *Gaygusuz v Austria*, 1996-IV, the applicant was a Turkish national who had worked in Austria between 1973 and 1984. Up until March 1987 he received a number of social security benefits, including unemployment and sickness payments, from the Austrian authorities. He then applied for an advance on his pension in the form of emergency assistance. The authorities refused his request as the legislation required applicants to be Austrian nationals in order to be eligible for such assistance. In September 1987 the applicant returned to live in Turkey. Mr Gaygusuz complained to the Commission alleging, *inter alia*, a violation of Article 1 of Protocol 1 in combination with Article 14. A unanimous Commission upheld his claim. Likewise the Court was united in finding a violation of these Articles.

The Court considers that the right to emergency assistance—in so far as provided for in the applicable legislation—is a pecuniary right for the purposes of P1-1. That provision (P1-1) is therefore applicable without it being necessary to rely solely on the link between entitlement to emergency assistance and the obligation to pay 'taxes or other contributions'. . . .

Moreover the Contracting States enjoy a certain margin of appreciation in assessing whether and to what extent differences in otherwise similar situations justify a different treatment. However, very weighty reasons would have to be put forward before the Court could regard a difference of treatment based exclusively on the ground of nationality as compatible with the Convention. . . .

It considers, like the Commission, that the difference in treatment between Austrians and non-Austrians as regards entitlement to emergency assistance, of which Mr Gaygusuz was a victim, is not based on any 'objective and reasonable justification. [Paras 41, 42, and 50.]

7   The Court found discrimination based upon religion to have occurred in *Hoffmann v Austria* A.255-C (1993). The applicant had married a fellow Roman Catholic in 1980. Subsequently, they had two children who were baptized as Roman Catholics. The applicant left the Roman Catholic church and became a Jehovah's Witness. In 1983 the applicant began divorce proceedings against her (former) husband. While those proceedings were pending the applicant left her husband and took their children with her. Later the lower courts granted the applicant custody over the children. However, the Supreme Court granted parental rights to the husband as the children were being brought up in accordance with the applicant's new religious principles (governing such matters as opposition to blood transfusions). The applicant complained to the Commission alleging, *inter alia*, a breach of Article 8 in conjunction with Article 14 due to the denial of custody over the children because of her religion. The Commission, by 8 votes to 6, found a breach of those Articles. A closely divided Court (5 votes to 4) upheld the applicant's complaint.

The European Court therefore accepts that there has been a difference in treatment and that that difference was on the ground of religion; this conclusion is supported by the tone and phrasing of the Supreme Court's considerations regarding the practical consequences of the applicant's religion....

Notwithstanding any possible arguments to the contrary, a distinction based essentially on a difference in religion alone is not acceptable. [Paras 33 and 36.]

The dissentients generally considered that the Supreme Court had not discriminated against the applicant on the grounds of her religion, but had attached significance to the effects of the applicant's religious beliefs on the welfare of her children. This disagreement within the Court reveals the potentially narrow boundary between lawful differential treatment and unlawful discrimination under Article 14.

8   A unanimous Grand Chamber found unlawful religious discrimination to have taken place in *Thlimmenos v Greece*, judgment of 6 April 2000. The applicant was also a Jehovah's Witness. During 1983 he had been convicted, and sentenced to four years' imprisonment, by a military tribunal for refusing to wear a military uniform. His refusal was motivated by the pacifist beliefs of his religion. In 1988 the applicant sat a public examination for entry into the profession of chartered accountancy (he came second out of 60 candidates). However, the Executive Board of the Greek Institute of Chartered Accountants refused to admit him to the profession because of his earlier conviction. Subsequently, the applicant complained to the Commission alleging, *inter alia*, a breach of Article 14 in conjunction with Article 9. By 22 votes to 6, the Commission upheld the complaint.

41. The Court notes that the applicant was not appointed a chartered accountant as a result of his past conviction for insubordination consisting in his refusal to wear the military uniform. He was thus treated differently from the other persons who had applied for that post on the ground of his status as a convicted person. The Court considers that such difference of treatment does not generally come within the scope of Article 14 in so far as it relates to access to a particular profession, the right to freedom of profession not being guaranteed by the Convention.

42. However, the applicant does not complain of the distinction that the rules governing access to the profession make between convicted persons and others. His complaint rather concerns the fact that in the application of the relevant law no distinction is made between persons convicted of offences committed exclusively because of their religious beliefs and persons convicted of other offences. In this context the Court notes that the applicant is a member of the Jehovah's Witnesses, a religious group committed to pacifism, and that there is nothing in the file to disprove the applicant's claim that he refused to wear the military uniform only because he considered that his religion prevented him from doing so. In essence, the applicant's argument amounts to saying that he is discriminated against in the exercise of his freedom of religion, as guaranteed by Article 9 of the Convention, in that he was treated like any other person convicted of a felony although his own conviction resulted from the very exercise of this freedom. Seen in this perspective, the Court accepts that the 'set of facts' complained of by the applicant—his being treated as a person convicted of a felony for the purposes of an appointment to a chartered accountant's post despite the fact that the offence for which he had been convicted was prompted by his religious beliefs—'falls within the ambit of a Convention provision', namely Article 9.

43. In order to reach this conclusion, the Court, as opposed to the Commission, does not find it necessary to examine whether the applicant's initial conviction and the authorities' subsequent refusal to appoint him amounted to interference with his rights under Article 9 § 1. In particular, the Court does not have to address, in the present case, the question whether, notwithstanding the wording of Article 4 § 3 (b), the imposition of such sanctions on conscientious objectors to compulsory military service may in itself infringe the right to freedom of thought, conscience and religion guaranteed by Article 9 § 1.

44. The Court has so far considered that the right under Article 14 not to be discriminated against in the enjoyment of the rights guaranteed under the Convention is violated when States treat differently persons in analogous situations without providing an objective and reasonable justification (see the *Inze* judgment . . . § 41). However, the Court considers that this is not the only facet of the prohibition of discrimination in Article 14. The right not to be discriminated against in the enjoyment of the rights guaranteed under the Convention is also violated when States without an objective and reasonable justification fail to treat differently persons whose situations are significantly different.

45. It follows that Article 14 of the Convention is of relevance to the applicant's complaint and applies in the circumstances of this case in conjunction with Article 9 thereof.

46. The next question to be addressed is whether Article 14 of the Convention has been complied with. According to its case-law, the Court will have to examine whether the failure to treat the applicant differently from other persons convicted of a felony pursued a legitimate aim. If it did the Court will have to examine whether there was a reasonable relationship of proportionality between the means employed and the aim sought to be realised (see the *Inze* judgment cited above, ibid).

47. The Court considers that, as a matter of principle, States have a legitimate interest to exclude some offenders from the profession of chartered accountant. However, the Court also considers that, unlike other convictions for serious criminal offences, a conviction for refusing on religious or philosophical grounds to wear the military uniform cannot imply any dishonesty or moral turpitude likely to undermine the offender's ability to exercise this profession. Excluding the applicant on the ground that he was an unfit person was not, therefore, justified. The Court takes note of the Government's argument that persons who refuse to serve their country must be appropriately punished. However, it also notes that the applicant did serve a prison sentence for his refusal to wear the military uniform. In these circumstances, the Court considers that imposing a further sanction on the applicant was disproportionate. It follows that the applicant's exclusion from the profession of chartered accountants did not pursue a legitimate aim. As a result, the Court finds that there existed no objective and reasonable justification for not treating the applicant differently from other persons convicted of a felony.

48. It is true that the authorities had no option under the law but to refuse to appoint the applicant a chartered accountant. However, contrary to what the Government's representative appeared to argue at the hearing, this cannot absolve the respondent State from responsibility under the Convention. The Court has never excluded that legislation may be found to be in direct breach of the Convention (see, *inter alia, Chassagnou v France*, ECHR 1999-III). In the present case the Court considers that it was the State having enacted the relevant legislation which violated the applicant's right not to be discriminated against in the enjoyment of his right under Article 9 of the Convention. That State did so by failing to introduce appropriate exceptions to the rule barring persons convicted of a felony from the profession of chartered accountants.

49. The Court concludes, therefore, that there has been a violation of Article 14 of the Convention taken in conjunction with Article 9.

Apart from the clear finding of religious discrimination, the judgment is highly significant for the expansion of the concept of discrimination under the Convention elaborated in paragraph 44. Now, the failure to treat persons in different situations differently will also potentially be unlawful. This is the inverse aspect of the established form of discrimination under Article 14 (of treating persons in similar situations differently). States will, therefore, have to be more sensitive to the particular circumstances of individuals when legislating or administering programmes which impinge upon Convention rights.

An example of a situation where a State was able to justify refusing to accord different treatment to a person occurred in **Pretty v UK**, p 118. In respect of her complaint under

Article 14 the applicant contended that *Thlimmenos* obliged the domestic authorities to enable Mrs Pretty's husband lawfully to help her to commit suicide, because Mrs Pretty's physical disabilities prevented her from undertaking such an act on her own. The Chamber, unanimously, ruled that:

89. Even if the principle derived from the *Thlimmenos* case is applied to the applicant's situation however, there is, in the Court's view, objective and reasonable justification for not distinguishing in law between those who are and those who are not physically capable of committing suicide. Under Article 8 of the Convention, the Court has found that there are sound reasons for not introducing into the law exceptions to cater for those who are deemed not to be vulnerable. Similar cogent reasons exist under Article 14 for not seeking to distinguish between those who are able and those who are unable to commit suicide unaided. The borderline between the two categories will often be a very fine one and to seek to build into the law an exemption for those judged to be incapable of committing suicide would seriously undermine the protection of life which the 1961 Act was intended to safeguard and greatly increase the risk of abuse.

90. Consequently, there has been no violation of Article 14 in the present case.

9   The full-time Court has ruled that discriminatory treatment based upon a person's sexual orientation is contrary to Article 14. In *Salgueiro Da Silva Mouta v Portugal*, judgment of 21 December 1999, the applicant separated from his wife in 1990 and began living with a man in a homosexual relationship. During the following year, as part of divorce proceedings, the applicant agreed with his wife that she would have parental responsibility for their daughter but that he was to have contact rights in respect of his daughter. However, his ex-wife did not enable the applicant to have contact with his daughter. He then applied to the Lisbon Family Court for an order assigning parental responsibility to him. The Family Court granted such an order and the daughter lived with the applicant and his male partner for six months, until she was allegedly abducted by her mother. The applicant's ex-wife appealed against the Family Court decision to the Lisbon Court of Appeal which reversed the lower court's judgment because:

The fact that the child's father, who has come to terms with his homosexuality, wishes to live with another man is a reality which has to be accepted. It is well known that society is becoming more and more tolerant of such situations. However, it cannot be argued that an environment of this kind is the healthiest and best suited to a child's psychological, social and mental development, especially given the dominant model in our society, as the appellant rightly points out. The child should live in a family environment, a traditional Portuguese family, which is certainly not the set-up her father has decided to enter into, since he is living with another man as if they were man and wife. It is not our task here to determine whether homosexuality is or is not an illness or whether it is a sexual orientation towards persons of the same sex. In both cases it is an abnormality and children should not grow up in the shadow of abnormal situations; such are the dictates of human nature and let us remember that it is [the applicant] himself who acknowledged this when, in his initial application of 5 July 1990, he stated that he had definitively left the marital home to go and live with a boyfriend, a decision which is not normal according to common criteria.

The applicant complained to the Strasbourg Court that the decision to award parental responsibility to his ex-wife was based upon his sexual orientation and that constituted a violation of Article 14 combined with Article 8. The Chamber, unanimously, held that:

28....The Court is accordingly forced to conclude that there was a difference of treatment between the applicant and M.'s mother which was based on the applicant's sexual orientation, a concept which is undoubtedly covered by Article 14 of the Convention. The Court reiterates in that connection that the list set out in that provision is illustrative and not exhaustive, as is shown by the words 'any ground such as' (in French 'notamment') (see the *Engel and Others v the Netherlands* judgment of 8 June 1976, Series A No 22, pp 30–1, § 72).

2. Justification for the difference in treatment

29. In accordance with the case-law of the Convention institutions, a difference of treatment is discriminatory within the meaning of Article 14 if it has no objective and reasonable justification, that is if it does not pursue a legitimate aim or if there is not a reasonable relationship of proportionality between the means employed and the aim sought to be realised (see the *Karlheinz Schmidt v Germany* judgment of 18 July 1994, Series A No 291-B, pp 32–3, § 24).

30. The decision of the Court of Appeal undeniably pursued a legitimate aim, namely the protection of the health and rights of the child; it must now be examined whether the second requirement was also satisfied.

31. In the applicant's submission, the wording of the judgment clearly showed that the decision to award parental responsibility to the mother was based mainly on the father's sexual orientation, which inevitably gave rise to discrimination against him in relation to the other parent.

32. The Government submitted that the decision in question had, on the contrary, merely touched on the applicant's homosexuality. The considerations of the Court of Appeal to which the applicant referred, when viewed in context, were merely sociological, or even statistical, observations. Even if certain passages of the judgment could arguably have been worded differently, clumsy or unfortunate expressions could not in themselves amount to a violation of the Convention.

...

35. It is the Court's view that the above passages from the judgment in question, far from being merely clumsy or unfortunate as the Government maintained, or mere obiter dicta, suggest, quite to the contrary, that the applicant's homosexuality was a factor which was decisive in the final decision. That conclusion is supported by the fact that the Court of Appeal, when ruling on the applicant's right to contact, warned him not to adopt conduct which might make the child realise that her father was living with another man 'in conditions resembling those of man and wife' (ibid).

36. The Court is therefore forced to find, in the light of the foregoing, that the Court of Appeal made a distinction based on considerations regarding the applicant's sexual orientation, a distinction which is not acceptable under the Convention (see, *mutatis mutandis*, the *Hoffmann* judgment cited above, p 60, § 36).

The Court cannot therefore find that a reasonable relationship of proportionality existed between the means employed and the aim pursued; there has accordingly been a violation of Article 8 taken in conjunction with Article 14.

In the later case of **L and V v Austria**, judgment of 9 January 2003, the Court strengthened its protection against discriminatory treatment based upon sexual orientation by requiring 'particularly serious reasons' to justify the use of this criterion. The applicants had whilst in their twenties engaged in consensual homosexual acts with males between the ages of 14 and 18. Under Austrian law, prior to 2002, it was a criminal offence for males of 19 and over to engage in consensual homosexual acts with males aged between 14 and 18. Consensual heterosexual or lesbian acts between adults and persons over the age of 14 were not criminal at that time in Austria. The applicants complained to Strasbourg that their convictions by the Austrian courts, for which they were given suspended prison sentences, violated Article 14 combined with Article 8. The unanimous Chamber determined that:

49. What is decisive is whether there was an objective and reasonable justification why young men in the 14 to 18 age bracket needed protection against sexual relationships with adult men,

while young women in the same age bracket did not need such protection against relations with either adult men or women. In this connection the Court reiterates that the scope of the margin of appreciation left to the Contracting State will vary according to the circumstances, the subject matter and the background; in this respect, one of the relevant factors may be the existence or non-existence of common ground between the laws of the Contracting States...

50. In the present case the applicants pointed out, and this has not been contested by the Government, that there is an ever growing European consensus to apply equal ages of consent for heterosexual, lesbian and homosexual relations. Similarly, the Commission observed in *Sutherland* [Commission's report of 1 July 1997] that 'equality of treatment in respect of the age of consent is now recognised by the great majority of member States of the Council of Europe' (*loc cit*, § 59).

51. The Government relied on the Constitutional Court's judgment of 3 October 1989, which had considered Article 209 of the Criminal Code necessary to avoid 'a dangerous strain...be[ing] placed by homosexual experiences upon the sexual development of young males'. However, this approach has been outdated by the 1995 parliamentary debate on a possible repeal of that provision. As was rightly pointed out by the applicants, the vast majority of experts who gave evidence in Parliament clearly expressed themselves in favour of an equal age of consent, finding in particular that sexual orientation was in most cases established before the age of puberty and that the theory that male adolescents were 'recruited' into homosexuality had thus been disproved. Notwithstanding its knowledge of these changes in the scientific approach to the issue, Parliament decided in November 1996, that is, shortly before the applicants' convictions, in January and February 1997 respectively, to keep Article 209 on the statute book.

52. To the extent that Article 209 of the Criminal Code embodied a predisposed bias on the part of a heterosexual majority against a homosexual minority, these negative attitudes cannot of themselves be considered by the Court to amount to sufficient justification for the differential treatment any more than similar negative attitudes towards those of a different race, origin or colour...

53. In conclusion, the Court finds that the Government have not offered convincing and weighty reasons justifying the maintenance in force of Article 209 of the Criminal Code and, consequently, the applicants' convictions under this provision.

54. Accordingly, there has been a violation of Article 14 of the Convention taken in conjunction with Article 8.

A similar analysis was applied in **SL v Austria**, judgment of 9 January 2003, in respect of a 15-year-old male who complained that the above legislation prohibited him from engaging in consensual homosexual acts. In 2002 the Austrian Parliament amended the Criminal Code to prohibit sexual acts (heterosexual, homosexual, or lesbian) with persons under the age of 16 if that person is not mature enough to understand the meaning of the act.

The Commission opinion in **Sutherland** is examined at p 491.

In **Karner v Austria**, judgment of 24 July 2003, the Court treated differences of treatment on the basis of sexual orientation in the same way as differences on the basis of gender with the consequence that the respondent State was accorded a 'narrow' margin of appreciation when the Court examined if Article 14 had been breached. The applicant (who died after he had made his application to Strasbourg) had lived for a number of years with a homosexual partner in a flat rented by the latter. When the latter died the landlord brought proceedings against the applicant to terminate the tenancy. The applicant sought to rely on the statutory right to succeed to a tenancy given to a deceased tenant's 'life companion'. The Supreme Court ruled that that phrase did not apply to persons of the same sex. Before the Strasbourg Court the Austrian Government accepted that the applicant had been treated differently on the grounds of his sexual orientation, however the Government argued that this had been as a result of the reasonable justification that domestic law aimed to protect the traditional family. The Court (the Austrian *ad hoc* Judge dissented on the ground that as the applicant was deceased the case should have been struck-out) concluded that the applicant's claim fell within the applicant's right to respect for his home (under Article 8). As for the Government's submission in respect of Article 14:

41. The aim of protecting the family in the traditional sense is rather abstract and a broad variety of concrete measures may be used to implement it. In cases in which the margin of appreciation afforded to member States is narrow, as the position where there is a difference in treatment based on sex or sexual orientation, the principle of proportionality does not merely require that the measure chosen is in principle suited for realising the aim sought. It must also be shown that it was necessary to exclude persons living in a homosexual relationship from the scope of application of Section 14 of the Rent Act in order to achieve that aim. The Court cannot see that the Government has advanced any arguments that would allow of such a conclusion.

42. Accordingly, the Court finds that the Government have not offered convincing and weighty reasons justifying the narrow interpretation of Section 14(3) of the Rent Act that prevented a surviving partner of a couple of the same sex from relying on that provision.

43. Thus, there has been a violation of Article 14 of the Convention, taken together with Article 8.

10   A Grand Chamber adopted a more cautious approach than the original Chamber to the examination of whether there had been a racially motivated killing by military personnel in *Nachova and Others v Bulgaria*, judgment of 6 July 2005, see p 141.

1. Whether the respondent State is liable for deprivation of life on the basis of the victims' race or ethnic origin

144. The Court has established above that agents of the respondent State unlawfully killed Mr Angelov and Mr Petkov in violation of Article 2 of the Convention. The applicants have further alleged that there has been a separate violation of Article 14 of the Convention in that racial prejudice played a role in their deaths.

145. Discrimination is treating differently, without an objective and reasonable justification, persons in relevantly similar situations (see *Willis v the United Kingdom*, No 36042/97, § 48, ECHR 2002-IV). Racial violence is a particular affront to human dignity and, in view of its perilous consequences, requires from the authorities special vigilance and a vigorous reaction. It is for this reason that the authorities must use all available means to combat racism and racist violence, thereby reinforcing democracy's vision of a society in which diversity is not perceived as a threat but as a source of its enrichment. The Court will revert to that issue below.

146. Faced with the applicants' complaint of a violation of Article 14, as formulated, the Court's task is to establish whether or not racism was a causal factor in the shooting that led to the deaths of Mr Angelov and Mr Petkov so as to give rise to a breach of Article 14 of the Convention taken in conjunction with Article 2.

147. It notes in this connection that in assessing evidence, the Court has adopted the standard of proof 'beyond reasonable doubt'. However, it has never been its purpose to borrow the approach of the national legal systems that use that standard. Its role is not to rule on criminal guilt or civil liability but on Contracting States' responsibility under the Convention. The specificity of its task under Article 19 of the Convention—to ensure the observance by the Contracting States of their engagement to secure the fundamental rights enshrined in the Convention—conditions its approach to the issues of evidence and proof. In the proceedings before the Court, there are no procedural barriers to the admissibility of evidence or pre-determined formulae for its assessment. It adopts the conclusions that are, in its view, supported by the free evaluation of

all evidence, including such inferences as may flow from the facts and the parties' submissions. According to its established case-law, proof may follow from the coexistence of sufficiently strong, clear and concordant inferences or of similar unrebutted presumptions of fact. Moreover, the level of persuasion necessary for reaching a particular conclusion and, in this connection, the distribution of the burden of proof are intrinsically linked to the specificity of the facts, the nature of the allegation made and the Convention right at stake. The Court is also attentive to the seriousness that attaches to a ruling that a Contracting State has violated fundamental rights (see, among others, the following judgments: *Ireland v the United Kingdom*, judgment of 18 January 1978, Series A No 25, § 161; *Ribitsch v Austria*, judgment of 4 December 1995, Series A No 336, p 24, § 32; *Akdivar and Others v Turkey*, judgment of 16 September 1996, Reports 1996-IV, p 1211, § 68; *Tanli v Turkey*, No 26129/95, § 111, ECHR 2001-III; and *Ilaşcu and Others v Moldova and Russia* [GC], No 48787/99, § 26, 8 July 2004).

148. The applicants have referred to several separate facts and they maintain that sufficient inferences of a racist act can be drawn from them.

149. First, the applicants considered revealing the fact that Major G. had discharged bursts of automatic fire in a populated area, in disregard of the public's safety. Considering that there was no rational explanation for such behaviour, the applicants were of the view that racist hatred on the part of Major G. was the only plausible explanation and that he would not have acted in that manner in a non-Roma neighbourhood.

150. The Court notes, however, that the use of firearms in the circumstances at issue was regrettably not prohibited under the relevant domestic regulations, a flagrant deficiency which it has earlier condemned. The military police officers carried their automatic rifles 'in accordance with the rules' and were instructed to use all necessary means to effect the arrest. The possibility that Major G. was simply adhering strictly to the regulations and would have acted as he did in any similar context, regardless of the ethnicity of the fugitives, cannot therefore be excluded. While the relevant regulations were fundamentally flawed and fell well short of the Convention requirements on the protection of the right to life, there is nothing to suggest that Major G. would not have used his weapon in a non-Roma neighbourhood.

151. It is true, as the Court has found above, that Major G.'s conduct during the arrest operation calls for serious criticism in that he used grossly excessive force. Nonetheless, it cannot be excluded either that his reaction was shaped by the inadequacy of the legal framework governing the use of firearms and by the fact that he was trained to operate within that framework.

152. The applicants also stated that the military police officers' attitude had been strongly influenced by their knowledge of the victims' Roma origin. However, it is not possible to speculate on whether or not Mr Angelov's and Mr Petkov's Roma origin had any bearing on the officers' perception of them. Furthermore, there is evidence that some of the officers knew one or both of the victims personally.

153. The applicants referred to the statement given by Mr M. M., a neighbour of one of the victims, who reported that Major G. had shouted at him 'you damn Gypsies' immediately after the shooting. While such evidence of a racial slur being uttered in connection with a violent act should have led the authorities in this case to verify Mr M.M.'s statement, that statement is of itself an insufficient basis for concluding that the respondent State is liable for a racist killing.

154. Lastly, the applicants relied on information about numerous incidents involving the use of force against Roma by Bulgarian law enforcement officers that had not resulted in the conviction of those responsible.

155. It is true that a number of organisations, including intergovernmental bodies, have expressed concern about the occurrence of such incidents. However, the Court cannot lose sight of the

fact that its sole concern is to ascertain whether in the case at hand the killing of Mr Angelov and Mr Petkov was motivated by racism.

156. In its judgment the Chamber decided to shift the burden of proof to the respondent Government on account of the authorities' failure to carry out an effective investigation into the alleged racist motive for the killing. The inability of the Government to satisfy the Chamber that the events complained of were not shaped by racism resulted in its finding a substantive violation of Article 14 of the Convention, taken together with Article 2.

157. The Grand Chamber reiterates that in certain circumstances, where the events lie wholly, or in large part, within the exclusive knowledge of the authorities, as in the case of death of a person within their control in custody, the burden of proof may be regarded as resting on the authorities to provide a satisfactory and convincing explanation of, in particular, the causes of the detained person's death (see *Salman v Turkey* [GC], No 21986/93, § 100, ECHR 2000-VII). The Grand Chamber cannot exclude the possibility that in certain cases of alleged discrimination it may require the respondent Government to disprove an arguable allegation of discrimination and—if they fail to do so—find a violation of Article 14 of the Convention on that basis. However, where it is alleged—as here—that a violent act was motivated by racial prejudice, such an approach would amount to requiring the respondent Government to prove the absence of a particular subjective attitude on the part of the person concerned. While in the legal systems of many countries proof of the discriminatory effect of a policy or decision will dispense with the need to prove intent in respect of alleged discrimination in employment or the provision of services, that approach is difficult to transpose to a case where it is alleged that an act of violence was racially motivated. The Grand Chamber, departing from the Chamber's approach, does not consider that the alleged failure of the authorities to carry out an effective investigation into the alleged racist motive for the killing should shift the burden of proof to the respondent Government with regard to the alleged violation of Article 14 in conjunction with the substantive aspect of Article 2 of the Convention. The question of the authorities' compliance with their procedural obligation is a separate issue, to which the Court will revert below.

158. In sum, having assessed all relevant elements, the Court does not consider that it has been established that racist attitudes played a role in Mr Angelov's and Mr Petkov's deaths.

159. It thus finds that there has been no violation of Article 14 of the Convention taken together with Article 2 in its substantive aspect.

2. Procedural aspect: whether the respondent State complied with its obligation to investigate possible racist motives

(a) General principles

160. The Grand Chamber endorses the Chamber's analysis in the present case of the Contracting States' procedural obligation to investigate possible racist motives for acts of violence. The Chamber stated, in particular (§§ 156–9):

'... States have a general obligation under Article 2 of the Convention to conduct an effective investigation in cases of deprivation of life.

'... That obligation must be discharged without discrimination, as required by Article 14 of the Convention ... [W]here there is suspicion that racial attitudes induced a violent act it is particularly important that the official investigation is pursued with vigour and impartiality, having regard to the need to reassert continuously society's condemnation of racism and ethnic hatred and to maintain the confidence of minorities in the ability of the authorities to protect them from the threat of racist violence. Compliance with the State's positive obligations under Article 2 of the Convention requires that the domestic legal system must demonstrate its capacity to enforce criminal law against those who unlawfully took the life of another, irrespective of the victim's racial or ethnic origin (see *Menson and Others v the United Kingdom* (dec.), No 47916/99, ECHR 2003-V) ...

...[W]hen investigating violent incidents and, in particular, deaths at the hands of State agents, State authorities have the additional duty to take all reasonable steps to unmask any racist motive and to establish whether or not ethnic hatred or prejudice may have played a role in the events. Failing to do so and treating racially induced violence and brutality on an equal footing with cases that have no racist overtones would be to turn a blind eye to the specific nature of acts that are particularly destructive of fundamental rights. A failure to make a distinction in the way in which situations that are essentially different are handled may constitute unjustified treatment irreconcilable with Article 14 of the Convention (see, *mutatis mutandis*, *Thlimmenos v Greece* [GC], No 34369/97, § 44, ECHR 2000-IV). In order to maintain public confidence in their law enforcement machinery, Contracting States must ensure that in the investigation of incidents involving the use of force a distinction is made both in their legal systems and in practice between cases of excessive use of force and of racist killing.

'Admittedly, proving racial motivation will often be extremely difficult in practice. The respondent State's obligation to investigate possible racist overtones to a violent act is an obligation to use best endeavours and not absolute (see, *mutatis mutandis*, *Shanaghan v the United Kingdom*, No 37715/97, § 90, ECHR 2001-III, setting out the same standard with regard to the general obligation to investigate). The authorities must do what is reasonable in the circumstances to collect and secure the evidence, explore all practical means of discovering the truth and deliver fully reasoned, impartial and objective decisions, without omitting suspicious facts that may be indicative of a racially induced violence.'

161. The Grand Chamber would add that the authorities' duty to investigate the existence of a possible link between racist attitudes and an act of violence is an aspect of their procedural obligations arising under Article 2 of the Convention, but may also be seen as implicit in their responsibilities under Article 14 of the Convention taken in conjunction with Article 2 to secure the enjoyment of the right to life without discrimination. Owing to the interplay of the two provisions, issues such as those in the present case may fall to be examined under one of the two provisions only, with no separate issue arising under the other, or may require examination under both Articles. This is a question to be decided in each case on its facts and depending on the nature of the allegations made.

(b) Application of these principles in the present case

162. The Court has already found that the Bulgarian authorities violated Article 2 of the Convention in that they failed to conduct a meaningful investigation into the deaths of Mr Angelov and Mr Petkov. It considers that in the present case it must examine separately the complaint that there was also a failure to investigate a possible causal link between alleged racist attitudes and the killing of the two men.

163. The authorities investigating the deaths of Mr Angelov and Mr Petkov had before them the statement of Mr M.M., a neighbour of the victims, who stated that Major G. had shouted: 'You damn Gypsies' while pointing a gun at him immediately after the shooting. That statement, seen against the background of the many published accounts of the existence in Bulgaria of prejudice and hostility against Roma, called for verification.

164. The Grand Chamber considers—as the Chamber did—that any evidence of racist verbal abuse being uttered by law enforcement agents in connection with an operation involving the use of force against persons from an ethnic or other minority is highly relevant to the question whether or not unlawful, hatred-induced violence has taken place. Where such evidence comes to light in the investigation, it must be verified and—if confirmed—a thorough examination of all the facts should be undertaken in order to uncover any possible racist motives.

165. Furthermore, the fact that Major G. used grossly excessive force against two unarmed and non-violent men also called for a careful investigation.

166. In sum, the investigator and the prosecutors involved in the present case had before them plausible information which was sufficient to alert them to the need to carry out an initial verification

and, depending on the outcome, an investigation into possible racist overtones in the events that led to the death of the two men.

167. However, the authorities did nothing to verify Mr M.M.'s statement. They omitted to question witnesses about it. Major G. was not asked to explain why he had considered it necessary to use such a degree of force. No attempt was made to verify Major G.'s record and to ascertain, for example, whether he had previously been involved in similar incidents or whether he had ever been accused in the past of displaying anti-Roma sentiment. Those failings were compounded by the behaviour of the investigator and the prosecutors, who, as the Court has found above, disregarded relevant facts and terminated the investigation, thereby shielding Major G. from prosecution.

168. The Court thus finds that the authorities failed in their duty under Article 14 of the Convention taken together with Article 2 to take all possible steps to investigate whether or not discrimination may have played a role in the events. It follows that there has been a violation of Article 14 of the Convention taken together with Article 2 in its procedural aspect.

Judges Casadevall, Hedigan, Mularoni, Fura-Sandstrom, Gyulumyan, and Spielmann issued a partly dissenting opinion in which they expressed the view that:

2. We cannot subscribe to the new approach adopted by the Court which entails linking a possible violation of Article 14 to the substantive and procedural aspects of Article 2 individually. An overall approach would have been preferable, since it would have better reflected the special nature of Article 14, which has no independent existence as it applies solely to the rights and freedoms guaranteed by the Convention. Since Article 14 has no independent existence, we consider it artificial and unhelpful to distinguish between the substantive and procedural aspects, especially as in the instant case the Court found violations of both these aspects of Article 2.

Do you think the majority were unduly timorous in their application of Article 14?

11 A subsequent Grand Chamber enhanced the ability of persons to complain that they were the victims of indirect discrimination by allowing them to use statistical data to establish a prima facie case of discriminatory treatment. In ***DH and others v The Czech Republic***, judgment of 13 November 2007, the 18 applicants were Czech nationals of Roma ethnic origin who alleged that they had suffered indirect race/ethnic discrimination by being placed in special schools, thereby violating Article 14 in conjunction with Article 2 of Protocol 1. The Grand Chamber held that:

175. . . . The Court has also accepted that a general policy or measure that has disproportionately prejudicial effects on a particular group may be considered discriminatory notwithstanding that it is not specifically aimed at that group . . .

176. Discrimination on account of, *inter alia*, a person's ethnic origin is a form of racial discrimination. Racial discrimination is a particularly invidious kind of discrimination and, in view of its perilous consequences, required from the authorities special vigilance and a vigorous reaction. It is for this reason that the authorities must use all available means to combat racism, thereby reinforcing democracy's vision of a society in which diversity is not perceived as a threat but as a source of enrichment . . .

186. . . . the Court has noted in previous cases that applicants may have difficulty in proving discriminatory treatment (*Nachova and Others*, cited above, §§ 147 and 157). In order to guarantee those concerned the effective protection of their rights, less strict evidential rules should apply in cases of alleged indirect discrimination.

. . .

188. In these circumstances, the Court considers that when it comes to assessing the impact of a measure or practice on an individual or group, statistics which appear on critical examination to be reliable and significant will be sufficient to constitute the prima facie evidence the applicant is required to produce. This does not, however, mean that indirect discrimination cannot be proved without statistical evidence.

189. Where an applicant alleging indirect discrimination thus establishes a rebuttable presumption that the effect of a measure or practice is discriminatory, the burden then shifts to the respondent State, which must show that the difference in treatment is not discriminatory (see, *mutatis mutandis, Nachova and Others*, cited above, § 157). Regard being had in particular to the specificity of the facts and the nature of the allegations made in this type of case (ibid., § 147), it would be extremely difficult in practice for applicants to prove indirect discrimination without such a shift in the burden of proof.

190. In the present case, the statistical data submitted by the applicants was obtained from questionnaires that were sent out to the head teachers of special and primary schools in the town of Ostrava in 1999. It indicates that at the time 56% of all pupils placed in special schools in Ostrava were Roma. Conversely, Roma represented only 2.26% of the total number of pupils attending primary school in Ostrava. Further, whereas only 1.8% of non-Roma pupils were placed in special schools, the proportion of Roma pupils in Ostrava assigned to special schools was 50.3%. According to the Government, these figures are not sufficiently conclusive as they merely reflect the subjective opinions of the head teachers. The Government also noted that no official information on the ethnic origin of the pupils existed and that the Ostrava region had one of the largest Roma populations.

191. The Grand Chamber observes that these figures are not disputed by the Government and that they have not produced any alternative statistical evidence. In view of their comment that no official information on the ethnic origin of the pupils exists, the Court accepts that the statistics submitted by the applicants may not be entirely reliable. It nevertheless considers that these figures reveal a dominant trend that has been confirmed both by the respondent State and the independent supervisory bodies which have looked into the question.

. . .

194. Where it has been shown that legislation produces such a discriminatory effect, the Grand Chamber considers that, as with cases concerning employment or the provision of services, it is not necessary in cases in the educational sphere (see, *mutatis mutandis, Nachova and Others*, cited above, § 157) to prove any discriminatory intent on the part of the relevant authorities.

195. In these circumstances, the evidence submitted by the applicants can be regarded as sufficiently reliable and significant to give rise to a strong presumption of indirect discrimination. The burden of proof must therefore shift to the Government, which must show that the difference in the impact of the legislation was the result of objective factors unrelated to ethnic origin.

A majority of the Grand Chamber, 13 votes to 4, went on to find that the respondent State could not justify the 'disproportionately prejudicial effect on the Roma community' of the application of the special schools legislative scheme. The judgment in **DH** brought the Court's approach to analysing indirect discrimination into conformity with other European institutions (including the European Commission against Racism and Intolerance, and the European Court of Justice). However, R. Sandland has critically commented that:

In lay, rather than legal terms it may not be obvious why the Court has been prepared to find a violation of Article 14 taken together with Article 2 of Protocol No.1 on the basis of statistical evidence which strongly suggests wide-spread discrimination in the field of education but not, albeit that the statistical or general evidence is just as compelling, when Article 14 has been taken together with Article 2 or Article 3 in the field of policing. There is something anomalous about the situation in which the education rights of minorities are better protected than the right to life or to freedom from torture of minority groups. ['Developing a Jurisprudence of Difference: The Protection of the Human Rights of Travelling Peoples by the European Court of Human Rights' (2008) 8(3) *Human Rights Law Review* 475 at 514.]

After a visit, in November 2010, the Human Rights Commissioner (Thomas Hammarberg) observed that, '[t]here has been virtually no change on the ground in the Czech Republic since the European Court of Human Rights found three years ago that the country had discriminated against Roma children by educating them in schools for children with mental disabilities.' He welcomed the Government's creation of an action plan to promote inclusive education for all children. But, Roma children were still 12 times more likely to be studying in special schools than non-Roma pupils. The Commissioner called upon the Government to ensure a change of approach with the next year's school intake (Press release 22/11/2010).

Another Grand Chamber was deeply divided (9 votes to 8) when it concluded that there had been discrimination where only Roma children had been placed in separate classes in ordinary primary schools: *Orsus and others v Croatia*, judgment of 16 March 2010.

12 A unanimous Grand Chamber found no breach of Article 14 in conjunction with Article 1 of Protocol 1 where a woman who had been married in accordance with religious (Islamic) rites, but had not undergone a civil marriage, was denied a survivor's pension/related social security benefits (after the death of her husband) in *Serife Yigit v Turkey*, judgment of 2 November 2010. The Court considered that the Turkish Civil Code, since 1926, had clearly provided that a civil marriage was a prerequisite for a religious marriage and that the law had been designed to protect women (e.g. by establishing rights for wives on the death of their husbands). Therefore, the difference in treatment of the applicant and a wife who had undergone a valid civil marriage pursued a legitimate aim and the consequences for her were proportionate (she and her deceased husband had the opportunity to undertake a civil marriage during the 26 years of their religious marriage).

13 The Court's policy towards examining allegations of unlawful discrimination under Article 14, when it has already found a breach of a substantive Convention right in the same case, was explained in *Dudgeon v UK* A.45 (1981), see also p 491.

Where a substantive Article of the Convention has been invoked both on its own and together with Article 14 and a separate breach has been found of the substantive Article, it is not generally necessary for the Court also to examine the case under Article 14, though the position is otherwise if a clear inequality of treatment in the enjoyment of the right in question is a fundamental aspect of the case . . . [Para 67.]

An example of the latter situation occurred in *Aziz v Cyprus*, judgment of 22 June 2004. The applicant was a Cypriot national who lived in Nicosia. The authorities refused to register him on the electoral roll because he was a member of the Turkish-Cypriot community. Aziz alleged a breach of his right to vote contrary to Article 3 of Protocol 1 and a breach of Article 14 in that he was prevented from exercising his right to vote on the grounds of his national origins or association with a national minority. The Chamber was unanimous in finding a breach of Article 3 of Protocol 1 and also of Article 14 taken with that right.

36. The Court considers that, in the instant case, the complaint under Article 14 is not a mere restatement of the applicant's complaint under Article 3 of Protocol No 1. The Court notes that the applicant was a Cypriot national, resident in the Government-controlled area of Cyprus. It observes

that the difference in treatment in the present case resulted from the very fact that the applicant was a Turkish Cypriot. It emanated from the constitutional provisions regulating the voting rights between members of the Greek-Cypriot and Turkish-Cypriot communities that had become impossible to implement in practice.

37. Although the Court takes note of the Government's arguments, it considers that they cannot justify this difference on reasonable and objective grounds, particularly in the light of the fact that Turkish Cypriots in the applicant's situation are prevented from voting at any parliamentary election.

38. Thus, the Court concludes that there is a clear inequality of treatment in the enjoyment of the right in question, which must be considered a fundamental aspect of the case. There has accordingly been a violation of Article 14 of the Convention in conjunction with Article 3 of Protocol No 1.

Alternatively, where the Court has found a violation of Article 14 (in conjunction with a substantive right) it may decline to examine an argument that the substantive right alone has been breached; for example in *Thlimmenos* (Note 8) the Court refused to consider whether there had been a breach of Article 9.

14 The inherent weakness of Article 14, namely that it does not contain an independent prohibition of discrimination, has been addressed by Protocol 12 (which came into force on 1 April 2005 for the 11 member States which had by then ratified it). A Grand Chamber explained the Court's approach to interpreting the latter in the highly sensitive case of *Sejdic and Finci v Bosnia and Herzegovina*, judgment of 22 December 2009. During 1995, the USA and the EU secured the agreement of the three main groupings (the Bosniacs, Serbs, and Croats) to end the violent strife in Bosnia and Herzegovina (B&H), which had resulted in over 100,000 deaths/disappearances. The 'Dayton Peace Agreement' contained a constitution for B&H which divided powers and State offices between the three 'constituent peoples' of B&H (i.e. the above groups who had been involved in the fighting). The applicants were citizens of B&H, but they did not declare themselves to be members of any of the constituent peoples with the consequence that they were unable to stand for election to a number of public positions. The applicants contended, before the Court, that, *inter alia*, their inability to be candidates for the collective Presidency of B&H violated Article 1 of Protocol 12. The Grand Chamber held that:

55. The notion of discrimination has been interpreted consistently in the Court's jurisprudence concerning Article 14 of the Convention. In particular, this jurisprudence has made it clear that 'discrimination' means treating differently, without an objective and reasonable justification, persons in similar situations ... The authors used the same term, discrimination, in Article 1 of Protocol No. 12. Notwithstanding the difference in scope between those provisions, the meaning of this term in Article 1 of Protocol No. 12 was intended to be identical to that in Article 14 (see the Explanatory Report to Protocol No. 12, § 18). The Court does not therefore see any reason to depart from the settled interpretation of 'discrimination', noted above, in applying the same term under Article 1 of Protocol No. 12 ...

Subject to one dissent, the Grand Chamber went on to conclude that there had been a breach of Article 1 as the discriminatory provisions in the Dayton constitution could no longer be justified. The case was extremely controversial because the population of B&H had not been able to reach an agreed consensus to amend their constitution via the domestic political process.

ARTICLE 15 DEROGATION IN TIME OF EMERGENCY

From its early jurisprudence regarding Article 15, the Court has accorded domestic authorities a wide margin of appreciation to both assess the existence of a public emergency threatening the life of the nation and determine the form of the necessary measures of derogation (*Ireland*). This is a recognition of the practical limitations of judicial supervision from Strasbourg. States have not, thankfully, invoked Article 15 frequently. It has been utilized in the context of both domestic (*Brannigan and McBride*) and international terrorism (*A and others*). Despite the deferential approach of the Court it has been willing to find that national responses were not compatible with the requirements of Article 15 (e.g. in *Aksoy*). Furthermore, in *A and others* the Court adopted a supportive attitude towards a national supreme court's finding of a violation of Article 15.

Lawless v Ireland (No 3) A.3 (1961)
European Court of Human Rights

On a number of occasions since the establishment of the Irish Free State in 1921 armed groups, calling themselves the 'Irish Republican Army' (IRA), have been formed to use violence to end British sovereignty in Northern Ireland. During 1939 the IRA 'declared war on Great Britain' and the Irish Government responded by securing the passage of the Offences Against the State (Amendment) Act 1940 (No 2 of 1940) which granted powers of extra-judicial detention to Ministers of the State. During 1956 and 1957 there was a renewed outbreak of IRA violence, including the bombing of the Dublin to Belfast railway line and the ambushing of a Northern Irish police patrol near the border which resulted in one officer being killed. Consequently, the Irish Government issued a proclamation, on 5 July 1957, bringing the special powers of arrest and detention under the 1940 Act into force. A few days later the Irish Minister for External Affairs informed the Secretary General of the Council of Europe that the 1940 Act had been activated and that his letter should be regarded as notification of derogation under Article 15 of the Convention.

In 1956, during his trial in Ireland on charges of unlawful possession of firearms, the applicant admitted that he was a member of the IRA. He was acquitted of those charges, but convicted of possessing incriminating documents (relating to guerrilla warfare) by the Dublin District Court in May 1957 and sentenced to one month's imprisonment. On 13 July 1957, Lawless was detained on the order of the Minister of Justice, issued under the 1940 Act, as the latter considered Lawless to be engaged in activities prejudicial to the security of the State. Lawless was held in the Curragh Internment Camp. He was released from detention on 11 December 1957, after having given a verbal undertaking that he would not engage 'in any illegal activities under the Offences Against the State Acts'. Lawless complained to Strasbourg alleging a violation of a number of his Convention rights including those of liberty and a fair trial under Articles 5 and 6. The Irish Government, *inter alia*, sought to rely upon Article 15 to justify its actions.

22. Whereas it follows from these provisions that, without being released from all its undertakings assumed in the Convention, the Government of any High Contracting Party has the right, in case of war or public emergency threatening the life of the nation, to take measures derogating from its obligations under the Convention other than those named in Article 15, paragraph 2 (art 15-2), provided that such measures are strictly limited to what is required by the exigencies of the situation and also that they do not conflict with other obligations under international law; whereas it is for the Court to determine whether the conditions laid down in Article 15 (art 15) for the exercise of the exceptional right of derogation have been fulfilled in the present case;

(a) As to the existence of a public emergency threatening the life of the nation

23. Whereas the Irish Government, by a Proclamation dated 5 July 1957 and published in the Official Gazette on 8 July 1957, brought into force the extraordinary powers conferred upon it by Part II of the Offences against the State (Amendment) Act, 1940, 'to secure the preservation of public peace and order';

24. Whereas, by letter dated 20 July 1957 addressed to the Secretary-General of the Council of Europe, the Irish Government expressly stated that 'the detention of persons under the Act is considered necessary to prevent the commission of offences against public peace and order and to prevent the maintaining of military or armed forces other than those authorised by the Constitution';

25. Whereas, in reply to the Application introduced by G. R. Lawless before the Commission, the Irish Government adduced a series of facts from which they inferred the existence, during the period mentioned, of 'a public emergency threatening the life of the nation' within the meaning of Article 15 (art 15);

26. Whereas, before the Commission, G. R. Lawless submitted in support of his application that the aforesaid facts, even if proved to exist, would not have constituted a 'public emergency threatening the life of the nation' within the meaning of Article 15 (art 15); whereas, moreover, he disputed some of the facts adduced by the Irish Government;

27. Whereas the Commission, following the investigation carried out by it in accordance with Article 28 (art 28) of the Convention, expressed a majority opinion in its Report that in 'July 1957 there existed in Ireland a public emergency threatening the life of the nation within the meaning of Article 15, paragraph 1 (art 15-1), of the Convention';

28. Whereas, in the general context of Article 15 (art 15) of the Convention, the natural and customary meaning of the words 'other public emergency threatening the life of the nation' is sufficiently clear; whereas they refer to an exceptional situation of crisis or emergency which affects the whole population and constitutes a threat to the organised life of the community of which the State is composed; whereas, having thus established the natural and customary meaning of this conception, the Court must determine whether the facts and circumstances which led the Irish Government to make their Proclamation of 5 July 1957 come within this conception; whereas the Court, after an examination, find this to be the case; whereas the existence at the time of a 'public emergency threatening the life of the nation', was reasonably deduced by the Irish Government from a combination of several factors, namely: in the first place, the existence in the territory of the Republic of Ireland of a secret army engaged in unconstitutional activities and using violence to attain its purposes; secondly, the fact that this army was also operating outside the territory of the State, thus seriously jeopardising the relations of the Republic of Ireland with its neighbour; thirdly,

the steady and alarming increase in terrorist activities from the autumn of 1956 and throughout the first half of 1957;

29. Whereas, despite the gravity of the situation, the Government had succeeded, by using means available under ordinary legislation, in keeping public institutions functioning more or less normally, but whereas the homicidal ambush on the night 3 to 4 July 1957 in the territory of Northern Ireland near the border had brought to light, just before 12 July—a date, which, for historical reasons is particularly critical for the preservation of public peace and order—the imminent danger to the nation caused by the continuance of unlawful activities in Northern Ireland by the IRA and various associated groups, operating from the territory of the Republic of Ireland;

30. Whereas, in conclusion, the Irish Government were justified in declaring that there was a public emergency in the Republic of Ireland threatening the life of the nation and were hence entitled, applying the provisions of Article 15, paragraph 1 (art 15-1), of Convention for the purposes for which those provisions were made, to take measures derogating from their obligations under the Convention;

(b) As to whether the measures taken in derogation from obligations under the Convention were 'strictly required by the exigencies of the situation'

31. Whereas Article 15, paragraph 1 (art 15-1), provides that a High Contracting Party may derogate from its obligations under the Convention only 'to the extent strictly required by the exigencies of the situation'; whereas it is therefore necessary, in the present case, to examine whether the bringing into force of Part II of the 1940 Act was a measure strictly required by the emergency existing in 1957;

32. Whereas G. R. Lawless contended before the Commission that even if the situation in 1957 was such as to justify derogation from obligations under the Convention, the bringing into operation and the enforcement of Part II of the Offences against the State (Amendment) Act 1940 were disproportionate to the strict requirements of the situation;

33. Whereas the Irish Government, before both the Commission and the Court, contended that the measures taken under Part II of the 1940 Act were, in the circumstances, strictly required by the exigencies of the situation in accordance with Article 15, paragraph 1 (art 15-1), of the Convention;

34. Whereas while the majority of the Commission concurred with the Irish Government's submissions on this point, some members of the Commission drew from the facts established different legal conclusions;

35. Whereas it was submitted that in view of the means available to the Irish Government in 1957 for controlling the activities of the IRA and its splinter groups the Irish Government could have taken measures which would have rendered superfluous so grave a measure as detention without trial; whereas, in this connection, mention was made of the application of the ordinary criminal law, the institution of special criminal courts of the type provided for by the Offences against the State Act, 1939, or of military courts; whereas it would have been possible to consider other measures such as the sealing of the border between the Republic of Ireland and Northern Ireland;

36. Whereas, however, considering, in the judgment of the Court, that in 1957 the application of the ordinary law had proved unable to check the growing danger which threatened the Republic of Ireland; whereas the ordinary criminal courts, or even the special criminal courts or military courts, could not suffice to restore peace and order; whereas, in particular, the amassing of the necessary evidence to convict persons involved in activities of the IRA and its splinter groups was meeting with great difficulties caused by the military, secret and terrorist character of those groups and the fear they created among the population; whereas the fact that these groups operated mainly in Northern Ireland, their activities in the Republic of Ireland being virtually limited to the preparation of armed raids across the border was an additional impediment to the gathering of sufficient

evidence; whereas the sealing of the border would have had extremely serious repercussions on the population as a whole, beyond the extent required by the exigencies of the emergency;

Whereas it follows from the foregoing that none of the above-mentioned means would have made it possible to deal with the situation existing in Ireland in 1957; whereas, therefore, the administrative detention—as instituted under the Act (Amendment) of 1940—of individuals suspected of intending to take part in terrorist activities, appeared, despite its gravity, to be a measure required by the circumstances;

37. Whereas, moreover, the Offences against the State (Amendment) Act of 1940, was subject to a number of safeguards designed to prevent abuses in the operation of the system of administrative detention; whereas the application of the Act was thus subject to constant supervision by Parliament, which not only received precise details of its enforcement at regular intervals but could also at any time, by a Resolution, annul the Government's Proclamation which had brought the Act into force; whereas the Offences against the State (Amendment) Act 1940, provided for the establishment of a 'Detention Commission' made up of three members, which the Government did in fact set up, the members being an officer of the Defence Forces and two judges; whereas any person detained under this Act could refer his case to that Commission whose opinion, if favourable to the release of the person concerned, was binding upon the Government; whereas, moreover, the ordinary courts could themselves compel the Detention Commission to carry out its functions;

Whereas, in conclusion, immediately after the Proclamation which brought the power of detention into force, the Government publicly announced that it would release any person detained who gave an undertaking to respect the Constitution and the Law and not to engage in any illegal activity, and that the wording of this undertaking was later altered to one which merely required that the person detained would undertake to observe the law and refrain from activities contrary to the 1940 Act; whereas the persons arrested were informed immediately after their arrest that they would be released following the undertaking in question; whereas in a democratic country such as Ireland the existence of this guarantee of release given publicly by the Government constituted a legal obligation on the Government to release all persons who gave the undertaking;

Whereas, therefore, it follows from the foregoing that the detention without trial provided for by the 1940 Act, subject to the above-mentioned safeguards, appears to be a measure strictly required by the exigencies of the situation within the meaning of Article 15 (art 15) of the Convention;

38. Whereas, in the particular case of G. R. Lawless, there is nothing to show that the powers of detention conferred upon the Irish Government by the Offences against the State (Amendment) Act 1940, were employed against him, either within the meaning of Article 18 (art 18) of the Convention, for a purpose other than that for which they were granted, or within the meaning of Article 15 (art 15) of the Convention, by virtue of a measure going beyond what was strictly required by the situation at that time; whereas on the contrary, the Commission, after finding in its Decision of 30 August 1958 on the admissibility of the Application that the Applicant had in fact submitted his Application to it after having exhausted the domestic remedies, observed in its Report that the general conduct of G. R. Lawless, 'his association with persons known to be active members of the IRA, his conviction for carrying incriminating documents and other circumstances were such as to draw upon the Applicant the gravest suspicion that, whether or not he was any longer a member, he still was concerned with the activities of the IRA at the time of his arrest in July 1957; whereas the file also shows that, at the beginning of G. R. Lawless's detention under Act No 2 of 1940, the Irish Government informed him that he would be released if he gave a written undertaking 'to respect the Constitution of Ireland and the Laws' and not to 'be a member of or assist any organisation that is an unlawful organisation under the Offences against the State Act, 1939'; whereas in December 1957 the Government renewed its offer in a different form, which was accepted by G. R. Lawless, who gave a verbal undertaking before the Detention Commission not to 'take part in any activities that are illegal under the Offences against the State Acts 1939 and 1940' and was accordingly immediately released;

(c) As to whether the measures derogating from obligations under the Convention were 'inconsistent with ... other obligations under international law'

39. Whereas Article 15, paragraph 1 (art 15-1), of the Convention authorises a High Contracting Party to take measures derogating from the Convention only provided that they 'are not inconsistent with ... other obligations under international law';

40. Whereas, although neither the Commission nor the Irish Government have referred to this provision in the proceedings, the function of the Court, which is to ensure the observance of the engagements undertaken by the Contracting Parties in the Convention (Article 19 of the Convention) (art 19), requires it to determine proprio motu whether this condition has been fulfilled in the present case;

41. Whereas no facts have come to the knowledge of the Court which give it cause hold that the measure taken by the Irish Government derogating from the Convention may have conflicted with the said Government's other obligations under international law;

(d) As to whether the letter of 20th July 1957 from the Irish Government to the Secretary-General of the Council of Europe was a sufficient notification for the purposes of Article 15, paragraph 3 (art 15-3), of the Convention

42. Whereas Article 15, paragraph 3 (art 15-3), of the Convention provides that a Contracting Party availing itself of the right of derogation under paragraph 1 of the same Article (art 15-1) shall keep the Secretary-General of the Council of Europe fully informed of the measures which it has taken and the reasons therefor and shall also inform him when such measures have ceased to operate;

43. Whereas, in the present case, the Irish Government, on 20 July 1957, sent the Secretary-General of the Council of Europe a letter informing him—as is stated therein: 'in compliance with Article 15 (3) (art 15-3) of the Convention'—that Part II of the Offences against the State (Amendment) Act, 1940, had been brought into force on 8th July 1957; whereas copies of the Irish Government's Proclamation on the subject and of the 1940 Act itself were attached to the said letter; whereas the Irish Government explained in the said letter that the measure in question was 'considered necessary to prevent the commission of offences against public peace and order and to prevent the maintaining of military or armed forces other than those authorised by the Constitution';

44. Whereas G. R. Lawless contested before the Commission the Irish Government's right to rely on the letter of 20 July 1957 as a valid notice of derogation under Article 15, paragraph 3 (art 15-3), of the Convention; whereas, in substance, he contended before the Commission: that the letter had not the character of a notice of derogation, as the Government had not sent it for the purpose of registering a formal notice of derogation; that even if the letter were to be regarded as constituting such a notice, it did not comply with the strict requirements of Article 15, paragraph 3 (art 15-3), in that it neither adduced, as a ground for detention without trial, the existence of a time of war or other public emergency threatening the life of the nation nor properly defined the nature of the measure taken by the Government; whereas the Principal Delegate of the Commission, in the proceedings before the Court, made known a third contention of G. R. Lawless to the effect that the derogation, even if it had been duly notified to the Secretary-General on 20 July 1957, could not be enforced against persons within the jurisdiction of the Republic of Ireland in respect of the period before 23 October 1957, when it was first made public in Ireland;

45. Whereas the Commission expressed the opinion that the Irish Government had not delayed in bringing the enforcement of the special measures to the attention of the Secretary-General with explicit reference to Article 15, paragraph 3 (art 15-3), of the Convention; whereas the terms of the letter of 20 July 1957, to which were attached copies of the 1940 Act and of the Proclamation bringing it into force, were sufficient to indicate to the Secretary-General the nature of the measures taken and that consequently, while noting that the letter of 20 July did not contain a detailed

account of the reasons which had led the Irish Government to take the measures of derogation, it could not say that in the present case there had not been a sufficient compliance with the provisions of Article 15, paragraph 3 (art 15-3); whereas, with regard to G. R. Lawless' third contention the Delegates of the Commission added, in the proceedings before the Court, that Article 15, paragraph 3 (art 15-3), of the Convention required only that the Secretary-General of the Council of Europe be informed of the measures of derogation taken, without obliging the State concerned to promulgate the notice of derogation within the framework of its municipal laws;

46. Whereas the Irish Government, in their final submissions, asked the Court to state, in accordance with the Commission's opinion, that the letter of 20 July 1957 constituted a sufficient notification for the purposes of Article 15, paragraph 3 (art 15-3), of the Convention or, alternatively, to declare that there is nothing in the said paragraph 3 (art 15-3) which, in the present case, detracts from the Irish Government's right to rely on paragraph 1 of the said Article 15 (art 15-1);

47. Whereas the Court is called upon in the first instance, to examine whether, in pursuance of paragraph 3 of Article 15 (art 15-3) of the Convention, the Secretary-General of the Council of Europe was duly informed both of the measures taken and of the reason therefor; whereas the Court notes that a copy of the Offences against the State (Amendment) Act, 1940, and a copy of the Proclamation of 5 July, published on 8 July 1957, bringing into force Part II of the aforesaid Act were attached to the letter of 20 July; that it was explained in the letter of 20 July that the measures had been taken in order 'to prevent the commission of offences against public peace and order and to prevent the maintaining of military or armed forces other than those authorised by the Constitution'; that the Irish Government thereby gave the Secretary-General sufficient information of the measures taken and the reasons therefor; that, in the second place, the Irish Government brought this information to the Secretary-General's attention only 12 days after the entry into force of the measures derogating from their obligations under the Convention; and that the notification was therefore made without delay; whereas, in conclusion, the Convention does not contain any special provision to the effect that the Contracting State concerned must promulgate in its territory the notice of derogation addressed to the Secretary-General of the Council of Europe;

Whereas the Court accordingly finds that, in the present case, the Irish Government fulfilled their obligations as Party to the Convention under Article 15, paragraph 3 (art 15-3), of the Convention;

48. For these reasons,

THE COURT

Unanimously, . . .

(iv) States that the detention of G. R. Lawless from 13 July to 11 December 1957 was founded on the right of derogation duly exercised by the Irish Government in pursuance of Article 15 (art 15) of the Convention in July 1957;

(v) States that the communication addressed by the Irish Government to the Secretary-General of the Council of Europe on 20 July 1957 constituted sufficient notification within the meaning of Article 15, paragraph 3 (art 15-3), of the Convention;

Decides, accordingly, that in the present case the facts found do not disclose a breach by the Irish Government of their obligations under the European Convention for the Protection of Human Rights and Fundamental Freedoms; . . .

NOTES

1   The Court was composed of President Cassin and Judges: Maridakis, Rodenbourg, McGonigal, Balladore Pallieri, Arnalds, and Arik.

2   Judge Maridakis issued a concurring individual opinion in which he expressed the view that:

By 'public emergency threatening the life of the nation' it is to be understood a quite exceptional situation which imperils or might imperil the normal operation of public policy established in accordance with the lawfully expressed will of the citizens, in respect alike of the situation inside the country and of relations with foreign Powers.

3   The rather archaic language and style of the Court's judgment can be explained by the fact that this was the first case determined by that institution. Nevertheless, its interpretation of the terms 'other public emergency threatening the life of the nation', given in paragraph 28, has been applied in subsequent cases.

4   Although the Irish Government relied upon Article 15 to justify its extra-judicial measures designed to combat IRA terrorism in *Lawless*, when it brought a later complaint against the UK's use of extra-judicial powers of arrest and detention in Northern Ireland it sought to argue that the requirements of Article 15 had not been satisfied. The background to the *Ireland v UK* case has already been explained (p 145). The Court held that:

B. ON ARTICLE 5 TAKEN TOGETHER WITH ARTICLE 15 (ART 15+5)

202. The applicant Government maintain that the powers relating to extra-judicial deprivation of liberty which were applied in Northern Ireland from 9 August 1971 to March 1975 were not in complete conformity with Article 15 (art 15) and, accordingly, violated Article 5 (art 5).

   The Commission is unanimous in not accepting this claim and it is disputed by the respondent Government.

   ...

204. Article 5 (art 5) does not appear among the entrenched provisions listed in paragraph 2 of Article 15 (art 15-2) and is therefore one of the Articles subject to the 'right of derogation' reserved by the Contracting States, the exercise of which is regulated by paragraphs 1 and 3 (art 15-1, art 15-3).

1. On the 'public emergency threatening the life of the nation'

205. Article 15 (art 15) comes into play only 'in time of war or other public emergency threatening the life of the nation'. The existence of such an emergency is perfectly clear from the facts summarised above...and was not questioned by anyone before either the Commission or the Court. The crisis experienced at the time by the six counties therefore comes within the ambit of Article 15 (art 15).

2. On the 'extent strictly required'

206. The Contracting States may make use of their right of derogation only 'to the extent strictly required by the exigencies of the situation'. The Irish Government consider the 'extent strictly required' to have been exceeded, whereas the British Government and the Commission assert the contrary.

(a) The role of the Court

207. The limits on the Court's powers of review (see judgment of 23 July 1968 on the merits of the 'Belgian Linguistic' case, Series A No 6, p 35, para 10 *in fine*; Handyside judgment of 7 December 1976, Series A No 24, p 22, para 48) are particularly apparent where Article 15 (art 15) is concerned.

   It falls in the first place to each Contracting State, with its responsibility for 'the life of [its] nation', to determine whether that life is threatened by a 'public emergency' and, if so, how far it is necessary to go in attempting to overcome the emergency. By reason of their direct and continuous contact with the pressing needs of the moment, the national authorities are in principle in a better position than the international judge to decide both on the presence of such an emergency and on the nature and scope of derogations necessary to avert it. In this matter Article 15 para 1 (art 15-1) leaves those authorities a wide margin of appreciation.

Nevertheless, the States do not enjoy an unlimited power in this respect. The Court, which, with the Commission, is responsible for ensuring the observance of the States' engagements (Article 19) (art 19), is empowered to rule on whether the States have gone beyond the 'extent strictly required by the exigencies' of the crisis (*Lawless* judgment of 1 July 1961, Series A No 3, p 55, para 22, and pp 57–59, paras 36–38). The domestic margin of appreciation is thus accompanied by a European supervision.

(b) Questions of evidence

...

209. The Court is not bound, under the Convention or under the general principles applicable to international tribunals, by strict rules of evidence. In order to satisfy itself, the Court is entitled to rely on evidence of every kind, including, insofar as it deems them relevant, documents or statements emanating from governments, be they respondent or applicant, or from their institutions or officials....

(c) Questions concerning the merits

211. The Court has to decide whether the United Kingdom went beyond the 'extent strictly required'. For this purpose the Court must, as in the *Lawless* case (judgment of 1 July 1961, Series A No 3, pp 57–9, paras 36–37), enquire into the necessity for, on the one hand, deprivation of liberty contrary to paragraph 1 of Article 5 (art 5-1) and, on the other hand, the failure of guarantees to attain the level fixed by paragraphs 2 to 4 (art 5-2, art 5-3, art 5-4).

(i) On the necessity for derogation from paragraph 1 of Article 5 (art 5-1) by extra-judicial deprivation of liberty

212. Unquestionably, the exercise of the special powers was mainly, and before 5 February 1973 even exclusively, directed against the IRA as an underground military force. The intention was to combat an organisation which had played a considerable subversive rôle throughout the recent history of Ireland and which was creating, in August 1971 and thereafter, a particularly far-reaching and acute danger for the territorial integrity of the United Kingdom, the institutions of the six counties and the lives of the province's inhabitants ... Being confronted with a massive wave of violence and intimidation, the Northern Ireland Government and then, after the introduction of direct rule (30 March 1972), the British Government were reasonably entitled to consider that normal legislation offered insufficient resources for the campaign against terrorism and that recourse to measures outside the scope of the ordinary law, in the shape of extra-judicial deprivation of liberty, was called for. When the Irish Republic was faced with a serious crisis in 1957, it adopted the same approach and the Court did not conclude that the 'extent strictly required' had been exceeded (*Lawless* judgment of 1 July 1961, Series A No 3, pp 35–36, para 14, and pp 57–58, para 36).

However, under one of the provisions complained of, namely Regulation 10, a person who was in no way suspected of a crime or offence or of activities prejudicial to peace and order could be arrested for the sole purpose of obtaining from him information about others—and this sometimes occurred ... This sort of arrest can be justifiable only in a very exceptional situation, but the circumstances prevailing in Northern Ireland did fall into such a category. Many witnesses could not give evidence freely without running the greatest risks ... the competent authorities were entitled to take the view, without exceeding their margin of appreciation, that it was indispensable to arrest such witnesses so that they could be questioned in conditions of relative security and not be exposed to reprisals. Moreover and above all, Regulation 10 authorised deprivation of liberty only for a maximum of 48 hours.

213. ... it appears to the Court that the extra-judicial measures brought into operation could, in the situation described above, reasonably have been considered strictly required for the protection of public security and that, in the context of Article 15 (art 15), their intrinsic necessity, once recognised, could not be affected by the restriction of their field of application.

214. The Irish Government submit that experience shows extra-judicial deprivation of liberty to have been ineffectual. They contend that the policy introduced on 9 August 1971 not only failed to put a brake on terrorism but also had the result of increasing it...Consequently, the British Government, after attenuating the policy in varying degrees following the introduction of direct rule...abandoned it on 5 December 1975: since then, it appears that no one has been detained in the six counties under the emergency legislation, despite the persistence of an intense campaign of violence and even though the Emergency Provisions Amendment Act has remained in force...This, claim the applicant Government, confirms that extra-judicial deprivation of liberty was not an absolute necessity.

The Court cannot accept this argument.

It is certainly not the Court's function to substitute for the British Government's assessment any other assessment of what might be the most prudent or most expedient policy to combat terrorism. The Court must do no more than review the lawfulness, under the Convention, of the measures adopted by that Government from 9 August 1971 onwards. For this purpose the Court must arrive at its decision in the light, not of a purely retrospective examination of the efficacy of those measures, but of the conditions and circumstances reigning when they were originally taken and subsequently applied.

Adopting, as it must, this approach, the Court accepts that the limits of the margin of appreciation left to the Contracting States by Article 15 para 1 (art 15-1) were not overstepped by the United Kingdom when it formed the opinion that extra-judicial deprivation of liberty was necessary from August 1971 to March 1975.

(ii) On the necessity for derogation from the guarantees under paragraphs 2 to 4 of Article 5 (art 5-2, art 5-3, art 5-4)

215. The Court must now examine under Article 15 para 1 (art 15-1) the necessity for the far-reaching derogations found by it to have been made from paragraphs 2 to 4 of Article 5 (art 5-2, art 5-3, art 5-4)...

216. Neither Regulations 10 and 11 (1) nor section 10 of the Emergency Provisions Act afforded any remedy, judicial or administrative, against arrests effected thereunder. Although persons arrested under Regulation 11 (1) could, before 7 November 1972, apply to the Civil Authority for release on bail, the Terrorists Order deprived them of this right by revoking Regulation 11 (4) under which it arose. However, the duration of such arrests never exceeded 48 hours as regards Regulation 10, seventy-two hours as regards section 10 of the Emergency Provisions Act and, in practice, seventy-two hours as regards Regulation 11...

217. Similarly, Regulation 11 (2), Article 4 of the Terrorists Order and paragraph 11 of Schedule 1 to the Emergency Provisions Act did not provide for any remedy. Detention under Regulation 11 (2) sometimes continued for longer than twenty-eight days, but it was never to be for an indefinite period and the detainee could, if the administrative authority agreed, apply to the courts for release on bail (Regulation 11 (4) and the *McElduff* case, judgment of 12 October 1971). On the other hand, interim custody imposed under Article 4 of the Terrorists Order, or subsequently under paragraph 11 of Schedule 1 to the Emergency Provisions Act, continued until adjudication by the commissioner; the Chief Constable invariably referred the case to him within the initial twenty-eight day time-limit but the commissioner gave his decision after several weeks or even after six months...

218. Individuals deprived of their liberty under Regulation 12 (1), Article 5 of the Terrorists Order or paragraph 24 of Schedule 1 to the Emergency Provisions Act were in many cases interned or detained for some years. Nevertheless, the advisory committee set up by Regulation 12 (1) afforded, notwithstanding its non-judicial character, a certain measure of protection that cannot be discounted. By establishing commissioners and an appeal tribunal, the Terrorists Order brought further safeguards which were somewhat strengthened by the Emergency Provisions Act...

219. There was in addition the valuable, if limited, review effected by the courts, when the opportunity arose, by virtue of the common law ...

220. An overall examination of the legislation and practice at issue reveals that they evolved in the direction of increasing respect for individual liberty. The incorporation right from the start of more satisfactory judicial, or at least administrative, guarantees would certainly have been desirable, especially as Regulations 10 to 12 (1) dated back to 1956–1957 and were made under an Act of 1922, but it would be unrealistic to isolate the first from the later phases. When a State is struggling against a public emergency threatening the life of the nation, it would be rendered defenceless if it were required to accomplish everything at once, to furnish from the outset each of its chosen means of action with each of the safeguards reconcilable with the priority requirements for the proper functioning of the authorities and for restoring peace within the community. The interpretation of Article 15 (art 15) must leave a place for progressive adaptations.

The Northern Ireland Government sought in the first place—unsuccessfully—to meet the most pressing problem, to stem the wave of violence that was sweeping the region. After assuming direct responsibility for the future of the province, the British Government and Parliament lost little time in moderating in certain respects the severity of the laws applied in the early days. The Court asked itself whether those laws should not have been attenuated even more, especially as regards interim custody ... but does not consider that it can give an affirmative answer. It must not be forgotten that the crisis experienced at the time by the six counties was serious and, hence, of a kind that justified far-reaching derogations from paragraphs 2 to 4 of Article 5 (art 5-2, art 5-3, art 5-4). In view of the Contracting States' margin of appreciation, the Court does not find it established that the United Kingdom exceeded in this respect the 'extent strictly required' referred to in Article 15 para 1 (art 15-1).

221. According to the applicant Government, the non-contested violations of Article 3 (art 3) are relevant under Articles 5 and 15 (art 15+5) taken together. They claim that deprivation of liberty was sometimes imposed on the strength of information extracted in conditions contrary to Article 3 (art 3) and was thereby rendered unlawful under Article 15 (art 15). The Irish argument is also said to be confirmed by the existence of those violations since they would probably have been prevented by the impugned legislation if it had afforded genuine guarantees to the persons concerned.

The Court emphasises, as do the respondent Government and the Commission, that Articles 3 and 5 (art 3, art 5) embody quite separate obligations. Moreover, the violations of Article 3 (art 3) found in the present judgment fail to show that it was not necessary to apply the extra-judicial powers in force.

3. On the 'other obligations under international law'

222. Article 15 para 1 (art 15-1) *in fine* prohibits any derogation inconsistent 'with other obligations under international law'. There is nothing in the data before the Court to suggest that the United Kingdom disregarded such obligations in this case; in particular, the Irish Government never supplied to the Commission or the Court precise details on the claim formulated or outlined on this point in their application of 16 December 1971.

4. On the observance of paragraph 3 of Article 15 (art 15-3)

223. The Court finds proprio motu, in the light of its *Lawless* judgment of 1 July 1961 (Series A No 3, pp 61–62, para 47), that the British notices of derogation dated 20 August 1971, 23 January 1973 and 16 August 1973 ... fulfilled the requirements of Article 15 para 3 (art 15-3).

5. Conclusion

224. The Court has accordingly come to the conclusion that, since the requirements of Article 15 (art 15) were met, the derogations from Article 5 (art 5) were not, in the circumstances of the case, in breach of the Convention.

A significant aspect of the above judgment was the Court's express recognition, in paragraph 207, that States are to be accorded a wide margin of appreciation in determining if the threats encompassed by Article 15 have arisen in their territories and how they should respond to them. For an examination of this concept, see p 633.

....

Brannigan and McBride v UK A.258-B (1993)
European Court of Human Rights

Between 1972 and 1992 over 3,000 deaths were attributable to terrorism in Northern Ireland. Other parts of the UK have also been subject to a considerable amount of terrorist violence linked to the situation in Northern Ireland. Under section 12 of the Prevention of Terrorism (Temporary Provisions) Act 1984, police officers were given the power to arrest and detain, for questioning, persons whom officers had reasonable grounds for suspecting to be concerned in the commission, preparation, or instigation of acts of terrorism relating to Northern Ireland. Officers could detain such person for up to 48 hours. The Secretary of State (for Northern Ireland) could also authorize, under the section, the continued detention of such persons for a maximum of five additional days (hence no person could be detained for more than seven days in total without being charged in respect of a criminal offence). On 29 November 1988, in *Brogan v UK* (p 302), the Court ruled that the detention of persons for a minimum time of four days and six hours under section 12 violated Article 5(3) of the Convention. The Home Secretary made a statement to Parliament on 22 December 1988 in which he explained the difficulties of introducing judicial controls over the arrest and detention of terrorist suspects.

We must pay proper regard to the tremendous pressures that are already faced by the judiciary, especially in Northern Ireland, where most cases have to be considered. We are also concerned that information about terrorist intentions, which often forms part of the case for an extension of detention, does not find its way back to the terrorists as a consequence of judicial procedures, which at least in the United Kingdom legal tradition generally require someone accused and his legal advisers to know the information alleged against him . . .

In the meantime, the position cannot be left as it stands. I have already made clear to the House that we shall ensure that the police continue to have the powers they need to counter terrorism, and they continue to need to be able to detain suspects for up to seven days in some cases. To ensure that there can be no doubt about the ability of the police to deal effectively with such cases, the Government are today taking steps to give notice of derogation under Article 15 (art 15) of the European Convention of Human Rights, and Article 4 of the International Covenant on Civil and Political Rights. There is a public emergency within the meaning of these provisions in respect of terrorism connected with the affairs of Northern Ireland in the United Kingdom . . .

On 23 December 1988 the UK informed the Secretary General of the Council of Europe that the Government had availed itself of the right of derogation conferred by Article 15(1) to the extent that the exercise of powers under section 12 of the 1984 Act might be inconsistent with the obligations imposed by Article 5(3) of the Convention. The declaration stated:

. . . Following [the *Brogan* judgment], the Secretary of State for the Home Department informed Parliament on 6 December 1988 that, against the background of the terrorist campaign, and the over-riding need to bring terrorists to justice, the Government did not believe that the maximum period of detention should be reduced. He informed Parliament that the Government were examining the matter with a view to responding to the judgment. On 22 December 1988, the Secretary of State further informed Parliament that it remained the Government's wish, if it could be achieved, to find a judicial process under which extended detention might be reviewed and where appropriate authorised by a judge or other judicial officer. But a further period of reflection and consultation was necessary before the Government could bring forward a firm and final view. Since the judgment of 29 November 1988 as well as previously, the Government have found it necessary to continue to exercise, in relation to terrorism connected with the affairs of Northern Ireland, the powers described above enabling further detention without charge, for periods of up to five days, on the authority of the Secretary of State, to the extent strictly required by the exigencies of the situation to enable necessary enquiries and investigations properly to be completed in order to decide whether criminal proceedings should be instituted. To the extent that the exercise of these powers may be inconsistent with the obligations imposed by the Convention the Government have availed themselves of the right of derogation conferred by Article 15(1) of the Convention and will continue to do so until further notice...

The Government reviewed whether the powers of extended detention could be conferred on the normal courts, but concluded that it would not be appropriate to involve courts in such decisions for the reasons given in a Written Answer in Parliament by the Secretary of State, Mr David Waddington, on 14 November 1989:

Decisions to authorise the detention of terrorist suspects for periods beyond 48 hours may be, and often are, taken on the basis of information, the nature and source of which could not be revealed to a suspect or his legal adviser without serious risk to individuals assisting the police or the prospect of further valuable intelligence being lost. Any new procedure which avoided those dangers by allowing a court to make a decision on information not presented to the detainee or his legal adviser would represent a radical departure from the principles which govern judicial proceedings in this country and could seriously affect public trust and confidence in the independence of the judiciary. The Government would be most reluctant to introduce any new procedure which could have this effect. [Official Report, 14 November 1989, col 210.]

In a further notice dated 12 December 1989 the UK informed the Secretary General that a satisfactory procedure for the review of detention of terrorist suspects involving the judiciary had not been identified and that the derogation would therefore remain in place for as long as circumstances require. The first applicant was arrested by the police on 9 January 1989 and the Secretary of State authorized, under section 12, his continued detention until 15 January. During that time the applicant was interrogated on 43 occasions. The second applicant was arrested on 5 January 1989 and the Secretary of State authorized his detention until 9 January. The applicants complained to the Commission that their periods of detention violated Article 5(3) as interpreted by the Court in *Brogan*. By 8 votes to 5, the Commission found no breach of the Convention in the light of the UK's derogation of 23 December 1988.

37. The Government, noting that both of the applicants were detained for longer periods than the shortest period found by the Court to be in breach of Article 5 para 3 (art 5-3) in the case of *Brogan*, conceded that the requirement of promptness had not been respected in the present cases... They further accepted that, in the absence of an enforceable right to compensation in respect of the breach of Article 5 para 3 (art 5-3), Article 5 para 5 (art 5-5) had not been complied with.

Having regard to its judgment in the case of *Brogan*, the Court finds that Article 5 paras 3 and 5 (art 5-3, art 5-5) have not been respected...

38. However, the Government further submitted that the failure to observe these requirements of Article 5 (art 5) had been met by their derogation of 23 December 1988 under Article 15 (art 15) of the Convention.

The Court must therefore examine the validity of the Government's derogation in the light of this provision. It recalls at the outset that the question whether any derogation from the United Kingdom's obligations under the Convention might be permissible under Article 15 (art 15) by reason of the terrorist campaign in Northern Ireland was specifically left open by the Court in the *Brogan* case . . .

VALIDITY OF THE UNITED KINGDOM'S DEROGATION UNDER ARTICLE 15 (ART 15)

39. The applicants maintained that the derogation under Article 15 (art 15) was invalid. This was disputed by both the Government and the Commission. . . .

1. The Court's approach to the matter

41. The applicants argued that it would be inconsistent with Article 15 para 2 (art 15-2) if, in derogating from safeguards recognised as essential for the protection of non-derogable rights such as Articles 2 and 3 (art 2, art 3), the national authorities were to be afforded a wide margin of appreciation. This was especially so where the emergency was of a quasi-permanent nature such as that existing in Northern Ireland. To do so would also be inconsistent with the *Brogan* judgment where the Court had regarded judicial control as one of the fundamental principles of a democratic society and had already—they claimed—extended to the Government a margin of appreciation by taking into account in paragraph 58 (p 32) the context of terrorism in Northern Ireland (*loc cit.*).

42. In their written submissions, Amnesty International maintained that strict scrutiny was required by the Court when examining derogation from fundamental procedural guarantees which were essential for the protection of detainees at all times, but particularly in times of emergency. Liberty, Interights and the Committee on the Administration of Justice ('Liberty and Others') submitted for their part that, if States are to be allowed a margin of appreciation at all, it should be narrower the more permanent the emergency becomes.

43. The Court recalls that it falls to each Contracting State, with its responsibility for 'the life of [its] nation', to determine whether that life is threatened by a 'public emergency' and, if so, how far it is necessary to go in attempting to overcome the emergency. By reason of their direct and continuous contact with the pressing needs of the moment, the national authorities are in principle in a better position than the international judge to decide both on the presence of such an emergency and on the nature and scope of derogations necessary to avert it. Accordingly, in this matter a wide margin of appreciation should be left to the national authorities (see the *Ireland v UK* judgment of 18 January 1978, Series A No 25, pp 78–79, para 207).

Nevertheless, Contracting Parties do not enjoy an unlimited power of appreciation. It is for the Court to rule on whether *inter alia* the States have gone beyond the 'extent strictly required by the exigencies' of the crisis. The domestic margin of appreciation is thus accompanied by a European supervision (ibid). At the same time, in exercising its supervision the Court must give appropriate weight to such relevant factors as the nature of the rights affected by the derogation, the circumstances leading to, and the duration of, the emergency situation.

2. Existence of a public emergency threatening the life of the nation

44. Although the applicants did not dispute that there existed a public emergency 'threatening the life of the nation', they submitted that the burden rested on the Government to satisfy the Court that such an emergency really existed.

45. It was, however, suggested by Liberty and Others in their written submissions that at the relevant time there was no longer any evidence of an exceptional situation of crisis. They maintained that reconsideration of the position could only properly have led to a further derogation if there was a demonstrable deterioration in the situation since August 1984 when the Government withdrew their previous derogation. For the Standing Advisory Commission on Human Rights, on

the other hand, there was a public emergency in Northern Ireland at the relevant time of a sufficient magnitude to entitle the Government to derogate.

46. Both the Government and the Commission, referring to the existence of public disturbance in Northern Ireland, maintained that there was such an emergency.

47. Recalling its case-law in *Lawless v Ireland* (judgment of 1 July 1961, Series A No 3, p 56, para 28) and *Ireland v UK* (*loc. cit.*, Series A No 25, p 78, para 205) and making its own assessment, in the light of all the material before it as to the extent and impact of terrorist violence in Northern Ireland and elsewhere in the United Kingdom . . . the Court considers there can be no doubt that such a public emergency existed at the relevant time.

It does not judge it necessary to compare the situation which obtained in 1984 with that which prevailed in December 1988 since a decision to withdraw a derogation is, in principle, a matter within the discretion of the State and since it is clear that the Government believed that the legislation in question was in fact compatible with the Convention . . .

3. Were the measures strictly required by the exigencies of the situation?

(a) General considerations

48. The Court recalls that judicial control of interferences by the executive with the individual's right to liberty provided for by Article 5 (art 5) is implied by one of the fundamental principles of a democratic society, namely the rule of law (see the above-mentioned *Brogan* judgment, Series A No 145-B, p 32, para 58). It further observes that the notice of derogation invoked in the present case was lodged by the respondent Government soon after the judgment in the above-mentioned *Brogan* case where the Court had found the Government to be in breach of their obligations under Article 5 para 3 (art 5-3) by not bringing the applicants 'promptly' before a court.

The Court must scrutinise the derogation against this background and taking into account that the power of arrest and detention in question has been in force since 1974. However, it must be observed that the central issue in the present case is not the existence of the power to detain suspected terrorists for up to seven days—indeed a complaint under Article 5 para 1 (art 5-1) was withdrawn by the applicants . . .—but rather the exercise of this power without judicial intervention.

(b) Was the derogation a genuine response to an emergency situation?

49. For the applicants, the purported derogation was not a necessary response to any new or altered state of affairs but was the Government's reaction to the decision in *Brogan* and was lodged merely to circumvent the consequences of this judgment.

50. The Government and the Commission maintained that, while it was true that this judgment triggered off the derogation, the exigencies of the situation have at all times since 1974 required the powers of extended detention conferred by the Prevention of Terrorism legislation. It was the view of successive Governments that these powers were consistent with Article 5 para 3 (art 5-3) and that no derogation was necessary. However, both the measures and the derogation were direct responses to the emergency with which the United Kingdom was and continues to be confronted.

51. The Court first observes that the power of arrest and extended detention has been considered necessary by the Government since 1974 in dealing with the threat of terrorism. Following the *Brogan* judgment the Government were then faced with the option of either introducing judicial control of the decision to detain under section 12 of the 1984 Act or lodging a derogation from their Convention obligations in this respect. The adoption of the view by the Government that judicial control compatible with Article 5 para 3 (art 5-3) was not feasible because of the special difficulties associated with the investigation and prosecution of terrorist crime rendered derogation inevitable. Accordingly, the power of extended detention without such judicial control and the derogation of 23 December 1988 being clearly linked to the persistence of the emergency situation, there is no indication that the derogation was other than a genuine response.

(c) Was the derogation premature?

52. The applicants maintained that derogation was an interim measure which Article 15 (art 15) did not provide for since it appeared from the notice of derogation communicated to the Secretary General of the Council of Europe on 23 December 1988 that the Government had not reached a 'firm or final view' on the need to derogate from Article 5 para 3 (art 5-3) and required a further period of reflection and consultation. Following this period the Secretary of State for the Home Department confirmed the derogation in a statement to Parliament on 14 November 1989... Prior to this concluded view Article 15 (art 15) did not permit derogation. Furthermore, even at this date the Government had not properly examined whether the obligation in Article 5 para 3 (art 5-3) could be satisfied by an 'officer authorised by law to exercise judicial power'.

53. The Government contended that the validity of the derogation was not affected by their examination of the possibility of judicial control of extended detention since, as the Commission had pointed out, it was consistent with the requirements of Article 15 para 3 (art 15-3) to keep derogation measures under constant review.

54. The Court does not accept the applicants' argument that the derogation was premature.

While it is true that Article 15 (art 15) does not envisage an interim suspension of Convention guarantees pending consideration of the necessity to derogate, it is clear from the notice of derogation that 'against the background of the terrorist campaign, and the over-riding need to bring terrorists to justice, the Government did not believe that the maximum period of detention should be reduced'. However it remained the Government's wish 'to find a judicial process under which extended detention might be reviewed and where appropriate authorised by a judge or other judicial officer'...

The validity of the derogation cannot be called into question for the sole reason that the Government had decided to examine whether in the future a way could be found of ensuring greater conformity with Convention obligations. Indeed, such a process of continued reflection is not only in keeping with Article 15 para 3 (art 15-3) which requires permanent review of the need for emergency measures but is also implicit in the very notion of proportionality.

(d) Was the absence of judicial control of extended detention justified?

55. The applicants further considered that there was no basis for the Government's assertion that control of extended detention by a judge or other officer authorised by law to exercise judicial power was not possible or that a period of seven days' detention was necessary. They did not accept that the material required to satisfy a court of the justification for extended detention could be more sensitive than that needed in proceedings for habeas corpus. They and the Standing Advisory Commission on Human Rights also pointed out that the courts in Northern Ireland were frequently called on to deal with submissions based on confidential information—for example, in bail applications—and that there were sufficient procedural and evidential safeguards to protect confidentiality. Procedures also existed where judges were required to act on the basis of material which would not be disclosed either to the legal adviser or to his client. This was the case, for example, with claims by the executive to public interest immunity or application by the police to extend detention under the Police and Criminal Evidence (Northern Ireland) Order 1989...

56. On this point the Government responded that none of the above procedures involved both the non-disclosure of material to the detainee or his legal adviser and an executive act of the court. The only exception appeared in Schedule 7 to the Prevention of Terrorism (Temporary Provisions) Act 1989 where *inter alia* the court may make an order in relation to the production of, and search for, special material relevant to terrorist investigations. However, paragraph 8 of Schedule 7 provides that, where the disclosure of information to the court would be too sensitive or would prejudice the investigation, the power to make the order is conferred on the Secretary of State and not the court...

It was also emphasised that the Government had reluctantly concluded that, within the framework of the common-law system, it was not feasible to introduce a system which would be compatible with Article 5 para 3 (art 5-3) but would not weaken the effectiveness of the response to the terrorist threat. Decisions to prolong detention were taken on the basis of information the nature and source of which could not be revealed to a suspect or his legal adviser without risk to individuals assisting the police or the prospect of further valuable intelligence being lost. Moreover, involving the judiciary in the process of granting or approving extensions of detention created a real risk of undermining their independence as they would inevitably be seen as part of the investigation and prosecution process.

In addition, the Government did not accept that the comparison with habeas corpus was a valid one since judicial involvement in the grant or approval of extension would require the disclosure of a considerable amount of additional sensitive information which it would not be necessary to produce in habeas corpus proceedings. In particular, a court would have to be provided with details of the nature and extent of police inquiries following the arrest, including details of witnesses interviewed and information obtained from other sources as well as information about the future course of the police investigation.

Finally, Lords Shackleton and Jellicoe and Viscount Colville in their reports had concluded that arrest and extended detention were indispensable powers in combating terrorism. These reports also found that the training of terrorists in remaining silent under police questioning hampered and protracted the investigation of terrorist offences. In consequence, the police were required to undertake extensive checks and inquiries and to rely to a greater degree than usual on painstaking detective work and forensic examination...

57. The Commission was of the opinion that the Government had not overstepped their margin of appreciation in this regard.

58. The Court notes the opinions expressed in the various reports reviewing the operation of the Prevention of Terrorism legislation that the difficulties of investigating and prosecuting terrorist crime give rise to the need for an extended period of detention which would not be subject to judicial control... Moreover, these special difficulties were recognised in its above-mentioned *Brogan* judgment (see Series A No 145-B, p 33, para 61).

It further observes that it remains the view of the respondent Government that it is essential to prevent the disclosure to the detainee and his legal adviser of information on the basis of which decisions on the extension of detention are made and that, in the adversarial system of the common law, the independence of the judiciary would be compromised if judges or other judicial officers were to be involved in the granting or approval of extensions.

The Court also notes that the introduction of a 'judge or other officer authorised by law to exercise judicial power' into the process of extension of periods of detention would not of itself necessarily bring about a situation of compliance with Article 5 para 3 (art 5-3). That provision—like Article 5 para 4 (art 5-4)—must be understood to require the necessity of following a procedure that has a judicial character although that procedure need not necessarily be identical in each of the cases where the intervention of a judge is required...

59. It is not the Court's role to substitute its view as to what measures were most appropriate or expedient at the relevant time in dealing with an emergency situation for that of the Government which have direct responsibility for establishing the balance between the taking of effective measures to combat terrorism on the one hand, and respecting individual rights on the other (see the above-mentioned *Ireland v UK* judgment, Series A No 25, p 82, para 214, and the *Klass v Germany* judgment of 6 September 1978, Series A No 28, p 23, para 49). In the context of Northern Ireland, where the judiciary is small and vulnerable to terrorist attacks, public confidence in the independence of the judiciary is understandably a matter to which the Government attach great importance.

60. In the light of these considerations it cannot be said that the Government have exceeded their margin of appreciation in deciding, in the prevailing circumstances, against judicial control.

(e) Safeguards against abuse

61. The applicants, Amnesty International and Liberty and Others maintained that the safeguards against abuse of the detention power were negligible and that during the period of detention the detainee was completely cut off from the outside world and not permitted access to newspapers, radios or his family. Amnesty International, in particular, stressed that international standards such as the 1988 United Nations Body of Principles for the Protection of All Persons under Any Form of Detention or Imprisonment (General Assembly Resolution 43/173 of 9 December 1988) ruled out incommunicado detention by requiring access to lawyers and members of the family. Amnesty submitted that being brought promptly before a judicial authority was especially important since in Northern Ireland habeas corpus has been shown to be ineffective in practice. In their view Article 5 para 4 (art 5-4) should be considered non-derogable in times of public emergency.

In addition, it was contended that a decision to extend detention cannot in practical terms be challenged by habeas corpus or judicial review since it is taken completely in secret and, in nearly all cases, is granted. This is evident from the fact that, despite the thousands of extended detention orders, a challenge to such a decision has never been attempted.

62. Although submissions have been made by the applicants and the organisations concerning the absence of effective safeguards, the Court is satisfied that such safeguards do in fact exist and provide an important measure of protection against arbitrary behaviour and incommunicado detention.

63. In the first place, the remedy of habeas corpus is available to test the lawfulness of the original arrest and detention. There is no dispute that this remedy was open to the applicants had they or their legal advisers chosen to avail themselves of it and that it provides an important measure of protection against arbitrary detention (see the above-mentioned *Brogan* judgment, Series A No 145-B, pp 34–35, paras 63–65). The Court recalls, in this context, that the applicants withdrew their complaint of a breach of Article 5 para 4 (art 5-4) of the Convention ... In the second place, detainees have an absolute and legally enforceable right to consult a solicitor after forty-eight hours from the time of arrest. Both of the applicants were, in fact, free to consult a solicitor after this period ...

Moreover, within this period the exercise of this right can only be delayed where there exists reasonable grounds for doing so. It is clear from judgments of the High Court in Northern Ireland that the decision to delay access to a solicitor is susceptible to judicial review and that in such proceedings the burden of establishing reasonable grounds for doing so rests on the authorities. In these cases judicial review has been shown to be a speedy and effective manner of ensuring that access to a solicitor is not arbitrarily withheld ...

It is also not disputed that detainees are entitled to inform a relative or friend about their detention and to have access to a doctor.

65. In addition to the above basic safeguards the operation of the legislation in question has been kept under regular independent review and, until 1989, it was subject to regular renewal.

(f) Conclusion

66. Having regard to the nature of the terrorist threat in Northern Ireland, the limited scope of the derogation and the reasons advanced in support of it, as well as the existence of basic safeguards against abuse, the Court takes the view that the Government have not exceeded their margin of appreciation in considering that the derogation was strictly required by the exigencies of the situation.

4. Other obligations under international law

67. The Court recalls that under Article 15 para 1 (art 15-1) measures taken by the State derogating from Convention obligations must not be 'inconsistent with its other obligations under international law' ...

68. In this respect, before the Court the applicants contended for the first time that it was an essential requirement for a valid derogation under Article 4 of the 1966 United Nations International Covenant on Civil and Political Rights ('the Covenant'), to which the United Kingdom is a Party, that a public emergency must have been 'officially proclaimed'. Since such proclamation had never taken place the derogation was inconsistent with the United Kingdom's other obligations under international law. In their view this requirement involved a formal proclamation and not a mere statement in Parliament.

69. For the Government, it was open to question whether an official proclamation was necessary for the purposes of Article 4 of the Covenant, since the emergency existed prior to the ratification of the Covenant by the United Kingdom and has continued to the present day. In any event, the existence of the emergency and the fact of derogation were publicly and formally announced by the Secretary of State for the Home Department to the House of Commons on 22 December 1988. Moreover there had been no suggestion by the United Nations Human Rights Committee that the derogation did not satisfy the formal requirements of Article 4.

70. The Delegate of the Commission considered the Government's argument to be tenable.

71. The relevant part of Article 4 of the Covenant states:

In time of public emergency which threatens the life of the nation and the existence of which is officially proclaimed...'

72. The Court observes that it is not its role to seek to define authoritatively the meaning of the terms 'officially proclaimed' in Article 4 of the Covenant. Nevertheless it must examine whether there is any plausible basis for the applicant's argument in this respect.

73. In his statement of 22 December 1988 to the House of Commons the Secretary of State for the Home Department explained in detail the reasons underlying the Government's decision to derogate and announced that steps were being taken to give notice of derogation under both Article 15 (art 15) of the European Convention and Article 4 of the Covenant. He added that there was 'a public emergency within the meaning of these provisions in respect of terrorism connected with the affairs of Northern Ireland in the United Kingdom...'...

In the Court's view the above statement, which was formal in character and made public the Government's intentions as regards derogation, was well in keeping with the notion of an official proclamation. It therefore considers that there is no basis for the applicants' arguments in this regard.

5. Summary

74. In the light of the above examination, the Court concludes that the derogation lodged by the United Kingdom satisfies the requirements of Article 15 (art 15) and that therefore the applicants cannot validly complain of a violation of Article 5 para 3 (art 5-3). It follows that there was no obligation under Article 5 para 5 (art 5-5) to provide the applicants with an enforceable right to compensation....

FOR THESE REASONS, THE COURT
1. Holds by twenty-two votes to four that the United Kingdom's derogation satisfies the requirements of Article 15 (art 15) and that therefore the applicants cannot validly complain of a violation of Article 5 para 3 (art 5-3); ...

NOTES

1   The plenary Court was composed of President Ryssdal and Judges: Bernhardt, Thor Vilhjalmsson, Gölcüklü, Matscher, Macdonald, Russo, Spielmann, Valticos, Martens, Palm, Foighel, Pekkanen, Loizou, Morenilla, Bigi, Freeland, Baka, Lopes Rocha, Wildhaber, Mifsud Bonnici, and Gotchev.

2   Judge Pettiti in his dissenting opinion expressed the view that:

...The member States of the Council of Europe which went through serious periods of terrorism (for example Italy) confronted such terrorism while retaining judicial involvement in extended police custody. It would be possible to find in comparative law and in criminal procedure examples of judicial mechanisms protecting the use by the police of 'informers' who have to remain anonymous. In camera hearings can be envisaged. The British system too has recourse to the principle of immunity which makes it possible for the public prosecutor not to disclose certain prosecution evidence. It is thus possible to avoid the disadvantages of the ordinary procedural rules applicable at this stage (see the *Edwards v UK* judgment of 16 December 1992, Series A No 247-B). Is there not, on the part of the police, a desire to conceal from the courts some of their practices?...

In the *Brannigan and McBride* case, in my opinion, the Government's action fell outside the margin of appreciation which the Court is able to recognise. The fundamental principle which must prevail and which is consistent with British and European tradition is that detention cannot be extended from four days to seven days without the involvement of a judge, who is the guarantor of individual freedoms and fundamental rights.

3   In his dissent Judge Walsh observed:

2. The terms of Article 15 para 1 (art 15-1) of the Convention have been invoked as a justification for this step, namely that there is a 'time of war or other public emergency threatening the life of the nation'. In the present case 'the nation' is presumed to be the entire United Kingdom. While there is ample evidence of political violence in Northern Ireland which could be described as threatening the life of that region of the United Kingdom there is no evidence that the life of the rest of the United Kingdom, viz. the island of Great Britain, is threatened by 'the war or public emergency in Northern Ireland', which is separated by sea from Great Britain and of which it does not form a part.

3. Furthermore there is no evidence that the operation of the courts in either Northern Ireland or Great Britain has been restricted or affected by 'the war or public emergency' in Northern Ireland. It is the United Kingdom Government which wishes to restrict the operation of the courts by being unwilling to allow arrested persons to be brought before a judge as prescribed by Article 5 para 3 (art 5-3) of the Convention....

4   Judge De Meyer dissented because:

...The Government of the United Kingdom have tried to escape the consequences of [the *Brogan*] judgment by lodging once again a notice of derogation under Article 15 in order to continue the practice concerned. In my view, this is not permissible: they failed to convince me that such a far-reaching departure from the rule of respect for individual liberty could, either after or before the end of 1988, be 'strictly required by the exigencies of the situation'....

5   Judge Makarczyk's dissent considered it to be of vital importance that:

...the United Kingdom Government should attempt to prove before the Court...that extended administrative detention does in fact contribute to eliminate the reasons for which the extraordinary measures needed to be introduced—in other words the prevention and combating of terrorism. But, as far as I can see, no such attempt has been made either in the Government's memorial and the attached documents, or in the pleading before the Court. Instead, the Government's main arguments have centred on the alleged detrimental effects on the judiciary of control by a judge of extended detention without the normal judicial procedure....

6   While the Court was not willing formally to reduce the breadth of the margin of appreciation accorded to States under Article 15 when a public emergency was of long duration, the judgment (at paragraph 43) indicates that this is a significant consideration in the Court's assessment of the lawfulness of a particular derogation.

Aksoy v Turkey 1996-VI
European Court of Human Rights

The facts in regard to the applicant's complaint under Article 3 have been described at p 161. In response to the applicant's allegation that he had suffered a violation of Article 5(3), by being detained for at least 14 days without judicial supervision (see p 305), the Turkish Government sought to rely upon its notice of derogation submitted to the Secretary General in 1990 (and subsequently revised) covering specified provinces in south-east Turkey.

68. The Court recalls that it falls to each Contracting State, with its responsibility for 'the life of [its] nation', to determine whether that life is threatened by a 'public emergency' and, if so, how far it is necessary to go in attempting to overcome the emergency. By reason of their direct and continuous contact with the pressing needs of the moment, the national authorities are in principle better placed than the international judge to decide both on the presence of such an emergency and on the nature and scope of the derogations necessary to avert it. Accordingly, in this matter a wide margin of appreciation should be left to the national authorities.

Nonetheless, Contracting Parties do not enjoy an unlimited discretion. It is for the Court to rule whether, *inter alia*, the States have gone beyond the "extent strictly required by the exigencies" of the crisis. The domestic margin of appreciation is thus accompanied by a European supervision. In exercising this supervision, the Court must give appropriate weight to such relevant factors as the nature of the rights affected by the derogation and the circumstances leading to, and the duration of, the emergency situation (see the *Brannigan and McBride v the United Kingdom* judgment of 26 May 1993, Series A No 258-B, pp 49–50, para. 43).

2. Existence of a public emergency threatening the life of the nation

69. The Government, with whom the Commission agreed on this point, maintained that there was a public emergency 'threatening the life of the nation' in South-East Turkey. The applicant did not contest the issue, although he submitted that, essentially, it was a matter for the Convention organs to decide.

70. The Court considers, in the light of all the material before it, that the particular extent and impact of PKK terrorist activity in South-East Turkey has undoubtedly created, in the region concerned, a 'public emergency threatening the life of the nation' (see, *mutatis mutandis*, the *Lawless v Ireland* judgment of 1 July 1961, Series A No 3, p 56, para 28, the above-mentioned *Ireland v the United Kingdom* judgment [A. 25 (1978)], p 78, para 205, and the above-mentioned *Brannigan and McBride* judgment, p 50, para. 47).

3. Whether the measures were strictly required by the exigencies of the situation

(a) The length of the unsupervised detention

71. The Government asserted that the applicant had been arrested on 26 November 1992 along with thirteen others on suspicion of aiding and abetting PKK terrorists, being a member of the Kiziltepe branch of the PKK and distributing PKK tracts. He was held in custody for fourteen days, in accordance with Turkish law, which allows a person detained in connection with a collective offence to be held for up to thirty days in the state of emergency region.

72. They explained that the place in which the applicant was arrested and detained fell within the area covered by the Turkish derogation. This derogation was necessary and justified, in view of the extent and gravity of PKK terrorism in Turkey, particularly in the South East. The investigation of terrorist offences presented the authorities with special problems, as the Court had recognised

in the past, because the members of terrorist organisations were expert in withstanding interrogation, had secret support networks and access to substantial resources. A great deal of time and effort was required to secure and verify evidence in a large region confronted with a terrorist organisation that had strategic and technical support from neighbouring countries. These difficulties meant that it was impossible to provide judicial supervision during a suspect's detention in police custody.

73. The applicant submitted that he was detained on 24 November 1992 and released on 10 December 1992. He alleged that the post-dating of arrests was a common practice in the state of emergency region.

74. While he did not present detailed arguments against the validity of the Turkish derogation as a whole, he questioned whether the situation in South-East Turkey necessitated the holding of suspects for fourteen days or more without judicial supervision. He submitted that judges in South-East Turkey would not be put at risk if they were permitted and required to review the legality of detention at shorter intervals.

75. The Commission could not establish with any certainty whether the applicant was first detained on 24 November 1992, as he claimed, or on 26 November 1992, as alleged by the Government, and it therefore proceeded on the basis that he was held for at least fourteen days without being brought before a judge or other officer authorised by law to exercise judicial power.

76. The Court would stress the importance of Article 5 in the Convention system: it enshrines a fundamental human right, namely the protection of the individual against arbitrary interference by the State with his or her right to liberty. Judicial control of interferences by the executive with the individual's right to liberty is an essential feature of the guarantee embodied in Article 5 para. 3, which is intended to minimise the risk of arbitrariness and to ensure the rule of law (see the above-mentioned *Brogan and Others* judgment, p 32, para 58). Furthermore, prompt judicial intervention may lead to the detection and prevention of serious ill-treatment, which, as stated above (paragraph 62), is prohibited by the Convention in absolute and non-derogable terms.

77. In the *Brannigan and McBride* judgment (cited at paragraph 68 above), the Court held that the United Kingdom Government had not exceeded their margin of appreciation by derogating from their obligations under Article 5 of the Convention to the extent that individuals suspected of terrorist offences were allowed to be held for up to seven days without judicial control.

In the instant case, the applicant was detained for at least fourteen days without being brought before a judge or other officer. The Government have sought to justify this measure by reference to the particular demands of police investigations in a geographically vast area faced with a terrorist organisation receiving outside support (see paragraph 72 above).

78. Although the Court is of the view—which it has expressed on several occasions in the past (see, for example, the above-mentioned *Brogan and Others* judgment)—that the investigation of terrorist offences undoubtedly presents the authorities with special problems, it cannot accept that it is necessary to hold a suspect for fourteen days without judicial intervention. This period is exceptionally long, and left the applicant vulnerable not only to arbitrary interference with his right to liberty but also to torture. Moreover, the Government have not adduced any detailed reasons before the Court as to why the fight against terrorism in South-East Turkey rendered judicial intervention impracticable.

(b) Safeguards

79. The Government emphasised that both the derogation and the national legal system provided sufficient safeguards to protect human rights. Thus, the derogation itself was limited to the strict minimum required for the fight against terrorism; the permissible length of detention was prescribed by law and the consent of a public prosecutor was necessary if the police wished to remand a suspect in custody beyond these periods. Torture was prohibited by Article 243 of the Criminal

Code and Article 135 (a) stipulated that any statement made in consequence of the administration of torture or any other form of ill-treatment would have no evidential weight.

80. The applicant pointed out that long periods of unsupervised detention, together with the lack of safeguards provided for the protection of prisoners, facilitated the practice of torture. Thus, he was tortured with particular intensity on his third and fourth days in detention, and was held thereafter to allow his injuries to heal; throughout this time he was denied access to either a lawyer or a doctor. Moreover, he was kept blindfolded during interrogation, which meant that he could not identify those who mistreated him. The reports of Amnesty International ('Turkey: a Policy of Denial', February 1995), the European Committee for the Prevention of Torture and the United Nations Committee against Torture showed that the safeguards contained in the Turkish Criminal Code, which were in any case inadequate, were routinely ignored in the state of emergency region.

81. The Commission considered that the Turkish system offered insufficient safeguards to detainees, for example there appeared to be no speedy remedy of habeas corpus and no legally enforceable rights of access to a lawyer, doctor, friend or relative. In these circumstances, despite the serious terrorist threat in South-East Turkey, the measure which allowed the applicant to be detained for at least fourteen days without being brought before a judge or other officer exercising judicial functions exceeded the Government's margin of appreciation and could not be said to be strictly required by the exigencies of the situation.

82. In its above-mentioned *Brannigan and McBride* judgment the Court was satisfied that there were effective safeguards in operation in Northern Ireland which provided an important measure of protection against arbitrary behaviour and incommunicado detention. For example, the remedy of habeas corpus was available to test the lawfulness of the original arrest and detention, there was an absolute and legally enforceable right to consult a solicitor forty-eight hours after the time of arrest and detainees were entitled to inform a relative or friend about their detention and to have access to a doctor (*op cit*, pp 55–6, paras 62–3).

83. In contrast, however, the Court considers that in this case insufficient safeguards were available to the applicant, who was detained over a long period of time. In particular, the denial of access to a lawyer, doctor, relative or friend and the absence of any realistic possibility of being brought before a court to test the legality of the detention meant that he was left completely at the mercy of those holding him.

84. The Court has taken account of the unquestionably serious problem of terrorism in South-East Turkey and the difficulties faced by the State in taking effective measures against it. However, it is not persuaded that the exigencies of the situation necessitated the holding of the applicant on suspicion of involvement in terrorist offences for fourteen days or more in incommunicado detention without access to a judge or other judicial officer.

5. Conclusion

87. In conclusion, the Court finds that there has been a violation of Article 5 para. 3 of the Convention.

...

FOR THESE REASONS, THE COURT

...

3. Holds by eight votes to one that there has been a violation of Article 5(3) of the Convention;

NOTES

1 The composition of the Court has already been elaborated at p 163. Judge Gölcüklü dissented as he considered that Aksoy had not exhausted domestic remedies.

2   *Aksoy* is a rare example of the Court determining that the conditions of Article 15 had not been satisfied by the respondent State.

3   In the subsequent case of *Sakik and Others v Turkey*, judgment of 26 November 1997, the Court, unanimously, found that the above derogations were not applicable to the applicants' complaints as their detention had taken place outside the geographical areas specified in Turkey's derogations. The six applicants were former members of the Turkish National Assembly who were arrested, on the orders of the public prosecutor, as they left the parliament building in Ankara. They were held in police custody for between 12 and 14 days before being brought before a judge. The applicants complained, *inter alia*, of a breach of Article 5(3). The Turkish Government submitted that as it had exercised the right of derogation under Article 15 no breach of Article 5 had occurred.

35. The applicants submitted that the derogation in question did not apply to the measures imposed on them. The Commission agreed.

36. The Court notes that Legislative Decrees nos. 424, 425 and 430, which are referred to in the derogation of 6 August 1990 and the letter of 3 January 1991, apply, according to the descriptive summary of their content, only to the region where a state of emergency has been proclaimed, which, according to the derogation, does not include the city of Ankara. However, the applicants' arrest and detention took place in Ankara on the orders first of the public prosecutor attached to the Ankara National Security Court and later of the judges of that court.

37. The Government submitted that this was no bar to the derogation's applicability. The facts of the case constituted only the prolongation of a terrorist campaign being conducted from inside the area where the state of emergency had been proclaimed, in south-east Turkey. The terrorist threat was not confined to any particular part of Turkish territory. That had to be taken into account if the Turkish derogation was to be interpreted in the light of its object and purpose, namely to enable 'normality for the purposes of the Convention' to be restored throughout the country as quickly as possible.

38. In its *Aksoy v Turkey* judgment the Court has already noted the unquestionably serious problem of terrorism in south-east Turkey and the difficulties faced by the State in taking effective measures against it. It held in that connection that the particular extent and impact of Kurdish Workers' Party (PKK) activity in south-east Turkey had undoubtedly created, in the region concerned, a 'public emergency threatening the life of the nation' (see the judgment of 18 December 1996, Reports of Judgments and Decisions 1996-VI, pp 2281 and 2284, §§ 70 and 84).

39. It should be noted, however, that Article 15 authorises derogations from the obligations arising from the Convention only 'to the extent strictly required by the exigencies of the situation'.

40. In the present case the Court would be working against the object and purpose of that provision if, when assessing the territorial scope of the derogation concerned, it were to extend its effects to a part of Turkish territory not explicitly named in the notice of derogation. It follows that the derogation in question is inapplicable ratione loci to the facts of the case.

Consequently, it is not necessary to determine whether it satisfies the requirements of Article 15.

The Court went on to find violations of Article 5 paragraphs (3), (4), and (5). The judgment in *Sakik* reveals the Court interpreting the precise wording of derogations strictly.

4   In *A and others v UK*, see p 296, the Grand Chamber was faced with the highly extraordinary situation where the respondent government was seeking to challenge the findings of its highest national court that an Article 15 derogation was not a proportional measure.

158. . . . The Court does not consider that there is any reason of principle why, since the applicants have requested it to examine the lawfulness of their detention, the Government should not now have the chance to raise all the arguments open to them to defend the proceedings, even if this involves calling into question the conclusions of their own supreme court.

. . .

174. . . . Moreover, the domestic courts are part of the 'national authorities' to which the Court affords a wide margin of appreciation under Article 15. In the unusual circumstances of the present case, where the highest domestic court has examined the issues relating to the State's derogation and concluded that there was a public emergency threatening the life of the nation but that the measures taken in consequence were not strictly required by the exigencies of the situation, the Court considers that it would be justified in reaching a contrary conclusion only if satisfied that the national court had misinterpreted or misapplied Article 15 or the Court's jurisprudence under that Article or reached a conclusion which was manifestly unreasonable.

The Grand Chamber went on (unanimously) to conclude that there was a public emergency threatening the life of the nation in the UK from Al'Qaeda after the September 2001 attacks in the USA.

177. Although when the derogation was made no al'Qaeda attack had taken place within the territory of the UK, the Court does not consider that the national authorities can be criticised, in the light of the evidence available to them at the time, for fearing that such an attack was 'imminent', in that an atrocity might be committed without warning at any time. The requirement of imminence cannot be interpreted so narrowly as to require a State to wait for disaster to strike before taking measures to deal with it. Moreover, the danger of a terrorist attack was, tragically, shown by the bombings and attempted bombings in London in July 2005 to have been very real.

But the Grand Chamber did observe that it was 'striking' that the UK was the only member State to have made a derogation in the face of the threat from Al'Qaeda. The Grand Chamber also agreed with the House of Lords' assessment that the British derogation was disproportionate as it unjustifiably discriminated against non-nationals.

The above judgment reveals the Strasbourg Court adopting a highly supportive stance towards national courts that have found a breach of Article 15. The British derogation was withdrawn in March 2005.

INDEX